ECE/TRANS/202 (Vol. I)

Economic Commission for Europe
Committee on Inland Transport

ADR

applicable as from 1 January 2009

European Agreement

Concerning the International Carriage
of Dangerous Goods by Road

Volume I

UNITED NATIONS
New York and Geneva, 2008

NOTE

The designations employed and the presentation of the material in this publication do not imply the expression of any opinion whatsoever on the part of the Secretariat of the United Nations concerning the legal status of any country, territory, city or area, or of its authorities, or concerning the delimitation of its frontiers or boundaries.

ECE/TRANS/202 (Vol. I)

NO LOAN
Per
UNI
E|ECE
A2-1

UNITED NATIONS PUBLICATION
Sales No.: E.08.VIII.1
ISBN 978-92-1-139131-2
(complete set of 2 volumes)

Volumes I and II not to be sold separately.

FOREWORD

General

The European Agreement concerning the International Carriage of Dangerous Goods by Road (ADR) was done at Geneva on 30 September 1957 under the auspices of the United Nations Economic Commission for Europe, and it entered into force on 29 January 1968. The Agreement itself was amended by the Protocol amending article 14 (3) done at New York on 21 August 1975, which entered into force on 19 April 1985.

According to article 2 of the Agreement, dangerous goods barred from carriage by Annex A shall not be accepted for international transport, while international transport of other dangerous goods shall be authorized subject to compliance with:

- the conditions laid down in Annex A for the goods in question, in particular as regards their packaging and labelling; and

- the conditions laid down in Annex B, in particular as regards the construction, equipment and operation of the vehicle carrying the goods in question.

Nevertheless, according to article 4, each Contracting Party shall retain the right to regulate or prohibit, for reasons other than safety during carriage, the entry of dangerous goods into its territory. Contracting Parties also retain the right to arrange, by bilateral or multilateral agreements, that certain dangerous goods which are prohibited from carriage by Annex A be internationally carried, subject to certain conditions, on their territories, or that dangerous goods authorized to be carried internationally according to Annex A be carried on their territories under conditions less stringent than those specified in Annexes A and B.

Annexes A and B have been regularly amended and updated since the entry into force of ADR.

Structure of Annexes A and B

The Working Party on the Transport of Dangerous Goods (WP.15) of the Economic Commission for Europe's Committee on Inland Transport decided, at its fifty-first session (26-30 October 1992), to restructure Annexes A and B, on the basis of a proposal by the International Road Transport Union (TRANS/WP.15/124, paras. 100-108). The main objectives were to make the requirements more accessible and more user-friendly so that they could be applied more easily not only to international road transport operations under ADR, but also to domestic traffic in all European States through national or European Community legislation, and ultimately to ensure a consistent regulatory framework at European level. It was also considered necessary to identify more clearly the duties of the various participants in the transport chain, to group more systematically the requirements concerning these various participants, and to differentiate the legal requirements of ADR from the European or international standards that could be applied to meet such requirements.

The structure is consistent with that of the United Nations *Recommendations on the Transport of Dangerous Goods*, *Model Regulations*, the *International Maritime Dangerous Goods Code (IMDG Code)* and the *Regulations concerning the International Carriage of Dangerous Goods by Rail (RID)*.

It has been split into nine parts, but still grouped under two annexes to align with the wording of article 2 of the Agreement itself. The layout is as follows:

Annex A: General provisions and provisions concerning dangerous articles and substances

Part 1   General provisions
Part 2   Classification
Part 3   Dangerous goods list, special provisions and exemptions related to limited and excepted quantities
Part 4   Packing and tank provisions

Part 5   Consignment procedures
Part 6   Requirements for the construction and testing of packagings, intermediate bulk containers (IBCs), large packagings, tanks and bulk containers
Part 7   Provisions concerning the conditions of carriage, loading, unloading and handling

Annex B: Provisions concerning transport equipment and transport operations

Part 8   Requirements for vehicle crews, equipment, operation and documentation
Part 9   Requirements concerning the construction and approval of vehicles

Part 1, which contains general provisions and definitions, is an essential part, since it contains all definitions for terms used throughout the other parts, and it defines precisely the scope and applicability of ADR, including the possibility of exemptions, as well as the applicability of other regulations. It also contains provisions concerning training, derogations and transitional measures, the respective safety obligations of the various participants in a chain of transport of dangerous goods, control measures, safety advisers and transport of dangerous goods security. New provisions intended to harmonize the conditions for restricting the passage of vehicles carrying dangerous goods through road tunnels have been included in this version.

Central to the use of the restructured ADR is table A of Chapter 3.2 which contains the dangerous goods list in the numerical order of UN numbers. Once the UN number of a specific dangerous substance or article has been determined, the table provides cross-references to specific requirements to be applied for the carriage of that substance or article, and to the chapters or sections where these specific requirements may be found. Nevertheless, it should be borne in mind that the general requirements or class specific requirements of the various Parts have to be applied in addition to specific requirements, as relevant.

An alphabetical index which indicates the UN number assigned to specific dangerous goods has been prepared by the secretariat and added as table B of Chapter 3.2 to facilitate the access to table A when the UN number is unknown. This table B is not an official part of ADR and has been added in the publication for easy reference only.

When goods which are known or suspected to be dangerous cannot be found by name in any of tables A or B, they have to be classified in accordance with Part 2, which contains all relevant procedures and criteria to determine whether such goods are deemed to be dangerous or not and which UN number should be assigned.

Applicable texts

This version ("2009 ADR") takes into account all new amendments adopted by WP.15 in 2006, 2007 and 2008, circulated under the symbols ECE/TRANS/WP.15/195 and -/Corr.1 and ECE/TRANS/WP.15/195/Add.1, which, subject to acceptance by the Contracting Parties in accordance with article 14(3) of the Agreement, should enter into force on 1 January 2009.

Nevertheless, due to the transitional measures provided for in 1.6.1.1 of Annex A, the previous version ("2007 ADR") may continue to be used until 30 June 2009. Longer transitional measures are provided for the construction of new vehicles (see 1.6.5.4).

Territorial applicability

ADR is an Agreement between States, and there is no overall enforcing authority. In practice, highway checks are carried out by Contracting Parties, and non-compliance may then result in legal action by national authorities against offenders in accordance with their domestic legislation. ADR itself does not prescribe any penalties. At the time of publishing, the Contracting Parties are Albania, Austria, Azerbaijan, Belarus, Belgium, Bosnia and Herzegovina, Bulgaria, Croatia, Cyprus, Czech Republic, Denmark, Estonia, Finland, France, Germany, Greece, Hungary, Ireland, Italy, Kazakhstan, Latvia, Liechtenstein, Lithuania, Luxembourg, Malta, Moldova, Montenegro, Morocco, Netherlands, Norway, Poland, Portugal, Romania, Russian Federation, Serbia, Slovakia, Slovenia, Spain, Sweden, Switzerland, The former Yugoslav Republic of Macedonia, Ukraine and United Kingdom.

ADR applies to transport operations performed on the territory of at least two of the above-mentioned Contracting Parties. In addition, it should be noted that, in the interest of uniformity and free trading across the European Union (EU), Annexes A and B of ADR have also been adopted by EU Member States as the basis for regulation of the carriage of dangerous goods by road within and between their territories (Council directive 94/55/EC of 21 November 1994 on the approximation of the laws of the Member States with regard to the transport of dangerous goods by road, as amended). A number of non-EU countries have also adopted Annexes A and B of ADR as the basis for their national legislation.

Additional practical information

Any query concerning the application of ADR should be directed to the relevant competent authority. Additional information may be found on the UNECE Transport Division web site on the following page:

> http://www.unece.org/trans/danger/publi/adr/adr_e.html

This page, updated on a continuous basis, contains the links to the following information:

- Agreement (without annexes);
- Protocol of signature;
- Present status of ADR;
- Depositary notifications;
- Country information (Competent Authorities, notifications according to 1.9.4);
- Multilateral agreements;
- Publication details (Corrigenda);
- ADR 2009 (files);
- ADR 2001, 2003, 2005 and 2007 (files and amendments).

TABLE OF CONTENTS
VOLUME I

Page

Table of contents (cont'd)

Table of contents (cont'd)

TABLE OF CONTENTS
VOLUME II

Page

Table of contents (cont'd)

Table of contents (cont'd)

EUROPEAN AGREEMENT CONCERNING THE INTERNATIONAL CARRIAGE OF DANGEROUS GOODS BY ROAD (ADR)

THE CONTRACTING PARTIES,

DESIRING to increase the safety of international transport by road,

HAVE AGREED as follows:

Article 1

For the purpose of this Agreement,

(a)   the term "vehicle" shall mean motor vehicles, articulated vehicles, trailers and semi-trailers, as defined in article 4 of the Convention on Road Traffic of 19 September 1949, other than vehicles belonging to or under the orders of the armed forces of a Contracting Party;

(b)   the term "dangerous goods" shall mean those substances and articles the international carriage by road of which is prohibited by, or authorized only on certain conditions by, Annexes A and B;

(c)   the term "international transport" shall mean any transport operation performed on the territory of at least two Contracting Parties by vehicles defined in (a) above.

Article 2

1.   Subject to the provisions of article 4, paragraph 3, dangerous goods barred from carriage by Annex A shall not be accepted for international transport.

2.   International transport of other dangerous goods shall be authorized subject to compliance with:

(a)   the conditions laid down in Annex A for the goods in question, in particular as regards their packaging and labelling, and

(b)   the conditions laid down in Annex B, in particular as regards the construction, equipment and operation of the vehicle carrying the goods in question, subject to the provisions of article 4, paragraph 2.

Article 3

The Annexes to this Agreement shall form an integral part thereof.

Article 4

1.   Each Contracting Party shall retain the right to regulate or prohibit, for reasons other than safety during carriage, the entry of dangerous goods into its territory.

2.   Vehicles in service on the territory of a Contracting Party at the time of entry into force of this Agreement or brought into service on such territory within two months after its entry into force shall be allowed, for a period of three years from such entry into force, to perform the international transport of dangerous goods even if their construction and equipment do not entirely conform to the requirements laid down in Annex B for the transport operation in question. Under special clauses of Annex B, however, this period may be reduced.

3.	The Contracting Parties shall retain the right to arrange, by special bilateral or multilateral agreements, that certain of the dangerous goods which under this Agreement are barred from all international transport may, subject to certain conditions, be accepted for international transport on their territories, or that dangerous goods which under this Agreement are acceptable for international transport only on specified conditions may be accepted for international transport on their territories under conditions less stringent than those laid down in the Annexes to this Agreement. The special bilateral or multilateral agreements referred to in this paragraph shall be communicated to the Secretary-General of the United Nations, who shall communicate them to the Contracting Parties which are not signatories to the said agreements.

Article 5

The transport operations to which this Agreement applies shall remain subject to national or international regulations applicable in general to road traffic, international road transport and international trade.

Article 6

1.	Countries members of the Economic Commission for Europe and countries admitted to the Commission in a consultative capacity under paragraph 8 of the Commission's terms of reference may become Contracting Parties to this Agreement.

（a）	by signing it;

（b）	by ratifying it after signing it subject to ratification;

（c）	by acceding to it.

2.	Such countries as may participate in certain activities of the Economic Commission for Europe in accordance with paragraph 11 of the Commission's terms of reference may become Contracting Parties to this Agreement by acceding to it after its entry into force.

3.	The Agreement shall be open for signature until 15 December 1957. Thereafter, it shall be open for accession.

4.	Ratification or accession shall be effected by the depositing of an instrument with the Secretary-General of the United Nations.

Article 7

1.	This agreement shall enter into force one month after the date on which the number of countries mentioned in article 6, paragraph 1, which have signed it without reservation of ratification or have deposited their instruments of ratification or accession has reached a total of five. However, the Annexes thereto shall not apply until six months after the entry into force of the Agreement itself.

2.	For any country ratifying or acceding to this Agreement after five of the countries referred to in article 6, paragraph 1, have signed it without reservation of ratification or have deposited their instruments of ratification or accession, this Agreement shall enter into force one month after the said country has deposited its instrument of ratification or accession and the Annexes thereto shall apply for the said country either on the same date, if they are already in force by that date, or, if they are not in force by that date, on the date on which they apply under the provisions of paragraph 1 of this article.

Article 8

1.	Any contracting Party may denounce this Agreement by so notifying the Secretary-General of the United Nations.

2.	Denunciation shall take effect twelve months after the date of receipt by the Secretary-General of the notification of denunciation.

Article 9

1.   This Agreement shall cease to have effect if, after its entry into force, the number of Contracting Parties is less than five during twelve consecutive months.

2.   In the event of the conclusion of a worldwide agreement for the regulation of the transport of dangerous goods, any provision of this Agreement which is contrary to any provision of the said worldwide agreement shall, from the date on which the latter enters into force, automatically cease to apply to relations between the Parties to this Agreement which become parties to the worldwide agreement, and shall automatically be replaced by the relevant provision of the said worldwide agreement.

Article 10

1.   Any country may, at the time of signing this Agreement without reservation of ratification or of depositing its instrument of ratification or accession or at any time thereafter, declare by notification addressed to the Secretary-General of the United Nations that this Agreement shall extend to all or any of the territories for the international relations of which it is responsible. The Agreement and the annexes thereto shall extend to the territory or territories named in the notification one month after it is received by the Secretary-General.

2.   Any country which has made a declaration under paragraph 1 of this article extending this Agreement to any territory for whose international relations it is responsible may denounce the Agreement separately in respect of the said territory in accordance with the provisions of article 8.

Article 11

1.   Any dispute between two or more Contracting Parties concerning the interpretation or application of this Agreement shall so far as possible be settled by negotiation between them.

2.   Any dispute which is not settled by negotiation shall be submitted to arbitration if any one of the Contracting Parties in dispute so requests and shall be referred accordingly to one or more arbitrators selected by agreement between the Parties in dispute. If within three months from the date of the request for arbitration the Parties in dispute are unable to agree on the selection of an arbitrator or arbitrators, any of those Parties may request the Secretary-General of the United Nations to nominate a single arbitrator to whom the dispute shall be referred for decision.

3.   The decision of the arbitrator or arbitrators appointed under paragraph 2 of this article shall be binding on the Contracting Parties in dispute.

Article 12

1.   Each Contracting Party may, at the time of signing, ratifying, or acceding to, this Agreement, declare that it does not consider itself bound by article 11. Other Contracting Parties shall not be bound by article 11 in respect of any Contracting Party which has entered such a reservation.

2.   Any Contracting Party having entered a reservation as provided for in paragraph 1 of this article may at any time withdraw such reservation by notifying the Secretary-General of the United Nations.

Article 13

1.   After this Agreement has been in force for three years, any Contracting Party may, by notification to the Secretary-General of the United Nations, request that a conference be convened for the purpose of reviewing the text of the Agreement. The Secretary-General shall notify all Contracting Parties of the request and a review conference shall be convened by the Secretary-General if, within a period of four months following the date of notification by the Secretary-General, not less than one-fourth of the Contracting Parties notify him of their concurrence with the request.

2.   If a conference is convened in accordance with paragraph 1 of this article, the Secretary-General shall notify all the Contracting Parties and invite them to submit within a period of three months such proposals as they may wish the Conference to consider. The Secretary-General shall circulate to all Contracting Parties the provisional agenda for the conference, together with the texts of such proposals, at least three months before the date on which the conference is to meet.

3.   The Secretary-General shall invite to any conference convened in accordance with this article all countries referred to in article 6, paragraph 1, and countries which have become Contracting Parties under article 6, paragraph 2.

Article 14[1]

1.   Independently of the revision procedure provided for in article 13, any Contracting Party may propose one or more amendments to the Annexes to this Agreement. To that end it shall transmit the text thereof to the Secretary-General of the United Nations. The Secretary-General may also propose amendments to the Annexes to this Agreement for the purpose of ensuring concordance between those Annexes and other international agreements concerning the carriage of dangerous goods.

2.   The Secretary-General shall transmit any proposal made under paragraph 1 of this article to all Contracting Parties and inform thereof the other countries referred to in article 6, paragraph 1.

3.   Any proposed amendment to the Annexes shall be deemed to be accepted unless, within three months from the date on which the Secretary-General circulates it, at least one-third of the Contracting Parties, or five of them if one-third exceeds that figure, have given the Secretary-General written notification of their objection to the proposed amendment. If the amendment is deemed to be accepted, it shall enter into force for all the Contracting Parties, on the expiry of a further period of three months, except in the following cases:

   (a)   In cases where similar amendments have been or are likely to be made to the other international agreements referred to in paragraph 1 of this article, the amendment shall enter into force on the expiry of a period the duration of which shall be determined by the Secretary-General in such a way as to allow, wherever possible, the simultaneous entry into force of the amendment and those that have been made or are likely to be made to such other agreements; such period shall not, however, be of less than one month's duration;

   (b)   The Contracting Party submitting the proposed amendment may specify in its proposal, for the purpose of entry into force of the amendment, should it be accepted, a period of more than three months' duration.

4.   The Secretary-General shall, as soon as possible, notify all Contracting Parties and all the countries referred to in article 6, paragraph 1, of any objection which may be received from the Contracting Parties to a proposed amendment.

5.   If the proposed amendment to the Annexes is not deemed to be accepted, but if at least one Contracting Party other than the Contracting Party which proposed the amendment has given the Secretary-General written notification of its agreement to the proposal, a meeting of all the Contracting Parties and all the countries referred to in article 6, paragraph 1, shall be convened by the Secretary-General within three months after the expiry of the period of three months within which, under paragraph 3 of this article, notification must be given of objection to the amendment. The Secretary-General may also invite to such meeting representatives of:

   (a)   intergovernmental organizations which are concerned with transport matters;

---

[1]   ***Note by the Secretariat:*** *The text of Article 14, paragraph 3 incorporates a modification which entered into force on 19 April 1985 in accordance with a Protocol transmitted to Contracting Parties under cover of Depositary Notification C.N.229.1975.TREATIES-8 of 18 September 1975.*

(b)   international non-governmental organizations whose activities are directly related to the transport of dangerous goods in the territories of the Contracting Parties.

6.   Any amendment adopted by more than half the total number of Contracting Parties at a meeting convened in accordance with paragraph 5 of this article shall enter into force for all Contracting Parties in accordance with the procedure agreed at such meeting by the majority of the Contracting Parties attending it.

Article 15

In addition to the notifications provided for in articles 13 and 14, the Secretary-General of the United Nations shall notify the countries referred to in article 6, paragraph 1, and the countries which have become Contracting Parties under article 6, paragraph 2, of

(a)   signatures, ratifications and accessions in accordance with article 6;

(b)   the dates on which this Agreement and the Annexes thereto enter into force in accordance with article 7;

(c)   denunciations in accordance with article 8;

(d)   the termination of the Agreement in accordance with article 9;

(e)   notifications and denunciations received in accordance with article 10;

(f)   declarations and notifications received in accordance with article 12, paragraphs 1 and 2;

(g)   the acceptance and date of entry into force of amendments in accordance with article 14, paragraphs 3 and 6.

Article 16

1.   The Protocol of Signature of this Agreement shall have the same force, effect and duration as the Agreement itself, of which it shall be considered to be an integral part.

2.   No reservation to this Agreement, other than those entered in the Protocol of Signature and those made in accordance with article 12, shall be permitted.

Article 17

After 15 December 1957, the original of this Agreement shall be deposited with the Secretary-General of the United Nations, who shall transmit certified true copies thereof to each of the countries referred to in article 6, paragraph 1.

IN WITNESS WHEREOF the undersigned, being duly authorized thereto, have signed this Agreement.

DONE at Geneva, this thirtieth day of September one thousand nine hundred and fifty-seven, in a single copy, in the English and French languages for the text of the Agreement proper, and in the French language for the Annexes, each text being equally authentic for the Agreement proper.

The Secretary-General of the United Nations is requested to prepare an authoritative translation of the Annexes in the English language and attach it to the certified true copies referred to in article 17.

PROTOCOL OF SIGNATURE

PROTOCOL OF SIGNATURE

TO THE EUROPEAN AGREEMENT ON THE INTERNATIONAL
CARRIAGE OF DANGEROUS GOODS BY ROAD (ADR)

On proceeding to sign the European Agreement on the International Carriage of Dangerous Goods by Road (ADR) the undersigned, duly authorized,

1.   **CONSIDERING** that the conditions governing the carriage of dangerous goods by sea to or from the United Kingdom differ basically from those set forth in Annex A to ADR and that it is impossible to modify them so as to conform to the latter in the near future;

HAVING REGARD to the undertaking given by the United Kingdom to submit as an amendment to the said Annex A a special appendix containing special provisions for road-sea carriage of dangerous goods between the Continent and the United Kingdom;

HAVE AGREED that, until the entry into force of such special appendix, dangerous goods carried under ADR to or from the United Kingdom shall comply with the provisions of Annex A to ADR and also with the United Kingdom conditions for the carriage of dangerous goods by sea;

2.   **TAKE NOTE OF** a declaration by the representative of France to the effect that the Government of the French Republic reserves the right, notwithstanding the provisions of article 4, paragraph 2, to refuse to allow vehicles in service on the territory of another Contracting Party, whatever the date on which they were put into service, to be used for the carriage of dangerous goods on French territory unless such vehicles comply either with the conditions laid down for such carriage in Annex B or with the conditions laid down for the carriage of the goods in question in the French regulations governing the carriage of dangerous goods by road;

3.   **RECOMMEND** that, before submission in accordance with article 14, paragraph 1, or article 13, paragraph 2, proposed amendments to this Agreement or its Annexes shall as far as possible first be discussed at meetings of experts of the Contracting Parties and, if necessary, of the other countries mentioned in article 6, paragraph 1, of the Agreement and of the international organizations mentioned in article 14, paragraph 5, of the Agreement.

ANNEX A

GENERAL PROVISIONS AND PROVISIONS CONCERNING DANGEROUS SUBSTANCES AND ARTICLES

PART 1

General provisions

CHAPTER 1.1

SCOPE AND APPLICABILITY

1.1.1   **Structure**

Annexes A and B of ADR are grouped into nine parts. Annex A consists of Parts 1 to 7, and Annex B of Parts 8 and 9. Each part is subdivided into chapters and each chapter into sections and sub-sections. Within each part the number of the part is included with the numbers of the chapters, sections and sub-sections, for example Part 4, Chapter 2, Section 1 is numbered "4.2.1".

1.1.2   **Scope**

1.1.2.1   For the purposes of Article 2 of ADR, Annex A specifies:

(a)   Dangerous goods which are barred from international carriage;

(b)   Dangerous goods which are authorized for international carriage and the conditions attaching to them (including exemptions) particularly with regard to:

-     classification of goods, including classification criteria and relevant test methods;

-     use of packagings (including mixed packing);

-     use of tanks (including filling);

-     consignment procedures (including marking and labelling of packages and placarding and marking of means of transport as well as documentation and information required);

-     provisions concerning the construction, testing and approval of packagings and tanks;

-     use of means of transport (including loading, mixed loading and unloading).

1.1.2.2   Annex A contains certain provisions which, according to Article 2 of ADR, pertain to Annex B or to both Annexes A and B, as follows:

1.1.1	Structure
1.1.2.3	(Scope of Annex B)
1.1.2.4	
1.1.3.1	Exemptions related to the nature of the transport operation
1.1.3.6	Exemptions related to quantities carried per transport unit
1.1.4	Applicability of other regulations
1.1.4.5	Carriage other than by road
Chapter 1.2	Definitions and units of measurements
Chapter 1.3	Training of persons involved in the carriage of dangerous goods
Chapter 1.4	Safety obligations of the participants
Chapter 1.5	Derogations
Chapter 1.6	Transitional measures
Chapter 1.8	Checks and other support measures to ensure compliance with safety requirements

1.1.2.3   For the purposes of Article 2 of ADR, Annex B specifies the conditions regarding the construction, equipment and operation of vehicles carrying dangerous goods authorized for carriage:

- requirements for vehicle crews, equipment, operation and documentation;

- requirements concerning the construction and approval of vehicles.

1.1.2.4   In Article 1(c) of ADR, the word "vehicles" need not refer to one and the same vehicle. An international transport operation may be performed by several different vehicles provided that the operation takes place on the territory of at least two Contracting Parties to ADR between the consignor and the consignee indicated in the transport document.

1.1.3   Exemptions

1.1.3.1   *Exemptions related to the nature of the transport operation*

The provisions laid down in ADR do not apply to:

(a)   The carriage of dangerous goods by private individuals where the goods in question are packaged for retail sale and are intended for their personal or domestic use or for their leisure or sporting activities provided that measures have been taken to prevent any leakage of contents in normal conditions of carriage. When these goods are flammable liquids carried in refillable receptacles filled by, or for, a private individual, the total quantity shall not exceed 60 litres per receptacle and 240 litres per transport unit. Dangerous goods in IBCs, large packagings or tanks are not considered to be packaged for retail sale;

(b)   The carriage of machinery or equipment not specified in this Annex and which happen to contain dangerous goods in their internal or operational equipment, provided that measures have been taken to prevent any leakage of contents in normal conditions of carriage;

(c)   The carriage undertaken by enterprises which is ancillary to their main activity, such as deliveries to or returns from building or civil engineering sites, or in relation to surveying, repairs and maintenance, in quantities of not more than 450 litres per packaging and within the maximum quantities specified in 1.1.3.6. Measures shall be taken to prevent any leakage of contents in normal conditions of carriage. These exemptions do not apply to Class 7.

Carriage undertaken by such enterprises for their supply or external or internal distribution does not fall within the scope of this exemption;

(d)   The carriage undertaken by or under the supervision of the emergency services, insofar as such carriage is necessary in relation to the emergency response, in particular carriage undertaken:

- by breakdown vehicles carrying vehicles which have been involved in accidents or have broken down and contain dangerous goods; or

- to contain and recover the dangerous goods involved in an incident or accident and move them to a safe place;

(e)   Emergency transport intended to save human lives or protect the environment provided that all measures are taken to ensure that such transport is carried out in complete safety;

(f)   The carriage of uncleaned empty static storage vessels which have contained gases of Class 2, groups A, O or F, substances of Class 3 or Class 9 belonging to packing group II or III or pesticides of Class 6.1 belonging to packing group II or III, subject to the following conditions:

- All openings with the exception of pressure relief devices (when fitted) are hermetically closed;

- Measures have been taken to prevent any leakage of contents in normal conditions of carriage; and

- The load is fixed in cradles or crates or other handling devices or to the vehicle or container in such a way that they will not become loose or shift during normal conditions of carriage.

This exemption does not apply to static storage vessels which have contained desensitized explosives or substances the carriage of which is prohibited by ADR.

NOTE: For radioactive material, see 1.7.1.4.

1.1.3.2   *Exemptions related to the carriage of gases*

The provisions laid down in ADR do not apply to the carriage of:

(a)   Gases contained in the tanks of a vehicle, performing a transport operation and destined for its propulsion or for the operation of any of its equipment (e.g. refrigerating equipment);

(b)   Gases contained in the fuel tanks of vehicles transported. The fuel cock between gas tank and engine shall be closed and the electric contact open;

(c)   Gases of Groups A and O (according to 2.2.2.1), if the pressure of the gas in the receptacle or tank at a temperature of 20 °C does not exceed 200 kPa (2 bar) and if the gas is not a liquefied or a refrigerated liquefied gas. This includes every kind of receptacle or tank, e.g. also parts of machinery and apparatus;

(d)   Gases contained in the equipment used for the operation of the vehicle (e.g. fire extinguishers), including in spare parts (e.g. inflated pneumatic tyres); this exemption also applies to inflated pneumatic tyres carried as a load;

(e)   Gases contained in the special equipment of vehicles and necessary for the operation of this special equipment during transport (cooling systems, fish-tanks, heaters, etc.) as well as spare receptacles for such equipment or uncleaned empty exchange receptacles, transported in the same transport unit; and

(f)   Gases contained in foodstuffs or beverages.

1.1.3.3   *Exemptions related to the carriage of liquid fuels*

The provisions laid down in ADR do not apply to the carriage of:

(a)   Fuel contained in the tanks of a vehicle performing a transport operation and destined for its propulsion or for the operation of any of its equipment.

The fuel may be carried in fixed fuel tanks, directly connected to the vehicle's engine and/or auxiliary equipment, which comply with the pertinent legal provisions, or may be carried in portable fuel containers (such as jerricans).

The total capacity of the fixed tanks shall not exceed 1500 litres per transport unit and the capacity of a tank fitted to a trailer shall not exceed 500 litres. A maximum of 60 litres per transport unit may be carried in portable fuel containers. These restrictions shall not apply to vehicles operated by the emergency services;

(b)   Fuel contained in the tanks of vehicles or of other means of conveyance (such as boats) which are carried as a load, where it is destined for their propulsion or the operation of any of their equipment. Any fuel cocks between the engine or equipment and the fuel tank shall be closed during carriage unless it is essential for the equipment to remain operational. Where appropriate, the vehicles or other means of conveyance shall be loaded upright and secured against falling.

1.1.3.4   *Exemptions related to special provisions or to dangerous goods packed in limited or excepted quantities*

NOTE: For radioactive material, see 1.7.1.4.

1.1.3.4.1   Certain special provisions of Chapter 3.3 exempt partially or totally the carriage of specific dangerous goods from the requirements of ADR. The exemption applies when the special provision is referred to in Column (6) of Table A of Chapter 3.2 against the dangerous goods entry concerned.

1.1.3.4.2   Certain dangerous goods may be subject to exemptions provided that the conditions of Chapter 3.4 are met.

1.1.3.4.3   Certain dangerous goods may be subject to exemptions provided that the conditions of Chapter 3.5 are met.

1.1.3.5   *Exemptions related to empty uncleaned packagings*

Empty uncleaned packagings (including IBCs and large packagings) which have contained substances of Classes 2, 3, 4.1, 5.1, 6.1, 8 and 9 are not subject to the conditions of ADR if adequate measures have been taken to nullify any hazard. Hazards are nullified if adequate measures have been taken to nullify all hazards of Classes 1 to 9.

1.1.3.6   *Exemptions related to quantities carried per transport unit*

1.1.3.6.1   For the purposes of this sub-section, dangerous goods are assigned to transport categories 0, 1, 2, 3, or 4, as indicated in Column (15) of Table A of Chapter 3.2. Empty uncleaned packagings having contained substances assigned to transport category "0" are also assigned to transport category "0". Empty uncleaned packagings having contained substances assigned to a transport category other than "0" are assigned to transport category "4".

1.1.3.6.2 Where the quantity of dangerous goods carried on a transport unit does not exceed the values indicated in column (3) of the table in 1.1.3.6.3 for a given transport category (when the dangerous goods carried in the transport unit belong to the same category) or the value calculated in accordance with 1.1.3.6.4 (when the dangerous goods carried in the transport unit belong to different transport categories), they may be carried in packages in one transport unit without application of the following provisions:

- Chapter 1.10, except for Class 1 explosives of Division 1.4 of UN Nos. 0104, 0237, 0255, 0267, 0289, 0361, 0365, 0366, 0440, 0441, 0455, 0456 and 0500;
- Chapter 5.3;
- Section 5.4.3;
- Chapter 7.2, except for V5 and V8 of 7.2.4;
- CV1 of 7.5.11;
- Part 8 except for   8.1.2.1 (a),
                        8.1.4.2 to 8.1.4.5,
                        8.2.3,
                        8.3.3,
                        8.3.4,
                        8.3.5,
                        Chapter 8.4,
                        S1(3) and (6),
                        S2(1),
                        S4 and
                        S14 to S21 of Chapter 8.5;
- Part 9.

1.1.3.6.3   Where the dangerous goods carried in the transport unit belong to the same category, the maximum total quantity per transport unit is indicated in column (3) of the table below.

Transport category (1)	Substances or articles packing group or classification code/group or UN No. (2)	Maximum total quantity per transport unit (3)
0	Class 1: 1.1A/1.1L/1.2L/1.3L and UN No. 0190 Class 3: UN No. 3343 Class 4.2: Substances belonging to packing group I Class 4.3: UN Nos. 1183, 1242, 1295, 1340, 1390, 1403, 1928, 2813, 2965, 2968, 2988, 3129, 3130, 3131, 3134, 3148, 3396, 3398 and 3399 Class 5.1: UN No. 2426 Class 6.1: UN Nos. 1051, 1600, 1613, 1614, 2312, 3250 and 3294 Class 6.2: UN Nos. 2814 and 2900 Class 7: UN Nos. 2912 to 2919, 2977, 2978 and 3321 to 3333 Class 8: UN No. 2215 (MALEIC ANHYDRIDE, MOLTEN) Class 9: UN Nos. 2315, 3151, 3152 and 3432 and apparatus containing such substances or mixtures and empty uncleaned packagings, except those classified under UN No. 2908, having contained substances classified in this transport category.	0
1	Substances and articles belonging to packing group I and not classified in transport category 0 and substances and articles of the following classes: Class 1: 1.1B to 1.1J [a] /1.2B to 1.2J/1.3C/1.3G/1.3H/1.3J/1.5D [a] Class 2: groups T, TC [a], TO, TF, TOC and TFC aerosols: groups C, CO, FC, T, TF, TC, TO, TFC and TOC Class 4.1: UN Nos. 3221 to 3224 and 3231 to 3240 Class 5.2: UN Nos. 3101 to 3104 and 3111 to 3120	20
2	Substances or articles belonging to packing group II and not classified in transport categories 0, 1 or 4 and substances of the following classes: Class 1: 1.4B to 1.4G and 1.6N Class 2: group F aerosols: group F Class 4.1: UN Nos. 3225 to 3230 Class 5.2: UN Nos. 3105 to 3110 Class 6.1: substances and articles belonging to packing group III Class 9: UN No. 3245	333
3	Substances and articles belonging to packing group III and not classified in transport categories 0, 2 or 4 and substances and articles of the following classes: Class 2: groups A and O aerosols: groups A and O Class 3: UN No. 3473 Class 4.3: UN No. 3476 Class 8: UN Nos. 2794, 2795, 2800, 3028 and 3477 Class 9: UN Nos. 2990 and 3072	1 000
4	Class 1: 1.4S Class 4.1: UN Nos. 1331, 1345, 1944, 1945, 2254 and 2623 Class 4.2: UN Nos. 1361 and 1362 packing group III Class 7: UN Nos. 2908 to 2911 Class 9: UN No. 3268 and empty, uncleaned packagings having contained dangerous goods, except for those classified in transport category 0	unlimited

[a]   *For UN Nos. 0081, 0082, 0084, 0241, 0331, 0332, 0482, 1005 and 1017, the total maximum quantity per transport unit shall be 50 kg.*

In the above table, "maximum total quantity per transport unit" means:

- For articles, gross mass in kilograms (for articles of Class 1, net mass in kilograms of the explosive substance; for dangerous goods in machinery and equipment specified in this Annex, the total quantity of dangerous goods contained therein in kilograms or litres as appropriate);

- For solids, liquefied gases, refrigerated liquefied gases and dissolved gases, net mass in kilograms;

- For liquids and compressed gases, nominal capacity of receptacles (see definition in 1.2.1) in litres.

1.1.3.6.4 Where dangerous goods of different transport categories are carried in the same transport unit, the sum of:

- The quantity of substances and articles of transport category 1 multiplied by "50";

- The quantity of substances and articles of transport category 1 referred to in Note a to the table in 1.1.3.6.3 multiplied by "20";

- The quantity of substances and articles of transport category 2 multiplied by "3"; and

- The quantity of substances and articles of transport category 3;

shall not exceed "1 000".

1.1.3.6.5 For the purposes of this sub-section, dangerous goods exempted in accordance with 1.1.3.2 to 1.1.3.5 shall not be taken into account.

1.1.3.7 *Exemptions related to the carriage of lithium batteries*

The provisions laid down in ADR do not apply to:

(a) Lithium batteries installed in a vehicle, performing a transport operation and destined for its propulsion or for the operation of any of its equipment;

(b) Lithium batteries contained in equipment for the operation of this equipment used or intended for use during carriage (e.g. a laptop).

1.1.4 **Applicability of other regulations**

1.1.4.1 *(Reserved)*

1.1.4.2 *Carriage in a transport chain including maritime or air carriage*

1.1.4.2.1 Packages, containers, portable tanks and tank-containers, which do not entirely meet the requirements for packing, mixed packing, marking, labelling of packages or placarding and orange plate marking, of ADR, but are in conformity with the requirements of the IMDG Code or the ICAO Technical Instructions shall be accepted for carriage in a transport chain including maritime or air carriage subject to the following conditions:

(a) If the packages are not marked and labelled in accordance with ADR, they shall bear markings and danger labels in accordance with the requirements of the IMDG Code or the ICAO Technical Instructions;

(b)   The requirements of the IMDG Code or the ICAO Technical Instructions shall be applicable to mixed packing within a package;

(c)   For carriage in a transport chain including maritime carriage, if the containers, portable tanks or tank-containers are not marked and placarded in accordance with Chapter 5.3 of this Annex, they shall be marked and placarded in accordance with Chapter 5.3 of the IMDG Code. In such case, only 5.3.2.1.1 of this Annex is applicable to the marking of the vehicle itself. For empty, uncleaned portable tanks and tank-containers, this requirement shall apply up to and including the subsequent transfer to a cleaning station.

This derogation does not apply in the case of goods classified as dangerous goods in classes 1 to 9 of ADR and considered as non-dangerous goods according to the applicable requirements of the IMDG Code or the ICAO Technical Instructions.

1.1.4.2.2   Transport units composed of a vehicle or vehicles other than those carrying containers, portable tanks or tank containers as provided for in 1.1.4.2.1 (c), which are not placarded in accordance with the provisions of 5.3.1 of ADR but which are marked and placarded in accordance with Chapter 5.3 of the IMDG Code, shall be accepted for carriage in a transport chain including maritime transport provided that the orange-coloured plate marking provisions of 5.3.2 of ADR are complied with.

1.1.4.2.3   For carriage in a transport chain including maritime or air carriage, the information required under 5.4.1 and 5.4.2 and under any special provision of Chapter 3.3 may be substituted by the transport document and information required by the IMDG Code or the ICAO Technical Instructions respectively provided that any additional information required by ADR is also included.

NOTE: *For carriage in accordance with 1.1.4.2.1, see also 5.4.1.1.7. For carriage in containers, see also 5.4.2.*

1.1.4.3   *Use of IMO type portable tanks approved for maritime transport*

IMO type portable tanks (types 1, 2, 5 and 7) which do not meet the requirements of Chapters 6.7 or 6.8, but which have been built and approved before 1 January 2003 in accordance with the provisions (including transitional provisions) of the IMDG Code (Amdt. 29-98) may be used until 31 December 2009 provided they are found to meet the applicable inspection and test provisions of the IMDG Code (Amdt. 29-98) and that the instructions referred to in Columns (12) and (14) of Chapter 3.2 of the IMDG Code (Amdt. 33-06) are fully complied with. They may continue to be used after 31 December 2009 if they meet the applicable inspection and test provisions of the IMDG Code, but provided that the instructions of Columns (10) and (11) of Chapter 3.2 of ADR and of Chapter 4.2 are complied with. [1]

1.1.4.4   *(Reserved)*

---

[1]   *The International Maritime Organization (IMO) has issued "Guidance on the Continued Use of Existing IMO Type Portable Tanks and Road Tank Vehicles for the Transport of Dangerous Goods" as circular DSC.1/Circ.12 and Corrigenda. The text of this guidance can be found on the IMO website at: www.imo.org.*

1.1.4.5   *Carriage other than by road*

1.1.4.5.1   If the vehicle carrying out a transport operation subject to the requirements of ADR is conveyed over a section of the journey otherwise than by road haulage, then any national or international regulations which, on the said section, govern the carriage of dangerous goods by the mode of transport used for conveying the road vehicle shall alone be applicable to the said section of the journey.

1.1.4.5.2   In the cases referred to in 1.1.4.5.1 above, the involved ADR Contracting Parties may agree to apply the requirements of ADR to the section of a journey where a vehicle is conveyed otherwise than by road haulage, supplemented, if they consider it necessary, by additional requirements, unless such agreements between the involved ADR Contracting Parties would contravene clauses of the international conventions governing the carriage of dangerous goods by the mode of transport used for conveying the road vehicle on the said section of the journey, e.g. the International Convention for the Safety of Life at Sea (SOLAS), to which these ADR Contacting Parties would also be contracting parties.

These agreements shall be notified by the Contracting Party which has taken the initiative thereof to the Secretariat of the United Nations Economic Commission for Europe which shall bring them to the attention of the Contracting Parties.

1.1.4.5.3   In cases where a transport operation subject to the provisions of ADR is likewise subject over the whole or a part of the road journey to the provisions of an international convention which regulates the carriage of dangerous goods by a mode of transport other than road carriage by virtue of clauses extending the applicability of that convention to certain motor-vehicle services, then the provisions of that international convention shall apply over the journey in question concurrently with those of ADR which are not incompatible with them; the other clauses of ADR shall not apply over the journey in question.

CHAPTER 1.2

DEFINITIONS AND UNITS OF MEASUREMENT

1.2.1   **Definitions**

NOTE: *This section contains all general or specific definitions.*

For the purposes of ADR:

A

"ADN" means the European Agreement concerning the International Carriage of Dangerous Goods by Inland Waterways;

"Aerosol or aerosol dispenser" means any non-refillable receptacle meeting the requirements of 6.2.6, made of metal, glass or plastics and containing a gas, compressed, liquefied or dissolved under pressure, with or without a liquid, paste or powder, and fitted with a release device allowing the contents to be ejected as solid or liquid particles in suspension in a gas, as a foam, paste or powder or in a liquid state or in a gaseous state;

"Animal material" means animal carcasses, animal body parts, or animal foodstuffs;

"Applicant" means, in the case of conformity assessment, the manufacturer or its authorised representative in a country Contracting Party. In the case of periodic testing and exceptional checks, *applicant* means the testing facility, the operator or their authorised representative in a country Contracting Party;

NOTE: *Exceptionally a third party (for instance an operator in accordance with the definition of 1.2.1) may apply for the conformity assessment.*

"Approval"

> *Multilateral approval*, for the carriage of Class 7 material, means approval by the relevant competent authority of the country of origin of the design or shipment, as applicable, and by the competent authority of each country through or into which the consignment is to be carried. The term "through or into" specifically excludes "over", i.e. the approval and notification requirements shall not apply to a country over which radioactive material is carried in an aircraft, provided that there is no scheduled stop in that country;

> *Unilateral approval*, for the carriage of Class 7 material, means an approval of a design which is required to be given by the competent authority of the country of origin of the design only. If the country of origin is not a Contracting Party to ADR, the approval shall require validation by the competent authority of the first Contracting Party to ADR reached by the consignment (see 6.4.22.6);

"ASTM" means the American Society for Testing and Materials (ASTM International, 100 Barr Harbor Drive, PO Box C700, West Conshohocken, PA, 19428-2959, United States of America);

B

"Bag" means a flexible packaging made of paper, plastics film, textiles, woven material or other suitable material;

"Battery-vehicle" means a vehicle containing elements which are linked to each other by a manifold and permanently fixed to a transport unit. The following elements are considered to be elements of a battery-vehicle: cylinders, tubes, bundles of cylinders (also known as frames), pressure drums as well as tanks destined for the carriage of gases of Class 2 with a capacity of more than 450 litres;

"Body" (for all categories of IBC other than composite IBCs) means the receptacle proper, including openings and closures, but does not include service equipment;

"Box" means a packaging with complete rectangular or polygonal faces, made of metal, wood, plywood, reconstituted wood, fibreboard, plastics or other suitable material. Small holes for purposes of ease of handling or opening or to meet classification requirements, are permitted as long as they do not compromise the integrity of the packaging during carriage;

"Bulk containers" means containment systems (including any liner or coating) intended for the carriage of solid substances which are in direct contact with the containment system. Packagings, intermediate bulk containers (IBCs), large packagings and tanks are not included.

Bulk containers are:

- of a permanent character and accordingly strong enough to be suitable for repeated use;

- specially designed to facilitate the carriage of goods by one or more modes of carriage without intermediate reloading;

- fitted with devices permitting its ready handling;

- of a capacity of not less than 1.0 m^3;

Examples of bulk containers are containers, offshore bulk containers, skips, bulk bins, swap bodies, trough-shaped containers, roller containers, load compartments of vehicles;

"Bundle of cylinders" means an assembly of cylinders that are fastened together and which are interconnected by a manifold and carried as a unit. The total water capacity shall not exceed 3 000 litres except that bundles intended for the carriage of toxic gases of Class 2 (groups starting with letter T according to 2.2.2.1.3) shall be limited to 1 000 litres water capacity;

C

"Calculation pressure" means a theoretical pressure at least equal to the test pressure which, according to the degree of danger exhibited by the substance being carried, may to a greater or lesser degree exceed the working pressure. It is used solely to determine the thickness of the walls of the shell, independently of any external or internal reinforcing device (see also *"Discharge pressure"*, *"Filling pressure"*, *"Maximum working pressure (gauge pressure)"* and *"Test pressure"*);

NOTE: For portable tanks, see Chapter 6.7.

"Capacity of shell or shell compartment" for tanks, means the total inner volume of the shell or shell compartment expressed in litres or cubic metres. When it is impossible to completely fill the shell or the shell compartment because of its shape or construction, this reduced capacity shall be used for the determination of the degree of filling and for the marking of the tank;

"Carriage" means the change of place of dangerous goods, including stops made necessary by transport conditions and including any period spent by the dangerous goods in vehicles, tanks and containers made necessary by traffic conditions before, during and after the change of place.

This definition also covers the intermediate temporary storage of dangerous goods in order to change the mode or means of transport (transshipment). This shall apply provided that transport documents showing the place of dispatch and the place of reception are presented on request and provided that packages and tanks are not opened during intermediate storage, except to be checked by the competent authorities;

"Carriage in bulk" means the carriage of unpackaged solids or articles in vehicles or containers. The term does not apply to packaged goods nor to substances carried in tanks;

"Carrier" means the enterprise which carries out the transport operation with or without a transport contract;

"CGA" means the Compressed Gas Association (CGA, 4221 Walney Road, 5th Floor, Chantilly VA 20151-2923, United States of America);

"Closed container", see *"Container"*;

"Closed vehicle" means a vehicle having a body capable of being closed;

"Closure" means a device which closes an opening in a receptacle;

"Collective entry" means an entry for a well defined group of substances or articles (see 2.1.1.2, B, C and D);

"Combination packaging" means a combination of packagings for transport purposes, consisting of one or more inner packagings secured in an outer packing in accordance with 4.1.1.5;

NOTE: *The "inners" of "combination packagings" are always termed "inner packagings" and not "inner receptacles". A glass bottle is an example of such an "inner packaging".*

"Combustion heater" means a device directly using liquid or gaseous fuel and not using the waste heat from the engine used for propulsion of the vehicle;

"Competent authority" means the authority or authorities or any other body or bodies designated as such in each State and in each specific case in accordance with domestic law;

"Compliance assurance" (radioactive material) means a systematic programme of measures applied by a competent authority which is aimed at ensuring that the requirements of ADR are met in practice;

"Composite IBC with plastics inner receptacle" means an IBC comprising structural equipment in the form of a rigid outer casing encasing a plastics inner receptacle together with any service or other structural equipment. It is so constructed that the inner receptacle

and outer casing once assembled form, and are used as, an integrated single unit to be filled, stored, transported or emptied as such;

NOTE: "Plastics material", when used in connection with inner receptacles for composite IBCs, is taken to include other polymeric materials such as rubber.

"Composite packaging (plastics material)" is a packaging consisting of an inner plastics receptacle and an outer packaging (made of metal, fibreboard, plywood, etc.). Once assembled such a packaging remains thereafter an inseparable unit; it is filled, stored, despatched and emptied as such;

NOTE: See NOTE under "Composite packagings (glass, porcelain or stoneware)".

"Composite packaging (glass, porcelain or stoneware)" is a packaging consisting of an inner glass, porcelain or stoneware receptacle and an outer packaging (made of metal, wood, fibreboard, plastics material, expanded plastics material, etc.). Once assembled, such a packaging remains thereafter an inseparable unit; it is filled, stored, despatched and emptied as such;

NOTE: The "inners" of "composite packagings" are normally termed "inner receptacles". For example, the "inner" of a 6HA1 (composite packaging, plastics material) is such an "inner receptacle" since it is normally not designed to perform a containment function without its "outer packaging" and is not therefore an "inner packaging".

"Confinement system", for the carriage of Class 7 material, means the assembly of fissile material and packaging components specified by the designer and agreed to by the competent authority as intended to preserve criticality safety;

"Conformity assessment" means the process of verifying the conformity of a product according to the provisions of sections 1.8.6 and 1.8.7 related to type approval, supervision of manufacture and initial inspection and testing;

"Consignee" means the consignee according to the contract for carriage. If the consignee designates a third party in accordance with the provisions applicable to the contract for carriage, this person shall be deemed to be the consignee within the meaning of ADR. If the transport operation takes place without a contract for carriage, the enterprise which takes charge of the dangerous goods on arrival shall be deemed to be the consignee;

"Consignment" means any package or packages, or load of dangerous goods, presented by a consignor for carriage;

"Consignor" means the enterprise which consigns dangerous goods either on its own behalf or for a third party. If the transport operation is carried out under a contract for carriage, consignor means the consignor according to the contract for carriage;

"Container" means an article of transport equipment (lift van or other similar structure):

-       of a permanent character and accordingly strong enough to be suitable for repeated use;

-       specially designed to facilitate the carriage of goods, by one or more means of transport, without breakage of load;

-       fitted with devices permitting its ready stowage and handling, particularly when being transloaded from one means of transport to another;

-　so designed as to be easy to fill and empty;

-　having an internal volume of not less than 1 m3, except for containers for the carriage of radioactive material.

In addition:

"Small container" means a container which has either any overall outer dimension (length, width or height) less than 1.5 m, or an internal volume of not more than 3 m^3;

"Large container" means

(a)　A container which does not meet the definition of a small container;

(b)　In the meaning of the CSC, a container of a size such that the area enclosed by the four outer bottom corners is either

(i)　at least 14 m^2 (150 square feet); or

(ii)　at least 7 m^2 (75 square feet) if fitted with top corner fittings;

"Closed container" means a totally enclosed container having a rigid roof, rigid side walls, rigid end walls and a floor. The term includes containers with an opening roof where the roof can be closed during transport;

"Open container" means an open top container or a platform based container;

"Sheeted container" means an open container equipped with a sheet to protect the goods loaded;

A *"swap body"* is a container which, in accordance with EN 283:1991 has the following characteristics:

-　from the point of view of mechanical strength, it is only built for carriage on a wagon or a vehicle on land or by roll-on roll-of ship;

-　it cannot be stacked;

-　it can be removed from vehicles by means of equipment on board the vehicle and on its own supports, and can be reloaded;

NOTE: *The term "container" does not cover conventional packagings, IBCs, tank-containers or vehicles. Nevertheless, a container may be used as a packaging for the carriage of radioactive material.*

"Containment system", for the carriage of Class 7 material, means the assembly of components of the packaging specified by the designer as intended to retain the radioactive material during carriage;

"Control temperature" means the maximum temperature at which the organic peroxide or the self-reactive substance can be safely carried;

"Criticality safety index (CSI) assigned to a package, overpack or container containing fissile material", for the carriage of Class 7 material, means a number which is used to provide control over the accumulation of packages, overpacks or containers containing fissile material;

"CSC" means the International Convention for Safe Containers (Geneva, 1972) as amended and published by the International Maritime Organization (IMO), London;

"Crate" means an outer packaging with incomplete surfaces;

"Critical temperature" means the temperature above which the substance cannot exist in the liquid state;

"Cryogenic receptacle" means a transportable thermally insulated pressure receptacle for refrigerated liquefied gases of a water capacity of not more than 1 000 litres;

"Cylinder" means a transportable pressure receptacle of a water capacity not exceeding 150 litres (see also *"Bundle of cylinders"*);

D

"Dangerous goods" means those substances and articles the carriage of which is prohibited by ADR, or authorized only under the conditions prescribed therein;

"Dangerous reaction" means:

(a)   Combustion or evolution of considerable heat;

(b)   Evolution of flammable, asphyxiant, oxidizing or toxic gases;

(c)   The formation of corrosive substances;

(d)   The formation of unstable substances; or

(e)   Dangerous rise in pressure (for tanks only);

"Demountable tank" means a tank, other than a fixed tank, a portable tank, a tank-container or an element of a battery-vehicle or a MEGC which has a capacity of more than 450 litres, is not designed for the carriage of goods without breakage of load, and normally can only be handled when it is empty;

"Design", for the carriage of Class 7 material, means the description of special form radioactive material, low dispersible radioactive material, package or packaging which enables such an item to be fully identified. The description may include specifications, engineering drawings, reports demonstrating compliance with regulatory requirements, and other relevant documentation;

"Discharge pressure" means the maximum pressure actually built up in the tank when it is being discharged under pressure (see also *"Calculation pressure"*, *"Filling pressure"*, *"Maximum working pressure (gauge pressure)"* and *"Test pressure"*);

"Drum" means a flat-ended or convex-ended cylindrical packaging made out of metal, fibreboard, plastics, plywood or other suitable materials. This definition also includes packagings of other shapes, e.g. round, taper-necked packagings or pail-shaped packagings. Wooden barrels and jerricans are not covered by this definition;

E

"EC Directive" means provisions decided by the competent institutions of the European Community and which are binding, as to the result to be achieved, upon each Member State to which it is addressed, but shall leave to the national authorities the choice of form and methods;

"ECE Regulation" means a regulation annexed to the Agreement concerning the adoption of uniform technical prescriptions for wheeled vehicles equipment and parts which can be fitted and or used on wheeled vehicles and the conditions for reciprocal recognition of approvals granted on the basis of these prescriptions (1958 Agreement, as amended);

"Emergency temperature" means the temperature at which emergency procedures shall be implemented in the event of loss of temperature control;

"EN" (standard) means a European standard published by the European Committee for Standardization (CEN) (CEN – 36 rue de Stassart. B-1050 Brussels);

"Enterprise" means any natural person, any legal person, whether profit-making or not, any association or group of persons without legal personality, whether profit-making or not, or any official body, whether it has legal personality itself or is dependent upon an authority that has such personality;

"Exclusive use", for the carriage of Class 7 material, means the sole use, by a single consignor, of a vehicle or of a large container, in respect of which all initial, intermediate and final loading and unloading is carried out in accordance with the directions of the consignor or consignee;

F

"Fibreboard IBC" means a fibreboard body with or without separate top and bottom caps, if necessary an inner liner (but no inner packagings), and appropriate service and structural equipment;

"Filler" means any enterprise which loads dangerous goods into a tank (tank-vehicle, demountable tank, portable tank or tank-container) and/or into a vehicle, large container or small container for carriage in bulk, or into a battery-vehicle or MEGC;

"Filling pressure" means the maximum pressure actually built up in the tank when it is being filled under pressure (see also *"Calculation pressure"*, *"Discharge pressure"*, *"Maximum working pressure (gauge pressure)"* and *"Test pressure"*);

"Filling ratio" means the ratio of the mass of gas to the mass of water at 15 °C that would fill completely a pressure receptacle fitted ready for use;

"Fixed tank" means a tank having a capacity of more than 1 000 litres which is permanently attached to a vehicle (which then becomes a tank-vehicle) or is an integral part of the frame of such vehicle;

"Flammable component" (for aerosols) means flammable liquids, flammable solids or flammable gases and gas mixtures as defined in Notes 1 to 3 of sub-section 31.1.3 of Part III of the Manual of Tests and Criteria. This designation does not cover pyrophoric, self-heating or water-reactive substances. The chemical heat of combustion shall be determined by one of the following methods ASTM D 240, ISO/FDIS 13943:1999 (E/F) 86.1 to 86.3 or NFPA 30B;

"Flash-point" means the lowest temperature of a liquid at which its vapours form a flammable mixture with air;

"Flexible IBC" means a body constituted of film, woven fabric or any other flexible material or combinations thereof, and if necessary, an inner coating or liner, together with any appropriate service equipment and handling devices;

"Full load" means any load originating from one consignor for which the use of a vehicle or of a large container is exclusively reserved and all operations for the loading and unloading of which are carried out in conformity with the instructions of the consignor or of the consignee;

NOTE: *The corresponding term for Class 7 is "exclusive use".*

G

"Gas" means a substance which:

(a)   At 50 °C has a vapour pressure greater than 300 kPa (3 bar); or

(b)   Is completely gaseous at 20 °C under standard pressure of 101.3 kPa;

"Gas cartridge" means any non-refillable receptacle containing, under pressure, a gas or a mixture of gases. It may be fitted with a valve;

"GHS" means the second revised edition of the Globally Harmonized System of Classification and Labelling of Chemicals, published by the United Nations as document ST/SG/AC.10/30/Rev.2;

H

"Handling device" (for flexible IBCs) means any sling, loop, eye or frame attached to the body of the IBC or formed from the continuation of the IBC body material;

"Hermetically closed tank" means a tank intended for the carriage of liquid substances with a calculation pressure of at least 4 bar or intended for the carriage of solid substances (powdery or granular) regardless of its calculation pressure, the openings of which are hermetically closed and which:

-        is not equipped with safety valves, bursting discs, other similar safety devices or vacuum valves; or

-        is not equipped with safety valves, bursting discs or other similar safety devices, but is equipped with vacuum valves, in accordance with the requirements of 6.8.2.2.3; or

-        is equipped with safety valves preceded by a bursting disc according to 6.8.2.2.10, but is not equipped with vacuum valves; or

-        is equipped with safety valves preceded by a bursting disc according to 6.8.2.2.10 and vacuum valves, in accordance with the requirements of 6.8.2.2.3;

I

"IAEA" means the International Atomic Energy Agency (IAEA), (IAEA, P.O. Box 100 – A - 1400 Vienna);

"IBC", see *"Intermediate bulk container"*;

"ICAO" means the International Civil Aviation Organization (ICAO, 999 University Street, Montreal, Quebec H3C 5H7, Canada);

"ICAO Technical Instructions" means the Technical Instructions for the Safe Transport of Dangerous Goods by Air, which complement Annex 18 to the Chicago Convention on

International Civil Aviation (Chicago 1944), published by the International Civil Aviation Organization (ICAO) in Montreal;

"IMDG Code" means the International Maritime Dangerous Goods Code, for the implementation of Chapter VII, Part A, of the International Convention for the Safety of Life at Sea, 1974 (SOLAS Convention), published by the International Maritime Organization (IMO), London;

"IMO" means the International Maritime Organization (IMO, 4 Albert Embankment, London SE1 7SR, United Kingdom);

"Inner packaging" means a packaging for which an outer packaging is required for carriage;

"Inner receptacle" means a receptacle which requires an outer packaging in order to perform its containment function;

"Inspection body" means an independent inspection and testing body approved by the competent authority;

"Intermediate bulk container" *(IBC)* means a rigid, or flexible portable packaging, other than those specified in Chapter 6.1, that:

(a)   Has a capacity of:

    (i)   not more than 3 m^3 for solids and liquids of packing groups II and III;

    (ii)   not more than 1.5 m^3 for solids of packing group I when packed in flexible, rigid plastics, composite, fibreboard and wooden IBCs;

    (iii)   not more than 3 m^3 for solids of packing group I when packed in metal IBCs;

    (iv)   not more than 3 m^3 for radioactive material of Class 7;

(b)   Is designed for mechanical handling;

(c)   Is resistant to the stresses produced in handling and transport as determined by the tests specified in Chapter 6.5;

(see also *"Composite IBC with plastics inner receptacle"*, *"Fibreboard IBC"*, *"Flexible IBC"*, *"Metal IBC"*, *"Rigid plastics IBC"* and *"Wooden IBC"*).

NOTE 1:   *Portable tanks or tank-containers that meet the requirements of Chapter 6.7 or 6.8 respectively are not considered to be intermediate bulk containers (IBCs).*

NOTE 2:   *Intermediate bulk containers (IBCs) which meet the requirements of Chapter 6.5 are not considered to be containers for the purposes of ADR.*

"Remanufactured IBC" means a metal, rigid plastics or composite IBC that:

(a)   Is produced as a UN type from a non-UN type; or

(b)   Is converted from one UN design type to another UN design type.

Remanufactured IBCs are subject to the same requirements of ADR that apply to new IBCs of the same type (see also design type definition in 6.5.6.1.1);

"Repaired IBC" means a metal, rigid plastics or composite IBC that, as a result of impact or for any other cause (e.g. corrosion, embrittlement or other evidence of reduced strength as compared to the design type) is restored so as to conform to the design type and to be able to withstand the design type tests. For the purposes of ADR, the replacement of the rigid inner receptacle of a composite IBC with a receptacle conforming to the original manufacturer's specification is considered repair. However, routine maintenance of rigid IBCs is not considered repair. The bodies of rigid plastics IBCs and the inner receptacles of composite IBCs are not repairable. Flexible IBCs are not repairable unless approved by the competent authority;

"Routine maintenance of flexible IBCs" means the routine performance on plastics or textile flexible IBCs of operations, such as:

(a)   Cleaning; or

(b)   Replacement of non-integral components, such as non-integral liners and closure ties, with components conforming to the original manufacturer's specification;

provided that these operations do not adversely affect the containment function of the flexible IBC or alter the design type.

"Routine maintenance of rigid IBCs" means the routine performance on metal, rigid plastics or composite IBCs of operations such as:

(a)   Cleaning;

(b)   Removal and reinstallation or replacement of body closures (including associated gaskets), or of service equipment, conforming to the original manufacturer's specifications, provided that the leaktightness of the IBC is verified; or

(c)   Restoration of structural equipment not directly performing a dangerous goods containment or discharge pressure retention function so as to conform to the design type (e.g. the straightening of legs or lifting attachments) provided that the containment function of the IBC is not affected;

"Intermediate packaging" means a packaging placed between inner packagings or articles, and an outer packaging;

"ISO" (standard) means an international standard published by the International Organization for Standardization (ISO) (ISO - 1, rue de Varembé. CH-1204 Geneva 20);

J

"Jerrican" means a metal or plastics packaging of rectangular or polygonal cross-section with one or more orifices;

L

"Large container ", see *"Container"*;

"Large packaging" means a packaging consisting of an outer packaging which contains articles or inner packagings and which

(a)   Is designed for mechanical handling;

(b)   Exceeds 400 kg net mass or 450 litres capacity but has a volume of not more than 3 m³;

"Leakproofness test" means a test to determine the leakproofness of a tank, a packaging or an IBC and of the equipment and closure devices;

NOTE: *For portable tanks, see Chapter 6.7.*

"Light-gauge metal packaging" means a packaging of circular, elliptical, rectangular or polygonal cross-section (also conical) and taper-necked and pail-shaped packaging made of metal, having a wall thickness of less than 0.5 mm (e.g. tinplate), flat or convex bottomed and with one or more orifices, which is not covered by the definitions for drums or jerricans;

"Liner" means a tube or bag inserted into a packaging, including large packagings or IBCs, but not forming an integral part of it, including the closures of its openings;

"Liquid" means a substance which at 50 °C has a vapour pressure of not more than 300 kPa (3 bar), which is not completely gaseous at 20 °C and 101.3 kPa, and which

(a)   Has a melting point or initial melting point of 20 °C or less at a pressure of 101.3 kPa; or

(b)   Is liquid according to the ASTM D 4359-90 test method; or

(c)   Is not pasty according to the criteria applicable to the test for determining fluidity (penetrometer test) described in 2.3.4;

NOTE: *"Carriage in the liquid state", for the purpose of tank requirements, means:*

-    *Carriage of liquids according to the above definition; or*

-    *Solids handed over for carriage in the molten state.*

"Loader" means any enterprise which loads dangerous goods into a vehicle or large container;

M

"Manual of Tests and Criteria" means the fourth revised edition of the United Nations Recommendations on the Transport of Dangerous Goods, Manual of Tests and Criteria, published by the United Nations Organization (ST/SG/AC.10/11/Rev.4 as amended by documents ST/SG/AC.10/11/Rev.4/Amend.1 and ST/SG/AC.10/11/Rev.4/Amend.2);

"Mass of package" means gross mass of the package unless otherwise stated. The mass of containers and tanks used for the carriage of goods is not included in the gross mass;

"Maximum capacity" means the maximum inner volume of receptacles or packagings including intermediate bulk containers (IBCs) and large packagings expressed in cubic metres or litres;

"Maximum net mass" means the maximum net mass of contents in a single packaging or maximum combined mass of inner packagings and the contents thereof expressed in kilograms;

"Maximum normal operating pressure", for the carriage of Class 7 material, means the maximum pressure above atmospheric pressure at mean sea-level that would develop in the containment system in a period of one year under the conditions of temperature and solar radiation corresponding to environmental conditions in the absence of venting, external cooling by an ancillary system, or operational controls during carriage;

"Maximum permissible gross mass"

(a)   (for all categories of IBCs other than flexible IBCs) means the mass of the IBC and any service or structural equipment together with the maximum net mass;

(b)   (for tanks) means the tare of the tank and the heaviest load authorized for carriage;

NOTE: *For portable tanks, see Chapter 6.7.*

"Maximum permissible load" (for flexible IBCs) means the maximum net mass for which the IBC is intended and which it is authorized to carry;

"Maximum working pressure (gauge pressure)" means the highest of the following three pressures:

(a)   The highest effective pressure allowed in the tank during filling (maximum filling pressure allowed);

(b)   The highest effective pressure allowed in the tank during discharge (maximum discharge pressure allowed); and

(c)   The effective gauge pressure to which the tank is subjected by its contents (including such extraneous gases as it may contain) at the maximum working temperature.

Unless the special requirements prescribed in Chapter 4.3 provide otherwise, the numerical value of this working pressure (gauge pressure) shall not be lower than the vapour pressure (absolute pressure) of the filling substance at 50 °C.

For tanks equipped with safety valves (with or without bursting disc) other than tanks for the carriage of compressed, liquefied or dissolved gases of Class 2, the maximum working pressure (gauge pressure) shall however be equal to the prescribed opening pressure of such safety valves.

(See also *"Calculation pressure"*, *"Discharge pressure"*, *"Filling pressure"* and *"Test pressure"*);

NOTE 1:   *For portable tanks, see Chapter 6.7.*

NOTE 2:   *For closed cryogenic receptacles, see NOTE to 6.2.1.3.6.5.*

"MEGC", see *"Multiple-element gas container"*;

"Member of a vehicle crew" means a driver or any other person accompanying the driver for safety, security, training or operational reasons;

"MEMU", see *"Mobile explosives manufacturing unit"*;

"Metal IBC" means a metal body together with appropriate service and structural equipment;

"Mild steel" means a steel having a minimum tensile strength between 360 N/mm^2 and 440 N/mm^2;

NOTE: For portable tanks, see Chapter 6.7.

"Mobile explosives manufacturing unit" (MEMU) means a unit, or a vehicle mounted with a unit, for manufacturing and charging explosives from dangerous goods that are not explosives. The unit consists of various tanks and bulk containers and process equipment as well as pumps and related equipment. The MEMU may have special compartments for packaged explosives;

NOTE: Even though the definition of MEMU includes the expression "manufacturing and charging explosives" the requirements for MEMUs apply only to carriage and not to manufacturing and charging of explosives.

"Multiple-element gas container" (MEGC) means a unit containing elements which are linked to each other by a manifold and mounted on a frame. The following elements are considered to be elements of a multiple-element gas container: cylinders, tubes, pressure drums and bundles of cylinders as well as tanks for the carriage of gases of Class 2 having a capacity of more than 450 litres;

NOTE: For UN MEGCs, see Chapter 6.7.

N

"Nominal capacity of the receptacle" means the nominal volume of the dangerous substance contained in the receptacle expressed in litres. For compressed gas cylinders the nominal capacity shall be the water capacity of the cylinder;

"N.O.S. entry (not otherwise specified entry)" means a collective entry to which substances, mixtures, solutions or articles may be assigned if they:

(a)   Are not mentioned by name in Table A of Chapter 3.2; and

(b)   Exhibit chemical, physical and/or dangerous properties corresponding to the Class, classification code, packing group and the name and description of the n.o.s. entry;

O

"Offshore bulk container" means a bulk container specially designed for repeated use for carriage to, from and between offshore facilities. An offshore bulk container is designed and constructed in accordance with the guidelines for the approval of offshore containers handled in open seas specified by the International Maritime Organization (IMO) in document MSC/Circ.860;

"Open container", see *"Container"*;

"Open vehicle" means a vehicle the platform of which has no superstructure or is merely provided with side boards and a tailboard;

"Outer packaging" means the outer protection of the composite or combination packaging together with any absorbent materials, cushioning and any other components necessary to contain and protect inner receptacles or inner packagings;

"Overpack" means an enclosure used (by a single consignor in the case of Class 7) to contain one or more packages, consolidated into a single unit easier to handle and stow during carriage;

Examples of overpacks:

(a)   A loading tray such as a pallet, on which several packages are placed or stacked and secured by a plastics strip, shrink or stretch wrapping or other appropriate means; or

(b)   An outer protective packaging such as a box or a crate;

P

"Package" means the complete product of the packing operation, consisting of the packaging or large packaging or IBC and its contents prepared for dispatch. The term includes receptacles for gases as defined in this section as well as articles which, because of their size, mass or configuration may be carried unpackaged or carried in cradles, crates or handling devices. Except for the carriage of radioactive material, the term does not apply to goods which are carried in bulk, nor to substances carried in tanks;

NOTE: For radioactive material, see 2.2.7.2, 4.1.9.1.1 and Chapter 6.4.

"Packaging" means one or more receptacles and any other components or materials necessary for the receptacles to perform their containment and other safety functions (see also *"Combination packaging"*, *"Composite packaging (plastics material)"*, *"Composite packaging (glass, porcelain or stoneware)"*, *"Inner packaging"*, *"Intermediate bulk container (IBC)"*, *"Intermediate packaging"*, *"Large packaging"*, *"Light-gauge metal packaging"*, *"Outer packaging"*, *"Reconditioned packaging"*, *"Remanufactured packaging"*, *"Reused packaging"*, *"Salvage packaging"* and *"Sift-proof packaging")*;

"Packer" means any enterprise which puts dangerous goods into packagings, including large packagings and intermediate bulk containers (IBCs) and, where necessary, prepares packages for carriage;

"Packing group" means a group to which, for packing purposes, certain substances may be assigned in accordance with their degree of danger. The packing groups have the following meanings which are explained more fully in Part 2:

Packing group I: Substances presenting high danger;
Packing group II: Substances presenting medium danger; and
Packing group III: Substances presenting low danger;

NOTE: Certain articles containing dangerous goods are assigned to a packing group.

"Portable tank" means a multimodal tank having, when used for the carriage of Class 2 substances, a capacity of more than 450 litres in accordance with the definitions in Chapter 6.7 or the IMDG Code and indicated by a portable tank instruction (T-Code) in Column (10) of Table A of Chapter 3.2;

"Portable tank operator", see *"Tank-container/portable tank operator"*;

"Pressure drum" means a welded transportable pressure receptacle of a water capacity exceeding 150 litres and of not more than 1 000 litres, (e.g. cylindrical receptacles equipped with rolling hoops, spheres on skids);"

"Pressure receptacle" means a collective term that includes cylinders, tubes, pressure drums, closed cryogenic receptacles and bundles of cylinders;

"Pressurized gas cartridge", see *"Aerosol or aerosol dispenser"*;

"Protected IBC" (for metal IBCs) means an IBC provided with additional protection against impact, the protection taking the form of, for example, a multi-layer (sandwich) or double-wall construction, or a frame with a metal lattice-work casing;

Q

"Quality assurance" means a systematic programme of controls and inspections applied by any organization or body which is aimed at providing confidence that the safety prescriptions in ADR are met in practice;

R

"Radiation level", for the carriage of Class 7 material, means the corresponding dose rate expressed in millisieverts per hour;

"Radioactive contents", for the carriage of Class 7 material, mean the radioactive material together with any contaminated or activated solids, liquids, and gases within the packaging;

"Receptacle" (Class 1) includes boxes, bottles, cans, drums, jars and tubes, including any means of closure used in the inner or intermediate packaging;

"Receptacle" means a containment vessel for receiving and holding substances or articles, including any means of closing. This definition does not apply to shells (see also *"Cryogenic receptacle"*, *"Inner receptacle"*, *"Pressure receptacle"*, *"Rigid inner receptacle"* and *"Gas cartridge"*);

"Reconditioned packaging" means in particular

(a) Metal drums that are:

    (i) cleaned to original materials of construction, with all former contents, internal and external corrosion, and external coatings and labels removed;

    (ii) restored to original shape and contour, with chimes (if any) straightened and sealed and all non-integral gaskets replaced; and

    (iii) inspected after cleaning but before painting, with rejection of packagings with visible pitting, significant reduction in the material thickness, metal fatigue, damaged threads or closures or other significant defects;

(b) Plastics drums and jerricans that:

    (i) are cleaned to original materials of construction, with all former contents, external coatings and labels removed;

    (ii) have all non-integral gaskets replaced; and

    (iii) are inspected after cleaning with rejection of packagings with visible damage such as tears, creases or cracks, or damaged threads or closures or other significant defects;

"Recycled plastics material" means material recovered from used industrial packagings that has been cleaned and prepared for processing into new packagings;

"Reel" (Class 1) means a device made of plastics, wood, fibreboard, metal or other suitable material comprising a central spindle with, or without, side walls at each end of the spindle. Articles and substances can be wound onto the spindle and may be retained by side walls;

"Reference steel" means a steel with a tensile strength of 370 N/mm^2 and an elongation at fracture of 27%;

"Remanufactured IBC", see *"Intermediate Bulk Container (IBC)"*;

"Remanufactured packaging" means in particular

(a)   Metal drums that:

      (i)   are produced as a UN type complying with the requirements of Chapter 6.1 from a non-UN type;

      (ii)   are converted from one UN type complying with the requirements of Chapter 6.1 to another UN type; or

      (iii)   undergo the replacement of integral structural components (such as non-removable heads);

(b)   Plastics drums that:

      (i)   are converted from one UN type to another UN type (e.g. 1H1 to 1H2); or

      (ii)   undergo the replacement of integral structural components.

Remanufactured drums are subject to the requirements of Chapter 6.1 which apply to new drums of the same type;

"Repaired IBC", see *"Intermediate Bulk Container (IBC)"*;

"Reused packaging" means a packaging which has been examined and found free of defects affecting the ability to withstand the performance tests. The term includes those which are refilled with the same or similar compatible contents and are carried within distribution chains controlled by the consignor of the product;

"RID" means Regulations concerning the International Carriage of Dangerous Goods by Rail (Appendix C of COTIF (Convention concerning international carriage by rail));

"Rigid inner receptacle" (for composite IBCs) means a receptacle which retains its general shape when empty without its closures in place and without benefit of the outer casing. Any inner receptacle that is not "rigid" is considered to be "flexible";

"Rigid plastics IBC" means a rigid plastics body, which may have structural equipment together with appropriate service equipment;

"Routine maintenance of flexible IBCs", see *"Intermediate Bulk Container (IBC)"*;

"Routine maintenance of rigid IBCs", see *"Intermediate Bulk Container (IBC)"*;

S

"Safety valve" means a spring-loaded device which is activated automatically by pressure the purpose of which is to protect the tank against unacceptable excess internal pressure;

"SADT" see *"Self-accelerating decomposition temperature"*;

"Salvage packaging" means a special packaging into which damaged, defective or leaking dangerous goods packages, or dangerous goods that have spilled or leaked are placed for purposes of carriage for recovery or disposal;

"Self-accelerating decomposition temperature" (SADT), means the lowest temperature at which self-accelerating decomposition may occur with substance in the packaging as used during carriage. Provisions for determining the SADT and the effects of heating under confinement are contained in Part II of the Manual of Tests and Criteria;

"Service equipment"

(a)   Of the tank means filling and emptying, venting, safety, heating and heat insulating devices and measuring instruments;

(b)   Of the elements of a battery-vehicle or of a MEGC means filling and emptying devices, including the manifold, safety devices and measuring instruments;

(c)   Of an IBC means the filling and discharge devices and any pressure-relief or venting, safety, heating and heat insulating devices and measuring instruments;

NOTE: For portable tanks, see Chapter 6.7.

"Settled pressure" means the pressure of the contents of a pressure receptacle in thermal and diffusive equilibrium;

"Sheeted container", see *"Container"*;

"Sheeted vehicle" means an open vehicle provided with a sheet to protect the load;

"Shell" means the sheathing containing the substance (including the openings and their closures);

NOTE 1: This definition does not apply to receptacles.

NOTE 2: For portable tanks, see Chapter 6.7.

"Sift-proof packaging" means a packaging impermeable to dry contents, including fine solid material produced during carriage;

"Small container", see *"Container"*;

"Small receptacle containing gas", see *"Gas cartridge"*;

"Solid" means:

(a)   A substance with a melting point or initial melting point of more than 20 °C at a pressure of 101.3 kPa; or

(b)   A substance which is not liquid according to the ASTM D 4359-90 test method or which is pasty according to the criteria applicable to the test for determining fluidity (penetrometer test) described in 2.3.4;

"Structural equipment"

(a)   For tanks of a tank-vehicle or demountable tank, means the external or internal reinforcing, fastening, protective or stabilizing members of the shell;

(b)   For tanks of a tank-container, means the external or internal reinforcing, fastening, protective or stabilizing members of the shell;

(c)   For elements of a battery-vehicle or an MEGC means the external or internal reinforcing, fastening, protective or stabilizing members of the shell or receptacle;

(d)   For IBCs other than flexible IBCs means the reinforcing, fastening, handling, protective or stabilizing members of the body (including the base pallet for composite IBCs with plastics inner receptacle);

NOTE: For portable tanks, see Chapter 6.7.

"Swap-body", see *"Container"*;

T

"Tank" means a shell, including its service and structural equipment. When used alone, the term tank means a tank-container, portable tank, demountable tank or fixed tank as defined in this Part, including tanks forming elements of battery-vehicles or MEGCs (see also *"Demountable tank"*, *"Fixed tank"*, *"Portable tank"* and *"Multiple-element gas container"*);

NOTE: For portable tanks, see 6.7.4.1.

"Tank-container" means an article of transport equipment meeting the definition of a container, and comprising a shell and items of equipment, including the equipment to facilitate movement of the tank-container without significant change of attitude, used for the carriage of gases, liquid, powdery or granular substances and, when used for the carriage of Class 2 substances, having a capacity of more than 0.45 m^3 (450 litres);

NOTE: IBCs which meet the requirements of Chapter 6.5 are not considered to be tank-containers.

"Tank-container/portable tank operator" means any enterprise in whose name the tank-container/portable tank is registered;

"Tank record" means a file containing all the important technical information concerning a tank, a battery-vehicle or a MEGC, such as certificates referred to in 6.8.2.3, 6.8.2.4 and 6.8.3.4;

"Tank swap body" is considered to be a tank-container;

"Tank-vehicle" means a vehicle built to carry liquids, gases or powdery or granular substances and comprising one or more fixed tanks. In addition to the vehicle proper, or the units of running gear used in its stead, a tank-vehicle comprises one or more shells, their items of equipment and the fittings for attaching them to the vehicle or to the running-gear units;

"Technical name" means a recognized chemical name, if relevant a biological name, or other name currently used in scientific and technical handbooks, journals and texts (see 3.1.2.8.1.1);

"Test pressure" means the required pressure applied during a pressure test for initial or periodic inspection (see also *"Calculation pressure"*, *"Discharge pressure"*, *"Filling pressure"* and *"Maximum working pressure (gauge pressure)"*);

NOTE: *For portable tanks, see Chapter 6.7.*

"Transport index (TI) assigned to a package, overpack or container, or to unpackaged LSA-I or SCO-I", for the carriage of Class 7 material, means a number which is used to provide control over radiation exposure;

"Transport unit" means a motor vehicle without an attached trailer, or a combination consisting of a motor vehicle and an attached trailer;

"Tray" (Class 1) means a sheet of metal, plastics, fibreboard or other suitable material which is placed in the inner, intermediate or outer packaging and achieves a close-fit in such packaging. The surface of the tray may be shaped so that packagings or articles can be inserted, held secure and separated from each other;

"Tube" (Class 2) means a seamless transportable pressure receptacle of a water capacity exceeding 150 litres and of not more than 3 000 litres;

U

"UIC" means the International Union of Railways (UIC, 16 rue Jean Rey, F-75015 Paris, France);

"UNECE" means the United Nations Economic Commission for Europe (UNECE, Palais des Nations, 8-14 avenue de la Paix, CH-1211 Geneva 10, Switzerland);

"Undertaking", see *"Enterprise"*;

"UN Model Regulations" means the Model Regulations annexed to the fifteenth revised edition of the Recommendations on the Transport of Dangerous Goods published by the United Nations (ST/SG/AC.10/1/Rev.15);

"UN number" means the four-figure identification number of the substance or article taken from the UN Model Regulations;

V

"Vacuum-operated waste tank" means a fixed tank, demountable tank, tank-container or tank swap body primarily used for the carriage of dangerous wastes, with special constructional features and/or equipment to facilitate the loading and unloading of wastes as specified in Chapter 6.10. A tank which fully complies with the requirements of Chapter 6.7 or 6.8 is not considered to be a vacuum-operated waste tank;

"Vacuum valve" means a spring-loaded device which is activated automatically by pressure the purpose of which is to protect the tank against unacceptable negative internal pressure;

"Vehicle" see *"Battery-vehicle"*, *"Closed vehicle"*, *"Open vehicle"*, *"Sheeted vehicle"* and *"Tank-vehicle"*;

W

"Wastes" means substances, solutions, mixtures or articles for which no direct use is envisaged but which are transported for reprocessing, dumping, elimination by incineration or other methods of disposal;

"Wooden barrel" means a packaging made of natural wood, of round cross-section, having convex walls, consisting of staves and heads and fitted with hoops;

"Wooden IBC" means a rigid or collapsible wooden body, together with an inner liner (but no inner packaging) and appropriate service and structural equipment;

"Working pressure" means the settled pressure of a compressed gas at a reference temperature of 15 °C in a full pressure receptacle;

NOTE: *For tanks, see "Maximum working pressure".*

"Woven plastics" (for flexible IBCs) means a material made from stretch tapes or monofilaments of suitable plastics material.

1.2.2   Units of measurement

1.2.2.1   The following units of measurement [a] are applicable in ADR:

Measurement of	SI Unit [b]	Acceptable alternative unit	Relationship between units
Length	m (metre)	-	-
Area	m^2 (square metre)	-	-
Volume	m^3 (cubic metre)	l [c] (litre)	1 l = 10^{-3} m^3
Time	s (second)	min (minute)	1 min = 60 s
		h (hour)	1 h = 3 600 s
		d (day)	1 d = 86 400 s
Mass	kg (kilogram)	g (gramme)	1g = 10^{-3} kg
		t (ton)	1 t = 10^3 kg
Mass density	kg/m^3	kg/l	1 kg/l = 10^3 kg/m^3
Temperature	K (kelvin)	°C (degree Celsius)	0 °C = 273.15 K
Temperature difference	K (kelvin)	°C (degree Celsius)	1 °C = 1 K
Force	N (newton)	-	1 N = 1 kg.m/s^2
Pressure	Pa (pascal)		1 Pa = 1 N/m^2
		bar (bar)	1 bar = 10^5 Pa
Stress	N/m^2	N/mm^2	1 N/mm^2 = 1 MPa
Work		kWh (kilowatt hours)	1 kWh = 3.6 MJ
Energy	J (joule)		1 J = 1 N.m = 1 W.s
Quantity of heat		eV (electronvolt)	1 eV = 0.1602 H 10^{-18}J
Power	W (watt)	-	1 W = 1 J/s = 1 N.m/s
Kinematic viscosity	m^2/s	mm^2/s	1 mm^2/s = 10^{-6} m^2/s
Dynamic viscosity	Pa.s	mPa.s	1 mPa.s = 10^{-3} Pa.s
Activity	Bq (becquerel)		
Dose equivalent	Sv (sievert)		

[a]   *The following round figures are applicable for the conversion of the units hitherto used into SI Units.*

Force
1 kg   =   9.807 N
1 N   =   0.102 kg

Stress
1 kg/mm^2 =   9.807 N/mm^2
1 N/mm^2 =   0.102 kg/mm^2

Pressure
1 Pa   =   1 N/m^2 =   10^{-5} bar   =   1.02 × 10^{-5} kg/cm^2 = 0.75 × 10^{-2} torr
1 bar   =   10^5 Pa   =   1.02 kg/cm^2 =   750 torr
1 kg/cm^2 =   9.807 × 10^4 Pa   =   0.9807 bar   =   736 torr
1 torr   =   1.33 × 10^2 Pa   =   1.33 × 10^{-3} bar   =   1.36 × 10^{-3} kg/cm^2

Energy, Work, Quantity of heat
1 J   =   1 N.m   =   0.278 × 10^{-6} kWh   =   0.102 kgm   = 0.239 × 10^{-3} kcal
1 kWh   =   3.6 × 10^6 J   =   367 × 10^3 kgm   =   860 kcal
1 kgm   =   9.807 J   =   2.72 × 10^{-6} kWh   =   2.34 × 10^{-3} kcal
1 kcal   =   4.19 × 10^3 J   =   1.16 × 10^{-3} kWh   =   427 kgm

Power
1 W   =   0.102 kgm/s   =   0.86 kcal/h
1 kgm/s   =   9.807 W   =   8.43 kcal/h
1 kcal/h   =   1.16 W   =   0.119 kgm/s

Kinematic viscosity
1 m^2/s   =   10^4 St (Stokes)
1 St   =   10^{-4} m^2/s

Dynamic viscosity
1 Pa.s   =   1 N.s/m^2 =   10 P (poise)   =   0.102 kg.s/m^2
1 P   =   0.1 Pa.s   =   0.1 N.s/m^2 =   1.02 × 10^{-2} kg.s/m^2
1 kg.s/m^2 =   9.807 Pa.s   =   9.807 N.s/m^2 =   98.07 P

The decimal multiples and sub-multiples of a unit may be formed by prefixes or symbols, having the following meanings, placed before the name or symbol of the unit:

Factor		Prefix	Symbol
1 000 000 000 000 000 000	$= 10^{18}$	quintillion	exa	E
1 000 000 000 000 000	$= 10^{15}$	quadrillion	peta	P
1 000 000 000 000	$= 10^{12}$	trillion	tera	T
1 000 000 000	$= 10^{9}$	billion	giga	G
1 000 000	$= 10^{6}$	million	mega	M
1 000	$= 10^{3}$	thousand	kilo	k
100	$= 10^{2}$	hundred	hecto	h
10	$= 10^{1}$	ten	deca	da
0.1	$= 10^{-1}$	tenth	deci	d
0.01	$= 10^{-2}$	hundredth	centi	c
0.001	$= 10^{-3}$	thousandth	milli	m
0.000 001	$= 10^{-6}$	millionth	micro	μ
0.000 000 001	$= 10^{-9}$	billionth	nano	n
0.000 000 000 001	$= 10^{-12}$	trillionth	pico	p
0.000 000 000 000 001	$= 10^{-15}$	quadrillionth	femto	f
0.000 000 000 000 000 001	$= 10^{-18}$	quintillionth	atto	a

NOTE: *10^{9} billion is United Nations usage in English. By analogy, so is $10^{-9} = 1$ billionth.*

1.2.2.2   Unless expressly stated otherwise, the sign "%" in ADR represents:

(a)   In the case of mixtures of solids or of liquids, and also in the case of solutions and of solids wetted by a liquid, a percentage mass based on the total mass of the mixture, the solution or the wetted solid;

(b)   In the case of mixtures of compressed gases, when filled by pressure, the proportion of the volume indicated as a percentage of the total volume of the gaseous mixture, or, when filled by mass, the proportion of the mass indicated as a percentage of the total mass of the mixture;

(c)   In the case of mixtures of liquefied gases and dissolved gases, the proportion of the mass indicated as a percentage of the total mass of the mixture.

1.2.2.3   Pressures of all kinds relating to receptacles (such as test pressure, internal pressure, safety valve opening pressure) are always indicated in gauge pressure (pressure in excess of atmospheric pressure); however, the vapour pressure of substances is always expressed in absolute pressure.

1.2.2.4   Where ADR specifies a degree of filling for receptacles, this is always related to a reference temperature of the substances of 15 °C, unless some other temperature is indicated.

CHAPTER 1.3

TRAINING OF PERSONS INVOLVED IN THE CARRIAGE OF DANGEROUS GOODS

1.3.1　**Scope and applicability**

Persons employed by the participants referred to in Chapter 1.4, whose duties concern the carriage of dangerous goods, shall receive training in the requirements governing the carriage of such goods appropriate to their responsibilities and duties. Training requirements specific to security of dangerous goods in Chapter 1.10 shall also be addressed.

NOTE 1:　*With regard to the training for the safety adviser, see 1.8.3.*

NOTE 2:　*With regard to the training of the vehicle crew, see Chapter 8.2.*

NOTE 3:　*For training with regard to Class 7, see also 1.7.2.5.*

NOTE 4:　*The training shall be effected before taking on responsibilities concerning the carriage of dangerous goods.*

1.3.2　**Nature of the training**

The training shall take the following form, appropriate to the responsibility and duties of the individual concerned.

1.3.2.1　*General awareness training*

Personnel shall be familiar with the general requirements of the provisions for the carriage of dangerous goods.

1.3.2.2　*Function-specific training*

Personnel shall receive detailed training, commensurate directly with their duties and responsibilities in the requirements of the regulations concerning the carriage of dangerous goods.

Where the carriage of dangerous goods involves a multimodal transport operation, the personnel shall be made aware of the requirements concerning other transport modes.

1.3.2.3　*Safety training*

Commensurate with the degree of risk of injury or exposure arising from an incident involving the carriage of dangerous goods, including loading and unloading, personnel shall receive training covering the hazards and dangers presented by dangerous goods.

The training provided shall aim to make personnel aware of the safe handling and emergency response procedures.

1.3.2.4　*(Deleted)*

1.3.3   Documentation

Details of all the training undertaken shall be kept by both the employer and the employee and shall be verified upon commencing a new employment. The training shall be periodically supplemented with refresher training to take account of changes in regulations.

CHAPTER 1.4

SAFETY OBLIGATIONS OF THE PARTICIPANTS

1.4.1   General safety measures

1.4.1.1   The participants in the carriage of dangerous goods shall take appropriate measures according to the nature and the extent of foreseeable dangers, so as to avoid damage or injury and, if necessary, to minimize their effects. They shall, in all events, comply with the requirements of ADR in their respective fields.

1.4.1.2   When there is an immediate risk that public safety may be jeopardized, the participants shall immediately notify the emergency services and shall make available to them the information they require to take action.

1.4.1.3   ADR may specify certain of the obligations falling to the various participants.

If a Contracting Party considers that no lessening of safety is involved, it may in its domestic legislation transfer the obligations falling to a specific participant to one or several other participants, provided that the obligations of 1.4.2 and 1.4.3 are met. These derogations shall be communicated by the Contracting Party to the Secretariat of the United Nations Economic Commission for Europe which will bring them to the attention of the Contracting Parties.

The requirements of 1.2.1, 1.4.2 and 1.4.3 concerning the definitions of participants and their respective obligations shall not affect the provisions of domestic law concerning the legal consequences (criminal nature, liability, etc.) stemming from the fact that the participant in question is e.g. a legal entity, a self-employed worker, an employer or an employee.

1.4.2   Obligations of the main participants

NOTE: For radioactive material, see also 1.7.6.

1.4.2.1   *Consignor*

1.4.2.1.1   The consignor of dangerous goods is required to hand over for carriage only consignments which conform to the requirements of ADR. In the context of 1.4.1, he shall in particular:

(a)   Ascertain that the dangerous goods are classified and authorized for carriage in accordance with ADR;

(b)   Furnish the carrier with information and data and, if necessary, the required transport documents and accompanying documents (authorizations, approvals, notifications, certificates, etc.), taking into account in particular the requirements of Chapter 5.4 and of the tables in Part 3;

(c)   Use only packagings, large packagings, intermediate bulk containers (IBCs) and tanks (tank-vehicles, demountable tanks, battery-vehicles, MEGCs, portable tanks and tank-containers) approved for and suited to the carriage of the substances concerned and bearing the markings prescribed by ADR;

(d)   Comply with the requirements on the means of dispatch and on forwarding restrictions;

(e) Ensure that even empty uncleaned and not degassed tanks (tank-vehicles, demountable tanks, battery-vehicles, MEGCs, portable tanks and tank-containers) or empty uncleaned vehicles and large and small bulk containers are appropriately marked and labelled and that empty uncleaned tanks are closed and present the same degree of leakproofness as if they were full.

1.4.2.1.2 If the consignor uses the services of other participants (packer, loader, filler, etc.), he shall take appropriate measures to ensure that the consignment meets the requirements of ADR. He may, however, in the case of 1.4.2.1.1 (a), (b), (c) and (e), rely on the information and data made available to him by other participants.

1.4.2.1.3 When the consignor acts on behalf of a third party, the latter shall inform the consignor in writing that dangerous goods are involved and make available to him all the information and documents he needs to perform his obligations.

1.4.2.2 *Carrier*

1.4.2.2.1 In the context of 1.4.1, where appropriate, the carrier shall in particular:

(a) Ascertain that the dangerous goods to be carried are authorized for carriage in accordance with ADR;

(b) Ascertain that the prescribed documentation is on board the transport unit;

(c) Ascertain visually that the vehicles and loads have no obvious defects, leakages or cracks, missing equipment, etc.;

(d) Ascertain that the date of the next test for tank-vehicles, battery-vehicles, demountable tanks, portable tanks, tank-containers and MEGCs has not expired;

NOTE: *Tanks, battery-vehicles and MEGCs may however be carried after the expiry of this date under the conditions of 4.1.6.10 (in the case of battery-vehicles and MEGCs containing pressure receptacles as elements), 4.2.4.4, 4.3.2.4.4, 6.7.2.19.6, 6.7.3.15.6 or 6.7.4.14.6.*

(e) verify that the vehicles are not overloaded;

(f) ascertain that the danger labels and markings prescribed for the vehicles have been affixed;

(g) ascertain that the equipment prescribed in the written instructions for the driver is on board the vehicle.

Where appropriate, this shall be done on the basis of the transport documents and accompanying documents, by a visual inspection of the vehicle or the containers and, where appropriate, the load.

1.4.2.2.2 The carrier may, however, in the case of 1.4.2.2.1 (a), (b), (e) and (f), rely on information and data made available to him by other participants.

1.4.2.2.3 If the carrier observes an infringement of the requirements of ADR, in accordance with 1.4.2.2.1, he shall not forward the consignment until the matter has been rectified.

1.4.2.2.4 If, during the journey, an infringement which could jeopardize the safety of the operation is observed, the consignment shall be halted as soon as possible bearing in mind the requirements of traffic safety, of the safe immobilisation of the consignment, and of public safety. The transport operation may only be continued once the consignment complies with applicable regulations. The competent authority(ies) concerned by the rest of the journey may grant an authorization to pursue the transport operation.

In case the required compliance cannot be achieved and no authorization is granted for the rest of the journey, the competent authority(ies) shall provide the carrier with the necessary administrative assistance. The same shall apply in case the carrier informs this/these competent authority(ies) that the dangerous nature of the goods carried was not communicated to him by the consignor and that he wishes, by virtue of the law applicable in particular to the contract of carriage, to unload, destroy or render the goods harmless.

1.4.2.2.5   *(Reserved)*

1.4.2.3   *Consignee*

1.4.2.3.1   The consignee has the obligation not to defer acceptance of the goods without compelling reasons and to verify, after unloading, that the requirements of ADR concerning him have been complied with.

In the context of 1.4.1, he shall in particular:

(a)   Carry out in the cases provided for by ADR the prescribed cleaning and decontamination of the vehicles and containers;

(b)   Ensure that the containers once completely unloaded, cleaned and decontaminated, no longer bear danger markings conforming to Chapter 5.3.

1.4.2.3.2   If the consignee makes use of the services of other participants (unloader, cleaner, decontamination facility, etc.) he shall take appropriate measures to ensure that the requirements of ADR have been complied with.

1.4.2.3.3   If these verifications bring to light an infringement of the requirements of ADR, the consignee shall return the container to the carrier only after the infringement has been remedied.

1.4.3   **Obligations of the other participants**

A non-exhaustive list of the other participants and their respective obligations is given below. The obligations of the other participants flow from section 1.4.1 above insofar as they know or should have known that their duties are performed as part of a transport operation subject to ADR.

1.4.3.1   *Loader*

1.4.3.1.1   In the context of 1.4.1, the loader has the following obligations in particular:

(a)   He shall hand the dangerous goods over to the carrier only if they are authorized for carriage in accordance with ADR;

(b)   He shall, when handing over for carriage packed dangerous goods or uncleaned empty packagings, check whether the packaging is damaged. He shall not hand over a package the packaging of which is damaged, especially if it is not leakproof, and there are leakages or the possibility of leakages of the dangerous substance, until the damage has been repaired; this obligation also applies to empty uncleaned packagings;

(c)   He shall, when loading dangerous goods in a vehicle, or a large or small container, comply with the special requirements concerning loading and handling;

(d)   He shall, after loading dangerous goods into a container comply with the requirements concerning danger markings conforming to Chapter 5.3;

(e)   He shall, when loading packages, comply with the prohibitions on mixed loading taking into account dangerous goods already in the vehicle or large container and requirements concerning the separation of foodstuffs, other articles of consumption or animal feedstuffs.

1.4.3.1.2   The loader may, however, in the case of 1.4.3.1.1 (a), (d) and (e), rely on information and data made available to him by other participants.

1.4.3.2   *Packer*

In the context of 1.4.1, the packer shall comply with in particular:

(a)   The requirements concerning packing conditions, or mixed packing conditions; and

(b)   When he prepares packages for carriage, the requirements concerning marking and labelling of the packages.

1.4.3.3   *Filler*

In the context of 1.4.1, the filler has the following obligations in particular:

(a)   He shall ascertain prior to the filling of tanks that both they and their equipment are technically in a satisfactory condition;

(b)   He shall ascertain that the date of the next test for tank-vehicles, battery-vehicles, demountable tanks, portable tanks, tank-containers and MEGCs has not expired;

(c)   He shall only fill tanks with the dangerous goods authorized for carriage in those tanks;

(d)   He shall, in filling the tank, comply with the requirements concerning dangerous goods in adjoining compartments;

(e)   He shall, during the filling of the tank, observe the maximum permissible degree of filling or the maximum permissible mass of contents per litre of capacity for the substance being filled;

(f)   He shall, after filling the tank, check the leakproofness of the closing devices;

(g)   He shall ensure that no dangerous residue of the filling substance adheres to the outside of the tanks filled by him;

(h)   He shall, in preparing the dangerous goods for carriage, ensure that the orange plates and placards or labels prescribed are affixed on the tanks, on the vehicles and on the large and small containers for carriage in bulk in accordance with the requirements;

(i)   *(Reserved)*;

(j)   He shall, when filling vehicles or containers with dangerous goods in bulk, ascertain that the relevant provisions of Chapter 7.3 are complied with.

1.4.3.4   *Tank-container/portable tank operator*

In the context of 1.4.1, the tank-container/portable tank operator shall in particular:

(a)   Ensure compliance with the requirements for construction, equipment, tests and marking;

(b)   Ensure that the maintenance of shells and their equipment is carried out in such a way as to ensure that, under normal operating conditions, the tank-container/portable tank satisfies the requirements of ADR until the next inspection;

(c)   Have an exceptional check made when the safety of the shell or its equipment is liable to be impaired by a repair, an alteration or an accident.

1.4.3.5   *(Reserved)*

CHAPTER 1.5

DEROGATIONS

1.5.1   **Temporary derogations**

1.5.1.1   In accordance with Article 4, paragraph 3 of ADR, the competent authorities of the Contracting Parties may agree directly among themselves to authorize certain transport operations in their territories by temporary derogation from the requirements of ADR, provided that safety is not compromised thereby. The authority which has taken the initiative with respect to the temporary derogation shall notify such derogations to the Secretariat of the United Nations Economic Commission for Europe which shall bring them to the attention of the Contracting Parties [1].

     NOTE: "Special arrangement" in accordance with 1.7.4 is not considered to be a temporary derogation in accordance with this section.

1.5.1.2   The period of validity of the temporary derogation shall not be more than five years from the date of its entry into force. The temporary derogation shall automatically cease as from the date of the entry into force of a relevant amendment to ADR.

1.5.1.3   Transport operations on the basis of temporary derogations shall constitute transport operations in the sense of ADR.

1.5.2   *(Reserved)*

---

[1]   ***Note by the Secretariat:*** *The special agreements concluded under this Chapter may be consulted on the web site of the Secretariat of the United Nations Economic Commission for Europe (http://www.unece.org/trans/danger/danger.htm).*

CHAPTER 1.6

TRANSITIONAL MEASURES

1.6.1   **General**

1.6.1.1   Unless otherwise provided, the substances and articles of ADR may be carried until 30 June 2009 in accordance with the requirements of ADR applicable up to 31 December 2008.

1.6.1.2   (a)   The danger labels and placards which until 31 December 2004 conformed to models No. 7A, 7B, 7C, 7D or 7E prescribed up to that date may be used until 31 December 2010.

               (b)   The danger labels and placards which until 31 December 2006 conformed to model No. 5.2 prescribed up to that date may be used until 31 December 2010.

1.6.1.3   Substances and articles of Class 1, belonging to the armed forces of a Contracting Party, that were packaged prior to 1 January 1990 in accordance with the requirements of ADR in effect at that time may be carried after 31 December 1989 provided the packagings maintain their integrity and are declared in the transport document as military goods packaged prior to 1 January 1990. The other requirements applicable as from 1 January 1990 for this class shall be complied with.

1.6.1.4   Substances and articles of Class 1 that were packaged between 1 January 1990 and 31 December 1996 in accordance with the requirements of ADR in effect at that time may be carried after 31 December 1996, provided the packagings maintain their integrity and are declared in the transport document as goods of Class 1 packaged between 1 January 1990 and 31 December 1996.

1.6.1.5   *(Reserved)*

1.6.1.6   Intermediate bulk containers (IBCs) manufactured before 1 January 2003 in accordance with the requirements of marginal 3612 (1) applicable up to 30 June 2001 and which do not conform to the requirements of 6.5.2.1.1 regarding the height of letters, numerals and symbols applicable as from 1 July 2001 may continue to be used.

1.6.1.7   Type approvals for drums, jerricans and composite packagings made of high or medium molecular mass polyethylene issued before 1 July 2005 in accordance with the requirements of 6.1.5.2.6 in force up to 31 December 2004, but which are not in accordance with the requirements of 4.1.1.19, continue to be valid until 31 December 2009. Any such packagings manufactured and marked on the basis of these type approvals may be used until the end of their period of use determined in 4.1.1.15.

1.6.1.8   Existing orange-coloured plates which meet the requirements of sub-section 5.3.2.2 applicable up to 31 December 2004 may continue to be used.

1.6.1.9   *(Deleted)*

1.6.1.10   Lithium cells and batteries manufactured before 1 July 2003 which had been tested in accordance with the requirements applicable until 31 December 2002 but which had not been tested in accordance with the requirements applicable as from 1 January 2003, and appliances containing such lithium cells or batteries, may continue to be carried up to 30 June 2013 if all the other applicable requirements are fulfilled.

1.6.1.11	Type approvals for drums, jerricans and composite packagings made of high or medium molecular mass polyethylene, and for high molecular mass polyethylene IBCs, issued before 1 July 2007 in accordance with the requirements of 6.1.6.1 (a) in force up to 31 December 2006, but which are not in accordance with the requirements of 6.1.6.1 (a) applicable as from 1 January 2007, continue to be valid.
1.6.1.12	Notwithstanding the provisions of section 1.9.5, Contracting Parties may continue to apply, until 31 December 2009 at the latest, restrictions to the passage of vehicles through road tunnels in accordance with the provisions of national law.
1.6.1.13	For vehicles first registered or which first entered into service before 1 January 2009, the requirements of 5.3.2.2.1 and 5.3.2.2.2 that the plate, numbers and letters shall remain affixed irrespective of the orientation of the vehicle may not be applied until 31 December 2009.
1.6.1.14	IBCs manufactured before 1 January 2011 in accordance with the requirements in force up to 31 December 2010 and conforming to a design type which has not passed the vibration test of 6.5.6.13 may still be used.
1.6.1.15	IBCs manufactured, remanufactured or repaired before 1 January 2011 need not be marked with the maximum permitted stacking load in accordance with 6.5.2.2.2. Such IBCs, not marked in accordance with 6.5.2.2.2, may still be used after 31 December 2010 but must be marked in accordance with 6.5.2.2.2 if they are remanufactured or repaired after that date.
1.6.1.16	Animal material affected by pathogens included in Category B, other than those which would be assigned to Category A if they were in culture (see 2.2.62.1.12.2), may be carried in accordance with provisions determined by the competent authority until 31 December 2014 [1].
1.6.1.17	Substances of classes 1 to 9 other than those assigned to UN Nos. 3077 or 3082 to which the classification criteria of 2.2.9.1.10 have not been applied and which are not marked in accordance with 5.2.1.8 and 5.3.6 may still be carried until 31 December 2010 without application of the provisions concerning the carriage of environmentally hazardous substances.
1.6.1.18	The provisions of sections 3.4.9 to 3.4.13 need only be applied as from 1 January 2011.

1.6.2   Pressure receptacles and receptacles for Class 2

1.6.2.1	Receptacles built before 1 January 1997 and which do not conform to the requirements of ADR applicable as from 1 January 1997, but the carriage of which was permitted under the requirements of ADR applicable up to 31 December 1996, may continue to be transported after that date if the periodic test requirements in packing instructions P200 and P203 are complied with.
1.6.2.2	Cylinders in accordance with the definition in 1.2.1 which were submitted to an initial inspection or periodic inspection before 1 January 1997 may be transported empty and uncleaned without a label until the date of the next refilling or the next periodic inspection.

---

[1]   *Regulations for dead infected animals are contained e.g. in Regulation (EC) No. 1774/2002 of the European Parliament and of the Council of 3 October 2002 laying down health rules concerning animal by-products not intended for human consumption (Official Journal of the European Communities, No. L 273 of 10.10.2002, p. 1).*

1.6.2.3	Receptacles intended for the carriage of Class 2 substances constructed before 1 January 2003, may continue to bear, after 1 January 2003, the markings conforming to the requirements applicable until 31 December 2002.
1.6.2.4	Pressure receptacles designed and constructed in accordance with technical codes no longer recognized according to 6.2.5 may still be used.
1.6.2.5	Pressure receptacles and their closures designed and constructed in accordance with standards applicable at the time of their construction (see 6.2.4) according to the provisions of ADR which were applicable at that time may still be used.
1.6.2.6	Pressure receptacles for substances other than those of Class 2, built before 1 July 2009 in accordance with the requirements of 4.1.4.4 in force up to 31 December 2008, but which do not conform to the requirements of 4.1.3.6 applicable as from 1 January 2009, may continue to be used provided that the requirements of 4.1.4.4 in force up to 31 December 2008 are complied with.
1.6.2.7	Contracting Parties may continue to apply the requirements of 6.2.1.4.1 to 6.2.1.4.4 applicable until 31 December 2008 instead of those of 1.8.6, 1.8.7, 6.2.2.9, 6.2.3.6 to 6.2.3.8 until 30 June 2011.

1.6.3   **Fixed tanks (tank-vehicles), demountable tanks and battery-vehicles**

1.6.3.1	Fixed tanks (tank-vehicles), demountable tanks and battery-vehicles built before the entry into force of the requirements applicable as from 1 October 1978 may be kept in service if the equipment of the shell meets the requirements of Chapter 6.8. The thickness of the shell wall, except in the case of shells intended for the carriage of refrigerated liquefied gases of Class 2, shall be appropriate to a calculation pressure of not less than 0.4 MPa (4 bar) (gauge pressure) in the case of mild steel or of not less than 200 kPa (2 bar) (gauge pressure) in the case of aluminium and aluminium alloys. For other than circular cross-sections of tanks, the diameter to be used as a basis for calculation shall be that of a circle whose area is equal to that of the actual cross-section of the tank.
1.6.3.2	The periodic tests for fixed tanks (tank-vehicles), demountable tanks and battery-vehicles kept in service under these transitional requirements shall be conducted in accordance with the requirements of 6.8.2.4 and 6.8.3.4 and with the pertinent special requirements for the various classes. Unless the earlier requirements prescribed a higher test pressure, a test pressure of 200 kPa (2 bar) (gauge pressure) shall suffice for aluminium shells and aluminium alloy shells.
1.6.3.3	Fixed tanks (tank-vehicles), demountable tanks and battery-vehicles which meet the transitional requirements in 1.6.3.1 and 1.6.3.2 may be used until 30 September 1993 for the carriage of the dangerous goods for which they have been approved. This transitional period shall not apply to fixed tanks (tank-vehicles), demountable tanks and battery-vehicles intended for the carriage of substances of Class 2, or to fixed tanks (tank-vehicles), demountable tanks and battery-vehicles whose wall thickness and items of equipment meet the requirements of Chapter 6.8.
1.6.3.4	(a) Fixed tanks (tank-vehicles), demountable tanks and battery-vehicles constructed before 1 May 1985 in accordance with the requirements of ADR in force between 1 October 1978 and 30 April 1985 but not conforming to the requirements applicable as from 1 May 1985 may continue to be used after that date;

(b)   Fixed tanks (tank-vehicles), demountable tanks and battery-vehicles, constructed between 1 May 1985 and the entry into force of the requirements applicable as from 1 January 1988 which do not conform to those requirements but were constructed according to the requirements of ADR in force until that date, may continue to be used after that date.

1.6.3.5   Fixed tanks (tank-vehicles), demountable tanks and battery-vehicles, constructed before 1 January 1993 in accordance with the requirements in force up to 31 December 1992 but which do not conform to the requirements applicable as from 1 January 1993 may still be used.

1.6.3.6   (a)   Fixed tanks (tank-vehicles), demountable tanks and battery-vehicles constructed between 1 January 1978 and 31 December 1984, if used after 31 December 2004, shall conform to the requirements of marginal 211 127 (5), applicable as from 1 January 1990, concerning shell thickness and protection against damage;

            (b)   Fixed tanks (tank-vehicles), demountable tanks and battery-vehicles constructed between 1 January 1985 and 31 December 1989, if used after 31 December 2010, shall conform to the requirements of marginal 211 127 (5), applicable as from 1 January 1990, concerning shell thickness and protection against damage.

1.6.3.7   Fixed tanks (tank-vehicles), demountable tanks and battery-vehicles constructed before 1 January 1999 in accordance with the requirements in force up to 31 December 1998 but which do not, however, conform to the requirements applicable as from 1 January 1999 may still be used.

1.6.3.8   Fixed tanks (tank-vehicles), demountable tanks and battery-vehicles intended for the carriage of substances of Class 2, which were built prior to 1 January 1997, may carry markings conforming to the requirements applicable up to 31 December 1996, until the next periodic test.

            When, because of amendments to ADR, some proper shipping names of gases have been modified, it is not necessary to modify the names on the plate or on the shell itself (see 6.8.3.5.2 or 6.8.3.5.3), provided that the names of the gases on the fixed tanks (tank-vehicles), demountable tanks and battery-vehicles or on the plates [see 6.8.3.5.6 (b) or (c)] are adapted at the first periodic test thereafter.

1.6.3.9 and 1.6.3.10   *(Reserved)*

1.6.3.11   Fixed tanks (tank-vehicles) and demountable tanks constructed before 1 January 1997 in accordance with the requirements in force up to 31 December 1996 but which do not, however, conform to the requirements of marginals 211 332 and 211 333 applicable as from 1 January 1997, may still be used.

1.6.3.12   *(Reserved)*

1.6.3.13   *(Deleted)*

1.6.3.14   *(Reserved)*

1.6.3.15   Fixed tanks (tank-vehicles) and demountable tanks constructed before 1 July 2007 in accordance with the requirements in force up to 31 December 2006 but which do not, however, conform to the requirements of 6.8.2.2.3 applicable as from 1 January 2007 may continue to be used until the next periodic inspection.

1.6.3.16 For fixed tanks (tank-vehicles), demountable tanks and battery-vehicles constructed before 1 January 2007 which do not conform to the requirements of 4.3.2, 6.8.2.3, 6.8.2.4 and 6.8.3.4 concerning the tank record, the retention of files for the tank record shall start at the latest at the next periodic inspection.

1.6.3.17 Fixed tanks (tank-vehicles) and demountable tanks intended for the carriage of substances of Class 3, packing group I having a vapour pressure of not more than 175 kPa (1.75 bar) (absolute) at 50 °C, constructed before 1 July 2007 in accordance with the requirements applicable up to 31 December 2006, to which tank code L1.5BN had been assigned in accordance with the requirements applicable up to 31 December 2006, may continue to be used for the carriage of the substances mentioned above, until 31 December 2018.

1.6.3.18 Fixed tanks (tank-vehicles), demountable tanks and battery-vehicles constructed before 1 January 2003 in accordance with the requirements in force up to 30 June 2001, but which do not, however, conform to the requirements applicable as from 1 July 2001, may still be used.

1.6.3.19 Fixed tanks (tank-vehicles) and demountable tanks constructed before 1 January 2003 in accordance with the requirements of 6.8.2.1.21 in force up to 31 December 2002 but which do not, however, conform to the requirements applicable as from 1 January 2003 may still be used.

1.6.3.20 Fixed tanks (tank-vehicles) and demountable tanks constructed before 1 July 2003 in accordance with the requirements in force up to 31 December 2002 but which do not, however, conform to the requirements of 6.8.2.1.7 applicable as from 1 January 2003 and special provision TE15 of 6.8.4 (b) applicable from 1 January 2003 to 31 December 2006 may still be used.

1.6.3.21 *(Deleted)*

1.6.3.22 to 1.6.3.24 *(Reserved)*

1.6.3.25 The type of the test ("P" or "L") required by 6.8.2.5.1 need not be added to the tank plate until the first test after 1 January 2007 is performed.

1.6.3.26 Fixed tanks (tank-vehicles) and demountable tanks constructed before 1 January 2007 in accordance with the requirements in force up to 31 December 2006 but which do not, however, conform to the requirements applicable as from 1 January 2007 regarding the marking of the external design pressure in accordance with 6.8.2.5.1, may still be used.

1.6.3.27 to 1.6.3.29 *(Reserved)*

1.6.3.30 Vacuum-operated waste fixed tanks (tank-vehicles) and demountable tanks constructed before 1 July 2005 in accordance with the requirements applicable up to 31 December 2004 but which do not conform to the requirements of 6.10.3.9 applicable as from 1 January 2005, may still be used.

1.6.3.31 Fixed tanks (tank-vehicles), demountable tanks and tanks forming elements of battery-vehicles designed and constructed in accordance with a technical code which was recognized at the time of their construction according to the provisions of 6.8.2.7 which were applicable at that time may still be used.

1.6.3.32 Fixed tanks (tank vehicles) and demountable tanks constructed before 1 July 2007 in accordance with the requirements in force up to 31 December 2006, equipped with manhole cover assemblies in accordance with the provisions of standard EN 13317:2002 referred to in the table of paragraph 6.8.2.6, applicable until 31 December 2006, including those of the figure and table B.2 of annex B of the said standard which are no longer accepted as from 1 January 2007, or the material of which does not meet the requirements of EN 13094:2004, paragraph 5.2, may still be used.

1.6.3.33   When the shell of a fixed tank (tank-vehicle) or demountable tank was already divided by partitions or surge plates into sections of not more than 7 500 litres capacity before 1 January 2009, the capacity of the shell need not be supplemented with the symbol "S" in the particulars required by 6.8.2.5.1 until the next periodic inspection according to 6.8.2.4.2 is performed.

1.6.3.34   Notwithstanding the provisions of 4.3.2.2.4, fixed tanks (tank-vehicles) and demountable tanks intended for the carriage of liquefied gases or refrigerated liquefied gases, which meet the applicable construction requirements of ADR but which were divided, before 1 July 2009, by partitions or surge plates into sections of more than 7 500 litres capacity may still be filled to more than 20% and less than 80% of their capacity.

1.6.3.35   Contracting Parties need not apply the requirements of 1.8.6, 1.8.7 and 6.8.4 TA4 and TT9 before 1 July 2011.

1.6.3.36 to 1.6.3.39   *(Reserved)*

1.6.3.40   *Fibre-reinforced plastics (FRP) tanks*

FRP tanks which have been constructed before 1 July 2002 in conformity with a design type approved before 1 July 2001 in accordance with the requirements of Appendix B.1c which were in force until 30 June 2001 may continue to be used until the end of their lifetime provided that all the requirements in force up to 30 June 2001 have been and continue to be complied with.

However, as from 1 July 2001, no new design type may be approved in accordance with the requirements in force until 30 June 2001.

1.6.4   Tank-containers, portable tanks and MEGCs

1.6.4.1   Tank-containers constructed before 1 January 1988 in accordance with the requirements in force up to 31 December 1987 but which do not, however, conform to the requirements applicable as from 1 January 1988, may still be used.

1.6.4.2   Tank-containers constructed before 1 January 1993 in accordance with the requirements in force up to 31 December 1992 but which do not, however, conform to the requirements applicable as from 1 January 1993, may still be used.

1.6.4.3   Tank-containers constructed before 1 January 1999 in accordance with the requirements in force up to 31 December 1998 but which do not, however, conform to the requirements applicable as from 1 January 1999, may still be used.

1.6.4.4   *(Reserved)*

1.6.4.5   When, because of amendments to ADR, some proper shipping names of gases have been modified, it is not necessary to modify the names on the plate or on the shell itself (see 6.8.3.5.2 or 6.8.3.5.3), provided that the names of the gases on the tank-containers and MEGCs or on the plates [see 6.8.3.5.6 (b) or (c)] are adapted at the first periodic test thereafter.

1.6.4.6	Tank-containers constructed before 1 January 2007 in accordance with the requirements in force up to 31 December 2006 but which do not, however, conform to the requirements applicable as from 1 January 2007 regarding the marking of the external design pressure in accordance with 6.8.2.5.1, may still be used.
1.6.4.7	Tank-containers constructed before 1 January 1997 in accordance with the requirements in force up to 31 December 1996 but which do not, however, conform to the requirements of marginals 212 332 and 212 333 applicable as from 1 January 1997, may still be used.
1.6.4.8	*(Reserved)*
1.6.4.9	Tank-containers and MEGCs designed and constructed in accordance with a technical code which was recognized at the time of their construction according to the provisions of 6.8.2.7 which were applicable at that time may still be used.
1.6.4.10	*(Deleted)*
1.6.4.11	*(Reserved)*
1.6.4.12	Tank-containers and MEGCs constructed before 1 January 2003 in accordance with the requirements applicable up to 30 June 2001, but which do not, however, conform to the requirements applicable as from 1 July 2001, may still be used.
1.6.4.13	Tank-containers constructed before 1 July 2003 in accordance with the requirements in force up to 31 December 2002 but which do not, however, conform to the requirements of 6.8.2.1.7 applicable as from 1 January 2003 and special provision TE15 of 6.8.4 (b) applicable from 1 January 2003 to 31 December 2006 may still be used.
1.6.4.14	*(Reserved)*
1.6.4.15	The type of the test ("P" or "L") required by 6.8.2.5.1 need not be added to the tank plate until the first test after 1 January 2007 is performed.
1.6.4.16	*(Deleted)*
1.6.4.17	Tank-containers constructed before 1 July 2007 in accordance with the requirements in force up to 31 December 2006 but which do not conform to the requirements of 6.8.2.2.3 applicable as from 1 January 2007 may continue to be used until the next periodic inspection.
1.6.4.18	For tank-containers and MEGCs constructed before 1 January 2007 which do not conform to the requirements of 4.3.2, 6.8.2.3, 6.8.2.4 and 6.8.3.4 concerning the tank record, the retention of files for the tank record shall start at the latest at the next periodic inspection.
1.6.4.19	Tank-containers intended for the carriage of substances of Class 3, packing group I having a vapour pressure of not more than 175 kPa (1.75 bar) (absolute) at 50 °C, constructed before 1 July 2007 in accordance with the requirements applicable up to 31 December 2006, to which tank code L1.5BN had been assigned in accordance with the requirements applicable up to 31 December 2006, may continue to be used for the carriage of the substances mentioned above until 31 December 2016.
1.6.4.20	Vacuum-operated waste tank-containers constructed before 1 July 2005 in accordance with the requirements applicable up to 31 December 2004 but which do not conform to the requirements of 6.10.3.9 applicable as from 1 January 2005, may still be used.

1.6.4.21 to 1.6.4.29   *(Reserved)*

1.6.4.30   Portable tanks and UN MEGCs which do not meet the design requirements applicable as from 1 January 2007 but which have been constructed according to a design approval certificate which has been issued before 1 January 2008 may continue to be used.

1.6.4.31   For substances where TP35 is assigned in column (11) of Table A of Chapter 3.2, portable tank instruction T14 prescribed in ADR applicable up to 31 December 2008 may continue to be applied until 31 December 2014.

1.6.4.32   When the shell of a tank-container was already divided by partitions or surge plates into sections of not more than 7 500 litres capacity before 1 January 2009, the capacity of the shell need not be supplemented with the symbol "S" in the particulars required by 6.8.2.5.1 until the next periodic inspection according to 6.8.2.4.2 is performed.

1.6.4.33   Notwithstanding the provisions of 4.3.2.2.4, tank-containers intended for the carriage of liquefied gases or refrigerated liquefied gases, which meet the applicable construction requirements of ADR but which were divided, before 1 July 2009, by partitions or surge plates into sections of more than 7 500 litres capacity may still be filled to more than 20% and less than 80% of their capacity.

1.6.4.34   Contracting Parties need not apply the requirements of 1.8.6, 1.8.7 and 6.8.4 TA4 and TT9 before 1 July 2011.

1.6.5   Vehicles

1.6.5.1 and 1.6.5.2   *(Reserved)*

1.6.5.3   *(Deleted)*

1.6.5.4   As regards the construction of EX/II, EX/III, FL, OX and AT vehicles, the requirements of Part 9 in force up to 31 December 2008 may be applied until 31 March 2010.

1.6.5.5   Vehicles registered or entering into service before 1 January 2003 the electric equipment of which does not comply with the requirements of 9.2.2, 9.3.7 or 9.7.8 but complies with the requirements applicable until 30 June 2001 may still be used.

1.6.5.6   *(Deleted)*

1.6.5.7   Complete or completed vehicles which have been type-approved before 31 December 2002 according to ECE Regulation No. 105 [2] as amended by the 01 series of amendments or the corresponding provisions of Directive 98/91/EC [3] and which do not comply with the requirements of Chapter 9.2 but comply with the requirements applicable to the construction of base vehicles (marginals 220 100 to 220 540 of Appendix B.2) applicable until 30 June 2001 may continue to be approved and used provided they are first registered or they entered into service before 1 July 2003.

---

[2]   *ECE Regulation No. 105 (Uniform provisions concerning the approval of vehicles intended for the carriage of dangerous goods with regard to their specific constructional features).*

[3]   *Directive 98/91/EC of the European Parliament and of the Council of 14 December 1998 relating to motor vehicles and their trailers intended for the transport of dangerous goods by road and amending Directive 70/156/EEC relating to the type approval of motor vehicles and their trailers (Official Journal of the European Communities No. L 011 of 16 January 1999, pp. 0025-0036).*

1.6.5.8	EX/II and EX/III vehicles which have been first approved before 1 July 2005 and which comply with the requirements of Part 9 in force up to 31 December 2004 but which do not however conform to the requirements applicable as from 1 January 2005 may still be used.
1.6.5.9	Tank-vehicles with fixed tanks with a capacity of more than 3 m³ intended for the carriage of dangerous goods in the liquid or molten state tested with a pressure of less than 4 bar, which do not comply with the requirements of 9.7.5.2, first registered (or which entered into service if the registration is not mandatory) before 1 July 2004, may still be used.
1.6.5.10	Certificates of approval which conform to the model shown in 9.1.3.5 applicable up to 31 December 2006 and those which conform to the model shown in 9.1.3.5 applicable from 1 January 2007 to 31 December 2008 may continue to be used.
1.6.5.11	MEMUs which have been constructed and approved before 1 January 2009 in accordance with the provisions of national law but which do not, however, conform to the construction and approval requirements applicable as from 1 January 2009 may be used with the approval of the competent authorities in the countries of use.

1.6.6   **Class 7**

1.6.6.1   *Packages not requiring competent authority approval of design under the 1985 and 1985 (as amended 1990) editions of IAEA Safety Series No. 6*

Excepted packages, Industrial packages Type IP-1, Type IP-2 and Type IP-3 and Type A packages that did not require approval of design by the competent authority and which meet the requirements of the 1985 or 1985 (as amended 1990) Editions of IAEA Regulations for the Safe Transport of Radioactive Material (IAEA Safety Series No. 6) may continue to be used subject to the mandatory programme of quality assurance in accordance with the requirements of 1.7.3 and the activity limits and material restrictions of 2.2.7.2.2, 2.2.7.2.4.1, 2.2.7.2.4.4, 2.2.7.2.4.5, 2.2.7.2.4.6, special provision 336 of Chapter 3.3 and 4.1.9.3.

Any packaging modified, unless to improve safety, or manufactured after 31 December 2003, shall meet the requirements of ADR. Packages prepared for carriage not later than 31 December 2003 under the 1985 or 1985 (as amended 1990) Editions of IAEA Safety Series No. 6 may continue in transport. Packages prepared for carriage after this date shall meet the requirements of ADR.

1.6.6.2   *Packages approved under the 1973, 1973 (as amended), 1985 and 1985 (as amended 1990) editions of IAEA Safety Series No. 6*

1.6.6.2.1   Packagings manufactured to a package design approved by the competent authority under the provisions of the 1973 or 1973 (as amended) Editions of IAEA Safety Series No. 6 may continue to be used, subject to: multilateral approval of package design, the mandatory programme of quality assurance in accordance with the applicable requirements of 1.7.3 and the activity limits and material restrictions of 2.2.7.2.2, 2.2.7.2.4.1, 2.2.7.2.4.4, 2.2.7.2.4.5, 2.2.7.2.4.6, special provision 337 of Chapter 3.3 and 4.1.9.3. No new manufacture of such packaging shall be permitted to commence. Changes in the design of the packaging or in the nature or quantity of the authorized radioactive contents which, as determined by the competent authority, would significantly affect safety shall require that the requirements of ADR be met. A serial number according to the provision of 5.2.1.7.5 shall be assigned to and marked on the outside of each packaging.

1.6.6.2.2 Packagings manufactured to a package design approved by the competent authority under the provisions of the 1985 or 1985 (as amended 1990) Editions of IAEA Safety Series No. 6 may continue to be used, subject to: the multilateral approval of package design; the mandatory programme of quality assurance in accordance with the requirements of 1.7.3 and the activity limits and material restrictions of 2.2.7.2.2, 2.2.7.2.4.1, 2.2.7.2.4.4, 2.2.7.2.4.5, 2.2.7.2.4.6, special provision 337 of Chapter 3.3 and 4.1.9.3. Changes in the design of the packaging or in the nature or quantity of the authorized radioactive contents which, as determined by the competent authority, would significantly affect safety shall require that the requirements of these Regulations be met. All packagings for which manufacture begins after 31 December 2006 shall meet the requirements of ADR.

1.6.6.3 *Special form radioactive material approved under the 1973, 1973 (as amended), 1985 and 1985 (as amended 1990) Editions of IAEA Safety Series No. 6*

Special form radioactive material manufactured to a design which had received unilateral approval by the competent authority under the 1973, 1973 (as amended), 1985 or 1985 (as amended 1990) Editions of IAEA Safety Series No. 6 may continue to be used when in compliance with the mandatory programme of quality assurance in accordance with the applicable requirements of 1.7.3. All special form radioactive material manufactured after 31 December 2003 shall meet the requirements of ADR.

CHAPTER 1.7

GENERAL PROVISIONS CONCERNING CLASS 7

1.7.1 **Scope and application**

NOTE 1: *In the event of accidents or incidents during the carriage of radioactive material, emergency provisions, as established by relevant national and/or international organizations, shall be observed to protect persons, property and the environment. Appropriate guidelines for such provisions are contained in "Planning and Preparing for Emergency Response to Transport Accidents Involving Radioactive Material", Safety Standard Series No. TS-G-1.2 (ST-3), IAEA, Vienna (2002).*

NOTE 2: *Emergency procedures shall take into account the formation of other dangerous substances that may result from the reaction between the contents of a consignment and the environment in the event of an accident.*

1.7.1.1 ADR establishes standards of safety which provide an acceptable level of control of the radiation, criticality and thermal hazards to persons, property and the environment that are associated with the carriage of radioactive material. These standards are based on the IAEA Regulations for the Safe Transport of Radioactive Material, 2005 edition, Safety Standards Series No. TS-R-1, IAEA, Vienna (2005). Explanatory material on the 1996 edition of TS-R-1 can be found in the "Advisory Material for the IAEA Regulations for the Safe Transport of Radioactive Material", Safety Standards Series No. TS-G-1.1 (ST-2) IAEA, Vienna (2002).

1.7.1.2 The objective of ADR is to protect persons, property and the environment from the effects of radiation during the carriage of radioactive material. This protection is achieved by requiring:

(a) Containment of the radioactive contents;

(b) Control of external radiation levels;

(c) Prevention of criticality; and

(d) Prevention of damage caused by heat.

These requirements are satisfied firstly by applying a graded approach to contents limits for packages and vehicles and to performance standards applied to package designs depending upon the hazard of the radioactive contents. Secondly, they are satisfied by imposing requirements on the design and operation of packages and on the maintenance of packagings, including a consideration of the nature of the radioactive contents. Finally, they are satisfied by requiring administrative controls including, where appropriate, approval by competent authorities.

1.7.1.3 ADR applies to the carriage of radioactive material by road including carriage which is incidental to the use of the radioactive material. Carriage comprises all operations and conditions associated with and involved in the movement of radioactive material; these include the design, manufacture, maintenance and repair of packaging, and the preparation, consigning, loading, carriage including in-transit storage, unloading and receipt at the final destination of loads of radioactive material and packages. A graded approach is applied to the performance standards in ADR that is characterized by three general severity levels:

(a)   Routine conditions of carriage (incident free);

(b)   Normal conditions of carriage (minor mishaps);

(c)   Accident conditions of carriage.

1.7.1.4   The provisions laid down in ADR do not apply to the carriage of:

(a)   Radioactive material that is an integral part of the means of transport;

(b)   Radioactive material moved within an establishment which is subject to appropriate safety regulations in force in the establishment and where the movement does not involve public roads or railways;

(c)   Radioactive material implanted or incorporated into a person or live animal for diagnosis or treatment;

(d)   Radioactive material in consumer products which have received regulatory approval, following their sale to the end user;

(e)   Natural material and ores containing naturally occurring radionuclides which are either in their natural state, or have only been processed for purposes other than for extraction of the radionuclides, and which are not intended to be processed for use of these radionuclides provided the activity concentration of the material does not exceed 10 times the values specified in 2.2.7.2.2.1 (b), or calculated in accordance with 2.2.7.2.2.2 to 2.2.7.2.2.6;

(f)   Non-radioactive solid objects with radioactive substances present on any surfaces in quantities not in excess of the limit set out in the definition for "contamination" in 2.2.7.1.2.

1.7.1.5   *Specific provisions for the carriage of excepted packages*

Excepted packages as specified in 2.2.7.2.4.1 shall be subject only to the following provisions of Parts 5 to 7:

(a)   The applicable requirements in 5.1.2, 5.1.3.2, 5.1.4, 5.2.1.2, 5.2.1.7.1 to 5.2.1.7.3, 5.2.1.9, 5.4.1.1.1 (a), (g) and (h) and 7.5.11 CV33 (5.2);

(b)   The requirements for excepted packages specified in 6.4.4; and

(c)   If the excepted package contains fissile material, one of the fissile exceptions provided by 2.2.7.2.3.5 shall apply and the requirement of 6.4.7.2 shall be met.

Excepted packages are subject to the relevant provisions of all other parts of ADR.

1.7.2   Radiation protection programme

1.7.2.1   The carriage of radioactive material shall be subject to a Radiation protection programme which shall consist of systematic arrangements aimed at providing adequate consideration of radiation protection measures.

1.7.2.2   Doses to persons shall be below the relevant dose limits. Protection and safety shall be optimized in order that the magnitude of individual doses, the number of persons exposed, and the likelihood of incurring exposure shall be kept as low as reasonably achievable, economic and social factors being taken into account within the restriction that the doses to individuals be subject to dose constraints. A structured and systematic approach shall be adopted and shall include consideration of the interfaces between carriage and other activities.

1.7.2.3 The nature and extent of the measures to be employed in the programme shall be related to the magnitude and likelihood of radiation exposures. The programme shall incorporate the requirements in 1.7.2.2, 1.7.2.4 and 1.7.2.5. Programme documents shall be available, on request, for inspection by the relevant competent authority.

1.7.2.4 For occupational exposures arising from transport activities, where it is assessed that the effective dose:

(a) Is likely to be between 1 mSv and 6 mSv in a year, a dose assessment programme via work place monitoring or individual monitoring shall be conducted;

(b) Is likely to exceed 6 mSv in a year, individual monitoring shall be conducted.

When individual monitoring or work place monitoring is conducted, appropriate records shall be kept.

NOTE: For occupational exposures arising from transport activities, where it is assessed that the effective dose is most unlikely to exceed 1 mSv in a year, no special work patterns, detailed monitoring, dose assessment programmes or individual record keeping need be required.

1.7.2.5 Workers (see 7.5.11, CV33 Note 3) shall receive appropriate training concerning radiation protection including the precautions to be observed in order to restrict their occupational exposure and the exposure of other persons who might be affected by their actions.

1.7.3 **Quality assurance**

Quality assurance programmes based on international, national or other standards acceptable to the competent authority shall be established and implemented for the design, manufacture, testing, documentation, use, maintenance and inspection of all special form radioactive material, low dispersible radioactive material and packages and for carriage and in-transit storage operations to ensure compliance with the relevant provisions of ADR. Certification that the design specification has been fully implemented shall be available to the competent authority. The manufacturer, consignor or user shall be prepared to provide facilities for competent authority inspection during manufacture and use and to demonstrate to any cognizant competent authority that:

(a) The manufacturing methods and materials used are in accordance with the approved design specifications; and

(b) All packagings are periodically inspected and, as necessary, repaired and maintained in good condition so that they continue to comply with all relevant requirements and specifications, even after repeated use.

Where competent authority approval is required, such approval shall take into account and be contingent upon the adequacy of the quality assurance programme.

1.7.4   **Special arrangement**

1.7.4.1   Special arrangement shall mean those provisions, approved by the competent authority, under which consignments which do not satisfy all the requirements of ADR applicable to radioactive material may be transported.

NOTE: Special arrangement is not considered to be a temporary derogation in accordance with 1.5.1.

1.7.4.2   Consignments for which conformity with any provision applicable to Class 7 is impracticable shall not be transported except under special arrangement. Provided the competent authority is satisfied that conformity with the Class 7 provisions of ADR is impracticable and that the requisite standards of safety established by ADR have been demonstrated through alternative means the competent authority may approve special arrangement transport operations for single or a planned series of multiple consignments. The overall level of safety in carriage shall be at least equivalent to that which would be provided if all the applicable requirements had been met. For international consignments of this type, multilateral approval shall be required.

1.7.5   **Radioactive material possessing other dangerous properties**

In addition to the radioactive and fissile properties, any subsidiary risk of the contents of the package, such as explosiveness, flammability, pyrophoricity, chemical toxicity and corrosiveness, shall also be taken into account in the documentation, packing, labelling, marking, placarding, stowage, segregation and carriage, in order to be in compliance with all relevant provisions for dangerous goods of ADR.

1.7.6   **Non-compliance**

1.7.6.1   In the event of a non-compliance with any limit in ADR applicable to radiation level or contamination,

(a)   The consignor shall be informed of the non-compliance by:

(i)   the carrier if the non-compliance is identified during carriage; or

(ii)   the consignee if the non-compliance is identified at receipt;

(b)   The carrier, consignor or consignee, as appropriate shall:

(i)   take immediate steps to mitigate the consequences of the non-compliance;

(ii)   investigate the non-compliance and its causes, circumstances and consequences;

(iii)   take appropriate action to remedy the causes and circumstances that led to the non-compliance and to prevent a recurrence of similar circumstances that led to the non-compliance; and

(iv)   communicate to the competent authority(ies) on the causes of the non-compliance and on corrective or preventive actions taken or to be taken; and

(c)   The communication of the non-compliance to the consignor and competent authority(ies), respectively, shall be made as soon as practicable and it shall be immediate whenever an emergency exposure situation has developed or is developing.

CHAPTER 1.8

CHECKS AND OTHER SUPPORT MEASURES TO ENSURE COMPLIANCE WITH SAFETY REQUIREMENTS

1.8.1 **Administrative controls of dangerous goods**

1.8.1.1 The competent authorities of the Contracting Parties may, on their national territory, at any time, conduct spot checks to verify whether the requirements concerning the carriage of dangerous goods have been met including, in accordance with 1.10.1.5, those concerning security measures.

    These checks shall, however, be made without endangering persons, property or the environment and without major disruption of road services.

1.8.1.2 Participants in the carriage of dangerous goods (Chapter 1.4) shall, without delay, in the context of their respective obligations, provide the competent authorities and their agents with the necessary information for carrying out the checks.

1.8.1.3 The competent authorities may also, for the purposes of carrying out checks on the premises of the enterprises participating in the carriage of dangerous goods (Chapter 1.4), make inspections, consult the necessary documents and remove samples of dangerous goods or packagings for examination, provided that safety is not jeopardized thereby. The participants in the carriage of dangerous goods (Chapter 1.4) shall also make the vehicles or parts of vehicles and the equipment and installations accessible for the purpose of checking where this is possible and reasonable. They may, if they deem necessary, designate a person from the enterprise to accompany the representative of the competent authority.

1.8.1.4 If the competent authorities observe that the requirements of ADR have not been met, they may prohibit a consignment or interrupt a transport operation until the defects observed are rectified, or they may prescribe other appropriate measures. Immobilization may take place on the spot or at another place selected by the authorities for safety reasons. These measures shall not cause a major disruption in road services.

1.8.2 **Mutual administrative support**

1.8.2.1 The Contracting Parties shall agree on mutual administrative support for the implementation of ADR.

1.8.2.2 When a Contracting Party has reasons to observe that the safety of the carriage of dangerous goods on its territory is compromised as a result of very serious or repeated infringements by an enterprise which has its headquarters on the territory of another Contracting Party, it shall notify the competent authorities of this Contracting Party of such infringements. The competent authorities of the Contracting Party on the territory of which the very serious or repeated infringements were observed may request the competent authorities of the Contracting Party on the territory of which the enterprise has its headquarters to take appropriate measures against the offender(s). The transmission of data referring to persons shall not be permitted unless it is necessary for the prosecution of very serious or repeated infringements.

1.8.2.3 The authorities notified shall communicate to the competent authorities of the Contracting Party on the territory of which the infringements were observed, the measures which have, if necessary, been taken with respect to the enterprise.

1.8.3   **Safety adviser**

1.8.3.1   Each undertaking, the activities of which include the carriage, or the related packing, loading, filling or unloading, of dangerous goods by road shall appoint one or more safety advisers for the carriage of dangerous goods, responsible for helping to prevent the risks inherent in such activities with regard to persons, property and the environment.

1.8.3.2   The competent authorities of the Contracting Parties may provide that these requirements shall not apply to undertakings:

      (a)   The activities of which concern quantities in each transport unit smaller than those referred to in 1.1.3.6, 1.7.1.4 and in Chapters 3.3, 3.4 and 3.5; or

      (b)   The main or secondary activities of which are not the carriage or the related loading or unloading of dangerous goods but which occasionally engage in the national carriage or the related loading or unloading of dangerous goods posing little danger or risk of pollution.

1.8.3.3   The main task of the adviser shall be, under the responsibility of the head of the undertaking, to seek by all appropriate means and by all appropriate action, within the limits of the relevant activities of that undertaking, to facilitate the conduct of those activities in accordance with the requirements applicable and in the safest possible way.

With regard to the undertaking's activities, the adviser has the following duties in particular:

- monitoring compliance with the requirements governing the carriage of dangerous goods;

- advising his undertaking on the carriage of dangerous goods;

- preparing an annual report to the management of his undertaking or a local public authority, as appropriate, on the undertaking's activities in the carriage of dangerous goods. Such annual reports shall be preserved for five years and made available to the national authorities at their request.

The adviser's duties also include monitoring the following practices and procedures relating to the relevant activities of the undertaking:

- the procedures for compliance with the requirements governing the identification of dangerous goods being transported;

- the undertaking's practice in taking account, when purchasing means of transport, of any special requirements in connection with the dangerous goods being transported;

- the procedures for checking the equipment used in connection with the carriage, loading or unloading of dangerous goods;

- the proper training of the undertaking's employees and the maintenance of records of such training;

- the implementation of proper emergency procedures in the event of any accident or incident that may affect safety during the carriage, loading or unloading of dangerous goods;

- investigating and, where appropriate, preparing reports on serious accidents, incidents or serious infringements recorded during the carriage, loading or unloading of dangerous goods;

- the implementation of appropriate measures to avoid the recurrence of accidents, incidents or serious infringements;

- the account taken of the legal prescriptions and special requirements associated with the carriage of dangerous goods in the choice and use of sub-contractors or third parties;

- verification that employees involved in the carriage, loading or unloading of dangerous goods have detailed operational procedures and instructions;

- the introduction of measures to increase awareness of the risks inherent in the carriage, loading and unloading of dangerous goods;

- the implementation of verification procedures to ensure the presence on board the means of transport of the documents and safety equipment which must accompany transport and the compliance of such documents and equipment with the regulations;

- the implementation of verification procedures to ensure compliance with the requirements governing loading and unloading;

- the existence of the security plan indicated in 1.10.3.2.

1.8.3.4   The adviser may also be the head of the undertaking, a person with other duties in the undertaking, or a person not directly employed by that undertaking, provided that that person is capable of performing the duties of adviser.

1.8.3.5   Each undertaking concerned shall, on request, inform the competent authority or the body designated for that purpose by each Contracting Party of the identity of its adviser.

1.8.3.6   Whenever an accident affects persons, property or the environment or results in damage to property or the environment during carriage, loading or unloading carried out by the undertaking concerned, the adviser shall, after collecting all the relevant information, prepare an accident report to the management of the undertaking or to a local public authority, as appropriate. That report shall not replace any report by the management of the undertaking which might be required under any other international or national legislation.

1.8.3.7   An adviser shall hold a vocational training certificate, valid for transport by road. That certificate shall be issued by the competent authority or the body designated for that purpose by each Contracting Party.

1.8.3.8   To obtain a certificate, a candidate shall undergo training and pass an examination approved by the competent authority of the Contracting Party.

1.8.3.9   The main aims of the training shall be to provide candidates with sufficient knowledge of the risks inherent in the carriage of dangerous goods, of the laws, regulations and administrative provisions applicable to the modes of transport concerned and of the duties listed in 1.8.3.3.

1.8.3.10   The examination shall be organized by the competent authority or by an examining body designated by the competent authority. The examining body shall not be a training provider.

The examining body shall be designated in writing. This approval may be of limited duration and shall be based on the following criteria:

- competence of the examining body;

- specifications of the form of the examinations the examining body is proposing;

- measures intended to ensure that examinations are impartial;

- independence of the body from all natural or legal persons employing safety advisers.

1.8.3.11 The aim of the examination is to ascertain whether candidates possess the necessary level of knowledge to carry out the duties incumbent upon a safety adviser as listed in 1.8.3.3, for the purpose of obtaining the certificate prescribed in sub-section 1.8.3.7, and it shall cover at least the following subjects:

(a) Knowledge of the types of consequences which may be caused by an accident involving dangerous goods and knowledge of the main causes of accidents;

(b) Requirements under national law, international conventions and agreements, with regard to the following in particular:

- classification of dangerous goods (procedure for classifying solutions and mixtures, structure of the list of substances, classes of dangerous goods and principles for their classification, nature of dangerous goods transported, physical, chemical and toxicological properties of dangerous goods);

- general packing provisions, provisions for tanks and tank-containers (types, code, marking, construction, initial and periodic inspection and testing);

- marking and labelling, placarding and orange plates marking (marking and labelling of packages, placing and removal of placards and orange plates);

- particulars in transport documents (information required);

- method of consignment and restrictions on dispatch (full load, carriage in bulk, carriage in intermediate bulk containers, carriage in containers, carriage in fixed or demountable tanks);

- transport of passengers;

- prohibitions and precautions relating to mixed loading;

- segregation of goods;

- limitation of the quantities carried and quantities exemptions;

- handling and stowage (loading and unloading - filling ratios -, stowage and segregation);

- cleaning and/or degassing before loading and after unloading;

- crews, vocational training;

- vehicle documents (transport documents, instructions in writing, vehicle approval certificate, driver training certificate, copies of any derogations, other documents);

-   instructions in writing (implementation of the instructions and crew protection equipment);

-   supervision requirements (parking);

-   traffic regulations and restrictions;

-   operational discharges or accidental leaks of pollutants;

-   requirements relating to transport equipment.

1.8.3.12   *Examinations*

1.8.3.12.1   The examination shall consist of a written test which may be supplemented by an oral examination.

1.8.3.12.2   The use in the written test of documentation other than international or national regulations is not permitted.

1.8.3.12.3   Electronic media may be used only if provided by the examining body. There shall be no means of a candidate introducing further data to the electronic media provided; the candidate may only answer the questions posed.

1.8.3.12.4   The written test shall consist of two parts:

(a)   Candidates shall receive a questionnaire. It shall include at least 20 open questions covering at least the subjects mentioned in the list in 1.8.3.11. However, multiple choice questions may be used. In this case, two multiple choice questions count as one open question. Amongst these subjects particular attention shall be paid to the following subjects:

-   general preventive and safety measures;

-   classification of dangerous goods;

-   general packing provisions, including tanks, tank-containers, tank-vehicles, etc.;

-   danger markings and labels;

-   information in transport document;

-   handling and stowage;

-   crew, vocational training;

-   vehicle documents and transport certificates;

-   instructions in writing;

-   requirements concerning transport equipment;

(b)   Candidates shall undertake a case study in keeping with the duties of the adviser referred to in 1.8.3.3, in order to demonstrate that they have the necessary qualifications to fulfil the task of adviser.

1.8.3.13   The Contracting Parties may decide that candidates who intend working for undertakings specializing in the carriage of certain types of dangerous goods need only be questioned on the substances relating to their activities. These types of goods are:

-    Class 1;

-    Class 2;

-    Class 7;

-    Classes 3, 4.1, 4.2, 4.3, 5.1, 5.2, 6.1, 6.2, 8 and 9;

-    UN Nos. 1202, 1203, 1223, 3475, and aviation fuel classified under UN Nos. 1268 or 1863.

The certificate prescribed in 1.8.3.7 shall clearly indicate that it is only valid for one type of the dangerous goods referred to in this sub-section and on which the adviser has been questioned under the conditions defined in 1.8.3.12.

Certificates of training as safety advisers issued before 1 January 2009 for UN Nos. 1202, 1203 and 1223 are also valid for UN No. 3475 and aviation fuel classified under UN Nos. 1268 or 1863.

1.8.3.14   The competent authority or the examining body shall keep a running list of the questions that have been included in the examination.

1.8.3.15   The certificate prescribed in 1.8.3.7 shall take the form laid down in 1.8.3.18 and shall be recognized by all Contracting Parties.

1.8.3.16   *Validity and renewal of certificates*

1.8.3.16.1   The certificate shall be valid for five years. The period of the validity of a certificate shall be extended from the date of its expiry for five years at a time where, during the year before its expiry, its holder has passed an examination. The examination shall be approved by the competent authority.

1.8.3.16.2   The aim of the examination is to ascertain that the holder has the necessary knowledge to carry out the duties set out in 1.8.3.3. The knowledge required is set out in 1.8.3.11 (b) and shall include the amendments to the regulations introduced since the award of the last certificate. The examination shall be held and supervised on the same basis as in 1.8.3.10 and 1.8.3.12 to 1.8.3.14. However, holders need not undertake the case study specified in 1.8.3.12.4 (b).

1.8.3.17   The requirements set out in 1.8.3.1 to 1.8.3.16 shall be considered to have been fulfilled if the relevant conditions of Council Directive 96/35/EC of 3 June 1996 on the appointment and vocational qualification of safety advisers for the transport of dangerous goods by road, rail and inland waterway [1] and of Directive 2000/18/EC of the European Parliament and of the Council of 17 April 2000 on minimum examination requirements for safety advisers for the transport of dangerous goods by road, rail or inland waterway [2] are applied.

---

[1]   *Official Journal of the European Communities, No. L145 of 19 June 1996, page 10.*

[2]   *Official Journal of the European Communities, No. L118 of 19 May 2000, page 41.*

1.8.3.18   *Form of certificate*

Certificate of training as safety adviser for the transport of dangerous goods

Certificate No: ....

Distinguishing sign of the State issuing the certificate: ....

Surname: ....

Forename(s): ....

Date and place of birth: ....

Nationality: ....

Signature of holder: ....

Valid until .... for undertakings which transport dangerous goods and for undertakings which carry out related loading or unloading:

□ by road   □ by rail   □ by inland waterway

Issued by: ....

Date: ....   Signature: ....

Extended until: ....   By: ....

Date: ....   Signature: ....

1.8.4　　　　**List of competent authorities and bodies designated by them**

The Contracting Parties shall communicate to the Secretariat of the United Nations Economic Commission for Europe the addresses of the authorities and bodies designated by them which are competent in accordance with national law to implement ADR, referring in each case to the relevant requirement of ADR and giving the addresses to which the relevant applications should be made.

The Secretariat of the United Nations Economic Commission for Europe shall establish a list on the basis of the information received and shall keep it up-to-date. It shall communicate this list and the amendments thereto to the Contracting Parties.

1.8.5　　　　**Notifications of occurrences involving dangerous goods**

1.8.5.1　　　If a serious accident or incident takes place during loading, filling, carriage or unloading of dangerous goods on the territory of a Contracting Party, the loader, filler, carrier or consignee, respectively, shall ascertain that a report conforming to the model prescribed in 1.8.5.4 is made to the competent authority of the Contracting Party concerned.

1.8.5.2　　　The Contracting Party shall in turn, if necessary, make a report to the Secretariat of the United Nations Economic Commission for Europe with a view to informing the other Contracting Parties.

1.8.5.3　　　An occurrence subject to report in accordance with 1.8.5.1 has occurred if dangerous goods were released or if there was an imminent risk of loss of product, if personal injury, material or environmental damage occurred, or if the authorities were involved and one or more of the following criteria has/have been met:

Personal injury means an occurrence in which death or injury directly relating to the dangerous goods carried has occurred, and where the injury

(a)　　Requires intensive medical treatment;

(b)　　Requires a stay in hospital of at least one day; or

(c)　　Results in the inability to work for at least three consecutive days.

Loss of product means the release of dangerous goods

(a)　　Of transport category 0 or 1 in quantities of 50 kg / 50 l or more;

(b)　　Of transport category 2 in quantities of 333 kg / 333 l or more; or

(c)　　Of transport category 3 or 4 in quantities of 1 000 kg / 1 000 l or more.

The loss of product criterion also applies if there was an imminent risk of loss of product in the above-mentioned quantities. As a rule, this has to be assumed if, owing to structural damage, the means of containment is no longer suitable for further carriage or if, for any other reason, a sufficient level of safety is no longer ensured (e.g. owing to distortion of tanks or containers, overturning of a tank or fire in the immediate vicinity).

If dangerous goods of Class 6.2 are involved, the obligation to report applies without quantity limitation.

In occurrences involving Class 7 material, the criteria for loss of product are:

(a)   Any release of radioactive material from the packages;

(b)   Exposure leading to a breach of the limits set out in the regulations for protection of workers and members of the public against ionizing radiation (Schedule II of IAEA Safety Series No. 115 – "International Basic Safety Standards for Protection Against Ionizing Radiation and for Safety of Radiation Sources"); or

(c)   Where there is reason to believe that there has been a significant degradation in any package safety function (containment, shielding, thermal protection or criticality) that may have rendered the package unsuitable for continued carriage without additional safety measures.

NOTE: See the requirements of 7.5.11 CV33 (6) for undeliverable consignments.

Material damage or environmental damage means the release of dangerous goods, irrespective of the quantity, where the estimated amount of damage exceeds 50,000 Euros. Damage to any directly involved means of carriage containing dangerous goods and to the modal infrastructure shall not be taken into account for this purpose.

Involvement of authorities means the direct involvement of the authorities or emergency services during the occurrence involving dangerous goods and the evacuation of persons or closure of public traffic routes (roads/railways) for at least three hours owing to the danger posed by the dangerous goods.

If necessary, the competent authority may request further relevant information.

1.8.5.4   *Model for report on occurrences during the carriage of dangerous goods*

**Report on occurrences during the carriage of dangerous goods
in accordance with RID/ADR section 1.8.5**

- 71 -

Carrier/Railway infrastructure operator:
....
Address:
....
Contact name: ....………   Telephone: ....   Fax: ....…………

(The competent authority shall remove this cover sheet before forwarding the report)

1. Mode	
□ Rail Wagon number (optional)	□ Road Vehicle registration (optional) ....

2. Date and location of occurrence	
Year: .... Month:	Day: .... Time: ....
Rail □ Station □ Shunting/marshalling yard □ Loading/unloading/transhipment site Location / Country: .... or □ Open line: Description of line: .... Kilometres:	Road □ Built-up area □ Loading/unloading/transhipment site □ Open road Location / Country: ....

3. Topography
□ Gradient/incline □ Tunnel □ Bridge/Underpass □ Crossing

4. Particular weather conditions
□ Rain □ Snow □ Ice □ Fog □ Thunderstorm □ Storm Temperature: ..... °C

5. Description of occurrence
□ Derailment/Leaving the road □ Collision □ Overturning/Rolling over □ Fire □ Explosion □ Loss □ Technical fault Additional description of occurrence: ....

6. Dangerous goods involved

UN Number [1]	Class	Packing Group	Estimated quantity of loss of products (kg or l) [2]	Means of containment [3]	Means of containment material	Type of failure of means of containment [4]

[1] For dangerous goods assigned to collective entries to which special provision 274 applies, also the technical name shall be indicated.

[2] For Class 7, indicate values according to the criteria in 1.8.5.3.

[3] Indicate the appropriate number
1 Packaging
2 IBC
3 Large packaging
4 Small container
5 Wagon
6 Vehicle
7 Tank-wagon
8 Tank-vehicle
9 Battery-wagon
10 Battery-vehicle
11 Wagon with demountable tanks
12 Demountable tank
13 Large container
14 Tank-container
15 MEGC
16 Portable tank

[4] Indicate the appropriate number
1 Loss
2 Fire
3 Explosion
4 Structural failure

7. Cause of occurrence (if clearly known)

☐ Technical fault
☐ Faulty load securing
☐ Operational cause (rail operation)
☐ Other:
....
....
....

8. Consequences of occurrence

Personal injury in connection with the dangerous goods involved:
☐ Deaths (number: ......)
☐ Injured (number: ......)

Loss of product:
☐ Yes
☐ No
☐ Imminent risk of loss of product

Material/Environmental damage:
☐ Estimated level of damage ≤ 50,000 Euros
☐ Estimated level of damage > 50,000 Euros

Involvement of authorities:
☐ Yes ☐ Evacuation of persons for a duration of at least three hours caused by the dangerous goods involved
☐ Closure of public traffic routes for a duration of at least three hours caused by the dangerous goods involved
☐ No

If necessary, the competent authority may request further relevant information.

1.8.6 **Administrative controls for application of the conformity assessments, periodic inspections, and exceptional checks described in 1.8.7**

1.8.6.1 The competent authority may approve inspection bodies for conformity assessments, periodic inspections, exceptional checks and surveillance of the in-house inspection service as specified in section 1.8.7.

1.8.6.2 The competent authority shall ensure the monitoring of the inspection bodies and shall revoke or restrict the approval given, if it notes that an approved body is no longer in compliance with the approval and the requirements of 1.8.6.4 or does not follow the procedures specified in the provisions of ADR.

1.8.6.3 If the approval is revoked or restricted or when the inspection body has ceased activity, the competent authority shall take the appropriate steps to ensure that the files are either processed by another inspection body or kept available.

1.8.6.4 The inspection body shall:

(a) Have a staff with an organisational structure, capable, trained, competent and skilled, to satisfactorily perform its technical functions;

(b) Have access to suitable and adequate facilities and equipment;

(c) Operate in an impartial manner and be free from any influence which could prevent it from doing so;

(d) Ensure commercial confidentiality of the commercial and proprietary activities of the manufacturer and other bodies;

(e) Maintain clear demarcation between actual inspection body functions and unrelated functions;

(f) Have a documented quality system;

(g) Ensure that the tests and inspections specified in the relevant standard and in ADR are performed; and

(h) Maintain an effective and appropriate report and record system in accordance with 1.8.7.

The inspection body shall additionally be accredited according to the standard EN ISO/IEC 17020:2004, as specified in 6.2.3.6 and TA4 and TT9 of 6.8.4.

An inspection body starting a new activity may be approved temporarily. Before temporary designation, the competent authority shall ensure that the inspection body meets the requirements of the standard EN ISO/IEC 17020:2004. The inspection body shall be accredited in its first year of activity to be able to continue this new activity.

1.8.7   **Procedures for conformity assessment and periodic inspection**

NOTE: In this section, "relevant body" means a body assigned in 6.2.2.9 when certifying UN pressure receptacles, in 6.2.3.6 when approving non-UN pressure receptacles and in special provisions TA4 and TT9 of 6.8.4.

1.8.7.1   *General provisions*

1.8.7.1.1   The procedures in section 1.8.7 shall be applied according to the table in 6.2.3.6 when approving non-UN pressure receptacles and according to TA4 and TT9 of 6.8.4 when approving tanks, battery-vehicles and MEGCs.

The procedures in section 1.8.7 may be applied according to the table in 6.2.2.9 when certifying UN pressure receptacles.

1.8.7.1.2   Each application for

(a)   The type approval in accordance with 1.8.7.2 or;

(b)   The supervision of manufacture in accordance with 1.8.7.3 and the initial inspection and test in accordance with 1.8.7.4; or

(c)   The periodic inspection and exceptional checks in accordance with 1.8.7.5

shall be lodged by the applicant with a single competent authority, its delegate or an approved inspection body of his choice.

1.8.7.1.3   The application shall include:

(a)   The name and address of the applicant;

(b)   For conformity assessment where the applicant is not the manufacturer, the name and address of the manufacturer;

(c)   A written declaration that the same application has not been lodged with any other competent authority, its delegate or inspection body;

(d)   The relevant technical documentation specified in 1.8.7.7;

(e)   A statement allowing the competent authority, its delegate or inspection body access for inspection purposes to the locations of manufacture, inspection, testing and storage and providing it with all necessary information.

1.8.7.1.4   Where the applicant can demonstrate to the satisfaction of the competent authority or its delegated inspection body conformity with 1.8.7.6 the applicant may establish an in-house inspection service which may perform part or all of the inspections and tests when specified in 6.2.2.9 or 6.2.3.6.

1.8.7.2   *Type approval*

1.8.7.2.1   The applicant shall:

(a)   In the case of pressure receptacles, place at the disposal of the relevant body representative samples of the production envisaged. The relevant body may request further samples if required by the test programme;

(b) In the case of tanks, battery-vehicles or MEGCs, give access to the prototype for type testing.

1.8.7.2.2 The relevant body shall:

(a) Examine the technical documentation specified in 1.8.7.7.1 to verify that the design is in accordance with the relevant provisions of ADR, and the prototype or the prototype lot has been manufactured in conformity with the technical documentation and is representative of the design;

(b) Perform the examinations and witness the tests specified in ADR, to determine that the provisions have been applied and fulfilled, and the procedures adopted by the manufacturer meet the requirements;

(c) Check the certificate(s) issued by the materials manufacturer(s) against the relevant provisions of ADR;

(d) As applicable, approve the procedures for the permanent joining of parts or check that they have been previously approved, and verify that the staff undertaking the permanent joining of parts and the non-destructive tests are qualified or approved;

(e) Agree with the applicant the location and testing facilities where the examinations and necessary tests are to be carried out.

The relevant body shall issue a type-examination report to the applicant.

1.8.7.2.3 Where the type satisfies all applicable provisions, the competent authority, its delegate or the inspection body, shall issue a type approval certificate.

This certificate shall contain:

(a) The name and address of the issuer;

(b) The name and address of the manufacturer;

(c) A reference to the version of ADR and standards used for the type examination;

(d) Any requirements resulting from the examination;

(e) The necessary data for identification of the type and variation, as defined by the relevant standard; and

(f) The reference to the type examination report(s).

A list of the relevant parts of the technical documentation shall be annexed to the certificate (see 1.8.7.7.1).

1.8.7.3 *Supervision of manufacture*

1.8.7.3.1 The manufacturing process shall be subject to a survey by the relevant body to ensure the product is produced in conformity with the provisions of the type approval.

1.8.7.3.2 The applicant shall take all the necessary measures to ensure that the manufacturing process complies with the applicable provisions of ADR and of the type approval certificate and its annexes.

1.8.7.3.3   The relevant body shall:

(a)   Verify the conformity with the technical documentation specified in 1.8.7.7.2;

(b)   Verify that the manufacturing process produces products in conformity with the requirements and the documentation which apply to it;

(c)   Verify the traceability of materials and check the material certificate(s) against the specifications;

(d)   As applicable, verify that the personnel undertaking the permanent joining of parts and the non-destructive tests are qualified or approved;

(e)   Agree with the applicant on the location where the examinations and necessary tests are to be carried out; and

(f)   Record the results of its survey.

1.8.7.4   *Initial inspection and tests*

1.8.7.4.1   The applicant shall:

(a)   Affix the marks specified in ADR; and

(b)   Supply to the relevant body the technical documentation specified in 1.8.7.7.

1.8.7.4.2   The relevant body shall:

(a)   Perform the necessary examinations and tests in order to verify that the product is manufactured in accordance with the type approval and the relevant provisions;

(b)   Check the certificates supplied by the manufacturers of service equipment against the service equipment;

(c)   Issue an initial inspection and test report to the applicant relating to the detailed tests and verifications carried out and the verified technical documentation; and

(d)   Draw up a written certificate of conformity of the manufacture and affix its registered mark when the manufacture satisfies the provisions.

The certificate and report may cover a number of items of the same type (group certificate or report).

1.8.7.4.3   The certificate shall contain as a minimum:

(a)   The name and address of the relevant body;

(b)   The name and address of the manufacturer and the name and address of the applicant, if not the manufacturer;

(c)   A reference to the version of the ADR and standards used for the initial inspections and tests;

(d)   The results of the inspections and tests;

(e)   The data for identification of the inspected product(s), at least the serial number or for non refillable cylinders the batch number; and

(f)   The type approval number.

1.8.7.5   *Periodic inspection and exceptional checks*

The relevant body shall:

(a)   Perform the identification and verify the conformity with the documentation;

(b)   Carry out the inspections and witness the tests in order to check that the requirements are met;

(c)   Issue reports of the results of the inspections and tests, which may cover a number of items; and

(d)   Ensure that the required marks are applied.

1.8.7.6   *Surveillance of the applicant's in-house inspection service*

1.8.7.6.1   The applicant shall:

(a)   Implement an in-house inspection service with a quality system for inspections and tests documented in 1.8.7.7.5 and subject to surveillance;

(b)   Fulfil the obligations arising out of the quality system as approved and to ensure that it remains satisfactory and efficient;

(c)   Appoint trained and competent personnel for the in-house inspection service; and

(d)   Affix the registered mark of the inspection body where appropriate.

1.8.7.6.2   The inspection body shall carry out an initial audit. If satisfactory the inspection body shall issue an authorisation for a period not exceeding three years. The following provisions shall be met:

(a)   This audit shall confirm that the inspections and tests performed on the product are in compliance with the requirements of ADR;

(b)   The inspection body may authorise the in-house inspection service of the applicant to affix the registered mark of the inspection body to each approved product;

(c)   The authorisation may be renewed after a satisfactory audit in the last year prior to the expiry. The new period of validity shall begin with the date of expiry of the authorisation; and

(d)   The auditors of the inspection body shall be competent to carry out the assessment of conformity of the product covered by the quality system.

1.8.7.6.3   The inspection body shall carry out periodic audits within the duration of the authorisation to make sure that the applicant maintains and applies the quality system. The following provisions shall be met:

(a)   A minimum of two audits shall be carried out in a 12 month period;

(b)   The inspection body may require additional visits, training, technical changes, modifications of the quality system, restrict or prohibit the inspections and tests to be done by the applicant;

(c)   The inspection body shall assess any changes in the quality system and decide whether the modified quality system will still satisfy the requirements of the initial audit or whether a full reassessment is required;

(d)   The auditors of the inspection body shall be competent to carry out the assessment of conformity of the product covered by the quality system; and

(e)   The inspection body shall provide the applicant with a visit or audit report and, if a test has taken place, with a test report.

1.8.7.6.4   In cases of non conformity with the relevant requirements the inspection body shall ensure that corrective measures are taken. If corrective measures are not taken in due time, the inspection body shall suspend or withdraw the permission for the in-house inspection service to carry out its activities. The notice of suspension or withdrawal shall be transmitted to the competent authority. A report shall be provided to the applicant giving detailed reasons for the decisions taken by the inspection body.

1.8.7.7   *Documents*

The technical documentation shall enable an assessment to be made of conformity with the relevant requirements.

1.8.7.7.1   *Documents for type approval*

The applicant shall provide as appropriate:

(a)   The list of standards used for the design and manufacture;

(b)   A description of the type including all variations;

(c)   The instructions according to the relevant column of table A of Chapter 3.2 or a list of dangerous goods to be transported for dedicated products;

(d)   A general assembly drawing or drawings;

(e)   The detailed drawings, including the dimensions used for the calculations, of the product, the service equipment, the structural equipment, the marking and/or the labelling necessary to verify the conformity;

(f)   The calculation notes, results and conclusions;

(g)   The list of the service equipment with the relevant technical data and information on the safety devices including the calculation of the relief capacity if relevant;

(h)   The list of material requested in the standard for manufacture used for every part, sub-part, lining, service and structural equipment and the corresponding material specifications or the corresponding declaration of conformity to ADR;

(i)   The approved qualification of permanent joining process;

(j)   The description of the heat treatment process(es); and

(k)   The procedures, descriptions and records of all relevant tests listed in the standards or ADR for the type approval and for the manufacture.

1.8.7.7.2   *Documents for the supervision of manufacture*

The applicant shall make available as appropriate:

(a)   The documents listed in 1.8.7.7.1;

(b)   The manufacturing procedures including test procedures;

(c)   The manufacturing records;

(d)   The approved qualifications of permanent joining operators;

(e)   The approved qualifications of the non destructive test operators;

(f)   The reports of the destructive and non destructive tests;

(g)   The heat treatment records; and

(h)   The calibration records.

1.8.7.7.3   *Documents for initial inspection and tests*

The applicant shall make available as appropriate:

(a)   The documents listed in 1.8.7.7.1 and 1.8.7.7.2;

(b)   The material certificates of the product and any sub-parts;

(c)   The declarations of conformity and material certificates of the service equipment; and

(d)   A declaration of conformity including the description of the product and all the variations adopted from the type approval.

1.8.7.7.4   *Documents for periodic inspections and exceptional checks*

The applicant shall make available as appropriate:

(a)   For pressure receptacles, the documents specifying special requirements when the manufacturing and periodic inspections and tests standards so require;

(b)   For tanks:

(i)   the tank record; and

(ii)   one or more of the documents mentioned in 1.8.7.7.1 to 1.8.7.7.3.

1.8.7.7.5   *Documents for the assessment of in-house inspection service*

The applicant for in-house inspection service shall make available the quality system documentation as appropriate:

(a)   The organisational structure and responsibilities;

(b)   The relevant inspection and test, quality control, quality assurance and process operation instructions, and systematic actions that will be used;

(c)   The quality records, such as inspection reports, test data, calibration data and certificates;

(d)   The management reviews to ensure the effective operation of the quality system arising from the audits in accordance with 1.8.7.6;

(e)   The process describing how customer and regulation requirements are met;

(f)   The process for control of documents and their revision;

(g)   The procedures for dealing with non-conforming products; and

(h)   The training programmes and qualification procedures for relevant personnel.

1.8.7.8   *Products manufactured, approved, inspected and tested according to standards*

The requirements of 1.8.7.7 are considered to have been complied with if the following standards, as relevant, are applied:

Applicable subsection and paragraph	References	Title of the document
1.8.7.7.1 to 1.8.7.7.4	EN 12972:2007	Tanks for transport of dangerous goods - Testing, inspection and marking of metallic tanks

CHAPTER 1.9

TRANSPORT RESTRICTIONS BY THE COMPETENT AUTHORITIES

1.9.1   In accordance with Article 4, paragraph 1 of ADR, the entry of dangerous goods into the territory of Contracting Parties may be subject to regulations or prohibitions imposed for reasons other than safety during carriage. Such regulations or prohibitions shall be published in an appropriate form.

1.9.2   Subject to the provisions of 1.9.3, a Contracting Party may apply to vehicles engaged in the international carriage of dangerous goods by road on its territory certain additional provisions not included in ADR, provided that those provisions do not conflict with Article 2, paragraph 2 of the Agreement, and are contained in its domestic legislation applying equally to vehicles engaged in the domestic carriage of dangerous goods by road on the territory of that Contracting Party.

1.9.3   Additional provisions falling within the scope of 1.9.2 are as follows:

(a)   Additional safety requirements or restrictions concerning vehicles using certain structures such as bridges, vehicles using combined transport modes such as ferries or trains, or vehicles entering or leaving ports or other transport terminals;

(b)   Requirements for vehicles to follow prescribed routes to avoid commercial or residential areas, environmentally sensitive areas, industrial zones containing hazardous installations or roads presenting severe physical hazards;

(c)   Emergency requirements regarding routeing or parking of vehicles carrying dangerous goods resulting from extreme weather conditions, earthquake, accident, industrial action, civil disorder or military hostilities;

(d)   Restrictions on movement of dangerous goods traffic on certain days of the week or year.

1.9.4   The competent authority of the Contracting Party applying on its territory any additional provisions within the scope of 1.9.3 (a) and (d) above shall notify the Secretariat of the United Nations Economic Commission for Europe of the additional provisions, which Secretariat shall bring them to the attention of the Contracting Parties.

1.9.5   **Tunnel restrictions**

NOTE: Provisions concerning restrictions for the passage of vehicles through road tunnels are also included in Chapter 8.6.

1.9.5.1   *General provisions*

When applying restrictions to the passage of vehicles carrying dangerous goods through tunnels, the competent authority shall assign the road tunnel to one of the tunnel categories defined in 1.9.5.2.2. Account should be taken of the tunnel characteristics, risk assessment including availability and suitability of alternative routes and modes and traffic management considerations. The same tunnel may be assigned to more than one tunnel category, e.g. depending on the hours of the day, or the day of the week etc.

1.9.5.2   *Categorization*

1.9.5.2.1   The categorization shall be based on the assumption that in tunnels there are three major dangers which may cause numerous victims or serious damage to the tunnel structure:

(a)   Explosions;

(b)   Release of toxic gas or volatile toxic liquid;

(c)   Fires.

1.9.5.2.2   The five tunnel categories are the following:

Tunnel category A:

No restrictions for the transport of dangerous goods;

Tunnel category B:

Restriction for dangerous goods which may lead to a very large explosion;

The following dangerous goods are considered to fulfil this criterion [1]:

Class 1:   Compatibility groups A and L; Class 3:   Classification code D (UN Nos. 1204, 2059, 3064, 3343, 3357 and 3379); Class 4.1:   Classification codes D and DT; and   Self-reactive substances, type B (UN Nos. 3221, 3222, 3231 and 3232); Class 5.2:   Organic peroxides, type B (UN Nos. 3101, 3102, 3111 and 3112).
When the total net explosive mass per transport unit is greater than 1000 kg: Class 1:   Divisions 1.1, 1.2 and 1.5 (except compatibility groups A and L).
When carried in tanks: Class 2:   Classification codes F, TF and TFC; Class 4.2:   Packing group I; Class 4.3:   Packing group I; Class 5.1:   Packing group I.

Tunnel category C:

Restriction for dangerous goods which may lead to a very large explosion, a large explosion or a large toxic release;

The following dangerous goods are considered to fulfil this criterion [1]:

-     the dangerous goods restricted in tunnel category B, and

-     the following dangerous goods:

---

[1]   *The assessment is based on the intrinsic dangerous properties of the goods, the type of containment and the quantity carried.*

Class 1:	Divisions 1.1, 1.2 and 1.5 (except compatibility groups A and L); and Division 1.3 (compatibility groups H and J);
Class 7:	UN Nos. 2977 and 2978.
When the net explosive mass per transport unit is greater than 5000 kg:	
Class 1:	Division 1.3 (compatibility groups C and G).
When carried in tanks:	
Class 2:	Classification codes 2A, 2O, 3A and 3O, and classification codes containing the letter T only or letter groups TC, TO and TOC
Class 3:	Packing group I for classification codes FC, FT1, FT2 and FTC;
Class 6.1:	Packing group I
Class 8:	Packing group I for classification codes CT1, CFT and COT.

Tunnel category D:

Restriction for dangerous goods which may lead to a very large explosion, to a large explosion, to a large toxic release or to a large fire;

The following dangerous goods are considered to fulfil this criterion [1]:

- the dangerous goods restricted in tunnel category C, and

- the following dangerous goods:

Class 1:	Division 1.3 (compatibility groups C and G);
Class 2:	Classification codes F, FC, T, TF, TC, TO, TFC and TOC;
Class 4.1:	Self-reactive substances, types C, D, E and F; and UN Nos. 2956, 3241, 3242 and 3251;
Class 5.2:	Organic peroxides, types C, D, E and F;
Class 6.1:	Packing group I for classification codes TF1 and TFC; and Toxic by inhalation entries (UN Nos. 3381 to 3390);
Class 8:	Packing group I for classification codes CT1, CFT and COT;
Class 9:	Classification codes M9 and M10.
When carried in bulk or in tanks:	
Class 3	
Class 4.2:	Packing group II;
Class 4.3:	Packing group II;
Class 6.1:	Packing group II; and Packing group III for classification code TF2;
Class 8:	Packing group I for classification codes CF1, CFT and CW1; and Packing group II for classification codes CF1 and CFT
Class 9:	Classification codes M2 and M3.

Tunnel category E:

Restriction for all dangerous goods other than UN Nos. 2919, 3291, 3331, 3359 and 3373.

NOTE: *For the dangerous goods assigned to UN Nos. 2919 and 3331, restrictions to the passage through tunnels may, however, be part of the special arrangement approved by the competent authority(ies) on the basis of 1.7.4.2.*

---

[1] *The assessment is based on the intrinsic dangerous properties of the goods, the type of containment and the quantity carried.*

1.9.5.3   *Provisions for road signs and notification of restrictions*

1.9.5.3.1   Contracting Parties shall indicate tunnel prohibitions and alternative routes by means of signs and signals.

1.9.5.3.2   For this purpose, they may use signs C, 3h and D, 10a, 10b and 10c and signals according to the Vienna Convention on Road Signs and Signals (Vienna, 1968) and the European Agreement supplementing the Convention on Road Signs and Signals (Geneva, 1971) as interpreted by the Resolution on Road Signs and Signals (R.E.2) of the UNECE Inland Transport Committee Principal Working Party on Road Transport, as amended.

1.9.5.3.3   In order to facilitate international understanding of signs, the system of signs and signals prescribed in the Vienna Convention is based on the use of shapes, and colours characteristic of each class of signs and wherever possible, on the use of graphic symbols rather than inscriptions. Where Contracting Parties consider it necessary to modify the signs and symbols prescribed, the modifications made shall not alter their essential characteristics. Where Contracting Parties do not apply the Vienna Convention, the prescribed signs and symbols may be modified, provided that the modifications made shall not alter their essential intent.

1.9.5.3.4   Traffic signs and signals intended to prohibit access of vehicles carrying dangerous goods to road tunnels shall be affixed at a place where the choice of alternative routes is possible.

1.9.5.3.5   When access to tunnels is restricted or alternative routes are prescribed, the signs shall be displayed with additional panels as follows:

No sign: no restriction

Sign with additional panel bearing the letter B: applies to vehicles carrying dangerous goods not allowed in tunnels of category B;

Sign with additional panel bearing the letter C: applies to vehicles carrying dangerous goods not allowed in tunnels of category C;

Sign with additional panel bearing the letter D: applies to vehicles carrying dangerous goods not allowed in tunnels of category D;

Sign with additional panel bearing the letter E: applies to vehicles carrying dangerous goods not allowed in tunnels of category E.

1.9.5.3.6   Tunnel restrictions shall not apply when dangerous goods are carried in accordance with 1.1.3

1.9.5.3.7   Restrictions shall be published officially and made publicly available. Contracting Parties shall notify the secretariat of UNECE of such restrictions and the secretariat shall make this information publicly available on its website.

1.9.5.3.8   When Contracting Parties apply specific operating measures designed to reduce the risks and related to some or all vehicles using tunnels, such as declaration before entering or passage in convoys escorted by accompanying vehicles, such operating measures shall be published officially and made publicly available.

CHAPTER 1.10

SECURITY PROVISIONS

NOTE: *For the purposes of this Chapter, security means measures or precautions to be taken to minimise theft or misuse of dangerous goods that may endanger persons, property or the environment.*

1.10.1   General provisions

1.10.1.1   All persons engaged in the carriage of dangerous goods shall consider the security requirements set out in this Chapter commensurate with their responsibilities.

1.10.1.2   Dangerous goods shall only be offered for carriage to carriers that have been appropriately identified.

1.10.1.3   Areas within temporary storage terminals, temporary storage sites, vehicle depots, berthing areas and marshalling yards used for the temporary storage during carriage of dangerous goods shall be properly secured, well lit and, where possible and appropriate, not accessible to the general public.

1.10.1.4   Each member of a vehicle crew shall carry with them means of identification, which includes their photograph, during carriage of dangerous goods.

1.10.1.5   Safety inspections in accordance with 1.8.1 and 7.5.1.1 shall cover appropriate security measures.

1.10.1.6   The competent authority shall maintain up-to-date registers of all valid training certificates for drivers stipulated in 8.2.1 issued by it or by any recognized organization.

1.10.2   Security training

1.10.2.1   The training and the refresher training specified in Chapter 1.3 shall also include elements of security awareness. The security refresher training need not be linked to regulatory changes only.

1.10.2.2   Security awareness training shall address the nature of security risks, recognising security risks, methods to address and reduce such risks and actions to be taken in the event of a security breach. It shall include awareness of security plans (if appropriate) commensurate with the responsibilities and duties of individuals and their part in implementing security plans.

1.10.3   Provisions for high consequence dangerous goods

1.10.3.1   "High consequence dangerous goods" are those which have the potential for misuse in a terrorist incident and which may, as a result, produce serious consequences such as mass casualties or mass destruction. The list of high consequence dangerous goods is provided in Table 1.10.5.

1.10.3.2 *Security plans*

1.10.3.2.1 Carriers, consignors and other participants specified in 1.4.2 and 1.4.3 engaged in the carriage of high consequence dangerous goods (see Table 1.10.5) shall adopt, implement and comply with a security plan that addresses at least the elements specified in 1.10.3.2.2.

1.10.3.2.2 The security plan shall comprise at least the following elements:

(a) Specific allocation of responsibilities for security to competent and qualified persons with appropriate authority to carry out their responsibilities;

(b) Records of dangerous goods or types of dangerous goods concerned;

(c) Review of current operations and assessment of security risks, including any stops necessary to the transport operation, the keeping of dangerous goods in the vehicle, tank or container before, during and after the journey and the intermediate temporary storage of dangerous goods during the course of intermodal transfer or transhipment between units as appropriate;

(d) Clear statement of measures that are to be taken to reduce security risks, commensurate with the responsibilities and duties of the participant, including:

- training;

- security policies (e.g. response to higher threat conditions, new employee/employment verification, etc.);

- operating practices (e.g. choice/use of routes where known, access to dangerous goods in intermediate temporary storage (as defined in (c)), proximity to vulnerable infrastructure etc.);

- equipment and resources that are to be used to reduce security risks;

(e) Effective and up to date procedures for reporting and dealing with security threats, breaches of security or security incidents;

(f) Procedures for the evaluation and testing of security plans and procedures for periodic review and update of the plans;

(g) Measures to ensure the physical security of transport information contained in the security plan; and

(h) Measures to ensure that the distribution of information relating to the transport operation contained in the security plan is limited to those who need to have it. Such measures shall not preclude the provision of information required elsewhere in ADR.

NOTE: Carriers, consignors and consignees should co-operate with each other and with competent authorities to exchange threat information, apply appropriate security measures and respond to security incidents.

1.10.3.3 Devices, equipment or arrangements to prevent the theft of the vehicle carrying high consequence dangerous goods (see Table 1.10.5) and its cargo, shall be applied and measures taken to ensure that these are operational and effective at all times. The application of these protective measures shall not jeopardize emergency response.

NOTE: When appropriate and already fitted, the use of transport telemetry or other tracking methods or devices should be used to monitor the movement of high consequence dangerous goods (see Table 1.10.5).

1.10.4   In accordance with the provisions of 1.1.3.6, the requirements of 1.10.1, 1.10.2, 1.10.3 and 8.1.2.1 (d) do not apply when the quantities carried in packages on a transport unit do not exceed those referred to in 1.1.3.6.3, except for UN Nos. 0104, 0237, 0255, 0267, 0289, 0361, 0365, 0366, 0440, 0441, 0455, 0456 and 0500 (see first indent of 1.1.3.6.2). In addition, the requirements of 1.10.1, 1.10.2, 1.10.3 and 8.1.2.1 (d) do not apply when the quantities carried in tanks or in bulk on a transport unit do not exceed those referred to in 1.1.3.6.3.

1.10.5   High consequence dangerous goods are those listed in the table below and carried in quantities greater than those indicated therein.

Table 1.10.5: List of high consequence dangerous goods

Class	Division	Substance or article	Quantity		
			Tank (l) [c]	Bulk (kg) [d]	Packages (kg)
1	1.1	Explosives	[a]	[a]	0
	1.2	Explosives	[a]	[a]	0
	1.3	Compatibility group C explosives	[a]	[a]	0
	1.4	Explosives of UN Nos. 0104, 0237, 0255, 0267, 0289, 0361, 0365, 0366, 0440, 0441, 0455, 0456 and 0500	[a]	[a]	0
	1.5	Explosives	0	[a]	0
2		Flammable gases (classification codes including only the letter F)	3000	[a]	[b]
		Toxic gases (classification codes including letters T, TF, TC, TO, TFC or TOC) excluding aerosols	0	[a]	0
3		Flammable liquids of packing groups I and II	3000	[a]	[b]
		Desensitized explosives	0	[a]	0
4.1		Desensitized explosives	[a]	[a]	0
4.2		Packing group I substances	3000	[a]	[b]
4.3		Packing group I substances	3000	[a]	[b]
5.1		Oxidizing liquids of packing group I	3000	[a]	[b]
		Perchlorates, ammonium nitrate, ammonium nitrate fertilisers and ammonium nitrate emulsions or suspensions or gels	3000	3000	[b]
6.1		Toxic substances of packing group I	0	[a]	0
6.2		Infectious substances of Category A (UN Nos. 2814 and 2900)	[a]	0	0
7		Radioactive material	3000 A_1 (special form) or 3000 A_2, as applicable, in Type B(U), B(M) or C packages		
8		Corrosive substances of packing group I	3000	[a]	[b]

[a]   *Not relevant.*

[b]   *The provisions of 1.10.3 do not apply, whatever the quantity is.*

[c]   *A value indicated in this column is applicable only if carriage in tanks is authorized, in accordance with Chapter 3.2, Table A, column (10) or (12). For substances that are not authorized for carriage in tanks, the instruction in this column is not relevant.*

[d]   *A value indicated in this column is applicable only if carriage in bulk is authorized, in accordance with Chapter 3.2, Table A, column (10) or (17). For substances that are not authorized for carriage in bulk, the instruction in this column is not relevant.*

1.10.6   For radioactive material, the provisions of this Chapter are deemed to be complied with when the provisions of the Convention on Physical Protection of Nuclear Material and of IAEA INFCIRC/225 (Rev.4) are applied.

PART 2

Classification

CHAPTER 2.1

GENERAL PROVISIONS

2.1.1 **Introduction**

2.1.1.1   The classes of dangerous goods according to ADR are the following:

Class 1   Explosive substances and articles
Class 2   Gases
Class 3   Flammable liquids
Class 4.1   Flammable solids, self-reactive substances and solid desensitized explosives
Class 4.2   Substances liable to spontaneous combustion
Class 4.3   Substances which, in contact with water, emit flammable gases
Class 5.1   Oxidizing substances
Class 5.2   Organic peroxides
Class 6.1   Toxic substances
Class 6.2   Infectious substances
Class 7   Radioactive material
Class 8   Corrosive substances
Class 9   Miscellaneous dangerous substances and articles

2.1.1.2   Each entry in the different classes has been assigned a UN number. The following types of entries are used:

A.   Single entries for well defined substances or articles including entries for substances covering several isomers, e.g.:

UN No. 1090   ACETONE
UN No. 1104   AMYL ACETATES
UN No. 1194   ETHYL NITRITE SOLUTION

B.   Generic entries for a well defined group of substances or articles, which are not n.o.s. entries, e.g.:

UN No. 1133   ADHESIVES
UN No. 1266   PERFUMERY PRODUCTS
UN No. 2757   CARBAMATE PESTICIDE, SOLID, TOXIC
UN No. 3101   ORGANIC PEROXIDE TYPE B, LIQUID

C.   Specific n.o.s. entries covering a group of substances or articles of a particular chemical or technical nature, not otherwise specified, e.g.:

UN No. 1477   NITRATES, INORGANIC, N.O.S.
UN No. 1987   ALCOHOLS, N.O.S.

D.   General n.o.s. entries covering a group of substances or articles having one or more dangerous properties, not otherwise specified, e.g.:

UN No. 1325   FLAMMABLE SOLID, ORGANIC, N.O.S.
UN No. 1993   FLAMMABLE LIQUID, N.O.S.

The entries defined under B., C. and D. are defined as collective entries.

2.1.1.3   For packing purposes, substances other than those of Classes 1, 2, 5.2, 6.2 and 7, and other than self-reactive substances of Class 4.1 are assigned to packing groups in accordance with the degree of danger they present:

Packing group I: Substances presenting high danger;
Packing group II: Substances presenting medium danger;
Packing group III: Substances presenting low danger.

The packing group(s) to which a substance is assigned is (are) indicated in Table A of Chapter 3.2.

2.1.2   Principles of classification

2.1.2.1   The dangerous goods covered by the heading of a class are defined on the basis of their properties according to sub-section 2.2.x.1 of the relevant class. Assignment of dangerous goods to a class and a packing group is made according to the criteria mentioned in the same sub-section 2.2.x.1. Assignment of one or several subsidiary risk(s) to a dangerous substance or article is made according to the criteria of the class or classes corresponding to those risks, as mentioned in the appropriate sub-section(s) 2.2.x.1.

2.1.2.2   All dangerous goods entries are listed in Table A of Chapter 3.2 in the numerical order of their UN Number. This table contains relevant information on the goods listed, such as name, class, packing group(s), label(s) to be affixed, packing and carriage provisions [1].

2.1.2.3   Dangerous goods which are listed or defined in sub-section 2.2.x.2 of each class are not to be accepted for carriage.

2.1.2.4   Goods not mentioned by name, i.e. goods not listed as single entries in Table A of Chapter 3.2 and not listed or defined in one of the above-mentioned sub-sections 2.2.x.2 shall be assigned to the relevant class in accordance with the procedure of section 2.1.3. In addition, the subsidiary risk (if any) and the packing group (if any) shall be determined. Once the class, subsidiary risk (if any) and packing group (if any) have been established the relevant UN number shall be determined. The decision trees in sub-sections 2.2.x.3 (list of collective entries) at the end of each class indicate the relevant parameters for selecting the relevant collective entry (UN number). In all cases the most specific collective entry covering the properties of the substance or article shall be selected, according to the hierarchy indicated in 2.1.1.2 by the letters B, C and D respectively. If the substance or article cannot be classified under entries of type B or C according to 2.1.1.2, then, and only then shall it be classified under an entry of type D.

2.1.2.5   On the basis of the test procedures of Chapter 2.3 and the criteria set out in sub-sections 2.2.x.1 of classes when it is so specified, it may be determined that a substance, solution or mixture of a certain class, mentioned by name in Table A of Chapter 3.2, does not meet the criteria of that class. In such a case, the substance, solution or mixture is deemed not to belong to that class.

2.1.2.6   For the purposes of classification, substances with a melting point or initial melting point of 20 °C or lower at a pressure of 101.3 kPa shall be considered to be liquids. A viscous substance for which a specific melting point cannot be determined shall be subjected to the ASTM D 4359-90 test or to the test for determining fluidity (penetrometer test) prescribed in 2.3.4.

---

[1]   *Note by the Secretariat: An alphabetic list of these entries has been prepared by the secretariat and is reproduced in Table B of Chapter 3.2. This table is not an official part of the ADR.*

2.1.3 **Classification of substances, including solutions and mixtures (such as preparations and wastes), not mentioned by name**

2.1.3.1   Substances including solutions and mixtures not mentioned by name shall be classified according to their degree of danger on the basis of the criteria mentioned in sub-section 2.2.x.1 of the various classes. The danger(s) presented by a substance shall be determined on the basis of its physical and chemical characteristics and physiological properties. Such characteristics and properties shall also be taken into account when such experience leads to a more stringent assignment.

2.1.3.2   A substance not mentioned by name in Table A of Chapter 3.2 presenting a single hazard shall be classified in the relevant class under a collective entry listed in sub-section 2.2.x.3 of that class.

2.1.3.3   A solution or mixture containing only one dangerous substance mentioned by name in Table A of Chapter 3.2, together with one or more non-dangerous substance(s), shall be regarded as the dangerous substance listed by name, unless:

(a)   The solution or mixture is specifically mentioned by name in Table A of Chapter 3.2; or

(b)   It is quite clear from the entry for the dangerous substance that it is applicable only to the pure or technically pure substance; or

(c)   The class, physical state or packing group of the solution or mixture is different from that of the dangerous substance.

In the cases referred to under (b) or (c) above, the solution or mixture shall be classified as a substance not mentioned by name in the relevant class under a collective entry listed in sub-section 2.2.x.3 of that class taking account of the subsidiary risks presented by that solution or mixture, if any, unless the solution or mixture do not meet the criteria of any class, in which case they are not subject to ADR.

2.1.3.4   Solutions and mixtures containing substances belonging to one of the entries mentioned in 2.1.3.4.1 or 2.1.3.4.2 shall be classified in accordance with the provisions of these paragraphs.

2.1.3.4.1   Solutions and mixtures containing one of the following substances mentioned by name shall always be classified under the same entry as the substance they contain, provided they do not have the hazard characteristics as indicated in 2.1.3.5.3:

-   Class 3

    UN No. 1921 PROPYLENEIMINE, STABILIZED; UN No. 2481 ETHYL ISOCYANATE; UN No. 3064 NITROGLYCERIN SOLUTION IN ALCOHOL with more than 1% but not more than 5% nitroglycerin;

-   Class 6.1

    UN No. 1051 HYDROGEN CYANIDE, STABILIZED, containing less than 3% water; UN No. 1185 ETHYLENEIMINE, STABILIZED; UN No. 1259 NICKEL CARBONYL; UN No. 1613 HYDROCYANIC ACID, AQUEOUS SOLUTION (HYDROGEN CYANIDE, AQUEOUS SOLUTION), with not more than 20% hydrogen cyanide; UN No. 1614 HYDROGEN CYANIDE, STABILIZED, containing not more than 3% water and absorbed in a porous inert material; UN No. 1994 IRON PENTACARBONYL; UN No. 2480 METHYL ISOCYANATE; UN No. 3294 HYDROGEN CYANIDE, SOLUTION IN ALCOHOL, with not more than 45% hydrogen cyanide;

-     <u>Class 8</u>

        UN No. 1052 HYDROGEN FLUORIDE, ANHYDROUS; UN No. 1744 BROMINE or UN No. 1744 BROMINE SOLUTION; UN No. 1790 HYDROFLUORIC ACID with more than 85% hydrogen fluoride; UN No. 2576 PHOSPHORUS OXYBROMIDE, MOLTEN;

2.1.3.4.2   Solutions and mixtures containing a substance belonging to one of the following entries of Class 9:

UN No. 2315 POLYCHLORINATED BIPHENYLS, LIQUID;

UN No. 3151 POLYHALOGENATED BIPHENYLS, LIQUID;

UN No. 3151 POLYHALOGENATED TERPHENYLS, LIQUID;

UN No. 3152 POLYHALOGENATED BIPHENYLS, SOLID;

UN No. 3152 POLYHALOGENATED TERPHENYLS, SOLID; or

UN No. 3432 POLYCHLORINATED BIPHENYLS, SOLID

shall always be classified under the same entry of Class 9 provided that:

-     they do not contain any additional dangerous component other than components of packing group III of classes 3, 4.1, 4.2, 4.3, 5.1, 6.1 or 8; and

-     they do not have the hazard characteristics as indicated in 2.1.3.5.3.

2.1.3.5   Substances not mentioned by name in Table A of Chapter 3.2, having more than one hazard characteristic and solutions or mixtures containing several dangerous substances shall be classified under a collective entry (see 2.1.2.4) and packing group of the appropriate class in accordance with their hazard characteristics. Such classification according to the hazard characteristics shall be carried out as follows:

2.1.3.5.1   The physical and chemical characteristics and physiological properties shall be determined by measurement or calculation and the substance, solution or mixture shall be classified according to the criteria mentioned in sub-section 2.2.x.1 of the various classes.

2.1.3.5.2   If this determination is not possible without disproportionate cost or effort (as for some kinds of wastes), the substance, solution or mixture shall be classified in the class of the component presenting the major hazard.

2.1.3.5.3   If the hazard characteristics of the substance, solution or mixture fall within more than one class or group of substances listed below then the substance, solution or mixture shall be classified in the class or group of substances corresponding to the major hazard on the basis of the following order of precedence:

(a)   Material of Class 7 (apart from radioactive material in excepted packages where the other hazardous properties take precedence);

(b)   Substances of Class 1;

(c)   Substances of Class 2;

(d)   Liquid desensitized explosives of Class 3;

(e)   Self-reactive substances and solid desensitized explosives of Class 4.1;

(f)   Pyrophoric substances of Class 4.2;

(g) Substances of Class 5.2;

(h) Substances of Class 6.1 or Class 3 which, on the basis of their inhalation toxicity, are to be classified under Packing group I (Substances meeting the classification criteria of Class 8 and having an inhalation toxicity of dust and mist (LC_{50}) in the range of Packing group I and a toxicity through oral ingestion or dermal contact only in the range of Packing group III or less, shall be allocated to Class 8);

(i) Infectious substances of Class 6.2.

2.1.3.5.4 If the hazard characteristics of the substance fall within more than one class or group of substances not listed in 2.1.3.5.3 above, the substance shall be classified in accordance with the same procedure but the relevant class shall be selected according to the precedence of hazards table in 2.1.3.10.

2.1.3.5.5 If the substance to be carried is a waste, with a composition that is not precisely known, its assignment to a UN number and packing group in accordance with 2.1.3.5.2 may be based on the consignor's knowledge of the waste, including all available technical and safety data as requested by safety and environmental legislation in force [2].

In case of doubt, the highest danger level shall be taken.

If however, on the basis of the knowledge of the composition of the waste and the physical and chemical properties of the identified components, it is possible to demonstrate that the properties of the waste do not correspond to the properties of the packing group I level, the waste may be classified by default in the most appropriate n.o.s. entry of packing group II.

This procedure may not be used for wastes containing substances mentioned in 2.1.3.5.3, substances of Class 4.3, substances of the case mentioned in 2.1.3.7 or substances which are not accepted for carriage in accordance with 2.2.x.2.

2.1.3.6 The most specific applicable collective entry (see 2.1.2.4) shall always be used, i.e. a general n.o.s. entry shall only be used if a generic entry or a specific n.o.s. entry cannot be used.

2.1.3.7 Solutions and mixtures of oxidizing substances or substances with an oxidizing subsidiary risk may have explosive properties. In such a case they are not to be accepted for carriage unless they meet the requirements for Class 1.

2.1.3.8 Substances of classes 1 to 9, other than those assigned to UN Nos. 3077 or 3082, meeting the criteria of 2.2.9.1.10 are additionally to their hazards of classes 1 to 9 considered to be environmentally hazardous substances. Other substances meeting the criteria of 2.2.9.1.10 are to be assigned to UN Nos. 3077 or 3082 as appropriate.

---

[2] *Such legislation is for instance the Commission Decision 2000/532/EC of 3 May 2000 replacing Decision 94/3/EC establishing a list of wastes pursuant to Article 1(a) of Council Directive 75/442/EEC on waste (replaced by the Directive of the European Parliament and of the Council 2006/12/EC (Official Journal of the European Communities No. L 114 of 27 April 2006, page 9)) and Council Decision 94/904/EC establishing a list of hazardous wastes pursuant to Article 1(4) of Council Directive 91/689/EEC on hazardous wastes (Official Journal of the European Communities No. L 226 of 6 September 2000, page 3).*

2.1.3.9   Wastes that do not meet the criteria for classification in classes 1 to 9 but are covered by the *Basel Convention on the Control of Transboundary Movements of Hazardous Wastes and their Disposal* may be carried under UN Nos. 3077 or 3082.

2.1.3.10 Table of precedence of hazards

Class and packing group	4.1, II	4.1, III	4.2, II	4.2, III	4.3, I	4.3, II	4.3, III	5.1, I	5.1, II	5.1, III	6.1, I DERMAL	6.1, I ORAL	6.1, II	6.1, III	8, I	8, II	8, III	9
3, I	SOL 4.1 / LIQ 3,I	SOL 4.1 / LIQ 3,I	SOL 4.2 / LIQ 3,I	SOL 4.2 / LIQ 3,I	4.3,I	4.3,I	4.3,I	SOL 5.1,I / LIQ 3,I	SOL 5.1,I / LIQ 3,I	SOL 5.1,I / LIQ 3,I	3,I	3,I	3,I	3,I	8,I	3,I	3,I	3,I
3, II	SOL 4.1 / LIQ 3,II	SOL 4.1 / LIQ 3,II	SOL 4.2 / LIQ 3,II	SOL 4.2 / LIQ 3,II	4.3,I	4.3,II	4.3,II	SOL 5.1,I / LIQ 3,II	SOL 5.1,II / LIQ 3,II	SOL 5.1,II / LIQ 3,II	3,II	3,II	3,II	3,II	8,I	3,II	3,II	3,II
3, III	SOL 4.1 / LIQ 3,III	SOL 4.1 / LIQ 3,III	SOL 4.2 / LIQ 3,III	SOL 4.2 / LIQ 3,III	4.3,I	4.3,II	4.3,III	SOL 5.1,I / LIQ 3,II	SOL 5.1,II / LIQ 3,II	SOL 5.1,III / LIQ 3,II	6.1,I	6.1,I	6.1,II	3,III[a]	8,I	8,II	3,III	3,III
4.1, II			4.2,II	4.2,II	4.3,I	4.3,II	4.3,II	5.1,I	4.1,II	4.1,II	6.1,I	6.1,I	SOL 4.1,II / LIQ 6.1,II	SOL 4.1,II / LIQ 6.1,II	8,I	SOL 4.1,II / LIQ 8,II	SOL 4.1,II / LIQ 8,II	4.1,II
4.1, III			4.2,II	4.2,III	4.3,I	4.3,II	4.3,III	5.1,I	4.1,III	4.1,III	6.1,I	6.1,I	6.1,II	SOL 4.1,III / LIQ 6.1,III	8,I	8,II	SOL 4.1,III / LIQ 8,III	4.1,III
4.2, II				4.2,II	4.3,I	4.3,II	4.3,II	5.1,I	4.2,II	4.2,II	6.1,I	6.1,I	4.2,II	4.2,II	8,I	4.2,II	4.2,II	4.2,II
4.2, III					4.3,I	4.3,II	4.3,III	5.1,I	5.1,II	4.2,III	6.1,I	6.1,I	6.1,II	4.2,III	8,I	8,II	4.2,III	4.2,III
4.3, I						4.3,I	4.3,I	4.3,I	4.3,I	4.3,I	6.1,I	4.3,I	4.3,I	4.3,I	4.3,I	4.3,I	4.3,I	4.3,I
4.3, II							4.3,II	5.1,I	4.3,II	4.3,II	6.1,I	4.3,II	4.3,II	4.3,II	8,I	4.3,II	4.3,II	4.3,II
4.3, III								5.1,I	5.1,II	4.3,III	6.1,I	4.3,III	4.3,III	4.3,III	8,I	8,II	4.3,III	4.3,III
5.1, I									5.1,I	5.1,I	6.1,I	5.1,I	5.1,I	5.1,I	5.1,I	5.1,I	5.1,I	5.1,I
5.1, II										5.1,II	6.1,I	5.1,II	5.1,II	5.1,II	8,I	5.1,II	5.1,II	5.1,II
5.1, III											6.1,I	5.1,III	6.1,II	5.1,III	8,I	8,II	5.1,III	5.1,III
6.1, I DERMAL															SOL 6.1,I / LIQ 8,I	6.1,I	6.1,I	6.1,I
6.1, I ORAL															SOL 6.1,I / LIQ 8,I	6.1,I	6.1,I	6.1,I
6.1, II INHAL															SOL 6.1,II / LIQ 8,I	6.1,II	6.1,II	6.1,II
6.1, II DERMAL															SOL 6.1,I / LIQ 8,I	SOL 6.1,II / LIQ 8,II	SOL 6.1,II / LIQ 8,II	6.1,II
6.1, II ORAL															8,I	SOL 6.1,II / LIQ 8,II	SOL 6.1,III / LIQ 8,III	6.1,II
6.1, III															8,I	8,II	8,III	6.1,III
8, I																8,I	8,I	8,I
8, II																	8,II	8,II
8, III																		8,III

SOL = Solid substances and mixtures
LIQ = Liquid substances, mixtures and solutions
DERMAL = Dermal toxicity
ORAL = Oral toxicity
INHAL = Inhalation toxicity
[a] Class 6.1 for pesticides

NOTE 1: Examples to explain the use of the table

Classification of a single substance

Description of the substance to be classified:

An amine not mentioned by name meeting the criteria for Class 3, packing group II as well as those for Class 8, packing group I.

Procedure:

The intersection of line 3 II with column 8 I gives 8 I.
This amine has therefore to be classified in Class 8 under:

UN No. 2734 AMINES LIQUID, CORROSIVE, FLAMMABLE, N.O.S. or UN No. 2734 POLYAMINES, LIQUID, CORROSIVE, FLAMMABLE, N.O.S.
packing group I

Classification of a mixture

Description of the mixture to be classified:

Mixture consisting of a flammable liquid classified in Class 3, packing group III, a toxic substance in Class 6.1, packing group II and a corrosive substance in Class 8, packing group I.

Procedure:

The intersection of line 3 III with column 6.1 II gives 6.1 II.
The intersection of line 6.1 II with column 8 I gives 8 I LIQ.
This mixture not further defined has therefore to be classified in Class 8 under:

UN No. 2922 CORROSIVE LIQUID, TOXIC, N.O.S. packing group I.

NOTE 2: Examples for the classification of mixtures and solutions under a class and a packing group:

A phenol solution of Class 6.1, (II), in benzene of Class 3, (II) is to be classified in Class 3, (II); this solution is to be classified under UN No. 1992 FLAMMABLE LIQUID, TOXIC, N.O.S., Class 3, (II), by virtue of the toxicity of the phenol.

A solid mixture of sodium arsenate of Class 6.1, (II) and sodium hydroxide of Class 8, (II) is to be classified under UN No. 3290 TOXIC SOLID, CORROSIVE, INORGANIC, N.O.S., in Class 6.1 (II).

A solution of crude or refined naphthalene of Class 4.1, (III) in petrol of Class 3, (II), is to be classified under UN No. 3295 HYDROCARBONS, LIQUID, N.O.S. in Class 3, (II).

A mixture of hydrocarbons of Class 3, (III), and of polychlorinated biphenyls (PCB) of Class 9, (II), is to be classified under UN No. 2315 POLYCHLORINATED BIPHENYLS LIQUID or UN No. 3432 POLYCHLORINATED BIPHENYLS SOLID in Class 9, (II).

A mixture of propyleneimine of Class 3, and polychlorinated biphenyls (PCB) of Class 9, (II), is to be classified under UN No. 1921 PROPYLENEIMINE, INHIBITED in Class 3.

2.1.4 Classification of samples

2.1.4.1 When the class of a substance is uncertain and it is being carried for further testing, a tentative class, proper shipping name and UN number shall be assigned on the basis of the consignor's knowledge of the substance and application of:

(a) the classification criteria of Chapter 2.2; and

(b) the requirements of this Chapter.

The most severe packing group possible for the proper shipping name chosen shall be used.

Where this provision is used the proper shipping name shall be supplemented with the word "SAMPLE" (e.g., "FLAMMABLE LIQUID, N.O.S., SAMPLE"). In certain instances, where a specific proper shipping name is provided for a sample of a substance considered to meet certain classification criteria (e.g., GAS SAMMPLE, NON-PRESSURIZED, FLAMMABLE, UN No. 3167) that proper shipping name shall be used. When an N.O.S. entry is used to carry the sample, the proper shipping name need not be supplemented with the technical name as required by special provision 274 of Chapter 3.3.

2.1.4.2 Samples of the substance shall be carried in accordance with the requirements applicable to the tentative assigned proper shipping name provided:

(a) The substance is not considered to be a substance not accepted for carriage by sub-sections 2.2.x.2 of Chapter 2.2 or by Chapter 3.2;

(b) The substance is not considered to meet the criteria for Class 1 or considered to be an infectious substance or a radioactive material;

(c) The substance is in compliance with 2.2.41.1.15 or 2.2.52.1.9 if it is a self-reactive substance or an organic peroxide, respectively;

(d) The sample is carried in a combination packaging with a net mass per package not exceeding 2.5 kg; and

(e) The sample is not packed together with other goods.

CHAPTER 2.2

CLASS SPECIFIC PROVISIONS

2.2.1   **Class 1**   **Explosive substances and articles**

2.2.1.1   *Criteria*

2.2.1.1.1   The heading of Class 1 covers:

(a)   Explosive substances: solid or liquid substances (or mixtures of substances) capable by chemical reaction of producing gases at such a temperature and pressure and at such a speed as to cause damage to the surroundings.

Pyrotechnic substances: substances or mixtures of substances designed to produce an effect by heat, light, sound, gas or smoke or a combination of these as the result of non-detonating self-sustaining exothermic chemical reactions;

NOTE 1: Substances which are not themselves explosive but which may form an explosive mixture of gas, vapour or dust are not substances of Class 1.

NOTE 2: Also excluded from Class 1 are: water- or alcohol-wetted explosives of which the water or alcohol content exceeds the limits specified and those containing plasticizers - these explosives are assigned to Class 3 or Class 4.1 - and those explosives which, on the basis of their predominant hazard, are assigned to Class 5.2.

(b)   Explosive articles: articles containing one or more explosive or pyrotechnic substances;

NOTE: Devices containing explosive or pyrotechnic substances in such small quantity or of such a character that their inadvertent or accidental ignition or initiation during carriage would not cause any manifestation external to the device by projection, fire, smoke, heat or loud noise are not subject to the requirements of Class 1.

(c)   Substances and articles not mentioned above which are manufactured with a view to producing a practical effect by explosion or a pyrotechnic effect.

2.2.1.1.2   Any substance or article having or suspected of having explosive properties shall be considered for assignment to Class 1 in accordance with the tests, procedures and criteria prescribed in Part I, Manual of Tests and Criteria.

A substance or article assigned to Class 1 can only be accepted for carriage when it has been assigned to a name or n.o.s. entry listed in Table A of Chapter 3.2 and meets the criteria of the Manual of Tests and Criteria.

2.2.1.1.3   The substances and articles of Class 1 shall be assigned to a UN Number and a name or n.o.s. entry listed in Table A of Chapter 3.2. Interpretation of the names of substances and articles in Table A of Chapter 3.2 shall be based upon the glossary in 2.2.1.1.8.

Samples of new or existing explosive substances or articles carried for purposes including: testing, classification, research and development quality control, or as a commercial sample, other than initiating explosive, may be assigned to UN No. 0190 SAMPLES, EXPLOSIVE.

The assignment of explosive substances and articles not mentioned by name as such in Table A of Chapter 3.2 to an n.o.s entry of Class 1 or UN No. 0190 SAMPLES, EXPLOSIVE as well as the assignment of certain substances the carriage of which is subject to a specific authorization by the competent authority according to the special provisions referred to in Column (6) of Table A of Chapter 3.2 shall be made by the competent authority of the country of origin. This competent authority shall also approve in writing the conditions of carriage of these substances and articles. If the country of origin is not a Contracting Party to ADR, the classification and the conditions of carriage shall be recognized by the competent authority of the first country Contracting Party to ADR reached by the consignment.

2.2.1.1.4 Substances and articles of Class 1 shall have been assigned to a division in accordance with 2.2.1.1.5 and to a compatibility group in accordance with 2.2.1.1.6. The division shall be based on the results of the tests described in 2.3.0 and 2.3.1 applying the definitions in 2.2.1.1.5. The compatibility group shall be determined in accordance with the definitions in 2.2.1.1.6. The classification code shall consist of the division number and the compatibility group letter.

2.2.1.1.5 *Definition of divisions*

Division 1.1 Substances and articles which have a mass explosion hazard (a mass explosion is an explosion which affects almost the entire load virtually instantaneously).

Division 1.2 Substances and articles which have a projection hazard but not a mass explosion hazard.

Division 1.3 Substances and articles which have a fire hazard and either a minor blast hazard or a minor projection hazard or both, but not a mass explosion hazard:

(a) combustion of which gives rise to considerable radiant heat; or

(b) which burn one after another, producing minor blast or projection effects or both.

Division 1.4 Substances and articles which present only a slight risk of explosion in the event of ignition or initiation during carriage. The effects are largely confined to the package and no projection of fragments of appreciable size or range is to be expected. An external fire shall not cause virtually instantaneous explosion of almost the entire contents of the package.

Division 1.5 Very insensitive substances having a mass explosion hazard which are so insensitive that there is very little probability of initiation or of transition from burning to detonation under normal conditions of carriage. As a minimum requirement they must not explode in the external fire test.

Division 1.6 Extremely insensitive articles which do not have a mass explosion hazard. The articles contain only extremely insensitive detonating substances and demonstrate a negligible probability of accidental initiation or propagation.

NOTE: The risk from articles of Division 1.6 is limited to the explosion of a single article.

2.2.1.1.6   *Definition of compatibility groups of substances and articles*

A   Primary explosive substance.

B   Article containing a primary explosive substance and not having two or more effective protective features. Some articles, such as detonators for blasting, detonator assemblies for blasting and primers, cap-type, are included, even though they do not contain primary explosives.

C   Propellant explosive substance or other deflagrating explosive substance or article containing such explosive substance.

D   Secondary detonating explosive substance or black powder or article containing a secondary detonating explosive substance, in each case without means of initiation and without a propelling charge, or article containing a primary explosive substance and having two or more effective protective features.

E   Article containing a secondary detonating explosive substance, without means of initiation, with a propelling charge (other than one containing a flammable liquid or gel or hypergolic liquids).

F   Article containing a secondary detonating explosive substance with its own means of initiation, with a propelling charge (other than one containing a flammable liquid or gel or hypergolic liquids) or without a propelling charge.

G   Pyrotechnic substance, or article containing a pyrotechnic substance, or article containing both an explosive substance and an illuminating, incendiary, tear- or smoke-producing substance (other than a water-activated article or one which contains white phosphorus, phosphides, a pyrophoric substance, a flammable liquid or gel or hypergolic liquids).

H   Article containing both an explosive substance and white phosphorus.

J   Article containing both an explosive substance and a flammable liquid or gel.

K   Article containing both an explosive substance and a toxic chemical agent.

L   Explosive substance or article containing an explosive substance and presenting a special risk (e.g. due to water activation or the presence of hypergolic liquids, phosphides or a pyrophoric substance) necessitating isolation of each type.

N   Articles containing only extremely insensitive detonating substances.

S   Substance or article so packed or designed that any hazardous effects arising from accidental functioning are confined within the package unless the package has been degraded by fire, in which case all blast or projection effects are limited to the extent that they do not significantly hinder or prevent fire-fighting or other emergency response efforts in the immediate vicinity of the package.

NOTE 1: Each substance or article, packed in a specified packaging, may be assigned to one compatibility group only. Since the criterion of compatibility group S is empirical, assignment to this group is necessarily linked to the tests for assignment of a classification code.

NOTE 2: Articles of compatibility groups D and E may be fitted or packed together with their own means of initiation provided that such means have at least two effective protective features designed to prevent an explosion in the event of accidental functioning of the means of initiation. Such packages shall be assigned to compatibility groups D or E.

NOTE 3: *Articles of compatibility groups D and E may be packed together with their own means of initiation, which do not have two effective protective features (i.e. means of initiation assigned to compatibility group B), provided that they comply with mixed packing provision MP 21 of Section 4.1.10. Such packages shall be assigned to compatibility groups D or E.*

NOTE 4: *Articles may be fitted or packed together with their own means of ignition provided that the means of ignition cannot function during normal conditions of carriage.*

NOTE 5: *Articles of compatibility groups C, D and E may be packed together. Such packages shall be assigned to compatibility group E.*

2.2.1.1.7   *Assignment of fireworks to divisions*

2.2.1.1.7.1   Fireworks shall normally be assigned to divisions 1.1, 1.2, 1.3, and 1.4 on the basis of test data derived from Test Series 6 of the Manual of Tests and Criteria. However, since the range of such articles is very extensive and the availability of test facilities may be limited, assignment to divisions may also be made in accordance with the procedure in 2.2.1.1.7.2.

2.2.1.1.7.2   Assignment of fireworks to UN Nos. 0333, 0334, 0335 and 0336 may be made on the basis of analogy, without the need for Test Series 6 testing, in accordance with the default fireworks classification table in 2.2.1.1.7.5. Such assignment shall be made with the agreement of the competent authority. Items not specified in the table shall be classified on the basis of test data derived from Test Series 6.

NOTE 1: *The addition of other types of fireworks to column 1 of the table in 2.2.1.1.7.5 shall only be made on the basis of full test data submitted to the UN Sub-Committee of Experts on the Transport of Dangerous Goods for consideration.*

NOTE 2: *Test data derived by competent authorities which validates, or contradicts the assignment of fireworks specified in column 4 of the table in 2.2.1.1.7.5 to divisions in column 5 should be submitted to the UN Sub-Committee of Experts on the Transport of Dangerous Goods for information.*

2.2.1.1.7.3   Where fireworks of more than one division are packed in the same package, they shall be classified on the basis of the most dangerous division unless test data derived from Test Series 6 indicate otherwise.

2.2.1.1.7.4   The classification shown in the table in 2.2.1.1.7.5 applies only for articles packed in fibreboard boxes (4G).

2.2.1.1.7.5   *Default fireworks classification table* [1]

NOTE 1: *References to percentages in the table, unless otherwise stated, are to the mass of all pyrotechnic composition (e.g. rocket motors, lifting charge, bursting charge and effect charge).*

---

[1]   *This table contains a list of firework classifications which may be used in the absence of Test Series 6 data (see 2.2.1.1.7.2).*

NOTE 2: *"Flash composition" in this table refers to pyrotechnic compositions in powder form or as pyrotechnic units as presented in the fireworks, that are used to produce an aural effect, or used as a bursting charge or lifting charge, unless the time taken for the pressure rise is demonstrated to be more than 8 ms for 0.5 g of pyrotechnic composition in Test Series 2(c)(i) "Time/pressure test" of the Manual of Tests and Criteria.*

NOTE 3: *Dimensions in mm refer to:*

- *for spherical and peanut shells the diameter of the sphere of the shell;*
- *for cylinder shells the length of the shell;*
- *for a shell in mortar, Roman candle, shot tube firework or mine the inside diameter of the tube comprising or containing the firework;*
- *for a bag mine or cylinder mine, the inside diameter of the mortar intended to contain the mine.*

Type	Includes: / Synonym:	Definition	Specification	Classification
Shell, spherical or cylindrical	Spherical display shell: aerial shell, colour shell, dye shell, multi-break shell, multi-effect shell, nautical shell, parachute shell, smoke shell, star shell; report shell: maroon, salute, sound shell, thunderclap, aerial shell kit	Device with or without propellant charge, with delay fuse and bursting charge, pyrotechnic unit(s) or loose pyrotechnic composition and designed to be projected from a mortar	All report shells	1.1G
			Colour shell: ≥ 180 mm	1.1G
			Colour shell: < 180 mm with > 25% flash composition, as loose powder and/or report effects	1.1G
			Colour shell: < 180 mm with ≤ 25% flash composition, as loose powder and/or report effects	1.3G
			Colour shell: ≤ 50 mm, or ≤ 60 g pyrotechnic composition, with ≤ 2% flash composition as loose powder and/or report effects	1.4G
	Peanut shell	Device with two or more spherical aerial shells in a common wrapper propelled by the same propellant charge with separate external delay fuses	The most hazardous spherical aerial shell determines the classification	
	Preloaded mortar, shell in mortar	Assembly comprising a spherical or cylindrical shell inside a mortar from which the shell is designed to be projected	All report shells	1.1G
			Colour shell: ≥ 180 mm	1.1G
			Colour shell: > 25% flash composition as loose powder and/or report effects	1.1G
			Colour shell: > 50 mm and < 180 mm	1.2G
			Colour shell: ≤ 50 mm, or ≤ 60 g pyrotechnic composition, with ≤ 25% flash composition as loose powder and/or report effects	1.3G

Type	Includes: / Synonym:	Definition	Specification	Classification
Shell, spherical or cylindrical *(cont'd)*	Shell of shells (spherical) *(Reference to percentages for shell of shells are to the gross mass of the fireworks article)*	Device without propellant charge, with delay fuse and bursting charge, containing report shells and inert materials and designed to be projected from a mortar	> 120 mm	1.1G
		Device without propellant charge, with delay fuse and bursting charge, containing report shells ≤ 25g flash composition per report unit, with ≤ 33% flash composition and ≥ 60% inert materials and designed to be projected from a mortar	≤ 120 mm	1.3G
		Device without propellant charge, with delay fuse and bursting charge, containing colour shells and/or pyrotechnic units and designed to be projected from a mortar	> 300 mm	1.1G
		Device without propellant charge, with delay fuse and bursting charge, containing colour shells ≤ 70mm and/or pyrotechnic units, with ≤ 25% flash composition and ≤ 60% pyrotechnic composition and designed to be projected from a mortar	> 200 mm and ≤ 300 mm	1.3G
		Device with propellant charge, with delay fuse and bursting charge, containing colour shells ≤ 70 mm and/or pyrotechnic units, with ≤ 25% flash composition and ≤ 60% pyrotechnic composition and designed to be projected from a mortar	≤ 200 mm	1.3G
Battery/ combination	Barrage, bombardos, cakes, finale box, flowerbed, hybrid, multiple tubes, shell cakes, banger batteries, flash banger batteries	Assembly including several elements either containing the same type or several types each corresponding to one of the types of fireworks listed in this table, with one or two points of ignition	The most hazardous firework type determines the classification	

Type	Includes: / Synonym:	Definition	Specification	Classification
Roman candle	Exhibition candle, candle, bombettes	Tube containing a series of pyrotechnic units consisting of alternate pyrotechnic composition, propellant charge, and transmitting fuse	≥ 50 mm inner diameter, containing flash composition, or < 50 mm with > 25% flash composition	1.1G
			≥ 50 mm inner diameter, containing no flash composition	1.2G
			< 50 mm inner diameter and ≤ 25% flash composition	1.3G
			≤ 30 mm inner diameter, each pyrotechnic unit ≤ 25 g and ≤ 5% flash composition	1.4G
Shot tube	Single shot Roman candle, small preloaded mortar	Tube containing a pyrotechnic unit consisting of pyrotechnic composition, propellant charge with or without transmitting fuse	≤ 30 mm inner diameter and pyrotechnic unit > 25 g, or > 5% and ≤ 25% flash composition	1.3G
			≤ 30 mm inner diameter, pyrotechnic unit ≤ 25 g and ≤ 5% flash composition	1.4G
Rocket	Avalanche rocket, signal rocket, whistling rocket, bottle rocket, sky rocket, missile type rocket, table rocket	Tube containing pyrotechnic composition and/or pyrotechnic units, equipped with stick(s) or other means for stabilization of flight, and designed to be propelled into the air	Flash composition effects only	1.1G
			Flash composition > 25% of the pyrotechnic composition	1.1G
			> 20 g pyrotechnic composition and flash composition ≤ 25%	1.3G
			≤ 20 g pyrotechnic composition, black powder bursting charge and ≤ 0.13 g flash composition per report and ≤ 1 g in total	1.4G

Type	Includes: / Synonym:	Definition	Specification	Classification
Mine	Pot-a-feu, ground mine, bag mine, cylinder mine	Tube containing propellant charge and pyrotechnic units and designed to be placed on the ground or to be fixed in the ground. The principal effect is ejection of all the pyrotechnic units in a single burst producing a widely dispersed visual and/or aural effect in the air or:	> 25% flash composition, as loose powder and/ or report effects	1.1G
			≥ 180 mm and ≤ 25% flash composition, as loose powder and/ or report effects	1.1G
		Cloth or paper bag or cloth or paper cylinder containing propellant charge and pyrotechnic units, designed to be placed in a mortar and to function as a mine	< 180 mm and ≤ 25% flash composition, as loose powder and/ or report effects	1.3G
			≤ 150 g pyrotechnic composition, containing ≤ 5% flash composition as loose powder and/ or report effects. Each pyrotechnic unit ≤ 25 g, each report effect < 2g; each whistle, if any, ≤ 3 g	1.4G
Fountain	Volcanos, gerbs, showers, lances, Bengal fire, flitter sparkle, cylindrical fountains, cone fountains, illuminating torch	Non-metallic case containing pressed or consolidated pyrotechnic composition producing sparks and flame	≥ 1 kg pyrotechnic composition	1.3G
			< 1 kg pyrotechnic composition	1.4G
Sparkler	Handheld sparklers, non-handheld sparklers, wire sparklers	Rigid wire partially coated (along one end) with slow burning pyrotechnic composition with or without an ignition tip	Perchlorate based sparklers: > 5 g per item or > 10 items per pack	1.3G
			Perchlorate based sparklers: ≤ 5 g per item and ≤ 10 items per pack; Nitrate based sparklers: ≤ 30 g per item	1.4G

Type	Includes: / Synonym:	Definition	Specification	Classification
Bengal stick	Dipped stick	Non-metallic stick partially coated (along one end) with slow-burning pyrotechnic composition and designed to be held in the hand	Perchlorate based items: > 5 g per item or > 10 items per pack	1.3 G
			Perchlorate based items: ≤ 5 g per item and ≤ 10 items per pack; nitrate based items: ≤ 30 g per item	1.4G
Low hazard fireworks and novelties	Table bombs, throwdowns, crackling granules, smokes, fog, snakes, glow worm, serpents, snaps, party poppers	Device designed to produce very limited visible and/ or audible effect which contains small amounts of pyrotechnic and/or explosive composition.	Throwdowns and snaps may contain up to 1.6 mg of silver fulminate; snaps and party poppers may contain up to 16 mg of potassium chlorate/red phosphorous mixture; other articles may contain up to 5 g of pyrotechnic composition, but no flash composition	1.4G
Spinner	Aerial spinner, helicopter, chaser, ground spinner	Non-metallic tube or tubes containing gas- or spark-producing pyrotechnic composition, with or without noise producing composition, with or without aerofoils attached	Pyrotechnic composition per item > 20 g, containing ≤ 3% flash composition as report effects, or whistle composition ≤ 5 g	1.3G
			Pyrotechnic composition per item ≤ 20 g, containing ≤ 3% flash composition as report effects, or whistle composition ≤ 5 g	1.4G
Wheels	Catherine wheels, Saxon	Assembly including drivers containing pyrotechnic composition and provided with a means of attaching it to a support so that it can rotate	≥ 1 kg total pyrotechnic composition, no report effect, each whistle (if any) ≤ 25 g and ≤ 50 g whistle composition per wheel	1.3G
			< 1 kg total pyrotechnic composition, no report effect, each whistle (if any) ≤ 5 g and ≤ 10 g whistle composition per wheel	1.4G

Type	Includes: / Synonym:	Definition	Specification	Classification
Aerial wheel	Flying Saxon, UFO's, rising crown	Tubes containing propellant charges and sparks- flame- and/or noise producing pyrotechnic compositions, the tubes being fixed to a supporting ring	> 200 g total pyrotechnic composition or > 60 g pyrotechnic composition per driver, ≤ 3% flash composition as report effects, each whistle (if any) ≤ 25 g and ≤ 50 g whistle composition per wheel	1.3G
			≤ 200 g total pyrotechnic composition and ≤ 60 g pyrotechnic composition per driver, ≤ 3% flash composition as report effects, each whistle (if any) ≤ 5 g and ≤ 10 g whistle composition per wheel	1.4G
Selection pack	Display selection box, display selection pack, garden selection box, indoor selection box; assortment	A pack of more than one type each corresponding to one of the types of fireworks listed in this table	The most hazardous firework type determines the classification	
Firecracker	Celebration cracker, celebration roll, string cracker	Assembly of tubes (paper or cardboard) linked by a pyrotechnic fuse, each tube intended to produce an aural effect	Each tube ≤ 140 mg of flash composition or ≤ 1 g black powder	1.4G
Banger	Salute, flash banger, lady cracker	Non-metallic tube containing report composition intended to produce an aural effect	> 2 g flash composition per item	1.1G
			≤ 2 g flash composition per item and ≤ 10 g per inner packaging	1.3G
			≤ 1 g flash composition per item and ≤ 10 g per inner packaging or ≤ 10 g black powder per item	1.4G

2.2.1.1.8   *Glossary of names*

NOTE 1: *The descriptions in the glossary are not intended to replace the test procedures, nor to determine the hazard classification of a substance or article of Class 1. Assignment to the correct division and a decision on whether Compatibility Group S is appropriate shall be based on testing of the product in accordance with the Manual of Tests and Criteria, Part I or by analogy with similar products which have already been tested and assigned in accordance with the procedures of the Manual of Tests and Criteria.*

NOTE 2: *The figures given after the names refer to the relevant UN numbers (Column 1 of Table A of Chapter 3.2). For the classification code, see 2.2.1.1.4.*

AIR BAG INFLATORS or AIR BAG MODULES or SEAT-BELT PRETENSIONERS: UN No. 0503

Articles which contain pyrotechnic substances and are used as life-saving vehicle airbags or seat-belts.

AMMUNITION, ILLUMINATING, with or without burster, expelling charge or propelling charge: UN Nos. 0171, 0254, 0297

Ammunition designed to produce a single source of intense light for lighting up an area. The term includes illuminating cartridges, grenades and projectiles; and illuminating and target identification bombs.

NOTE: *The following articles: CARTRIDGES, SIGNAL; SIGNAL DEVICES HAND; SIGNALS, DISTRESS; FLARES, AERIAL; FLARES, SURFACE are not included in this definition. They are listed separately.*

AMMUNITION, INCENDIARY, liquid or gel, with burster, expelling charge or propelling charge: UN No. 0247

Ammunition containing liquid or gelatinous incendiary substance. Except when the incendiary substance is an explosive <u>per se</u>, it also contains one or more of the following: a propelling charge with primer and igniter charge; a fuze with burster or expelling charge.

AMMUNITION, INCENDIARY, WHITE PHOSPHORUS with burster, expelling charge or propelling charge: UN Nos. 0243, 0244

Ammunition containing white phosphorus as incendiary substance. It also contains one or more of the following: a propelling charge with primer and igniter charge; a fuze with burster or expelling charge.

AMMUNITION, INCENDIARY with or without burster, expelling charge or propelling charge: UN Nos. 0009, 0010, 0300

Ammunition containing incendiary composition. Except when the composition is an explosive <u>per se</u>, it also contains one or more of the following: a propelling charge with primer and igniter charge; a fuze with burster or expelling charge.

AMMUNITION, PRACTICE: UN Nos. 0362, 0488

Ammunition without a main bursting charge, containing a burster or expelling charge. Normally it also contains a fuze and a propelling charge.

NOTE: *GRENADES, PRACTICE are not included in this definition. They are listed separately.*

AMMUNITION, PROOF: UN No. 0363

Ammunition containing pyrotechnic substances, used to test the performance or strength of new ammunition, weapon components or assemblies.

AMMUNITION, SMOKE, WHITE PHOSPHORUS, with burster, expelling charge or propelling charge: UN Nos. 0245, 0246

Ammunition containing white phosphorus as a smoke-producing substance. It also contains one or more of the following: a propelling charge with primer and igniter charge; a fuze with burster or expelling charge. The term includes grenades, smoke.

AMMUNITION, SMOKE with or without burster, expelling charge or propelling charge: UN Nos. 0015, 0016, 0303

Ammunition containing a smoke-producing substance such as chlorosulphonic acid mixture or titanium tetrachloride; or a smoke-producing pyrotechnic composition based on hexachloroethane or red phosphorus. Except when the substance is an explosive per se, the ammunition also contains one or more of the following: a propelling charge with primer and igniter charge; a fuze with burster or expelling charge. The term includes grenades, smoke.

NOTE: SIGNALS, SMOKE are not included in this definition. They are listed separately.

AMMUNITION, TEAR-PRODUCING, with burster, expelling charge or propelling charge: UN Nos. 0018, 0019, 0301

Ammunition containing a tear-producing substance. It also contains one or more of the following: a pyrotechnic substance; a propelling charge with primer and igniter charge; a fuze with burster or expelling charge.

ARTICLES, EXPLOSIVE, EXTREMELY INSENSITIVE (ARTICLES EEI): UN No. 0486

Articles containing only extremely insensitive detonating substances (EIDS) which demonstrate a negligible probability of accidental initiation or propagation under normal conditions of transport, and which have passed Test Series 7.

ARTICLES, PYROPHORIC: UN No. 0380

Articles which contain a pyrophoric substance (capable of spontaneous ignition when exposed to air) and an explosive substance or component. The term excludes articles containing white phosphorus.

ARTICLES, PYROTECHNIC, for technical purposes: UN Nos. 0428, 0429, 0430, 0431, 0432

Articles which contain pyrotechnic substances and are used for technical purposes such as heat generation, gas generation, theatrical effects, etc.

NOTE: The following articles: all ammunition; CARTRIDGES, SIGNAL; CUTTERS, CABLE, EXPLOSIVE; FIREWORKS; FLARES, AERIAL; FLARES, SURFACE; RELEASE DEVICES, EXPLOSIVE; RIVETS, EXPLOSIVE; SIGNAL DEVICES, HAND; SIGNALS, DISTRESS; SIGNALS, RAILWAY TRACK, EXPLOSIVES; SIGNALS, SMOKE are not included in this definition. They are listed separately.

BLACK POWDER (GUNPOWDER), COMPRESSED or BLACK POWDER (GUNPOWDER), IN PELLETS: UN No. 0028

Substance consisting of a pelletized form of black powder.

BLACK POWDER (GUNPOWDER), granular or as meal: UN No. 0027

Substance consisting of an intimate mixture of charcoal or other carbon and either potassium nitrate or sodium nitrate, with or without sulphur.

BOMBS, WITH FLAMMABLE LIQUID, with bursting charge: UN Nos. 0399, 0400

Articles which are dropped from aircraft, consisting of a tank filled with inflammable liquid and bursting charge.

BOMBS, PHOTO-FLASH: UN No. 0038

Explosive articles which are dropped from aircraft to provide brief, intense illumination for photography. They contain a charge of detonating explosive without means of initiation or with means of initiation containing two or more effective protective features.

BOMBS, PHOTO-FLASH: UN No. 0037

Explosive articles which are dropped from aircraft to provide brief, intense illumination for photography. They contain a charge of detonating explosive with means of initiation not containing two or more effective protective features.

BOMBS, PHOTO-FLASH: UN Nos. 0039, 0299

Explosive articles which are dropped from aircraft to provide brief, intense illumination for photography. They contain a photo-flash composition.

BOMBS with bursting charge: UN Nos. 0034; 0035

Explosive articles which are dropped from aircraft, without means of initiation or with means of initiation containing two or more effective protective features.

BOMBS with bursting charge: UN Nos. 0033, 0291

Explosive articles which are dropped from aircraft, with means of initiation not containing two or more effective protective features.

BOOSTERS WITH DETONATOR: UN Nos. 0225, 0268

Articles consisting of a charge of detonating explosive with means of initiation. They are used to increase the initiating power of detonators or detonating cord.

BOOSTERS without detonator: UN Nos. 0042, 0283

Articles consisting of a charge of detonating explosive without means of initiation. They are used to increase the initiating power of detonators or detonating cord.

BURSTERS, explosive: UN No. 0043

Articles consisting of a small charge of explosive used to open projectiles or other ammunition in order to disperse their contents.

CARTRIDGES, FLASH: UN Nos. 0049, 0050

Articles consisting of a casing, a primer and flash powder, all assembled in one piece ready for firing.

CARTRIDGES FOR WEAPONS, BLANK: UN Nos. 0326, 0413, 0327, 0338, 0014

Ammunition consisting of a closed cartridge case with a centre or rim fire primer and a charge of smokeless or black powder but no projectile. It produces a loud noise and is used for training, saluting, propelling charge, starter pistols, etc. The term includes ammunition, blank.

CARTRIDGES FOR WEAPONS, INERT PROJECTILE: UN Nos. 0328, 0417, 0339, 0012

Ammunition consisting of a projectile without bursting charge but with a propelling charge with or without a primer. The articles may include a tracer, provided that the predominant hazard is that of the propelling charge.

CARTRIDGES FOR WEAPONS with bursting charge: UN Nos. 0006, 0321, 0412

Ammunition consisting of a projectile with a bursting charge without means of initiation or with means of initiation containing two or more effective protective features; and a propelling charge with or without a primer. The term includes fixed (assembled) ammunition, semi-fixed (partially assembled) ammunition and separate loading ammunition when the components are packed together.

CARTRIDGES FOR WEAPONS with bursting charge: UN Nos. 0005, 0007, 0348

Ammunition consisting of a projectile with a bursting charge with means of initiation not containing two or more effective protective features; and a propelling charge with or without a primer. The term includes fixed (assembled) ammunition, semi-fixed (partially assembled) ammunition and separate loading ammunition when the components are packed together.

CARTRIDGES, OIL WELL: UN Nos. 0277, 0278

Articles consisting of a thin casing of fibreboard, metal or other material containing only propellant powder which projects a hardened projectile to perforate an oil well casing.

NOTE: CHARGES, SHAPED are not included in this definition. They are listed separately.

CARTRIDGES, POWER DEVICE: UN Nos. 0275, 0276, 0323, 0381

Articles designed to accomplish mechanical actions. They consist of a casing with a charge of deflagrating explosive and a means of ignition. The gaseous products of the deflagration produce inflation, linear or rotary motion or activate diaphragms, valves or switches or project fastening devices or extinguishing agents.

CARTRIDGES, SIGNAL: UN Nos. 0054, 0312, 0405

Articles designed to fire coloured flares or other signals from signal pistols, etc.

CARTRIDGES, SMALL ARMS: UN Nos. 0417, 0339, 0012

Ammunition consisting of a cartridge case fitted with a centre or rim fire primer and containing both a propelling charge and solid projectile. They are designed to be fired in weapons of calibre not larger than 19.1 mm. Shot-gun cartridges of any calibre are included in this description.

NOTE: *CARTRIDGES, SMALL ARMS, BLANK, are not included in this definition. They are listed separately. Some military small arms cartridges are not included in this definition. They are listed under CARTRIDGES FOR WEAPONS, INERT PROJECTILE.*

CARTRIDGES, SMALL ARMS, BLANK: UN Nos. 0014, 0327, 0338

Ammunition consisting of a closed cartridge case with a centre or rim fire primer and a charge of smokeless or black powder. The cartridge cases contain no projectiles. The cartridges are designed to be fired from weapons with a calibre of at most 19.1 mm and serve to produce a loud noise and are used for training, saluting, propelling charge, starter pistols, etc.

CASES, CARTRIDGE, EMPTY, WITH PRIMER: UN Nos. 0379; 0055

Articles consisting of a cartridge case made from metal, plastics or other non-inflammable material, in which the only explosive component is the primer.

CASES, COMBUSTIBLE, EMPTY, WITHOUT PRIMER: UN Nos. 0447, 0446

Articles consisting of a cartridge case made partly or entirely from nitrocellulose.

CHARGES, BURSTING, PLASTICS BONDED: UN Nos. 0457, 0458, 0459, 0460

Articles consisting of a charge of detonating explosive, plastics bonded, manufactured in a specific form without a casing and without means of initiation. They are designed as components of ammunition such as warheads.

CHARGES, DEMOLITION: UN No. 0048

Articles containing a charge of a detonating explosive in a casing of fibreboard, plastics, metal or other material. The articles are without means of initiation or with means of initiation containing two or more effective protective features.

NOTE: *The following articles: BOMBS; MINES; PROJECTILES are not included in this definition. They are listed separately.*

CHARGES, DEPTH: UN No. 0056

Articles consisting of a charge of detonating explosive contained in a drum or projectile without means of initiation or with means of initiation containing two or more effective protective features. They are designed to detonate under water.

CHARGES, EXPLOSIVE, COMMERCIAL without detonator: UN Nos. 0442, 0443, 0444, 0445

Articles consisting of a charge of detonating explosive without means of initiation, used for explosive welding, jointing, forming and other metallurgical processes.

CHARGES, PROPELLING, FOR CANNON: UN Nos. 0242, 0279, 0414

Charges of propellant in any physical form for separate-loading ammunition for cannon.

CHARGES, PROPELLING: UN Nos. 0271, 0272, 0415, 0491

Articles consisting of a charge of a propellant charge in any physical form, with or without a casing, as a component of rocket motors or for reducing the drag of projectiles.

CHARGES, SHAPED, without detonator: UN Nos. 0059, 0439, 0440, 0441

Articles consisting of a casing containing a charge of detonating explosive with a cavity lined with rigid material, without means of initiation. They are designed to produce a powerful, penetrating jet effect.

CHARGES, SHAPED, FLEXIBLE, LINEAR: UN Nos. 0237, 0288

Articles consisting of a V-shaped core of a detonating explosive clad by a flexible sheath.

CHARGES, SUPPLEMENTARY, EXPLOSIVE: UN No. 0060

Articles consisting of a small removable booster placed in the cavity of a projectile between the fuze and the bursting charge.

COMPONENTS, EXPLOSIVE TRAIN, N.O.S.: UN Nos. 0382, 0383, 0384, 0461

Articles containing an explosive designed to transmit detonation or deflagration within an explosive train.

CONTRIVANCES, WATER-ACTIVATED with burster, expelling charge or propelling charge: UN Nos. 0248, 0249

Articles whose functioning depends upon physico-chemical reaction of their contents with water.

CORD, DETONATING, flexible: UN Nos. 0065, 0289

Article consisting of a core of detonating explosive enclosed in spun fabric and a plastics or other covering. The covering is not necessary if the spun fabric is sift-proof.

CORD (FUSE) DETONATING, metal clad: UN Nos. 0102, 0290

Article consisting of a core of detonating explosive clad by a soft metal tube with or without protective covering.

CORD (FUSE) DETONATING, MILD EFFECT, metal clad: UN No. 0104

Article consisting of a core of detonating explosive clad by a soft metal tube with or without a protective covering. The quantity of explosive substance is so small that only a mild effect is manifested outside the cord.

CORD, IGNITER: UN No. 0066

Article consisting of textile yarns covered with black powder or another fast burning pyrotechnic composition and of a flexible protective covering; or it consists of a core of black powder surrounded by a flexible woven fabric. It burns progressively along its length with an external flame and is used to transmit ignition from a device to a charge or primer.

CUTTERS, CABLE, EXPLOSIVE: UN No. 0070

Articles consisting of a knife-edged device which is driven by a small charge of deflagrating explosive into an anvil.

DETONATOR ASSEMBLIES, NON-ELECTRIC for blasting: UN Nos. 0360, 0361, 0500

Non-electric detonators assembled with and activated by such means as safety fuse, shock tube, flash tube or detonating cord. They may be of instantaneous design or incorporate delay elements. Detonating relays incorporating detonating cord are included.

DETONATORS, ELECTRIC for blasting: UN Nos. 0030, 0255, 0456

Articles specially designed for the initiation of blasting explosives. These detonators may be constructed to detonate instantaneously or may contain a delay element. Electric detonators are activated by an electric current.

DETONATORS FOR AMMUNITION: UN Nos. 0073, 0364, 0365, 0366

Articles consisting of a small metal or plastics tube containing explosives such as lead azide, PETN or combinations of explosives. They are designed to start a detonation train.

DETONATORS, NON-ELECTRIC for blasting: UN Nos. 0029, 0267, 0455

Articles specially designed for the initiation of blasting explosives. These detonators may be constructed to detonate instantaneously or may contain a delay element. Non-electric detonators are activated by such means as shock tube, flash tube, safety fuse, other igniferous device or flexible detonating cord. Detonating relays without detonating cord are included.

EXPLOSIVE, BLASTING, TYPE A: UN No. 0081

Substances consisting of liquid organic nitrates such as nitroglycerine or a mixture of such ingredients with one or more of the following: nitrocellulose; ammonium nitrate or other inorganic nitrates; aromatic nitro-derivatives, or combustible materials, such as wood-meal and aluminium powder. They may contain inert components such as kieselguhr, and additives such as colouring agents and stabilizers. Such explosives shall be in powdery, gelatinous or elastic form. The term includes dynamite; gelatine, blasting and gelatine dynamites.

EXPLOSIVE, BLASTING, TYPE B: UN Nos. 0082, 0331

Substances consisting of

(a)   a mixture of ammonium nitrate or other inorganic nitrates with an explosive such as trinitrotoluene, with or without other substances such as wood-meal and aluminium powder; or

(b)   a mixture of ammonium nitrate or other inorganic nitrates with other combustible substances which are not explosive ingredients. In both cases they may contain inert components such as kieselguhr, and additives such as colouring agents and stabilizers. Such explosives must not contain nitroglycerine, similar liquid organic nitrates or chlorates.

EXPLOSIVE, BLASTING, TYPE C: UN No. 0083

Substances consisting of a mixture of either potassium or sodium chlorate or potassium, sodium or ammonium perchlorate with organic nitro-derivatives or combustible materials such as wood-meal or aluminium powder or a hydrocarbon. They may contain inert components such as kieselguhr and additives such as colouring agents and stabilizers. Such explosives must not contain nitroglycerine or similar liquid organic nitrates.

EXPLOSIVE, BLASTING, TYPE D: UN No. 0084

Substances consisting of a mixture of organic nitrated compounds and combustible materials such as hydrocarbons and aluminium powder. They may contain inert components such as kieselguhr and additives such as colouring agents and stabilizers. Such explosives must not contain nitroglycerine, similar liquid organic nitrates, chlorates and ammonium nitrate. The term generally includes plastic explosives.

EXPLOSIVES, BLASTING, TYPE E: UN Nos. 0241, 0332

Substances consisting of water as an essential ingredient and high proportions of ammonium nitrate or other oxidizers, some or all of which are in solution. The other constituents may include nitro-derivatives such as trinitrotoluene, hydrocarbons or aluminium powder. They may contain inert components such as kieselguhr and additives such as colouring agents and stabilizers. The term includes explosives, emulsion, explosives, slurry and explosives, watergel.

FIREWORKS: UN Nos. 0333, 0334, 0335, 0336, 0337

Pyrotechnic articles designed for entertainment.

FLARES, AERIAL: UN Nos. 0093, 0403, 0404, 0420, 0421;

Articles containing pyrotechnic substances which are designed to be dropped from an aircraft to illuminate, identify, signal or warn.

FLARES, SURFACE: UN Nos. 0092, 0418, 0419

Articles containing pyrotechnic substances which are designed for use on the surface to illuminate, identify, signal or warn.

FLASH POWDER: UN Nos. 0094, 0305

Pyrotechnic substance which, when ignited, produces an intense light.

FRACTURING DEVICES, EXPLOSIVE without detonator, for oil wells: UN No. 0099

Articles consisting of a charge of detonating explosive contained in a casing without means of initiation. They are used to fracture the rock around a drill shaft to assist the flow of crude oil from the rock.

FUSE, IGNITER, tubular, metal clad: UN No. 0103

Article consisting of a metal tube with a core of deflagrating explosive.

FUSE, NON-DETONATING: UN No. 0101

Article consisting of cotton yarns impregnated with fine black powder (quickmatch). It burns with an external flame and is used in ignition trains for fireworks, etc.

FUSE, SAFETY: UN No. 0105

Article consisting of a core of fine grained black powder surrounded by a flexible woven fabric with one or more protective outer coverings. When ignited, it burns at a predetermined rate without any external explosive effect.

FUZES, DETONATING: UN Nos. 0106, 0107, 0257, 0367

Articles with explosive components designed to produce a detonation in ammunition. They incorporate mechanical, electrical, chemical or hydrostatic components to initiate the detonation. They generally incorporate protective features.

FUZES, DETONATING with protective features: UN Nos. 0408, 0409, 0410

Articles with explosive components designed to produce a detonation in ammunition. They incorporate mechanical, electrical, chemical or hydrostatic components to initiate the detonation. The detonating fuze must incorporate two or more effective protective features.

FUZES, IGNITING: UN Nos. 0316, 0317, 0368

Articles with primary explosive components designed to produce a deflagration in ammunition. They incorporate mechanical, electrical, chemical or hydrostatic components to start the deflagration. They generally incorporate protective features.

GRENADES, hand or rifle, with bursting charge: UN Nos. 0284, 0285

Articles which are designed to be thrown by hand or to be projected by a rifle. They are without means of initiation or with means of initiation containing two or more effective protective features.

GRENADES, hand or rifle, with bursting charge: UN Nos. 0292, 0293

Articles which are designed to be thrown by hand or to be projected by a rifle. They are with means of initiation not containing two or more effective protective features.

GRENADES, PRACTICE, hand or rifle: UN Nos. 0110, 0372, 0318, 0452

Articles without a main bursting charge which are designed to be thrown by hand or to be projected by a rifle. They contain the priming device and may contain a spotting charge.

HEXOTONAL: UN No. 0393

Substance consisting of an intimate mixture of cyclotrimethylene-trinitramine (RDX), trinitrotoluene (TNT) and aluminium.

HEXOLITE (HEXOTOL), dry or wetted with less than 15% water, by mass: UN No. 0118

Substance consisting of an intimate mixture of cyclotrimethylene-trinitramine (RDX) and trinitrotoluene (TNT). The term includes "Composition B".

IGNITERS: UN Nos. 0121, 0314, 0315, 0325, 0454

Articles containing one or more explosive substances designed to produce a deflagration in an explosive train. They may be actuated chemically, electrically or mechanically.

NOTE: The following articles: CORD, IGNITER; FUSE, IGNITER; FUSE, NON-DETONATING; FUZES, IGNITING; LIGHTERS, FUSE; PRIMERS, CAP TYPE; PRIMERS, TUBULAR are not included in this definition. They are listed separately.

JET PERFORATING GUNS, CHARGED, oil well, without detonator: UN Nos. 0124, 0494

Articles consisting of a steel tube or metallic strip, into which are inserted shaped charges connected by detonating cord, without means of initiation.

LIGHTERS, FUSE: UN No. 0131

Articles of various design actuated by friction, percussion or electricity and used to ignite safety fuse.

MINES with bursting charge: UN Nos. 0137, 0138

Articles consisting normally of metal or composition receptacles filled with a detonating explosive, without means of initiation or with means of initiation containing two or more effective protective features. They are designed to be operated by the passage of ships, vehicles or personnel. The term includes "Bangalore torpedoes".

MINES with bursting charge: UN Nos. 0136, 0294

Articles consisting normally of metal or composition receptacles filled with a detonating explosive, with means of initiation not containing two or more effective protective features. They are designed to be operated by the passage of ships, vehicles or personnel. The term includes "Bangalore torpedoes".

OCTOLITE (OCTOL), dry or wetted with less than 15% water, by mass: UN No. 0266

Substance consisting of an intimate mixture of cyclotetramethylene-tetranitramine (HMX) and trinitrotoluene (TNT).

OCTONAL: UN No. 0496

Substance consisting of an intimate mixture of cyclotetramethylenetetranitramine (HMX), trinitrotoluene (TNT) and aluminium.

PENTOLITE, dry or wetted with less than 15% water, by mass: UN No. 0151

Substance consisting of an intimate mixture of pentaerythrite tetranitrate (PETN) and trinitrotoluene (TNT).

POWDER CAKE (POWDER PASTE), WETTED with not less than 17% alcohol, by mass; POWDER CAKE (POWDER PASTE), WETTED with not less than 25% water, by mass: UN Nos. 0433, 0159

Substance consisting of nitrocellulose impregnated with not more than 60% of nitroglycerine or other liquid organic nitrates or a mixture of these.

POWDER, SMOKELESS: UN Nos. 0160, 0161

Substance based on nitrocellulose used as propellant. The term includes propellants with a single base (nitrocellulose (NC) alone), those with a double base (such as NC and nitroglycerine/(NG)) and those with a triple base (such as NC/NG/nitroguanidine).

NOTE: Cast, pressed or bag-charges of smokeless powder are listed under CHARGES, PROPELLING or CHARGES, PROPELLING, FOR CANON.

PRIMERS, CAP TYPE: UN Nos. 0044, 0377, 0378

Articles consisting of a metal or plastics cap containing a small amount of primary explosive mixture that is readily ignited by impact. They serve as igniting elements in small arms cartridges and in percussion primers for propelling charges.

PRIMERS, TUBULAR: UN Nos. 0319, 0320, 0376

Articles consisting of a primer for ignition and an auxiliary charge of deflagrating explosive such as black powder used to ignite the propelling charge in a cartridge case for cannon, etc.

PROJECTILES, inert with tracer: UN Nos. 0345, 0424, 0425

Articles such as a shell or bullet, which are projected from a cannon or other gun, rifle or other small arm.

PROJECTILES with burster or expelling charge: UN Nos. 0346, 0347

Articles such as a shell or bullet, which are projected from a cannon or other gun. They are without means of initiation or with means of initiation containing two or more effective protective features. They are used to scatter dyes for spotting or other inert materials.

PROJECTILES with burster or expelling charge: UN Nos. 0426, 0427

Articles such as a shell or bullet, which are projected from a cannon or other gun. They are with means of initiation not containing two or more effective protective features. They are used to scatter dyes for spotting or other inert materials.

PROJECTILES with burster or expelling charge: UN Nos. 0434, 0435

Articles such as a shell or bullet, which are projected from a cannon or other gun, rifle or other small arm. They are used to scatter dyes for spotting or other inert materials.

PROJECTILES with bursting charge: UN Nos. 0168, 0169, 0344

Articles such as a shell or bullet, which are projected from a cannon or other gun. They are without means of initiation or with means of initiation containing two or more effective protective features.

PROJECTILES with bursting charge: UN Nos. 0167, 0324

Articles such as a shell or bullet, which are projected from a cannon or other gun. They are with means of initiation not containing two or more effective protective features.

PROPELLANT, LIQUID: UN Nos. 0495, 0497

Substance consisting of a deflagrating liquid explosive, used for propulsion.

PROPELLANT, SOLID: UN Nos. 0498, 0499, 0501

Substance consisting of a deflagrating solid explosive, used for propulsion.

RELEASE DEVICES, EXPLOSIVE: UN No. 0173

Articles consisting of a small charge of explosive with means of initiation and rods or links. They sever the rods or links to release equipment quickly.

RIVETS, EXPLOSIVE: UN No. 0174

Articles consisting of a small charge of explosive inside a metallic rivet.

ROCKET MOTORS: UN Nos. 0186, 0280, 0281

Articles consisting of a charge of explosive, generally a solid propellant, contained in a cylinder fitted with one or more nozzles. They are designed to propel a rocket or a guided missile.

ROCKET MOTORS, LIQUID FUELLED: UN Nos. 0395, 0396

Articles consisting of a liquid fuel within a cylinder fitted with one or more nozzles. They are designed to propel a rocket or a guided missile.

ROCKET MOTORS WITH HYPERGOLIC LIQUIDS with or without expelling charge: UN Nos. 0322, 0250

Articles consisting of a hypergolic fuel contained in a cylinder fitted with one or more nozzles. They are designed to propel a rocket or a guided missile.

ROCKETS, LINE THROWING: UN Nos. 0238, 0240, 0453

Articles consisting of a rocket motor which is designed to extend a line.

ROCKETS, LIQUID FUELLED with bursting charge: UN Nos. 0397, 0398

Articles consisting of a liquid fuel within a cylinder fitted with one or more nozzles and fitted with a warhead. The term includes guided missiles.

ROCKETS with bursting charge: UN Nos. 0181, 0182

Articles consisting of a rocket motor and a warhead without means of initiation or with means of initiation containing two or more effective protective features. The term includes guided missiles.

ROCKETS with bursting charge: UN Nos. 0180, 0295

Articles consisting of a rocket motor and a warhead with means of initiation not containing two or more effective protective features. The term includes guided missiles.

ROCKETS with expelling charge: UN Nos. 0436, 0437, 0438

Articles consisting of a rocket motor and a charge to expel the payload from a rocket head. The term includes guided missiles.

ROCKETS with inert head: UN Nos. 0183, 0502

Articles consisting of a rocket motor and an inert head. The term includes guided missiles.

SAMPLES, EXPLOSIVE, other than initiating explosive UN No. 0190

New or existing explosive substances or articles, not yet assigned to a name in Table A of Chapter 3.2 and carried in conformity with the instructions of the competent authority and generally in small quantities, inter alia, for the purposes of testing, classification, research and development, or quality control, or as commercial samples.

NOTE: Explosive substances or articles already assigned to another name in Table A of Chapter 3.2 are not included in this definition.

SIGNAL DEVICES, HAND: UN Nos. 0191, 0373

Portable articles containing pyrotechnic substances which produce visual signals or warnings. The term includes small surface flares such as highway or railway flares and small distress flares.

SIGNALS, DISTRESS, ship: UN Nos. 0194, 0195, 0505, 0506

Articles containing pyrotechnic substances designed to produce signals by means of sound, flame or smoke or any combination thereof.

SIGNALS, RAILWAY TRACK, EXPLOSIVE: UN Nos. 0192, 0193, 0492, 0493

Articles containing a pyrotechnic substance which explodes with a loud report when the article is crushed. They are designed to be placed on a rail.

SIGNALS, SMOKE: UN Nos. 0196, 0197, 0313, 0487, 0507

Articles containing pyrotechnic substances which emit smoke. In addition they may contain devices for emitting audible signals.

SOUNDING DEVICES, EXPLOSIVE: UN Nos. 0374, 0375

Articles consisting of a charge of detonating explosive, without means of initiation or with means of initiation containing two or more effective protective features. They are dropped from ships and function when they reach a predetermined depth or the sea bed.

SOUNDING DEVICES, EXPLOSIVE: UN Nos. 0204, 0296

Articles consisting of a charge of detonating explosive with means of initiation not containing two or more effective protective features. They are dropped from ships and function when they reach a predetermined depth or the sea bed.

SUBSTANCES, EXPLOSIVE, VERY INSENSITIVE (Substances, EVI), N.O.S.: UN No. 0482

Substances presenting a mass explosion hazard but which are so insensitive that there is very little probability of initiation or of transition from burning to detonation under normal conditions of transport, and which have passed Test Series 5.

TORPEDOES, LIQUID FUELLED with inert head: UN No. 0450

Articles consisting of a liquid explosive system to propel the torpedo through the water, with an inert head.

TORPEDOES, LIQUID FUELLED with or without bursting charge: UN No. 0449

Articles consisting of either a liquid explosive system to propel the torpedo through the water, with or without a warhead; or a liquid non-explosive system to propel the torpedo through the water, with a warhead.

TORPEDOES with bursting charge: UN No. 0451

Articles consisting of a non-explosive system to propel the torpedo through the water, and a warhead without means of initiation or with means of initiation containing two or more effective protective features.

TORPEDOES with bursting charge: UN No. 0329

Articles consisting of an explosive system to propel the torpedo through the water, and a warhead without means of initiation or with means of initiation containing two or more effective protective features.

TORPEDOES with bursting charge: UN No. 0330

Articles consisting of an explosive or non-explosive system to propel the torpedo through the water, and a warhead with means of initiation not containing two or more effective protective features.

TRACERS FOR AMMUNITION: UN Nos. 0212, 0306

Sealed articles containing pyrotechnic substances, designed to reveal the trajectory of a projectile.

TRITONAL: UN No. 0390

Substance consisting of trinitrotoluene (TNT) mixed with aluminium.

WARHEADS, ROCKET with burster or expelling charge: UN No. 0370

Articles consisting of an inert payload and a small charge of detonating or deflagrating explosive, without means of initiation or with means of initiation containing two or more effective protective features. They are designed to be fitted to a rocket motor to scatter inert material. The term includes warheads for guided missiles.

WARHEADS, ROCKET with burster or expelling charge: UN No. 0371

Articles consisting of an inert payload and a small charge of detonating or deflagrating explosive, with means of initiation not containing two or more effective protective features. They are designed to be fitted to a rocket motor to scatter inert material. The term includes warheads for guided missiles.

WARHEADS, ROCKET with bursting charge: UN Nos. 0286, 0287

Articles consisting of a detonating explosive, without means of initiation or with means of initiation containing two or more effective protective features. They are designed to be fitted to a rocket. The term includes warheads for guided missiles.

WARHEADS, ROCKET with bursting charge: UN No. 0369

Articles consisting of a detonating explosive, with means of initiation not containing two or more effective protective features. They are designed to be fitted to a rocket. The term includes warheads for guided missiles.

WARHEADS, TORPEDO with bursting charge: UN No. 0221

Articles consisting of a detonating explosive, without means of initiation or with means of initiation containing two or more effective protective features. They are designed to be fitted to a torpedo.

2.2.1.2   *Substances and articles not accepted for carriage*

2.2.1.2.1   Explosive substances which are unduly sensitive according to the criteria of the Manual of Tests and Criteria, Part I, or are liable to spontaneous reaction, as well as explosive substances and articles which cannot be assigned to a name or n.o.s. entry listed in Table A of Chapter 3.2, shall not be accepted for carriage.

2.2.1.2.2   Articles of compatibility group K shall not be accepted for carriage (1.2K, UN No. 0020 and 1.3K, UN No. 0021).

2.2.1.3   *List of collective entries*

Classification code (see 2.2.1.1.4)	UN No.	Name of the substance or article
1.1A	0473	SUBSTANCES, EXPLOSIVE, N.O.S.
1.1B	0461	COMPONENTS, EXPLOSIVE TRAIN, N.O.S.
1.1C	0474	SUBSTANCES, EXPLOSIVE, N.O.S.
	0497	PROPELLANT, LIQUID
	0498	PROPELLANT, SOLID
	0462	ARTICLES, EXPLOSIVE, N.O.S.
1.1D	0475	SUBSTANCES, EXPLOSIVE, N.O.S.
	0463	ARTICLES, EXPLOSIVE, N.O.S.
1.1E	0464	ARTICLES, EXPLOSIVE, N.O.S.
1.1F	0465	ARTICLES, EXPLOSIVE, N.O.S.
1.1G	0476	SUBSTANCES, EXPLOSIVE, N.O.S.
1.1L	0357	SUBSTANCES, EXPLOSIVE, N.O.S.
	0354	ARTICLES, EXPLOSIVE, N.O.S.
1.2B	0382	COMPONENTS, EXPLOSIVE TRAIN, N.O.S.
1.2C	0466	ARTICLES, EXPLOSIVE, N.O.S.
1.2D	0467	ARTICLES, EXPLOSIVE, N.O.S.
1.2E	0468	ARTICLES, EXPLOSIVE, N.O.S.
1.2F	0469	ARTICLES, EXPLOSIVE, N.O.S.
1.2L	0358	SUBSTANCES, EXPLOSIVE, N.O.S.
	0248	CONTRIVANCES, WATER-ACTIVATED with burster, expelling charge or propelling charge
	0355	ARTICLES, EXPLOSIVE, N.O.S.
1.3C	0132	DEFLAGRATING METAL SALTS OF AROMATIC NITRO-DERIVATIVES, N.O.S.
	0477	SUBSTANCES, EXPLOSIVE, N.O.S.
	0495	PROPELLANT, LIQUID
	0499	PROPELLANT, SOLID
	0470	ARTICLES, EXPLOSIVE, N.O.S.
1.3G	0478	SUBSTANCES, EXPLOSIVE, N.O.S.
1.3L	0359	SUBSTANCES, EXPLOSIVE, N.O.S.
	0249	CONTRIVANCES, WATER-ACTIVATED with burster, expelling charge or propelling charge
	0356	ARTICLES, EXPLOSIVE, N.O.S.
1.4B	0350	ARTICLES, EXPLOSIVE, N.O.S.
	0383	COMPONENTS, EXPLOSIVE TRAIN, N.O.S.
1.4C	0479	SUBSTANCES, EXPLOSIVE, N.O.S.
	0501	PROPELLANT, SOLID
	0351	ARTICLES, EXPLOSIVE, N.O.S.

Classification code (see 2.2.1.1.4)	UN No.	Name of the substance or article
1.4D	0480	SUBSTANCES, EXPLOSIVE, N.O.S.
	0352	ARTICLES, EXPLOSIVE, N.O.S.
1.4E	0471	ARTICLES, EXPLOSIVE, N.O.S.
1.4F	0472	ARTICLES, EXPLOSIVE, N.O.S.
1.4G	0485	SUBSTANCES, EXPLOSIVE, N.O.S.
	0353	ARTICLES, EXPLOSIVE, N.O.S.
1.4S	0481	SUBSTANCES, EXPLOSIVE, N.O.S.
	0349	ARTICLES, EXPLOSIVE, N.O.S.
	0384	COMPONENTS, EXPLOSIVE TRAIN, N.O.S.
1.5D	0482	SUBSTANCES, EXPLOSIVE, VERY INSENSITIVE (SUBSTANCES, EVI) N.O.S.
1.6N	0486	ARTICLES, EXPLOSIVE, EXTREMELY INSENSITIVE (ARTICLES, EEI)
	0190	SAMPLES, EXPLOSIVE other than initiating explosive
		NOTE: Division and Compatibility Group shall be defined as directed by the competent authority and according to the principles in 2.2.1.1.4.

2.2.2   **Class 2**   **Gases**

2.2.2.1   *Criteria*

2.2.2.1.1   The heading of Class 2 covers pure gases, mixtures of gases, mixtures of one or more gases with one or more other substances and articles containing such substances.

A gas is a substance which:

(a)   at 50 °C has a vapour pressure greater than 300 kPa (3 bar); or

(b)   is completely gaseous at 20 °C at the standard pressure of 101.3 kPa.

NOTE 1: UN No. 1052 HYDROGEN FLUORIDE, ANHYDROUS is nevertheless classified in Class 8.

NOTE 2: A pure gas may contain other components deriving from its production process or added to preserve the stability of the product, provided that the level of these components does not change its classification or its conditions of carriage, such as filling ratio, filling pressure, test pressure.

NOTE 3: N.O.S. entries in 2.2.2.3 may cover pure gases as well as mixtures.

NOTE 4: Carbonated beverages are not subject to the provisions of ADR.

2.2.2.1.2   The substances and articles of Class 2 are subdivided as follows:

1.   *Compressed gas:* a gas which when packaged under pressure for carriage is entirely gaseous at -50 °C; this category includes all gases with a critical temperature less than or equal to -50 °C;

2.   *Liquefied gas:* a gas which when packaged under pressure for carriage is partially liquid at temperatures above -50 °C. A distinction is made between:

High pressure liquefied gas: a gas with a critical temperature above -50 °C and equal to or below +65 °C; and

Low pressure liquefied gas: a gas with a critical temperature above +65 °C;

3.   *Refrigerated liquefied gas*: a gas which when packaged for carriage is made partially liquid because of its low temperature;

4.   *Dissolved gas:* a gas which when packaged under pressure for carriage is dissolved in a liquid phase solvent;

5.   Aerosol dispensers and receptacles, small, containing gas (gas cartridges);

6.   Other articles containing gas under pressure;

7.   Non-pressurized gases subject to special requirements (gas samples).

2.2.2.1.3   Substances and articles (except aerosols) of Class 2 are assigned to one of the following groups according to their hazardous properties, as follows:

A   asphyxiant;

O   oxidizing;

F   flammable;

T   toxic;

TF   toxic, flammable;

TC   toxic, corrosive;

TO   toxic, oxidizing;

TFC   toxic, flammable, corrosive;

TOC   toxic, oxidizing, corrosive.

For gases and gas mixtures presenting hazardous properties associated with more than one group according to the criteria, the groups designated by letter T take precedence over all other groups. The groups designated by letter F take precedence over the groups designated by letters A or O.

NOTE 1: In the UN Model Regulations, the IMDG Code and the ICAO Technical Instructions, gases are assigned to one of the following three divisions, based on the primary hazard:

Division 2.1:	*flammable gases (corresponding to the groups designated by the capital letter F);*
Division 2.2:	*non-flammable, non-toxic gases (corresponding to the groups designated by the capital letters A or O);*
Division 2.3:	*toxic gases (corresponding to the groups designated by the capital letter T i.e. T, TF, TC, TO, TFC and TOC).*

NOTE 2: Receptacles, small containing gas (UN No. 2037) shall be assigned to the groups A to TOC according to the hazard of the contents. For aerosols (UN No. 1950), see 2.2.2.1.6.

NOTE 3: Corrosive gases are considered to be toxic, and are therefore assigned to the group TC, TFC or TOC.

NOTE 4: Mixtures containing more than 21% oxygen by volume shall be classified as oxidizing.

2.2.2.1.4   If a mixture of Class 2 mentioned by name in Table A of Chapter 3.2 meets different criteria as mentioned in 2.2.2.1.2 and 2.2.2.1.5, this mixture shall be classified according to the criteria and assigned to an appropriate N.O.S. entry.

2.2.2.1.5   Substances and articles (except aerosols) of Class 2 which are not mentioned by name in Table A of Chapter 3.2 shall be classified under a collective entry listed in 2.2.2.3 in accordance with 2.2.2.1.2 and 2.2.2.1.3. The following criteria shall apply:

Asphyxiant gases

Gases which are non-oxidizing, non-flammable and non-toxic and which dilute or replace oxygen normally in the atmosphere.

Flammable gases

Gases which at 20 °C and a standard pressure of 101.3 kPa:

(a)   are ignitable when in a mixture of 13% or less by volume with air; or

(b)   have a flammable range with air of at least 12 percentage points regardless of the lower flammable limit.

Flammability shall be determined by tests or by calculation, in accordance with methods adopted by ISO (see ISO 10156:1996).

Where insufficient data are available to use these methods, tests by a comparable method recognized by the competent authority of the country of origin may be used.

If the country of origin is not a Contracting Party to ADR these methods shall be recognized by the competent authority of the first country Contracting Party to ADR reached by the consignment.

Oxidizing gases

Gases, which may, generally by providing oxygen, cause or contribute to the combustion of other material more than air does. Oxidizing ability is determined either by tests or by calculation methods adopted by ISO (see ISO 10156:1996 and ISO 10156-2:2005).

Toxic gases

NOTE: *Gases meeting the criteria for toxicity in part or completely owing to their corrosivity are to be classified as toxic. See also the criteria under the heading "Corrosive gases" for a possible subsidiary corrosivity risk.*

Gases which:

(a)   are known to be so toxic or corrosive to humans as to pose a hazard to health; or

(b)   are presumed to be toxic or corrosive to humans because they have a LC_{50} value for acute toxicity equal to or less than 5 000 ml/m³ (ppm) when tested in accordance with 2.2.61.1.

In the case of gas mixtures (including vapours of substances from other classes) the following formula may be used:

$$LC_{50} \text{ Toxic (mixture)} = \frac{1}{\sum\limits_{i=1}^{n} \dfrac{f_i}{T_i}}$$

where f_i =   mole fraction of the ith component substance of the mixture;

T_i = toxicity index of the ith component substance of the mixture.

The T_i equals the LC_{50} value as found in packing instruction P200 of 4.1.4.1.

When no LC_{50} value is listed in packing instruction P200 of 4.1.4.1, a LC_{50} value available in scientific literature shall be used. When the LC_{50} value is unknown, the toxicity index is determined by using the lowest LC_{50} value of substances of similar physiological and chemical effects, or through testing if this is the only practical possibility.

Corrosive gases

Gases or gas mixtures meeting the criteria for toxicity completely owing to their corrosivity are to be classified as toxic with a subsidiary corrosivity risk.

A gas mixture that is considered to be toxic due to the combined effects of corrosivity and toxicity has a subsidiary risk of corrosivity when the mixture is known by human experience to be destructive to the skin, eyes or mucous membranes or when the LC_{50} value of the corrosive components of the mixture is equal to or less than 5 000 ml/m³ (ppm) when the LC_{50} is calculated by the formula:

$$LC_{50} \text{ Corrosive (mixture)} = \frac{1}{\sum_{i=1}^{n} \frac{f_{ci}}{T_{ci}}}$$

where fc_i = mole fraction of the ith corrosive component substance of the mixture;

Tc_i = toxicity index of the ith corrosive component substance of the mixture.

The Tc_i equals the LC_{50} value as found in packing instruction P200 of 4.1.4.1.

When no LC_{50} value is listed in packing instruction P200 of 4.1.4.1, a LC_{50} value available in scientific literature shall be used.

When the LC_{50} value is unknown the toxicity index is determined by using the lowest LC_{50} value of substances of similar physiological and chemical effects, or through testing if this is the only practical possibility.

2.2.2.1.6   *Aerosols*

Aerosols (UN No. 1950) are assigned to one of the following groups according to their hazardous properties, as follows:

A   asphyxiant;

O   oxidizing;

F   flammable;

T   toxic;

C   corrosive;

CO   corrosive, oxidizing;

FC   flammable, corrosive;

TF   toxic, flammable;

TC   toxic, corrosive;

TO   toxic, oxidizing;

TFC   toxic, flammable, corrosive;

TOC   toxic, oxidizing, corrosive.

The classification depends on the nature of the contents of the aerosol dispenser.

NOTE: Gases, which meet the definition of toxic gases according to 2.2.2.1.5 or of pyrophoric gases according to packing instruction P200 in 4.1.4.1, shall not be used as a propellant in an aerosol dispenser. Aerosols with contents meeting the criteria for packing group I for toxicity or corrosivity shall not be accepted for carriage (see also 2.2.2.2.2).

The following criteria shall apply:

(a)   Assignment to group A shall apply when the contents do not meet the criteria for any other group according to sub-paragraphs (b) to (f) below;

(b)   Assignment to group O shall apply when the aerosol contains an oxidizing gas according to 2.2.2.1.5;

(c)   Assignment to group F shall apply if the contents include 85% by mass or more flammable components and the chemical heat of combustion is 30 kJ/g or more.

It shall not apply if the contents contain 1% by mass or less flammable components and the heat of combustion is less than 20 kJ/g.

Otherwise the aerosol shall be tested for flammability in accordance with the tests described in the *Manual of Tests and Criteria*, Part III, section 31. Extremely flammable and flammable aerosols shall be assigned to group F;

NOTE: Flammable components are flammable liquids, flammable solids or flammable gases and gas mixtures as defined in Notes 1 to 3 of sub-section 31.1.3 of Part III of the Manual of Tests and Criteria. This designation does not cover pyrophoric, self-heating or water-reactive substances. The chemical heat of combustion shall be determined by one of the following methods ASTM D 240, ISO/FDIS 13943: 1999 (E/F) 86.1 to 86.3 or NFPA 30B.

(d)   Assignment to group T shall apply when the contents, other than the propellant of aerosol dispensers to be ejected, are classified as Class 6.1, packing groups II or III;

(e)   Assignment to group C shall apply when the contents, other than the propellant of aerosol dispensers to be ejected, meet the criteria for Class 8, packing groups II or III;

(f)   When the criteria for more than one group amongst groups O, F, T, and C are met, assignment to groups CO, FC, TF, TC TO, TFC or TOC shall apply, as relevant.

2.2.2.2   *Gases not accepted for carriage*

2.2.2.2.1   Chemically unstable substances of Class 2 shall not be accepted for carriage, unless the necessary steps have been taken to prevent all possibility of a dangerous reaction e.g. decomposition, dismutation or polymerisation under normal conditions during transport. To this end particular care shall be taken to ensure that receptacles and tanks do not contain any substances liable to promote these reactions.

2.2.2.2.2   The following substances and mixtures shall not be accepted for carriage:

- UN No. 2186 HYDROGEN CHLORIDE, REFRIGERATED LIQUID;

- UN No. 2421 NITROGEN TRIOXIDE;

- UN No. 2455 METHYL NITRITE;

- Refrigerated liquefied gases which cannot be assigned to classification codes 3A, 3O or 3F;

- Dissolved gases which cannot be classified under UN Nos. 1001, 2073 or 3318;

- Aerosols where gases which are toxic according to 2.2.2.1.5 or pyrophoric according to packing instruction P200 in 4.1.4.1 are used as propellants;

- Aerosols with contents meeting the criteria for packing group I for toxicity or corrosivity (see 2.2.61 and 2.2.8);

- Receptacles, small, containing gases which are very toxic (LC_{50} lower than 200 ppm) or pyrophoric according to packing instruction P200 in 4.1.4.1.

2.2.2.3   *List of collective entries*

Compressed gases		
Classification code	**UN No.**	**Name of the substance or article**
1 A	1956	COMPRESSED GAS, N.O.S.
1 O	3156	COMPRESSED GAS, OXIDIZING, N.O.S.
1 F	1964	HYDROCARBON GAS MIXTURE, COMPRESSED, N.O.S.
	1954	COMPRESSED GAS, FLAMMABLE, N.O.S.
1T	1955	COMPRESSED GAS, TOXIC, N.O.S.
1 TF	1953	COMPRESSED GAS, TOXIC, FLAMMABLE, N.O.S.
1 TC	3304	COMPRESSED GAS, TOXIC, CORROSIVE, N.O.S.
1 TO	3303	COMPRESSED GAS, TOXIC, OXIDIZING, N.O.S.
1 TFC	3305	COMPRESSED GAS, TOXIC, FLAMMABLE, CORROSIVE, N.O.S.
1 TOC	3306	COMPRESSED GAS, TOXIC, OXIDIZING, CORROSIVE, N.O.S.

Liquefied gases		
Classification code	**UN No.**	**Name of the substance or article**
2 A	1058	LIQUEFIED GASES, non-flammable, charged with nitrogen, carbon dioxide or air
	1078	REFRIGERANT GAS, N.O.S.
		such as mixtures of gases, indicated by the letter R..., which as:
		Mixture F1, have a vapour pressure at 70 °C not exceeding 1.3 MPa (13 bar) and a density at 50 °C not lower than that of dichlorofluoromethane (1.30 kg/l);
		Mixture F2, have a vapour pressure at 70 °C not exceeding 1.9 MPa (19 bar) and a density at 50 °C not lower than that of dichlorodifluoromethane (1.21 kg/l);
		Mixture F3, have a vapour pressure at 70 °C not exceeding 3 MPa (30 bar) and a density at 50 °C not lower than that of chlorodifluoromethane (1.09 kg/l).
		NOTE: Trichlorofluoromethane (Refrigerant R 11), 1,1,2-trichloro-1,2,2-trifluoroethane (Refrigerant R 113), 1,1,1-trichloro-2,2,2-trifluoroethane (Refrigerant R 113a), 1-chloro-1,2,2-trifluoroethane (Refrigerant R 133) and 1-chloro-1,1,2-trifluoroethane (Refrigerant R 133b) are not substances of Class 2. They may, however, enter into the composition of mixtures F1 to F3.
	1968	INSECTICIDE GAS, N.O.S.
	3163	LIQUEFIED GAS, N.O.S.
2 O	3157	LIQUEFIED GAS, OXIDIZING, N.O.S.
2 F	1010	BUTADIENES AND HYDROCARBON MIXTURE, STABILIZED, having a vapour pressure at 70 °C not exceeding 1.1 MPa (11 bar) and a density at 50 °C not lower than 0.525 kg/l.
		NOTE: Butadienes, stabilized are also classified under UN No. 1010, see Table A of Chapter 3.2.
	1060	METHYLACETYLENE AND PROPADIENE MIXTURE, STABILIZED
		such as mixtures of methylacetylene and propadiene with hydrocarbons, which as:
		Mixture P1, contain not more than 63% methylacetylene and propadiene by volume and not more than 24% propane and propylene by volume, the percentage of C_4- saturated hydrocarbons being not less than 14% by volume; and as
		Mixture P2, contain not more than 48% methylacetylene and propadiene by volume and not more than 50% propane and propylene by volume, the percentage of C_4- saturated hydrocarbons being not less than 5% by volume,
		as well as mixtures of propadiene with 1 to 4% methylacetylene.

Liquefied gases *(cont'd)*		
Classification code	**UN No.**	**Name of the substance or article**
2 F *(cont'd)*	1965	HYDROCARBON GAS MIXTURE, LIQUEFIED, N.O.S such as mixtures, which as: Mixture A, have a vapour pressure at 70 °C not exceeding 1.1 MPa (11 bar) and a density at 50 °C not lower than 0.525 kg/l; Mixture A01, have a vapour pressure at 70 °C not exceeding 1.6 MPa (16 bar) and a relative density at 50 °C not lower than 0.516 kg/l; Mixture A02, have a vapour pressure at 70 °C not exceeding 1.6 MPa (16 bar) and a relative density at 50 °C not lower than 0.505 kg/l; Mixture A0, have a vapour pressure at 70 °C not exceeding 1.6 MPa (16 bar) and a density at 50 °C not lower than 0.495 kg/l; Mixture A1, have a vapour pressure at 70 °C not exceeding 2.1 MPa (21 bar) and a density at 50 °C not lower than 0.485 kg/l; Mixture B1 have a vapour pressure at 70 °C not exceeding 2.6 MPa (26 bar) and a relative density at 50 °C not lower than 0.474 kg/l; Mixture B2 have a vapour pressure at 70 °C not exceeding 2.6 MPa (26 bar) and a relative density at 50 °C not lower than 0.463 kg/l; Mixture B, have a vapour pressure at 70 °C not exceeding 2.6 MPa (26 bar) and a density at 50 °C not lower than 0.450 kg/l; Mixture C, have a vapour pressure at 70 °C not exceeding 3.1 MPa (31 bar) and a relative density at 50 °C not lower than 0.440 kg/l; ***NOTE 1:*** *In the case of the foregoing mixtures, the use of the following names customary in the trade is permitted for describing these substances: for mixtures A, A01, A02 and A0: BUTANE; for mixture C: PROPANE.* ***NOTE 2:*** *UN No. 1075 PETROLEUM GASES, LIQUEFIED may be used as an alternative entry for UN No. 1965 HYDROCARBON GAS MIXTURE LIQUEFIED, N.O.S. for carriage prior to or following maritime or air carriage.*
	3354	INSECTICIDE GAS, FLAMMABLE, N.O.S.
	3161	LIQUEFIED GAS, FLAMMABLE, N.O.S.
2 T	1967	INSECTICIDE GAS, TOXIC, N.O.S.
	3162	LIQUEFIED GAS, TOXIC, N.O.S.
2 TF	3355	INSECTICIDE GAS, TOXIC, FLAMMABLE, N.O.S.
	3160	LIQUEFIED GAS, TOXIC, FLAMMABLE, N.O.S.
2 TC	3308	LIQUEFIED GAS, TOXIC, CORROSIVE, N.O.S.
2 TO	3307	LIQUEFIED GAS, TOXIC, OXIDIZING, N.O.S.
2 TFC	3309	LIQUEFIED GAS, TOXIC, FLAMMABLE, CORROSIVE, N.O.S.
2 TOC	3310	LIQUEFIED GAS, TOXIC, OXIDIZING, CORROSIVE, N.O.S.

Refrigerated liquefied gases		
Classification code	**UN No.**	**Name of the substance or article**
3 A	3158	GAS, REFRIGERATED LIQUID, N.O.S.
3 O	3311	GAS, REFRIGERATED LIQUID, OXIDIZING, N.O.S.
3 F	3312	GAS, REFRIGERATED LIQUID, FLAMMABLE, N.O.S.

Dissolved gases		
Classification code	**UN No.**	**Name of the substance or article**
4		Only substances listed in Table A of Chapter 3.2 are to be accepted for carriage.

Aerosols and receptacles, small, containing gas		
Classification code	**UN No.**	**Name of the substance or article**
5	1950	AEROSOLS
	2037	RECEPTACLES, SMALL CONTAINING GAS (GAS CARTRIDGES) without a release device, non-refillable

Other articles containing gas under pressure		
Classification code	**UN No.**	**Name of the substance or article**
6A	2857	REFRIGERATING MACHINES containing non-flammable, non-toxic gases or ammonia solutions (UN 2672)
	3164	ARTICLES, PRESSURIZED, PNEUMATIC (containing non-flammable gas) or
	3164	ARTICLES, PRESSURIZED, HYDRAULIC (containing non-flammable gas)
6F	3150	DEVICES, SMALL, HYDROCARBON GAS POWERED or
	3150	HYDROCARBON GAS REFILLS FOR SMALL DEVICES, with release device
	3478	FUEL CELL CARTRIDGES, containing liquefied flammable gas or
	3478	FUEL CELL CARTRIDGES CONTAINED IN EQUIPMENT, containing liquefied flammable gas or
	3478	FUEL CELL CARTRIDGES PACKED WITH EQUIPMENT, containing liquefied flammable gas
	3479	FUEL CELL CARTRIDGES, containing hydrogen in metal hydride or
	3479	FUEL CELL CARTRIDGES CONTAINED IN EQUIPMENT, containing hydrogen in metal hydride or
	3479	FUEL CELL CARTRIDGES PACKED WITH EQUIPMENT, containing hydrogen in metal hydride

Gas samples		
Classification code	**UN No.**	**Name of the substance or article**
7 F	3167	GAS SAMPLE, NON-PRESSURIZED, FLAMMABLE, N.O.S., not refrigerated liquid
7 T	3169	GAS SAMPLE, NON-PRESSURIZED, TOXIC, N.O.S., not refrigerated liquid
7 TF	3168	GAS SAMPLE, NON-PRESSURIZED, TOXIC, FLAMMABLE, N.O.S., not refrigerated liquid

2.2.3   **Class 3**   **Flammable liquids**

2.2.3.1   *Criteria*

2.2.3.1.1   The heading of Class 3 covers substances and articles containing substances of this Class which:

- are liquids according to subparagraph (a) of the definition for "liquid" in 1.2.1;

- have at 50 °C a vapour pressure of not more than 300 kPa (3 bar) and are not completely gaseous at 20 °C and at standard pressure of 101.3 kPa; and

- have a flash-point of not more than 60 °C (see 2.3.3.1 for the relevant test).

The heading of Class 3 also covers liquid substances and molten solid substances with a flash-point of more than 60°C and which are carried or handed over for carriage whilst heated at temperatures equal to or higher than their flash-point. These substances are assigned to UN No. 3256.

The heading of Class 3 also covers liquid desensitized explosives. Liquid desensitized explosives are explosive substances which are dissolved or suspended in water or other liquid substances, to form an homogeneous liquid mixture to suppress their explosive properties. Such entries in Table A of Chapter 3.2 are UN Nos. 1204, 2059, 3064, 3343, 3357 and 3379.

NOTE 1: Substances having a flash-point above 35 °C, non-toxic and non-corrosive, which do not sustain combustion according to the criteria of sub-section 32.2.5 of Part III of the Manual of Tests and Criteria, are not substances of Class 3; if, however, these substances are handed over for carriage and carried whilst heated at temperatures equal to or higher than their flash-point, they are substances of Class 3.

NOTE 2: By derogation from paragraph 2.2.3.1.1 above, diesel fuel, gasoil, heating oil (light) having a flash-point above 60 °C and not more than 100 °C shall be deemed substances of Class 3, UN No. 1202.

NOTE 3: Liquids which are highly toxic on inhalation, having a flash-point below 23 °C and toxic substances, having a flash-point of 23 °C or above are substances of Class 6.1 (see 2.2.61.1).

NOTE 4: Flammable liquid substances and preparations used as pesticides, which are highly toxic, toxic or slightly toxic and have a flash-point of 23 °C or above are substances of Class 6.1 (see 2.2.61.1).

2.2.3.1.2   The substances and articles of Class 3 are subdivided as follows:

F   Flammable liquids, without subsidiary risk:

    F1   Flammable liquids having a flash-point of or below 60 °C;
    F2   Flammable liquids having a flash-point above 60 °C which are carried or handed over for carriage at or above their flash-point (elevated temperature substances);

FT   Flammable liquids, toxic:

    FT1   Flammable liquids, toxic;
    FT2   Pesticides;

FC   Flammable liquids, corrosive;

FTC   Flammable liquids, toxic, corrosive;

D   Liquid desensitized explosives.

2.2.3.1.3   Substances and articles classified in Class 3 are listed in Table A of Chapter 3.2. Substances not mentioned by name in Table A of Chapter 3.2 shall be assigned to the relevant entry of 2.2.3.3 and the relevant packing group in accordance with the provisions of this section. Flammable liquids shall be assigned to one of the following packing groups according to the degree of danger they present for carriage:

Packing group	Flash point (closed cup)	Initial boiling point
I	--	$\leq 35°C$
II [a]	$< 23°C$	$> 35°C$
III [a]	$\geq 23°C \leq 60°C$	$> 35°C$

[a]   *See also 2.2.3.1.4.*

For a liquid with (a) subsidiary risk(s), the packing group determined in accordance with the table above and the packing group based on the severity of the subsidiary risk(s) shall be considered; the classification and packing group shall then be determined in accordance with the table of precedence of hazards in 2.1.3.10.

2.2.3.1.4   Liquid or viscous mixtures and preparations, including those containing no more than 20% nitrocellulose with a nitrogen content not exceeding 12.6% (by dry mass), shall be assigned to packing group III only if the following requirements are met:

(a)   the height of the separated layer of solvent is less than 3% of the total height of the sample in the solvent-separation test (see Manual of Tests and Criteria, Part III, sub-section 32.5.1); and

(b)   the viscosity [2] and flash-point are in accordance with the following table:

Kinematic viscosity (extrapolated) v (at near-zero shear rate) mm^2/s at 23 °C	Flow time t in accordance with ISO 2431:1993		Flash-point in °C
	in s	Jet diameter in mm	
$20 < v \leq 80$	$20 < t \leq 60$	4	above 17
$80 < v \leq 135$	$60 < t \leq 100$	4	above 10
$135 < v \leq 220$	$20 < t \leq 32$	6	above 5
$220 < v \leq 300$	$32 < t \leq 44$	6	above -1
$300 < v \leq 700$	$44 < t \leq 100$	6	above -5
$700 < v$	$100 < t$	6	-5 and below

---

[2]   *Viscosity determination: Where the substance concerned is non-Newtonian, or where a flow cup method of viscosity determination is otherwise unsuitable, a variable shear-rate viscometer shall be used to determine the dynamic viscosity coefficient of the substance, at 23 °C, at a number of shear rates. The values obtained are plotted against shear rate and then extrapolated to zero shear rate. The dynamic viscosity thus obtained, divided by the density, gives the apparent kinematic viscosity at near-zero shear rate.*

NOTE: Mixtures containing more than 20% but not more than 55% nitrocellulose with a nitrogen content not exceeding 12.6% by dry mass are substances assigned to UN No. 2059.

Mixtures having a flash-point below 23 °C and containing:

- *more than 55% nitrocellulose, whatever their nitrogen content; or*

- *not more than 55% nitrocellulose with a nitrogen content above 12.6% by dry mass,*

are substances of Class 1 (UN Nos. 0340 or 0342) or of Class 4.1 (UN Nos. 2555, 2556 or 2557).

2.2.3.1.5   Non-toxic, non-corrosive and non-environmentally hazardous solutions and homogeneous mixtures having a flash-point of 23 °C or above (viscous substances, such as paints or varnishes, excluding substances containing more than 20% nitrocellulose) packed in receptacles of less than 450 litres capacity, are not subject to ADR if, in the solvent-separation test (see Manual of Tests and Criteria, Part III, sub-section 32.5.1), the height of the separated layer of solvent is less than 3% of the total height, and if the substances at 23 °C have, in the flow cup conforming to ISO 2431:1993 having a jet 6 mm in diameter, a flow time of:

(a)   not less than 60 seconds; or

(b)   not less than 40 seconds and contain not more than 60% of substances of Class 3.

2.2.3.1.6   If substances of Class 3, as a result of admixtures, come into categories of risk different from those to which the substances mentioned by name in Table A of Chapter 3.2 belong, these mixtures or solutions shall be assigned to the entries to which they belong on the basis of their actual degree of danger.

NOTE: For the classification of solutions and mixtures (such as preparations and wastes) see also 2.1.3.

2.2.3.1.7   On the basis of the test procedures in accordance with 2.3.3.1 and 2.3.4, and the criteria set out in 2.2.3.1.1, it may also be determined whether the nature of a solution or a mixture mentioned by name or containing a substance mentioned by name is such that the solution or mixture is not subject to the provisions for this Class (see also 2.1.3).

2.2.3.2   *Substances not accepted for carriage*

2.2.3.2.1   Substances of Class 3 which are liable to form peroxides easily (as happens with ethers or with certain heterocyclic oxygenated substances) shall not be accepted for carriage if their peroxide content, calculated as hydrogen peroxide (H_2O_2), exceeds 0.3%. The peroxide content shall be determined as indicated in 2.3.3.2.

2.2.3.2.2   The chemically unstable substances of Class 3 shall not be accepted for carriage unless the necessary steps have been taken to prevent their dangerous decomposition or polymerization during carriage. To this end, it shall be ensured in particular that receptacles and tanks do not contain any substance liable to promote these reactions.

2.2.3.2.3   Liquid desensitized explosives other than those listed in Table A of Chapter 3.2 shall not be accepted for carriage as substances of Class 3.

2.2.3.3   *List of collective entries*

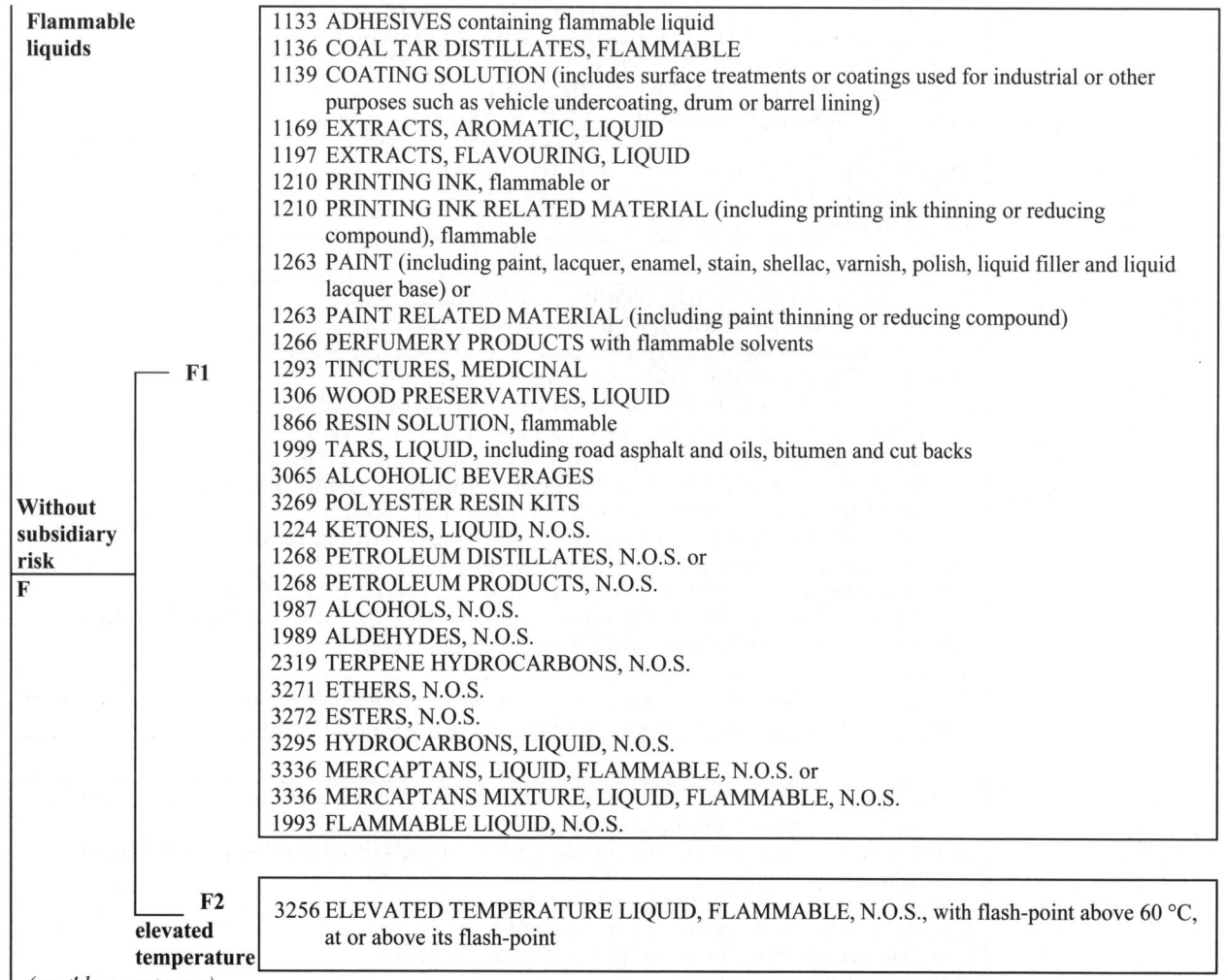

Flammable liquids		1133 ADHESIVES containing flammable liquid 1136 COAL TAR DISTILLATES, FLAMMABLE 1139 COATING SOLUTION (includes surface treatments or coatings used for industrial or other purposes such as vehicle undercoating, drum or barrel lining) 1169 EXTRACTS, AROMATIC, LIQUID 1197 EXTRACTS, FLAVOURING, LIQUID 1210 PRINTING INK, flammable or 1210 PRINTING INK RELATED MATERIAL (including printing ink thinning or reducing compound), flammable 1263 PAINT (including paint, lacquer, enamel, stain, shellac, varnish, polish, liquid filler and liquid lacquer base) or 1263 PAINT RELATED MATERIAL (including paint thinning or reducing compound) 1266 PERFUMERY PRODUCTS with flammable solvents
	F1	1293 TINCTURES, MEDICINAL 1306 WOOD PRESERVATIVES, LIQUID 1866 RESIN SOLUTION, flammable 1999 TARS, LIQUID, including road asphalt and oils, bitumen and cut backs 3065 ALCOHOLIC BEVERAGES 3269 POLYESTER RESIN KITS 1224 KETONES, LIQUID, N.O.S. 1268 PETROLEUM DISTILLATES, N.O.S. or
Without subsidiary risk **F**		1268 PETROLEUM PRODUCTS, N.O.S. 1987 ALCOHOLS, N.O.S. 1989 ALDEHYDES, N.O.S. 2319 TERPENE HYDROCARBONS, N.O.S. 3271 ETHERS, N.O.S. 3272 ESTERS, N.O.S. 3295 HYDROCARBONS, LIQUID, N.O.S. 3336 MERCAPTANS, LIQUID, FLAMMABLE, N.O.S. or 3336 MERCAPTANS MIXTURE, LIQUID, FLAMMABLE, N.O.S. 1993 FLAMMABLE LIQUID, N.O.S.
	F2 **elevated temperature**	3256 ELEVATED TEMPERATURE LIQUID, FLAMMABLE, N.O.S., with flash-point above 60 °C, at or above its flash-point

(cont'd on next page)

FT1	1228 MERCAPTANS, LIQUID, FLAMMABLE, TOXIC, N.O.S. or 1228 MERCAPTAN MIXTURE, LIQUID, FLAMMABLE, TOXIC, N.O.S. 1986 ALCOHOLS, FLAMMABLE, TOXIC, N.O.S. 1988 ALDEHYDES, FLAMMABLE, TOXIC, N.O.S. 2478 ISOCYANATES, FLAMMABLE, TOXIC, N.O.S. or 2478 ISOCYANATE SOLUTION, FLAMMABLE, TOXIC, N.O.S. 3248 MEDICINE, LIQUID, FLAMMABLE, TOXIC, N.O.S. 3273 NITRILES, FLAMMABLE, TOXIC, N.O.S. 1992 FLAMMABLE LIQUID, TOXIC, N.O.S.

Toxic FT

FT2 **pesticide** **(f.p<23 °C)**	2758 CARBAMATE PESTICIDE, LIQUID, FLAMMABLE, TOXIC 2760 ARSENICAL PESTICIDE, LIQUID, FLAMMABLE, TOXIC 2762 ORGANOCHLORINE PESTICIDE, LIQUID, FLAMMABLE, TOXIC 2764 TRIAZINE PESTICIDE, LIQUID, FLAMMABLE, TOXIC 2772 THIOCARBAMATE PESTICIDE, LIQUID, FLAMMABLE, TOXIC 2776 COPPER BASED PESTICIDE, LIQUID, FLAMMABLE, TOXIC 2778 MERCURY BASED PESTICIDE, LIQUID, FLAMMABLE, TOXIC 2780 SUBSTITUTED NITROPHENOL PESTICIDE, LIQUID, FLAMMABLE, TOXIC 2782 BIPYRIDILIUM PESTICIDE, LIQUID, FLAMMABLE, TOXIC 2784 ORGANOPHOSPHORUS PESTICIDE, LIQUID, FLAMMABLE, TOXIC 2787 ORGANOTIN PESTICIDE, LIQUID, FLAMMABLE, TOXIC 3024 COUMARIN DERIVATIVE PESTICIDE, LIQUID, FLAMMABLE, TOXIC 3346 PHENOXYACETIC ACID DERIVATIVE PESTICIDE, LIQUID, FLAMMABLE, TOXIC 3350 PYRETHROID PESTICIDE, LIQUID, FLAMMABLE TOXIC 3021 PESTICIDE, LIQUID, FLAMMABLE, TOXIC, N.O.S. *NOTE: The classification of a pesticide under an entry shall be effected on the basis of the active ingredient, of the physical state of the pesticide and any subsidiary risks it may exhibit.*

Corrosive

FC	3469 PAINT, FLAMMABLE, CORROSIVE (including paint, lacquer, enamel, stain, shellac, varnish, polish, liquid filler and liquid lacquer base) or 3469 PAINT RELATED MATERIAL, FLAMMABLE, CORROSIVE (including paint thinning or reducing compound) 2733 AMINES, FLAMMABLE, CORROSIVE, N.O.S. or 2733 POLYAMINES, FLAMMABLE, CORROSIVE, N.O.S. 2985 CHLOROSILANES, FLAMMABLE, CORROSIVE, N.O.S. 3274 ALCOHOLATES SOLUTION, N.O.S., in alcohol 2924 FLAMMABLE LIQUID, CORROSIVE, N.O.S.

Toxic, corrosive

FTC	3286 FLAMMABLE LIQUID, TOXIC, CORROSIVE, N.O.S.

Liquid desensitised explosive

D	3343 NITROGLYCERIN MIXTURE, DESENSITIZED, LIQUID, FLAMMABLE, N.O.S. with not more than 30% nitroglycerin by mass 3357 NITROGLYCERIN MIXTURE, DESENSITIZED, LIQUID, N.O.S. with not more than 30% nitroglycerin by mass 3379 DESENSITIZED EXPLOSIVE, LIQUID, N.O.S.

2.2.41   **Class 4.1**   **Flammable solids, self-reactive substances and solid desensitized explosives**

2.2.41.1   *Criteria*

2.2.41.1.1   The heading of Class 4.1 covers flammable substances and articles, desensitized explosives which are solids according to subparagraph (a) of the definition "solid" in 1.2.1 and self-reactive liquids or solids.

The following are assigned to Class 4.1:

-    readily flammable solid substances and articles (see paragraphs 2.2.41.1.3 to 2.2.41.1.8);

-    self-reactive solids or liquids (see paragraphs 2.2.41.1.9 to 2.2.41.1.17);

-    solid desensitized explosives (see 2.2.41.1.18);

-    substances related to self-reactive substances (see 2.2.41.1.19).

2.2.41.1.2   The substances and articles of Class 4.1 are subdivided as follows:

F   Flammable solids, without subsidiary risk:

    F1   Organic;
    F2   Organic, molten;
    F3   Inorganic;

FO   Flammable solids, oxidizing;

FT   Flammable solids, toxic:

    FT1   Organic, toxic;
    FT2   Inorganic, toxic;

FC   Flammable solids, corrosive:

    FC1   Organic, corrosive;
    FC2   Inorganic, corrosive;

D   Solid desensitized explosives without subsidiary risk;

DT   Solid desensitized explosives, toxic;

SR   Self-reactive substances:

    SR1   Not requiring temperature control;
    SR2   Requiring temperature control.

Flammable solids

Definition and properties

2.2.41.1.3   *Flammable solids* are readily combustible solids and solids which may cause fire through friction.

Readily combustible solids are powdered, granular, or pasty substances which are dangerous if they can be easily ignited by brief contact with an ignition source, such as a burning match, and if the flame spreads rapidly. The danger may come not only from the fire but also from toxic combustion products. Metal powders are especially dangerous because of the difficulty of extinguishing a fire since normal extinguishing agents such as carbon dioxide or water can increase the hazard.

Classification

2.2.41.1.4   Substances and articles classified as flammable solids of Class 4.1 are listed in Table A of Chapter 3.2. The assignment of organic substances and articles not mentioned by name in Table A of Chapter 3.2 to the relevant entry of sub-section 2.2.41.3 in accordance with the provisions of Chapter 2.1 can be based on experience or on the results of the test procedures in accordance with Part III, sub-section 33.2.1 of the Manual of Tests and Criteria. The assignment of inorganic substances not mentioned by name shall be based on the results of the test procedures in accordance with Part III, sub-section 33.2.1 of the Manual of Tests and Criteria; experience shall also be taken into account when it leads to a more stringent assignment.

2.2.41.1.5   When substances not mentioned by name are assigned to one of the entries listed in 2.2.41.3 on the basis of the test procedures in accordance with the Manual of Tests and Criteria, Part III, sub-section 33.2.1, the following criteria apply:

(a)   With the exception of metal powders or powders of metal alloys, powdery, granular or pasty substances shall be classified as readily flammable substances of Class 4.1 if they can be easily ignited by brief contact with an ignition source (e.g. a burning match), or if, in the event of ignition, the flame spreads rapidly, the burning time is less than 45 seconds for a measured distance of 100 mm or the rate of burning is greater than 2.2 mm/s;

(b)   Metal powders or powders of metal alloys shall be assigned to Class 4.1 if they can be ignited by a flame and the reaction spreads over the whole length of the sample in 10 minutes or less.

Solids which may cause fire through friction shall be classified in Class 4.1 by analogy with existing entries (e.g. matches) or in accordance with any appropriate special provision.

2.2.41.1.6   On the basis of the test procedure in accordance with the Manual of Tests and Criteria, Part III, Section 33.2.1 and the criteria set out in 2.2.41.1.4 and 2.2.41.1.5, it may also be determined whether the nature of a substance mentioned by name is such that the substance is not subject to the provisions for this Class.

2.2.41.1.7   If substances of Class 4.1, as a result of admixtures, come into different categories of risk from those to which the substances mentioned by name in Table A of Chapter 3.2 belong, these mixtures shall be assigned to the entries to which they belong on the basis of their actual degree of danger.

NOTE: *For the classification of solutions and mixtures (such as preparations and wastes), see also 2.1.3.*

2.2.41.1.8 Flammable solids classified under the various entries in Table A of Chapter 3.2 shall be assigned to packing groups II or III on the basis of test procedures of the Manual of Tests and Criteria, Part III, sub-section 33.2.1, in accordance with the following criteria:

(a) Readily flammable solids which, when tested, have a burning time of less than 45 seconds over a measured distance of 100 mm shall be assigned to:

Packing group II: if the flame passes the wetted zone;

Packing group III: if the wetted zone stops the flame for at least four minutes;

(b) Metal powders or powders of metal alloys shall be assigned to:

Packing group II: if, when tested, the reaction spreads over the whole length of the sample in five minutes or less;

Packing group III: if, when tested, the reaction spreads over the whole length of the sample in more than five minutes.

For solids which may cause fire through friction, the packing group shall be assigned by analogy with existing entries or in accordance with any special provision.

Self-reactive substances

Definitions

2.2.41.1.9 For the purposes of ADR, *self-reactive substances* are thermally unstable substances liable to undergo a strongly exothermic decomposition even without participation of oxygen (air). Substances are not considered to be self-reactive substances of Class 4.1, if:

(a) they are explosives according to the criteria of Class 1;

(b) they are oxidizing substances according to the classification procedure for Class 5.1 (see 2.2.51.1) except that mixtures of oxidizing substances which contain 5% or more of combustible organic substances shall be subjected to the classification procedure defined in Note 2;

(c) they are organic peroxides according to the criteria of Class 5.2 (see 2.2.52.1);

(d) their heat of decomposition is less than 300 J/g; or

(e) their self-accelerating decomposition temperature (SADT) (see Note 3 below) is greater than 75 °C for a 50 kg package.

NOTE 1: *The heat of decomposition can be determined using any internationally recognised method e.g. differential scanning calorimetry and adiabatic calorimetry.*

NOTE 2: *Mixtures of oxidizing substances meeting the criteria of Class 5.1 which contain 5% or more of combustible organic substances, which do not meet the criteria mentioned in (a), (c), (d) or (e) above, shall be subjected to the self-reactive substance classification procedure.*

A mixture showing the properties of a self-reactive substance, type B to F, shall be classified as a self-reactive substance of Class 4.1.

A mixture showing the properties of a self-reactive substance, type G, according to the principle given in sub-section 20.4.3 (g) of Part II of the Manual of Tests and Criteria shall be considered for classification as a substance of Class 5.1 (see 2.2.51.1).

NOTE 3: *The self-accelerating decomposition temperature (SADT) is the lowest temperature at which self-accelerating decomposition may occur with a substance in the packaging as used during carriage. Requirements for the determination of the SADT are given in the Manual of Tests and Criteria, Part II, Chapter 20 and section 28.4.*

NOTE 4: *Any substance which shows the properties of a self-reactive substance shall be classified as such, even if this substance gives a positive test result according to 2.2.42.1.5 for inclusion in Class 4.2.*

Properties

2.2.41.1.10 The decomposition of self-reactive substances can be initiated by heat, contact with catalytic impurities (e.g. acids, heavy-metal compounds, bases), friction or impact. The rate of decomposition increases with temperature and varies with the substance. Decomposition, particularly if no ignition occurs, may result in the evolution of toxic gases or vapours. For certain self-reactive substances, the temperature shall be controlled. Some self-reactive substances may decompose explosively, particularly if confined. This characteristic may be modified by the addition of diluents or by the use of appropriate packagings. Certain self-reactive substances burn vigorously. Self-reactive substances are, for example, some compounds of the types listed below:

aliphatic azo compounds (-C-N=N-C-);
organic azides (-C-N$_3$);
diazonium salts (-CN$_2^+$ Z$^-$);
N-nitroso compounds (-N-N=O); and
aromatic sulphohydrazides (-SO$_2$-NH-NH$_2$).

This list is not exhaustive and substances with other reactive groups and some mixtures of substances may have similar properties.

Classification

2.2.41.1.11 Self-reactive substances are classified into seven types according to the degree of danger they present. The types of self-reactive substances range from type A, which is not accepted for carriage in the packaging in which it is tested, to type G, which is not subject to the provisions for self-reactive substances of Class 4.1. The classification of types B to F is directly related to the maximum quantity allowed in one packaging. The principles to be applied for classification as well as the applicable classification procedures, test methods and criteria and an example of a suitable test report are given in Part II of the Manual of Tests and Criteria.

2.2.41.1.12 Self-reactive substances which have already been classified and are already permitted for carriage in packagings are listed in 2.2.41.4, those already permitted for carriage in IBCs are listed in 4.1.4.2, packing instruction IBC520 and those already permitted for carriage in tanks according to Chapter 4.2 are listed in 4.2.5.2, portable tank instruction T23. Each permitted substance listed is assigned to a generic entry of Table A of Chapter 3.2 (UN Nos. 3221 to 3240), and appropriate subsidiary risks and remarks providing relevant transport information are given.

The collective entries specify:

-       self-reactive substances types B to F, see 2.2.41.1.11 above;

-	physical state (liquid/solid); and

-	temperature control (when required), see 2.2.41.1.17 below.

The classification of the self-reactive substances listed in 2.2.41.4 is based on the technically pure substance (except where a concentration of less than 100% is specified).

2.2.41.1.13	Classification of self-reactive substances not listed in 2.2.41.4, 4.1.4.2, packing instruction IBC520 or 4.2.5.2, portable tank instruction T23 and assignment to a collective entry shall be made by the competent authority of the country of origin on the basis of a test report. The statement of approval shall contain the classification and the relevant conditions of carriage. If the country of origin is not a Contracting Party to ADR, the classification and the conditions of carriage shall be recognized by the competent authority of the first country Contracting Party to ADR reached by the consignment.

2.2.41.1.14	Activators, such as zinc compounds, may be added to some self-reactive substances to change their reactivity. Depending on both the type and the concentration of the activator, this may result in a decrease in thermal stability and a change in explosive properties. If either of these properties is altered, the new formulation shall be assessed in accordance with the classification procedure.

2.2.41.1.15	Samples of self-reactive substances or formulations of self-reactive substances not listed in 2.2.41.4, for which a complete set of test results is not available and which are to be carried for further testing or evaluation, shall be assigned to one of the appropriate entries for self-reactive substances type C provided the following conditions are met:

-	the available data indicate that the sample would be no more dangerous than self-reactive substances type B;

-	the sample is packaged in accordance with packing method OP2 and the quantity per transport unit is limited to 10 kg;

-	the available data indicate that the control temperature, if any, is sufficiently low to prevent any dangerous decomposition and sufficiently high to prevent any dangerous phase separation.

Desensitization

2.2.41.1.16	In order to ensure safety during carriage, self-reactive substances are in many cases desensitized by use of a diluent. Where a percentage of a substance is stipulated, this refers to the percentage by mass, rounded to the nearest whole number. If a diluent is used, the self-reactive substance shall be tested with the diluent present in the concentration and form used in carriage. Diluents which may allow a self-reactive substance to concentrate to a dangerous extent in the event of leakage from a packaging shall not be used. Any diluent shall be compatible with the self-reactive substance. In this regard, compatible diluents are those solids or liquids which have no detrimental influence on the thermal stability and hazard type of the self-reactive substance. Liquid diluents in formulations requiring temperature control (see 2.2.41.1.14) shall have a boiling point of at least 60 °C and a flash-point not less than 5 °C. The boiling point of the liquid shall be at least 50 °C higher than the control temperature of the self-reactive substance.

Temperature control requirements

2.2.41.1.17	Certain self-reactive substances may only be carried under temperature controlled conditions. The control temperature is the maximum temperature at which the self-reactive substance can be safely carried. It is assumed that the temperature of the immediate surroundings of a package only exceeds 55 °C during carriage for a relatively short time in a 24 hour period. In the event of loss of temperature control, it may be necessary to implement emergency procedures. The emergency temperature is the temperature at which such procedures shall be implemented.

The control and emergency temperatures are derived from the SADT (see table 1). The SADT shall be determined in order to decide whether a substance shall be subjected to temperature control during carriage. Provisions for the determination of the SADT are given in the Manual of Tests and Criteria, Part II, Chapter 20 and Section 28.4.

Table 1: Derivation of control and emergency temperatures

Type of receptacle	SADT [a]	Control temperature	Emergency temperature
Single packagings and IBCs	20 °C or less	20 °C below SADT	10 °C below SADT
	over 20 °C to 35 °C	15 °C below SADT	10 °C below SADT
	over 35 °C	10 °C below SADT	5 °C below SADT
Tanks	not greater than 50 °C	10 °C below SADT	5 °C below SADT

[a]   *SADT of the substance as packaged for carriage.*

Self-reactive substances with an SADT not greater than 55 °C shall be subject to temperature control during carriage. Where applicable, control and emergency temperatures are listed in 2.2.41.4. The actual temperature during carriage may be lower than the control temperature but shall be selected so as to avoid dangerous separation of phases.

Solid desensitized explosives

2.2.41.1.18   Solid desensitized explosives are substances which are wetted with water or alcohols or are diluted with other substances to suppress their explosive properties. Such entries in Table A of Chapter 3.2 are: UN Nos. 1310, 1320, 1321, 1322, 1336, 1337, 1344, 1347, 1348, 1349, 1354, 1355, 1356, 1357, 1517, 1571, 2555, 2556, 2557, 2852, 2907, 3317, 3319, 3344, 3364, 3365, 3366, 3367, 3368, 3369, 3370, 3376, 3380 and 3474.

Substances related to self-reactive substances

2.2.41.1.19   Substances that:

(a)   have been provisionally accepted into Class 1 according to Test Series 1 and 2 but exempted from Class 1 by Test Series 6;

(b)   are not self-reactive substances of Class 4.1; and

(c)   are not substances of Classes 5.1 or 5.2;

are also assigned to Class 4.1. UN Nos. 2956, 3241, 3242 and 3251 are such entries.

2.2.41.2   *Substances not accepted for carriage*

2.2.41.2.1   The chemically unstable substances of Class 4.1 shall not be accepted for carriage unless the necessary steps have been taken to prevent their dangerous decomposition or polymerization during carriage. To this end, it shall in particular be ensured that receptacles and tanks do not contain any substance liable to promote these reactions.

2.2.41.2.2 Flammable solids, oxidizing, assigned to UN No. 3097 shall not be accepted for carriage unless they meet the requirements for Class 1 (see also 2.1.3.7).

2.2.41.2.3 The following substances shall not be accepted for carriage:

-   Self-reactive substances of type A (see Manual of Tests and Criteria, Part II, paragraph 20.4.2 (a));

-   Phosphorus sulphides which are not free from yellow and white phosphorus;

-   Solid densitized explosives other than those listed in Table A of Chapter 3.2;

-   Inorganic flammable substances in the molten form other than UN No. 2448 SULPHUR, MOLTEN.

2.2.41.3 *List of collective entries*

Flammable solids	**without subsidiary risk**	organic	**F1**	3175	SOLIDS CONTAINING FLAMMABLE LIQUID, N.O.S.
				1353	FIBRES IMPREGNATED WITH WEAKLY NITRATED NITROCELLULOSE, N.O.S. or
				1353	FABRICS IMPREGNATED WITH WEAKLY NITRATED NITROCELLULOSE, N.O.S.
				1325	FLAMMABLE SOLID, ORGANIC, N.O.S.
		organic molten	**F2**	3176	FLAMMABLE SOLID, ORGANIC, MOLTEN, N.O.S.
		inorganic	**F3**	3089	METAL POWDER, FLAMMABLE, N.O.S. [a] [b]
				3181	METAL SALTS OF ORGANIC COMPOUNDS, FLAMMABLE, N.O.S.
				3182	METAL HYDRIDES, FLAMMABLE, N.O.S. [c]
				3178	FLAMMABLE SOLID, INORGANIC, N.O.S.
	oxidizing		**FO**	3097	FLAMMABLE SOLID, OXIDIZING, N.O.S. (not allowed, see para. 2.2.41.2.2)
	toxic **FT**	organic	**FT1**	2926	FLAMMABLE SOLID, TOXIC, ORGANIC, N.O.S.
		inorganic	**FT2**	3179	FLAMMABLE SOLID, TOXIC, INORGANIC, N.O.S.
	corrosive **FC**	organic	**FC1**	2925	FLAMMABLE SOLID, CORROSIVE, ORGANIC, N.O.S.
		inorganic	**FC2**	3180	FLAMMABLE SOLID, CORROSIVE, INORGANIC, N.O.S.
Solid desen-sitized explosives	without subsidiary risk		**D**	3319	NITROGLYCERIN MIXTURE, DESENSITIZED, SOLID, N.O.S. with more than 2% but not more than 10% nitroglycerin by mass
				3344	PENTAERYTHRITE TETRANITRATE (PENTAERYTHRITOL TETRANITRATE, PETN) MIXTURE, DESENSITIZED, SOLID, N.O.S. with more than 10% but not more than 20% PETN by mass
				3380	DESENSITIZED EXPLOSIVE, SOLID, N.O.S.
	toxic		**DT**		Only substances listed in Table A of Chapter 3.2 are to be accepted for carriage as substances of Class 4.1
Self-reactive substances SR	not requiring temperature control		**SR1**		SELF-REACTIVE LIQUID TYPE A } Not accepted for carriage,
					SELF-REACTIVE SOLID TYPE A } see 2.2.41.2.3
				3221	SELF-REACTIVE LIQUID TYPE B
				3222	SELF-REACTIVE SOLID TYPE B
				3223	SELF-REACTIVE LIQUID TYPE C
				3224	SELF-REACTIVE SOLID TYPE C
				3225	SELF-REACTIVE LIQUID TYPE D
				3226	SELF-REACTIVE SOLID TYPE D
				3227	SELF-REACTIVE LIQUID TYPE E
				3228	SELF-REACTIVE SOLID TYPE E
				3229	SELF-REACTIVE LIQUID TYPE F
				3230	SELF-REACTIVE SOLID TYPE F
					SELF-REACTIVE LIQUID TYPE G } Not subject to the provisions applicable to
					SELF-REACTIVE SOLID TYPE G } Class 4.1, see 2.2.41.1.11
	requiring temperature control		**SR2**	3231	SELF-REACTIVE LIQUID TYPE B, TEMPERATURE CONTROLLED
				3232	SELF-REACTIVE SOLID TYPE B, TEMPERATURE CONTROLLED
				3233	SELF-REACTIVE LIQUID TYPE C, TEMPERATURE CONTROLLED
				3234	SELF-REACTIVE SOLID TYPE C, TEMPERATURE CONTROLLED
				3235	SELF-REACTIVE LIQUID TYPE D, TEMPERATURE CONTROLLED
				3236	SELF-REACTIVE SOLID TYPE D, TEMPERATURE CONTROLLED
				3237	SELF-REACTIVE LIQUID TYPE E, TEMPERATURE CONTROLLED
				3238	SELF-REACTIVE SOLID TYPE E, TEMPERATURE CONTROLLED
				3239	SELF-REACTIVE LIQUID TYPE F, TEMPERATURE CONTROLLED
				3240	SELF-REACTIVE SOLID TYPE F, TEMPERATURE CONTROLLED

---

[a] *Metals and metal alloys in powdered or other flammable form, liable to spontaneous combustion, are substances of Class 4.2.*

[b] *Metals and metal alloys in powdered or other flammable form, which in contact with water, emit flammable gases, are substances of Class 4.3.*

[c] *Metals hydrides which, in contact with water, emit flammable gases, are substances of Class 4.3. Aluminium borohydride or aluminium borohydride in devices are substances of Class 4.2, UN No. 2870.*

2.2.41.4　　*List of currently assigned self-reactive substances in packagings*

In the column "Packing Method" codes "OP1" to "OP8" refer to packing methods in 4.1.4.1, packing instruction P520 (see also 4.1.7.1). Self-reactive substances to be carried shall fulfil the classification and the control and emergency temperatures (derived from the SADT) as listed. For substances permitted in IBCs, see 4.1.4.2, packing instruction IBC520 and, for those permitted in tanks according to Chapter 4.2, see 4.2.5.2, portable tank instruction T23.

NOTE: *The classification given in this table is based on the technically pure substance (except where a concentration of less than 100% is specified). For other concentrations, the substance may be classified differently following the procedures given in Part II of the Manual of Tests and Criteria and in 2.2.41.1.17.*

SELF-REACTIVE SUBSTANCE	Concen-tration (%)	Packing method	Control tempera-ture (°C)	Emergency tempera-ture (°C)	UN generic entry	Remarks
ACETONE-PYROGALLOL COPOLYMER 2-DIAZO-1-NAPHTHOL-5-SULPHONATE	100	OP8			3228	
AZODICARBONAMIDE FORMULATION TYPE B, TEMPERATURE CONTROLLED	< 100	OP5			3232	(1) (2)
AZODICARBONAMIDE FORMULATION TYPE C	< 100	OP6			3224	(3)
AZODICARBONAMIDE FORMULATION TYPE C, TEMPERATURE CONTROLLED	< 100	OP6			3234	(4)
AZODICARBONAMIDE FORMULATION TYPE D	< 100	OP7			3226	(5)
AZODICARBONAMIDE FORMULATION TYPE D, TEMPERATURE CONTROLLED	< 100	OP7			3236	(6)
2,2' -AZODI(2,4-DIMETHYL- 4-METHOXY-VALERONITRILE)	100	OP7	-5	+5	3236	
2,2' -AZODI(2,4-DIMETHYL- VALERONITRILE)	100	OP7	+10	+15	3236	
2,2' -AZODI(ETHYL- 2-METHYL-PROPIONATE)	100	OP7	+20	+25	3235	
1,1-AZODI(HEXAHYDROBENZONITRILE)	100	OP7			3226	
2,2' -AZODI(ISOBUTYRONITRILE	100	OP6	+40	+45	3234	
2,2' -AZODI(ISOBUTYRONITRILE) as a water based paste	≤ 50%	OP6			3224	
2,2' -AZODI(2-METHYLBUTYRONITRILE)	100	OP7	+35	+40	3236	
BENZENE-1,3-DISULPHONYL HYDRAZIDE, as a paste	52	OP7			3226	
BENZENE SULPHONYL HYDRAZIDE	100	OP7			3226	
4-(BENZYL(ETHYL)AMINO)-3-ETHOXY-BENZENEDIAZONIUM ZINC CHLORIDE	100	OP7			3226	
4-(BENZYL(METHYL)AMINO)-3-ETHOXY-BENZENEDIAZONIUM ZINC CHLORIDE	100	OP7	+40	+45	3236	
3-CHLORO-4-DIETHYLAMINOBENZENE-DIAZONIUM ZINC CHLORIDE	100	OP7			3226	
2-DIAZO-1-NAPHTHOL-4-SULPHONYL CHLORIDE	100	OP5			3222	(2)
2-DIAZO-1-NAPHTHOL-5-SULPHONYL CHLORIDE	100	OP5			3222	(2)
2-DIAZO-1-NAPHTHOL SULPHONIC ACID ESTER MIXTURE, TYPE D	< 100	OP7			3226	(9)
2,5-DIBUTOXY-4-(4-MORPHOLINYL)-BENZENEDIAZONIUM, TETRACHLOROZINCATE (2:1)	100	OP8			3228	
2,5-DIETHOXY-4-MORPHOLINO-BENZENEDIAZONIUM ZINC CHLORIDE	67-100	OP7	+35	+40	3236	
2,5-DIETHOXY-4-MORPHOLINO-BENZENEDIAZONIUM ZINC CHLORIDE	66	OP7	+40	+45	3236	
2,5-DIETHOXY-4-MORPHOLINO-BENZENEDIAZONIUM TETRAFLUOROBORATE	100	OP7	+30	+35	3236	

SELF-REACTIVE SUBSTANCE	Concen-tration (%)	Packing method	Control tempera-ture (°C)	Emergency tempera-ture (°C)	UN generic entry	Remarks
2,5-DIETHOXY-4-(4-MORPHOLINYL)-BENZENEDIAZONIUM SULPHATE	100	OP7			3226	
2,5-DIETHOXY-4-(PHENYLSULPHONYL)-BENZENEDIAZONIUM ZINC CHLORIDE	67	OP7	+40	+45	3236	
DIETHYLENEGLYCOL BIS (ALLYL CARBONATE) + DI- ISOPROPYL-PEROXYDICARBONATE	$\geq 88 + \leq 12$	OP8	-10	0	3237	
2,5-DIMETHOXY-4-(4-METHYL-PHENYLSULPHONYL)BENZENE- DIAZONIUM ZINC CHLORIDE	79	OP7	+40	+45	3236	
4-(DIMETHYLAMINO)-BENZENE-DIAZONIUM TRICHLOROZINCATE (-1)	100	OP8			3228	
4-DIMETHYLAMINO-6-(2-DIMETHYL-AMINOETHOXY) TOLUENE- 2-DIAZONIUM ZINC CHLORIDE	100	OP7	+40	+45	3236	
N,N'-DINITROSO-N,N'- DIMETHYL TEREPHTHALAMIDE, as a paste	72	OP6			3224	
N,N'-DINITROSOPENTAMETHYLENE-TETRAMINE	82	OP6			3224	(7)
DIPHENYLOXIDE-4,4'-DISULPHONYL HYDRAZIDE	100	OP7			3226	
4-DIPROPYLAMINOBENZENE- DIAZONIUM ZINC CHLORIDE	100	OP7			3226	
2-(N,N-ETHOXYCARBONYL-PHENYLAMINO)-3-METHOXY-4-(N-METHYL-N-CYCLOHEXYLAMINO) BENZENEDIAZONIUM ZINC CHLORIDE	63-92	OP7	+ 40	+ 45	3236	
2-(N,N-ETHOXYCARBONYL-PHENYLAMINO)-3-METHOXY-4-(N-METHYL-N-CYCLOHEXYLAMINO) BENZENEDIAZONIUM ZINC CHLORIDE	62	OP7	+ 35	+ 40	3236	
N-FORMYL-2-(NITROMETHYLENE) -1,3-PERHYDROTHIAZINE	100	OP7	+45	+50	3236	
2-(2-HYDROXYETHOXY)-1-(PYRROLIDIN-1-YL)BENZENE-4- DIAZONIUM ZINC CHLORIDE	100	OP7	+ 45	+ 50	3236	
3-(2-HYDROXYETHOXY)-4- (PYRROLIDIN-1-YL) BENZENE DIAZONIUM ZINC CHLORIDE	100	OP7	+40	+45	3236	
2-(N,N-METHYLAMINOETHYLCARBONYL)-4-(3,4-DIMETHYLPHENYLSULPHONYL) BENZENEDIAZONIUM HYDROGEN SULPHATE	96	OP7	+45	+50	3236	
4-METHYLBENZENESULPHONYLHYDRAZIDE	100	OP7			3226	
3-METHYL-4-(PYRROLIDIN-1-YL) BENZENEDIAZONIUM TETRAFLUOROBORATE	95	OP6	+45	+50	3234	
4-NITROSOPHENOL	100	OP7	+35	+40	3236	
SELF-REACTIVE LIQUID, SAMPLE		OP2			3223	(8)
SELF-REACTIVE LIQUID, SAMPLE, TEMPERATURE CONTROLLED		OP2			3233	(8)
SELF-REACTIVE SOLID, SAMPLE		OP2			3224	(8)
SELF-REACTIVE SOLID, SAMPLE, TEMPERATURE CONTROLLED		OP2			3234	(8)
SODIUM 2-DIAZO-1-NAPHTHOL- 4-SULPHONATE	100	OP7			3226	
SODIUM 2-DIAZO-1-NAPHTHOL- 5-SULPHONATE	100	OP7			3226	
TETRAMINE PALLADIUM (II) NITRATE	100	OP6	+30	+35	3234	

Remarks

(1)   Azodicarbonamide formulations which fulfil the criteria of paragraph 20.4.2 (b) of the Manual of Tests and Criteria. The control and emergency temperatures shall be determined by the procedure given in 2.2.41.1.17.

(2)   "EXPLOSIVE" subsidiary risk label required (Model No. 1, see 5.2.2.2.2).

(3)   Azodicarbonamide formulations which fulfil the criteria of paragraph 20.4.2 (c) of the Manual of Tests and Criteria.

(4)   Azodicarbonamide formulations which fulfil the criteria of paragraph 20.4.2 (c) of the Manual of Tests and Criteria. The control and emergency temperatures shall be determined by the procedure given in 2.2.41.1.17.

(5)   Azodicarbonamide formulations which fulfil the criteria of paragraph 20.4.2 (d) of the Manual of Tests and Criteria.

(6)   Azodicarbonamide formulations which fulfil the criteria of paragraph 20.4.2 (d) of the Manual of Tests and Criteria. The control and emergency temperatures shall be determined by the procedure given in 2.2.41.1.17.

(7)   With a compatible diluent having a boiling point of not less than 150 °C.

(8)   See 2.2.41.1.15.

(9)   This entry applies to mixtures of esters of 2-diazo-1-naphthol-4-sulphonic acid and 2-diazo-1-naphthol-5-sulphonic acid which fulfil the criteria of paragraph 20.4.2 (d) of the *Manual of Test and Criteria*.

2.2.42 **Class 4.2** **Substances liable to spontaneous combustion**

2.2.42.1 *Criteria*

2.2.42.1.1 The heading of Class 4.2 covers:

- *Pyrophoric substances* which are substances, including mixtures and solutions (liquid or solid), which even in small quantities ignite on contact with air within five minutes. These are the Class 4.2 substances the most liable to spontaneous combustion; and

- *Self-heating substances and articles* which are substances and articles, including mixtures and solutions, which, on contact with air, without energy supply, are liable to self-heating. These substances will ignite only in large amounts (kilogrammes) and after long periods of time (hours or days).

2.2.42.1.2 The substances and articles of Class 4.2 are subdivided as follows:

S   Substances liable to spontaneous combustion, without subsidiary risk:

    S1   Organic, liquid;
    S2   Organic, solid;
    S3   Inorganic, liquid;
    S4   Inorganic, solid;
    S5   Organometallic;

SW   Substances liable to spontaneous combustion, which, in contact with water, emit flammable gases;

SO   Substances liable to spontaneous combustion, oxidizing;

ST   Substances liable to spontaneous combustion, toxic:

    ST1   Organic, toxic, liquid;
    ST2   Organic, toxic, solid;
    ST3   Inorganic, toxic, liquid;
    ST4   Inorganic, toxic, solid;

SC   Substances liable to spontaneous combustion, corrosive:

    SC1   Organic, corrosive, liquid;
    SC2   Organic, corrosive, solid;
    SC3   Inorganic, corrosive, liquid;
    SC4   Inorganic, corrosive, solid.

Properties

2.2.42.1.3 Self-heating of these substances, leading to spontaneous combustion, is caused by reaction of the substance with oxygen (in the air) and the heat developed not being conducted away rapidly enough to the surroundings. Spontaneous combustion occurs when the rate of heat production exceeds the rate of heat loss and the auto-ignition temperature is reached.

Classification

2.2.42.1.4   Substances and articles classified in Class 4.2 are listed in Table A of Chapter 3.2. The assignment of substances and articles not mentioned by name in Table A of Chapter 3.2 to the relevant specific N.O.S. entry of 2.2.42.3 in accordance with the provisions of Chapter 2.1 can be based on experience or the results of the test procedures in accordance with the Manual of Tests and Criteria, Part III, Section 33.3. Assignment to general N.O.S. entries of Class 4.2 shall be based on the results of the test procedures in accordance with the Manual of Tests and Criteria, Part III, section 33.3; experience shall also be taken into account when it leads to a more stringent assignment.

2.2.42.1.5   When substances or articles not mentioned by name are assigned to one of the entries listed in 2.2.42.3 on the basis of the test procedures in accordance with the Manual of Tests and Criteria, Part III, section 33.3, the following criteria shall apply:

(a)   Solids liable to spontaneous combustion (pyrophoric) shall be assigned to Class 4.2 when they ignite on falling from a height of 1 m or within five minutes;

(b)   Liquids liable to spontaneous combustion (pyrophoric) shall be assigned to Class 4.2 when:

(i)   on being poured on an inert carrier, they ignite within five minutes, or

(ii)   in the event of a negative result of the test according to (i), when poured on a dry, indented filter paper (Whatman No. 3 filter), they ignite or carbonize it within five minutes;

(c)   Substances in which, in a 10 cm sample cube, at 140 °C test temperature, spontaneous combustion or a rise in temperature to over 200 °C is observed within 24 hours shall be assigned to Class 4.2. This criterion is based on the temperature of the spontaneous combustion of charcoal, which is at 50 °C for a sample cube of 27 m^3. Substances with a temperature of spontaneous combustion higher than 50 °C for a volume of 27 m^3 are not to be assigned to Class 4.2.

NOTE 1: *Substances carried in packages with a volume of not more than 3 m^3 are exempted from Class 4.2 if, tested with a 10 cm sample cube at 120 °C, no spontaneous combustion nor a rise in temperature to over 180 °C is observed within 24 hours.*

NOTE 2: *Substances carried in packages with a volume of not more than 450 litres are exempted from Class 4.2 if, tested with a 10 cm sample cube at 100 °C, no spontaneous combustion nor a rise in temperature to over 160 °C is observed within 24 hours.*

NOTE 3: *Since organometallic substances can be classified in Class 4.2 or 4.3 with additional subsidiary risks, depending on their properties, a specific classification flow chart for these substances is given in 2.3.5.*

2.2.42.1.6   If substances of Class 4.2, as a result of admixtures, come into different categories of risk from those to which the substances mentioned by name in Table A of Chapter 3.2 belong, these mixtures shall be assigned to the entries to which they belong on the basis of their actual degree of danger.

NOTE: *For the classification of solutions and mixtures (such as preparations and wastes), see also 2.1.3.*

2.2.42.1.7 On the basis of the test procedure in the Manual of Tests and Criteria, Part III, section 33.3 and the criteria set out in 2.2.42.1.5, it may also be determined whether the nature of a substance mentioned by name is such that the substance is not subject to the provisions for this Class.

Assignment of packing groups

2.2.42.1.8 Substances and articles classified under the various entries in Table A of Chapter 3.2 shall be assigned to packing groups I, II or III on the basis of test procedures of the Manual of Tests and Criteria, Part III, section 33.3, in accordance with the following criteria:

(a) Substances liable to spontaneous combustion (pyrophoric) shall be assigned to packing group I;

(b) Self-heating substances and articles in which, in a 2.5 cm sample cube, at 140 °C test temperature, spontaneous combustion or a rise in temperature to over 200 °C is observed within 24 hours, shall be assigned to packing group II;

Substances with a temperature of spontaneous combustion higher than 50 °C for a volume of 450 litres are not to be assigned to packing group II;

(c) Slightly self-heating substances in which, in a 2.5 cm sample cube, the phenomena referred to under (b) are not observed, in the given conditions, but in which in a 10 cm sample cube at 140 °C test temperature spontaneous combustion or a rise in temperature to over 200 °C is observed within 24 hours, shall be assigned to packing group III.

2.2.42.2 *Substances not accepted for carriage*

The following substances shall not be accepted for carriage:

- UN No. 3255 tert-BUTYL HYPOCHLORITE; and

- Self-heating solids, oxidizing, assigned to UN No. 3127 unless they meet the requirements for Class 1 (see 2.1.3.7).

2.2.42.3 *List of collective entries*

Substances liable to spontaneous combustion	**organic**	**liquid**	**S1**	2845	PYROPHORIC LIQUID, ORGANIC, N.O.S.
				3183	SELF-HEATING LIQUID, ORGANIC, N.O.S.
Without subsidiary risk **S**		**solid**	**S2**	1373	FIBRES or FABRICS, ANIMAL or VEGETABLE or SYNTHETIC, N.O.S. with oil
				2006	PLASTICS, NITROCELLULOSE-BASED, SELF-HEATING, N.O.S.
				3313	ORGANIC PIGMENTS, SELF HEATING
				2846	PYROPHORIC SOLID, ORGANIC, N.O.S.
				3088	SELF-HEATING SOLID, ORGANIC, N.O.S.
	inorganic	**liquid**	**S3**	3194	PYROPHORIC LIQUID, INORGANIC, N.O.S.
				3186	SELF-HEATING LIQUID, INORGANIC, N.O.S.
		solid	**S4**	1383	PYROPHORIC METAL, N.O.S. or
				1383	PYROPHORIC ALLOY, N.O.S.
				1378	METAL CATALYST, WETTED with a visible excess of liquid
				2881	METAL CATALYST, DRY
				3189[a]	METAL POWDER, SELF-HEATING, N.O.S.
				3205	ALKALINE EARTH METAL ALCOHOLATES, N.O.S.
				3200	PYROPHORIC SOLID, INORGANIC, N.O.S.
				3190	SELF-HEATING SOLID, INORGANIC, N.O.S.
	organometallic		**S5**	3392	ORGANOMETALLIC SUBSTANCE, LIQUID, PYROPHORIC
				3391	ORGANOMETALLIC SUBSTANCE, SOLID, PYROPHORIC
				3400	ORGANOMETALLIC SUBSTANCE, SOLID, SELF-HEATING
Water-reactive			**SW**	3394	ORGANOMETALLIC SUBSTANCE, LIQUID, PYROPHORIC, WATER-REACTIVE
				3393	ORGANOMETALLIC SUBSTANCE, SOLID, PYROPHORIC, WATER-REACTIVE
Oxidizing			**SO**	3127	SELF-HEATING SOLID, OXIDIZING, N.O.S. (not allowed, see 2.2.42.2)
Toxic **ST**	**organic**	**liquid**	**ST1**	3184	SELF-HEATING LIQUID, TOXIC, ORGANIC, N.O.S.
		solid	**ST2**	3128	SELF-HEATING SOLID, TOXIC, ORGANIC, N.O.S.
	inorganic	**liquid**	**ST3**	3187	SELF-HEATING LIQUID, TOXIC, INORGANIC, N.O.S.
		solid	**ST4**	3191	SELF-HEATING SOLID, TOXIC, INORGANIC, N.O.S.
Corrosive **SC**	**organic**	**liquid**	**SC1**	3185	SELF-HEATING LIQUID, CORROSIVE, ORGANIC, N.O.S.
		solid	**SC2**	3126	SELF-HEATING SOLID, CORROSIVE, ORGANIC, N.O.S.
	inorganic	**liquid**	**SC3**	3188	SELF-HEATING LIQUID, CORROSIVE, INORGANIC, N.O.S.
		solid	**SC4**	3206	ALKALI METAL ALCOHOLATES, SELF-HEATING, CORROSIVE, N.O.S.
				3192	SELF-HEATING SOLID, CORROSIVE, INORGANIC, N.O.S.

---

[a]   *Dust and powder of metals, non toxic in a non-spontaneous combustible form which nevertheless, in contact with water, emit flammable gases, are substances of Class 4.3.*

2.2.43   **Class 4.3   Substances which, in contact with water, emit flammable gases**

2.2.43.1   *Criteria*

2.2.43.1.1   The heading of Class 4.3 covers substances which react with water to emit flammable gases liable to form explosive mixtures with air, and articles containing such substances.

2.2.43.1.2   Substances and articles of Class 4.3 are subdivided as follows:

W   Substances which, in contact with water, emit flammable gases, without subsidiary risk, and articles containing such substances:

W1   Liquid;
W2   Solid;
W3   Articles;

WF1   Substances which, in contact with water, emit flammable gases, liquid, flammable;

WF2   Substances which, in contact with water, emit flammable gases, solid, flammable;

WS   Substances which, in contact with water, emit flammable gases, solid, self-heating;

WO   Substances which, in contact with water, emit flammable gases, oxidizing, solid;

WT   Substances which, in contact with water, emit flammable gases, toxic:

WT1   Liquid;
WT2   Solid;

WC   Substances which, in contact with water, emit flammable gases, corrosive:

WC1   Liquid;
WC2   Solid;

WFC   Substances which, in contact with water, emit flammable gases, flammable, corrosive.

Properties

2.2.43.1.3   Certain substances in contact with water may emit flammable gases that can form explosive mixtures with air. Such mixtures are easily ignited by all ordinary sources of ignition, for example naked lights, sparking handtools or unprotected light bulbs. The resulting blast wave and flames may endanger people and the environment. The test method referred to in 2.2.43.1.4 below is used to determine whether the reaction of a substance with water leads to the development of a dangerous amount of gases which may be flammable. This test method shall not be applied to pyrophoric substances.

Classification

2.2.43.1.4   Substances and articles classified in Class 4.3 are listed in Table A of Chapter 3.2. The assignment of substances and articles not mentioned by name in Table A of Chapter 3.2 to the relevant entry of 2.2.43.3 in accordance with the provisions of Chapter 2.1 shall be based on the results of the test procedure in accordance with the Manual of Tests and Criteria, Part III, Section 33.4; experience shall also be taken into account when it leads to a more stringent assignment.

2.2.43.1.5　　When substances not mentioned by name are assigned to one of the entries listed in 2.2.43.3 on the basis of the test procedure in accordance with the Manual of Tests and Criteria, Part III, Section 33.4, the following criteria shall apply:

A substance shall be assigned to Class 4.3 if:

(a)　spontaneous ignition of the gas emitted takes place in any step of the test procedure; or

(b)　there is an evolution of flammable gas at a rate greater than 1 litre per kilogramme of the substance to be tested per hour.

NOTE:　Since organometallic substances can be classified in Class 4.2 or 4.3 with additional subsidiary risks, depending on their properties, a specific classification flow chart for these substances is given in 2.3.5.

2.2.43.1.6　　If substances of Class 4.3, as a result of admixtures, come into different categories of risk from those to which the substances mentioned by name in Table A of Chapter 3.2 belong, these mixtures shall be assigned to the entries to which they belong on the basis of their actual degree of danger.

NOTE: For the classification of solutions and mixtures (such as preparations and wastes) see also 2.1.3.

2.2.43.1.7　　On the basis of the test procedures in accordance with the Manual of Tests and Criteria, Part III, Section 33.4, and the criteria set out in paragraph 2.2.43.1.5, it may also be determined whether the nature of a substance mentioned by name is such that the substance is not subject to the provisions for this Class.

Assignment of packing groups

2.2.43.1.8　　Substances and articles classified under the various entries in Table A of Chapter 3.2 shall be assigned to packing groups I, II or III on the basis of test procedures of the Manual of Tests and Criteria, Part III, section 33.4, in accordance with the following criteria:

(a)　Packing group I shall be assigned to any substance which reacts vigorously with water at ambient temperature and generally demonstrates a tendency for the gas produced to ignite spontaneously, or one which reacts readily with water at ambient temperatures such that the rate of evolution of flammable gas is equal to or greater than 10 litres per kilogramme of substance over any one minute period;

(b)　Packing group II shall be assigned to any substance which reacts readily with water at ambient temperature such that the maximum rate of evolution of flammable gas is equal to or greater than 20 litres per kilogramme of substance per hour, and which does not meet the criteria of packing group I;

(c)　Packing group III shall be assigned to any substance which reacts slowly with water at ambient temperature such that the maximum rate of evolution of flammable gas is greater than 1 litre per kilogramme of substance per hour, and which does not meet the criteria of packing groups I or II.

2.2.43.2　　Substances not accepted for carriage

Water-reactive solids, oxidizing, assigned to UN No. 3133 shall not be accepted for carriage unless they meet the requirements for Class 1 (see also 2.1.3.7).

2.2.43.3 *List of collective entries*

Substances which, in contact with water, emit flammable gases			1389 ALKALI METAL AMALGAM, LIQUID 1391 ALKALI METAL DISPERSION having a flash-point above 60 °C or 1391 ALKALINE EARTH METAL DISPERSION having a flash-point above 60 °C 1392 ALKALINE EARTH METAL AMALGAM, LIQUID 1420 POTASSIUM METAL ALLOYS, LIQUID
	liquid	W1	1421 ALKALI METAL ALLOY, LIQUID, N.O.S. 1422 POTASSIUM SODIUM ALLOYS, LIQUID 3398 ORGANOMETALLIC SUBSTANCE, LIQUID, WATER-REACTIVE 3148 WATER-REACTIVE LIQUID, N.O.S.
Without subsidiary risk W	solid	W2 ª	1390 ALKALI METAL AMIDES 3401 ALKALI METAL AMALGAM, SOLID 3402 ALKALINE EARTH METAL AMALGAM, SOLID 3170 ALUMINIUM SMELTING BY-PRODUCTS or 3170 ALUMINIUM REMELTING BY-PRODUCTS 3403 POTASSIUM METAL ALLOYS, SOLID 3404 POTASSIUM SODIUM ALLOYS, SOLID 1393 ALKALINE EARTH METAL ALLOY, N.O.S. 1409 METAL HYDRIDES, WATER-REACTIVE, N.O.S. 3208 METALLIC SUBSTANCE, WATER-REACTIVE, N.O.S. 3395 ORGANOMETALLIC SUBSTANCE, SOLID, WATER-REACTIVE 2813 WATER-REACTIVE SOLID, N.O.S.
	articles	W3	3292 BATTERIES, CONTAINING SODIUM or 3292 CELLS, CONTAINING SODIUM
Liquid, flammable		WF1	1391 ALKALI METAL DISPERSION having a flash-point of not more than 60 °C or 1391 ALKALINE EARTH METAL DISPERSION having a flash-point of not more than 60 °C 3399 ORGANOMETALLIC SUBSTANCE, LIQUID, WATER-REACTIVE, FLAMMABLE
Solid, flammable		WF2	3396 ORGANOMETALLIC SUBSTANCE, SOLID, WATER-REACTIVE, FLAMMABLE 3132 WATER-REACTIVE SOLID, FLAMMABLE, N.O.S.
Solid, self-heating		WS ᵇ	3397 ORGANOMETALLIC SUBSTANCE, SOLID, WATER-REACTIVE, SELF-HEATING 3209 METALLIC SUBSTANCE, WATER-REACTIVE, SELF-HEATING, N.O.S. 3135 WATER-REACTIVE SOLID, SELF-HEATING, N.O.S.
Solid, oxidizing		WO	3133 WATER-REACTIVE SOLID, OXIDIZING, N.O.S. (not allowed, see 2.2.43.2)
Toxic WT	liquid	WT1	3130 WATER-REACTIVE LIQUID, TOXIC, N.O.S.
	solid	WT2	3134 WATER-REACTIVE SOLID, TOXIC, N.O.S.
Corrosive WC	liquid	WC1	3129 WATER-REACTIVE LIQUID, CORROSIVE, N.O.S.
	solid	WC2	3131 WATER-REACTIVE SOLID, CORROSIVE, N.O.S.
Flammable, corrosive		WFC ᶜ	2988 CHLOROSILANES, WATER-REACTIVE, FLAMMABLE, CORROSIVE, NO.S. (No other collective entry with this classification code available, if need be, classification under a collective entry with a classification code to be determined according to the table of precedence of hazard in 2.1.3.10.)

ª   *Metals and metal alloys which, in contact with water, do not emit flammable gases and are not pyrophoric or self-heating, but which are readily flammable, are substances of Class 4.1. Alkaline-earth metals and alkaline-earth metal alloys in pyrophoric form are substances of Class 4.2 Dust and powders of metals in pyrophoric form are substances of Class 4.2. Metals and metal alloys in pyrophoric form are substances of Class 4.2. Compounds of phosphorus with heavy metals such as iron, copper, etc. are not subject to the provisions of ADR.*

ᵇ   *Metals and metal alloys in pyrophoric form are substances of Class 4.2.*

ᶜ   *Chlorosilanes, having a flash-point of less than 23 °C and which, in contact with water, do not emit flammable gases, are substances of Class 3. Chlorosilanes, having a flash-point equal to or greater than 23 °C and which, in contact with water, do not emit flammable gases, are substances of Class 8.*

2.2.51   **Class 5.1   Oxidizing substances**

2.2.51.1   *Criteria*

2.2.51.1.1   The heading of Class 5.1 covers substances which, while in themselves not necessarily combustible, may, generally by yielding oxygen, cause or contribute to the combustion of other material, and articles containing such substances.

2.2.51.1.2   The substances of Class 5.1 and articles containing such substances are subdivided as follows:

O   Oxidizing substances without subsidiary risk or articles containing such substances:

O1   Liquid;
O2   Solid;
O3   Articles;

OF   Oxidizing substances, solid, flammable;

OS   Oxidizing substances, solid, self-heating;

OW   Oxidizing substances, solid which, in contact with water, emit flammable gases;

OT   Oxidizing substances, toxic:

OT1   Liquid;
OT2   Solid;

OC   Oxidizing substances, corrosive:

OC1   Liquid;
OC2   Solid;

OTC   Oxidizing substances, toxic, corrosive.

2.2.51.1.3   Substances and articles classified in Class 5.1 are listed in Table A of Chapter 3.2. The assignment of substances and articles not mentioned by name in Table A of Chapter 3.2 to the relevant entry of 2.2.51.3 in accordance with the provisions of Chapter 2.1 can be based on the tests, methods and criteria in paragraphs 2.2.51.1.6-2.2.51.1.9 below and the Manual of Tests and Criteria, Part III, Section 34.4. In the event of divergence between test results and known experience, judgement based on known experience shall take precedence over test results.

2.2.51.1.4   If substances of Class 5.1, as a result of admixtures, come into different categories of risk from those to which the substances mentioned by name in Table A of Chapter 3.2 belong, these mixtures or solutions shall be assigned to the entries to which they belong on the basis of their actual degree of danger.

NOTE: For the classification of solutions and mixtures (such as preparations and wastes), see also Section 2.1.3.

2.2.51.1.5   On the basis of the test procedures in the Manual of Tests and Criteria, Part III, Section 34.4 and the criteria set out in 2.2.51.1.6 to 2.2.51.1.9 it may also be determined whether the nature of a substance mentioned by name in Table A of Chapter 3.2 is such that the substance is not subject to the provisions for this class.

Oxidizing solids

Classification

2.2.51.1.6   When oxidizing solid substances not mentioned by name in Table A of Chapter 3.2 are assigned to one of the entries listed in 2.2.51.3 on the basis of the test procedure in accordance with the Manual of Tests and Criteria, Part III, sub-section 34.4.1, the following criteria shall apply:

A solid substance shall be assigned to Class 5.1 if, in the 4:1 or the 1:1 sample-to-cellulose ratio (by mass) tested, it ignites or burns or exhibits mean burning times equal to or less than that of a 3:7 mixture (by mass) of potassium bromate and cellulose.

Assignment of packing groups

2.2.51.1.7   Oxidizing solids classified under the various entries in Table A of Chapter 3.2 shall be assigned to packing groups I, II or III on the basis of test procedures of the Manual of Tests and Criteria, Part III, sub-section 34.4.1, in accordance with the following criteria:

(a)   Packing group I: any substance which, in the 4:1 or 1:1 sample-to-cellulose ratio (by mass) tested, exhibits a mean burning time less than the mean burning time of a 3:2 mixture, by mass, of potassium bromate and cellulose;

(b)   Packing group II: any substance which, in the 4:1 or 1:1 sample-to-cellulose ratio (by mass) tested, exhibits a mean burning time equal to or less than the mean burning time of a 2:3 mixture (by mass) of potassium bromate and cellulose and the criteria for packing group I are not met;

(c)   Packing group III: any substance which, in the 4:1 or 1:1 sample-to-cellulose ratio (by mass) tested, exhibits a mean burning time equal to or less than the mean burning time of a 3:7 mixture (by mass) of potassium bromate and cellulose and the criteria for packing groups I and II are not met.

Oxidizing liquids

Classification

2.2.51.1.8   When oxidizing liquid substances not mentioned by name in Table A of Chapter 3.2 are assigned to one of the entries listed in sub-section 2.2.51.3 on the basis of the test procedure in accordance with the Manual of Tests and Criteria, Part III, sub-section 34.4.2, the following criteria shall apply:

A liquid substance shall be assigned to Class 5.1 if, in the 1:1 mixture, by mass, of substance and cellulose tested, it exhibits a pressure rise of 2070 kPa gauge or more and a mean pressure rise time equal to or less than the mean pressure rise time of a 1:1 mixture, by mass, of 65% aqueous nitric acid and cellulose.

Assignment of packing groups

2.2.51.1.9   Oxidizing liquids classified under the various entries in Table A of Chapter 3.2 shall be assigned to packing groups I, II or III on the basis of test procedures of the Manual of Tests and Criteria, Part III, section 34.4.2, in accordance with the following criteria:

(a) Packing group I: any substance which, in the 1:1 mixture, by mass, of substance and cellulose tested, spontaneously ignites; or the mean pressure rise time of a 1:1 mixture, by mass, of substance and cellulose is less than that of a 1:1 mixture, by mass, of 50% perchloric acid and cellulose;

(b) Packing group II: any substance which, in the 1:1 mixture, by mass, of substance and cellulose tested, exhibits a mean pressure rise time less than or equal to the mean pressure rise time of a 1:1 mixture, by mass, of 40% aqueous sodium chlorate solution and cellulose; and the criteria for packing group I are not met;

(c) Packing group III: any substance which, in the 1:1 mixture, by mass, of substance and cellulose tested, exhibits a mean pressure rise time less than or equal to the mean pressure rise time of a 1:1 mixture, by mass, of 65% aqueous nitric acid and cellulose; and the criteria for packing groups I and II are not met.

2.2.51.2 *Substances not accepted for carriage*

2.2.51.2.1 The chemically unstable substances of Class 5.1 shall not be accepted for carriage unless the necessary steps have been taken to prevent their dangerous decomposition or polymerization during carriage. To this end it shall in particular be ensured that receptacles and tanks do not contain any material liable to promote these reactions.

2.2.51.2.2 The following substances and mixtures shall not be accepted for carriage:

- oxidizing solids, self-heating, assigned to UN No. 3100, oxidizing solids, water-reactive, assigned to UN No. 3121 and oxidizing solids, flammable, assigned to UN No. 3137, unless they meet the requirements for Class 1 (see also 2.1.3.7);

- hydrogen peroxide, not stabilized or hydrogen peroxide, aqueous solutions, not stabilized containing more than 60% hydrogen peroxide;

- tetranitromethane not free from combustible impurities;

- perchloric acid solutions containing more than 72% (mass) acid, or mixtures of perchloric acid with any liquid other than water;

- chloric acid solution containing more than 10% chloric acid or mixtures of chloric acid with any liquid other than water;

- halogenated fluor compounds other than UN Nos. 1745 BROMINE PENTAFLUORIDE; 1746 BROMINE TRIFLUORIDE and 2495 IODINE PENTAFLUORIDE of Class 5.1 as well as UN Nos. 1749 CHLORINE TRIFLUORIDE and 2548 CHLORINE PENTAFLUORIDE of Class 2;

- ammonium chlorate and its aqueous solutions and mixtures of a chlorate with an ammonium salt;

- ammonium chlorite and its aqueous solutions and mixtures of a chlorite with an ammonium salt;

- mixtures of a hypochlorite with an ammonium salt;

- ammonium bromate and its aqueous solutions and mixtures of a bromate with an ammonium salt;

- ammonium permanganate and its aqueous solutions and mixtures of a permanganate with an ammonium salt;

- ammonium nitrate containing more than 0.2% combustible substances (including any organic substance calculated as carbon) unless it is a constituent of a substance or article of Class 1;

- fertilizers having an ammonium nitrate content (in determining the ammonium nitrate content, all nitrate ions for which a molecular equivalent of ammonium ions is present in the mixture shall be calculated as ammonium nitrate) or a content in combustible substances exceeding the values specified in special provision 307 except under the conditions applicable to Class 1;

- ammonium nitrite and its aqueous solutions and mixtures of an inorganic nitrite with an ammonium salt;

- mixtures of potassium nitrate, sodium nitrite and an ammonium salt.

2.2.51.3   *List of collective entries*

Oxidizing substances	liquid	**O1**	3210	CHLORATES, INORGANIC, AQUEOUS SOLUTION, N.O.S.
			3211	PERCHLORATES, INORGANIC, AQUEOUS SOLUTION, N.O.S.
			3213	BROMATES, INORGANIC, AQUEOUS SOLUTION, N.O.S.
			3214	PERMANGANATES, INORGANIC, AQUEOUS SOLUTION, N.O.S.
			3216	PERSULPHATES, INORGANIC, AQUEOUS SOLUTION, N.O.S.
			3218	NITRATES, INORGANIC, AQUEOUS SOLUTION, N.O.S.
			3219	NITRITES, INORGANIC, AQUEOUS SOLUTION, N.O.S.
			3139	OXIDIZING LIQUID, N.O.S.
			1450	BROMATES, INORGANIC, N.O.S
			1461	CHLORATES, INORGANIC, N.O.S.
			1462	CHLORITES, INORGANIC, N.O.S.
			1477	NITRATES, INORGANIC, N.O.S
			1481	PERCHLORATES, INORGANIC, N.O.S.
Without subsidiary risk	solid	**O2**	1482	PERMANGANATES, INORGANIC, N.O.S.
O			1483	PEROXIDES, INORGANIC, N.O.S
			2627	NITRITES, INORGANIC, N.O.S.
			3212	HYPOCHLORITES, INORGANIC, N.O.S.
			3215	PERSULPHATES, INORGANIC, N.O.S.
			1479	OXIDIZING SOLID, N.O.S.
	articles	**O3**	3356	OXYGEN GENERATOR, CHEMICAL
Solid, flammable		**OF**	3137	OXIDIZING SOLID, FLAMMABLE, N.O.S. (not allowed, see 2.2.51.2)
Solid, self-heating		**OS**	3100	OXIDIZING SOLID, SELF-HEATING, N.O.S. (not allowed, see 2.2.51.2)
Solid, water reactive		**OW**	3121	OXIDIZING SOLID, WATER REACTIVE, N.O.S. (not allowed, see 2.2.51.2)
Toxic	liquid	**OT1**	3099	OXIDIZING LIQUID, TOXIC, N.O.S.
OT	solid	**OT2**	3087	OXIDIZING SOLID, TOXIC, N.O.S.
Corrosive	liquid	**OC1**	3098	OXIDIZING LIQUID, CORROSIVE, N.O.S.
OC	solid	**OC2**	3085	OXIDIZING SOLID, CORROSIVE, N.O.S.
Toxic, corrosive		**OTC**	(No collective entry with this classification code available; if need be, classification under a collective entry with a classification code to be determined according to the table of precedence of hazard in 2.1.3.10.)	

2.2.52   **Class 5.2**   **Organic peroxides**

2.2.52.1   *Criteria*

2.2.52.1.1   The heading of Class 5.2 covers organic peroxides and formulations of organic peroxides.

2.2.52.1.2   The substances of Class 5.2 are subdivided as follows:

P1   Organic peroxides, not requiring temperature control;
P2   Organic peroxides, requiring temperature control.

Definition

2.2.52.1.3   *Organic peroxides* are organic substances which contain the bivalent -O-O- structure and may be considered derivatives of hydrogen peroxide, where one or both of the hydrogen atoms have been replaced by organic radicals.

Properties

2.2.52.1.4   Organic peroxides are liable to exothermic decomposition at normal or elevated temperatures. The decomposition can be initiated by heat, contact with impurities (e.g. acids, heavy-metal compounds, amines), friction or impact. The rate of decomposition increases with temperature and varies with the organic peroxide formulation. Decomposition may result in the evolution of harmful, or flammable, gases or vapours. For certain organic peroxides the temperature shall be controlled during carriage. Some organic peroxides may decompose explosively, particularly if confined. This characteristic may be modified by the addition of diluents or by the use of appropriate packagings. Many organic peroxides burn vigorously. Contact of organic peroxides with the eyes is to be avoided. Some organic peroxides will cause serious injury to the cornea, even after brief contact, or will be corrosive to the skin.

NOTE: *Test methods for determining the flammability of organic peroxides are set out in the Manual of Tests and Criteria, Part III, sub-section 32.4. Because organic peroxides may react vigorously when heated, it is recommended to determine their flash-point using small sample sizes such as described in ISO 3679:1983.*

Classification

2.2.52.1.5   Any organic peroxide shall be considered for classification in Class 5.2 unless the organic peroxide formulation contains:

(a)   Not more than 1.0% available oxygen from the organic peroxides when containing not more than 1.0% hydrogen peroxide;

(b)   Not more than 0.5% available oxygen from the organic peroxides when containing more than 1.0% but not more than 7.0% hydrogen peroxide.

NOTE: *The available oxygen content (%) of an organic peroxide formulation is given by the formula*

$$16 \times \sum (n_i \times c_i/m_i)$$

where:
n_i =   *number of peroxygen groups per molecule of organic peroxide i;*
c_i =   *concentration (mass %) of organic peroxide i; and*
m_i =   *molecular mass of organic peroxide i.*

2.2.52.1.6   Organic peroxides are classified into seven types according to the degree of danger they present. The types of organic peroxide range from type A, which is not accepted for carriage in the packaging in which it is tested, to type G, which is not subject to the provisions of Class 5.2. The classification of types B to F is directly related to the maximum quantity allowed in one packaging. The principles to be applied to the classification of substances not listed in 2.2.52.4 are set out in the Manual of Tests and Criteria, Part II.

2.2.52.1.7   Organic peroxides which have already been classified and are already permitted for carriage in packagings are listed in 2.2.52.4, those already permitted for carriage in IBCs are listed in 4.1.4.2, packing instruction IBC520 and those already permitted for carriage in tanks in accordance with Chapters 4.2 and 4.3 are listed in 4.2.5.2, portable tank instruction T23. Each permitted substance listed is assigned to a generic entry of Table A of Chapter 3.2 (UN Nos. 3101 to 3120) and appropriate subsidiary risks and remarks providing relevant transport information are given.

These generic entries specify:

-    the type (B to F) of organic peroxide (see 2.2.52.1.6 above);

-    physical state (liquid/solid); and

-    temperature control (when required), see 2.2.52.1.15 to 2.2.52.1.18.

Mixtures of these formulations may be classified as the same type of organic peroxide as that of the most dangerous component and be carried under the conditions of carriage given for this type. However, as two stable components can form a thermally less stable mixture, the self-accelerating decomposition temperature (SADT) of the mixture shall be determined and, if necessary, the control and emergency temperatures derived from the SADT in accordance with 2.2.52.1.16.

2.2.52.1.8   Classification of organic peroxides, formulations or mixtures of organic peroxides not listed in 2.2.52.4, 4.1.4.2 packing instruction IBC520 or 4.2.5.2, portable tank instruction T23, and assignment to a collective entry shall be made by the competent authority of the country of origin. The statement of approval shall contain the classification and the relevant conditions of carriage. If the country of origin is not a Contracting Party to ADR, the classification and conditions of carriage shall be recognized by the competent authority of the first country Contracting Party to ADR reached by the consignment.

2.2.52.1.9   Samples of organic peroxides or formulations of organic peroxides not listed in 2.2.52.4, for which a complete set of test results is not available and which are to be carried for further testing or evaluation, shall be assigned to one of the appropriate entries for organic peroxides type C provided the following conditions are met:

-    the available data indicate that the sample would be no more dangerous than organic peroxides type B;

-    the sample is packaged in accordance with packing method OP2 and the quantity per transport unit is limited to 10 kg;

-    the available data indicate that the control temperature, if any, is sufficiently low to prevent any dangerous decomposition and sufficiently high to prevent any dangerous phase separation.

Desensitization of organic peroxides

2.2.52.1.10　In order to ensure safety during carriage, organic peroxides are in many cases desensitized by organic liquids or solids, inorganic solids or water. Where a percentage of a substance is stipulated, this refers to the percentage by mass, rounded to the nearest whole number. In general, desensitization shall be such that, in case of spillage, the organic peroxide will not concentrate to a dangerous extent.

2.2.52.1.11　Unless otherwise stated for the individual organic peroxide formulation, the following definition(s) shall apply to diluents used for desensitization:

-　diluents type A are organic liquids which are compatible with the organic peroxide and which have a boiling point of not less than 150 °C. Type A diluents may be used for desensitizing all organic peroxides;

-　diluents type B are organic liquids which are compatible with the organic peroxide and which have a boiling point of less than 150 °C but not less than 60 °C and a flash-point of not less than 5 °C.

Type B diluents may be used for desensitization of all organic peroxides provided that the boiling point of the liquid is at least 60 °C higher than the SADT in a 50 kg package.

2.1.52.1.12　Diluents, other than type A or type B, may be added to organic peroxide formulations as listed in 2.2.52.4 provided that they are compatible. However, replacement of all or part of a type A or type B diluent by another diluent with differing properties requires that the organic peroxide formulation be re-assessed in accordance with the normal acceptance procedure for Class 5.2.

2.2.52.1.13　Water may only be used for the desensitization of organic peroxides which are listed in 2.2.52.4 or in the competent authority decision according to 2.2.52.1.8 as being "with water" or "as a stable dispersion in water". Samples of organic peroxides or formulations of organic peroxides not listed in 2.2.52.4 may also be desensitized with water provided the requirements of 2.2.52.1.9 are met.

2.2.52.1.14　Organic and inorganic solids may be used for desensitization of organic peroxides provided that they are compatible. Compatible liquids and solids are those which have no detrimental influence on the thermal stability and hazard type of the organic peroxide formulation.

Temperature control requirements

2.2.52.1.15　Certain organic peroxides may only be carried under temperature-controlled conditions. The control temperature is the maximum temperature at which the organic peroxide can be safely carried. It is assumed that the temperature of the immediate surroundings of a package only exceeds 55 °C during carriage for a relatively short time in a 24 hour period. In the event of loss of temperature control, it may be necessary to implement emergency procedures. The emergency temperature is the temperature at which such procedures shall be implemented.

2.2.52.1.16　The control and emergency temperatures are derived from the SADT which is defined as the lowest temperature at which self-accelerating decomposition may occur with a substance in the packaging as used during carriage (see Table 1). The SADT shall be determined in order to decide whether a substance shall be subjected to temperature control during carriage. Provisions for the determination of the SADT are given in the Manual of Tests and Criteria, Part II, Sections 20 and 28.4.

Table 1: Derivation of control and emergency temperatures

Type of receptacle	SADT [a]	Control temperature	Emergency temperature
Single packagings and IBCs	20 °C or less	20 °C below SADT	10 °C below SADT
	over 20 °C to 35 °C	15 °C below SADT	10 °C below SADT
	over 35 °C	10 °C below SADT	5 °C below SADT
Tanks	not greater than 50 °C	10 °C below SADT	5 °C below SADT

[a]   *SADT of the substance as packaged for carriage*

2.2.52.1.17   The following organic peroxides shall be subject to temperature control during carriage:

-        organic peroxides types B and C with an SADT ≤ 50 °C;

-        organic peroxides type D showing a medium effect when heated under confinement with an SADT ≤ 50 °C or showing a low or no effect when heated under confinement with an SADT ≤ 45 °C; and

-        organic peroxides types E and F with an SADT ≤ 45 °C.

NOTE: Provisions for the determination of the effects of heating under confinement are given in the Manual of Tests and Criteria, Part II, Section 20 and Sub-section 28.4.

2.2.52.1.18   Where applicable, control and emergency temperatures are listed in 2.2.52.4. The actual temperature during carriage may be lower than the control temperature but shall be selected so as to avoid dangerous separation of phases.

2.2.52.2   *Substances not accepted for carriage*

Organic peroxides, type A, shall not be accepted for carriage under the provisions of Class 5.2 (see Manual of Tests and Criteria, Part II, paragraph 20.4.3 (a)).

2.2.52.3   *List of collective entries*

Organic peroxides		ORGANIC PEROXIDE TYPE A, LIQUID ORGANIC PEROXIDE TYPE A, SOLID	} Not accepted for carriage, } see 2.2.52.2
	3101	ORGANIC PEROXIDE TYPE B, LIQUID	
	3102	ORGANIC PEROXIDE TYPE B, SOLID	
	3103	ORGANIC PEROXIDE TYPE C, LIQUID	
	3104	ORGANIC PEROXIDE TYPE C, SOLID	
Not requiring temperature control **P1**	3105	ORGANIC PEROXIDE TYPE D, LIQUID	
	3106	ORGANIC PEROXIDE TYPE D, SOLID	
	3107	ORGANIC PEROXIDE TYPE E, LIQUID	
	3108	ORGANIC PEROXIDE TYPE E, SOLID	
	3109	ORGANIC PEROXIDE TYPE F, LIQUID	
	3110	ORGANIC PEROXIDE TYPE F, SOLID	
		ORGANIC PEROXIDE TYPE G, LIQUID ORGANIC PEROXIDE TYPE G, SOLID	} Not subject to the provisions } applicable to Class 5.2, see 2.2.52.1.6

	3111	ORGANIC PEROXIDE TYPE B, LIQUID, TEMPERATURE CONTROLLED
	3112	ORGANIC PEROXIDE TYPE B, SOLID, TEMPERATURE CONTROLLED
	3113	ORGANIC PEROXIDE TYPE C, LIQUID, TEMPERATURE CONTROLLED
	3114	ORGANIC PEROXIDE TYPE C, SOLID, TEMPERATURE CONTROLLED
Requiring temperature control **P2**	3115	ORGANIC PEROXIDE TYPE D, LIQUID, TEMPERATURE CONTROLLED
	3116	ORGANIC PEROXIDE TYPE D, SOLID, TEMPERATURE CONTROLLED
	3117	ORGANIC PEROXIDE TYPE E, LIQUID, TEMPERATURE CONTROLLED
	3118	ORGANIC PEROXIDE TYPE E, SOLID, TEMPERATURE CONTROLLED
	3119	ORGANIC PEROXIDE TYPE F, LIQUID, TEMPERATURE CONTROLLED
	3120	ORGANIC PEROXIDE TYPE F, SOLID, TEMPERATURE CONTROLLED

2.2.52.4   *List of currently assigned organic peroxides in packagings*

In the column "Packing Method", codes "OP1" to "OP8" refer to packing methods in 4.1.4.1, packing instruction P520 (see also 4.1.7.1). Organic peroxides to be carried shall fulfil the classification and the control and emergency temperatures (derived from the SADT) as listed. For substances permitted in IBCs, see 4.1.4.2, packing instruction IBC520 and, for those permitted in tanks according to Chapters 4.2 and 4.3, see 4.2.5.2, portable tank instruction T23.

ORGANIC PEROXIDE	Concentration (%)	Diluent type A (%)	Diluent type B (%) 1)	Inert solid (%)	Water	Packing Method	Control temperature (°C)	Emergency temperature (°C)	Number (Generic entry)	Subsidiary risks and remarks
ACETYL ACETONE PEROXIDE	≤ 42	≥ 48			≥ 8	OP7			3105	2)
"	≤ 32 as a paste					OP7			3106	20)
ACETYL CYCLOHEXANESULPHONYL PEROXIDE	≤ 82		≥ 68		≥ 12	OP4	-10	0	3112	3)
"	≤ 32					OP7	-10	0	3115	
tert-AMYL HYDROPEROXIDE	≤ 88	≥ 6			≥ 6	OP8			3107	
tert-AMYL PEROXYACETATE	≤ 62	≥ 38				OP7			3105	
tert-AMYL PEROXYBENZOATE	≤ 100					OP5			3103	
tert-AMYL PEROXY-2-ETHYLHEXANOATE	≤ 100					OP7	+20	+25	3115	
tert-AMYL PEROXY-2-ETHYLHEXYL CARBONATE	≤ 100					OP7			3105	
tert-AMYL PEROXY ISOPROPYL CARBONATE	≤ 77	≥ 23				OP5			3103	
tert-AMYL PEROXYNEODECANOATE	≤ 77		≥ 23			OP7	0	+10	3115	
"	≤ 47	≥ 53				OP8	0	+10	3119	
tert-AMYL PEROXYPIVALATE	≤ 77		≥ 23			OP5	+10	+15	3113	
tert-AMYLPEROXY-3,5,5-TRIMETHYLHEXANOATE	≤ 100					OP7			3105	3)
tert-BUTYL CUMYL PEROXIDE	> 42 - 100					OP8			3107	
"	≤ 52			≥ 48		OP8			3108	
n-BUTYL-4,4-DI-(tert-BUTYLPEROXY)VALERATE	> 52 - 100					OP5			3103	
"	≤ 52			≥ 48		OP8			3108	
tert-BUTYL HYDROPEROXIDE	>79 - 90				≥ 10	OP5			3103	13)
"	≤ 80	≥ 20				OP7			3105	4) 13)
"	≤ 79				> 14	OP8			3107	13) 23)
"	≤ 72				≥ 28	OP8			3109	13)
tert-BUTYL HYDROPEROXIDE + DI-tert-BUTYLPEROXIDE	< 82 + >9				≥ 7	OP5			3103	13)

ORGANIC PEROXIDE	Concentration (%)	Diluent type A (%)	Diluent type B (%) 1)	Inert solid (%)	Water	Packing Method	Control temperature (°C)	Emergency temperature (°C)	Number (Generic entry)	Subsidiary risks and remarks
tert-BUTYL MONOPEROXYMALEATE	> 52 - 100					OP5			3102	3)
"	≤ 52	≥ 48				OP6			3103	
"	≤ 52			≥ 48		OP8			3108	
"	≤ 52 as a paste					OP8			3108	
tert-BUTYL PEROXYACETATE	> 52 - 77	≥ 23				OP5			3101	3)
"	> 32 - 52	≥ 48				OP6			3103	
"	≤ 32		≥ 68			OP8			3109	
tert-BUTYL PEROXYBENZOATE	> 77 - 100					OP5			3103	
"	> 52 - 77	≥ 23				OP7			3105	
"	≤ 52			≥ 48		OP7			3106	
tert-BUTYL PEROXYBUTYL FUMARATE	≤ 52	≥ 48				OP7			3105	
tert-BUTYL PEROXYCROTONATE	≤ 77	≥ 23				OP7			3105	
tert-BUTYL PEROXYDIETHYLACETATE	≤ 100					OP5	+20	+25	3113	
tert-BUTYL PEROXY-2-ETHYLHEXANOATE	> 52 – 100					OP6	+20	+25	3113	
"	> 32 - 52		≥ 48			OP8	+30	+35	3117	
"	≤ 52			≥ 48		OP8	+20	+25	3118	
"	≤ 32		≥ 68			OP8	+40	+45	3119	
tert-BUTYL PEROXY-2-ETHYLHEXANOATE + 2,2-DI-(tert-BUTYLPEROXY)BUTANE	≤ 12 + ≤ 14	≥ 14		≥ 60		OP7			3106	
"	≤ 31 + ≤ 36		≥ 33			OP7	+35	+40	3115	
tert-BUTYL PEROXY-2-ETHYLHEXYLCARBONATE	≤ 100					OP7			3105	
tert-BUTYL PEROXYISOBUTYRATE	> 52 - 77		≥ 23			OP5	+15	+20	3111	3)
"	≤ 52		≥ 48			OP7	+15	+20	3115	
tert-BUTYLPEROXY ISOPROPYLCARBONATE	≤ 77	≥ 23				OP5			3103	

ORGANIC PEROXIDE	Concentration (%)	Diluent type A (%)	Diluent type B (%) 1)	Inert solid (%)	Water	Packing Method	Control temperature (°C)	Emergency temperature (°C)	Number (Generic entry)	Subsidiary risks and remarks
1-(2-tert-BUTYLPEROXY ISOPROPYL)-3-ISOPROPENYLBENZENE	≤ 77	≥ 23				OP7			3105	
"	≤ 42			≥ 58		OP8			3108	
tert-BUTYL PEROXY-2-METHYLBENZOATE	≤ 100					OP5			3103	
tert-BUTYL PEROXYNEODECANOATE	> 77 - 100					OP7	-5	+5	3115	
"	≤ 77		≥ 23			OP7	0	+10	3115	
"	≤ 52 as a stable dispersion in water					OP8	0	+10	3119	
"	≤ 42 as a stable dispersion in water (frozen)					OP8	0	+10	3118	
"	≤ 32	≥ 68				OP8	0	+10	3119	
tert-BUTYL PEROXYNEOHEPTANOATE	≤ 77	≥ 23				OP7	0	+10	3115	
"	≤ 42 as a stable dispersion in water					OP8	0	+10	3117	
tert-BUTYL PEROXYPIVALATE	> 67 - 77	≥ 23				OP5	0	+10	3113	
"	> 27 - 67		≥ 33			OP7	0	+10	3115	
"	≤ 27		≥ 73			OP8	+30	+35	3119	
tert-BUTYLPEROXY STEARYLCARBONATE	≤ 100					OP7			3106	
tert-BUTYL PEROXY-3,5,5-TRIMETHYLHEXANOATE	> 32 - 100					OP7			3105	
"	≤ 42			≥ 58		OP7			3106	
"	≤ 32		≥ 68			OP8			3109	
3-CHLOROPEROXYBENZOIC ACID	> 57 - 86			≥ 14		OP1			3102	3)
"	≤ 57			≥ 3	≥ 40	OP7			3106	
"	≤ 77			≥ 6	≥ 17	OP7			3106	
CUMYL HYDROPEROXIDE	> 90 - 98	≤ 10				OP8			3107	13)
"	≤ 90	≥ 10				OP8			3109	13) 18)

ORGANIC PEROXIDE	Concentration (%)	Diluent type A (%)	Diluent type B (%) 1)	Inert solid (%)	Water	Packing Method	Control temperature (°C)	Emergency temperature (°C)	Number (Generic entry)	Subsidiary risks and remarks
CUMYL PEROXYNEODECANOATE	≤87	≥13				OP7	-10	0	3115	
"	≤77		≥23			OP7	-10	0	3115	
"	≤52 as a stable dispersion in water					OP8	-10	0	3119	
CUMYL PEROXYNEOHEPTANOATE	≤77	≥23				OP7	-10	0	3115	
CUMYL PEROXYPIVALATE	≤77		≥23			OP7	-5	+5	3115	
CYCLOHEXANONE PEROXIDE(S)	≤91				≥9	OP6			3104	13)
"	≤72	≥28				OP7			3105	5)
"	≤72 as a paste					OP7			3106	5) 20)
"	≤32			≥68					Exempt	29)
DIACETONE ALCOHOL PEROXIDES	≤57		≥26		≥8	OP7	+40	+45	3115	6)
DIACETYL PEROXIDE	≤27		≥73			OP7	+20	+25	3115	7) 13)
DI-tert-AMYL PEROXIDE	≤100					OP8			3107	
2,2-DI-(tert-AMYLPEROXY)BUTANE	≤57	≥43				OP7			3105	
1,1-DI-(tert-AMYLPEROXY)CYCLOHEXANE	≤82	≥18				OP6			3103	
DIBENZOYL PEROXIDE	>51 - 100			≤48		OP2			3102	3)
"	>77 - 94				≥6	OP4			3102	3)
"	≤77				≥23	OP6			3104	
"	≤62			≥28	≥10	OP7			3106	
"	>52 – 62 as a paste					OP7			3106	20)
"	>35 - 52			≥48		OP7			3106	
"	>36 - 42	≥18			≤40	OP8			3107	
"	≤56.5 as a paste				≥15	OP8			3108	
"	≤52 as a paste					OP8			3108	20)
"	≤42 as a stable dispersion in water					OP8			3109	
"	≤35			≥65					Exempt	29)

ORGANIC PEROXIDE	Concentration (%)	Diluent type A (%)	Diluent type B (%) 1)	Inert solid (%)	Water	Packing Method	Control temperature (°C)	Emergency temperature (°C)	Number (Generic entry)	Subsidiary risks and remarks
DI-(4-tert-BUTYLCYCLOHEXYL) PEROXYDICARBONATE	≤ 100					OP6	+30	+35	3114	
"	≤ 42 as a stable dispersion in water					OP8	+30	+35	3119	
DI-tert-BUTYL PEROXIDE	> 52 - 100					OP8			3107	
"	≤ 52		≥ 48			OP8			3109	25)
DI-tert-BUTYL PEROXYAZELATE	≤ 52	≥ 48				OP7			3105	
2,2-DI-(tert-BUTYLPEROXY)BUTANE	≤ 52	≥ 48				OP6			3103	
1,6-Di-(tert-BUTYLPEROXYCARBONYLOXY) HEXANE	≤ 72	≥ 28				OP5			3103	
1,1-DI-(tert-BUTYLPEROXY) CYCLOHEXANE	> 80 - 100					OP5			3101	3)
"	≤ 72		≥ 28			OP5			3103	30)
"	> 52 - 80	≥ 20				OP5			3103	
"	> 42 - 52	≥ 48				OP7			3105	
"	≤ 42	≥ 13		≥ 45		OP7			3106	
"	≤ 42	≥ 58				OP8			3109	
"	≤ 27	≥ 25				OP8			3107	21)
"	≤ 13	≥ 13	≥ 74			OP8			3109	
1,1-DI-(tert-BUTYLPEROXY) CYCLOHEXANE + tert-BUTYL PEROXY-2-ETHYLHEXANOATE	≤ 43 + ≤ 16	≥ 41				OP 7			3105	
DI-n-BUTYL PEROXYDICARBONATE	> 27 - 52		≥ 48			OP7	-15	-5	3115	
"	≤ 27		≥ 73			OP8	-10	0	3117	
"	≤ 42 as a stable dispersion in water (frozen)					OP8	-15	-5	3118	
DI-sec-BUTYL PEROXYDICARBONATE	> 52 - 100					OP4	-20	-10	3113	
"	≤ 52		≥ 48			OP7	-15	-5	3115	

ORGANIC PEROXIDE	Concentration (%)	Diluent type A (%)	Diluent type B (%) 1)	Inert solid (%)	Water	Packing Method	Control temperature (°C)	Emergency temperature (°C)	Number (Generic entry)	Subsidiary risks and remarks
DI-(2-tert-BUTYLPEROXYISOPROPYL)BENZENE(S)	> 42 - 100			≤ 57		OP7			3106	
"	≤ 42			≥ 58					Exempt	29)
DI-(tert-BUTYLPEROXY) PHTHALATE	> 42 - 52	≥ 48				OP7			3105	
"	≤ 52 as a paste					OP7			3106	20)
"	≤ 42	≥ 58				OP8			3107	
2,2-DI-(tert-BUTYLPEROXY)PROPANE	≤ 52	≥ 48				OP7			3105	
"	≤ 42	≥ 13		≥ 45		OP7			3106	
1,1-DI-(tert-BUTYLPEROXY)-3,3,5-TRIMETHYLCYCLOHEXANE	> 90 - 100					OP5			3101	3)
"	≤ 90		≥ 10			OP5			3103	30)
"	> 57 - 90	≥ 10				OP5			3103	
"	≤ 77		≥ 23			OP5			3103	
"	≤ 57			≥ 43		OP8			3110	
"	≤ 57	≥ 43				OP8			3107	
"	≤ 32	≥ 26	≥ 42			OP8			3107	
DICETYL PEROXYDICARBONATE	≤ 100					OP7	+30	+35	3116	
"	≤ 42 as a stable dispersion in water					OP8	+30	+35	3119	
DI-4-CHLOROBENZOYL PEROXIDE	≤ 77				≥ 23	OP5			3102	3)
"	≤ 52 as a paste					OP7			3106	20)
"	≤ 32			≥ 68					Exempt	29)
DICUMYL PEROXIDE	> 52 - 100					OP8			3110	12)
"	≤ 52			≥ 48					Exempt	29)
DICYCLOHEXYL PEROXYDICARBONATE	> 91 - 100					OP3	+10	+15	3112	3)
"	≤ 91				≥ 9	OP5	+10	+15	3114	
"	≤ 42 as a stable dispersion in water					OP8	+15	+20	3119	

ORGANIC PEROXIDE	Concentration (%)	Diluent type A (%)	Diluent type B (%) 1)	Inert solid (%)	Water	Packing Method	Control temperature (°C)	Emergency temperature (°C)	Number (Generic entry)	Subsidiary risks and remarks
DIDECANOYL PEROXIDE	≤ 100					OP6	+30	+35	3114	
2,2-DI-(4,4-DI (tert-BUTYLPEROXY) CYCLOHEXYL) PROPANE	≤ 42			≥ 58		OP7			3106	
"	≤ 22		≥ 78			OP8			3107	
DI-2,4-DICHLOROBENZOYL PEROXIDE	≤ 77				≥ 23	OP5			3102	3)
"	≤ 52 as a paste					OP8	+ 20	+ 25	3118	
"	≤ 52 as a paste with silicon oil					OP7			3106	
DI-(2-ETHOXYETHYL) PEROXYDICARBONATE	≤ 52		≥ 48			OP7	-10	0	3115	
DI-(2-ETHYLHEXYL) PEROXYDICARBONATE	> 77 – 100					OP5	-20	-10	3113	
"	≤ 77		≥ 23			OP7	-15	-5	3115	
"	≤ 62 as a stable dispersion in water					OP8	-15	-5	3119	
"	≤ 52 as a stable dispersion in water (frozen)					OP8	-15	-5	3120	
2,2-DIHYDROPEROXYPROPANE	≤ 27			≥ 73		OP5			3102	3)
DI-(1-HYDROXYCYCLOHEXYL) PEROXIDE	≤ 100					OP7			3106	
DIISOBUTYRYL PEROXIDE	> 32 – 52		≥ 48			OP5	-20	-10	3111	3)
"	≤ 32		≥ 68			OP7	-20	-10	3115	
DIISOPROPYLBENZENE DIHYDROPEROXIDE	≤ 82	≥ 5			≥ 5	OP7			3106	24)
DIISOPROPYL PEROXYDICARBONATE	> 52-100					OP2	-15	-5	3112	3)
"	≤ 52		≥ 48			OP7	-20	-10	3115	
"	≤ 28	≥ 72				OP7	-15	-5	3115	
DILAUROYL PEROXIDE	≤ 100					OP7			3106	
"	≤ 42 as a stable dispersion in water					OP8			3109	
DI-(3-METHOXYBUTYL) PEROXYDICARBONATE	≤ 52		≥ 48			OP7	-5	+5	3115	

ORGANIC PEROXIDE	Concentration (%)	Diluent type A (%)	Diluent type B (%) 1)	Inert solid (%)	Water	Packing Method	Control temperature (°C)	Emergency temperature (°C)	Number (Generic entry)	Subsidiary risks and remarks
DI-(2-METHYLBENZOYL) PEROXIDE	≤ 87				≥ 13	OP5	+30	+35	3112	3)
DI-(3-METHYLBENZOYL) PEROXIDE + BENZOYL (3-METHYLBENZOYL) PEROXIDE + DIBENZOYL PEROXIDE	≤ 20 + ≤ 18 + ≤ 4		≥ 58			OP7	+35	+40	3115	
DI-(4-METHYLBENZOYL) PEROXIDE	≤ 52 as a paste with silicon oil					OP7			3106	
2,5-DIMETHYL-2,5-DI-(BENZOYLPEROXY)HEXANE	> 82-100					OP5			3102	3)
"	≤ 82			≥ 18		OP7			3106	
"	≤ 82				≥ 18	OP5			3104	
2,5-DIMETHYL-2,5-DI-(tert-BUTYLPEROXY)HEXANE	> 52 – 100					OP7			3105	
"	≤ 77			≥ 23		OP8			3108	
"	≤ 52	≥ 48				OP8			3109	
"	≤ 47 as a paste					OP8			3108	
2,5-DIMETHYL-2,5-DI-(tert-BUTYLPEROXY)HEXYNE-3	> 86-100					OP5			3101	3)
"	>52-86	≥ 14				OP5			3103	26)
"	≤ 52			≥ 48		OP7			3106	
2,5-DIMETHYL-2,5-DI-(2-ETHYLHEXANOYLPEROXY)HEXANE	≤ 100					OP5	+20	+25	3113	
2,5-DIMETHYL-2,5-DIHYDROPEROXYHEXANE	≤ 82				≥ 18	OP6			3104	
2,5-DIMETHYL-2,5-DI-(3,5,5-TRIMETHYLHEXANOYLPEROXY)HEXANE	≤ 77	≥ 23				OP7			3105	
1,1-DIMETHYL-3-HYDROXYBUTYL PEROXYNEOHEPTANOATE	≤ 52	≥ 48				OP8	0	+10	3117	
DIMYRISTYL PEROXYDICARBONATE	≤ 100					OP7	+20	+25	3116	
"	≤ 42 as a stable dispersion in water					OP8	+20	+25	3119	

ORGANIC PEROXIDE	Concentration (%)	Diluent type A (%)	Diluent type B (%) 1)	Inert solid (%)	Water	Packing Method	Control temperature (°C)	Emergency temperature (°C)	Number (Generic entry)	Subsidiary risks and remarks
DI-(2-NEODECANOYLPEROXYISOPROPYL) BENZENE	≤ 52	≥ 48				OP7	-10	0	3115	
DI-n-NONANOYL PEROXIDE	≤ 100					OP7	0	+10	3116	
DI-n-OCTANOYL PEROXIDE	≤ 100					OP5	+10	+15	3114	
DI-(2-PHENOXYETHYL) PEROXYDICARBONATE	>85-100					OP5			3102	3)
"	≤ 85				≥ 15	OP7			3106	
DIPROPIONYL PEROXIDE	≤ 27		≥ 73			OP8	+15	+20	3117	
DI-n-PROPYL PEROXYDICARBONATE	≤ 100					OP3	-25	-15	3113	
"	≤ 77		≥ 23			OP5	-20	-10	3113	
DISUCCINIC ACID PEROXIDE	> 72-100					OP4			3102	3) 17)
"	≤ 72				≥ 28	OP7	+10	+15	3116	
DI-(3,5,5-TRIMETHYLHEXANOYL) PEROXIDE	> 38-82	≥ 18				OP7	0	+10	3115	
"	≤ 52 as a stable dispersion in water					OP8	+10	+15	3119	
"	≤ 38	≥ 62				OP8	+20	+25	3119	
ETHYL 3,3-DI-(tert-AMYLPEROXY)BUTYRATE	≤ 67	≥ 33				OP7			3105	
ETHYL 3,3-DI-(tert-BUTYLPEROXY)BUTYRATE	> 77 - 100					OP5			3103	
"	≤ 77	≥ 23				OP7			3105	
"	≤ 52			≥ 48		OP7			3106	
1-(2-ETHYLHEXANOYLPEROXY)-1,3-DIMETHYLBUTYL PEROXYPIVALATE	≤ 52	≥ 45	≥ 10			OP7	-20	-10	3115	
tert-HEXYL PEROXYNEODECANOATE	≤ 71	≥ 29				OP7	0	+10	3115	
tert-HEXYL PEROXYPIVALATE	≤ 72		≥ 28			OP7	+10	+15	3115	
3-HYDROXY-1,1-DIMETHYLBUTYL PEROXYNEODECANOATE	≤ 77	≥ 23				OP 7	- 5	+ 5	3115	
"	≤ 52	≥ 48				OP 8	- 5	+ 5	3117	
"	≤ 52 as a stable dispersion in water					OP 8	- 5	+ 5	3119	

ORGANIC PEROXIDE	Concentration (%)	Diluent type A (%)	Diluent type B (%) 1)	Inert solid (%)	Water	Packing Method	Control temperature (°C)	Emergency temperature (°C)	Number (Generic entry)	Subsidiary risks and remarks
ISOPROPYL sec-BUTYL PEROXYDICARBONATE +DI-sec-BUTYL PEROXYDICARBONATE +DI-ISOPROPYL PEROXYDICARBONATE	≤ 32 + ≤ 15 – 18 ≤ 12 – 15	≥ 38				OP7	-20	-10	3115	
"	≤ 52 + ≤ 28 + ≤ 22					OP5	-20	-10	3111	3)
ISOPROPYLCUMYL HYDROPEROXIDE	≤ 72	≥ 28				OP8			3109	13)
p-MENTHYL HYDROPEROXIDE	> 72 - 100					OP7			3105	13)
"	≤ 72	≥ 28				OP8			3109	27)
METHYLCYCLOHEXANONE PEROXIDE(S)	≤ 67		≥ 33			OP7	+35	+40	3115	
METHYL ETHYL KETONE PEROXIDE(S)	see remark 8)	≥ 48				OP5			3101	3) 8) 13)
"	see remark 9)	≥ 55				OP7			3105	9)
"	see remark 10)	≥ 60				OP8			3107	10)
METHYL ISOBUTYL KETONE PEROXIDE(S)	≤ 62	≥ 19				OP7			3105	22)
METHYL ISOPROPYL KETONE PEROXIDE(S)	see remark 31)	≥ 70				OP8			3109	31)
ORGANIC PEROXIDE, LIQUID, SAMPLE						OP2			3103	11)
ORGANIC PEROXIDE, LIQUID, SAMPLE, TEMPERATURE CONTROLLED						OP2			3113	11)
ORGANIC PEROXIDE, SOLID, SAMPLE						OP2			3104	11)
ORGANIC PEROXIDE, SOLID, SAMPLE, TEMPERATURE CONTROLLED						OP2			3114	11)
3,3,5,7,7-PENTAMETHYL-1,2,4-TRIOXEPANE	≤ 100					OP8			3107	
PEROXYACETIC ACID, TYPE D, stabilized	≤ 43					OP7			3105	13) 14) 19)
PEROXYACETIC ACID, TYPE E, stabilized	≤ 43					OP8			3107	13) 15) 19)
PEROXYACETIC ACID, TYPE F, stabilized	≤ 43					OP8			3109	13) 16) 19)
PEROXYLAURIC ACID	≤ 100					OP8	+35	+40	3118	11)
PINANYL HYDROPEROXIDE	> 56 – 100					OP7			3105	13)
"	≤ 56	≥ 44				OP8			3109	
POLYETHER POLY-tert-BUTYLPEROXY-CARBONATE	≤ 52		≥ 48			OP8			3107	

ORGANIC PEROXIDE	Concentration (%)	Diluent type A (%)	Diluent type B (%) 1)	Inert solid (%)	Water	Packing Method	Control temperature (°C)	Emergency temperature (°C)	Number (Generic entry)	Subsidiary risks and remarks
1,1,3,3-TETRAMETHYLBUTYL HYDROPEROXIDE	≤ 100					OP7			3105	
1,1,3,3-TETRAMETHYLBUTYL PEROXY-2-ETHYLHEXANOATE	≤ 100					OP7	+15	+20	3115	
1,1,3,3- TETRAMETHYLBUTYL PEROXYNEODECANOATE	≤ 72		≥ 28			OP7	-5	+5	3115	
"	≤ 52 as a stable dispersion in water					OP8	-5	+5	3119	
1,1,3,3-TETRAMETHYLBUTYL PEROXYPIVALATE	≤ 77	≥ 23				OP7	0	+10	3115	
3,6,9-TRIETHYL-3,6,9-TRIMETHYL -1,4,7 TRIPEROXONANE	≤ 42	≥ 58				OP7			3105	28)

Remarks (refer to the last column of the Table in 2.2.52.4):

1)   Diluent type B may always be replaced by diluent type A. The boiling point of diluent type B shall be at least 60°C higher than the SADT of the organic peroxide.

2)   Available oxygen ≤ 4.7%.

3)   "EXPLOSIVE" subsidiary risk label required (Model No.1, see 5.2.2.2.2).

4)   Diluent may be replaced by di-tert-butyl peroxide.

5)   Available oxygen ≤ 9%.

6)   With ≤ 9% hydrogen peroxide; available oxygen ≤ 10%.

7)   Only non-metallic packagings allowed.

8)   Available oxygen > 10% and ≤ 10.7%, with or without water.

9)   Available oxygen ≤ 10% , with or without water.

10)   Available oxygen ≤ 8.2% , with or without water.

11)   See 2.2.52.1.9.

12)   Up to 2000 kg per receptacle assigned to ORGANIC PEROXIDE TYPE F on the basis of large scale trials.

13)   "CORROSIVE" subsidiary risk label required (Model No.8, see 5.2.2.2.2).

14)   Peroxyacetic acid formulations which fulfil the criteria of the Manual of Tests and Criteria, paragraph 20.4.3 (d).

15)   Peroxyacetic acid formulations which fulfil the criteria of the Manual of Tests and Criteria, paragraph 20.4.3 (e).

16)   Peroxyacetic acid formulations which fulfil the criteria of the Manual of Tests and Criteria, paragraph 20.4.3 (f).

17)   Addition of water to this organic peroxide will decrease its thermal stability.

18)   No "CORROSIVE" subsidiary risk label (Model No.8, see 5.2.2.2.2) required for concentrations below 80%.

19)   Mixtures with hydrogen peroxide, water and acid(s).

20)   With diluent type A, with or without water.

21)   With ≥ 25% diluent type A by mass, and in addition ethylbenzene.

22)   With ≥ 19%, diluent type A by mass, and in addition methyl isobutyl ketone.

23)   With < 6% di-tert-butyl peroxide.

24)   With ≤ 8% 1-isopropylhydroperoxy-4-isopropylhydroxybenzene.

25)   Diluent type B with boiling point > 110 °C.

26)   With < 0.5% hydroperoxides content.

27)   For concentrations more than 56%, "CORROSIVE" subsidiary risk label required (Model No.8, see 5.2.2.2.2).

28)   Available active oxygen ≤ 7.6% in diluent type A having a 95% boil-off point in the range of 200 - 260 °C.

29)   Not subject to the requirements of ADR for Class 5.2.

30)   Diluent type B with boiling point > 130 °C.

31)   Active oxygen ≤ 6.7%.

2.2.61   **Class 6.1**   **Toxic substances**

2.2.61.1   *Criteria*

2.2.61.1.1   The heading of Class 6.1 covers substances of which it is known by experience or regarding which it is presumed from experiments on animals that in relatively small quantities they are able by a single action or by action of short duration to cause damage to human health, or death, by inhalation, by cutaneous absorption or by ingestion.

2.2.61.1.2   Substances of Class 6.1 are subdivided as follows:

T   Toxic substances without subsidiary risk:

    T1   Organic, liquid;
    T2   Organic, solid;
    T3   Organometallic substances;
    T4   Inorganic, liquid;
    T5   Inorganic, solid;
    T6   Liquid, used as pesticides;
    T7   Solid, used as pesticides;
    T8   Samples;
    T9   Other toxic substances;

TF   Toxic substances, flammable:

    TF1   Liquid;
    TF2   Liquid, used as pesticides;
    TF3   Solid;

TS   Toxic substances, self-heating, solid;

TW   Toxic substances, which, in contact with water, emit flammable gases:

    TW1   Liquid;
    TW2   Solid;

TO   Toxic substances, oxidizing:

    TO1   Liquid;
    TO2   Solid;

TC   Toxic substances, corrosive:

    TC1   Organic, liquid;
    TC2   Organic, solid;
    TC3   Inorganic, liquid;
    TC4   Inorganic, solid;

TFC   Toxic substances, flammable, corrosive.

2.2.61.1.3   For the purposes of ADR:

LD_{50} (median lethal dose) for acute oral toxicity is the statistically derived single dose of a substance that can be expected to cause death within 14 days in 50 per cent of young adult albino rats when administered by the oral route. The LD_{50} value is expressed in terms of mass of test substance per mass of test animal (mg/kg);

LD_{50} for acute dermal toxicity is that dose of the substance which, administered by continuous contact for 24 hours with the bare skin of albino rabbits, is most likely to cause death within 14 days in one half of the animals tested. The number of animals tested shall be sufficient to give a statistically significant result and be in conformity with good pharmacological practice. The result is expressed in milligrams per kg body mass;

LC_{50} for acute toxicity on inhalation is that concentration of vapour, mist or dust which, administered by continuous inhalation to both male and female young adult albino rats for one hour, is most likely to cause death within 14 days in one half of the animals tested. A solid substance shall be tested if at least 10% (by mass) of its total mass is likely to be dust in a respirable range, e.g. the aerodynamic diameter of that particle-fraction is 10 μm or less. A liquid substance shall be tested if a mist is likely to be generated in a leakage of the transport containment. Both for solid and liquid substances more than 90% (by mass) of a specimen prepared for inhalation toxicity shall be in the respirable range as defined above. The result is expressed in milligrams per litre of air for dusts and mists or in millilitres per cubic metre of air (parts per million) for vapours.

Classification and assignment of packing groups

2.2.61.1.4   Substances of Class 6.1 shall be classified in three packing groups according to the degree of danger they present for carriage, as follows:

Packing group I: highly toxic substances
Packing group II: toxic substances
Packing group III: slightly toxic substances.

2.2.61.1.5   Substances, mixtures, solutions and articles classified in Class 6.1 are listed in Table A of Chapter 3.2. The assignment of substances, mixtures and solutions not mentioned by name in Table A of Chapter 3.2 to the relevant entry of sub-section 2.2.61.3 and to the relevant packing group in accordance with the provisions of Chapter 2.1, shall be made according to the following criteria in 2.2.61.1.6 to 2.2.61.1.11.

2.2.61.1.6   To assess the degree of toxicity, account shall be taken of human experience of instances of accidental poisoning, as well as special properties possessed by any individual substances: liquid state, high volatility, any special likelihood of cutaneous absorption, and special biological effects.

2.2.61.1.7   In the absence of observations on humans, the degree of toxicity shall be assessed using the available data from animal experiments in accordance with the table below:

	Packing group	Oral toxicity LD_{50} (mg/kg)	Dermal toxicity LD_{50} (mg/kg)	Inhalation toxicity by dusts and mists LC_{50} (mg/l)
Highly toxic	I	≤ 5	≤ 50	≤ 0.2
Toxic	II	> 5 and ≤ 50	> 50 and ≤ 200	> 0.2 and ≤ 2
Slightly toxic	III [a]	> 50 and ≤ 300	> 200 and $\leq$ 1 000	> 2 and ≤ 4

[a]   *Tear gas substances shall be included in packing group II even if data concerning their toxicity correspond to packing group III criteria.*

2.2.61.1.7.1   Where a substance exhibits different degrees of toxicity for two or more kinds of exposure, it shall be classified under the highest such degree of toxicity.

2.2.61.1.7.2   Substances meeting the criteria of Class 8 and with an inhalation toxicity of dusts and mists (LC_{50}) leading to packing group I shall only be accepted for an allocation to Class 6.1 if the toxicity through oral ingestion or dermal contact is at least in the range of packing groups I or II. Otherwise an assignment to Class 8 shall be made if appropriate (see 2.2.8.1.5).

2.2.61.1.7.3   The criteria for inhalation toxicity of dusts and mists are based on LC_{50} data relating to 1-hour exposure, and where such information is available it shall be used. However, where only LC_{50} data relating to 4-hour exposure are available, such figures can be multiplied by four and the product substituted in the above criteria, i.e. LC_{50} value multiplied by four (4 hour) is considered the equivalent of LC_{50} (1 hour).

Inhalation toxicity of vapours

2.2.61.1.8   Liquids giving off toxic vapours shall be classified into the following groups where "V" is the saturated vapour concentration (in ml/m^3 of air) (volatility) at 20 °C and standard atmospheric pressure:

	Packing group	
Highly toxic	I	Where $V \geq 10\ LC_{50}$ and $LC_{50} \leq 1\ 000$ ml/m^3
Toxic	II	Where $V \geq LC_{50}$ and $LC_{50} \leq 3\ 000$ ml/m^3 and the criteria for packing group I are not met
Slightly toxic	III[a]	Where $V \geq 1/5\ LC_{50}$ and $LC_{50} \leq 5\ 000$ ml/m^3 and the criteria for packing groups I and II are not met

[a]   *Tear gas substances shall be included in packing group II even if data concerning their toxicity correspond to packing group III criteria.*

These criteria for inhalation toxicity of vapours are based on LC_{50} data relating to 1-hour exposure, and where such information is available, it shall be used.

However, where only LC_{50} data relating to 4-hour exposure to the vapours are available, such figures can be multiplied by two and the product substituted in the above criteria, i.e. LC_{50} (4 hour) $\times$ 2 is considered the equivalent of LC_{50} (1 hour).

In this figure, the criteria are expressed in graphical form, as an aid to easy classification. However, due to approximations inherent in the use of graphs, substances falling on or near group borderlines shall be checked using numerical criteria.

GROUP BORDERLINES INHALATION TOXICITY OF VAPOURS

Mixtures of liquids

2.2.61.1.9   Mixtures of liquids which are toxic on inhalation shall be assigned to packing groups according to the following criteria:

2.2.61.1.9.1   If LC_{50} is known for each of the toxic substances constituting the mixture, the packing group may be determined as follows:

(a)   calculation of the LC_{50} of the mixture:

$$LC_{50} \text{ (mixture)} = \frac{1}{\displaystyle\sum_{i=1}^{1} \frac{f_i}{LC_{50i}}}$$

where f_i =   molar fraction of constituent i of the mixture;

            LC_{50i} =   average lethal concentration of constituent i in ml/m^3.

(b)   calculation of volatility of each mixture constituent:

$$V_i = P_i \times \frac{10^6}{101.3} \ (ml/m^3)$$

where P_i =   partial pressure of constituent i in kPa at 20 °C and at standard atmospheric pressure.

(c)   calculation of the ratio of volatility to LC_{50}:

$$R = \sum_{i=1}^{n} \frac{V_i}{LC_{50i}}$$

(d)   the values calculated for LC_{50} (mixture) and R are then used to determine the packing group of the mixture:

Packing group I $R \geq 10$ and LC_{50} (mixture) $\leq 1\ 000\ ml/m^3$;

Packing group II $R \geq 1$ and LC_{50} (mixture) $\leq 3\ 000\ ml/m^3$, if the mixture does not meet the criteria for packing group I;

Packing group III $R \geq 1/5$ and LC_{50} (mixture) $\leq 5\ 000\ ml/m^3$, if the mixture does not meet the criteria of packing groups I or II.

2.2.61.1.9.2   In the absence of LC_{50} data on the toxic constituent substances, the mixture may be assigned to a group based on the following simplified threshold toxicity tests. When these threshold tests are used, the most restrictive group shall be determined and used for carrying the mixture.

2.2.61.1.9.3   A mixture is assigned to packing group I only if it meets both of the following criteria:

(a)   A sample of the liquid mixture is vaporized and diluted with air to create a test atmosphere of 1 000 ml/m^3 vaporized mixture in air. Ten albino rats (5 male and 5 female) are exposed to the test atmosphere for 1 hour and observed for 14 days. If five or more of the animals die within the 14-day observation period, the mixture is presumed to have an LC_{50} equal to or less than 1 000 ml/m^3;

(b)   A sample of vapour in equilibrium with the liquid mixture is diluted with 9 equal volumes of air to form a test atmosphere. Ten albino rats (5 male and 5 female) are exposed to the test atmosphere for 1 hour and observed for 14 days. If five or more of the animals die within the 14-day observation period, the mixture is presumed to have a volatility equal to or greater than 10 times the mixture LC_{50}.

2.2.61.1.9.4   A mixture is assigned to packing group II only if it meets both of the following criteria, and does not meet the criteria for packing group I:

(a)   A sample of the liquid mixture is vaporized and diluted with air to create a test atmosphere of 3 000 ml/m^3 vaporized mixture in air. Ten albino rats (5 male and 5 female) are exposed to the test atmosphere for 1 hour and observed for 14 days. If five or more of the animals die within the 14-day observation period, the mixture is presumed to have an LC_{50} equal to or less than 3 000 ml/m^3;

(b)   A sample of the vapour in equilibrium with the liquid mixture is used to form a test atmosphere. Ten albino rats (5 male and 5 female) are exposed to the test atmosphere for 1 hour and observed for 14 days. If five or more of the animals die within the 14-day observation period, the mixture is presumed to have a volatility equal to or greater than the mixture LC_{50}.

2.2.61.1.9.5   A mixture is assigned to packing group III only if it meets both of the following criteria, and does not meet the criteria for packing groups I or II:

(a)   A sample of the liquid mixture is vaporized and diluted with air to create a test atmosphere of 5 000 ml/m^3 vaporized mixture in air. Ten albino rats (5 male and 5 female) are exposed to the test atmosphere for 1 hour and observed for 14 days. If five or more of the animals die within the 14-day observation period, the mixture is presumed to have an LC_{50} equal to or less than 5 000 ml/m^3;

(b)   The vapour concentration (volatility) of the liquid mixture is measured and if the vapour concentration is equal to or greater than 1 000 ml/m^3, the mixture is presumed to have a volatility equal to or greater than 1/5 the mixture LC_{50}.

Methods for determining oral and dermal toxicity of mixtures

2.2.61.1.10   When classifying and assigning the appropriate packing group to mixtures in Class 6.1 in accordance with the oral and dermal toxicity criteria (see 2.2.61.1.3), it is necessary to determine the acute LD_{50} of the mixture.

2.2.61.1.10.1   If a mixture contains only one active substance, and the LD_{50} of that constituent is known, in the absence of reliable acute oral and dermal toxicity data on the actual mixture to be carried, the oral or dermal LD_{50} may be obtained by the following method:

$$LD_{50} \text{ value of preparation} = \frac{LD_{50} \text{ value of active substance} \times 100}{\text{percentage of active substance by mass}}$$

2.2.61.1.10.2　If a mixture contains more than one active constituent, there are three possible approaches that may be used to determine the oral or dermal LD_{50} of the mixture. The preferred method is to obtain reliable acute oral and dermal toxicity data on the actual mixture to be carried. If reliable, accurate data are not available, then either of the following methods may be performed:

(a)　Classify the formulation according to the most hazardous constituent of the mixture as if that constituent were present in the same concentration as the total concentration of all active constituents; or

(b)　Apply the formula:

$$\frac{C_A}{T_A} + \frac{C_B}{T_B} + ... + \frac{C_Z}{T_Z} = \frac{100}{T_M}$$

where:

C　=　the percentage concentration of constituent A, B, ..., Z in the mixture;

T　=　the oral LD_{50} values of constituent A, B, ... Z;

T_M　=　the oral LD_{50} value of the mixture.

NOTE: This formula can also be used for dermal toxicities provided that this information is available on the same species for all constituents. The use of this formula does not take into account any potentiation or protective phenomena.

Classification of pesticides

2.2.61.1.11　All active pesticide substances and their preparations for which the LC_{50} and/or LD_{50} values are known and which are classified in Class 6.1 shall be classified under appropriate packing groups in accordance with the criteria given in 2.2.61.1.6 to 2.2.61.1.9. Substances and preparations which are characterized by subsidiary risks shall be classified according to the precedence of hazard Table in 2.1.3.10 with the assignment of appropriate packing groups.

2.2.61.1.11.1　If the oral or dermal LD_{50} value for a pesticide preparation is not known, but the LD_{50} value of its active substance(s) is known, the LD_{50} value for the preparation may be obtained by applying the procedures in 2.2.61.1.10.

NOTE: LD_{50} toxicity data for a number of common pesticides may be obtained from the most current edition of the document "The WHO Recommended Classification of Pesticides by Hazard and Guidelines to Classification" available from the International Programme on Chemical Safety, World Health Organisation (WHO), 1211 Geneva 27, Switzerland. While that document may be used as a source of LD_{50} data for pesticides, its classification system shall not be used for purposes of transport classification of, or assignment of packing groups to, pesticides, which shall be in accordance with the requirements of ADR.

2.2.61.1.11.2　The proper shipping name used in the carriage of the pesticide shall be selected on the basis of the active ingredient, of the physical state of the pesticide and any subsidiary risks it may exhibit (see 3.1.2).

2.2.61.1.12　If substances of Class 6.1, as a result of admixtures, come into categories of risk different from those to which the substances mentioned by name in Table A of Chapter 3.2 belong, these mixtures or solutions shall be assigned to the entries to which they belong on the basis of their actual degree of danger.

NOTE: For the classification of solutions and mixtures (such as preparations and wastes), see also 2.1.3.

2.2.61.1.13   On the basis of the criteria of 2.2.61.1.6 to 2.2.61.1.11, it may also be determined whether the nature of a solution or mixture mentioned by name or containing a substance mentioned by name is such that the solution or mixture is not subject to the requirements for this Class.

2.2.61.1.14   Substances, solutions and mixtures, with the exception of substances and preparations used as pesticides, which do not meet the criteria of Directives 67/548/EEC [3] or 1999/45/EC [4] as amended and which are not therefore classified as highly toxic, toxic or harmful according to these directives, as amended, may be considered as substances not belonging to Class 6.1.

2.2.61.2   *Substances not accepted for carriage*

2.2.61.2.1   Chemically unstable substances of Class 6.1 shall not be accepted for carriage unless the necessary steps have been taken to prevent their dangerous decomposition or polymerization during carriage. To this end, it shall in particular be ensured that receptacles and tanks do not contain any substance(s) likely to cause such a reaction.

2.2.61.2.2   The following substances and mixtures shall not be accepted for carriage:

- Hydrogen cyanide, anhydrous or in solution, which do not meet the descriptions of UN Nos. 1051, 1613, 1614 and 3294;

- metal carbonyls, having a flash-point below 23 °C, other than UN Nos. 1259 NICKEL CARBONYL and 1994 IRON PENTACARBONYL;

- 2,3,7,8-TETRACHLORODIBENZO-P-DIOXINE   (TCDD)   in   concentrations considered highly toxic in accordance with the criteria in 2.2.61.1.7;

- UN No. 2249 DICHLORODIMETHYL ETHER, SYMMETRICAL;

- preparations of phosphides without additives inhibiting the emission of toxic flammable gases.

---

[3]   *Council Directive 67/548/EEC of 27 June 1967 on the approximation of laws, regulations and administrative provisions relating to the classification, packaging and labelling of dangerous substances (Official Journal of the European Communities No. L 196 of 16.08.1967, page 1).*

[4]   *Directive 1999/45/EC of the European Parliament and of the Council of 31 May 1999 on the approximation of laws, regulations and administrative provisions of the Member States relating to the classification, packaging and labelling of dangerous preparations (Official Journal of the European Communities No. L 200 of 30 July 1999, pages 1 to 68).*

2.2.61.3   *List of collective entries*

Toxic substances <u>without</u> subsidiary risk(s)

Organic			
	liquid [a]	**T1**	1583 CHLOROPICRIN MIXTURE, N.O.S. 1602 DYE, LIQUID, TOXIC, N.O.S., or 1602 DYE INTERMEDIATE, LIQUID, TOXIC, N.O.S. 1693 TEAR GAS SUBSTANCE, LIQUID, N.O.S. 1851 MEDICINE, LIQUID, TOXIC, N.O.S. 2206 ISOCYANATES, TOXIC, N.O.S. or 2206 ISOCYANATE SOLUTION, TOXIC, N.O.S. 3140 ALKALOIDS, LIQUID, N.O.S. or 3140 ALKALOID SALTS, LIQUID, N.O.S. 3142 DISINFECTANT, LIQUID, TOXIC, N.O.S. 3144 NICOTINE COMPOUND, LIQUID, N.O.S. or 3144 NICOTINE PREPARATION, LIQUID, N.O.S. 3172 TOXINS, EXTRACTED FROM LIVING SOURCES, LIQUID, N.O.S. 3276 NITRILES, TOXIC, LIQUID, N.O.S 3278 ORGANOPHOSPHORUS COMPOUND, TOXIC, LIQUID, N.O.S. 3381 TOXIC BY INHALATION LIQUID, N.O.S. with an inhalation toxicity lower than or equal to 200 ml/m^3 and saturated vapour concentration greater than or equal to 500 LC_{50} 3382 TOXIC BY INHALATION LIQUID, N.O.S. with an inhalation toxicity lower than or equal to 1000 ml/m^3 and saturated vapour concentration greater than or equal to 10 LC_{50} 2810 TOXIC LIQUID, ORGANIC, N.O.S.
	solid [a, b]	**T2**	1544 ALKALOIDS, SOLID, N.O.S. or 1544 ALKALOID SALTS, SOLID, N.O.S. 1601 DISINFECTANT, SOLID, TOXIC, N.O.S. 1655 NICOTINE COMPOUND, SOLID, N.O.S., or 1655 NICOTINE PREPARATION, SOLID, N.O.S. 3448 TEAR GAS SUBSTANCE, SOLID, N.O.S. 3143 DYE, SOLID, TOXIC, N.O.S. or 3143 DYE INTERMEDIATE, SOLID, TOXIC, N.O.S. 3462 TOXINS, EXTRACTED FROM LIVING SOURCES, SOLID, N.O.S. 3249 MEDICINE, SOLID, TOXIC, N.O.S. 3464 ORGANOPHOSPHORUS COMPOUND, TOXIC, SOLID, N.O.S. 3439 NITRILES, TOXIC, SOLID, N.O.S. 2811 TOXIC SOLID, ORGANIC, N.O.S.
Organometallic [c, d]		**T3**	2026 PHENYLMERCURIC COMPOUND, N.O.S. 2788 ORGANOTIN COMPOUND, LIQUID, N.O.S. 3146 ORGANOTIN COMPOUND, SOLID, N.O.S. 3280 ORGANOARSENIC COMPOUND, LIQUID, N.O.S. 3465 ORGANOARSENIC COMPOUND, SOLID, N.O.S. 3281 METAL CARBONYLS, LIQUID, N.O.S. 3466 METAL CARBONYLS, SOLID, N.O.S. 3282 ORGANOMETALLIC COMPOUND, TOXIC, LIQUID, N.O.S. 3467 ORGANOMETALLIC COMPOUND, TOXIC, SOLID, N.O.S.

(cont'd on next page)

[a]   *Substances and preparations containing alkaloids or nicotine used as pesticides shall be classified under UN No. 2588 PESTICIDES, SOLID, TOXIC, N.O.S., UN No. 2902 PESTICIDES, LIQUID, TOXIC, N.O.S. or UN No. 2903 PESTICIDES, LIQUID, TOXIC, FLAMMABLE, N.O.S.*

[b]   *Active substances and triturations or mixtures of substances intended for laboratories and experiments and for the manufacture of pharmaceutical products with other substances shall be classified according to their toxicity (see 2.2.61.1.7 to 2.2.61.1.11).*

[c]   *Self-heating substances, slightly toxic and spontaneously combustible organometallic compounds, are substances of Class 4.2.*

[d]   *Water-reactive substances, slightly toxic, and water-reactive organometallic compounds, are substances of Class 4.3.*

Toxic substances <u>without</u> subsidiary risk(s) *(cont'd)*

Inorganic	liquid ^{e} **T4**	1556	ARSENIC COMPOUND, LIQUID, N.O.S., inorganic including: Arsenates, n.o.s., Arsenites, n.o.s.; and Arsenic sulphides, n.o.s.
		1935	CYANIDE SOLUTION, N.O.S.
		2024	MERCURY COMPOUND, LIQUID, N.O.S.
		3141	ANTIMONY COMPOUND, INORGANIC, LIQUID, N.O.S.
		3440	SELENIUM COMPOUND, LIQUID, N.O.S.
		3381	TOXIC BY INHALATION LIQUID, N.O.S. with an inhalation toxicity lower than or equal to 200 ml/m^3 and saturated vapour concentration greater than or equal to 500 LC$_{50}$
		3382	TOXIC BY INHALATION LIQUID, N.O.S. with an inhalation toxicity lower than or equal to 1000 ml/m^3 and saturated vapour concentration greater than or equal to 10 LC$_{50}$
		3287	TOXIC LIQUID, INORGANIC, N.O.S.

solids $^{f, g}$ **T5**	1549	ANTIMONY COMPOUND, INORGANIC, SOLID, N.O.S
	1557	ARSENIC COMPOUND, SOLID, N.O.S., including: Arsenates, n.o.s.; Arsenites, n.o.s.; and Arsenic sulphides, n.o.s.
	1564	BARIUM COMPOUND, N.O.S.
	1566	BERYLLIUM COMPOUND, N.O.S.
	1588	CYANIDES, INORGANIC, SOLID, N.O.S.
	1707	THALLIUM COMPOUND, N.O.S.
	2025	MERCURY COMPOUND, SOLID, N.O.S.
	2291	LEAD COMPOUND, SOLUBLE, N.O.S.
	2570	CADMIUM COMPOUND
	2630	SELENATES or
	2630	SELENITES
	2856	FLUOROSILICATES, N.O.S.
	3283	SELENIUM COMPOUND, SOLID, N.O.S.
	3284	TELLURIUM COMPOUND, N.O.S.
	3285	VANADIUM COMPOUND, N.O.S.
	3288	TOXIC SOLID, INORGANIC, N.O.S.

liquid^h **T6**	2992	CARBAMATE PESTICIDE, LIQUID, TOXIC
	2994	ARSENICAL PESTICIDE, LIQUID, TOXIC
	2996	ORGANOCHLORINE PESTICIDE, LIQUID, TOXIC
	2998	TRIAZINE PESTICIDE, LIQUID, TOXIC
	3006	THIOCARBAMATE PESTICIDE, LIQUID, TOXIC
	3010	COPPER BASED PESTICIDE, LIQUID, TOXIC
	3012	MERCURY BASED PESTICIDE, LIQUID, TOXIC
	3014	SUBSTITUTED NITROPHENOL PESTICIDE, LIQUID, TOXIC
	3016	BIPYRIDILIUM PESTICIDE, LIQUID, TOXIC
	3018	ORGANOPHOSPHORUS PESTICIDE, LIQUID, TOXIC
	3020	ORGANOTIN PESTICIDE, LIQUID, TOXIC
	3026	COUMARIN DERIVATIVE PESTICIDE, LIQUID, TOXIC
	3348	PHENOXYACETIC ACID DERIVATIVE PESTICIDE, LIQUID, TOXIC
	3352	PYRETHROID PESTICIDE, LIQUID, TOXIC
Pesticides	2902	PESTICIDE, LIQUID, TOXIC, N.O.S.

(cont'd on next page)

---

^{e} *Mercury fulminate, wetted with not less than 20% water, or mixture of alcohol and water by mass is a substance of Class 1, UN No. 0135.*

^{f} *Ferricyanides, ferrocyanides, alkaline thiocyanates and ammonium thiocyanates are not subject to the provisions of ADR.*

^{g} *Lead salts and lead pigments which, when mixed in a ratio of 1:1,000 with 0.07M hydrochloric acid and stirred for one hour at a temperature of 23 °C ± 2 °C, exhibit a solubility of 5% or less, are not subject to the provisions of ADR.*

^{h} *Articles impregnated with this pesticide, such as fibreboard plates, paper strips, cotton-wool balls, sheets of plastics material, in hermetically closed wrappings, are not subject to the provisions of ADR.*

2.2.61.3   *List of collective entries (cont'd)*

Toxic substances **without** subsidiary risk(s) *(cont'd)*

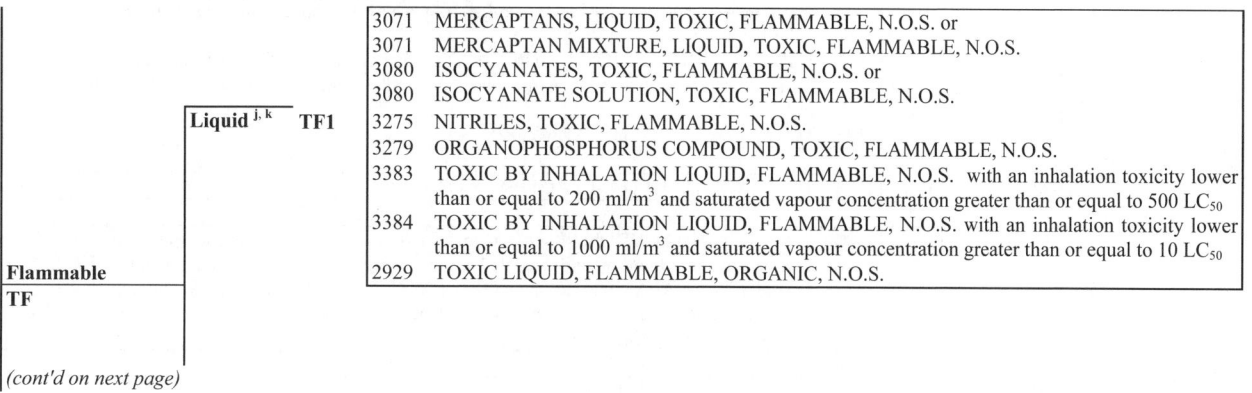

Pesticides *(cont'd)*		
Solid[h] T7	2757	CARBAMATE PESTICIDE, SOLID, TOXIC
	2759	ARSENICAL PESTICIDE, SOLID, TOXIC
	2761	ORGANOCHLORINE PESTICIDE, SOLID, TOXIC
	2763	TRIAZINE PESTICIDE, SOLID, TOXIC
	2771	THIOCARBAMATE PESTICIDE, SOLID, TOXIC
	2775	COPPER BASED PESTICIDE, SOLID, TOXIC
	2777	MERCURY BASED PESTICIDE, SOLID, TOXIC
	2779	SUBSTITUTED NITROPHENOL PESTICIDE, SOLID, TOXIC
	2781	BIPYRIDILIUM PESTICIDE, SOLID, TOXIC
	2783	ORGANOPHOSPHORUS PESTICIDE, SOLID, TOXIC
	2786	ORGANOTIN PESTICIDE, SOLID, TOXIC
	3027	COUMARIN DERIVATIVE PESTICIDE, SOLID, TOXIC
	3048	ALUMINIUM PHOSPHIDE PESTICIDE
	3345	PHENOXYACETIC ACID DERIVATIVE PESTICIDE, SOLID, TOXIC
	3349	PYRETHROID PESTICIDE, SOLID, TOXIC
	2588	PESTICIDE, SOLID, TOXIC, N.O.S.

Samples T8	3315	CHEMICAL SAMPLE, TOXIC

Other toxic substances [i] T9	3243	SOLIDS CONTAINING TOXIC LIQUID, N.O.S.

Toxic substances **with** subsidiary risk(s)

Liquid [j, k] TF1	3071	MERCAPTANS, LIQUID, TOXIC, FLAMMABLE, N.O.S. or
	3071	MERCAPTAN MIXTURE, LIQUID, TOXIC, FLAMMABLE, N.O.S.
	3080	ISOCYANATES, TOXIC, FLAMMABLE, N.O.S. or
	3080	ISOCYANATE SOLUTION, TOXIC, FLAMMABLE, N.O.S.
	3275	NITRILES, TOXIC, FLAMMABLE, N.O.S.
	3279	ORGANOPHOSPHORUS COMPOUND, TOXIC, FLAMMABLE, N.O.S.
	3383	TOXIC BY INHALATION LIQUID, FLAMMABLE, N.O.S. with an inhalation toxicity lower than or equal to 200 ml/m³ and saturated vapour concentration greater than or equal to 500 LC_{50}
	3384	TOXIC BY INHALATION LIQUID, FLAMMABLE, N.O.S. with an inhalation toxicity lower than or equal to 1000 ml/m³ and saturated vapour concentration greater than or equal to 10 LC_{50}
Flammable TF	2929	TOXIC LIQUID, FLAMMABLE, ORGANIC, N.O.S.

(cont'd on next page)

---

[h]   *Articles impregnated with this pesticide, such as fibreboard plates, paper strips, cotton-wool balls, sheets of plastics material, in hermetically closed wrappings, are not subject to the provisions of ADR.*

[i]   *Mixtures of solids which are not subject to the provisions of ADR and of toxic liquids may be carried under UN No. 3243 without first applying the classification criteria of Class 6.1, provided there is no free liquid visible at the time the substance is loaded or at the time the packaging, container or transport unit is closed. Each packaging shall correspond to a design type that has passed a leakproofness test at the packing group II level. This entry shall not be used for solids containing a packing group I liquid.*

[j]   *Highly toxic or toxic, flammable liquids having a flash-point below 23 °C excluding substances which are highly toxic on inhalation, i.e. UN Nos. 1051, 1092, 1098, 1143, 1163, 1182, 1185, 1238, 1239, 1244, 1251, 1259, 1613, 1614, 1695, 1994, 2334, 2382, 2407, 2438, 2480, 2482, 2484, 2485, 2606, 2929, 3279 and 3294 are substances of Class 3.*

[k]   *Flammable liquids, slightly toxic, with the exception of substances and preparations used as pesticides, having a flash-point between 23 °C and 60 °C inclusive, are substances of Class 3.*

Toxic substances <u>with</u> subsidiary risk(s) (cont'd)

Flammable TF *(cont'd)*			2991	CARBAMATE PESTICIDE, LIQUID, TOXIC, FLAMMABLE
			2993	ARSENICAL PESTICIDE, LIQUID, TOXIC, FLAMMABLE
			2995	ORGANOCHLORINE PESTICIDE, LIQUID, TOXIC, FLAMMABLE
			2997	TRIAZINE PESTICIDE, LIQUID, TOXIC, FLAMMABLE
			3005	THIOCARBAMATE PESTICIDE, LIQUID, TOXIC, FLAMMABLE
			3009	COPPER BASED PESTICIDE, LIQUID, TOXIC, FLAMMABLE
	pesticides, liquid **TF2**		3011	MERCURY BASED PESTICIDE, LIQUID, TOXIC, FLAMMABLE
			3013	SUBSTITUTED NITROPHENOL PESTICIDE, LIQUID, TOXIC, FLAMMABLE
	(flash-point not less than 23 °C)		3015	BIPYRIDILIUM PESTICIDE, LIQUID, TOXIC, FLAMMABLE
			3017	ORGANOPHOSPHORUS PESTICIDE, LIQUID, TOXIC, FLAMMABLE
			3019	ORGANOTIN PESTICIDE, LIQUID, TOXIC, FLAMMABLE
			3025	COUMARIN DERIVATIVE PESTICIDE, LIQUID, TOXIC, FLAMMABLE
			3347	PHENOXYACETIC ACID DERIVATIVE PESTICIDE, LIQUID, TOXIC, FLAMMABLE
			3351	PYRETHROID PESTICIDE, LIQUID, TOXIC, FLAMMABLE
			2903	PESTICIDE, LIQUID, TOXIC, FLAMMABLE, N.O.S.
	solid **TF3**		1700	TEAR GAS CANDLES
			2930	TOXIC SOLID, FLAMMABLE, ORGANIC, N.O.S.
Solid, self-heating [c] **TS**			3124	TOXIC SOLID, SELF-HEATING, N.O.S.
	liquid **TW1**		3385	TOXIC BY INHALATION LIQUID, WATER-REACTIVE, N.O.S. with an inhalation toxicity lower than or equal to 200 ml/m^3 and saturated vapour concentration greater than or equal to 500 LC$_{50}$
			3386	TOXIC BY INHALATION LIQUID, WATER-REACTIVE, N.O.S. with an inhalation toxicity lower than or equal to 1000 ml/m^3 and saturated vapour concentration greater than or equal to 10 LC$_{50}$
			3123	TOXIC LIQUID, WATER-REACTIVE, N.O.S.
Water-reactive [d] **TW**	**solid** [n] **TW2**		3125	TOXIC SOLID, WATER-REACTIVE, N.O.S.
	liquid **TO1**		3387	TOXIC BY INHALATION LIQUID, OXIDIZING, N.O.S. with an inhalation toxicity lower than or equal to 200 ml/m^3 and saturated vapour concentration greater than or equal to 500 LC$_{50}$
			3388	TOXIC BY INHALATION LIQUID, OXIDIZING, N.O.S. with an inhalation toxicity lower than or equal to 1000 ml/m^3 and saturated vapour concentration greater than or equal to 10 LC$_{50}$
			3122	TOXIC LIQUID, OXIDIZING, N.O.S.
Oxidizing [l] **TO**	**solid** **TO2**		3086	TOXIC SOLID, OXIDIZING, N.O.S.
	liquid **TC1**		3277	CHLOROFORMATES, TOXIC, CORROSIVE, N.O.S.
			3361	CHLOROSILANES, TOXIC, CORROSIVE, N.O.S.
	organic		3389	TOXIC BY INHALATION LIQUID, CORROSIVE, N.O.S. with an inhalation toxicity lower than or equal to 200 ml/m^3 and saturated vapour concentration greater than or equal to 500 LC$_{50}$
			3390	TOXIC BY INHALATION LIQUID, CORROSIVE, N.O.S. with an inhalation toxicity lower than or equal to 1000 ml/m^3 and saturated vapour concentration greater than or equal to 10 LC$_{50}$
Corrosive [m] **TC**			2927	TOXIC LIQUID, CORROSIVE, ORGANIC, N.O.S.
	solid **TC2**		2928	TOXIC SOLID, CORROSIVE, ORGANIC, N.O.S.

(cont'd on next page)

---

[c]   *Self-heating substances, slightly toxic and spontaneously combustible organometallic compounds, are substances of Class 4.2.*

[d]   *Water-reactive substances, slightly toxic, and water-reactive organometallic compounds, are substances of Class 4.3.*

[l]   *Oxidizing substances, slightly toxic, are substances of Class 5.1.*

[m]   *Substances slightly toxic and slightly corrosive, are substances of Class 8.*

[n]   *Metal phosphides assigned to UN Nos. 1360, 1397, 1432, 1714, 2011 and 2013 are substances of Class 4.3.*

2.2.61.3   *List of collective entries (cont'd)*

Toxic substances <u>with</u> subsidiary risk(s) (cont'd)

| | | | 3389 | TOXIC BY INHALATION LIQUID, CORROSIVE, N.O.S. with an inhalation toxicity lower than or equal to 200 ml/m³ and saturated vapour concentration greater than or equal to 500 LC_{50} |

(Structured representation of the diagram:)

Corrosive [m]
TC *(cont'd)*

inorganic

liquid — **TC3**

3389	TOXIC BY INHALATION LIQUID, CORROSIVE, N.O.S. with an inhalation toxicity lower than or equal to 200 ml/m³ and saturated vapour concentration greater than or equal to 500 LC_{50}
3390	TOXIC BY INHALATION LIQUID, CORROSIVE, N.O.S. with an inhalation toxicity lower than or equal to 1000 ml/m³ and saturated vapour concentration greater than or equal to 10 LC_{50}
3289	TOXIC LIQUID, CORROSIVE, INORGANIC, N.O.S.

solid — **TC4**

| 3290 | TOXIC SOLID, CORROSIVE, INORGANIC, N.O.S. |

Flammable, corrosive
TFC

2742	CHLOROFORMATES, TOXIC, CORROSIVE, FLAMMABLE, N.O.S.
3362	CHLOROSILANES, TOXIC, CORROSIVE, FLAMMABLE, N.O.S.
	(No other collective entry available; if need be, classification under a collective entry with a classification code to be determined according to the table of precedence of hazards in 2.1.3.10)

---

[m]   *Substances slightly toxic and slightly corrosive, are substances of Class 8.*

2.2.62   **Class 6.2**   **Infectious substances**

2.2.62.1   *Criteria*

2.2.62.1.1   The heading of Class 6.2 covers infectious substances. For the purposes of ADR, infectious substances are substances which are known or are reasonably expected to contain pathogens. Pathogens are defined as microorganisms (including bacteria, viruses, rickettsiae, parasites, fungi) and other agents such as prions, which can cause disease in humans or animals.

> *NOTE 1: Genetically modified microorganisms and organisms, biological products, diagnostic specimens and infected live animals shall be assigned to this Class if they meet the conditions for this class.*

> *NOTE 2: Toxins from plant, animal or bacterial sources which do not contain any infectious substances or organisms or which are not contained in them are substances of Class 6.1, UN Nos. 3172 or 3462.*

2.2.62.1.2   Substances of Class 6.2 are subdivided as follows:

    I1   Infectious substances affecting humans;

    I2   Infectious substances affecting animals only;

    I3   Clinical waste;

    I4   Biological substances.

Definitions

2.2.62.1.3   For the purposes of ADR,

"Biological products" are those products derived from living organisms which are manufactured and distributed in accordance with the requirements of appropriate national authorities, which may have special licensing requirements, and are used either for prevention, treatment, or diagnosis of disease in humans or animals, or for development, experimental or investigational purposes related thereto. They include, but are not limited to, finished or unfinished products such as vaccines;

"Cultures" are the result of a process by which pathogens are intentionally propagated. This definition does not include human or animal patient specimens as defined in this paragraph;

"Genetically modified microorganisms and organisms" are microorganisms and organisms in which genetic material has been purposely altered through genetic engineering in a way that does not occur naturally;

"Medical or clinical wastes" are wastes derived from the medical treatment of animals or humans or from bio-research;

"Patient specimens" are human or animal materials, collected directly from humans or animals, including, but not limited to, excreta, secreta, blood and its components, tissue and tissue fluid swabs, and body parts being carried for purposes such as research, diagnosis, investigational activities, disease treatment and prevention.

Classification

2.2.62.1.4   Infectious substances shall be classified in Class 6.2 and assigned to UN Nos. 2814, 2900, 3291 or 3373, as appropriate.

Infectious substances are divided into the following categories:

2.2.62.1.4.1   <u>Category A</u>: An infectious substance which is carried in a form that, when exposure to it occurs, is capable of causing permanent disability, life-threatening or fatal disease in otherwise healthy humans or animals. Indicative examples of substances that meet these criteria are given in the table in this paragraph.

NOTE: An exposure occurs when an infectious substance is released outside of the protective packaging, resulting in physical contact with humans or animals.

(a)   Infectious substances meeting these criteria which cause disease in humans or both in humans and animals shall be assigned to UN No. 2814. Infectious substances which cause disease only in animals shall be assigned to UN No. 2900;

(b)   Assignment to UN No. 2814 or UN No. 2900 shall be based on the known medical history and symptoms of the source human or animal, endemic local conditions, or professional judgement concerning individual circumstances of the source human or animal.

NOTE 1:   The proper shipping name for UN No. 2814 is "INFECTIOUS SUBSTANCE, AFFECTING HUMANS".   The proper shipping name for UN No. 2900 is "INFECTIOUS SUBSTANCE, AFFECTING ANIMALS only".

NOTE 2:   The following table is not exhaustive. Infectious substances, including new or emerging pathogens, which do not appear in the table but which meet the same criteria shall be assigned to Category A.   In addition, if there is doubt as to whether or not a substance meets the criteria it shall be included in Category A.

NOTE 3:   In the following table, the microorganisms written in italics are bacteria, mycoplasmas, rickettsia or fungi.

INDICATIVE EXAMPLES OF INFECTIOUS SUBSTANCES INCLUDED IN CATEGORY A IN ANY FORM UNLESS OTHERWISE INDICATED (2.2.62.1.4.1)	
UN Number and name	**Microorganism**
UN No. 2814 Infectious substances affecting humans	*Bacillus anthracis (cultures only)*
	Brucella abortus (cultures only)
	Brucella melitensis (cultures only)
	Brucella suis (cultures only)
	Burkholderia mallei - Pseudomonas mallei – Glanders *(cultures only)*
	Burkholderia pseudomallei – Pseudomonas pseudomallei (cultures only)
	Chlamydia psittaci - avian strains (cultures only)
	Clostridium botulinum (cultures only)
	Coccidioides immitis (cultures only)
	Coxiella burnetii (cultures only)
	Crimean-Congo haemorrhagic fever virus
	Dengue virus (cultures only)
	Eastern equine encephalitis virus (cultures only)
	Escherichia coli, verotoxigenic (cultures only) [a]
	Ebola virus
	Flexal virus
	Francisella tularensis (cultures only)
	Guanarito virus
	Hantaan virus
	Hantavirus causing haemorrhagic fever with renal syndrome
	Hendra virus
	Hepatitis B virus (cultures only)
	Herpes B virus (cultures only)
	Human immunodeficiency virus (cultures only)
	Highly pathogenic avian influenza virus (cultures only)
	Japanese Encephalitis virus (cultures only)
	Junin virus
	Kyasanur Forest disease virus
	Lassa virus
	Machupo virus
	Marburg virus
	Monkeypox virus
	Mycobacterium tuberculosis (cultures only) [a]
	Nipah virus
	Omsk haemorrhagic fever virus
	Poliovirus (cultures only)
	Rabies virus (cultures only)
	Rickettsia prowazekii (cultures only)
	Rickettsia rickettsii (cultures only)
	Rift Valley fever virus (cultures only)
	Russian spring-summer encephalitis virus (cultures only)
	Sabia virus
	Shigella dysenteriae type 1 (cultures only) [a]
	Tick-borne encephalitis virus (cultures only)
	Variola virus
	Venezuelan equine encephalitis virus (cultures only)
	West Nile virus (cultures only)
	Yellow fever virus (cultures only)
	Yersinia pestis (cultures only)

[a]   *Nevertheless, when the cultures are intended for diagnostic or clinical purposes, they may be classified as infectious substances of Category B.*

INDICATIVE EXAMPLES OF INFECTIOUS SUBSTANCES INCLUDED IN CATEGORY A IN ANY FORM UNLESS OTHERWISE INDICATED (2.2.62.1.4.1)	
UN Number and name	**Microorganism**
UN No. 2900 Infectious substances affecting animals only	African swine fever virus (cultures only) Avian paramyxovirus Type 1 - Velogenic Newcastle disease virus (cultures only) Classical swine fever virus (cultures only) Foot and mouth disease virus (cultures only) Lumpy skin disease virus (cultures only) *Mycoplasma mycoides* - Contagious bovine pleuropneumonia (cultures only) Peste des petits ruminants virus (cultures only) Rinderpest virus (cultures only) Sheep-pox virus (cultures only) Goatpox virus (cultures only) Swine vesicular disease virus (cultures only) Vesicular stomatitis virus (cultures only)

2.2.62.1.4.2   Category B: An infectious substance which does not meet the criteria for inclusion in Category A. Infectious substances in Category B shall be assigned to UN No. 3373.

> *NOTE: The proper shipping name of UN No. 3373 is "BIOLOGICAL SUBSTANCE, CATEGORY B ".*

2.2.62.1.5   *Exemptions*

2.2.62.1.5.1   Substances which do not contain infectious substances or substances which are unlikely to cause disease in humans or animals are not subject to the provisions of ADR unless they meet the criteria for inclusion in another class.

2.2.62.1.5.2   Substances containing microorganisms which are non-pathogenic to humans or animals are not subject to ADR unless they meet the criteria for inclusion in another class.

2.2.62.1.5.3   Substances in a form that any present pathogens have been neutralized or inactivated such that they no longer pose a health risk are not subject to ADR unless they meet the criteria for inclusion in another class.

2.2.62.1.5.4   Substances where the concentration of pathogens is at a level naturally encountered (including foodstuff and water samples) and which are not considered to pose a significant risk of infection are not subject to ADR unless they meet the criteria for inclusion in another class.

2.2.62.1.5.5   Dried blood spots, collected by applying a drop of blood onto absorbent material, or faecal occult blood screening tests and blood or blood components which have been collected for the purposes of transfusion or for the preparation of blood products to be used for transfusion or transplantation and any tissues or organs intended for use in transplantation are not subject to the provisions of ADR.

2.2.62.1.5.6   Human or animal specimens for which there is minimal likelihood that pathogens are present are not subject to ADR if the specimen is carried in a packaging which will prevent any leakage and which is marked with the words "Exempt human specimen" or "Exempt animal specimen", as appropriate.

The packaging is deemed to comply with the above requirements if it meets the following conditions:

(a)   The packaging consists of three components:

(i)   a leak-proof primary receptacle(s);

(ii)   a leak-proof secondary packaging; and

(iii)   an outer packaging of adequate strength for its capacity, mass and intended use, and with at least one surface having minimum dimensions of 100 mm × 100 mm;

(b)   For liquids, absorbent material in sufficient quantity to absorb the entire contents is placed between the primary receptacle(s) and the secondary packaging so that, during carriage, any release or leak of a liquid substance will not reach the outer packaging and will not compromise the integrity of the cushioning material;

(c)   When multiple fragile primary receptacles are placed in a single secondary packaging, they are either individually wrapped or separated to prevent contact between them.

NOTE 1: An element of professional judgment is required to determine if a substance is exempt under this paragraph. That judgment should be based on the known medical history, symptoms and individual circumstances of the source, human or animal, and endemic local conditions. Examples of specimens which may be carried under this paragraph include the blood or urine tests to monitor cholesterol levels, blood glucose levels, hormone levels, or prostate specific antibodies (PSA); those required to monitor organ function such as heart, liver or kidney function for humans or animals with non-infectious diseases, or for therapeutic drug monitoring; those conducted for insurance or employment purposes and are intended to determine the presence of drugs or alcohol; pregnancy test; biopsies to detect cancer; and antibody detection in humans or animals in the absence of any concern for infection (e.g. evaluation of vaccine induced immunity, diagnosis of autoimmune disease, etc.).

NOTE 2: For air transport, packagings for specimens exempted under this paragraph shall meet the conditions in (a) to (c).

2.2.62.1.6 to 2.2.62.1.8   *(Reserved)*

2.2.62.1.9   *Biological products*

For the purposes of ADR, biological products are divided into the following groups:

(a)   those which are manufactured and packaged in accordance with the requirements of appropriate national authorities and carried for the purposes of final packaging or distribution, and use for personal health care by medical professionals or individuals. Substances in this group are not subject to the provisions of ADR;

(b)   those which do not fall under paragraph (a) and are known or reasonably believed to contain infectious substances and which meet the criteria for inclusion in Category A or Category B. Substances in this group shall be assigned to UN Nos. 2814, 2900 or 3373, as appropriate.

NOTE: Some licensed biological products may present a biohazard only in certain parts of the world. In that case, competent authorities may require these biological products to be in compliance with local requirements for infectious substances or may impose other restrictions.

2.2.62.1.10   *Genetically modified microorganisms and organisms*

Genetically modified microorganisms not meeting the definition of infectious substance shall be classified according to section 2.2.9.

2.2.62.1.11   *Medical or clinical wastes*

2.2.62.1.11.1   Medical or clinical wastes containing Category A infectious substances shall be assigned to UN No. 2814 or UN No. 2900 as appropriate.   Medical or clinical wastes containing infectious substances in Category B shall be assigned to UN No. 3291.

NOTE: Medical or clinical wastes assigned to number 18 01 03 (Wastes from human or animal health care and/or related research – wastes from natal care, diagnosis, treatment or prevention of disease in humans – wastes whose collection and disposal is subject to special requirements in order to prevent infection) or 18 02 02 (Wastes from human or animal health care and/or related research – wastes from research, diagnosis, treatment or prevention of disease involving animals – wastes whose collection and disposal is subject to special requirements in order to prevent infection) according to the list of wastes annexed to the Commission Decision 2000/532/EC [5] as amended, shall be classified according to the provisions set out in this paragraph, based on the medical or veterinary diagnosis concerning the patient or the animal.

2.2.62.1.11.2   Medical or clinical wastes which are reasonably believed to have a low probability of containing infectious substances shall be assigned to UN No. 3291. For the assignment, international, regional or national waste catalogues may be taken into account.

NOTE 1: The proper shipping name for UN No. 3291 is "CLINICAL WASTE, UNSPECIFIED, N.O.S." or "(BIO) MEDICAL WASTE, N.O.S". or "REGULATED MEDICAL WASTE, N.O.S.".

NOTE 2: Notwithstanding the classification criteria set out above, medical or clinical wastes assigned to number 18 01 04 (Wastes from human or animal health care and/or related research – wastes from natal care, diagnosis, treatment or prevention of disease in humans – wastes whose collection and disposal is not subject to special requirements in order to prevent infection) or 18 02 03 (Wastes from human or animal health care and/or related research – wastes from research, diagnosis, treatment or prevention of disease involving animals – wastes whose collection and disposal is not subject to special requirements in order to prevent infection) according to the list of wastes annexed to the Commission Decision 2000/532/EC [5] as amended, are not subject to the provisions of ADR.

2.2.62.1.11.3   Decontaminated medical or clinical wastes which previously contained infectious substances are not subject to the provisions of ADR unless they meet the criteria for inclusion in another class.

2.2.62.1.11.4   Medical or clinical wastes assigned to UN No. 3291 are assigned to packing group II.

---

[5]   *Commission Decision 2000/532/EC of 3 May 2000 replacing Decision 94/3/EC establishing a list of wastes pursuant to Article 1(a) of Council Directive 75/442/EEC on waste (replaced by the Directive 2006/12/EC of the European Parliament and of the Council (Official Journal of the European Communities No. L 114 of 27 April 2006, page 9)) and Council Decision 94/904/EC establishing a list of hazardous waste pursuant to Article 1(4) of Council Directive 91/689/EEC on hazardous waste (Official Journal of the European Communities No. L 226 of 6 September 2000, page 3).*

2.2.62.1.12   *Infected animals*

2.2.62.1.12.1   Unless an infectious substance cannot be consigned by any other means, live animals shall not be used to consign such a substance. A live animal which has been intentionally infected and is known or suspected to contain an infectious substance shall only be carried under terms and conditions approved by the competent authority [6].

2.2.62.1.12.2   Animal material affected by pathogens of Category A or by pathogens which would be assigned to Category A in cultures only, shall be assigned to UN 2814 or UN 2900 as appropriate. Animal material affected by pathogens of Category B, other than those which would be assigned to Category A if they were in cultures, shall be assigned to UN 3373.

2.2.62.2   *Substances not accepted for carriage*

Live vertebrate or invertebrate animals shall not be used to carry an infectious agent unless the agent cannot be carried by other means or unless this carriage has been approved by the competent authority (see 2.2.62.1.12.1).

2.2.62.3   *List of collective entries*

Effects on humans	I1	2814	INFECTIOUS SUBSTANCE, AFFECTING HUMANS
Effects on animals only	I2	2900	INFECTIOUS SUBSTANCE, AFFECTING ANIMALS only
Clinical waste	I3	3291 3291 3291	CLINICAL WASTE, UNSPECIFIED, N.O.S. or (BIO) MEDICAL WASTE, N.O.S. or REGULATED MEDICAL WASTE, N.O.S.
Biological substances	I4	3373	BIOLOGICAL SUBSTANCE, CATEGORY B

---

[6]   *Regulations governing the carriage of live animals are contained in, e.g. Directive 91/628/EEC of 19 November 1991 on the protection of animals during transport (Official Journal of the European Communities No. L 340 of 11.12.1991, p.17) and in the Recommendations of the Council of Europe (Ministerial Committee) on the carriage of certain animal species.*

2.2.7 **Class 7** **Radioactive material**

2.2.7.1 *Definitions*

2.2.7.1.1 *Radioactive material* means any material containing radionuclides where both the activity concentration and the total activity in the consignment exceed the values specified in 2.2.7.2.2.1 to 2.2.7.2.2.6.

2.2.7.1.2 *Contamination*

Contamination means the presence of a radioactive substance on a surface in quantities in excess of 0.4 Bq/cm^2 for beta and gamma emitters and low toxicity alpha emitters, or 0.04 Bq/cm^2 for all other alpha emitters.

Non-fixed contamination means contamination that can be removed from a surface during routine conditions of carriage.

Fixed contamination means contamination other than non-fixed contamination.

2.2.7.1.3 *Definitions of specific terms*

A_1 and A_2

A_1 means the activity value of special form radioactive material which is listed in the Table in 2.2.7.2.2.1 or derived in 2.2.7.2.2.2 and is used to determine the activity limits for the requirements of ADR.

A_2 means the activity value of radioactive material, other than special form radioactive material, which is listed in the Table in 2.2.7.2.2.1 or derived in 2.2.7.2.2.2 and is used to determine the activity limits for the requirements of ADR.

Fissile material means uranium-233, uranium-235, plutonium-239, plutonium-241, or any combination of these radionuclides. Excepted from this definition is:

(a) Natural uranium or depleted uranium which is unirradiated; and

(b) Natural uranium or depleted uranium which has been irradiated in thermal reactors only.

Low dispersible radioactive material means either a solid radioactive material or a solid radioactive material in a sealed capsule, that has limited dispersibility and is not in powder form.

Low specific activity (LSA) material means radioactive material which by its nature has a limited specific activity, or radioactive material for which limits of estimated average specific activity apply. External shielding materials surrounding the LSA material shall not be considered in determining the estimated average specific activity.

Low toxicity alpha emitters are: natural uranium; depleted uranium; natural thorium; uranium-235 or uranium-238; thorium-232; thorium-228 and thorium-230 when contained in ores or physical and chemical concentrates; or alpha emitters with a half-life of less than 10 days.

Special form radioactive material means either:

(a)   An indispersible solid radioactive material; or

(b)   A sealed capsule containing radioactive material.

Specific activity of a radionuclide means the activity per unit mass of that nuclide. The specific activity of a material shall mean the activity per unit mass of the material in which the radionuclides are essentially uniformly distributed.

Surface contaminated object (SCO) means a solid object which is not itself radioactive but which has radioactive material distributed on its surfaces.

Unirradiated thorium means thorium containing not more than 10^{-7} g of uranium-233 per gram of thorium-232.

Unirradiated uranium means uranium containing not more than 2×10^3 Bq of plutonium per gram of uranium-235, not more than 9×10^6 Bq of fission products per gram of uranium-235 and not more than 5×10^{-3} g of uranium-236 per gram of uranium-235.

Uranium - natural, depleted, enriched means the following:

> *Natural uranium* means uranium (which may be chemically separated) containing the naturally occurring distribution of uranium isotopes (approximately 99.28% uranium-238, and 0.72% uranium-235 by mass).

> *Depleted uranium* means uranium containing a lesser mass percentage of uranium-235 than in natural uranium.

> *Enriched uranium* means uranium containing a greater mass percentage of uranium-235 than 0.72%.

> In all cases, a very small mass percentage of uranium-234 is present.

2.2.7.2   *Classification*

2.2.7.2.1   *General provisions*

2.2.7.2.1.1   Radioactive material shall be assigned to one of the UN number specified in Table 2.2.7.2.1.1 depending on the activity level of the radionuclides contained in a package, the fissile or non-fissile properties of these radionuclides, the type of package to be presented for carriage, and the nature or form of the contents of the package, or special arrangements governing the carriage operation, in accordance with the provisions laid down in 2.2.7.2.2 to 2.2.7.2.5.

Table 2.2.7.2.1.1   Assignment of UN numbers

Excepted packages (1.7.1.5)	
UN 2908	RADIOACTIVE MATERIAL, EXCEPTED PACKAGE - EMPTY PACKAGING
UN 2909	RADIOACTIVE MATERIAL, EXCEPTED PACKAGE - ARTICLES MANUFACTURED FROM NATURAL URANIUM or DEPLETED URANIUM or NATURAL THORIUM
UN 2910	RADIOACTIVE MATERIAL, EXCEPTED PACKAGE - LIMITED QUANTITY OF MATERIAL
UN 2911	RADIOACTIVE MATERIAL, EXCEPTED PACKAGE - INSTRUMENTS or ARTICLES
Low specific activity radioactive material (2.2.7.2.3.1)	
UN 2912	RADIOACTIVE MATERIAL, LOW SPECIFIC ACTIVITY (LSA-I), non-fissile or fissile-excepted
UN 3321	RADIOACTIVE MATERIAL, LOW SPECIFIC ACTIVITY (LSA-II), non fissile or fissile-excepted
UN 3322	RADIOACTIVE MATERIAL, LOW SPECIFIC ACTIVITY (LSA-III), non fissile or fissile-excepted
UN 3324	RADIOACTIVE MATERIAL, LOW SPECIFIC ACTIVITY (LSA-II), FISSILE
UN 3325	RADIOACTIVE MATERIAL, LOW SPECIFIC ACTIVITY, (LSA-III), FISSILE
Surface contaminated objects (2.2.7.2.3.2)	
UN 2913	RADIOACTIVE MATERIAL, SURFACE CONTAMINATED OBJECTS (SCO-I or SCO-II), non-fissile or fissile-excepted
UN 3326	RADIOACTIVE MATERIAL, SURFACE CONTAMINATED OBJECTS (SCO-I or SCO-II), FISSILE
Type A packages (2.2.7.2.4.4)	
UN 2915	RADIOACTIVE MATERIAL, TYPE A PACKAGE, non-special form, non-fissile or fissile-excepted
UN 3327	RADIOACTIVE MATERIAL, TYPE A PACKAGE, FISSILE, non-special form
UN 3332	RADIOACTIVE MATERIAL, TYPE A PACKAGE, SPECIAL FORM, non fissile or fissile-excepted
UN 3333	RADIOACTIVE MATERIAL, TYPE A PACKAGE, SPECIAL FORM, FISSILE
Type B(U) packages (2.2.7.2.4.6)	
UN 2916	RADIOACTIVE MATERIAL, TYPE B(U) PACKAGE, non-fissile or fissile-excepted
UN 3328	RADIOACTIVE MATERIAL, TYPE B(U) PACKAGE, FISSILE
Type B(M) packages (2.2.7.2.4.6)	
UN 2917	RADIOACTIVE MATERIAL, TYPE B(M) PACKAGE, non-fissile or fissile-excepted
UN 3329	RADIOACTIVE MATERIAL, TYPE B(M) PACKAGE, FISSILE
Type C packages (2.2.7.2.4.6)	
UN 3323	RADIOACTIVE MATERIAL, TYPE C PACKAGE, non fissile or fissile-excepted
UN 3330	RADIOACTIVE MATERIAL, TYPE C PACKAGE, FISSILE
Special arrangement (2.2.7.2.5)	
UN 2919	RADIOACTIVE MATERIAL, TRANSPORTED UNDER SPECIAL ARRANGEMENT, non-fissile or fissile-excepted
UN 3331	RADIOACTIVE MATERIAL, TRANSPORTED UNDER SPECIAL ARRANGEMENT, FISSILE
Uranium hexafluoride (2.2.7.2.4.5)	
UN 2977	RADIOACTIVE MATERIAL, URANIUM HEXAFLUORIDE, FISSILE
UN 2978	RADIOACTIVE MATERIAL, URANIUM HEXAFLUORIDE, non-fissile or fissile-excepted

2.2.7.2.2   *Determination of activity level*

2.2.7.2.2.1   The following basic values for individual radionuclides are given in Table 2.2.7.2.2.1:

(a) A_1 and A_2 in TBq;

(b)   Activity concentration for exempt material in Bq/g; and

(c)   Activity limits for exempt consignments in Bq.

Table 2.2.7.2.2.1: Basic radionuclides values for individual radionuclides

Radionuclide (atomic number)	A_1 (TBq)	A_2 (TBq)	Activity concentration for exempt material (Bq/g)	Activity limit for an exempt consignment (Bq)
Actinium (89)				
Ac-225 (a)	8×10^{-1}	6×10^{-3}	1×10^{1}	1×10^{4}
Ac-227 (a)	9×10^{-1}	9×10^{-5}	1×10^{-1}	1×10^{3}
Ac-228	6×10^{-1}	5×10^{-1}	1×10^{1}	1×10^{6}
Silver (47)				
Ag-105	2×10^{0}	2×10^{0}	1×10^{2}	1×10^{6}
Ag-108m (a)	7×10^{-1}	7×10^{-1}	1×10^{1} (b)	1×10^{6} (b)
Ag-110m (a)	4×10^{-1}	4×10^{-1}	1×10^{1}	1×10^{6}
Ag-111	2×10^{0}	6×10^{-1}	1×10^{3}	1×10^{6}
Aluminium (13)				
Al-26	1×10^{-1}	1×10^{-1}	1×10^{1}	1×10^{5}
Americium (95)				
Am-241	1×10^{1}	1×10^{-3}	1×10^{0}	1×10^{4}
Am-242m (a)	1×10^{1}	1×10^{-3}	1×10^{0} (b)	1×10^{4} (b)
Am-243 (a)	5×10^{0}	1×10^{-3}	1×10^{0} (b)	1×10^{3} (b)
Argon (18)				
Ar-37	4×10^{1}	4×10^{1}	1×10^{6}	1×10^{8}
Ar-39	4×10^{1}	2×10^{1}	1×10^{7}	1×10^{4}
Ar-41	3×10^{-1}	3×10^{-1}	1×10^{2}	1×10^{9}
Arsenic (33)				
As-72	3×10^{-1}	3×10^{-1}	1×10^{1}	1×10^{5}
As-73	4×10^{1}	4×10^{1}	1×10^{3}	1×10^{7}
As-74	1×10^{0}	9×10^{-1}	1×10^{1}	1×10^{6}

Radionuclide (atomic number)	A_1 (TBq)	A_2 (TBq)	Activity concentration for exempt material (Bq/g)	Activity limit for an exempt consignment (Bq)
As-76	3×10^{-1}	3×10^{-1}	1×10^2	1×10^5
As-77	2×10^1	7×10^{-1}	1×10^3	1×10^6
Astatine (85)				
At-211 (a)	2×10^1	5×10^{-1}	1×10^3	1×10^7
Gold (79)				
Au-193	7×10^0	2×10^0	1×10^2	1×10^7
Au-194	1×10^0	1×10^0	1×10^1	1×10^6
Au-195	1×10^1	6×10^0	1×10^2	1×10^7
Au-198	1×10^0	6×10^{-1}	1×10^2	1×10^6
Au-199	1×10^1	6×10^{-1}	1×10^2	1×10^6
Barium (56)				
Ba-131 (a)	2×10^0	2×10^0	1×10^2	1×10^6
Ba-133	3×10^0	3×10^0	1×10^2	1×10^6
Ba-133m	2×10^1	6×10^{-1}	1×10^2	1×10^6
Ba-140 (a)	5×10^{-1}	3×10^{-1}	1×10^1 (b)	1×10^5 (b)
Beryllium (4)				
Be-7	2×10^1	2×10^1	1×10^3	1×10^7
Be-10	4×10^1	6×10^{-1}	1×10^4	1×10^6
Bismuth (83)				
Bi-205	7×10^{-1}	7×10^{-1}	1×10^1	1×10^6
Bi-206	3×10^{-1}	3×10^{-1}	1×10^1	1×10^5
Bi-207	7×10^{-1}	7×10^{-1}	1×10^1	1×10^6
Bi-210	1×10^0	6×10^{-1}	1×10^3	1×10^6
Bi-210m (a)	6×10^{-1}	2×10^{-2}	1×10^1	1×10^5
Bi-212 (a)	7×10^{-1}	6×10^{-1}	1×10^1 (b)	1×10^5 (b)
Berkelium (97)				
Bk-247	8×10^0	8×10^{-4}	1×10^0	1×10^4
Bk-249 (a)	4×10^1	3×10^{-1}	1×10^3	1×10^6
Bromine (35)				
Br-76	4×10^{-1}	4×10^{-1}	1×10^1	1×10^5
Br-77	3×10^0	3×10^0	1×10^2	1×10^6

Radionuclide (atomic number)	A_1 (TBq)	A_2 (TBq)	Activity concentration for exempt material (Bq/g)	Activity limit for an exempt consignment (Bq)
Br-82	4×10^{-1}	4×10^{-1}	1×10^1	1×10^6
Carbon (6)				
C-11	1×10^0	6×10^{-1}	1×10^1	1×10^6
C-14	4×10^1	3×10^0	1×10^4	1×10^7
Calcium (20)				
Ca-41	Unlimited	Unlimited	1×10^5	1×10^7
Ca-45	4×10^1	1×10^0	1×10^4	1×10^7
Ca-47 (a)	3×10^0	3×10^{-1}	1×10^1	1×10^6
Cadmium (48)				
Cd-109	3×10^1	2×10^0	1×10^4	1×10^6
Cd-113m	4×10^1	5×10^{-1}	1×10^3	1×10^6
Cd-115 (a)	3×10^0	4×10^{-1}	1×10^2	1×10^6
Cd-115m	5×10^{-1}	5×10^{-1}	1×10^3	1×10^6
Cerium (58)				
Ce-139	7×10^0	2×10^0	1×10^2	1×10^6
Ce-141	2×10^1	6×10^{-1}	1×10^2	1×10^7
Ce-143	9×10^{-1}	6×10^{-1}	1×10^2	1×10^6
Ce-144 (a)	2×10^{-1}	2×10^{-1}	1×10^2 (b)	1×10^5 (b)
Californium (98)				
Cf-248	4×10^1	6×10^{-3}	1×10^1	1×10^4
Cf-249	3×10^0	8×10^{-4}	1×10^0	1×10^3
Cf-250	2×10^1	2×10^{-3}	1×10^1	1×10^4
Cf-251	7×10^0	7×10^{-4}	1×10^0	1×10^3
Cf-252	1×10^{-1}	3×10^{-3}	1×10^1	1×10^4
Cf-253 (a)	4×10^1	4×10^{-2}	1×10^2	1×10^5
Cf-254	1×10^{-3}	1×10^{-3}	1×10^0	1×10^3
Chlorine (17)				
Cl-36	1×10^1	6×10^{-1}	1×10^4	1×10^6
Cl-38	2×10^{-1}	2×10^{-1}	1×10^1	1×10^5

Radionuclide (atomic number)	A_1 (TBq)	A_2 (TBq)	Activity concentration for exempt material (Bq/g)	Activity limit for an exempt consignment (Bq)
Curium (96)				
Cm-240	4×10^1	2×10^{-2}	1×10^2	1×10^5
Cm-241	2×10^0	1×10^0	1×10^2	1×10^6
Cm-242	4×10^1	1×10^{-2}	1×10^2	1×10^5
Cm-243	9×10^0	1×10^{-3}	1×10^0	1×10^4
Cm-244	2×10^1	2×10^{-3}	1×10^1	1×10^4
Cm-245	9×10^0	9×10^{-4}	1×10^0	1×10^3
Cm-246	9×10^0	9×10^{-4}	1×10^0	1×10^3
Cm-247 (a)	3×10^0	1×10^{-3}	1×10^0	1×10^4
Cm-248	2×10^{-2}	3×10^{-4}	1×10^0	1×10^3
Cobalt (27)				
Co-55	5×10^{-1}	5×10^{-1}	1×10^1	1×10^6
Co-56	3×10^{-1}	3×10^{-1}	1×10^1	1×10^5
Co-57	1×10^1	1×10^1	1×10^2	1×10^6
Co-58	1×10^0	1×10^0	1×10^1	1×10^6
Co-58m	4×10^1	4×10^1	1×10^4	1×10^7
Co-60	4×10^{-1}	4×10^{-1}	1×10^1	1×10^5
Chromium (24)				
Cr-51	3×10^1	3×10^1	1×10^3	1×10^7
Caesium (55)				
Cs-129	4×10^0	4×10^0	1×10^2	1×10^5
Cs-131	3×10^1	3×10^1	1×10^3	1×10^6
Cs-132	1×10^0	1×10^0	1×10^1	1×10^5
Cs-134	7×10^{-1}	7×10^{-1}	1×10^1	1×10^4
Cs-134m	4×10^1	6×10^{-1}	1×10^3	1×10^5
Cs-135	4×10^1	1×10^0	1×10^4	1×10^7
Cs-136	5×10^{-1}	5×10^{-1}	1×10^1	1×10^5
Cs-137 (a)	2×10^0	6×10^{-1}	1×10^1 (b)	1×10^4 (b)

Radionuclide (atomic number)	A_1 (TBq)	A_2 (TBq)	Activity concentration for exempt material (Bq/g)	Activity limit for an exempt consignment (Bq)
Copper (29)				
Cu-64	6×10^0	1×10^0	1×10^2	1×10^6
Cu-67	1×10^1	7×10^{-1}	1×10^2	1×10^6
Dysprosium (66)				
Dy-159	2×10^1	2×10^1	1×10^3	1×10^7
Dy-165	9×10^{-1}	6×10^{-1}	1×10^3	1×10^6
Dy-166 (a)	9×10^{-1}	3×10^{-1}	1×10^3	1×10^6
Erbium (68)				
Er-169	4×10^1	1×10^0	1×10^4	1×10^7
Er-171	8×10^{-1}	5×10^{-1}	1×10^2	1×10^6
Europium (63)				
Eu-147	2×10^0	2×10^0	1×10^2	1×10^6
Eu-148	5×10^{-1}	5×10^{-1}	1×10^1	1×10^6
Eu-149	2×10^1	2×10^1	1×10^2	1×10^7
Eu-150(short lived)	2×10^0	7×10^{-1}	1×10^3	1×10^6
Eu-150(long lived)	7×10^{-1}	7×10^{-1}	1×10^1	1×10^6
Eu-152	1×10^0	1×10^0	1×10^1	1×10^6
Eu-152m	8×10^{-1}	8×10^{-1}	1×10^2	1×10^6
Eu-154	9×10^{-1}	6×10^{-1}	1×10^1	1×10^6
Eu-155	2×10^1	3×10^0	1×10^2	1×10^7
Eu-156	7×10^{-1}	7×10^{-1}	1×10^1	1×10^6
Fluorine (9)				
F-18	1×10^0	6×10^{-1}	1×10^1	1×10^6
Iron (26)				
Fe-52 (a)	3×10^{-1}	3×10^{-1}	1×10^1	1×10^6
Fe-55	4×10^1	4×10^1	1×10^4	1×10^6
Fe-59	9×10^{-1}	9×10^{-1}	1×10^1	1×10^6
Fe-60 (a)	4×10^1	2×10^{-1}	1×10^2	1×10^5
Gallium (31)				
Ga-67	7×10^0	3×10^0	1×10^2	1×10^6
Ga-68	5×10^{-1}	5×10^{-1}	1×10^1	1×10^5

Radionuclide (atomic number)	A_1 (TBq)	A_2 (TBq)	Activity concentration for exempt material (Bq/g)	Activity limit for an exempt consignment (Bq)
Ga-72	4×10^{-1}	4×10^{-1}	1×10^1	1×10^5
Gadolinium (64)				
Gd-146 (a)	5×10^{-1}	5×10^{-1}	1×10^1	1×10^6
Gd-148	2×10^1	2×10^{-3}	1×10^1	1×10^4
Gd-153	1×10^1	9×10^0	1×10^2	1×10^7
Gd-159	3×10^0	6×10^{-1}	1×10^3	1×10^6
Germanium (32)				
Ge-68 (a)	5×10^{-1}	5×10^{-1}	1×10^1	1×10^5
Ge-71	4×10^1	4×10^1	1×10^4	1×10^8
Ge-77	3×10^{-1}	3×10^{-1}	1×10^1	1×10^5
Hafnium (72)				
Hf-172 (a)	6×10^{-1}	6×10^{-1}	1×10^1	1×10^6
Hf-175	3×10^0	3×10^0	1×10^2	1×10^6
Hf-181	2×10^0	5×10^{-1}	1×10^1	1×10^6
Hf-182	Unlimited	Unlimited	1×10^2	1×10^6
Mercury (80)				
Hg-194 (a)	1×10^0	1×10^0	1×10^1	1×10^6
Hg-195m (a)	3×10^0	7×10^{-1}	1×10^2	1×10^6
Hg-197	2×10^1	1×10^1	1×10^2	1×10^7
Hg-197m	1×10^1	4×10^{-1}	1×10^2	1×10^6
Hg-203	5×10^0	1×10^0	1×10^2	1×10^5
Holmium (67)				
Ho-166	4×10^{-1}	4×10^{-1}	1×10^3	1×10^5
Ho-166m	6×10^{-1}	5×10^{-1}	1×10^1	1×10^6
Iodine (53)				
I-123	6×10^0	3×10^0	1×10^2	1×10^7
I-124	1×10^0	1×10^0	1×10^1	1×10^6
I-125	2×10^1	3×10^0	1×10^3	1×10^6
I-126	2×10^0	1×10^0	1×10^2	1×10^6
I-129	Unlimited	Unlimited	1×10^2	1×10^5
I-131	3×10^0	7×10^{-1}	1×10^2	1×10^6

Radionuclide (atomic number)	A_1 (TBq)	A_2 (TBq)	Activity concentration for exempt material (Bq/g)	Activity limit for an exempt consignment (Bq)
I-132	4×10^{-1}	4×10^{-1}	1×10^1	1×10^5
I-133	7×10^{-1}	6×10^{-1}	1×10^1	1×10^6
I-134	3×10^{-1}	3×10^{-1}	1×10^1	1×10^5
I-135 (a)	6×10^{-1}	6×10^{-1}	1×10^1	1×10^6
Indium (49)				
In-111	3×10^0	3×10^0	1×10^2	1×10^6
In-113m	4×10^0	2×10^0	1×10^2	1×10^6
In-114m (a)	1×10^1	5×10^{-1}	1×10^2	1×10^6
In-115m	7×10^0	1×10^0	1×10^2	1×10^6
Iridium (77)				
Ir-189 (a)	1×10^1	1×10^1	1×10^2	1×10^7
Ir-190	7×10^{-1}	7×10^{-1}	1×10^1	1×10^6
Ir-192	1×10^0(c)	6×10^{-1}	1×10^1	1×10^4
Ir-194	3×10^{-1}	3×10^{-1}	1×10^2	1×10^5
Potassium (19)				
K-40	9×10^{-1}	9×10^{-1}	1×10^2	1×10^6
K-42	2×10^{-1}	2×10^{-1}	1×10^2	1×10^6
K-43	7×10^{-1}	6×10^{-1}	1×10^1	1×10^6
Krypton (36)				
Kr-79	4×10^0	1×10^0	1×10^3	1×10^5
Kr-81	4×10^1	4×10^1	1×10^4	1×10^7
Kr-85	1×10^1	1×10^1	1×10^5	1×10^4
Kr-85m	8×10^0	3×10^0	1×10^3	1×10^{10}
Kr-87	2×10^{-1}	2×10^{-1}	1×10^2	1×10^9
Lanthanum (57)				
La-137	3×10^1	6×10^0	1×10^3	1×10^7
La-140	4×10^{-1}	4×10^{-1}	1×10^1	1×10^5
Lutetium (71)				
Lu-172	6×10^{-1}	6×10^{-1}	1×10^1	1×10^6
Lu-173	8×10^0	8×10^0	1×10^2	1×10^7
Lu-174	9×10^0	9×10^0	1×10^2	1×10^7

Radionuclide (atomic number)	A_1 (TBq)	A_2 (TBq)	Activity concentration for exempt material (Bq/g)	Activity limit for an exempt consignment (Bq)
Lu-174m	2×10^1	1×10^1	1×10^2	1×10^7
Lu-177	3×10^1	7×10^{-1}	1×10^3	1×10^7
Magnesium (12)				
Mg-28 (a)	3×10^{-1}	3×10^{-1}	1×10^1	1×10^5
Manganese (25)				
Mn-52	3×10^{-1}	3×10^{-1}	1×10^1	1×10^5
Mn-53	Unlimited	Unlimited	1×10^4	1×10^9
Mn-54	1×10^0	1×10^0	1×10^1	1×10^6
Mn-56	3×10^{-1}	3×10^{-1}	1×10^1	1×10^5
Molybdenum (42)				
Mo-93	4×10^1	2×10^1	1×10^3	1×10^8
Mo-99 (a)	1×10^0	6×10^{-1}	1×10^2	1×10^6
Nitrogen (7)				
N-13	9×10^{-1}	6×10^{-1}	1×10^2	1×10^9
Sodium (11)				
Na-22	5×10^{-1}	5×10^{-1}	1×10^1	1×10^6
Na-24	2×10^{-1}	2×10^{-1}	1×10^1	1×10^5
Niobium (41)				
Nb-93m	4×10^1	3×10^1	1×10^4	1×10^7
Nb-94	7×10^{-1}	7×10^{-1}	1×10^1	1×10^6
Nb-95	1×10^0	1×10^0	1×10^1	1×10^6
Nb-97	9×10^{-1}	6×10^{-1}	1×10^1	1×10^6
Neodymium (60)				
Nd-147	6×10^0	6×10^{-1}	1×10^2	1×10^6
Nd-149	6×10^{-1}	5×10^{-1}	1×10^2	1×10^6
Nickel (28)				
Ni-59	Unlimited	Unlimited	1×10^4	1×10^8
Ni-63	4×10^1	3×10^1	1×10^5	1×10^8
Ni-65	4×10^{-1}	4×10^{-1}	1×10^1	1×10^6
Neptunium (93)				
Np-235	4×10^1	4×10^1	1×10^3	1×10^7

Radionuclide (atomic number)	A_1 (TBq)	A_2 (TBq)	Activity concentration for exempt material (Bq/g)	Activity limit for an exempt consignment (Bq)
Np-236(short-lived)	2×10^1	2×10^0	1×10^3	1×10^7
Np-236(long-lived)	9×10^0	2×10^{-2}	1×10^2	1×10^5
Np-237	2×10^1	2×10^{-3}	1×10^0 (b)	1×10^3 (b)
Np-239	7×10^0	4×10^{-1}	1×10^2	1×10^7
Osmium (76)				
Os-185	1×10^0	1×10^0	1×10^1	1×10^6
Os-191	1×10^1	2×10^0	1×10^2	1×10^7
Os-191m	4×10^1	3×10^1	1×10^3	1×10^7
Os-193	2×10^0	6×10^{-1}	1×10^2	1×10^6
Os-194 (a)	3×10^{-1}	3×10^{-1}	1×10^2	1×10^5
Phosphorus (15)				
P-32	5×10^{-1}	5×10^{-1}	1×10^3	1×10^5
P-33	4×10^1	1×10^0	1×10^5	1×10^8
Protactinium (91)				
Pa-230 (a)	2×10^0	7×10^{-2}	1×10^1	1×10^6
Pa-231	4×10^0	4×10^{-4}	1×10^0	1×10^3
Pa-233	5×10^0	7×10^{-1}	1×10^2	1×10^7
Lead (82)				
Pb-201	1×10^0	1×10^0	1×10^1	1×10^6
Pb-202	4×10^1	2×10^1	1×10^3	1×10^6
Pb-203	4×10^0	3×10^0	1×10^2	1×10^6
Pb-205	Unlimited	Unlimited	1×10^4	1×10^7
Pb-210 (a)	1×10^0	5×10^{-2}	1×10^1 (b)	1×10^4 (b)
Pb-212 (a)	7×10^{-1}	2×10^{-1}	1×10^1 (b)	1×10^5 (b)
Palladium (46)				
Pd-103 (a)	4×10^1	4×10^1	1×10^3	1×10^8
Pd-107	Unlimited	Unlimited	1×10^5	1×10^8
Pd-109	2×10^0	5×10^{-1}	1×10^3	1×10^6
Promethium (61)				
Pm-143	3×10^0	3×10^0	1×10^2	1×10^6
Pm-144	7×10^{-1}	7×10^{-1}	1×10^1	1×10^6

Radionuclide (atomic number)	A_1 (TBq)	A_2 (TBq)	Activity concentration for exempt material (Bq/g)	Activity limit for an exempt consignment (Bq)
Pm-145	3×10^1	1×10^1	1×10^3	1×10^7
Pm-147	4×10^1	2×10^0	1×10^4	1×10^7
Pm-148m (a)	8×10^{-1}	7×10^{-1}	1×10^1	1×10^6
Pm-149	2×10^0	6×10^{-1}	1×10^3	1×10^6
Pm-151	2×10^0	6×10^{-1}	1×10^2	1×10^6
Polonium (84)				
Po-210	4×10^1	2×10^{-2}	1×10^1	1×10^4
Praseodymium (59)				
Pr-142	4×10^{-1}	4×10^{-1}	1×10^2	1×10^5
Pr-143	3×10^0	6×10^{-1}	1×10^4	1×10^6
Platinum (78)				
Pt-188 (a)	1×10^0	8×10^{-1}	1×10^1	1×10^6
Pt-191	4×10^0	3×10^0	1×10^2	1×10^6
Pt-193	4×10^1	4×10^1	1×10^4	1×10^7
Pt-193m	4×10^1	5×10^{-1}	1×10^3	1×10^7
Pt-195m	1×10^1	5×10^{-1}	1×10^2	1×10^6
Pt-197	2×10^1	6×10^{-1}	1×10^3	1×10^6
Pt-197m	1×10^1	6×10^{-1}	1×10^2	1×10^6
Plutonium (94)				
Pu-236	3×10^1	3×10^{-3}	1×10^1	1×10^4
Pu-237	2×10^1	2×10^1	1×10^3	1×10^7
Pu-238	1×10^1	1×10^{-3}	1×10^0	1×10^4
Pu-239	1×10^1	1×10^{-3}	1×10^0	1×10^4
Pu-240	1×10^1	1×10^{-3}	1×10^0	1×10^3
Pu-241 (a)	4×10^1	6×10^{-2}	1×10^2	1×10^5
Pu-242	1×10^1	1×10^{-3}	1×10^0	1×10^4
Pu-244 (a)	4×10^{-1}	1×10^{-3}	1×10^0	1×10^4
Radium (88)				
Ra-223 (a)	4×10^{-1}	7×10^{-3}	1×10^2 (b)	1×10^5 (b)
Ra-224 (a)	4×10^{-1}	2×10^{-2}	1×10^1 (b)	1×10^5 (b)
Ra-225 (a)	2×10^{-1}	4×10^{-3}	1×10^2	1×10^5

Radionuclide (atomic number)	A_1 (TBq)	A_2 (TBq)	Activity concentration for exempt material (Bq/g)	Activity limit for an exempt consignment (Bq)
Ra-226 (a)	2×10^{-1}	3×10^{-3}	1×10^{1} (b)	1×10^{4} (b)
Ra-228 (a)	6×10^{-1}	2×10^{-2}	1×10^{1} (b)	1×10^{5} (b)
Rubidium (37)				
Rb-81	2×10^{0}	8×10^{-1}	1×10^{1}	1×10^{6}
Rb-83 (a)	2×10^{0}	2×10^{0}	1×10^{2}	1×10^{6}
Rb-84	1×10^{0}	1×10^{0}	1×10^{1}	1×10^{6}
Rb-86	5×10^{-1}	5×10^{-1}	1×10^{2}	1×10^{5}
Rb-87	Unlimited	Unlimited	1×10^{4}	1×10^{7}
Rb(nat)	Unlimited	Unlimited	1×10^{4}	1×10^{7}
Rhenium (75)				
Re-184	1×10^{0}	1×10^{0}	1×10^{1}	1×10^{6}
Re-184m	3×10^{0}	1×10^{0}	1×10^{2}	1×10^{6}
Re-186	2×10^{0}	6×10^{-1}	1×10^{3}	1×10^{6}
Re-187	Unlimited	Unlimited	1×10^{6}	1×10^{9}
Re-188	4×10^{-1}	4×10^{-1}	1×10^{2}	1×10^{5}
Re-189 (a)	3×10^{0}	6×10^{-1}	1×10^{2}	1×10^{6}
Re(nat)	Unlimited	Unlimited	1×10^{6}	1×10^{9}
Rhodium (45)				
Rh-99	2×10^{0}	2×10^{0}	1×10^{1}	1×10^{6}
Rh-101	4×10^{0}	3×10^{0}	1×10^{2}	1×10^{7}
Rh-102	5×10^{-1}	5×10^{-1}	1×10^{1}	1×10^{6}
Rh-102m	2×10^{0}	2×10^{0}	1×10^{2}	1×10^{6}
Rh-103m	4×10^{1}	4×10^{1}	1×10^{4}	1×10^{8}
Rh-105	1×10^{1}	8×10^{-1}	1×10^{2}	1×10^{7}
Radon (86)				
Rn-222 (a)	3×10^{-1}	4×10^{-3}	1×10^{1} (b)	1×10^{8} (b)
Ruthenium (44)				
Ru-97	5×10^{0}	5×10^{0}	1×10^{2}	1×10^{7}
Ru-103 (a)	2×10^{0}	2×10^{0}	1×10^{2}	1×10^{6}
Ru-105	1×10^{0}	6×10^{-1}	1×10^{1}	1×10^{6}
Ru-106 (a)	2×10^{-1}	2×10^{-1}	1×10^{2} (b)	1×10^{5} (b)

Radionuclide (atomic number)	A_1 (TBq)	A_2 (TBq)	Activity concentration for exempt material (Bq/g)	Activity limit for an exempt consignment (Bq)
Sulphur (16)				
S-35	4×10^1	3×10^0	1×10^5	1×10^8
Antimony (51)				
Sb-122	4×10^{-1}	4×10^{-1}	1×10^2	1×10^4
Sb-124	6×10^{-1}	6×10^{-1}	1×10^1	1×10^6
Sb-125	2×10^0	1×10^0	1×10^2	1×10^6
Sb-126	4×10^{-1}	4×10^{-1}	1×10^1	1×10^5
Scandium (21)				
Sc-44	5×10^{-1}	5×10^{-1}	1×10^1	1×10^5
Sc-46	5×10^{-1}	5×10^{-1}	1×10^1	1×10^6
Sc-47	1×10^1	7×10^{-1}	1×10^2	1×10^6
Sc-48	3×10^{-1}	3×10^{-1}	1×10^1	1×10^5
Selenium (34)				
Se-75	3×10^0	3×10^0	1×10^2	1×10^6
Se-79	4×10^1	2×10^0	1×10^4	1×10^7
Silicon (14)				
Si-31	6×10^{-1}	6×10^{-1}	1×10^3	1×10^6
Si-32	4×10^1	5×10^{-1}	1×10^3	1×10^6
Samarium (62)				
Sm-145	1×10^1	1×10^1	1×10^2	1×10^7
Sm-147	Unlimited	Unlimited	1×10^1	1×10^4
Sm-151	4×10^1	1×10^1	1×10^4	1×10^8
Sm-153	9×10^0	6×10^{-1}	1×10^2	1×10^6
Tin (50)				
Sn-113 (a)	4×10^0	2×10^0	1×10^3	1×10^7
Sn-117m	7×10^0	4×10^{-1}	1×10^2	1×10^6
Sn-119m	4×10^1	3×10^1	1×10^3	1×10^7
Sn-121m (a)	4×10^1	9×10^{-1}	1×10^3	1×10^7
Sn-123	8×10^{-1}	6×10^{-1}	1×10^3	1×10^6
Sn-125	4×10^{-1}	4×10^{-1}	1×10^2	1×10^5
Sn-126 (a)	6×10^{-1}	4×10^{-1}	1×10^1	1×10^5

Radionuclide (atomic number)	A_1 (TBq)	A_2 (TBq)	Activity concentration for exempt material (Bq/g)	Activity limit for an exempt consignment (Bq)
Strontium (38)				
Sr-82 (a)	2×10^{-1}	2×10^{-1}	1×10^1	1×10^5
Sr-85	2×10^0	2×10^0	1×10^2	1×10^6
Sr-85m	5×10^0	5×10^0	1×10^2	1×10^7
Sr-87m	3×10^0	3×10^0	1×10^2	1×10^6
Sr-89	6×10^{-1}	6×10^{-1}	1×10^3	1×10^6
Sr-90 (a)	3×10^{-1}	3×10^{-1}	1×10^2 (b)	1×10^4 (b)
Sr-91 (a)	3×10^{-1}	3×10^{-1}	1×10^1	1×10^5
Sr-92 (a)	1×10^0	3×10^{-1}	1×10^1	1×10^6
Tritium (1)				
T(H-3)	4×10^1	4×10^1	1×10^6	1×10^9
Tantalum (73)				
Ta-178(long-lived)	1×10^0	8×10^{-1}	1×10^1	1×10^6
Ta-179	3×10^1	3×10^1	1×10^3	1×10^7
Ta-182	9×10^{-1}	5×10^{-1}	1×10^1	1×10^4
Terbium (65)				
Tb-157	4×10^1	4×10^1	1×10^4	1×10^7
Tb-158	1×10^0	1×10^0	1×10^1	1×10^6
Tb-160	1×10^0	6×10^{-1}	1×10^1	1×10^6
Technetium (43)				
Tc-95m (a)	2×10^0	2×10^0	1×10^1	1×10^6
Tc-96	4×10^{-1}	4×10^{-1}	1×10^1	1×10^6
Tc-96m (a)	4×10^{-1}	4×10^{-1}	1×10^3	1×10^7
Tc-97	Unlimited	Unlimited	1×10^3	1×10^8
Tc-97m	4×10^1	1×10^0	1×10^3	1×10^7
Tc-98	8×10^{-1}	7×10^{-1}	1×10^1	1×10^6
Tc-99	4×10^1	9×10^{-1}	1×10^4	1×10^7
Tc-99m	1×10^1	4×10^0	1×10^2	1×10^7
Tellurium (52)				
Te-121	2×10^0	2×10^0	1×10^1	1×10^6
Te-121m	5×10^0	3×10^0	1×10^2	1×10^6

Radionuclide (atomic number)	A_1 (TBq)	A_2 (TBq)	Activity concentration for exempt material (Bq/g)	Activity limit for an exempt consignment (Bq)
Te-123m	8×10^0	1×10^0	1×10^2	1×10^7
Te-125m	2×10^1	9×10^{-1}	1×10^3	1×10^7
Te-127	2×10^1	7×10^{-1}	1×10^3	1×10^6
Te-127m (a)	2×10^1	5×10^{-1}	1×10^3	1×10^7
Te-129	7×10^{-1}	6×10^{-1}	1×10^2	1×10^6
Te-129m (a)	8×10^{-1}	4×10^{-1}	1×10^3	1×10^6
Te-131m (a)	7×10^{-1}	5×10^{-1}	1×10^1	1×10^6
Te-132 (a)	5×10^{-1}	4×10^{-1}	1×10^2	1×10^7
Thorium (90)				
Th-227	1×10^1	5×10^{-3}	1×10^1	1×10^4
Th-228 (a)	5×10^{-1}	1×10^{-3}	1×10^0 (b)	1×10^4 (b)
Th-229	5×10^0	5×10^{-4}	1×10^0 (b)	1×10^3 (b)
Th-230	1×10^1	1×10^{-3}	1×10^0	1×10^4
Th-231	4×10^1	2×10^{-2}	1×10^3	1×10^7
Th-232	Unlimited	Unlimited	1×10^1	1×10^4
Th-234 (a)	3×10^{-1}	3×10^{-1}	1×10^3 (b)	1×10^5 (b)
Th(nat)	Unlimited	Unlimited	1×10^0 (b)	1×10^3 (b)
Titanium (22)				
Ti-44 (a)	5×10^{-1}	4×10^{-1}	1×10^1	1×10^5
Thallium (81)				
Tl-200	9×10^{-1}	9×10^{-1}	1×10^1	1×10^6
Tl-201	1×10^1	4×10^0	1×10^2	1×10^6
Tl-202	2×10^0	2×10^0	1×10^2	1×10^6
Tl-204	1×10^1	7×10^{-1}	1×10^4	1×10^4
Thulium (69)				
Tm-167	7×10^0	8×10^{-1}	1×10^2	1×10^6
Tm-170	3×10^0	6×10^{-1}	1×10^3	1×10^6
Tm-171	4×10^1	4×10^1	1×10^4	1×10^8
Uranium (92)				
U-230 (fast lung absorption) (a)(d)	4×10^1	1×10^{-1}	1×10^1 (b)	1×10^5 (b)
U-230 (medium lung absorption) (a)(e)	4×10^1	4×10^{-3}	1×10^1	1×10^4

Radionuclide (atomic number)	A_1 (TBq)	A_2 (TBq)	Activity concentration for exempt material (Bq/g)	Activity limit for an exempt consignment (Bq)
U-230 (slow lung absorption) (a)(f)	3×10^1	3×10^{-3}	1×10^1	1×10^4
U-232 (fast lung absorption) (d)	4×10^1	1×10^{-2}	1×10^0 (b)	1×10^3 (b)
U-232 (medium lung absorption) (e)	4×10^1	7×10^{-3}	1×10^1	1×10^4
U-232 (slow lung absorption) (f)	1×10^1	1×10^{-3}	1×10^1	1×10^4
U-233 (fast lung absorption) (d)	4×10^1	9×10^{-2}	1×10^1	1×10^4
U-233 (medium lung absorption) (e)	4×10^1	2×10^{-2}	1×10^2	1×10^5
U-233 (slow lung absorption) (f)	4×10^1	6×10^{-3}	1×10^1	1×10^5
U-234 (fast lung absorption) (d)	4×10^1	9×10^{-2}	1×10^1	1×10^4
U-234 (medium lung absorption) (e)	4×10^1	2×10^{-2}	1×10^2	1×10^5
U-234 (slow lung absorption) (f)	4×10^1	6×10^{-3}	1×10^1	1×10^5
U-235 (all lung absorption types) (a)(d)(e)(f)	Unlimited	Unlimited	1×10^1 (b)	1×10^4 (b)
U-236 (fast lung absorption) (d)	Unlimited	Unlimited	1×10^1	1×10^4
U-236 (medium lung absorption) (e)	4×10^1	2×10^{-2}	1×10^2	1×10^5
U-236 (slow lung absorption) (f)	4×10^1	6×10^{-3}	1×10^1	1×10^4
U-238 (all lung absorption types) (d)(e)(f)	Unlimited	Unlimited	1×10^1 (b)	1×10^4 (b)
U (nat)	Unlimited	Unlimited	1×10^0 (b)	1×10^3 (b)
U (enriched to 20% or less) (g)	Unlimited	Unlimited	1×10^0	1×10^3
U (dep)	Unlimited	Unlimited	1×10^0	1×10^3
Vanadium (23)				
V-48	4×10^{-1}	4×10^{-1}	1×10^1	1×10^5
V-49	4×10^1	4×10^1	1×10^4	1×10^7
Tungsten (74)				
W-178 (a)	9×10^0	5×10^0	1×10^1	1×10^6
W-181	3×10^1	3×10^1	1×10^3	1×10^7
W-185	4×10^1	8×10^{-1}	1×10^4	1×10^7
W-187	2×10^0	6×10^{-1}	1×10^2	1×10^6
W-188 (a)	4×10^{-1}	3×10^{-1}	1×10^2	1×10^5

Radionuclide (atomic number)	A_1 (TBq)	A_2 (TBq)	Activity concentration for exempt material (Bq/g)	Activity limit for an exempt consignment (Bq)
Xenon (54)				
Xe-122 (a)	4×10^{-1}	4×10^{-1}	1×10^2	1×10^9
Xe-123	2×10^0	7×10^{-1}	1×10^2	1×10^9
Xe-127	4×10^0	2×10^0	1×10^3	1×10^5
Xe-131m	4×10^1	4×10^1	1×10^4	1×10^4
Xe-133	2×10^1	1×10^1	1×10^3	1×10^4
Xe-135	3×10^0	2×10^0	1×10^3	1×10^{10}
Yttrium (39)				
Y-87 (a)	1×10^0	1×10^0	1×10^1	1×10^6
Y-88	4×10^{-1}	4×10^{-1}	1×10^1	1×10^6
Y-90	3×10^{-1}	3×10^{-1}	1×10^3	1×10^5
Y-91	6×10^{-1}	6×10^{-1}	1×10^3	1×10^6
Y-91m	2×10^0	2×10^0	1×10^2	1×10^6
Y-92	2×10^{-1}	2×10^{-1}	1×10^2	1×10^5
Y-93	3×10^{-1}	3×10^{-1}	1×10^2	1×10^5
Ytterbium (70)				
Yb-169	4×10^0	1×10^0	1×10^2	1×10^7
Yb-175	3×10^1	9×10^{-1}	1×10^3	1×10^7
Zinc (30)				
Zn-65	2×10^0	2×10^0	1×10^1	1×10^6
Zn-69	3×10^0	6×10^{-1}	1×10^4	1×10^6
Zn-69m (a)	3×10^0	6×10^{-1}	1×10^2	1×10^6
Zirconium (40)				
Zr-88	3×10^0	3×10^0	1×10^2	1×10^6
Zr-93	Unlimited	Unlimited	1×10^3 (b)	1×10^7 (b)
Zr-95 (a)	2×10^0	8×10^{-1}	1×10^1	1×10^6
Zr-97 (a)	4×10^{-1}	4×10^{-1}	1×10^1 (b)	1×10^5 (b)

(a) A_1 and/or A_2 values for these parent radionuclides include contributions from daughter radionuclides with half-lives less than 10 days, as listed in the following:

Mg-28	Al-28
Ar-42	K-42
Ca-47	Sc-47
Ti-44	Sc-44
Fe-52	Mn-52m
Fe-60	Co-60m
Zn-69m	Zn-69
Ge-68	Ga-68
Rb-83	Kr-83m
Sr-82	Rb-82
Sr-90	Y-90
Sr-91	Y-91m
Sr-92	Y-92
Y-87	Sr-87m
Zr-95	Nb-95m
Zr-97	Nb-97m, Nb-97
Mo-99	Tc-99m
Tc-95m	Tc-95
Tc-96m	Tc-96
Ru-103	Rh-103m
Ru-106	Rh-106
Pd-103	Rh-103m
Ag-108m	Ag-108
Ag-110m	Ag-110
Cd-115	In-115m
In-114m	In-114
Sn-113	In-113m
Sn-121m	Sn-121
Sn-126	Sb-126m
Te-118	Sb-118
Te-127m	Te-127
Te-129m	Te-129
Te-131m	Te-131
Te-132	I-132
I-135	Xe-135m
Xe-122	I-122
Cs-137	Ba-137m
Ba-131	Cs-131
Ba-140	La-140
Ce-144	Pr-144m, Pr-144
Pm-148m	Pm-148
Gd-146	Eu-146
Dy-166	Ho-166
Hf-172	Lu-172
W-178	Ta-178
W-188	Re-188
Re-189	Os-189m
Os-194	Ir-194
Ir-189	Os-189m
Pt-188	Ir-188
Hg-194	Au-194
Hg-195m	Hg-195
Pb-210	Bi-210
Pb-212	Bi-212, Tl-208, Po-212
Bi-210m	Tl-206

Bi-212	Tl-208, Po-212
At-211	Po-211
Rn-222	Po-218, Pb-214, At-218, Bi-214, Po-214
Ra-223	Rn-219, Po-215, Pb-211, Bi-211, Po-211, Tl-207
Ra-224	Rn-220, Po-216, Pb-212, Bi-212, Tl-208, Po-212
Ra-225	Ac-225, Fr-221, At-217, Bi-213, Tl-209, Po-213, Pb-209
Ra-226	Rn-222, Po-218, Pb-214, At-218, Bi-214, Po-214
Ra-228	Ac-228
Ac-225	Fr-221, At-217, Bi-213, Tl-209, Po-213, Pb-209
Ac-227	Fr-223
Th-228	Ra-224, Rn-220, Po-216, Pb-212, Bi-212, Tl-208, Po-212
Th-234	Pa-234m, Pa-234
Pa-230	Ac-226, Th-226, Fr-222, Ra-222, Rn-218, Po-214
U-230	Th-226, Ra-222, Rn-218, Po-214
U-235	Th-231
Pu-241	U-237
Pu-244	U-240, Np-240m
Am-242m	Am-242, Np-238
Am-243	Np-239
Cm-247	Pu-243
Bk-249	Am-245
Cf-253	Cm-249

(b) Parent nuclides and their progeny included in secular equilibrium are listed in the following:

Sr-90	Y-90
Zr-93	Nb-93m
Zr-97	Nb-97
Ru-106	Rh-106
Ag-108m	Ag-108
Cs-137	Ba-137m
Ce-144	Pr-144
Ba-140	La-140
Bi-212	Tl-208 (0.36), Po-212 (0.64)
Pb-210	Bi-210, Po-210
Pb-212	Bi-212, Tl-208 (0.36), Po-212 (0.64)
Rn-222	Po-218, Pb-214, Bi-214, Po-214
Ra-223	Rn-219, Po-215, Pb-211, Bi-211, Tl-207
Ra-224	Rn-220, Po-216, Pb-212, Bi-212, Tl-208 (0.36), Po-212 (0.64)
Ra-226	Rn-222, Po-218, Pb-214, Bi-214, Po-214, Pb-210, Bi-210, Po-210
Ra-228	Ac-228
Th-228	Ra-224, Rn-220, Po-216, Pb212, Bi-212, Tl208 (0.36), Po-212 (0.64)
Th-229	Ra-225, Ac-225, Fr-221, At-217, Bi-213, Po-213, Pb-209
Th-nat	Ra-228, Ac-228, Th-228, Ra-224, Rn-220, Po-216, Pb-212, Bi-212, l208 (0.36), Po-212 (0.64)
Th-234	Pa-234m
U-230	Th-226, Ra-222, Rn-218, Po-214
U-232	Th-228, Ra-224, Rn-220, Po-216, Pb-212, Bi-212, Tl-208 (0.36), Po-212 (0.64)
U-235	Th-231
U-238	Th-234, Pa-234m
U-nat	Th-234, Pa-234m, U-234, Th-230, Ra-226, Rn-222, Po-218, Pb-214, Bi-214, Po-214, Pb-210, Bi-210, Po-210
Np-237	Pa-233
Am-242m	Am-242
Am-243	Np-239

(c)   The quantity may be determined from a measurement of the rate of decay or a measurement of the radiation level at a prescribed distance from the source.

(d)   These values apply only to compounds of uranium that take the chemical form of UF_6, UO_2F_2 and $UO_2(NO_3)_2$ in both normal and accident conditions of carriage.

(e)   These values apply only to compounds of uranium that take the chemical form of UO_3, UF_4, UCl_4 and hexavalent compounds in both normal and accident conditions of carriage.

(f)   These values apply to all compounds of uranium other than those specified in (d) and (e) above.

(g)   These values apply to unirradiated uranium only.

2.2.7.2.2.2   For individual radionuclides which are not listed in Table 2.2.7.2.2.1 the determination of the basic radionuclide values referred to in 2.2.7.2.2.1 shall require multilateral approval. It is permissible to use an A_2 value calculated using a dose coefficient for the appropriate lung absorption type as recommended by the International Commission on Radiological Protection, if the chemical forms of each radionuclide under both normal and accident conditions of carriage are taken into consideration. Alternatively, the radionuclide values in Table 2.2.7.2.2.2 may be used without obtaining competent authority approval.

Table 2.2.7.2.2.2: Basic radionuclide values for unknown radionuclides or mixtures

Radioactive contents	A_1	A_2	Activity concentration for exempt material	Activity limit for exempt consignments
	(TBq)	(TBq)	(Bq/g)	(Bq)
Only beta or gamma emitting nuclides are known to be present	0.1	0.02	1×10^1	1×10^4
Alpha emitting nuclides but no neutron emitters are known to be present	0.2	9×10^{-5}	1×10^{-1}	1×10^3
Neutron emitting nuclides are known to be present or no relevant data are available	0.001	9×10^{-5}	1×10^{-1}	1×10^3

2.2.7.2.2.3   In the calculations of A_1 and A_2 for a radionuclide not in Table 2.2.7.2.2.1, a single radioactive decay chain in which the radionuclides are present in their naturally occurring proportions, and in which no daughter nuclide has a half-life either longer than 10 days or longer than that of the parent nuclide, shall be considered as a single radionuclide; and the activity to be taken into account and the A_1 or A_2 value to be applied shall be those corresponding to the parent nuclide of that chain. In the case of radioactive decay chains in which any daughter nuclide has a half-life either longer than 10 days or greater than that of the parent nuclide, the parent and such daughter nuclides shall be considered as mixtures of different nuclides.

2.2.7.2.2.4   For mixtures of radionuclides, the determination of the basic radionuclide values referred to in 2.2.7.2.2.1 may be determined as follows:

$$X_m = \frac{1}{\sum_i \dfrac{f(i)}{X(i)}}$$

where,

f(i)   is the fraction of activity or activity concentration of radionuclide i in the mixture;

X(i)   is the appropriate value of A1 or A2, or the activity concentration for exempt material or the activity limit for an exempt consignment as appropriate for the radionuclide i; and

X_m is the derived value of A_1 or A_2, or the activity concentration for exempt material or the activity limit for an exempt consignment in the case of a mixture.

2.2.7.2.2.5   When the identity of each radionuclide is known but the individual activities of some of the radionuclides are not known, the radionuclides may be grouped and the lowest radionuclide value, as appropriate, for the radionuclides in each group may be used in applying the formulas in 2.2.7.2.2.4 and 2.2.7.2.4.4. Groups may be based on the total alpha activity and the total beta/gamma activity when these are known, using the lowest radionuclide values for the alpha emitters or beta/gamma emitters, respectively.

2.2.7.2.2.6   For individual radionuclides or for mixtures of radionuclides for which relevant data are not available, the values shown in Table 2.2.7.2.2.2 shall be used.

2.2.7.2.3   *Determination of other material characteristics*

2.2.7.2.3.1   Low specific activity (LSA) material

2.2.7.2.3.1.1   *(Reserved)*

2.2.7.2.3.1.2   LSA material shall be in one of three groups:

(a)   LSA-I

     (i)   uranium and thorium ores and concentrates of such ores, and other ores containing naturally occurring radionuclides which are intended to be processed for the use of these radionuclides;

     (ii)   natural uranium, depleted uranium, natural thorium or their compounds or mixtures, providing they are unirradiated and in solid or liquid form;

     (iii)   radioactive material for which the A_2 value is unlimited, excluding material classified as fissile according to 2.2.7.2.3.5; or

     (iv)   other radioactive material in which the activity is distributed throughout and the estimated average specific activity does not exceed 30 times the values for activity concentration specified in 2.2.7.2.2.1 to 2.2.7.2.2.6, excluding material classified as fissile according to 2.2.7.2.3.5;

(b) LSA-II

    (i)   water with tritium concentration up to 0.8 TBq/l; or

    (ii)   other material in which the activity is distributed throughout and the estimated average specific activity does not exceed 10^{-4} A2/g for solids and gases, and 10^{-5} A2/g for liquids;

(c) LSA-III - Solids (e.g. consolidated wastes, activated materials), excluding powders, in which:

    (i)   the radioactive material is distributed throughout a solid or a collection of solid objects, or is essentially uniformly distributed in a solid compact binding agent (such as concrete, bitumen, ceramic, etc.);

    (ii)   the radioactive material is relatively insoluble, or it is intrinsically contained in a relatively insoluble matrix, so that, even under loss of packaging, the loss of radioactive material per package by leaching when placed in water for seven days would not exceed 0.1 A2; and

    (iii)   the estimated average specific activity of the solid, excluding any shielding material, does not exceed 2×10^{-3} A2/g.

2.2.7.2.3.1.3   LSA-III material shall be a solid of such a nature that if the entire contents of a package were subjected to the test specified in 2.2.7.2.3.1.4 the activity in the water would not exceed $0.1\ A_2$.

2.2.7.2.3.1.4   LSA-III material shall be tested as follows:

A solid material sample representing the entire contents of the package shall be immersed for 7 days in water at ambient temperature. The volume of water to be used in the test shall be sufficient to ensure that at the end of the 7 day test period the free volume of the unabsorbed and unreacted water remaining shall be at least 10% of the volume of the solid test sample itself. The water shall have an initial pH of 6-8 and a maximum conductivity of 1 mS/m at 20 °C. The total activity of the free volume of water shall be measured following the 7 day immersion of the test sample.

2.2.7.2.3.1.5   Demonstration of compliance with the performance standards in 2.2.7.2.3.1.4 shall be in accordance with 6.4.12.1 and 6.4.12.2.

2.2.7.2.3.2   Surface contaminated object (SCO)

SCO is classified in one of two groups:

(a) SCO-I: A solid object on which:

    (i)   the non-fixed contamination on the accessible surface averaged over 300 cm2 (or the area of the surface if less than 300 cm2) does not exceed 4 Bq/cm2 for beta and gamma emitters and low toxicity alpha emitters, or 0.4 Bq/cm2 for all other alpha emitters; and

    (ii)   the fixed contamination on the accessible surface averaged over 300 cm2 (or the area of the surface if less than 300 cm2) does not exceed 4×10^4 Bq/cm2 for beta and gamma emitters and low toxicity alpha emitters, or 4×10^3 Bq/cm2 for all other alpha emitters; and

(iii)   the non-fixed contamination plus the fixed contamination on the inaccessible surface averaged over 300 cm2 (or the area of the surface if less than 300 cm2) does not exceed 4×10^4 Bq/cm2 for beta and gamma emitters and low toxicity alpha emitters, or 4×10^3 Bq/cm2 for all other alpha emitters;

(b)   SCO-II: A solid object on which either the fixed or non-fixed contamination on the surface exceeds the applicable limits specified for SCO-I in (a) above and on which:

    (i)   the non-fixed contamination on the accessible surface averaged over 300 cm2 (or the area of the surface if less than 300 cm2) does not exceed 400 Bq/cm2 for beta and gamma emitters and low toxicity alpha emitters, or 40 Bq/cm2 for all other alpha emitters; and

    (ii)   the fixed contamination on the accessible surface, averaged over 300 cm2 (or the area of the surface if less than 300 cm2) does not exceed 8×10^5 Bq/cm2 for beta and gamma emitters and low toxicity alpha emitters, or 8×10^4 Bq/cm2 for all other alpha emitters; and

    (iii)   the non-fixed contamination plus the fixed contamination on the inaccessible surface averaged over 300 cm2 (or the area of the surface if less than 300 cm2) does not exceed 8×10^5 Bq/cm2 for beta and gamma emitters and low toxicity alpha emitters, or 8×10^4 Bq/cm2 for all other alpha emitters.

2.2.7.2.3.3   Special form radioactive material

2.2.7.2.3.3.1   Special form radioactive material shall have at least one dimension not less than 5 mm. When a sealed capsule constitutes part of the special form radioactive material, the capsule shall be so manufactured that it can be opened only by destroying it. The design for special form radioactive material requires unilateral approval.

2.2.7.2.3.3.2   Special form radioactive material shall be of such a nature or shall be so designed that if it is subjected to the tests specified in 2.2.7.2.3.3.4 to 2.2.7.2.3.3.8, it shall meet the following requirements:

(a)   It would not break or shatter under the impact, percussion and bending tests 2.2.7.2.3.3.5 (a), (b), (c) and 2.2.7.2.3.3.6 (a) as applicable;

(b)   It would not melt or disperse in the applicable heat test 2.2.7.2.3.3.5 (d) or 2.2.7.2.3.3.6 (b) as applicable; and

(c)   The activity in the water from the leaching tests specified in 2.2.7.2.3.3.7 and 2.2.7.2.3.3.8 would not exceed 2 kBq; or alternatively for sealed sources, the leakage rate for the volumetric leakage assessment test specified in ISO 9978:1992 "Radiation Protection - Sealed Radioactive Sources - Leakage Test Methods", would not exceed the applicable acceptance threshold acceptable to the competent authority.

2.2.7.2.3.3.3   Demonstration of compliance with the performance standards in 2.2.7.2.3.3.2 shall be in accordance with 6.4.12.1 and 6.4.12.2.

2.2.7.2.3.3.4   Specimens that comprise or simulate special form radioactive material shall be subjected to the impact test, the percussion test, the bending test, and the heat test specified in 2.2.7.2.3.3.5 or alternative tests as authorized in 2.2.7.2.3.3.6. A different specimen may be used for each of the tests. Following each test, a leaching assessment or volumetric leakage test shall be performed on the specimen by a method no less sensitive than the methods given in 2.2.7.2.3.3.7 for indispersible solid material or 2.2.7.2.3.3.8 for encapsulated material.

2.2.7.2.3.3.5   The relevant test methods are:

(a)   Impact test: The specimen shall drop onto the target from a height of 9 m. The target shall be as defined in 6.4.14;

(b)   Percussion test: The specimen shall be placed on a sheet of lead which is supported by a smooth solid surface and struck by the flat face of a mild steel bar so as to cause an impact equivalent to that resulting from a free drop of 1.4 kg through 1 m. The lower part of the bar shall be 25 mm in diameter with the edges rounded off to a radius of (3.0 ± 0.3) mm. The lead, of hardness number 3.5 to 4.5 on the Vickers scale and not more than 25 mm thick, shall cover an area greater than that covered by the specimen. A fresh surface of lead shall be used for each impact. The bar shall strike the specimen so as to cause maximum damage;

(c)   Bending test: The test shall apply only to long, slender sources with both a minimum length of 10 cm and a length to minimum width ratio of not less than 10. The specimen shall be rigidly clamped in a horizontal position so that one half of its length protrudes from the face of the clamp. The orientation of the specimen shall be such that the specimen will suffer maximum damage when its free end is struck by the flat face of a steel bar. The bar shall strike the specimen so as to cause an impact equivalent to that resulting from a free vertical drop of 1.4 kg through 1 m. The lower part of the bar shall be 25 mm in diameter with the edges rounded off to a radius of (3.0 ± 0.3) mm;

(d)   Heat test: The specimen shall be heated in air to a temperature of 800 °C and held at that temperature for a period of 10 minutes and shall then be allowed to cool.

2.2.7.2.3.3.6   Specimens that comprise or simulate radioactive material enclosed in a sealed capsule may be excepted from:

(a)   The tests prescribed in 2.2.7.2.3.3.5 (a) and (b) provided the mass of the special form radioactive material:

(i)   is less than 200 g and they are alternatively subjected to the Class 4 impact test prescribed in ISO 2919:1999 "Radiation protection - Sealed radioactive sources - General requirements and classification"; or

(ii)   is less than 500 g and they are alternatively subjected to the Class 5 impact test prescribed in ISO 2919:1999 "Radiation protection - Sealed radioactive sources - General requirements and classification"; and

(b)   The test prescribed in 2.2.7.2.3.3.5 (d) provided they are alternatively subjected to the Class 6 temperature test specified in ISO 2919:1999 "Radiation protection - Sealed radioactive sources - General requirements and classification".

2.2.7.2.3.3.7   For specimens which comprise or simulate indispersible solid material, a leaching assessment shall be performed as follows:

(a)   The specimen shall be immersed for 7 days in water at ambient temperature. The volume of water to be used in the test shall be sufficient to ensure that at the end of the 7 day test period the free volume of the unabsorbed and unreacted water remaining shall be at least 10% of the volume of the solid test sample itself. The water shall have an initial pH of 6-8 and a maximum conductivity of 1 mS/m at 20 °C;

(b)   The water with specimen shall then be heated to a temperature of (50 ± 5) °C and maintained at this temperature for 4 hours;

(c)   The activity of the water shall then be determined;

(d)   The specimen shall then be kept for at least 7 days in still air at not less than 30 °C and relative humidity not less than 90%;

(e)   The specimen shall then be immersed in water of the same specification as in (a) above and the water with the specimen heated to (50 ± 5) °C and maintained at this temperature for 4 hours;

(f)   The activity of the water shall then be determined.

2.2.7.2.3.3.8   For specimens which comprise or simulate radioactive material enclosed in a sealed capsule, either a leaching assessment or a volumetric leakage assessment shall be performed as follows:

(a)   The leaching assessment shall consist of the following steps:

(i)   the specimen shall be immersed in water at ambient temperature. The water shall have an initial pH of 6-8 with a maximum conductivity of 1 mS/m at 20 °C;

(ii)   the water and specimen shall be heated to a temperature of (50 ± 5) °C and maintained at this temperature for 4 hours;

(iii)   the activity of the water shall then be determined;

(iv)   the specimen shall then be kept for at least 7 days in still air at not less than 30 °C and relative humidity of not less than 90%;

(v)   the process in (i), (ii) and (iii) shall be repeated;

(b)   The alternative volumetric leakage assessment shall comprise any of the tests prescribed in ISO 9978:1992 "Radiation Protection - Sealed radioactive sources - Leakage test methods", which are acceptable to the competent authority.

2.2.7.2.3.4   Low dispersible radioactive material

2.2.7.2.3.4.1   The design for low dispersible radioactive material shall require multilateral approval. Low dispersible radioactive material shall be such that the total amount of this radioactive material in a package shall meet the following requirements:

(a)   The radiation level at 3 m from the unshielded radioactive material does not exceed 10 mSv/h;

(b)   If subjected to the tests specified in 6.4.20.3 and 6.4.20.4, the airborne release in gaseous and particulate forms of up to 100 μm aerodynamic equivalent diameter would not exceed 100 A2. A separate specimen may be used for each test; and

(c)   If subjected to the test specified in 2.2.7.2.3.1.4 the activity in the water would not exceed 100 A2. In the application of this test, the damaging effects of the tests specified in (b) above shall be taken into account.

2.2.7.2.3.4.2   Low dispersible radioactive material shall be tested as follows:

A specimen that comprises or simulates low dispersible radioactive material shall be subjected to the enhanced thermal test specified in 6.4.20.3 and the impact test specified in 6.4.20.4. A different specimen may be used for each of the tests. Following each test, the specimen shall be subjected to the leach test specified in 2.2.7.2.3.1.4. After each test it shall be determined if the applicable requirements of 2.2.7.2.3.4.1 have been met.

2.2.7.2.3.4.3   Demonstration of compliance with the performance standards in 2.2.7.2.3.4.1 and 2.2.7.2.3.4.2 shall be in accordance with 6.4.12.1 and 6.4.12.2.

2.2.7.2.3.5   Fissile material

Packages containing fissile radionuclides shall be classified under the relevant entry of table 2.2.7.2.1.1 for fissile material unless one of the conditions (a) to (d) of this paragraph is met. Only one type of exception is allowed per consignment.

(a)   A mass limit per consignment such that:

$$\frac{\text{mass of uranium235 (g)}}{X} + \frac{\text{mass of other fissile material (g)}}{Y} < 1$$

where X and Y are the mass limits defined in Table 2.2.7.2.3.5, provided that the smallest external dimension of each package is not less than 10 cm and that either:

(i)   each individual package contains not more than 15 g of fissile material; for unpackaged material, this quantity limitation shall apply to the consignment being carried in or on the vehicle; or

(ii)   the fissile material is a homogeneous hydrogenous solution or mixture where the ratio of fissile nuclides to hydrogen is less than 5% by mass; or

(iii)   there are not more than 5 g of fissile material in any 10 litre volume of material.

Neither beryllium nor deuterium shall be present in quantities exceeding 1% of the applicable consignment mass limits provided in Table 2.2.7.2.3.5, except for deuterium in natural concentration in hydrogen.

(b)   Uranium enriched in uranium-235 to a maximum of 1% by mass, and with a total plutonium and uranium-233 content not exceeding 1% of the mass of uranium-235, provided that the fissile material is distributed essentially homogeneously throughout the material. In addition, if uranium-235 is present in metallic, oxide or carbide forms, it shall not form a lattice arrangement;

(c)   Liquid solutions of uranyl nitrate enriched in uranium-235 to a maximum of 2% by mass, with a total plutonium and uranium-233 content not exceeding 0.002% of the mass of uranium, and with a minimum nitrogen to uranium atomic ratio (N/U) of 2;

(d)   Packages containing, individually, a total plutonium mass not more than 1 kg, of which not more than 20% by mass may consist of plutonium-239, plutonium-241 or any combination of those radionuclides.

Table 2.2.7.2.3.5: Consignment mass limits for exceptions from the requirements for packages containing fissile material

Fissile material	Fissile material mass (g) mixed with substances having an average hydrogen density less than or equal to water	Fissile material mass (g) mixed with substances having an average hydrogen density greater than water
Uranium-235 (X)	400	290
Other fissile material (Y)	250	180

2.2.7.2.4   *Classification of packages or unpacked material*

The quantity of radioactive material in a package shall not exceed the relevant limits for the package type as specified below.

2.2.7.2.4.1   Classification as excepted package

2.2.7.2.4.1.1   Packages may be classified as excepted packages if:

(a)   They are empty packagings having contained radioactive material;

(b)   They contain instruments or articles in limited quantities;

(c)   They contain articles manufactured of natural uranium, depleted uranium or natural thorium; or

(d)   They contain radioactive material in limited quantities.

2.2.7.2.4.1.2   A package containing radioactive material may be classified as an excepted package provided that the radiation level at any point on its external surface does not exceed 5 µSv/h.

Table 2.2.7.2.4.1.2: Activity limits for excepted packages

| Physical state of contents | Instruments or articles | | Materials |
	Item limits [a]	Package limits [a]	Package limits [a]
(1)	(2)	(3)	(4)
Solids			
special form	$10^{-2} A_1$	A_1	$10^{-3} A_1$
other form	$10^{-2} A_2$	A_2	$10^{-3} A_2$
Liquids	$10^{-3} A_2$	$10^{-1} A_2$	$10^{-4} A_2$
Gases			
tritium	$2 \times 10^{-2} A_2$	$2 \times 10^{-1} A_2$	$2 \times 10^{-2} A_2$
special form	$10^{-3} A_1$	$10^{-2} A_1$	$10^{-3} A_1$
other forms	$10^{-3} A_2$	$10^{-2} A_2$	$10^{-3} A_2$

[a]   *For mixtures of radionuclides, see 2.2.7.2.2.4 to 2.2.7.2.2.6.*

2.2.7.2.4.1.3   Radioactive material which is enclosed in or is included as a component part of an instrument or other manufactured article may be classified under UN No. 2911 RADIOACTIVE MATERIAL, EXCEPTED PACKAGE - INSTRUMENTS or ARTICLES provided that:

(a)   The radiation level at 10 cm from any point on the external surface of any unpackaged instrument or article is not greater than 0.1 mSv/h; and

(b)   Each instrument or manufactured article bears the marking "RADIOACTIVE" except:

   (i)   radioluminescent time-pieces or devices;

   (ii)   consumer products that either have received regulatory approval according to 1.7.1.4 (d) or do not individually exceed the activity limit for an exempt consignment in Table 2.2.7.2.2.1 (column 5), provided such products are carried in a package that bears the marking "RADIOACTIVE" on an internal surface in such a manner that warning of the presence of radioactive material is visible on opening the package; and

(c)   The active material is completely enclosed by non-active components (a device performing the sole function of containing radioactive material shall not be considered to be an instrument or manufactured article); and

(d)   The limits specified in columns 2 and 3 of Table 2.2.7.2.4.1.2 are met for each individual item and each package, respectively.

2.2.7.2.4.1.4   Radioactive material with an activity not exceeding the limit specified in column 4 of Table 2.2.7.2.4.1.2, may be classified under UN No. 2910 RADIOACTIVE MATERIAL, EXCEPTED PACKAGE - LIMITED QUANTITY OF MATERIAL provided that:

(a)   The package retains its radioactive contents under routine conditions of carriage; and

(b)   The package bears the marking "RADIOACTIVE" on an internal surface in such a manner that a warning of the presence of radioactive material is visible on opening the package.

2.2.7.2.4.1.5   An empty packaging which had previously contained radioactive material with an activity not exceeding the limit specified in column 4 of Table 2.2.7.2.4.1.2 may be classified under UN No. 2908 RADIOACTIVE MATERIAL, EXCEPTED PACKAGE - EMPTY PACKAGING, provided that:

(a)   It is in a well-maintained condition and securely closed;

(b)   The outer surface of any uranium or thorium in its structure is covered with an inactive sheath made of metal or some other substantial material;

(c)   The level of internal non-fixed contamination, when averaged over any 300 cm2, does not exceed:

   (i)   400 Bq/cm2 for beta and gamma emitters and low toxicity alpha emitters; and

   (ii)   40 Bq/cm2 for all other alpha emitters; and

(d)   Any labels which may have been displayed on it in conformity with 5.2.2.1.11.1 are no longer visible.

2.2.7.2.4.1.6   Articles manufactured of natural uranium, depleted uranium or natural thorium and articles in which the sole radioactive material is unirradiated natural uranium, unirradiated depleted uranium or unirradiated natural thorium may be classified under UN No. 2909 RADIOACTIVE MATERIAL, EXCEPTED PACKAGE - ARTICLES MANUFACTURED FROM NATURAL URANIUM or DEPLETED URANIUM or NATURAL THORIUM, provided that the outer surface of the uranium or thorium is enclosed in an inactive sheath made of metal or some other substantial material.

2.2.7.2.4.2   Classification as Low specific activity (LSA) material

Radioactive material may only be classified as LSA material if the conditions of 2.2.7.2.3.1 and 4.1.9.2 are met.

2.2.7.2.4.3   Classification as Surface contaminated object (SCO)

Radioactive material may be classified as SCO if the conditions of 2.2.7.2.3.2 and 4.1.9.2 are met.

2.2.7.2.4.4   Classification as Type A package

Packages containing radioactive material may be classified as Type A packages provided that the following conditions are met:

Type A packages shall not contain activities greater than the following:

(a)   For special form radioactive material - A1; or

(b)   For all other radioactive material - A2.

For mixtures of radionuclides whose identities and respective activities are known, the following condition shall apply to the radioactive contents of a Type A package:

$$\Sigma_i \frac{B(i)}{A_1(i)} + \Sigma_j \frac{C(j)}{A_2(j)} \leq 1$$

where $B(i)$ is the activity of radionuclide i as special form radioactive material;

$A_1(i)$ is the A_1 value for radionuclide i;

$C(j)$ is the activity of radionuclide j as other than special form radioactive material; and

$A_2(j)$ is the A_2 value for radionuclide j.

2.2.7.2.4.5   Classification of Uranium hexafluoride

Uranium hexafluoride shall only be assigned to UN Nos. 2977 RADIOACTIVE MATERIAL, URANIUM HEXAFLUORIDE, FISSILE, or 2978 RADIOACTIVE MATERIAL, URANIUM HEXAFLUORIDE, non-fissile or fissile-excepted.

2.2.7.2.4.5.1   Packages containing uranium hexafluoride shall not contain:

(a)   A mass of uranium hexafluoride different from that authorized for the package design;

(b)   A mass of uranium hexafluoride greater than a value that would lead to an ullage smaller than 5% at the maximum temperature of the package as specified for the plant systems where the package shall be used; or

(c)   Uranium hexafluoride other than in solid form or at an internal pressure above atmospheric pressure when presented for carriage.

2.2.7.2.4.6   Classification as Type B(U), Type B(M) or Type C packages

2.2.7.2.4.6.1 Packages not otherwise classified in 2.2.7.2.4 (2.2.7.2.4.1 to 2.2.7.2.4.5) shall be classified in accordance with the competent authority approval certificate for the package issued by the country of origin of design.

2.2.7.2.4.6.2 A package may only be classified as a Type B(U) if it does not contain:

(a) Activities greater than those authorized for the package design;

(b) Radionuclides different from those authorized for the package design; or

(c) Contents in a form, or a physical or chemical state different from those authorized for the package design;

as specified in the certificate of approval.

2.2.7.2.4.6.3 A package may only be classified as a Type B(M) if it does not contain:

(a) Activities greater than those authorized for the package design;

(b) Radionuclides different from those authorized for the package design; or

(c) Contents in a form, or a physical or chemical state different from those authorized for the package design;

as specified in the certificate of approval.

2.2.7.2.4.6.4 A package may only be classified as a Type C if it does not contain:

(a) Activities greater than those authorized for the package design;

(b) Radionuclides different from those authorized for the package design; or

(c) Contents in a form, or physical or chemical state different from those authorized for the package design;

as specified in the certificate of approval.

2.2.7.2.5 *Special arrangements*

Radioactive material shall be classified as transported under special arrangement when it is intended to be carried in accordance with 1.7.4.

2.2.8   **Class 8**   **Corrosive substances**

2.2.8.1   *Criteria*

2.2.8.1.1   The heading of Class 8 covers substances and articles containing substances of this class which by chemical action attack epithelial tissue - of skin or mucous membranes - with which they are in contact, or which in the event of leakage are capable of damaging or destroying other goods, or means of transport. The heading of this class also covers other substances which form a corrosive liquid only in the presence of water, or which produce corrosive vapour or mist in the presence of natural moisture of the air.

2.2.8.1.2   Substances and articles of Class 8 are subdivided as follows:

    C1-C10   Corrosive substances without subsidiary risk:

            C1-C4   Acid substances:
                    C1   Inorganic, liquid;
                    C2   Inorganic, solid;
                    C3   Organic, liquid;
                    C4   Organic, solid;

            C5-C8   Basic substances:
                    C5   Inorganic, liquid;
                    C6   Inorganic, solid;
                    C7   Organic, liquid;
                    C8   Organic, solid;

            C9-C10   Other corrosive substances:
                    C9   Liquid;
                    C10   Solid;

    C11   Articles;

    CF   Corrosive substances, flammable:
            CF1   Liquid;
            CF2   Solid;

    CS   Corrosive substances, self-heating:
            CS1   Liquid;
            CS2   Solid;

    CW   Corrosive substances which, in contact with water, emit flammable gases:
            CW1   Liquid;
            CW2   Solid;

    CO   Corrosive substances, oxidizing:
            CO1   Liquid;
            CO2   Solid;

    CT   Corrosive substances, toxic:
            CT1   Liquid;
            CT2   Solid;

    CFT   Corrosive substances, flammable, liquid, toxic;

    COT   Corrosive substances, oxidizing, toxic.

2.2.8.1.3   Substances of Class 8 shall be classified in three packing groups according to the degree of danger they present for carriage, as follows:

Packing group I: highly corrosive substances
Packing group II: corrosive substances
Packing group III: slightly corrosive substances.

2.2.8.1.4   Substances and articles classified in Class 8 are listed in Table A of Chapter 3.2. Allocation of substances to packing groups I, II and III has been made on the basis of experience taking into account such additional factors as inhalation risk (see 2.2.8.1.5) and reactivity with water (including the formation of dangerous decomposition products).

2.2.8.1.5   A substance or preparation meeting the criteria of Class 8 having an inhalation toxicity of dusts and mists (LC_{50}) in the range of packing group I, but toxicity through oral ingestion or dermal contact only in the range of packing group III or less, shall be allocated to Class 8.

2.2.8.1.6   Substances, including mixtures, not mentioned by name in Table A of Chapter 3.2 can be assigned to the relevant entry of sub-section 2.2.8.3, and to the relevant packing group on the basis of the length of time of contact necessary to produce full thickness destruction of human skin in accordance with the criteria of (a) to (c) below.

Liquids, and solids which may become liquid during carriage, which are judged not to cause full thickness destruction of human skin shall still be considered for their potential to cause corrosion to certain metal surfaces. In assigning the packing group, account shall be taken of human experience in instances of accidental exposure. In the absence of human experience, the grouping shall be based on data obtained from experiments in accordance with OECD Guideline 404 [7].

(a)   Packing group I is assigned to substances that cause full thickness destruction of intact skin tissue within an observation period up to 60 minutes starting after the exposure time of 3 minutes or less;

(b)   Packing group II is assigned to substances that cause full thickness destruction of intact skin tissue within an observation period up to 14 days starting after the exposure time of more than 3 minutes but not more than 60 minutes;

(c)   Packing group III is assigned to substances that:

-    cause full thickness destruction of intact skin tissue within an observation period up to 14 days starting after the exposure time of more than 60 minutes but not more than 4 hours; or

-    are judged not to cause full thickness destruction of intact skin tissue, but which exhibit a corrosion rate on either steel or aluminium surfaces exceeding 6.25 mm a year at a test temperature of 55 °C when tested on both materials. For the purposes of testing steel, type S235JR+CR (1.0037 resp. St 37-2), S275J2G3+CR (1.0144 resp. St 44-3), ISO 3574, Unified Numbering System (UNS) G10200 or SAE 1020, and for testing aluminium, non-clad, types 7075-T6 or AZ5GU-T6 shall be used. An acceptable test is prescribed in the Manual of Tests and Criteria, Part III, Section 37.

NOTE: Where an initial test on either steel or aluminium indicates the substance being tested is corrosive the follow up test on the other metal is not required.

---

[7]   *OECD guidelines for Testing of Chemicals, No. 404 "Acute Dermal Irritation/Corrosion" (1992).*

2.2.8.1.7   If substances of Class 8, as a result of admixtures, come into categories of risk different from those to which the substances mentioned by name in Table A of Chapter 3.2 belong, these mixtures or solutions shall be assigned to the entries to which they belong, on the basis of their actual degree of danger.

NOTE: For the classification of solutions and mixtures (such as preparations and wastes), see also 2.1.3.

2.2.8.1.8   On the basis of the criteria set out in paragraph 2.2.8.1.6, it may also be determined whether the nature of a solution or mixture mentioned by name or containing a substance mentioned by name is such that the solution or mixture is not subject to the provisions for this class.

2.2.8.1.9   Substances, solutions and mixtures, which

-       do not meet the criteria of Directives 67/548/EEC [3] or 1999/45/EC [4] as amended and therefore are not classified as corrosive according to these directives, as amended; and

-       do not exhibit a corrosive effect on steel or aluminium;

may be considered as substances not belonging to Class 8.

NOTE: UN No. 1910 calcium oxide and UN No. 2812 sodium aluminate, listed in the UN Model Regulations, are not subject to the provisions of ADR.

2.2.8.2   *Substances not accepted for carriage*

2.2.8.2.1   The chemically unstable substances of Class 8 shall not be accepted for carriage unless the necessary steps have been taken to prevent their dangerous decomposition or polymerization during carriage. To this end it shall in particular be ensured that receptacles and tanks do not contain any substance liable to promote these reactions.

2.2.8.2.2   The following substances shall not be accepted for carriage:

-       UN No. 1798 NITROHYDROCHLORIC ACID;

-       chemically unstable mixtures of spent sulphuric acid;

-       chemically unstable mixtures of nitrating acid or mixtures of residual sulphuric and nitric acids, not denitrated;

-       perchloric acid aqueous solution with more than 72% pure acid, by mass, or mixtures of perchloric acid with any liquid other than water.

---

[3]   *Council Directive 67/548/EEC of 27 June 1967 on the approximation of laws, regulations and administrative provisions relating to the classification, packaging and labelling of dangerous substances (Official Journal of the European Communities No. L 196 of 16.08.1967, page 1).*

[4]   *Directive 1999/45/EC of the European Parliament and of the Council of 31 May 1999 on the approximation of laws, regulations and administrative provisions of the Member States relating to the classification, packaging and labelling of dangerous preparations (Official Journal of the European Communities No. L 200 of 30 July 1999, pages 1 to 68).*

2.2.8.3   *List of collective entries*

Corrosive substances <u>without</u> subsidiary risk

		liquid	C1	2584	ALKYLSULPHONIC ACIDS, LIQUID with more than 5% free sulphuric acid or
				2584	ARYLSULPHONIC ACIDS, LIQUID with more than 5% free sulphuric acid
				2693	BISULPHITES, AQUEOUS SOLUTION, N.O.S.
				2837	BISULPHATES, AQUEOUS SOLUTION
	inorganic			3264	CORROSIVE LIQUID, ACIDIC, INORGANIC, N.O.S.
				1740	HYDROGENDIFLUORIDES, SOLID, N.O.S.
				2583	ALKYLSULPHONIC ACIDS, SOLID with more than 5% free sulphuric acid or
				2583	ARYLSULPHONIC ACIDS, SOLID with more than 5% free sulphuric acid
Acid		solid	C2	3260	CORROSIVE SOLID, ACIDIC, INORGANIC, N.O.S.
C1-C4		liquid	C3	2586	ALKYLSULPHONIC ACIDS, LIQUID with not more than 5% free sulphuric acid or
				2586	ARYLSULPHONIC ACIDS, LIQUID with not more than 5% free sulphuric acid
				2987	CHLOROSILANES, CORROSIVE, N.O.S.
				3145	ALKYLPHENOLS, LIQUID, N.O.S. (including C_2-C_{12} homologues)
	organic			3265	CORROSIVE LIQUID, ACIDIC, ORGANIC, N.O.S
				2430	ALKYLPHENOLS, SOLID, N.O.S. (including C_2-C_{12} homologues)
				2585	ALKYLSULPHONIC ACIDS, SOLID with not more than 5% free sulphuric acid or
				2585	ARYLSULPHONIC ACIDS, SOLID with not more than 5% free sulphuric acid
		solid	C4	3261	CORROSIVE SOLID, ACIDIC, ORGANIC, N.O.S.
		liquid	C5	1719	CAUSTIC ALKALI LIQUID, N.O.S.
				2797	BATTERY FLUID, ALKALI
	inorganic			3266	CORROSIVE LIQUID, BASIC, INORGANIC, N.O.S.
		solid	C6	3262	CORROSIVE SOLID, BASIC, INORGANIC, N.O.S.
Basic		liquid	C7	2735	AMINES, LIQUID, CORROSIVE, N.O.S. or
C5-C8				2735	POLYAMINES, LIQUID, CORROSIVE, N.O.S.
	organic			3267	CORROSIVE LIQUID, BASIC, ORGANIC, N.O.S.
				3259	AMINES, SOLID, CORROSIVE, N.O.S., or
				3259	POLYAMINES, SOLID, CORROSIVE, N.O.S.
		solid	C8	3263	CORROSIVE SOLID, BASIC, ORGANIC, N.O.S.
		liquid	C9	1903	DISINFECTANT, LIQUID, CORROSIVE, N.O.S
				2801	DYE, LIQUID, CORROSIVE, N.O.S. or
				2801	DYE INTERMEDIATE, LIQUID, CORROSIVE, N.O.S.
				3066	PAINT (including paint, enamel, stain, shellac, varnish, polish, liquid filler and lacquer base) or
Other corrosive substances				3066	PAINT RELATED MATERIAL (including paint thinning or reducing compound)
C9-C10				1760	CORROSIVE LIQUID, N.O.S.
				3147	DYE, SOLID, CORROSIVE, N.O.S. or
				3147	DYE INTERMEDIATE, SOLID, CORROSIVE, N.O.S.
				3244	SOLIDS CONTAINING CORROSIVE LIQUID, N.O.S.
		solid[a]	C10	1759	CORROSIVE SOLID, N.O.S.
				2794	BATTERIES, WET, FILLED WITH ACID, electric storage
				2795	BATTERIES, WET, FILLED WITH ALKALI, electric storage
Articles			C11	2800	BATTERIES, WET, NON-SPILLABLE, electric storage
				3028	BATTERIES, DRY, CONTAINING POTASSIUM HYDROXIDE SOLID, electric storage

(cont'd on next page)

---

[a]   *Mixtures of solids which are not subject to the provisions of ADR and of corrosive liquids may be carried under UN No. 3244 without being subject to the classification criteria of Class 8, provided there is no free liquid visible at the time the substance is loaded or at the time the packaging, container or transport unit is closed. Each packaging shall correspond to a design type which has passed the leakproofness test for Packing group II level.*

Corrosive substances <u>with</u> subsidiary risk(s)

(cont'd)	liquid	CF1	3470	PAINT, CORROSIVE, FLAMMABLE (including paint, enamel, stain, shellac, varnish, polish, liquid filler and lacquer base) or
			3470	PAINT RELATED MATERIAL, CORROSIVE, FLAMMABLE (including paint thinning or reducing compound)
			2734	AMINES, LIQUID, CORROSIVE, FLAMMABLE, N.O.S. or
			2734	POLYAMINES, LIQUID, CORROSIVE, FLAMMABLE, N.O.S.
			2986	CHLOROSILANES, CORROSIVE, FLAMMABLE, N.O.S.
Flammable ᵇ			2920	CORROSIVE LIQUID, FLAMMABLE, N.O.S.
CF	solid	CF2	2921	CORROSIVE SOLID, FLAMMABLE, N.O.S.
Self-heating	liquid	CS1	3301	CORROSIVE LIQUID, SELF-HEATING, N.O.S.
CS	solid	CS2	3095	CORROSIVE SOLID, SELF-HEATING, N.O.S.
Water-reactive	liquid ᵇ	CW1	3094	CORROSIVE LIQUID, WATER-REACTIVE, N.O.S.
CW	solid	CW2	3096	CORROSIVE SOLID, WATER-REACTIVE, N.O.S.
Oxidizing	liquid	CO1	3093	CORROSIVE LIQUID, OXIDIZING, N.O.S.
CO	solid	CO2	3084	CORROSIVE SOLID, OXIDIZING, N.O.S.
Toxic ᵈ	liquid ᶜ	CT1	3471	HYDROGENDIFLUORIDES SOLUTION, N.O.S.
			2922	CORROSIVE LIQUID, TOXIC, N.O.S.
CT	solid ᵉ	CT2	2923	CORROSIVE SOLID, TOXIC, N.O.S.
Flammable, liquid, toxic ᵈ		CFT		No collective entry with this classification code available; if need be, classification under a collective entry with a classification code to be determined according to table of precedence of hazard in 2.1.3.10.
Oxidizing, toxic ᵈ, ᵉ		COT		No collective entry with this classification code available; if need be, classification under a collective entry with a classification code to be determined according to table of precedence of hazard in 2.1.3.10.

ᵇ   *Chlorosilanes which, in contact with water or moist air, emit flammable gases, are substances of Class 4.3.*

ᶜ   *Chloroformates having predominantly toxic properties are substances of Class 6.1.*

ᵈ   *Corrosive substances which are highly toxic by inhalation, as defined in 2.2.61.1.4 to 2.2.61.1.9 are substances of Class 6.1.*

ᵉ   *UN No. 2505 AMMONIUM FLUORIDE, UN No. 1812 POTASSIUM FLUORIDE, SOLID, UN No. 1690 SODIUM FLUORIDE, SOLID, UN No. 2674 SODIUM FLUOROSILICATE, UN No. 2856 FLUOROSILICATES, N.O.S., UN No. 3415 SODIUM FLUORIDE SOLUTION and UN No. 3422 POTASSIUM FLUORIDE SOLUTION are substances of Class 6.1.*

2.2.9   **Class 9**   **Miscellaneous dangerous substances and articles**

2.2.9.1   *Criteria*

2.2.9.1.1   The heading of Class 9 covers substances and articles which, during carriage, present a danger not covered by the heading of other classes.

2.2.9.1.2   The substances and articles of Class 9 are subdivided as follows:

       M1   Substances which, on inhalation as fine dust, may endanger health;

       M2   Substances and apparatus which, in the event of fire, may form dioxins;

       M3   Substances evolving flammable vapour;

       M4   Lithium batteries;

       M5   Life-saving appliances;

       M6-M8   Environmentally hazardous substances:

             M6   Pollutant to the aquatic environment, liquid;
             M7   Pollutant to the aquatic environment, solid;
             M8   Genetically modified microorganisms and organisms;

       M9-M10   Elevated temperature substances:

             M9   Liquid;
             M10   Solid;

       M11   Other substances presenting a danger during carriage, but not meeting the definitions of another class.

Definitions and classification

2.2.9.1.3   Substances and articles classified in Class 9 are listed in Table A of Chapter 3.2. The assignment of substances and articles not mentioned by name in Table A of Chapter 3.2 to the relevant entry of that Table or of sub-section 2.2.9.3 shall be done in accordance with 2.2.9.1.4 to 2.2.9.1.14 below.

Substances which, on inhalation as fine dust, may endanger health

2.2.9.1.4   Substances which, on inhalation as fine dust, may endanger health include asbestos and mixtures containing asbestos.

Substances and apparatus which, in the event of fire, may form dioxins

2.2.9.1.5   Substances and apparatus which, in the event of fire, may form dioxins include polychlorinated biphenyls (PCBs) and terphenyls (PCTs) and polyhalogenated biphenyls and terphenyls and mixtures containing these substances, as well as apparatus such as transformers, condensers and apparatus containing those substances or mixtures.

NOTE: *Mixtures with a PCB or PCT content of not more than 50 mg/kg are not subject to the provisions of ADR.*

Substances evolving flammable vapour

2.2.9.1.6   Substances evolving flammable vapour include polymers containing flammable liquids with a flash-point not exceeding 55 °C.

Lithium batteries

2.2.9.1.7   The term "lithium battery" covers all cells and batteries containing lithium in any form. They may be assigned to Class 9 if they meet the requirements of special provision 230 of Chapter 3.3. They are not subject to the provisions of ADR if they meet the requirements of special provision 188 of Chapter 3.3. They shall be classified in accordance with the procedures of Section 38.3 of the Manual of Tests and Criteria.

Life-saving appliances

2.2.9.1.8   Life-saving appliances include life-saving appliances and motor vehicle components which meet the descriptions of special provisions 235 or 296 of Chapter 3.3.

Environmentally hazardous substances

2.2.9.1.9   *(Deleted)*

Pollutants to the aquatic environment

2.2.9.1.10   *Environmentally hazardous substances (aquatic environment)*

2.2.9.1.10.1   General definitions

2.2.9.1.10.1.1   Environmentally hazardous substances include, inter alia, liquid or solid substances pollutant to the aquatic environment and solutions and mixtures of such substances (such as preparations and wastes).

For the purposes of 2.2.9.1.10, "*substance*" means chemical elements and their compounds in the natural state or obtained by any production process, including any additive necessary to preserve the stability of the product and any impurities deriving from the process used, but excluding any solvent which may be separated without affecting the stability of the substance or changing its composition.

2.2.9.1.10.1.2   The aquatic environment may be considered in terms of the aquatic organisms that live in the water, and the aquatic ecosystem of which they are part [8]. The basis, therefore, of the identification of hazard is the aquatic toxicity of the substance or mixture, although this may be modified by further information on the degradation and bioaccumulation behaviour.

2.2.9.1.10.1.3   While the following classification procedure is intended to apply to all substances and mixtures, it is recognised that in some cases, e.g. metals or poorly soluble inorganic compounds, special guidance will be necessary [9].

2.2.9.1.10.1.4   The following definitions apply for acronyms or terms used in this section:

-    BCF: Bioconcentration Factor;
-    BOD: Biochemical Oxygen Demand;

---

[8]   *This does not address aquatic pollutants for which there may be a need to consider effects beyond the aquatic environment such as the impacts on human health etc.*
[9]   *This can be found in Annex 10 of the GHS.*

-   COD: Chemical Oxygen Demand;
-   GLP: Good Laboratory Practices;
-   EC_{50}: the effective concentration of substance that causes 50% of the maximum response;
-   ErC_{50}: EC_{50} in terms of reduction of growth;
-   Kow: octanol/water partition coefficient;
-   LC_{50} (50% lethal concentration): the concentration of a substance in water which causes the death of 50% (one half) in a group of test animals;
-   $L(E)C_{50}$: LC_{50} or EC_{50};
-   NOEC: No Observed Effect Concentration;
-   OECD Test Guidelines: Test guidelines published by the Organization for Economic Cooperation and Development (OECD).

2.2.9.1.10.2   Definitions and data requirements

2.2.9.1.10.2.1   The basic elements for classification of environmentally hazardous substances (aquatic environment) are:

-   Acute aquatic toxicity;
-   Potential for or actual bioaccumulation;
-   Degradation (biotic or abiotic) for organic chemicals; and
-   Chronic aquatic toxicity.

2.2.9.1.10.2.2   While data from internationally harmonised test methods are preferred, in practice, data from national methods may also be used where they are considered as equivalent. In general, it has been agreed that freshwater and marine species toxicity data can be considered as equivalent data and are preferably to be derived using OECD Test Guidelines or equivalent according to the principles of Good Laboratory Practices (GLP). Where such data are not available, classification shall be based on the best available data.

2.2.9.1.10.2.3   Acute aquatic toxicity shall normally be determined using a fish 96 hour LC_{50} (OECD Test Guideline 203 or equivalent), a crustacea species 48 hour EC_{50} (OECD Test Guideline 202 or equivalent) and/or an algal species 72 or 96 hour EC_{50} (OECD Test Guideline 201 or equivalent). These species are considered as surrogate for all aquatic organisms and data on other species such as Lemna may also be considered if the test methodology is suitable.

2.2.9.1.10.2.4   Bioaccumulation means net result of uptake, transformation and elimination of a substance in an organism due to all routes of exposure (i.e. air, water, sediment/soil and food).

The potential for bioaccumulation shall normally be determined by using the octanol/water partition coefficient, usually reported as a log K_{ow} determined according to OECD Test Guideline 107 or 117. While this represents a potential to bioaccumulate, an experimentally determined Bioconcentration Factor (BCF) provides a better measure and shall be used in preference when available. A BCF shall be determined according to OECD Test Guideline 305.

2.2.9.1.10.2.5   Environmental degradation may be biotic or abiotic (e.g. hydrolysis) and the criteria used reflect this fact. Ready biodegradation is most easily defined using the OECD biodegradability tests (OECD Test Guideline 301 (A - F)). A pass level in these tests may be considered as indicative of rapid degradation in most environments. These are freshwater tests and thus the use of the results from OECD Test Guideline 306, which is more suitable for marine environments, has also been included. Where such data are not available, a BOD(5 days)/COD ratio ≥ 0.5 is considered as indicative of rapid degradation.

Abiotic degradation such as hydrolysis, primary degradation, both abiotic and biotic, degradation in non-aquatic media and proven rapid degradation in the environment may all be considered in defining rapid degradability [10].

Substances are considered rapidly degradable in the environment if the following criteria are met:

(a)   In 28-day ready biodegradation studies, the following levels of degradation are achieved:

  (i)   Tests based on dissolved organic carbon: 70%;

  (ii)   Tests based on oxygen depletion or carbon dioxide generation: 60% of theoretical maxima;

These levels of biodegradation shall be achieved within 10 days of the start of degradation which point is taken as the time when 10% of the substance has been degraded; or

(b)   In those cases where only BOD and COD data are available, when the ratio of BOD5/COD is $\geq$ 0.5; or

(c)   If other convincing scientific evidence is available to demonstrate that the substance or mixture can be degraded (biotically and/or abiotically) in the aquatic environment to a level above 70% within a 28 day period.

2.2.9.1.10.2.6   Chronic toxicity data are less available than acute data and the range of testing procedures less standardised. Data generated according to the OECD Test Guidelines 210 (Fish Early Life Stage) or 211 (Daphnia Reproduction) and 201 (Algal Growth Inhibition) may be accepted. Other validated and internationally accepted tests may also be used. The "No Observed Effect Concentrations" (NOECs) or other equivalent L(E)Cx shall be used.

2.2.9.1.10.3   Substance classification categories and criteria

Substances shall be classified as "environmentally hazardous substances (aquatic environment)", if they satisfy the criteria for Acute 1, Chronic 1 or Chronic 2, according to the following tables:

Acute toxicity

Category: Acute 1	
Acute toxicity:	
96 hr LC_{50} (for fish)	$\leq$ 1 mg/l and/or
48 hr EC_{50} (for crustacea)	$\leq$ 1 mg/l and/or
72 or 96hr ErC_{50} (for algae or other aquatic plants)	$\leq$ 1 mg/l

---

[10]   *Special guidance on data interpretation is provided in Chapter 4.1 and Annex 9 of the GHS.*

Chronic toxicity

Category: Chronic 1

Acute toxicity:

96 hr LC_{50} (for fish)	≤ 1 mg/l and/or
48 hr EC_{50} (for crustacea)	≤ 1 mg/l and/or
72 or 96hr ErC_{50} (for algae or other aquatic plants)	≤ 1 mg/l

and the substance is not rapidly degradable and/or the log $K_{ow} \geq 4$ (unless the experimentally determined BCF < 500)

Category: Chronic 2

Acute toxicity:

96 hr LC_{50} (for fish)	>1 to ≤ 10 mg/l and/or
48 hr EC_{50} (for crustacea)	>1 to ≤ 10 mg/l and/or
72 or 96hr ErC_{50} (for algae or other aquatic plants)	>1 to ≤ 10 mg/l

and the substance is not rapidly degradable and/or the log $K_{ow} \geq 4$ (unless the experimentally determined BCF < 500), unless the chronic toxicity NOECs are > 1 mg/l

---

The classification flowchart below outlines the process to be followed:

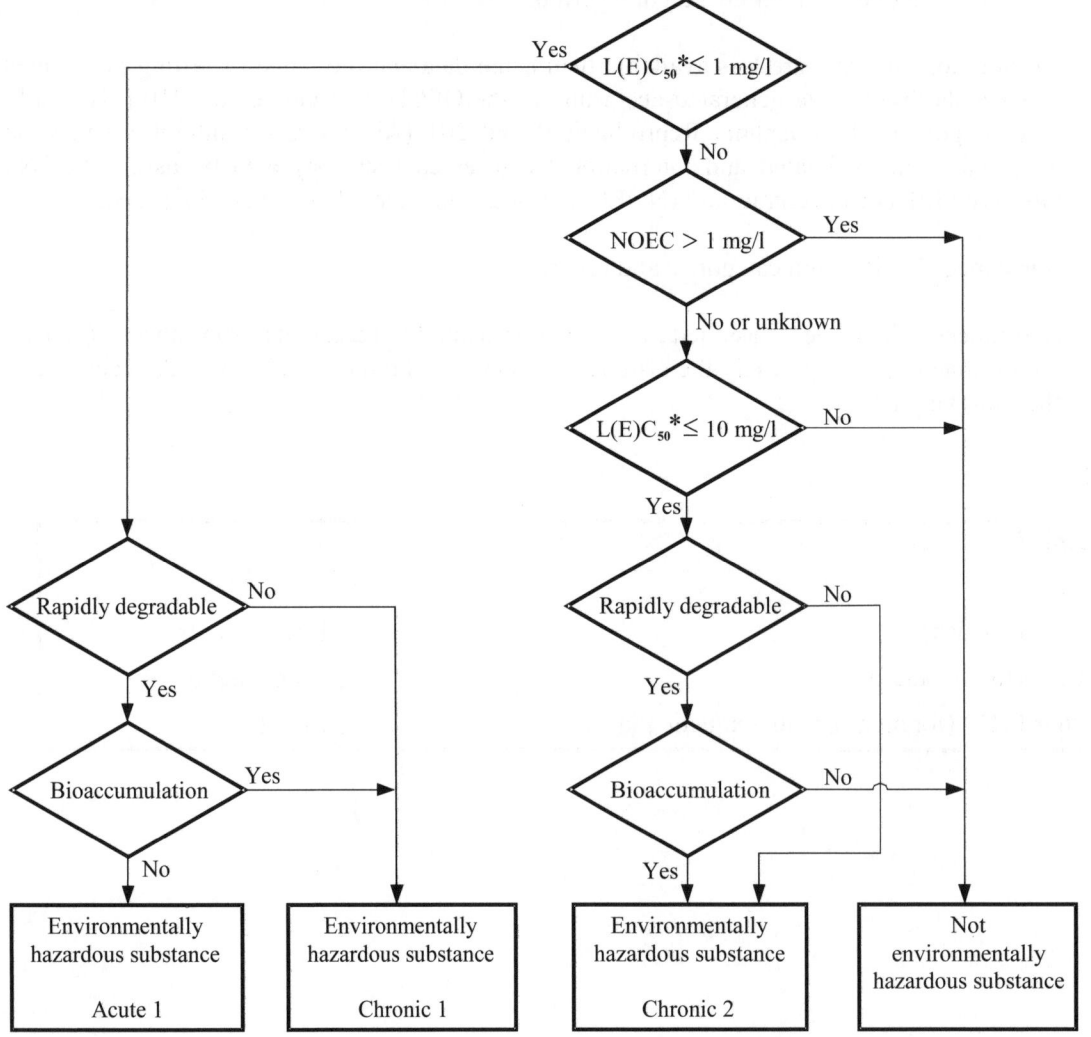

*   *Lowest value of 96-hour LC_{50}, 48-hour EC_{50} or 72-hour or 96-hour ErC_{50}, as appropriate.*

2.2.9.1.10.4   Mixtures classification categories and criteria

2.2.9.1.10.4.1   The classification system for mixtures covers the classification categories which are used for substances meaning acute category 1 and chronic categories 1 and 2. In order to make use of all available data for purposes of classifying the aquatic environmental hazards of the mixture, the following assumption is made and is applied where appropriate:

The "relevant ingredients" of a mixture are those which are present in a concentration of 1% (by mass) or greater, unless there is a presumption (e.g. in the case of highly toxic ingredients) that an ingredient present at less than 1% can still be relevant for classifying the mixture for aquatic environmental hazards.

2.2.9.1.10.4.2   The approach for classification of aquatic environmental hazards is tiered, and is dependent upon the type of information available for the mixture itself and for its ingredients. Elements of the tiered approach include:

(a)   Classification based on tested mixtures;

(b)   Classification based on bridging principles;

(c)   The use of "summation of classified ingredients" and/or an "additivity formula".

Figure 2.2.9.1.10.4.2 below outlines the process to be followed.

Figure 2.2.9.1.10.4.2: Tiered approach to classification of mixtures for acute and chronic aquatic environmental hazards

2.2.9.1.10.4.3 Classification of mixtures when data are available for the complete mixture

2.2.9.1.10.4.3.1 When the mixture as a whole has been tested to determine its aquatic toxicity, it shall be classified according to the criteria that have been agreed for substances, but only for acute toxicity. The classification is based on the data for fish, crustacea and algae/plants. Classification of mixtures by using LC_{50} or EC_{50} data for the mixture as a whole is not possible for chronic categories since both toxicity data and environmental fate data are needed, and there are no degradability and bioaccumulation data for mixtures as a whole. It is not possible to apply the criteria for chronic classification because the data from degradability and bio-accumulation tests of mixtures cannot be interpreted; they are meaningful only for single substances.

2.2.9.1.10.4.3.2 When there are acute toxicity test data (LC_{50} or EC_{50}) available for the mixture as a whole, these data as well as information with respect to the classification of ingredients for chronic toxicity shall be used to complete the classification for tested mixtures as follows. When chronic (long term) toxicity data (NOEC) are also available, they shall be used as well.

    (a) $L(E)C_{50}$ (LC_{50} or EC_{50}) of the tested mixture $\leq$ 1 mg/l and NOEC of the tested mixture $\leq$ 1.0 mg/l or unknown:

-    classify mixture as category acute 1;

-    apply summation of classified ingredients approach (see 2.2.9.1.10.4.6.3 and 2.2.9.1.10.4.6.4) for chronic classification (chronic 1, 2, or no need of chronic classification);

    (b) $L(E)C_{50}$ of the tested mixture $\leq$ 1 mg/l and NOEC of the tested mixture > 1.0 mg/l:

-    classify mixture as category acute 1;

-    apply summation of classified ingredients approach (see 2.2.9.1.10.4.6.3 and 2.2.9.1.10.4.6.4) for classification as category chronic 1. If the mixture is not classified as category chronic 1, then there is no need for chronic classification;

    (c) $L(E)C_{50}$ of the tested mixture > 1 mg/l, or above the water solubility, and NOEC of the tested mixture $\leq$ 1.0 mg/l or unknown:

-    no need to classify for acute toxicity;

-    apply summation of classified ingredients approach (see 2.2.9.1.10.4.6.3 and 2.2.9.1.10.4.6.4) for chronic classification or no need for chronic classification;

    (d) $L(E)C_{50}$ of the tested mixture > 1 mg/l, or above the water solubility, and NOEC of the tested mixture > 1.0 mg/l:

-    No need to classify for acute or chronic toxicity.

2.2.9.1.10.4.4 Bridging principles

2.2.9.1.10.4.4.1 Where the mixture itself has not been tested to determine its aquatic environmental hazard, but there are sufficient data on the individual ingredients and similar tested mixtures to adequately characterise the hazards of the mixture, these data shall be used in accordance with the following agreed bridging rules. This ensures that the classification process uses the available data to the greatest extent possible in characterising the hazards of the mixture without the necessity for additional testing in animals.

2.2.9.1.10.4.4.2   Dilution

2.2.9.1.10.4.4.2.1   If a mixture is formed by diluting another classified mixture or a substance with a diluent which has an equivalent or lower aquatic hazard classification than the least toxic original ingredient and which is not expected to affect the aquatic hazards of other ingredients, then the mixture shall be classified as equivalent to the original mixture or substance.

2.2.9.1.10.4.4.2.2   If a mixture is formed by diluting another classified mixture or a substance with water or other totally non-toxic material, the toxicity of the mixture shall be calculated from the original mixture or substance.

2.2.9.1.10.4.4.3   Batching

The aquatic hazard classification of one production batch of a complex mixture shall be assumed to be substantially equivalent to that of another production batch of the same commercial product and produced by or under the control of the same manufacturer, unless there is reason to believe there is significant variation such that the aquatic hazard classification of the batch has changed. If the latter occurs, new classification is necessary.

2.2.9.1.10.4.4.4   Concentration of mixtures which are classified with the most severe classification categories (chronic 1 and acute 1)

If a mixture is classified as chronic 1 and/or acute 1, and ingredients of the mixture which are classified as chronic 1 and/or acute 1 are further concentrated, the more concentrated mixture shall be classified with the same classification category as the original mixture without additional testing.

2.2.9.1.10.4.4.5   Interpolation within one toxicity category

If mixtures A and B are in the same classification category and mixture C is made in which the toxicologically active ingredients have concentrations intermediate to those in mixtures A and B, then mixture C shall be in the same category as A and B. Note that the identity of the ingredients is the same in all three mixtures.

2.2.9.1.10.4.4.6   Substantially similar mixtures

Given the following:

(a)   two mixtures:

(i)   A + B;

(ii)   C + B;

(b)   the concentration of ingredient B is the same in both mixtures;

(c)   the concentration of ingredient A in mixture (i) equals that of ingredient C in mixture (ii);

(d)   classification for A and C are available and are the same, i.e. they are in the same hazard category and are not expected to affect the aquatic toxicity of B,

then there shall be no need to test mixture (ii) if mixture (i) is already characterised by testing and both mixtures are classified in the same category.

2.2.9.1.10.4.5   Classification of mixtures when data are available for all ingredients or only for some ingredients of the mixture

2.2.9.1.10.4.5.1 The classification of a mixture shall be based on summation of the concentrations of its classified ingredients. The percentage of ingredients classified as "Acute" or "Chronic" will feed straight into the summation method. Details of the summation method are described in 2.2.9.1.10.4.6.1 to 2.2.9.1.10.4.6.4.

2.2.9.1.10.4.5.2 Mixtures may be made of a combination of both ingredients that are classified (as Acute 1 and/or Chronic 1, 2) and those for which adequate test data are available. When adequate toxicity data are available for more than one ingredient in the mixture, the combined toxicity of those ingredients shall be calculated using the following additivity formula, and the calculated toxicity shall be used to assign that portion of the mixture an acute toxicity hazard which is then subsequently used in applying the summation method.

$$\frac{\sum C_i}{L(E)C_{50m}} = \sum_n \frac{C_i}{L(E)C_{50i}}$$

where:

C_i	=	concentration of ingredient i (mass percentage);
$L(E)C_{50i}$	=	(mg/l) LC_{50} or EC_{50} for ingredient i;
n	=	number of ingredients, and i is running from 1 to n;
$L(E)C_{50m}$	=	$L(E)C_{50}$ of the part of the mixture with test data.

2.2.9.1.10.4.5.3 When applying the additivity formula for part of the mixture, it is preferable to calculate the toxicity of this part of the mixture using for each substance toxicity values that relate to the same species (i.e. fish, daphnia or algae) and then to use the highest toxicity (lowest value) obtained (i.e. use the most sensitive of the three species). However, when toxicity data for each ingredient are not available in the same species, the toxicity value of each ingredient shall be selected in the same manner that toxicity values are selected for the classification of substances, i.e. the higher toxicity (from the most sensitive test organism) is used. The calculated acute toxicity shall then be used to classify this part of the mixture as Acute 1 using the same criteria described for substances.

2.2.9.1.10.4.5.4 If a mixture is classified in more than one way, the method yielding the more conservative result shall be used.

2.2.9.1.10.4.6   Summation method

2.2.9.1.10.4.6.1 Classification procedure

In general a more severe classification for mixtures overrides a less severe classification, e.g. a classification with chronic 1 overrides a classification with chronic 2. As a consequence the classification procedure is already completed if the results of the classification is chronic 1. A more severe classification than chronic 1 is not possible; therefore, it is not necessary to pursue the classification procedure further.

2.2.9.1.10.4.6.2 Classification for the acute category 1

2.2.9.1.10.4.6.2.1   All ingredients classified as acute 1 shall be considered. If the sum of these ingredients is greater than or equal to 25% the whole mixture shall be classified as category acute 1. If the result of the calculation is a classification of the mixture as category acute 1, the classification process is completed.

2.2.9.1.10.4.6.2.2 The classification of mixtures for acute hazards based on this summation of classified ingredients, is summarised in Table 2.2.9.1.10.4.6.2.2 below.

Table 2.2.9.1.10.4.6.2.2 : Classification of a mixture for acute hazards, based on summation of classified ingredients

Sum of ingredients classified as:	Mixture is classified as:
Acute $1 \times M^a \geq 25\%$	Acute 1

^a   *For explanation of the M factor, see 2.2.9.1.10.4.6.4.*

2.2.9.1.10.4.6.3 Classification for the chronic categories 1, 2

2.2.9.1.10.4.6.3.1 First, all ingredients classified as chronic 1 are considered. If the sum of these ingredients is greater than or equal to 25% the mixture shall be classified as category chronic 1. If the result of the calculation is a classification of the mixture as category chronic 1 the classification procedure is completed.

2.2.9.1.10.4.6.3.2 In cases where the mixture is not classified as chronic 1, classification of the mixture as chronic 2 is considered. A mixture shall be classified as chronic 2 if 10 times the sum of all ingredients classified as chronic 1 plus the sum of all ingredients classified as chronic 2 is greater than or equal to 25%. If the result of the calculation is classification of the mixture as chronic 2, the classification process is completed.

2.2.9.1.10.4.6.3.3 The classification of mixtures for chronic hazards, based on this summation of classified ingredients, is summarised in Table 2.2.9.1.10.4.6.3.3 below.

Table 2.2.9.1.10.4.6.3.3: Classification of a mixture for chronic hazards, based on summation of classified ingredients

Sum of ingredients classified as:		Mixture is classified as:
Chronic $1 \times M^a$	$\geq 25\%$	Chronic 1
$(M \times 10 \times$ Chronic 1$)+$Chronic 2	$\geq 25\%$	Chronic 2

^a   *For explanation of the M factor, see 2.2.9.1.10.4.6.4.*

2.2.9.1.10.4.6.4 Mixtures with highly toxic ingredients

Category acute 1 ingredients with toxicities well below 1 mg/l may influence the toxicity of the mixture and are given increased weight in applying the summation method. When a mixture contains ingredients classified as acute or chronic 1, the tiered approach described in 2.2.9.1.10.4.6.2 and 2.2.9.1.10.4.6.3 shall be applied using a weighted sum by multiplying the concentrations of acute 1 ingredients by a factor, instead of merely adding up the percentages. This means that the concentration of "Acute 1" in the left column of Table 2.2.9.1.10.4.6.2.2 and the concentration of "Chronic 1" in the left column of Table 2.2.9.1.10.4.6.3.3 are multiplied by the appropriate multiplying factor. The multiplying factors to be applied to these ingredients are defined using the toxicity value, as summarised in Table 2.2.9.1.10.4.6.4 below. Therefore, in order to classify a mixture containing acute 1 and/or chronic 1 ingredients, the classifier needs to be informed of the value of the M factor in order to apply the summation method. Alternatively, the additivity formula (see 2.2.9.1.10.4.5.2) may be used when toxicity data are available for all highly toxic ingredients in the mixture and there is convincing evidence that all other ingredients, including those for which specific acute toxicity data are not available, are of low or no toxicity and do not significantly contribute to the environmental hazard of the mixture.

Table 2.2.9.1.10.4.6.4 : Multiplying factors for highly toxic ingredients of mixtures

L(E)C$_{50}$ value	Multiplying factor (M)
$0.1 < L(E)C_{50} \leq 1$	1
$0.01 < L(E)C_{50} \leq 0.1$	10
$0.001 < L(E)C_{50} \leq 0.01$	100
$0.0001 < L(E)C_{50} \leq 0.001$	1000
$0.00001 < L(E)C_{50} \leq 0.0001$	10000
(continue in factor 10 intervals)	

2.2.9.1.10.4.6.5   Classification of mixtures with ingredients without any useable information

In the event that no useable information on acute and/or chronic aquatic hazard is available for one or more relevant ingredients, it is concluded that the mixture cannot be attributed (a) definitive hazard category(ies). In this situation the mixture shall be classified based on the known ingredients only with the additional statement that: "x percent of the mixture consists of ingredient(s) of unknown hazard to the aquatic environment.

2.2.9.1.10.5   Substances or mixtures dangerous to the aquatic environment not otherwise classified under ADR

2.2.9.1.10.5.1   Substances or mixtures dangerous to the aquatic environment not otherwise classified under ADR shall be designated:

UN No. 3077 ENVIRONMENTALLY HAZARDOUS SUBSTANCE, SOLID, N.O.S. or
UN No. 3082 ENVIRONMENTALLY HAZARDOUS SUBSTANCE, LIQUID, N.O.S.

They shall be assigned to packing group III.

2.2.9.1.10.5.2   Notwithstanding the provisions of 2.2.9.1.10,

    (a)   Substances which cannot be assigned to entries other than UN Nos. 3077 and 3082 in Class 9 or to other entries in classes 1 to 8, but which are identified in Council Directive 67/548/EEC of 27 June 1967 on the approximation of laws, regulations and administrative provisions relating to the classification, packaging and labelling of dangerous substances [11], as amended, as substances to which letter N "Environmentally hazardous" (R50; R50/53; R51/53) has been allocated; and

    (b)   Solutions and mixtures (such as preparations and wastes) of substances to which letter N "Environmentally hazardous" (R50; R50/53; R51/53) has been allocated in Directive 67/548/EEC, as amended, and which, according to Directive 1999/45/EC of the European Parliament and of the Council of 31 May 1999 concerning the approximation of the laws, regulations and administrative provisions of the Member States relating to the classification, packaging and labelling of dangerous preparations [12], as amended, are also allocated letter N "Environmentally hazardous" (R50; R50/53; R51/53), and which cannot be assigned to entries other than UN Nos. 3077 and 3082 in Class 9 or to other entries in classes 1 to 8;

shall be assigned to UN Nos. 3077 or 3082 of Class 9 as appropriate.

---

[11]   *Official Journal of the European Communities No.196, of 16 August 1967, pp. 1 – 5.*
[12]   *Official Journal of the European Communities No. L 200, of 30 July 1999, pp. 1 – 68.*

Genetically modified microorganisms or organisms

2.2.9.1.11   Genetically modified microorganisms (GMMOs) and genetically modified organisms (GMOs) are microorganisms and organisms in which genetic material has been purposely altered through genetic engineering in a way that does not occur naturally. They are assigned to Class 9 (UN No. 3245) if they do not meet the definition of infectious substances, but are capable of altering animals, plants or microbiological substances in a way not normally the result of natural reproduction.

NOTE 1:   GMMOs and GMOs which are infectious are substances of Class 6.2, UN Nos. 2814, 2900 or 3373.

NOTE 2:   GMMOs or GMOs are not subject to the provisions of ADR when authorized for use by the competent authorities of the countries of origin, transit and destination [13].

NOTE 3:   Live animals shall not be used to carry genetically modified microorganisms classified in Class 9 unless the substance can be carried no other way.

2.2.9.1.12   *(Deleted)*

Elevated temperature substances

2.2.9.1.13   Elevated temperature substances include substances which are carried or handed over for carriage in the liquid state at or above 100 °C and, in the case of those with a flash-point, below their flash-point. They also include solids which are carried or handed over for carriage at or above 240 °C.

NOTE: Elevated temperature substances may be assigned to Class 9 only if they do not meet the criteria of any other class.

Other substances presenting a danger during carriage but not meeting the definitions of another class.

2.2.9.1.14   The following other miscellaneous substances not meeting the definitions of another class are assigned to Class 9:

Solid ammonia compounds having a flash-point below 60 °C;
Low hazard dithionites;
Highly volatile liquids;
Substances emitting noxious fumes;
Substances containing allergens;
Chemical kits and first aid kits;

NOTE: UN No. 1845 carbon dioxide, solid (dry ice), UN No. 2071 ammonium nitrate fertilizers, UN No. 2216 fish meal (fish scrap), stabilized, UN No. 2807 magnetized material, UN No. 3166 engine, internal combustion or vehicle, flammable gas powered or vehicle, flammable liquid powered, UN No. 3171 battery-powered vehicle or 3171 battery-powered equipment (wet battery), UN No. 3334 aviation regulated liquid, n.o.s., UN No. 3335 aviation regulated solid, n.o.s. and UN No. 3363 dangerous goods in machinery or dangerous goods in apparatus listed in the UN Model Regulations, are not subject to the provisions of ADR.

---

[13]   *See in particular Part C of Directive 2001/18/EC of the European Parliament and of the Council on the deliberate release into the environment of genetically modified organisms and repealing Council Directive 90/220/EEC (Official Journal of the European Communities, No. L 106, of 17 April 2001, pp. 8-14), which sets out the authorization procedures for the European Community.*

2.2.9.1.15   When indicated in column (4) of Table A of Chapter 3.2, substances and articles of Class 9 are assigned to one of the following packing groups according to their degree of danger:

Packing group II: substances presenting medium danger;
Packing group III: substances presenting low danger.

2.2.9.2   ***Substances and articles not accepted for carriage***

The following substances and articles shall not be accepted for carriage:

-      Lithium batteries which do not meet the relevant conditions of special provisions 188, 230 or 636 of Chapter 3.3;

-      Uncleaned empty containment vessels for apparatus such as transformers, condensers and hydraulic apparatus containing substances assigned to UN Nos. 2315, 3151, 3152 or 3432.

2.2.9.3 *List of collective entries*

Substances which, on inhalation as fine dust, may endanger health	**M1**	2212 BLUE ASBESTOS (crocidolite) or 2212 BROWN ASBESTOS (amosite, mysorite) 2590 WHITE ASBESTOS (chrysotile, actinolite, anthophyllite, tremolite)
Substances and apparatus which, in the event of fire, may form dioxins	**M2**	2315 POLYCHLORINATED BIPHENYLS, LIQUID 3432 POLYCHLORINATED BIPHENYLS, SOLID 3151 POLYHALOGENATED BIPHENYLS, LIQUID or 3151 POLYHALOGENATED TERPHENYLS, LIQUID 3152 POLYHALOGENATED BIPHENYLS, SOLID or 3152 POLYHALOGENATED TERPHENYLS, SOLID
Substances evolving flammable vapour	**M3**	2211 POLYMERIC BEADS, EXPANDABLE, evolving flammable vapour 3314 PLASTICS MOULDING COMPOUND in dough, sheet or extruded rope form evolving flammable vapour
Lithium batteries	**M4**	3090 LITHIUM METAL BATTERIES (including lithium alloy batteries) 3091 LITHIUM METAL BATTERIES CONTAINED IN EQUIPMENT (including lithium alloy batteries) or 3091 LITHIUM METAL BATTERIES PACKED WITH EQUIPMENT (including lithium alloy batteries) 3480 LITHIUM ION BATTERIES (including lithium ion polymer batteries) 3481 LITHIUM ION BATTERIES CONTAINED IN EQUIPMENT (including lithium ion polymer batteries) or 3481 LITHIUM ION BATTERIES PACKED WITH EQUIPMENT (including lithium ion polymer batteries)
Live-saving appliances	**M5**	2990 LIFE-SAVING APPLIANCES, SELF-INFLATING 3072 LIFE-SAVING APPLIANCES NOT SELF-INFLATING containing dangerous goods as equipment 3268 AIR BAG INFLATORS or 3268 AIR BAG MODULES or 3268 SEAT-BELT PRETENSIONERS
Environmentally hazardous substances — **pollutant to the aquatic environment, liquid**	**M6**	3082 ENVIRONMENTALLY HAZARDOUS SUBSTANCE, LIQUID, N.O.S.
Environmentally hazardous substances — **pollutant to the aquatic environment, solid**	**M7**	3077 ENVIRONMENTALLY HAZARDOUS SUBSTANCE, SOLID, N.O.S.
genetically modified micro-organisms and organisms	**M8**	3245 GENETICALLY MODIFIED MICROORGANISMS or 3245 GENETICALLY MODIFIED ORGANISMS
Elevated temperature substances — **liquid**	**M9**	3257 ELEVATED TEMPERATURE LIQUID, N.O.S., at or above 100 °C and below its flash-point (including molten metal, molten salts, etc.)
Elevated temperature substances — **solid**	**M10**	3258 ELEVATED TEMPERATURE SOLID, N.O.S., at or above 240 °C
Other substances or articles presenting a danger during carriage, but not meeting the definitions of another class	**M11**	No collective entry available. Only substances listed in Table A of Chapter 3.2 are subject to the provisions for Class 9 under this classification code, as follows: 1841 ACETALDEHYDE AMMONIA 1931 ZINC DITHIONITE (ZINC HYDROSULPHITE) 1941 DIBROMODIFLUOROMETHANE 1990 BENZALDEHYDE 2969 CASTOR BEANS, or 2969 CASTOR MEAL, or 2969 CASTOR POMACE, or 2969 CASTOR FLAKE 3316 CHEMICAL KIT, or 3316 FIRST AID KIT 3359 FUMIGATED UNIT

CHAPTER 2.3

TEST METHODS

2.3.0   **General**

Unless otherwise provided for in Chapter 2.2 or in this Chapter, the test methods to be used for the classification of dangerous goods are those described in the Manual of Tests and Criteria.

2.3.1   **Exudation test for blasting explosives of Type A**

2.3.1.1   Blasting explosives of type A (UN No. 0081) shall, if they contain more than 40% liquid nitric ester, in addition to the testing specified in the Manual of Tests and Criteria, satisfy the following exudation test.

2.3.1.2   The apparatus for testing blasting explosive for exudation (figs. 1 to 3) consists of a hollow bronze cylinder. This cylinder, which is closed at one end by a plate of the same metal, has an internal diameter of 15.7 mm and a depth of 40 mm. It is pierced by 20 holes 0.5 mm in diameter (four sets of five holes) on the circumference. A bronze piston, cylindrically fashioned over a length of 48 mm and having a total length of 52 mm, slides into the vertically placed cylinder. The piston, whose diameter is 15.6 mm, is loaded with a mass of 2 220 g so that a pressure of 120 kPa (1.20 bar) is exerted on the base of the cylinder.

2.3.1.3   A small plug of blasting explosive weighing 5 to 8 g, 30 mm long and 15 mm in diameter, is wrapped in very fine gauze and placed in the cylinder; the piston and its loading mass are then placed on it so that the blasting explosive is subjected to a pressure of 120 kPa (1.20 bar). The time taken for the appearance of the first signs of oily droplets (nitroglycerine) at the outer orifices of the cylinder holes is noted.

2.3.1.4   The blasting explosive is considered satisfactory if the time elapsing before the appearance of the liquid exudations is more than five minutes, the test having been carried out at a temperature of 15 °C to 25 °C.

Test of blasting explosive for exudation

Fig.1: Bell-form charge, mass 2220 g, capable of being suspended from a bronze piston

Fig.2: Cylindrical bronze piston, dimensions in mm

Fig.3: Hollow bronze cylinder, closed at one end; Plan and cut dimensions in mm

Fig. 1 to 3

(1) 4 series of 5 holes at 0.5 N
(2) copper
(3) iron plate with centre cone at the inferior face
(4) 4 openings, approximately 46x56, set at even intervals on the periphery

2.3.2   **Tests relating to nitrated cellulose mixtures of Class 4.1**

2.3.2.1   Nitrocellulose heated for half an hour at 132 °C shall not give off visible yellowish-brown nitrous fumes (nitrous gases). The ignition temperature shall be above 180 °C. See 2.3.2.3 to 2.3.2.8, 2.3.2.9 (a) and 2.3.2.10 below.

2.3.2.2   3 g of plasticized nitrocellulose, heated for one hour at 132 °C, shall not give off visible yellowish-brown nitrous fumes (nitrous gases). The ignition temperature shall be above 170 °C. See 2.3.2.3 to 2.3.2.8, 2.3.2.9 (b) and 2.3.2.10 below.

2.3.2.3   The test procedures set out below are to be applied when differences of opinion arise as to the acceptability of substances for carriage by road.

2.3.2.4   If other methods or test procedures are used to verify the conditions of stability prescribed above in this section, those methods shall lead to the same findings as could be reached by the methods specified below.

2.3.2.5   In carrying out the stability tests by heating described below, the temperature of the oven containing the sample under test shall not deviate by more than 2 °C from the prescribed temperature; the prescribed duration of a 30-minute or 60-minute test shall be observed to within two minutes. The oven shall be such that the required temperature is restored not more than five minutes after insertion of the sample.

2.3.2.6   Before undergoing the tests in 2.3.2.9 and 2.3.2.10, the samples shall be dried for not less than 15 hours at the ambient temperature in a vacuum desiccator containing fused and granulated calcium chloride, the sample substance being spread in a thin layer; for this purpose, substances which are neither in powder form nor fibrous shall be ground, or grated, or cut into small pieces. The pressure in the desiccator shall be brought below 6.5 kPa (0.065 bar).

2.3.2.7   Before being dried as prescribed in 2.3.2.6 above, substances conforming to 2.3.2.2 shall undergo preliminary drying in a well-ventilated oven, with its temperature set at 70 °C, until the loss of mass per quarter-hour is less than 0.3% of the original mass.

2.3.2.8   Weakly nitrated nitrocellulose conforming to 2.3.2.1 shall first undergo preliminary drying as prescribed in 2.3.2.7 above; drying shall then be completed by keeping the nitrocellulose for at least 15 hours over concentrated sulphuric acid in a desiccator.

2.3.2.9   *Test of chemical stability under heat*

(a)   *Test of the substance listed in paragraph 2.3.2.1 above.*

(i)   In each of two glass test tubes having the following dimensions:

length	350	mm
internal diameter	16	mm
thickness of wall	1.5	mm

is placed 1 g of substance dried over calcium chloride (if necessary the drying shall be carried out after reducing the substance to pieces weighing not more than 0.05 g each).

Both test tubes, completely covered with loose-fitting closures, are then so placed in an oven that at least four-fifths of their length is visible, and are kept at a constant temperature of 132 °C for 30 minutes. It is observed whether nitrous gases in the form of yellowish-brown fumes clearly visible against a white background are given off during this time;

(ii)   In the absence of such fumes the substance is deemed to be stable;

(b)   *Test of plasticized nitrocellulose (see 2.3.2.2)*

   (i)   3 g of plasticized nitrocellulose are placed in glass test tubes, similar to those referred to in (a), which are then placed in an oven kept at a constant temperature of 132 °C;

   (ii)   The test tubes containing the plasticized nitrocellulose are kept in the oven for one hour. During this time no yellowish-brown nitrous fumes (nitrous gases) shall be visible. Observation and appraisal as in (a).

2.3.2.10   *Ignition temperature (see 2.3.2.1 and 2.3.2.2)*

(a)   The ignition temperature is determined by heating 0.2 g of substance enclosed in a glass test tube immersed in a Wood's alloy bath. The test tube is placed in the bath when the latter has reached 100 °C. The temperature of the bath is then progressively increased by 5 °C per minute;

(b)   The test tubes must have the following dimensions:

length	125 mm
internal diameter	15 mm
thickness of wall	0.5 mm

and shall be immersed to a depth of 20 mm;

(c)   The test shall be repeated three times, the temperature at which ignition of the substance occurs, i.e., slow or rapid combustion, deflagration or detonation, being noted each time;

(d)   The lowest temperature recorded in the three tests is the ignition temperature.

2.3.3   **Tests relating to flammable liquids of Classes 3, 6.1 and 8**

2.3.3.1   *Test for determining flash-point*

2.3.3.1.1   The flash-point shall be determined by means of one of the following types of apparatus:

(a)   Abel;

(b)   Abel-Pensky;

(c)   Tag;

(d)   Pensky-Martens;

(e)   Apparatus in accordance with ISO 3679: 1983 or ISO 3680: 1983.

2.3.3.1.2   To determine the flash-point of paints, gums and similar viscous products containing solvents, only apparatus and test methods suitable for determining the flash-point for viscous liquids shall be used, in accordance with the following standards:

(a)   International Standard ISO 3679: 1983;

(b)   International Standard ISO 3680: 1983;

(c)   International Standard ISO 1523: 1983;

(d)   German Standard DIN 53213: 1978, Part 1.

2.3.3.1.3   The test procedure shall be either according to an equilibrium method or according to a non-equilibrium method.

2.3.3.1.4   For the procedure according to an equilibrium method, see:

(a)   International Standard ISO 1516: 1981;

(b)   International Standard ISO 3680: 1983;

(c)   International Standard ISO 1523: 1983;

(d)   International Standard ISO 3679: 1983.

2.3.3.1.5   The procedure according to a non-equilibrium method shall be:

(a)   for the Abel apparatus, see:

(i)   British Standard BS 2000 Part 170: 1995;

(ii)   French Standard NF MO7-011: 1988;

(iii)   French Standard NF T66-009: 1969;

(b)   for the Abel-Pensky apparatus, see:

(i)   German Standard DIN 51755, Part 1: 1974 (for temperatures from 5 °C to 65 °C);

(ii)   German Standard DIN 51755, Part 2: 1978 (for temperatures below 5 °C);

(iii)   French Standard NF MO7-036: 1984;

(c)   for the Tag apparatus, see American Standard ASTM D 56: 1993;

(d)   for the Pensky-Martens apparatus, see:

(i)   International Standard ISO 2719: 1988;

(ii)   European Standard EN 22719 in each of its national versions (e.g. BS 2000, part 404/EN 22719): 1994;

(iii)   American Standard ASTM D 93: 1994;

(iv)   Institute of Petroleum Standard IP 34: 1988.

2.3.3.1.6   The test methods listed in 2.3.3.1.4 and 2.3.3.1.5 shall only be used for flash-point ranges which are specified in the individual methods. The possibility of chemical reactions between the substance and the sample holder shall be considered when selecting the method to be used. The apparatus shall, as far as is consistent with safety, be placed in a draught-free position. For safety, a method utilizing a small sample size, around 2 ml, shall be used for organic peroxides and self-reactive substances (also known as "energetic" substances), or for toxic substances.

2.3.3.1.7   When the flash-point, determined by a non-equilibrium method in accordance with 2.3.3.1.5 is found to be 23 ± 2 °C or 60 ± 2 °C, it shall be confirmed for each temperature range by an equilibrium method in accordance with 2.3.3.1.4.

2.3.3.1.8   In the event of a dispute as to the classification of a flammable liquid, the classification proposed by the consignor shall be accepted if a check-test of the flash-point, yields a result not differing by more than 2 °C from the limits (23 °C and 60 °C respectively) stated in 2.2.3.1. If the difference is more than 2 °C, a second check-test shall be carried out, and the lowest figure of the flash-points obtained in either check-test shall be adopted.

2.3.3.2 *Test for determining peroxide content*

To determine the peroxide content of a liquid, the procedure is as follows:

A quantity p (about 5 g, weighed to the nearest 0.01 g) of the liquid to be titrated is placed in an Erlenmeyer flask; 20 cm^3 of acetic anhydride and about 1 g of powdered solid potassium iodide are added; the flask is shaken and, after 10 minutes, heated for 3 minutes to about 60 °C. When it has been left to cool for 5 minutes, 25 cm^3 of water are added. After this, it is left standing for half an hour, then the liberated iodine is titrated with a decinormal solution of sodium thiosulphate, no indicator being added; complete discoloration indicates the end of the reaction. If n is the number of cm^3 of thiosulphate solution required, the percentage of peroxide (calculated as H_2O_2) present in the sample is obtained by the formula:

$$\frac{17n}{100p}$$

2.3.4 Test for determining fluidity

To determine the fluidity of liquid, viscous or pasty substances and mixtures, the following test method shall be used.

2.3.4.1 *Test apparatus*

Commercial penetrometer conforming to ISO 2137:1985, with a guide rod of 47.5 g $\pm$ 0.05 g; sieve disc of duralumin with conical bores and a mass of 102.5 g $\pm$ 0.05 g (see Figure 1); penetration vessel with an inside diameter of 72 mm to 80 mm for reception of the sample.

2.3.4.2 *Test procedure*

The sample is poured into the penetration vessel not less than half an hour before the measurement. The vessel is then hermetically closed and left standing until the measurement. The sample in the hermetically closed penetration vessel is heated to 35 °C $\pm$ 0.5 °C and is placed on the penetrometer table immediately prior to measurement (not more than two minutes). The point S of the sieve disc is then brought into contact with the surface of the liquid and the rate of penetration is measured.

2.3.4.3 *Evaluation of test results*

A substance is pasty if, after the centre S has been brought into contact with the surface of the sample, the penetration indicated by the dial gauge:

(a)   after a loading time of 5 s $\pm$ 0.1 s, is less than 15.0 mm $\pm$ 0.3 mm; or

(b)   after a loading time of 5 s $\pm$ 0.1 s, is greater than 15.0 mm $\pm$ 0.3 mm, but the additional penetration after another 55 s $\pm$ 0.5 s is less than 5.0 mm $\pm$ 0.5 mm.

NOTE: In the case of samples having a flow point, it is often impossible to produce a steady level surface in the penetration vessel and, hence, to establish satisfactory initial measuring conditions for the contact of the point S. Furthermore, with some samples, the impact of the sieve disc can cause an elastic deformation of the surface and, in the first few seconds, simulate a deeper penetration. In all these cases, it may be appropriate to make the evaluation in paragraph (b) above.

Figure 1 – Penetrometer

Adjust mass to
102.5g± 0.05g

Ø 3.2 ±0.02

Ø 9 ±0.5

Ø 7.4 ±0.02

16⁰52'

Ø 3.2

82.6

12.7 ±3

12.7

10.3

Press fit

S S

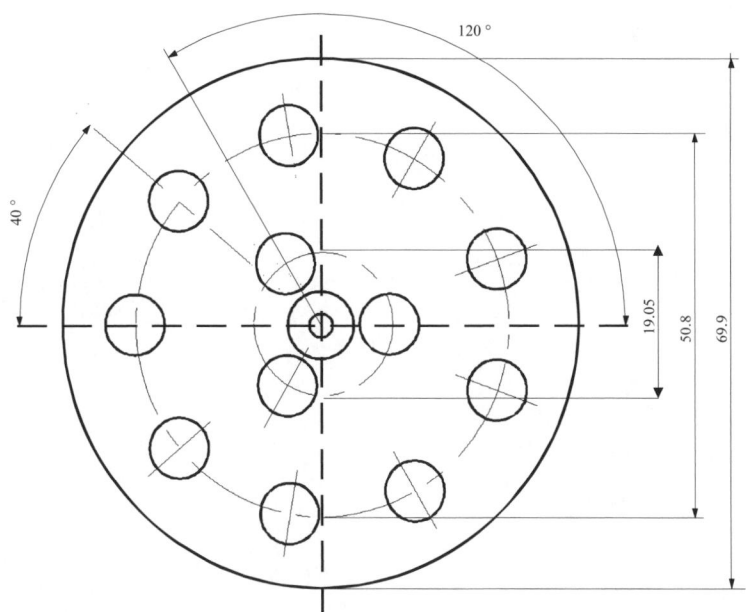

120 °

40 °

19.05

50.8

69.9

Tolerances not specified are ± 0.1 mm.

- 263 -

2.3.5 **Classification of organometallic substances in Classes 4.2 and 4.3**

Depending on their properties as determined in accordance with tests N.1 to N.5 of the Manual of Tests end Criteria, Part III, section 33, organometallic substances may be classified in Class 4.2 or 4.3, as appropriate, in accordance with the flowchart scheme given in Figure 2.3.5.

NOTE 1: *Depending on their other properties and on the precedence of hazard table (see 2.1.3.10), organometallic substances may have to be classified in other classes as appropriate.*

NOTE 2: *Flammable solutions with organometallic compounds in concentrations which are not liable to spontaneous combustion or, in contact with water, do not emit flammable gases in dangerous quantities, are substances of Class 3.*

Figure 2.3.5: Flowchart scheme for the classification of organometallic substances in Classes 4.2 and 4.3 [b]

---

[a]   *If applicable and testing is relevant, taking into account reactivity properties, class 6.1 and 8 properties should be considered according to the precedence of hazard table of 2.1.3.10.*

[b]   *Test methods N.1 to N.5 can be found in the Manual of Tests and Criteria, Part III, Section 33.*

PART 3

Dangerous goods list, special provisions and exemptions related to limited and excepted quantities

CHAPTER 3.1

GENERAL

3.1.1 Introduction

In addition to the provisions referred to or given in the tables of this Part, the general requirements of each Part, Chapter and/or Section are to be observed. These general requirements are not given in the tables. When a general requirement is contradictory to a special provision, the special provision prevails.

3.1.2 Proper shipping name

NOTE: For proper shipping names used for the carriage of samples, see 2.1.4.1.

3.1.2.1 The proper shipping name is that portion of the entry most accurately describing the goods in Table A in Chapter 3.2, which is shown in upper case characters (plus any numbers, Greek letters, "sec", "tert", and the letters "m", "n", "o", "p", which form an integral part of the name). An alternative proper shipping name may be shown in brackets following the main proper shipping name [e.g., ETHANOL (ETHYL ALCOHOL)]. Portions of an entry appearing in lower case need not be considered as part of the proper shipping name.

3.1.2.2 When conjunctions such as "and" or "or" are in lower case or when segments of the name are punctuated by commas, the entire name of the entry need not necessarily be shown in the transport document or package markings. This is the case particularly when a combination of several distinct entries are listed under a single UN Number. Examples illustrating the selection of the proper shipping name for such entries are:

(a) UN 1057 LIGHTERS or LIGHTER REFILLS - The proper shipping name is the most appropriate of the following possible combinations:

LIGHTERS

LIGHTER REFILLS;

(b) UN 2793 FERROUS METAL BORINGS, SHAVINGS, TURNINGS or CUTTINGS in a form liable to self-heating. The proper shipping name is the most appropriate of the following combinations:

FERROUS METAL BORINGS

FERROUS METAL SHAVINGS

FERROUS METAL TURNINGS

FERROUS METAL CUTTINGS.

3.1.2.3 Proper shipping names may be used in the singular or plural as appropriate. In addition, when qualifying words are used as part of the proper shipping name, their sequence on documentation or package markings is optional. For instance, "DIMETHYLAMINE AQUEOUS SOLUTION" may alternatively be shown "AQUEOUS SOLUTION OF DIMETHYLAMINE". Commercial or military names for goods of Class 1 which contain the proper shipping name supplemented by additional descriptive text may be used.

3.1.2.4 Many substances have an entry for both the liquid and solid state (see definitions for liquid and solid in 1.2.1), or for the solid and solution. These are allocated separate UN numbers which are not necessarily adjacent to each other [1].

3.1.2.5 Unless it is already included in capital letters in the name indicated in Table A in Chapter 3.2, the qualifying word "MOLTEN" shall be added as part of the proper shipping name when a substance, which is a solid in accordance with the definition in 1.2.1, is offered for carriage in the molten state (e.g. ALKYLPHENOL, SOLID, N.O.S., MOLTEN).

3.1.2.6 Except for self-reactive substances and organic peroxides and unless it is already included in capital letters in the name indicated in Column (2) of Table A of Chapter 3.2, the word "STABILIZED" shall be added as part of the proper shipping name of a substance which without stabilization would be forbidden from carriage in accordance with paragraphs 2.2.X.2 due to it being liable to dangerously react under conditions normally encountered in carriage (e.g.: "TOXIC LIQUID, ORGANIC, N.O.S., STABILIZED").

When temperature control is used to stabilize such substances to prevent the development of any dangerous excess pressure, then:

(a) For liquids: where the SADT is less than or equal to 50 °C, the provisions of 2.2.41.1.17, the special provision V8 of Chapter 7.2, the special provision S4 of Chapter 8.5 and the requirements of Chapter 9.6 shall apply; for carriage in IBCs and tanks, all the provisions applicable to UN No. 3239 apply (see in particular 4.1.7.2, packing instruction IBC520 et 4.2.1.13);

(b) For gases: the conditions of carriage shall be approved by the competent authority.

3.1.2.7 Hydrates may be carried under the proper shipping name for the anhydrous substance.

3.1.2.8 *Generic or "not otherwise specified" (N.O.S.) names*

3.1.2.8.1 Generic and "not otherwise specified" proper shipping names that are assigned to special provision 274 in Column (6) of Table A in Chapter 3.2 shall be supplemented with the technical name of the goods unless a national law or international convention prohibits its disclosure if it is a controlled substance. For explosives of Class 1, the dangerous goods description may be supplemented by additional descriptive text to indicate commercial or military names. Technical names shall be entered in brackets immediately following the proper shipping name. An appropriate modifier, such as "contains" or "containing" or other qualifying words such as "mixture", "solution", etc. and the percentage of the technical constituent may also be used. For example: "UN 1993 FLAMMABLE LIQUID, N.O.S. (CONTAINS XYLENE AND BENZENE), 3, II".

3.1.2.8.1.1 The technical name shall be a recognized chemical name, if relevant a biological name, or other name currently used in scientific and technical handbooks, journals and texts. Trade names shall not be used for this purpose. In the case of pesticides, only ISO common name(s), other name(s) in the World Health Organization (WHO) Recommended Classification of Pesticides by Hazard and Guidelines to Classification, or the name(s) of the active substance(s) may be used.

---

[1] *Details are provided in the alphabetical index (Table B of Chapter 3.2), e.g.:*

NITROXYLENES, LIQUID   6.1   1665;
NITROXYLENES, SOLID   6.1   3447.

3.1.2.8.1.2   When a mixture of dangerous goods is described by one of the "N.O.S." or "generic" entries to which special provision 274 has been allocated in Column (6) of Table A in Chapter 3.2, not more than the two constituents which most predominantly contribute to the hazard or hazards of a mixture need to be shown, excluding controlled substances when their disclosure is prohibited by national law or international convention. If a package containing a mixture is labelled with any subsidiary risk label, one of the two technical names shown in parentheses shall be the name of the constituent which compels the use of the subsidiary risk label.

NOTE: See 5.4.1.2.2.

3.1.2.8.1.3   Examples illustrating the selection of the proper shipping name supplemented with the technical name of goods for such N.O.S. entries are:

UN 2902   PESTICIDE, LIQUID, TOXIC, N.O.S. (drazoxolon);
UN 3394   ORGANOMETALLIC SUBSTANCE, LIQUID, PYROPHORIC, WATER-REACTIVE (trimethylgallium).

3.1.2.9   *Mixtures and solutions containing one dangerous substance*

When mixtures and solutions have to be regarded as the dangerous substance mentioned by name in accordance with the classification requirements of 2.1.3.3, the qualifying word "SOLUTION" or "MIXTURE", as appropriate, shall be added as part of the proper shipping name, e.g. "ACETONE SOLUTION". In addition, the concentration of the solution or mixture may also be indicated, e.g. "ACETONE 75% SOLUTION".

CHAPTER 3.2

DANGEROUS GOODS LIST

3.2.1   **Table A: Dangerous Goods List**

Explanations

As a rule, each row of Table A of this Chapter deals with the substance(s) or article(s) covered by a specific UN number. However, when substances or articles belonging to the same UN number have different chemical properties, physical properties and/or carriage conditions, several consecutive rows may be used for that UN number.

Each column of Table A is dedicated to a specific subject as indicated in the explanatory notes below. The intersection of columns and rows (cell) contains information concerning the subject treated in that column, for the substance(s) or article(s) of that row:

-      The first four cells identify the substance(s) or article(s) belonging to that row (additional information in that respect may be given by the special provisions referred to in Column (6);

-      The following cells give the applicable special provisions, either in the form of complete information or in coded form. The codes cross-refer to detailed information that is to be found in the Part, Chapter, Section and/or Sub-section indicated in the explanatory notes below. An empty cell means either that there is no special provision and that only the general requirements apply, or that the carriage restriction indicated in the explanatory notes is in force.

The applicable general requirements are not referred to in the corresponding cells. The explanatory notes below indicate for every column the Part(s), Chapter(s), Section(s) and/or Sub-section(s) where these are to be found.

Explanatory notes for each column:

Column (1)   "UN No."

                    Contains the UN number:

-      of the dangerous substance or article if the substance or article has been assigned its own specific UN number; or

-      of the generic or n.o.s. entry to which the dangerous substances or articles not mentioned by name shall be assigned in accordance with the criteria ("decision trees") of Part 2.

Column (2)   "Name and description"

                    Contains, in upper case characters, the name of the substance or article, if the substance or article has been assigned its own specific UN number, or of the generic or n.o.s. entry to which it has been assigned in accordance with the criteria ("decision trees") of Part 2. This name shall be used as the proper shipping name or, when applicable, as part of the proper shipping name (see 3.1.2 for further details on the proper shipping name).

A descriptive text in lower case characters is added after the proper shipping name to clarify the scope of the entry if the classification and/or carriage conditions of the substance or article may be different under certain conditions.

Column (3a)   "Class"

Contains the number of the class, whose heading covers the dangerous substance or article. This class number is assigned in accordance with the procedures and criteria of Part 2.

Column (3b)   "Classification code"

Contains the classification code of the dangerous substance or article.

-    For dangerous substances or articles of Class 1, the code consists of a division number and compatibility group letter, which are assigned in accordance with the procedures and criteria of 2.2.1.1.4;

-    For dangerous substances or articles of Class 2, the code consists of a number and hazardous property group, which are explained in 2.2.2.1.2 and 2.2.2.1.3;

-    For dangerous substances or articles of Classes 3, 4.1, 4.2, 4.3, 5.1, 5.2, 6.1, 6.2, 8 and 9, the codes are explained in 2.2.x.1.2 [1];

-    Dangerous substances or articles of Class 7 do not have a classification code.

Column (4)   "Packing group"

Contains the packing group number(s) (I, II or III) assigned to the dangerous substance. These packing group numbers are assigned on the basis of the procedures and criteria of Part 2. Certain articles and substances are not assigned to packing groups.

Column (5)   "Labels"

Contains the model number of the labels/placards (see 5.2.2.2 and 5.3.1.7) that have to be affixed to packages, containers, tank-containers, portable tanks, MEGCs and vehicles. However, for substances or articles of Class 7, 7X means label model No.7A, 7B or 7C as appropriate according to the category (see 5.1.5.3.4 and 5.2.2.1.11.1) or placard No. 7D (see 5.3.1.1.3 and 5.3.1.7.2).

The general provisions on labelling/placarding (e.g. number of labels, their location) are to be found in 5.2.2.1 for packages, and in 5.3.1, for containers, tank-containers, MEGCs, portable tanks and vehicles.

NOTE: Special provisions, indicated in Column (6), may change the above labelling provisions.

---

[1]   *x = the class number of the dangerous substance or article, without dividing point if applicable.*

Column (6)   "Special provisions"

Contains the numeric codes of special provisions that have to be met. These provisions concern a wide array of subjects, mainly connected with the contents of Columns (1) to (5) (e.g. carriage prohibitions, exemptions from requirements, explanations concerning the classification of certain forms of the dangerous goods concerned and additional labelling or marking provisions), and are listed in Chapter 3.3 in numerical order. If Column (6) is empty, no special provisions apply to the contents of Columns (1) to (5) for the dangerous goods concerned.

Column (7a)   "Limited Quantities"

Contains an alphanumeric code with the following meaning:

-   "LQ0" signifies that no exemption from the provisions of ADR exists for the dangerous goods packed in limited quantities;

-   All the other alphanumeric codes starting with the letters "LQ" signify that the provisions of ADR are not applicable if the conditions indicated in Chapter 3.4 are fulfilled.

Column (7b)   "Excepted Quantities"

Contains an alphanumeric code with the following meaning:

-   "E0" signifies that no exemption from the provisions of ADR exists for the dangerous goods packed in excepted quantities;

-   All the other alphanumerical codes starting with the letter "E" signify that the provisions of ADR are not applicable if the conditions indicated in Chapter 3.5 are fulfilled.

Column (8)   "Packing instructions"

Contains the alphanumeric codes of the applicable packing instructions:

-   Alphanumeric codes starting with the letter "P", which refers to packing instructions for packagings and receptacles (except IBCs and large packagings), or "R", which refers to packing instructions for light gauge metal packagings. These are listed in 4.1.4.1 in numerical order, and specify the packagings and receptacles that are authorized. They also indicate which of the general packing provisions of 4.1.1, 4.1.2 and 4.1.3, and which of the special packing provisions of 4.1.5, 4.1.6, 4.1.7, 4.1.8 and 4.1.9 have to be met. If Column (8) does not contain a code starting with the letters "P" or "R", the dangerous goods concerned may not be carried in packagings;

-   Alphanumeric codes starting with the letters "IBC" refer to packing instructions for IBCs. These are listed in 4.1.4.2 in numerical order, and specify the IBCs that are authorized. They also indicate which of the general packing provisions of 4.1.1, 4.1.2 and 4.1.3, and which of the special packing provisions of 4.1.5, 4.1.6, 4.1.7, 4.1.8 and 4.1.9 have to be met. If Column (8) does not contain a code starting with the letters "IBC", the dangerous goods concerned may not be carried in IBCs;

-       Alphanumeric codes starting with the letters "LP" refer to packing instructions for large packagings. These are listed in 4.1.4.3 in numerical order, and specify the large packagings that are authorized. They also indicate which of the general packing provisions of 4.1.1, 4.1.2 and 4.1.3, and which of the special packing provisions of 4.1.5, 4.1.6, 4.1.7, 4.1.8 and 4.1.9 have to be met. If Column (8) does not contain a code starting with the letters "LP", the dangerous goods concerned cannot be carried in large packagings;

NOTE: Special packing provisions, indicated in Column (9a), may change the above packing instructions.

Column (9a)   "Special packing provisions"

Contains the alphanumeric codes of the applicable special packing provisions:

-       Alphanumeric codes starting with the letters "PP" or "RR" refer to special packing provisions for packagings and receptacles (except IBCs and large packagings) that have additionally to be met. These are to be found in 4.1.4.1, at the end of the relevant packing instruction (with the letter "P" or "R") referred to in Column (8). If Column (9a) does not contain a code starting with the letters "PP" or "RR", none of the special packing provisions listed at the end of the relevant packing instruction apply;

-       Alphanumeric codes starting with the letter "B" or the letters "BB" refer to special packing provisions for IBCs that have additionally to be met. These are to be found in 4.1.4.2, at the end of the relevant packing instruction (with the letters "IBC") referred to in Column (8). If Column (9a) does not contain a code starting with the letter "B" or the letters "BB", none of the special packing provisions listed at the end of the relevant packing instruction apply;

-       Alphanumeric codes starting with the letter "L" refer to special packing provisions for large packagings that have additionally to be met. These are to be found in 4.1.4.3, at the end of the relevant packing instruction (with the letters "LP") referred to in Column (8). If Column (9a) does not contain a code starting with the letter "L", none of the special packing provisions listed at the end of the relevant packing instruction apply.

Column (9b)   "Mixed packing provisions"

Contains the alphanumeric codes starting with the letters "MP" of the applicable mixed packing provisions. These are listed in 4.1.10 in numerical order. If Column (9b) does not contain a code starting with the letters "MP", only the general requirements apply (see 4.1.1.5 and 4.1.1.6).

Column (10)   "Portable tank and bulk container instructions"

Contains an alphanumeric code assigned to a portable tank instruction, in accordance with 4.2.5.2.1 to 4.2.5.2.4 and 4.2.5.2.6. This portable tank instruction corresponds to the least stringent provisions that are acceptable for the carriage of the substance in portable tanks. The codes identifying the other portable tank instructions that are also permitted for the carriage of the substance are to be found in 4.2.5.2.5. If no code is given, carriage in portable tanks is not permitted unless a competent authority approval is granted as detailed in 6.7.1.3.

The general requirements for the design, construction, equipment, type approval, testing and marking of portable tanks are to be found in Chapter 6.7. The general requirements for the use (e.g. filling) are to be found in 4.2.1 to 4.2.4.

The indication of a "(M)" means that the substance may be carried in UN MEGCs.

NOTE: Special provisions, indicated in Column (11), may change the above requirements.

May also contain alphanumeric codes starting with the letters "BK" referring to types of bulk containers described in Chapter 6.11 which may be used for the carriage of bulk goods in accordance with 7.3.1.1 (a) and 7.3.2.

Column (11)   "Portable tank and bulk container special provisions"

Contains the alphanumeric codes of the portable tank special provisions that have additionally to be met. These codes, starting with the letters "TP" refer to special provisions for the construction or use of these portable tanks. They are to be found in 4.2.5.3.

NOTE: If technically relevant, these special provisions are not only applicable to the portable tanks specified in column (10), but also to the portable tanks that may be used according to the table in 4.2.5.2.5.

Column (12)   "Tank codes for ADR tanks"

Contains an alphanumeric code describing a tank type, in accordance with 4.3.3.1.1 (for gases of Class 2) or 4.3.4.1.1 (for substances of Classes 3 to 9). This tank type corresponds to the least stringent tank provisions that are acceptable for the carriage of the relevant substance in ADR tanks. The codes describing the other permitted tank types are to be found in 4.3.3.1.2 (for gases of Class 2) or 4.3.4.1.2 (for substances of Classes 3 to 9). If no code is given, carriage in ADR tanks is not permitted.

If in this column a tank code for solids (S) and for liquids (L) is indicated, this means that this substance may be offered for carriage in tanks in the solid or the liquid (molten) state. In general this provision is applicable to substances having melting points from 20 °C to 180 °C.

If for a solid, only a tank code for liquids (L) is indicated in this column, this means that this substance is only offered for carriage in tanks in the liquid (molten) state.

The general requirements for the construction, equipment, type approval, testing and marking that are not indicated in the tank code are to be found in 6.8.1, 6.8.2, 6.8.3 and 6.8.5. The general requirements for the use (e.g. maximum degree of filling, minimum test pressure) are to be found in 4.3.1 to 4.3.4.

The indication of a "(M)" after the tank code means that the substance can also be carried in battery-vehicles or MEGCs.

The indication of a (+) after the tank code means that the alternative use of the tanks is permitted only where this is specified in the certificate of type approval.

For fibre-reinforced plastic tanks, see 4.4.1 and Chapter 6.9; for vacuum operated waste tanks, see 4.5.1 and Chapter 6.10.

NOTE: Special provisions, indicated in Column (13), may change the above requirements.

Column (13)   "Special provisions for ADR tanks"

Contains the alphanumeric codes of the special provisions for ADR tanks that have additionally to be met:

- Alphanumeric codes starting with the letters "TU" refer to special provisions for the use of these tanks. These are to be found in 4.3.5;

- Alphanumeric codes starting with the letters "TC" refer to special provisions for the construction of these tanks. These are to be found in 6.8.4 (a);

- Alphanumeric codes starting with the letters "TE" refer to special provisions concerning the items of equipment of these tanks. These are to be found in 6.8.4 (b);

- Alphanumeric codes starting with the letters "TA" refer to special provisions for the type approval of these tanks. These are to be found in 6.8.4 (c);

- Alphanumeric codes starting with the letters "TT" refer to special provisions for the testing of these tanks. These are to be found in 6.8.4 (d);

- Alphanumeric codes starting with the letters "TM" refer to special provisions for the marking of these tanks. These are to be found in 6.8.4 (e).

NOTE: If technically relevant, these special provisions are not only applicable to the tanks specified in column (12), but also to the tanks that may be used according to the hierarchies in 4.3.3.1.2 and 4.3.4.1.2.

Column (14)   "Vehicle for tank carriage"

Contains a code designating the vehicle (including the drawing vehicle of trailers or semi-trailers) (see 9.1.1) to be used for the carriage of the substance in tank in accordance with 7.4.2. The requirements concerning the construction and approval of vehicles are to be found in Chapters 9.1, 9.2 and 9.7.

Column (15)   "Transport category / (Tunnel restriction code)"

Contains at the top of the cell a figure indicating the transport category to which the substance or article is assigned for the purposes of exemption related to quantities carried per transport unit (see 1.1.3.6).

Contains at the bottom of the cell, between brackets, the tunnel restriction code that refers to the applicable restriction for the passage of vehicles carrying the substance or article through road tunnels. These are to be found in Chapter 8.6. When no tunnel restriction code has been assigned, this is indicated by the mention '(–)'.

Column (16)   "Special provisions for carriage - Packages"
Contains the alphanumeric code(s), starting with letter "V", of the applicable special provisions (if any) for carriage in packages. These are listed in 7.2.4. General provisions concerning the carriage in packages are to be found in Chapters 7.1 and 7.2.

NOTE: In addition, special provisions indicated in Column (18), concerning loading, unloading and handling, shall be observed.

Column (17)   "Special provisions for carriage - Bulk"

Contains the alphanumeric code(s), starting with letters "VV", of the applicable special provisions for carriage in bulk. These are listed in 7.3.3. If no code is given, carriage in bulk is not permitted. General Provisions concerning the carriage in bulk are to be found in Chapters 7.1 and 7.3.

NOTE: In addition, special provisions indicated in Column (18), concerning loading, unloading and handling, shall be observed.

Column (18)   "Special provisions for carriage - Loading and unloading"

Contains the alphanumeric code(s), starting with letters "CV", of the applicable special provisions for loading, unloading and handling. These are listed in 7.5.11. If no code is given, only the general provisions apply (see 7.5.1 to 7.5.10).

Column (19)   "Special provisions for carriage - Operation"

Contains the alphanumeric code(s), starting with letter "S", of the applicable special provisions for operation which are listed in Chapter 8.5. These provisions shall be applied in addition to the requirements of Chapters 8.1 to 8.4 but in the event of conflict with the requirements of Chapters 8.1 to 8.4, the special provisions shall take precedence.

Column (20)   "Hazard identification number"

Contains a two or three figure number (preceded in certain cases by the letter "X") for substances and articles of classes 2 to 9, and for substances and articles of Class 1, the classification code (see column (3b)). In the cases described in 5.3.2.1, this number shall appear in the upper half of the orange-coloured marking. The meaning of the hazard identification numbers is explained in 5.3.2.3.

TABLE A

DANGEROUS GOODS LIST

UN No.	Name and description	Class	Classification code	Packing group	Labels	Special provisions	Limited and excepted quantities		Packaging			Portable tanks and bulk containers	
									Packing instructions	Special packing provisions	Mixed packing provisions	Instructions	Special provisions
	3.1.2	2.2	2.2	2.1.1.3	5.2.2	3.3	3.4.6	3.5.1.2	4.1.4	4.1.4	4.1.10	4.2.5.2 7.3.2	4.2.5.3
(1)	(2)	(3a)	(3b)	(4)	(5)	(6)	(7a)	(7b)	(8)	(9a)	(9b)	(10)	(11)
0004	AMMONIUM PICRATE dry or wetted with less than 10% water, by mass	1	1.1D		1		LQ0	E0	P112(a) P112(b) P112(c)	PP26	MP20		
0005	CARTRIDGES FOR WEAPONS with bursting charge	1	1.1F		1		LQ0	E0	P130		MP23		
0006	CARTRIDGES FOR WEAPONS with bursting charge	1	1.1E		1		LQ0	E0	P130 LP101	PP67 L1	MP21		
0007	CARTRIDGES FOR WEAPONS with bursting charge	1	1.2F		1		LQ0	E0	P130		MP23		
0009	AMMUNITION, INCENDIARY with or without burster, expelling charge or propelling charge	1	1.2G		1		LQ0	E0	P130 LP101	PP67 L1	MP23		
0010	AMMUNITION, INCENDIARY with or without burster, expelling charge or propelling charge	1	1.3G		1		LQ0	E0	P130 LP101	PP67 L1	MP23		
0012	CARTRIDGES FOR WEAPONS, INERT PROJECTILE or CARTRIDGES, SMALL ARMS	1	1.4S		1.4		LQ0	E0	P130		MP23 MP24		
0014	CARTRIDGES FOR WEAPONS, BLANK or CARTRIDGES, SMALL ARMS, BLANK	1	1.4S		1.4		LQ0	E0	P130		MP23 MP24		
0015	AMMUNITION, SMOKE with or without burster, expelling charge or propelling charge	1	1.2G		1		LQ0	E0	P130 LP101	PP67 L1	MP23		
0015	AMMUNITION, SMOKE with or without burster, expelling charge or propelling charge, containing corrosive substances	1	1.2G		1 +8		LQ0	E0	P130 LP101	PP67 L1	MP23		
0016	AMMUNITION, SMOKE with or without burster, expelling charge or propelling charge	1	1.3G		1		LQ0	E0	P130 LP101	PP67 L1	MP23		
0016	AMMUNITION, SMOKE with or without burster, expelling charge or propelling charge, containing corrosive substances	1	1.3G		1 +8		LQ0	E0	P130 LP101	PP67 L1	MP23		
0018	AMMUNITION, TEAR-PRODUCING with burster, expelling charge or propelling charge	1	1.2G		1 +6.1 +8		LQ0	E0	P130 LP101	PP67 L1	MP23		
0019	AMMUNITION, TEAR-PRODUCING with burster, expelling charge or propelling charge	1	1.3G		1 +6.1 +8		LQ0	E0	P130 LP101	PP67 L1	MP23		
0020	AMMUNITION, TOXIC with burster, expelling charge or propelling charge	1	1.2K	CARRIAGE PROHIBITED									
0021	AMMUNITION, TOXIC with burster, expelling charge or propelling charge	1	1.3K	CARRIAGE PROHIBITED									
0027	BLACK POWDER (GUNPOWDER), granular or as a meal	1	1.1D		1		LQ0	E0	P113	PP50	MP20 MP24		
0028	BLACK POWDER (GUNPOWDER), COMPRESSED or BLACK POWDER (GUNPOWDER), IN PELLETS	1	1.1D		1		LQ0	E0	P113	PP51	MP20 MP24		
0029	DETONATORS, NON-ELECTRIC for blasting	1	1.1B		1		LQ0	E0	P131	PP68	MP23		
0030	DETONATORS, ELECTRIC for blasting	1	1.1B		1		LQ0	E0	P131		MP23		

ADR tank		Vehicle for tank carriage	Transport category	Special provisions for carriage				Hazard identifi-cation No.	UN No.	Name and description
Tank code	Special provisions		(Tunnel restriction code)	Packages	Bulk	Loading, unloading and handling	Operation			
4.3	4.3.5, 6.8.4	9.1.1.2	1.1.3.6 (8.6)	7.2.4	7.3.3	7.5.11	8.5	5.3.2.3		3.1.2
(12)	(13)	(14)	(15)	(16)	(17)	(18)	(19)	(20)	(1)	(2)
			1 (B1000C)	V2 V3		CV1 CV2 CV3	S1		0004	AMMONIUM PICRATE dry or wetted with less than 10% water, by mass
			1 (B1000C)	V2		CV1 CV2 CV3	S1		0005	CARTRIDGES FOR WEAPONS with bursting charge
			1 (B1000C)	V2		CV1 CV2 CV3	S1		0006	CARTRIDGES FOR WEAPONS with bursting charge
			1 (B1000C)	V2		CV1 CV2 CV3	S1		0007	CARTRIDGES FOR WEAPONS with bursting charge
			1 (B1000C)	V2		CV1 CV2 CV3	S1		0009	AMMUNITION, INCENDIARY with or without burster, expelling charge or propelling charge
			1 (C5000D)	V2		CV1 CV2 CV3	S1		0010	AMMUNITION, INCENDIARY with or without burster, expelling charge or propelling charge
			4 (E)			CV1 CV2 CV3	S1		0012	CARTRIDGES FOR WEAPONS, INERT PROJECTILE or CARTRIDGES, SMALL ARMS
			4 (E)			CV1 CV2 CV3	S1		0014	CARTRIDGES FOR WEAPONS, BLANK or CARTRIDGES, SMALL ARMS, BLANK
			1 (B1000C)	V2		CV1 CV2 CV3	S1		0015	AMMUNITION, SMOKE with or without burster, expelling charge or propelling charge
			1 (B1000C)	V2		CV1 CV2 CV3	S1		0015	AMMUNITION, SMOKE with or without burster, expelling charge or propelling charge, containing corrosive substances
			1 (C5000D)	V2		CV1 CV2 CV3	S1		0016	AMMUNITION, SMOKE with or without burster, expelling charge or propelling charge
			1 (C5000D)	V2		CV1 CV2 CV3	S1		0016	AMMUNITION, SMOKE with or without burster, expelling charge or propelling charge, containing corrosive substances
			1 (B1000C)	V2		CV1 CV2 CV3 CV28	S1		0018	AMMUNITION, TEAR-PRODUCING with burster, expelling charge or propelling charge
			1 (C5000D)	V2		CV1 CV2 CV3 CV28	S1		0019	AMMUNITION, TEAR-PRODUCING with burster, expelling charge or propelling charge
CARRIAGE PROHIBITED									0020	AMMUNITION, TOXIC with burster, expelling charge or propelling charge
CARRIAGE PROHIBITED									0021	AMMUNITION, TOXIC with burster, expelling charge or propelling charge
			1 (B1000C)	V2 V3		CV1 CV2 CV3	S1		0027	BLACK POWDER (GUNPOWDER), granular or as a meal
			1 (B1000C)	V2		CV1 CV2 CV3	S1		0028	BLACK POWDER (GUNPOWDER), COMPRESSED or BLACK POWDER (GUNPOWDER), IN PELLETS
			1 (B1000C)	V2		CV1 CV2 CV3	S1		0029	DETONATORS, NON-ELECTRIC for blasting
			1 (B1000C)	V2		CV1 CV2 CV3	S1		0030	DETONATORS, ELECTRIC for blasting

UN No.	Name and description	Class	Classification code	Packing group	Labels	Special provisions	Limited and excepted quantities		Packaging			Portable tanks and bulk containers	
									Packing instructions	Special packing provisions	Mixed packing provisions	Instructions	Special provisions
	3.1.2	2.2	2.2	2.1.1.3	5.2.2	3.3	3.4.6	3.5.1.2	4.1.4	4.1.4	4.1.10	4.2.5.2 7.3.2	4.2.5.3
(1)	(2)	(3a)	(3b)	(4)	(5)	(6)	(7a)	(7b)	(8)	(9a)	(9b)	(10)	(11)
0033	BOMBS with bursting charge	1	1.1F		1		LQ0	E0	P130		MP23		
0034	BOMBS with bursting charge	1	1.1D		1		LQ0	E0	P130 LP101	PP67 L1	MP21		
0035	BOMBS with bursting charge	1	1.2D		1		LQ0	E0	P130 LP101	PP67 L1	MP21		
0037	BOMBS, PHOTO-FLASH	1	1.1F		1		LQ0	E0	P130		MP23		
0038	BOMBS, PHOTO-FLASH	1	1.1D		1		LQ0	E0	P130 LP101	PP67 L1	MP21		
0039	BOMBS, PHOTO-FLASH	1	1.2G		1		LQ0	E0	P130 LP101	PP67 L1	MP23		
0042	BOOSTERS without detonator	1	1.1D		1		LQ0	E0	P132(a) P132(b)		MP21		
0043	BURSTERS, explosive	1	1.1D		1		LQ0	E0	P133	PP69	MP21		
0044	PRIMERS, CAP TYPE	1	1.4S		1.4		LQ0	E0	P133		MP23 MP24		
0048	CHARGES, DEMOLITION	1	1.1D		1		LQ0	E0	P130 LP101	PP67 L1	MP21		
0049	CARTRIDGES, FLASH	1	1.1G		1		LQ0	E0	P135		MP23		
0050	CARTRIDGES, FLASH	1	1.3G		1		LQ0	E0	P135		MP23		
0054	CARTRIDGES, SIGNAL	1	1.3G		1		LQ0	E0	P135		MP23 MP24		
0055	CASES, CARTRIDGE, EMPTY, WITH PRIMER	1	1.4S		1.4		LQ0	E0	P136		MP23		
0056	CHARGES, DEPTH	1	1.1D		1		LQ0	E0	P130 LP101	PP67 L1	MP21		
0059	CHARGES, SHAPED without detonator	1	1.1D		1		LQ0	E0	P137	PP70	MP21		
0060	CHARGES, SUPPLEMENTARY, EXPLOSIVE	1	1.1D		1		LQ0	E0	P132(a) P132(b)		MP21		
0065	CORD, DETONATING, flexible	1	1.1D		1		LQ0	E0	P139	PP71 PP72	MP21		
0066	CORD, IGNITER	1	1.4G		1.4		LQ0	E0	P140		MP23		
0070	CUTTERS, CABLE, EXPLOSIVE	1	1.4S		1.4		LQ0	E0	P134 LP102		MP23		
0072	CYCLOTRIMETHYLENE-TRINITRAMINE (CYCLONITE; HEXOGEN; RDX), WETTED with not less than 15% water, by mass	1	1.1D		1	266	LQ0	E0	P112(a)	PP45	MP20		
0073	DETONATORS FOR AMMUNITION	1	1.1B		1		LQ0	E0	P133		MP23		

ADR tank		Vehicle for tank carriage	Transport category (Tunnel restriction code)	Special provisions for carriage				Hazard identification No.	UN No.	Name and description
Tank code	Special provisions			Packages	Bulk	Loading, unloading and handling	Operation			
4.3	4.3.5, 6.8.4	9.1.1.2	1.1.3.6 (8.6)	7.2.4	7.3.3	7.5.11	8.5	5.3.2.3		3.1.2
(12)	(13)	(14)	(15)	(16)	(17)	(18)	(19)	(20)	(1)	(2)
			1 (B1000C)	V2		CV1 CV2 CV3	S1		0033	BOMBS with bursting charge
			1 (B1000C)	V2		CV1 CV2 CV3	S1		0034	BOMBS with bursting charge
			1 (B1000C)	V2		CV1 CV2 CV3	S1		0035	BOMBS with bursting charge
			1 (B1000C)	V2		CV1 CV2 CV3	S1		0037	BOMBS, PHOTO-FLASH
			1 (B1000C)	V2		CV1 CV2 CV3	S1		0038	BOMBS, PHOTO-FLASH
			1 (B1000C)	V2		CV1 CV2 CV3	S1		0039	BOMBS, PHOTO-FLASH
			1 (B1000C)	V2		CV1 CV2 CV3	S1		0042	BOOSTERS without detonator
			1 (B1000C)	V2		CV1 CV2 CV3	S1		0043	BURSTERS, explosive
			4 (E)			CV1 CV2 CV3	S1		0044	PRIMERS, CAP TYPE
			1 (B1000C)	V2		CV1 CV2 CV3	S1		0048	CHARGES, DEMOLITION
			1 (B1000C)	V2		CV1 CV2 CV3	S1		0049	CARTRIDGES, FLASH
			1 (C5000D)	V2		CV1 CV2 CV3	S1		0050	CARTRIDGES, FLASH
			1 (C5000D)	V2		CV1 CV2 CV3	S1		0054	CARTRIDGES, SIGNAL
			4 (E)			CV1 CV2 CV3	S1		0055	CASES, CARTRIDGE, EMPTY, WITH PRIMER
			1 (B1000C)	V2		CV1 CV2 CV3	S1		0056	CHARGES, DEPTH
			1 (B1000C)	V2		CV1 CV2 CV3	S1		0059	CHARGES, SHAPED without detonator
			1 (B1000C)	V2		CV1 CV2 CV3	S1		0060	CHARGES, SUPPLEMENTARY, EXPLOSIVE
			1 (B1000C)	V2		CV1 CV2 CV3	S1		0065	CORD, DETONATING, flexible
			2 (E)	V2		CV1 CV2 CV3	S1		0066	CORD, IGNITER
			4 (E)			CV1 CV2 CV3	S1		0070	CUTTERS, CABLE, EXPLOSIVE
			1 (B1000C)	V2		CV1 CV2 CV3	S1		0072	CYCLOTRIMETHYLENE-TRINITRAMINE (CYCLONITE; HEXOGEN; RDX), WETTED with not less than 15% water, by mass
			1 (B1000C)	V2		CV1 CV2 CV3	S1		0073	DETONATORS FOR AMMUNITION

UN No.	Name and description	Class	Classifi-cation code	Packing group	Labels	Special provi-sions	Limited and excepted quantities		Packaging			Portable tanks and bulk containers	
									Packing instruc-tions	Special packing provisions	Mixed packing provisions	Instruc-tions	Special provisions
	3.1.2	2.2	2.2	2.1.1.3	5.2.2	3.3	3.4.6	3.5.1.2	4.1.4	4.1.4	4.1.10	4.2.5.2 7.3.2	4.2.5.3
(1)	(2)	(3a)	(3b)	(4)	(5)	(6)	(7a)	(7b)	(8)	(9a)	(9b)	(10)	(11)
0074	DIAZODINITROPHENOL, WETTED with not less than 40% water, or mixture of alcohol and water, by mass	1	1.1A		1	266	LQ0	E0	P110(b)	PP42	MP20		
0075	DIETHYLENEGLYCOL DINITRATE, DESENSITIZED with not less than 25% non-volatile, water-insoluble phlegmatizer, by mass	1	1.1D		1	266	LQ0	E0	P115	PP53 PP54 PP57 PP58	MP20		
0076	DINITROPHENOL, dry or wetted with less than 15% water, by mass	1	1.1D		1 +6.1		LQ0	E0	P112(a) P112(b) P112(c)	PP26	MP20		
0077	DINITROPHENOLATES, alkali metals, dry or wetted with less than 15% water, by mass	1	1.3C		1 +6.1		LQ0	E0	P114(a) P114(b)	PP26	MP20		
0078	DINITRORESORCINOL, dry or wetted with less than 15% water, by mass	1	1.1D		1		LQ0	E0	P112(a) P112(b) P112(c)	PP26	MP20		
0079	HEXANITRODIPHENYL-AMINE (DIPICRYLAMINE; HEXYL)	1	1.1D		1		LQ0	E0	P112(b) P112(c)		MP20		
0081	EXPLOSIVE, BLASTING, TYPE A	1	1.1D		1	616 617	LQ0	E0	P116	PP63 PP66	MP20		
0082	EXPLOSIVE, BLASTING, TYPE B	1	1.1D		1	617	LQ0	E0	P116 IBC100	PP61 PP62 PP65 B9	MP20		
0083	EXPLOSIVE, BLASTING, TYPE C	1	1.1D		1	267 617	LQ0	E0	P116		MP20		
0084	EXPLOSIVE, BLASTING, TYPE D	1	1.1D		1	617	LQ0	E0	P116		MP20		
0092	FLARES, SURFACE	1	1.3G		1		LQ0	E0	P135		MP23		
0093	FLARES, AERIAL	1	1.3G		1		LQ0	E0	P135		MP23		
0094	FLASH POWDER	1	1.1G		1		LQ0	E0	P113	PP49	MP20		
0099	FRACTURING DEVICES, EXPLOSIVE without detonator, for oil wells	1	1.1D		1		LQ0	E0	P134 LP102		MP21		
0101	FUSE, NON-DETONATING	1	1.3G		1		LQ0	E0	P140	PP74 PP75	MP23		
0102	CORD (FUSE), DETONATING, metal clad	1	1.2D		1		LQ0	E0	P139	PP71	MP21		
0103	FUSE, IGNITER, tubular, metal clad	1	1.4G		1.4		LQ0	E0	P140		MP23		
0104	CORD (FUSE), DETONATING, MILD EFFECT, metal clad	1	1.4D		1.4		LQ0	E0	P139	PP71	MP21		
0105	FUSE, SAFETY	1	1.4S		1.4		LQ0	E0	P140	PP73	MP23		
0106	FUZES, DETONATING	1	1.1B		1		LQ0	E0	P141		MP23		
0107	FUZES, DETONATING	1	1.2B		1		LQ0	E0	P141		MP23		

ADR tank		Vehicle for tank carriage	Transport category (Tunnel restriction code)	Special provisions for carriage				Hazard identifi-cation No.	UN No.	Name and description
Tank code	Special provisions			Packages	Bulk	Loading, unloading and handling	Operation			
4.3	4.3.5, 6.8.4	9.1.1.2	1.1.3.6 (8.6)	7.2.4	7.3.3	7.5.11	8.5	5.3.2.3		3.1.2
(12)	(13)	(14)	(15)	(16)	(17)	(18)	(19)	(20)	(1)	(2)
			0 (B)	V2		CV1 CV2 CV3	S1		0074	DIAZODINITROPHENOL, WETTED with not less than 40% water, or mixture of alcohol and water, by mass
			1 (B1000C)	V2		CV1 CV2 CV3	S1		0075	DIETHYLENEGLYCOL DINITRATE, DESENSITIZED with not less than 25% non-volatile, water-insoluble phlegmatizer, by mass
			1 (B1000C)	V2 V3		CV1 CV2 CV3 CV28	S1		0076	DINITROPHENOL, dry or wetted with less than 15% water, by mass
			1 (C5000D)	V2 V3		CV1 CV2 CV3 CV28	S1		0077	DINITROPHENOLATES, alkali metals, dry or wetted with less than 15% water, by mass
			1 (B1000C)	V2 V3		CV1 CV2 CV3	S1		0078	DINITRORESORCINOL, dry or wetted with less than 15% water, by mass
			1 (B1000C)	V2 V3		CV1 CV2 CV3	S1		0079	HEXANITRODIPHENYL-AMINE (DIPICRYLAMINE; HEXYL)
			1 (B1000C)	V2 V3		CV1 CV2 CV3	S1		0081	EXPLOSIVE, BLASTING, TYPE A
			1 (B1000C)	V2 V3		CV1 CV2 CV3	S1		0082	EXPLOSIVE, BLASTING, TYPE B
			1 (B1000C)	V2 V3		CV1 CV2 CV3	S1		0083	EXPLOSIVE, BLASTING, TYPE C
			1 (B1000C)	V2		CV1 CV2 CV3	S1		0084	EXPLOSIVE, BLASTING, TYPE D
			1 (C5000D)	V2		CV1 CV2 CV3	S1		0092	FLARES, SURFACE
			1 (C5000D)	V2		CV1 CV2 CV3	S1		0093	FLARES, AERIAL
			1 (B1000C)	V2 V3		CV1 CV2 CV3	S1		0094	FLASH POWDER
			1 (B1000C)	V2		CV1 CV2 CV3	S1		0099	FRACTURING DEVICES, EXPLOSIVE without detonator, for oil wells
			1 (C5000D)	V2		CV1 CV2 CV3	S1		0101	FUSE, NON-DETONATING
			1 (B1000C)	V2		CV1 CV2 CV3	S1		0102	CORD (FUSE), DETONATING, metal clad
			2 (E)	V2		CV1 CV2 CV3	S1		0103	FUSE, IGNITER, tubular, metal clad
			2 (E)	V2		CV1 CV2 CV3	S1		0104	CORD (FUSE), DETONATING, MILD EFFECT, metal clad
			4 (E)			CV1 CV2 CV3	S1		0105	FUSE, SAFETY
			1 (B1000C)	V2		CV1 CV2 CV3	S1		0106	FUZES, DETONATING
			1 (B1000C)	V2		CV1 CV2 CV3	S1		0107	FUZES, DETONATING

UN No.	Name and description	Class	Classifi-cation code	Packing group	Labels	Special provi-sions	Limited and excepted quantities		Packaging			Portable tanks and bulk containers	
									Packing instruc-tions	Special packing provisions	Mixed packing provisions	Instruc-tions	Special provisions
3.1.2		2.2	2.2	2.1.1.3	5.2.2	3.3	3.4.6	3.5.1.2	4.1.4	4.1.4	4.1.10	4.2.5.2 7.3.2	4.2.5.3
(1)	(2)	(3a)	(3b)	(4)	(5)	(6)	(7a)	(7b)	(8)	(9a)	(9b)	(10)	(11)
0110	GRENADES, PRACTICE, hand or rifle	1	1.4S		1.4		LQ0	E0	P141		MP23		
0113	GUANYLNITROSAMINO-GUANYLIDENE HYDRAZINE, WETTED with not less than 30% water, by mass	1	1.1A		1	266	LQ0	E0	P110(b)	PP42	MP20		
0114	GUANYLNITROSAMINO-GUANYLTETRAZENE (TETRAZENE), WETTED with not less than 30% water, or mixture of alcohol and water, by mass	1	1.1A		1	266	LQ0	E0	P110(b)	PP42	MP20		
0118	HEXOLITE (HEXOTOL), dry or wetted with less than 15% water, by mass	1	1.1D		1		LQ0	E0	P112(a) P112(b) P112(c)		MP20		
0121	IGNITERS	1	1.1G		1		LQ0	E0	P142		MP23		
0124	JET PERFORATING GUNS, CHARGED, oil well, without detonator	1	1.1D		1		LQ0	E0	P101		MP21		
0129	LEAD AZIDE, WETTED with not less than 20% water, or mixture of alcohol and water, by mass	1	1.1A		1	266	LQ0	E0	P110(b)	PP42	MP20		
0130	LEAD STYPHNATE (LEAD TRINITRORESORCINATE), WETTED with not less than 20% water, or mixture of alcohol and water, by mass	1	1.1A		1	266	LQ0	E0	P110(b)	PP42	MP20		
0131	LIGHTERS, FUSE	1	1.4S		1.4		LQ0	E0	P142		MP23		
0132	DEFLAGRATING METAL SALTS OF AROMATIC NITRODERIVATIVES, N.O.S.	1	1.3C		1	274	LQ0	E0	P114(a) P114(b)	PP26	MP2		
0133	MANNITOL HEXANITRATE (NITROMANNITE), WETTED with not less than 40% water, or mixture of alcohol and water, by mass	1	1.1D		1	266	LQ0	E0	P112(a)		MP20		
0135	MERCURY FULMINATE, WETTED with not less than 20% water, or mixture of alcohol and water, by mass	1	1.1A		1	266	LQ0	E0	P110(b)	PP42	MP20		
0136	MINES with bursting charge	1	1.1F		1		LQ0	E0	P130		MP23		
0137	MINES with bursting charge	1	1.1D		1		LQ0	E0	P130 LP101	PP67 L1	MP21		
0138	MINES with bursting charge	1	1.2D		1		LQ0	E0	P130 LP101	PP67 L1	MP21		
0143	NITROGLYCERIN, DESENSITIZED with not less than 40% non-volatile water-insoluble phlegmatizer, by mass	1	1.1D		1 +6.1	266 271	LQ0	E0	P115	PP53 PP54 PP57 PP58	MP20		
0144	NITROGLYCERIN SOLUTION IN ALCOHOL with more than 1% but not more than 10% nitroglycerin	1	1.1D		1	500	LQ0	E0	P115	PP45 PP55 PP56 PP59 PP60	MP20		
0146	NITROSTARCH, dry or wetted with less than 20% water, by mass	1	1.1D		1		LQ0	E0	P112(a) P112(b) P112(c)		MP20		

| ADR tank | | Vehicle for tank carriage | Transport category (Tunnel restriction code) | Special provisions for carriage | | | | Hazard identifi-cation No. | UN No. | Name and description |
| Tank code | Special provisions | | | Packages | Bulk | Loading, unloading and handling | Operation | | | |
4.3	4.3.5, 6.8.4	9.1.1.2	1.1.3.6 (8.6)	7.2.4	7.3.3	7.5.11	8.5	5.3.2.3		3.1.2
(12)	(13)	(14)	(15)	(16)	(17)	(18)	(19)	(20)	(1)	(2)
			4 (E)			CV1 CV2 CV3	S1		0110	GRENADES, PRACTICE, hand or rifle
			0 (B)	V2		CV1 CV2 CV3	S1		0113	GUANYLNITROSAMINO-GUANYLIDENE HYDRAZINE, WETTED with not less than 30% water, by mass
			0 (B)	V2		CV1 CV2 CV3	S1		0114	GUANYLNITROSAMINO-GUANYLTETRAZENE (TETRAZENE), WETTED with not less than 30% water, or mixture of alcohol and water, by mass
			1 (B1000C)	V2 V3		CV1 CV2 CV3	S1		0118	HEXOLITE (HEXOTOL), dry or wetted with less than 15% water, by mass
			1 (B1000C)	V2		CV1 CV2 CV3	S1		0121	IGNITERS
			1 (B1000C)	V2		CV1 CV2 CV3	S1		0124	JET PERFORATING GUNS, CHARGED, oil well, without detonator
			0 (B)	V2		CV1 CV2 CV3	S1		0129	LEAD AZIDE, WETTED with not less than 20% water, or mixture of alcohol and water, by mass
			0 (B)	V2		CV1 CV2 CV3	S1		0130	LEAD STYPHNATE (LEAD TRINITRORESORCINATE), WETTED with not less than 20% water, or mixture of alcohol and water, by mass
			4 (E)			CV1 CV2 CV3	S1		0131	LIGHTERS, FUSE
			1 (C5000D)	V2 V3		CV1 CV2 CV3	S1		0132	DEFLAGRATING METAL SALTS OF AROMATIC NITRODERIVATIVES, N.O.S.
			1 (B1000C)	V2		CV1 CV2 CV3	S1		0133	MANNITOL HEXANITRATE (NITROMANNITE), WETTED with not less than 40% water, or mixture of alcohol and water, by mass
			0 (B)	V2		CV1 CV2 CV3	S1		0135	MERCURY FULMINATE, WETTED with not less than 20% water, or mixture of alcohol and water, by mass
			1 (B1000C)	V2		CV1 CV2 CV3	S1		0136	MINES with bursting charge
			1 (B1000C)	V2		CV1 CV2 CV3	S1		0137	MINES with bursting charge
			1 (B1000C)	V2		CV1 CV2 CV3	S1		0138	MINES with bursting charge
			1 (B1000C)	V2		CV1 CV2 CV3 CV28	S1		0143	NITROGLYCERIN, DESENSITIZED with not less than 40% non-volatile water-insoluble phlegmatizer, by mass
			1 (B1000C)	V2		CV1 CV2 CV3	S1		0144	NITROGLYCERIN SOLUTION IN ALCOHOL with more than 1% but not more than 10% nitroglycerin
			1 (B1000C)	V2 V3		CV1 CV2 CV3	S1		0146	NITROSTARCH, dry or wetted with less than 20% water, by mass

UN No.	Name and description	Class	Classification code	Packing group	Labels	Special provisions	Limited and excepted quantities		Packaging			Portable tanks and bulk containers	
							quantities		Packing instructions	Special packing provisions	Mixed packing provisions	Instructions	Special provisions
	3.1.2	2.2	2.2	2.1.1.3	5.2.2	3.3	3.4.6	3.5.1.2	4.1.4	4.1.4	4.1.10	4.2.5.2 7.3.2	4.2.5.3
(1)	(2)	(3a)	(3b)	(4)	(5)	(6)	(7a)	(7b)	(8)	(9a)	(9b)	(10)	(11)
0147	NITRO UREA	1	1.1D		1		LQ0	E0	P112(b)		MP20		
0150	PENTAERYTHRITE TETRANITRATE (PENTAERYTHRITOL TETRANITRATE; PETN), WETTED with not less than 25% water, by mass, or DESENSITIZED with not less than 15% phlegmatizer, by mass	1	1.1D		1	266	LQ0	E0	P112(a) P112(b)		MP20		
0151	PENTOLITE, dry or wetted with less than 15% water, by mass	1	1.1D		1		LQ0	E0	P112(a) P112(b) P112(c)		MP20		
0153	TRINITROANILINE (PICRAMIDE)	1	1.1D		1		LQ0	E0	P112(b) P112(c)		MP20		
0154	TRINITROPHENOL (PICRIC ACID), dry or wetted with less than 30% water, by mass	1	1.1D		1		LQ0	E0	P112(a) P112(b) P112(c)	PP26	MP20		
0155	TRINITROCHLORO-BENZENE (PICRYL CHLORIDE)	1	1.1D		1		LQ0	E0	P112(b) P112(c)		MP20		
0159	POWDER CAKE (POWDER PASTE), WETTED with not less than 25% water, by mass	1	1.3C		1	266	LQ0	E0	P111	PP43	MP20		
0160	POWDER, SMOKELESS	1	1.1C		1		LQ0	E0	P114(b)	PP50 PP52	MP20 MP24		
0161	POWDER, SMOKELESS	1	1.3C		1		LQ0	E0	P114(b)	PP50 PP52	MP20 MP24		
0167	PROJECTILES with bursting charge	1	1.1F		1		LQ0	E0	P130		MP23		
0168	PROJECTILES with bursting charge	1	1.1D		1		LQ0	E0	P130 LP101	PP67 L1	MP21		
0169	PROJECTILES with bursting charge	1	1.2D		1		LQ0	E0	P130 LP101	PP67 L1	MP21		
0171	AMMUNITION, ILLUMINATING with or without burster, expelling charge or propelling charge	1	1.2G		1		LQ0	E0	P130 LP101	PP67 L1	MP23		
0173	RELEASE DEVICES, EXPLOSIVE	1	1.4S		1.4		LQ0	E0	P134 LP102		MP23		
0174	RIVETS, EXPLOSIVE	1	1.4S		1.4		LQ0	E0	P134 LP102		MP23		
0180	ROCKETS with bursting charge	1	1.1F		1		LQ0	E0	P130		MP23		
0181	ROCKETS with bursting charge	1	1.1E		1		LQ0	E0	P130 LP101	PP67 L1	MP21		
0182	ROCKETS with bursting charge	1	1.2E		1		LQ0	E0	P130 LP101	PP67 L1	MP21		
0183	ROCKETS with inert head	1	1.3C		1		LQ0	E0	P130 LP101	PP67 L1	MP22		
0186	ROCKET MOTORS	1	1.3C		1		LQ0	E0	P130 LP101	PP67 L1	MP22 MP24		
0190	SAMPLES, EXPLOSIVE, other than initiating explosive	1				16 274	LQ0	E0	P101		MP2		

ADR tank		Vehicle for tank carriage	Transport category (Tunnel restriction code)	Special provisions for carriage				Hazard identifi-cation No.	UN No.	Name and description
Tank code	Special provisions			Packages	Bulk	Loading, unloading and handling	Operation			
4.3	4.3.5, 6.8.4	9.1.1.2	1.1.3.6 (8.6)	7.2.4	7.3.3	7.5.11	8.5	5.3.2.3		3.1.2
(12)	(13)	(14)	(15)	(16)	(17)	(18)	(19)	(20)	(1)	(2)
			1 (B1000C)	V2 V3		CV1 CV2 CV3	S1		0147	NITRO UREA
			1 (B1000C)	V2 V3		CV1 CV2 CV3	S1		0150	PENTAERYTHRITE TETRANITRATE (PENTAERYTHRITOL TETRANITRATE; PETN), WETTED with not less than 25% water, by mass, or DESENSITIZED with not less than 15% phlegmatizer, by mass
			1 (B1000C)	V2 V3		CV1 CV2 CV3	S1		0151	PENTOLITE, dry or wetted with less than 15% water, by mass
			1 (B1000C)	V2 V3		CV1 CV2 CV3	S1		0153	TRINITROANILINE (PICRAMIDE)
			1 (B1000C)	V2 V3		CV1 CV2 CV3	S1		0154	TRINITROPHENOL (PICRIC ACID), dry or wetted with less than 30% water, by mass
			1 (B1000C)	V2 V3		CV1 CV2 CV3	S1		0155	TRINITROCHLORO-BENZENE (PICRYL CHLORIDE)
			1 (C5000D)	V2		CV1 CV2 CV3	S1		0159	POWDER CAKE (POWDER PASTE), WETTED with not less than 25% water, by mass
			1 (B1000C)	V2 V3		CV1 CV2 CV3	S1		0160	POWDER, SMOKELESS
			1 (C5000D)	V2 V3		CV1 CV2 CV3	S1		0161	POWDER, SMOKELESS
			1 (B1000C)	V2		CV1 CV2 CV3	S1		0167	PROJECTILES with bursting charge
			1 (B1000C)	V2		CV1 CV2 CV3	S1		0168	PROJECTILES with bursting charge
			1 (B1000C)	V2		CV1 CV2 CV3	S1		0169	PROJECTILES with bursting charge
			1 (B1000C)	V2		CV1 CV2 CV3	S1		0171	AMMUNITION, ILLUMINATING with or without burster, expelling charge or propelling charge
			4 (E)			CV1 CV2 CV3	S1		0173	RELEASE DEVICES, EXPLOSIVE
			4 (E)			CV1 CV2 CV3	S1		0174	RIVETS, EXPLOSIVE
			1 (B1000C)	V2		CV1 CV2 CV3	S1		0180	ROCKETS with bursting charge
			1 (B1000C)	V2		CV1 CV2 CV3	S1		0181	ROCKETS with bursting charge
			1 (B1000C)	V2		CV1 CV2 CV3	S1		0182	ROCKETS with bursting charge
			1 (C5000D)	V2		CV1 CV2 CV3	S1		0183	ROCKETS with inert head
			1 (C5000D)	V2		CV1 CV2 CV3	S1		0186	ROCKET MOTORS
			0 (E)	V2		CV1 CV2 CV3	S1		0190	SAMPLES, EXPLOSIVE, other than initiating explosive

UN No.	Name and description	Class	Classifi-cation code	Packing group	Labels	Special provi-sions	Limited and excepted quantities		Packaging			Portable tanks and bulk containers	
									Packing instruc-tions	Special packing provisions	Mixed packing provisions	Instruc-tions	Special provisions
	3.1.2	2.2	2.2	2.1.1.3	5.2.2	3.3	3.4.6	3.5.1.2	4.1.4	4.1.4	4.1.10	4.2.5.2 7.3.2	4.2.5.3
(1)	(2)	(3a)	(3b)	(4)	(5)	(6)	(7a)	(7b)	(8)	(9a)	(9b)	(10)	(11)
0191	SIGNAL DEVICES, HAND	1	1.4G		1.4		LQ0	E0	P135		MP23 MP24		
0192	SIGNALS, RAILWAY TRACK, EXPLOSIVE	1	1.1G		1		LQ0	E0	P135		MP23		
0193	SIGNALS, RAILWAY TRACK, EXPLOSIVE	1	1.4S		1.4		LQ0	E0	P135		MP23		
0194	SIGNALS, DISTRESS, ship	1	1.1G		1		LQ0	E0	P135		MP23 MP24		
0195	SIGNALS, DISTRESS, ship	1	1.3G		1		LQ0	E0	P135		MP23 MP24		
0196	SIGNALS, SMOKE	1	1.1G		1		LQ0	E0	P135		MP23		
0197	SIGNALS, SMOKE	1	1.4G		1.4		LQ0	E0	P135		MP23 MP24		
0204	SOUNDING DEVICES, EXPLOSIVE	1	1.2F		1		LQ0	E0	P134 LP102		MP23		
0207	TETRANITROANILINE	1	1.1D		1		LQ0	E0	P112(b) P112(c)		MP20		
0208	TRINITROPHENYLMETHYL-NITRAMINE (TETRYL)	1	1.1D		1		LQ0	E0	P112(b) P112(c)		MP20		
0209	TRINITROTOLUENE (TNT), dry or wetted with less than 30% water, by mass	1	1.1D		1		LQ0	E0	P112(b) P112(c)	PP46	MP20		
0212	TRACERS FOR AMMUNITION	1	1.3G		1		LQ0	E0	P133	PP69	MP23		
0213	TRINITROANISOLE	1	1.1D		1		LQ0	E0	P112(b) P112(c)		MP20		
0214	TRINITROBENZENE, dry or wetted with less than 30% water, by mass	1	1.1D		1		LQ0	E0	P112(a) P112(b) P112(c)		MP20		
0215	TRINITROBENZOIC ACID, dry or wetted with less than 30% water, by mass	1	1.1D		1		LQ0	E0	P112(a) P112(b) P112(c)		MP20		
0216	TRINITRO-m-CRESOL	1	1.1D		1		LQ0	E0	P112(b) P112(c)	PP26	MP20		
0217	TRINITRONAPHTHALENE	1	1.1D		1		LQ0	E0	P112(b) P112(c)		MP20		
0218	TRINITROPHENETOLE	1	1.1D		1		LQ0	E0	P112(b) P112(c)		MP20		
0219	TRINITRORESORCINOL (STYPHNIC ACID), dry or wetted with less than 20% water, or mixture of alcohol and water, by mass	1	1.1D		1		LQ0	E0	P112(a) P112(b) P112(c)	PP26	MP20		
0220	UREA NITRATE, dry or wetted with less than 20% water, by mass	1	1.1D		1		LQ0	E0	P112(a) P112(b) P112(c)		MP20		
0221	WARHEADS, TORPEDO with bursting charge	1	1.1D		1		LQ0	E0	P130 LP101	PP67 L1	MP21		
0222	AMMONIUM NITRATE with more than 0.2% combustible substances, including any organic substance calculated as carbon, to the exclusion of any other added substance	1	1.1D		1		LQ0	E0	P112(b) P112(c)	PP47	MP20		

ADR tank		Vehicle for tank carriage	Transport category (Tunnel restriction code)	Special provisions for carriage				Hazard identifi-cation No.	UN No.	Name and description
Tank code	Special provisions			Packages	Bulk	Loading, unloading and handling	Operation			
4.3	4.3.5, 6.8.4	9.1.1.2	1.1.3.6 (8.6)	7.2.4	7.3.3	7.5.11	8.5	5.3.2.3		3.1.2
(12)	(13)	(14)	(15)	(16)	(17)	(18)	(19)	(20)	(1)	(2)
			2 (E)	V2		CV1 CV2 CV3	S1		0191	SIGNAL DEVICES, HAND
			1 (B1000C)	V2		CV1 CV2 CV3	S1		0192	SIGNALS, RAILWAY TRACK, EXPLOSIVE
			4 (E)			CV1 CV2 CV3	S1		0193	SIGNALS, RAILWAY TRACK, EXPLOSIVE
			1 (B1000C)	V2		CV1 CV2 CV3	S1		0194	SIGNALS, DISTRESS, ship
			1 (C5000D)	V2		CV1 CV2 CV3	S1		0195	SIGNALS, DISTRESS, ship
			1 (B1000C)	V2		CV1 CV2 CV3	S1		0196	SIGNALS, SMOKE
			2 (E)	V2		CV1 CV2 CV3	S1		0197	SIGNALS, SMOKE
			1 (B1000C)	V2		CV1 CV2 CV3	S1		0204	SOUNDING DEVICES, EXPLOSIVE
			1 (B1000C)	V2 V3		CV1 CV2 CV3	S1		0207	TETRANITROANILINE
			1 (B1000C)	V2 V3		CV1 CV2 CV3	S1		0208	TRINITROPHENYLMETHYL-NITRAMINE (TETRYL)
			1 (B1000C)	V2 V3		CV1 CV2 CV3	S1		0209	TRINITROTOLUENE (TNT), dry or wetted with less than 30% water, by mass
			1 (C5000D)	V2		CV1 CV2 CV3	S1		0212	TRACERS FOR AMMUNITION
			1 (B1000C)	V2 V3		CV1 CV2 CV3	S1		0213	TRINITROANISOLE
			1 (B1000C)	V2 V3		CV1 CV2 CV3	S1		0214	TRINITROBENZENE, dry or wetted with less than 30% water, by mass
			1 (B1000C)	V2 V3		CV1 CV2 CV3	S1		0215	TRINITROBENZOIC ACID, dry or wetted with less than 30% water, by mass
			1 (B1000C)	V2 V3		CV1 CV2 CV3	S1		0216	TRINITRO-m-CRESOL
			1 (B1000C)	V2 V3		CV1 CV2 CV3	S1		0217	TRINITRONAPHTHALENE
			1 (B1000C)	V2 V3		CV1 CV2 CV3	S1		0218	TRINITROPHENETOLE
			1 (B1000C)	V2 V3		CV1 CV2 CV3	S1		0219	TRINITRORESORCINOL (STYPHNIC ACID), dry or wetted with less than 20% water, or mixture of alcohol and water, by mass
			1 (B1000C)	V2 V3		CV1 CV2 CV3	S1		0220	UREA NITRATE, dry or wetted with less than 20% water, by mass
			1 (B1000C)	V2		CV1 CV2 CV3	S1		0221	WARHEADS, TORPEDO with bursting charge
			1 (B1000C)	V2 V3		CV1 CV2 CV3	S1		0222	AMMONIUM NITRATE with more than 0.2% combustible substances, including any organic substance calculated as carbon, to the exclusion of any other added substance

UN No.	Name and description	Class	Classifi-cation code	Packing group	Labels	Special provi-sions	Limited and excepted quantities		Packaging			Portable tanks and bulk containers	
									Packing instruc-tions	Special packing provisions	Mixed packing provisions	Instruc-tions	Special provisions
	3.1.2	2.2	2.2	2.1.1.3	5.2.2	3.3	3.4.6	3.5.1.2	4.1.4	4.1.4	4.1.10	4.2.5.2 7.3.2	4.2.5.3
(1)	(2)	(3a)	(3b)	(4)	(5)	(6)	(7a)	(7b)	(8)	(9a)	(9b)	(10)	(11)
0224	BARIUM AZIDE, dry or wetted with less than 50% water, by mass	1	1.1A		1 +6.1		LQ0	E0	P110(b)	PP42	MP20		
0225	BOOSTERS WITH DETONATOR	1	1.1B		1		LQ0	E0	P133	PP69	MP23		
0226	CYCLOTETRAMETHYLENE-TETRANITRAMINE (HMX; OCTOGEN), WETTED with not less than 15% water, by mass	1	1.1D		1	266	LQ0	E0	P112(a)	PP45	MP20		
0234	SODIUM DINITRO-o-CRESOLATE, dry or wetted with less than 15% water, by mass	1	1.3C		1		LQ0	E0	P114(a) P114(b)	PP26	MP20		
0235	SODIUM PICRAMATE, dry or wetted with less than 20% water, by mass	1	1.3C		1		LQ0	E0	P114(a) P114(b)	PP26	MP20		
0236	ZIRCONIUM PICRAMATE, dry or wetted with less than 20% water, by mass	1	1.3C		1		LQ0	E0	P114(a) P114(b)	PP26	MP20		
0237	CHARGES, SHAPED, FLEXIBLE, LINEAR	1	1.4D		1.4		LQ0	E0	P138		MP21		
0238	ROCKETS, LINE-THROWING	1	1.2G		1		LQ0	E0	P130		MP23 MP24		
0240	ROCKETS, LINE-THROWING	1	1.3G		1		LQ0	E0	P130		MP23 MP24		
0241	EXPLOSIVE, BLASTING, TYPE E	1	1.1D		1	617	LQ0	E0	P116 IBC100	PP61 PP62 PP65 B10	MP20		
0242	CHARGES, PROPELLING, FOR CANNON	1	1.3C		1		LQ0	E0	P130		MP22		
0243	AMMUNITION, INCENDIARY, WHITE PHOSPHORUS with burster, expelling charge or propelling charge	1	1.2H		1		LQ0	E0	P130 LP101	PP67 L1	MP23		
0244	AMMUNITION, INCENDIARY, WHITE PHOSPHORUS with burster, expelling charge or propelling charge	1	1.3H		1		LQ0	E0	P130 LP101	PP67 L1	MP23		
0245	AMMUNITION, SMOKE, WHITE PHOSPHORUS with burster, expelling charge or propelling charge	1	1.2H		1		LQ0	E0	P130 LP101	PP67 L1	MP23		
0246	AMMUNITION, SMOKE, WHITE PHOSPHORUS with burster, expelling charge or propelling charge	1	1.3H		1		LQ0	E0	P130 LP101	PP67 L1	MP23		
0247	AMMUNITION, INCENDIARY, liquid or gel, with burster, expelling charge or propelling charge	1	1.3J		1		LQ0	E0	P101		MP23		
0248	CONTRIVANCES, WATER-ACTIVATED with burster, expelling charge or propelling charge	1	1.2L		1	274	LQ0	E0	P144	PP77	MP1		
0249	CONTRIVANCES, WATER-ACTIVATED with burster, expelling charge or propelling charge	1	1.3L		1	274	LQ0	E0	P144	PP77	MP1		

ADR tank		Vehicle for tank carriage	Transport category (Tunnel restriction code)	Special provisions for carriage				Hazard identifi-cation No.	UN No.	Name and description
Tank code	Special provisions			Packages	Bulk	Loading, unloading and handling	Operation			
4.3	4.3.5, 6.8.4	9.1.1.2	1.1.3.6 (8.6)	7.2.4	7.3.3	7.5.11	8.5	5.3.2.3		3.1.2
(12)	(13)	(14)	(15)	(16)	(17)	(18)	(19)	(20)	(1)	(2)
			0 (B)	V2 V3		CV1 CV2 CV3 CV28	S1		0224	BARIUM AZIDE, dry or wetted with less than 50% water, by mass
			1 (B1000C)	V2		CV1 CV2 CV3	S1		0225	BOOSTERS WITH DETONATOR
			1 (B1000C)	V2		CV1 CV2 CV3	S1		0226	CYCLOTETRAMETHYLENE-TETRANITRAMINE (HMX; OCTOGEN), WETTED with not less than 15% water, by mass
			1 (C5000D)	V2 V3		CV1 CV2 CV3	S1		0234	SODIUM DINITRO-o-CRESOLATE, dry or wetted with less than 15% water, by mass
			1 (C5000D)	V2 V3		CV1 CV2 CV3	S1		0235	SODIUM PICRAMATE, dry or wetted with less than 20% water, by mass
			1 (C5000D)	V2 V3		CV1 CV2 CV3	S1		0236	ZIRCONIUM PICRAMATE, dry or wetted with less than 20% water, by mass
			2 (E)	V2		CV1 CV2 CV3	S1		0237	CHARGES, SHAPED, FLEXIBLE, LINEAR
			1 (B1000C)	V2		CV1 CV2 CV3	S1		0238	ROCKETS, LINE-THROWING
			1 (C5000D)	V2		CV1 CV2 CV3	S1		0240	ROCKETS, LINE-THROWING
			1 (B1000C)	V2		CV1 CV2 CV3	S1		0241	EXPLOSIVE, BLASTING, TYPE E
			1 (C5000D)	V2		CV1 CV2 CV3	S1		0242	CHARGES, PROPELLING, FOR CANNON
			1 (B1000C)	V2		CV1 CV2 CV3	S1		0243	AMMUNITION, INCENDIARY, WHITE PHOSPHORUS with burster, expelling charge or propelling charge
			1 (C)	V2		CV1 CV2 CV3	S1		0244	AMMUNITION, INCENDIARY, WHITE PHOSPHORUS with burster, expelling charge or propelling charge
			1 (B1000C)	V2		CV1 CV2 CV3	S1		0245	AMMUNITION, SMOKE, WHITE PHOSPHORUS with burster, expelling charge or propelling charge
			1 (C)	V2		CV1 CV2 CV3	S1		0246	AMMUNITION, SMOKE, WHITE PHOSPHORUS with burster, expelling charge or propelling charge
			1 (C)	V2		CV1 CV2 CV3	S1		0247	AMMUNITION, INCENDIARY, liquid or gel, with burster, expelling charge or propelling charge
			0 (B)	V2		CV1 CV2 CV3 CV4	S1		0248	CONTRIVANCES, WATER-ACTIVATED with burster, expelling charge or propelling charge
			0 (B)	V2		CV1 CV2 CV3 CV4	S1		0249	CONTRIVANCES, WATER-ACTIVATED with burster, expelling charge or propelling charge

UN No.	Name and description	Class	Classifi-cation code	Packing group	Labels	Special provi-sions	Limited and excepted quantities		Packaging			Portable tanks and bulk containers	
									Packing instruc-tions	Special packing provisions	Mixed packing provisions	Instruc-tions	Special provisions
	3.1.2	2.2	2.2	2.1.1.3	5.2.2	3.3	3.4.6	3.5.1.2	4.1.4	4.1.4	4.1.10	4.2.5.2 7.3.2	4.2.5.3
(1)	(2)	(3a)	(3b)	(4)	(5)	(6)	(7a)	(7b)	(8)	(9a)	(9b)	(10)	(11)
0250	ROCKET MOTORS WITH HYPERGOLIC LIQUIDS with or without expelling charge	1	1.3L		1		LQ0	E0	P101		MP1		
0254	AMMUNITION, ILLUMINATING with or without burster, expelling charge or propelling charge	1	1.3G		1		LQ0	E0	P130 LP101	PP67 L1	MP23		
0255	DETONATORS, ELECTRIC for blasting	1	1.4B		1.4		LQ0	E0	P131		MP23		
0257	FUZES, DETONATING	1	1.4B		1.4		LQ0	E0	P141		MP23		
0266	OCTOLITE (OCTOL), dry or wetted with less than 15% water, by mass	1	1.1D		1		LQ0	E0	P112(a) P112(b) P112(c)		MP20		
0267	DETONATORS, NON-ELECTRIC for blasting	1	1.4B		1.4		LQ0	E0	P131	PP68	MP23		
0268	BOOSTERS WITH DETONATOR	1	1.2B		1		LQ0	E0	P133	PP69	MP23		
0271	CHARGES, PROPELLING	1	1.1C		1		LQ0	E0	P143	PP76	MP22		
0272	CHARGES, PROPELLING	1	1.3C		1		LQ0	E0	P143	PP76	MP22		
0275	CARTRIDGES, POWER DEVICE	1	1.3C		1		LQ0	E0	P134 LP102		MP22		
0276	CARTRIDGES, POWER DEVICE	1	1.4C		1.4		LQ0	E0	P134 LP102		MP22		
0277	CARTRIDGES, OIL WELL	1	1.3C		1		LQ0	E0	P134 LP102		MP22		
0278	CARTRIDGES, OIL WELL	1	1.4C		1.4		LQ0	E0	P134 LP102		MP22		
0279	CHARGES, PROPELLING, FOR CANNON	1	1.1C		1		LQ0	E0	P130		MP22		
0280	ROCKET MOTORS	1	1.1C		1		LQ0	E0	P130 LP101	PP67 L1	MP22		
0281	ROCKET MOTORS	1	1.2C		1		LQ0	E0	P130 LP101	PP67 L1	MP22		
0282	NITROGUANIDINE (PICRITE), dry or wetted with less than 20% water, by mass	1	1.1D		1		LQ0	E0	P112(a) P112(b) P112(c)		MP20		
0283	BOOSTERS without detonator	1	1.2D		1		LQ0	E0	P132(a) P132(b)		MP21		
0284	GRENADES, hand or rifle, with bursting charge	1	1.1D		1		LQ0	E0	P141		MP21		
0285	GRENADES, hand or rifle, with bursting charge	1	1.2D		1		LQ0	E0	P141		MP21		
0286	WARHEADS, ROCKET with bursting charge	1	1.1D		1		LQ0	E0	P130 LP101	PP67 L1	MP21		
0287	WARHEADS, ROCKET with bursting charge	1	1.2D		1		LQ0	E0	P130 LP101	PP67 L1	MP21		
0288	CHARGES, SHAPED, FLEXIBLE, LINEAR	1	1.1D		1		LQ0	E0	P138		MP21		

ADR tank		Vehicle for tank carriage	Transport category (Tunnel restriction code)	Special provisions for carriage				Hazard identifi-cation No.	UN No.	Name and description
Tank code	Special provisions			Packages	Bulk	Loading, unloading and handling	Operation			
4.3	4.3.5, 6.8.4	9.1.1.2	1.1.3.6 (8.6)	7.2.4	7.3.3	7.5.11	8.5	5.3.2.3		3.1.2
(12)	(13)	(14)	(15)	(16)	(17)	(18)	(19)	(20)	(1)	(2)
			0 (B)	V2		CV1 CV2 CV3 CV4	S1		0250	ROCKET MOTORS WITH HYPERGOLIC LIQUIDS with or without expelling charge
			1 (C5000D)	V2		CV1 CV2 CV3	S1		0254	AMMUNITION, ILLUMINATING with or without burster, expelling charge or propelling charge
			2 (E)	V2		CV1 CV2 CV3	S1		0255	DETONATORS, ELECTRIC for blasting
			2 (E)	V2		CV1 CV2 CV3	S1		0257	FUZES, DETONATING
			1 (B1000C)	V2 V3		CV1 CV2 CV3	S1		0266	OCTOLITE (OCTOL), dry or wetted with less than 15% water, by mass
			2 (E)	V2		CV1 CV2 CV3	S1		0267	DETONATORS, NON-ELECTRIC for blasting
			1 (B1000C)	V2		CV1 CV2 CV3	S1		0268	BOOSTERS WITH DETONATOR
			1 (B1000C)	V2		CV1 CV2 CV3	S1		0271	CHARGES, PROPELLING
			1 (C5000D)	V2		CV1 CV2 CV3	S1		0272	CHARGES, PROPELLING
			1 (C5000D)	V2		CV1 CV2 CV3	S1		0275	CARTRIDGES, POWER DEVICE
			2 (E)	V2		CV1 CV2 CV3	S1		0276	CARTRIDGES, POWER DEVICE
			1 (C5000D)	V2		CV1 CV2 CV3	S1		0277	CARTRIDGES, OIL WELL
			2 (E)	V2		CV1 CV2 CV3	S1		0278	CARTRIDGES, OIL WELL
			1 (B1000C)	V2		CV1 CV2 CV3	S1		0279	CHARGES, PROPELLING, FOR CANNON
			1 (B1000C)	V2		CV1 CV2 CV3	S1		0280	ROCKET MOTORS
			1 (B1000C)	V2		CV1 CV2 CV3	S1		0281	ROCKET MOTORS
			1 (B1000C)	V2 V3		CV1 CV2 CV3	S1		0282	NITROGUANIDINE (PICRITE), dry or wetted with less than 20% water, by mass
			1 (B1000C)	V2		CV1 CV2 CV3	S1		0283	BOOSTERS without detonator
			1 (B1000C)	V2		CV1 CV2 CV3	S1		0284	GRENADES, hand or rifle, with bursting charge
			1 (B1000C)	V2		CV1 CV2 CV3	S1		0285	GRENADES, hand or rifle, with bursting charge
			1 (B1000C)	V2		CV1 CV2 CV3	S1		0286	WARHEADS, ROCKET with bursting charge
			1 (B1000C)	V2		CV1 CV2 CV3	S1		0287	WARHEADS, ROCKET with bursting charge
			1 (B1000C)	V2		CV1 CV2 CV3	S1		0288	CHARGES, SHAPED, FLEXIBLE, LINEAR

UN No.	Name and description	Class	Classifi-cation code	Packing group	Labels	Special provi-sions	Limited and excepted quantities		Packaging			Portable tanks and bulk containers	
									Packing instruc-tions	Special packing provisions	Mixed packing provisions	Instruc-tions	Special provisions
	3.1.2	2.2	2.2	2.1.1.3	5.2.2	3.3	3.4.6	3.5.1.2	4.1.4	4.1.4	4.1.10	4.2.5.2 7.3.2	4.2.5.3
(1)	(2)	(3a)	(3b)	(4)	(5)	(6)	(7a)	(7b)	(8)	(9a)	(9b)	(10)	(11)
0289	CORD, DETONATING, flexible	1	1.4D		1.4		LQ0	E0	P139	PP71 PP72	MP21		
0290	CORD (FUSE), DETONATING, metal clad	1	1.1D		1		LQ0	E0	P139	PP71	MP21		
0291	BOMBS with bursting charge	1	1.2F		1		LQ0	E0	P130		MP23		
0292	GRENADES, hand or rifle, with bursting charge	1	1.1F		1		LQ0	E0	P141		MP23		
0293	GRENADES, hand or rifle, with bursting charge	1	1.2F		1		LQ0	E0	P141		MP23		
0294	MINES with bursting charge	1	1.2F		1		LQ0	E0	P130		MP23		
0295	ROCKETS with bursting charge	1	1.2F		1		LQ0	E0	P130		MP23		
0296	SOUNDING DEVICES, EXPLOSIVE	1	1.1F		1		LQ0	E0	P134 LP102		MP23		
0297	AMMUNITION, ILLUMINATING with or without burster, expelling charge or propelling charge	1	1.4G		1.4		LQ0	E0	P130 LP101	PP67 L1	MP23		
0299	BOMBS, PHOTO-FLASH	1	1.3G		1		LQ0	E0	P130 LP101	PP67 L1	MP23		
0300	AMMUNITION, INCENDIARY with or without burster, expelling charge or propelling charge	1	1.4G		1.4		LQ0	E0	P130 LP101	PP67 L1	MP23		
0301	AMMUNITION, TEAR-PRODUCING with burster, expelling charge or propelling charge	1	1.4G		1.4 +6.1 +8		LQ0	E0	P130 LP101	PP67 L1	MP23		
0303	AMMUNITION, SMOKE with or without burster, expelling charge or propelling charge	1	1.4G		1.4		LQ0	E0	P130 LP101	PP67 L1	MP23		
0303	AMMUNITION, SMOKE with or without burster, expelling charge or propelling charge, containing corrosive substances	1	1.4G		1.4 +8		LQ0	E0	P130 LP101	PP67 L1	MP23		
0305	FLASH POWDER	1	1.3G		1		LQ0	E0	P113	PP49	MP20		
0306	TRACERS FOR AMMUNITION	1	1.4G		1.4		LQ0	E0	P133	PP69	MP23		
0312	CARTRIDGES, SIGNAL	1	1.4G		1.4		LQ0	E0	P135		MP23 MP24		
0313	SIGNALS, SMOKE	1	1.2G		1		LQ0	E0	P135		MP23		
0314	IGNITERS	1	1.2G		1		LQ0	E0	P142		MP23		
0315	IGNITERS	1	1.3G		1		LQ0	E0	P142		MP23		
0316	FUZES, IGNITING	1	1.3G		1		LQ0	E0	P141		MP23		
0317	FUZES, IGNITING	1	1.4G		1.4		LQ0	E0	P141		MP23		

ADR tank		Vehicle for tank carriage	Transport category (Tunnel restriction code)	Special provisions for carriage				Hazard identifi-cation No.	UN No.	Name and description
Tank code	Special provisions			Packages	Bulk	Loading, unloading and handling	Operation			
4.3	4.3.5, 6.8.4	9.1.1.2	1.1.3.6 (8.6)	7.2.4	7.3.3	7.5.11	8.5	5.3.2.3		3.1.2
(12)	(13)	(14)	(15)	(16)	(17)	(18)	(19)	(20)	(1)	(2)
			2 (E)	V2		CV1 CV2 CV3	S1		0289	CORD, DETONATING, flexible
			1 (B1000C)	V2		CV1 CV2 CV3	S1		0290	CORD (FUSE), DETONATING, metal clad
			1 (B1000C)	V2		CV1 CV2 CV3	S1		0291	BOMBS with bursting charge
			1 (B1000C)	V2		CV1 CV2 CV3	S1		0292	GRENADES, hand or rifle, with bursting charge
			1 (B1000C)	V2		CV1 CV2 CV3	S1		0293	GRENADES, hand or rifle, with bursting charge
			1 (B1000C)	V2		CV1 CV2 CV3	S1		0294	MINES with bursting charge
			1 (B1000C)	V2		CV1 CV2 CV3	S1		0295	ROCKETS with bursting charge
			1 (B1000C)	V2		CV1 CV2 CV3	S1		0296	SOUNDING DEVICES, EXPLOSIVE
			2 (E)	V2		CV1 CV2 CV3	S1		0297	AMMUNITION, ILLUMINATING with or without burster, expelling charge or propelling charge
			1 (C5000D)	V2		CV1 CV2 CV3	S1		0299	BOMBS, PHOTO-FLASH
			2 (E)	V2		CV1 CV2 CV3	S1		0300	AMMUNITION, INCENDIARY with or without burster, expelling charge or propelling charge
			2 (E)	V2		CV1 CV2 CV3 CV28	S1		0301	AMMUNITION, TEAR-PRODUCING with burster, expelling charge or propelling charge
			2 (E)	V2		CV1 CV2 CV3	S1		0303	AMMUNITION, SMOKE with or without burster, expelling charge or propelling charge
			2 (E)	V2		CV1 CV2 CV3	S1		0303	AMMUNITION, SMOKE with or without burster, expelling charge or propelling charge, containing corrosive substances
			1 (C5000D)	V2 V3		CV1 CV2 CV3	S1		0305	FLASH POWDER
			2 (E)	V2		CV1 CV2 CV3	S1		0306	TRACERS FOR AMMUNITION
			2 (E)	V2		CV1 CV2 CV3	S1		0312	CARTRIDGES, SIGNAL
			1 (B1000C)	V2		CV1 CV2 CV3	S1		0313	SIGNALS, SMOKE
			1 (B1000C)	V2		CV1 CV2 CV3	S1		0314	IGNITERS
			1 (C5000D)	V2		CV1 CV2 CV3	S1		0315	IGNITERS
			1 (C5000D)	V2		CV1 CV2 CV3	S1		0316	FUZES, IGNITING
			2 (E)	V2		CV1 CV2 CV3	S1		0317	FUZES, IGNITING

UN No.	Name and description	Class	Classifi-cation code	Packing group	Labels	Special provi-sions	Limited and excepted quantities		Packaging			Portable tanks and bulk containers	
									Packing instruc-tions	Special packing provisions	Mixed packing provisions	Instruc-tions	Special provisions
	3.1.2	2.2	2.2	2.1.1.3	5.2.2	3.3	3.4.6	3.5.1.2	4.1.4	4.1.4	4.1.10	4.2.5.2 7.3.2	4.2.5.3
(1)	(2)	(3a)	(3b)	(4)	(5)	(6)	(7a)	(7b)	(8)	(9a)	(9b)	(10)	(11)
0318	GRENADES, PRACTICE, hand or rifle	1	1.3G		1		LQ0	E0	P141		MP23		
0319	PRIMERS, TUBULAR	1	1.3G		1		LQ0	E0	P133		MP23		
0320	PRIMERS, TUBULAR	1	1.4G		1.4		LQ0	E0	P133		MP23		
0321	CARTRIDGES FOR WEAPONS with bursting charge	1	1.2E		1		LQ0	E0	P130 LP101	PP67 L1	MP21		
0322	ROCKET MOTORS WITH HYPERGOLIC LIQUIDS with or without expelling charge	1	1.2L		1		LQ0	E0	P101		MP1		
0323	CARTRIDGES, POWER DEVICE	1	1.4S		1.4		LQ0	E0	P134 LP102		MP23		
0324	PROJECTILES with bursting charge	1	1.2F		1		LQ0	E0	P130		MP23		
0325	IGNITERS	1	1.4G		1.4		LQ0	E0	P142		MP23		
0326	CARTRIDGES FOR WEAPONS, BLANK	1	1.1C		1		LQ0	E0	P130		MP22		
0327	CARTRIDGES FOR WEAPONS, BLANK or CARTRIDGES, SMALL ARMS, BLANK	1	1.3C		1		LQ0	E0	P130		MP22		
0328	CARTRIDGES FOR WEAPONS, INERT PROJECTILE	1	1.2C		1		LQ0	E0	P130 LP101	PP67 L1	MP22		
0329	TORPEDOES with bursting charge	1	1.1E		1		LQ0	E0	P130 LP101	PP67 L1	MP21		
0330	TORPEDOES with bursting charge	1	1.1F		1		LQ0	E0	P130		MP23		
0331	EXPLOSIVE, BLASTING, TYPE B (AGENT, BLASTING, TYPE B)	1	1.5D		1.5	617	LQ0	E0	P116 IBC100	PP61 PP62 PP64 PP65	MP20	T1	TP1 TP17 TP32
0332	EXPLOSIVE, BLASTING, TYPE E (AGENT, BLASTING, TYPE E)	1	1.5D		1.5	617	LQ0	E0	P116 IBC100	PP61 PP62 PP65	MP20	T1	TP1 TP17 TP32
0333	FIREWORKS	1	1.1G		1	645	LQ0	E0	P135		MP23 MP24		
0334	FIREWORKS	1	1.2G		1	645	LQ0	E0	P135		MP23 MP24		
0335	FIREWORKS	1	1.3G		1	645	LQ0	E0	P135		MP23 MP24		
0336	FIREWORKS	1	1.4G		1.4	645 651	LQ0	E0	P135		MP23 MP24		
0337	FIREWORKS	1	1.4S		1.4	645	LQ0	E0	P135		MP23 MP24		
0338	CARTRIDGES FOR WEAPONS, BLANK or CARTRIDGES, SMALL ARMS, BLANK	1	1.4C		1.4		LQ0	E0	P130		MP22		

ADR tank		Vehicle for tank carriage	Transport category (Tunnel restriction code)	Special provisions for carriage				Hazard identifi- cation No.	UN No.	Name and description
Tank code	Special provisions			Packages	Bulk	Loading, unloading and handling	Operation			
4.3	4.3.5, 6.8.4	9.1.1.2	1.1.3.6 (8.6)	7.2.4	7.3.3	7.5.11	8.5	5.3.2.3		3.1.2
(12)	(13)	(14)	(15)	(16)	(17)	(18)	(19)	(20)	(1)	(2)
			1 (C5000D)	V2		CV1 CV2 CV3	S1		0318	GRENADES, PRACTICE, hand or rifle
			1 (C5000D)	V2		CV1 CV2 CV3	S1		0319	PRIMERS, TUBULAR
			2 (E)	V2		CV1 CV2 CV3	S1		0320	PRIMERS, TUBULAR
			1 (B1000C)	V2		CV1 CV2 CV3	S1		0321	CARTRIDGES FOR WEAPONS with bursting charge
			0 (B)	V2		CV1 CV2 CV3	S1		0322	ROCKET MOTORS WITH HYPERGOLIC LIQUIDS with or without expelling charge
			4 (E)			CV1 CV2 CV3	S1		0323	CARTRIDGES, POWER DEVICE
			1 (B1000C)	V2		CV1 CV2 CV3	S1		0324	PROJECTILES with bursting charge
			2 (E)	V2		CV1 CV2 CV3	S1		0325	IGNITERS
			1 (B1000C)	V2		CV1 CV2 CV3	S1		0326	CARTRIDGES FOR WEAPONS, BLANK
			1 (C5000D)	V2		CV1 CV2 CV3	S1		0327	CARTRIDGES FOR WEAPONS, BLANK or CARTRIDGES, SMALL ARMS, BLANK
			1 (B1000C)	V2		CV1 CV2 CV3	S1		0328	CARTRIDGES FOR WEAPONS, INERT PROJECTILE
			1 (B1000C)	V2		CV1 CV2 CV3	S1		0329	TORPEDOES with bursting charge
			1 (B1000C)	V2		CV1 CV2 CV3	S1		0330	TORPEDOES with bursting charge
		EX/III	1 (B1000C)	V2		CV1 CV2 CV3	S1	1.5D	0331	EXPLOSIVE, BLASTING, TYPE B (AGENT, BLASTING, TYPE B)
		EX/III	1 (B1000C)	V2		CV1 CV2 CV3	S1	1.5D	0332	EXPLOSIVE, BLASTING, TYPE E (AGENT, BLASTING, TYPE E)
			1 (B1000C)	V2 V3		CV1 CV2 CV3	S1		0333	FIREWORKS
			1 (B1000C)	V2 V3		CV1 CV2 CV3	S1		0334	FIREWORKS
			1 (C5000D)	V2 V3		CV1 CV2 CV3	S1		0335	FIREWORKS
			2 (E)	V2		CV1 CV2 CV3	S1		0336	FIREWORKS
			4 (E)			CV1 CV2 CV3	S1		0337	FIREWORKS
			2 (E)	V2		CV1 CV2 CV3	S1		0338	CARTRIDGES FOR WEAPONS, BLANK or CARTRIDGES, SMALL ARMS, BLANK

UN No.	Name and description	Class	Classifi-cation code	Packing group	Labels	Special provi-sions	Limited and excepted quantities		Packaging			Portable tanks and bulk containers	
									Packing instruc-tions	Special packing provisions	Mixed packing provisions	Instruc-tions	Special provisions
3.1.2		2.2	2.2	2.1.1.3	5.2.2	3.3	3.4.6	3.5.1.2	4.1.4	4.1.4	4.1.10	4.2.5.2 7.3.2	4.2.5.3
(1)	(2)	(3a)	(3b)	(4)	(5)	(6)	(7a)	(7b)	(8)	(9a)	(9b)	(10)	(11)
0339	CARTRIDGES FOR WEAPONS, INERT PROJECTILE or CARTRIDGES, SMALL ARMS	1	1.4C		1.4		LQ0	E0	P130		MP22		
0340	NITROCELLULOSE, dry or wetted with less than 25% water (or alcohol), by mass	1	1.1D		1		LQ0	E0	P112(a) P112(b)		MP20		
0341	NITROCELLULOSE, unmodified or plasticized with less than 18% plasticizing substance, by mass	1	1.1D		1		LQ0	E0	P112(b)		MP20		
0342	NITROCELLULOSE, WETTED with not less than 25% alcohol, by mass	1	1.3C		1	105	LQ0	E0	P114(a)	PP43	MP20		
0343	NITROCELLULOSE, PLASTICIZED with not less than 18% plasticizing substance, by mass	1	1.3C		1	105	LQ0	E0	P111		MP20		
0344	PROJECTILES with bursting charge	1	1.4D		1.4		LQ0	E0	P130 LP101	PP67 L1	MP21		
0345	PROJECTILES, inert with tracer	1	1.4S		1.4		LQ0	E0	P130 LP101	PP67 L1	MP23		
0346	PROJECTILES with burster or expelling charge	1	1.2D		1		LQ0	E0	P130 LP101	PP67 L1	MP21		
0347	PROJECTILES with burster or expelling charge	1	1.4D		1.4		LQ0	E0	P130 LP101	PP67 L1	MP21		
0348	CARTRIDGES FOR WEAPONS with bursting charge	1	1.4F		1.4		LQ0	E0	P130		MP23		
0349	ARTICLES, EXPLOSIVE, N.O.S.	1	1.4S		1.4	178 274	LQ0	E0	P101		MP2		
0350	ARTICLES, EXPLOSIVE, N.O.S.	1	1.4B		1.4	178 274	LQ0	E0	P101		MP2		
0351	ARTICLES, EXPLOSIVE, N.O.S.	1	1.4C		1.4	178 274	LQ0	E0	P101		MP2		
0352	ARTICLES, EXPLOSIVE, N.O.S.	1	1.4D		1.4	178 274	LQ0	E0	P101		MP2		
0353	ARTICLES, EXPLOSIVE, N.O.S.	1	1.4G		1.4	178 274	LQ0	E0	P101		MP2		
0354	ARTICLES, EXPLOSIVE, N.O.S.	1	1.1L		1	178 274	LQ0	E0	P101		MP1		
0355	ARTICLES, EXPLOSIVE, N.O.S.	1	1.2L		1	178 274	LQ0	E0	P101		MP1		
0356	ARTICLES, EXPLOSIVE, N.O.S.	1	1.3L		1	178 274	LQ0	E0	P101		MP1		
0357	SUBSTANCES, EXPLOSIVE, N.O.S.	1	1.1L		1	178 274	LQ0	E0	P101		MP1		
0358	SUBSTANCES, EXPLOSIVE, N.O.S.	1	1.2L		1	178 274	LQ0	E0	P101		MP1		

ADR tank		Vehicle for tank carriage	Transport category (Tunnel restriction code)	Special provisions for carriage				Hazard identifi-cation No.	UN No.	Name and description
Tank code	Special provisions			Packages	Bulk	Loading, unloading and handling	Operation			
4.3	4.3.5, 6.8.4	9.1.1.2	1.1.3.6 (8.6)	7.2.4	7.3.3	7.5.11	8.5	5.3.2.3		3.1.2
(12)	(13)	(14)	(15)	(16)	(17)	(18)	(19)	(20)	(1)	(2)
			2 (E)	V2		CV1 CV2 CV3	S1		0339	CARTRIDGES FOR WEAPONS, INERT PROJECTILE or CARTRIDGES, SMALL ARMS
			1 (B1000C)	V2 V3		CV1 CV2 CV3	S1		0340	NITROCELLULOSE, dry or wetted with less than 25% water (or alcohol), by mass
			1 (B1000C)	V2 V3		CV1 CV2 CV3	S1		0341	NITROCELLULOSE, unmodified or plasticized with less than 18% plasticizing substance, by mass
			1 (C5000D)	V2		CV1 CV2 CV3	S1		0342	NITROCELLULOSE, WETTED with not less than 25% alcohol, by mass
			1 (C5000D)	V2		CV1 CV2 CV3	S1		0343	NITROCELLULOSE, PLASTICIZED with not less than 18% plasticizing substance, by mass
			2 (E)	V2		CV1 CV2 CV3	S1		0344	PROJECTILES with bursting charge
			4 (E)			CV1 CV2 CV3	S1		0345	PROJECTILES, inert with tracer
			1 (B1000C)	V2		CV1 CV2 CV3	S1		0346	PROJECTILES with burster or expelling charge
			2 (E)	V2		CV1 CV2 CV3	S1		0347	PROJECTILES with burster or expelling charge
			2 (E)	V2		CV1 CV2 CV3	S1		0348	CARTRIDGES FOR WEAPONS with bursting charge
			4 (E)			CV1 CV2 CV3	S1		0349	ARTICLES, EXPLOSIVE, N.O.S.
			2 (E)	V2		CV1 CV2 CV3	S1		0350	ARTICLES, EXPLOSIVE, N.O.S.
			2 (E)	V2		CV1 CV2 CV3	S1		0351	ARTICLES, EXPLOSIVE, N.O.S.
			2 (E)	V2		CV1 CV2 CV3	S1		0352	ARTICLES, EXPLOSIVE, N.O.S.
			2 (E)	V2		CV1 CV2 CV3	S1		0353	ARTICLES, EXPLOSIVE, N.O.S.
			0 (B)	V2		CV1 CV2 CV3 CV4	S1		0354	ARTICLES, EXPLOSIVE, N.O.S.
			0 (B)	V2		CV1 CV2 CV3 CV4	S1		0355	ARTICLES, EXPLOSIVE, N.O.S.
			0 (B)	V2		CV1 CV2 CV3 CV4	S1		0356	ARTICLES, EXPLOSIVE, N.O.S.
			0 (B)	V2		CV1 CV2 CV3 CV4	S1		0357	SUBSTANCES, EXPLOSIVE, N.O.S.
			0 (B)	V2		CV1 CV2 CV3 CV4	S1		0358	SUBSTANCES, EXPLOSIVE, N.O.S.

UN No.	Name and description	Class	Classifi- cation code	Packing group	Labels	Special provi- sions	Limited and excepted quantities		Packaging			Portable tanks and bulk containers	
									Packing instruc- tions	Special packing provisions	Mixed packing provisions	Instruc- tions	Special provisions
	3.1.2	2.2	2.2	2.1.1.3	5.2.2	3.3	3.4.6	3.5.1.2	4.1.4	4.1.4	4.1.10	4.2.5.2 7.3.2	4.2.5.3
(1)	(2)	(3a)	(3b)	(4)	(5)	(6)	(7a)	(7b)	(8)	(9a)	(9b)	(10)	(11)
0359	SUBSTANCES, EXPLOSIVE, N.O.S.	1	1.3L		1	178 274	LQ0	E0	P101		MP1		
0360	DETONATOR ASSEMBLIES, NON-ELECTRIC for blasting	1	1.1B		1		LQ0	E0	P131		MP23		
0361	DETONATOR ASSEMBLIES, NON-ELECTRIC for blasting	1	1.4B		1.4		LQ0	E0	P131		MP23		
0362	AMMUNITION, PRACTICE	1	1.4G		1.4		LQ0	E0	P130 LP101	PP67 L1	MP23		
0363	AMMUNITION, PROOF	1	1.4G		1.4		LQ0	E0	P130 LP101	PP67 L1	MP23		
0364	DETONATORS FOR AMMUNITION	1	1.2B		1		LQ0	E0	P133		MP23		
0365	DETONATORS FOR AMMUNITION	1	1.4B		1.4		LQ0	E0	P133		MP23		
0366	DETONATORS FOR AMMUNITION	1	1.4S		1.4		LQ0	E0	P133		MP23		
0367	FUZES, DETONATING	1	1.4S		1.4		LQ0	E0	P141		MP23		
0368	FUZES, IGNITING	1	1.4S		1.4		LQ0	E0	P141		MP23		
0369	WARHEADS, ROCKET with bursting charge	1	1.1F		1		LQ0	E0	P130		MP23		
0370	WARHEADS, ROCKET with burster or expelling charge	1	1.4D		1.4		LQ0	E0	P130 LP101	PP67 L1	MP21		
0371	WARHEADS, ROCKET with burster or expelling charge	1	1.4F		1.4		LQ0	E0	P130		MP23		
0372	GRENADES, PRACTICE, hand or rifle	1	1.2G		1		LQ0	E0	P141		MP23		
0373	SIGNAL DEVICES, HAND	1	1.4S		1.4		LQ0	E0	P135		MP23 MP24		
0374	SOUNDING DEVICES, EXPLOSIVE	1	1.1D		1		LQ0	E0	P134 LP102		MP21		
0375	SOUNDING DEVICES, EXPLOSIVE	1	1.2D		1		LQ0	E0	P134 LP102		MP21		
0376	PRIMERS, TUBULAR	1	1.4S		1.4		LQ0	E0	P133		MP23		
0377	PRIMERS, CAP TYPE	1	1.1B		1		LQ0	E0	P133		MP23		
0378	PRIMERS, CAP TYPE	1	1.4B		1.4		LQ0	E0	P133		MP23		
0379	CASES, CARTRIDGE, EMPTY, WITH PRIMER	1	1.4C		1.4		LQ0	E0	P136		MP22		
0380	ARTICLES, PYROPHORIC	1	1.2L		1		LQ0	E0	P101		MP1		
0381	CARTRIDGES, POWER DEVICE	1	1.2C		1		LQ0	E0	P134 LP102		MP22		

ADR tank		Vehicle for tank carriage	Transport category (Tunnel restriction code)	Special provisions for carriage				Hazard identifi-cation No.	UN No.	Name and description
Tank code	Special provisions			Packages	Bulk	Loading, unloading and handling	Operation			
4.3	4.3.5, 6.8.4	9.1.1.2	1.1.3.6 (8.6)	7.2.4	7.3.3	7.5.11	8.5	5.3.2.3		3.1.2
(12)	(13)	(14)	(15)	(16)	(17)	(18)	(19)	(20)	(1)	(2)
			0 (B)	V2		CV1 CV2 CV3 CV4	S1		0359	SUBSTANCES, EXPLOSIVE, N.O.S.
			1 (B1000C)	V2		CV1 CV2 CV3	S1		0360	DETONATOR ASSEMBLIES, NON-ELECTRIC for blasting
			2 (E)	V2		CV1 CV2 CV3	S1		0361	DETONATOR ASSEMBLIES, NON-ELECTRIC for blasting
			2 (E)	V2		CV1 CV2 CV3	S1		0362	AMMUNITION, PRACTICE
			2 (E)	V2		CV1 CV2 CV3	S1		0363	AMMUNITION, PROOF
			1 (B1000C)	V2		CV1 CV2 CV3	S1		0364	DETONATORS FOR AMMUNITION
			2 (E)	V2		CV1 CV2 CV3	S1		0365	DETONATORS FOR AMMUNITION
			4 (E)			CV1 CV2 CV3	S1		0366	DETONATORS FOR AMMUNITION
			4 (E)			CV1 CV2 CV3	S1		0367	FUZES, DETONATING
			4 (E)			CV1 CV2 CV3	S1		0368	FUZES, IGNITING
			1 (B1000C)	V2		CV1 CV2 CV3	S1		0369	WARHEADS, ROCKET with bursting charge
			2 (E)	V2		CV1 CV2 CV3	S1		0370	WARHEADS, ROCKET with burster or expelling charge
			2 (E)	V2		CV1 CV2 CV3	S1		0371	WARHEADS, ROCKET with burster or expelling charge
			1 (B1000C)	V2		CV1 CV2 CV3	S1		0372	GRENADES, PRACTICE, hand or rifle
			4 (E)			CV1 CV2 CV3	S1		0373	SIGNAL DEVICES, HAND
			1 (B1000C)	V2		CV1 CV2 CV3	S1		0374	SOUNDING DEVICES, EXPLOSIVE
			1 (B1000C)	V2		CV1 CV2 CV3	S1		0375	SOUNDING DEVICES, EXPLOSIVE
			4 (E)			CV1 CV2 CV3	S1		0376	PRIMERS, TUBULAR
			1 (B1000C)	V2		CV1 CV2 CV3	S1		0377	PRIMERS, CAP TYPE
			2 (E)	V2		CV1 CV2 CV3	S1		0378	PRIMERS, CAP TYPE
			2 (E)	V2		CV1 CV2 CV3	S1		0379	CASES, CARTRIDGE, EMPTY, WITH PRIMER
			0 (B)	V2		CV1 CV2 CV3 CV4	S1		0380	ARTICLES, PYROPHORIC
			1 (B1000C)	V2		CV1 CV2 CV3	S1		0381	CARTRIDGES, POWER DEVICE

UN No.	Name and description	Class	Classifi-cation code	Packing group	Labels	Special provi-sions	Limited and excepted quantities		Packaging			Portable tanks and bulk containers	
									Packing instruc-tions	Special packing provisions	Mixed packing provisions	Instruc-tions	Special provisions
	3.1.2	2.2	2.2	2.1.1.3	5.2.2	3.3	3.4.6	3.5.1.2	4.1.4	4.1.4	4.1.10	4.2.5.2 7.3.2	4.2.5.3
(1)	(2)	(3a)	(3b)	(4)	(5)	(6)	(7a)	(7b)	(8)	(9a)	(9b)	(10)	(11)
0382	COMPONENTS, EXPLOSIVE TRAIN, N.O.S.	1	1.2B		1	178 274	LQ0	E0	P101		MP2		
0383	COMPONENTS, EXPLOSIVE TRAIN, N.O.S.	1	1.4B		1.4	178 274	LQ0	E0	P101		MP2		
0384	COMPONENTS, EXPLOSIVE TRAIN, N.O.S.	1	1.4S		1.4	178 274	LQ0	E0	P101		MP2		
0385	5-NITROBENZOTRIAZOL	1	1.1D		1		LQ0	E0	P112(b) P112(c)		MP20		
0386	TRINITROBENZENE-SULPHONIC ACID	1	1.1D		1		LQ0	E0	P112(b) P112(c)	PP26	MP20		
0387	TRINITROFLUORENONE	1	1.1D		1		LQ0	E0	P112(b) P112(c)		MP20		
0388	TRINITROTOLUENE (TNT) AND TRINITROBENZENE MIXTURE or TRINITROTOLUENE (TNT) AND HEXANITROSTILBENE MIXTURE	1	1.1D		1		LQ0	E0	P112(b) P112(c)		MP20		
0389	TRINITROTOLUENE (TNT) MIXTURE CONTAINING TRINITROBENZENE AND HEXANITROSTILBENE	1	1.1D		1		LQ0	E0	P112(b) P112(c)		MP20		
0390	TRITONAL	1	1.1D		1		LQ0	E0	P112(b) P112(c)		MP20		
0391	CYCLOTRIMETHYLENE-TRINITRAMINE (CYCLONITE; HEXOGEN; RDX) AND CYCLOTETRAMETHYLENE-TETRANITRAMINE (HMX; OCTOGEN) MIXTURE, WETTED with not less than 15% water, by mass or DESENSITIZED with not less than 10% phlegmatiser by mass	1	1.1D		1	266	LQ0	E0	P112(a) P112(b)		MP20		
0392	HEXANITROSTILBENE	1	1.1D		1		LQ0	E0	P112(b) P112(c)		MP20		
0393	HEXOTONAL	1	1.1D		1		LQ0	E0	P112(b)		MP20		
0394	TRINITRORESORCINOL (STYPHNIC ACID), WETTED with not less than 20% water, or mixture of alcohol and water, by mass	1	1.1D		1		LQ0	E0	P112(a)	PP26	MP20		
0395	ROCKET MOTORS, LIQUID FUELLED	1	1.2J		1		LQ0	E0	P101		MP23		
0396	ROCKET MOTORS, LIQUID FUELLED	1	1.3J		1		LQ0	E0	P101		MP23		
0397	ROCKETS, LIQUID FUELLED with bursting charge	1	1.1J		1		LQ0	E0	P101		MP23		
0398	ROCKETS, LIQUID FUELLED with bursting charge	1	1.2J		1		LQ0	E0	P101		MP23		
0399	BOMBS WITH FLAMMABLE LIQUID with bursting charge	1	1.1J		1		LQ0	E0	P101		MP23		
0400	BOMBS WITH FLAMMABLE LIQUID with bursting charge	1	1.2J		1		LQ0	E0	P101		MP23		

ADR tank		Vehicle for tank carriage	Transport category (Tunnel restriction code)	Special provisions for carriage				Hazard identifi-cation No.	UN No.	Name and description
Tank code	Special provisions			Packages	Bulk	Loading, unloading and handling	Operation			
4.3	4.3.5, 6.8.4	9.1.1.2	1.1.3.6 (8.6)	7.2.4	7.3.3	7.5.11	8.5	5.3.2.3		3.1.2
(12)	(13)	(14)	(15)	(16)	(17)	(18)	(19)	(20)	(1)	(2)
			1 (B1000C)	V2		CV1 CV2 CV3	S1		0382	COMPONENTS, EXPLOSIVE TRAIN, N.O.S.
			2 (E)	V2		CV1 CV2 CV3	S1		0383	COMPONENTS, EXPLOSIVE TRAIN, N.O.S.
			4 (E)			CV1 CV2 CV3	S1		0384	COMPONENTS, EXPLOSIVE TRAIN, N.O.S.
			1 (B1000C)	V2 V3		CV1 CV2 CV3	S1		0385	5-NITROBENZOTRIAZOL
			1 (B1000C)	V2 V3		CV1 CV2 CV3	S1		0386	TRINITROBENZENE-SULPHONIC ACID
			1 (B1000C)	V2 V3		CV1 CV2 CV3	S1		0387	TRINITROFLUORENONE
			1 (B1000C)	V2 V3		CV1 CV2 CV3	S1		0388	TRINITROTOLUENE (TNT) AND TRINITROBENZENE MIXTURE or TRINITROTOLUENE (TNT) AND HEXANITROSTILBENE MIXTURE
			1 (B1000C)	V2 V3		CV1 CV2 CV3	S1		0389	TRINITROTOLUENE (TNT) MIXTURE CONTAINING TRINITROBENZENE AND HEXANITROSTILBENE
			1 (B1000C)	V2 V3		CV1 CV2 CV3	S1		0390	TRITONAL
			1 (B1000C)	V2 V3		CV1 CV2 CV3	S1		0391	CYCLOTRIMETHYLENE-TRINITRAMINE (CYCLONITE; HEXOGEN; RDX) AND CYCLOTETRAMETHYLENE-TETRANITRAMINE (HMX; OCTOGEN) MIXTURE, WETTED with not less than 15% water, by mass or DESENSITIZED with not less than 10% phlegmatiser by mass
			1 (B1000C)	V2 V3		CV1 CV2 CV3	S1		0392	HEXANITROSTILBENE
			1 (B1000C)	V2 V3		CV1 CV2 CV3	S1		0393	HEXOTONAL
			1 (B1000C)	V2		CV1 CV2 CV3	S1		0394	TRINITRORESORCINOL (STYPHNIC ACID), WETTED with not less than 20% water, or mixture of alcohol and water, by mass
			1 (B1000C)	V2		CV1 CV2 CV3	S1		0395	ROCKET MOTORS, LIQUID FUELLED
			1 (C)	V2		CV1 CV2 CV3	S1		0396	ROCKET MOTORS, LIQUID FUELLED
			1 (B1000C)	V2		CV1 CV2 CV3	S1		0397	ROCKETS, LIQUID FUELLED with bursting charge
			1 (B1000C)	V2		CV1 CV2 CV3	S1		0398	ROCKETS, LIQUID FUELLED with bursting charge
			1 (B1000C)	V2		CV1 CV2 CV3	S1		0399	BOMBS WITH FLAMMABLE LIQUID with bursting charge
			1 (B1000C)	V2		CV1 CV2 CV3	S1		0400	BOMBS WITH FLAMMABLE LIQUID with bursting charge

UN No.	Name and description	Class	Classifi-cation code	Packing group	Labels	Special provi-sions	Limited and excepted quantities		Packaging			Portable tanks and bulk containers	
									Packing instruc-tions	Special packing provisions	Mixed packing provisions	Instruc-tions	Special provisions
	3.1.2	2.2	2.2	2.1.1.3	5.2.2	3.3	3.4.6	3.5.1.2	4.1.4	4.1.4	4.1.10	4.2.5.2 7.3.2	4.2.5.3
(1)	(2)	(3a)	(3b)	(4)	(5)	(6)	(7a)	(7b)	(8)	(9a)	(9b)	(10)	(11)
0401	DIPICRYL SULPHIDE, dry or wetted with less than 10% water, by mass	1	1.1D		1		LQ0	E0	P112(a) P112(b) P112(c)		MP20		
0402	AMMONIUM PERCHLORATE	1	1.1D		1	152	LQ0	E0	P112(b) P112(c)		MP20		
0403	FLARES, AERIAL	1	1.4G		1.4		LQ0	E0	P135		MP23		
0404	FLARES, AERIAL	1	1.4S		1.4		LQ0	E0	P135		MP23		
0405	CARTRIDGES, SIGNAL	1	1.4S		1.4		LQ0	E0	P135		MP23 MP24		
0406	DINITROSOBENZENE	1	1.3C		1		LQ0	E0	P114(b)		MP20		
0407	TETRAZOL-1-ACETIC ACID	1	1.4C		1.4		LQ0	E0	P114(b)		MP20		
0408	FUZES, DETONATING with protective features	1	1.1D		1		LQ0	E0	P141		MP21		
0409	FUZES, DETONATING with protective features	1	1.2D		1		LQ0	E0	P141		MP21		
0410	FUZES, DETONATING with protective features	1	1.4D		1.4		LQ0	E0	P141		MP21		
0411	PENTAERYTHRITE TETRANITRATE (PENTAERYTHRITOL TETRANITRATE; PETN) with not less than 7% wax, by mass	1	1.1D		1	131	LQ0	E0	P112(b) P112(c)		MP20		
0412	CARTRIDGES FOR WEAPONS with bursting charge	1	1.4E		1.4		LQ0	E0	P130 LP101	PP67 L1	MP21		
0413	CARTRIDGES FOR WEAPONS, BLANK	1	1.2C		1		LQ0	E0	P130		MP22		
0414	CHARGES, PROPELLING, FOR CANNON	1	1.2C		1		LQ0	E0	P130		MP22		
0415	CHARGES, PROPELLING	1	1.2C		1		LQ0	E0	P143	PP76	MP22		
0417	CARTRIDGES FOR WEAPONS, INERT PROJECTILE or CARTRIDGES, SMALL ARMS	1	1.3C		1		LQ0	E0	P130		MP22		
0418	FLARES, SURFACE	1	1.1G		1		LQ0	E0	P135		MP23		
0419	FLARES, SURFACE	1	1.2G		1		LQ0	E0	P135		MP23		
0420	FLARES, AERIAL	1	1.1G		1		LQ0	E0	P135		MP23		
0421	FLARES, AERIAL	1	1.2G		1		LQ0	E0	P135		MP23		
0424	PROJECTILES, inert with tracer	1	1.3G		1		LQ0	E0	P130 LP101	PP67 L1	MP23		
0425	PROJECTILES, inert with tracer	1	1.4G		1.4		LQ0	E0	P130 LP101	PP67 L1	MP23		

	ADR tank	Vehicle for tank carriage	Transport category (Tunnel restriction code)	Special provisions for carriage				Hazard identifi-cation No.	UN No.	Name and description
Tank code	Special provisions			Packages	Bulk	Loading, unloading and handling	Operation			
4.3	4.3.5, 6.8.4	9.1.1.2	1.1.3.6 (8.6)	7.2.4	7.3.3	7.5.11	8.5	5.3.2.3		3.1.2
(12)	(13)	(14)	(15)	(16)	(17)	(18)	(19)	(20)	(1)	(2)
			1 (B1000C)	V2 V3		CV1 CV2 CV3	S1		0401	DIPICRYL SULPHIDE, dry or wetted with less than 10% water, by mass
			1 (B1000C)	V2 V3		CV1 CV2 CV3	S1		0402	AMMONIUM PERCHLORATE
			2 (E)	V2		CV1 CV2 CV3	S1		0403	FLARES, AERIAL
			4 (E)			CV1 CV2 CV3	S1		0404	FLARES, AERIAL
			4 (E)			CV1 CV2 CV3	S1		0405	CARTRIDGES, SIGNAL
			1 (C5000D)	V2 V3		CV1 CV2 CV3	S1		0406	DINITROSOBENZENE
			2 (E)	V2		CV1 CV2 CV3	S1		0407	TETRAZOL-1-ACETIC ACID
			1 (B1000C)	V2		CV1 CV2 CV3	S1		0408	FUZES, DETONATING with protective features
			1 (B1000C)	V2		CV1 CV2 CV3	S1		0409	FUZES, DETONATING with protective features
			2 (E)	V2		CV1 CV2 CV3	S1		0410	FUZES, DETONATING with protective features
			1 (B1000C)	V2 V3		CV1 CV2 CV3	S1		0411	PENTAERYTHRITE TETRANITRATE (PENTAERYTHRITOL TETRANITRATE; PETN) with not less than 7% wax, by mass
			2 (E)	V2		CV1 CV2 CV3	S1		0412	CARTRIDGES FOR WEAPONS with bursting charge
			1 (B1000C)	V2		CV1 CV2 CV3	S1		0413	CARTRIDGES FOR WEAPONS, BLANK
			1 (B1000C)	V2		CV1 CV2 CV3	S1		0414	CHARGES, PROPELLING, FOR CANNON
			1 (B1000C)	V2		CV1 CV2 CV3	S1		0415	CHARGES, PROPELLING
			1 (C5000D)	V2		CV1 CV2 CV3	S1		0417	CARTRIDGES FOR WEAPONS, INERT PROJECTILE or CARTRIDGES, SMALL ARMS
			1 (B1000C)	V2		CV1 CV2 CV3	S1		0418	FLARES, SURFACE
			1 (B1000C)	V2		CV1 CV2 CV3	S1		0419	FLARES, SURFACE
			1 (B1000C)	V2		CV1 CV2 CV3	S1		0420	FLARES, AERIAL
			1 (B1000C)	V2		CV1 CV2 CV3	S1		0421	FLARES, AERIAL
			1 (C5000D)	V2		CV1 CV2 CV3	S1		0424	PROJECTILES, inert with tracer
			2 (E)	V2		CV1 CV2 CV3	S1		0425	PROJECTILES, inert with tracer

UN No.	Name and description	Class	Classifi-cation code	Packing group	Labels	Special provi-sions	Limited and excepted quantities		Packaging			Portable tanks and bulk containers	
									Packing instruc-tions	Special packing provisions	Mixed packing provisions	Instruc-tions	Special provisions
	3.1.2	2.2	2.2	2.1.1.3	5.2.2	3.3	3.4.6	3.5.1.2	4.1.4	4.1.4	4.1.10	4.2.5.2 7.3.2	4.2.5.3
(1)	(2)	(3a)	(3b)	(4)	(5)	(6)	(7a)	(7b)	(8)	(9a)	(9b)	(10)	(11)
0426	PROJECTILES with burster or expelling charge	1	1.2F		1		LQ0	E0	P130		MP23		
0427	PROJECTILES with burster or expelling charge	1	1.4F		1.4		LQ0	E0	P130		MP23		
0428	ARTICLES, PYROTECHNIC for technical purposes	1	1.1G		1		LQ0	E0	P135		MP23 MP24		
0429	ARTICLES, PYROTECHNIC for technical purposes	1	1.2G		1		LQ0	E0	P135		MP23 MP24		
0430	ARTICLES, PYROTECHNIC for technical purposes	1	1.3G		1		LQ0	E0	P135		MP23 MP24		
0431	ARTICLES, PYROTECHNIC for technical purposes	1	1.4G		1.4		LQ0	E0	P135		MP23 MP24		
0432	ARTICLES, PYROTECHNIC for technical purposes	1	1.4S		1.4		LQ0	E0	P135		MP23 MP24		
0433	POWDER CAKE (POWDER PASTE), WETTED with not less than 17% alcohol, by mass	1	1.1C		1	266	LQ0	E0	P111		MP20		
0434	PROJECTILES with burster or expelling charge	1	1.2G		1		LQ0	E0	P130 LP101	PP67 L1	MP23		
0435	PROJECTILES with burster or expelling charge	1	1.4G		1.4		LQ0	E0	P130 LP101	PP67 L1	MP23		
0436	ROCKETS with expelling charge	1	1.2C		1		LQ0	E0	P130 LP101	PP67 L1	MP22		
0437	ROCKETS with expelling charge	1	1.3C		1		LQ0	E0	P130 LP101	PP67 L1	MP22		
0438	ROCKETS with expelling charge	1	1.4C		1.4		LQ0	E0	P130 LP101	PP67 L1	MP22		
0439	CHARGES, SHAPED, without detonator	1	1.2D		1		LQ0	E0	P137	PP70	MP21		
0440	CHARGES, SHAPED, without detonator	1	1.4D		1.4		LQ0	E0	P137	PP70	MP21		
0441	CHARGES, SHAPED, without detonator	1	1.4S		1.4		LQ0	E0	P137	PP70	MP23		
0442	CHARGES, EXPLOSIVE, COMMERCIAL without detonator	1	1.1D		1		LQ0	E0	P137		MP21		
0443	CHARGES, EXPLOSIVE, COMMERCIAL without detonator	1	1.2D		1		LQ0	E0	P137		MP21		
0444	CHARGES, EXPLOSIVE, COMMERCIAL without detonator	1	1.4D		1.4		LQ0	E0	P137		MP21		
0445	CHARGES, EXPLOSIVE, COMMERCIAL without detonator	1	1.4S		1.4		LQ0	E0	P137		MP23		
0446	CASES, COMBUSTIBLE, EMPTY, WITHOUT PRIMER	1	1.4C		1.4		LQ0	E0	P136		MP22		
0447	CASES, COMBUSTIBLE, EMPTY, WITHOUT PRIMER	1	1.3C		1		LQ0	E0	P136		MP22		
0448	5-MERCAPTOTETRAZOL-1-ACETIC ACID	1	1.4C		1.4		LQ0	E0	P114(b)		MP20		
0449	TORPEDOES, LIQUID FUELLED with or without bursting charge	1	1.1J		1		LQ0	E0	P101		MP23		

ADR tank		Vehicle for tank carriage	Transport category (Tunnel restriction code)	Special provisions for carriage				Hazard identifi-cation No.	UN No.	Name and description
Tank code	Special provisions			Packages	Bulk	Loading, unloading and handling	Operation			
4.3	4.3.5, 6.8.4	9.1.1.2	1.1.3.6 (8.6)	7.2.4	7.3.3	7.5.11	8.5	5.3.2.3		3.1.2
(12)	(13)	(14)	(15)	(16)	(17)	(18)	(19)	(20)	(1)	(2)
			1 (B1000C)	V2		CV1 CV2 CV3	S1		0426	PROJECTILES with burster or expelling charge
			2 (E)	V2		CV1 CV2 CV3	S1		0427	PROJECTILES with burster or expelling charge
			1 (B1000C)	V2		CV1 CV2 CV3	S1		0428	ARTICLES, PYROTECHNIC for technical purposes
			1 (B1000C)	V2		CV1 CV2 CV3	S1		0429	ARTICLES, PYROTECHNIC for technical purposes
			1 (C5000D)	V2		CV1 CV2 CV3	S1		0430	ARTICLES, PYROTECHNIC for technical purposes
			2 (E)	V2		CV1 CV2 CV3	S1		0431	ARTICLES, PYROTECHNIC for technical purposes
			4 (E)			CV1 CV2 CV3	S1		0432	ARTICLES, PYROTECHNIC for technical purposes
			1 (B1000C)	V2		CV1 CV2 CV3	S1		0433	POWDER CAKE (POWDER PASTE), WETTED with not less than 17% alcohol, by mass
			1 (B1000C)	V2		CV1 CV2 CV3	S1		0434	PROJECTILES with burster or expelling charge
			2 (E)	V2		CV1 CV2 CV3	S1		0435	PROJECTILES with burster or expelling charge
			1 (B1000C)	V2		CV1 CV2 CV3	S1		0436	ROCKETS with expelling charge
			1 (C5000D)	V2		CV1 CV2 CV3	S1		0437	ROCKETS with expelling charge
			2 (E)	V2		CV1 CV2 CV3	S1		0438	ROCKETS with expelling charge
			1 (B1000C)	V2		CV1 CV2 CV3	S1		0439	CHARGES, SHAPED, without detonator
			2 (E)	V2		CV1 CV2 CV3	S1		0440	CHARGES, SHAPED, without detonator
			4 (E)	V2		CV1 CV2 CV3	S1		0441	CHARGES, SHAPED, without detonator
			1 (B1000C)	V2		CV1 CV2 CV3	S1		0442	CHARGES, EXPLOSIVE, COMMERCIAL without detonator
			1 (B1000C)	V2		CV1 CV2 CV3	S1		0443	CHARGES, EXPLOSIVE, COMMERCIAL without detonator
			2 (E)	V2		CV1 CV2 CV3	S1		0444	CHARGES, EXPLOSIVE, COMMERCIAL without detonator
			4 (E)			CV1 CV2 CV3	S1		0445	CHARGES, EXPLOSIVE, COMMERCIAL without detonator
			2 (E)	V2		CV1 CV2 CV3	S1		0446	CASES, COMBUSTIBLE, EMPTY, WITHOUT PRIMER
			1 (C5000D)	V2		CV1 CV2 CV3	S1		0447	CASES, COMBUSTIBLE, EMPTY, WITHOUT PRIMER
			2 (E)	V2		CV1 CV2 CV3	S1		0448	5-MERCAPTOTETRAZOL-1-ACETIC ACID
			1 (B1000C)	V2		CV1 CV2 CV3	S1		0449	TORPEDOES, LIQUID FUELLED with or without bursting charge

UN No.	Name and description	Class	Classifi-cation code	Packing group	Labels	Special provi-sions	Limited and excepted quantities		Packaging			Portable tanks and bulk containers	
									Packing instruc-tions	Special packing provisions	Mixed packing provisions	Instruc-tions	Special provisions
	3.1.2	2.2	2.2	2.1.1.3	5.2.2	3.3	3.4.6	3.5.1.2	4.1.4	4.1.4	4.1.10	4.2.5.2 7.3.2	4.2.5.3
(1)	(2)	(3a)	(3b)	(4)	(5)	(6)	(7a)	(7b)	(8)	(9a)	(9b)	(10)	(11)
0450	TORPEDOES, LIQUID FUELLED with inert head	1	1.3J		1		LQ0	E0	P101		MP23		
0451	TORPEDOES with bursting charge	1	1.1D		1		LQ0	E0	P130 LP101	PP67 L1	MP21		
0452	GRENADES, PRACTICE, hand or rifle	1	1.4G		1.4		LQ0	E0	P141		MP23		
0453	ROCKETS, LINE-THROWING	1	1.4G		1.4		LQ0	E0	P130		MP23		
0454	IGNITERS	1	1.4S		1.4		LQ0	E0	P142		MP23		
0455	DETONATORS, NON-ELECTRIC for blasting	1	1.4S		1.4		LQ0	E0	P131	PP68	MP23		
0456	DETONATORS, ELECTRIC for blasting	1	1.4S		1.4		LQ0	E0	P131		MP23		
0457	CHARGES, BURSTING, PLASTICS BONDED	1	1.1D		1		LQ0	E0	P130		MP21		
0458	CHARGES, BURSTING, PLASTICS BONDED	1	1.2D		1		LQ0	E0	P130		MP21		
0459	CHARGES, BURSTING, PLASTICS BONDED	1	1.4D		1.4		LQ0	E0	P130		MP21		
0460	CHARGES, BURSTING, PLASTICS BONDED	1	1.4S		1.4		LQ0	E0	P130		MP23		
0461	COMPONENTS, EXPLOSIVE TRAIN, N.O.S.	1	1.1B		1	178 274	LQ0	E0	P101		MP2		
0462	ARTICLES, EXPLOSIVE, N.O.S.	1	1.1C		1	178 274	LQ0	E0	P101		MP2		
0463	ARTICLES, EXPLOSIVE, N.O.S.	1	1.1D		1	178 274	LQ0	E0	P101		MP2		
0464	ARTICLES, EXPLOSIVE, N.O.S.	1	1.1E		1	178 274	LQ0	E0	P101		MP2		
0465	ARTICLES, EXPLOSIVE, N.O.S.	1	1.1F		1	178 274	LQ0	E0	P101		MP2		
0466	ARTICLES, EXPLOSIVE, N.O.S.	1	1.2C		1	178 274	LQ0	E0	P101		MP2		
0467	ARTICLES, EXPLOSIVE, N.O.S.	1	1.2D		1	178 274	LQ0	E0	P101		MP2		
0468	ARTICLES, EXPLOSIVE, N.O.S.	1	1.2E		1	178 274	LQ0	E0	P101		MP2		
0469	ARTICLES, EXPLOSIVE, N.O.S.	1	1.2F		1	178 274	LQ0	E0	P101		MP2		
0470	ARTICLES, EXPLOSIVE, N.O.S.	1	1.3C		1	178 274	LQ0	E0	P101		MP2		
0471	ARTICLES, EXPLOSIVE, N.O.S.	1	1.4E		1.4	178 274	LQ0	E0	P101		MP2		
0472	ARTICLES, EXPLOSIVE, N.O.S.	1	1.4F		1.4	178 274	LQ0	E0	P101		MP2		
0473	SUBSTANCES, EXPLOSIVE, N.O.S.	1	1.1A		1	178 274	LQ0	E0	P101		MP2		

ADR tank		Vehicle for tank carriage	Transport category (Tunnel restriction code)	Special provisions for carriage				Hazard identifi- cation No.	UN No.	Name and description
Tank code	Special provisions			Packages	Bulk	Loading, unloading and handling	Operation			
4.3	4.3.5, 6.8.4	9.1.1.2	1.1.3.6 (8.6)	7.2.4	7.3.3	7.5.11	8.5	5.3.2.3		3.1.2
(12)	(13)	(14)	(15)	(16)	(17)	(18)	(19)	(20)	(1)	(2)
			1 (C)	V2		CV1 CV2 CV3	S1		0450	TORPEDOES, LIQUID FUELLED with inert head
			1 (B1000C)	V2		CV1 CV2 CV3	S1		0451	TORPEDOES with bursting charge
			2 (E)	V2		CV1 CV2 CV3	S1		0452	GRENADES, PRACTICE, hand or rifle
			2 (E)	V2		CV1 CV2 CV3	S1		0453	ROCKETS, LINE-THROWING
			4 (E)			CV1 CV2 CV3	S1		0454	IGNITERS
			4 (E)			CV1 CV2 CV3	S1		0455	DETONATORS, NON-ELECTRIC for blasting
			4 (E)			CV1 CV2 CV3	S1		0456	DETONATORS, ELECTRIC for blasting
			1 (B1000C)	V2		CV1 CV2 CV3	S1		0457	CHARGES, BURSTING, PLASTICS BONDED
			1 (B1000C)	V2		CV1 CV2 CV3	S1		0458	CHARGES, BURSTING, PLASTICS BONDED
			2 (E)	V2		CV1 CV2 CV3	S1		0459	CHARGES, BURSTING, PLASTICS BONDED
			4 (E)			CV1 CV2 CV3	S1		0460	CHARGES, BURSTING, PLASTICS BONDED
			1 (B1000C)	V2		CV1 CV2 CV3	S1		0461	COMPONENTS, EXPLOSIVE TRAIN, N.O.S.
			1 (B1000C)	V2		CV1 CV2 CV3	S1		0462	ARTICLES, EXPLOSIVE, N.O.S.
			1 (B1000C)	V2		CV1 CV2 CV3	S1		0463	ARTICLES, EXPLOSIVE, N.O.S.
			1 (B1000C)	V2		CV1 CV2 CV3	S1		0464	ARTICLES, EXPLOSIVE, N.O.S.
			1 (B1000C)	V2		CV1 CV2 CV3	S1		0465	ARTICLES, EXPLOSIVE, N.O.S.
			1 (B1000C)	V2		CV1 CV2 CV3	S1		0466	ARTICLES, EXPLOSIVE, N.O.S.
			1 (B1000C)	V2		CV1 CV2 CV3	S1		0467	ARTICLES, EXPLOSIVE, N.O.S.
			1 (B1000C)	V2		CV1 CV2 CV3	S1		0468	ARTICLES, EXPLOSIVE, N.O.S.
			1 (B1000C)	V2		CV1 CV2 CV3	S1		0469	ARTICLES, EXPLOSIVE, N.O.S.
			1 (C5000D)	V2		CV1 CV2 CV3	S1		0470	ARTICLES, EXPLOSIVE, N.O.S.
			2 (E)	V2		CV1 CV2 CV3	S1		0471	ARTICLES, EXPLOSIVE, N.O.S.
			2 (E)	V2		CV1 CV2 CV3	S1		0472	ARTICLES, EXPLOSIVE, N.O.S.
			0 (B)	V2		CV1 CV2 CV3	S1		0473	SUBSTANCES, EXPLOSIVE, N.O.S.

UN No.	Name and description	Class	Classifi-cation code	Packing group	Labels	Special provi-sions	Limited and excepted quantities		Packaging			Portable tanks and bulk containers	
									Packing instruc-tions	Special packing provisions	Mixed packing provisions	Instruc-tions	Special provisions
	3.1.2	2.2	2.2	2.1.1.3	5.2.2	3.3	3.4.6	3.5.1.2	4.1.4	4.1.4	4.1.10	4.2.5.2 7.3.2	4.2.5.3
(1)	(2)	(3a)	(3b)	(4)	(5)	(6)	(7a)	(7b)	(8)	(9a)	(9b)	(10)	(11)
0474	SUBSTANCES, EXPLOSIVE, N.O.S.	1	1.1C		1	178 274	LQ0	E0	P101		MP2		
0475	SUBSTANCES, EXPLOSIVE, N.O.S.	1	1.1D		1	178 274	LQ0	E0	P101		MP2		
0476	SUBSTANCES, EXPLOSIVE, N.O.S.	1	1.1G		1	178 274	LQ0	E0	P101		MP2		
0477	SUBSTANCES, EXPLOSIVE, N.O.S.	1	1.3C		1	178 274	LQ0	E0	P101		MP2		
0478	SUBSTANCES, EXPLOSIVE, N.O.S.	1	1.3G		1	178 274	LQ0	E0	P101		MP2		
0479	SUBSTANCES, EXPLOSIVE, N.O.S.	1	1.4C		1.4	178 274	LQ0	E0	P101		MP2		
0480	SUBSTANCES, EXPLOSIVE, N.O.S.	1	1.4D		1.4	178 274	LQ0	E0	P101		MP2		
0481	SUBSTANCES, EXPLOSIVE, N.O.S.	1	1.4S		1.4	178 274	LQ0	E0	P101		MP2		
0482	SUBSTANCES, EXPLOSIVE, VERY INSENSITIVE (SUBSTANCES, EVI), N.O.S.	1	1.5D		1.5	178 274	LQ0	E0	P101		MP2		
0483	CYCLOTRIMETHYLENE-TRINITRAMINE (CYCLONITE; HEXOGEN; RDX), DESENSITIZED	1	1.1D		1		LQ0	E0	P112(b) P112(c)		MP20		
0484	CYCLOTETRAMETHYLENE-TETRANITRAMINE (HMX; OCTOGEN), DESENSITIZED	1	1.1D		1		LQ0	E0	P112(b) P112(c)		MP20		
0485	SUBSTANCES, EXPLOSIVE, N.O.S.	1	1.4G		1.4	178 274	LQ0	E0	P101		MP2		
0486	ARTICLES, EXPLOSIVE, EXTREMELY INSENSITIVE (ARTICLES, EEI)	1	1.6N		1.6		LQ0	E0	P101		MP23		
0487	SIGNALS, SMOKE	1	1.3G		1		LQ0	E0	P135		MP23		
0488	AMMUNITION, PRACTICE	1	1.3G		1		LQ0	E0	P130 LP101	PP67 L1	MP23		
0489	DINITROGLYCOLURIL (DINGU)	1	1.1D		1		LQ0	E0	P112(b) P112(c)		MP20		
0490	NITROTRIAZOLONE (NTO)	1	1.1D		1		LQ0	E0	P112(b) P112(c)		MP20		
0491	CHARGES, PROPELLING	1	1.4C		1.4		LQ0	E0	P143	PP76	MP22		
0492	SIGNALS, RAILWAY TRACK, EXPLOSIVE	1	1.3G		1		LQ0	E0	P135		MP23		
0493	SIGNALS, RAILWAY TRACK, EXPLOSIVE	1	1.4G		1.4		LQ0	E0	P135		MP23		
0494	JET PERFORATING GUNS, CHARGED, oil well, without detonator	1	1.4D		1.4		LQ0	E0	P101		MP21		
0495	PROPELLANT, LIQUID	1	1.3C		1	224	LQ0	E0	P115	PP53 PP54 PP57 PP58	MP20		
0496	OCTONAL	1	1.1D		1		LQ0	E0	P112(b) P112(c)		MP20		

ADR tank		Vehicle for tank carriage	Transport category (Tunnel restriction code)	Special provisions for carriage				Hazard identifi-cation No.	UN No.	Name and description
Tank code	Special provisions			Packages	Bulk	Loading, unloading and handling	Operation			
4.3	4.3.5, 6.8.4	9.1.1.2	1.1.3.6 (8.6)	7.2.4	7.3.3	7.5.11	8.5	5.3.2.3		3.1.2
(12)	(13)	(14)	(15)	(16)	(17)	(18)	(19)	(20)	(1)	(2)
			1 (B1000C)	V2 V3		CV1 CV2 CV3	S1		0474	SUBSTANCES, EXPLOSIVE, N.O.S.
			1 (B1000C)	V2 V3		CV1 CV2 CV3	S1		0475	SUBSTANCES, EXPLOSIVE, N.O.S.
			1 (B1000C)	V2 V3		CV1 CV2 CV3	S1		0476	SUBSTANCES, EXPLOSIVE, N.O.S.
			1 (C5000D)	V2 V3		CV1 CV2 CV3	S1		0477	SUBSTANCES, EXPLOSIVE, N.O.S.
			1 (C5000D)	V2 V3		CV1 CV2 CV3	S1		0478	SUBSTANCES, EXPLOSIVE, N.O.S.
			2 (E)	V2		CV1 CV2 CV3	S1		0479	SUBSTANCES, EXPLOSIVE, N.O.S.
			2 (E)	V2		CV1 CV2 CV3	S1		0480	SUBSTANCES, EXPLOSIVE, N.O.S.
			4 (E)			CV1 CV2 CV3	S1		0481	SUBSTANCES, EXPLOSIVE, N.O.S.
			1 (B1000C)	V2		CV1 CV2 CV3	S1		0482	SUBSTANCES, EXPLOSIVE, VERY INSENSITIVE (SUBSTANCES, EVI), N.O.S.
			1 (B1000C)	V2 V3		CV1 CV2 CV3	S1		0483	CYCLOTRIMETHYLENE-TRINITRAMINE (CYCLONITE; HEXOGEN; RDX), DESENSITIZED
			1 (B1000C)	V2 V3		CV1 CV2 CV3	S1		0484	CYCLOTETRAMETHYLENE-TETRANITRAMINE (HMX; OCTOGEN), DESENSITIZED
			2 (E)	V2 V3		CV1 CV2 CV3	S1		0485	SUBSTANCES, EXPLOSIVE, N.O.S.
			2 (E)	V2		CV1 CV2 CV3	S1		0486	ARTICLES, EXPLOSIVE, EXTREMELY INSENSITIVE (ARTICLES, EEI)
			1 (C5000D)	V2		CV1 CV2 CV3	S1		0487	SIGNALS, SMOKE
			1 (C5000D)	V2		CV1 CV2 CV3	S1		0488	AMMUNITION, PRACTICE
			1 (B1000C)	V2 V3		CV1 CV2 CV3	S1		0489	DINITROGLYCOLURIL (DINGU)
			1 (B1000C)	V2 V3		CV1 CV2 CV3	S1		0490	NITROTRIAZOLONE (NTO)
			2 (E)	V2		CV1 CV2 CV3	S1		0491	CHARGES, PROPELLING
			1 (C5000D)	V2		CV1 CV2 CV3	S1		0492	SIGNALS, RAILWAY TRACK, EXPLOSIVE
			2 (E)	V2		CV1 CV2 CV3	S1		0493	SIGNALS, RAILWAY TRACK, EXPLOSIVE
			2 (E)	V2		CV1 CV2 CV3	S1		0494	JET PERFORATING GUNS, CHARGED, oil well, without detonator
			1 (C5000D)	V2		CV1 CV2 CV3	S1		0495	PROPELLANT, LIQUID
			1 (B1000C)	V2 V3		CV1 CV2 CV3	S1		0496	OCTONAL

UN No.	Name and description	Class	Classifi-cation code	Packing group	Labels	Special provi-sions	Limited and excepted quantities		Packaging			Portable tanks and bulk containers	
									Packing instruc-tions	Special packing provisions	Mixed packing provisions	Instruc-tions	Special provisions
	3.1.2	2.2	2.2	2.1.1.3	5.2.2	3.3	3.4.6	3.5.1.2	4.1.4	4.1.4	4.1.10	4.2.5.2 7.3.2	4.2.5.3
(1)	(2)	(3a)	(3b)	(4)	(5)	(6)	(7a)	(7b)	(8)	(9a)	(9b)	(10)	(11)
0497	PROPELLANT, LIQUID	1	1.1C		1	224	LQ0	E0	P115	PP53 PP54 PP57 PP58	MP20		
0498	PROPELLANT, SOLID	1	1.1C		1		LQ0	E0	P114(b)		MP20		
0499	PROPELLANT, SOLID	1	1.3C		1		LQ0	E0	P114(b)		MP20		
0500	DETONATOR ASSEMBLIES, NON-ELECTRIC for blasting	1	1.4S		1.4		LQ0	E0	P131		MP23		
0501	PROPELLANT, SOLID	1	1.4C		1.4		LQ0	E0	P114(b)		MP20		
0502	ROCKETS with inert head	1	1.2C		1		LQ0	E0	P130 LP101	PP67 L1	MP22		
0503	AIR BAG INFLATORS or AIR BAG MODULES or SEAT-BELT PRETENSIONERS	1	1.4G		1.4	235 289	LQ0	E0	P135		MP23		
0504	1H-TETRAZOLE	1	1.1D		1		LQ0	E0	P112(c)	PP48	MP20		
0505	SIGNALS, DISTRESS, ship	1	1.4G		1.4		LQ0	E0	P135		MP23 MP24		
0506	SIGNALS, DISTRESS, ship	1	1.4S		1.4		LQ0	E0	P135		MP23 MP24		
0507	SIGNALS, SMOKE	1	1.4S		1.4		LQ0	E0	P135		MP23 MP24		
0508	1-HYDROXY-BENZOTRIAZOLE, ANHYDROUS, dry or wetted with less than 20% water, by mass	1	1.3C		1		LQ0	E0	P114(b)	PP48 PP50	MP20		
1001	ACETYLENE, DISSOLVED	2	4F		2.1		LQ0	E0	P200		MP9		
1002	AIR, COMPRESSED	2	1A		2.2	292	LQ1	E1	P200		MP9	(M)	
1003	AIR, REFRIGERATED LIQUID	2	3O		2.2 +5.1		LQ0	E0	P203		MP9	T75	TP5 TP22
1005	AMMONIA, ANHYDROUS	2	2TC		2.3 +8	23	LQ0	E0	P200		MP9	(M) T50	
1006	ARGON, COMPRESSED	2	1A		2.2		LQ1	E1	P200		MP9	(M)	
1008	BORON TRIFLUORIDE	2	2TC		2.3 +8		LQ0	E0	P200		MP9	(M)	
1009	BROMOTRIFLUORO-METHANE (REFRIGERANT GAS R 13B1)	2	2A		2.2		LQ1	E1	P200		MP9	(M) T50	
1010	BUTADIENES, STABILIZED or BUTADIENES AND HYDROCARBON MIXTURE, STABILIZED, having a vapour pressure at 70 °C not exceeding 1.1 Mpa (11 bar) and a density at 50 °C not lower than 0.525 kg/l	2	2F		2.1	618	LQ0	E0	P200		MP9	(M) T50	
1011	BUTANE	2	2F		2.1	652	LQ0	E0	P200		MP9	(M) T50	

	ADR tank	Vehicle for tank carriage	Transport category (Tunnel restriction code)	Special provisions for carriage				Hazard identification No.	UN No.	Name and description
Tank code	Special provisions			Packages	Bulk	Loading, unloading and handling	Operation			
4.3	4.3.5, 6.8.4	9.1.1.2	1.1.3.6 (8.6)	7.2.4	7.3.3	7.5.11	8.5	5.3.2.3		3.1.2
(12)	(13)	(14)	(15)	(16)	(17)	(18)	(19)	(20)	(1)	(2)
			1 (B1000C)	V2		CV1 CV2 CV3	S1		0497	PROPELLANT, LIQUID
			1 (B1000C)	V2		CV1 CV2 CV3	S1		0498	PROPELLANT, SOLID
			1 (C5000D)	V2		CV1 CV2 CV3	S1		0499	PROPELLANT, SOLID
			4 (E)			CV1 CV2 CV3	S1		0500	DETONATOR ASSEMBLIES, NON-ELECTRIC for blasting
			2 (E)	V2		CV1 CV2 CV3	S1		0501	PROPELLANT, SOLID
			1 (B1000C)	V2		CV1 CV2 CV3	S1		0502	ROCKETS with inert head
			2 (E)	V2		CV1 CV2 CV3	S1		0503	AIR BAG INFLATORS or AIR BAG MODULES or SEAT-BELT PRETENSIONERS
			1 (B1000C)	V2 V3		CV1 CV2 CV3	S1		0504	1H-TETRAZOLE
			2 (E)	V2		CV1 CV2 CV3	S1		0505	SIGNALS, DISTRESS, ship
			4 (E)			CV1 CV2 CV3	S1		0506	SIGNALS, DISTRESS, ship
			4 (E)			CV1 CV2 CV3	S1		0507	SIGNALS, SMOKE
			1 (C5000D)	V2 V3		CV1 CV2 CV3	S1		0508	1-HYDROXY-BENZOTRIAZOLE, ANHYDROUS, dry or wetted with less than 20% water, by mass
PxBN(M)	TU17 TA4 TT9	FL	2 (B/D)			CV9 CV10 CV36	S2	239	1001	ACETYLENE, DISSOLVED
CxBN(M)	TA4 TT9	AT	3 (E)			CV9 CV10		20	1002	AIR, COMPRESSED
RxBN	TU7 TU19 TA4 TT9	AT	3 (C/E)	V5		CV9 CV11 CV36	S20	225	1003	AIR, REFRIGERATED LIQUID
PxBH(M)	TA4 TT8 TT9	AT	1 (C/D)			CV9 CV10 CV36	S14	268	1005	AMMONIA, ANHYDROUS
CxBN(M)	TA4 TT9	AT	3 (E)			CV9 CV10 CV36		20	1006	ARGON, COMPRESSED
PxBH(M)	TA4 TT9	AT	1 (C/D)			CV9 CV10 CV36	S14	268	1008	BORON TRIFLUORIDE
PxBN(M)	TA4 TT9	AT	3 (C/E)			CV9 CV10 CV36		20	1009	BROMOTRIFLUORO-METHANE (REFRIGERANT GAS R 13B1)
PxBN(M)	TA4 TT9	FL	2 (B/D)			CV9 CV10 CV36	S2 S20	239	1010	BUTADIENES, STABILIZED or BUTADIENES AND HYDROCARBON MIXTURE, STABILIZED, having a vapour pressure at 70 °C not exceeding 1.1 Mpa (11 bar) and a density at 50 °C not lower than 0.525 kg/l
PxBN(M)	TA4 TT9	FL	2 (B/D)			CV9 CV10 CV36	S2 S20	23	1011	BUTANE

UN No.	Name and description	Class	Classification code	Packing group	Labels	Special provisions	Limited and excepted quantities		Packaging			Portable tanks and bulk containers	
									Packing instructions	Special packing provisions	Mixed packing provisions	Instructions	Special provisions
	3.1.2	2.2	2.2	2.1.1.3	5.2.2	3.3	3.4.6	3.5.1.2	4.1.4	4.1.4	4.1.10	4.2.5.2 7.3.2	4.2.5.3
(1)	(2)	(3a)	(3b)	(4)	(5)	(6)	(7a)	(7b)	(8)	(9a)	(9b)	(10)	(11)
1012	BUTYLENES MIXTURE or 1-BUTYLENE or cis-2-BUTYLENE or trans-2-BUTYLENE	2	2F		2.1		LQ0	E0	P200		MP9	(M) T50	
1013	CARBON DIOXIDE	2	2A		2.2	584 653	LQ1	E1	P200		MP9	(M)	
1016	CARBON MONOXIDE, COMPRESSED	2	1TF		2.3 +2.1		LQ0	E0	P200		MP9	(M)	
1017	CHLORINE	2	2TOC		2.3 +5.1 +8		LQ0	E0	P200		MP9	(M) T50	TP19
1018	CHLORODIFLUORO-METHANE (REFRIGERANT GAS R 22)	2	2A		2.2		LQ1	E1	P200		MP9	(M) T50	
1020	CHLOROPENTAFLUORO-ETHANE (REFRIGERANT GAS R 115)	2	2A		2.2		LQ1	E1	P200		MP9	(M) T50	
1021	1-CHLORO-1,2,2,2-TETRAFLUOROETHANE (REFRIGERANT GAS R 124)	2	2A		2.2		LQ1	E1	P200		MP9	(M) T50	
1022	CHLOROTRIFLUORO-METHANE (REFRIGERANT GAS R 13)	2	2A		2.2		LQ1	E1	P200		MP9	(M)	
1023	COAL GAS, COMPRESSED	2	1TF		2.3 +2.1		LQ0	E0	P200		MP9	(M)	
1026	CYANOGEN	2	2TF		2.3 +2.1		LQ0	E0	P200		MP9	(M)	
1027	CYCLOPROPANE	2	2F		2.1		LQ0	E0	P200		MP9	(M) T50	
1028	DICHLORODIFLUORO-METHANE (REFRIGERANT GAS R 12)	2	2A		2.2		LQ1	E1	P200		MP9	(M) T50	
1029	DICHLOROFLUORO-METHANE (REFRIGERANT GAS R 21)	2	2A		2.2		LQ1	E1	P200		MP9	(M) T50	
1030	1,1-DIFLUOROETHANE (REFRIGERANT GAS R 152a)	2	2F		2.1		LQ0	E0	P200		MP9	(M) T50	
1032	DIMETHYLAMINE, ANHYDROUS	2	2F		2.1		LQ0	E0	P200		MP9	(M) T50	
1033	DIMETHYL ETHER	2	2F		2.1		LQ0	E0	P200		MP9	(M) T50	
1035	ETHANE	2	2F		2.1		LQ0	E0	P200		MP9	(M)	
1036	ETHYLAMINE	2	2F		2.1		LQ0	E0	P200		MP9	(M) T50	
1037	ETHYL CHLORIDE	2	2F		2.1		LQ0	E0	P200		MP9	(M) T50	
1038	ETHYLENE, REFRIGERATED LIQUID	2	3F		2.1		LQ0	E0	P203		MP9	T75	TP5
1039	ETHYL METHYL ETHER	2	2F		2.1		LQ0	E0	P200		MP9	(M)	
1040	ETHYLENE OXIDE	2	2TF		2.3 +2.1		LQ0	E0	P200		MP9	(M)	
1040	ETHYLENE OXIDE WITH NITROGEN up to a total pressure of 1 MPa (10 bar) at 50 °C	2	2TF		2.3 +2.1		LQ0	E0	P200		MP9	(M) T50	TP20

ADR tank		Vehicle for tank carriage	Transport category (Tunnel restriction code)	Special provisions for carriage				Hazard identifi-cation No.	UN No.	Name and description
Tank code	Special provisions			Packages	Bulk	Loading, unloading and handling	Operation			
4.3	4.3.5, 6.8.4	9.1.1.2	1.1.3.6 (8.6)	7.2.4	7.3.3	7.5.11	8.5	5.3.2.3		3.1.2
(12)	(13)	(14)	(15)	(16)	(17)	(18)	(19)	(20)	(1)	(2)
PxBN(M)	TA4 TT9	FL	2 (B/D)			CV9 CV10 CV36	S2 S20	23	1012	BUTYLENES MIXTURE or 1-BUTYLENE or cis-2-BUTYLENE or trans-2-BUTYLENE
PxBN(M)	TA4 TT9	AT	3 (C/E)			CV9 CV10 CV36		20	1013	CARBON DIOXIDE
CxBH(M)	TA4 TT9	FL	1 (B/D)			CV9 CV10 CV36	S2 S14	263	1016	CARBON MONOXIDE, COMPRESSED
P22DH(M)	TA4 TT9	AT	1 (C/D)			CV9 CV10 CV36	S14	265	1017	CHLORINE
PxBN(M)	TA4 TT9	AT	3 (C/E)			CV9 CV10 CV36		20	1018	CHLORODIFLUORO-METHANE (REFRIGERANT GAS R 22)
PxBN(M)	TA4 TT9	AT	3 (C/E)			CV9 CV10 CV36		20	1020	CHLOROPENTAFLUORO-ETHANE (REFRIGERANT GAS R 115)
PxBN(M)	TA4 TT9	AT	3 (C/E)			CV9 CV10 CV36		20	1021	1-CHLORO-1,2,2,2-TETRAFLUOROETHANE (REFRIGERANT GAS R 124)
PxBN(M)	TA4 TT9	AT	3 (C/E)			CV9 CV10 CV36		20	1022	CHLOROTRIFLUORO-METHANE (REFRIGERANT GAS R 13)
CxBH(M)	TA4 TT9	FL	1 (B/D)			CV9 CV10 CV36	S2 S14	263	1023	COAL GAS, COMPRESSED
PxBH(M)	TA4 TT9	FL	1 (B/D)			CV9 CV10 CV36	S2 S14	263	1026	CYANOGEN
PxBN(M)	TA4 TT9	FL	2 (B/D)			CV9 CV10 CV36	S2 S20	23	1027	CYCLOPROPANE
PxBN(M)	TA4 TT9	AT	3 (C/E)			CV9 CV10 CV36		20	1028	DICHLORODIFLUORO-METHANE (REFRIGERANT GAS R 12)
PxBN(M)	TA4 TT9	AT	3 (C/E)			CV9 CV10 CV36		20	1029	DICHLOROFLUORO-METHANE (REFRIGERANT GAS R 21)
PxBN(M)	TA4 TT9	FL	2 (B/D)			CV9 CV10 CV36	S2 S20	23	1030	1,1-DIFLUOROETHANE (REFRIGERANT GAS R 152a)
PxBN(M)	TA4 TT9	FL	2 (B/D)			CV9 CV10 CV36	S2 S20	23	1032	DIMETHYLAMINE, ANHYDROUS
PxBN(M)	TA4 TT9	FL	2 (B/D)			CV9 CV10 CV36	S2 S20	23	1033	DIMETHYL ETHER
PxBN(M)	TA4 TT9	FL	2 (B/D)			CV9 CV10 CV36	S2 S20	23	1035	ETHANE
PxBN(M)	TA4 TT9	FL	2 (B/D)			CV9 CV10 CV36	S2 S20	23	1036	ETHYLAMINE
PxBN(M)	TA4 TT9	FL	2 (B/D)			CV9 CV10 CV36	S2 S20	23	1037	ETHYL CHLORIDE
RxBN	TU18 TA4 TT9	FL	2 (B/D)	V5		CV9 CV11 CV36	S2 S17	223	1038	ETHYLENE, REFRIGERATED LIQUID
PxBN(M)	TA4 TT9	FL	2 (B/D)			CV9 CV10 CV36	S2 S20	23	1039	ETHYL METHYL ETHER
		FL	1 (B/D)			CV9 CV10 CV36	S2 S14	263	1040	ETHYLENE OXIDE
PxBH(M)	TA4 TT9	FL	1 (B/D)			CV9 CV10 CV36	S2 S14	263	1040	ETHYLENE OXIDE WITH NITROGEN up to a total pressure of 1 MPa (10 bar) at 50 °C

UN No.	Name and description	Class	Classifi-cation code	Packing group	Labels	Special provi-sions	Limited and excepted quantities		Packaging			Portable tanks and bulk containers	
							quantities		Packing instruc-tions	Special packing provisions	Mixed packing provisions	Instruc-tions	Special provisions
	3.1.2	2.2	2.2	2.1.1.3	5.2.2	3.3	3.4.6	3.5.1.2	4.1.4	4.1.4	4.1.10	4.2.5.2 7.3.2	4.2.5.3
(1)	(2)	(3a)	(3b)	(4)	(5)	(6)	(7a)	(7b)	(8)	(9a)	(9b)	(10)	(11)
1041	ETHYLENE OXIDE AND CARBON DIOXIDE MIXTURE with more than 9% but not more than 87% ethylene oxide	2	2F		2.1		LQ0	E0	P200		MP9	(M) T50	
1043	FERTILIZER AMMONIATING SOLUTION with free ammonia	2	4A		2.2	642							
1044	FIRE EXTINGUISHERS with compressed or liquefied gas	2	6A		2.2	225 594	LQ0	E0	P003		MP9		
1045	FLUORINE, COMPRESSED	2	1TOC		2.3 +5.1 +8		LQ0	E0	P200		MP9		
1046	HELIUM, COMPRESSED	2	1A		2.2		LQ1	E1	P200		MP9	(M)	
1048	HYDROGEN BROMIDE, ANHYDROUS	2	2TC		2.3 +8		LQ0	E0	P200		MP9	(M)	
1049	HYDROGEN, COMPRESSED	2	1F		2.1		LQ0	E0	P200		MP9	(M)	
1050	HYDROGEN CHLORIDE, ANHYDROUS	2	2TC		2.3 +8		LQ0	E0	P200		MP9	(M)	
1051	HYDROGEN CYANIDE, STABILIZED containing less than 3% water	6.1	TF1	I	6.1 +3	603	LQ0	E5	P200		MP2		
1052	HYDROGEN FLUORIDE, ANHYDROUS	8	CT1	I	8 +6.1		LQ0	E0	P200		MP2	T10	TP2
1053	HYDROGEN SULPHIDE	2	2TF		2.3 +2.1		LQ0	E0	P200		MP9	(M)	
1055	ISOBUTYLENE	2	2F		2.1		LQ0	E0	P200		MP9	(M) T50	
1056	KRYPTON, COMPRESSED	2	1A		2.2		LQ1	E1	P200		MP9	(M)	
1057	LIGHTERS or LIGHTER REFILLS containing flammable gas	2	6F		2.1	201 654	LQ0	E0	P002	PP84 RR5	MP9		
1058	LIQUEFIED GASES, non-flammable, charged with nitrogen, carbon dioxide or air	2	2A		2.2		LQ1	E1	P200		MP9	(M)	
1060	METHYLACETYLENE AND PROPADIENE MIXTURE, STABILIZED such as mixture P1 or mixture P2	2	2F		2.1	581	LQ0	E0	P200		MP9	(M) T50	
1061	METHYLAMINE, ANHYDROUS	2	2F		2.1		LQ0	E0	P200		MP9	(M) T50	
1062	METHYL BROMIDE with not more than 2% chloropicrin	2	2T		2.3	23	LQ0	E0	P200		MP9	(M) T50	
1063	METHYL CHLORIDE (REFRIGERANT GAS R 40)	2	2F		2.1		LQ0	E0	P200		MP9	(M) T50	
1064	METHYL MERCAPTAN	2	2TF		2.3 +2.1		LQ0	E0	P200		MP9	(M) T50	
1065	NEON, COMPRESSED	2	1A		2.2		LQ1	E1	P200		MP9	(M)	
1066	NITROGEN, COMPRESSED	2	1A		2.2		LQ1	E1	P200		MP9	(M)	

ADR tank		Vehicle for tank carriage	Transport category (Tunnel restriction code)	Special provisions for carriage				Hazard identifi-cation No.	UN No.	Name and description
Tank code	Special provisions			Packages	Bulk	Loading, unloading and handling	Operation			
4.3	4.3.5, 6.8.4	9.1.1.2	1.1.3.6 (8.6)	7.2.4	7.3.3	7.5.11	8.5	5.3.2.3		3.1.2
(12)	(13)	(14)	(15)	(16)	(17)	(18)	(19)	(20)	(1)	(2)
PxBN(M)	TA4 TT9	FL	2 (B/D)			CV9 CV10 CV36	S2 S20	239	1041	ETHYLENE OXIDE AND CARBON DIOXIDE MIXTURE with more than 9% but not more than 87% ethylene oxide
			(E)						1043	FERTILIZER AMMONIATING SOLUTION with free ammonia
			3 (E)			CV9			1044	FIRE EXTINGUISHERS with compressed or liquefied gas
			1 (D)			CV9 CV10 CV36	S14		1045	FLUORINE, COMPRESSED
CxBN(M)	TA4 TT9	AT	3 (E)			CV9 CV10 CV36		20	1046	HELIUM, COMPRESSED
PxBH(M)	TA4 TT9	AT	1 (C/D)			CV9 CV10 CV36	S14	268	1048	HYDROGEN BROMIDE, ANHYDROUS
CxBN(M)	TA4 TT9	FL	2 (B/D)			CV9 CV10 CV36	S2 S20	23	1049	HYDROGEN, COMPRESSED
PxBH(M)	TA4 TT9	AT	1 (C/D)			CV9 CV10 CV36	S14	268	1050	HYDROGEN CHLORIDE, ANHYDROUS
			0 (D)			CV1 CV13 CV28	S2 S9 S10 S14		1051	HYDROGEN CYANIDE, STABILIZED containing less than 3% water
L21DH(+)	TU14 TU34 TC1 TE21 TA4 TT9 TM3	AT	1 (C/D)			CV13 CV28 CV34	S14	886	1052	HYDROGEN FLUORIDE, ANHYDROUS
PxDH(M)	TA4 TT9	FL	1 (B/D)			CV9 CV10 CV36	S2 S14	263	1053	HYDROGEN SULPHIDE
PxBN(M)	TA4 TT9	FL	2 (B/D)			CV9 CV10 CV36	S2 S20	23	1055	ISOBUTYLENE
CxBN(M)	TA4 TT9	AT	3 (E)			CV9 CV10 CV36		20	1056	KRYPTON, COMPRESSED
			2 (D)			CV9	S2		1057	LIGHTERS or LIGHTER REFILLS containing flammable gas
PxBN(M)	TA4 TT9	AT	3 (C/E)			CV9 CV10 CV36		20	1058	LIQUEFIED GASES, non-flammable, charged with nitrogen, carbon dioxide or air
PxBN(M)	TA4 TT9	FL	2 (B/D)			CV9 CV10 CV36	S2 S20	239	1060	METHYLACETYLENE AND PROPADIENE MIXTURE, STABILIZED such as mixture P1 or mixture P2
PxBN(M)	TA4 TT9	FL	2 (B/D)			CV9 CV10 CV36	S2 S20	23	1061	METHYLAMINE, ANHYDROUS
PxBH(M)	TA4 TT9	AT	1 (C/D)			CV9 CV10 CV36	S14	26	1062	METHYL BROMIDE with not more than 2% chloropicrin
PxBN(M)	TA4 TT9	FL	2 (B/D)			CV9 CV10 CV36	S2 S20	23	1063	METHYL CHLORIDE (REFRIGERANT GAS R 40)
PxDH(M)	TA4 TT9	FL	1 (B/D)			CV9 CV10 CV36	S2 S14	263	1064	METHYL MERCAPTAN
CxBN(M)	TA4 TT9	AT	3 (E)			CV9 CV10 CV36		20	1065	NEON, COMPRESSED
CxBN(M)	TA4 TT9	AT	3 (E)			CV9 CV10 CV36		20	1066	NITROGEN, COMPRESSED

UN No.	Name and description	Class	Classifi-cation code	Packing group	Labels	Special provi-sions	Limited and excepted quantities		Packaging			Portable tanks and bulk containers	
									Packing instruc-tions	Special packing provisions	Mixed packing provisions	Instruc-tions	Special provisions
	3.1.2	2.2	2.2	2.1.1.3	5.2.2	3.3	3.4.6	3.5.1.2	4.1.4	4.1.4	4.1.10	4.2.5.2 7.3.2	4.2.5.3
(1)	(2)	(3a)	(3b)	(4)	(5)	(6)	(7a)	(7b)	(8)	(9a)	(9b)	(10)	(11)
1067	DINITROGEN TETROXIDE (NITROGEN DIOXIDE)	2	2TOC		2.3 +5.1 +8		LQ0	E0	P200		MP9	T50	TP21
1069	NITROSYL CHLORIDE	2	2TC		2.3 +8		LQ0	E0	P200		MP9		
1070	NITROUS OXIDE	2	2O		2.2 +5.1	584	LQ0	E0	P200		MP9	(M)	
1071	OIL GAS, COMPRESSED	2	1TF		2.3 +2.1		LQ0	E0	P200		MP9	(M)	
1072	OXYGEN, COMPRESSED	2	1O		2.2 +5.1		LQ0	E0	P200		MP9	(M)	
1073	OXYGEN, REFRIGERATED LIQUID	2	3O		2.2 +5.1		LQ0	E0	P203		MP9	T75	TP5 TP22
1075	PETROLEUM GASES, LIQUEFIED	2	2F		2.1	274 583 639	LQ0	E0	P200		MP9	(M) T50	
1076	PHOSGENE	2	2TC		2.3 +8		LQ0	E0	P200		MP9		
1077	PROPYLENE	2	2F		2.1		LQ0	E0	P200		MP9	(M) T50	
1078	REFRIGERANT GAS, N.O.S., such as mixture F1, mixture F2 or mixture F3	2	2A		2.2	274 582	LQ1	E1	P200		MP9	(M) T50	
1079	SULPHUR DIOXIDE	2	2TC		2.3 +8		LQ0	E0	P200		MP9	(M) T50	TP19
1080	SULPHUR HEXAFLUORIDE	2	2A		2.2		LQ1	E1	P200		MP9	(M)	
1081	TETRAFLUOROETHYLENE, STABILIZED	2	2F		2.1		LQ0	E0	P200		MP9	(M)	
1082	TRIFLUOROCHLORO-ETHYLENE, STABILIZED	2	2TF		2.3 +2.1		LQ0	E0	P200		MP9	(M) T50	
1083	TRIMETHYLAMINE, ANHYDROUS	2	2F		2.1		LQ0	E0	P200		MP9	(M) T50	
1085	VINYL BROMIDE, STABILIZED	2	2F		2.1		LQ0	E0	P200		MP9	(M) T50	
1086	VINYL CHLORIDE, STABILIZED	2	2F		2.1		LQ0	E0	P200		MP9	(M) T50	
1087	VINYL METHYL ETHER, STABILIZED	2	2F		2.1		LQ0	E0	P200		MP9	(M) T50	
1088	ACETAL	3	F1	II	3		LQ4	E2	P001 IBC02 R001		MP19	T4	TP1
1089	ACETALDEHYDE	3	F1	I	3		LQ3	E3	P001		MP7 MP17	T11	TP2 TP7
1090	ACETONE	3	F1	II	3		LQ4	E2	P001 IBC02 R001		MP19	T4	TP1
1091	ACETONE OILS	3	F1	II	3		LQ4	E2	P001 IBC02 R001		MP19	T4	TP1 TP8
1092	ACROLEIN, STABILIZED	6.1	TF1	I	6.1 +3		LQ0	E5	P601		MP8 MP17	T22	TP2 TP7 TP35
1093	ACRYLONITRILE, STABILIZED	3	FT1	I	3 +6.1		LQ0	E0	P001		MP7 MP17	T14	TP2

- 322 -

ADR tank		Vehicle for tank carriage	Transport category (Tunnel restriction code)	Special provisions for carriage				Hazard identifi-cation No.	UN No.	Name and description
Tank code	Special provisions			Packages	Bulk	Loading, unloading and handling	Operation			
4.3	4.3.5, 6.8.4	9.1.1.2	1.1.3.6 (8.6)	7.2.4	7.3.3	7.5.11	8.5	5.3.2.3		3.1.2
(12)	(13)	(14)	(15)	(16)	(17)	(18)	(19)	(20)	(1)	(2)
PxBH(M)	TU17 TA4 TT9	AT	1 (C/D)			CV9 CV10 CV36	S14	265	1067	DINITROGEN TETROXIDE (NITROGEN DIOXIDE)
			1 (D)			CV9 CV10 CV36	S14		1069	NITROSYL CHLORIDE
PxBN(M)	TA4 TT9	AT	3 (C/E)			CV9 CV10 CV36		25	1070	NITROUS OXIDE
CxBH(M)	TA4 TT9	FL	1 (B/D)			CV9 CV10 CV36	S2 S14	263	1071	OIL GAS, COMPRESSED
CxBN(M)	TA4 TT9	AT	3 (E)			CV9 CV10 CV36		25	1072	OXYGEN, COMPRESSED
RxBN	TU7 TU19 TA4 TT9	AT	3 (C/E)	V5		CV9 CV11 CV36	S20	225	1073	OXYGEN, REFRIGERATED LIQUID
PxBN(M)	TA4 TT9	FL	2 (B/D)			CV9 CV10 CV36	S2 S20	23	1075	PETROLEUM GASES, LIQUEFIED
P22DH(M)	TU17 TA4 TT9	AT	1 (C/D)			CV9 CV10 CV36	S14	268	1076	PHOSGENE
PxBN(M)	TA4 TT9	FL	2 (B/D)			CV9 CV10 CV36	S2 S20	23	1077	PROPYLENE
PxBN(M)	TA4 TT9	AT	3 (C/E)			CV9 CV10 CV36		20	1078	REFRIGERANT GAS, N.O.S., such as mixture F1, mixture F2 or mixture F3
PxDH(M)	TA4 TT9	AT	1 (C/D)			CV9 CV10 CV36	S14	268	1079	SULPHUR DIOXIDE
PxBN(M)	TA4 TT9	AT	3 (C/E)			CV9 CV10 CV36		20	1080	SULPHUR HEXAFLUORIDE
		FL	2 (B/D)			CV9 CV10 CV36	S2 S20	239	1081	TETRAFLUOROETHYLENE, STABILIZED
PxBH(M)	TA4 TT9	FL	1 (B/D)			CV9 CV10 CV36	S2 S14	263	1082	TRIFLUOROCHLORO-ETHYLENE, STABILIZED
PxBN(M)	TA4 TT9	FL	2 (B/D)			CV9 CV10 CV36	S2 S20	23	1083	TRIMETHYLAMINE, ANHYDROUS
PxBN(M)	TA4 TT9	FL	2 (B/D)			CV9 CV10 CV36	S2 S20	239	1085	VINYL BROMIDE, STABILIZED
PxBN(M)	TA4 TT9	FL	2 (B/D)			CV9 CV10 CV36	S2 S20	239	1086	VINYL CHLORIDE, STABILIZED
PxBN(M)	TA4 TT9	FL	2 (B/D)			CV9 CV10 CV36	S2 S20	239	1087	VINYL METHYL ETHER, STABILIZED
LGBF		FL	2 (D/E)				S2 S20	33	1088	ACETAL
L4BN	TU8	FL	1 (D/E)				S2 S20	33	1089	ACETALDEHYDE
LGBF		FL	2 (D/E)				S2 S20	33	1090	ACETONE
LGBF		FL	2 (D/E)				S2 S20	33	1091	ACETONE OILS
L10CH	TU14 TU15 TE19 TE21	FL	1 (C/D)			CV1 CV13 CV28	S2 S9 S14	663	1092	ACROLEIN, STABILIZED
L10CH	TU14 TU15 TE21	FL	1 (C/E)			CV13 CV28	S2 S22	336	1093	ACRYLONITRILE, STABILIZED

- 323 -

UN No.	Name and description	Class	Classification code	Packing group	Labels	Special provisions	Limited and excepted quantities		Packaging			Portable tanks and bulk containers	
							quantities		Packing instructions	Special packing provisions	Mixed packing provisions	Instructions	Special provisions
	3.1.2	2.2	2.2	2.1.1.3	5.2.2	3.3	3.4.6	3.5.1.2	4.1.4	4.1.4	4.1.10	4.2.5.2 7.3.2	4.2.5.3
(1)	(2)	(3a)	(3b)	(4)	(5)	(6)	(7a)	(7b)	(8)	(9a)	(9b)	(10)	(11)
1098	ALLYL ALCOHOL	6.1	TF1	I	6.1 +3		LQ0	E5	P602		MP8 MP17	T20	TP2 TP35
1099	ALLYL BROMIDE	3	FT1	I	3 +6.1		LQ0	E0	P001		MP7 MP17	T14	TP2
1100	ALLYL CHLORIDE	3	FT1	I	3 +6.1		LQ0	E0	P001		MP7 MP17	T14	TP2
1104	AMYL ACETATES	3	F1	III	3		LQ7	E1	P001 IBC03 LP01 R001		MP19	T2	TP1
1105	PENTANOLS	3	F1	II	3		LQ4	E2	P001 IBC02 R001		MP19	T4	TP1 TP29
1105	PENTANOLS	3	F1	III	3		LQ7	E1	P001 IBC03 LP01 R001		MP19	T2	TP1
1106	AMYLAMINE	3	FC	II	3 +8		LQ4	E2	P001 IBC02		MP19	T7	TP1
1106	AMYLAMINE	3	FC	III	3 +8		LQ7	E1	P001 IBC03 R001		MP19	T4	TP1
1107	AMYL CHLORIDE	3	F1	II	3		LQ4	E2	P001 IBC02 R001		MP19	T4	TP1
1108	1-PENTENE (n-AMYLENE)	3	F1	I	3		LQ3	E3	P001		MP7 MP17	T11	TP2
1109	AMYL FORMATES	3	F1	III	3		LQ7	E1	P001 IBC03 LP01 R001		MP19	T2	TP1
1110	n-AMYL METHYL KETONE	3	F1	III	3		LQ7	E1	P001 IBC03 LP01 R001		MP19	T2	TP1
1111	AMYL MERCAPTAN	3	F1	II	3		LQ4	E2	P001 IBC02 R001		MP19	T4	TP1
1112	AMYL NITRATE	3	F1	III	3		LQ7	E1	P001 IBC03 LP01 R001		MP19	T2	TP1
1113	AMYL NITRITE	3	F1	II	3		LQ4	E2	P001 IBC02 R001		MP19	T4	TP1
1114	BENZENE	3	F1	II	3		LQ4	E2	P001 IBC02 R001		MP19	T4	TP1
1120	BUTANOLS	3	F1	II	3		LQ4	E2	P001 IBC02 R001		MP19	T4	TP1 TP29
1120	BUTANOLS	3	F1	III	3		LQ7	E1	P001 IBC03 LP01 R001		MP19	T2	TP1
1123	BUTYL ACETATES	3	F1	II	3		LQ4	E2	P001 IBC02 R001		MP19	T4	TP1
1123	BUTYL ACETATES	3	F1	III	3		LQ7	E1	P001 IBC03 LP01 R001		MP19	T2	TP1
1125	n-BUTYLAMINE	3	FC	II	3 +8		LQ4	E2	P001 IBC02		MP19	T7	TP1
1126	1-BROMOBUTANE	3	F1	II	3		LQ4	E2	P001 IBC02 R001		MP19	T4	TP1
1127	CHLOROBUTANES	3	F1	II	3		LQ4	E2	P001 IBC02 R001		MP19	T4	TP1

ADR tank		Vehicle for tank carriage	Transport category (Tunnel restriction code)	Special provisions for carriage				Hazard identifi-cation No.	UN No.	Name and description
Tank code	Special provisions			Packages	Bulk	Loading, unloading and handling	Operation			
4.3	4.3.5, 6.8.4	9.1.1.2	1.1.3.6 (8.6)	7.2.4	7.3.3	7.5.11	8.5	5.3.2.3		3.1.2
(12)	(13)	(14)	(15)	(16)	(17)	(18)	(19)	(20)	(1)	(2)
L10CH	TU14 TU15 TE19 TE21	FL	1 (C/D)			CV1 CV13 CV28	S2 S9 S14	663	1098	ALLYL ALCOHOL
L10CH	TU14 TU15 TE21	FL	1 (C/E)			CV13 CV28	S2 S22	336	1099	ALLYL BROMIDE
L10CH	TU14 TU15 TE21	FL	1 (C/E)			CV13 CV28	S2 S22	336	1100	ALLYL CHLORIDE
LGBF		FL	3 (D/E)				S2	30	1104	AMYL ACETATES
LGBF		FL	2 (D/E)				S2 S20	33	1105	PENTANOLS
LGBF		FL	3 (D/E)				S2	30	1105	PENTANOLS
L4BH		FL	2 (D/E)				S2 S20	338	1106	AMYLAMINE
L4BN		FL	3 (D/E)				S2	38	1106	AMYLAMINE
LGBF		FL	2 (D/E)				S2 S20	33	1107	AMYL CHLORIDE
L4BN		FL	1 (D/E)				S2 S20	33	1108	1-PENTENE (n-AMYLENE)
LGBF		FL	3 (D/E)				S2	30	1109	AMYL FORMATES
LGBF		FL	3 (D/E)				S2	30	1110	n-AMYL METHYL KETONE
LGBF		FL	2 (D/E)				S2 S20	33	1111	AMYL MERCAPTAN
LGBF		FL	3 (D/E)				S2	30	1112	AMYL NITRATE
LGBF		FL	2 (D/E)				S2 S20	33	1113	AMYL NITRITE
LGBF		FL	2 (D/E)				S2 S20	33	1114	BENZENE
LGBF		FL	2 (D/E)				S2 S20	33	1120	BUTANOLS
LGBF		FL	3 (D/E)				S2	30	1120	BUTANOLS
LGBF		FL	2 (D/E)				S2 S20	33	1123	BUTYL ACETATES
LGBF		FL	3 (D/E)				S2	30	1123	BUTYL ACETATES
L4BH		FL	2 (D/E)				S2 S20	338	1125	n-BUTYLAMINE
LGBF		FL	2 (D/E)				S2 S20	33	1126	1-BROMOBUTANE
LGBF		FL	2 (D/E)				S2 S20	33	1127	CHLOROBUTANES

UN No.	Name and description	Class	Classifi-cation code	Packing group	Labels	Special provi-sions	Limited and excepted quantities		Packaging			Portable tanks and bulk containers	
							quantities		Packing instruc-tions	Special packing provisions	Mixed packing provisions	Instruc-tions	Special provisions
	3.1.2	2.2	2.2	2.1.1.3	5.2.2	3.3	3.4.6	3.5.1.2	4.1.4	4.1.4	4.1.10	4.2.5.2 7.3.2	4.2.5.3
(1)	(2)	(3a)	(3b)	(4)	(5)	(6)	(7a)	(7b)	(8)	(9a)	(9b)	(10)	(11)
1128	n-BUTYL FORMATE	3	F1	II	3		LQ4	E2	P001 IBC02 R001		MP19	T4	TP1
1129	BUTYRALDEHYDE	3	F1	II	3		LQ4	E2	P001 IBC02 R001		MP19	T4	TP1
1130	CAMPHOR OIL	3	F1	III	3		LQ7	E1	P001 IBC03 LP01 R001		MP19	T2	TP1
1131	CARBON DISULPHIDE	3	FT1	I	3 +6.1		LQ0	E0	P001	PP31	MP7 MP17	T14	TP2 TP7
1133	ADHESIVES containing flammable liquid	3	F1	I	3		LQ3	E3	P001		MP7 MP17	T11	TP1 TP8 TP27
1133	ADHESIVES containing flammable liquid (vapour pressure at 50 °C more than 110 kPa)	3	F1	II	3	640C	LQ6	E2	P001	PP1	MP19	T4	TP1 TP8
1133	ADHESIVES containing flammable liquid (vapour pressure at 50 °C not more than 110 kPa)	3	F1	II	3	640D	LQ6	E2	P001 IBC02 R001	PP1	MP19	T4	TP1 TP8
1133	ADHESIVES containing flammable liquid	3	F1	III	3	640E	LQ7	E1	P001 IBC03 LP01 R001	PP1	MP19	T2	TP1
1133	ADHESIVES containing flammable liquid (having a flash point below 23 °C and viscous according to 2.2.3.1.4) (boiling point not more than 35 °C)	3	F1	III	3	640F	LQ7	E1	P001 LP01 R001	PP1	MP19	T2	TP1
1133	ADHESIVES containing flammable liquid (having a flash point below 23 °C and viscous according to 2.2.3.1.4) (vapour pressure at 50 °C more than 110 kPa, boiling point of more than 35 °C)	3	F1	III	3	640G	LQ7	E1	P001 LP01 R001	PP1	MP19	T2	TP1
1133	ADHESIVES containing flammable liquid (having a flash point below 23 °C and viscous according to 2.2.3.1.4) (vapour pressure at 50 °C not more than 110 kPa)	3	F1	III	3	640H	LQ7	E1	P001 IBC02 LP01 R001	PP1	MP19	T2	TP1
1134	CHLOROBENZENE	3	F1	III	3		LQ7	E1	P001 IBC03 LP01 R001		MP19	T2	TP1
1135	ETHYLENE CHLOROHYDRIN	6.1	TF1	I	6.1 +3		LQ0	E5	P001		MP8 MP17	T14	TP2
1136	COAL TAR DISTILLATES, FLAMMABLE	3	F1	II	3		LQ4	E2	P001 IBC02 R001		MP19	T4	TP1
1136	COAL TAR DISTILLATES, FLAMMABLE	3	F1	III	3		LQ7	E1	P001 IBC03 LP01 R001		MP19	T4	TP1 TP29
1139	COATING SOLUTION (includes surface treatments or coatings used for industrial or other purposes such as vehicle under coating, drum or barrel lining)	3	F1	I	3		LQ3	E3	P001		MP7 MP17	T11	TP1 TP8 TP27

ADR tank		Vehicle for tank carriage	Transport category (Tunnel restriction code)	Special provisions for carriage				Hazard identifi-cation No.	UN No.	Name and description
Tank code	Special provisions	9.1.1.2	1.1.3.6 (8.6)	Packages	Bulk	Loading, unloading and handling	Operation	5.3.2.3		
4.3	4.3.5, 6.8.4			7.2.4	7.3.3	7.5.11	8.5			3.1.2
(12)	(13)	(14)	(15)	(16)	(17)	(18)	(19)	(20)	(1)	(2)
LGBF		FL	2 (D/E)				S2 S20	33	1128	n-BUTYL FORMATE
LGBF		FL	2 (D/E)				S2 S20	33	1129	BUTYRALDEHYDE
LGBF		FL	3 (D/E)				S2	30	1130	CAMPHOR OIL
L10CH	TU14 TU15 TE21	FL	1 (C/E)			CV13 CV28	S2 S22	336	1131	CARBON DISULPHIDE
L4BN		FL	1 (D/E)				S2 S20	33	1133	ADHESIVES containing flammable liquid
L1.5BN		FL	2 (D/E)				S2 S20	33	1133	ADHESIVES containing flammable liquid (vapour pressure at 50 °C more than 110 kPa)
LGBF		FL	2 (D/E)				S2 S20	33	1133	ADHESIVES containing flammable liquid (vapour pressure at 50 °C not more than 110 kPa)
LGBF		FL	3 (D/E)				S2	30	1133	ADHESIVES containing flammable liquid
L4BN		FL	3 (D/E)				S2	33	1133	ADHESIVES containing flammable liquid (having a flash point below 23 °C and viscous according to 2.2.3.1.4) (boiling point not more than 35 °C)
L1.5BN		FL	3 (D/E)				S2	33	1133	ADHESIVES containing flammable liquid (having a flash point below 23 °C and viscous according to 2.2.3.1.4) (vapour pressure at 50 °C more than 110 kPa, boiling point of more than 35 °C)
LGBF		FL	3 (D/E)				S2	33	1133	ADHESIVES containing flammable liquid (having a flash point below 23 °C and viscous according to 2.2.3.1.4) (vapour pressure at 50 °C not more than 110 kPa)
LGBF		FL	3 (D/E)				S2	30	1134	CHLOROBENZENE
L10CH	TU14 TU15 TE19 TE21	FL	1 (C/D)			CV1 CV13 CV28	S2 S9 S14	663	1135	ETHYLENE CHLOROHYDRIN
LGBF		FL	2 (D/E)				S2 S20	33	1136	COAL TAR DISTILLATES, FLAMMABLE
LGBF		FL	3 (D/E)				S2	30	1136	COAL TAR DISTILLATES, FLAMMABLE
L4BN		FL	1 (D/E)				S2 S20	33	1139	COATING SOLUTION (includes surface treatments or coatings used for industrial or other purposes such as vehicle under coating, drum or barrel lining)

UN No.	Name and description	Class	Classifi-cation code	Packing group	Labels	Special provi-sions	Limited and excepted quantities		Packaging			Portable tanks and bulk containers	
									Packing instruc-tions	Special packing provisions	Mixed packing provisions	Instruc-tions	Special provisions
	3.1.2	2.2	2.2	2.1.1.3	5.2.2	3.3	3.4.6	3.5.1.2	4.1.4	4.1.4	4.1.10	4.2.5.2 7.3.2	4.2.5.3
(1)	(2)	(3a)	(3b)	(4)	(5)	(6)	(7a)	(7b)	(8)	(9a)	(9b)	(10)	(11)
1139	COATING SOLUTION (includes surface treatments or coatings used for industrial or other purposes such as vehicle under coating, drum or barrel lining) (vapour pressure at 50 °C more than 110 kPa)	3	F1	II	3	640C	LQ6	E2	P001		MP19	T4	TP1 TP8
1139	COATING SOLUTION (includes surface treatments or coatings used for industrial or other purposes such as vehicle under coating, drum or barrel lining) (vapour pressure at 50 °C not more than 110 kPa)	3	F1	II	3	640D	LQ6	E2	P001 IBC02 R001		MP19	T4	TP1 TP8
1139	COATING SOLUTION (includes surface treatments or coatings used for industrial or other purposes such as vehicle under coating, drum or barrel lining)	3	F1	III	3	640E	LQ7	E1	P001 IBC03 LP01 R001		MP19	T2	TP1
1139	COATING SOLUTION (includes surface treatments or coatings used for industrial or other purposes such as vehicle under coating, drum or barrel lining) (having a flash-point below 23 °C and viscous according to 2.2.3.1.4) (boiling point not more than 35 °C)	3	F1	III	3	640F	LQ7	E1	P001 LP01 R001		MP19	T2	TP1
1139	COATING SOLUTION (includes surface treatments or coatings used for industrial or other purposes such as vehicle under coating, drum or barrel lining) (having a flash-point below 23 °C and viscous according to 2.2.3.1.4) (vapour pressure at 50 °C more than 110 kPa, boiling point of more than 35 °C)	3	F1	III	3	640G	LQ7	E1	P001 LP01 R001		MP19	T2	TP1
1139	COATING SOLUTION (includes surface treatments or coatings used for industrial or other purposes such as vehicle under coating, drum or barrel lining) (having a flash-point below 23 °C and viscous according to 2.2.3.1.4) (vapour pressure at 50 °C not more than 110 kPa)	3	F1	III	3	640H	LQ7	E1	P001 IBC02 LP01 R001		MP19	T2	TP1
1143	CROTONALDEHYDE or CROTONALDEHYDE, STABILIZED	6.1	TF1	I	6.1 +3	324	LQ0	E5	P001		MP8 MP17	T20	TP2 TP35
1144	CROTONYLENE	3	F1	I	3		LQ3	E3	P001		MP7 MP17	T11	TP2
1145	CYCLOHEXANE	3	F1	II	3		LQ4	E2	P001 IBC02 R001		MP19	T4	TP1
1146	CYCLOPENTANE	3	F1	II	3		LQ4	E2	P001 IBC02 R001		MP19	T7	TP1
1147	DECAHYDRO-NAPHTHALENE	3	F1	III	3		LQ7	E1	P001 IBC03 LP01 R001		MP19	T2	TP1
1148	DIACETONE ALCOHOL	3	F1	II	3		LQ4	E2	P001 IBC02 R001		MP19	T4	TP1
1148	DIACETONE ALCOHOL	3	F1	III	3		LQ7	E1	P001 IBC03 LP01 R001		MP19	T2	TP1

ADR tank		Vehicle for tank carriage	Transport category (Tunnel restriction code)	Special provisions for carriage				Hazard identifi-cation No.	UN No.	Name and description
Tank code	Special provisions			Packages	Bulk	Loading, unloading and handling	Operation			
4.3	4.3.5, 6.8.4	9.1.1.2	1.1.3.6 (8.6)	7.2.4	7.3.3	7.5.11	8.5	5.3.2.3		3.1.2
(12)	(13)	(14)	(15)	(16)	(17)	(18)	(19)	(20)	(1)	(2)
L1.5BN		FL	2 (D/E)				S2 S20	33	1139	COATING SOLUTION (includes surface treatments or coatings used for industrial or other purposes such as vehicle under coating, drum or barrel lining) (vapour pressure at 50 °C more than 110 kPa)
LGBF		FL	2 (D/E)				S2 S20	33	1139	COATING SOLUTION (includes surface treatments or coatings used for industrial or other purposes such as vehicle under coating, drum or barrel lining) (vapour pressure at 50 °C not more than 110 kPa)
LGBF		FL	3 (D/E)				S2	30	1139	COATING SOLUTION (includes surface treatments or coatings used for industrial or other purposes such as vehicle under coating, drum or barrel lining)
L4BN		FL	3 (D/E)				S2	33	1139	COATING SOLUTION (includes surface treatments or coatings used for industrial or other purposes such as vehicle under coating, drum or barrel lining) (having a flash-point below 23 °C and viscous according to 2.2.3.1.4) (boiling point not more than 35 °C)
L1.5BN		FL	3 (D/E)				S2	33	1139	COATING SOLUTION (includes surface treatments or coatings used for industrial or other purposes such as vehicle under coating, drum or barrel lining) (having a flash-point below 23 °C and viscous according to 2.2.3.1.4) (vapour pressure at 50 °C more than 110 kPa, boiling point of more than 35 °C)
LGBF		FL	3 (D/E)				S2	33	1139	COATING SOLUTION (includes surface treatments or coatings used for industrial or other purposes such as vehicle under coating, drum or barrel lining) (having a flash-point below 23 °C and viscous according to 2.2.3.1.4) (vapour pressure at 50 °C not more than 110 kPa)
L10CH	TU14 TU15 TE19 TE21	FL	1 (C/D)			CV1 CV13 CV28	S2 S9 S14	663	1143	CROTONALDEHYDE or CROTONALDEHYDE, STABILIZED
L4BN		FL	1 (D/E)				S2 S20	339	1144	CROTONYLENE
LGBF		FL	2 (D/E)				S2 S20	33	1145	CYCLOHEXANE
LGBF		FL	2 (D/E)				S2 S20	33	1146	CYCLOPENTANE
LGBF		FL	3 (D/E)				S2	30	1147	DECAHYDRO-NAPHTHALENE
LGBF		FL	2 (D/E)				S2 S20	33	1148	DIACETONE ALCOHOL
LGBF		FL	3 (D/E)				S2	30	1148	DIACETONE ALCOHOL

UN No.	Name and description	Class	Classification code	Packing group	Labels	Special provisions	Limited and excepted quantities		Packaging			Portable tanks and bulk containers	
							quantities		Packing instructions	Special packing provisions	Mixed packing provisions	Instructions	Special provisions
	3.1.2	2.2	2.2	2.1.1.3	5.2.2	3.3	3.4.6	3.5.1.2	4.1.4	4.1.4	4.1.10	4.2.5.2 7.3.2	4.2.5.3
(1)	(2)	(3a)	(3b)	(4)	(5)	(6)	(7a)	(7b)	(8)	(9a)	(9b)	(10)	(11)
1149	DIBUTYL ETHERS	3	F1	III	3		LQ7	E1	P001 IBC03 LP01 R001		MP19	T2	TP1
1150	1,2-DICHLOROETHYLENE	3	F1	II	3		LQ4	E2	P001 IBC02 R001		MP19	T7	TP2
1152	DICHLOROPENTANES	3	F1	III	3		LQ7	E1	P001 IBC03 LP01 R001		MP19	T2	TP1
1153	ETHYLENE GLYCOL DIETHYL ETHER	3	F1	II	3		LQ4	E2	P001 IBC02 R001		MP19	T4	TP1
1153	ETHYLENE GLYCOL DIETHYL ETHER	3	F1	III	3		LQ7	E1	P001 IBC03 LP01 R001		MP19	T2	TP1
1154	DIETHYLAMINE	3	FC	II	3 +8		LQ4	E2	P001 IBC02		MP19	T7	TP1
1155	DIETHYL ETHER (ETHYL ETHER)	3	F1	I	3		LQ3	E3	P001		MP7 MP17	T11	TP2
1156	DIETHYL KETONE	3	F1	II	3		LQ4	E2	P001 IBC02 R001		MP19	T4	TP1
1157	DIISOBUTYL KETONE	3	F1	III	3		LQ7	E1	P001 IBC03 LP01 R001		MP19	T2	TP1
1158	DIISOPROPYLAMINE	3	FC	II	3 +8		LQ4	E2	P001 IBC02		MP19	T7	TP1
1159	DIISOPROPYL ETHER	3	F1	II	3		LQ4	E2	P001 IBC02 R001		MP19	T4	TP1
1160	DIMETHYLAMINE AQUEOUS SOLUTION	3	FC	II	3 +8		LQ4	E2	P001 IBC02		MP19	T7	TP1
1161	DIMETHYL CARBONATE	3	F1	II	3		LQ4	E2	P001 IBC02 R001		MP19	T4	TP1
1162	DIMETHYLDICHLORO-SILANE	3	FC	II	3 +8		LQ4	E2	P010		MP19	T10	TP2 TP7
1163	DIMETHYLHYDRAZINE, UNSYMMETRICAL	6.1	TFC	I	6.1 +3 +8		LQ0	E5	P602		MP8 MP17	T20	TP2 TP35
1164	DIMETHYL SULPHIDE	3	F1	II	3		LQ4	E2	P001 IBC02	B8	MP19	T7	TP2
1165	DIOXANE	3	F1	II	3		LQ4	E2	P001 IBC02 R001		MP19	T4	TP1
1166	DIOXOLANE	3	F1	II	3		LQ4	E2	P001 IBC02 R001		MP19	T4	TP1
1167	DIVINYL ETHER, STABILIZED	3	F1	I	3		LQ3	E3	P001		MP7 MP17	T11	TP2
1169	EXTRACTS, AROMATIC, LIQUID	3	F1	I	3		LQ3	E3	P001		MP7 MP17		
1169	EXTRACTS, AROMATIC, LIQUID (vapour pressure at 50 °C more than 110 kPa)	3	F1	II	3	601 640C	LQ6	E2	P001		MP19	T4	TP1 TP8
1169	EXTRACTS, AROMATIC, LIQUID (vapour pressure at 50 °C not more than 110 kPa)	3	F1	II	3	601 640D	LQ6	E2	P001 IBC02 R001		MP19	T4	TP1 TP8
1169	EXTRACTS, AROMATIC, LIQUID	3	F1	III	3	601 640E	LQ7	E1	P001 IBC03 LP01 R001		MP19	T2	TP1
1169	EXTRACTS, AROMATIC, LIQUID (having a flash-point below 23 °C and viscous according to 2.2.3.1.4) (boiling point not more than 35 °C)	3	F1	III	3	601 640F	LQ7	E1	P001 LP01 R001		MP19	T2	TP1

ADR tank		Vehicle for tank carriage	Transport category (Tunnel restriction code)	Special provisions for carriage				Hazard identifi-cation No.	UN No.	Name and description
Tank code	Special provisions			Packages	Bulk	Loading, unloading and handling	Operation			
4.3	4.3.5, 6.8.4	9.1.1.2	1.1.3.6 (8.6)	7.2.4	7.3.3	7.5.11	8.5	5.3.2.3		3.1.2
(12)	(13)	(14)	(15)	(16)	(17)	(18)	(19)	(20)	(1)	(2)
LGBF		FL	3 (D/E)				S2	30	1149	DIBUTYL ETHERS
LGBF		FL	2 (D/E)				S2 S20	33	1150	1,2-DICHLOROETHYLENE
LGBF		FL	3 (D/E)				S2	30	1152	DICHLOROPENTANES
LGBF		FL	2 (D/E)				S2 S20	33	1153	ETHYLENE GLYCOL DIETHYL ETHER
LGBF		FL	3 (D/E)				S2	30	1153	ETHYLENE GLYCOL DIETHYL ETHER
L4BH		FL	2 (D/E)				S2 S20	338	1154	DIETHYLAMINE
L4BN		FL	1 (D/E)				S2 S20	33	1155	DIETHYL ETHER (ETHYL ETHER)
LGBF		FL	2 (D/E)				S2 S20	33	1156	DIETHYL KETONE
LGBF		FL	3 (D/E)				S2	30	1157	DIISOBUTYL KETONE
L4BH		FL	2 (D/E)				S2 S20	338	1158	DIISOPROPYLAMINE
LGBF		FL	2 (D/E)				S2 S20	33	1159	DIISOPROPYL ETHER
L4BH		FL	2 (D/E)				S2 S20	338	1160	DIMETHYLAMINE AQUEOUS SOLUTION
LGBF		FL	2 (D/E)				S2 S20	33	1161	DIMETHYL CARBONATE
L4BH		FL	2 (D/E)				S2 S20	X338	1162	DIMETHYLDICHLORO-SILANE
L10CH	TU14 TU15 TE19 TE21	FL	1 (C/D)			CV1 CV13 CV28	S2 S9 S14	663	1163	DIMETHYLHYDRAZINE, UNSYMMETRICAL
L1.5BN		FL	2 (D/E)				S2 S20	33	1164	DIMETHYL SULPHIDE
LGBF		FL	2 (D/E)				S2 S20	33	1165	DIOXANE
LGBF		FL	2 (D/E)				S2 S20	33	1166	DIOXOLANE
L4BN		FL	1 (D/E)				S2 S20	339	1167	DIVINYL ETHER, STABILIZED
L4BN		FL	1 (D/E)				S2 S20	33	1169	EXTRACTS, AROMATIC, LIQUID
L1.5BN		FL	2 (D/E)				S2 S20	33	1169	EXTRACTS, AROMATIC, LIQUID (vapour pressure at 50 °C more than 110 kPa)
LGBF		FL	2 (D/E)				S2 S20	33	1169	EXTRACTS, AROMATIC, LIQUID (vapour pressure at 50 °C not more than 110 kPa)
LGBF		FL	3 (D/E)				S2	30	1169	EXTRACTS, AROMATIC, LIQUID
L4BN		FL	3 (D/E)				S2	33	1169	EXTRACTS, AROMATIC, LIQUID (having a flash-point below 23 °C and viscous according to 2.2.3.1.4) (boiling point not more than 35 °C)

UN No.	Name and description	Class	Classifi-cation code	Packing group	Labels	Special provi-sions	Limited and excepted quantities		Packaging			Portable tanks and bulk containers	
									Packing instruc-tions	Special packing provisions	Mixed packing provisions	Instruc-tions	Special provisions
	3.1.2	2.2	2.2	2.1.1.3	5.2.2	3.3	3.4.6	3.5.1.2	4.1.4	4.1.4	4.1.10	4.2.5.2 7.3.2	4.2.5.3
(1)	(2)	(3a)	(3b)	(4)	(5)	(6)	(7a)	(7b)	(8)	(9a)	(9b)	(10)	(11)
1169	EXTRACTS, AROMATIC, LIQUID (having a flash-point below 23 °C and viscous according to 2.2.3.1.4) (vapour pressure at 50 °C more than 110 kPa, boiling point of more than 35 °C)	3	F1	III	3	601 640G	LQ7	E1	P001 LP01 R001		MP19	T2	TP1
1169	EXTRACTS, AROMATIC, LIQUID (having a flash-point below 23 °C and viscous according to 2.2.3.1.4) (vapour pressure at 50 °C not more than 110 kPa)	3	F1	III	3	601 640H	LQ7	E1	P001 IBC02 LP01 R001		MP19	T2	TP1
1170	ETHANOL (ETHYL ALCOHOL) or ETHANOL SOLUTION (ETHYL ALCOHOL SOLUTION)	3	F1	II	3	144 601	LQ4	E2	P001 IBC02 R001		MP19	T4	TP1
1170	ETHANOL SOLUTION (ETHYL ALCOHOL SOLUTION)	3	F1	III	3	144 601	LQ7	E1	P001 IBC03 LP01 R001		MP19	T2	TP1
1171	ETHYLENE GLYCOL MONOETHYL ETHER	3	F1	III	3		LQ7	E1	P001 IBC03 LP01 R001		MP19	T2	TP1
1172	ETHYLENE GLYCOL MONOETHYL ETHER ACETATE	3	F1	III	3		LQ7	E1	P001 IBC03 LP01 R001		MP19	T2	TP1
1173	ETHYL ACETATE	3	F1	II	3		LQ4	E2	P001 IBC02 R001		MP19	T4	TP1
1175	ETHYLBENZENE	3	F1	II	3		LQ4	E2	P001 IBC02 R001		MP19	T4	TP1
1176	ETHYL BORATE	3	F1	II	3		LQ4	E2	P001 IBC02 R001		MP19	T4	TP1
1177	2-ETHYLBUTYL ACETATE	3	F1	III	3		LQ7	E1	P001 IBC03 LP01 R001		MP19	T2	TP1
1178	2-ETHYLBUTYRALDEHYDE	3	F1	II	3		LQ4	E2	P001 IBC02 R001		MP19	T4	TP1
1179	ETHYL BUTYL ETHER	3	F1	II	3		LQ4	E2	P001 IBC02 R001		MP19	T4	TP1
1180	ETHYL BUTYRATE	3	F1	III	3		LQ7	E1	P001 IBC03 LP01 R001		MP19	T2	TP1
1181	ETHYL CHLOROACETATE	6.1	TF1	II	6.1 +3		LQ17	E4	P001 IBC02		MP15	T7	TP2
1182	ETHYL CHLOROFORMATE	6.1	TFC	I	6.1 +3 +8		LQ0	E5	P602		MP8 MP17	T14	TP2
1183	ETHYLDICHLOROSILANE	4.3	WFC	I	4.3 +3 +8		LQ0	E0	P401	RR7	MP2	T14	TP2 TP7
1184	ETHYLENE DICHLORIDE	3	FT1	II	3 +6.1		LQ0	E2	P001 IBC02		MP19	T7	TP1
1185	ETHYLENEIMINE, STABILIZED	6.1	TF1	I	6.1 +3		LQ0	E5	P601		MP2	T22	TP2
1188	ETHYLENE GLYCOL MONOMETHYL ETHER	3	F1	III	3		LQ7	E1	P001 IBC03 LP01 R001		MP19	T2	TP1

ADR tank		Vehicle for tank carriage	Transport category (Tunnel restriction code)	Special provisions for carriage				Hazard identifi-cation No.	UN No.	Name and description
Tank code	Special provisions			Packages	Bulk	Loading, unloading and handling	Operation			
4.3	4.3.5, 6.8.4	9.1.1.2	1.1.3.6 (8.6)	7.2.4	7.3.3	7.5.11	8.5	5.3.2.3		3.1.2
(12)	(13)	(14)	(15)	(16)	(17)	(18)	(19)	(20)	(1)	(2)
L1.5BN		FL	3 (D/E)				S2	33	1169	EXTRACTS, AROMATIC, LIQUID (having a flash-point below 23 °C and viscous according to 2.2.3.1.4) (vapour pressure at 50 °C more than 110 kPa, boiling point of more than 35 °C)
LGBF		FL	3 (D/E)				S2	33	1169	EXTRACTS, AROMATIC, LIQUID (having a flash-point below 23 °C and viscous according to 2.2.3.1.4) (vapour pressure at 50 °C not more than 110 kPa)
LGBF		FL	2 (D/E)				S2 S20	33	1170	ETHANOL (ETHYL ALCOHOL) or ETHANOL SOLUTION (ETHYL ALCOHOL SOLUTION)
LGBF		FL	3 (D/E)				S2	30	1170	ETHANOL SOLUTION (ETHYL ALCOHOL SOLUTION)
LGBF		FL	3 (D/E)				S2	30	1171	ETHYLENE GLYCOL MONOETHYL ETHER
LGBF		FL	3 (D/E)				S2	30	1172	ETHYLENE GLYCOL MONOETHYL ETHER ACETATE
LGBF		FL	2 (D/E)				S2 S20	33	1173	ETHYL ACETATE
LGBF		FL	2 (D/E)				S2 S20	33	1175	ETHYLBENZENE
LGBF		FL	2 (D/E)				S2 S20	33	1176	ETHYL BORATE
LGBF		FL	3 (D/E)				S2	30	1177	2-ETHYLBUTYL ACETATE
LGBF		FL	2 (D/E)				S2 S20	33	1178	2-ETHYLBUTYRALDEHYDE
LGBF		FL	2 (D/E)				S2 S20	33	1179	ETHYL BUTYL ETHER
LGBF		FL	3 (D/E)				S2	30	1180	ETHYL BUTYRATE
L4BH	TU15 TE19	FL	2 (D/E)			CV13 CV28	S2 S9 S19	63	1181	ETHYL CHLOROACETATE
L10CH	TU14 TU15 TE19 TE21	FL	1 (C/D)			CV1 CV13 CV28	S2 S9 S14	663	1182	ETHYL CHLOROFORMATE
L10DH	TU14 TU23 TE21 TM2 TM3	FL	0 (B/E)	V1		CV23	S2 S20	X338	1183	ETHYLDICHLOROSILANE
L4BH	TU15	FL	2 (D/E)			CV13 CV28	S2 S19	336	1184	ETHYLENE DICHLORIDE
L15CH	TU14 TU15 TE19 TE21	FL	1 (C/D)			CV1 CV13 CV28	S2 S9 S14	663	1185	ETHYLENEIMINE, STABILIZED
LGBF		FL	3 (D/E)				S2	30	1188	ETHYLENE GLYCOL MONOMETHYL ETHER

UN No.	Name and description	Class	Classification code	Packing group	Labels	Special provisions	Limited and excepted quantities		Packaging			Portable tanks and bulk containers	
							quantities		Packing instructions	Special packing provisions	Mixed packing provisions	Instructions	Special provisions
	3.1.2	2.2	2.2	2.1.1.3	5.2.2	3.3	3.4.6	3.5.1.2	4.1.4	4.1.4	4.1.10	4.2.5.2 7.3.2	4.2.5.3
(1)	(2)	(3a)	(3b)	(4)	(5)	(6)	(7a)	(7b)	(8)	(9a)	(9b)	(10)	(11)
1189	ETHYLENE GLYCOL MONOMETHYL ETHER ACETATE	3	F1	III	3		LQ7	E1	P001 IBC03 LP01 R001		MP19	T2	TP1
1190	ETHYL FORMATE	3	F1	II	3		LQ4	E2	P001 IBC02 R001		MP19	T4	TP1
1191	OCTYL ALDEHYDES	3	F1	III	3		LQ7	E1	P001 IBC03 LP01 R001		MP19	T2	TP1
1192	ETHYL LACTATE	3	F1	III	3		LQ7	E1	P001 IBC03 LP01 R001		MP19	T2	TP1
1193	ETHYL METHYL KETONE (METHYL ETHYL KETONE)	3	F1	II	3		LQ4	E2	P001 IBC02 R001		MP19	T4	TP1
1194	ETHYL NITRITE SOLUTION	3	FT1	I	3 +6.1		LQ0	E0	P001		MP7 MP17		
1195	ETHYL PROPIONATE	3	F1	II	3		LQ4	E2	P001 IBC02 R001		MP19	T4	TP1
1196	ETHYLTRICHLOROSILANE	3	FC	II	3 +8		LQ4	E2	P010		MP19	T10	TP2 TP7
1197	EXTRACTS, FLAVOURING, LIQUID	3	F1	I	3		LQ3	E3	P001		MP7 MP17		
1197	EXTRACTS, FLAVOURING, LIQUID (vapour pressure at 50 °C more than 110 kPa)	3	F1	II	3	601 640C	LQ6	E2	P001		MP19	T4	TP1 TP8
1197	EXTRACTS, FLAVOURING, LIQUID (vapour pressure at 50 °C not more than 110 kPa)	3	F1	II	3	601 640D	LQ6	E2	P001 IBC02 R001		MP19	T4	TP1 TP8
1197	EXTRACTS, FLAVOURING, LIQUID	3	F1	III	3	601 640E	LQ7	E1	P001 IBC03 LP01 R001		MP19	T2	TP1
1197	EXTRACTS, FLAVOURING, LIQUID (having a flash-point below 23 °C and viscous according to 2.2.3.1.4) (boiling point not more than 35 °C)	3	F1	III	3	601 640F	LQ7	E1	P001 LP01 R001		MP19	T2	TP1
1197	EXTRACTS, FLAVOURING, LIQUID (having a flash-point below 23 °C and viscous according to 2.2.3.1.4) (vapour pressure at 50 °C more than 110 kPa, boiling point of more than 35 °C)	3	F1	III	3	601 640G	LQ7	E1	P001 LP01 R001		MP19	T2	TP1
1197	EXTRACTS, FLAVOURING, LIQUID (having a flash-point below 23 °C and viscous according to 2.2.3.1.4) (vapour pressure at 50 °C not more than 110 kPa)	3	F1	III	3	601 640H	LQ7	E1	P001 IBC02 LP01 R001		MP19	T2	TP1
1198	FORMALDEHYDE SOLUTION, FLAMMABLE	3	FC	III	3 +8		LQ7	E1	P001 IBC03 R001		MP19	T4	TP1
1199	FURALDEHYDES	6.1	TF1	II	6.1 +3		LQ0	E4	P001 IBC02		MP15	T7	TP2
1201	FUSEL OIL	3	F1	II	3		LQ4	E2	P001 IBC02 R001		MP19	T4	TP1
1201	FUSEL OIL	3	F1	III	3		LQ7	E1	P001 IBC03 LP01 R001		MP19	T2	TP1
1202	GAS OIL or DIESEL FUEL or HEATING OIL, LIGHT (flash-point not more than 60 °C)	3	F1	III	3	640K	LQ7	E1	P001 IBC03 LP01 R001		MP19	T2	TP1

ADR tank		Vehicle for tank carriage	Transport category (Tunnel restriction code)	Special provisions for carriage				Hazard identifi- cation No.	UN No.	Name and description
Tank code	Special provisions			Packages	Bulk	Loading, unloading and handling	Operation			
4.3	4.3.5, 6.8.4	9.1.1.2	1.1.3.6 (8.6)	7.2.4	7.3.3	7.5.11	8.5	5.3.2.3		3.1.2
(12)	(13)	(14)	(15)	(16)	(17)	(18)	(19)	(20)	(1)	(2)
LGBF		FL	3 (D/E)				S2	30	1189	ETHYLENE GLYCOL MONOMETHYL ETHER ACETATE
LGBF		FL	2 (D/E)				S2 S20	33	1190	ETHYL FORMATE
LGBF		FL	3 (D/E)				S2	30	1191	OCTYL ALDEHYDES
LGBF		FL	3 (D/E)				S2	30	1192	ETHYL LACTATE
LGBF		FL	2 (D/E)				S2 S20	33	1193	ETHYL METHYL KETONE (METHYL ETHYL KETONE)
L10CH	TU14 TU15 TE21	FL	1 (C/E)			CV13 CV28	S2 S22	336	1194	ETHYL NITRITE SOLUTION
LGBF		FL	2 (D/E)				S2 S20	33	1195	ETHYL PROPIONATE
L4BH		FL	2 (D/E)				S2 S20	X338	1196	ETHYLTRICHLOROSILANE
L4BN		FL	1 (D/E)				S2 S20	33	1197	EXTRACTS, FLAVOURING, LIQUID
L1.5BN		FL	2 (D/E)				S2 S20	33	1197	EXTRACTS, FLAVOURING, LIQUID (vapour pressure at 50 °C more than 110 kPa)
LGBF		FL	2 (D/E)				S2 S20	33	1197	EXTRACTS, FLAVOURING, LIQUID (vapour pressure at 50 °C not more than 110 kPa)
LGBF		FL	3 (D/E)				S2	30	1197	EXTRACTS, FLAVOURING, LIQUID
L4BN		FL	3 (D/E)				S2	33	1197	EXTRACTS, FLAVOURING, LIQUID (having a flash-point below 23 °C and viscous according to 2.2.3.1.4) (boiling point not more than 35 °C)
L1.5BN		FL	3 (D/E)				S2	33	1197	EXTRACTS, FLAVOURING, LIQUID (having a flash-point below 23 °C and viscous according to 2.2.3.1.4) (vapour pressure at 50 °C more than 110 kPa, boiling point of more than 35 °C)
LGBF		FL	3 (D/E)				S2	33	1197	EXTRACTS, FLAVOURING, LIQUID (having a flash-point below 23 °C and viscous according to 2.2.3.1.4) (vapour pressure at 50 °C not more than 110 kPa)
L4BN		FL	3 (D/E)				S2	38	1198	FORMALDEHYDE SOLUTION, FLAMMABLE
L4BH	TU15 TE19	FL	2 (D/E)			CV13 CV28	S2 S9 S19	63	1199	FURALDEHYDES
LGBF		FL	2 (D/E)				S2 S20	33	1201	FUSEL OIL
LGBF		FL	3 (D/E)				S2	30	1201	FUSEL OIL
LGBF		FL	3 (D/E)				S2	30	1202	GAS OIL or DIESEL FUEL or HEATING OIL, LIGHT (flash-point not more than 60 °C)

UN No.	Name and description	Class	Classifi- cation code	Packing group	Labels	Special provi- sions	Limited and excepted quantities		Packaging			Portable tanks and bulk containers	
									Packing instruc- tions	Special packing provisions	Mixed packing provisions	Instruc- tions	Special provisions
	3.1.2	2.2	2.2	2.1.1.3	5.2.2	3.3	3.4.6	3.5.1.2	4.1.4	4.1.4	4.1.10	4.2.5.2 7.3.2	4.2.5.3
(1)	(2)	(3a)	(3b)	(4)	(5)	(6)	(7a)	(7b)	(8)	(9a)	(9b)	(10)	(11)
1202	DIESEL FUEL complying with standard EN 590:2004 or GAS OIL or HEATING OIL, LIGHT with a flash-point as specified in EN 590:2004	3	F1	III	3	640L	LQ7	E1	P001 IBC03 LP01 R001		MP19	T2	TP1
1202	GAS OIL or DIESEL FUEL or HEATING OIL, LIGHT (flash-point more than 60 °C and not more than 100 °C)	3	F1	III	3	640M	LQ7	E1	P001 IBC03 LP01 R001		MP19	T2	TP1
1203	MOTOR SPIRIT or GASOLINE or PETROL	3	F1	II	3	243 534	LQ4	E2	P001 IBC02 R001	BB2	MP19	T4	TP1
1204	NITROGLYCERIN SOLUTION IN ALCOHOL with not more than 1% nitroglycerin	3	D	II	3	601	LQ0	E0	P001 IBC02	PP5	MP2		
1206	HEPTANES	3	F1	II	3		LQ4	E2	P001 IBC02 R001		MP19	T4	TP1
1207	HEXALDEHYDE	3	F1	III	3		LQ7	E1	P001 IBC03 LP01 R001		MP19	T2	TP1
1208	HEXANES	3	F1	II	3		LQ4	E2	P001 IBC02 R001		MP19	T4	TP1
1210	PRINTING INK, flammable or PRINTING INK RELATED MATERIAL (including printing ink thinning or reducing compound), flammable	3	F1	I	3	163	LQ3	E3	P001		MP7 MP17	T11	TP1 TP8
1210	PRINTING INK, flammable or PRINTING INK RELATED MATERIAL (including printing ink thinning or reducing compound), flammable (vapour pressure at 50 °C more than 110 kPa)	3	F1	II	3	163 640C	LQ6	E2	P001	PP1	MP19	T4	TP1 TP8
1210	PRINTING INK, flammable or PRINTING INK RELATED MATERIAL (including printing ink thinning or reducing compound), flammable (vapour pressure at 50 °C not more than 110 kPa)	3	F1	II	3	163 640D	LQ6	E2	P001 IBC02 R001	PP1	MP19	T4	TP1 TP8
1210	PRINTING INK, flammable or PRINTING INK RELATED MATERIAL (including printing ink thinning or reducing compound), flammable	3	F1	III	3	163 640E	LQ7	E1	P001 IBC03 LP01 R001	PP1	MP19	T2	TP1
1210	PRINTING INK, flammable or PRINTING INK RELATED MATERIAL (including printing ink thinning or reducing compound), flammable (having a flash-point below 23 °C and viscous according to 2.2.3.1.4) (boiling point not more than 35 °C)	3	F1	III	3	163 640F	LQ7	E1	P001 LP01 R001	PP1	MP19	T2	TP1

ADR tank		Vehicle for tank carriage	Transport category (Tunnel restriction code)	Special provisions for carriage				Hazard identifi-cation No.	UN No.	Name and description
Tank code	Special provisions			Packages	Bulk	Loading, unloading and handling	Operation			
4.3	4.3.5, 6.8.4	9.1.1.2	1.1.3.6 (8.6)	7.2.4	7.3.3	7.5.11	8.5	5.3.2.3		3.1.2
(12)	(13)	(14)	(15)	(16)	(17)	(18)	(19)	(20)	(1)	(2)
LGBF		AT	3 (D/E)				S2	30	1202	DIESEL FUEL complying with standard EN 590:2004 or GAS OIL or HEATING OIL, LIGHT with a flash-point as specified in EN 590:2004
LGBV		AT	3 (D/E)					30	1202	GAS OIL or DIESEL FUEL or HEATING OIL, LIGHT (flash-point more than 60 °C and not more than 100 °C)
LGBF	TU9	FL	2 (D/E)				S2 S20	33	1203	MOTOR SPIRIT or GASOLINE or PETROL
			2 (B)				S2 S14		1204	NITROGLYCERIN SOLUTION IN ALCOHOL with not more than 1% nitroglycerin
LGBF		FL	2 (D/E)				S2 S20	33	1206	HEPTANES
LGBF		FL	3 (D/E)				S2	30	1207	HEXALDEHYDE
LGBF		FL	2 (D/E)				S2 S20	33	1208	HEXANES
L4BN		FL	1 (D/E)				S2 S20	33	1210	PRINTING INK, flammable or PRINTING INK RELATED MATERIAL (including printing ink thinning or reducing compound), flammable
L1.5BN		FL	2 (D/E)				S2 S20	33	1210	PRINTING INK, flammable or PRINTING INK RELATED MATERIAL (including printing ink thinning or reducing compound), flammable (vapour pressure at 50 °C more than 110 kPa)
LGBF		FL	2 (D/E)				S2 S20	33	1210	PRINTING INK, flammable or PRINTING INK RELATED MATERIAL (including printing ink thinning or reducing compound), flammable (vapour pressure at 50 °C not more than 110 kPa)
LGBF		FL	3 (D/E)				S2	30	1210	PRINTING INK, flammable or PRINTING INK RELATED MATERIAL (including printing ink thinning or reducing compound), flammable
L4BN		FL	3 (D/E)				S2	33	1210	PRINTING INK, flammable or PRINTING INK RELATED MATERIAL (including printing ink thinning or reducing compound), flammable (having a flash-point below 23 °C and viscous according to 2.2.3.1.4) (boiling point not more than 35 °C)

UN No.	Name and description	Class	Classifi-cation code	Packing group	Labels	Special provi-sions	Limited and excepted quantities		Packaging			Portable tanks and bulk containers	
									Packing instruc-tions	Special packing provisions	Mixed packing provisions	Instruc-tions	Special provisions
	3.1.2	2.2	2.2	2.1.1.3	5.2.2	3.3	3.4.6	3.5.1.2	4.1.4	4.1.4	4.1.10	4.2.5.2 7.3.2	4.2.5.3
(1)	(2)	(3a)	(3b)	(4)	(5)	(6)	(7a)	(7b)	(8)	(9a)	(9b)	(10)	(11)
1210	PRINTING INK, flammable or PRINTING INK RELATED MATERIAL (including printing ink thinning or reducing compound), flammable (having a flash-point below 23 °C and viscous according to 2.2.3.1.4) (vapour pressure at 50 °C more than 110 kPa, boiling point of more than 35 °C)	3	F1	III	3	163 640G	LQ7	E1	P001 LP01 R001	PP1	MP19	T2	TP1
1210	PRINTING INK, flammable or PRINTING INK RELATED MATERIAL (including printing ink thinning or reducing compound), flammable (having a flash-point below 23 °C and viscous according to 2.2.3.1.4) (vapour pressure at 50 °C not more than 110 kPa)	3	F1	III	3	163 640H	LQ7	E1	P001 IBC02 LP01 R001	PP1	MP19	T2	TP1
1212	ISOBUTANOL (ISOBUTYL ALCOHOL)	3	F1	III	3		LQ7	E1	P001 IBC03 LP01 R001		MP19	T2	TP1
1213	ISOBUTYL ACETATE	3	F1	II	3		LQ4	E2	P001 IBC02 R001		MP19	T4	TP1
1214	ISOBUTYLAMINE	3	FC	II	3 +8		LQ4	E2	P001 IBC02		MP19	T7	TP1
1216	ISOOCTENES	3	F1	II	3		LQ4	E2	P001 IBC02 R001		MP19	T4	TP1
1218	ISOPRENE, STABILIZED	3	F1	I	3		LQ3	E3	P001		MP7 MP17	T11	TP2
1219	ISOPROPANOL (ISOPROPYL ALCOHOL)	3	F1	II	3	601	LQ4	E2	P001 IBC02 R001		MP19	T4	TP1
1220	ISOPROPYL ACETATE	3	F1	II	3		LQ4	E2	P001 IBC02 R001		MP19	T4	TP1
1221	ISOPROPYLAMINE	3	FC	I	3 +8		LQ3	E0	P001		MP7 MP17	T11	TP2
1222	ISOPROPYL NITRATE	3	F1	II	3		LQ4	E2	P001 IBC02 R001	B7	MP19		
1223	KEROSENE	3	F1	III	3		LQ7	E1	P001 IBC03 LP01 R001		MP19	T2	TP2
1224	KETONES, LIQUID, N.O.S. (vapour pressure at 50 °C more than 110 kPa)	3	F1	II	3	274 640C	LQ4	E2	P001		MP19	T7	TP1 TP8 TP28
1224	KETONES, LIQUID, N.O.S. (vapour pressure at 50 °C not more than 110 kPa)	3	F1	II	3	274 640D	LQ4	E2	P001 IBC02 R001		MP19	T7	TP1 TP8 TP28
1224	KETONES, LIQUID, N.O.S.	3	F1	III	3	274	LQ7	E1	P001 IBC03 LP01 R001		MP19	T4	TP1 TP29
1228	MERCAPTANS, LIQUID, FLAMMABLE, TOXIC, N.O.S. or MERCAPTAN MIXTURE, LIQUID, FLAMMABLE, TOXIC, N.O.S.	3	FT1	II	3 +6.1	274	LQ0	E2	P001 IBC02		MP19	T11	TP2 TP27
1228	MERCAPTANS, LIQUID, FLAMMABLE, TOXIC, N.O.S. or MERCAPTAN MIXTURE, LIQUID, FLAMMABLE, TOXIC, N.O.S.	3	FT1	III	3 +6.1	274	LQ7	E1	P001 IBC03 R001		MP19	T7	TP1 TP28

ADR tank		Vehicle for tank carriage	Transport category (Tunnel restriction code)	Special provisions for carriage				Hazard identifi-cation No.	UN No.	Name and description
Tank code	Special provisions			Packages	Bulk	Loading, unloading and handling	Operation			
4.3	4.3.5, 6.8.4	9.1.1.2	1.1.3.6 (8.6)	7.2.4	7.3.3	7.5.11	8.5	5.3.2.3		3.1.2
(12)	(13)	(14)	(15)	(16)	(17)	(18)	(19)	(20)	(1)	(2)
L1.5BN		FL	3 (D/E)				S2	33	1210	PRINTING INK, flammable or PRINTING INK RELATED MATERIAL (including printing ink thinning or reducing compound), flammable (having a flash-point below 23 °C and viscous according to 2.2.3.1.4) (vapour pressure at 50 °C more than 110 kPa, boiling point of more than 35 °C)
LGBF		FL	3 (D/E)				S2	33	1210	PRINTING INK, flammable or PRINTING INK RELATED MATERIAL (including printing ink thinning or reducing compound), flammable (having a flash-point below 23 °C and viscous according to 2.2.3.1.4) (vapour pressure at 50 °C not more than 110 kPa)
LGBF		FL	3 (D/E)				S2	30	1212	ISOBUTANOL (ISOBUTYL ALCOHOL)
LGBF		FL	2 (D/E)				S2 S20	33	1213	ISOBUTYL ACETATE
L4BH		FL	2 (D/E)				S2 S20	338	1214	ISOBUTYLAMINE
LGBF		FL	2 (D/E)				S2 S20	33	1216	ISOOCTENES
L4BN		FL	1 (D/E)				S2 S20	339	1218	ISOPRENE, STABILIZED
LGBF		FL	2 (D/E)				S2 S20	33	1219	ISOPROPANOL (ISOPROPYL ALCOHOL)
LGBF		FL	2 (D/E)				S2 S20	33	1220	ISOPROPYL ACETATE
L10CH	TU14 TE21	FL	1 (C/E)				S2 S20	338	1221	ISOPROPYLAMINE
			2 (E)				S2 S20		1222	ISOPROPYL NITRATE
LGBF		FL	3 (D/E)				S2	30	1223	KEROSENE
L1.5BN		FL	2 (D/E)				S2 S20	33	1224	KETONES, LIQUID, N.O.S. (vapour pressure at 50 °C more than 110 kPa)
LGBF		FL	2 (D/E)				S2 S20	33	1224	KETONES, LIQUID, N.O.S. (vapour pressure at 50 °C not more than 110 kPa)
LGBF		FL	3 (D/E)				S2	30	1224	KETONES, LIQUID, N.O.S.
L4BH	TU15	FL	2 (D/E)			CV13 CV28	S2 S19	336	1228	MERCAPTANS, LIQUID, FLAMMABLE, TOXIC, N.O.S. or MERCAPTAN MIXTURE, LIQUID, FLAMMABLE, TOXIC, N.O.S.
L4BH	TU15	FL	3 (D/E)			CV13 CV28	S2	36	1228	MERCAPTANS, LIQUID, FLAMMABLE, TOXIC, N.O.S. or MERCAPTAN MIXTURE, LIQUID, FLAMMABLE, TOXIC, N.O.S.

UN No.	Name and description	Class	Classification code	Packing group	Labels	Special provisions	Limited quantities	Excepted quantities	Packing instructions	Special packing provisions	Mixed packing provisions	Instructions	Special provisions
3.1.2	3.1.2	2.2	2.2	2.1.1.3	5.2.2	3.3	3.4.6	3.5.1.2	4.1.4	4.1.4	4.1.10	4.2.5.2 7.3.2	4.2.5.3
(1)	(2)	(3a)	(3b)	(4)	(5)	(6)	(7a)	(7b)	(8)	(9a)	(9b)	(10)	(11)
1229	MESITYL OXIDE	3	F1	III	3		LQ7	E1	P001 IBC03 LP01 R001		MP19	T2	TP1
1230	METHANOL	3	FT1	II	3 +6.1	279	LQ0	E2	P001 IBC02		MP19	T7	TP2
1231	METHYL ACETATE	3	F1	II	3		LQ4	E2	P001 IBC02 R001		MP19	T4	TP1
1233	METHYLAMYL ACETATE	3	F1	III	3		LQ7	E1	P001 IBC03 LP01 R001		MP19	T2	TP1
1234	METHYLAL	3	F1	II	3		LQ4	E2	P001 IBC02	B8	MP19	T7	TP2
1235	METHYLAMINE, AQUEOUS SOLUTION	3	FC	II	3 +8		LQ4	E2	P001 IBC02		MP19	T7	TP1
1237	METHYL BUTYRATE	3	F1	II	3		LQ4	E2	P001 IBC02 R001		MP19	T4	TP1
1238	METHYL CHLOROFORMATE	6.1	TFC	I	6.1 +3 +8		LQ0	E5	P602		MP8 MP17	T22	TP2 TP35
1239	METHYL CHLOROMETHYL ETHER	6.1	TF1	I	6.1 +3		LQ0	E5	P602		MP8 MP17	T22	TP2 TP35
1242	METHYLDICHLOROSILANE	4.3	WFC	I	4.3 +3 +8		LQ0	E0	P401	RR7	MP2	T14	TP2 TP7
1243	METHYL FORMATE	3	F1	I	3		LQ3	E3	P001		MP7 MP17	T11	TP2
1244	METHYLHYDRAZINE	6.1	TFC	I	6.1 +3 +8		LQ0	E5	P602		MP8 MP17	T22	TP2 TP35
1245	METHYL ISOBUTYL KETONE	3	F1	II	3		LQ4	E2	P001 IBC02 R001		MP19	T4	TP1
1246	METHYL ISOPROPENYL KETONE, STABILIZED	3	F1	II	3		LQ4	E2	P001 IBC02 R001		MP19	T4	TP1
1247	METHYL METHACRYLATE MONOMER, STABILIZED	3	F1	II	3		LQ4	E2	P001 IBC02 R001		MP19	T4	TP1
1248	METHYL PROPIONATE	3	F1	II	3		LQ4	E2	P001 IBC02 R001		MP19	T4	TP1
1249	METHYL PROPYL KETONE	3	F1	II	3		LQ4	E2	P001 IBC02 R001		MP19	T4	TP1
1250	METHYLTRICHLORO-SILANE	3	FC	II	3 +8		LQ4	E2	P010		MP19	T10	TP2 TP7
1251	METHYL VINYL KETONE, STABILIZED	6.1	TFC	I	6.1 +3 +8		LQ0	E5	P601	RR7	MP8 MP17	T14	TP2
1259	NICKEL CARBONYL	6.1	TF1	I	6.1 +3		LQ0	E5	P601		MP2		
1261	NITROMETHANE	3	F1	II	3		LQ4	E2	P001 R001	RR2	MP19		
1262	OCTANES	3	F1	II	3		LQ4	E2	P001 IBC02 R001		MP19	T4	TP1
1263	PAINT (including paint, lacquer, enamel, stain, shellac, varnish, polish, liquid filler and liquid lacquer base) or PAINT RELATED MATERIAL (including paint thinning and reducing compound)	3	F1	I	3	163 650	LQ3	E3	P001		MP7 MP17	T11	TP1 TP8 TP27

ADR tank		Vehicle for tank carriage	Transport category (Tunnel restriction code)	Special provisions for carriage				Hazard identifi-cation No.	UN No.	Name and description
Tank code	Special provisions			Packages	Bulk	Loading, unloading and handling	Operation			
4.3	4.3.5, 6.8.4	9.1.1.2	1.1.3.6 (8.6)	7.2.4	7.3.3	7.5.11	8.5	5.3.2.3		3.1.2
(12)	(13)	(14)	(15)	(16)	(17)	(18)	(19)	(20)	(1)	(2)
LGBF		FL	3 (D/E)				S2	30	1229	MESITYL OXIDE
L4BH	TU15	FL	2 (D/E)			CV13 CV28	S2 S19	336	1230	METHANOL
LGBF		FL	2 (D/E)				S2 S20	33	1231	METHYL ACETATE
LGBF		FL	3 (D/E)				S2	30	1233	METHYLAMYL ACETATE
L1.5BN		FL	2 (D/E)				S2 S20	33	1234	METHYLAL
L4BH		FL	2 (D/E)				S2 S20	338	1235	METHYLAMINE, AQUEOUS SOLUTION
LGBF		FL	2 (D/E)				S2 S20	33	1237	METHYL BUTYRATE
L10CH	TU14 TU15 TE19 TE21	FL	1 (C/D)			CV1 CV13 CV28	S2 S9 S14	663	1238	METHYL CHLOROFORMATE
L10CH	TU14 TU15 TE19 TE21	FL	1 (C/D)			CV1 CV13 CV28	S2 S9 S14	663	1239	METHYL CHLOROMETHYL ETHER
L10DH	TU14 TU24 TE21 TM2 TM3	FL	0 (B/E)	V1		CV23	S2 S20	X338	1242	METHYLDICHLOROSILANE
L4BN		FL	1 (D/E)				S2 S20	33	1243	METHYL FORMATE
L10CH	TU14 TU15 TE19 TE21	FL	1 (C/D)			CV1 CV13 CV28	S2 S9 S14	663	1244	METHYLHYDRAZINE
LGBF		FL	2 (D/E)				S2 S20	33	1245	METHYL ISOBUTYL KETONE
LGBF		FL	2 (D/E)				S2 S20	339	1246	METHYL ISOPROPENYL KETONE, STABILIZED
LGBF		FL	2 (D/E)				S2 S20	339	1247	METHYL METHACRYLATE MONOMER, STABILIZED
LGBF		FL	2 (D/E)				S2 S20	33	1248	METHYL PROPIONATE
LGBF		FL	2 (D/E)				S2 S20	33	1249	METHYL PROPYL KETONE
L4BH		FL	2 (D/E)				S2 S20	X338	1250	METHYLTRICHLORO-SILANE
L10CH	TU14 TU15 TE19 TE21	FL	1 (C/D)			CV1 CV13 CV28	S2 S9 S14	639	1251	METHYL VINYL KETONE, STABILIZED
L15CH	TU14 TU15 TU31 TE19 TE21 TM3	FL	1 (C/D)			CV1 CV13 CV28	S2 S9 S14	663	1259	NICKEL CARBONYL
			2 (E)				S2 S20		1261	NITROMETHANE
LGBF		FL	2 (D/E)				S2 S20	33	1262	OCTANES
L4BN		FL	1 (D/E)				S2 S20	33	1263	PAINT (including paint, lacquer, enamel, stain, shellac, varnish, polish, liquid filler and liquid lacquer base) or PAINT RELATED MATERIAL (including paint thinning and reducing compound)

UN No.	Name and description	Class	Classification code	Packing group	Labels	Special provisions	Limited and excepted quantities		Packaging			Portable tanks and bulk containers	
									Packing instructions	Special packing provisions	Mixed packing provisions	Instructions	Special provisions
	3.1.2	2.2	2.2	2.1.1.3	5.2.2	3.3	3.4.6	3.5.1.2	4.1.4	4.1.4	4.1.10	4.2.5.2 7.3.2	4.2.5.3
(1)	(2)	(3a)	(3b)	(4)	(5)	(6)	(7a)	(7b)	(8)	(9a)	(9b)	(10)	(11)
1263	PAINT (including paint, lacquer, enamel, stain, shellac, varnish, polish, liquid filler and liquid lacquer base) or PAINT RELATED MATERIAL (including paint thinning and reducing compound) (vapour pressure at 50 °C more than 110 kPa)	3	F1	II	3	163 640C 650	LQ6	E2	P001	PP1	MP19	T4	TP1 TP8 TP28
1263	PAINT (including paint, lacquer, enamel, stain, shellac, varnish, polish, liquid filler and liquid lacquer base) or PAINT RELATED MATERIAL (including paint thinning and reducing compound) (vapour pressure at 50 °C not more than 110 kPa)	3	F1	II	3	163 640D 650	LQ6	E2	P001 IBC02 R001	PP1	MP19	T4	TP1 TP8 TP28
1263	PAINT (including paint, lacquer, enamel, stain, shellac, varnish, polish, liquid filler and liquid lacquer base) or PAINT RELATED MATERIAL (including paint thinning and reducing compound)	3	F1	III	3	163 640E 650	LQ7	E1	P001 IBC03 LP01 R001	PP1	MP19	T2	TP1 TP29
1263	PAINT (including paint, lacquer, enamel, stain, shellac, varnish, polish, liquid filler and liquid lacquer base) or PAINT RELATED MATERIAL (including paint thinning and reducing compound) (having a flash-point below 23 °C and viscous according to 2.2.3.1.4) (boiling point not more than 35 °C)	3	F1	III	3	163 640F 650	LQ7	E1	P001 LP01 R001	PP1	MP19	T2	TP1 TP29
1263	PAINT (including paint, lacquer, enamel, stain, shellac, varnish, polish, liquid filler and liquid lacquer base) or PAINT RELATED MATERIAL (including paint thinning and reducing compound) (having a flash-point below 23 °C and viscous according to 2.2.3.1.4) (vapour pressure at 50 °C more than 110 kPa, boiling point of more than 35 °C)	3	F1	III	3	163 640G 650	LQ7	E1	P001 LP01 R001	PP1	MP19	T2	TP1 TP29
1263	PAINT (including paint, lacquer, enamel, stain, shellac, varnish, polish, liquid filler and liquid lacquer base) or PAINT RELATED MATERIAL (including paint thinning and reducing compound) (having a flash-point below 23 °C and viscous according to 2.2.3.1.4) (vapour pressure at 50 °C not more than 110 kPa)	3	F1	III	3	163 640H 650	LQ7	E1	P001 IBC02 LP01 R001	PP1	MP19	T2	TP1 TP29
1264	PARALDEHYDE	3	F1	III	3		LQ7	E1	P001 IBC03 LP01 R001		MP19	T2	TP1
1265	PENTANES, liquid	3	F1	I	3		LQ3	E3	P001		MP7 MP17	T11	TP2
1265	PENTANES, liquid	3	F1	II	3		LQ4	E2	P001 IBC02	B8	MP19	T4	TP1
1266	PERFUMERY PRODUCTS with flammable solvents	3	F1	I	3		LQ3	E3	P001		MP7 MP17		

ADR tank		Vehicle for tank carriage	Transport category (Tunnel restriction code)	Special provisions for carriage				Hazard identifi-cation No.	UN No.	Name and description
Tank code	Special provisions			Packages	Bulk	Loading, unloading and handling	Operation			
4.3	4.3.5, 6.8.4	9.1.1.2	1.1.3.6 (8.6)	7.2.4	7.3.3	7.5.11	8.5	5.3.2.3		3.1.2
(12)	(13)	(14)	(15)	(16)	(17)	(18)	(19)	(20)	(1)	(2)
L1.5BN		FL	2 (D/E)				S2 S20	33	1263	PAINT (including paint, lacquer, enamel, stain, shellac, varnish, polish, liquid filler and liquid lacquer base) or PAINT RELATED MATERIAL (including paint thinning and reducing compound) (vapour pressure at 50 °C more than 110 kPa)
LGBF		FL	2 (D/E)				S2 S20	33	1263	PAINT (including paint, lacquer, enamel, stain, shellac, varnish, polish, liquid filler and liquid lacquer base) or PAINT RELATED MATERIAL (including paint thinning and reducing compound) (vapour pressure at 50 °C not more than 110 kPa)
LGBF		FL	3 (D/E)				S2	30	1263	PAINT (including paint, lacquer, enamel, stain, shellac, varnish, polish, liquid filler and liquid lacquer base) or PAINT RELATED MATERIAL (including paint thinning and reducing compound)
L4BN		FL	3 (D/E)				S2	33	1263	PAINT (including paint, lacquer, enamel, stain, shellac, varnish, polish, liquid filler and liquid lacquer base) or PAINT RELATED MATERIAL (including paint thinning and reducing compound) (having a flash-point below 23 °C and viscous according to 2.2.3.1.4) (boiling point not more than 35 °C)
L1.5BN		FL	3 (D/E)				S2	33	1263	PAINT (including paint, lacquer, enamel, stain, shellac, varnish, polish, liquid filler and liquid lacquer base) or PAINT RELATED MATERIAL (including paint thinning and reducing compound) (having a flash-point below 23 °C and viscous according to 2.2.3.1.4) (vapour pressure at 50 °C more than 110 kPa, boiling point of more than 35 °C)
LGBF		FL	3 (D/E)				S2	33	1263	PAINT (including paint, lacquer, enamel, stain, shellac, varnish, polish, liquid filler and liquid lacquer base) or PAINT RELATED MATERIAL (including paint thinning and reducing compound) (having a flash-point below 23 °C and viscous according to 2.2.3.1.4) (vapour pressure at 50 °C not more than 110 kPa)
LGBF		FL	3 (D/E)				S2	30	1264	PARALDEHYDE
L4BN		FL	1 (D/E)				S2 S20	33	1265	PENTANES, liquid
L1.5BN		FL	2 (D/E)				S2 S20	33	1265	PENTANES, liquid
L4BN		FL	1 (D/E)				S2 S20	33	1266	PERFUMERY PRODUCTS with flammable solvents

UN No.	Name and description	Class	Classifi-cation code	Packing group	Labels	Special provi-sions	Limited and excepted quantities		Packaging			Portable tanks and bulk containers	
									Packing instruc-tions	Special packing provisions	Mixed packing provisions	Instruc-tions	Special provisions
	3.1.2	2.2	2.2	2.1.1.3	5.2.2	3.3	3.4.6	3.5.1.2	4.1.4	4.1.4	4.1.10	4.2.5.2 7.3.2	4.2.5.3
(1)	(2)	(3a)	(3b)	(4)	(5)	(6)	(7a)	(7b)	(8)	(9a)	(9b)	(10)	(11)
1266	PERFUMERY PRODUCTS with flammable solvents (vapour pressure at 50 °C more than 110 kPa)	3	F1	II	3	640C	LQ6	E2	P001		MP19	T4	TP1 TP8
1266	PERFUMERY PRODUCTS with flammable solvents (vapour pressure at 50 °C not more than 110 kPa)	3	F1	II	3	640D	LQ6	E2	P001 IBC02 R001		MP19	T4	TP1 TP8
1266	PERFUMERY PRODUCTS with flammable solvents	3	F1	III	3	640E	LQ7	E1	P001 IBC03 LP01 R001		MP19	T2	TP1
1266	PERFUMERY PRODUCTS with flammable solvents (having a flash-point below 23 °C and viscous according to 2.2.3.1.4) (boiling point not more than 35 °C)	3	F1	III	3	640F	LQ7	E1	P001 LP01 R001		MP19	T2	TP1
1266	PERFUMERY PRODUCTS with flammable solvents (having a flash-point below 23 °C and viscous according to 2.2.3.1.4) (vapour pressure at 50 °C more than 110 kPa, boiling point of more than 35 °C)	3	F1	III	3	640G	LQ7	E1	P001 LP01 R001		MP19	T2	TP1
1266	PERFUMERY PRODUCTS with flammable solvents (having a flash-point below 23 °C and viscous according to 2.2.3.1.4) (vapour pressure at 50 °C not more than 110 kPa)	3	F1	III	3	640H	LQ7	E1	P001 IBC02 LP01 R001		MP19	T2	TP1
1267	PETROLEUM CRUDE OIL	3	F1	I	3	649	LQ3	E3	P001		MP7 MP17	T11	TP1 TP8
1267	PETROLEUM CRUDE OIL (vapour pressure at 50 °C more than 110 kPa)	3	F1	II	3	640C 649	LQ4	E2	P001		MP19	T4	TP1 TP8
1267	PETROLEUM CRUDE OIL (vapour pressure at 50 °C not more than 110 kPa)	3	F1	II	3	640D 649	LQ4	E2	P001 IBC02 R001		MP19	T4	TP1 TP8
1267	PETROLEUM CRUDE OIL	3	F1	III	3		LQ7	E1	P001 IBC03 LP01 R001		MP19	T2	TP1
1268	PETROLEUM DISTILLATES, N.O.S. or PETROLEUM PRODUCTS, N.O.S.	3	F1	I	3	649	LQ3	E3	P001		MP7 MP17	T11	TP1 TP8
1268	PETROLEUM DISTILLATES, N.O.S. or PETROLEUM PRODUCTS, N.O.S. (vapour pressure at 50 °C more than 110 kPa)	3	F1	II	3	640C 649	LQ4	E2	P001		MP19	T7	TP1 TP8 TP28
1268	PETROLEUM DISTILLATES, N.O.S. or PETROLEUM PRODUCTS, N.O.S. (vapour pressure at 50 °C not more than 110 kPa)	3	F1	II	3	640D 649	LQ4	E2	P001 IBC02 R001		MP19	T7	TP1 TP8 TP28
1268	PETROLEUM DISTILLATES, N.O.S. or PETROLEUM PRODUCTS, N.O.S.	3	F1	III	3		LQ7	E1	P001 IBC03 LP01 R001		MP19	T4	TP1 TP29
1272	PINE OIL	3	F1	III	3		LQ7	E1	P001 IBC03 LP01 R001		MP19	T2	TP1
1274	n-PROPANOL (PROPYL ALCOHOL, NORMAL)	3	F1	II	3		LQ4	E2	P001 IBC02 R001		MP19	T4	TP1
1274	n-PROPANOL (PROPYL ALCOHOL, NORMAL)	3	F1	III	3		LQ7	E1	P001 IBC03 LP01 R001		MP19	T2	TP1

ADR tank		Vehicle for tank carriage	Transport category (Tunnel restriction code)	Special provisions for carriage				Hazard identifi-cation No.	UN No.	Name and description
Tank code	Special provisions			Packages	Bulk	Loading, unloading and handling	Operation			
4.3	4.3.5, 6.8.4	9.1.1.2	1.1.3.6 (8.6)	7.2.4	7.3.3	7.5.11	8.5	5.3.2.3		3.1.2
(12)	(13)	(14)	(15)	(16)	(17)	(18)	(19)	(20)	(1)	(2)
L1.5BN		FL	2 (D/E)				S2 S20	33	1266	PERFUMERY PRODUCTS with flammable solvents (vapour pressure at 50 °C more than 110 kPa)
LGBF		FL	2 (D/E)				S2 S20	33	1266	PERFUMERY PRODUCTS with flammable solvents (vapour pressure at 50 °C not more than 110 kPa)
LGBF		FL	3 (D/E)				S2	30	1266	PERFUMERY PRODUCTS with flammable solvents
L4BN		FL	3 (D/E)				S2	33	1266	PERFUMERY PRODUCTS with flammable solvents (having a flash-point below 23 °C and viscous according to 2.2.3.1.4) (boiling point not more than 35 °C)
L1.5BN		FL	3 (D/E)				S2	33	1266	PERFUMERY PRODUCTS with flammable solvents (having a flash-point below 23 °C and viscous according to 2.2.3.1.4) (vapour pressure at 50 °C more than 110 kPa, boiling point of more than 35 °C)
LGBF		FL	3 (D/E)				S2	33	1266	PERFUMERY PRODUCTS with flammable solvents (having a flash-point below 23 °C and viscous according to 2.2.3.1.4) (vapour pressure at 50 °C not more than 110 kPa)
L4BN		FL	1 (D/E)				S2 S20	33	1267	PETROLEUM CRUDE OIL
L1.5BN		FL	2 (D/E)				S2 S20	33	1267	PETROLEUM CRUDE OIL (vapour pressure at 50 °C more than 110 kPa)
LGBF		FL	2 (D/E)				S2 S20	33	1267	PETROLEUM CRUDE OIL (vapour pressure at 50 °C not more than 110 kPa)
LGBF		FL	3 (D/E)				S2	30	1267	PETROLEUM CRUDE OIL
L4BN		FL	1 (D/E)				S2 S20	33	1268	PETROLEUM DISTILLATES, N.O.S. or PETROLEUM PRODUCTS, N.O.S.
L1.5BN		FL	2 (D/E)				S2 S20	33	1268	PETROLEUM DISTILLATES, N.O.S. or PETROLEUM PRODUCTS, N.O.S. (vapour pressure at 50 °C more than 110 kPa)
LGBF		FL	2 (D/E)				S2 S20	33	1268	PETROLEUM DISTILLATES, N.O.S. or PETROLEUM PRODUCTS, N.O.S. (vapour pressure at 50 °C not more than 110 kPa)
LGBF		FL	3 (D/E)				S2	30	1268	PETROLEUM DISTILLATES, N.O.S. or PETROLEUM PRODUCTS, N.O.S.
LGBF		FL	3 (D/E)				S2	30	1272	PINE OIL
LGBF		FL	2 (D/E)				S2 S20	33	1274	n-PROPANOL (PROPYL ALCOHOL, NORMAL)
LGBF		FL	3 (D/E)				S2	30	1274	n-PROPANOL (PROPYL ALCOHOL, NORMAL)

UN No.	Name and description	Class	Classifi-cation code	Packing group	Labels	Special provi-sions	Limited and excepted quantities		Packaging			Portable tanks and bulk containers	
									Packing instruc-tions	Special packing provisions	Mixed packing provisions	Instruc-tions	Special provisions
	3.1.2	2.2	2.2	2.1.1.3	5.2.2	3.3	3.4.6	3.5.1.2	4.1.4	4.1.4	4.1.10	4.2.5.2 7.3.2	4.2.5.3
(1)	(2)	(3a)	(3b)	(4)	(5)	(6)	(7a)	(7b)	(8)	(9a)	(9b)	(10)	(11)
1275	PROPIONALDEHYDE	3	F1	II	3		LQ4	E2	P001 IBC02 R001		MP19	T7	TP1
1276	n-PROPYL ACETATE	3	F1	II	3		LQ4	E2	P001 IBC02 R001		MP19	T4	TP1
1277	PROPYLAMINE	3	FC	II	3 +8		LQ4	E2	P001 IBC02		MP19	T7	TP1
1278	1-CHLOROPROPANE	3	F1	II	3		LQ4	E2	P001 IBC02	B8	MP19	T7	TP2
1279	1,2-DICHLOROPROPANE	3	F1	II	3		LQ4	E2	P001 IBC02 R001		MP19	T4	TP1
1280	PROPYLENE OXIDE	3	F1	I	3		LQ3	E3	P001		MP7 MP17	T11	TP2 TP7
1281	PROPYL FORMATES	3	F1	II	3		LQ4	E2	P001 IBC02 R001		MP19	T4	TP1
1282	PYRIDINE	3	F1	II	3		LQ4	E2	P001 IBC02 R001		MP19	T4	TP2
1286	ROSIN OIL	3	F1	I	3		LQ3	E3	P001		MP7 MP17		
1286	ROSIN OIL (vapour pressure at 50 °C more than 110 kPa)	3	F1	II	3	640C	LQ6	E2	P001		MP19	T4	TP1
1286	ROSIN OIL (vapour pressure at 50 °C not more than 110 kPa)	3	F1	II	3	640D	LQ6	E2	P001 IBC02 R001		MP19	T4	TP1
1286	ROSIN OIL	3	F1	III	3	640E	LQ7	E1	P001 IBC03 LP01 R001		MP19	T2	TP1
1286	ROSIN OIL (having a flash-point below 23 °C and viscous according to 2.2.3.1.4) (boiling point not more than 35 °C)	3	F1	III	3	640F	LQ7	E1	P001 LP01 R001		MP19	T2	TP1
1286	ROSIN OIL (having a flash-point below 23 °C and viscous according to 2.2.3.1.4) (vapour pressure at 50 °C more than 110 kPa, boiling point of more than 35 °C)	3	F1	III	3	640G	LQ7	E1	P001 LP01 R001		MP19	T2	TP1
1286	ROSIN OIL (having a flash-point below 23 °C and viscous according to 2.2.3.1.4) (vapour pressure at 50 °C not more than 110 kPa)	3	F1	III	3	640H	LQ7	E1	P001 IBC02 LP01 R001		MP19	T2	TP1
1287	RUBBER SOLUTION	3	F1	I	3		LQ3	E3	P001		MP7 MP17		
1287	RUBBER SOLUTION (vapour pressure at 50 °C more than 110 kPa)	3	F1	II	3	640C	LQ6	E2	P001		MP19	T4	TP1 TP8
1287	RUBBER SOLUTION (vapour pressure at 50 °C not more than 110 kPa)	3	F1	II	3	640D	LQ6	E2	P001 IBC02 R001		MP19	T4	TP1 TP8
1287	RUBBER SOLUTION	3	F1	III	3	640E	LQ7	E1	P001 IBC03 LP01 R001		MP19	T2	TP1
1287	RUBBER SOLUTION (having a flash-point below 23 °C and viscous according to 2.2.3.1.4) (boiling point not more than 35 °C)	3	F1	III	3	640F	LQ7	E1	P001 LP01 R001		MP19	T2	TP1
1287	RUBBER SOLUTION (having a flash-point below 23 °C and viscous according to 2.2.3.1.4) (vapour pressure at 50 °C more than 110 kPa, boiling point of more than 35 °C)	3	F1	III	3	640G	LQ7	E1	P001 LP01 R001		MP19	T2	TP1

ADR tank		Vehicle for tank carriage	Transport category (Tunnel restriction code)	Special provisions for carriage				Hazard identifi-cation No.	UN No.	Name and description
Tank code	Special provisions			Packages	Bulk	Loading, unloading and handling	Operation			
4.3	4.3.5, 6.8.4	9.1.1.2	1.1.3.6 (8.6)	7.2.4	7.3.3	7.5.11	8.5	5.3.2.3		3.1.2
(12)	(13)	(14)	(15)	(16)	(17)	(18)	(19)	(20)	(1)	(2)
LGBF		FL	2 (D/E)				S2 S20	33	1275	PROPIONALDEHYDE
LGBF		FL	2 (D/E)				S2 S20	33	1276	n-PROPYL ACETATE
L4BH		FL	2 (D/E)				S2 S20	338	1277	PROPYLAMINE
L1.5BN		FL	2 (D/E)				S2 S20	33	1278	1-CHLOROPROPANE
LGBF		FL	2 (D/E)				S2 S20	33	1279	1,2-DICHLOROPROPANE
L4BN		FL	1 (D/E)				S2 S20	33	1280	PROPYLENE OXIDE
LGBF		FL	2 (D/E)				S2 S20	33	1281	PROPYL FORMATES
LGBF		FL	2 (D/E)				S2 S20	33	1282	PYRIDINE
L4BN		FL	1 (D/E)				S2 S20	33	1286	ROSIN OIL
L1.5BN		FL	2 (D/E)				S2 S20	33	1286	ROSIN OIL (vapour pressure at 50 °C more than 110 kPa)
LGBF		FL	2 (D/E)				S2 S20	33	1286	ROSIN OIL (vapour pressure at 50 °C not more than 110 kPa)
LGBF		FL	3 (D/E)				S2	30	1286	ROSIN OIL
L4BN		FL	3 (D/E)				S2	33	1286	ROSIN OIL (having a flash-point below 23 °C and viscous according to 2.2.3.1.4) (boiling point not more than 35 °C)
L1.5BN		FL	3 (D/E)				S2	33	1286	ROSIN OIL (having a flash-point below 23 °C and viscous according to 2.2.3.1.4) (vapour pressure at 50 °C more than 110 kPa, boiling point of more than 35 °C)
LGBF		FL	3 (D/E)				S2	33	1286	ROSIN OIL (having a flash-point below 23 °C and viscous according to 2.2.3.1.4) (vapour pressure at 50 °C not more than 110 kPa)
L4BN		FL	1 (D/E)				S2 S20	33	1287	RUBBER SOLUTION
L1.5BN		FL	2 (D/E)				S2 S20	33	1287	RUBBER SOLUTION (vapour pressure at 50 °C more than 110 kPa)
LGBF		FL	2 (D/E)				S2 S20	33	1287	RUBBER SOLUTION (vapour pressure at 50 °C not more than 110 kPa)
LGBF		FL	3 (D/E)				S2	30	1287	RUBBER SOLUTION
L4BN		FL	3 (D/E)				S2	33	1287	RUBBER SOLUTION (having a flash-point below 23 °C and viscous according to 2.2.3.1.4) (boiling point not more than 35 °C)
L1.5BN		FL	3 (D/E)				S2	33	1287	RUBBER SOLUTION (having a flash-point below 23 °C and viscous according to 2.2.3.1.4) (vapour pressure at 50 °C more than 110 kPa, boiling point of more than 35 °C)

UN No.	Name and description	Class	Classification code	Packing group	Labels	Special provisions	Limited quantities	Excepted quantities	Packing instructions	Special packing provisions	Mixed packing provisions	Instructions	Special provisions
	3.1.2	2.2	2.2	2.1.1.3	5.2.2	3.3	3.4.6	3.5.1.2	4.1.4	4.1.4	4.1.10	4.2.5.2 7.3.2	4.2.5.3
(1)	(2)	(3a)	(3b)	(4)	(5)	(6)	(7a)	(7b)	(8)	(9a)	(9b)	(10)	(11)
1287	RUBBER SOLUTION (having a flash-point below 23 °C and viscous according to 2.2.3.1.4) (vapour pressure at 50 °C not more than 110 kPa)	3	F1	III	3	640H	LQ7	E1	P001 IBC02 LP01 R001		MP19	T2	TP1
1288	SHALE OIL	3	F1	II	3		LQ4	E2	P001 IBC02 R001		MP19	T4	TP1 TP8
1288	SHALE OIL	3	F1	III	3		LQ7	E1	P001 IBC03 LP01 R001		MP19	T2	TP1
1289	SODIUM METHYLATE SOLUTION in alcohol	3	FC	II	3 +8		LQ4	E2	P001 IBC02		MP19	T7	TP1 TP8
1289	SODIUM METHYLATE SOLUTION in alcohol	3	FC	III	3 +8		LQ7	E1	P001 IBC02 R001		MP19	T4	TP1
1292	TETRAETHYL SILICATE	3	F1	III	3		LQ7	E1	P001 IBC03 LP01 R001		MP19	T2	TP1
1293	TINCTURES, MEDICINAL	3	F1	II	3	601	LQ4	E2	P001 IBC02 R001		MP19	T4	TP1 TP8
1293	TINCTURES, MEDICINAL	3	F1	III	3	601	LQ7	E1	P001 IBC03 LP01 R001		MP19	T2	TP1
1294	TOLUENE	3	F1	II	3		LQ4	E2	P001 IBC02 R001		MP19	T4	TP1
1295	TRICHLOROSILANE	4.3	WFC	I	4.3 +3 +8		LQ0	E0	P401	RR7	MP2	T14	TP2 TP7
1296	TRIETHYLAMINE	3	FC	II	3 +8		LQ4	E2	P001 IBC02		MP19	T7	TP1
1297	TRIMETHYLAMINE, AQUEOUS SOLUTION, not more than 50% trimethylamine, by mass	3	FC	I	3 +8		LQ3	E0	P001		MP7 MP17	T11	TP1
1297	TRIMETHYLAMINE, AQUEOUS SOLUTION, not more than 50% trimethylamine, by mass	3	FC	II	3 +8		LQ4	E2	P001 IBC02		MP19	T7	TP1
1297	TRIMETHYLAMINE, AQUEOUS SOLUTION, not more than 50% trimethylamine, by mass	3	FC	III	3 +8		LQ7	E1	P001 IBC03 R001		MP19	T7	TP1
1298	TRIMETHYLCHLORO-SILANE	3	FC	II	3 +8		LQ4	E2	P010		MP19	T10	TP2 TP7
1299	TURPENTINE	3	F1	III	3		LQ7	E1	P001 IBC03 LP01 R001		MP19	T2	TP1
1300	TURPENTINE SUBSTITUTE	3	F1	II	3		LQ4	E2	P001 IBC02 R001		MP19	T4	TP1
1300	TURPENTINE SUBSTITUTE	3	F1	III	3		LQ7	E1	P001 IBC03 LP01 R001		MP19	T2	TP1
1301	VINYL ACETATE, STABILIZED	3	F1	II	3		LQ4	E2	P001 IBC02 R001		MP19	T4	TP1
1302	VINYL ETHYL ETHER, STABILIZED	3	F1	I	3		LQ3	E3	P001		MP7 MP17	T11	TP2
1303	VINYLIDENE CHLORIDE, STABILIZED	3	F1	I	3		LQ3	E3	P001		MP7 MP17	T12	TP2 TP7
1304	VINYL ISOBUTYL ETHER, STABILIZED	3	F1	II	3		LQ4	E2	P001 IBC02 R001		MP19	T4	TP1

ADR tank		Vehicle for tank carriage	Transport category	Special provisions for carriage				Hazard identifi-cation No.	UN No.	Name and description
Tank code	Special provisions		(Tunnel restriction code)	Packages	Bulk	Loading, unloading and handling	Operation			
4.3	4.3.5, 6.8.4	9.1.1.2	1.1.3.6 (8.6)	7.2.4	7.3.3	7.5.11	8.5	5.3.2.3		3.1.2
(12)	(13)	(14)	(15)	(16)	(17)	(18)	(19)	(20)	(1)	(2)
LGBF		FL	3 (D/E)				S2	33	1287	RUBBER SOLUTION (having a flash-point below 23 °C and viscous according to 2.2.3.1.4) (vapour pressure at 50 °C not more than 110 kPa)
LGBF		FL	2 (D/E)				S2 S20	33	1288	SHALE OIL
LGBF		FL	3 (D/E)				S2	30	1288	SHALE OIL
L4BH		FL	2 (D/E)				S2 S20	338	1289	SODIUM METHYLATE SOLUTION in alcohol
L4BN		FL	3 (D/E)				S2	38	1289	SODIUM METHYLATE SOLUTION in alcohol
LGBF		FL	3 (D/E)				S2	30	1292	TETRAETHYL SILICATE
LGBF		FL	2 (D/E)				S2 S20	33	1293	TINCTURES, MEDICINAL
LGBF		FL	3 (D/E)				S2	30	1293	TINCTURES, MEDICINAL
LGBF		FL	2 (D/E)				S2 S20	33	1294	TOLUENE
L10DH	TU14 TU25 TE21 TM2 TM3	FL	0 (B/E)	V1		CV23	S2 S20	X338	1295	TRICHLOROSILANE
L4BH		FL	2 (D/E)				S2 S20	338	1296	TRIETHYLAMINE
L10CH	TU14 TE21	FL	1 (C/E)				S2 S20	338	1297	TRIMETHYLAMINE, AQUEOUS SOLUTION, not more than 50% trimethylamine, by mass
L4BH		FL	2 (D/E)				S2 S20	338	1297	TRIMETHYLAMINE, AQUEOUS SOLUTION, not more than 50% trimethylamine, by mass
L4BN		FL	3 (D/E)				S2	38	1297	TRIMETHYLAMINE, AQUEOUS SOLUTION, not more than 50% trimethylamine, by mass
L4BH		FL	2 (D/E)				S2 S20	X338	1298	TRIMETHYLCHLORO-SILANE
LGBF		FL	3 (D/E)				S2	30	1299	TURPENTINE
LGBF		FL	2 (D/E)				S2 S20	33	1300	TURPENTINE SUBSTITUTE
LGBF		FL	3 (D/E)				S2	30	1300	TURPENTINE SUBSTITUTE
LGBF		FL	2 (D/E)				S2 S20	339	1301	VINYL ACETATE, STABILIZED
L4BN		FL	1 (D/E)				S2 S20	339	1302	VINYL ETHYL ETHER, STABILIZED
L4BN		FL	1 (D/E)				S2 S20	339	1303	VINYLIDENE CHLORIDE, STABILIZED
LGBF		FL	2 (D/E)				S2 S20	339	1304	VINYL ISOBUTYL ETHER, STABILIZED

UN No.	Name and description	Class	Classification code	Packing group	Labels	Special provisions	Limited and excepted quantities		Packaging			Portable tanks and bulk containers	
							quantities		Packing instructions	Special packing provisions	Mixed packing provisions	Instructions	Special provisions
	3.1.2	2.2	2.2	2.1.1.3	5.2.2	3.3	3.4.6	3.5.1.2	4.1.4	4.1.4	4.1.10	4.2.5.2 7.3.2	4.2.5.3
(1)	(2)	(3a)	(3b)	(4)	(5)	(6)	(7a)	(7b)	(8)	(9a)	(9b)	(10)	(11)
1305	VINYLTRICHLOROSILANE	3	FC	II	3 +8		LQ4	E2	P010		MP19	T10	TP2 TP7
1306	WOOD PRESERVATIVES, LIQUID (vapour pressure at 50 °C more than 110 kPa)	3	F1	II	3	640C	LQ6	E2	P001		MP19	T4	TP1 TP8
1306	WOOD PRESERVATIVES, LIQUID (vapour pressure at 50 °C not more than 110 kPa)	3	F1	II	3	640D	LQ6	E2	P001 IBC02 R001		MP19	T4	TP1 TP8
1306	WOOD PRESERVATIVES, LIQUID	3	F1	III	3	640E	LQ7	E1	P001 IBC03 LP01 R001		MP19	T2	TP1
1306	WOOD PRESERVATIVES, LIQUID (having a flash-point below 23 °C and viscous according to 2.2.3.1.4) (boiling point not more than 35 °C)	3	F1	III	3	640F	LQ7	E1	P001 LP01 R001		MP19	T2	TP1
1306	WOOD PRESERVATIVES, LIQUID (having a flash-point below 23 °C and viscous according to 2.2.3.1.4) (vapour pressure at 50 °C more than 110 kPa, boiling point of more than 35 °C)	3	F1	III	3	640G	LQ7	E1	P001 LP01 R001		MP19	T2	TP1
1306	WOOD PRESERVATIVES, LIQUID (having a flash-point below 23 °C and viscous according to 2.2.3.1.4) (vapour pressure at 50 °C not more than 110 kPa)	3	F1	III	3	640H	LQ7	E1	P001 IBC02 LP01 R001		MP19	T2	TP1
1307	XYLENES	3	F1	II	3		LQ4	E2	P001 IBC02 R001		MP19	T4	TP1
1307	XYLENES	3	F1	III	3		LQ7	E1	P001 IBC03 LP01 R001		MP19	T2	TP1
1308	ZIRCONIUM SUSPENDED IN A FLAMMABLE LIQUID	3	F1	I	3		LQ3	E3	P001	PP33	MP7 MP17		
1308	ZIRCONIUM SUSPENDED IN A FLAMMABLE LIQUID (vapour pressure at 50 °C more than 110 kPa)	3	F1	II	3	640C	LQ4	E2	P001 R001	PP33	MP19		
1308	ZIRCONIUM SUSPENDED IN A FLAMMABLE LIQUID (vapour pressure at 50 °C not more than 110 kPa)	3	F1	II	3	640D	LQ4	E2	P001 R001	PP33	MP19		
1308	ZIRCONIUM SUSPENDED IN A FLAMMABLE LIQUID	3	F1	III	3		LQ7	E1	P001 R001		MP19		
1309	ALUMINIUM POWDER, COATED	4.1	F3	II	4.1		LQ8	E2	P002 IBC08	PP38 B4	MP11	T3	TP33
1309	ALUMINIUM POWDER, COATED	4.1	F3	III	4.1		LQ9	E1	P002 IBC08 LP02 R001	PP11 B3	MP11	T1	TP33
1310	AMMONIUM PICRATE, WETTED with not less than 10% water, by mass	4.1	D	I	4.1		LQ0	E0	P406	PP26	MP2		
1312	BORNEOL	4.1	F1	III	4.1		LQ9	E1	P002 IBC08 LP02 R001	B3	MP10	T1	TP33
1313	CALCIUM RESINATE	4.1	F3	III	4.1		LQ9	E1	P002 IBC06 R001		MP11	T1	TP33
1314	CALCIUM RESINATE, FUSED	4.1	F3	III	4.1		LQ9	E1	P002 IBC04 R001		MP11	T1	TP33

ADR tank		Vehicle for tank carriage	Transport category (Tunnel restriction code)	Special provisions for carriage				Hazard identifi-cation No.	UN No.	Name and description
Tank code	Special provisions			Packages	Bulk	Loading, unloading and handling	Operation			
4.3	4.3.5, 6.8.4	9.1.1.2	1.1.3.6 (8.6)	7.2.4	7.3.3	7.5.11	8.5	5.3.2.3		3.1.2
(12)	(13)	(14)	(15)	(16)	(17)	(18)	(19)	(20)	(1)	(2)
L4BH		FL	2 (D/E)				S2 S20	X338	1305	VINYLTRICHLOROSILANE
L1.5BN		FL	2 (D/E)				S2 S20	33	1306	WOOD PRESERVATIVES, LIQUID (vapour pressure at 50 °C more than 110 kPa)
LGBF		FL	2 (D/E)				S2 S20	33	1306	WOOD PRESERVATIVES, LIQUID (vapour pressure at 50 °C not more than 110 kPa)
LGBF		FL	3 (D/E)				S2	30	1306	WOOD PRESERVATIVES, LIQUID
L4BN		FL	3 (D/E)				S2	33	1306	WOOD PRESERVATIVES, LIQUID (having a flash-point below 23 °C and viscous according to 2.2.3.1.4) (boiling point not more than 35 °C)
L1.5BN		FL	3 (D/E)				S2	33	1306	WOOD PRESERVATIVES, LIQUID (having a flash-point below 23 °C and viscous according to 2.2.3.1.4) (vapour pressure at 50 °C more than 110 kPa, boiling point of more than 35 °C)
LGBF		FL	3 (D/E)				S2	33	1306	WOOD PRESERVATIVES, LIQUID (having a flash-point below 23 °C and viscous according to 2.2.3.1.4) (vapour pressure at 50 °C not more than 110 kPa)
LGBF		FL	2 (D/E)				S2 S20	33	1307	XYLENES
LGBF		FL	3 (D/E)				S2	30	1307	XYLENES
L4BN		FL	1 (D/E)				S2 S20	33	1308	ZIRCONIUM SUSPENDED IN A FLAMMABLE LIQUID
L1.5BN		FL	2 (D/E)				S2 S20	33	1308	ZIRCONIUM SUSPENDED IN A FLAMMABLE LIQUID (vapour pressure at 50 °C more than 110 kPa)
LGBF		FL	2 (D/E)				S2 S20	33	1308	ZIRCONIUM SUSPENDED IN A FLAMMABLE LIQUID (vapour pressure at 50 °C not more than 110 kPa)
LGBF		FL	3 (D/E)				S2	30	1308	ZIRCONIUM SUSPENDED IN A FLAMMABLE LIQUID
SGAN		AT	2 (E)	V11				40	1309	ALUMINIUM POWDER, COATED
SGAV		AT	3 (E)		VV1			40	1309	ALUMINIUM POWDER, COATED
			1 (B)				S14		1310	AMMONIUM PICRATE, WETTED with not less than 10% water, by mass
SGAV		AT	3 (E)		VV1			40	1312	BORNEOL
SGAV		AT	3 (E)	V12	VV1			40	1313	CALCIUM RESINATE
SGAV		AT	3 (E)		VV1			40	1314	CALCIUM RESINATE, FUSED

UN No.	Name and description	Class	Classifi-cation code	Packing group	Labels	Special provi-sions	Limited and excepted quantities		Packaging			Portable tanks and bulk containers	
									Packing instruc-tions	Special packing provisions	Mixed packing provisions	Instruc-tions	Special provisions
	3.1.2	2.2	2.2	2.1.1.3	5.2.2	3.3	3.4.6	3.5.1.2	4.1.4	4.1.4	4.1.10	4.2.5.2 7.3.2	4.2.5.3
(1)	(2)	(3a)	(3b)	(4)	(5)	(6)	(7a)	(7b)	(8)	(9a)	(9b)	(10)	(11)
1318	COBALT RESINATE, PRECIPITATED	4.1	F3	III	4.1		LQ9	E1	P002 IBC06 R001		MP11	T1	TP33
1320	DINITROPHENOL, WETTED with not less than 15% water, by mass	4.1	DT	I	4.1 +6.1		LQ0	E0	P406	PP26	MP2		
1321	DINITROPHENOLATES, WETTED with not less than 15% water, by mass	4.1	DT	I	4.1 +6.1		LQ0	E0	P406	PP26	MP2		
1322	DINITRORESORCINOL, WETTED with not less than 15% water, by mass	4.1	D	I	4.1		LQ0	E0	P406	PP26	MP2		
1323	FERROCERIUM	4.1	F3	II	4.1	249	LQ8	E2	P002 IBC08	B4	MP11	T3	TP33
1324	FILMS, NITROCELLULOSE BASE, gelatin coated, except scrap	4.1	F1	III	4.1		LQ9	E1	P002 R001	PP15	MP11		
1325	FLAMMABLE SOLID, ORGANIC, N.O.S.	4.1	F1	II	4.1	274	LQ8	E2	P002 IBC08	B4	MP10	T3	TP33
1325	FLAMMABLE SOLID, ORGANIC, N.O.S.	4.1	F1	III	4.1	274	LQ9	E1	P002 IBC08 LP02 R001	B3	MP10	T1	TP33
1326	HAFNIUM POWDER, WETTED with not less than 25% water	4.1	F3	II	4.1	586	LQ8	E2	P410 IBC06	PP40	MP11	T3	TP33
1327	Hay, Straw or Bhusa	4.1	F1		NOT SUBJECT TO ADR								
1328	HEXAMETHYLENETE-TRAMINE	4.1	F1	III	4.1		LQ9	E1	P002 IBC08 R001	B3	MP10	T1	TP33
1330	MANGANESE RESINATE	4.1	F3	III	4.1		LQ9	E1	P002 IBC06 R001		MP11	T1	TP33
1331	MATCHES, 'STRIKE ANYWHERE'	4.1	F1	III	4.1	293	LQ9	E1	P407	PP27	MP12		
1332	METALDEHYDE	4.1	F1	III	4.1		LQ9	E1	P002 IBC08 LP02 R001	B3	MP10	T1	TP33
1333	CERIUM, slabs, ingots or rods	4.1	F3	II	4.1		LQ8	E2	P002 IBC08	B4	MP11		
1334	NAPHTHALENE, CRUDE or NAPHTHALENE, REFINED	4.1	F1	III	4.1	501	LQ9	E1	P002 IBC08 LP02 R001	B3	MP10	T1 BK1 BK2	TP33
1336	NITROGUANIDINE (PICRITE), WETTED with not less than 20% water, by mass	4.1	D	I	4.1		LQ0	E0	P406		MP2		
1337	NITROSTARCH, WETTED with not less than 20% water, by mass	4.1	D	I	4.1		LQ0	E0	P406		MP2		
1338	PHOSPHORUS, AMORPHOUS	4.1	F3	III	4.1		LQ9	E1	P410 IBC08 R001	B3	MP11	T1	TP33
1339	PHOSPHORUS HEPTASULPHIDE, free from yellow and white phosphorus	4.1	F3	II	4.1	602	LQ8	E2	P410 IBC04		MP11	T3	TP33
1340	PHOSPHORUS PENTASULPHIDE, free from yellow and white phosphorus	4.3	WF2	II	4.3 +4.1	602	LQ11	E2	P410 IBC04		MP14	T3	TP33
1341	PHOSPHORUS SESQUISULPHIDE, free from yellow and white phosphorus	4.1	F3	II	4.1	602	LQ8	E2	P410 IBC04		MP11	T3	TP33
1343	PHOSPHORUS TRISULPHIDE, free from yellow and white phosphorus	4.1	F3	II	4.1	602	LQ8	E2	P410 IBC04		MP11	T3	TP33

ADR tank		Vehicle for tank carriage	Transport category (Tunnel restriction code)	Special provisions for carriage				Hazard identifi-cation No.	UN No.	Name and description
Tank code	Special provisions			Packages	Bulk	Loading, unloading and handling	Operation			
4.3	4.3.5, 6.8.4	9.1.1.2	1.1.3.6 (8.6)	7.2.4	7.3.3	7.5.11	8.5	5.3.2.3		3.1.2
(12)	(13)	(14)	(15)	(16)	(17)	(18)	(19)	(20)	(1)	(2)
SGAV		AT	3 (E)	V12	VV1			40	1318	COBALT RESINATE, PRECIPITATED
			1 (B)			CV28	S14		1320	DINITROPHENOL, WETTED with not less than 15% water, by mass
			1 (B)			CV28	S14		1321	DINITROPHENOLATES, WETTED with not less than 15% water, by mass
			1 (B)				S14		1322	DINITRORESORCINOL, WETTED with not less than 15% water, by mass
SGAN		AT	2 (E)	V11				40	1323	FERROCERIUM
			3 (E)						1324	FILMS, NITROCELLULOSE BASE, gelatin coated, except scrap
SGAN		AT	2 (E)	V11				40	1325	FLAMMABLE SOLID, ORGANIC, N.O.S.
SGAV		AT	3 (E)		VV1			40	1325	FLAMMABLE SOLID, ORGANIC, N.O.S.
SGAN		AT	2 (E)	V11 V12				40	1326	HAFNIUM POWDER, WETTED with not less than 25% water
NOT SUBJECT TO ADR									1327	Hay, Straw or Bhusa
SGAV		AT	3 (E)		VV1			40	1328	HEXAMETHYLENETE-TRAMINE
SGAV		AT	3 (E)	V12	VV1			40	1330	MANGANESE RESINATE
			4 (E)						1331	MATCHES, 'STRIKE ANYWHERE'
SGAV		AT	3 (E)		VV1			40	1332	METALDEHYDE
			2 (E)	V11					1333	CERIUM, slabs, ingots or rods
SGAV		AT	3 (E)		VV2			40	1334	NAPHTHALENE, CRUDE or NAPHTHALENE, REFINED
			1 (B)				S14		1336	NITROGUANIDINE (PICRITE), WETTED with not less than 20% water, by mass
			1 (B)				S14		1337	NITROSTARCH, WETTED with not less than 20% water, by mass
SGAV		AT	3 (E)		VV1			40	1338	PHOSPHORUS, AMORPHOUS
SGAN		AT	2 (E)					40	1339	PHOSPHORUS HEPTASULPHIDE, free from yellow and white phosphorus
SGAN		AT	0 (D/E)	V1		CV23		423	1340	PHOSPHORUS PENTASULPHIDE, free from yellow and white phosphorus
SGAN		AT	2 (E)					40	1341	PHOSPHORUS SESQUISULPHIDE, free from yellow and white phosphorus
SGAN		AT	2 (E)					40	1343	PHOSPHORUS TRISULPHIDE, free from yellow and white phosphorus

UN No. 3.1.2	Name and description 3.1.2	Class 2.2	Classifi-cation code 2.2	Packing group 2.1.1.3	Labels 5.2.2	Special provi-sions 3.3	Limited and excepted quantities 3.4.6	3.5.1.2	Packing instruc-tions 4.1.4	Special packing provisions 4.1.4	Mixed packing provisions 4.1.10	Portable tanks and bulk containers Instruc-tions 4.2.5.2 7.3.2	Special provisions 4.2.5.3
(1)	(2)	(3a)	(3b)	(4)	(5)	(6)	(7a)	(7b)	(8)	(9a)	(9b)	(10)	(11)
1344	TRINITROPHENOL (PICRIC ACID), WETTED with not less than 30% water, by mass	4.1	D	I	4.1		LQ0	E0	P406	PP26	MP2		
1345	RUBBER SCRAP or RUBBER SHODDY, powdered or granulated	4.1	F1	II	4.1		LQ8	E2	P002 IBC08	B4	MP11	T3	TP33
1346	SILICON POWDER, AMORPHOUS	4.1	F3	III	4.1	32	LQ9	E1	P002 IBC08 LP02 R001	B3	MP11	T1	TP33
1347	SILVER PICRATE, WETTED with not less than 30% water, by mass	4.1	D	I	4.1		LQ0	E0	P406	PP25 PP26	MP2		
1348	SODIUM DINITRO-o-CRESOLATE, WETTED with not less than 15% water, by mass	4.1	DT	I	4.1 +6.1		LQ0	E0	P406	PP26	MP2		
1349	SODIUM PICRAMATE, WETTED with not less than 20% water, by mass	4.1	D	I	4.1		LQ0	E0	P406	PP26	MP2		
1350	SULPHUR	4.1	F3	III	4.1	242	LQ9	E1	P002 IBC08 LP02 R001	B3	MP11	T1 BK1 BK2	TP33
1352	TITANIUM POWDER, WETTED with not less than 25% water	4.1	F3	II	4.1	586	LQ8	E2	P410 IBC06	PP40	MP11	T3	TP33
1353	FIBRES or FABRICS IMPREGNATED WITH WEAKLY NITRATED NITROCELLULOSE, N.O.S.	4.1	F1	III	4.1	274 502	LQ9	E1	P410 IBC08 R001	B3	MP11		
1354	TRINITROBENZENE, WETTED with not less than 30% water, by mass	4.1	D	I	4.1		LQ0	E0	P406		MP2		
1355	TRINITROBENZOIC ACID, WETTED with not less than 30% water, by mass	4.1	D	I	4.1		LQ0	E0	P406		MP2		
1356	TRINITROTOLUENE (TNT), WETTED with not less than 30% water, by mass	4.1	D	I	4.1		LQ0	E0	P406		MP2		
1357	UREA NITRATE, WETTED with not less than 20% water, by mass	4.1	D	I	4.1	227	LQ0	E0	P406		MP2		
1358	ZIRCONIUM POWDER, WETTED with not less than 25% water	4.1	F3	II	4.1	586	LQ8	E2	P410 IBC06	PP40	MP11	T3	TP33
1360	CALCIUM PHOSPHIDE	4.3	WT2	I	4.3 +6.1		LQ0	E0	P403		MP2		
1361	CARBON, animal or vegetable origin	4.2	S2	II	4.2		LQ0	E2	P002 IBC06	PP12	MP14	T3	TP33
1361	CARBON, animal or vegetable origin	4.2	S2	III	4.2		LQ0	E1	P002 IBC08 LP02 R001	PP12 B3	MP14	T1	TP33
1362	CARBON, ACTIVATED	4.2	S2	III	4.2	646	LQ0	E1	P002 IBC08 LP02 R001	PP11 B3	MP14	T1	TP33
1363	COPRA	4.2	S2	III	4.2		LQ0	E1	P003 IBC08 LP02 R001	PP20 B3 B6	MP14		
1364	COTTON WASTE, OILY	4.2	S2	III	4.2		LQ0	E1	P003 IBC08 LP02 R001	PP19 B3 B6	MP14		
1365	COTTON, WET	4.2	S2	III	4.2		LQ0	E1	P003 IBC08 LP02 R001	PP19 B3 B6	MP14		

ADR tank		Vehicle for tank carriage	Transport category (Tunnel restriction code)	Special provisions for carriage				Hazard identifi-cation No.	UN No.	Name and description
Tank code	Special provisions			Packages	Bulk	Loading, unloading and handling	Operation			
4.3	4.3.5, 6.8.4	9.1.1.2	1.1.3.6 (8.6)	7.2.4	7.3.3	7.5.11	8.5	5.3.2.3		3.1.2
(12)	(13)	(14)	(15)	(16)	(17)	(18)	(19)	(20)	(1)	(2)
			1 (B)				S14		1344	TRINITROPHENOL (PICRIC ACID), WETTED with not less than 30% water, by mass
SGAN		AT	4 (E)	V11				40	1345	RUBBER SCRAP or RUBBER SHODDY, powdered or granulated
SGAV		AT	3 (E)		VV1			40	1346	SILICON POWDER, AMORPHOUS
			1 (B)				S14		1347	SILVER PICRATE, WETTED with not less than 30% water, by mass
			1 (B)			CV28	S14		1348	SODIUM DINITRO-o-CRESOLATE, WETTED with not less than 15% water, by mass
			1 (B)				S14		1349	SODIUM PICRAMATE, WETTED with not less than 20% water, by mass
SGAV		AT	3 (E)		VV1			40	1350	SULPHUR
SGAN		AT	2 (E)	V11 V12				40	1352	TITANIUM POWDER, WETTED with not less than 25% water
			3 (E)						1353	FIBRES or FABRICS IMPREGNATED WITH WEAKLY NITRATED NITROCELLULOSE, N.O.S.
			1 (B)				S14		1354	TRINITROBENZENE, WETTED with not less than 30% water, by mass
			1 (B)				S14		1355	TRINITROBENZOIC ACID, WETTED with not less than 30% water, by mass
			1 (B)				S14		1356	TRINITROTOLUENE (TNT), WETTED with not less than 30% water, by mass
			1 (B)				S14		1357	UREA NITRATE, WETTED with not less than 20% water, by mass
SGAN		AT	2 (E)	V11 V12				40	1358	ZIRCONIUM POWDER, WETTED with not less than 25% water
			1 (E)	V1		CV23 CV28	S20		1360	CALCIUM PHOSPHIDE
SGAN	TU11	AT	2 (D/E)	V1 V12 V13				40	1361	CARBON, animal or vegetable origin
SGAV		AT	4 (E)	V1 V13	VV4			40	1361	CARBON, animal or vegetable origin
SGAV		AT	4 (E)	V1	VV4			40	1362	CARBON, ACTIVATED
			3 (E)	V1	VV4			40	1363	COPRA
			3 (E)	V1	VV4			40	1364	COTTON WASTE, OILY
			3 (E)	V1	VV4			40	1365	COTTON, WET

UN No.	Name and description	Class	Classification code	Packing group	Labels	Special provisions	Limited and excepted quantities		Packaging			Portable tanks and bulk containers	
							quantities		Packing instructions	Special packing provisions	Mixed packing provisions	Instructions	Special provisions
	3.1.2	2.2	2.2	2.1.1.3	5.2.2	3.3	3.4.6	3.5.1.2	4.1.4	4.1.4	4.1.10	4.2.5.2 7.3.2	4.2.5.3
(1)	(2)	(3a)	(3b)	(4)	(5)	(6)	(7a)	(7b)	(8)	(9a)	(9b)	(10)	(11)
1369	p-NITROSODIMETHYL-ANILINE	4.2	S2	II	4.2		LQ0	E2	P410 IBC06		MP14	T3	TP33
1372	Fibres, animal or fibres, vegetable burnt, wet or damp	4.2	S2	NOT SUBJECT TO ADR									
1373	FIBRES or FABRICS, ANIMAL or VEGETABLE or SYNTHETIC, N.O.S. with oil	4.2	S2	III	4.2	274	LQ0	E1	P410 IBC08 R001	B3	MP14	T1	TP33
1374	FISH MEAL (FISH SCRAP), UNSTABILIZED	4.2	S2	II	4.2	300	LQ0	E2	P410 IBC08	B4	MP14	T3	TP33
1376	IRON OXIDE, SPENT or IRON SPONGE, SPENT obtained from coal gas purification	4.2	S4	III	4.2	592	LQ0	E1	P002 IBC08 LP02 R001	B3	MP14	T1 BK2	TP33
1378	METAL CATALYST, WETTED with a visible excess of liquid	4.2	S4	II	4.2	274	LQ0	E2	P410 IBC01	PP39	MP14	T3	TP33
1379	PAPER, UNSATURATED OIL TREATED, incompletely dried (including carbon paper)	4.2	S2	III	4.2		LQ0	E1	P410 IBC08 R001	B3	MP14		
1380	PENTABORANE	4.2	ST3	I	4.2 +6.1		LQ0	E0	P601		MP2		
1381	PHOSPHORUS, WHITE or YELLOW, UNDER WATER or IN SOLUTION	4.2	ST3	I	4.2 +6.1	503	LQ0	E0	P405		MP2	T9	TP3 TP31
1381	PHOSPHORUS, WHITE or YELLOW, DRY	4.2	ST4	I	4.2 +6.1	503	LQ0	E0	P405		MP2	T9	TP3 TP31
1382	POTASSIUM SULPHIDE, ANHYDROUS or POTASSIUM SULPHIDE with less than 30% water of crystallization	4.2	S4	II	4.2	504	LQ0	E2	P410 IBC06		MP14	T3	TP33
1383	PYROPHORIC METAL, N.O.S. or PYROPHORIC ALLOY, N.O.S.	4.2	S4	I	4.2	274	LQ0	E0	P404		MP13	T21	TP7 TP33
1384	SODIUM DITHIONITE (SODIUM HYDROSULPHITE)	4.2	S4	II	4.2		LQ0	E2	P410 IBC06		MP14	T3	TP33
1385	SODIUM SULPHIDE, ANHYDROUS or SODIUM SULPHIDE with less than 30% water of crystallization	4.2	S4	II	4.2	504	LQ0	E2	P410 IBC06		MP14	T3	TP33
1386	SEED CAKE with more than 1.5% oil and not more than 11% moisture	4.2	S2	III	4.2		LQ0	E1	P003 IBC08 LP02 R001	PP20 B3 B6	MP14		
1387	Wool waste, wet	4.2	S2	NOT SUBJECT TO ADR									
1389	ALKALI METAL AMALGAM, LIQUID	4.3	W1	I	4.3	182 274	LQ0	E0	P402	RR8	MP2		
1390	ALKALI METAL AMIDES	4.3	W2	II	4.3	182 274 505	LQ11	E2	P410 IBC07		MP14	T3	TP33
1391	ALKALI METAL DISPERSION or ALKALINE EARTH METAL DISPERSION having a flash-point above 60 °C	4.3	W1	I	4.3	182 183 274 506	LQ0	E0	P402	RR8	MP2		
1391	ALKALI METAL DISPERSION or ALKALINE EARTH METAL DISPERSION having a flash-point of not more than 60 °C	4.3	WF1	I	4.3 +3	182 183 274 506	LQ0	E0	P402	RR8	MP2		
1392	ALKALINE EARTH METAL AMALGAM, LIQUID	4.3	W1	I	4.3	183 274 506	LQ0	E0	P402		MP2		
1393	ALKALINE EARTH METAL ALLOY, N.O.S.	4.3	W2	II	4.3	183 274 506	LQ11	E2	P410 IBC07		MP14	T3	TP33
1394	ALUMINIUM CARBIDE	4.3	W2	II	4.3		LQ11	E2	P410 IBC07		MP14	T3	TP33

ADR tank		Vehicle for tank carriage	Transport category (Tunnel restriction code)	Special provisions for carriage				Hazard identification No.	UN No.	Name and description
Tank code	Special provisions			Packages	Bulk	Loading, unloading and handling	Operation			
4.3	4.3.5, 6.8.4	9.1.1.2	1.1.3.6 (8.6)	7.2.4	7.3.3	7.5.11	8.5	5.3.2.3		3.1.2
(12)	(13)	(14)	(15)	(16)	(17)	(18)	(19)	(20)	(1)	(2)
SGAN		AT	2 (D/E)	V1 V12				40	1369	p-NITROSODIMETHYL-ANILINE
NOT SUBJECT TO ADR									1372	Fibres, animal or fibres, vegetable burnt, wet or damp
			3 (E)	V1	VV4			40	1373	FIBRES or FABRICS, ANIMAL or VEGETABLE or SYNTHETIC, N.O.S. with oil
		AT	2 (D/E)	V1				40	1374	FISH MEAL (FISH SCRAP), UNSTABILIZED
SGAV		AT	3 (E)	V1	VV4			40	1376	IRON OXIDE, SPENT or IRON SPONGE, SPENT obtained from coal gas purification
SGAN		AT	2 (D/E)	V1				40	1378	METAL CATALYST, WETTED with a visible excess of liquid
			3 (E)	V1	VV4			40	1379	PAPER, UNSATURATED OIL TREATED, incompletely dried (including carbon paper)
L21DH	TU14 TC1 TE21 TM1	AT	0 (B/E)	V1		CV28	S20	333	1380	PENTABORANE
L10DH(+)	TU14 TU16 TU21 TE3 TE21	AT	0 (B/E)	V1		CV28	S20	46	1381	PHOSPHORUS, WHITE or YELLOW, UNDER WATER or IN SOLUTION
L10DH(+)	TU14 TU16 TU21 TE3 TE21	AT	0 (B/E)	V1		CV28	S20	46	1381	PHOSPHORUS, WHITE or YELLOW, DRY
SGAN		AT	2 (D/E)	V1 V12				40	1382	POTASSIUM SULPHIDE, ANHYDROUS or POTASSIUM SULPHIDE with less than 30% water of crystallization
		AT	0 (B/E)	V1			S20	43	1383	PYROPHORIC METAL, N.O.S. or PYROPHORIC ALLOY, N.O.S.
SGAN		AT	2 (D/E)	V1 V12				40	1384	SODIUM DITHIONITE (SODIUM HYDROSULPHITE)
SGAN		AT	2 (D/E)	V1 V12				40	1385	SODIUM SULPHIDE, ANHYDROUS or SODIUM SULPHIDE with less than 30% water of crystallization
			3 (E)	V1	VV4			40	1386	SEED CAKE with more than 1.5% oil and not more than 11% moisture
NOT SUBJECT TO ADR									1387	Wool waste, wet
L10BN(+)	TU1 TE5 TT3 TM2	AT	1 (B/E)	V1		CV23	S20	X323	1389	ALKALI METAL AMALGAM, LIQUID
SGAN		AT	0 (D/E)	V1 V12		CV23		423	1390	ALKALI METAL AMIDES
L10BN(+)	TU1 TE5 TT3 TM2	AT	1 (B/E)	V1		CV23	S20	X323	1391	ALKALI METAL DISPERSION or ALKALINE EARTH METAL DISPERSION having a flash-point above 60 °C
L10BN(+)	TU1 TE5 TT3 TM2	FL	1 (B/E)	V1		CV23	S2 S20	X323	1391	ALKALI METAL DISPERSION or ALKALINE EARTH METAL DISPERSION having a flash-point of not more than 60 °C
L10BN(+)	TU1 TE5 TT3 TM2	AT	1 (B/E)	V1		CV23	S20	X323	1392	ALKALINE EARTH METAL AMALGAM, LIQUID
SGAN		AT	2 (D/E)	V1 V12		CV23		423	1393	ALKALINE EARTH METAL ALLOY, N.O.S.
SGAN		AT	2 (D/E)	V1 V12	VV5	CV23		423	1394	ALUMINIUM CARBIDE

UN No.	Name and description	Class	Classifi-cation code	Packing group	Labels	Special provi-sions	Limited and excepted quantities		Packaging			Portable tanks and bulk containers	
									Packing instruc-tions	Special packing provisions	Mixed packing provisions	Instruc-tions	Special provisions
	3.1.2	2.2	2.2	2.1.1.3	5.2.2	3.3	3.4.6	3.5.1.2	4.1.4	4.1.4	4.1.10	4.2.5.2 7.3.2	4.2.5.3
(1)	(2)	(3a)	(3b)	(4)	(5)	(6)	(7a)	(7b)	(8)	(9a)	(9b)	(10)	(11)
1395	ALUMINIUM FERROSILICON POWDER	4.3	WT2	II	4.3 +6.1		LQ11	E2	P410 IBC05	PP40	MP14	T3	TP33
1396	ALUMINIUM POWDER, UNCOATED	4.3	W2	II	4.3		LQ12	E2	P410 IBC07	PP40	MP14	T3	TP33
1396	ALUMINIUM POWDER, UNCOATED	4.3	W2	III	4.3		LQ12	E1	P410 IBC08 R001	B4	MP14	T1	TP33
1397	ALUMINIUM PHOSPHIDE	4.3	WT2	I	4.3 +6.1	507	LQ0	E0	P403		MP2		
1398	ALUMINIUM SILICON POWDER, UNCOATED	4.3	W2	III	4.3	37	LQ12	E1	P410 IBC08 R001	B4	MP14	T1	TP33
1400	BARIUM	4.3	W2	II	4.3		LQ11	E2	P410 IBC07		MP14	T3	TP33
1401	CALCIUM	4.3	W2	II	4.3		LQ11	E2	P410 IBC07		MP14	T3	TP33
1402	CALCIUM CARBIDE	4.3	W2	I	4.3		LQ0	E0	P403 IBC04		MP2	T9	TP7 TP33
1402	CALCIUM CARBIDE	4.3	W2	II	4.3		LQ11	E2	P410 IBC07		MP14	T3	TP33
1403	CALCIUM CYANAMIDE with more than 0.1% calcium carbide	4.3	W2	III	4.3	38	LQ12	E1	P410 IBC08 R001	B4	MP14	T1	TP33
1404	CALCIUM HYDRIDE	4.3	W2	I	4.3		LQ0	E0	P403		MP2		
1405	CALCIUM SILICIDE	4.3	W2	II	4.3		LQ11	E2	P410 IBC07		MP14	T3	TP33
1405	CALCIUM SILICIDE	4.3	W2	III	4.3		LQ12	E1	P410 IBC08 R001	B4	MP14	T1	TP33
1407	CAESIUM	4.3	W2	I	4.3		LQ0	E0	P403 IBC04		MP2		
1408	FERROSILICON with 30% or more but less than 90% silicon	4.3	WT2	III	4.3 +6.1	39	LQ12	E1	P003 IBC08 R001	PP20 B4 B6	MP14	T1 BK2	TP33
1409	METAL HYDRIDES, WATER-REACTIVE, N.O.S.	4.3	W2	I	4.3	274 508	LQ0	E0	P403		MP2		
1409	METAL HYDRIDES, WATER-REACTIVE, N.O.S.	4.3	W2	II	4.3	274 508	LQ11	E2	P410 IBC04		MP14	T3	TP33
1410	LITHIUM ALUMINIUM HYDRIDE	4.3	W2	I	4.3		LQ0	E0	P403		MP2		
1411	LITHIUM ALUMINIUM HYDRIDE, ETHEREAL	4.3	WF1	I	4.3 +3		LQ0	E0	P402	RR8	MP2		
1413	LITHIUM BOROHYDRIDE	4.3	W2	I	4.3		LQ0	E0	P403		MP2		
1414	LITHIUM HYDRIDE	4.3	W2	I	4.3		LQ0	E0	P403		MP2		
1415	LITHIUM	4.3	W2	I	4.3		LQ0	E0	P403 IBC04		MP2		
1417	LITHIUM SILICON	4.3	W2	II	4.3		LQ11	E2	P410 IBC07		MP14	T3	TP33
1418	MAGNESIUM POWDER or MAGNESIUM ALLOYS POWDER	4.3	WS	I	4.3 +4.2		LQ0	E0	P403		MP2		
1418	MAGNESIUM POWDER or MAGNESIUM ALLOYS POWDER	4.3	WS	II	4.3 +4.2		LQ11	E2	P410 IBC05		MP14	T3	TP33
1418	MAGNESIUM POWDER or MAGNESIUM ALLOYS POWDER	4.3	WS	III	4.3 +4.2		LQ12	E1	P410 IBC08 R001	B4	MP14	T1	TP33
1419	MAGNESIUM ALUMINIUM PHOSPHIDE	4.3	WT2	I	4.3 +6.1		LQ0	E0	P403		MP2		
1420	POTASSIUM METAL ALLOYS, LIQUID	4.3	W1	I	4.3		LQ0	E0	P402		MP2		
1421	ALKALI METAL ALLOY, LIQUID, N.O.S.	4.3	W1	I	4.3	182 274	LQ0	E0	P402	RR8	MP2		
1422	POTASSIUM SODIUM ALLOYS, LIQUID	4.3	W1	I	4.3		LQ0	E0	P402		MP2	T9	TP3 TP7 TP31

ADR tank		Vehicle for tank carriage	Transport category (Tunnel restriction code)	Special provisions for carriage				Hazard identifi-cation No.	UN No.	Name and description
Tank code	Special provisions			Packages	Bulk	Loading, unloading and handling	Operation			
4.3	4.3.5, 6.8.4	9.1.1.2	1.1.3.6 (8.6)	7.2.4	7.3.3	7.5.11	8.5	5.3.2.3		3.1.2
(12)	(13)	(14)	(15)	(16)	(17)	(18)	(19)	(20)	(1)	(2)
SGAN		AT	2 (D/E)	V1		CV23 CV28		462	1395	ALUMINIUM FERROSILICON POWDER
SGAN		AT	2 (D/E)	V1 V12		CV23		423	1396	ALUMINIUM POWDER, UNCOATED
SGAN		AT	3 (E)	V1	VV5	CV23		423	1396	ALUMINIUM POWDER, UNCOATED
			1 (E)	V1		CV23 CV28	S20		1397	ALUMINIUM PHOSPHIDE
SGAN		AT	3 (E)	V1	VV5	CV23		423	1398	ALUMINIUM SILICON POWDER, UNCOATED
SGAN		AT	2 (D/E)	V1 V12		CV23		423	1400	BARIUM
SGAN		AT	2 (D/E)	V1 V12		CV23		423	1401	CALCIUM
		AT	1 (B/E)	V1		CV23	S20	X423	1402	CALCIUM CARBIDE
SGAN		AT	2 (D/E)	V1 V12	VV5	CV23		423	1402	CALCIUM CARBIDE
SGAN		AT	0 (E)	V1		CV23		423	1403	CALCIUM CYANAMIDE with more than 0.1% calcium carbide
			1 (E)	V1		CV23	S20		1404	CALCIUM HYDRIDE
SGAN		AT	2 (D/E)	V1 V12	VV7	CV23		423	1405	CALCIUM SILICIDE
SGAN		AT	3 (E)	V1	VV5 VV7	CV23		423	1405	CALCIUM SILICIDE
L10CH(+)	TU2 TU14 TE5 TE21 TT3 TM2	AT	1 (B/E)	V1		CV23	S20	X423	1407	CAESIUM
SGAN		AT	3 (E)	V1	VV1	CV23 CV28		462	1408	FERROSILICON with 30% or more but less than 90% silicon
			1 (E)	V1		CV23	S20		1409	METAL HYDRIDES, WATER-REACTIVE, N.O.S.
SGAN		AT	2 (D/E)	V1		CV23		423	1409	METAL HYDRIDES, WATER-REACTIVE, N.O.S.
			1 (E)	V1		CV23	S20		1410	LITHIUM ALUMINIUM HYDRIDE
			1 (E)	V1		CV23	S2 S20		1411	LITHIUM ALUMINIUM HYDRIDE, ETHEREAL
			1 (E)	V1		CV23	S20		1413	LITHIUM BOROHYDRIDE
			1 (E)	V1		CV23	S20		1414	LITHIUM HYDRIDE
L10BN(+)	TU1 TE5 TT3 TM2	AT	1 (B/E)	V1		CV23	S20	X423	1415	LITHIUM
SGAN		AT	2 (D/E)	V1 V12		CV23		423	1417	LITHIUM SILICON
			1 (E)	V1		CV23	S20		1418	MAGNESIUM POWDER or MAGNESIUM ALLOYS POWDER
SGAN		AT	2 (D/E)	V1		CV23		423	1418	MAGNESIUM POWDER or MAGNESIUM ALLOYS POWDER
SGAN		AT	3 (E)	V1	VV5	CV23		423	1418	MAGNESIUM POWDER or MAGNESIUM ALLOYS POWDER
			1 (E)	V1		CV23 CV28	S20		1419	MAGNESIUM ALUMINIUM PHOSPHIDE
L10BN(+)	TU1 TE5 TT3 TM2	AT	1 (B/E)	V1		CV23	S20	X323	1420	POTASSIUM METAL ALLOYS, LIQUID
L10BN(+)	TU1 TE5 TT3 TM2	AT	1 (B/E)	V1		CV23	S20	X323	1421	ALKALI METAL ALLOY, LIQUID, N.O.S.
L10BN(+)	TU1 TE5 TT3 TM2	AT	1 (B/E)	V1		CV23	S20	X323	1422	POTASSIUM SODIUM ALLOYS, LIQUID

UN No.	Name and description	Class	Classifi-cation code	Packing group	Labels	Special provisions	Limited and excepted quantities		Packaging			Portable tanks and bulk containers	
									Packing instruc-tions	Special packing provisions	Mixed packing provisions	Instruc-tions	Special provisions
	3.1.2	2.2	2.2	2.1.1.3	5.2.2	3.3	3.4.6	3.5.1.2	4.1.4	4.1.4	4.1.10	4.2.5.2 7.3.2	4.2.5.3
(1)	(2)	(3a)	(3b)	(4)	(5)	(6)	(7a)	(7b)	(8)	(9a)	(9b)	(10)	(11)
1423	RUBIDIUM	4.3	W2	I	4.3		LQ0	E0	P403 IBC04		MP2		
1426	SODIUM BOROHYDRIDE	4.3	W2	I	4.3		LQ0	E0	P403		MP2		
1427	SODIUM HYDRIDE	4.3	W2	I	4.3		LQ0	E0	P403		MP2		
1428	SODIUM	4.3	W2	I	4.3		LQ0	E0	P403 IBC04		MP2	T9	TP7 TP33
1431	SODIUM METHYLATE	4.2	SC4	II	4.2 +8		LQ0	E2	P410 IBC05		MP14	T3	TP33
1432	SODIUM PHOSPHIDE	4.3	WT2	I	4.3 +6.1		LQ0	E0	P403		MP2		
1433	STANNIC PHOSPHIDES	4.3	WT2	I	4.3 +6.1		LQ0	E0	P403		MP2		
1435	ZINC ASHES	4.3	W2	III	4.3		LQ12	E1	P002 IBC08 R001	B4	MP14	T1	TP33
1436	ZINC POWDER or ZINC DUST	4.3	WS	I	4.3 +4.2		LQ0	E0	P403		MP2		
1436	ZINC POWDER or ZINC DUST	4.3	WS	II	4.3 +4.2		LQ11	E2	P410 IBC07	PP40	MP14	T3	TP33
1436	ZINC POWDER or ZINC DUST	4.3	WS	III	4.3 +4.2		LQ12	E1	P410 IBC08 R001	B4	MP14	T1	TP33
1437	ZIRCONIUM HYDRIDE	4.1	F3	II	4.1		LQ8	E2	P410 IBC04	PP40	MP11	T3	TP33
1438	ALUMINIUM NITRATE	5.1	O2	III	5.1		LQ12	E1	P002 IBC08 LP02 R001	B3	MP10	T1 BK1 BK2	TP33
1439	AMMONIUM DICHROMATE	5.1	O2	II	5.1		LQ11	E2	P002 IBC08	B4	MP2	T3	TP33
1442	AMMONIUM PERCHLORATE	5.1	O2	II	5.1	152	LQ11	E2	P002 IBC06		MP2	T3	TP33
1444	AMMONIUM PERSULPHATE	5.1	O2	III	5.1		LQ12	E1	P002 IBC08 LP02 R001	B3	MP10	T1	TP33
1445	BARIUM CHLORATE, SOLID	5.1	OT2	II	5.1 +6.1		LQ11	E2	P002 IBC06		MP2	T3	TP33
1446	BARIUM NITRATE	5.1	OT2	II	5.1 +6.1		LQ11	E2	P002 IBC08	B4	MP2	T3	TP33
1447	BARIUM PERCHLORATE, SOLID	5.1	OT2	II	5.1 +6.1		LQ11	E2	P002 IBC06		MP2	T3	TP33
1448	BARIUM PERMANGANATE	5.1	OT2	II	5.1 +6.1		LQ11	E2	P002 IBC06		MP2	T3	TP33
1449	BARIUM PEROXIDE	5.1	OT2	II	5.1 +6.1		LQ11	E2	P002 IBC06		MP2	T3	TP33
1450	BROMATES, INORGANIC, N.O.S.	5.1	O2	II	5.1	274 604	LQ11	E2	P002 IBC08	B4	MP2	T3	TP33
1451	CAESIUM NITRATE	5.1	O2	III	5.1		LQ12	E1	P002 IBC08 LP02 R001	B3	MP10	T1	TP33
1452	CALCIUM CHLORATE	5.1	O2	II	5.1		LQ11	E2	P002 IBC08	B4	MP2	T3	TP33
1453	CALCIUM CHLORITE	5.1	O2	II	5.1		LQ11	E2	P002 IBC08	B4	MP2	T3	TP33
1454	CALCIUM NITRATE	5.1	O2	III	5.1	208	LQ12	E1	P002 IBC08 LP02 R001	B3	MP10	T1 BK1 BK2	TP33
1455	CALCIUM PERCHLORATE	5.1	O2	II	5.1		LQ11	E2	P002 IBC06		MP2	T3	TP33
1456	CALCIUM PERMANGANATE	5.1	O2	II	5.1		LQ11	E2	P002 IBC06		MP2	T3	TP33
1457	CALCIUM PEROXIDE	5.1	O2	II	5.1		LQ11	E2	P002 IBC06		MP2	T3	TP33
1458	CHLORATE AND BORATE MIXTURE	5.1	O2	II	5.1		LQ11	E2	P002 IBC08	B4	MP2	T3	TP33

ADR tank		Vehicle for tank carriage	Transport category (Tunnel restriction code)	Special provisions for carriage				Hazard identification No.	UN No.	Name and description
Tank code	Special provisions			Packages	Bulk	Loading, unloading and handling	Operation			
4.3	4.3.5, 6.8.4	9.1.1.2	1.1.3.6 (8.6)	7.2.4	7.3.3	7.5.11	8.5	5.3.2.3		3.1.2
(12)	(13)	(14)	(15)	(16)	(17)	(18)	(19)	(20)	(1)	(2)
L10CH(+)	TU2 TU14 TE5 TE21 TT3 TM2	AT	1 (B/E)	V1		CV23	S20	X423	1423	RUBIDIUM
			1 (E)	V1		CV23	S20		1426	SODIUM BOROHYDRIDE
			1 (E)	V1		CV23	S20		1427	SODIUM HYDRIDE
L10BN(+)	TU1 TE5 TT3 TM2	AT	1 (B/E)	V1		CV23	S20	X423	1428	SODIUM
SGAN		AT	2 (D/E)	V1				48	1431	SODIUM METHYLATE
			1 (E)	V1		CV23 CV28	S20		1432	SODIUM PHOSPHIDE
			1 (E)	V1		CV23 CV28	S20		1433	STANNIC PHOSPHIDES
SGAN		AT	3 (E)	V1	VV5	CV23		423	1435	ZINC ASHES
			1 (E)	V1		CV23	S20		1436	ZINC POWDER or ZINC DUST
SGAN		AT	2 (D/E)	V1 V12		CV23		423	1436	ZINC POWDER or ZINC DUST
SGAN		AT	3 (E)	V1	VV5	CV23		423	1436	ZINC POWDER or ZINC DUST
SGAN		AT	2 (E)					40	1437	ZIRCONIUM HYDRIDE
SGAV	TU3	AT	3 (E)		VV8	CV24		50	1438	ALUMINIUM NITRATE
SGAN	TU3	AT	2 (E)	V11		CV24		50	1439	AMMONIUM DICHROMATE
			2 (E)	V11 V12	VV8	CV24	S23	50	1442	AMMONIUM PERCHLORATE
SGAV	TU3	AT	3 (E)		VV8	CV24		50	1444	AMMONIUM PERSULPHATE
SGAN	TU3	AT	2 (E)	V11 V12		CV24 CV28		56	1445	BARIUM CHLORATE, SOLID
SGAN	TU3	AT	2 (E)	V11		CV24 CV28		56	1446	BARIUM NITRATE
SGAN	TU3	AT	2 (E)	V11 V12		CV24 CV28	S23	56	1447	BARIUM PERCHLORATE, SOLID
SGAN	TU3	AT	2 (E)	V11 V12		CV24 CV28		56	1448	BARIUM PERMANGANATE
SGAN	TU3	AT	2 (E)	V11 V12		CV24 CV28		56	1449	BARIUM PEROXIDE
SGAV	TU3	AT	2 (E)	V11	VV8	CV24		50	1450	BROMATES, INORGANIC, N.O.S.
SGAV	TU3	AT	3 (E)		VV8	CV24		50	1451	CAESIUM NITRATE
SGAV	TU3	AT	2 (E)	V11	VV8	CV24		50	1452	CALCIUM CHLORATE
SGAN	TU3	AT	2 (E)	V11		CV24		50	1453	CALCIUM CHLORITE
SGAV	TU3	AT	3 (E)		VV8	CV24		50	1454	CALCIUM NITRATE
SGAV	TU3	AT	2 (E)	V11 V12	VV8	CV24	S23	50	1455	CALCIUM PERCHLORATE
SGAN	TU3	AT	2 (E)	V11 V12		CV24		50	1456	CALCIUM PERMANGANATE
SGAN	TU3	AT	2 (E)	V11 V12		CV24		50	1457	CALCIUM PEROXIDE
SGAV	TU3	AT	2 (E)	V11	VV8	CV24		50	1458	CHLORATE AND BORATE MIXTURE

UN No.	Name and description	Class	Classification code	Packing group	Labels	Special provisions	Limited and excepted quantities		Packaging			Portable tanks and bulk containers	
									Packing instructions	Special packing provisions	Mixed packing provisions	Instructions	Special provisions
	3.1.2	2.2	2.2	2.1.1.3	5.2.2	3.3	3.4.6	3.5.1.2	4.1.4	4.1.4	4.1.10	4.2.5.2 7.3.2	4.2.5.3
(1)	(2)	(3a)	(3b)	(4)	(5)	(6)	(7a)	(7b)	(8)	(9a)	(9b)	(10)	(11)
1458	CHLORATE AND BORATE MIXTURE	5.1	O2	III	5.1		LQ12	E1	P002 IBC08 LP02 R001	B3	MP2	T1	TP33
1459	CHLORATE AND MAGNESIUM CHLORIDE MIXTURE, SOLID	5.1	O2	II	5.1		LQ11	E2	P002 IBC08	B4	MP2	T3	TP33
1459	CHLORATE AND MAGNESIUM CHLORIDE MIXTURE, SOLID	5.1	O2	III	5.1		LQ12	E1	P002 IBC08 LP02 R001	B3	MP2	T1	TP33
1461	CHLORATES, INORGANIC, N.O.S.	5.1	O2	II	5.1	274 605	LQ11	E2	P002 IBC06		MP2	T3	TP33
1462	CHLORITES, INORGANIC, N.O.S.	5.1	O2	II	5.1	274 509 606	LQ11	E2	P002 IBC06		MP2	T3	TP33
1463	CHROMIUM TRIOXIDE, ANHYDROUS	5.1	OTC	II	5.1 +6.1 +8	510	LQ11	E2	P002 IBC08	B4	MP2	T3	TP33
1465	DIDYMIUM NITRATE	5.1	O2	III	5.1		LQ12	E1	P002 IBC08 LP02 R001	B3	MP10	T1	TP33
1466	FERRIC NITRATE	5.1	O2	III	5.1		LQ12	E1	P002 IBC08 LP02 R001	B3	MP10	T1	TP33
1467	GUANIDINE NITRATE	5.1	O2	III	5.1		LQ12	E1	P002 IBC08 LP02 R001	B3	MP10	T1	TP33
1469	LEAD NITRATE	5.1	OT2	II	5.1 +6.1		LQ11	E2	P002 IBC08	B4	MP2	T3	TP33
1470	LEAD PERCHLORATE, SOLID	5.1	OT2	II	5.1 +6.1		LQ11	E2	P002 IBC06		MP2	T3	TP33
1471	LITHIUM HYPOCHLORITE, DRY or LITHIUM HYPOCHLORITE MIXTURE	5.1	O2	II	5.1		LQ11	E2	P002 IBC08	B4	MP10		
1472	LITHIUM PEROXIDE	5.1	O2	II	5.1		LQ11	E2	P002 IBC06		MP2	T3	TP33
1473	MAGNESIUM BROMATE	5.1	O2	II	5.1		LQ11	E2	P002 IBC08	B4	MP2	T3	TP33
1474	MAGNESIUM NITRATE	5.1	O2	III	5.1	332	LQ12	E1	P002 IBC08 LP02 R001	B3	MP10	T1 BK1 BK2	TP33
1475	MAGNESIUM PERCHLORATE	5.1	O2	II	5.1		LQ11	E2	P002 IBC06		MP2	T3	TP33
1476	MAGNESIUM PEROXIDE	5.1	O2	II	5.1		LQ11	E2	P002 IBC06		MP2	T3	TP33
1477	NITRATES, INORGANIC, N.O.S.	5.1	O2	II	5.1	274 511	LQ11	E2	P002 IBC08	B4	MP10	T3	TP33
1477	NITRATES, INORGANIC, N.O.S.	5.1	O2	III	5.1	274 511	LQ12	E1	P002 IBC08 LP02 R001	B3	MP10	T1	TP33
1479	OXIDIZING SOLID, N.O.S.	5.1	O2	I	5.1	274	LQ0	E0	P503 IBC05		MP2		
1479	OXIDIZING SOLID, N.O.S.	5.1	O2	II	5.1	274	LQ11	E2	P002 IBC08	B4	MP2	T3	TP33
1479	OXIDIZING SOLID, N.O.S.	5.1	O2	III	5.1	274	LQ12	E1	P002 IBC08 LP02 R001	B3	MP2	T1	TP33
1481	PERCHLORATES, INORGANIC, N.O.S.	5.1	O2	II	5.1	274	LQ11	E2	P002 IBC06		MP2	T3	TP33
1481	PERCHLORATES, INORGANIC, N.O.S.	5.1	O2	III	5.1	274	LQ12	E1	P002 IBC08 LP02 R001	B3	MP2	T1	TP33
1482	PERMANGANATES, INORGANIC, N.O.S.	5.1	O2	II	5.1	274 608	LQ11	E2	P002 IBC06		MP2	T3	TP33

ADR tank		Vehicle for tank carriage	Transport category (Tunnel restriction code)	Special provisions for carriage				Hazard identifi-cation No.	UN No.	Name and description
Tank code	Special provisions			Packages	Bulk	Loading, unloading and handling	Operation			
4.3	4.3.5, 6.8.4	9.1.1.2	1.1.3.6 (8.6)	7.2.4	7.3.3	7.5.11	8.5	5.3.2.3		3.1.2
(12)	(13)	(14)	(15)	(16)	(17)	(18)	(19)	(20)	(1)	(2)
SGAV	TU3	AT	3 (E)		VV8	CV24		50	1458	CHLORATE AND BORATE MIXTURE
SGAV	TU3	AT	2 (E)	V11	VV8	CV24		50	1459	CHLORATE AND MAGNESIUM CHLORIDE MIXTURE, SOLID
SGAV	TU3	AT	3 (E)		VV8	CV24		50	1459	CHLORATE AND MAGNESIUM CHLORIDE MIXTURE, SOLID
SGAV	TU3	AT	2 (E)	V11 V12	VV8	CV24		50	1461	CHLORATES, INORGANIC, N.O.S.
SGAN	TU3	AT	2 (E)	V11 V12		CV24		50	1462	CHLORITES, INORGANIC, N.O.S.
SGAN	TU3	AT	2 (E)	V11 V12		CV24 CV28		568	1463	CHROMIUM TRIOXIDE, ANHYDROUS
SGAV	TU3	AT	3 (E)		VV8	CV24		50	1465	DIDYMIUM NITRATE
SGAV	TU3	AT	3 (E)		VV8	CV24		50	1466	FERRIC NITRATE
SGAV	TU3	AT	3 (E)		VV8	CV24		50	1467	GUANIDINE NITRATE
SGAN	TU3	AT	2 (E)	V11		CV24 CV28		56	1469	LEAD NITRATE
SGAN	TU3	AT	2 (E)	V11 V12		CV24 CV28	S23	56	1470	LEAD PERCHLORATE, SOLID
SGAN	TU3	AT	2 (E)	V11		CV24		50	1471	LITHIUM HYPOCHLORITE, DRY or LITHIUM HYPOCHLORITE MIXTURE
SGAN	TU3	AT	2 (E)	V11 V12		CV24		50	1472	LITHIUM PEROXIDE
SGAV	TU3	AT	2 (E)	V11	VV8	CV24		50	1473	MAGNESIUM BROMATE
SGAV	TU3	AT	3 (E)		VV8	CV24		50	1474	MAGNESIUM NITRATE
SGAV	TU3	AT	2 (E)	V11 V12	VV8	CV24	S23	50	1475	MAGNESIUM PERCHLORATE
SGAN	TU3	AT	2 (E)	V11 V12		CV24		50	1476	MAGNESIUM PEROXIDE
SGAN	TU3	AT	2 (E)	V11		CV24		50	1477	NITRATES, INORGANIC, N.O.S.
SGAV	TU3	AT	3 (E)		VV8	CV24		50	1477	NITRATES, INORGANIC, N.O.S.
			1 (E)	V10		CV24	S20		1479	OXIDIZING SOLID, N.O.S.
SGAN	TU3	AT	2 (E)	V11		CV24		50	1479	OXIDIZING SOLID, N.O.S.
SGAN	TU3	AT	3 (E)			CV24		50	1479	OXIDIZING SOLID, N.O.S.
SGAV	TU3	AT	2 (E)	V11 V12	VV8	CV24	S23	50	1481	PERCHLORATES, INORGANIC, N.O.S.
SGAV	TU3	AT	3 (E)		VV8	CV24	S23	50	1481	PERCHLORATES, INORGANIC, N.O.S.
SGAN	TU3	AT	2 (E)	V11 V12		CV24		50	1482	PERMANGANATES, INORGANIC, N.O.S.

UN No.	Name and description	Class	Classification code	Packing group	Labels	Special provisions	Limited and excepted quantities		Packaging			Portable tanks and bulk containers	
									Packing instructions	Special packing provisions	Mixed packing provisions	Instructions	Special provisions
	3.1.2	2.2	2.2	2.1.1.3	5.2.2	3.3	3.4.6	3.5.1.2	4.1.4	4.1.4	4.1.10	4.2.5.2 7.3.2	4.2.5.3
(1)	(2)	(3a)	(3b)	(4)	(5)	(6)	(7a)	(7b)	(8)	(9a)	(9b)	(10)	(11)
1482	PERMANGANATES, INORGANIC, N.O.S.	5.1	O2	III	5.1	274 608	LQ12	E1	P002 IBC08 LP02 R001	B3	MP2	T1	TP33
1483	PEROXIDES, INORGANIC, N.O.S.	5.1	O2	II	5.1	274	LQ11	E2	P002 IBC06		MP2	T3	TP33
1483	PEROXIDES, INORGANIC, N.O.S.	5.1	O2	III	5.1	274	LQ12	E1	P002 IBC08 LP02 R001	B3	MP2	T1	TP33
1484	POTASSIUM BROMATE	5.1	O2	II	5.1		LQ11	E2	P002 IBC08	B4	MP2	T3	TP33
1485	POTASSIUM CHLORATE	5.1	O2	II	5.1		LQ11	E2	P002 IBC08	B4	MP2	T3	TP33
1486	POTASSIUM NITRATE	5.1	O2	III	5.1		LQ12	E1	P002 IBC08 LP02 R001	B3	MP10	T1 BK1 BK2	TP33
1487	POTASSIUM NITRATE AND SODIUM NITRITE MIXTURE	5.1	O2	II	5.1	607	LQ11	E2	P002 IBC08	B4	MP10	T3	TP33
1488	POTASSIUM NITRITE	5.1	O2	II	5.1		LQ11	E2	P002 IBC08	B4	MP10	T3	TP33
1489	POTASSIUM PERCHLORATE	5.1	O2	II	5.1		LQ11	E2	P002 IBC06		MP2	T3	TP33
1490	POTASSIUM PERMANGANATE	5.1	O2	II	5.1		LQ11	E2	P002 IBC08	B4	MP2	T3	TP33
1491	POTASSIUM PEROXIDE	5.1	O2	I	5.1		LQ0	E0	P503 IBC06		MP2		
1492	POTASSIUM PERSULPHATE	5.1	O2	III	5.1		LQ12	E1	P002 IBC08 LP02 R001	B3	MP10	T1	TP33
1493	SILVER NITRATE	5.1	O2	II	5.1		LQ11	E2	P002 IBC08	B4	MP10	T3	TP33
1494	SODIUM BROMATE	5.1	O2	II	5.1		LQ11	E2	P002 IBC08	B4	MP2	T3	TP33
1495	SODIUM CHLORATE	5.1	O2	II	5.1		LQ11	E2	P002 IBC08	B4	MP2	T3 BK1 BK2	TP33
1496	SODIUM CHLORITE	5.1	O2	II	5.1		LQ11	E2	P002 IBC08	B4	MP2	T3	TP33
1498	SODIUM NITRATE	5.1	O2	III	5.1		LQ12	E1	P002 IBC08 LP02 R001	B3	MP10	T1 BK1 BK2	TP33
1499	SODIUM NITRATE AND POTASSIUM NITRATE MIXTURE	5.1	O2	III	5.1		LQ12	E1	P002 IBC08 LP02 R001	B3	MP10	T1 BK1 BK2	TP33
1500	SODIUM NITRITE	5.1	OT2	III	5.1 +6.1		LQ12	E1	P002 IBC08 R001	B3	MP10	T1	TP33
1502	SODIUM PERCHLORATE	5.1	O2	II	5.1		LQ11	E2	P002 IBC06		MP2	T3	TP33
1503	SODIUM PERMANGANATE	5.1	O2	II	5.1		LQ11	E2	P002 IBC06		MP2	T3	TP33
1504	SODIUM PEROXIDE	5.1	O2	I	5.1		LQ0	E0	P503 IBC05		MP2		
1505	SODIUM PERSULPHATE	5.1	O2	III	5.1		LQ12	E1	P002 IBC08 LP02 R001	B3	MP10	T1	TP33
1506	STRONTIUM CHLORATE	5.1	O2	II	5.1		LQ11	E2	P002 IBC08	B4	MP2	T3	TP33
1507	STRONTIUM NITRATE	5.1	O2	III	5.1		LQ12	E1	P002 IBC08 LP02 R001	B3	MP10	T1	TP33
1508	STRONTIUM PERCHLORATE	5.1	O2	II	5.1		LQ11	E2	P002 IBC06		MP2	T3	TP33

ADR tank		Vehicle for tank carriage	Transport category (Tunnel restriction code)	Special provisions for carriage				Hazard identification No.	UN No.	Name and description
Tank code	Special provisions			Packages	Bulk	Loading, unloading and handling	Operation			
4.3	4.3.5, 6.8.4	9.1.1.2	1.1.3.6 (8.6)	7.2.4	7.3.3	7.5.11	8.5	5.3.2.3		3.1.2
(12)	(13)	(14)	(15)	(16)	(17)	(18)	(19)	(20)	(1)	(2)
SGAN	TU3	AT	3 (E)			CV24		50	1482	PERMANGANATES, INORGANIC, N.O.S.
SGAN	TU3	AT	2 (E)	V11 V12		CV24		50	1483	PEROXIDES, INORGANIC, N.O.S.
SGAN	TU3	AT	3 (E)			CV24		50	1483	PEROXIDES, INORGANIC, N.O.S.
SGAV	TU3	AT	2 (E)	V11	VV8	CV24		50	1484	POTASSIUM BROMATE
SGAV	TU3	AT	2 (E)	V11	VV8	CV24		50	1485	POTASSIUM CHLORATE
SGAV	TU3	AT	3 (E)		VV8	CV24		50	1486	POTASSIUM NITRATE
SGAV	TU3	AT	2 (E)	V11	VV8	CV24		50	1487	POTASSIUM NITRATE AND SODIUM NITRITE MIXTURE
SGAV	TU3	AT	2 (E)	V11	VV8	CV24		50	1488	POTASSIUM NITRITE
SGAV	TU3	AT	2 (E)	V11 V12	VV8	CV24	S23	50	1489	POTASSIUM PERCHLORATE
SGAN	TU3	AT	2 (E)	V11		CV24		50	1490	POTASSIUM PERMANGANATE
			1 (E)	V10 V12		CV24	S20		1491	POTASSIUM PEROXIDE
SGAV	TU3	AT	3 (E)		VV8	CV24		50	1492	POTASSIUM PERSULPHATE
SGAV	TU3	AT	2 (E)	V11	VV8	CV24		50	1493	SILVER NITRATE
SGAV	TU3	AT	2 (E)	V11	VV8	CV24		50	1494	SODIUM BROMATE
SGAV	TU3	AT	2 (E)	V11	VV8	CV24		50	1495	SODIUM CHLORATE
SGAN	TU3	AT	2 (E)	V11		CV24		50	1496	SODIUM CHLORITE
SGAV	TU3	AT	3 (E)		VV8	CV24		50	1498	SODIUM NITRATE
SGAV	TU3	AT	3 (E)		VV8	CV24		50	1499	SODIUM NITRATE AND POTASSIUM NITRATE MIXTURE
SGAN	TU3	AT	3 (E)			CV24 CV28		56	1500	SODIUM NITRITE
SGAV	TU3	AT	2 (E)	V11 V12	VV8	CV24	S23	50	1502	SODIUM PERCHLORATE
SGAN	TU3	AT	2 (E)	V11 V12		CV24		50	1503	SODIUM PERMANGANATE
			1 (E)	V10		CV24	S20		1504	SODIUM PEROXIDE
SGAV	TU3	AT	3 (E)		VV8	CV24		50	1505	SODIUM PERSULPHATE
SGAV	TU3	AT	2 (E)	V11	VV8	CV24		50	1506	STRONTIUM CHLORATE
SGAV	TU3	AT	3 (E)		VV8	CV24		50	1507	STRONTIUM NITRATE
SGAV	TU3	AT	2 (E)	V11 V12	VV8	CV24	S23	50	1508	STRONTIUM PERCHLORATE

UN No.	Name and description	Class	Classifi-cation code	Packing group	Labels	Special provi-sions	Limited and excepted quantities		Packaging			Portable tanks and bulk containers	
									Packing instruc-tions	Special packing provisions	Mixed packing provisions	Instruc-tions	Special provisions
3.1.2	3.1.2	2.2	2.2	2.1.1.3	5.2.2	3.3	3.4.6	3.5.1.2	4.1.4	4.1.4	4.1.10	4.2.5.2 7.3.2	4.2.5.3
(1)	(2)	(3a)	(3b)	(4)	(5)	(6)	(7a)	(7b)	(8)	(9a)	(9b)	(10)	(11)
1509	STRONTIUM PEROXIDE	5.1	O2	II	5.1		LQ11	E2	P002 IBC06		MP2	T3	TP33
1510	TETRANITROMETHANE	5.1	OT1	I	5.1 +6.1	609	LQ0	E0	P602		MP2		
1511	UREA HYDROGEN PEROXIDE	5.1	OC2	III	5.1 +8		LQ12	E1	P002 IBC08 R001	B3	MP2	T1	TP33
1512	ZINC AMMONIUM NITRITE	5.1	O2	II	5.1		LQ11	E2	P002 IBC08	B4	MP10	T3	TP33
1513	ZINC CHLORATE	5.1	O2	II	5.1		LQ11	E2	P002 IBC08	B4	MP2	T3	TP33
1514	ZINC NITRATE	5.1	O2	II	5.1		LQ11	E2	P002 IBC08	B4	MP10	T3	TP33
1515	ZINC PERMANGANATE	5.1	O2	II	5.1		LQ11	E2	P002 IBC06		MP2	T3	TP33
1516	ZINC PEROXIDE	5.1	O2	II	5.1		LQ11	E2	P002 IBC06		MP2	T3	TP33
1517	ZIRCONIUM PICRAMATE, WETTED with not less than 20% water, by mass	4.1	D	I	4.1		LQ0	E0	P406	PP26	MP2		
1541	ACETONE CYANOHYDRIN, STABILIZED	6.1	T1	I	6.1		LQ0	E5	P602		MP8 MP17	T14	TP2
1544	ALKALOIDS, SOLID, N.O.S. or ALKALOID SALTS, SOLID, N.O.S.	6.1	T2	I	6.1	43 274	LQ0	E5	P002 IBC07		MP18	T6	TP33
1544	ALKALOIDS, SOLID, N.O.S. or ALKALOID SALTS, SOLID, N.O.S.	6.1	T2	II	6.1	43 274	LQ18	E4	P002 IBC08	B4	MP10	T3	TP33
1544	ALKALOIDS, SOLID, N.O.S. or ALKALOID SALTS, SOLID, N.O.S.	6.1	T2	III	6.1	43 274	LQ9	E1	P002 IBC08 LP02 R001	B3	MP10	T1	TP33
1545	ALLYL ISOTHIOCYANATE, STABILIZED	6.1	TF1	II	6.1 +3		LQ17	E4	P001 IBC02		MP15	T7	TP2
1546	AMMONIUM ARSENATE	6.1	T5	II	6.1		LQ18	E4	P002 IBC08	B4	MP10	T3	TP33
1547	ANILINE	6.1	T1	II	6.1	279	LQ17	E4	P001 IBC02		MP15	T7	TP2
1548	ANILINE HYDROCHLORIDE	6.1	T2	III	6.1		LQ9	E1	P002 IBC08 LP02 R001	B3	MP10	T1	TP33
1549	ANTIMONY COMPOUND, INORGANIC, SOLID, N.O.S.	6.1	T5	III	6.1	45 274 512	LQ9	E1	P002 IBC08 LP02 R001	B3	MP10	T1	TP33
1550	ANTIMONY LACTATE	6.1	T5	III	6.1		LQ9	E1	P002 IBC08 LP02 R001	B3	MP10	T1	TP33
1551	ANTIMONY POTASSIUM TARTRATE	6.1	T5	III	6.1		LQ9	E1	P002 IBC08 LP02 R001	B3	MP10	T1	TP33
1553	ARSENIC ACID, LIQUID	6.1	T4	I	6.1		LQ0	E5	P001		MP8 MP17	T20	TP2 TP7
1554	ARSENIC ACID, SOLID	6.1	T5	II	6.1		LQ18	E4	P002 IBC08	B4	MP10	T3	TP33
1555	ARSENIC BROMIDE	6.1	T5	II	6.1		LQ18	E4	P002 IBC08	B4	MP10	T3	TP33
1556	ARSENIC COMPOUND, LIQUID, N.O.S., inorganic, including: Arsenates, n.o.s., Arsenites, n.o.s.; and Arsenic sulphides, n.o.s.	6.1	T4	I	6.1	43 274	LQ0	E5	P001		MP8 MP17	T14	TP2 TP27

ADR tank		Vehicle for tank carriage	Transport category (Tunnel restriction code)	Special provisions for carriage				Hazard identifi-cation No.	UN No.	Name and description
Tank code	Special provisions			Packages	Bulk	Loading, unloading and handling	Operation			
4.3	4.3.5, 6.8.4	9.1.1.2	1.1.3.6 (8.6)	7.2.4	7.3.3	7.5.11	8.5	5.3.2.3		3.1.2
(12)	(13)	(14)	(15)	(16)	(17)	(18)	(19)	(20)	(1)	(2)
SGAN	TU3	AT	2 (E)	V11 V12		CV24		50	1509	STRONTIUM PEROXIDE
L4BN	TU3 TU28	AT	1 (B/E)	V5		CV24 CV28	S20	559	1510	TETRANITROMETHANE
SGAN	TU3	AT	3 (E)			CV24		58	1511	UREA HYDROGEN PEROXIDE
SGAN	TU3	AT	2 (E)	V11		CV24		50	1512	ZINC AMMONIUM NITRITE
SGAV	TU3	AT	2 (E)	V11	VV8	CV24		50	1513	ZINC CHLORATE
SGAN	TU3	AT	2 (E)	V11		CV24		50	1514	ZINC NITRATE
SGAN	TU3	AT	2 (E)	V11 V12		CV24		50	1515	ZINC PERMANGANATE
SGAN	TU3	AT	2 (E)	V11 V12		CV24		50	1516	ZINC PEROXIDE
			1 (B)				S14		1517	ZIRCONIUM PICRAMATE, WETTED with not less than 20% water, by mass
L10CH	TU14 TU15 TE19 TE21	AT	1 (C/E)			CV1 CV13 CV28	S9 S14	669	1541	ACETONE CYANOHYDRIN, STABILIZED
S10AH	TU15 TE19	AT	1 (C/E)	V10 V12		CV1 CV13 CV28	S9 S14	66	1544	ALKALOIDS, SOLID, N.O.S. or ALKALOID SALTS, SOLID, N.O.S.
SGAH L4BH	TU15 TE19	AT	2 (D/E)	V11		CV13 CV28	S9 S19	60	1544	ALKALOIDS, SOLID, N.O.S. or ALKALOID SALTS, SOLID, N.O.S.
SGAH L4BH	TU15 TE19	AT	2 (E)		VV9	CV13 CV28	S9	60	1544	ALKALOIDS, SOLID, N.O.S. or ALKALOID SALTS, SOLID, N.O.S.
L4BH	TU15 TE19	FL	2 (D/E)			CV13 CV28	S2 S9 S19	639	1545	ALLYL ISOTHIOCYANATE, STABILIZED
SGAH	TU15 TE19	AT	2 (D/E)	V11		CV13 CV28	S9 S19	60	1546	AMMONIUM ARSENATE
L4BH	TU15 TE19	AT	2 (D/E)			CV13 CV28	S9 S19	60	1547	ANILINE
SGAH	TU15 TE19	AT	2 (E)		VV9	CV13 CV28	S9	60	1548	ANILINE HYDROCHLORIDE
SGAH L4BH	TU15 TE19	AT	2 (E)		VV9	CV13 CV28	S9	60	1549	ANTIMONY COMPOUND, INORGANIC, SOLID, N.O.S.
SGAH L4BH	TU15 TE19	AT	2 (E)		VV9	CV13 CV28	S9	60	1550	ANTIMONY LACTATE
SGAH L4BH	TU15 TE19	AT	2 (E)		VV9	CV13 CV28	S9	60	1551	ANTIMONY POTASSIUM TARTRATE
L10CH	TU14 TU15 TE19 TE21	AT	1 (C/E)			CV1 CV13 CV28	S9 S14	66	1553	ARSENIC ACID, LIQUID
SGAH L4BH	TU15 TE19	AT	2 (D/E)	V11		CV13 CV28	S9 S19	60	1554	ARSENIC ACID, SOLID
SGAH L4BH	TU15 TE19	AT	2 (D/E)	V11		CV13 CV28	S9 S19	60	1555	ARSENIC BROMIDE
L10CH	TU14 TU15 TE19 TE21	AT	1 (C/E)			CV1 CV13 CV28	S9 S14	66	1556	ARSENIC COMPOUND, LIQUID, N.O.S., inorganic, including: Arsenates, n.o.s., Arsenites, n.o.s.; and Arsenic sulphides, n.o.s.

UN No.	Name and description	Class	Classifi-cation code	Packing group	Labels	Special provi-sions	Limited and excepted quantities		Packaging			Portable tanks and bulk containers	
							quantities		Packing instruc-tions	Special packing provisions	Mixed packing provisions	Instruc-tions	Special provisions
	3.1.2	2.2	2.2	2.1.1.3	5.2.2	3.3	3.4.6	3.5.1.2	4.1.4	4.1.4	4.1.10	4.2.5.2 7.3.2	4.2.5.3
(1)	(2)	(3a)	(3b)	(4)	(5)	(6)	(7a)	(7b)	(8)	(9a)	(9b)	(10)	(11)
1556	ARSENIC COMPOUND, LIQUID, N.O.S., inorganic, including: Arsenates, n.o.s., Arsenites, n.o.s.; and Arsenic sulphides, n.o.s.	6.1	T4	II	6.1	43 274	LQ17	E4	P001 IBC02		MP15	T11	TP2 TP27
1556	ARSENIC COMPOUND, LIQUID, N.O.S., inorganic, including: Arsenates, n.o.s., Arsenites, n.o.s.; and Arsenic sulphides, n.o.s.	6.1	T4	III	6.1	43 274	LQ7	E1	P001 IBC03 LP01 R001		MP19	T7	TP2 TP28
1557	ARSENIC COMPOUND, SOLID, N.O.S., inorganic, including: Arsenates, n.o.s.; Arsenites, n.o.s.; and Arsenic sulphides, n.o.s.	6.1	T5	I	6.1	43 274	LQ0	E5	P002 IBC07		MP18	T6	TP33
1557	ARSENIC COMPOUND, SOLID, N.O.S., inorganic, including: Arsenates, n.o.s.; Arsenites, n.o.s.; and Arsenic sulphides, n.o.s.	6.1	T5	II	6.1	43 274	LQ18	E4	P002 IBC08	B4	MP10	T3	TP33
1557	ARSENIC COMPOUND, SOLID, N.O.S., inorganic, including: Arsenates, n.o.s.; Arsenites, n.o.s.; and Arsenic sulphides, n.o.s.	6.1	T5	III	6.1	43 274	LQ9	E1	P002 IBC08 LP02 R001	B3	MP10	T1	TP33
1558	ARSENIC	6.1	T5	II	6.1		LQ18	E4	P002 IBC08	B4	MP10	T3	TP33
1559	ARSENIC PENTOXIDE	6.1	T5	II	6.1		LQ18	E4	P002 IBC08	B4	MP10	T3	TP33
1560	ARSENIC TRICHLORIDE	6.1	T4	I	6.1		LQ0	E5	P602		MP8 MP17	T14	TP2
1561	ARSENIC TRIOXIDE	6.1	T5	II	6.1		LQ18	E4	P002 IBC08	B4	MP10	T3	TP33
1562	ARSENICAL DUST	6.1	T5	II	6.1		LQ18	E4	P002 IBC08	B4	MP10	T3	TP33
1564	BARIUM COMPOUND, N.O.S.	6.1	T5	II	6.1	177 274 513 587	LQ18	E4	P002 IBC08	B4	MP10	T3	TP33
1564	BARIUM COMPOUND, N.O.S.	6.1	T5	III	6.1	177 274 513 587	LQ9	E1	P002 IBC08 LP02 R001	B3	MP10	T1	TP33
1565	BARIUM CYANIDE	6.1	T5	I	6.1		LQ0	E5	P002 IBC07		MP18	T6	TP33
1566	BERYLLIUM COMPOUND, N.O.S.	6.1	T5	II	6.1	274 514	LQ18	E4	P002 IBC08	B4	MP10	T3	TP33
1566	BERYLLIUM COMPOUND, N.O.S.	6.1	T5	III	6.1	274 514	LQ9	E1	P002 IBC08 LP02 R001	B3	MP10	T1	TP33
1567	BERYLLIUM POWDER	6.1	TF3	II	6.1 +4.1		LQ18	E4	P002 IBC08	B4	MP10	T3	TP33
1569	BROMOACETONE	6.1	TF1	II	6.1 +3		LQ17	E4	P602		MP15	T20	TP2
1570	BRUCINE	6.1	T2	I	6.1	43	LQ0	E5	P002 IBC07		MP18	T6	TP33
1571	BARIUM AZIDE, WETTED with not less than 50% water, by mass	4.1	DT	I	4.1 +6.1	568	LQ0	E0	P406		MP2		
1572	CACODYLIC ACID	6.1	T5	II	6.1		LQ18	E4	P002 IBC08	B4	MP10	T3	TP33
1573	CALCIUM ARSENATE	6.1	T5	II	6.1		LQ18	E4	P002 IBC08	B4	MP10	T3	TP33
1574	CALCIUM ARSENATE AND CALCIUM ARSENITE MIXTURE, SOLID	6.1	T5	II	6.1		LQ18	E4	P002 IBC08	B4	MP10	T3	TP33

ADR tank		Vehicle for tank carriage	Transport category (Tunnel restriction code)	Special provisions for carriage				Hazard identifi- cation No.	UN No.	Name and description
Tank code	Special provisions			Packages	Bulk	Loading, unloading and handling	Operation			
4.3	4.3.5, 6.8.4	9.1.1.2	1.1.3.6 (8.6)	7.2.4	7.3.3	7.5.11	8.5	5.3.2.3		3.1.2
(12)	(13)	(14)	(15)	(16)	(17)	(18)	(19)	(20)	(1)	(2)
L4BH	TU15 TE19	AT	2 (D/E)			CV13 CV28	S9 S19	60	1556	ARSENIC COMPOUND, LIQUID, N.O.S., inorganic, including: Arsenates, n.o.s., Arsenites, n.o.s.; and Arsenic sulphides, n.o.s.
L4BH	TU15 TE19	AT	2 (E)			CV13 CV28	S9	60	1556	ARSENIC COMPOUND, LIQUID, N.O.S., inorganic, including: Arsenates, n.o.s., Arsenites, n.o.s.; and Arsenic sulphides, n.o.s.
S10AH L10CH	TU15 TE19	AT	1 (C/E)	V10 V12		CV1 CV13 CV28	S9 S14	66	1557	ARSENIC COMPOUND, SOLID, N.O.S., inorganic, including: Arsenates, n.o.s.; Arsenites, n.o.s.; and Arsenic sulphides, n.o.s.
SGAH L4BH	TU15 TE19	AT	2 (D/E)	V11		CV13 CV28	S9 S19	60	1557	ARSENIC COMPOUND, SOLID, N.O.S., inorganic, including: Arsenates, n.o.s.; Arsenites, n.o.s.; and Arsenic sulphides, n.o.s.
SGAH L4BH	TU15 TE19	AT	2 (E)		VV9	CV13 CV28	S9	60	1557	ARSENIC COMPOUND, SOLID, N.O.S., inorganic, including: Arsenates, n.o.s.; Arsenites, n.o.s.; and Arsenic sulphides, n.o.s.
SGAH	TU15 TE19	AT	2 (D/E)	V11		CV13 CV28	S9 S19	60	1558	ARSENIC
SGAH	TU15 TE19	AT	2 (D/E)	V11		CV13 CV28	S9 S19	60	1559	ARSENIC PENTOXIDE
L10CH	TU14 TU15 TE19 TE21	AT	1 (C/E)			CV1 CV13 CV28	S9 S14	66	1560	ARSENIC TRICHLORIDE
SGAH	TU15 TE19	AT	2 (D/E)	V11		CV13 CV28	S9 S19	60	1561	ARSENIC TRIOXIDE
SGAH	TU15 TE19	AT	2 (D/E)	V11		CV13 CV28	S9 S19	60	1562	ARSENICAL DUST
SGAH L4BH	TU15 TE19	AT	2 (D/E)	V11		CV13 CV28	S9 S19	60	1564	BARIUM COMPOUND, N.O.S.
SGAH L4BH	TU15 TE19	AT	2 (E)		VV9	CV13 CV28	S9	60	1564	BARIUM COMPOUND, N.O.S.
S10AH	TU15 TE19	AT	1 (C/E)	V10 V12		CV1 CV13 CV28	S9 S14	66	1565	BARIUM CYANIDE
SGAH L4BH	TU15 TE19	AT	2 (D/E)	V11		CV13 CV28	S9 S19	60	1566	BERYLLIUM COMPOUND, N.O.S.
SGAH L4BH	TU15 TE19	AT	2 (E)		VV9	CV13 CV28	S9	60	1566	BERYLLIUM COMPOUND, N.O.S.
SGAH	TU15 TE19	AT	2 (D/E)	V11		CV13 CV28	S9 S19	64	1567	BERYLLIUM POWDER
L4BH	TU15 TE19	FL	2 (D/E)			CV13 CV28	S2 S9 S19	63	1569	BROMOACETONE
S10AH L10CH	TU14 TU15 TE19 TE21	AT	1 (C/E)	V10 V12		CV1 CV13 CV28	S9 S14	66	1570	BRUCINE
			1 (B)			CV28	S14		1571	BARIUM AZIDE, WETTED with not less than 50% water, by mass
SGAH	TU15 TE19	AT	2 (D/E)	V11		CV13 CV28	S9 S19	60	1572	CACODYLIC ACID
SGAH	TU15 TE19	AT	2 (D/E)	V11		CV13 CV28	S9 S19	60	1573	CALCIUM ARSENATE
SGAH	TU15 TE19	AT	2 (D/E)	V11		CV13 CV28	S9 S19	60	1574	CALCIUM ARSENATE AND CALCIUM ARSENITE MIXTURE, SOLID

UN No.	Name and description	Class	Classifi-cation code	Packing group	Labels	Special provi-sions	Limited and excepted quantities		Packaging			Portable tanks and bulk containers	
									Packing instruc-tions	Special packing provisions	Mixed packing provisions	Instruc-tions	Special provisions
	3.1.2	2.2	2.2	2.1.1.3	5.2.2	3.3	3.4.6	3.5.1.2	4.1.4	4.1.4	4.1.10	4.2.5.2 7.3.2	4.2.5.3
(1)	(2)	(3a)	(3b)	(4)	(5)	(6)	(7a)	(7b)	(8)	(9a)	(9b)	(10)	(11)
1575	CALCIUM CYANIDE	6.1	T5	I	6.1		LQ0	E5	P002 IBC07		MP18	T6	TP33
1577	CHLORODINITRO-BENZENES, LIQUID	6.1	T1	II	6.1	279	LQ17	E4	P001 IBC02		MP15	T7	TP2
1578	CHLORONITROBENZENES, SOLID	6.1	T2	II	6.1	279	LQ18	E4	P002 IBC08	B4	MP10	T3	TP33
1579	4-CHLORO-o-TOLUIDINE HYDROCHLORIDE, SOLID	6.1	T2	III	6.1		LQ9	E1	P002 IBC08 LP02 R001	B3	MP10	T1	TP33
1580	CHLOROPICRIN	6.1	T1	I	6.1		LQ0	E5	P602		MP8 MP17	T14	TP2
1581	CHLOROPICRIN AND METHYL BROMIDE MIXTURE with more than 2% chloropicrin	2	2T		2.3		LQ0	E0	P200		MP9	(M) T50	
1582	CHLOROPICRIN AND METHYL CHLORIDE MIXTURE	2	2T		2.3		LQ0	E0	P200		MP9	(M) T50	
1583	CHLOROPICRIN MIXTURE, N.O.S.	6.1	T1	I	6.1	274 315 515	LQ0	E5	P602		MP8 MP17		
1583	CHLOROPICRIN MIXTURE, N.O.S.	6.1	T1	II	6.1	274 515	LQ17	E4	P001 IBC02		MP15		
1583	CHLOROPICRIN MIXTURE, N.O.S.	6.1	T1	III	6.1	274 515	LQ7	E1	P001 IBC03 LP01 R001		MP19		
1585	COPPER ACETOARSENITE	6.1	T5	II	6.1		LQ18	E4	P002 IBC08	B4	MP10	T3	TP33
1586	COPPER ARSENITE	6.1	T5	II	6.1		LQ18	E4	P002 IBC08	B4	MP10	T3	TP33
1587	COPPER CYANIDE	6.1	T5	II	6.1		LQ18	E4	P002 IBC08	B4	MP10	T3	TP33
1588	CYANIDES, INORGANIC, SOLID, N.O.S.	6.1	T5	I	6.1	47 274	LQ0	E5	P002 IBC07		MP18	T6	TP33
1588	CYANIDES, INORGANIC, SOLID, N.O.S.	6.1	T5	II	6.1	47 274	LQ18	E4	P002 IBC08	B4	MP10	T3	TP33
1588	CYANIDES, INORGANIC, SOLID, N.O.S.	6.1	T5	III	6.1	47 274	LQ9	E1	P002 IBC08 LP02 R001	B3	MP10	T1	TP33
1589	CYANOGEN CHLORIDE, STABILIZED	2	2TC		2.3 +8		LQ0	E0	P200		MP9		
1590	DICHLOROANILINES, LIQUID	6.1	T1	II	6.1	279	LQ17	E4	P001 IBC02		MP15	T7	TP2
1591	o-DICHLOROBENZENE	6.1	T1	III	6.1	279	LQ7	E1	P001 IBC03 LP01 R001		MP19	T4	TP1
1593	DICHLOROMETHANE	6.1	T1	III	6.1	516	LQ7	E1	P001 IBC03 LP01 R001	B8	MP19	T7	TP2
1594	DIETHYL SULPHATE	6.1	T1	II	6.1		LQ17	E4	P001 IBC02		MP15	T7	TP2
1595	DIMETHYL SULPHATE	6.1	TC1	I	6.1 +8		LQ0	E5	P602		MP8 MP17	T20	TP2 TP35
1596	DINITROANILINES	6.1	T2	II	6.1		LQ18	E4	P002 IBC08	B4	MP10	T3	TP33
1597	DINITROBENZENES, LIQUID	6.1	T1	II	6.1		LQ17	E4	P001 IBC02		MP15	T7	TP2
1597	DINITROBENZENES, LIQUID	6.1	T1	III	6.1		LQ7	E1	P001 IBC03 LP01 R001		MP19	T7	TP2

ADR tank		Vehicle for tank carriage	Transport category (Tunnel restriction code)	Special provisions for carriage				Hazard identifi-cation No.	UN No.	Name and description
Tank code	Special provisions			Packages	Bulk	Loading, unloading and handling	Operation			
4.3	4.3.5, 6.8.4	9.1.1.2	1.1.3.6 (8.6)	7.2.4	7.3.3	7.5.11	8.5	5.3.2.3		3.1.2
(12)	(13)	(14)	(15)	(16)	(17)	(18)	(19)	(20)	(1)	(2)
S10AH	TU15 TE19	AT	1 (C/E)	V10 V12		CV1 CV13 CV28	S9 S14	66	1575	CALCIUM CYANIDE
L4BH	TU15 TE19	AT	2 (D/E)			CV13 CV28	S9 S19	60	1577	CHLORODINITRO-BENZENES, LIQUID
SGAH	TU15 TE19	AT	2 (D/E)	V11		CV13 CV28	S9 S19	60	1578	CHLORONITROBENZENES, SOLID
SGAH L4BH	TU15 TE19	AT	2 (E)		VV9	CV13 CV28	S9	60	1579	4-CHLORO-o-TOLUIDINE HYDROCHLORIDE, SOLID
L10CH	TU14 TU15 TE19 TE21	AT	1 (C/E)			CV1 CV13 CV28	S9 S14	66	1580	CHLOROPICRIN
PxBH(M)	TA4 TT9	AT	1 (C/D)			CV9 CV10 CV36	S14	26	1581	CHLOROPICRIN AND METHYL BROMIDE MIXTURE with more than 2% chloropicrin
PxBH(M)	TA4 TT9	AT	1 (C/D)			CV9 CV10 CV36	S14	26	1582	CHLOROPICRIN AND METHYL CHLORIDE MIXTURE
L10CH	TU14 TU15 TE19 TE21	AT	1 (C/E)			CV1 CV13 CV28	S9 S14	66	1583	CHLOROPICRIN MIXTURE, N.O.S.
L4BH	TU15 TE19	AT	2 (D/E)			CV13 CV28	S9 S19	60	1583	CHLOROPICRIN MIXTURE, N.O.S.
L4BH	TU15 TE19	AT	2 (E)			CV13 CV28	S9	60	1583	CHLOROPICRIN MIXTURE, N.O.S.
SGAH	TU15 TE19	AT	2 (D/E)	V11		CV13 CV28	S9 S19	60	1585	COPPER ACETOARSENITE
SGAH	TU15 TE19	AT	2 (D/E)	V11		CV13 CV28	S9 S19	60	1586	COPPER ARSENITE
SGAH	TU15 TE19	AT	2 (D/E)	V11		CV13 CV28	S9 S19	60	1587	COPPER CYANIDE
S10AH	TU15 TE19	AT	1 (C/E)	V10 V12		CV1 CV13 CV28	S9 S14	66	1588	CYANIDES, INORGANIC, SOLID, N.O.S.
SGAH	TU15 TE19	AT	2 (D/E)	V11		CV13 CV28	S9 S19	60	1588	CYANIDES, INORGANIC, SOLID, N.O.S.
SGAH	TU15 TE19	AT	2 (E)		VV9	CV13 CV28	S9	60	1588	CYANIDES, INORGANIC, SOLID, N.O.S.
			1 (D)			CV9 CV10 CV36	S14		1589	CYANOGEN CHLORIDE, STABILIZED
L4BH	TU15 TE19	AT	2 (D/E)			CV13 CV28	S9 S19	60	1590	DICHLOROANILINES, LIQUID
L4BH	TU15 TE19	AT	2 (E)			CV13 CV28	S9	60	1591	o-DICHLOROBENZENE
L4BH	TU15 TE19	AT	2 (E)			CV13 CV28	S9	60	1593	DICHLOROMETHANE
L4BH	TU15 TE19	AT	2 (D/E)			CV13 CV28	S9 S19	60	1594	DIETHYL SULPHATE
L10CH	TU14 TU15 TE19 TE21	AT	1 (C/E)			CV1 CV13 CV28	S9 S14	668	1595	DIMETHYL SULPHATE
SGAH L4BH	TU15 TE19	AT	2 (D/E)	V11		CV13 CV28	S9 S19	60	1596	DINITROANILINES
L4BH	TU15 TE19	AT	2 (D/E)			CV13 CV28	S9 S19	60	1597	DINITROBENZENES, LIQUID
L4BH	TU15 TE19	AT	2 (E)			CV13 CV28	S9	60	1597	DINITROBENZENES, LIQUID

UN No.	Name and description	Class	Classification code	Packing group	Labels	Special provisions	Limited and excepted quantities		Packaging			Portable tanks and bulk containers	
									Packing instructions	Special packing provisions	Mixed packing provisions	Instructions	Special provisions
	3.1.2	2.2	2.2	2.1.1.3	5.2.2	3.3	3.4.6	3.5.1.2	4.1.4	4.1.4	4.1.10	4.2.5.2 7.3.2	4.2.5.3
(1)	(2)	(3a)	(3b)	(4)	(5)	(6)	(7a)	(7b)	(8)	(9a)	(9b)	(10)	(11)
1598	DINITRO-o-CRESOL	6.1	T2	II	6.1	43	LQ18	E4	P002 IBC08	B4	MP10	T3	TP33
1599	DINITROPHENOL SOLUTION	6.1	T1	II	6.1		LQ17	E4	P001 IBC02		MP15	T7	TP2
1599	DINITROPHENOL SOLUTION	6.1	T1	III	6.1		LQ7	E1	P001 IBC03 LP01 R001		MP19	T4	TP1
1600	DINITROTOLUENES, MOLTEN	6.1	T1	II	6.1		LQ0	E0				T7	TP3
1601	DISINFECTANT, SOLID, TOXIC, N.O.S.	6.1	T2	I	6.1	274	LQ0	E5	P002 IBC07		MP18	T6	TP33
1601	DISINFECTANT, SOLID, TOXIC, N.O.S.	6.1	T2	II	6.1	274	LQ18	E4	P002 IBC08	B4	MP10	T3	TP33
1601	DISINFECTANT, SOLID, TOXIC, N.O.S.	6.1	T2	III	6.1	274	LQ9	E1	P002 IBC08 LP02 R001	B3	MP10	T1	TP33
1602	DYE, LIQUID, TOXIC, N.O.S. or DYE INTERMEDIATE, LIQUID, TOXIC, N.O.S.	6.1	T1	I	6.1	274	LQ0	E5	P001		MP8 MP17		
1602	DYE, LIQUID, TOXIC, N.O.S. or DYE INTERMEDIATE, LIQUID, TOXIC, N.O.S.	6.1	T1	II	6.1	274	LQ17	E4	P001 IBC02		MP15		
1602	DYE, LIQUID, TOXIC, N.O.S. or DYE INTERMEDIATE, LIQUID, TOXIC, N.O.S.	6.1	T1	III	6.1	274	LQ7	E1	P001 IBC03 LP01 R001		MP19		
1603	ETHYL BROMOACETATE	6.1	TF1	II	6.1 +3		LQ17	E4	P001 IBC02		MP15	T7	TP2
1604	ETHYLENEDIAMINE	8	CF1	II	8 +3		LQ22	E2	P001 IBC02		MP15	T7	TP2
1605	ETHYLENE DIBROMIDE	6.1	T1	I	6.1		LQ0	E5	P602		MP8 MP17	T14	TP2
1606	FERRIC ARSENATE	6.1	T5	II	6.1		LQ18	E4	P002 IBC08	B4	MP10	T3	TP33
1607	FERRIC ARSENITE	6.1	T5	II	6.1		LQ18	E4	P002 IBC08	B4	MP10	T3	TP33
1608	FERROUS ARSENATE	6.1	T5	II	6.1		LQ18	E4	P002 IBC08	B4	MP10	T3	TP33
1611	HEXAETHYL TETRAPHOSPHATE	6.1	T1	II	6.1		LQ17	E4	P001 IBC02		MP15	T7	TP2
1612	HEXAETHYL TETRAPHOSPHATE AND COMPRESSED GAS MIXTURE	2	1T		2.3		LQ0	E0	P200		MP9	(M)	
1613	HYDROCYANIC ACID, AQUEOUS SOLUTION (HYDROGEN CYANIDE, AQUEOUS SOLUTION) with not more than 20% hydrogen cyanide	6.1	TF1	I	6.1 +3	48	LQ0	E5	P601		MP8 MP17	T14	TP2
1614	HYDROGEN CYANIDE, STABILIZED, containing less than 3% water and absorbed in a porous inert material	6.1	TF1	I	6.1 +3	603	LQ0	E5	P099 P601	RR10	MP2		
1616	LEAD ACETATE	6.1	T5	III	6.1		LQ9	E1	P002 IBC08 LP02 R001	B3	MP10	T1	TP33
1617	LEAD ARSENATES	6.1	T5	II	6.1		LQ18	E4	P002 IBC08	B4	MP10	T3	TP33
1618	LEAD ARSENITES	6.1	T5	II	6.1		LQ18	E4	P002 IBC08	B4	MP10	T3	TP33
1620	LEAD CYANIDE	6.1	T5	II	6.1		LQ18	E4	P002 IBC08	B4	MP10	T3	TP33
1621	LONDON PURPLE	6.1	T5	II	6.1	43	LQ18	E4	P002 IBC08	B4	MP10	T3	TP33
1622	MAGNESIUM ARSENATE	6.1	T5	II	6.1		LQ18	E4	P002 IBC08	B4	MP10	T3	TP33

ADR tank		Vehicle for tank carriage	Transport category (Tunnel restriction code)	Special provisions for carriage				Hazard identification No.	UN No.	Name and description
Tank code	Special provisions			Packages	Bulk	Loading, unloading and handling	Operation			
4.3	4.3.5, 6.8.4	9.1.1.2	1.1.3.6 (8.6)	7.2.4	7.3.3	7.5.11	8.5	5.3.2.3		3.1.2
(12)	(13)	(14)	(15)	(16)	(17)	(18)	(19)	(20)	(1)	(2)
SGAH L4BH	TU15 TE19	AT	2 (D/E)	V11		CV13 CV28	S9 S19	60	1598	DINITRO-o-CRESOL
L4BH	TU15 TE19	AT	2 (D/E)			CV13 CV28	S9 S19	60	1599	DINITROPHENOL SOLUTION
L4BH	TU15 TE19	AT	2 (E)			CV13 CV28	S9	60	1599	DINITROPHENOL SOLUTION
L4BH	TU15 TE19	AT	0 (D/E)			CV13	S9 S19	60	1600	DINITROTOLUENES, MOLTEN
S10AH L10CH	TU15 TE19	AT	1 (C/E)	V10 V12		CV1 CV13 CV28	S9 S14	66	1601	DISINFECTANT, SOLID, TOXIC, N.O.S.
SGAH L4BH	TU15 TE19	AT	2 (D/E)	V11		CV13 CV28	S9 S19	60	1601	DISINFECTANT, SOLID, TOXIC, N.O.S.
SGAH L4BH	TU15 TE19	AT	2 (E)		VV9	CV13 CV28	S9	60	1601	DISINFECTANT, SOLID, TOXIC, N.O.S.
L10CH	TU14 TU15 TE19 TE21	AT	1 (C/E)			CV1 CV13 CV28	S9 S14	66	1602	DYE, LIQUID, TOXIC, N.O.S. or DYE INTERMEDIATE, LIQUID, TOXIC, N.O.S.
L4BH	TU15 TE19	AT	2 (D/E)			CV13 CV28	S9 S19	60	1602	DYE, LIQUID, TOXIC, N.O.S. or DYE INTERMEDIATE, LIQUID, TOXIC, N.O.S.
L4BH	TU15 TE19	AT	2 (E)			CV13 CV28	S9	60	1602	DYE, LIQUID, TOXIC, N.O.S. or DYE INTERMEDIATE, LIQUID, TOXIC, N.O.S.
L4BH	TU15 TE19	FL	2 (D/E)			CV13 CV28	S2 S9 S19	63	1603	ETHYL BROMOACETATE
L4BN		FL	2 (D/E)				S2	83	1604	ETHYLENEDIAMINE
L10CH	TU14 TU15 TE19 TE21	AT	1 (C/E)			CV1 CV13 CV28	S9 S14	66	1605	ETHYLENE DIBROMIDE
SGAH	TU15 TE19	AT	2 (D/E)	V11		CV13 CV28	S9 S19	60	1606	FERRIC ARSENATE
SGAH	TU15 TE19	AT	2 (D/E)	V11		CV13 CV28	S9 S19	60	1607	FERRIC ARSENITE
SGAH	TU15 TE19	AT	2 (D/E)	V11		CV13 CV28	S9 S19	60	1608	FERROUS ARSENATE
L4BH	TU15 TE19	AT	2 (D/E)			CV13 CV28	S9 S19	60	1611	HEXAETHYL TETRAPHOSPHATE
CxBH(M)	TA4 TT9	AT	1 (C/D)			CV9 CV10 CV36	S14	26	1612	HEXAETHYL TETRAPHOSPHATE AND COMPRESSED GAS MIXTURE
L15DH(+)	TU14 TU15 TE19 TE21	FL	0 (C/D)			CV1 CV13 CV28	S2 S9 S14	663	1613	HYDROCYANIC ACID, AQUEOUS SOLUTION (HYDROGEN CYANIDE, AQUEOUS SOLUTION) with not more than 20% hydrogen cyanide
			0 (D)			CV1 CV13 CV28	S2 S9 S10 S14		1614	HYDROGEN CYANIDE, STABILIZED, containing less than 3% water and absorbed in a porous inert material
SGAH L4BH	TU15 TE19	AT	2 (E)		VV9	CV13 CV28	S9	60	1616	LEAD ACETATE
SGAH	TU15 TE19	AT	2 (D/E)	V11		CV13 CV28	S9 S19	60	1617	LEAD ARSENATES
SGAH	TU15 TE19	AT	2 (D/E)	V11		CV13 CV28	S9 S19	60	1618	LEAD ARSENITES
SGAH	TU15 TE19	AT	2 (D/E)	V11		CV13 CV28	S9 S19	60	1620	LEAD CYANIDE
SGAH	TU15 TE19	AT	2 (D/E)	V11		CV13 CV28	S9 S19	60	1621	LONDON PURPLE
SGAH	TU15 TE19	AT	2 (D/E)	V11		CV13 CV28	S9 S19	60	1622	MAGNESIUM ARSENATE

UN No.	Name and description	Class	Classification code	Packing group	Labels	Special provisions	Limited and excepted quantities		Packaging			Portable tanks and bulk containers	
							Limited quantities	Excepted quantities	Packing instructions	Special packing provisions	Mixed packing provisions	Instructions	Special provisions
	3.1.2	2.2	2.2	2.1.1.3	5.2.2	3.3	3.4.6	3.5.1.2	4.1.4	4.1.4	4.1.10	4.2.5.2 7.3.2	4.2.5.3
(1)	(2)	(3a)	(3b)	(4)	(5)	(6)	(7a)	(7b)	(8)	(9a)	(9b)	(10)	(11)
1623	MERCURIC ARSENATE	6.1	T5	II	6.1		LQ18	E4	P002 IBC08	B4	MP10	T3	TP33
1624	MERCURIC CHLORIDE	6.1	T5	II	6.1		LQ18	E4	P002 IBC08	B4	MP10	T3	TP33
1625	MERCURIC NITRATE	6.1	T5	II	6.1		LQ18	E4	P002 IBC08	B4	MP10	T3	TP33
1626	MERCURIC POTASSIUM CYANIDE	6.1	T5	I	6.1		LQ0	E5	P002 IBC07		MP18	T6	TP33
1627	MERCUROUS NITRATE	6.1	T5	II	6.1		LQ18	E4	P002 IBC08	B4	MP10	T3	TP33
1629	MERCURY ACETATE	6.1	T5	II	6.1		LQ18	E4	P002 IBC08	B4	MP10	T3	TP33
1630	MERCURY AMMONIUM CHLORIDE	6.1	T5	II	6.1		LQ18	E4	P002 IBC08	B4	MP10	T3	TP33
1631	MERCURY BENZOATE	6.1	T5	II	6.1		LQ18	E4	P002 IBC08	B4	MP10	T3	TP33
1634	MERCURY BROMIDES	6.1	T5	II	6.1		LQ18	E4	P002 IBC08	B4	MP10	T3	TP33
1636	MERCURY CYANIDE	6.1	T5	II	6.1		LQ18	E4	P002 IBC08	B4	MP10	T3	TP33
1637	MERCURY GLUCONATE	6.1	T5	II	6.1		LQ18	E4	P002 IBC08	B4	MP10	T3	TP33
1638	MERCURY IODIDE	6.1	T5	II	6.1		LQ18	E4	P002 IBC08	B4	MP10	T3	TP33
1639	MERCURY NUCLEATE	6.1	T5	II	6.1		LQ18	E4	P002 IBC08	B4	MP10	T3	TP33
1640	MERCURY OLEATE	6.1	T5	II	6.1		LQ18	E4	P002 IBC08	B4	MP10	T3	TP33
1641	MERCURY OXIDE	6.1	T5	II	6.1		LQ18	E4	P002 IBC08	B4	MP10	T3	TP33
1642	MERCURY OXYCYANIDE, DESENSITIZED	6.1	T5	II	6.1		LQ18	E4	P002 IBC08	B4	MP10	T3	TP33
1643	MERCURY POTASSIUM IODIDE	6.1	T5	II	6.1		LQ18	E4	P002 IBC08	B4	MP10	T3	TP33
1644	MERCURY SALICYLATE	6.1	T5	II	6.1		LQ18	E4	P002 IBC08	B4	MP10	T3	TP33
1645	MERCURY SULPHATE	6.1	T5	II	6.1		LQ18	E4	P002 IBC08	B4	MP10	T3	TP33
1646	MERCURY THIOCYANATE	6.1	T5	II	6.1		LQ18	E4	P002 IBC08	B4	MP10	T3	TP33
1647	METHYL BROMIDE AND ETHYLENE DIBROMIDE MIXTURE, LIQUID	6.1	T1	I	6.1		LQ0	E5	P602		MP8 MP17	T20	TP2
1648	ACETONITRILE	3	F1	II	3		LQ4	E2	P001 IBC02 R001		MP19	T7	TP2
1649	MOTOR FUEL ANTI-KNOCK MIXTURE having a flash-point above 60 °C	6.1	T3	I	6.1		LQ0	E5	P602		MP8 MP17	T14	TP2
1649	MOTOR FUEL ANTI-KNOCK MIXTURE having a flash-point of not more than 60 °C	6.1	TF1	I	6.1 +3		LQ0	E5	P602		MP8 MP17	T14	TP2
1650	beta-NAPHTHYLAMINE, SOLID	6.1	T2	II	6.1		LQ18	E4	P002 IBC08	B4	MP10	T3	TP33
1651	NAPHTHYLTHIOUREA	6.1	T2	II	6.1	43	LQ18	E4	P002 IBC08	B4	MP10	T3	TP33
1652	NAPHTHYLUREA	6.1	T2	II	6.1		LQ18	E4	P002 IBC08	B4	MP10	T3	TP33
1653	NICKEL CYANIDE	6.1	T5	II	6.1		LQ18	E4	P002 IBC08	B4	MP10	T3	TP33
1654	NICOTINE	6.1	T1	II	6.1		LQ17	E4	P001 IBC02		MP15		
1655	NICOTINE COMPOUND, SOLID, N.O.S. or NICOTINE PREPARATION, SOLID, N.O.S.	6.1	T2	I	6.1	43 274	LQ0	E5	P002 IBC07		MP18	T6	TP33
1655	NICOTINE COMPOUND, SOLID, N.O.S. or NICOTINE PREPARATION, SOLID, N.O.S.	6.1	T2	II	6.1	43 274	LQ18	E4	P002 IBC08	B4	MP10	T3	TP33

ADR tank		Vehicle for tank carriage	Transport category (Tunnel restriction code)	Special provisions for carriage				Hazard identifi-cation No.	UN No.	Name and description
Tank code	Special provisions			Packages	Bulk	Loading, unloading and handling	Operation			
4.3	4.3.5, 6.8.4	9.1.1.2	1.1.3.6 (8.6)	7.2.4	7.3.3	7.5.11	8.5	5.3.2.3		3.1.2
(12)	(13)	(14)	(15)	(16)	(17)	(18)	(19)	(20)	(1)	(2)
SGAH	TU15 TE19	AT	2 (D/E)	V11		CV13 CV28	S9 S19	60	1623	MERCURIC ARSENATE
SGAH	TU15 TE19	AT	2 (D/E)	V11		CV13 CV28	S9 S19	60	1624	MERCURIC CHLORIDE
SGAH	TU15 TE19	AT	2 (D/E)	V11		CV13 CV28	S9 S19	60	1625	MERCURIC NITRATE
S10AH	TU15 TE19	AT	1 (C/E)	V10 V12		CV1 CV13 CV28	S9 S14	66	1626	MERCURIC POTASSIUM CYANIDE
SGAH	TU15 TE19	AT	2 (D/E)	V11		CV13 CV28	S9 S19	60	1627	MERCUROUS NITRATE
SGAH	TU15 TE19	AT	2 (D/E)	V11		CV13 CV28	S9 S19	60	1629	MERCURY ACETATE
SGAH	TU15 TE19	AT	2 (D/E)	V11		CV13 CV28	S9 S19	60	1630	MERCURY AMMONIUM CHLORIDE
SGAH	TU15 TE19	AT	2 (D/E)	V11		CV13 CV28	S9 S19	60	1631	MERCURY BENZOATE
SGAH	TU15 TE19	AT	2 (D/E)	V11		CV13 CV28	S9 S19	60	1634	MERCURY BROMIDES
SGAH	TU15 TE19	AT	2 (D/E)	V11		CV13 CV28	S9 S19	60	1636	MERCURY CYANIDE
SGAH	TU15 TE19	AT	2 (D/E)	V11		CV13 CV28	S9 S19	60	1637	MERCURY GLUCONATE
SGAH	TU15 TE19	AT	2 (D/E)	V11		CV13 CV28	S9 S19	60	1638	MERCURY IODIDE
SGAH	TU15 TE19	AT	2 (D/E)	V11		CV13 CV28	S9 S19	60	1639	MERCURY NUCLEATE
SGAH	TU15 TE19	AT	2 (D/E)	V11		CV13 CV28	S9 S19	60	1640	MERCURY OLEATE
SGAH	TU15 TE19	AT	2 (D/E)	V11		CV13 CV28	S9 S19	60	1641	MERCURY OXIDE
SGAH	TU15 TE19	AT	2 (D/E)	V11		CV13 CV28	S9 S19	60	1642	MERCURY OXYCYANIDE, DESENSITIZED
SGAH	TU15 TE19	AT	2 (D/E)	V11		CV13 CV28	S9 S19	60	1643	MERCURY POTASSIUM IODIDE
SGAH	TU15 TE19	AT	2 (D/E)	V11		CV13 CV28	S9 S19	60	1644	MERCURY SALICYLATE
SGAH	TU15 TE19	AT	2 (D/E)	V11		CV13 CV28	S9 S19	60	1645	MERCURY SULPHATE
SGAH	TU15 TE19	AT	2 (D/E)	V11		CV13 CV28	S9 S19	60	1646	MERCURY THIOCYANATE
L10CH	TU14 TU15 TE19 TE21	AT	1 (C/E)			CV1 CV13 CV28	S9 S14	66	1647	METHYL BROMIDE AND ETHYLENE DIBROMIDE MIXTURE, LIQUID
LGBF		FL	2 (D/E)				S2 S20	33	1648	ACETONITRILE
L10CH	TU14 TU15 TE19 TE21 TT6	AT	1 (C/E)			CV1 CV13 CV28	S9 S14	66	1649	MOTOR FUEL ANTI-KNOCK MIXTURE having a flash-point above 60 °C
L10CH	TU14 TU15 TE19 TE21 TT6	FL	1 (C/D)			CV1 CV13 CV28	S2 S9 S14	663	1649	MOTOR FUEL ANTI-KNOCK MIXTURE having a flash-point of not more than 60 °C
SGAH L4BH	TU15 TE19	AT	2 (D/E)	V11		CV13 CV28	S9 S19	60	1650	beta-NAPHTHYLAMINE, SOLID
SGAH	TU15 TE19	AT	2 (D/E)	V11		CV13 CV28	S9 S19	60	1651	NAPHTHYLTHIOUREA
SGAH	TU15 TE19	AT	2 (D/E)	V11		CV13 CV28	S9 S19	60	1652	NAPHTHYLUREA
SGAH L4BH	TU15 TE19	AT	2 (D/E)	V11		CV13 CV28	S9 S19	60	1653	NICKEL CYANIDE
L4BH	TU15 TE19	AT	2 (D/E)			CV13 CV28	S9 S19	60	1654	NICOTINE
S10AH L10CH	TU15 TE19	AT	1 (C/E)	V10 V12		CV1 CV13 CV28	S9 S14	66	1655	NICOTINE COMPOUND, SOLID, N.O.S. or NICOTINE PREPARATION, SOLID, N.O.S.
SGAH L4BH	TU15 TE19	AT	2 (D/E)	V11		CV13 CV28	S9 S19	60	1655	NICOTINE COMPOUND, SOLID, N.O.S. or NICOTINE PREPARATION, SOLID, N.O.S.

UN No.	Name and description	Class	Classifi-cation code	Packing group	Labels	Special provi-sions	Limited and excepted quantities		Packaging			Portable tanks and bulk containers	
									Packing instruc-tions	Special packing provisions	Mixed packing provisions	Instruc-tions	Special provisions
3.1.2		2.2	2.2	2.1.1.3	5.2.2	3.3	3.4.6	3.5.1.2	4.1.4	4.1.4	4.1.10	4.2.5.2 7.3.2	4.2.5.3
(1)	(2)	(3a)	(3b)	(4)	(5)	(6)	(7a)	(7b)	(8)	(9a)	(9b)	(10)	(11)
1655	NICOTINE COMPOUND, SOLID, N.O.S. or NICOTINE PREPARATION, SOLID, N.O.S.	6.1	T2	III	6.1	43 274	LQ9	E1	P002 IBC08 LP02 R001	B3	MP10	T1	TP33
1656	NICOTINE HYDROCHLORIDE, LIQUID or SOLUTION	6.1	T1	II	6.1	43	LQ17	E4	P001 IBC02		MP15		
1656	NICOTINE HYDROCHLORIDE, LIQUID or SOLUTION	6.1	T1	III	6.1	43	LQ7	E1	P001 IBC03 LP01 R001		MP19		
1657	NICOTINE SALICYLATE	6.1	T2	II	6.1		LQ18	E4	P002 IBC08	B4	MP10	T3	TP33
1658	NICOTINE SULPHATE, SOLUTION	6.1	T1	II	6.1		LQ17	E4	P001 IBC02		MP15	T7	TP2
1658	NICOTINE SULPHATE, SOLUTION	6.1	T1	III	6.1		LQ7	E1	P001 IBC03 LP01 R001		MP19	T7	TP2
1659	NICOTINE TARTRATE	6.1	T2	II	6.1		LQ18	E4	P002 IBC08	B4	MP10	T3	TP33
1660	NITRIC OXIDE, COMPRESSED	2	1TOC		2.3 +5.1 +8		LQ0	E0	P200		MP9		
1661	NITROANILINES (o-, m-, p-)	6.1	T2	II	6.1	279	LQ18	E4	P002 IBC08	B4	MP10	T3	TP33
1662	NITROBENZENE	6.1	T1	II	6.1	279	LQ17	E4	P001 IBC02		MP15	T7	TP2
1663	NITROPHENOLS (o-, m-, p-)	6.1	T2	III	6.1	279	LQ9	E1	P002 IBC08 LP02 R001	B3	MP10	T1	TP33
1664	NITROTOLUENES, LIQUID	6.1	T1	II	6.1		LQ17	E4	P001 IBC02		MP15	T7	TP2
1665	NITROXYLENES, LIQUID	6.1	T1	II	6.1		LQ17	E4	P001 IBC02		MP15	T7	TP2
1669	PENTACHLOROETHANE	6.1	T1	II	6.1		LQ17	E4	P001 IBC02		MP15	T7	TP2
1670	PERCHLOROMETHYL MERCAPTAN	6.1	T1	I	6.1		LQ0	E5	P602		MP8 MP17	T14	TP2
1671	PHENOL, SOLID	6.1	T2	II	6.1	279	LQ18	E4	P002 IBC08	B4	MP10	T3	TP33
1672	PHENYLCARBYLAMINE CHLORIDE	6.1	T1	I	6.1		LQ0	E5	P602		MP8 MP17	T14	TP2
1673	PHENYLENEDIAMINES (o-, m-, p-)	6.1	T2	III	6.1	279	LQ9	E1	P002 IBC08 LP02 R001	B3	MP10	T1	TP33
1674	PHENYLMERCURIC ACETATE	6.1	T3	II	6.1	43	LQ18	E4	P002 IBC08	B4	MP10	T3	TP33
1677	POTASSIUM ARSENATE	6.1	T5	II	6.1		LQ18	E4	P002 IBC08	B4	MP10	T3	TP33
1678	POTASSIUM ARSENITE	6.1	T5	II	6.1		LQ18	E4	P002 IBC08	B4	MP10	T3	TP33
1679	POTASSIUM CUPROCYANIDE	6.1	T5	II	6.1		LQ18	E4	P002 IBC08	B4	MP10	T3	TP33
1680	POTASSIUM CYANIDE, SOLID	6.1	T5	I	6.1		LQ0	E5	P002 IBC07		MP18	T6	TP33
1683	SILVER ARSENITE	6.1	T5	II	6.1		LQ18	E4	P002 IBC08	B4	MP10	T3	TP33
1684	SILVER CYANIDE	6.1	T5	II	6.1		LQ18	E4	P002 IBC08	B4	MP10	T3	TP33
1685	SODIUM ARSENATE	6.1	T5	II	6.1		LQ18	E4	P002 IBC08	B4	MP10	T3	TP33
1686	SODIUM ARSENITE, AQUEOUS SOLUTION	6.1	T4	II	6.1	43	LQ17	E4	P001 IBC02		MP15	T7	TP2

| ADR tank | | Vehicle for tank carriage | Transport category (Tunnel restriction code) | Special provisions for carriage | | | | Hazard identifi-cation No. | UN No. | Name and description |
| Tank code | Special provisions | | | Packages | Bulk | Loading, unloading and handling | Operation | | | |
4.3	4.3.5, 6.8.4	9.1.1.2	1.1.3.6 (8.6)	7.2.4	7.3.3	7.5.11	8.5	5.3.2.3		3.1.2
(12)	(13)	(14)	(15)	(16)	(17)	(18)	(19)	(20)	(1)	(2)
SGAH L4BH	TU15 TE19	AT	2 (E)		VV9	CV13 CV28	S9	60	1655	NICOTINE COMPOUND, SOLID, N.O.S. or NICOTINE PREPARATION, SOLID, N.O.S.
L4BH	TU15 TE19	AT	2 (D/E)			CV13 CV28	S9 S19	60	1656	NICOTINE HYDROCHLORIDE, LIQUID or SOLUTION
L4BH	TU15 TE19	AT	2 (E)			CV13 CV28	S9	60	1656	NICOTINE HYDROCHLORIDE, LIQUID or SOLUTION
SGAH L4BH	TU15 TE19	AT	2 (D/E)	V11		CV13 CV28	S9 S19	60	1657	NICOTINE SALICYLATE
L4BH	TU15 TE19	AT	2 (D/E)			CV13 CV28	S9 S19	60	1658	NICOTINE SULPHATE, SOLUTION
L4BH	TU15 TE19	AT	2 (E)			CV13 CV28	S9	60	1658	NICOTINE SULPHATE, SOLUTION
SGAH L4BH	TU15 TE19	AT	2 (D/E)	V11		CV13 CV28	S9 S19	60	1659	NICOTINE TARTRATE
			1 (D)			CV9 CV10 CV36	S14		1660	NITRIC OXIDE, COMPRESSED
SGAH L4BH	TU15 TE19	AT	2 (D/E)	V11		CV13 CV28	S9 S19	60	1661	NITROANILINES (o-, m-, p-)
L4BH	TU15 TE19	AT	2 (D/E)			CV13 CV28	S9 S19	60	1662	NITROBENZENE
SGAH L4BH	TU15 TE19	AT	2 (E)		VV9	CV13 CV28	S9	60	1663	NITROPHENOLS (o-, m-, p-)
L4BH	TU15 TE19	AT	2 (D/E)			CV13 CV28	S9 S19	60	1664	NITROTOLUENES, LIQUID
L4BH	TU15 TE19	AT	2 (D/E)			CV13 CV28	S9 S19	60	1665	NITROXYLENES, LIQUID
L4BH	TU15 TE19	AT	2 (D/E)			CV13 CV28	S9 S19	60	1669	PENTACHLOROETHANE
L10CH	TU14 TU15 TE19 TE21	AT	1 (C/E)			CV1 CV13 CV28	S9 S14	66	1670	PERCHLOROMETHYL MERCAPTAN
SGAH	TU15 TE19	AT	2 (D/E)	V11		CV13 CV28	S9 S19	60	1671	PHENOL, SOLID
L10CH	TU14 TU15 TE19 TE21	AT	1 (C/E)			CV1 CV13 CV28	S9 S14	66	1672	PHENYLCARBYLAMINE CHLORIDE
SGAH L4BH	TU15 TE19	AT	2 (E)		VV9	CV13 CV28	S9	60	1673	PHENYLENEDIAMINES (o-, m-, p-)
SGAH L4BH	TU15 TE19	AT	2 (D/E)	V11		CV13 CV28	S9 S19	60	1674	PHENYLMERCURIC ACETATE
SGAH	TU15 TE19	AT	2 (D/E)	V11		CV13 CV28	S9 S19	60	1677	POTASSIUM ARSENATE
SGAH	TU15 TE19	AT	2 (D/E)	V11		CV13 CV28	S9 S19	60	1678	POTASSIUM ARSENITE
SGAH	TU15 TE19	AT	2 (D/E)	V11		CV13 CV28	S9 S19	60	1679	POTASSIUM CUPROCYANIDE
S10AH	TU15 TE19	AT	1 (C/E)	V10 V12		CV1 CV13 CV28	S9 S14	66	1680	POTASSIUM CYANIDE, SOLID
SGAH	TU15 TE19	AT	2 (D/E)	V11		CV13 CV28	S9 S19	60	1683	SILVER ARSENITE
SGAH	TU15 TE19	AT	2 (D/E)	V11		CV13 CV28	S9 S19	60	1684	SILVER CYANIDE
SGAH	TU15 TE19	AT	2 (D/E)	V11		CV13 CV28	S9 S19	60	1685	SODIUM ARSENATE
L4BH	TU15 TE19	AT	2 (D/E)			CV13 CV28	S9 S19	60	1686	SODIUM ARSENITE, AQUEOUS SOLUTION

UN No.	Name and description	Class	Classifi-cation code	Packing group	Labels	Special provi-sions	Limited and excepted quantities		Packaging			Portable tanks and bulk containers	
									Packing instruc-tions	Special packing provisions	Mixed packing provisions	Instruc-tions	Special provisions
	3.1.2	2.2	2.2	2.1.1.3	5.2.2	3.3	3.4.6	3.5.1.2	4.1.4	4.1.4	4.1.10	4.2.5.2 7.3.2	4.2.5.3
(1)	(2)	(3a)	(3b)	(4)	(5)	(6)	(7a)	(7b)	(8)	(9a)	(9b)	(10)	(11)
1686	SODIUM ARSENITE, AQUEOUS SOLUTION	6.1	T4	III	6.1	43	LQ7	E1	P001 IBC03 LP01 R001		MP19	T4	TP2
1687	SODIUM AZIDE	6.1	T5	II	6.1		LQ18	E4	P002 IBC08	B4	MP10		
1688	SODIUM CACODYLATE	6.1	T5	II	6.1		LQ18	E4	P002 IBC08	B4	MP10	T3	TP33
1689	SODIUM CYANIDE, SOLID	6.1	T5	I	6.1		LQ0	E5	P002 IBC07		MP18	T6	TP33
1690	SODIUM FLUORIDE, SOLID	6.1	T5	III	6.1		LQ9	E1	P002 IBC08 LP02 R001	B3	MP10	T1	TP33
1691	STRONTIUM ARSENITE	6.1	T5	II	6.1		LQ18	E4	P002 IBC08	B4	MP10	T3	TP33
1692	STRYCHNINE or STRYCHNINE SALTS	6.1	T2	I	6.1		LQ0	E5	P002 IBC07		MP18	T6	TP33
1693	TEAR GAS SUBSTANCE, LIQUID, N.O.S.	6.1	T1	I	6.1	274	LQ0	E5	P001		MP8 MP17		
1693	TEAR GAS SUBSTANCE, LIQUID, N.O.S.	6.1	T1	II	6.1	274	LQ17	E4	P001 IBC02		MP15		
1694	BROMOBENZYL CYANIDES, LIQUID	6.1	T1	I	6.1	138	LQ0	E5	P001		MP8 MP17	T14	TP2
1695	CHLOROACETONE, STABILIZED	6.1	TFC	I	6.1 +3 +8		LQ0	E5	P001		MP8 MP17	T20	TP2 TP35
1697	CHLOROACETOPHENONE, SOLID	6.1	T2	II	6.1		LQ18	E4	P002 IBC08	B4	MP10	T3	TP33
1698	DIPHENYLAMINE CHLOROARSINE	6.1	T3	I	6.1		LQ0	E5	P002		MP18	T6	TP33
1699	DIPHENYLCHLORO-ARSINE, LIQUID	6.1	T3	I	6.1		LQ0	E5	P001		MP8 MP17		
1700	TEAR GAS CANDLES	6.1	TF3	II	6.1 +4.1		LQ18	E0	P600				
1701	XYLYL BROMIDE, LIQUID	6.1	T1	II	6.1		LQ17	E4	P001 IBC02		MP15	T7	TP2
1702	1,1,2,2-TETRACHLOROETHANE	6.1	T1	II	6.1		LQ17	E4	P001 IBC02		MP15	T7	TP2
1704	TETRAETHYL DITHIOPYROPHOSPHATE	6.1	T2	II	6.1	43	LQ18	E4	P001 IBC02		MP10	T7	TP2
1707	THALLIUM COMPOUND, N.O.S.	6.1	T5	II	6.1	43 274	LQ18	E4	P002 IBC08	B4	MP10	T3	TP33
1708	TOLUIDINES, LIQUID	6.1	T1	II	6.1	279	LQ17	E4	P001 IBC02		MP15	T7	TP2
1709	2,4-TOLUYLENEDIAMINE, SOLID	6.1	T2	III	6.1		LQ9	E1	P002 IBC08 LP02 R001	B3	MP10	T1	TP33
1710	TRICHLOROETHYLENE	6.1	T1	III	6.1		LQ7	E1	P001 IBC03 LP01 R001		MP19	T4	TP1
1711	XYLIDINES, LIQUID	6.1	T1	II	6.1		LQ17	E4	P001 IBC02		MP15	T7	TP2
1712	ZINC ARSENATE, ZINC ARSENITE or ZINC ARSENATE AND ZINC ARSENITE MIXTURE	6.1	T5	II	6.1		LQ18	E4	P002 IBC08	B4	MP10	T3	TP33
1713	ZINC CYANIDE	6.1	T5	I	6.1		LQ0	E5	P002 IBC07		MP18	T6	TP33
1714	ZINC PHOSPHIDE	4.3	WT2	I	4.3 +6.1		LQ0	E0	P403		MP2		

ADR tank		Vehicle for tank carriage	Transport category (Tunnel restriction code)	Special provisions for carriage				Hazard identifi-cation No.	UN No.	Name and description
Tank code	Special provisions			Packages	Bulk	Loading, unloading and handling	Operation			
4.3	4.3.5, 6.8.4	9.1.1.2	1.1.3.6 (8.6)	7.2.4	7.3.3	7.5.11	8.5	5.3.2.3		3.1.2
(12)	(13)	(14)	(15)	(16)	(17)	(18)	(19)	(20)	(1)	(2)
L4BH	TU15 TE19	AT	2 (E)			CV13 CV28	S9	60	1686	SODIUM ARSENITE, AQUEOUS SOLUTION
			2 (D/E)	V11		CV13 CV28	S9 S19		1687	SODIUM AZIDE
SGAH	TU15 TE19	AT	2 (D/E)	V11		CV13 CV28	S9 S19	60	1688	SODIUM CACODYLATE
S10AH	TU15 TE19	AT	1 (C/E)	V10 V12		CV1 CV13 CV28	S9 S14	66	1689	SODIUM CYANIDE, SOLID
SGAH	TU15 TE19	AT	2 (E)		VV9	CV13 CV28	S9	60	1690	SODIUM FLUORIDE, SOLID
SGAH	TU15 TE19	AT	2 (D/E)	V11		CV13 CV28	S9 S19	60	1691	STRONTIUM ARSENITE
S10AH	TU15 TE19	AT	1 (C/E)	V10 V12		CV1 CV13 CV28	S9 S14	66	1692	STRYCHNINE or STRYCHNINE SALTS
L10CH	TU14 TU15 TE19 TE21	AT	1 (C/E)			CV1 CV13 CV28	S9 S14	66	1693	TEAR GAS SUBSTANCE, LIQUID, N.O.S.
L4BH	TU15 TE19	AT	2 (D/E)			CV13 CV28	S9 S19	60	1693	TEAR GAS SUBSTANCE, LIQUID, N.O.S.
L10CH	TU14 TU15 TE19 TE21	AT	1 (C/E)			CV1 CV13 CV28	S9 S14	66	1694	BROMOBENZYL CYANIDES, LIQUID
L10CH	TU14 TU15 TE19 TE21	FL	1 (C/D)			CV1 CV13 CV28	S2 S9 S14	663	1695	CHLOROACETONE, STABILIZED
SGAH L4BH	TU15 TE19	AT	2 (D/E)	V11		CV13 CV28	S9 S19	60	1697	CHLOROACETOPHENONE, SOLID
S10AH	TU15 TE19	AT	1 (C/E)			CV1 CV13 CV28	S9 S14	66	1698	DIPHENYLAMINE CHLOROARSINE
L10CH	TU14 TU15 TE19 TE21	AT	1 (C/E)			CV1 CV13 CV28	S9 S14	66	1699	DIPHENYLCHLORO-ARSINE, LIQUID
			2 (D/E)			CV13 CV28	S9 S19		1700	TEAR GAS CANDLES
L4BH	TU15 TE19	AT	2 (D/E)			CV13 CV28	S9 S19	60	1701	XYLYL BROMIDE, LIQUID
L4BH	TU15 TE19	AT	2 (D/E)			CV13 CV28	S9 S19	60	1702	1,1,2,2-TETRACHLOROETHANE
SGAH L4BH	TU15 TE19	AT	2 (D/E)	V11		CV13 CV28	S9 S19	60	1704	TETRAETHYL DITHIOPYROPHOSPHATE
SGAH L4BH	TU15 TE19	AT	2 (D/E)	V11		CV13 CV28	S9 S19	60	1707	THALLIUM COMPOUND, N.O.S.
L4BH	TU15 TE19	AT	2 (D/E)			CV13 CV28	S9 S19	60	1708	TOLUIDINES, LIQUID
SGAH L4BH	TU15 TE19	AT	2 (E)		VV9	CV13 CV28	S9	60	1709	2,4-TOLUYLENEDIAMINE, SOLID
L4BH	TU15 TE19	AT	2 (E)			CV13 CV28	S9	60	1710	TRICHLOROETHYLENE
L4BH	TU15 TE19	AT	2 (D/E)			CV13 CV28	S9 S19	60	1711	XYLIDINES, LIQUID
SGAH	TU15 TE19	AT	2 (D/E)	V11		CV13 CV28	S9 S19	60	1712	ZINC ARSENATE, ZINC ARSENITE or ZINC ARSENATE AND ZINC ARSENITE MIXTURE
S10AH	TU15 TE19	AT	1 (C/E)	V10 V12		CV1 CV13 CV28	S9 S14	66	1713	ZINC CYANIDE
			1 (E)	V1		CV23 CV28	S14		1714	ZINC PHOSPHIDE

UN No. 3.1.2	Name and description 3.1.2	Class 2.2	Classification code 2.2	Packing group 2.1.1.3	Labels 5.2.2	Special provisions 3.3	Limited and excepted quantities 3.4.6	Limited and excepted quantities 3.5.1.2	Packaging Packing instructions 4.1.4	Packaging Special packing provisions 4.1.4	Packaging Mixed packing provisions 4.1.10	Portable tanks and bulk containers Instructions 4.2.5.2 7.3.2	Portable tanks and bulk containers Special provisions 4.2.5.3
(1)	(2)	(3a)	(3b)	(4)	(5)	(6)	(7a)	(7b)	(8)	(9a)	(9b)	(10)	(11)
1715	ACETIC ANHYDRIDE	8	CF1	II	8 +3		LQ22	E2	P001 IBC02		MP15	T7	TP2
1716	ACETYL BROMIDE	8	C3	II	8		LQ22	E2	P001 IBC02		MP15	T8	TP2
1717	ACETYL CHLORIDE	3	FC	II	3 +8		LQ4	E2	P001 IBC02		MP19	T8	TP2
1718	BUTYL ACID PHOSPHATE	8	C3	III	8		LQ7	E1	P001 IBC03 LP01 R001		MP19	T4	TP1
1719	CAUSTIC ALKALI LIQUID, N.O.S.	8	C5	II	8	274	LQ22	E2	P001 IBC02		MP15	T11	TP2 TP27
1719	CAUSTIC ALKALI LIQUID, N.O.S.	8	C5	III	8	274	LQ7	E1	P001 IBC03 R001		MP19	T7	TP1 TP28
1722	ALLYL CHLOROFORMATE	6.1	TFC	I	6.1 +3 +8		LQ0	E5	P001		MP8 MP17	T14	TP2
1723	ALLYL IODIDE	3	FC	II	3 +8		LQ4	E2	P001 IBC02		MP19	T7	TP2
1724	ALLYLTRICHLOROSILANE, STABILIZED	8	CF1	II	8 +3		LQ22	E2	P010		MP15	T10	TP2 TP7
1725	ALUMINIUM BROMIDE, ANHYDROUS	8	C2	II	8	588	LQ23	E2	P002 IBC08	B4	MP10	T3	TP33
1726	ALUMINIUM CHLORIDE, ANHYDROUS	8	C2	II	8	588	LQ23	E2	P002 IBC08	B4	MP10	T3	TP33
1727	AMMONIUM HYDROGENDIFLUORIDE, SOLID	8	C2	II	8		LQ23	E2	P002 IBC08	B4	MP10	T3	TP33
1728	AMYLTRICHLOROSILANE	8	C3	II	8		LQ22	E2	P010		MP15	T10	TP2 TP7
1729	ANISOYL CHLORIDE	8	C4	II	8		LQ23	E2	P002 IBC08	B4	MP10	T3	TP33
1730	ANTIMONY PENTACHLORIDE, LIQUID	8	C1	II	8		LQ22	E2	P001 IBC02		MP15	T7	TP2
1731	ANTIMONY PENTACHLORIDE SOLUTION	8	C1	II	8		LQ22	E2	P001 IBC02		MP15	T7	TP2
1731	ANTIMONY PENTACHLORIDE SOLUTION	8	C1	III	8		LQ7	E1	P001 IBC03 LP01 R001		MP19	T4	TP1
1732	ANTIMONY PENTAFLUORIDE	8	CT1	II	8 +6.1		LQ22	E2	P001 IBC02		MP15	T7	TP2
1733	ANTIMONY TRICHLORIDE	8	C2	II	8		LQ23	E2	P002 IBC08	B4	MP10	T3	TP33
1736	BENZOYL CHLORIDE	8	C3	II	8		LQ22	E2	P001 IBC02		MP15	T8	TP2
1737	BENZYL BROMIDE	6.1	TC1	II	6.1 +8		LQ17	E4	P001 IBC02		MP15	T8	TP2
1738	BENZYL CHLORIDE	6.1	TC1	II	6.1 +8		LQ17	E4	P001 IBC02		MP15	T8	TP2
1739	BENZYL CHLOROFORMATE	8	C9	I	8		LQ0	E0	P001		MP8 MP17	T10	TP2
1740	HYDROGENDIFLUORIDES, SOLID, N.O.S.	8	C2	II	8	274 517	LQ23	E2	P002 IBC08	B4	MP10	T3	TP33
1740	HYDROGENDIFLUORIDES, SOLID, N.O.S.	8	C2	III	8	274 517	LQ24	E1	P002 IBC08 LP02 R001	B3	MP10	T1	TP33
1741	BORON TRICHLORIDE	2	2TC		2.3 +8		LQ0	E0	P200		MP9	(M)	
1742	BORON TRIFLUORIDE ACETIC ACID COMPLEX, LIQUID	8	C3	II	8		LQ22	E2	P001 IBC02		MP15	T8	TP2
1743	BORON TRIFLUORIDE PROPIONIC ACID COMPLEX, LIQUID	8	C3	II	8		LQ22	E2	P001 IBC02		MP15	T8	TP2

ADR tank		Vehicle for tank carriage	Transport category (Tunnel restriction code)	Special provisions for carriage				Hazard identification No.	UN No.	Name and description
Tank code	Special provisions			Packages	Bulk	Loading, unloading and handling	Operation			
4.3	4.3.5, 6.8.4	9.1.1.2	1.1.3.6 (8.6)	7.2.4	7.3.3	7.5.11	8.5	5.3.2.3		3.1.2
(12)	(13)	(14)	(15)	(16)	(17)	(18)	(19)	(20)	(1)	(2)
L4BN		FL	2 (D/E)				S2	83	1715	ACETIC ANHYDRIDE
L4BN		AT	2 (E)					80	1716	ACETYL BROMIDE
L4BH		FL	2 (D/E)				S2 S20	X338	1717	ACETYL CHLORIDE
L4BN		AT	3 (E)					80	1718	BUTYL ACID PHOSPHATE
L4BN		AT	2 (E)					80	1719	CAUSTIC ALKALI LIQUID, N.O.S.
L4BN		AT	3 (E)					80	1719	CAUSTIC ALKALI LIQUID, N.O.S.
L10CH	TU14 TU15 TE19 TE21	FL	1 (C/D)			CV1 CV13 CV28	S2 S9 S14	668	1722	ALLYL CHLOROFORMATE
L4BH		FL	2 (D/E)				S2 S20	338	1723	ALLYL IODIDE
L4BN		FL	2 (D/E)				S2	X839	1724	ALLYLTRICHLOROSILANE, STABILIZED
SGAN		AT	2 (E)	V11				80	1725	ALUMINIUM BROMIDE, ANHYDROUS
SGAN		AT	2 (E)	V11				80	1726	ALUMINIUM CHLORIDE, ANHYDROUS
SGAN		AT	2 (E)	V11				80	1727	AMMONIUM HYDROGENDIFLUORIDE, SOLID
L4BN		AT	2 (E)					X80	1728	AMYLTRICHLOROSILANE
SGAN L4BN		AT	2 (E)	V11				80	1729	ANISOYL CHLORIDE
L4BN		AT	2 (E)					X80	1730	ANTIMONY PENTACHLORIDE, LIQUID
L4BN		AT	2 (E)					80	1731	ANTIMONY PENTACHLORIDE SOLUTION
L4BN		AT	3 (E)					80	1731	ANTIMONY PENTACHLORIDE SOLUTION
L4BN		AT	2 (E)			CV13 CV28		86	1732	ANTIMONY PENTAFLUORIDE
SGAN L4BN		AT	2 (E)	V11				80	1733	ANTIMONY TRICHLORIDE
L4BN		AT	2 (E)					80	1736	BENZOYL CHLORIDE
L4BH	TU15 TE19	AT	2 (D/E)			CV13 CV28	S9 S19	68	1737	BENZYL BROMIDE
L4BH	TU15 TE19	AT	2 (D/E)			CV13 CV28	S9 S19	68	1738	BENZYL CHLORIDE
L10BH		AT	1 (E)				S20	88	1739	BENZYL CHLOROFORMATE
SGAN		AT	2 (E)	V11				80	1740	HYDROGENDIFLUORIDES, SOLID, N.O.S.
SGAV		AT	3 (E)		VV9			80	1740	HYDROGENDIFLUORIDES, SOLID, N.O.S.
		AT	1 (C/D)			CV9 CV10 CV36	S14	268	1741	BORON TRICHLORIDE
L4BN		AT	2 (E)					80	1742	BORON TRIFLUORIDE ACETIC ACID COMPLEX, LIQUID
L4BN		AT	2 (E)					80	1743	BORON TRIFLUORIDE PROPIONIC ACID COMPLEX, LIQUID

- 381 -

UN No.	Name and description	Class	Classification code	Packing group	Labels	Special provisions	Limited and excepted quantities		Packaging			Portable tanks and bulk containers	
									Packing instructions	Special packing provisions	Mixed packing provisions	Instructions	Special provisions
	3.1.2	2.2	2.2	2.1.1.3	5.2.2	3.3	3.4.6	3.5.1.2	4.1.4	4.1.4	4.1.10	4.2.5.2 7.3.2	4.2.5.3
(1)	(2)	(3a)	(3b)	(4)	(5)	(6)	(7a)	(7b)	(8)	(9a)	(9b)	(10)	(11)
1744	BROMINE or BROMINE SOLUTION	8	CT1	I	8 +6.1		LQ0	E0	P804		MP2	T22	TP2 TP10
1745	BROMINE PENTAFLUORIDE	5.1	OTC	I	5.1 +6.1 +8		LQ0	E0	P200		MP2	T22	TP2
1746	BROMINE TRIFLUORIDE	5.1	OTC	I	5.1 +6.1 +8		LQ0	E0	P200		MP2	T22	TP2
1747	BUTYLTRICHLOROSILANE	8	CF1	II	8 +3		LQ22	E2	P010		MP15	T10	TP2 TP7
1748	CALCIUM HYPOCHLORITE, DRY or CALCIUM HYPOCHLORITE MIXTURE, DRY with more than 39% available chlorine (8.8% available oxygen)	5.1	O2	II	5.1	313 314 589	LQ11	E2	P002 IBC08	B4 B13	MP10		
1748	CALCIUM HYPOCHLORITE, DRY or CALCIUM HYPOCHLORITE MIXTURE, DRY with more than 39% available chlorine (8.8% available oxygen)	5.1	O2	III	5.1	316 589	LQ12	E1	P002 IBC08 R001	B4	MP10		
1749	CHLORINE TRIFLUORIDE	2	2TOC		2.3 +5.1 +8		LQ0	E0	P200		MP9	(M)	
1750	CHLOROACETIC ACID SOLUTION	6.1	TC1	II	6.1 +8		LQ17	E4	P001 IBC02		MP15	T7	TP2
1751	CHLOROACETIC ACID, SOLID	6.1	TC2	II	6.1 +8		LQ18	E4	P002 IBC08	B4	MP10	T3	TP33
1752	CHLOROACETYL CHLORIDE	6.1	TC1	I	6.1 +8		LQ0	E5	P001		MP8 MP17	T20	TP2 TP35
1753	CHLOROPHENYL-TRICHLOROSILANE	8	C3	II	8		LQ22	E2	P010		MP15	T10	TP2 TP7
1754	CHLOROSULPHONIC ACID (with or without sulphur trioxide)	8	C1	I	8		LQ0	E0	P001		MP8 MP17	T20	TP2
1755	CHROMIC ACID SOLUTION	8	C1	II	8	518	LQ22	E2	P001 IBC02		MP15	T8	TP2
1755	CHROMIC ACID SOLUTION	8	C1	III	8	518	LQ7	E1	P001 IBC02 LP01 R001		MP19	T4	TP1
1756	CHROMIC FLUORIDE, SOLID	8	C2	II	8		LQ23	E2	P002 IBC08	B4	MP10	T3	TP33
1757	CHROMIC FLUORIDE SOLUTION	8	C1	II	8		LQ22	E2	P001 IBC02		MP15	T7	TP2
1757	CHROMIC FLUORIDE SOLUTION	8	C1	III	8		LQ7	E1	P001 IBC03 LP01 R001		MP19	T4	TP1
1758	CHROMIUM OXYCHLORIDE	8	C1	I	8		LQ0	E0	P001		MP8 MP17	T10	TP2
1759	CORROSIVE SOLID, N.O.S.	8	C10	I	8	274	LQ0	E0	P002 IBC07		MP18	T6	TP33
1759	CORROSIVE SOLID, N.O.S.	8	C10	II	8	274	LQ23	E2	P002 IBC08	B4	MP10	T3	TP33
1759	CORROSIVE SOLID, N.O.S.	8	C10	III	8	274	LQ24	E1	P002 IBC08 LP02 R001	B3	MP10	T1	TP33
1760	CORROSIVE LIQUID, N.O.S.	8	C9	I	8	274	LQ0	E0	P001		MP8 MP17	T14	TP2 TP27
1760	CORROSIVE LIQUID, N.O.S.	8	C9	II	8	274	LQ22	E2	P001 IBC02		MP15	T11	TP2 TP27
1760	CORROSIVE LIQUID, N.O.S.	8	C9	III	8	274	LQ7	E1	P001 IBC03 LP01 R001		MP19	T7	TP1 TP28

ADR tank		Vehicle for tank carriage	Transport category (Tunnel restriction code)	Special provisions for carriage				Hazard identifi-cation No.	UN No.	Name and description
Tank code	Special provisions			Packages	Bulk	Loading, unloading and handling	Operation			
4.3	4.3.5, 6.8.4	9.1.1.2	1.1.3.6 (8.6)	7.2.4	7.3.3	7.5.11	8.5	5.3.2.3		3.1.2
(12)	(13)	(14)	(15)	(16)	(17)	(18)	(19)	(20)	(1)	(2)
L21DH(+)	TU14 TU33 TC5 TE21 TT2 TM3 TM5	AT	1 (C/D)			CV13 CV28	S14	886	1744	BROMINE or BROMINE SOLUTION
L10DH	TU3	AT	1 (B/E)			CV24 CV28	S14	568	1745	BROMINE PENTAFLUORIDE
L10DH	TU3	AT	1 (B/E)			CV24 CV28	S14	568	1746	BROMINE TRIFLUORIDE
L4BN		FL	2 (D/E)				S2	X83	1747	BUTYLTRICHLOROSILANE
SGAN	TU3	AT	2 (E)	V11		CV24 CV35		50	1748	CALCIUM HYPOCHLORITE, DRY or CALCIUM HYPOCHLORITE MIXTURE, DRY with more than 39% available chlorine (8.8% available oxygen)
SGAV	TU3	AT	3 (E)			CV24 CV35		50	1748	CALCIUM HYPOCHLORITE, DRY or CALCIUM HYPOCHLORITE MIXTURE, DRY with more than 39% available chlorine (8.8% available oxygen)
PxBH(M)	TA4 TT9	AT	1 (C/D)			CV9 CV10 CV36	S14	265	1749	CHLORINE TRIFLUORIDE
L4BH	TU15 TE19	AT	2 (D/E)			CV13 CV28	S9 S19	68	1750	CHLOROACETIC ACID SOLUTION
SGAH	TU15 TE19	AT	2 (D/E)	V11		CV13 CV28	S9 S19	68	1751	CHLOROACETIC ACID, SOLID
L10CH	TU14 TU15 TE19 TE21	AT	1 (C/E)			CV1 CV13 CV28	S9 S14	668	1752	CHLOROACETYL CHLORIDE
L4BN		AT	2 (E)					X80	1753	CHLOROPHENYL-TRICHLOROSILANE
L10BH		AT	1 (E)				S20	X88	1754	CHLOROSULPHONIC ACID (with or without sulphur trioxide)
L4BN		AT	2 (E)					80	1755	CHROMIC ACID SOLUTION
L4BN		AT	3 (E)					80	1755	CHROMIC ACID SOLUTION
SGAN		AT	2 (E)	V11				80	1756	CHROMIC FLUORIDE, SOLID
L4BN		AT	2 (E)					80	1757	CHROMIC FLUORIDE SOLUTION
L4BN		AT	3 (E)					80	1757	CHROMIC FLUORIDE SOLUTION
L10BH		AT	1 (E)				S20	X88	1758	CHROMIUM OXYCHLORIDE
S10AN L10BH		AT	1 (E)	V10 V12			S20	88	1759	CORROSIVE SOLID, N.O.S.
SGAN L4BN		AT	2 (E)	V11				80	1759	CORROSIVE SOLID, N.O.S.
SGAV L4BN		AT	3 (E)		VV9			80	1759	CORROSIVE SOLID, N.O.S.
L10BH		AT	1 (E)				S20	88	1760	CORROSIVE LIQUID, N.O.S.
L4BN		AT	2 (E)					80	1760	CORROSIVE LIQUID, N.O.S.
L4BN		AT	3 (E)					80	1760	CORROSIVE LIQUID, N.O.S.

UN No.	Name and description	Class	Classification code	Packing group	Labels	Special provisions	Limited and excepted quantities		Packaging			Portable tanks and bulk containers	
							quantities		Packing instructions	Special packing provisions	Mixed packing provisions	Instructions	Special provisions
	3.1.2	2.2	2.2	2.1.1.3	5.2.2	3.3	3.4.6	3.5.1.2	4.1.4	4.1.4	4.1.10	4.2.5.2 7.3.2	4.2.5.3
(1)	(2)	(3a)	(3b)	(4)	(5)	(6)	(7a)	(7b)	(8)	(9a)	(9b)	(10)	(11)
1761	CUPRIETHYLENEDIAMINE SOLUTION	8	CT1	II	8 +6.1		LQ22	E2	P001 IBC02		MP15	T7	TP2
1761	CUPRIETHYLENEDIAMINE SOLUTION	8	CT1	III	8 +6.1		LQ7	E1	P001 IBC03 R001		MP19	T7	TP1 TP28
1762	CYCLOHEXENYL-TRICHLOROSILANE	8	C3	II	8		LQ22	E2	P010		MP15	T10	TP2 TP7
1763	CYCLOHEXYLTRICHLORO-SILANE	8	C3	II	8		LQ22	E2	P010		MP15	T10	TP2 TP7
1764	DICHLOROACETIC ACID	8	C3	II	8		LQ22	E2	P001 IBC02		MP15	T8	TP2
1765	DICHLOROACETYL CHLORIDE	8	C3	II	8		LQ22	E2	P001 IBC02		MP15	T7	TP2
1766	DICHLOROPHENYL-TRICHLOROSILANE	8	C3	II	8		LQ22	E2	P010		MP15	T10	TP2 TP7
1767	DIETHYLDICHLORO-SILANE	8	CF1	II	8 +3		LQ22	E2	P010		MP15	T10	TP2 TP7
1768	DIFLUOROPHOSPHORIC ACID, ANHYDROUS	8	C1	II	8		LQ22	E2	P001 IBC02		MP15	T8	TP2
1769	DIPHENYLDICHLORO-SILANE	8	C3	II	8		LQ22	E2	P010		MP15	T10	TP2 TP7
1770	DIPHENYLMETHYL BROMIDE	8	C10	II	8		LQ23	E2	P002 IBC08	B4	MP10	T3	TP33
1771	DODECYLTRICHLORO-SILANE	8	C3	II	8		LQ22	E2	P010		MP15	T10	TP2 TP7
1773	FERRIC CHLORIDE, ANHYDROUS	8	C2	III	8	590	LQ24	E1	P002 IBC08 LP02 R001	B3	MP10	T1	TP33
1774	FIRE EXTINGUISHER CHARGES, corrosive liquid	8	C11	II	8		LQ22	E0	P001	PP4			
1775	FLUOROBORIC ACID	8	C1	II	8		LQ22	E2	P001 IBC02		MP15	T7	TP2
1776	FLUOROPHOSPHORIC ACID, ANHYDROUS	8	C1	II	8		LQ22	E2	P001 IBC02		MP15	T8	TP2
1777	FLUOROSULPHONIC ACID	8	C1	I	8		LQ0	E0	P001		MP8 MP17	T10	TP2
1778	FLUOROSILICIC ACID	8	C1	II	8		LQ22	E2	P001 IBC02		MP15	T8	TP2
1779	FORMIC ACID with more than 85% acid by mass	8	CF1	II	8 +3		LQ22	E2	P001 IBC02		MP15	T7	TP2
1780	FUMARYL CHLORIDE	8	C3	II	8		LQ22	E2	P001 IBC02		MP15	T7	TP2
1781	HEXADECYLTRICHLORO-SILANE	8	C3	II	8		LQ22	E2	P010		MP15	T10	TP2 TP7
1782	HEXAFLUORO-PHOSPHORIC ACID	8	C1	II	8		LQ22	E2	P001 IBC02		MP15	T8	TP2
1783	HEXAMETHYLENE-DIAMINE SOLUTION	8	C7	II	8		LQ22	E2	P001 IBC02		MP15	T7	TP2
1783	HEXAMETHYLENE-DIAMINE SOLUTION	8	C7	III	8		LQ7	E1	P001 IBC03 LP01 R001		MP19	T4	TP1
1784	HEXYLTRICHLOROSILANE	8	C3	II	8		LQ22	E2	P010		MP15	T10	TP2 TP7
1786	HYDROFLUORIC ACID AND SULPHURIC ACID MIXTURE	8	CT1	I	8 +6.1		LQ0	E0	P001		MP8 MP17	T10	TP2
1787	HYDRIODIC ACID	8	C1	II	8		LQ22	E2	P001 IBC02		MP15	T7	TP2
1787	HYDRIODIC ACID	8	C1	III	8		LQ7	E1	P001 IBC03 LP01 R001		MP19	T4	TP1
1788	HYDROBROMIC ACID	8	C1	II	8	519	LQ22	E2	P001 IBC02		MP15	T7	TP2
1788	HYDROBROMIC ACID	8	C1	III	8	519	LQ7	E1	P001 IBC03 LP01 R001		MP19	T4	TP1
1789	HYDROCHLORIC ACID	8	C1	II	8	520	LQ22	E2	P001 IBC02		MP15	T8	TP2

ADR tank		Vehicle for tank carriage	Transport category (Tunnel restriction code)	Special provisions for carriage				Hazard identifi-cation No.	UN No.	Name and description
Tank code	Special provisions			Packages	Bulk	Loading, unloading and handling	Operation			
4.3	4.3.5, 6.8.4	9.1.1.2	1.1.3.6 (8.6)	7.2.4	7.3.3	7.5.11	8.5	5.3.2.3		3.1.2
(12)	(13)	(14)	(15)	(16)	(17)	(18)	(19)	(20)	(1)	(2)
L4BN		AT	2 (E)			CV13 CV28		86	1761	CUPRIETHYLENEDIAMINE SOLUTION
L4BN		AT	3 (E)			CV13 CV28		86	1761	CUPRIETHYLENEDIAMINE SOLUTION
L4BN		AT	2 (E)					X80	1762	CYCLOHEXENYL-TRICHLOROSILANE
L4BN		AT	2 (E)					X80	1763	CYCLOHEXYLTRICHLORO-SILANE
L4BN		AT	2 (E)					80	1764	DICHLOROACETIC ACID
L4BN		AT	2 (E)					X80	1765	DICHLOROACETYL CHLORIDE
L4BN		AT	2 (E)					X80	1766	DICHLOROPHENYL-TRICHLOROSILANE
L4BN		FL	2 (D/E)				S2	X83	1767	DIETHYLDICHLORO-SILANE
L4BN		AT	2 (E)					80	1768	DIFLUOROPHOSPHORIC ACID, ANHYDROUS
L4BN		AT	2 (E)					X80	1769	DIPHENYLDICHLORO-SILANE
SGAN L4BN		AT	2 (E)	V11				80	1770	DIPHENYLMETHYL BROMIDE
L4BN		AT	2 (E)					X80	1771	DODECYLTRICHLORO-SILANE
SGAV		AT	3 (E)		VV9			80	1773	FERRIC CHLORIDE, ANHYDROUS
			2 (E)						1774	FIRE EXTINGUISHER CHARGES, corrosive liquid
L4BN		AT	2 (E)					80	1775	FLUOROBORIC ACID
L4BN		AT	2 (E)					80	1776	FLUOROPHOSPHORIC ACID, ANHYDROUS
L10BH		AT	1 (E)				S20	88	1777	FLUOROSULPHONIC ACID
L4BN		AT	2 (E)					80	1778	FLUOROSILICIC ACID
L4BN		FL	2 (D/E)				S2	83	1779	FORMIC ACID with more than 85% acid by mass
L4BN		AT	2 (E)					80	1780	FUMARYL CHLORIDE
L4BN		AT	2 (E)					X80	1781	HEXADECYLTRICHLORO-SILANE
L4BN		AT	2 (E)					80	1782	HEXAFLUORO-PHOSPHORIC ACID
L4BN		AT	2 (E)					80	1783	HEXAMETHYLENE-DIAMINE SOLUTION
L4BN		AT	3 (E)					80	1783	HEXAMETHYLENE-DIAMINE SOLUTION
L4BN		AT	2 (E)					X80	1784	HEXYLTRICHLOROSILANE
L10DH	TU14 TE21	AT	1 (C/D)			CV13 CV28	S14	886	1786	HYDROFLUORIC ACID AND SULPHURIC ACID MIXTURE
L4BN		AT	2 (E)					80	1787	HYDRIODIC ACID
L4BN		AT	3 (E)					80	1787	HYDRIODIC ACID
L4BN		AT	2 (E)					80	1788	HYDROBROMIC ACID
L4BN		AT	3 (E)					80	1788	HYDROBROMIC ACID
L4BN		AT	2 (E)					80	1789	HYDROCHLORIC ACID

UN No.	Name and description	Class	Classifi-cation code	Packing group	Labels	Special provi-sions	Limited and excepted quantities		Packaging			Portable tanks and bulk containers	
									Packing instruc-tions	Special packing provisions	Mixed packing provisions	Instruc-tions	Special provisions
3.1.2	3.1.2	2.2	2.2	2.1.1.3	5.2.2	3.3	3.4.6	3.5.1.2	4.1.4	4.1.4	4.1.10	4.2.5.2 7.3.2	4.2.5.3
(1)	(2)	(3a)	(3b)	(4)	(5)	(6)	(7a)	(7b)	(8)	(9a)	(9b)	(10)	(11)
1789	HYDROCHLORIC ACID	8	C1	III	8	520	LQ7	E1	P001 IBC03 LP01 R001		MP19	T4	TP1
1790	HYDROFLUORIC ACID with more than 85% hydrogen fluoride	8	CT1	I	8 +6.1	640I	LQ0	E0	P802		MP2	T10	TP2
1790	HYDROFLUORIC ACID with more than 60% but not more than 85% hydrogen fluoride	8	CT1	I	8 +6.1	640J	LQ0	E0	P001	PP81	MP8 MP17	T10	TP2
1790	HYDROFLUORIC ACID with not more than 60% hydrogen fluoride	8	CT1	II	8 +6.1		LQ22	E2	P001 IBC02		MP15	T8	TP2
1791	HYPOCHLORITE SOLUTION	8	C9	II	8	521	LQ22	E2	P001 IBC02	PP10 B5	MP15	T7	TP2 TP24
1791	HYPOCHLORITE SOLUTION	8	C9	III	8	521	LQ7	E1	P001 IBC02 LP01 R001	B5	MP19	T4	TP2 TP24
1792	IODINE MONOCHLORIDE	8	C1	II	8		LQ22	E2	P001 IBC02		MP15	T7	TP2
1793	ISOPROPYL ACID PHOSPHATE	8	C3	III	8		LQ7	E1	P001 IBC02 LP01 R001		MP19	T4	TP1
1794	LEAD SULPHATE with more than 3% free acid	8	C2	II	8	591	LQ23	E2	P002 IBC08	B4	MP10	T3	TP33
1796	NITRATING ACID MIXTURE with more than 50% nitric acid	8	CO1	I	8 +5.1		LQ0	E0	P001		MP8 MP17	T10	TP2
1796	NITRATING ACID MIXTURE with not more than 50% nitric acid	8	C1	II	8		LQ22	E2	P001 IBC02		MP15	T8	TP2
1798	NITROHYDROCHLORIC ACID	8	COT	CARRIAGE PROHIBITED									
1799	NONYLTRICHLOROSILANE	8	C3	II	8		LQ22	E2	P010		MP15	T10	TP2 TP7
1800	OCTADECYLTRICHLORO-SILANE	8	C3	II	8		LQ22	E2	P010		MP15	T10	TP2 TP7
1801	OCTYLTRICHLOROSILANE	8	C3	II	8		LQ22	E2	P010		MP15	T10	TP2 TP7
1802	PERCHLORIC ACID with not more than 50% acid, by mass	8	CO1	II	8 +5.1	522	LQ22	E2	P001 IBC02		MP3	T7	TP2
1803	PHENOLSULPHONIC ACID, LIQUID	8	C3	II	8		LQ22	E2	P001 IBC02		MP15	T7	TP2
1804	PHENYLTRICHLORO-SILANE	8	C3	II	8		LQ22	E2	P010		MP15	T10	TP2 TP7
1805	PHOSPHORIC ACID, SOLUTION	8	C1	III	8		LQ7	E1	P001 IBC03 LP01 R001		MP19	T4	TP1
1806	PHOSPHORUS PENTACHLORIDE	8	C2	II	8		LQ23	E2	P002 IBC08	B4	MP10	T3	TP33
1807	PHOSPHORUS PENTOXIDE	8	C2	II	8		LQ23	E2	P002 IBC08	B4	MP10	T3	TP33
1808	PHOSPHORUS TRIBROMIDE	8	C1	II	8		LQ22	E2	P001 IBC02		MP15	T7	TP2
1809	PHOSPHORUS TRICHLORIDE	6.1	TC3	I	6.1 +8		LQ0	E5	P001		MP8 MP17	T20	TP2 TP35
1810	PHOSPHORUS OXYCHLORIDE	8	C1	II	8		LQ22	E2	P001		MP15	T7	TP2
1811	POTASSIUM HYDROGENDIFLUORIDE, SOLID	8	CT2	II	8 +6.1		LQ23	E2	P002 IBC08	B4	MP10	T3	TP33
1812	POTASSIUM FLUORIDE, SOLID	6.1	T5	III	6.1		LQ9	E1	P002 IBC08 LP02 R001	B3	MP10	T1	TP33

ADR tank		Vehicle for tank carriage	Transport category (Tunnel restriction code)	Special provisions for carriage				Hazard identification No.	UN No.	Name and description
Tank code	Special provisions			Packages	Bulk	Loading, unloading and handling	Operation			
4.3	4.3.5, 6.8.4	9.1.1.2	1.1.3.6 (8.6)	7.2.4	7.3.3	7.5.11	8.5	5.3.2.3		3.1.2
(12)	(13)	(14)	(15)	(16)	(17)	(18)	(19)	(20)	(1)	(2)
L4BN		AT	3 (E)					80	1789	HYDROCHLORIC ACID
L21DH(+)	TU14 TU34 TC1 TE21 TA4 TT9 TM3	AT	1 (C/D)			CV13 CV28	S14	886	1790	HYDROFLUORIC ACID with more than 85% hydrogen fluoride
L10DH	TU14 TE21	AT	1 (C/D)			CV13 CV28	S14	886	1790	HYDROFLUORIC ACID with more than 60% but not more than 85% hydrogen fluoride
L4DH	TU14 TE21	AT	2 (E)			CV13 CV28		86	1790	HYDROFLUORIC ACID with not more than 60% hydrogen fluoride
L4BV(+)	TE11	AT	2 (E)					80	1791	HYPOCHLORITE SOLUTION
L4BV(+)	TE11	AT	3 (E)					80	1791	HYPOCHLORITE SOLUTION
L4BN		AT	2 (E)					80	1792	IODINE MONOCHLORIDE
L4BN		AT	3 (E)					80	1793	ISOPROPYL ACID PHOSPHATE
SGAN		AT	2 (E)	V11	VV9			80	1794	LEAD SULPHATE with more than 3% free acid
L10BH	TC6 TT1	AT	1 (E)			CV24	S14	885	1796	NITRATING ACID MIXTURE with more than 50% nitric acid
L4BN		AT	2 (E)					80	1796	NITRATING ACID MIXTURE with not more than 50% nitric acid
CARRIAGE PROHIBITED									1798	NITROHYDROCHLORIC ACID
L4BN		AT	2 (E)					X80	1799	NONYLTRICHLOROSILANE
L4BN		AT	2 (E)					X80	1800	OCTADECYLTRICHLORO-SILANE
L4BN		AT	2 (E)					X80	1801	OCTYLTRICHLOROSILANE
L4BN		AT	2 (E)			CV24		85	1802	PERCHLORIC ACID with not more than 50% acid, by mass
L4BN		AT	2 (E)					80	1803	PHENOLSULPHONIC ACID, LIQUID
L4BN		AT	2 (E)					X80	1804	PHENYLTRICHLORO-SILANE
L4BN		AT	3 (E)					80	1805	PHOSPHORIC ACID, SOLUTION
SGAN		AT	2 (E)	V11				80	1806	PHOSPHORUS PENTACHLORIDE
SGAN		AT	2 (E)	V11				80	1807	PHOSPHORUS PENTOXIDE
L4BN		AT	2 (E)					X80	1808	PHOSPHORUS TRIBROMIDE
L10CH	TU14 TU15 TE19 TE21	AT	1 (C/E)			CV1 CV13 CV28	S9 S14	668	1809	PHOSPHORUS TRICHLORIDE
L4BN		AT	2 (E)					X80	1810	PHOSPHORUS OXYCHLORIDE
SGAN		AT	2 (E)	V11		CV13 CV28		86	1811	POTASSIUM HYDROGENDIFLUORIDE, SOLID
SGAH	TU15 TE19	AT	2 (E)		VV9	CV13 CV28	S9	60	1812	POTASSIUM FLUORIDE, SOLID

UN No.	Name and description	Class	Classification code	Packing group	Labels	Special provisions	Limited and excepted quantities		Packaging			Portable tanks and bulk containers	
									Packing instructions	Special packing provisions	Mixed packing provisions	Instructions	Special provisions
	3.1.2	2.2	2.2	2.1.1.3	5.2.2	3.3	3.4.6	3.5.1.2	4.1.4	4.1.4	4.1.10	4.2.5.2 7.3.2	4.2.5.3
(1)	(2)	(3a)	(3b)	(4)	(5)	(6)	(7a)	(7b)	(8)	(9a)	(9b)	(10)	(11)
1813	POTASSIUM HYDROXIDE, SOLID	8	C6	II	8		LQ23	E2	P002 IBC08	B4	MP10	T3	TP33
1814	POTASSIUM HYDROXIDE SOLUTION	8	C5	II	8		LQ22	E2	P001 IBC02		MP15	T7	TP2
1814	POTASSIUM HYDROXIDE SOLUTION	8	C5	III	8		LQ7	E1	P001 IBC03 LP01 R001		MP19	T4	TP1
1815	PROPIONYL CHLORIDE	3	FC	II	3 +8		LQ4	E2	P001 IBC02		MP19	T7	TP1
1816	PROPYLTRICHLORO-SILANE	8	CF1	II	8 +3		LQ22	E2	P010		MP15	T10	TP2 TP7
1817	PYROSULPHURYL CHLORIDE	8	C1	II	8		LQ22	E2	P001 IBC02		MP15	T8	TP2
1818	SILICON TETRACHLORIDE	8	C1	II	8		LQ0	E2	P010		MP15	T10	TP2 TP7
1819	SODIUM ALUMINATE SOLUTION	8	C5	II	8		LQ22	E2	P001 IBC02		MP15	T7	TP2
1819	SODIUM ALUMINATE SOLUTION	8	C5	III	8		LQ7	E1	P001 IBC03 LP01 R001		MP19	T4	TP1
1823	SODIUM HYDROXIDE, SOLID	8	C6	II	8		LQ23	E2	P002 IBC08	B4	MP10	T3	TP33
1824	SODIUM HYDROXIDE SOLUTION	8	C5	II	8		LQ22	E2	P001 IBC02		MP15	T7	TP2
1824	SODIUM HYDROXIDE SOLUTION	8	C5	III	8		LQ7	E1	P001 IBC03 LP01 R001		MP19	T4	TP1
1825	SODIUM MONOXIDE	8	C6	II	8		LQ23	E2	P002 IBC08	B4	MP10	T3	TP33
1826	NITRATING ACID MIXTURE, SPENT, with more than 50% nitric acid	8	CO1	I	8 +5.1	113	LQ0	E0	P001		MP8 MP17	T10	TP2
1826	NITRATING ACID MIXTURE, SPENT, with not more than 50% nitric acid	8	C1	II	8	113	LQ22	E2	P001 IBC02		MP15	T8	TP2
1827	STANNIC CHLORIDE, ANHYDROUS	8	C1	II	8		LQ22	E2	P001 IBC02		MP15	T7	TP2
1828	SULPHUR CHLORIDES	8	C1	I	8		LQ0	E0	P602		MP8 MP17	T20	TP2
1829	SULPHUR TRIOXIDE, STABILIZED	8	C1	I	8	623	LQ0	E0	P001		MP8 MP17	T20	TP4 TP25 TP26
1830	SULPHURIC ACID with more than 51% acid	8	C1	II	8		LQ22	E2	P001 IBC02		MP15	T8	TP2
1831	SULPHURIC ACID, FUMING	8	CT1	I	8 +6.1		LQ0	E0	P602		MP8 MP17	T20	TP2
1832	SULPHURIC ACID, SPENT	8	C1	II	8	113	LQ22	E2	P001 IBC02		MP15	T8	TP2
1833	SULPHUROUS ACID	8	C1	II	8		LQ22	E2	P001 IBC02		MP15	T7	TP2
1834	SULPHURYL CHLORIDE	8	C1	I	8		LQ0	E0	P602		MP8 MP17	T20	TP2
1835	TETRAMETHYL-AMMONIUM HYDROXIDE SOLUTION	8	C7	II	8		LQ22	E2	P001 IBC02		MP15	T7	TP2
1835	TETRAMETHYL-AMMONIUM HYDROXIDE SOLUTION	8	C7	III	8		LQ7	E1	P001 IBC03 LP01 R001		MP19	T7	TP2
1836	THIONYL CHLORIDE	8	C1	I	8		LQ0	E0	P802		MP8 MP17	T10	TP2
1837	THIOPHOSPHORYL CHLORIDE	8	C1	II	8		LQ22	E2	P001 IBC02		MP15	T7	TP2
1838	TITANIUM TETRACHLORIDE	8	C1	II	8		LQ22	E2	P001 IBC02		MP15	T10	TP2
1839	TRICHLOROACETIC ACID	8	C4	II	8		LQ23	E2	P002 IBC08	B4	MP10	T3	TP33

ADR tank		Vehicle for tank	Transport category	Special provisions for carriage				Hazard identifi-	UN No.	Name and description
Tank code	Special provisions	carriage	(Tunnel restriction code)	Packages	Bulk	Loading, unloading and handling	Operation	cation No.		
4.3	4.3.5, 6.8.4	9.1.1.2	1.1.3.6 (8.6)	7.2.4	7.3.3	7.5.11	8.5	5.3.2.3		3.1.2
(12)	(13)	(14)	(15)	(16)	(17)	(18)	(19)	(20)	(1)	(2)
SGAN		AT	2 (E)	V11				80	1813	POTASSIUM HYDROXIDE, SOLID
L4BN		AT	2 (E)					80	1814	POTASSIUM HYDROXIDE SOLUTION
L4BN		AT	3 (E)					80	1814	POTASSIUM HYDROXIDE SOLUTION
L4BH		FL	2 (D/E)				S2 S20	338	1815	PROPIONYL CHLORIDE
L4BN		FL	2 (D/E)				S2	X83	1816	PROPYLTRICHLORO-SILANE
L4BN		AT	2 (E)					X80	1817	PYROSULPHURYL CHLORIDE
L4BN		AT	2 (E)					X80	1818	SILICON TETRACHLORIDE
L4BN		AT	2 (E)					80	1819	SODIUM ALUMINATE SOLUTION
L4BN		AT	3 (E)					80	1819	SODIUM ALUMINATE SOLUTION
SGAN		AT	2 (E)	V11				80	1823	SODIUM HYDROXIDE, SOLID
L4BN		AT	2 (E)					80	1824	SODIUM HYDROXIDE SOLUTION
L4BN		AT	3 (E)					80	1824	SODIUM HYDROXIDE SOLUTION
SGAN		AT	2 (E)	V11				80	1825	SODIUM MONOXIDE
L10BH		AT	1 (E)			CV24	S14	885	1826	NITRATING ACID MIXTURE, SPENT, with more than 50% nitric acid
L4BN		AT	2 (E)					80	1826	NITRATING ACID MIXTURE, SPENT, with not more than 50% nitric acid
L4BN		AT	2 (E)					X80	1827	STANNIC CHLORIDE, ANHYDROUS
L10BH		AT	1 (E)				S20	X88	1828	SULPHUR CHLORIDES
L10BH	TU32 TE13 TT5 TM3	AT	1 (E)				S20	X88	1829	SULPHUR TRIOXIDE, STABILIZED
L4BN		AT	2 (E)					80	1830	SULPHURIC ACID with more than 51% acid
L10BH		AT	1 (C/D)			CV13 CV28	S14	X886	1831	SULPHURIC ACID, FUMING
L4BN		AT	2 (E)					80	1832	SULPHURIC ACID, SPENT
L4BN		AT	2 (E)					80	1833	SULPHUROUS ACID
L10BH		AT	1 (E)				S20	X88	1834	SULPHURYL CHLORIDE
L4BN		AT	2 (E)					80	1835	TETRAMETHYL-AMMONIUM HYDROXIDE SOLUTION
L4BN		AT	3 (E)					80	1835	TETRAMETHYL-AMMONIUM HYDROXIDE SOLUTION
L10BH		AT	1 (E)				S20	X88	1836	THIONYL CHLORIDE
L4BN		AT	2 (E)					X80	1837	THIOPHOSPHORYL CHLORIDE
L4BN		AT	2 (E)					X80	1838	TITANIUM TETRACHLORIDE
SGAN L4BN		AT	2 (E)	V11				80	1839	TRICHLOROACETIC ACID

UN No.	Name and description	Class	Classifi-cation code	Packing group	Labels	Special provi-sions	Limited and excepted quantities		Packaging			Portable tanks and bulk containers	
									Packing instruc-tions	Special packing provisions	Mixed packing provisions	Instruc-tions	Special provisions
	3.1.2	2.2	2.2	2.1.1.3	5.2.2	3.3	3.4.6	3.5.1.2	4.1.4	4.1.4	4.1.10	4.2.5.2 7.3.2	4.2.5.3
(1)	(2)	(3a)	(3b)	(4)	(5)	(6)	(7a)	(7b)	(8)	(9a)	(9b)	(10)	(11)
1840	ZINC CHLORIDE SOLUTION	8	C1	III	8		LQ7	E1	P001 IBC03 LP01 R001		MP19	T4	TP1
1841	ACETALDEHYDE AMMONIA	9	M11	III	9		LQ27	E1	P002 IBC08 LP02 R001	B3 B6	MP10	T1	TP33
1843	AMMONIUM DINITRO-o-CRESOLATE, SOLID	6.1	T2	II	6.1		LQ18	E4	P002 IBC08	B4	MP10	T3	TP33
1845	Carbon dioxide, solid (Dry ice)	9	M11				NOT SUBJECT TO ADR						
1846	CARBON TETRACHLORIDE	6.1	T1	II	6.1		LQ17	E4	P001 IBC02		MP15	T7	TP2
1847	POTASSIUM SULPHIDE, HYDRATED with not less than 30% water of crystallization	8	C6	II	8	523	LQ23	E2	P002 IBC08	B4	MP10	T3	TP33
1848	PROPIONIC ACID with not less than 10% and less than 90% acid by mass	8	C3	III	8		LQ7	E1	P001 IBC03 LP01 R001		MP19	T4	TP1
1849	SODIUM SULPHIDE, HYDRATED with not less than 30% water	8	C6	II	8	523	LQ23	E2	P002 IBC08	B4	MP10	T3	TP33
1851	MEDICINE, LIQUID, TOXIC, N.O.S.	6.1	T1	II	6.1	221 274 601	LQ17	E4	P001		MP15		
1851	MEDICINE, LIQUID, TOXIC, N.O.S.	6.1	T1	III	6.1	221 274 601	LQ7	E1	P001 LP01 R001		MP19		
1854	BARIUM ALLOYS, PYROPHORIC	4.2	S4	I	4.2		LQ0	E0	P404		MP13	T21	TP7 TP33
1855	CALCIUM, PYROPHORIC or CALCIUM ALLOYS, PYROPHORIC	4.2	S4	I	4.2		LQ0	E0	P404		MP13		
1856	Rags, oily	4.2	S2				NOT SUBJECT TO ADR						
1857	Textile waste, wet	4.2	S2				NOT SUBJECT TO ADR						
1858	HEXAFLUOROPROPYLENE (REFRIGERANT GAS R 1216)	2	2A		2.2		LQ1	E1	P200		MP9	(M) T50	
1859	SILICON TETRAFLUORIDE	2	2TC		2.3 +8		LQ0	E0	P200		MP9	(M)	
1860	VINYL FLUORIDE, STABILIZED	2	2F		2.1		LQ0	E0	P200		MP9	(M)	
1862	ETHYL CROTONATE	3	F1	II	3		LQ4	E2	P001 IBC02 R001		MP19	T4	TP2
1863	FUEL, AVIATION, TURBINE ENGINE	3	F1	I	3		LQ3	E3	P001		MP7 MP17	T11	TP1 TP8 TP28
1863	FUEL, AVIATION, TURBINE ENGINE (vapour pressure at 50 °C more than 110 kPa)	3	F1	II	3	640C	LQ4	E2	P001		MP19	T4	TP1 TP8
1863	FUEL, AVIATION, TURBINE ENGINE (vapour pressure at 50 °C not more than 110 kPa)	3	F1	II	3	640D	LQ4	E2	P001 IBC02 R001		MP19	T4	TP1 TP8
1863	FUEL, AVIATION, TURBINE ENGINE	3	F1	III	3		LQ7	E1	P001 IBC03 LP01 R001		MP19	T2	TP1
1865	n-PROPYL NITRATE	3	F1	II	3		LQ4	E2	P001 IBC02 R001	B7	MP19		
1866	RESIN SOLUTION, flammable	3	F1	I	3		LQ3	E3	P001		MP7 MP17	T11	TP1 TP8 TP28
1866	RESIN SOLUTION, flammable (vapour pressure at 50 °C more than 110 kPa)	3	F1	II	3	640C	LQ6	E2	P001	PP1	MP19	T4	TP1 TP8

ADR tank		Vehicle for tank carriage	Transport category (Tunnel restriction code)	Special provisions for carriage				Hazard identification No.	UN No.	Name and description
Tank code	Special provisions			Packages	Bulk	Loading, unloading and handling	Operation			
4.3	4.3.5, 6.8.4	9.1.1.2	1.1.3.6 (8.6)	7.2.4	7.3.3	7.5.11	8.5	5.3.2.3		3.1.2
(12)	(13)	(14)	(15)	(16)	(17)	(18)	(19)	(20)	(1)	(2)
L4BN		AT	3 (E)					80	1840	ZINC CHLORIDE SOLUTION
SGAV		AT	3 (E)		VV3			90	1841	ACETALDEHYDE AMMONIA
SGAH	TU15 TE19	AT	2 (D/E)	V11		CV13 CV28	S9 S19	60	1843	AMMONIUM DINITRO-o-CRESOLATE, SOLID
NOT SUBJECT TO ADR									1845	Carbon dioxide, solid (Dry ice)
L4BH	TU15 TE19	AT	2 (D/E)			CV13 CV28	S9 S19	60	1846	CARBON TETRACHLORIDE
SGAN L4BN		AT	2 (E)	V11				80	1847	POTASSIUM SULPHIDE, HYDRATED with not less than 30% water of crystallization
L4BN		AT	3 (E)					80	1848	PROPIONIC ACID with not less than 10% and less than 90% acid by mass
SGAN L4BN		AT	2 (E)	V11				80	1849	SODIUM SULPHIDE, HYDRATED with not less than 30% water
L4BH	TU15 TE19	AT	2 (D/E)			CV13 CV28	S9 S19	60	1851	MEDICINE, LIQUID, TOXIC, N.O.S.
L4BH	TU15 TE19	AT	2 (E)			CV13 CV28	S9	60	1851	MEDICINE, LIQUID, TOXIC, N.O.S.
		AT	0 (B/E)	V1			S20	43	1854	BARIUM ALLOYS, PYROPHORIC
			0 (E)	V1			S20		1855	CALCIUM, PYROPHORIC or CALCIUM ALLOYS, PYROPHORIC
NOT SUBJECT TO ADR									1856	Rags, oily
NOT SUBJECT TO ADR									1857	Textile waste, wet
PxBN(M)	TA4 TT9	AT	3 (C/E)			CV9 CV10 CV36		20	1858	HEXAFLUOROPROPYLENE (REFRIGERANT GAS R 1216)
PxBH(M)	TA4 TT9	AT	1 (C/D)			CV9 CV10 CV36	S14	268	1859	SILICON TETRAFLUORIDE
PxBN(M)	TA4 TT9	FL	2 (B/D)			CV9 CV10 CV36	S2 S20	239	1860	VINYL FLUORIDE, STABILIZED
LGBF		FL	2 (D/E)				S2 S20	33	1862	ETHYL CROTONATE
L4BN		FL	1 (D/E)				S2 S20	33	1863	FUEL, AVIATION, TURBINE ENGINE
L1.5BN		FL	2 (D/E)				S2 S20	33	1863	FUEL, AVIATION, TURBINE ENGINE (vapour pressure at 50 °C more than 110 kPa)
LGBF		FL	2 (D/E)				S2 S20	33	1863	FUEL, AVIATION, TURBINE ENGINE (vapour pressure at 50 °C not more than 110 kPa)
LGBF		FL	3 (D/E)				S2	30	1863	FUEL, AVIATION, TURBINE ENGINE
			2 (E)				S2 S20		1865	n-PROPYL NITRATE
L4BN		FL	1 (D/E)				S2 S20	33	1866	RESIN SOLUTION, flammable
L1.5BN		FL	2 (D/E)				S2 S20	33	1866	RESIN SOLUTION, flammable (vapour pressure at 50 °C more than 110 kPa)

UN No.	Name and description	Class	Classifi-cation code	Packing group	Labels	Special provi-sions	Limited quantities	Excepted quantities	Packing instructions	Special packing provisions	Mixed packing provisions	Instructions	Special provisions
3.1.2	3.1.2	2.2	2.2	2.1.1.3	5.2.2	3.3	3.4.6	3.5.1.2	4.1.4	4.1.4	4.1.10	4.2.5.2 7.3.2	4.2.5.3
(1)	(2)	(3a)	(3b)	(4)	(5)	(6)	(7a)	(7b)	(8)	(9a)	(9b)	(10)	(11)
1866	RESIN SOLUTION, flammable (vapour pressure at 50 °C not more than 110 kPa)	3	F1	II	3	640D	LQ6	E2	P001 IBC02 R001	PP1	MP19	T4	TP1 TP8
1866	RESIN SOLUTION, flammable	3	F1	III	3	640E	LQ7	E1	P001 IBC03 LP01 R001	PP1	MP19	T2	TP1
1866	RESIN SOLUTION, flammable (having a flash-point below 23 °C and viscous according to 2.2.3.1.4) (boiling point not more than 35 °C)	3	F1	III	3	640F	LQ7	E1	P001 LP01 R001	PP1	MP19	T2	TP1
1866	RESIN SOLUTION, flammable (having a flash-point below 23 °C and viscous according to 2.2.3.1.4) (vapour pressure at 50 °C more than 110 kPa, boiling point of more than 35 °C)	3	F1	III	3	640G	LQ7	E1	P001 LP01 R001	PP1	MP19	T2	TP1
1866	RESIN SOLUTION, flammable (having a flash-point below 23 °C and viscous according to 2.2.3.1.4) (vapour pressure at 50 °C not more than 110 kPa)	3	F1	III	3	640H	LQ7	E1	P001 IBC02 LP01 R001	PP1	MP19	T2	TP1
1868	DECABORANE	4.1	FT2	II	4.1 +6.1		LQ0	E2	P002 IBC06		MP10	T3	TP33
1869	MAGNESIUM or MAGNESIUM ALLOYS with more than 50% magnesium in pellets, turnings or ribbons	4.1	F3	III	4.1	59	LQ9	E1	P002 IBC08 LP02 R001	B3	MP11	T1	TP33
1870	POTASSIUM BOROHYDRIDE	4.3	W2	I	4.3		LQ0	E0	P403		MP2		
1871	TITANIUM HYDRIDE	4.1	F3	II	4.1		LQ8	E2	P410 IBC04	PP40	MP11	T3	TP33
1872	LEAD DIOXIDE	5.1	OT2	III	5.1 +6.1		LQ12	E1	P002 IBC08 LP02 R001	B3	MP2	T1	TP33
1873	PERCHLORIC ACID with more than 50% but not more than 72% acid, by mass	5.1	OC1	I	5.1 +8	60	LQ0	E0	P502	PP28	MP3	T10	TP1
1884	BARIUM OXIDE	6.1	T5	III	6.1		LQ9	E1	P002 IBC08 LP02 R001	B3	MP10	T1	TP33
1885	BENZIDINE	6.1	T2	II	6.1		LQ18	E4	P002 IBC08	B4	MP10	T3	TP33
1886	BENZYLIDENE CHLORIDE	6.1	T1	II	6.1		LQ17	E4	P001 IBC02		MP15	T7	TP2
1887	BROMOCHLOROMETHANE	6.1	T1	III	6.1		LQ7	E1	P001 IBC03 LP01 R001		MP19	T4	TP1
1888	CHLOROFORM	6.1	T1	III	6.1		LQ7	E1	P001 IBC03 LP01 R001		MP19	T7	TP2
1889	CYANOGEN BROMIDE	6.1	TC2	I	6.1 +8		LQ0	E5	P002		MP18	T6	TP33
1891	ETHYL BROMIDE	6.1	T1	II	6.1		LQ17	E4	P001 IBC02	B8	MP15	T7	TP2
1892	ETHYLDICHLOROARSINE	6.1	T3	I	6.1		LQ0	E5	P602		MP8 MP17	T14	TP2
1894	PHENYLMERCURIC HYDROXIDE	6.1	T3	II	6.1		LQ18	E4	P002 IBC08	B4	MP10	T3	TP33
1895	PHENYLMERCURIC NITRATE	6.1	T3	II	6.1		LQ18	E4	P002 IBC08	B4	MP10	T3	TP33

ADR tank		Vehicle for tank carriage	Transport category (Tunnel restriction code)	Special provisions for carriage				Hazard identifi-cation No.	UN No.	Name and description
Tank code	Special provisions			Packages	Bulk	Loading, unloading and handling	Operation			
4.3	4.3.5, 6.8.4	9.1.1.2	1.1.3.6 (8.6)	7.2.4	7.3.3	7.5.11	8.5	5.3.2.3		3.1.2
(12)	(13)	(14)	(15)	(16)	(17)	(18)	(19)	(20)	(1)	(2)
LGBF		FL	2 (D/E)				S2 S20	33	1866	RESIN SOLUTION, flammable (vapour pressure at 50 °C not more than 110 kPa)
LGBF		FL	3 (D/E)				S2	30	1866	RESIN SOLUTION, flammable
L4BN		FL	3 (D/E)				S2	33	1866	RESIN SOLUTION, flammable (having a flash-point below 23 °C and viscous according to 2.2.3.1.4) (boiling point not more than 35 °C)
L1.5BN		FL	3 (D/E)				S2	33	1866	RESIN SOLUTION, flammable (having a flash-point below 23 °C and viscous according to 2.2.3.1.4) (vapour pressure at 50 °C more than 110 kPa, boiling point of more than 35 °C)
LGBF		FL	3 (D/E)				S2	33	1866	RESIN SOLUTION, flammable (having a flash-point below 23 °C and viscous according to 2.2.3.1.4) (vapour pressure at 50 °C not more than 110 kPa)
SGAN		AT	2 (E)	V11 V12		CV28		46	1868	DECABORANE
SGAV		AT	3 (E)		VV1			40	1869	MAGNESIUM or MAGNESIUM ALLOYS with more than 50% magnesium in pellets, turnings or ribbons
			1 (E)	V1		CV23	S20		1870	POTASSIUM BOROHYDRIDE
SGAN		AT	2 (E)					40	1871	TITANIUM HYDRIDE
SGAN	TU3	AT	3 (E)			CV24 CV28		56	1872	LEAD DIOXIDE
L4DN(+)	TU3 TU28	AT	1 (B/E)			CV24	S20	558	1873	PERCHLORIC ACID with more than 50% but not more than 72% acid, by mass
SGAH L4BH	TU15 TE19	AT	2 (E)		VV9	CV13 CV28	S9	60	1884	BARIUM OXIDE
SGAH L4BH	TU15 TE19	AT	2 (D/E)	V11		CV13 CV28	S9 S19	60	1885	BENZIDINE
L4BH	TU15 TE19	AT	2 (D/E)			CV13 CV28	S9 S19	60	1886	BENZYLIDENE CHLORIDE
L4BH	TU15 TE19	AT	2 (E)			CV13 CV28	S9	60	1887	BROMOCHLOROMETHANE
L4BH	TU15 TE19	AT	2 (E)			CV13 CV28	S9	60	1888	CHLOROFORM
S10AH L10CH	TU14 TU15 TE19 TE21	AT	1 (C/E)			CV1 CV13 CV28	S9 S14	668	1889	CYANOGEN BROMIDE
L4BH	TU15 TE19	AT	2 (D/E)			CV13 CV28	S9 S19	60	1891	ETHYL BROMIDE
L10CH	TU14 TU15 TE19 TE21	AT	1 (C/E)			CV1 CV13 CV28	S9 S14	66	1892	ETHYLDICHLOROARSINE
SGAH	TU15 TE19	AT	2 (D/E)	V11		CV13 CV28	S9 S19	60	1894	PHENYLMERCURIC HYDROXIDE
SGAH	TU15 TE19	AT	2 (D/E)	V11		CV13 CV28	S9 S19	60	1895	PHENYLMERCURIC NITRATE

UN No.	Name and description	Class	Classifi-cation code	Packing group	Labels	Special provi-sions	Limited and excepted quantities		Packaging			Portable tanks and bulk containers	
									Packing instruc-tions	Special packing provisions	Mixed packing provisions	Instruc-tions	Special provisions
	3.1.2	2.2	2.2	2.1.1.3	5.2.2	3.3	3.4.6	3.5.1.2	4.1.4	4.1.4	4.1.10	4.2.5.2 7.3.2	4.2.5.3
(1)	(2)	(3a)	(3b)	(4)	(5)	(6)	(7a)	(7b)	(8)	(9a)	(9b)	(10)	(11)
1897	TETRACHLOROETHYLENE	6.1	T1	III	6.1		LQ7	E1	P001 IBC03 LP01 R001		MP19	T4	TP1
1898	ACETYL IODIDE	8	C3	II	8		LQ22	E2	P001 IBC02		MP15	T7	TP2
1902	DIISOOCTYL ACID PHOSPHATE	8	C3	III	8		LQ7	E1	P001 IBC03 LP01 R001		MP19	T4	TP1
1903	DISINFECTANT, LIQUID, CORROSIVE, N.O.S.	8	C9	I	8	274	LQ0	E0	P001		MP8 MP17		
1903	DISINFECTANT, LIQUID, CORROSIVE, N.O.S.	8	C9	II	8	274	LQ22	E2	P001 IBC02		MP15		
1903	DISINFECTANT, LIQUID, CORROSIVE, N.O.S.	8	C9	III	8	274	LQ7	E1	P001 IBC03 LP01 R001		MP19		
1905	SELENIC ACID	8	C2	I	8		LQ0	E0	P002 IBC07		MP18	T6	TP33
1906	SLUDGE ACID	8	C1	II	8		LQ22	E2	P001 IBC02		MP15	T8	TP2 TP28
1907	SODA LIME with more than 4% sodium hydroxide	8	C6	III	8	62	LQ24	E1	P002 IBC08 LP02 R001	B3	MP10	T1	TP33
1908	CHLORITE SOLUTION	8	C9	II	8	521	LQ22	E2	P001 IBC02		MP15	T7	TP2 TP24
1908	CHLORITE SOLUTION	8	C9	III	8	521	LQ7	E1	P001 IBC03 LP01 R001		MP19	T4	TP2 TP24
1910	Calcium oxide	8	C6				NOT SUBJECT TO ADR						
1911	DIBORANE	2	2TF		2.3 +2.1		LQ0	E0	P200		MP9		
1912	METHYL CHLORIDE AND METHYLENE CHLORIDE MIXTURE	2	2F		2.1	228	LQ0	E0	P200		MP9	(M) T50	
1913	NEON, REFRIGERATED LIQUID	2	3A		2.2	593	LQ1	E1	P203		MP9	T75	TP5
1914	BUTYL PROPIONATES	3	F1	III	3		LQ7	E1	P001 IBC03 LP01 R001		MP19	T2	TP1
1915	CYCLOHEXANONE	3	F1	III	3		LQ7	E1	P001 IBC03 LP01 R001		MP19	T2	TP1
1916	2,2'-DICHLORODIETHYL ETHER	6.1	TF1	II	6.1 +3		LQ17	E4	P001 IBC02		MP15	T7	TP2
1917	ETHYL ACRYLATE, STABILIZED	3	F1	II	3		LQ4	E2	P001 IBC02 R001		MP19	T4	TP1
1918	ISOPROPYLBENZENE	3	F1	III	3		LQ7	E1	P001 IBC03 LP01 R001		MP19	T2	TP1
1919	METHYL ACRYLATE, STABILIZED	3	F1	II	3		LQ4	E2	P001 IBC02 R001		MP19	T4	TP1
1920	NONANES	3	F1	III	3		LQ7	E1	P001 IBC03 LP01 R001		MP19	T2	TP1
1921	PROPYLENEIMINE, STABILIZED	3	FT1	I	3 +6.1		LQ0	E0	P001		MP2	T14	TP2
1922	PYRROLIDINE	3	FC	II	3 +8		LQ4	E2	P001 IBC02		MP19	T7	TP1

ADR tank		Vehicle for tank carriage	Transport category (Tunnel restriction code)	Special provisions for carriage				Hazard identification No.	UN No.	Name and description
Tank code	Special provisions			Packages	Bulk	Loading, unloading and handling	Operation			
4.3	4.3.5, 6.8.4	9.1.1.2	1.1.3.6 (8.6)	7.2.4	7.3.3	7.5.11	8.5	5.3.2.3		3.1.2
(12)	(13)	(14)	(15)	(16)	(17)	(18)	(19)	(20)	(1)	(2)
L4BH	TU15 TE19	AT	2 (E)			CV13 CV28	S9	60	1897	TETRACHLOROETHYLENE
L4BN		AT	2 (E)					80	1898	ACETYL IODIDE
L4BN		AT	3 (E)					80	1902	DIISOOCTYL ACID PHOSPHATE
L10BH		AT	1 (E)				S20	88	1903	DISINFECTANT, LIQUID, CORROSIVE, N.O.S.
L4BN		AT	2 (E)					80	1903	DISINFECTANT, LIQUID, CORROSIVE, N.O.S.
L4BN		AT	3 (E)					80	1903	DISINFECTANT, LIQUID, CORROSIVE, N.O.S.
S10AN		AT	1 (E)	V10 V12			S20	88	1905	SELENIC ACID
L4BN		AT	2 (E)					80	1906	SLUDGE ACID
SGAV		AT	3 (E)		VV9			80	1907	SODA LIME with more than 4% sodium hydroxide
L4BV(+)	TE11	AT	2 (E)					80	1908	CHLORITE SOLUTION
L4BV(+)	TE11	AT	3 (E)					80	1908	CHLORITE SOLUTION
NOT SUBJECT TO ADR									1910	Calcium oxide
			1 (D)			CV9 CV10 CV36	S2 S14		1911	DIBORANE
PxBN(M)	TA4 TT9	FL	2 (B/D)			CV9 CV10 CV36	S2 S20	23	1912	METHYL CHLORIDE AND METHYLENE CHLORIDE MIXTURE
RxBN	TU19 TA4 TT9	AT	3 (C/E)	V5		CV9 CV11 CV36	S20	22	1913	NEON, REFRIGERATED LIQUID
LGBF		FL	3 (D/E)				S2	30	1914	BUTYL PROPIONATES
LGBF		FL	3 (D/E)				S2	30	1915	CYCLOHEXANONE
L4BH	TU15 TE19	FL	2 (D/E)			CV13 CV28	S2 S9 S19	63	1916	2,2'-DICHLORODIETHYL ETHER
LGBF		FL	2 (D/E)				S2 S20	339	1917	ETHYL ACRYLATE, STABILIZED
LGBF		FL	3 (D/E)				S2	30	1918	ISOPROPYLBENZENE
LGBF		FL	2 (D/E)				S2 S20	339	1919	METHYL ACRYLATE, STABILIZED
LGBF		FL	3 (D/E)				S2	30	1920	NONANES
L15CH	TU14 TU15 TE21	FL	1 (C/E)			CV13 CV28	S2 S22	336	1921	PROPYLENEIMINE, STABILIZED
L4BH		FL	2 (D/E)				S2 S20	338	1922	PYRROLIDINE

UN No.	Name and description	Class	Classification code	Packing group	Labels	Special provisions	Limited and excepted quantities		Packaging			Portable tanks and bulk containers	
									Packing instructions	Special packing provisions	Mixed packing provisions	Instructions	Special provisions
	3.1.2	2.2	2.2	2.1.1.3	5.2.2	3.3	3.4.6	3.5.1.2	4.1.4	4.1.4	4.1.10	4.2.5.2 7.3.2	4.2.5.3
(1)	(2)	(3a)	(3b)	(4)	(5)	(6)	(7a)	(7b)	(8)	(9a)	(9b)	(10)	(11)
1923	CALCIUM DITHIONITE (CALCIUM HYDROSULPHITE)	4.2	S4	II	4.2		LQ0	E2	P410 IBC06		MP14	T3	TP33
1928	METHYL MAGNESIUM BROMIDE IN ETHYL ETHER	4.3	WF1	I	4.3 +3		LQ0	E0	P402	RR8	MP2		
1929	POTASSIUM DITHIONITE (POTASSIUM HYDROSULPHITE)	4.2	S4	II	4.2		LQ0	E2	P410 IBC06		MP14	T3	TP33
1931	ZINC DITHIONITE (ZINC HYDROSULPHITE)	9	M11	III	9		LQ27	E1	P002 IBC08 LP02 R001	B3	MP10	T1	TP33
1932	ZIRCONIUM SCRAP	4.2	S4	III	4.2	524 592	LQ0	E1	P002 IBC08 LP02 R001	B3	MP14	T1	TP33
1935	CYANIDE SOLUTION, N.O.S.	6.1	T4	I	6.1	274 525	LQ0	E5	P001		MP8 MP17	T14	TP2 TP27
1935	CYANIDE SOLUTION, N.O.S.	6.1	T4	II	6.1	274 525	LQ17	E4	P001 IBC02		MP15	T11	TP2 TP27
1935	CYANIDE SOLUTION, N.O.S.	6.1	T4	III	6.1	274 525	LQ7	E1	P001 IBC03 LP01 R001		MP19	T7	TP2 TP28
1938	BROMOACETIC ACID SOLUTION	8	C3	II	8		LQ22	E2	P001 IBC02		MP15	T7	TP2
1938	BROMOACETIC ACID SOLUTION	8	C3	III	8		LQ7	E1	P001 IBC02 LP01 R001		MP19	T7	TP2
1939	PHOSPHORUS OXYBROMIDE	8	C2	II	8		LQ23	E2	P002 IBC08	B4	MP10	T3	TP33
1940	THIOGLYCOLIC ACID	8	C3	II	8		LQ22	E2	P001 IBC02		MP15	T7	TP2
1941	DIBROMODIFLUORO-METHANE	9	M11	III	9		LQ28	E1	P001 LP01 R001		MP15	T11	TP2
1942	AMMONIUM NITRATE with not more than 0.2% total combustible material, including any organic substance calculated as carbon, to the exclusion of any other added substance	5.1	O2	III	5.1	306 611	LQ12	E1	P002 IBC08 LP02 R001	B3	MP10	T1 BK1 BK2	TP33
1944	MATCHES, SAFETY (book, card or strike on box)	4.1	F1	III	4.1	293	LQ9	E1	P407 R001		MP11		
1945	MATCHES, WAX 'VESTA'	4.1	F1	III	4.1	293	LQ9	E1	P407 R001		MP11		
1950	AEROSOLS, asphyxiant	2	5A		2.2	190 327 625	LQ2	E0	P003 LP02	PP17 PP87 RR6 L2	MP9		
1950	AEROSOLS, corrosive	2	5C		2.2 +8	190 327 625	LQ2	E0	P003 LP02	PP17 PP87 RR6 L2	MP9		
1950	AEROSOLS, corrosive, oxidizing	2	5CO		2.2 +5.1 +8	190 327 625	LQ2	E0	P003 LP02	PP17 PP87 RR6 L2	MP9		
1950	AEROSOLS, flammable	2	5F		2.1	190 327 625	LQ2	E0	P003 LP02	PP17 PP87 RR6 L2	MP9		
1950	AEROSOLS, flammable, corrosive	2	5FC		2.1 +8	190 327 625	LQ2	E0	P003 LP02	PP17 PP87 RR6 L2	MP9		

ADR tank		Vehicle for tank carriage	Transport category (Tunnel restriction code)	Special provisions for carriage				Hazard identifi-cation No.	UN No.	Name and description
Tank code	Special provisions			Packages	Bulk	Loading, unloading and handling	Operation			
4.3	4.3.5, 6.8.4	9.1.1.2	1.1.3.6 (8.6)	7.2.4	7.3.3	7.5.11	8.5	5.3.2.3		3.1.2
(12)	(13)	(14)	(15)	(16)	(17)	(18)	(19)	(20)	(1)	(2)
SGAN		AT	2 (D/E)	V1 V12				40	1923	CALCIUM DITHIONITE (CALCIUM HYDROSULPHITE)
L10DH	TU4 TU14 TU22 TE21 TM2	FL	0 (B/E)	V1		CV23	S2 S20	X323	1928	METHYL MAGNESIUM BROMIDE IN ETHYL ETHER
SGAN		AT	2 (D/E)	V1 V12				40	1929	POTASSIUM DITHIONITE (POTASSIUM HYDROSULPHITE)
SGAV		AT	3 (E)		VV3			90	1931	ZINC DITHIONITE (ZINC HYDROSULPHITE)
SGAN		AT	3 (E)	V1	VV4			40	1932	ZIRCONIUM SCRAP
L10CH	TU14 TU15 TE19 TE21	AT	1 (C/E)			CV1 CV13 CV28	S9 S14	66	1935	CYANIDE SOLUTION, N.O.S.
L4BH	TU15 TE19	AT	2 (D/E)			CV13 CV28	S9 S19	60	1935	CYANIDE SOLUTION, N.O.S.
L4BH	TU15 TE19	AT	2 (E)			CV13 CV28	S9	60	1935	CYANIDE SOLUTION, N.O.S.
L4BN		AT	2 (E)					80	1938	BROMOACETIC ACID SOLUTION
L4BN		AT	3 (E)					80	1938	BROMOACETIC ACID SOLUTION
SGAN		AT	2 (E)	V11				80	1939	PHOSPHORUS OXYBROMIDE
L4BN		AT	2 (E)					80	1940	THIOGLYCOLIC ACID
L4BN		AT	3 (E)					90	1941	DIBROMODIFLUORO-METHANE
SGAV	TU3	AT	3 (E)		VV8	CV24	S23	50	1942	AMMONIUM NITRATE with not more than 0.2% total combustible material, including any organic substance calculated as carbon, to the exclusion of any other added substance
			4 (E)						1944	MATCHES, SAFETY (book, card or strike on box)
			4 (E)						1945	MATCHES, WAX 'VESTA'
			3 (E)	V14		CV9 CV12			1950	AEROSOLS, asphyxiant
			1 (E)	V14		CV9 CV12			1950	AEROSOLS, corrosive
			1 (E)	V14		CV9 CV12			1950	AEROSOLS, corrosive, oxidizing
			2 (D)	V14		CV9 CV12	S2		1950	AEROSOLS, flammable
			1 (D)	V14		CV9 CV12	S2		1950	AEROSOLS, flammable, corrosive

UN No.	Name and description	Class	Classification code	Packing group	Labels	Special provisions	Limited and excepted quantities		Packaging			Portable tanks and bulk containers	
							quantities		Packing instructions	Special packing provisions	Mixed packing provisions	Instructions	Special provisions
3.1.2		2.2	2.2	2.1.1.3	5.2.2	3.3	3.4.6	3.5.1.2	4.1.4	4.1.4	4.1.10	4.2.5.2 7.3.2	4.2.5.3
(1)	(2)	(3a)	(3b)	(4)	(5)	(6)	(7a)	(7b)	(8)	(9a)	(9b)	(10)	(11)
1950	AEROSOLS, oxidizing	2	5O		2.2 +5.1	190 327 625	LQ2	E0	P003 LP02	PP17 PP87 RR6 L2	MP9		
1950	AEROSOLS, toxic	2	5T		2.2 +6.1	190 327 625	LQ1	E0	P003 LP02	PP17 PP87 RR6 L2	MP9		
1950	AEROSOLS, toxic, corrosive	2	5TC		2.2 +6.1 +8	190 327 625	LQ1	E0	P003 LP02	PP17 PP87 RR6 L2	MP9		
1950	AEROSOLS, toxic, flammable	2	5TF		2.1 +6.1	190 327 625	LQ1	E0	P003 LP02	PP17 PP87 RR6 L2	MP9		
1950	AEROSOLS, toxic, flammable, corrosive	2	5TFC		2.1 +6.1 +8	190 327 625	LQ1	E0	P003 LP02	PP17 PP87 RR6 L2	MP9		
1950	AEROSOLS, toxic, oxidizing	2	5TO		2.2 +5.1 +6.1	190 327 625	LQ1	E0	P003 LP02	PP17 PP87 RR6 L2	MP9		
1950	AEROSOLS, toxic, oxidizing, corrosive	2	5TOC		2.2 +5.1 +6.1 +8	190 327 625	LQ1	E0	P003 LP02	PP17 PP87 RR6 L2	MP9		
1951	ARGON, REFRIGERATED LIQUID	2	3A		2.2	593	LQ1	E1	P203		MP9	T75	TP5
1952	ETHYLENE OXIDE AND CARBON DIOXIDE MIXTURE with not more than 9% ethylene oxide	2	2A		2.2		LQ1	E1	P200		MP9	(M)	
1953	COMPRESSED GAS, TOXIC, FLAMMABLE, N.O.S.	2	1TF		2.3 +2.1	274	LQ0	E0	P200		MP9	(M)	
1954	COMPRESSED GAS, FLAMMABLE, N.O.S.	2	1F		2.1	274	LQ0	E0	P200		MP9	(M)	
1955	COMPRESSED GAS, TOXIC, N.O.S.	2	1T		2.3	274	LQ0	E0	P200		MP9	(M)	
1956	COMPRESSED GAS, N.O.S.	2	1A		2.2	274 292 567	LQ1	E1	P200		MP9	(M)	
1957	DEUTERIUM, COMPRESSED	2	1F		2.1		LQ0	E0	P200		MP9	(M)	
1958	1,2-DICHLORO-1,1,2,2-TETRAFLUOROETHANE (REFRIGERANT GAS R 114)	2	2A		2.2		LQ1	E1	P200		MP9	(M) T50	
1959	1,1-DIFLUOROETHYLENE (REFRIGERANT GAS R 1132a)	2	2F		2.1		LQ0	E0	P200		MP9	(M)	
1961	ETHANE, REFRIGERATED LIQUID	2	3F		2.1		LQ0	E0	P203		MP9	T75	TP5
1962	ETHYLENE	2	2F		2.1		LQ0	E0	P200		MP9	(M)	
1963	HELIUM, REFRIGERATED LIQUID	2	3A		2.2	593	LQ1	E1	P203		MP9	T75	TP5 TP34
1964	HYDROCARBON GAS MIXTURE, COMPRESSED, N.O.S.	2	1F		2.1	274	LQ0	E0	P200		MP9	(M)	

(12)	(13)	(14)	(15)	(16)	(17)	(18)	(19)	(20)	(1)	(2)
Tank code 4.3	Special provisions 4.3.5, 6.8.4	Vehicle for tank carriage 9.1.1.2	Transport category (Tunnel restriction code) 1.1.3.6 (8.6)	Packages 7.2.4	Bulk 7.3.3	Loading, unloading and handling 7.5.11	Operation 8.5	Hazard identification No. 5.3.2.3	UN No.	Name and description 3.1.2
			3 (E)	V14		CV9 CV12			1950	AEROSOLS, oxidizing
			1 (D)	V14		CV9 CV12 CV28			1950	AEROSOLS, toxic
			1 (D)	V14		CV9 CV12 CV28			1950	AEROSOLS, toxic, corrosive
			1 (D)	V14		CV9 CV12 CV28	S2		1950	AEROSOLS, toxic, flammable
			1 (D)	V14		CV9 CV12 CV28	S2		1950	AEROSOLS, toxic, flammable, corrosive
			1 (D)	V14		CV9 CV12 CV28			1950	AEROSOLS, toxic, oxidizing
			1 (D)	V14		CV9 CV12 CV28			1950	AEROSOLS, toxic, oxidizing, corrosive
RxBN	TU19 TA4 TT9	AT	3 (C/E)	V5		CV9 CV11 CV36	S20	22	1951	ARGON, REFRIGERATED LIQUID
PxBN(M)	TA4 TT9	AT	3 (C/E)			CV9 CV10 CV36		20	1952	ETHYLENE OXIDE AND CARBON DIOXIDE MIXTURE with not more than 9% ethylene oxide
CxBH(M)	TU6 TA4 TT9	FL	1 (B/D)			CV9 CV10 CV36	S2 S14	263	1953	COMPRESSED GAS, TOXIC, FLAMMABLE, N.O.S.
CxBN(M)	TA4 TT9	FL	2 (B/D)			CV9 CV10 CV36	S2 S20	23	1954	COMPRESSED GAS, FLAMMABLE, N.O.S.
CxBH(M)	TU6 TA4 TT9	AT	1 (C/D)			CV9 CV10 CV36	S14	26	1955	COMPRESSED GAS, TOXIC, N.O.S.
CxBN(M)	TA4 TT9	AT	3 (E)			CV9 CV10 CV36		20	1956	COMPRESSED GAS, N.O.S.
CxBN(M)	TA4 TT9	FL	2 (B/D)			CV9 CV10 CV36	S2 S20	23	1957	DEUTERIUM, COMPRESSED
PxBN(M)	TA4 TT9	AT	3 (C/E)			CV9 CV10 CV36		20	1958	1,2-DICHLORO-1,1,2,2-TETRAFLUOROETHANE (REFRIGERANT GAS R 114)
PxBN(M)	TA4 TT9	FL	2 (B/D)			CV9 CV10 CV36	S2 S20	239	1959	1,1-DIFLUOROETHYLENE (REFRIGERANT GAS R 1132a)
RxBN	TU18 TA4 TT9	FL	2 (B/D)	V5		CV9 CV11 CV36	S2 S17	223	1961	ETHANE, REFRIGERATED LIQUID
PxBN(M)	TA4 TT9	FL	2 (B/D)			CV9 CV10 CV36	S2 S20	23	1962	ETHYLENE
RxBN	TU19 TA4 TT9	AT	3 (C/E)	V5		CV9 CV11 CV36	S20	22	1963	HELIUM, REFRIGERATED LIQUID
CxBN(M)	TA4 TT9	FL	2 (B/D)			CV9 CV10 CV36	S2 S20	23	1964	HYDROCARBON GAS MIXTURE, COMPRESSED, N.O.S.

UN No.	Name and description	Class	Classification code	Packing group	Labels	Special provisions	Limited and excepted quantities		Packaging			Portable tanks and bulk containers	
									Packing instructions	Special packing provisions	Mixed packing provisions	Instructions	Special provisions
3.1.2		2.2	2.2	2.1.1.3	5.2.2	3.3	3.4.6	3.5.1.2	4.1.4	4.1.4	4.1.10	4.2.5.2 7.3.2	4.2.5.3
(1)	(2)	(3a)	(3b)	(4)	(5)	(6)	(7a)	(7b)	(8)	(9a)	(9b)	(10)	(11)
1965	HYDROCARBON GAS MIXTURE, LIQUEFIED, N.O.S. such as mixtures A, A01, A02, A0, A1, B1, B2, B or C	2	2F		2.1	274 583 652	LQ0	E0	P200		MP9	(M) T50	
1966	HYDROGEN, REFRIGERATED LIQUID	2	3F		2.1		LQ0	E0	P203		MP9	T75	TP5 TP23 TP34
1967	INSECTICIDE GAS, TOXIC, N.O.S.	2	2T		2.3	274	LQ0	E0	P200		MP9	(M)	
1968	INSECTICIDE GAS, N.O.S.	2	2A		2.2	274	LQ1	E1	P200		MP9	(M)	
1969	ISOBUTANE	2	2F		2.1		LQ0	E0	P200		MP9	(M) T50	
1970	KRYPTON, REFRIGERATED LIQUID	2	3A		2.2	593	LQ1	E1	P203		MP9	T75	TP5
1971	METHANE, COMPRESSED or NATURAL GAS, COMPRESSED with high methane content	2	1F		2.1		LQ0	E0	P200		MP9	(M)	
1972	METHANE, REFRIGERATED LIQUID or NATURAL GAS, REFRIGERATED LIQUID with high methane content	2	3F		2.1		LQ0	E0	P203		MP9	T75	TP5
1973	CHLORODIFLUORO-METHANE AND CHLOROPENTAFLUORO-ETHANE MIXTURE with fixed boiling point, with approximately 49% chlorodifluoromethane (REFRIGERANT GAS R 502)	2	2A		2.2		LQ1	E1	P200		MP9	(M) T50	
1974	CHLORODIFLUOROBROMO-METHANE (REFRIGERANT GAS R 12B1)	2	2A		2.2		LQ1	E1	P200		MP9	(M) T50	
1975	NITRIC OXIDE AND DINITROGEN TETROXIDE MIXTURE (NITRIC OXIDE AND NITROGEN DIOXIDE MIXTURE)	2	2TOC		2.3 +5.1 +8		LQ0	E0	P200		MP9		
1976	OCTAFLUOROCYCLO-BUTANE (REFRIGERANT GAS RC 318)	2	2A		2.2		LQ1	E1	P200		MP9	(M) T50	
1977	NITROGEN, REFRIGERATED LIQUID	2	3A		2.2	593	LQ1	E1	P203		MP9	T75	TP5
1978	PROPANE	2	2F		2.1	652	LQ0	E0	P200		MP9	(M) T50	
1982	TETRAFLUOROMETHANE (REFRIGERANT GAS R 14)	2	2A		2.2		LQ1	E1	P200		MP9	(M)	
1983	1-CHLORO-2,2,2-TRIFLUOROETHANE (REFRIGERANT GAS R 133a)	2	2A		2.2		LQ1	E1	P200		MP9	(M) T50	
1984	TRIFLUOROMETHANE (REFRIGERANT GAS R 23)	2	2A		2.2		LQ1	E1	P200		MP9	(M)	
1986	ALCOHOLS, FLAMMABLE, TOXIC, N.O.S.	3	FT1	I	3 +6.1	274	LQ0	E0	P001		MP7 MP17	T14	TP2 TP27
1986	ALCOHOLS, FLAMMABLE, TOXIC, N.O.S.	3	FT1	II	3 +6.1	274	LQ0	E2	P001 IBC02		MP19	T11	TP2 TP27
1986	ALCOHOLS, FLAMMABLE, TOXIC, N.O.S.	3	FT1	III	3 +6.1	274	LQ7	E1	P001 IBC03 R001		MP19	T7	TP1 TP28

ADR tank		Vehicle for tank carriage	Transport category (Tunnel restriction code)	Special provisions for carriage				Hazard identifi-cation No.	UN No.	Name and description
Tank code	Special provisions	9.1.1.2	1.1.3.6 (8.6)	Packages	Bulk	Loading, unloading and handling	Operation	5.3.2.3		
4.3	4.3.5, 6.8.4	9.1.1.2		7.2.4	7.3.3	7.5.11	8.5			3.1.2
(12)	(13)	(14)	(15)	(16)	(17)	(18)	(19)	(20)	(1)	(2)
PxBN(M)	TA4 TT9	FL	2 (B/D)			CV9 CV10 CV36	S2 S20	23	1965	HYDROCARBON GAS MIXTURE, LIQUEFIED, N.O.S. such as mixtures A, A01, A02, A0, A1, B1, B2, B or C
RxBN	TU18 TA4 TT9	FL	2 (B/D)	V5		CV9 CV11 CV36	S2 S17	223	1966	HYDROGEN, REFRIGERATED LIQUID
PxBH(M)	TU6 TA4 TT9	AT	1 (C/D)			CV9 CV10 CV36	S14	26	1967	INSECTICIDE GAS, TOXIC, N.O.S.
PxBN(M)	TA4 TT9	AT	3 (C/E)			CV9 CV10 CV36		20	1968	INSECTICIDE GAS, N.O.S.
PxBN(M)	TA4 TT9	FL	2 (B/D)			CV9 CV10 CV36	S2 S20	23	1969	ISOBUTANE
RxBN	TU19 TA4 TT9	AT	3 (C/E)	V5		CV9 CV11 CV36	S20	22	1970	KRYPTON, REFRIGERATED LIQUID
CxBN(M)	TA4 TT9	FL	2 (B/D)			CV9 CV10 CV36	S2 S20	23	1971	METHANE, COMPRESSED or NATURAL GAS, COMPRESSED with high methane content
RxBN	TU18 TA4 TT9	FL	2 (B/D)	V5		CV9 CV11 CV36	S2 S17	223	1972	METHANE, REFRIGERATED LIQUID or NATURAL GAS, REFRIGERATED LIQUID with high methane content
PxBN(M)	TA4 TT9	AT	3 (C/E)			CV9 CV10 CV36		20	1973	CHLORODIFLUORO-METHANE AND CHLOROPENTAFLUORO-ETHANE MIXTURE with fixed boiling point, with approximately 49% chlorodifluoromethane (REFRIGERANT GAS R 502)
PxBN(M)	TA4 TT9	AT	3 (C/E)			CV9 CV10 CV36		20	1974	CHLORODIFLUOROBROMO-METHANE (REFRIGERANT GAS R 12B1)
			1 (D)			CV9 CV10 CV36	S14		1975	NITRIC OXIDE AND DINITROGEN TETROXIDE MIXTURE (NITRIC OXIDE AND NITROGEN DIOXIDE MIXTURE)
PxBN(M)	TA4 TT9	AT	3 (C/E)			CV9 CV10 CV36		20	1976	OCTAFLUOROCYCLO-BUTANE (REFRIGERANT GAS RC 318)
RxBN	TU19 TA4 TT9	AT	3 (C/E)	V5		CV9 CV11 CV36	S20	22	1977	NITROGEN, REFRIGERATED LIQUID
PxBN(M)	TA4 TT9	FL	2 (B/D)			CV9 CV10 CV36	S2 S20	23	1978	PROPANE
PxBN(M)	TA4 TT9	AT	3 (C/E)			CV9 CV10 CV36		20	1982	TETRAFLUOROMETHANE (REFRIGERANT GAS R 14)
PxBN(M)	TA4 TT9	AT	3 (C/E)			CV9 CV10 CV36		20	1983	1-CHLORO-2,2,2-TRIFLUOROETHANE (REFRIGERANT GAS R 133a)
PxBN(M)	TA4 TT9	AT	3 (C/E)			CV9 CV10 CV36		20	1984	TRIFLUOROMETHANE (REFRIGERANT GAS R 23)
L10CH	TU14 TU15 TE21	FL	1 (C/E)			CV13 CV28	S2 S22	336	1986	ALCOHOLS, FLAMMABLE, TOXIC, N.O.S.
L4BH	TU15	FL	2 (D/E)			CV13 CV28	S2 S22	336	1986	ALCOHOLS, FLAMMABLE, TOXIC, N.O.S.
L4BH	TU15	FL	3 (D/E)			CV13 CV28	S2	36	1986	ALCOHOLS, FLAMMABLE, TOXIC, N.O.S.

UN No.	Name and description	Class	Classification code	Packing group	Labels	Special provisions	Limited and excepted quantities		Packaging			Portable tanks and bulk containers	
									Packing instructions	Special packing provisions	Mixed packing provisions	Instructions	Special provisions
	3.1.2	2.2	2.2	2.1.1.3	5.2.2	3.3	3.4.6	3.5.1.2	4.1.4	4.1.4	4.1.10	4.2.5.2 7.3.2	4.2.5.3
(1)	(2)	(3a)	(3b)	(4)	(5)	(6)	(7a)	(7b)	(8)	(9a)	(9b)	(10)	(11)
1987	ALCOHOLS, N.O.S. (vapour pressure at 50 °C more than 110 kPa)	3	F1	II	3	274 601 640C	LQ4	E2	P001		MP19	T7	TP1 TP8 TP28
1987	ALCOHOLS, N.O.S. (vapour pressure at 50 °C not more than 110 kPa)	3	F1	II	3	274 601 640D	LQ4	E2	P001 IBC02 R001		MP19	T7	TP1 TP8 TP28
1987	ALCOHOLS, N.O.S.	3	F1	III	3	274 601	LQ7	E1	P001 IBC03 LP01 R001		MP19	T4	TP1 TP29
1988	ALDEHYDES, FLAMMABLE, TOXIC, N.O.S.	3	FT1	I	3 +6.1	274	LQ0	E0	P001		MP7 MP17	T14	TP2 TP27
1988	ALDEHYDES, FLAMMABLE, TOXIC, N.O.S.	3	FT1	II	3 +6.1	274	LQ0	E2	P001 IBC02		MP19	T11	TP2 TP27
1988	ALDEHYDES, FLAMMABLE, TOXIC, N.O.S.	3	FT1	III	3 +6.1	274	LQ7	E1	P001 IBC03 R001		MP19	T7	TP1 TP28
1989	ALDEHYDES, N.O.S.	3	F1	I	3	274	LQ3	E3	P001		MP7 MP17	T11	TP1 TP27
1989	ALDEHYDES, N.O.S. (vapour pressure at 50 °C more than 110 kPa)	3	F1	II	3	274 640C	LQ4	E2	P001		MP19	T7	TP1 TP8 TP28
1989	ALDEHYDES, N.O.S. (vapour pressure at 50 °C not more than 110 kPa)	3	F1	II	3	274 640D	LQ4	E2	P001 IBC02 R001		MP19	T7	TP1 TP8 TP28
1989	ALDEHYDES, N.O.S.	3	F1	III	3	274	LQ7	E1	P001 IBC03 LP01 R001		MP19	T4	TP1 TP29
1990	BENZALDEHYDE	9	M11	III	9		LQ28	E1	P001 IBC03 LP01 R001		MP15	T2	TP1
1991	CHLOROPRENE, STABILIZED	3	FT1	I	3 +6.1		LQ0	E0	P001		MP7 MP17	T14	TP2 TP6
1992	FLAMMABLE LIQUID, TOXIC, N.O.S.	3	FT1	I	3 +6.1	274	LQ0	E0	P001		MP7 MP17	T14	TP2 TP27
1992	FLAMMABLE LIQUID, TOXIC, N.O.S.	3	FT1	II	3 +6.1	274	LQ0	E2	P001 IBC02		MP19	T7	TP2
1992	FLAMMABLE LIQUID, TOXIC, N.O.S.	3	FT1	III	3 +6.1	274	LQ7	E1	P001 IBC03 R001		MP19	T7	TP1 TP28
1993	FLAMMABLE LIQUID, N.O.S.	3	F1	I	3	274	LQ3	E3	P001		MP7 MP17	T11	TP1 TP27
1993	FLAMMABLE LIQUID, N.O.S. (vapour pressure at 50 °C more than 110 kPa)	3	F1	II	3	274 601 640C	LQ4	E2	P001		MP19	T7	TP1 TP8 TP28
1993	FLAMMABLE LIQUID, N.O.S. (vapour pressure at 50 °C not more than 110 kPa)	3	F1	II	3	274 601 640D	LQ4	E2	P001 IBC02 R001		MP19	T7	TP1 TP8 TP28
1993	FLAMMABLE LIQUID, N.O.S.	3	F1	III	3	274 601 640E	LQ7	E1	P001 IBC03 LP01 R001		MP19	T4	TP1 TP29
1993	FLAMMABLE LIQUID, N.O.S. (having a flash-point below 23 °C and viscous according to 2.2.3.1.4) (boiling point not more than 35 °C)	3	F1	III	3	274 601 640F	LQ7	E1	P001 LP01 R001		MP19	T4	TP1 TP29
1993	FLAMMABLE LIQUID, N.O.S. (having a flash-point below 23 °C and viscous according to 2.2.3.1.4) (vapour pressure at 50 °C more than 110 kPa, boiling point of more than 35 °C)	3	F1	III	3	274 601 640G	LQ7	E1	P001 LP01 R001		MP19	T4	TP1 TP29

ADR tank		Vehicle for tank carriage	Transport category (Tunnel restriction code)	Special provisions for carriage				Hazard identifi-cation No.	UN No.	Name and description
Tank code	Special provisions			Packages	Bulk	Loading, unloading and handling	Operation			
4.3	4.3.5, 6.8.4	9.1.1.2	1.1.3.6 (8.6)	7.2.4	7.3.3	7.5.11	8.5	5.3.2.3		3.1.2
(12)	(13)	(14)	(15)	(16)	(17)	(18)	(19)	(20)	(1)	(2)
L1.5BN		FL	2 (D/E)				S2 S20	33	1987	ALCOHOLS, N.O.S. (vapour pressure at 50 °C more than 110 kPa)
LGBF		FL	2 (D/E)				S2 S20	33	1987	ALCOHOLS, N.O.S. (vapour pressure at 50 °C not more than 110 kPa)
LGBF		FL	3 (D/E)				S2	30	1987	ALCOHOLS, N.O.S.
L10CH	TU14 TU15 TE21	FL	1 (C/E)			CV13 CV28	S2 S22	336	1988	ALDEHYDES, FLAMMABLE, TOXIC, N.O.S.
L4BH	TU15	FL	2 (D/E)			CV13 CV28	S2 S22	336	1988	ALDEHYDES, FLAMMABLE, TOXIC, N.O.S.
L4BH	TU15	FL	3 (D/E)			CV13 CV28	S2	36	1988	ALDEHYDES, FLAMMABLE, TOXIC, N.O.S.
L4BN		FL	1 (D/E)				S2 S20	33	1989	ALDEHYDES, N.O.S.
L1.5BN		FL	2 (D/E)				S2 S20	33	1989	ALDEHYDES, N.O.S. (vapour pressure at 50 °C more than 110 kPa)
LGBF		FL	2 (D/E)				S2 S20	33	1989	ALDEHYDES, N.O.S. (vapour pressure at 50 °C not more than 110 kPa)
LGBF		FL	3 (D/E)				S2	30	1989	ALDEHYDES, N.O.S.
LGBV		AT	3 (E)					90	1990	BENZALDEHYDE
L10CH	TU14 TU15 TE21	FL	1 (C/E)			CV13 CV28	S2 S22	336	1991	CHLOROPRENE, STABILIZED
L10CH	TU14 TU15 TE21	FL	1 (C/E)			CV13 CV28	S2 S22	336	1992	FLAMMABLE LIQUID, TOXIC, N.O.S.
L4BH	TU15	FL	2 (D/E)			CV13 CV28	S2 S19	336	1992	FLAMMABLE LIQUID, TOXIC, N.O.S.
L4BH	TU15	FL	3 (D/E)			CV13 CV28	S2	36	1992	FLAMMABLE LIQUID, TOXIC, N.O.S.
L4BN		FL	1 (D/E)				S2 S20	33	1993	FLAMMABLE LIQUID, N.O.S.
L1.5BN		FL	2 (D/E)				S2 S20	33	1993	FLAMMABLE LIQUID, N.O.S. (vapour pressure at 50 °C more than 110 kPa)
LGBF		FL	2 (D/E)				S2 S20	33	1993	FLAMMABLE LIQUID, N.O.S. (vapour pressure at 50 °C not more than 110 kPa)
LGBF		FL	3 (D/E)				S2	30	1993	FLAMMABLE LIQUID, N.O.S.
L4BN		FL	3 (D/E)				S2	33	1993	FLAMMABLE LIQUID, N.O.S. (having a flash-point below 23 °C and viscous according to 2.2.3.1.4) (boiling point not more than 35 °C)
L1.5BN		FL	3 (D/E)				S2	33	1993	FLAMMABLE LIQUID, N.O.S. (having a flash-point below 23 °C and viscous according to 2.2.3.1.4) (vapour pressure at 50 °C more than 110 kPa, boiling point of more than 35 °C)

UN No. 3.1.2	Name and description 3.1.2	Class 2.2	Classification code 2.2	Packing group 2.1.1.3	Labels 5.2.2	Special provisions 3.3	Limited and excepted quantities 3.4.6	Limited and excepted quantities 3.5.1.2	Packaging Packing instructions 4.1.4	Packaging Special packing provisions 4.1.4	Packaging Mixed packing provisions 4.1.10	Portable tanks and bulk containers Instructions 4.2.5.2 7.3.2	Portable tanks and bulk containers Special provisions 4.2.5.3
(1)	(2)	(3a)	(3b)	(4)	(5)	(6)	(7a)	(7b)	(8)	(9a)	(9b)	(10)	(11)
1993	FLAMMABLE LIQUID, N.O.S. (having a flash-point below 23 °C and viscous according to 2.2.3.1.4) (vapour pressure at 50 °C not more than 110 kPa)	3	F1	III	3	274 601 640H	LQ7	E1	P001 IBC02 LP01 R001		MP19	T4	TP1 TP29
1994	IRON PENTACARBONYL	6.1	TF1	I	6.1 +3		LQ0	E5	P601		MP2	T22	TP2
1999	TARS, LIQUID, including road asphalt and oils, bitumen and cut backs (vapour pressure at 50 °C more than 110 kPa)	3	F1	II	3	640C	LQ6	E2	P001		MP19	T3	TP3 TP29
1999	TARS, LIQUID, including road asphalt and oils, bitumen and cut backs (vapour pressure at 50 °C not more than 110 kPa)	3	F1	II	3	640D	LQ6	E2	P001 IBC02 R001		MP19	T3	TP3 TP29
1999	TARS, LIQUID, including road asphalt and oils, bitumen and cut backs	3	F1	III	3	640E	LQ7	E1	P001 IBC03 LP01 R001		MP19	T1	TP3
1999	TARS, LIQUID, including road asphalt and oils, bitumen and cut backs (having a flash-point below 23 °C and viscous according to 2.2.3.1.4) (boiling point not more than 35 °C)	3	F1	III	3	640F	LQ7	E1	P001 LP01 R001		MP19	T1	TP3
1999	TARS, LIQUID, including road asphalt and oils, bitumen and cut backs (having a flash-point below 23 °C and viscous according to 2.2.3.1.4) (vapour pressure at 50 °C more than 110 kPa, boiling point of more than 35 °C)	3	F1	III	3	640G	LQ7	E1	P001 LP01 R001		MP19	T1	TP3
1999	TARS, LIQUID, including road asphalt and oils, bitumen and cut backs (having a flash-point below 23 °C and viscous according to 2.2.3.1.4) (vapour pressure at 50 °C not more than 110 kPa)	3	F1	III	3	640H	LQ7	E1	P001 IBC02 LP01 R001		MP19	T1	TP3
2000	CELLULOID in block, rods, rolls, sheets, tubes, etc., except scrap	4.1	F1	III	4.1	502	LQ9	E1	P002 LP02 R001	PP7	MP11		
2001	COBALT NAPHTHENATES, POWDER	4.1	F3	III	4.1		LQ9	E1	P002 IBC08 LP02 R001	B3	MP11	T1	TP33
2002	CELLULOID, SCRAP	4.2	S2	III	4.2	526 592	LQ0	E1	P002 IBC08 LP02 R001	PP8 B3	MP14		
2004	MAGNESIUM DIAMIDE	4.2	S4	II	4.2		LQ0	E2	P410 IBC06		MP14	T3	TP33
2006	PLASTICS, NITROCELLULOSE-BASED, SELF-HEATING, N.O.S.	4.2	S2	III	4.2	274 528	LQ0	E1	P002 R001		MP14		
2008	ZIRCONIUM POWDER, DRY	4.2	S4	I	4.2	524 540	LQ0	E0	P404		MP13	T21	TP7 TP33
2008	ZIRCONIUM POWDER, DRY	4.2	S4	II	4.2	524 540	LQ0	E2	P410 IBC06		MP14	T3	TP33
2008	ZIRCONIUM POWDER, DRY	4.2	S4	III	4.2	524 540	LQ0	E1	P002 IBC08 LP02 R001	B3	MP14	T1	TP33
2009	ZIRCONIUM, DRY, finished sheets, strip or coiled wire	4.2	S4	III	4.2	524 592	LQ0	E1	P002 LP02 R001		MP14		
2010	MAGNESIUM HYDRIDE	4.3	W2	I	4.3		LQ0	E0	P403		MP2		

ADR tank		Vehicle for tank carriage	Transport category (Tunnel restriction code)	Special provisions for carriage				Hazard identifi-cation No.	UN No.	Name and description
Tank code	Special provisions			Packages	Bulk	Loading, unloading and handling	Operation			
4.3	4.3.5, 6.8.4	9.1.1.2	1.1.3.6 (8.6)	7.2.4	7.3.3	7.5.11	8.5	5.3.2.3		3.1.2
(12)	(13)	(14)	(15)	(16)	(17)	(18)	(19)	(20)	(1)	(2)
LGBF		FL	3 (D/E)				S2	33	1993	FLAMMABLE LIQUID, N.O.S. (having a flash-point below 23 °C and viscous according to 2.2.3.1.4) (vapour pressure at 50 °C not more than 110 kPa)
L15CH	TU14 TU15 TU31 TE19 TE21 TM3	FL	1 (C/D)			CV1 CV13 CV28	S2 S9 S14	663	1994	IRON PENTACARBONYL
L1.5BN		FL	2 (D/E)				S2 S20	33	1999	TARS, LIQUID, including road asphalt and oils, bitumen and cut backs (vapour pressure at 50 °C more than 110 kPa)
LGBF		FL	2 (D/E)				S2 S20	33	1999	TARS, LIQUID, including road asphalt and oils, bitumen and cut backs (vapour pressure at 50 °C not more than 110 kPa)
LGBF		FL	3 (D/E)				S2	30	1999	TARS, LIQUID, including road asphalt and oils, bitumen and cut backs
L4BN		FL	3 (D/E)				S2	33	1999	TARS, LIQUID, including road asphalt and oils, bitumen and cut backs (having a flash-point below 23 °C and viscous according to 2.2.3.1.4) (boiling point not more than 35 °C)
L1.5BN		FL	3 (D/E)				S2	33	1999	TARS, LIQUID, including road asphalt and oils, bitumen and cut backs (having a flash-point below 23 °C and viscous according to 2.2.3.1.4) (vapour pressure at 50 °C more than 110 kPa, boiling point of more than 35 °C)
LGBF		FL	3 (D/E)				S2	33	1999	TARS, LIQUID, including road asphalt and oils, bitumen and cut backs (having a flash-point below 23 °C and viscous according to 2.2.3.1.4) (vapour pressure at 50 °C not more than 110 kPa)
			3 (E)						2000	CELLULOID in block, rods, rolls, sheets, tubes, etc., except scrap
SGAV		AT	3 (E)		VV1			40	2001	COBALT NAPHTHENATES, POWDER
			3 (E)	V1					2002	CELLULOID, SCRAP
SGAN		AT	2 (D/E)	V1 V12				40	2004	MAGNESIUM DIAMIDE
			3 (E)	V1					2006	PLASTICS, NITROCELLULOSE-BASED, SELF-HEATING, N.O.S.
		AT	0 (B/E)	V1			S20	43	2008	ZIRCONIUM POWDER, DRY
SGAN		AT	2 (D/E)	V1 V12				40	2008	ZIRCONIUM POWDER, DRY
SGAN		AT	3 (E)	V1	VV4			40	2008	ZIRCONIUM POWDER, DRY
			3 (E)	V1	VV4			40	2009	ZIRCONIUM, DRY, finished sheets, strip or coiled wire
			1 (E)	V1		CV23	S20		2010	MAGNESIUM HYDRIDE

UN No.	Name and description	Class	Classification code	Packing group	Labels	Special provisions	Limited and excepted quantities		Packaging			Portable tanks and bulk containers	
									Packing instructions	Special packing provisions	Mixed packing provisions	Instructions	Special provisions
	3.1.2	2.2	2.2	2.1.1.3	5.2.2	3.3	3.4.6	3.5.1.2	4.1.4	4.1.4	4.1.10	4.2.5.2 7.3.2	4.2.5.3
(1)	(2)	(3a)	(3b)	(4)	(5)	(6)	(7a)	(7b)	(8)	(9a)	(9b)	(10)	(11)
2011	MAGNESIUM PHOSPHIDE	4.3	WT2	I	4.3 +6.1		LQ0	E0	P403		MP2		
2012	POTASSIUM PHOSPHIDE	4.3	WT2	I	4.3 +6.1		LQ0	E0	P403		MP2		
2013	STRONTIUM PHOSPHIDE	4.3	WT2	I	4.3 +6.1		LQ0	E0	P403		MP2		
2014	HYDROGEN PEROXIDE, AQUEOUS SOLUTION with not less than 20% but not more than 60% hydrogen peroxide (stabilized as necessary)	5.1	OC1	II	5.1 +8		LQ10	E2	P504 IBC02	PP10 B5	MP15	T7	TP2 TP6 TP24
2015	HYDROGEN PEROXIDE, AQUEOUS SOLUTION, STABILIZED with more than 70% hydrogen peroxide	5.1	OC1	I	5.1 +8	640N	LQ0	E0	P501		MP2	T9	TP2 TP6 TP24
2015	HYDROGEN PEROXIDE, AQUEOUS SOLUTION, STABILIZED with more than 60% hydrogen peroxide and not more than 70% hydrogen peroxide	5.1	OC1	I	5.1 +8	640O	LQ0	E0	P501		MP2	T9	TP2 TP6 TP24
2016	AMMUNITION, TOXIC, NON-EXPLOSIVE without burster or expelling charge, non-fuzed	6.1	T2	II	6.1		LQ0	E0	P600		MP10		
2017	AMMUNITION, TEAR-PRODUCING, NON-EXPLOSIVE without burster or expelling charge, non-fuzed	6.1	TC2	II	6.1 +8		LQ0	E0	P600				
2018	CHLOROANILINES, SOLID	6.1	T2	II	6.1		LQ18	E4	P002 IBC08	B4	MP10	T3	TP33
2019	CHLOROANILINES, LIQUID	6.1	T1	II	6.1		LQ17	E4	P001 IBC02		MP15	T7	TP2
2020	CHLOROPHENOLS, SOLID	6.1	T2	III	6.1	205	LQ9	E1	P002 IBC08 LP02 R001	B3	MP10	T1	TP33
2021	CHLOROPHENOLS, LIQUID	6.1	T1	III	6.1		LQ7	E1	P001 IBC03 LP01 R001		MP19	T4	TP1
2022	CRESYLIC ACID	6.1	TC1	II	6.1 +8		LQ17	E4	P001 IBC02		MP15	T7	TP2
2023	EPICHLOROHYDRIN	6.1	TF1	II	6.1 +3	279	LQ17	E4	P001 IBC02		MP15	T7	TP2
2024	MERCURY COMPOUND, LIQUID, N.O.S.	6.1	T4	I	6.1	43 274	LQ0	E5	P001		MP8 MP17		
2024	MERCURY COMPOUND, LIQUID, N.O.S.	6.1	T4	II	6.1	43 274	LQ17	E4	P001 IBC02		MP15		
2024	MERCURY COMPOUND, LIQUID, N.O.S.	6.1	T4	III	6.1	43 274	LQ7	E1	P001 IBC03 LP01 R001		MP19		
2025	MERCURY COMPOUND, SOLID, N.O.S.	6.1	T5	I	6.1	43 274 529 585	LQ0	E5	P002 IBC07		MP18	T6	TP33
2025	MERCURY COMPOUND, SOLID, N.O.S.	6.1	T5	II	6.1	43 274 529 585	LQ18	E4	P002 IBC08	B4	MP10	T3	TP33
2025	MERCURY COMPOUND, SOLID, N.O.S.	6.1	T5	III	6.1	43 274 529 585	LQ9	E1	P002 IBC08 LP02 R001	B3	MP10	T1	TP33
2026	PHENYLMERCURIC COMPOUND, N.O.S.	6.1	T3	I	6.1	43 274	LQ0	E5	P002 IBC07		MP18	T6	TP33
2026	PHENYLMERCURIC COMPOUND, N.O.S.	6.1	T3	II	6.1	43 274	LQ18	E4	P002 IBC08	B4	MP10	T3	TP33

ADR tank		Vehicle for tank carriage	Transport category (Tunnel restriction code)	Special provisions for carriage				Hazard identifi-cation No.	UN No.	Name and description
Tank code	Special provisions			Packages	Bulk	Loading, unloading and handling	Operation			
4.3	4.3.5, 6.8.4	9.1.1.2	1.1.3.6 (8.6)	7.2.4	7.3.3	7.5.11	8.5	5.3.2.3		3.1.2
(12)	(13)	(14)	(15)	(16)	(17)	(18)	(19)	(20)	(1)	(2)
			1 (E)	V1		CV23 CV28	S20		2011	MAGNESIUM PHOSPHIDE
			1 (E)	V1		CV23 CV28	S20		2012	POTASSIUM PHOSPHIDE
			1 (E)	V1		CV23 CV28	S20		2013	STRONTIUM PHOSPHIDE
L4BV(+)	TU3 TC2 TE8 TE11 TT1	AT	2 (E)			CV24		58	2014	HYDROGEN PEROXIDE, AQUEOUS SOLUTION with not less than 20% but not more than 60% hydrogen peroxide (stabilized as necessary)
L4DV(+)	TU3 TU28 TC2 TE8 TE9 TT1	OX	1 (B/E)	V5		CV24	S20	559	2015	HYDROGEN PEROXIDE, AQUEOUS SOLUTION, STABILIZED with more than 70% hydrogen peroxide
L4BV(+)	TU3 TU28 TC2 TE7 TE8 TE9 TT1	OX	1 (B/E)	V5		CV24	S20	559	2015	HYDROGEN PEROXIDE, AQUEOUS SOLUTION, STABILIZED with more than 60% hydrogen peroxide and not more than 70% hydrogen peroxide
			2 (D/E)			CV13 CV28	S9 S19		2016	AMMUNITION, TOXIC, NON-EXPLOSIVE without burster or expelling charge, non-fuzed
			2 (D/E)			CV13 CV28	S9 S19		2017	AMMUNITION, TEAR-PRODUCING, NON-EXPLOSIVE without burster or expelling charge, non-fuzed
SGAH L4BH	TU15 TE19	AT	2 (D/E)	V11		CV13 CV28	S9 S19	60	2018	CHLOROANILINES, SOLID
L4BH	TU15 TE19	AT	2 (D/E)			CV13 CV28	S9 S19	60	2019	CHLOROANILINES, LIQUID
SGAH	TU15 TE19	AT	2 (E)		VV9	CV13 CV28	S9	60	2020	CHLOROPHENOLS, SOLID
L4BH	TU15 TE19	AT	2 (E)			CV13 CV28	S9	60	2021	CHLOROPHENOLS, LIQUID
L4BH	TU15 TE19	AT	2 (D/E)			CV13 CV28	S9 S19	68	2022	CRESYLIC ACID
L4BH	TU15 TE19	FL	2 (D/E)			CV13 CV28	S2 S9 S19	63	2023	EPICHLOROHYDRIN
L10CH	TU14 TU15 TE19 TE21	AT	1 (C/E)			CV1 CV13 CV28	S9 S14	66	2024	MERCURY COMPOUND, LIQUID, N.O.S.
L4BH	TU15 TE19	AT	2 (D/E)			CV13 CV28	S9 S19	60	2024	MERCURY COMPOUND, LIQUID, N.O.S.
L4BH	TU15 TE19	AT	2 (E)			CV13 CV28	S9	60	2024	MERCURY COMPOUND, LIQUID, N.O.S.
S10AH	TU15 TE19	AT	1 (C/E)	V10 V12		CV1 CV13 CV28	S9 S14	66	2025	MERCURY COMPOUND, SOLID, N.O.S.
SGAH	TU15 TE19	AT	2 (D/E)	V11		CV13 CV28	S9 S19	60	2025	MERCURY COMPOUND, SOLID, N.O.S.
SGAH	TU15 TE19	AT	2 (E)		VV9	CV13 CV28	S9	60	2025	MERCURY COMPOUND, SOLID, N.O.S.
S10AH L10CH	TU14 TU15 TE19 TE21	AT	1 (C/E)	V10 V12		CV1 CV13 CV28	S9 S14	66	2026	PHENYLMERCURIC COMPOUND, N.O.S.
SGAH L4BH	TU15 TE19	AT	2 (D/E)	V11		CV13 CV28	S9 S19	60	2026	PHENYLMERCURIC COMPOUND, N.O.S.

UN No.	Name and description	Class	Classifi-cation code	Packing group	Labels	Special provi-sions	Limited and excepted quantities		Packaging			Portable tanks and bulk containers	
							quantities		Packing instruc-tions	Special packing provisions	Mixed packing provisions	Instruc-tions	Special provisions
	3.1.2	2.2	2.2	2.1.1.3	5.2.2	3.3	3.4.6	3.5.1.2	4.1.4	4.1.4	4.1.10	4.2.5.2 7.3.2	4.2.5.3
(1)	(2)	(3a)	(3b)	(4)	(5)	(6)	(7a)	(7b)	(8)	(9a)	(9b)	(10)	(11)
2026	PHENYLMERCURIC COMPOUND, N.O.S.	6.1	T3	III	6.1	43 274	LQ9	E1	P002 IBC08 LP02 R001	B3	MP10	T1	TP33
2027	SODIUM ARSENITE, SOLID	6.1	T5	II	6.1	43	LQ18	E4	P002 IBC08	B4	MP10	T3	TP33
2028	BOMBS, SMOKE, NON-EXPLOSIVE with corrosive liquid, without initiating device	8	C11	II	8		LQ0	E0	P803				
2029	HYDRAZINE, ANHYDROUS	8	CFT	I	8 +3 +6.1		LQ0	E0	P001		MP8 MP17		
2030	HYDRAZINE AQUEOUS SOLUTION, with more than 37% hydrazine by mass, having a flash-point above 60 °C	8	CT1	I	8 +6.1	530	LQ0	E0	P001		MP8 MP17	T10	TP2
2030	HYDRAZINE AQUEOUS SOLUTION, with more than 37% hydrazine by mass, having a flash-point of not more than 60 °C	8	CFT	I	8 +3 +6.1	530	LQ0	E0	P001		MP8 MP17	T10	TP2
2030	HYDRAZINE AQUEOUS SOLUTION, with more than 37% hydrazine by mass	8	CT1	II	8 +6.1	530	LQ22	E2	P001 IBC02		MP15	T7	TP2
2030	HYDRAZINE AQUEOUS SOLUTION, with more than 37% hydrazine by mass	8	CT1	III	8 +6.1	530	LQ7	E1	P001 IBC03 LP01 R001		MP19	T4	TP1
2031	NITRIC ACID, other than red fuming, with more than 70% nitric acid	8	CO1	I	8 +5.1		LQ0	E0	P001	PP81	MP8 MP17	T10	TP2
2031	NITRIC ACID, other than red fuming, with at least 65%, but not more than 70% nitric acid	8	CO1	II	8 +5.1		LQ22	E2	P001 IBC02	PP81 B15	MP15	T8	TP2
2031	NITRIC ACID, other than red fuming, with less than 65% nitric acid	8	C1	II	8		LQ22	E2	P001 IBC02	PP81 B15	MP15	T8	TP2
2032	NITRIC ACID, RED FUMING	8	COT	I	8 +5.1 +6.1		LQ0	E0	P602		MP8 MP17	T20	TP2
2033	POTASSIUM MONOXIDE	8	C6	II	8		LQ23	E2	P002 IBC08	B4	MP10	T3	TP33
2034	HYDROGEN AND METHANE MIXTURE, COMPRESSED	2	1F		2.1		LQ0	E0	P200		MP9	(M)	
2035	1,1,1-TRIFLUOROETHANE (REFRIGERANT GAS R 143a)	2	2F		2.1		LQ0	E0	P200		MP9	(M) T50	
2036	XENON	2	2A		2.2		LQ1	E1	P200		MP9	(M)	
2037	RECEPTACLES, SMALL, CONTAINING GAS (GAS CARTRIDGES) without a release device, non-refillable	2	5A		2.2	191 303	LQ2	E0	P003	PP17 RR6	MP9		
2037	RECEPTACLES, SMALL, CONTAINING GAS (GAS CARTRIDGES) without a release device, non-refillable	2	5F		2.1	191 303	LQ2	E0	P003	PP17 RR6	MP9		
2037	RECEPTACLES, SMALL, CONTAINING GAS (GAS CARTRIDGES) without a release device, non-refillable	2	5O		2.2 +5.1	191 303	LQ2	E0	P003	PP17 RR6	MP9		
2037	RECEPTACLES, SMALL, CONTAINING GAS (GAS CARTRIDGES) without a release device, non-refillable	2	5T		2.3	303	LQ1	E0	P003	PP17 RR6	MP9		

ADR tank		Vehicle for tank carriage	Transport category (Tunnel restriction code)	Special provisions for carriage				Hazard identifi-cation No.	UN No.	Name and description
Tank code	Special provisions			Packages	Bulk	Loading, unloading and handling	Operation			
4.3	4.3.5, 6.8.4	9.1.1.2	1.1.3.6 (8.6)	7.2.4	7.3.3	7.5.11	8.5	5.3.2.3		3.1.2
(12)	(13)	(14)	(15)	(16)	(17)	(18)	(19)	(20)	(1)	(2)
SGAH L4BH	TU15 TE19	AT	2 (E)		VV9	CV13 CV28	S9	60	2026	PHENYLMERCURIC COMPOUND, N.O.S.
SGAH	TU15 TE19	AT	2 (D/E)	V11		CV13 CV28	S9 S19	60	2027	SODIUM ARSENITE, SOLID
			2 (E)						2028	BOMBS, SMOKE, NON-EXPLOSIVE with corrosive liquid, without initiating device
			1 (E)			CV13 CV28	S2 S14		2029	HYDRAZINE, ANHYDROUS
L10BH		AT	1 (C/D)			CV13 CV28	S14	886	2030	HYDRAZINE AQUEOUS SOLUTION, with more than 37% hydrazine by mass, having a flash-point above 60 °C
L10BH		FL	1 (C/D)			CV13 CV28	S2 S14	886	2030	HYDRAZINE AQUEOUS SOLUTION, with more than 37% hydrazine by mass, having a flash-point of not more than 60 °C
L4BN		AT	2 (E)			CV13 CV28		86	2030	HYDRAZINE AQUEOUS SOLUTION, with more than 37% hydrazine by mass
L4BN		AT	3 (E)			CV13 CV28		86	2030	HYDRAZINE AQUEOUS SOLUTION, with more than 37% hydrazine by mass
L10BH	TC6 TT1	AT	1 (E)			CV24	S14	885	2031	NITRIC ACID, other than red fuming, with more than 70% nitric acid
L4BN		AT	2 (E)					85	2031	NITRIC ACID, other than red fuming, with at least 65%, but not more than 70% nitric acid
L4BN		AT	2 (E)					80	2031	NITRIC ACID, other than red fuming, with less than 65% nitric acid
L10BH	TC6 TT1	AT	1 (C/D)			CV13 CV24 CV28	S14	856	2032	NITRIC ACID, RED FUMING
SGAN		AT	2 (E)	V11				80	2033	POTASSIUM MONOXIDE
CxBN(M)	TA4 TT9	FL	2 (B/D)			CV9 CV10 CV36	S2 S20	23	2034	HYDROGEN AND METHANE MIXTURE, COMPRESSED
PxBN(M)	TA4 TT9	FL	2 (B/D)			CV9 CV10 CV36	S2 S20	23	2035	1,1,1-TRIFLUOROETHANE (REFRIGERANT GAS R 143a)
PxBN(M)	TA4 TT9	AT	3 (C/E)			CV9 CV10 CV36		20	2036	XENON
			3 (E)			CV9 CV12			2037	RECEPTACLES, SMALL, CONTAINING GAS (GAS CARTRIDGES) without a release device, non-refillable
			2 (D)			CV9 CV12	S2		2037	RECEPTACLES, SMALL, CONTAINING GAS (GAS CARTRIDGES) without a release device, non-refillable
			3 (E)			CV9 CV12			2037	RECEPTACLES, SMALL, CONTAINING GAS (GAS CARTRIDGES) without a release device, non-refillable
			1 (D)			CV9 CV12			2037	RECEPTACLES, SMALL, CONTAINING GAS (GAS CARTRIDGES) without a release device, non-refillable

UN No.	Name and description	Class	Classification code	Packing group	Labels	Special provisions	Limited and excepted quantities		Packaging			Portable tanks and bulk containers	
									Packing instructions	Special packing provisions	Mixed packing provisions	Instructions	Special provisions
	3.1.2	2.2	2.2	2.1.1.3	5.2.2	3.3	3.4.6	3.5.1.2	4.1.4	4.1.4	4.1.10	4.2.5.2 7.3.2	4.2.5.3
(1)	(2)	(3a)	(3b)	(4)	(5)	(6)	(7a)	(7b)	(8)	(9a)	(9b)	(10)	(11)
2037	RECEPTACLES, SMALL, CONTAINING GAS (GAS CARTRIDGES) without a release device, non-refillable	2	5TC		2.3 +8	303	LQ1	E0	P003	PP17 RR6	MP9		
2037	RECEPTACLES, SMALL, CONTAINING GAS (GAS CARTRIDGES) without a release device, non-refillable	2	5TF		2.3 +2.1	303	LQ1	E0	P003	PP17 RR6	MP9		
2037	RECEPTACLES, SMALL, CONTAINING GAS (GAS CARTRIDGES) without a release device, non-refillable	2	5TFC		2.3 +2.1 +8	303	LQ1	E0	P003	PP17 RR6	MP9		
2037	RECEPTACLES, SMALL, CONTAINING GAS (GAS CARTRIDGES) without a release device, non-refillable	2	5TO		2.3 +5.1	303	LQ1	E0	P003	PP17 RR6	MP9		
2037	RECEPTACLES, SMALL, CONTAINING GAS (GAS CARTRIDGES) without a release device, non-refillable	2	5TOC		2.3 +5.1 +8	303	LQ1	E0	P003	PP17 RR6	MP9		
2038	DINITROTOLUENES, LIQUID	6.1	T1	II	6.1		LQ17	E4	P001 IBC02		MP15	T7	TP2
2044	2,2-DIMETHYLPROPANE	2	2F		2.1		LQ0	E0	P200		MP9	(M)	
2045	ISOBUTYRALDEHYDE (ISOBUTYL ALDEHYDE)	3	F1	II	3		LQ4	E2	P001 IBC02 R001		MP19	T4	TP1
2046	CYMENES	3	F1	III	3		LQ7	E1	P001 IBC03 LP01 R001		MP19	T2	TP1
2047	DICHLOROPROPENES	3	F1	II	3		LQ4	E2	P001 IBC02 R001		MP19	T4	TP1
2047	DICHLOROPROPENES	3	F1	III	3		LQ7	E1	P001 IBC03 LP01 R001		MP19	T2	TP1
2048	DICYCLOPENTADIENE	3	F1	III	3		LQ7	E1	P001 IBC03 LP01 R001		MP19	T2	TP1
2049	DIETHYLBENZENE	3	F1	III	3		LQ7	E1	P001 IBC03 LP01 R001		MP19	T2	TP1
2050	DIISOBUTYLENE, ISOMERIC COMPOUNDS	3	F1	II	3		LQ4	E2	P001 IBC02 R001		MP19	T4	TP1
2051	2-DIMETHYLAMINO-ETHANOL	8	CF1	II	8 +3		LQ22	E2	P001 IBC02		MP15	T7	TP2
2052	DIPENTENE	3	F1	III	3		LQ7	E1	P001 IBC03 LP01 R001		MP19	T2	TP1
2053	METHYL ISOBUTYL CARBINOL	3	F1	III	3		LQ7	E1	P001 IBC03 LP01 R001		MP19	T2	TP1
2054	MORPHOLINE	8	CF1	I	8 +3		LQ0	E0	P001		MP8 MP17	T10	TP2
2055	STYRENE MONOMER, STABILIZED	3	F1	III	3		LQ7	E1	P001 IBC03 LP01		MP19	T2	TP1
2056	TETRAHYDROFURAN	3	F1	II	3		LQ4	E2	P001 IBC02 R001		MP19	T4	TP1
2057	TRIPROPYLENE	3	F1	II	3		LQ4	E2	P001 IBC02 R001		MP19	T4	TP1

ADR tank		Vehicle for tank carriage	Transport category (Tunnel restriction code)	Special provisions for carriage				Hazard identifi- cation No.	UN No.	Name and description
Tank code	Special provisions			Packages	Bulk	Loading, unloading and handling	Operation			
4.3	4.3.5, 6.8.4	9.1.1.2	1.1.3.6 (8.6)	7.2.4	7.3.3	7.5.11	8.5	5.3.2.3		3.1.2
(12)	(13)	(14)	(15)	(16)	(17)	(18)	(19)	(20)	(1)	(2)
			1 (D)			CV9 CV12			2037	RECEPTACLES, SMALL, CONTAINING GAS (GAS CARTRIDGES) without a release device, non-refillable
			1 (D)			CV9 CV12	S2		2037	RECEPTACLES, SMALL, CONTAINING GAS (GAS CARTRIDGES) without a release device, non-refillable
			1 (D)			CV9 CV12	S2		2037	RECEPTACLES, SMALL, CONTAINING GAS (GAS CARTRIDGES) without a release device, non-refillable
			1 (D)			CV9 CV12			2037	RECEPTACLES, SMALL, CONTAINING GAS (GAS CARTRIDGES) without a release device, non-refillable
			1 (D)			CV9 CV12			2037	RECEPTACLES, SMALL, CONTAINING GAS (GAS CARTRIDGES) without a release device, non-refillable
L4BH	TU15 TE19	AT	2 (D/E)			CV13 CV28	S9 S19	60	2038	DINITROTOLUENES, LIQUID
PxBN(M)	TA4 TT9	FL	2 (B/D)			CV9 CV10 CV36	S2 S20	23	2044	2,2-DIMETHYLPROPANE
LGBF		FL	2 (D/E)				S2 S20	33	2045	ISOBUTYRALDEHYDE (ISOBUTYL ALDEHYDE)
LGBF		FL	3 (D/E)				S2	30	2046	CYMENES
LGBF		FL	2 (D/E)				S2 S20	33	2047	DICHLOROPROPENES
LGBF		FL	3 (D/E)				S2	30	2047	DICHLOROPROPENES
LGBF		FL	3 (D/E)				S2	30	2048	DICYCLOPENTADIENE
LGBF		FL	3 (D/E)				S2	30	2049	DIETHYLBENZENE
LGBF		FL	2 (D/E)				S2 S20	33	2050	DIISOBUTYLENE, ISOMERIC COMPOUNDS
L4BN		FL	2 (D/E)				S2	83	2051	2-DIMETHYLAMINO-ETHANOL
LGBF		FL	3 (D/E)				S2	30	2052	DIPENTENE
LGBF		FL	3 (D/E)				S2	30	2053	METHYL ISOBUTYL CARBINOL
L10BH		FL	1 (D/E)				S2 S14	883	2054	MORPHOLINE
LGBF		FL	3 (D/E)				S2	39	2055	STYRENE MONOMER, STABILIZED
LGBF		FL	2 (D/E)				S2 S20	33	2056	TETRAHYDROFURAN
LGBF		FL	2 (D/E)				S2 S20	33	2057	TRIPROPYLENE

UN No.	Name and description	Class	Classification code	Packing group	Labels	Special provisions	Limited and excepted quantities		Packaging			Portable tanks and bulk containers	
							quantities		Packing instructions	Special packing provisions	Mixed packing provisions	Instructions	Special provisions
	3.1.2	2.2	2.2	2.1.1.3	5.2.2	3.3	3.4.6	3.5.1.2	4.1.4	4.1.4	4.1.10	4.2.5.2 7.3.2	4.2.5.3
(1)	(2)	(3a)	(3b)	(4)	(5)	(6)	(7a)	(7b)	(8)	(9a)	(9b)	(10)	(11)
2057	TRIPROPYLENE	3	F1	III	3		LQ7	E1	P001 IBC03 LP01 R001		MP19	T2	TP1
2058	VALERALDEHYDE	3	F1	II	3		LQ4	E2	P001 IBC02 R001		MP19	T4	TP1
2059	NITROCELLULOSE SOLUTION, FLAMMABLE with not more than 12.6% nitrogen, by dry mass, and not more than 55% nitrocellulose	3	D	I	3	198 531	LQ3	E0	P001		MP7 MP17	T11	TP1 TP8 TP27
2059	NITROCELLULOSE SOLUTION, FLAMMABLE with not more than 12.6% nitrogen, by dry mass, and not more than 55% nitrocellulose (vapour pressure at 50 °C more than 110 kPa)	3	D	II	3	198 531 640C	LQ4	E0	P001 IBC02		MP19	T4	TP1 TP8
2059	NITROCELLULOSE SOLUTION, FLAMMABLE with not more than 12.6% nitrogen, by dry mass, and not more than 55% nitrocellulose (vapour pressure at 50 °C not more than 110 kPa)	3	D	II	3	198 531 640D	LQ4	E0	P001 IBC02 R001		MP19	T4	TP1 TP8
2059	NITROCELLULOSE SOLUTION, FLAMMABLE with not more than 12.6% nitrogen, by dry mass, and not more than 55% nitrocellulose	3	D	III	3	198 531	LQ7	E0	P001 IBC03 LP01 R001		MP19	T2	TP1
2067	AMMONIUM NITRATE BASED FERTILIZER	5.1	O2	III	5.1	186 306 307	LQ12	E1	P002 IBC08 LP02 R001	B3	MP10	T1 BK1 BK2	TP33
2071	Ammonium nitrate based fertilizer, uniform mixtures of the nitrogen/phosphate, nitrogen/potash or nitrogen/phosphate/potash type, containing not more than 70% ammonium nitrate and not more than 0.4% total combustible/organic material calculated as carbon or with not more than 45% ammonium nitrate and unrestricted combustible material	9	M11	NOT SUBJECT TO ADR										
2073	AMMONIA SOLUTION, relative density less than 0.880 at 15 °C in water, with more than 35% but not more than 50% ammonia	2	4A		2.2	532	LQ1	E1	P200		MP9	(M)	
2074	ACRYLAMIDE, SOLID	6.1	T2	III	6.1		LQ9	E1	P002 IBC08 LP02 R001	B3	MP10	T1	TP33
2075	CHLORAL, ANHYDROUS, STABILIZED	6.1	T1	II	6.1		LQ17	E4	P001 IBC02		MP15	T7	TP2
2076	CRESOLS, LIQUID	6.1	TC1	II	6.1 +8		LQ17	E4	P001 IBC02		MP15	T7	TP2
2077	alpha-NAPHTHYLAMINE	6.1	T2	III	6.1		LQ9	E1	P002 IBC08 LP02 R001	B3	MP10	T1	TP33
2078	TOLUENE DIISOCYANATE	6.1	T1	II	6.1	279	LQ17	E4	P001 IBC02		MP15	T7	TP2
2079	DIETHYLENETRIAMINE	8	C7	II	8		LQ22	E2	P001 IBC02		MP15	T7	TP2
2186	HYDROGEN CHLORIDE, REFRIGERATED LIQUID	2	3TC	CARRIAGE PROHIBITED										

ADR tank		Vehicle for tank carriage	Transport category (Tunnel restriction code)	Special provisions for carriage				Hazard identifi-cation No.	UN No.	Name and description
Tank code	Special provisions			Packages	Bulk	Loading, unloading and handling	Operation			
4.3	4.3.5, 6.8.4	9.1.1.2	1.1.3.6 (8.6)	7.2.4	7.3.3	7.5.11	8.5	5.3.2.3		3.1.2
(12)	(13)	(14)	(15)	(16)	(17)	(18)	(19)	(20)	(1)	(2)
LGBF		FL	3 (D/E)				S2	30	2057	TRIPROPYLENE
LGBF		FL	2 (D/E)				S2 S20	33	2058	VALERALDEHYDE
L4BN		FL	1 (B)				S2 S14	33	2059	NITROCELLULOSE SOLUTION, FLAMMABLE with not more than 12.6% nitrogen, by dry mass, and not more than 55% nitrocellulose
L1.5BN		FL	2 (B)				S2 S14	33	2059	NITROCELLULOSE SOLUTION, FLAMMABLE with not more than 12.6% nitrogen, by dry mass, and not more than 55% nitrocellulose (vapour pressure at 50 °C more than 110 kPa)
LGBF		FL	2 (B)				S2 S14	33	2059	NITROCELLULOSE SOLUTION, FLAMMABLE with not more than 12.6% nitrogen, by dry mass, and not more than 55% nitrocellulose (vapour pressure at 50 °C not more than 110 kPa)
LGBF		FL	3 (B)				S2 S14	30	2059	NITROCELLULOSE SOLUTION, FLAMMABLE with not more than 12.6% nitrogen, by dry mass, and not more than 55% nitrocellulose
SGAV	TU3	AT	3 (E)		VV8	CV24	S23	50	2067	AMMONIUM NITRATE BASED FERTILIZER
NOT SUBJECT TO ADR									2071	Ammonium nitrate based fertilizer, uniform mixtures of the nitrogen/phosphate, nitrogen/potash or nitrogen/phosphate/potash type, containing not more than 70% ammonium nitrate and not more than 0.4% total combustible/organic material calculated as carbon or with not more than 45% ammonium nitrate and unrestricted combustible material
PxBN(M)	TA4 TT9	AT	3 (E)			CV9 CV10		20	2073	AMMONIA SOLUTION, relative density less than 0.880 at 15 °C in water, with more than 35% but not more than 50% ammonia
SGAH L4BH	TU15 TE19	AT	2 (E)		VV9	CV13 CV28	S9	60	2074	ACRYLAMIDE, SOLID
L4BH	TU15 TE19	AT	2 (D/E)			CV13 CV28	S9 S19	69	2075	CHLORAL, ANHYDROUS, STABILIZED
L4BH	TU15 TE19	AT	2 (D/E)			CV13 CV28	S9 S19	68	2076	CRESOLS, LIQUID
SGAH L4BH	TU15 TE19	AT	2 (E)		VV9	CV13 CV28	S9	60	2077	alpha-NAPHTHYLAMINE
L4BH	TU15 TE19	AT	2 (D/E)			CV13 CV28	S9 S19	60	2078	TOLUENE DIISOCYANATE
L4BN		AT	2 (E)					80	2079	DIETHYLENETRIAMINE
CARRIAGE PROHIBITED									2186	HYDROGEN CHLORIDE, REFRIGERATED LIQUID

UN No.	Name and description	Class	Classification code	Packing group	Labels	Special provisions	Limited and excepted quantities		Packaging			Portable tanks and bulk containers	
									Packing instructions	Special packing provisions	Mixed packing provisions	Instructions	Special provisions
	3.1.2	2.2	2.2	2.1.1.3	5.2.2	3.3	3.4.6	3.5.1.2	4.1.4	4.1.4	4.1.10	4.2.5.2 7.3.2	4.2.5.3
(1)	(2)	(3a)	(3b)	(4)	(5)	(6)	(7a)	(7b)	(8)	(9a)	(9b)	(10)	(11)
2187	CARBON DIOXIDE, REFRIGERATED LIQUID	2	3A		2.2	593	LQ1	E1	P203		MP9	T75	TP5
2188	ARSINE	2	2TF		2.3 +2.1		LQ0	E0	P200		MP9		
2189	DICHLOROSILANE	2	2TFC		2.3 +2.1 +8		LQ0	E0	P200		MP9	(M)	
2190	OXYGEN DIFLUORIDE, COMPRESSED	2	1TOC		2.3 +5.1 +8		LQ0	E0	P200		MP9		
2191	SULPHURYL FLUORIDE	2	2T		2.3		LQ0	E0	P200		MP9	(M)	
2192	GERMANE	2	2TF		2.3 +2.1	632	LQ0	E0	P200		MP9	(M)	
2193	HEXAFLUOROETHANE (REFRIGERANT GAS R 116)	2	2A		2.2		LQ1	E1	P200		MP9	(M)	
2194	SELENIUM HEXAFLUORIDE	2	2TC		2.3 +8		LQ0	E0	P200		MP9		
2195	TELLURIUM HEXAFLUORIDE	2	2TC		2.3 +8		LQ0	E0	P200		MP9		
2196	TUNGSTEN HEXAFLUORIDE	2	2TC		2.3 +8		LQ0	E0	P200		MP9		
2197	HYDROGEN IODIDE, ANHYDROUS	2	2TC		2.3 +8		LQ0	E0	P200		MP9	(M)	
2198	PHOSPHORUS PENTAFLUORIDE	2	2TC		2.3 +8		LQ0	E0	P200		MP9		
2199	PHOSPHINE	2	2TF		2.3 +2.1	632	LQ0	E0	P200		MP9		
2200	PROPADIENE, STABILIZED	2	2F		2.1		LQ0	E0	P200		MP9	(M)	
2201	NITROUS OXIDE, REFRIGERATED LIQUID	2	3O		2.2 +5.1		LQ0	E0	P203		MP9	T75	TP5 TP22
2202	HYDROGEN SELENIDE, ANHYDROUS	2	2TF		2.3 +2.1		LQ0	E0	P200		MP9		
2203	SILANE	2	2F		2.1	632	LQ0	E0	P200		MP9	(M)	
2204	CARBONYL SULPHIDE	2	2TF		2.3 +2.1		LQ0	E0	P200		MP9	(M)	
2205	ADIPONITRILE	6.1	T1	III	6.1		LQ7	E1	P001 IBC03 LP01 R001		MP19	T3	TP1
2206	ISOCYANATES, TOXIC, N.O.S. or ISOCYANATE SOLUTION, TOXIC, N.O.S.	6.1	T1	II	6.1	274 551	LQ17	E4	P001 IBC02		MP15	T11	TP2 TP27
2206	ISOCYANATES, TOXIC, N.O.S. or ISOCYANATE SOLUTION, TOXIC, N.O.S.	6.1	T1	III	6.1	274 551	LQ7	E1	P001 IBC03 LP01 R001		MP19	T7	TP1 TP28
2208	CALCIUM HYPOCHLORITE MIXTURE, DRY with more than 10% but not more than 39% available chlorine	5.1	O2	III	5.1	313 314	LQ12	E1	P002 IBC08 LP02 R001	B3 B13	MP10		

ADR tank		Vehicle for tank carriage	Transport category (Tunnel restriction code)	Special provisions for carriage				Hazard identification No.	UN No.	Name and description
Tank code	Special provisions			Packages	Bulk	Loading, unloading and handling	Operation			
4.3	4.3.5, 6.8.4	9.1.1.2	1.1.3.6 (8.6)	7.2.4	7.3.3	7.5.11	8.5	5.3.2.3		3.1.2
(12)	(13)	(14)	(15)	(16)	(17)	(18)	(19)	(20)	(1)	(2)
RxBN	TU19 TA4 TT9	AT	3 (C/E)	V5		CV9 CV11 CV36	S20	22	2187	CARBON DIOXIDE, REFRIGERATED LIQUID
			1 (D)			CV9 CV10 CV36	S2 S14		2188	ARSINE
PxBH(M)	TA4 TT9	FL	1 (B/D)			CV9 CV10 CV36	S2 S14	263	2189	DICHLOROSILANE
			1 (D)			CV9 CV10 CV36	S14		2190	OXYGEN DIFLUORIDE, COMPRESSED
PxBH(M)	TA4 TT9	AT	1 (C/D)			CV9 CV10 CV36	S14	26	2191	SULPHURYL FLUORIDE
		FL	1 (B/D)			CV9 CV10 CV36	S2 S14	263	2192	GERMANE
PxBN(M)	TA4 TT9	AT	3 (C/E)			CV9 CV10 CV36		20	2193	HEXAFLUOROETHANE (REFRIGERANT GAS R 116)
			1 (D)			CV9 CV10 CV36	S14		2194	SELENIUM HEXAFLUORIDE
			1 (D)			CV9 CV10 CV36	S14		2195	TELLURIUM HEXAFLUORIDE
			1 (D)			CV9 CV10 CV36	S14		2196	TUNGSTEN HEXAFLUORIDE
PxBH(M)	TA4 TT9	AT	1 (C/D)			CV9 CV10 CV36	S14	268	2197	HYDROGEN IODIDE, ANHYDROUS
			1 (D)			CV9 CV10 CV36	S14		2198	PHOSPHORUS PENTAFLUORIDE
			1 (D)			CV9 CV10 CV36	S2 S14		2199	PHOSPHINE
PxBN(M)	TA4 TT9	FL	2 (B/D)			CV9 CV10 CV36	S2 S20	239	2200	PROPADIENE, STABILIZED
RxBN	TU7 TU19 TA4 TT9	AT	3 (C/E)	V5		CV9 CV11 CV36	S20	225	2201	NITROUS OXIDE, REFRIGERATED LIQUID
			1 (D)			CV9 CV10 CV36	S2 S14		2202	HYDROGEN SELENIDE, ANHYDROUS
PxBN(M)	TA4 TT9	FL	2 (B/D)			CV9 CV10 CV36	S2 S20	23	2203	SILANE
PxBH(M)	TA4 TT9	FL	1 (B/D)			CV9 CV10 CV36	S2 S14	263	2204	CARBONYL SULPHIDE
L4BH	TU15 TE19	AT	2 (E)			CV13 CV28	S9	60	2205	ADIPONITRILE
L4BH	TU15 TE19	AT	2 (D/E)			CV13 CV28	S9 S19	60	2206	ISOCYANATES, TOXIC, N.O.S. or ISOCYANATE SOLUTION, TOXIC, N.O.S.
L4BH	TU15 TE19	AT	2 (E)			CV13 CV28	S9	60	2206	ISOCYANATES, TOXIC, N.O.S. or ISOCYANATE SOLUTION, TOXIC, N.O.S.
SGAN	TU3	AT	3 (E)			CV24 CV35		50	2208	CALCIUM HYPOCHLORITE MIXTURE, DRY with more than 10% but not more than 39% available chlorine

UN No.	Name and description	Class	Classification code	Packing group	Labels	Special provisions	Limited and excepted quantities		Packaging			Portable tanks and bulk containers	
									Packing instructions	Special packing provisions	Mixed packing provisions	Instructions	Special provisions
	3.1.2	2.2	2.2	2.1.1.3	5.2.2	3.3	3.4.6	3.5.1.2	4.1.4	4.1.4	4.1.10	4.2.5.2 7.3.2	4.2.5.3
(1)	(2)	(3a)	(3b)	(4)	(5)	(6)	(7a)	(7b)	(8)	(9a)	(9b)	(10)	(11)
2209	FORMALDEHYDE SOLUTION with not less than 25% formaldehyde	8	C9	III	8	533	LQ7	E1	P001 IBC03 LP01 R001		MP19	T4	TP1
2210	MANEB or MANEB PREPARATION with not less than 60% maneb	4.2	SW	III	4.2 +4.3	273	LQ0	E1	P002 IBC06 R001		MP14	T1	TP33
2211	POLYMERIC BEADS, EXPANDABLE, evolving flammable vapour	9	M3	III	None	207 633	LQ27	E1	P002 IBC08 R001	PP14 B3 B6	MP10	T1	TP33
2212	BLUE ASBESTOS (crocidolite) or BROWN ASBESTOS (amosite, mysorite)	9	M1	II	9	168	LQ25	E2	P002 IBC08	PP37 B4	MP10	T3	TP33
2213	PARAFORMALDEHYDE	4.1	F1	III	4.1		LQ9	E1	P002 IBC08 LP02 R001	PP12 B3	MP10	T1 BK1 BK2	TP33
2214	PHTHALIC ANHYDRIDE with more than 0.05% of maleic anhydride	8	C4	III	8	169	LQ24	E1	P002 IBC08 LP02 R001	B3	MP10	T1	TP33
2215	MALEIC ANHYDRIDE, MOLTEN	8	C3	III	8		LQ0	E0				T4	TP3
2215	MALEIC ANHYDRIDE	8	C4	III	8		LQ24	E1	P002 IBC08 R001	B3	MP10	T1	TP33
2216	Fish meal (Fish scrap), stabilized	9	M11	NOT SUBJECT TO ADR									
2217	SEED CAKE with not more than 1.5% oil and not more than 11% moisture	4.2	S2	III	4.2	142	LQ0	E1	P002 IBC08 LP02 R001	PP20 B3 B6	MP14		
2218	ACRYLIC ACID, STABILIZED	8	CF1	II	8 +3		LQ22	E2	P001 IBC02		MP15	T7	TP2
2219	ALLYL GLYCIDYL ETHER	3	F1	III	3		LQ7	E1	P001 IBC03 LP01 R001		MP19	T2	TP1
2222	ANISOLE	3	F1	III	3		LQ7	E1	P001 IBC03 LP01 R001		MP19	T2	TP1
2224	BENZONITRILE	6.1	T1	II	6.1		LQ17	E4	P001 IBC02		MP15	T7	TP2
2225	BENZENESULPHONYL CHLORIDE	8	C3	III	8		LQ7	E1	P001 IBC03 LP01 R001		MP19	T4	TP1
2226	BENZOTRICHLORIDE	8	C9	II	8		LQ22	E2	P001 IBC02		MP15	T7	TP2
2227	n-BUTYL METHACRYLATE, STABILIZED	3	F1	III	3		LQ7	E1	P001 IBC03 LP01 R001		MP19	T2	TP1
2232	2-CHLOROETHANAL	6.1	T1	I	6.1		LQ0	E5	P001		MP8 MP17	T14	TP2
2233	CHLOROANISIDINES	6.1	T2	III	6.1		LQ9	E1	P002 IBC08 LP02 R001	B3	MP10	T1	TP33
2234	CHLOROBENZOTRI-FLUORIDES	3	F1	III	3		LQ7	E1	P001 IBC03 LP01 R001		MP19	T2	TP1
2235	CHLOROBENZYL CHLORIDES, LIQUID	6.1	T1	III	6.1		LQ7	E1	P001 IBC03 LP01 R001		MP19	T4	TP1

ADR tank		Vehicle for tank carriage	Transport category (Tunnel restriction code)	Special provisions for carriage				Hazard identifi-cation No.	UN No.	Name and description
Tank code	Special provisions			Packages	Bulk	Loading, unloading and handling	Operation			
4.3	4.3.5, 6.8.4	9.1.1.2	1.1.3.6 (8.6)	7.2.4	7.3.3	7.5.11	8.5	5.3.2.3		3.1.2
(12)	(13)	(14)	(15)	(16)	(17)	(18)	(19)	(20)	(1)	(2)
L4BN		AT	3 (E)					80	2209	FORMALDEHYDE SOLUTION with not less than 25% formaldehyde
SGAN		AT	3 (E)	V1 V12	VV4			40	2210	MANEB or MANEB PREPARATION with not less than 60% maneb
SGAN	TE20	AT	3 (D/E)		VV3			90	2211	POLYMERIC BEADS, EXPANDABLE, evolving flammable vapour
SGAH	TU15	AT	2 (E)	V11		CV1 CV13 CV28	S19	90	2212	BLUE ASBESTOS (crocidolite) or BROWN ASBESTOS (amosite, mysorite)
SGAV		AT	3 (E)	V13	VV1			40	2213	PARAFORMALDEHYDE
SGAV L4BN		AT	3 (E)		VV9			80	2214	PHTHALIC ANHYDRIDE with more than 0.05% of maleic anhydride
L4BN		AT	0 (E)					80	2215	MALEIC ANHYDRIDE, MOLTEN
SGAV		AT	3 (E)		VV9			80	2215	MALEIC ANHYDRIDE
NOT SUBJECT TO ADR									2216	Fish meal (Fish scrap), stabilized
			3 (E)	V1	VV4			40	2217	SEED CAKE with not more than 1.5% oil and not more than 11% moisture
L4BN		FL	2 (D/E)				S2	839	2218	ACRYLIC ACID, STABILIZED
LGBF		FL	3 (D/E)				S2	30	2219	ALLYL GLYCIDYL ETHER
LGBF		FL	3 (D/E)				S2	30	2222	ANISOLE
L4BH	TU15 TE19	AT	2 (D/E)			CV13 CV28	S9 S19	60	2224	BENZONITRILE
L4BN		AT	3 (E)					80	2225	BENZENESULPHONYL CHLORIDE
L4BN		AT	2 (E)					80	2226	BENZOTRICHLORIDE
LGBF		FL	3 (D/E)				S2	39	2227	n-BUTYL METHACRYLATE, STABILIZED
L10CH	TU14 TU15 TE19 TE21	AT	1 (C/E)			CV1 CV13 CV28	S9 S14	66	2232	2-CHLOROETHANAL
SGAH L4BH	TU15 TE19	AT	2 (E)		VV9	CV13 CV28	S9	60	2233	CHLOROANISIDINES
LGBF		FL	3 (D/E)				S2	30	2234	CHLOROBENZOTRI-FLUORIDES
L4BH	TU15 TE19	AT	2 (E)			CV13 CV28	S9	60	2235	CHLOROBENZYL CHLORIDES, LIQUID

UN No.	Name and description	Class	Classification code	Packing group	Labels	Special provisions	Limited and excepted quantities		Packaging			Portable tanks and bulk containers	
							quantities		Packing instructions	Special packing provisions	Mixed packing provisions	Instructions	Special provisions
	3.1.2	2.2	2.2	2.1.1.3	5.2.2	3.3	3.4.6	3.5.1.2	4.1.4	4.1.4	4.1.10	4.2.5.2 7.3.2	4.2.5.3
(1)	(2)	(3a)	(3b)	(4)	(5)	(6)	(7a)	(7b)	(8)	(9a)	(9b)	(10)	(11)
2236	3-CHLORO-4-METHYLPHENYL ISOCYANATE, LIQUID	6.1	T1	II	6.1		LQ17	E4	P001 IBC02		MP15		
2237	CHLORONITROANILINES	6.1	T2	III	6.1		LQ9	E1	P002 IBC08 LP02 R001	B3	MP10	T1	TP33
2238	CHLOROTOLUENES	3	F1	III	3		LQ7	E1	P001 IBC03 LP01 R001		MP19	T2	TP1
2239	CHLOROTOLUIDINES, SOLID	6.1	T2	III	6.1		LQ9	E1	P002 IBC08 LP02 R001	B3	MP10	T1	TP33
2240	CHROMOSULPHURIC ACID	8	C1	I	8		LQ0	E0	P001		MP8 MP17	T10	TP2
2241	CYCLOHEPTANE	3	F1	II	3		LQ4	E2	P001 IBC02 R001		MP19	T4	TP1
2242	CYCLOHEPTENE	3	F1	II	3		LQ4	E2	P001 IBC02 R001		MP19	T4	TP1
2243	CYCLOHEXYL ACETATE	3	F1	III	3		LQ7	E1	P001 IBC03 LP01 R001		MP19	T2	TP1
2244	CYCLOPENTANOL	3	F1	III	3		LQ7	E1	P001 IBC03 LP01 R001		MP19	T2	TP1
2245	CYCLOPENTANONE	3	F1	III	3		LQ7	E1	P001 IBC03 LP01 R001		MP19	T2	TP1
2246	CYCLOPENTENE	3	F1	II	3		LQ4	E2	P001 IBC02	B8	MP19	T7	TP2
2247	n-DECANE	3	F1	III	3		LQ7	E1	P001 IBC03 LP01 R001		MP19	T2	TP1
2248	DI-n-BUTYLAMINE	8	CF1	II	8 +3		LQ22	E2	P001 IBC02		MP15	T7	TP2
2249	DICHLORODIMETHYL ETHER, SYMMETRICAL	6.1	TF1			CARRIAGE PROHIBITED							
2250	DICHLOROPHENYL ISOCYANATES	6.1	T2	II	6.1		LQ18	E4	P002 IBC08	B4	MP10	T3	TP33
2251	BICYCLO[2.2.1]HEPTA-2,5-DIENE, STABILIZED (2,5-NORBORNADIENE, STABILIZED)	3	F1	II	3		LQ4	E2	P001 IBC02 R001		MP19	T7	TP2
2252	1,2-DIMETHOXYETHANE	3	F1	II	3		LQ4	E2	P001 IBC02 R001		MP19	T4	TP1
2253	N,N-DIMETHYLANILINE	6.1	T1	II	6.1		LQ17	E4	P001 IBC02		MP15	T7	TP2
2254	MATCHES, FUSEE	4.1	F1	III	4.1	293	LQ9	E1	P407 R001		MP11		
2256	CYCLOHEXENE	3	F1	II	3		LQ4	E2	P001 IBC02 R001		MP19	T4	TP1
2257	POTASSIUM	4.3	W2	I	4.3		LQ0	E0	P403 IBC04		MP2	T9	TP7 TP33
2258	1,2-PROPYLENEDIAMINE	8	CF1	II	8 +3		LQ22	E2	P001 IBC02		MP15	T7	TP2
2259	TRIETHYLENETETRAMINE	8	C7	II	8		LQ22	E2	P001 IBC02		MP15	T7	TP2
2260	TRIPROPYLAMINE	3	FC	III	3 +8		LQ7	E1	P001 IBC03 R001		MP19	T4	TP1
2261	XYLENOLS, SOLID	6.1	T2	II	6.1		LQ18	E4	P002 IBC08	B4	MP10	T3	TP33

ADR tank		Vehicle for tank carriage	Transport category (Tunnel restriction code)	Special provisions for carriage				Hazard identifi- cation No.	UN No.	Name and description
Tank code	Special provisions			Packages	Bulk	Loading, unloading and handling	Operation			
4.3	4.3.5, 6.8.4	9.1.1.2	1.1.3.6 (8.6)	7.2.4	7.3.3	7.5.11	8.5	5.3.2.3		3.1.2
(12)	(13)	(14)	(15)	(16)	(17)	(18)	(19)	(20)	(1)	(2)
L4BH	TU15 TE19	AT	2 (D/E)			CV13 CV28	S9 S19	60	2236	3-CHLORO-4-METHYLPHENYL ISOCYANATE, LIQUID
SGAH L4BH	TU15 TE19	AT	2 (E)		VV9	CV13 CV28	S9	60	2237	CHLORONITROANILINES
LGBF		FL	3 (D/E)				S2	30	2238	CHLOROTOLUENES
SGAH L4BH	TU15 TE19	AT	2 (E)		VV9	CV13 CV28	S9	60	2239	CHLOROTOLUIDINES, SOLID
L10BH		AT	1 (E)				S20	88	2240	CHROMOSULPHURIC ACID
LGBF		FL	2 (D/E)				S2 S20	33	2241	CYCLOHEPTANE
LGBF		FL	2 (D/E)				S2 S20	33	2242	CYCLOHEPTENE
LGBF		FL	3 (D/E)				S2	30	2243	CYCLOHEXYL ACETATE
LGBF		FL	3 (D/E)				S2	30	2244	CYCLOPENTANOL
LGBF		FL	3 (D/E)				S2	30	2245	CYCLOPENTANONE
L1.5BN		FL	2 (D/E)				S2 S20	33	2246	CYCLOPENTENE
LGBF		FL	3 (D/E)				S2	30	2247	n-DECANE
L4BN		FL	2 (D/E)				S2	83	2248	DI-n-BUTYLAMINE
CARRIAGE PROHIBITED									2249	DICHLORODIMETHYL ETHER, SYMMETRICAL
SGAH L4BH	TU15 TE19	AT	2 (D/E)	V11		CV13 CV28	S9 S19	60	2250	DICHLOROPHENYL ISOCYANATES
LGBF		FL	2 (D/E)				S2 S20	339	2251	BICYCLO[2.2.1]HEPTA-2,5-DIENE, STABILIZED (2,5-NORBORNADIENE, STABILIZED)
LGBF		FL	2 (D/E)				S2 S20	33	2252	1,2-DIMETHOXYETHANE
L4BH	TU15 TE19	AT	2 (D/E)			CV13 CV28	S9 S19	60	2253	N,N-DIMETHYLANILINE
			4 (E)						2254	MATCHES, FUSEE
LGBF		FL	2 (D/E)				S2 S20	33	2256	CYCLOHEXENE
L10BN(+)	TU1 TE5 TT3 TM2	AT	1 (B/E)	V1		CV23	S20	X423	2257	POTASSIUM
L4BN		FL	2 (D/E)				S2	83	2258	1,2-PROPYLENEDIAMINE
L4BN		AT	2 (E)					80	2259	TRIETHYLENETETRAMINE
L4BN		FL	3 (D/E)				S2	38	2260	TRIPROPYLAMINE
SGAH L4BH	TU15 TE19	AT	2 (D/E)	V11		CV13 CV28	S9 S19	60	2261	XYLENOLS, SOLID

UN No.	Name and description	Class	Classification code	Packing group	Labels	Special provisions	Limited and excepted quantities		Packaging			Portable tanks and bulk containers	
									Packing instructions	Special packing provisions	Mixed packing provisions	Instructions	Special provisions
	3.1.2	2.2	2.2	2.1.1.3	5.2.2	3.3	3.4.6	3.5.1.2	4.1.4	4.1.4	4.1.10	4.2.5.2 7.3.2	4.2.5.3
(1)	(2)	(3a)	(3b)	(4)	(5)	(6)	(7a)	(7b)	(8)	(9a)	(9b)	(10)	(11)
2262	DIMETHYLCARBAMOYL CHLORIDE	8	C3	II	8		LQ22	E2	P001 IBC02		MP15	T7	TP2
2263	DIMETHYL-CYCLOHEXANES	3	F1	II	3		LQ4	E2	P001 IBC02 R001		MP19	T4	TP1
2264	N,N-DIMETHYL-CYCLOHEXYLAMINE	8	CF1	II	8 +3		LQ22	E2	P001 IBC02		MP15	T7	TP2
2265	N,N-DIMETHYL-FORMAMIDE	3	F1	III	3		LQ7	E1	P001 IBC03 LP01 R001		MP19	T2	TP2
2266	DIMETHYL-N-PROPYLAMINE	3	FC	II	3 +8		LQ4	E2	P001 IBC02		MP19	T7	TP2
2267	DIMETHYL THIOPHOSPHORYL CHLORIDE	6.1	TC1	II	6.1 +8		LQ17	E4	P001 IBC02		MP15	T7	TP2
2269	3,3'-IMINODIPROPYLAMINE	8	C7	III	8		LQ7	E1	P001 IBC03 LP01 R001		MP19	T4	TP2
2270	ETHYLAMINE, AQUEOUS SOLUTION with not less than 50% but not more than 70% ethylamine	3	FC	II	3 +8		LQ4	E2	P001 IBC02		MP19	T7	TP1
2271	ETHYL AMYL KETONE	3	F1	III	3		LQ7	E1	P001 IBC03 LP01 R001		MP19	T2	TP1
2272	N-ETHYLANILINE	6.1	T1	III	6.1		LQ7	E1	P001 IBC03 LP01 R001		MP19	T4	TP1
2273	2-ETHYLANILINE	6.1	T1	III	6.1		LQ7	E1	P001 IBC03 LP01 R001		MP19	T4	TP1
2274	N-ETHYL-N-BENZYLANILINE	6.1	T1	III	6.1		LQ7	E1	P001 IBC03 LP01 R001		MP19	T4	TP1
2275	2-ETHYLBUTANOL	3	F1	III	3		LQ7	E1	P001 IBC03 LP01 R001		MP19	T2	TP1
2276	2-ETHYLHEXYLAMINE	3	FC	III	3 +8		LQ7	E1	P001 IBC03 R001		MP19	T4	TP1
2277	ETHYL METHACRYLATE, STABILIZED	3	F1	II	3		LQ4	E2	P001 IBC02 R001		MP19	T4	TP1
2278	n-HEPTENE	3	F1	II	3		LQ4	E2	P001 IBC02 R001		MP19	T4	TP1
2279	HEXACHLOROBUTADIENE	6.1	T1	III	6.1		LQ7	E1	P001 IBC03 LP01 R001		MP19	T4	TP1
2280	HEXAMETHYLENE-DIAMINE, SOLID	8	C8	III	8		LQ24	E1	P002 IBC08 LP02 R001	B3	MP10	T1	TP33
2281	HEXAMETHYLENE DIISOCYANATE	6.1	T1	II	6.1		LQ17	E4	P001 IBC02		MP15	T7	TP2
2282	HEXANOLS	3	F1	III	3		LQ7	E1	P001 IBC03 LP01 R001		MP19	T2	TP1
2283	ISOBUTYL METHACRYLATE, STABILIZED	3	F1	III	3		LQ7	E1	P001 IBC03 LP01 R001		MP19	T2	TP1

ADR tank		Vehicle for tank carriage	Transport category (Tunnel restriction code)	Special provisions for carriage				Hazard identifi-cation No.	UN No.	Name and description
Tank code	Special provisions			Packages	Bulk	Loading, unloading and handling	Operation			
4.3	4.3.5, 6.8.4	9.1.1.2	1.1.3.6 (8.6)	7.2.4	7.3.3	7.5.11	8.5	5.3.2.3		3.1.2
(12)	(13)	(14)	(15)	(16)	(17)	(18)	(19)	(20)	(1)	(2)
L4BN		AT	2 (E)					80	2262	DIMETHYLCARBAMOYL CHLORIDE
LGBF		FL	2 (D/E)				S2 S20	33	2263	DIMETHYL-CYCLOHEXANES
L4BN		FL	2 (D/E)				S2	83	2264	N,N-DIMETHYL-CYCLOHEXYLAMINE
LGBF		FL	3 (D/E)				S2	30	2265	N,N-DIMETHYL-FORMAMIDE
L4BH		FL	2 (D/E)				S2 S20	338	2266	DIMETHYL-N-PROPYLAMINE
L4BH	TU15 TE19	AT	2 (D/E)			CV13 CV28	S9 S19	68	2267	DIMETHYL THIOPHOSPHORYL CHLORIDE
L4BN		AT	3 (E)					80	2269	3,3'-IMINODIPROPYLAMINE
L4BH		FL	2 (D/E)				S2 S20	338	2270	ETHYLAMINE, AQUEOUS SOLUTION with not less than 50% but not more than 70% ethylamine
LGBF		FL	3 (D/E)				S2	30	2271	ETHYL AMYL KETONE
L4BH	TU15 TE19	AT	2 (E)			CV13 CV28	S9	60	2272	N-ETHYLANILINE
L4BH	TU15 TE19	AT	2 (E)			CV13 CV28	S9	60	2273	2-ETHYLANILINE
L4BH	TU15 TE19	AT	2 (E)			CV13 CV28	S9	60	2274	N-ETHYL-N-BENZYLANILINE
LGBF		FL	3 (D/E)				S2	30	2275	2-ETHYLBUTANOL
L4BN		FL	3 (D/E)				S2	38	2276	2-ETHYLHEXYLAMINE
LGBF		FL	2 (D/E)				S2 S20	339	2277	ETHYL METHACRYLATE, STABILIZED
LGBF		FL	2 (D/E)				S2 S20	33	2278	n-HEPTENE
L4BH	TU15 TE19	AT	2 (E)			CV13 CV28	S9	60	2279	HEXACHLOROBUTADIENE
SGAV L4BN		AT	3 (E)		VV9			80	2280	HEXAMETHYLENE-DIAMINE, SOLID
L4BH	TU15 TE19	AT	2 (D/E)			CV13 CV28	S9 S19	60	2281	HEXAMETHYLENE DIISOCYANATE
LGBF		FL	3 (D/E)				S2	30	2282	HEXANOLS
LGBF		FL	3 (D/E)				S2	39	2283	ISOBUTYL METHACRYLATE, STABILIZED

UN No.	Name and description	Class	Classifi-cation code	Packing group	Labels	Special provi-sions	Limited and excepted quantities		Packaging			Portable tanks and bulk containers	
									Packing instruc-tions	Special packing provisions	Mixed packing provisions	Instruc-tions	Special provisions
	3.1.2	2.2	2.2	2.1.1.3	5.2.2	3.3	3.4.6	3.5.1.2	4.1.4	4.1.4	4.1.10	4.2.5.2 7.3.2	4.2.5.3
(1)	(2)	(3a)	(3b)	(4)	(5)	(6)	(7a)	(7b)	(8)	(9a)	(9b)	(10)	(11)
2284	ISOBUTYRONITRILE	3	FT1	II	3 +6.1		LQ0	E2	P001 IBC02		MP19	T7	TP2
2285	ISOCYANATOBENZO-TRIFLUORIDES	6.1	TF1	II	6.1 +3		LQ17	E4	P001 IBC02		MP15	T7	TP2
2286	PENTAMETHYLHEPTANE	3	F1	III	3		LQ7	E1	P001 IBC03 LP01 R001		MP19	T2	TP1
2287	ISOHEPTENE	3	F1	II	3		LQ4	E2	P001 IBC02 R001		MP19	T4	TP1
2288	ISOHEXENE	3	F1	II	3		LQ4	E2	P001 IBC02 R001	B8	MP19	T11	TP1
2289	ISOPHORONEDIAMINE	8	C7	III	8		LQ7	E1	P001 IBC03 LP01 R001		MP19	T4	TP1
2290	ISOPHORONE DIISOCYANATE	6.1	T1	III	6.1		LQ7	E1	P001 IBC03 LP01 R001		MP19	T4	TP2
2291	LEAD COMPOUND, SOLUBLE, N.O.S.	6.1	T5	III	6.1	199 274 535	LQ9	E1	P002 IBC08 LP02 R001	B3	MP10	T1	TP33
2293	4-METHOXY-4-METHYLPENTAN-2-ONE	3	F1	III	3		LQ7	E1	P001 IBC03 LP01 R001		MP19	T2	TP1
2294	N-METHYLANILINE	6.1	T1	III	6.1		LQ7	E1	P001 IBC03 LP01 R001		MP19	T4	TP1
2295	METHYL CHLOROACETATE	6.1	TF1	I	6.1 +3		LQ0	E5	P001		MP8 MP17	T14	TP2
2296	METHYLCYCLOHEXANE	3	F1	II	3		LQ4	E2	P001 IBC02 R001		MP19	T4	TP1
2297	METHYLCYCLO-HEXANONE	3	F1	III	3		LQ7	E1	P001 IBC03 LP01 R001		MP19	T2	TP1
2298	METHYLCYCLOPENTANE	3	F1	II	3		LQ4	E2	P001 IBC02 R001		MP19	T4	TP1
2299	METHYL DICHLOROACETATE	6.1	T1	III	6.1		LQ7	E1	P001 IBC03 LP01 R001		MP19	T4	TP1
2300	2-METHYL-5-ETHYLPYRIDINE	6.1	T1	III	6.1		LQ7	E1	P001 IBC03 LP01 R001		MP19	T4	TP1
2301	2-METHYLFURAN	3	F1	II	3		LQ4	E2	P001 IBC02 R001		MP19	T4	TP1
2302	5-METHYLHEXAN-2-ONE	3	F1	III	3		LQ7	E1	P001 IBC03 LP01 R001		MP19	T2	TP1
2303	ISOPROPENYLBENZENE	3	F1	III	3		LQ7	E1	P001 IBC03 LP01 R001		MP19	T2	TP1
2304	NAPHTHALENE, MOLTEN	4.1	F2	III	4.1	536	LQ0	E0				T1	TP3
2305	NITROBENZENE-SULPHONIC ACID	8	C4	II	8		LQ23	E2	P002 IBC08	B4	MP10	T3	TP33
2306	NITROBENZOTRI-FLUORIDES, LIQUID	6.1	T1	II	6.1		LQ17	E4	P001 IBC02		MP15	T7	TP2

ADR tank		Vehicle for tank carriage	Transport category (Tunnel restriction code)	Special provisions for carriage				Hazard identifi- cation No.	UN No.	Name and description
Tank code	Special provisions			Packages	Bulk	Loading, unloading and handling	Operation			
4.3	4.3.5, 6.8.4	9.1.1.2	1.1.3.6 (8.6)	7.2.4	7.3.3	7.5.11	8.5	5.3.2.3		3.1.2
(12)	(13)	(14)	(15)	(16)	(17)	(18)	(19)	(20)	(1)	(2)
L4BH	TU15	FL	2 (D/E)			CV13 CV28	S2 S19	336	2284	ISOBUTYRONITRILE
L4BH	TU15 TE19	FL	2 (D/E)			CV13 CV28	S2 S9 S19	63	2285	ISOCYANATOBENZO-TRIFLUORIDES
LGBF		FL	3 (D/E)				S2	30	2286	PENTAMETHYLHEPTANE
LGBF		FL	2 (D/E)				S2 S20	33	2287	ISOHEPTENE
LGBF		FL	2 (D/E)				S2 S20	33	2288	ISOHEXENE
L4BN		AT	3 (E)					80	2289	ISOPHORONEDIAMINE
L4BH	TU15 TE19	AT	2 (E)			CV13 CV28	S9	60	2290	ISOPHORONE DIISOCYANATE
SGAH L4BH	TU15 TE19	AT	2 (E)		VV9	CV13 CV28	S9	60	2291	LEAD COMPOUND, SOLUBLE, N.O.S.
LGBF		FL	3 (D/E)				S2	30	2293	4-METHOXY-4-METHYLPENTAN-2-ONE
L4BH	TU15 TE19	AT	2 (E)			CV13 CV28	S9	60	2294	N-METHYLANILINE
L10CH	TU14 TU15 TE19 TE21	FL	1 (C/D)			CV1 CV13 CV28	S2 S9 S14	663	2295	METHYL CHLOROACETATE
LGBF		FL	2 (D/E)				S2 S20	33	2296	METHYLCYCLOHEXANE
LGBF		FL	3 (D/E)				S2	30	2297	METHYLCYCLO-HEXANONE
LGBF		FL	2 (D/E)				S2 S20	33	2298	METHYLCYCLOPENTANE
L4BH	TU15 TE19	AT	2 (E)			CV13 CV28	S9	60	2299	METHYL DICHLOROACETATE
L4BH	TU15 TE19	AT	2 (E)			CV13 CV28	S9	60	2300	2-METHYL-5-ETHYLPYRIDINE
LGBF		FL	2 (D/E)				S2 S20	33	2301	2-METHYLFURAN
LGBF		FL	3 (D/E)				S2	30	2302	5-METHYLHEXAN-2-ONE
LGBF		FL	3 (D/E)				S2	30	2303	ISOPROPENYLBENZENE
LGBV	TU27 TE4 TE6	AT	3 (E)					44	2304	NAPHTHALENE, MOLTEN
SGAN L4BN		AT	2 (E)	V11				80	2305	NITROBENZENE-SULPHONIC ACID
L4BH	TU15 TE19	AT	2 (D/E)			CV13 CV28	S9 S19	60	2306	NITROBENZOTRI-FLUORIDES, LIQUID

UN No.	Name and description	Class	Classification code	Packing group	Labels	Special provisions	Limited and excepted quantities		Packaging			Portable tanks and bulk containers	
							quantities		Packing instructions	Special packing provisions	Mixed packing provisions	Instructions	Special provisions
	3.1.2	2.2	2.2	2.1.1.3	5.2.2	3.3	3.4.6	3.5.1.2	4.1.4	4.1.4	4.1.10	4.2.5.2 7.3.2	4.2.5.3
(1)	(2)	(3a)	(3b)	(4)	(5)	(6)	(7a)	(7b)	(8)	(9a)	(9b)	(10)	(11)
2307	3-NITRO-4-CHLORO-BENZOTRIFLUORIDE	6.1	T1	II	6.1		LQ17	E4	P001 IBC02		MP10	T7	TP2
2308	NITROSYLSULPHURIC ACID, LIQUID	8	C1	II	8		LQ22	E2	P001 IBC02		MP15	T8	TP2
2309	OCTADIENES	3	F1	II	3		LQ4	E2	P001 IBC02 R001		MP19	T4	TP1
2310	PENTANE-2,4-DIONE	3	FT1	III	3 +6.1		LQ7	E1	P001 IBC03 R001		MP19	T4	TP1
2311	PHENETIDINES	6.1	T1	III	6.1	279	LQ7	E1	P001 IBC03 LP01 R001		MP19	T4	TP1
2312	PHENOL, MOLTEN	6.1	T1	II	6.1		LQ0	E0				T7	TP3
2313	PICOLINES	3	F1	III	3		LQ7	E1	P001 IBC03 LP01 R001		MP19	T4	TP1
2315	POLYCHLORINATED BIPHENYLS, LIQUID	9	M2	II	9	305	LQ26	E2	P906 IBC02		MP15	T4	TP1
2316	SODIUM CUPROCYANIDE, SOLID	6.1	T5	I	6.1		LQ0	E5	P002 IBC07		MP18	T6	TP33
2317	SODIUM CUPROCYANIDE SOLUTION	6.1	T4	I	6.1		LQ0	E5	P001		MP8 MP17	T14	TP2
2318	SODIUM HYDROSULPHIDE with less than 25% water of crystallization	4.2	S4	II	4.2	504	LQ0	E2	P410 IBC06		MP14	T3	TP33
2319	TERPENE HYDROCARBONS, N.O.S.	3	F1	III	3		LQ7	E1	P001 IBC03 LP01 R001		MP19	T4	TP1 TP29
2320	TETRAETHYLENE-PENTAMINE	8	C7	III	8		LQ7	E1	P001 IBC03 LP01 R001		MP19	T4	TP1
2321	TRICHLOROBENZENES, LIQUID	6.1	T1	III	6.1		LQ7	E1	P001 IBC03 LP01 R001		MP19	T4	TP1
2322	TRICHLOROBUTENE	6.1	T1	II	6.1		LQ17	E4	P001 IBC02		MP15	T7	TP2
2323	TRIETHYL PHOSPHITE	3	F1	III	3		LQ7	E1	P001 IBC03 LP01 R001		MP19	T2	TP1
2324	TRIISOBUTYLENE	3	F1	III	3		LQ7	E1	P001 IBC03 LP01 R001		MP19	T4	TP1
2325	1,3,5-TRIMETHYLBENZENE	3	F1	III	3		LQ7	E1	P001 IBC03 LP01 R001		MP19	T2	TP1
2326	TRIMETHYLCYCLO-HEXYLAMINE	8	C7	III	8		LQ7	E1	P001 IBC03 LP01 R001		MP19	T4	TP1
2327	TRIMETHYLHEXA-METHYLENEDIAMINES	8	C7	III	8		LQ7	E1	P001 IBC03 LP01 R001		MP19	T4	TP1
2328	TRIMETHYLHEXA-METHYLENE DIISOCYANATE	6.1	T1	III	6.1		LQ7	E1	P001 IBC03 LP01 R001		MP19	T4	TP2

ADR tank		Vehicle for tank carriage	Transport category (Tunnel restriction code)	Special provisions for carriage				Hazard identifi-cation No.	UN No.	Name and description
Tank code	Special provisions			Packages	Bulk	Loading, unloading and handling	Operation			
4.3	4.3.5, 6.8.4	9.1.1.2	1.1.3.6 (8.6)	7.2.4	7.3.3	7.5.11	8.5	5.3.2.3		3.1.2
(12)	(13)	(14)	(15)	(16)	(17)	(18)	(19)	(20)	(1)	(2)
L4BH	TU15 TE19	AT	2 (D/E)			CV13 CV28	S9 S19	60	2307	3-NITRO-4-CHLORO-BENZOTRIFLUORIDE
L4BN		AT	2 (E)					X80	2308	NITROSYLSULPHURIC ACID, LIQUID
LGBF		FL	2 (D/E)				S2 S20	33	2309	OCTADIENES
L4BH	TU15	FL	3 (D/E)			CV13 CV28	S2	36	2310	PENTANE-2,4-DIONE
L4BH	TU15 TE19	AT	2 (E)			CV13 CV28	S9	60	2311	PHENETIDINES
L4BH	TU15 TE19	AT	0 (D/E)			CV13	S9 S19	60	2312	PHENOL, MOLTEN
LGBF		FL	3 (D/E)				S2	30	2313	PICOLINES
L4BH	TU15	AT	0 (D/E)		VV15	CV1 CV13 CV28	S19	90	2315	POLYCHLORINATED BIPHENYLS, LIQUID
S10AH	TU15 TE19	AT	1 (C/E)	V10 V12		CV1 CV13 CV28	S9 S14	66	2316	SODIUM CUPROCYANIDE, SOLID
L10CH	TU14 TU15 TE19 TE21	AT	1 (C/E)			CV1 CV13 CV28	S9 S14	66	2317	SODIUM CUPROCYANIDE SOLUTION
SGAN		AT	2 (D/E)	V1 V12				40	2318	SODIUM HYDROSULPHIDE with less than 25% water of crystallization
LGBF		FL	3 (D/E)				S2	30	2319	TERPENE HYDROCARBONS, N.O.S.
L4BN		AT	3 (E)					80	2320	TETRAETHYLENE-PENTAMINE
L4BH	TU15 TE19	AT	2 (E)			CV13 CV28	S9	60	2321	TRICHLOROBENZENES, LIQUID
L4BH	TU15 TE19	AT	2 (D/E)			CV13 CV28	S9 S19	60	2322	TRICHLOROBUTENE
LGBF		FL	3 (D/E)				S2	30	2323	TRIETHYL PHOSPHITE
LGBF		FL	3 (D/E)				S2	30	2324	TRIISOBUTYLENE
LGBF		FL	3 (D/E)				S2	30	2325	1,3,5-TRIMETHYLBENZENE
L4BN		AT	3 (E)					80	2326	TRIMETHYLCYCLO-HEXYLAMINE
L4BN		AT	3 (E)					80	2327	TRIMETHYLHEXA-METHYLENEDIAMINES
L4BH	TU15 TE19	AT	2 (E)			CV13 CV28	S9	60	2328	TRIMETHYLHEXA-METHYLENE DIISOCYANATE

UN No.	Name and description	Class	Classification code	Packing group	Labels	Special provisions	Limited and excepted quantities		Packaging			Portable tanks and bulk containers	
							quantities		Packing instructions	Special packing provisions	Mixed packing provisions	Instructions	Special provisions
	3.1.2	2.2	2.2	2.1.1.3	5.2.2	3.3	3.4.6	3.5.1.2	4.1.4	4.1.4	4.1.10	4.2.5.2 7.3.2	4.2.5.3
(1)	(2)	(3a)	(3b)	(4)	(5)	(6)	(7a)	(7b)	(8)	(9a)	(9b)	(10)	(11)
2329	TRIMETHYL PHOSPHITE	3	F1	III	3		LQ7	E1	P001 IBC03 LP01 R001		MP19	T2	TP1
2330	UNDECANE	3	F1	III	3		LQ7	E1	P001 IBC03 LP01 R001		MP19	T2	TP1
2331	ZINC CHLORIDE, ANHYDROUS	8	C2	III	8		LQ24	E1	P002 IBC08 LP02 R001	B3	MP10	T1	TP33
2332	ACETALDEHYDE OXIME	3	F1	III	3		LQ7	E1	P001 IBC03 LP01 R001		MP19	T4	TP1
2333	ALLYL ACETATE	3	FT1	II	3 +6.1		LQ0	E2	P001 IBC02		MP19	T7	TP1
2334	ALLYLAMINE	6.1	TF1	I	6.1 +3		LQ0	E5	P602		MP8 MP17	T20	TP2 TP35
2335	ALLYL ETHYL ETHER	3	FT1	II	3 +6.1		LQ0	E2	P001 IBC02		MP19	T7	TP1
2336	ALLYL FORMATE	3	FT1	I	3 +6.1		LQ0	E0	P001		MP7 MP17	T14	TP2
2337	PHENYL MERCAPTAN	6.1	TF1	I	6.1 +3		LQ0	E5	P001		MP8 MP17	T20	TP2 TP35
2338	BENZOTRIFLUORIDE	3	F1	II	3		LQ4	E2	P001 IBC02 R001		MP19	T4	TP1
2339	2-BROMOBUTANE	3	F1	II	3		LQ4	E2	P001 IBC02 R001		MP19	T4	TP1
2340	2-BROMOETHYL ETHYL ETHER	3	F1	II	3		LQ4	E2	P001 IBC02 R001		MP19	T4	TP1
2341	1-BROMO-3-METHYLBUTANE	3	F1	III	3		LQ7	E1	P001 IBC03 LP01 R001		MP19	T2	TP1
2342	BROMOMETHYL-PROPANES	3	F1	II	3		LQ4	E2	P001 IBC02 R001		MP19	T4	TP1
2343	2-BROMOPENTANE	3	F1	II	3		LQ4	E2	P001 IBC02 R001		MP19	T4	TP1
2344	BROMOPROPANES	3	F1	II	3		LQ4	E2	P001 IBC02 R001		MP19	T4	TP1
2344	BROMOPROPANES	3	F1	III	3		LQ7	E1	P001 IBC03 LP01 R001		MP19	T2	TP1
2345	3-BROMOPROPYNE	3	F1	II	3		LQ4	E2	P001 IBC02 R001		MP19	T4	TP1
2346	BUTANEDIONE	3	F1	II	3		LQ4	E2	P001 IBC02 R001		MP19	T4	TP1
2347	BUTYL MERCAPTAN	3	F1	II	3		LQ4	E2	P001 IBC02 R001		MP19	T4	TP1
2348	BUTYL ACRYLATES, STABILIZED	3	F1	III	3		LQ7	E1	P001 IBC03 LP01 R001		MP19	T2	TP1
2350	BUTYL METHYL ETHER	3	F1	II	3		LQ4	E2	P001 IBC02 R001		MP19	T4	TP1

ADR tank		Vehicle for tank carriage	Transport category (Tunnel restriction code)	Special provisions for carriage				Hazard identification No.	UN No.	Name and description
Tank code	Special provisions			Packages	Bulk	Loading, unloading and handling	Operation			
4.3	4.3.5, 6.8.4	9.1.1.2	1.1.3.6 (8.6)	7.2.4	7.3.3	7.5.11	8.5	5.3.2.3		3.1.2
(12)	(13)	(14)	(15)	(16)	(17)	(18)	(19)	(20)	(1)	(2)
LGBF		FL	3 (D/E)				S2	30	2329	TRIMETHYL PHOSPHITE
LGBF		FL	3 (D/E)				S2	30	2330	UNDECANE
SGAV		AT	3 (E)		VV9			80	2331	ZINC CHLORIDE, ANHYDROUS
LGBF		FL	3 (D/E)				S2	30	2332	ACETALDEHYDE OXIME
L4BH	TU15	FL	2 (D/E)			CV13 CV28	S2 S19	336	2333	ALLYL ACETATE
L10CH	TU14 TU15 TE19 TE21	FL	1 (C/D)			CV1 CV13 CV28	S2 S9 S14	663	2334	ALLYLAMINE
L4BH	TU15	FL	2 (D/E)			CV13 CV28	S2 S19	336	2335	ALLYL ETHYL ETHER
L10CH	TU14 TU15 TE21	FL	1 (C/E)			CV13 CV28	S2 S22	336	2336	ALLYL FORMATE
L10CH	TU14 TU15 TE19 TE21	FL	1 (C/D)			CV1 CV13 CV28	S2 S9 S14	663	2337	PHENYL MERCAPTAN
LGBF		FL	2 (D/E)				S2 S20	33	2338	BENZOTRIFLUORIDE
LGBF		FL	2 (D/E)				S2 S20	33	2339	2-BROMOBUTANE
LGBF		FL	2 (D/E)				S2 S20	33	2340	2-BROMOETHYL ETHYL ETHER
LGBF		FL	3 (D/E)				S2	30	2341	1-BROMO-3-METHYLBUTANE
LGBF		FL	2 (D/E)				S2 S20	33	2342	BROMOMETHYL-PROPANES
LGBF		FL	2 (D/E)				S2 S20	33	2343	2-BROMOPENTANE
LGBF		FL	2 (D/E)				S2 S20	33	2344	BROMOPROPANES
LGBF		FL	3 (D/E)				S2	30	2344	BROMOPROPANES
LGBF		FL	2 (D/E)				S2 S20	33	2345	3-BROMOPROPYNE
LGBF		FL	2 (D/E)				S2 S20	33	2346	BUTANEDIONE
LGBF		FL	2 (D/E)				S2 S20	33	2347	BUTYL MERCAPTAN
LGBF		FL	3 (D/E)				S2	39	2348	BUTYL ACRYLATES, STABILIZED
LGBF		FL	2 (D/E)				S2 S20	33	2350	BUTYL METHYL ETHER

UN No.	Name and description	Class	Classifi-cation code	Packing group	Labels	Special provi-sions	Limited and excepted quantities		Packaging			Portable tanks and bulk containers	
									Packing instruc-tions	Special packing provisions	Mixed packing provisions	Instruc-tions	Special provisions
	3.1.2	2.2	2.2	2.1.1.3	5.2.2	3.3	3.4.6	3.5.1.2	4.1.4	4.1.4	4.1.10	4.2.5.2 7.3.2	4.2.5.3
(1)	(2)	(3a)	(3b)	(4)	(5)	(6)	(7a)	(7b)	(8)	(9a)	(9b)	(10)	(11)
2351	BUTYL NITRITES	3	F1	II	3		LQ4	E2	P001 IBC02 R001		MP19	T4	TP1
2351	BUTYL NITRITES	3	F1	III	3		LQ7	E1	P001 IBC03 LP01 R001		MP19	T2	TP1
2352	BUTYL VINYL ETHER, STABILIZED	3	F1	II	3		LQ4	E2	P001 IBC02 R001		MP19	T4	TP1
2353	BUTYRYL CHLORIDE	3	FC	II	3 +8		LQ4	E2	P001 IBC02		MP19	T8	TP2
2354	CHLOROMETHYL ETHYL ETHER	3	FT1	II	3 +6.1		LQ0	E2	P001 IBC02		MP19	T7	TP1
2356	2-CHLOROPROPANE	3	F1	I	3		LQ3	E3	P001		MP7 MP17	T11	TP2
2357	CYCLOHEXYLAMINE	8	CF1	II	8 +3		LQ22	E2	P001 IBC02		MP15	T7	TP2
2358	CYCLOOCTATETRAENE	3	F1	II	3		LQ4	E2	P001 IBC02 R001		MP19	T4	TP1
2359	DIALLYLAMINE	3	FTC	II	3 +6.1 +8		LQ0	E2	P001 IBC02		MP19	T7	TP1
2360	DIALLYL ETHER	3	FT1	II	3 +6.1		LQ0	E2	P001 IBC02		MP19	T7	TP1
2361	DIISOBUTYLAMINE	3	FC	III	3 +8		LQ7	E1	P001 IBC03 R001		MP19	T4	TP1
2362	1,1-DICHLOROETHANE	3	F1	II	3		LQ4	E2	P001 IBC02 R001		MP19	T4	TP1
2363	ETHYL MERCAPTAN	3	F1	I	3		LQ3	E3	P001		MP7 MP17	T11	TP2
2364	n-PROPYLBENZENE	3	F1	III	3		LQ7	E1	P001 IBC03 LP01 R001		MP19	T2	TP1
2366	DIETHYL CARBONATE	3	F1	III	3		LQ7	E1	P001 IBC03 LP01 R001		MP19	T2	TP1
2367	alpha-METHYL-VALERALDEHYDE	3	F1	II	3		LQ4	E2	P001 IBC02 R001		MP19	T4	TP1
2368	alpha-PINENE	3	F1	III	3		LQ7	E1	P001 IBC03 LP01 R001		MP19	T2	TP1
2370	1-HEXENE	3	F1	II	3		LQ4	E2	P001 IBC02 R001		MP19	T4	TP1
2371	ISOPENTENES	3	F1	I	3		LQ3	E3	P001		MP7 MP17	T11	TP2
2372	1,2-DI-(DIMETHYLAMINO) ETHANE	3	F1	II	3		LQ4	E2	P001 IBC02 R001		MP19	T4	TP1
2373	DIETHOXYMETHANE	3	F1	II	3		LQ4	E2	P001 IBC02 R001		MP19	T4	TP1
2374	3,3-DIETHOXYPROPENE	3	F1	II	3		LQ4	E2	P001 IBC02 R001		MP19	T4	TP1
2375	DIETHYL SULPHIDE	3	F1	II	3		LQ4	E2	P001 IBC02 R001		MP19	T7	TP1
2376	2,3-DIHYDROPYRAN	3	F1	II	3		LQ4	E2	P001 IBC02 R001		MP19	T4	TP1
2377	1,1-DIMETHOXYETHANE	3	F1	II	3		LQ4	E2	P001 IBC02 R001		MP19	T7	TP1

ADR tank		Vehicle for tank carriage	Transport category (Tunnel restriction code)	Special provisions for carriage				Hazard identifi-cation No.	UN No.	Name and description
Tank code	Special provisions			Packages	Bulk	Loading, unloading and handling	Operation			
4.3	4.3.5, 6.8.4	9.1.1.2	1.1.3.6 (8.6)	7.2.4	7.3.3	7.5.11	8.5	5.3.2.3		3.1.2
(12)	(13)	(14)	(15)	(16)	(17)	(18)	(19)	(20)	(1)	(2)
LGBF		FL	2 (D/E)				S2 S20	33	2351	BUTYL NITRITES
LGBF		FL	3 (D/E)				S2	30	2351	BUTYL NITRITES
LGBF		FL	2 (D/E)				S2 S20	339	2352	BUTYL VINYL ETHER, STABILIZED
L4BH		FL	2 (D/E)				S2 S20	338	2353	BUTYRYL CHLORIDE
L4BH	TU15	FL	2 (D/E)			CV13 CV28	S2 S19	336	2354	CHLOROMETHYL ETHYL ETHER
L4BN		FL	1 (D/E)				S2 S20	33	2356	2-CHLOROPROPANE
L4BN		FL	2 (D/E)				S2	83	2357	CYCLOHEXYLAMINE
LGBF		FL	2 (D/E)				S2 S20	33	2358	CYCLOOCTATETRAENE
L4BH	TU15	FL	2 (D/E)			CV13 CV28	S2 S19	338	2359	DIALLYLAMINE
L4BH	TU15	FL	2 (D/E)			CV13 CV28	S2 S19	336	2360	DIALLYL ETHER
L4BN		FL	3 (D/E)				S2	38	2361	DIISOBUTYLAMINE
LGBF		FL	2 (D/E)				S2 S20	33	2362	1,1-DICHLOROETHANE
L4BN		FL	1 (D/E)				S2 S20	33	2363	ETHYL MERCAPTAN
LGBF		FL	3 (D/E)				S2	30	2364	n-PROPYLBENZENE
LGBF		FL	3 (D/E)				S2	30	2366	DIETHYL CARBONATE
LGBF		FL	2 (D/E)				S2 S20	33	2367	alpha-METHYL-VALERALDEHYDE
LGBF		FL	3 (D/E)				S2	30	2368	alpha-PINENE
LGBF		FL	2 (D/E)				S2 S20	33	2370	1-HEXENE
L4BN		FL	1 (D/E)				S2 S20	33	2371	ISOPENTENES
LGBF		FL	2 (D/E)				S2 S20	33	2372	1,2-DI-(DIMETHYLAMINO) ETHANE
LGBF		FL	2 (D/E)				S2 S20	33	2373	DIETHOXYMETHANE
LGBF		FL	2 (D/E)				S2 S20	33	2374	3,3-DIETHOXYPROPENE
LGBF		FL	2 (D/E)				S2 S20	33	2375	DIETHYL SULPHIDE
LGBF		FL	2 (D/E)				S2 S20	33	2376	2,3-DIHYDROPYRAN
LGBF		FL	2 (D/E)				S2 S20	33	2377	1,1-DIMETHOXYETHANE

UN No.	Name and description	Class	Classifi-cation code	Packing group	Labels	Special provi-sions	Limited and excepted quantities		Packaging			Portable tanks and bulk containers	
									Packing instruc-tions	Special packing provisions	Mixed packing provisions	Instruc-tions	Special provisions
	3.1.2	2.2	2.2	2.1.1.3	5.2.2	3.3	3.4.6	3.5.1.2	4.1.4	4.1.4	4.1.10	4.2.5.2 7.3.2	4.2.5.3
(1)	(2)	(3a)	(3b)	(4)	(5)	(6)	(7a)	(7b)	(8)	(9a)	(9b)	(10)	(11)
2378	2-DIMETHYLAMINO-ACETONITRILE	3	FT1	II	3 +6.1		LQ0	E2	P001 IBC02		MP19	T7	TP1
2379	1,3-DIMETHYLBUTYLAMINE	3	FC	II	3 +8		LQ4	E2	P001 IBC02		MP19	T7	TP1
2380	DIMETHYLDIETHOXY-SILANE	3	F1	II	3		LQ4	E2	P001 IBC02 R001		MP19	T4	TP1
2381	DIMETHYL DISULPHIDE	3	F1	II	3		LQ4	E2	P001 IBC02 R001		MP19	T4	TP1
2382	DIMETHYLHYDRAZINE, SYMMETRICAL	6.1	TF1	I	6.1 +3		LQ0	E5	P001		MP8 MP17	T14	TP2
2383	DIPROPYLAMINE	3	FC	II	3 +8		LQ4	E2	P001 IBC02		MP19	T7	TP1
2384	DI-n-PROPYL ETHER	3	F1	II	3		LQ4	E2	P001 IBC02 R001		MP19	T4	TP1
2385	ETHYL ISOBUTYRATE	3	F1	II	3		LQ4	E2	P001 IBC02 R001		MP19	T4	TP1
2386	1-ETHYLPIPERIDINE	3	FC	II	3 +8		LQ4	E2	P001 IBC02		MP19	T7	TP1
2387	FLUOROBENZENE	3	F1	II	3		LQ4	E2	P001 IBC02 R001		MP19	T4	TP1
2388	FLUOROTOLUENES	3	F1	II	3		LQ4	E2	P001 IBC02 R001		MP19	T4	TP1
2389	FURAN	3	F1	I	3		LQ3	E3	P001		MP7 MP17	T12	TP2
2390	2-IODOBUTANE	3	F1	II	3		LQ4	E2	P001 IBC02 R001		MP19	T4	TP1
2391	IODOMETHYLPROPANES	3	F1	II	3		LQ4	E2	P001 IBC02 R001		MP19	T4	TP1
2392	IODOPROPANES	3	F1	III	3		LQ7	E1	P001 IBC03 LP01 R001		MP19	T2	TP1
2393	ISOBUTYL FORMATE	3	F1	II	3		LQ4	E2	P001 IBC02 R001		MP19	T4	TP1
2394	ISOBUTYL PROPIONATE	3	F1	III	3		LQ7	E1	P001 IBC03 LP01 R001		MP19	T2	TP1
2395	ISOBUTYRYL CHLORIDE	3	FC	II	3 +8		LQ4	E2	P001 IBC02		MP19	T7	TP2
2396	METHACRYLALDEHYDE, STABILIZED	3	FT1	II	3 +6.1		LQ0	E2	P001 IBC02		MP19	T7	TP1
2397	3-METHYLBUTAN-2-ONE	3	F1	II	3		LQ4	E2	P001 IBC02 R001		MP19	T4	TP1
2398	METHYL tert-BUTYL ETHER	3	F1	II	3		LQ4	E2	P001 IBC02 R001		MP19	T7	TP1
2399	1-METHYLPIPERIDINE	3	FC	II	3 +8		LQ4	E2	P001 IBC02		MP19	T7	TP1
2400	METHYL ISOVALERATE	3	F1	II	3		LQ4	E2	P001 IBC02 R001		MP19	T4	TP1
2401	PIPERIDINE	8	CF1	I	8 +3		LQ0	E0	P001		MP8 MP17	T10	TP2
2402	PROPANETHIOLS	3	F1	II	3		LQ4	E2	P001 IBC02 R001		MP19	T4	TP1
2403	ISOPROPENYL ACETATE	3	F1	II	3		LQ4	E2	P001 IBC02 R001		MP19	T4	TP1

ADR tank		Vehicle for tank carriage	Transport category (Tunnel restriction code)	Special provisions for carriage				Hazard identifi- cation No.	UN No.	Name and description
Tank code	Special provisions			Packages	Bulk	Loading, unloading and handling	Operation			
4.3	4.3.5, 6.8.4	9.1.1.2	1.1.3.6 (8.6)	7.2.4	7.3.3	7.5.11	8.5	5.3.2.3		3.1.2
(12)	(13)	(14)	(15)	(16)	(17)	(18)	(19)	(20)	(1)	(2)
L4BH	TU15	FL	2 (D/E)			CV13 CV28	S2 S19	336	2378	2-DIMETHYLAMINO-ACETONITRILE
L4BH		FL	2 (D/E)				S2 S20	338	2379	1,3-DIMETHYLBUTYLAMINE
LGBF		FL	2 (D/E)				S2 S20	33	2380	DIMETHYLDIETHOXY-SILANE
LGBF		FL	2 (D/E)				S2 S20	33	2381	DIMETHYL DISULPHIDE
L10CH	TU14 TU15 TE19 TE21	FL	1 (C/D)			CV1 CV13 CV28	S2 S9 S14	663	2382	DIMETHYLHYDRAZINE, SYMMETRICAL
L4BH		FL	2 (D/E)				S2 S20	338	2383	DIPROPYLAMINE
LGBF		FL	2 (D/E)				S2 S20	33	2384	DI-n-PROPYL ETHER
LGBF		FL	2 (D/E)				S2 S20	33	2385	ETHYL ISOBUTYRATE
L4BH		FL	2 (D/E)				S2 S20	338	2386	1-ETHYLPIPERIDINE
LGBF		FL	2 (D/E)				S2 S20	33	2387	FLUOROBENZENE
LGBF		FL	2 (D/E)				S2 S20	33	2388	FLUOROTOLUENES
L4BN		FL	1 (D/E)				S2 S20	33	2389	FURAN
LGBF		FL	2 (D/E)				S2 S20	33	2390	2-IODOBUTANE
LGBF		FL	2 (D/E)				S2 S20	33	2391	IODOMETHYLPROPANES
LGBF		FL	3 (D/E)				S2	30	2392	IODOPROPANES
LGBF		FL	2 (D/E)				S2 S20	33	2393	ISOBUTYL FORMATE
LGBF		FL	3 (D/E)				S2	30	2394	ISOBUTYL PROPIONATE
L4BH		FL	2 (D/E)				S2 S20	338	2395	ISOBUTYRYL CHLORIDE
L4BH	TU15	FL	2 (D/E)			CV13 CV28	S2 S19	336	2396	METHACRYLALDEHYDE, STABILIZED
LGBF		FL	2 (D/E)				S2 S20	33	2397	3-METHYLBUTAN-2-ONE
LGBF		FL	2 (D/E)				S2 S20	33	2398	METHYL tert-BUTYL ETHER
L4BH		FL	2 (D/E)				S2 S20	338	2399	1-METHYLPIPERIDINE
LGBF		FL	2 (D/E)				S2 S20	33	2400	METHYL ISOVALERATE
L10BH		FL	1 (D/E)				S2 S14	883	2401	PIPERIDINE
LGBF		FL	2 (D/E)				S2 S20	33	2402	PROPANETHIOLS
LGBF		FL	2 (D/E)				S2 S20	33	2403	ISOPROPENYL ACETATE

UN No.	Name and description	Class	Classification code	Packing group	Labels	Special provisions	Limited and excepted quantities		Packaging			Portable tanks and bulk containers	
									Packing instructions	Special packing provisions	Mixed packing provisions	Instructions	Special provisions
	3.1.2	2.2	2.2	2.1.1.3	5.2.2	3.3	3.4.6	3.5.1.2	4.1.4	4.1.4	4.1.10	4.2.5.2 7.3.2	4.2.5.3
(1)	(2)	(3a)	(3b)	(4)	(5)	(6)	(7a)	(7b)	(8)	(9a)	(9b)	(10)	(11)
2404	PROPIONITRILE	3	FT1	II	3 +6.1		LQ0	E2	P001 IBC02		MP19	T7	TP1
2405	ISOPROPYL BUTYRATE	3	F1	III	3		LQ7	E1	P001 IBC03 LP01 R001		MP19	T2	TP1
2406	ISOPROPYL ISOBUTYRATE	3	F1	II	3		LQ4	E2	P001 IBC02 R001		MP19	T4	TP1
2407	ISOPROPYL CHLOROFORMATE	6.1	TFC	I	6.1 +3 +8		LQ0	E5	P602		MP8 MP17		
2409	ISOPROPYL PROPIONATE	3	F1	II	3		LQ4	E2	P001 IBC02 R001		MP19	T4	TP1
2410	1,2,3,6-TETRAHYDROPYRIDINE	3	F1	II	3		LQ4	E2	P001 IBC02 R001		MP19	T4	TP1
2411	BUTYRONITRILE	3	FT1	II	3 +6.1		LQ0	E2	P001 IBC02		MP19	T7	TP1
2412	TETRAHYDROTHIOPHENE	3	F1	II	3		LQ4	E2	P001 IBC02 R001		MP19	T4	TP1
2413	TETRAPROPYL ORTHOTITANATE	3	F1	III	3		LQ7	E1	P001 IBC03 LP01 R001		MP19	T4	TP1
2414	THIOPHENE	3	F1	II	3		LQ4	E2	P001 IBC02 R001		MP19	T4	TP1
2416	TRIMETHYL BORATE	3	F1	II	3		LQ4	E2	P001 IBC02 R001		MP19	T7	TP1
2417	CARBONYL FLUORIDE	2	2TC		2.3 +8		LQ0	E0	P200		MP9	(M)	
2418	SULPHUR TETRAFLUORIDE	2	2TC		2.3 +8		LQ0	E0	P200		MP9		
2419	BROMOTRIFLUORO-ETHYLENE	2	2F		2.1		LQ0	E0	P200		MP9	(M)	
2420	HEXAFLUOROACETONE	2	2TC		2.3 +8		LQ0	E0	P200		MP9	(M)	
2421	NITROGEN TRIOXIDE	2	2TOC		CARRIAGE PROHIBITED								
2422	OCTAFLUOROBUT-2-ENE (REFRIGERANT GAS R 1318)	2	2A		2.2		LQ1	E1	P200		MP9	(M)	
2424	OCTAFLUOROPROPANE (REFRIGERANT GAS R 218)	2	2A		2.2		LQ1	E1	P200		MP9	(M) T50	
2426	AMMONIUM NITRATE, LIQUID, hot concentrated solution, in a concentration of more than 80% but not more than 93%	5.1	O1		5.1	252 644	LQ0	E0				T7	TP1 TP16 TP17
2427	POTASSIUM CHLORATE, AQUEOUS SOLUTION	5.1	O1	II	5.1		LQ10	E2	P504 IBC02		MP2	T4	TP1
2427	POTASSIUM CHLORATE, AQUEOUS SOLUTION	5.1	O1	III	5.1		LQ13	E1	P504 IBC02 R001		MP2	T4	TP1
2428	SODIUM CHLORATE, AQUEOUS SOLUTION	5.1	O1	II	5.1		LQ10	E2	P504 IBC02		MP2	T4	TP1
2428	SODIUM CHLORATE, AQUEOUS SOLUTION	5.1	O1	III	5.1		LQ13	E1	P504 IBC02 R001		MP2	T4	TP1
2429	CALCIUM CHLORATE, AQUEOUS SOLUTION	5.1	O1	II	5.1		LQ10	E2	P504 IBC02		MP2	T4	TP1

ADR tank		Vehicle for tank carriage	Transport category (Tunnel restriction code)	Special provisions for carriage				Hazard identifi-cation No.	UN No.	Name and description
Tank code	Special provisions			Packages	Bulk	Loading, unloading and handling	Operation			
4.3	4.3.5, 6.8.4	9.1.1.2	1.1.3.6 (8.6)	7.2.4	7.3.3	7.5.11	8.5	5.3.2.3		3.1.2
(12)	(13)	(14)	(15)	(16)	(17)	(18)	(19)	(20)	(1)	(2)
L4BH	TU15	FL	2 (D/E)			CV13 CV28	S2 S19	336	2404	PROPIONITRILE
LGBF		FL	3 (D/E)				S2	30	2405	ISOPROPYL BUTYRATE
LGBF		FL	2 (D/E)				S2 S20	33	2406	ISOPROPYL ISOBUTYRATE
			1 (D)			CV1 CV13 CV28	S2 S9 S14		2407	ISOPROPYL CHLOROFORMATE
LGBF		FL	2 (D/E)				S2 S20	33	2409	ISOPROPYL PROPIONATE
LGBF		FL	2 (D/E)				S2 S20	33	2410	1,2,3,6-TETRAHYDROPYRIDINE
L4BH	TU15	FL	2 (D/E)			CV13 CV28	S2 S19	336	2411	BUTYRONITRILE
LGBF		FL	2 (D/E)				S2 S20	33	2412	TETRAHYDROTHIOPHENE
LGBF		FL	3 (D/E)				S2	30	2413	TETRAPROPYL ORTHOTITANATE
LGBF		FL	2 (D/E)				S2 S20	33	2414	THIOPHENE
LGBF		FL	2 (D/E)				S2 S20	33	2416	TRIMETHYL BORATE
PxBH(M)	TA4 TT9	AT	1 (C/D)			CV9 CV10 CV36	S14	268	2417	CARBONYL FLUORIDE
			1 (D)			CV9 CV10 CV36	S14		2418	SULPHUR TETRAFLUORIDE
PxBN(M)	TA4 TT9	FL	2 (B/D)			CV9 CV10 CV36	S2 S20	23	2419	BROMOTRIFLUORO-ETHYLENE
PxBH(M)	TA4 TT9	AT	1 (C/D)			CV9 CV10 CV36	S14	268	2420	HEXAFLUOROACETONE
CARRIAGE PROHIBITED									2421	NITROGEN TRIOXIDE
PxBN(M)	TA4 TT9	AT	3 (C/E)			CV9 CV10 CV36		20	2422	OCTAFLUOROBUT-2-ENE (REFRIGERANT GAS R 1318)
PxBN(M)	TA4 TT9	AT	3 (C/E)			CV9 CV10 CV36		20	2424	OCTAFLUOROPROPANE (REFRIGERANT GAS R 218)
L4BV(+)	TU3 TU12 TU29 TC3 TE9 TE10 TA1	AT	0 (E)				S23	59	2426	AMMONIUM NITRATE, LIQUID, hot concentrated solution, in a concentration of more than 80% but not more than 93%
L4BN	TU3	AT	2 (E)			CV24		50	2427	POTASSIUM CHLORATE, AQUEOUS SOLUTION
LGBV	TU3	AT	3 (E)			CV24		50	2427	POTASSIUM CHLORATE, AQUEOUS SOLUTION
L4BN	TU3	AT	2 (E)			CV24		50	2428	SODIUM CHLORATE, AQUEOUS SOLUTION
LGBV	TU3	AT	3 (E)			CV24		50	2428	SODIUM CHLORATE, AQUEOUS SOLUTION
L4BN	TU3	AT	2 (E)			CV24		50	2429	CALCIUM CHLORATE, AQUEOUS SOLUTION

UN No.	Name and description	Class	Classification code	Packing group	Labels	Special provisions	Limited and excepted quantities		Packaging			Portable tanks and bulk containers	
									Packing instructions	Special packing provisions	Mixed packing provisions	Instructions	Special provisions
	3.1.2	2.2	2.2	2.1.1.3	5.2.2	3.3	3.4.6	3.5.1.2	4.1.4	4.1.4	4.1.10	4.2.5.2 7.3.2	4.2.5.3
(1)	(2)	(3a)	(3b)	(4)	(5)	(6)	(7a)	(7b)	(8)	(9a)	(9b)	(10)	(11)
2429	CALCIUM CHLORATE, AQUEOUS SOLUTION	5.1	O1	III	5.1		LQ13	E1	P504 IBC02 R001		MP2	T4	TP1
2430	ALKYLPHENOLS, SOLID, N.O.S. (including C_2-C_{12} homologues)	8	C4	I	8	274	LQ0	E0	P002 IBC07		MP18	T6	TP33
2430	ALKYLPHENOLS, SOLID, N.O.S. (including C_2-C_{12} homologues)	8	C4	II	8	274	LQ23	E2	P002 IBC08	B4	MP10	T3	TP33
2430	ALKYLPHENOLS, SOLID, N.O.S. (including C_2-C_{12} homologues)	8	C4	III	8	274	LQ24	E1	P002 IBC08 LP02 R001	B3	MP10	T1	TP33
2431	ANISIDINES	6.1	T1	III	6.1		LQ7	E1	P001 IBC03 LP01 R001		MP19	T4	TP1
2432	N,N-DIETHYLANILINE	6.1	T1	III	6.1	279	LQ7	E1	P001 IBC03 LP01 R001		MP19	T4	TP1
2433	CHLORONITROTOLUENES, LIQUID	6.1	T1	III	6.1		LQ7	E1	P001 IBC03 LP01 R001		MP19	T4	TP1
2434	DIBENZYL-DICHLOROSILANE	8	C3	II	8		LQ22	E2	P010		MP15	T10	TP2 TP7
2435	ETHYLPHENYL-DICHLOROSILANE	8	C3	II	8		LQ22	E2	P010		MP15	T10	TP2 TP7
2436	THIOACETIC ACID	3	F1	II	3		LQ4	E2	P001 IBC02 R001		MP19	T4	TP1
2437	METHYLPHENYL-DICHLOROSILANE	8	C3	II	8		LQ22	E2	P010		MP15	T10	TP2 TP7
2438	TRIMETHYLACETYL CHLORIDE	6.1	TFC	I	6.1 +3 +8		LQ0	E5	P001		MP8 MP17	T14	TP2
2439	SODIUM HYDROGENDIFLUORIDE	8	C2	II	8		LQ23	E2	P002 IBC08	B4	MP10	T3	TP33
2440	STANNIC CHLORIDE PENTAHYDRATE	8	C2	III	8		LQ24	E1	P002 IBC08 LP02 R001	B3	MP10	T1	TP33
2441	TITANIUM TRICHLORIDE, PYROPHORIC or TITANIUM TRICHLORIDE MIXTURE, PYROPHORIC	4.2	SC4	I	4.2 +8	537	LQ0	E0	P404		MP13		
2442	TRICHLOROACETYL CHLORIDE	8	C3	II	8		LQ22	E2	P001		MP15	T7	TP2
2443	VANADIUM OXYTRICHLORIDE	8	C1	II	8		LQ22	E2	P001 IBC02		MP15	T7	TP2
2444	VANADIUM TETRACHLORIDE	8	C1	I	8		LQ0	E0	P802		MP8 MP17	T10	TP2
2446	NITROCRESOLS, SOLID	6.1	T2	III	6.1		LQ9	E1	P002 IBC08 LP02 R001	B3	MP10	T1	TP33
2447	PHOSPHORUS, WHITE, MOLTEN	4.2	ST3	I	4.2 +6.1		LQ0	E0				T21	TP3 TP7 TP26
2448	SULPHUR, MOLTEN	4.1	F3	III	4.1	538	LQ0	E0				T1	TP3
2451	NITROGEN TRIFLUORIDE	2	2O		2.2 +5.1		LQ0	E0	P200		MP9	(M)	
2452	ETHYLACETYLENE, STABILIZED	2	2F		2.1		LQ0	E0	P200		MP9	(M)	

ADR tank		Vehicle for tank carriage	Transport category (Tunnel restriction code)	Special provisions for carriage				Hazard identifi-cation No.	UN No.	Name and description
Tank code	Special provisions			Packages	Bulk	Loading, unloading and handling	Operation			
4.3	4.3.5, 6.8.4	9.1.1.2	1.1.3.6 (8.6)	7.2.4	7.3.3	7.5.11	8.5	5.3.2.3		3.1.2
(12)	(13)	(14)	(15)	(16)	(17)	(18)	(19)	(20)	(1)	(2)
LGBV	TU3	AT	3 (E)			CV24		50	2429	CALCIUM CHLORATE, AQUEOUS SOLUTION
S10AN L10BH		AT	1 (E)	V10 V12			S20	88	2430	ALKYLPHENOLS, SOLID, N.O.S. (including C$_2$-C$_{12}$ homologues)
SGAN L4BN		AT	2 (E)	V11				80	2430	ALKYLPHENOLS, SOLID, N.O.S. (including C$_2$-C$_{12}$ homologues)
SGAV L4BN		AT	3 (E)		VV9			80	2430	ALKYLPHENOLS, SOLID, N.O.S. (including C$_2$-C$_{12}$ homologues)
L4BH	TU15 TE19	AT	2 (E)			CV13 CV28	S9	60	2431	ANISIDINES
L4BH	TU15 TE19	AT	2 (E)			CV13 CV28	S9	60	2432	N,N-DIETHYLANILINE
L4BH	TU15 TE19	AT	2 (E)			CV13 CV28	S9	60	2433	CHLORONITROTOLUENES, LIQUID
L4BN		AT	2 (E)					X80	2434	DIBENZYL-DICHLOROSILANE
L4BN		AT	2 (E)					X80	2435	ETHYLPHENYL-DICHLOROSILANE
LGBF		FL	2 (D/E)				S2 S20	33	2436	THIOACETIC ACID
L4BN		AT	2 (E)					X80	2437	METHYLPHENYL-DICHLOROSILANE
L10CH	TU14 TU15 TE19 TE21	FL	1 (C/D)			CV1 CV13 CV28	S2 S9 S14	663	2438	TRIMETHYLACETYL CHLORIDE
SGAN		AT	2 (E)	V11				80	2439	SODIUM HYDROGENDIFLUORIDE
SGAV		AT	3 (E)		VV9			80	2440	STANNIC CHLORIDE PENTAHYDRATE
			0 (E)	V1			S20		2441	TITANIUM TRICHLORIDE, PYROPHORIC or TITANIUM TRICHLORIDE MIXTURE, PYROPHORIC
L4BN		AT	2 (E)					X80	2442	TRICHLOROACETYL CHLORIDE
L4BN		AT	2 (E)					80	2443	VANADIUM OXYTRICHLORIDE
L10BH		AT	1 (E)				S20	X88	2444	VANADIUM TETRACHLORIDE
SGAH L4BH	TU15 TE19	AT	2 (E)		VV9	CV13 CV28	S9	60	2446	NITROCRESOLS, SOLID
L10DH(+)	TU14 TU16 TU21 TE3 TE21	AT	0 (B/E)				S20	446	2447	PHOSPHORUS, WHITE, MOLTEN
LGBV(+)	TU27 TE4 TE6	AT	3 (E)					44	2448	SULPHUR, MOLTEN
PxBN(M)	TA4 TT9	AT	3 (C/E)			CV9 CV10 CV36		25	2451	NITROGEN TRIFLUORIDE
PxBN(M)	TA4 TT9	FL	2 (B/D)			CV9 CV10 CV36	S2 S20	239	2452	ETHYLACETYLENE, STABILIZED

UN No.	Name and description	Class	Classifi-cation code	Packing group	Labels	Special provisions	Limited and excepted quantities		Packaging			Portable tanks and bulk containers	
									Packing instruc-tions	Special packing provisions	Mixed packing provisions	Instruc-tions	Special provisions
	3.1.2	2.2	2.2	2.1.1.3	5.2.2	3.3	3.4.6	3.5.1.2	4.1.4	4.1.4	4.1.10	4.2.5.2 7.3.2	4.2.5.3
(1)	(2)	(3a)	(3b)	(4)	(5)	(6)	(7a)	(7b)	(8)	(9a)	(9b)	(10)	(11)
2453	ETHYL FLUORIDE (REFRIGERANT GAS R 161)	2	2F		2.1		LQ0	E0	P200		MP9	(M)	
2454	METHYL FLUORIDE (REFRIGERANT GAS R 41)	2	2F		2.1		LQ0	E0	P200		MP9	(M)	
2455	METHYL NITRITE	2	2A	CARRIAGE PROHIBITED									
2456	2-CHLOROPROPENE	3	F1	I	3		LQ3	E3	P001		MP7 MP17	T11	TP2
2457	2,3-DIMETHYLBUTANE	3	F1	II	3		LQ4	E2	P001 IBC02 R001		MP19	T7	TP1
2458	HEXADIENES	3	F1	II	3		LQ4	E2	P001 IBC02 R001		MP19	T4	TP1
2459	2-METHYL-1-BUTENE	3	F1	I	3		LQ3	E3	P001		MP7 MP17	T11	TP2
2460	2-METHYL-2-BUTENE	3	F1	II	3		LQ4	E2	P001 IBC02	B8	MP19	T7	TP1
2461	METHYLPENTADIENE	3	F1	II	3		LQ4	E2	P001 IBC02 R001		MP19	T4	TP1
2463	ALUMINIUM HYDRIDE	4.3	W2	I	4.3		LQ0	E0	P403		MP2		
2464	BERYLLIUM NITRATE	5.1	OT2	II	5.1 +6.1		LQ11	E2	P002 IBC08	B4	MP2	T3	TP33
2465	DICHLOROISOCYANURIC ACID, DRY or DICHLOROISOCYANURIC ACID SALTS	5.1	O2	II	5.1	135	LQ11	E2	P002 IBC08	B4	MP10	T3	TP33
2466	POTASSIUM SUPEROXIDE	5.1	O2	I	5.1		LQ0	E0	P503 IBC06		MP2		
2468	TRICHLOROISOCYANURIC ACID, DRY	5.1	O2	II	5.1		LQ11	E2	P002 IBC08	B4	MP10	T3	TP33
2469	ZINC BROMATE	5.1	O2	III	5.1		LQ12	E1	P002 IBC08 LP02 R001	B3	MP10	T1	TP33
2470	PHENYLACETONITRILE, LIQUID	6.1	T1	III	6.1		LQ7	E1	P001 IBC03 LP01 R001		MP19	T4	TP1
2471	OSMIUM TETROXIDE	6.1	T5	I	6.1		LQ0	E5	P002 IBC07	PP30	MP18	T6	TP33
2473	SODIUM ARSANILATE	6.1	T3	III	6.1		LQ9	E1	P002 IBC08 LP02 R001	B3	MP10	T1	TP33
2474	THIOPHOSGENE	6.1	T1	II	6.1	279	LQ17	E4	P001		MP15	T7	TP2
2475	VANADIUM TRICHLORIDE	8	C2	III	8		LQ24	E1	P002 IBC08 LP02 R001	B3	MP10	T1	TP33
2477	METHYL ISOTHIOCYANATE	6.1	TF1	I	6.1 +3		LQ0	E5	P001		MP8 MP17	T14	TP2
2478	ISOCYANATES, FLAMMABLE, TOXIC, N.O.S. or ISOCYANATE SOLUTION, FLAMMABLE, TOXIC, N.O.S.	3	FT1	II	3 +6.1	274 539	LQ0	E2	P001 IBC02		MP19	T11	TP2 TP27
2478	ISOCYANATES, FLAMMABLE, TOXIC, N.O.S. or ISOCYANATE SOLUTION, FLAMMABLE, TOXIC, N.O.S.	3	FT1	III	3 +6.1	274	LQ7	E1	P001 IBC03 R001		MP19	T7	TP1 TP28
2480	METHYL ISOCYANATE	6.1	TF1	I	6.1 +3		LQ0	E5	P601		MP2	T22	TP2

ADR tank		Vehicle for tank carriage	Transport category (Tunnel restriction code)	Special provisions for carriage				Hazard identifi- cation No.	UN No.	Name and description
Tank code	Special provisions			Packages	Bulk	Loading, unloading and handling	Operation			
4.3	4.3.5, 6.8.4	9.1.1.2	1.1.3.6 (8.6)	7.2.4	7.3.3	7.5.11	8.5	5.3.2.3		3.1.2
(12)	(13)	(14)	(15)	(16)	(17)	(18)	(19)	(20)	(1)	(2)
PxBN(M)	TA4 TT9	FL	2 (B/D)			CV9 CV10 CV36	S2 S20	23	2453	ETHYL FLUORIDE (REFRIGERANT GAS R 161)
PxBN(M)	TA4 TT9	FL	2 (B/D)			CV9 CV10 CV36	S2 S20	23	2454	METHYL FLUORIDE (REFRIGERANT GAS R 41)
CARRIAGE PROHIBITED									2455	METHYL NITRITE
L4BN		FL	1 (D/E)				S2 S20	33	2456	2-CHLOROPROPENE
LGBF		FL	2 (D/E)				S2 S20	33	2457	2,3-DIMETHYLBUTANE
LGBF		FL	2 (D/E)				S2 S20	33	2458	HEXADIENES
L4BN		FL	1 (D/E)				S2 S20	33	2459	2-METHYL-1-BUTENE
L1.5BN		FL	2 (D/E)				S2 S20	33	2460	2-METHYL-2-BUTENE
LGBF		FL	2 (D/E)				S2 S20	33	2461	METHYLPENTADIENE
			1 (E)	V1		CV23	S20		2463	ALUMINIUM HYDRIDE
SGAN	TU3	AT	2 (E)	V11		CV24 CV28		56	2464	BERYLLIUM NITRATE
SGAN	TU3	AT	2 (E)	V11		CV24		50	2465	DICHLOROISOCYANURIC ACID, DRY or DICHLOROISOCYANURIC ACID SALTS
			1 (E)	V10 V12		CV24	S20		2466	POTASSIUM SUPEROXIDE
SGAN	TU3	AT	2 (E)	V11		CV24		50	2468	TRICHLOROISOCYANURIC ACID, DRY
SGAV	TU3	AT	3 (E)		VV8	CV24		50	2469	ZINC BROMATE
L4BH	TU15 TE19	AT	2 (E)			CV13 CV28	S9	60	2470	PHENYLACETONITRILE, LIQUID
S10AH	TU15 TE19	AT	1 (C/E)	V10 V12		CV1 CV13 CV28	S9 S14	66	2471	OSMIUM TETROXIDE
SGAH L4BH	TU15 TE19	AT	2 (E)		VV9	CV13 CV28	S9	60	2473	SODIUM ARSANILATE
L4BH	TU15 TE19	AT	2 (D/E)			CV13 CV28	S9 S19	60	2474	THIOPHOSGENE
SGAV		AT	3 (E)		VV9			80	2475	VANADIUM TRICHLORIDE
L10CH	TU14 TU15 TE19 TE21	FL	1 (C/D)			CV1 CV13 CV28	S2 S9 S14	663	2477	METHYL ISOTHIOCYANATE
L4BH	TU15	FL	2 (D/E)			CV13 CV28	S2 S19	336	2478	ISOCYANATES, FLAMMABLE, TOXIC, N.O.S. or ISOCYANATE SOLUTION, FLAMMABLE, TOXIC, N.O.S.
L4BH	TU15	FL	3 (D/E)			CV13 CV28	S2	36	2478	ISOCYANATES, FLAMMABLE, TOXIC, N.O.S. or ISOCYANATE SOLUTION, FLAMMABLE, TOXIC, N.O.S.
L15CH	TU14 TU15 TE19 TE21	FL	1 (D)			CV1 CV13 CV28	S2 S9 S14	663	2480	METHYL ISOCYANATE

UN No. 3.1.2	Name and description 3.1.2	Class 2.2	Classification code 2.2	Packing group 2.1.1.3	Labels 5.2.2	Special provisions 3.3	Limited quantities 3.4.6	Excepted quantities 3.5.1.2	Packing instructions 4.1.4	Special packing provisions 4.1.4	Mixed packing provisions 4.1.10	Instructions 4.2.5.2 7.3.2	Special provisions 4.2.5.3
(1)	(2)	(3a)	(3b)	(4)	(5)	(6)	(7a)	(7b)	(8)	(9a)	(9b)	(10)	(11)
2481	ETHYL ISOCYANATE	3	FT1	I	3 +6.1		LQ0	E0	P601		MP2	T14	TP2
2482	n-PROPYL ISOCYANATE	6.1	TF1	I	6.1 +3		LQ0	E5	P001		MP8 MP17	T14	TP2
2483	ISOPROPYL ISOCYANATE	3	FT1	I	3 +6.1		LQ0	E0	P001		MP7 MP17	T14	TP2
2484	tert-BUTYL ISOCYANATE	6.1	TF1	I	6.1 +3		LQ0	E5	P001		MP8 MP17	T14	TP2
2485	n-BUTYL ISOCYANATE	6.1	TF1	I	6.1 +3		LQ0	E5	P001		MP8 MP17	T14	TP2
2486	ISOBUTYL ISOCYANATE	3	FT1	II	3 +6.1		LQ0	E2	P001		MP19	T8	TP2
2487	PHENYL ISOCYANATE	6.1	TF1	I	6.1 +3		LQ0	E5	P001		MP8 MP17	T14	TP2
2488	CYCLOHEXYL ISOCYANATE	6.1	TF1	I	6.1 +3		LQ0	E5	P001		MP8 MP17	T14	TP2
2490	DICHLOROISOPROPYL ETHER	6.1	T1	II	6.1		LQ17	E4	P001 IBC02		MP15	T7	TP2
2491	ETHANOLAMINE or ETHANOLAMINE SOLUTION	8	C7	III	8		LQ7	E1	P001 IBC03 LP01 R001		MP19	T4	TP1
2493	HEXAMETHYLENEIMINE	3	FC	II	3 +8		LQ4	E2	P001 IBC02		MP19	T7	TP1
2495	IODINE PENTAFLUORIDE	5.1	OTC	I	5.1 +6.1 +8		LQ0	E0	P200		MP2		
2496	PROPIONIC ANHYDRIDE	8	C3	III	8		LQ7	E1	P001 IBC03 LP01 R001		MP19	T4	TP1
2498	1,2,3,6-TETRAHYDROBENZAL-DEHYDE	3	F1	III	3		LQ7	E1	P001 IBC03 LP01 R001		MP19	T2	TP1
2501	TRIS-(1-AZIRIDINYL) PHOSPHINE OXIDE SOLUTION	6.1	T1	II	6.1		LQ17	E4	P001 IBC02		MP15	T7	TP2
2501	TRIS-(1-AZIRIDINYL) PHOSPHINE OXIDE SOLUTION	6.1	T1	III	6.1		LQ7	E1	P001 IBC03 LP01 R001		MP19	T4	TP1
2502	VALERYL CHLORIDE	8	CF1	II	8 +3		LQ22	E2	P001 IBC02		MP15	T7	TP2
2503	ZIRCONIUM TETRACHLORIDE	8	C2	III	8		LQ24	E1	P002 IBC08 LP02 R001	B3	MP10	T1	TP33
2504	TETRABROMOETHANE	6.1	T1	III	6.1		LQ7	E1	P001 IBC03 LP01 R001		MP19	T4	TP1
2505	AMMONIUM FLUORIDE	6.1	T5	III	6.1		LQ9	E1	P002 IBC08 LP02 R001	B3	MP10	T1	TP33
2506	AMMONIUM HYDROGEN SULPHATE	8	C2	II	8		LQ23	E2	P002 IBC08	B4	MP10	T3	TP33
2507	CHLOROPLATINIC ACID, SOLID	8	C2	III	8		LQ24	E1	P002 IBC08 LP02 R001	B3	MP10	T1	TP33
2508	MOLYBDENUM PENTACHLORIDE	8	C2	III	8		LQ24	E1	P002 IBC08 LP02 R001	B3	MP10	T1	TP33

ADR tank Tank code 4.3 (12)	Special provisions 4.3.5, 6.8.4 (13)	Vehicle for tank carriage 9.1.1.2 (14)	Transport category (Tunnel restriction code) 1.1.3.6 (8.6) (15)	Packages 7.2.4 (16)	Bulk 7.3.3 (17)	Loading, unloading and handling 7.5.11 (18)	Operation 8.5 (19)	Hazard identification No. 5.3.2.3 (20)	UN No. (1)	Name and description 3.1.2 (2)
L15CH	TU14 TU15 TE19 TE21	FL	1 (C/E)			CV13 CV28	S2 S22	336	2481	ETHYL ISOCYANATE
L10CH	TU14 TU15 TE19 TE21	FL	1 (C/D)			CV1 CV13 CV28	S2 S9 S14	663	2482	n-PROPYL ISOCYANATE
L10CH	TU14 TU15 TE21	FL	1 (C/E)			CV13 CV28	S2 S22	336	2483	ISOPROPYL ISOCYANATE
L10CH	TU14 TU15 TE19 TE21	FL	1 (C/D)			CV1 CV13 CV28	S2 S9 S14	663	2484	tert-BUTYL ISOCYANATE
L10CH	TU14 TU15 TE19 TE21	FL	1 (C/D)			CV1 CV13 CV28	S2 S9 S14	663	2485	n-BUTYL ISOCYANATE
L4BH	TU15	FL	2 (D/E)			CV13 CV28	S2 S19	336	2486	ISOBUTYL ISOCYANATE
L10CH	TU14 TU15 TE19 TE21	FL	1 (C/D)			CV1 CV13 CV28	S2 S9 S14	663	2487	PHENYL ISOCYANATE
L10CH	TU14 TU15 TE19 TE21	FL	1 (C/D)			CV1 CV13 CV28	S2 S9 S14	663	2488	CYCLOHEXYL ISOCYANATE
L4BH	TU15 TE19	AT	2 (D/E)			CV13 CV28	S9 S19	60	2490	DICHLOROISOPROPYL ETHER
L4BN		AT	3 (E)					80	2491	ETHANOLAMINE or ETHANOLAMINE SOLUTION
L4BH		FL	2 (D/E)				S2 S20	338	2493	HEXAMETHYLENEIMINE
L10DH	TU3	AT	1 (B/E)			CV24 CV28	S20	568	2495	IODINE PENTAFLUORIDE
L4BN		AT	3 (E)					80	2496	PROPIONIC ANHYDRIDE
LGBF		FL	3 (D/E)				S2	30	2498	1,2,3,6-TETRAHYDROBENZAL-DEHYDE
L4BH	TU15 TE19	AT	2 (D/E)			CV13 CV28	S9 S19	60	2501	TRIS-(1-AZIRIDINYL) PHOSPHINE OXIDE SOLUTION
L4BH	TU15 TE19	AT	2 (E)			CV13 CV28	S9	60	2501	TRIS-(1-AZIRIDINYL) PHOSPHINE OXIDE SOLUTION
L4BN		FL	2 (D/E)				S2	83	2502	VALERYL CHLORIDE
SGAV		AT	3 (E)		VV9			80	2503	ZIRCONIUM TETRACHLORIDE
L4BH	TU15 TE19	AT	2 (E)			CV13 CV28	S9	60	2504	TETRABROMOETHANE
SGAH	TU15 TE19	AT	2 (E)		VV9	CV13 CV28	S9	60	2505	AMMONIUM FLUORIDE
SGAV		AT	2 (E)	V11	VV9			80	2506	AMMONIUM HYDROGEN SULPHATE
SGAV		AT	3 (E)		VV9			80	2507	CHLOROPLATINIC ACID, SOLID
SGAV		AT	3 (E)		VV9			80	2508	MOLYBDENUM PENTACHLORIDE

UN No.	Name and description	Class	Classification code	Packing group	Labels	Special provisions	Limited and excepted quantities		Packaging			Portable tanks and bulk containers	
									Packing instructions	Special packing provisions	Mixed packing provisions	Instructions	Special provisions
	3.1.2	2.2	2.2	2.1.1.3	5.2.2	3.3	3.4.6	3.5.1.2	4.1.4	4.1.4	4.1.10	4.2.5.2 7.3.2	4.2.5.3
(1)	(2)	(3a)	(3b)	(4)	(5)	(6)	(7a)	(7b)	(8)	(9a)	(9b)	(10)	(11)
2509	POTASSIUM HYDROGEN SULPHATE	8	C2	II	8		LQ23	E2	P002 IBC08	B4	MP10	T3	TP33
2511	2-CHLOROPROPIONIC ACID	8	C3	III	8		LQ7	E1	P001 IBC03 LP01 R001		MP19	T4	TP2
2512	AMINOPHENOLS (o-, m-, p-)	6.1	T2	III	6.1	279	LQ9	E1	P002 IBC08 LP02 R001	B3	MP10	T1	TP33
2513	BROMOACETYL BROMIDE	8	C3	II	8		LQ22	E2	P001 IBC02		MP15	T8	TP2
2514	BROMOBENZENE	3	F1	III	3		LQ7	E1	P001 IBC03 LP01 R001		MP19	T2	TP1
2515	BROMOFORM	6.1	T1	III	6.1		LQ7	E1	P001 IBC03 LP01 R001		MP19	T4	TP1
2516	CARBON TETRABROMIDE	6.1	T2	III	6.1		LQ9	E1	P002 IBC08 LP02 R001	B3	MP10	T1	TP33
2517	1-CHLORO-1,1-DIFLUOROETHANE (REFRIGERANT GAS R 142b)	2	2F		2.1		LQ0	E0	P200		MP9	(M) T50	
2518	1,5,9-CYCLODODECATRIENE	6.1	T1	III	6.1		LQ7	E1	P001 IBC03 LP01 R001		MP19	T4	TP1
2520	CYCLOOCTADIENES	3	F1	III	3		LQ7	E1	P001 IBC03 LP01 R001		MP19	T2	TP1
2521	DIKETENE, STABILIZED	6.1	TF1	I	6.1 +3		LQ0	E5	P001		MP8 MP17	T14	TP2
2522	2-DIMETHYLAMINOETHYL METHACRYLATE	6.1	T1	II	6.1		LQ17	E4	P001 IBC02		MP15	T7	TP2
2524	ETHYL ORTHOFORMATE	3	F1	III	3		LQ7	E1	P001 IBC03 LP01 R001		MP19	T2	TP1
2525	ETHYL OXALATE	6.1	T1	III	6.1		LQ7	E1	P001 IBC03 LP01 R001		MP19	T4	TP1
2526	FURFURYLAMINE	3	FC	III	3 +8		LQ7	E1	P001 IBC03 R001		MP19	T4	TP1
2527	ISOBUTYL ACRYLATE, STABILIZED	3	F1	III	3		LQ7	E1	P001 IBC03 LP01 R001		MP19	T2	TP1
2528	ISOBUTYL ISOBUTYRATE	3	F1	III	3		LQ7	E1	P001 IBC03 LP01 R001		MP19	T2	TP1
2529	ISOBUTYRIC ACID	3	FC	III	3 +8		LQ7	E1	P001 IBC03 R001		MP19	T4	TP1
2531	METHACRYLIC ACID, STABILIZED	8	C3	II	8		LQ22	E2	P001 IBC02 LP01		MP15	T7	TP2 TP18 TP30
2533	METHYL TRICHLOROACETATE	6.1	T1	III	6.1		LQ7	E1	P001 IBC03 LP01 R001		MP19	T4	TP1

ADR tank		Vehicle for tank carriage	Transport category (Tunnel restriction code)	Special provisions for carriage				Hazard identifi-cation No.	UN No.	Name and description
Tank code	Special provisions			Packages	Bulk	Loading, unloading and handling	Operation			
4.3	4.3.5, 6.8.4	9.1.1.2	1.1.3.6 (8.6)	7.2.4	7.3.3	7.5.11	8.5	5.3.2.3		3.1.2
(12)	(13)	(14)	(15)	(16)	(17)	(18)	(19)	(20)	(1)	(2)
SGAV		AT	2 (E)	V11	VV9			80	2509	POTASSIUM HYDROGEN SULPHATE
L4BN		AT	3 (E)					80	2511	2-CHLOROPROPIONIC ACID
SGAH L4BH	TU15 TE19	AT	2 (E)		VV9	CV13 CV28	S9	60	2512	AMINOPHENOLS (o-, m-, p-)
L4BN		AT	2 (E)					X80	2513	BROMOACETYL BROMIDE
LGBF		FL	3 (D/E)				S2	30	2514	BROMOBENZENE
L4BH	TU15 TE19	AT	2 (E)			CV13 CV28	S9	60	2515	BROMOFORM
SGAH L4BH	TU15 TE19	AT	2 (E)		VV9	CV13 CV28	S9	60	2516	CARBON TETRABROMIDE
PxBN(M)	TA4 TT9	FL	2 (B/D)			CV9 CV10 CV36	S2 S20	23	2517	1-CHLORO-1,1-DIFLUOROETHANE (REFRIGERANT GAS R 142b)
L4BH	TU15 TE19	AT	2 (E)			CV13 CV28	S9	60	2518	1,5,9-CYCLODODECATRIENE
LGBF		FL	3 (D/E)				S2	30	2520	CYCLOOCTADIENES
L10CH	TU14 TU15 TE19 TE21	FL	1 (C/D)			CV1 CV13 CV28	S2 S9 S14	663	2521	DIKETENE, STABILIZED
L4BH	TU15 TE19	AT	2 (D/E)			CV13 CV28	S9 S19	69	2522	2-DIMETHYLAMINOETHYL METHACRYLATE
LGBF		FL	3 (D/E)				S2	30	2524	ETHYL ORTHOFORMATE
L4BH	TU15 TE19	AT	2 (E)			CV13 CV28	S9	60	2525	ETHYL OXALATE
L4BN		FL	3 (D/E)				S2	38	2526	FURFURYLAMINE
LGBF		FL	3 (D/E)				S2	39	2527	ISOBUTYL ACRYLATE, STABILIZED
LGBF		FL	3 (D/E)				S2	30	2528	ISOBUTYL ISOBUTYRATE
L4BN		FL	3 (D/E)				S2	38	2529	ISOBUTYRIC ACID
L4BN		AT	2 (E)					89	2531	METHACRYLIC ACID, STABILIZED
L4BH	TU15 TE19	AT	2 (E)			CV13 CV28	S9	60	2533	METHYL TRICHLOROACETATE

UN No.	Name and description	Class	Classification code	Packing group	Labels	Special provisions	Limited and excepted quantities		Packaging			Portable tanks and bulk containers	
									Packing instructions	Special packing provisions	Mixed packing provisions	Instructions	Special provisions
	3.1.2	2.2	2.2	2.1.1.3	5.2.2	3.3	3.4.6	3.5.1.2	4.1.4	4.1.4	4.1.10	4.2.5.2 7.3.2	4.2.5.3
(1)	(2)	(3a)	(3b)	(4)	(5)	(6)	(7a)	(7b)	(8)	(9a)	(9b)	(10)	(11)
2534	METHYLCHLOROSILANE	2	2TFC		2.3 +2.1 +8		LQ0	E0	P200		MP9	(M)	
2535	4-METHYLMORPHOLINE (N-METHYLMORPHOLINE)	3	FC	II	3 +8		LQ4	E2	P001 IBC02		MP19	T7	TP1
2536	METHYLTETRAHYDRO-FURAN	3	F1	II	3		LQ4	E2	P001 IBC02 R001		MP19	T4	TP1
2538	NITRONAPHTHALENE	4.1	F1	III	4.1		LQ9	E1	P002 IBC08 LP02 R001	B3	MP10	T1	TP33
2541	TERPINOLENE	3	F1	III	3		LQ7	E1	P001 IBC03 LP01 R001		MP19	T2	TP1
2542	TRIBUTYLAMINE	6.1	T1	II	6.1		LQ17	E4	P001 IBC02		MP15	T7	TP2
2545	HAFNIUM POWDER, DRY	4.2	S4	I	4.2	540	LQ0	E0	P404		MP13		
2545	HAFNIUM POWDER, DRY	4.2	S4	II	4.2	540	LQ0	E2	P410 IBC06		MP14	T3	TP33
2545	HAFNIUM POWDER, DRY	4.2	S4	III	4.2	540	LQ0	E1	P002 IBC08 LP02 R001	B3	MP14	T1	TP33
2546	TITANIUM POWDER, DRY	4.2	S4	I	4.2	540	LQ0	E0	P404		MP13		
2546	TITANIUM POWDER, DRY	4.2	S4	II	4.2	540	LQ0	E2	P410 IBC06		MP14	T3	TP33
2546	TITANIUM POWDER, DRY	4.2	S4	III	4.2	540	LQ0	E1	P002 IBC08 LP02 R001	B3	MP14	T1	TP33
2547	SODIUM SUPEROXIDE	5.1	O2	I	5.1		LQ0	E0	P503 IBC06		MP2		
2548	CHLORINE PENTAFLUORIDE	2	2TOC		2.3 +5.1 +8		LQ0	E0	P200		MP9		
2552	HEXAFLUOROACETONE HYDRATE, LIQUID	6.1	T1	II	6.1		LQ17	E4	P001 IBC02		MP15	T7	TP2
2554	METHYLALLYL CHLORIDE	3	F1	II	3		LQ4	E2	P001 IBC02 R001		MP19	T4	TP1
2555	NITROCELLULOSE WITH WATER (not less than 25% water, by mass)	4.1	D	II	4.1	541	LQ0	E0	P406		MP2		
2556	NITROCELLULOSE WITH ALCOHOL (not less than 25% alcohol, by mass, and not more than 12.6% nitrogen, by dry mass)	4.1	D	II	4.1	541	LQ0	E0	P406		MP2		
2557	NITROCELLULOSE, with not more than 12.6% nitrogen, by dry mass, MIXTURE WITH or WITHOUT PLASTICIZER, WITH or WITHOUT PIGMENT	4.1	D	II	4.1	241 541	LQ0	E0	P406		MP2		
2558	EPIBROMOHYDRIN	6.1	TF1	I	6.1 +3		LQ0	E5	P001		MP8 MP17	T14	TP2
2560	2-METHYLPENTAN-2-OL	3	F1	III	3		LQ7	E1	P001 IBC03 LP01 R001		MP19	T2	TP1
2561	3-METHYL-1-BUTENE	3	F1	I	3		LQ3	E3	P001		MP7 MP17	T11	TP2
2564	TRICHLOROACETIC ACID SOLUTION	8	C3	II	8		LQ22	E2	P001 IBC02		MP15	T7	TP2

ADR tank		Vehicle for tank carriage	Transport category (Tunnel restriction code)	Special provisions for carriage				Hazard identifi-cation No.	UN No.	Name and description
Tank code	Special provisions			Packages	Bulk	Loading, unloading and handling	Operation			
4.3	4.3.5, 6.8.4	9.1.1.2	1.1.3.6 (8.6)	7.2.4	7.3.3	7.5.11	8.5	5.3.2.3		3.1.2
(12)	(13)	(14)	(15)	(16)	(17)	(18)	(19)	(20)	(1)	(2)
		FL	1 (B/D)			CV9 CV10 CV36	S2 S14	263	2534	METHYLCHLOROSILANE
L4BH		FL	2 (D/E)				S2 S20	338	2535	4-METHYLMORPHOLINE (N-METHYLMORPHOLINE)
LGBF		FL	2 (D/E)				S2 S20	33	2536	METHYLTETRAHYDRO-FURAN
SGAV		AT	3 (E)		VV1			40	2538	NITRONAPHTHALENE
LGBF		FL	3 (D/E)				S2	30	2541	TERPINOLENE
L4BH	TU15 TE19	AT	2 (D/E)			CV13 CV28	S9 S19	60	2542	TRIBUTYLAMINE
			0 (E)	V1			S20		2545	HAFNIUM POWDER, DRY
SGAN		AT	2 (D/E)	V1 V12				40	2545	HAFNIUM POWDER, DRY
SGAN		AT	3 (E)	V1	VV4			40	2545	HAFNIUM POWDER, DRY
			0 (E)	V1			S20		2546	TITANIUM POWDER, DRY
SGAN		AT	2 (D/E)	V1 V12				40	2546	TITANIUM POWDER, DRY
SGAN		AT	3 (E)	V1	VV4			40	2546	TITANIUM POWDER, DRY
			1 (E)	V10 V12		CV24	S20		2547	SODIUM SUPEROXIDE
			1 (D)			CV9 CV10 CV36	S14		2548	CHLORINE PENTAFLUORIDE
L4BH	TU15 TE19	AT	2 (D/E)			CV13 CV28	S9 S19	60	2552	HEXAFLUOROACETONE HYDRATE, LIQUID
LGBF		FL	2 (D/E)				S2 S20	33	2554	METHYLALLYL CHLORIDE
			2 (B)				S14		2555	NITROCELLULOSE WITH WATER (not less than 25% water, by mass)
			2 (B)				S14		2556	NITROCELLULOSE WITH ALCOHOL (not less than 25% alcohol, by mass, and not more than 12.6% nitrogen, by dry mass)
			2 (B)				S14		2557	NITROCELLULOSE, with not more than 12.6% nitrogen, by dry mass, MIXTURE WITH or WITHOUT PLASTICIZER, WITH or WITHOUT PIGMENT
L10CH	TU14 TU15 TE19 TE21	FL	1 (C/D)			CV1 CV13 CV28	S2 S9 S14	663	2558	EPIBROMOHYDRIN
LGBF		FL	3 (D/E)				S2	30	2560	2-METHYLPENTAN-2-OL
L4BN		FL	1 (D/E)				S2 S20	33	2561	3-METHYL-1-BUTENE
L4BN		AT	2 (E)					80	2564	TRICHLOROACETIC ACID SOLUTION

UN No.	Name and description	Class	Classification code	Packing group	Labels	Special provisions	Limited and excepted quantities		Packaging			Portable tanks and bulk containers	
								quantities	Packing instructions	Special packing provisions	Mixed packing provisions	Instructions	Special provisions
	3.1.2	2.2	2.2	2.1.1.3	5.2.2	3.3	3.4.6	3.5.1.2	4.1.4	4.1.4	4.1.10	4.2.5.2 7.3.2	4.2.5.3
(1)	(2)	(3a)	(3b)	(4)	(5)	(6)	(7a)	(7b)	(8)	(9a)	(9b)	(10)	(11)
2564	TRICHLOROACETIC ACID SOLUTION	8	C3	III	8		LQ7	E1	P001 IBC03 LP01 R001		MP19	T4	TP1
2565	DICYCLOHEXYLAMINE	8	C7	III	8		LQ7	E1	P001 IBC03 LP01 R001		MP19	T4	TP1
2567	SODIUM PENTACHLOROPHENATE	6.1	T2	II	6.1		LQ18	E4	P002 IBC08	B4	MP10	T3	TP33
2570	CADMIUM COMPOUND	6.1	T5	I	6.1	274 596	LQ0	E5	P002 IBC07		MP18	T6	TP33
2570	CADMIUM COMPOUND	6.1	T5	II	6.1	274 596	LQ18	E4	P002 IBC08	B4	MP10	T3	TP33
2570	CADMIUM COMPOUND	6.1	T5	III	6.1	274 596	LQ9	E1	P002 IBC08 LP02 R001	B3	MP10	T1	TP33
2571	ALKYLSULPHURIC ACIDS	8	C3	II	8		LQ22	E2	P001 IBC02		MP15	T8	TP2 TP28
2572	PHENYLHYDRAZINE	6.1	T1	II	6.1		LQ17	E4	P001 IBC02		MP15	T7	TP2
2573	THALLIUM CHLORATE	5.1	OT2	II	5.1 +6.1		LQ11	E2	P002 IBC06		MP2	T3	TP33
2574	TRICRESYL PHOSPHATE with more than 3% ortho isomer	6.1	T1	II	6.1		LQ17	E4	P001 IBC02		MP15	T7	TP2
2576	PHOSPHORUS OXYBROMIDE, MOLTEN	8	C1	II	8		LQ0	E0				T7	TP3
2577	PHENYLACETYL CHLORIDE	8	C3	II	8		LQ22	E2	P001 IBC02		MP15	T7	TP2
2578	PHOSPHORUS TRIOXIDE	8	C2	III	8		LQ24	E1	P002 IBC08 LP02 R001	B3	MP10	T1	TP33
2579	PIPERAZINE	8	C8	III	8		LQ24	E1	P002 IBC08 LP02 R001	B3	MP10	T1	TP33
2580	ALUMINIUM BROMIDE SOLUTION	8	C1	III	8		LQ7	E1	P001 IBC03 LP01 R001		MP19	T4	TP1
2581	ALUMINIUM CHLORIDE SOLUTION	8	C1	III	8		LQ7	E1	P001 IBC03 LP01 R001		MP19	T4	TP1
2582	FERRIC CHLORIDE SOLUTION	8	C1	III	8		LQ7	E1	P001 IBC03 LP01 R001		MP19	T4	TP1
2583	ALKYLSULPHONIC ACIDS, SOLID or ARYLSULPHONIC ACIDS, SOLID with more than 5% free sulphuric acid	8	C2	II	8	274	LQ23	E2	P002 IBC08	B4	MP10	T3	TP33
2584	ALKYLSULPHONIC ACIDS, LIQUID or ARYLSULPHONIC ACIDS, LIQUID with more than 5% free sulphuric acid	8	C1	II	8	274	LQ22	E2	P001 IBC02		MP15	T8	TP2
2585	ALKYLSULPHONIC ACIDS, SOLID or ARYLSULPHONIC ACIDS, SOLID with not more than 5% free sulphuric acid	8	C4	III	8	274	LQ24	E1	P002 IBC08 LP02 R001	B3	MP10	T1	TP33

ADR tank		Vehicle for tank carriage	Transport category (Tunnel restriction code)	Special provisions for carriage				Hazard identifi-cation No.	UN No.	Name and description
Tank code	Special provisions			Packages	Bulk	Loading, unloading and handling	Operation			
4.3	4.3.5, 6.8.4	9.1.1.2	1.1.3.6 (8.6)	7.2.4	7.3.3	7.5.11	8.5	5.3.2.3		3.1.2
(12)	(13)	(14)	(15)	(16)	(17)	(18)	(19)	(20)	(1)	(2)
L4BN		AT	3 (E)					80	2564	TRICHLOROACETIC ACID SOLUTION
L4BN		AT	3 (E)					80	2565	DICYCLOHEXYLAMINE
SGAH	TU15 TE19	AT	2 (D/E)	V11		CV13 CV28	S9 S19	60	2567	SODIUM PENTACHLOROPHENATE
S10AH L10CH	TU14 TU15 TE19 TE21	AT	1 (C/E)	V10 V12		CV1 CV13 CV28	S9 S14	66	2570	CADMIUM COMPOUND
SGAH L4BH	TU15 TE19	AT	2 (D/E)	V11		CV13 CV28	S9 S19	60	2570	CADMIUM COMPOUND
SGAH L4BH	TU15 TE19	AT	2 (E)		VV9	CV13 CV28	S9	60	2570	CADMIUM COMPOUND
L4BN		AT	2 (E)					80	2571	ALKYLSULPHURIC ACIDS
L4BH	TU15 TE19	AT	2 (D/E)			CV13 CV28	S9 S19	60	2572	PHENYLHYDRAZINE
SGAN	TU3	AT	2 (E)	V11 V12		CV24 CV28		56	2573	THALLIUM CHLORATE
L4BH	TU15 TE19	AT	2 (D/E)			CV13 CV28	S9 S19	60	2574	TRICRESYL PHOSPHATE with more than 3% ortho isomer
L4BN		AT	2 (E)					80	2576	PHOSPHORUS OXYBROMIDE, MOLTEN
L4BN		AT	2 (E)					80	2577	PHENYLACETYL CHLORIDE
SGAV		AT	3 (E)		VV9			80	2578	PHOSPHORUS TRIOXIDE
SGAV L4BN		AT	3 (E)		VV9			80	2579	PIPERAZINE
L4BN		AT	3 (E)					80	2580	ALUMINIUM BROMIDE SOLUTION
L4BN		AT	3 (E)					80	2581	ALUMINIUM CHLORIDE SOLUTION
L4BN		AT	3 (E)					80	2582	FERRIC CHLORIDE SOLUTION
SGAN L4BN		AT	2 (E)	V11				80	2583	ALKYLSULPHONIC ACIDS, SOLID or ARYLSULPHONIC ACIDS, SOLID with more than 5% free sulphuric acid
L4BN		AT	2 (E)					80	2584	ALKYLSULPHONIC ACIDS, LIQUID or ARYLSULPHONIC ACIDS, LIQUID with more than 5% free sulphuric acid
SGAV		AT	3 (E)		VV9			80	2585	ALKYLSULPHONIC ACIDS, SOLID or ARYLSULPHONIC ACIDS, SOLID with not more than 5% free sulphuric acid

UN No.	Name and description	Class	Classification code	Packing group	Labels	Special provisions	Limited and excepted quantities		Packaging			Portable tanks and bulk containers	
									Packing instructions	Special packing provisions	Mixed packing provisions	Instructions	Special provisions
	3.1.2	2.2	2.2	2.1.1.3	5.2.2	3.3	3.4.6	3.5.1.2	4.1.4	4.1.4	4.1.10	4.2.5.2 7.3.2	4.2.5.3
(1)	(2)	(3a)	(3b)	(4)	(5)	(6)	(7a)	(7b)	(8)	(9a)	(9b)	(10)	(11)
2586	ALKYLSULPHONIC ACIDS, LIQUID or ARYLSULPHONIC ACIDS, LIQUID with not more than 5% free sulphuric acid	8	C3	III	8	274	LQ7	E1	P001 IBC03 LP01 R001		MP19	T4	TP1
2587	BENZOQUINONE	6.1	T2	II	6.1		LQ18	E4	P002 IBC08	B4	MP10	T3	TP33
2588	PESTICIDE, SOLID, TOXIC, N.O.S.	6.1	T7	I	6.1	61 274 648	LQ0	E5	P002 IBC02		MP18	T6	TP33
2588	PESTICIDE, SOLID, TOXIC, N.O.S.	6.1	T7	II	6.1	61 274 648	LQ18	E4	P002 IBC08	B4	MP10	T3	TP33
2588	PESTICIDE, SOLID, TOXIC, N.O.S.	6.1	T7	III	6.1	61 274 648	LQ9	E1	P002 IBC08 LP02 R001	B3	MP10	T1	TP33
2589	VINYL CHLOROACETATE	6.1	TF1	II	6.1 +3		LQ17	E4	P001 IBC02		MP15	T7	TP2
2590	WHITE ASBESTOS (chrysotile, actinolite, anthophyllite, tremolite)	9	M1	III	9	168 542	LQ27	E1	P002 IBC08 R001	PP37 B4	MP10	T1	TP33
2591	XENON, REFRIGERATED LIQUID	2	3A		2.2	593	LQ1	E1	P203		MP9	T75	TP5
2599	CHLOROTRIFLUORO-METHANE AND TRIFLUOROMETHANE AZEOTROPIC MIXTURE with approximately 60% chlorotrifluoromethane (REFRIGERANT GAS R 503)	2	2A		2.2		LQ1	E1	P200		MP9	(M)	
2601	CYCLOBUTANE	2	2F		2.1		LQ0	E0	P200		MP9	(M)	
2602	DICHLORODIFLUORO-METHANE AND 1,1-DIFLUOROETHANE AZEOTROPIC MIXTURE with approximately 74% dichlorodifluoromethane (REFRIGERANT GAS R 500)	2	2A		2.2		LQ1	E1	P200		MP9	(M) T50	
2603	CYCLOHEPTATRIENE	3	FT1	II	3 +6.1		LQ0	E2	P001 IBC02		MP19	T7	TP1
2604	BORON TRIFLUORIDE DIETHYL ETHERATE	8	CF1	I	8 +3		LQ0	E0	P001		MP8 MP17	T10	TP2
2605	METHOXYMETHYL ISOCYANATE	3	FT1	I	3 +6.1		LQ0	E0	P001		MP7 MP17	T14	TP2
2606	METHYL ORTHOSILICATE	6.1	TF1	I	6.1 +3		LQ0	E5	P001		MP8 MP17	T14	TP2
2607	ACROLEIN DIMER, STABILIZED	3	F1	III	3		LQ7	E1	P001 IBC03 LP01 R001		MP19	T2	TP1
2608	NITROPROPANES	3	F1	III	3		LQ7	E1	P001 IBC03 LP01 R001		MP19	T2	TP1
2609	TRIALLYL BORATE	6.1	T1	III	6.1		LQ7	E1	P001 IBC03 LP01 R001		MP19		
2610	TRIALLYLAMINE	3	FC	III	3 +8		LQ7	E1	P001 IBC03 R001		MP19	T4	TP1
2611	PROPYLENE CHLOROHYDRIN	6.1	TF1	II	6.1 +3		LQ17	E4	P001 IBC02		MP15	T7	TP2
2612	METHYL PROPYL ETHER	3	F1	II	3		LQ4	E2	P001 IBC02	B8	MP19	T7	TP2

ADR tank		Vehicle for tank carriage	Transport category (Tunnel restriction code)	Special provisions for carriage				Hazard identifi-cation No.	UN No.	Name and description
Tank code	Special provisions			Packages	Bulk	Loading, unloading and handling	Operation			
4.3	4.3.5, 6.8.4	9.1.1.2	1.1.3.6 (8.6)	7.2.4	7.3.3	7.5.11	8.5	5.3.2.3		3.1.2
(12)	(13)	(14)	(15)	(16)	(17)	(18)	(19)	(20)	(1)	(2)
L4BN		AT	3 (E)					80	2586	ALKYLSULPHONIC ACIDS, LIQUID or ARYLSULPHONIC ACIDS, LIQUID with not more than 5% free sulphuric acid
SGAH L4BH	TU15 TE19	AT	2 (D/E)	V11		CV13 CV28	S9 S19	60	2587	BENZOQUINONE
S10AH L10CH	TU14 TU15 TE19 TE21	AT	1 (C/E)			CV1 CV13 CV28	S9 S14	66	2588	PESTICIDE, SOLID, TOXIC, N.O.S.
SGAH L4BH	TU15 TE19	AT	2 (D/E)	V11		CV13 CV28	S9 S19	60	2588	PESTICIDE, SOLID, TOXIC, N.O.S.
SGAH L4BH	TU15 TE19	AT	2 (E)		VV9	CV13 CV28	S9	60	2588	PESTICIDE, SOLID, TOXIC, N.O.S.
L4BH	TU15 TE19	FL	2 (D/E)			CV13 CV28	S2 S9 S19	63	2589	VINYL CHLOROACETATE
SGAH	TU15	AT	3 (E)	V11		CV13 CV28		90	2590	WHITE ASBESTOS (chrysotile, actinolite, anthophyllite, tremolite)
RxBN	TU19 TA4 TT9	AT	3 (C/E)	V5		CV9 CV11 CV36	S20	22	2591	XENON, REFRIGERATED LIQUID
PxBN(M)	TA4 TT9	AT	3 (C/E)			CV9 CV10 CV36		20	2599	CHLOROTRIFLUORO-METHANE AND TRIFLUOROMETHANE AZEOTROPIC MIXTURE with approximately 60% chlorotrifluoromethane (REFRIGERANT GAS R 503)
PxBN(M)	TA4 TT9	FL	2 (B/D)			CV9 CV10 CV36	S2 S20	23	2601	CYCLOBUTANE
PxBN(M)	TA4 TT9	AT	3 (C/E)			CV9 CV10 CV36		20	2602	DICHLORODIFLUORO-METHANE AND 1,1-DIFLUOROETHANE AZEOTROPIC MIXTURE with approximately 74% dichlorodifluoromethane (REFRIGERANT GAS R 500)
L4BH	TU15	FL	2 (D/E)			CV13 CV28	S2 S19	336	2603	CYCLOHEPTATRIENE
L10BH		FL	1 (D/E)				S2 S14	883	2604	BORON TRIFLUORIDE DIETHYL ETHERATE
L10CH	TU14 TU15 TE21	FL	1 (C/E)			CV13 CV28	S2 S22	336	2605	METHOXYMETHYL ISOCYANATE
L10CH	TU14 TU15 TE19 TE21	FL	1 (C/D)			CV1 CV13 CV28	S2 S9 S14	663	2606	METHYL ORTHOSILICATE
LGBF		FL	3 (D/E)				S2	39	2607	ACROLEIN DIMER, STABILIZED
LGBF		FL	3 (D/E)				S2	30	2608	NITROPROPANES
L4BH	TU15 TE19	AT	2 (E)			CV13 CV28	S9	60	2609	TRIALLYL BORATE
L4BN		FL	3 (D/E)				S2	38	2610	TRIALLYLAMINE
L4BH	TU15 TE19	FL	2 (D/E)			CV13 CV28	S2 S9 S19	63	2611	PROPYLENE CHLOROHYDRIN
L1.5BN		FL	2 (D/E)				S2 S20	33	2612	METHYL PROPYL ETHER

UN No.	Name and description	Class	Classification code	Packing group	Labels	Special provisions	Limited and excepted quantities		Packaging			Portable tanks and bulk containers	
									Packing instructions	Special packing provisions	Mixed packing provisions	Instructions	Special provisions
	3.1.2	2.2	2.2	2.1.1.3	5.2.2	3.3	3.4.6	3.5.1.2	4.1.4	4.1.4	4.1.10	4.2.5.2 7.3.2	4.2.5.3
(1)	(2)	(3a)	(3b)	(4)	(5)	(6)	(7a)	(7b)	(8)	(9a)	(9b)	(10)	(11)
2614	METHALLYL ALCOHOL	3	F1	III	3		LQ7	E1	P001 IBC03 LP01 R001		MP19	T2	TP1
2615	ETHYL PROPYL ETHER	3	F1	II	3		LQ4	E2	P001 IBC02 R001		MP19	T4	TP1
2616	TRIISOPROPYL BORATE	3	F1	II	3		LQ4	E2	P001 IBC02 R001		MP19	T4	TP1
2616	TRIISOPROPYL BORATE	3	F1	III	3		LQ7	E1	P001 IBC03 LP01 R001		MP19	T2	TP1
2617	METHYLCYCLO-HEXANOLS, flammable	3	F1	III	3		LQ7	E1	P001 IBC03 LP01 R001		MP19	T2	TP1
2618	VINYLTOLUENES, STABILIZED	3	F1	III	3		LQ7	E1	P001 IBC03 LP01 R001		MP19	T2	TP1
2619	BENZYLDIMETHYLAMINE	8	CF1	II	8 +3		LQ22	E2	P001 IBC02		MP15	T7	TP2
2620	AMYL BUTYRATES	3	F1	III	3		LQ7	E1	P001 IBC03 LP01 R001		MP19	T2	TP1
2621	ACETYL METHYL CARBINOL	3	F1	III	3		LQ7	E1	P001 IBC03 LP01 R001		MP19	T2	TP1
2622	GLYCIDALDEHYDE	3	FT1	II	3 +6.1		LQ0	E2	P001 IBC02	B8	MP19	T7	TP1
2623	FIRELIGHTERS, SOLID with flammable liquid	4.1	F1	III	4.1		LQ9	E1	P002 LP02 R001	PP15	MP11		
2624	MAGNESIUM SILICIDE	4.3	W2	II	4.3		LQ11	E2	P410 IBC07		MP14	T3	TP33
2626	CHLORIC ACID, AQUEOUS SOLUTION with not more than 10% chloric acid	5.1	O1	II	5.1	613	LQ10	E2	P504 IBC02		MP2	T4	TP1
2627	NITRITES, INORGANIC, N.O.S.	5.1	O2	II	5.1	103 274	LQ11	E2	P002 IBC08	B4	MP10	T3	TP33
2628	POTASSIUM FLUOROACETATE	6.1	T2	I	6.1		LQ0	E5	P002 IBC07		MP18	T6	TP33
2629	SODIUM FLUOROACETATE	6.1	T2	I	6.1		LQ0	E5	P002 IBC07		MP18	T6	TP33
2630	SELENATES or SELENITES	6.1	T5	I	6.1	274	LQ0	E5	P002 IBC07		MP18	T6	TP33
2642	FLUOROACETIC ACID	6.1	T2	I	6.1		LQ0	E5	P002 IBC07		MP18	T6	TP33
2643	METHYL BROMOACETATE	6.1	T1	II	6.1		LQ17	E4	P001 IBC02		MP15	T7	TP2
2644	METHYL IODIDE	6.1	T1	I	6.1		LQ0	E5	P001		MP8 MP17	T14	TP2
2645	PHENACYL BROMIDE	6.1	T2	II	6.1		LQ18	E4	P002 IBC08	B4	MP10	T3	TP33
2646	HEXACHLOROCYCLO-PENTADIENE	6.1	T1	I	6.1		LQ0	E5	P001		MP8 MP17	T20	TP2 TP35
2647	MALONONITRILE	6.1	T2	II	6.1		LQ18	E4	P002 IBC08	B4	MP10	T3	TP33
2648	1,2-DIBROMOBUTAN-3-ONE	6.1	T1	II	6.1		LQ17	E4	P001 IBC02		MP15		
2649	1,3-DICHLOROACETONE	6.1	T2	II	6.1		LQ18	E4	P002 IBC08	B4	MP10	T3	TP33

ADR tank		Vehicle for tank carriage	Transport category (Tunnel restriction code)	Special provisions for carriage				Hazard identifi-cation No.	UN No.	Name and description
Tank code	Special provisions			Packages	Bulk	Loading, unloading and handling	Operation			
4.3	4.3.5, 6.8.4	9.1.1.2	1.1.3.6 (8.6)	7.2.4	7.3.3	7.5.11	8.5	5.3.2.3		3.1.2
(12)	(13)	(14)	(15)	(16)	(17)	(18)	(19)	(20)	(1)	(2)
LGBF		FL	3 (D/E)				S2	30	2614	METHALLYL ALCOHOL
LGBF		FL	2 (D/E)				S2 S20	33	2615	ETHYL PROPYL ETHER
LGBF		FL	2 (D/E)				S2 S20	33	2616	TRIISOPROPYL BORATE
LGBF		FL	3 (D/E)				S2	30	2616	TRIISOPROPYL BORATE
LGBF		FL	3 (D/E)				S2	30	2617	METHYLCYCLO-HEXANOLS, flammable
LGBF		FL	3 (D/E)				S2	39	2618	VINYLTOLUENES, STABILIZED
L4BN		FL	2 (D/E)				S2	83	2619	BENZYLDIMETHYLAMINE
LGBF		FL	3 (D/E)				S2	30	2620	AMYL BUTYRATES
LGBF		FL	3 (D/E)				S2	30	2621	ACETYL METHYL CARBINOL
L4BH	TU15	FL	2 (D/E)			CV13 CV28	S2 S19	336	2622	GLYCIDALDEHYDE
			4 (E)						2623	FIRELIGHTERS, SOLID with flammable liquid
SGAN		AT	2 (D/E)	V1 V12		CV23		423	2624	MAGNESIUM SILICIDE
L4BN	TU3	AT	2 (E)			CV24		50	2626	CHLORIC ACID, AQUEOUS SOLUTION with not more than 10% chloric acid
SGAN	TU3	AT	2 (E)	V11		CV24		50	2627	NITRITES, INORGANIC, N.O.S.
S10AH	TU15 TE19	AT	1 (C/E)	V10 V12		CV1 CV13 CV28	S9 S14	66	2628	POTASSIUM FLUOROACETATE
S10AH	TU15 TE19	AT	1 (C/E)	V10 V12		CV1 CV13 CV28	S9 S14	66	2629	SODIUM FLUOROACETATE
S10AH L10CH	TU14 TU15 TE19 TE21	AT	1 (C/E)	V10 V12		CV1 CV13 CV28	S9 S14	66	2630	SELENATES or SELENITES
S10AH L10CH	TU14 TU15 TE19 TE21	AT	1 (C/E)	V10 V12		CV1 CV13 CV28	S9 S14	66	2642	FLUOROACETIC ACID
L4BH	TU15 TE19	AT	2 (D/E)			CV13 CV28	S9 S19	60	2643	METHYL BROMOACETATE
L10CH	TU14 TU15 TE19 TE21	AT	1 (C/E)			CV1 CV13 CV28	S9 S14	66	2644	METHYL IODIDE
SGAH L4BH	TU15 TE19	AT	2 (D/E)	V11		CV13 CV28	S9 S19	60	2645	PHENACYL BROMIDE
L10CH	TU14 TU15 TE19 TE21	AT	1 (C/E)			CV1 CV13 CV28	S9 S14	66	2646	HEXACHLOROCYCLO-PENTADIENE
SGAH L4BH	TU15 TE19	AT	2 (D/E)	V11		CV13 CV28	S9 S19	60	2647	MALONONITRILE
L4BH	TU15 TE19	AT	2 (D/E)			CV13 CV28	S9 S19	60	2648	1,2-DIBROMOBUTAN-3-ONE
SGAH L4BH	TU15 TE19	AT	2 (D/E)	V11		CV13 CV28	S9 S19	60	2649	1,3-DICHLOROACETONE

UN No.	Name and description	Class	Classifi-cation code	Packing group	Labels	Special provi-sions	Limited and excepted quantities		Packaging			Portable tanks and bulk containers	
									Packing instruc-tions	Special packing provisions	Mixed packing provisions	Instruc-tions	Special provisions
	3.1.2	2.2	2.2	2.1.1.3	5.2.2	3.3	3.4.6	3.5.1.2	4.1.4	4.1.4	4.1.10	4.2.5.2 7.3.2	4.2.5.3
(1)	(2)	(3a)	(3b)	(4)	(5)	(6)	(7a)	(7b)	(8)	(9a)	(9b)	(10)	(11)
2650	1,1-DICHLORO-1-NITROETHANE	6.1	T1	II	6.1		LQ17	E4	P001 IBC02		MP15	T7	TP2
2651	4,4'-DIAMINODIPHENYL-METHANE	6.1	T2	III	6.1		LQ9	E1	P002 IBC08 LP02 R001	B3	MP10	T1	TP33
2653	BENZYL IODIDE	6.1	T1	II	6.1		LQ17	E4	P001 IBC02		MP15	T7	TP2
2655	POTASSIUM FLUOROSILICATE	6.1	T5	III	6.1		LQ9	E1	P002 IBC08 LP02 R001	B3	MP10	T1	TP33
2656	QUINOLINE	6.1	T1	III	6.1		LQ7	E1	P001 IBC03 LP01 R001		MP19	T4	TP1
2657	SELENIUM DISULPHIDE	6.1	T5	II	6.1		LQ18	E4	P002 IBC08	B4	MP10	T3	TP33
2659	SODIUM CHLOROACETATE	6.1	T2	III	6.1		LQ9	E1	P002 IBC08 LP02 R001	B3	MP10	T1	TP33
2660	NITROTOLUIDINES (MONO)	6.1	T2	III	6.1		LQ9	E1	P002 IBC08 LP02 R001	B3	MP10	T1	TP33
2661	HEXACHLOROACETONE	6.1	T1	III	6.1		LQ7	E1	P001 IBC03 LP01 R001		MP19	T4	TP1
2664	DIBROMOMETHANE	6.1	T1	III	6.1		LQ7	E1	P001 IBC03 LP01 R001		MP19	T4	TP1
2667	BUTYLTOLUENES	6.1	T1	III	6.1		LQ7	E1	P001 IBC03 LP01 R001		MP19	T4	TP1
2668	CHLOROACETONITRILE	6.1	TF1	II	6.1 +3		LQ17	E4	P001 IBC02		MP15	T7	TP2
2669	CHLOROCRESOLS SOLUTION	6.1	T1	II	6.1		LQ17	E4	P001 IBC02		MP15	T7	TP2
2669	CHLOROCRESOLS SOLUTION	6.1	T1	III	6.1		LQ7	E1	P001 IBC03 LP01 R001		MP19	T7	TP2
2670	CYANURIC CHLORIDE	8	C4	II	8		LQ23	E2	P002 IBC08	B4	MP10	T3	TP33
2671	AMINOPYRIDINES (o-, m-, p-)	6.1	T2	II	6.1		LQ18	E4	P002 IBC08	B4	MP10	T3	TP33
2672	AMMONIA SOLUTION, relative density between 0.880 and 0.957 at 15 °C in water, with more than 10% but not more than 35% ammonia	8	C5	III	8	543	LQ7	E1	P001 IBC03 LP01 R001		MP19	T7	TP1
2673	2-AMINO-4-CHLOROPHENOL	6.1	T2	II	6.1		LQ18	E4	P002 IBC08	B4	MP10	T3	TP33
2674	SODIUM FLUOROSILICATE	6.1	T5	III	6.1		LQ9	E1	P002 IBC08 LP02 R001	B3	MP10	T1	TP33
2676	STIBINE	2	2TF		2.3 +2.1		LQ0	E0	P200		MP9		
2677	RUBIDIUM HYDROXIDE SOLUTION	8	C5	II	8		LQ22	E2	P001 IBC02		MP15	T7	TP2
2677	RUBIDIUM HYDROXIDE SOLUTION	8	C5	III	8		LQ7	E1	P001 IBC03 LP01 R001		MP19	T4	TP1
2678	RUBIDIUM HYDROXIDE	8	C6	II	8		LQ23	E2	P002 IBC08	B4	MP10	T3	TP33

ADR tank		Vehicle for tank carriage	Transport category (Tunnel restriction code)	Special provisions for carriage				Hazard identification No.	UN No.	Name and description
Tank code	Special provisions			Packages	Bulk	Loading, unloading and handling	Operation			
4.3	4.3.5, 6.8.4	9.1.1.2	1.1.3.6 (8.6)	7.2.4	7.3.3	7.5.11	8.5	5.3.2.3		3.1.2
(12)	(13)	(14)	(15)	(16)	(17)	(18)	(19)	(20)	(1)	(2)
L4BH	TU15 TE19	AT	2 (D/E)			CV13 CV28	S9 S19	60	2650	1,1-DICHLORO-1-NITROETHANE
SGAH L4BH	TU15 TE19	AT	2 (E)		VV9	CV13 CV28	S9	60	2651	4,4'-DIAMINODIPHENYL-METHANE
L4BH	TU15 TE19	AT	2 (D/E)			CV13 CV28	S9 S19	60	2653	BENZYL IODIDE
SGAH L4BH	TU15 TE19	AT	2 (E)		VV9	CV13 CV28	S9	60	2655	POTASSIUM FLUOROSILICATE
L4BH	TU15 TE19	AT	2 (E)			CV13 CV28	S9	60	2656	QUINOLINE
SGAH L4BH	TU15 TE19	AT	2 (D/E)	V11		CV13 CV28	S9 S19	60	2657	SELENIUM DISULPHIDE
SGAH	TU15 TE19	AT	2 (E)		VV9	CV13 CV28	S9	60	2659	SODIUM CHLOROACETATE
SGAH L4BH	TU15 TE19	AT	2 (E)		VV9	CV13 CV28	S9	60	2660	NITROTOLUIDINES (MONO)
L4BH	TU15 TE19	AT	2 (E)			CV13 CV28	S9	60	2661	HEXACHLOROACETONE
L4BH	TU15 TE19	AT	2 (E)			CV13 CV28	S9	60	2664	DIBROMOMETHANE
L4BH	TU15 TE19	AT	2 (E)			CV13 CV28	S9	60	2667	BUTYLTOLUENES
L4BH	TU15 TE19	FL	2 (D/E)			CV13 CV28	S2 S9 S19	63	2668	CHLOROACETONITRILE
L4BH	TU15 TE19	AT	2 (D/E)			CV13 CV28	S9 S19	60	2669	CHLOROCRESOLS SOLUTION
L4BH	TU15 TE19	AT	2 (E)			CV13 CV28	S9	60	2669	CHLOROCRESOLS SOLUTION
SGAN L4BN		AT	2 (E)	V11				80	2670	CYANURIC CHLORIDE
SGAH L4BH	TU15 TE19	AT	2 (D/E)	V11		CV13 CV28	S9 S19	60	2671	AMINOPYRIDINES (o-, m-, p-)
L4BN		AT	3 (E)					80	2672	AMMONIA SOLUTION, relative density between 0.880 and 0.957 at 15 °C in water, with more than 10% but not more than 35% ammonia
SGAH L4BH	TU15 TE19	AT	2 (D/E)	V11		CV13 CV28	S9 S19	60	2673	2-AMINO-4-CHLOROPHENOL
SGAH L4BH	TU15 TE19	AT	2 (E)		VV9	CV13 CV28	S9	60	2674	SODIUM FLUOROSILICATE
			1 (D)			CV9 CV10 CV36	S2 S14		2676	STIBINE
L4BN		AT	2 (E)					80	2677	RUBIDIUM HYDROXIDE SOLUTION
L4BN		AT	3 (E)					80	2677	RUBIDIUM HYDROXIDE SOLUTION
SGAN		AT	2 (E)	V11				80	2678	RUBIDIUM HYDROXIDE

UN No. 3.1.2	Name and description 3.1.2	Class 2.2	Classification code 2.2	Packing group 2.1.1.3	Labels 5.2.2	Special provisions 3.3	Limited and excepted quantities 3.4.6	3.5.1.2	Packaging Packing instructions 4.1.4	Special packing provisions 4.1.4	Mixed packing provisions 4.1.10	Portable tanks and bulk containers Instructions 4.2.5.2 7.3.2	Special provisions 4.2.5.3
(1)	(2)	(3a)	(3b)	(4)	(5)	(6)	(7a)	(7b)	(8)	(9a)	(9b)	(10)	(11)
2679	LITHIUM HYDROXIDE SOLUTION	8	C5	II	8		LQ22	E2	P001 IBC02		MP15	T7	TP2
2679	LITHIUM HYDROXIDE SOLUTION	8	C5	III	8		LQ7	E1	P001 IBC03 LP01 R001		MP19	T4	TP2
2680	LITHIUM HYDROXIDE	8	C6	II	8		LQ23	E2	P002 IBC08	B4	MP10	T3	TP33
2681	CAESIUM HYDROXIDE SOLUTION	8	C5	II	8		LQ22	E2	P001 IBC02		MP15	T7	TP2
2681	CAESIUM HYDROXIDE SOLUTION	8	C5	III	8		LQ7	E1	P001 IBC03 LP01 R001		MP19	T4	TP1
2682	CAESIUM HYDROXIDE	8	C6	II	8		LQ23	E2	P002 IBC08	B4	MP10	T3	TP33
2683	AMMONIUM SULPHIDE SOLUTION	8	CFT	II	8 +3 +6.1		LQ22	E2	P001 IBC01		MP15	T7	TP2
2684	3-DIETHYLAMINOPROPYL-AMINE	3	FC	III	3 +8		LQ7	E1	P001 IBC03 R001		MP19	T4	TP1
2685	N,N-DIETHYLETHYLENE-DIAMINE	8	CF1	II	8 +3		LQ22	E2	P001 IBC02		MP15	T7	TP2
2686	2-DIETHYLAMINO-ETHANOL	8	CF1	II	8 +3		LQ22	E2	P001 IBC02		MP15	T7	TP2
2687	DICYCLOHEXYL-AMMONIUM NITRITE	4.1	F3	III	4.1		LQ9	E1	P002 IBC08 LP02 R001	B3	MP11	T1	TP33
2688	1-BROMO-3-CHLOROPROPANE	6.1	T1	III	6.1		LQ7	E1	P001 IBC03 LP01 R001		MP19	T4	TP1
2689	GLYCEROL alpha-MONOCHLOROHYDRIN	6.1	T1	III	6.1		LQ7	E1	P001 IBC03 LP01 R001		MP19	T4	TP1
2690	N,n-BUTYLIMIDAZOLE	6.1	T1	II	6.1		LQ17	E4	P001 IBC02		MP15	T7	TP2
2691	PHOSPHORUS PENTABROMIDE	8	C2	II	8		LQ23	E2	P002 IBC08	B4	MP10	T3	TP33
2692	BORON TRIBROMIDE	8	C1	I	8		LQ0	E0	P602		MP8 MP17	T20	TP2
2693	BISULPHITES, AQUEOUS SOLUTION, N.O.S.	8	C1	III	8	274	LQ7	E1	P001 IBC03 LP01 R001		MP19	T7	TP1 TP28
2698	TETRAHYDROPHTHALIC ANHYDRIDES with more than 0.05% of maleic anhydride	8	C4	III	8	169	LQ24	E1	P002 IBC08 LP02 R001	PP14 B3	MP10	T1	TP33
2699	TRIFLUOROACETIC ACID	8	C3	I	8		LQ0	E0	P001		MP8 MP17	T10	TP2
2705	1-PENTOL	8	C9	II	8		LQ22	E2	P001 IBC02		MP15	T7	TP2
2707	DIMETHYLDIOXANES	3	F1	II	3		LQ4	E2	P001 IBC02 R001		MP19	T4	TP1
2707	DIMETHYLDIOXANES	3	F1	III	3		LQ7	E1	P001 IBC03 LP01 R001		MP19	T2	TP1
2709	BUTYLBENZENES	3	F1	III	3		LQ7	E1	P001 IBC03 LP01 R001		MP19	T2	TP1
2710	DIPROPYL KETONE	3	F1	III	3		LQ7	E1	P001 IBC03 LP01 R001		MP19	T2	TP1

ADR tank		Vehicle for tank carriage	Transport category (Tunnel restriction code)	Special provisions for carriage				Hazard identifi-cation No.	UN No.	Name and description
Tank code	Special provisions			Packages	Bulk	Loading, unloading and handling	Operation			
4.3	4.3.5, 6.8.4	9.1.1.2	1.1.3.6 (8.6)	7.2.4	7.3.3	7.5.11	8.5	5.3.2.3		3.1.2
(12)	(13)	(14)	(15)	(16)	(17)	(18)	(19)	(20)	(1)	(2)
L4BN		AT	2 (E)					80	2679	LITHIUM HYDROXIDE SOLUTION
L4BN		AT	3 (E)					80	2679	LITHIUM HYDROXIDE SOLUTION
SGAN		AT	2 (E)	V11				80	2680	LITHIUM HYDROXIDE
L4BN		AT	2 (E)					80	2681	CAESIUM HYDROXIDE SOLUTION
L4BN		AT	3 (E)					80	2681	CAESIUM HYDROXIDE SOLUTION
SGAN		AT	2 (E)	V11				80	2682	CAESIUM HYDROXIDE
L4BN		FL	2 (D/E)			CV13 CV28	S2	86	2683	AMMONIUM SULPHIDE SOLUTION
L4BN		FL	3 (D/E)				S2	38	2684	3-DIETHYLAMINOPROPYL-AMINE
L4BN		FL	2 (D/E)				S2	83	2685	N,N-DIETHYLETHYLENE-DIAMINE
L4BN		FL	2 (D/E)				S2	83	2686	2-DIETHYLAMINO-ETHANOL
SGAV		AT	3 (E)		VV1			40	2687	DICYCLOHEXYL-AMMONIUM NITRITE
L4BH	TU15 TE19	AT	2 (E)			CV13 CV28	S9	60	2688	1-BROMO-3-CHLOROPROPANE
L4BH	TU15 TE19	AT	2 (E)			CV13 CV28	S9	60	2689	GLYCEROL alpha-MONOCHLOROHYDRIN
L4BH	TU15 TE19	AT	2 (D/E)			CV13 CV28	S9 S19	60	2690	N,n-BUTYLIMIDAZOLE
SGAN		AT	2 (E)	V11				80	2691	PHOSPHORUS PENTABROMIDE
L10BH		AT	1 (E)				S20	X88	2692	BORON TRIBROMIDE
L4BN		AT	3 (E)					80	2693	BISULPHITES, AQUEOUS SOLUTION, N.O.S.
SGAV L4BN		AT	3 (E)		VV9			80	2698	TETRAHYDROPHTHALIC ANHYDRIDES with more than 0.05% of maleic anhydride
L10BH		AT	1 (E)				S20	88	2699	TRIFLUOROACETIC ACID
L4BN		AT	2 (E)					80	2705	1-PENTOL
LGBF		FL	2 (D/E)				S2 S20	33	2707	DIMETHYLDIOXANES
LGBF		FL	3 (D/E)				S2	30	2707	DIMETHYLDIOXANES
LGBF		FL	3 (D/E)				S2	30	2709	BUTYLBENZENES
LGBF		FL	3 (D/E)				S2	30	2710	DIPROPYL KETONE

UN No.	Name and description	Class	Classification code	Packing group	Labels	Special provisions	Limited and excepted quantities		Packaging			Portable tanks and bulk containers	
							quantities		Packing instructions	Special packing provisions	Mixed packing provisions	Instructions	Special provisions
	3.1.2	2.2	2.2	2.1.1.3	5.2.2	3.3	3.4.6	3.5.1.2	4.1.4	4.1.4	4.1.10	4.2.5.2 7.3.2	4.2.5.3
(1)	(2)	(3a)	(3b)	(4)	(5)	(6)	(7a)	(7b)	(8)	(9a)	(9b)	(10)	(11)
2713	ACRIDINE	6.1	T2	III	6.1		LQ9	E1	P002 IBC08 LP02 R001	B3	MP10	T1	TP33
2714	ZINC RESINATE	4.1	F3	III	4.1		LQ9	E1	P002 IBC06 R001		MP11	T1	TP33
2715	ALUMINIUM RESINATE	4.1	F3	III	4.1		LQ9	E1	P002 IBC06 R001		MP11	T1	TP33
2716	1,4-BUTYNEDIOL	6.1	T2	III	6.1		LQ9	E1	P002 IBC08 LP02 R001	B3	MP10	T1	TP33
2717	CAMPHOR, synthetic	4.1	F1	III	4.1		LQ9	E1	P002 IBC08 LP02 R001	B3	MP10	T1	TP33
2719	BARIUM BROMATE	5.1	OT2	II	5.1 +6.1		LQ11	E2	P002 IBC08	B4	MP2	T3	TP33
2720	CHROMIUM NITRATE	5.1	O2	III	5.1		LQ12	E1	P002 IBC08 LP02 R001	B3	MP10	T1	TP33
2721	COPPER CHLORATE	5.1	O2	II	5.1		LQ11	E2	P002 IBC08	B4	MP2	T3	TP33
2722	LITHIUM NITRATE	5.1	O2	III	5.1		LQ12	E1	P002 IBC08 LP02 R001	B3	MP10	T1	TP33
2723	MAGNESIUM CHLORATE	5.1	O2	II	5.1		LQ11	E2	P002 IBC08	B4	MP2	T3	TP33
2724	MANGANESE NITRATE	5.1	O2	III	5.1		LQ12	E1	P002 IBC08 LP02 R001	B3	MP10	T1	TP33
2725	NICKEL NITRATE	5.1	O2	III	5.1		LQ12	E1	P002 IBC08 LP02 R001	B3	MP10	T1	TP33
2726	NICKEL NITRITE	5.1	O2	III	5.1		LQ12	E1	P002 IBC08 LP02 R001	B3	MP10	T1	TP33
2727	THALLIUM NITRATE	6.1	TO2	II	6.1 +5.1		LQ18	E4	P002 IBC06		MP10	T3	TP33
2728	ZIRCONIUM NITRATE	5.1	O2	III	5.1		LQ12	E1	P002 IBC08 LP02 R001	B3	MP10	T1	TP33
2729	HEXACHLOROBENZENE	6.1	T2	III	6.1		LQ9	E1	P002 IBC08 LP02 R001	B3	MP10	T1	TP33
2730	NITROANISOLES, LIQUID	6.1	T1	III	6.1	279	LQ7	E1	P001 IBC03 LP01 R001		MP19	T4	TP1
2732	NITROBROMOBENZENES, LIQUID	6.1	T1	III	6.1		LQ7	E1	P001 IBC03 LP01 R001		MP19	T4	TP1
2733	AMINES, FLAMMABLE, CORROSIVE, N.O.S. or POLYAMINES, FLAMMABLE, CORROSIVE, N.O.S.	3	FC	I	3 +8	274 544	LQ3	E0	P001		MP7 MP17	T14	TP1 TP27
2733	AMINES, FLAMMABLE, CORROSIVE, N.O.S. or POLYAMINES, FLAMMABLE, CORROSIVE, N.O.S.	3	FC	II	3 +8	274 544	LQ4	E2	P001 IBC02		MP19	T11	TP1 TP27

ADR tank		Vehicle for tank carriage	Transport category (Tunnel restriction code)	Special provisions for carriage				Hazard identification No.	UN No.	Name and description
Tank code	Special provisions			Packages	Bulk	Loading, unloading and handling	Operation			
4.3	4.3.5, 6.8.4	9.1.1.2	1.1.3.6 (8.6)	7.2.4	7.3.3	7.5.11	8.5	5.3.2.3		3.1.2
(12)	(13)	(14)	(15)	(16)	(17)	(18)	(19)	(20)	(1)	(2)
SGAH L4BH	TU15 TE19	AT	2 (E)		VV9	CV13 CV28	S9	60	2713	ACRIDINE
SGAV		AT	3 (E)	V12	VV1			40	2714	ZINC RESINATE
SGAV		AT	3 (E)	V12	VV1			40	2715	ALUMINIUM RESINATE
SGAH L4BH	TU15 TE19	AT	2 (E)		VV9	CV13 CV28	S9	60	2716	1,4-BUTYNEDIOL
SGAV		AT	3 (E)		VV1			40	2717	CAMPHOR, synthetic
SGAN	TU3	AT	2 (E)	V11		CV24 CV28		56	2719	BARIUM BROMATE
SGAV	TU3	AT	3 (E)		VV8	CV24		50	2720	CHROMIUM NITRATE
SGAV	TU3	AT	2 (E)	V11	VV8	CV24		50	2721	COPPER CHLORATE
SGAV	TU3	AT	3 (E)		VV8	CV24		50	2722	LITHIUM NITRATE
SGAV	TU3	AT	2 (E)	V11	VV8	CV24		50	2723	MAGNESIUM CHLORATE
SGAV	TU3	AT	3 (E)		VV8	CV24		50	2724	MANGANESE NITRATE
SGAV	TU3	AT	3 (E)		VV8	CV24		50	2725	NICKEL NITRATE
SGAV	TU3	AT	3 (E)		VV8	CV24		50	2726	NICKEL NITRITE
SGAH	TU15 TE19	AT	2 (D/E)	V11 V12		CV13 CV28	S9 S19	65	2727	THALLIUM NITRATE
SGAV	TU3	AT	3 (E)		VV8	CV24		50	2728	ZIRCONIUM NITRATE
SGAH	TU15 TE19	AT	2 (E)		VV9	CV13 CV28	S9	60	2729	HEXACHLOROBENZENE
L4BH	TU15 TE19	AT	2 (E)			CV13 CV28	S9	60	2730	NITROANISOLES, LIQUID
L4BH	TU15 TE19	AT	2 (E)			CV13 CV28	S9	60	2732	NITROBROMOBENZENES, LIQUID
L10CH	TU14 TE21	FL	1 (C/E)				S2 S20	338	2733	AMINES, FLAMMABLE, CORROSIVE, N.O.S. or POLYAMINES, FLAMMABLE, CORROSIVE, N.O.S.
L4BH		FL	2 (D/E)				S2 S20	338	2733	AMINES, FLAMMABLE, CORROSIVE, N.O.S. or POLYAMINES, FLAMMABLE, CORROSIVE, N.O.S.

UN No. 3.1.2	Name and description 3.1.2	Class 2.2	Classification code 2.2	Packing group 2.1.1.3	Labels 5.2.2	Special provisions 3.3	Limited and excepted quantities 3.4.6	3.5.1.2	Packing instructions 4.1.4	Special packing provisions 4.1.4	Mixed packing provisions 4.1.10	Portable tanks and bulk containers Instructions 4.2.5.2 7.3.2	Special provisions 4.2.5.3
(1)	(2)	(3a)	(3b)	(4)	(5)	(6)	(7a)	(7b)	(8)	(9a)	(9b)	(10)	(11)
2733	AMINES, FLAMMABLE, CORROSIVE, N.O.S. or POLYAMINES, FLAMMABLE, CORROSIVE, N.O.S.	3	FC	III	3 +8	274 544	LQ7	E1	P001 IBC03 R001		MP19	T7	TP1 TP28
2734	AMINES, LIQUID, CORROSIVE, FLAMMABLE, N.O.S. or POLYAMINES, LIQUID, CORROSIVE, FLAMMABLE, N.O.S.	8	CF1	I	8 +3	274	LQ0	E0	P001		MP8 MP17	T14	TP2 TP27
2734	AMINES, LIQUID, CORROSIVE, FLAMMABLE, N.O.S. or POLYAMINES, LIQUID, CORROSIVE, FLAMMABLE, N.O.S.	8	CF1	II	8 +3	274	LQ22	E2	P001 IBC02		MP15	T11	TP2 TP27
2735	AMINES, LIQUID, CORROSIVE, N.O.S. or POLYAMINES, LIQUID, CORROSIVE, N.O.S.	8	C7	I	8	274	LQ0	E0	P001		MP8 MP17	T14	TP2 TP27
2735	AMINES, LIQUID, CORROSIVE, N.O.S. or POLYAMINES, LIQUID, CORROSIVE, N.O.S.	8	C7	II	8	274	LQ22	E2	P001 IBC02		MP15	T11	TP1 TP27
2735	AMINES, LIQUID, CORROSIVE, N.O.S. or POLYAMINES, LIQUID, CORROSIVE, N.O.S.	8	C7	III	8	274	LQ7	E1	P001 IBC03 LP01 R001		MP19	T7	TP1 TP28
2738	N-BUTYLANILINE	6.1	T1	II	6.1		LQ17	E4	P001 IBC02		MP15	T7	TP2
2739	BUTYRIC ANHYDRIDE	8	C3	III	8		LQ7	E1	P001 IBC03 LP01 R001		MP19	T4	TP1
2740	n-PROPYL CHLOROFORMATE	6.1	TFC	I	6.1 +3 +8		LQ0	E5	P602		MP8 MP17	T20	TP2
2741	BARIUM HYPOCHLORITE with more than 22% available chlorine	5.1	OT2	II	5.1 +6.1		LQ11	E2	P002 IBC08	B4	MP2	T3	TP33
2742	CHLOROFORMATES, TOXIC, CORROSIVE, FLAMMABLE, N.O.S.	6.1	TFC	II	6.1 +3 +8	274 561	LQ17	E4	P001 IBC01		MP15		
2743	n-BUTYL CHLOROFORMATE	6.1	TFC	II	6.1 +3 +8		LQ17	E4	P001		MP15	T20	TP2
2744	CYCLOBUTYL CHLOROFORMATE	6.1	TFC	II	6.1 +3 +8		LQ17	E4	P001 IBC01		MP15	T7	TP2
2745	CHLOROMETHYL CHLOROFORMATE	6.1	TC1	II	6.1 +8		LQ17	E4	P001 IBC02		MP15	T7	TP2
2746	PHENYL CHLOROFORMATE	6.1	TC1	II	6.1 +8		LQ17	E4	P001 IBC02		MP15	T7	TP2
2747	tert-BUTYLCYCLOHEXYL CHLOROFORMATE	6.1	T1	III	6.1		LQ7	E1	P001 IBC03 LP01 R001		MP19	T4	TP1
2748	2-ETHYLHEXYL CHLOROFORMATE	6.1	TC1	II	6.1 +8		LQ17	E4	P001 IBC02		MP15	T7	TP2
2749	TETRAMETHYLSILANE	3	F1	I	3		LQ3	E3	P001		MP7 MP17	T14	TP2
2750	1,3-DICHLOROPROPANOL-2	6.1	T1	II	6.1		LQ17	E4	P001 IBC02		MP15	T7	TP2
2751	DIETHYLTHIO-PHOSPHORYL CHLORIDE	8	C3	II	8		LQ22	E2	P001 IBC02		MP15	T7	TP2
2752	1,2-EPOXY-3-ETHOXYPROPANE	3	F1	III	3		LQ7	E1	P001 IBC03 LP01 R001		MP19	T2	TP1
2753	N-ETHYLBENZYL-TOLUIDINES, LIQUID	6.1	T1	III	6.1		LQ7	E1	P001 IBC03 LP01 R001		MP19	T7	TP1

- 456 -

ADR tank		Vehicle for tank carriage	Transport category (Tunnel restriction code)	Special provisions for carriage				Hazard identifi-cation No.	UN No.	Name and description
Tank code	Special provisions			Packages	Bulk	Loading, unloading and handling	Operation			
4.3	4.3.5, 6.8.4	9.1.1.2	1.1.3.6 (8.6)	7.2.4	7.3.3	7.5.11	8.5	5.3.2.3		3.1.2
(12)	(13)	(14)	(15)	(16)	(17)	(18)	(19)	(20)	(1)	(2)
L4BN		FL	3 (D/E)				S2	38	2733	AMINES, FLAMMABLE, CORROSIVE, N.O.S. or POLYAMINES, FLAMMABLE, CORROSIVE, N.O.S.
L10BH		FL	1 (D/E)				S2 S14	883	2734	AMINES, LIQUID, CORROSIVE, FLAMMABLE, N.O.S. or POLYAMINES, LIQUID, CORROSIVE, FLAMMABLE, N.O.S.
L4BN		FL	2 (D/E)				S2	83	2734	AMINES, LIQUID, CORROSIVE, FLAMMABLE, N.O.S. or POLYAMINES, LIQUID, CORROSIVE, FLAMMABLE, N.O.S.
L10BH		AT	1 (E)				S20	88	2735	AMINES, LIQUID, CORROSIVE, N.O.S. or POLYAMINES, LIQUID, CORROSIVE, N.O.S.
L4BN		AT	2 (E)					80	2735	AMINES, LIQUID, CORROSIVE, N.O.S. or POLYAMINES, LIQUID, CORROSIVE, N.O.S.
L4BN		AT	3 (E)					80	2735	AMINES, LIQUID, CORROSIVE, N.O.S. or POLYAMINES, LIQUID, CORROSIVE, N.O.S.
L4BH	TU15 TE19	AT	2 (D/E)			CV13 CV28	S9 S19	60	2738	N-BUTYLANILINE
L4BN		AT	3 (E)					80	2739	BUTYRIC ANHYDRIDE
L10CH	TU14 TU15 TE19 TE21	FL	1 (C/D)			CV1 CV13 CV28	S2 S9 S14	668	2740	n-PROPYL CHLOROFORMATE
SGAN	TU3	AT	2 (E)	V11		CV24 CV28		56	2741	BARIUM HYPOCHLORITE with more than 22% available chlorine
L4BH	TU15 TE19	FL	2 (D/E)			CV13 CV28	S2 S9 S19	638	2742	CHLOROFORMATES, TOXIC, CORROSIVE, FLAMMABLE, N.O.S.
L4BH	TU15 TE19	FL	2 (D/E)			CV13 CV28	S2 S9 S19	638	2743	n-BUTYL CHLOROFORMATE
L4BH	TU15 TE19	FL	2 (D/E)			CV13 CV28	S2 S9 S19	638	2744	CYCLOBUTYL CHLOROFORMATE
L4BH	TU15 TE19	AT	2 (D/E)			CV13 CV28	S9 S19	68	2745	CHLOROMETHYL CHLOROFORMATE
L4BH	TU15 TE19	AT	2 (D/E)			CV13 CV28	S9 S19	68	2746	PHENYL CHLOROFORMATE
L4BH	TU15 TE19	AT	2 (E)			CV13 CV28	S9	60	2747	tert-BUTYLCYCLOHEXYL CHLOROFORMATE
L4BH	TU15 TE19	AT	2 (D/E)			CV13 CV28	S9 S19	68	2748	2-ETHYLHEXYL CHLOROFORMATE
L4BN		FL	1 (D/E)				S2 S20	33	2749	TETRAMETHYLSILANE
L4BH	TU15 TE19	AT	2 (D/E)			CV13 CV28	S9 S19	60	2750	1,3-DICHLOROPROPANOL-2
L4BN		AT	2 (E)					80	2751	DIETHYLTHIO-PHOSPHORYL CHLORIDE
LGBF		FL	3 (D/E)				S2	30	2752	1,2-EPOXY-3-ETHOXYPROPANE
L4BH	TU15 TE19	AT	2 (E)			CV13 CV28	S9	60	2753	N-ETHYLBENZYL-TOLUIDINES, LIQUID

UN No.	Name and description	Class	Classification code	Packing group	Labels	Special provisions	Limited and excepted quantities		Packaging			Portable tanks and bulk containers	
									Packing instructions	Special packing provisions	Mixed packing provisions	Instructions	Special provisions
	3.1.2	2.2	2.2	2.1.1.3	5.2.2	3.3	3.4.6	3.5.1.2	4.1.4	4.1.4	4.1.10	4.2.5.2 7.3.2	4.2.5.3
(1)	(2)	(3a)	(3b)	(4)	(5)	(6)	(7a)	(7b)	(8)	(9a)	(9b)	(10)	(11)
2754	N-ETHYLTOLUIDINES	6.1	T1	II	6.1		LQ17	E4	P001 IBC02		MP15	T7	TP2
2757	CARBAMATE PESTICIDE, SOLID, TOXIC	6.1	T7	I	6.1	61 274 648	LQ0	E5	P002 IBC07		MP18	T6	TP33
2757	CARBAMATE PESTICIDE, SOLID, TOXIC	6.1	T7	II	6.1	61 274 648	LQ18	E4	P002 IBC08	B4	MP10	T3	TP33
2757	CARBAMATE PESTICIDE, SOLID, TOXIC	6.1	T7	III	6.1	61 274 648	LQ9	E1	P002 IBC08 LP02 R001	B3	MP10	T1	TP33
2758	CARBAMATE PESTICIDE, LIQUID, FLAMMABLE, TOXIC, flash-point less than 23 °C	3	FT2	I	3 +6.1	61 274	LQ3	E0	P001		MP7 MP17	T14	TP2 TP27
2758	CARBAMATE PESTICIDE, LIQUID, FLAMMABLE, TOXIC, flash-point less than 23 °C	3	FT2	II	3 +6.1	61 274	LQ4	E2	P001 IBC02 R001		MP19	T11	TP2 TP27
2759	ARSENICAL PESTICIDE, SOLID, TOXIC	6.1	T7	I	6.1	61 274 648	LQ0	E5	P002 IBC07		MP18	T6	TP33
2759	ARSENICAL PESTICIDE, SOLID, TOXIC	6.1	T7	II	6.1	61 274 648	LQ18	E4	P002 IBC08	B4	MP10	T3	TP33
2759	ARSENICAL PESTICIDE, SOLID, TOXIC	6.1	T7	III	6.1	61 274 648	LQ9	E1	P002 IBC08 LP02 R001	B3	MP10	T1	TP33
2760	ARSENICAL PESTICIDE, LIQUID, FLAMMABLE, TOXIC, flash-point less than 23 °C	3	FT2	I	3 +6.1	61 274	LQ3	E0	P001		MP7 MP17	T14	TP2 TP27
2760	ARSENICAL PESTICIDE, LIQUID, FLAMMABLE, TOXIC, flash-point less than 23 °C	3	FT2	II	3 +6.1	61 274	LQ4	E2	P001 IBC02 R001		MP19	T11	TP2 TP27
2761	ORGANOCHLORINE PESTICIDE, SOLID, TOXIC	6.1	T7	I	6.1	61 274 648	LQ0	E5	P002 IBC07		MP18	T6	TP33
2761	ORGANOCHLORINE PESTICIDE, SOLID, TOXIC	6.1	T7	II	6.1	61 274 648	LQ18	E4	P002 IBC08	B4	MP10	T3	TP33
2761	ORGANOCHLORINE PESTICIDE, SOLID, TOXIC	6.1	T7	III	6.1	61 274 648	LQ9	E1	P002 IBC08 LP02 R001	B3	MP10	T1	TP33
2762	ORGANOCHLORINE PESTICIDE, LIQUID, FLAMMABLE, TOXIC, flash-point less than 23 °C	3	FT2	I	3 +6.1	61 274	LQ3	E0	P001		MP7 MP17	T14	TP2 TP27
2762	ORGANOCHLORINE PESTICIDE, LIQUID, FLAMMABLE, TOXIC, flash-point less than 23 °C	3	FT2	II	3 +6.1	61 274	LQ4	E2	P001 IBC02 R001		MP19	T11	TP2 TP27
2763	TRIAZINE PESTICIDE, SOLID, TOXIC	6.1	T7	I	6.1	61 274 648	LQ0	E5	P002 IBC07		MP18	T6	TP33
2763	TRIAZINE PESTICIDE, SOLID, TOXIC	6.1	T7	II	6.1	61 274 648	LQ18	E4	P002 IBC08	B4	MP10	T3	TP33
2763	TRIAZINE PESTICIDE, SOLID, TOXIC	6.1	T7	III	6.1	61 274 648	LQ9	E1	P002 IBC08 R001	B3	MP10	T1	TP33
2764	TRIAZINE PESTICIDE, LIQUID, FLAMMABLE, TOXIC, flash-point less than 23 °C	3	FT2	I	3 +6.1	61 274	LQ3	E0	P001		MP7 MP17	T14	TP2 TP27

ADR tank		Vehicle for tank carriage	Transport category (Tunnel restriction code)	Special provisions for carriage				Hazard identifi- cation No.	UN No.	Name and description
Tank code	Special provisions			Packages	Bulk	Loading, unloading and handling	Operation			
4.3	4.3.5, 6.8.4	9.1.1.2	1.1.3.6 (8.6)	7.2.4	7.3.3	7.5.11	8.5	5.3.2.3		3.1.2
(12)	(13)	(14)	(15)	(16)	(17)	(18)	(19)	(20)	(1)	(2)
L4BH	TU15 TE19	AT	2 (D/E)			CV13 CV28	S9 S19	60	2754	N-ETHYLTOLUIDINES
S10AH L10CH	TU14 TU15 TE19 TE21	AT	1 (C/E)	V10 V12		CV1 CV13 CV28	S9 S14	66	2757	CARBAMATE PESTICIDE, SOLID, TOXIC
SGAH L4BH	TU15 TE19	AT	2 (D/E)	V11		CV13 CV28	S9 S19	60	2757	CARBAMATE PESTICIDE, SOLID, TOXIC
SGAH L4BH	TU15 TE19	AT	2 (E)		VV9	CV13 CV28	S9	60	2757	CARBAMATE PESTICIDE, SOLID, TOXIC
L10CH	TU14 TU15 TE21	FL	1 (C/E)			CV13 CV28	S2 S22	336	2758	CARBAMATE PESTICIDE, LIQUID, FLAMMABLE, TOXIC, flash-point less than 23 °C
L4BH	TU15	FL	2 (D/E)			CV13 CV28	S2 S22	336	2758	CARBAMATE PESTICIDE, LIQUID, FLAMMABLE, TOXIC, flash-point less than 23 °C
S10AH L10CH	TU14 TU15 TE19 TE21	AT	1 (C/E)	V10 V12		CV1 CV13 CV28	S9 S14	66	2759	ARSENICAL PESTICIDE, SOLID, TOXIC
SGAH L4BH	TU15 TE19	AT	2 (D/E)	V11		CV13 CV28	S9 S19	60	2759	ARSENICAL PESTICIDE, SOLID, TOXIC
SGAH L4BH	TU15 TE19	AT	2 (E)		VV9	CV13 CV28	S9	60	2759	ARSENICAL PESTICIDE, SOLID, TOXIC
L10CH	TU14 TU15 TE21	FL	1 (C/E)			CV13 CV28	S2 S22	336	2760	ARSENICAL PESTICIDE, LIQUID, FLAMMABLE, TOXIC, flash-point less than 23 °C
L4BH	TU15	FL	2 (D/E)			CV13 CV28	S2 S22	336	2760	ARSENICAL PESTICIDE, LIQUID, FLAMMABLE, TOXIC, flash-point less than 23 °C
S10AH L10CH	TU14 TU15 TE19 TE21	AT	1 (C/E)	V10 V12		CV1 CV13 CV28	S9 S14	66	2761	ORGANOCHLORINE PESTICIDE, SOLID, TOXIC
SGAH L4BH	TU15 TE19	AT	2 (D/E)	V11		CV13 CV28	S9 S19	60	2761	ORGANOCHLORINE PESTICIDE, SOLID, TOXIC
SGAH L4BH	TU15 TE19	AT	2 (E)		VV9	CV13 CV28	S9	60	2761	ORGANOCHLORINE PESTICIDE, SOLID, TOXIC
L10CH	TU14 TU15 TE21	FL	1 (C/E)			CV13 CV28	S2 S22	336	2762	ORGANOCHLORINE PESTICIDE, LIQUID, FLAMMABLE, TOXIC, flash-point less than 23 °C
L4BH	TU15	FL	2 (D/E)			CV13 CV28	S2 S22	336	2762	ORGANOCHLORINE PESTICIDE, LIQUID, FLAMMABLE, TOXIC, flash-point less than 23 °C
S10AH L10CH	TU14 TU15 TE19 TE21	AT	1 (C/E)	V10 V12		CV1 CV13 CV28	S9 S14	66	2763	TRIAZINE PESTICIDE, SOLID, TOXIC
SGAH L4BH	TU15 TE19	AT	2 (D/E)	V11		CV13 CV28	S9 S19	60	2763	TRIAZINE PESTICIDE, SOLID, TOXIC
SGAH L4BH	TU15 TE19	AT	2 (E)		VV9	CV13 CV28	S9	60	2763	TRIAZINE PESTICIDE, SOLID, TOXIC
L10CH	TU14 TU15 TE21	FL	1 (C/E)			CV13 CV28	S2 S22	336	2764	TRIAZINE PESTICIDE, LIQUID, FLAMMABLE, TOXIC, flash-point less than 23 °C

UN No.	Name and description	Class	Classification code	Packing group	Labels	Special provisions	Limited and excepted quantities		Packaging			Portable tanks and bulk containers	
									Packing instructions	Special packing provisions	Mixed packing provisions	Instructions	Special provisions
	3.1.2	2.2	2.2	2.1.1.3	5.2.2	3.3	3.4.6	3.5.1.2	4.1.4	4.1.4	4.1.10	4.2.5.2 7.3.2	4.2.5.3
(1)	(2)	(3a)	(3b)	(4)	(5)	(6)	(7a)	(7b)	(8)	(9a)	(9b)	(10)	(11)
2764	TRIAZINE PESTICIDE, LIQUID, FLAMMABLE, TOXIC, flash-point less than 23 °C	3	FT2	II	3 +6.1	61 274	LQ4	E2	P001 IBC02 R001		MP19	T11	TP2 TP27
2771	THIOCARBAMATE PESTICIDE, SOLID, TOXIC	6.1	T7	I	6.1	61 274 648	LQ0	E5	P002 IBC07		MP18	T6	TP33
2771	THIOCARBAMATE PESTICIDE, SOLID, TOXIC	6.1	T7	II	6.1	61 274 648	LQ18	E4	P002 IBC08	B4	MP10	T3	TP33
2771	THIOCARBAMATE PESTICIDE, SOLID, TOXIC	6.1	T7	III	6.1	61 274 648	LQ9	E1	P002 IBC08 LP02 R001	B3	MP10	T1	TP33
2772	THIOCARBAMATE PESTICIDE, LIQUID, FLAMMABLE, TOXIC, flash-point less than 23 °C	3	FT2	I	3 +6.1	61 274	LQ3	E0	P001		MP7 MP17	T14	TP2 TP27
2772	THIOCARBAMATE PESTICIDE, LIQUID, FLAMMABLE, TOXIC, flash-point less than 23 °C	3	FT2	II	3 +6.1	61 274	LQ4	E2	P001 IBC02 R001		MP19	T11	TP2 TP27
2775	COPPER BASED PESTICIDE, SOLID, TOXIC	6.1	T7	I	6.1	61 274 648	LQ0	E5	P002 IBC07		MP18	T6	TP33
2775	COPPER BASED PESTICIDE, SOLID, TOXIC	6.1	T7	II	6.1	61 274 648	LQ18	E4	P002 IBC08	B4	MP10	T3	TP33
2775	COPPER BASED PESTICIDE, SOLID, TOXIC	6.1	T7	III	6.1	61 274 648	LQ9	E1	P002 IBC08 LP02 R001	B3	MP10	T1	TP33
2776	COPPER BASED PESTICIDE, LIQUID, FLAMMABLE, TOXIC, flash-point less than 23 °C	3	FT2	I	3 +6.1	61 274	LQ3	E0	P001		MP7 MP17	T14	TP2 TP27
2776	COPPER BASED PESTICIDE, LIQUID, FLAMMABLE, TOXIC, flash-point less than 23 °C	3	FT2	II	3 +6.1	61 274	LQ4	E2	P001 IBC02 R001		MP19	T11	TP2 TP27
2777	MERCURY BASED PESTICIDE, SOLID, TOXIC	6.1	T7	I	6.1	61 274 648	LQ0	E5	P002 IBC07		MP18	T6	TP33
2777	MERCURY BASED PESTICIDE, SOLID, TOXIC	6.1	T7	II	6.1	61 274 648	LQ18	E4	P002 IBC08	B4	MP10	T3	TP33
2777	MERCURY BASED PESTICIDE, SOLID, TOXIC	6.1	T7	III	6.1	61 274 648	LQ9	E1	P002 IBC08 LP02 R001	B3	MP10	T1	TP33
2778	MERCURY BASED PESTICIDE, LIQUID, FLAMMABLE, TOXIC, flash-point less than 23 °C	3	FT2	I	3 +6.1	61 274	LQ3	E0	P001		MP7 MP17	T14	TP2 TP27
2778	MERCURY BASED PESTICIDE, LIQUID, FLAMMABLE, TOXIC, flash-point less than 23 °C	3	FT2	II	3 +6.1	61 274	LQ4	E2	P001 IBC02 R001		MP19	T11	TP2 TP27
2779	SUBSTITUTED NITROPHENOL PESTICIDE, SOLID, TOXIC	6.1	T7	I	6.1	61 274 648	LQ0	E5	P002 IBC07		MP18	T6	TP33
2779	SUBSTITUTED NITROPHENOL PESTICIDE, SOLID, TOXIC	6.1	T7	II	6.1	61 274 648	LQ18	E4	P002 IBC08	B4	MP10	T3	TP33
2779	SUBSTITUTED NITROPHENOL PESTICIDE, SOLID, TOXIC	6.1	T7	III	6.1	61 274 648	LQ9	E1	P002 IBC08 LP02 R001	B3	MP10	T1	TP33

ADR tank		Vehicle for tank carriage	Transport category (Tunnel restriction code)	Special provisions for carriage				Hazard identifi-cation No.	UN No.	Name and description
Tank code	Special provisions			Packages	Bulk	Loading, unloading and handling	Operation			
4.3	4.3.5, 6.8.4	9.1.1.2	1.1.3.6 (8.6)	7.2.4	7.3.3	7.5.11	8.5	5.3.2.3		3.1.2
(12)	(13)	(14)	(15)	(16)	(17)	(18)	(19)	(20)	(1)	(2)
L4BH	TU15	FL	2 (D/E)			CV13 CV28	S2 S22	336	2764	TRIAZINE PESTICIDE, LIQUID, FLAMMABLE, TOXIC, flash-point less than 23 °C
S10AH L10CH	TU14 TU15 TE19 TE21	AT	1 (C/E)	V10 V12		CV1 CV13 CV28	S9 S14	66	2771	THIOCARBAMATE PESTICIDE, SOLID, TOXIC
SGAH L4BH	TU15 TE19	AT	2 (D/E)	V11		CV13 CV28	S9 S19	60	2771	THIOCARBAMATE PESTICIDE, SOLID, TOXIC
SGAH L4BH	TU15 TE19	AT	2 (E)		VV9	CV13 CV28	S9	60	2771	THIOCARBAMATE PESTICIDE, SOLID, TOXIC
L10CH	TU14 TU15 TE21	FL	1 (C/E)			CV13 CV28	S2 S22	336	2772	THIOCARBAMATE PESTICIDE, LIQUID, FLAMMABLE, TOXIC, flash-point less than 23 °C
L4BH	TU15	FL	2 (D/E)			CV13 CV28	S2 S22	336	2772	THIOCARBAMATE PESTICIDE, LIQUID, FLAMMABLE, TOXIC, flash-point less than 23 °C
S10AH L10CH	TU14 TU15 TE19 TE21	AT	1 (C/E)	V10 V12		CV1 CV13 CV28	S9 S14	66	2775	COPPER BASED PESTICIDE, SOLID, TOXIC
SGAH L4BH	TU15 TE19	AT	2 (D/E)	V11		CV13 CV28	S9 S19	60	2775	COPPER BASED PESTICIDE, SOLID, TOXIC
SGAH L4BH	TU15 TE19	AT	2 (E)		VV9	CV13 CV28	S9	60	2775	COPPER BASED PESTICIDE, SOLID, TOXIC
L10CH	TU14 TU15 TE21	FL	1 (C/E)			CV13 CV28	S2 S22	336	2776	COPPER BASED PESTICIDE, LIQUID, FLAMMABLE, TOXIC, flash-point less than 23 °C
L4BH	TU15	FL	2 (D/E)			CV13 CV28	S2 S22	336	2776	COPPER BASED PESTICIDE, LIQUID, FLAMMABLE, TOXIC, flash-point less than 23 °C
S10AH L10CH	TU14 TU15 TE19 TE21	AT	1 (C/E)	V10 V12		CV1 CV13 CV28	S9 S14	66	2777	MERCURY BASED PESTICIDE, SOLID, TOXIC
SGAH L4BH	TU15 TE19	AT	2 (D/E)	V11		CV13 CV28	S9 S19	60	2777	MERCURY BASED PESTICIDE, SOLID, TOXIC
SGAH L4BH	TU15 TE19	AT	2 (E)		VV9	CV13 CV28	S9	60	2777	MERCURY BASED PESTICIDE, SOLID, TOXIC
L10CH	TU14 TU15 TE21	FL	1 (C/E)			CV13 CV28	S2 S22	336	2778	MERCURY BASED PESTICIDE, LIQUID, FLAMMABLE, TOXIC, flash-point less than 23 °C
L4BH	TU15	FL	2 (D/E)			CV13 CV28	S2 S22	336	2778	MERCURY BASED PESTICIDE, LIQUID, FLAMMABLE, TOXIC, flash-point less than 23 °C
S10AH L10CH	TU14 TU15 TE19 TE21	AT	1 (C/E)	V10 V12		CV1 CV13 CV28	S9 S14	66	2779	SUBSTITUTED NITROPHENOL PESTICIDE, SOLID, TOXIC
SGAH L4BH	TU15 TE19	AT	2 (D/E)	V11		CV13 CV28	S9 S19	60	2779	SUBSTITUTED NITROPHENOL PESTICIDE, SOLID, TOXIC
SGAH L4BH	TU15 TE19	AT	2 (E)		VV9	CV13 CV28	S9	60	2779	SUBSTITUTED NITROPHENOL PESTICIDE, SOLID, TOXIC

UN No.	Name and description	Class	Classification code	Packing group	Labels	Special provisions	Limited and excepted quantities		Packaging			Portable tanks and bulk containers	
									Packing instructions	Special packing provisions	Mixed packing provisions	Instructions	Special provisions
	3.1.2	2.2	2.2	2.1.1.3	5.2.2	3.3	3.4.6	3.5.1.2	4.1.4	4.1.4	4.1.10	4.2.5.2 7.3.2	4.2.5.3
(1)	(2)	(3a)	(3b)	(4)	(5)	(6)	(7a)	(7b)	(8)	(9a)	(9b)	(10)	(11)
2780	SUBSTITUTED NITROPHENOL PESTICIDE, LIQUID, FLAMMABLE, TOXIC, flash-point less than 23 °C	3	FT2	I	3 +6.1	61 274	LQ3	E0	P001		MP7 MP17	T14	TP2 TP27
2780	SUBSTITUTED NITROPHENOL PESTICIDE, LIQUID, FLAMMABLE, TOXIC, flash-point less than 23 °C	3	FT2	II	3 +6.1	61 274	LQ4	E2	P001 IBC02 R001		MP19	T11	TP2 TP27
2781	BIPYRIDILIUM PESTICIDE, SOLID, TOXIC	6.1	T7	I	6.1	61 274 648	LQ0	E5	P002 IBC07		MP18	T6	TP33
2781	BIPYRIDILIUM PESTICIDE, SOLID, TOXIC	6.1	T7	II	6.1	61 274 648	LQ18	E4	P002 IBC08	B4	MP10	T3	TP33
2781	BIPYRIDILIUM PESTICIDE, SOLID, TOXIC	6.1	T7	III	6.1	61 274 648	LQ9	E1	P002 IBC08 LP02 R001	B3	MP10	T1	TP33
2782	BIPYRIDILIUM PESTICIDE, LIQUID, FLAMMABLE, TOXIC, flash-point less than 23 °C	3	FT2	I	3 +6.1	61 274	LQ3	E0	P001		MP7 MP17	T14	TP2 TP27
2782	BIPYRIDILIUM PESTICIDE, LIQUID, FLAMMABLE, TOXIC, flash-point less than 23 °C	3	FT2	II	3 +6.1	61 274	LQ4	E2	P001 IBC02 R001		MP19	T11	TP2 TP27
2783	ORGANOPHOSPHORUS PESTICIDE, SOLID, TOXIC	6.1	T7	I	6.1	61 274 648	LQ0	E5	P002 IBC07		MP18	T6	TP33
2783	ORGANOPHOSPHORUS PESTICIDE, SOLID, TOXIC	6.1	T7	II	6.1	61 274 648	LQ18	E4	P002 IBC08	B4	MP10	T3	TP33
2783	ORGANOPHOSPHORUS PESTICIDE, SOLID, TOXIC	6.1	T7	III	6.1	61 274 648	LQ9	E1	P002 IBC08 LP02 R001	B3	MP10	T1	TP33
2784	ORGANOPHOSPHORUS PESTICIDE, LIQUID, FLAMMABLE, TOXIC, flash-point less than 23 °C	3	FT2	I	3 +6.1	61 274	LQ3	E0	P001		MP7 MP17	T14	TP2 TP27
2784	ORGANOPHOSPHORUS PESTICIDE, LIQUID, FLAMMABLE, TOXIC, flash-point less than 23 °C	3	FT2	II	3 +6.1	61 274	LQ4	E2	P001 IBC02 R001		MP19	T11	TP2 TP27
2785	4-THIAPENTANAL	6.1	T1	III	6.1		LQ7	E1	P001 IBC03 LP01 R001		MP19	T4	TP1
2786	ORGANOTIN PESTICIDE, SOLID, TOXIC	6.1	T7	I	6.1	61 274 648	LQ0	E5	P002 IBC07		MP18	T6	TP33
2786	ORGANOTIN PESTICIDE, SOLID, TOXIC	6.1	T7	II	6.1	61 274 648	LQ18	E4	P002 IBC08	B4	MP10	T3	TP33
2786	ORGANOTIN PESTICIDE, SOLID, TOXIC	6.1	T7	III	6.1	61 274 648	LQ9	E1	P002 IBC08 LP02 R001	B3	MP10	T1	TP33
2787	ORGANOTIN PESTICIDE, LIQUID, FLAMMABLE, TOXIC, flash-point less than 23 °C	3	FT2	I	3 +6.1	61 274	LQ3	E0	P001		MP7 MP17	T14	TP2 TP27
2787	ORGANOTIN PESTICIDE, LIQUID, FLAMMABLE, TOXIC, flash-point less than 23 °C	3	FT2	II	3 +6.1	61 274	LQ4	E2	P001 IBC02 R001		MP19	T11	TP2 TP27
2788	ORGANOTIN COMPOUND, LIQUID, N.O.S.	6.1	T3	I	6.1	43 274	LQ0	E5	P001		MP8 MP17	T14	TP2 TP27

ADR tank		Vehicle for tank carriage	Transport category (Tunnel restriction code)	Special provisions for carriage				Hazard identifi-cation No.	UN No.	Name and description
Tank code	Special provisions			Packages	Bulk	Loading, unloading and handling	Operation			
4.3	4.3.5, 6.8.4	9.1.1.2	1.1.3.6 (8.6)	7.2.4	7.3.3	7.5.11	8.5	5.3.2.3		3.1.2
(12)	(13)	(14)	(15)	(16)	(17)	(18)	(19)	(20)	(1)	(2)
L10CH	TU14 TU15 TE21	FL	1 (C/E)			CV13 CV28	S2 S22	336	2780	SUBSTITUTED NITROPHENOL PESTICIDE, LIQUID, FLAMMABLE, TOXIC, flash-point less than 23 °C
L4BH	TU15	FL	2 (D/E)			CV13 CV28	S2 S22	336	2780	SUBSTITUTED NITROPHENOL PESTICIDE, LIQUID, FLAMMABLE, TOXIC, flash-point less than 23 °C
S10AH L10CH	TU14 TU15 TE19 TE21	AT	1 (C/E)	V10 V12		CV1 CV13 CV28	S9 S14	66	2781	BIPYRIDILIUM PESTICIDE, SOLID, TOXIC
SGAH L4BH	TU15 TE19	AT	2 (D/E)	V11		CV13 CV28	S9 S19	60	2781	BIPYRIDILIUM PESTICIDE, SOLID, TOXIC
SGAH L4BH	TU15 TE19	AT	2 (E)		VV9	CV13 CV28	S9	60	2781	BIPYRIDILIUM PESTICIDE, SOLID, TOXIC
L10CH	TU14 TU15 TE21	FL	1 (C/E)			CV13 CV28	S2 S22	336	2782	BIPYRIDILIUM PESTICIDE, LIQUID, FLAMMABLE, TOXIC, flash-point less than 23 °C
L4BH	TU15	FL	2 (D/E)			CV13 CV28	S2 S22	336	2782	BIPYRIDILIUM PESTICIDE, LIQUID, FLAMMABLE, TOXIC, flash-point less than 23 °C
S10AH L10CH	TU14 TU15 TE19 TE21	AT	1 (C/E)	V10 V12		CV1 CV13 CV28	S9 S14	66	2783	ORGANOPHOSPHORUS PESTICIDE, SOLID, TOXIC
SGAH L4BH	TU15 TE19	AT	2 (D/E)	V11		CV13 CV28	S9 S19	60	2783	ORGANOPHOSPHORUS PESTICIDE, SOLID, TOXIC
SGAH L4BH	TU15 TE19	AT	2 (E)		VV9	CV13 CV28	S9	60	2783	ORGANOPHOSPHORUS PESTICIDE, SOLID, TOXIC
L10CH	TU14 TU15 TE21	FL	1 (C/E)			CV13 CV28	S2 S22	336	2784	ORGANOPHOSPHORUS PESTICIDE, LIQUID, FLAMMABLE, TOXIC, flash-point less than 23 °C
L4BH	TU15	FL	2 (D/E)			CV13 CV28	S2 S22	336	2784	ORGANOPHOSPHORUS PESTICIDE, LIQUID, FLAMMABLE, TOXIC, flash-point less than 23 °C
L4BH	TU15 TE19	AT	2 (E)			CV13 CV28	S9	60	2785	4-THIAPENTANAL
S10AH L10CH	TU14 TU15 TE19 TE21	AT	1 (C/E)	V10 V12		CV1 CV13 CV28	S9 S14	66	2786	ORGANOTIN PESTICIDE, SOLID, TOXIC
SGAH L4BH	TU15 TE19	AT	2 (D/E)	V11		CV13 CV28	S9 S19	60	2786	ORGANOTIN PESTICIDE, SOLID, TOXIC
SGAH L4BH	TU15 TE19	AT	2 (E)		VV9	CV13 CV28	S9	60	2786	ORGANOTIN PESTICIDE, SOLID, TOXIC
L10CH	TU14 TU15 TE21	FL	1 (C/E)			CV13 CV28	S2 S22	336	2787	ORGANOTIN PESTICIDE, LIQUID, FLAMMABLE, TOXIC, flash-point less than 23 °C
L4BH	TU15	FL	2 (D/E)			CV13 CV28	S2 S22	336	2787	ORGANOTIN PESTICIDE, LIQUID, FLAMMABLE, TOXIC, flash-point less than 23 °C
L10CH	TU14 TU15 TE19 TE21	AT	1 (C/E)			CV1 CV13 CV28	S9 S14	66	2788	ORGANOTIN COMPOUND, LIQUID, N.O.S.

UN No.	Name and description	Class	Classification code	Packing group	Labels	Special provisions	Limited and excepted quantities		Packaging			Portable tanks and bulk containers	
							quantities		Packing instructions	Special packing provisions	Mixed packing provisions	Instructions	Special provisions
	3.1.2	2.2	2.2	2.1.1.3	5.2.2	3.3	3.4.6	3.5.1.2	4.1.4	4.1.4	4.1.10	4.2.5.2 7.3.2	4.2.5.3
(1)	(2)	(3a)	(3b)	(4)	(5)	(6)	(7a)	(7b)	(8)	(9a)	(9b)	(10)	(11)
2788	ORGANOTIN COMPOUND, LIQUID, N.O.S.	6.1	T3	II	6.1	43 274	LQ17	E4	P001 IBC02		MP15	T11	TP2 TP27
2788	ORGANOTIN COMPOUND, LIQUID, N.O.S.	6.1	T3	III	6.1	43 274	LQ7	E1	P001 IBC03 LP01 R001		MP19	T7	TP2 TP28
2789	ACETIC ACID, GLACIAL or ACETIC ACID SOLUTION, more than 80% acid, by mass	8	CF1	II	8 +3		LQ22	E2	P001 IBC02		MP15	T7	TP2
2790	ACETIC ACID SOLUTION, not less than 50% but not more than 80% acid, by mass	8	C3	II	8		LQ22	E2	P001 IBC02		MP15	T7	TP2
2790	ACETIC ACID SOLUTION, more than 10% and less than 50% acid, by mass	8	C3	III	8	597 647	LQ7	E1	P001 IBC03 LP01 R001		MP19	T4	TP1
2793	FERROUS METAL BORINGS, SHAVINGS, TURNINGS or CUTTINGS in a form liable to self-heating	4.2	S4	III	4.2	592	LQ0	E1	P003 IBC08 LP02 R001	PP20 B3 B6	MP14		
2794	BATTERIES, WET, FILLED WITH ACID, electric storage	8	C11		8	295 598	LQ0	E0	P801 P801a				
2795	BATTERIES, WET, FILLED WITH ALKALI, electric storage	8	C11		8	295 598	LQ0	E0	P801 P801a				
2796	SULPHURIC ACID with not more than 51% acid or BATTERY FLUID, ACID	8	C1	II	8		LQ22	E2	P001 IBC02		MP15	T8	TP2
2797	BATTERY FLUID, ALKALI	8	C5	II	8		LQ22	E2	P001 IBC02		MP15	T7	TP2 TP28
2798	PHENYLPHOSPHORUS DICHLORIDE	8	C3	II	8		LQ22	E2	P001 IBC02		MP15	T7	TP2
2799	PHENYLPHOSPHORUS THIODICHLORIDE	8	C3	II	8		LQ22	E2	P001 IBC02		MP15	T7	TP2
2800	BATTERIES, WET, NON-SPILLABLE, electric storage	8	C11		8	238 295 598	LQ0	E0	P003 P801a	PP16			
2801	DYE, LIQUID, CORROSIVE, N.O.S. or DYE INTERMEDIATE, LIQUID, CORROSIVE, N.O.S.	8	C9	I	8	274	LQ0	E0	P001		MP8 MP17	T14	TP2 TP27
2801	DYE, LIQUID, CORROSIVE, N.O.S. or DYE INTERMEDIATE, LIQUID, CORROSIVE, N.O.S.	8	C9	II	8	274	LQ22	E2	P001 IBC02		MP15	T11	TP2 TP27
2801	DYE, LIQUID, CORROSIVE, N.O.S. or DYE INTERMEDIATE, LIQUID, CORROSIVE, N.O.S.	8	C9	III	8	274	LQ7	E1	P001 IBC03 LP01 R001		MP19	T7	TP1 TP28
2802	COPPER CHLORIDE	8	C2	III	8		LQ24	E1	P002 IBC08 LP02 R001	B3	MP10	T1	TP33
2803	GALLIUM	8	C10	III	8		LQ24	E0	P800	PP41	MP10	T1	TP33
2805	LITHIUM HYDRIDE, FUSED SOLID	4.3	W2	II	4.3		LQ11	E2	P410 IBC04	PP40	MP14	T3	TP33
2806	LITHIUM NITRIDE	4.3	W2	I	4.3		LQ0	E0	P403 IBC04		MP2		
2807	Magnetized material	9	M11				NOT SUBJECT TO ADR						
2809	MERCURY	8	C9	III	8	599	LQ19	E0	P800		MP15		
2810	TOXIC LIQUID, ORGANIC, N.O.S.	6.1	T1	I	6.1	274 315 614	LQ0	E5	P001		MP8 MP17	T14	TP2 TP27
2810	TOXIC LIQUID, ORGANIC, N.O.S.	6.1	T1	II	6.1	274 614	LQ17	E4	P001 IBC02		MP15	T11	TP2 TP27

ADR tank		Vehicle for tank carriage	Transport category (Tunnel restriction code)	Special provisions for carriage				Hazard identifi-cation No.	UN No.	Name and description
Tank code	Special provisions			Packages	Bulk	Loading, unloading and handling	Operation			
4.3	4.3.5, 6.8.4	9.1.1.2	1.1.3.6 (8.6)	7.2.4	7.3.3	7.5.11	8.5	5.3.2.3		3.1.2
(12)	(13)	(14)	(15)	(16)	(17)	(18)	(19)	(20)	(1)	(2)
L4BH	TU15 TE19	AT	2 (D/E)			CV13 CV28	S9 S19	60	2788	ORGANOTIN COMPOUND, LIQUID, N.O.S.
L4BH	TU15 TE19	AT	2 (E)			CV13 CV28	S9	60	2788	ORGANOTIN COMPOUND, LIQUID, N.O.S.
L4BN		FL	2 (D/E)				S2	83	2789	ACETIC ACID, GLACIAL or ACETIC ACID SOLUTION, more than 80% acid, by mass
L4BN		AT	2 (E)					80	2790	ACETIC ACID SOLUTION, not less than 50% but not more than 80% acid, by mass
L4BN		AT	3 (E)					80	2790	ACETIC ACID SOLUTION, more than 10% and less than 50% acid, by mass
			3 (E)	V1	VV4			40	2793	FERROUS METAL BORINGS, SHAVINGS, TURNINGS or CUTTINGS in a form liable to self-heating
			3 (E)		VV14			80	2794	BATTERIES, WET, FILLED WITH ACID, electric storage
			3 (E)		VV14			80	2795	BATTERIES, WET, FILLED WITH ALKALI, electric storage
L4BN		AT	2 (E)					80	2796	SULPHURIC ACID with not more than 51% acid or BATTERY FLUID, ACID
L4BN		AT	2 (E)					80	2797	BATTERY FLUID, ALKALI
L4BN		AT	2 (E)					80	2798	PHENYLPHOSPHORUS DICHLORIDE
L4BN		AT	2 (E)					80	2799	PHENYLPHOSPHORUS THIODICHLORIDE
			3 (E)		VV14			80	2800	BATTERIES, WET, NON-SPILLABLE, electric storage
L10BH		AT	1 (E)				S20	88	2801	DYE, LIQUID, CORROSIVE, N.O.S. or DYE INTERMEDIATE, LIQUID, CORROSIVE, N.O.S.
L4BN		AT	2 (E)					80	2801	DYE, LIQUID, CORROSIVE, N.O.S. or DYE INTERMEDIATE, LIQUID, CORROSIVE, N.O.S.
L4BN		AT	3 (E)					80	2801	DYE, LIQUID, CORROSIVE, N.O.S. or DYE INTERMEDIATE, LIQUID, CORROSIVE, N.O.S.
SGAV		AT	3 (E)		VV9			80	2802	COPPER CHLORIDE
SGAV L4BN		AT	3 (E)		VV9			80	2803	GALLIUM
SGAN		AT	2 (D/E)	V1		CV23		423	2805	LITHIUM HYDRIDE, FUSED SOLID
			1 (E)	V1		CV23	S20		2806	LITHIUM NITRIDE
NOT SUBJECT TO ADR									2807	Magnetized material
L4BN		AT	3 (E)					80	2809	MERCURY
L10CH	TU14 TU15 TE19 TE21	AT	1 (C/E)			CV1 CV13 CV28	S9 S14	66	2810	TOXIC LIQUID, ORGANIC, N.O.S.
L4BH	TU15 TE19	AT	2 (D/E)			CV13 CV28	S9 S19	60	2810	TOXIC LIQUID, ORGANIC, N.O.S.

UN No.	Name and description	Class	Classifi-cation code	Packing group	Labels	Special provi-sions	Limited and excepted quantities		Packaging			Portable tanks and bulk containers	
									Packing instruc-tions	Special packing provisions	Mixed packing provisions	Instruc-tions	Special provisions
	3.1.2	2.2	2.2	2.1.1.3	5.2.2	3.3	3.4.6	3.5.1.2	4.1.4	4.1.4	4.1.10	4.2.5.2 7.3.2	4.2.5.3
(1)	(2)	(3a)	(3b)	(4)	(5)	(6)	(7a)	(7b)	(8)	(9a)	(9b)	(10)	(11)
2810	TOXIC LIQUID, ORGANIC, N.O.S.	6.1	T1	III	6.1	274 614	LQ7	E1	P001 IBC03 LP01 R001		MP19	T7	TP1 TP28
2811	TOXIC SOLID, ORGANIC, N.O.S.	6.1	T2	I	6.1	274 614	LQ0	E5	P002 IBC07		MP18	T6	TP33
2811	TOXIC SOLID, ORGANIC, N.O.S.	6.1	T2	II	6.1	274 614	LQ18	E4	P002 IBC08	B4	MP10	T3	TP33
2811	TOXIC SOLID, ORGANIC, N.O.S.	6.1	T2	III	6.1	274 614	LQ9	E1	P002 IBC08 LP02 R001	B3	MP10	T1	TP33
2812	Sodium aluminate, solid	8	C6	NOT SUBJECT TO ADR									
2813	WATER-REACTIVE SOLID, N.O.S.	4.3	W2	I	4.3	274	LQ0	E0	P403 IBC99	PP83	MP2	T9	TP7 TP33
2813	WATER-REACTIVE SOLID, N.O.S.	4.3	W2	II	4.3	274	LQ11	E2	P410 IBC07	PP83	MP14	T3	TP33
2813	WATER-REACTIVE SOLID, N.O.S.	4.3	W2	III	4.3	274	LQ12	E1	P410 IBC08 R001	PP83 B4	MP14	T1	TP33
2814	INFECTIOUS SUBSTANCE, AFFECTING HUMANS	6.2	I1		6.2	318	LQ0	E0	P620		MP5		
2814	INFECTIOUS SUBSTANCE, AFFECTING HUMANS, in refrigerated liquid nitrogen	6.2	I1		6.2 +2.2	318	LQ0	E0	P620		MP5		
2814	INFECTIOUS SUBSTANCE, AFFECTING HUMANS (animal material only)	6.2	I1		6.2	318	LQ0	E0	P620		MP5	BK1 BK2	
2815	N-AMINOETHYL-PIPERAZINE	8	C7	III	8		LQ7	E1	P001 IBC03 LP01 R001		MP19	T4	TP1
2817	AMMONIUM HYDROGENDIFLUORIDE SOLUTION	8	CT1	II	8 +6.1		LQ22	E2	P001 IBC02		MP15	T8	TP2
2817	AMMONIUM HYDROGENDIFLUORIDE SOLUTION	8	CT1	III	8 +6.1		LQ7	E1	P001 IBC03 R001		MP19	T4	TP1
2818	AMMONIUM POLYSULPHIDE SOLUTION	8	CT1	II	8 +6.1		LQ22	E2	P001 IBC02		MP15	T7	TP2
2818	AMMONIUM POLYSULPHIDE SOLUTION	8	CT1	III	8 +6.1		LQ7	E1	P001 IBC03 R001		MP19	T4	TP1
2819	AMYL ACID PHOSPHATE	8	C3	III	8		LQ7	E1	P001 IBC03 LP01 R001		MP19	T4	TP1
2820	BUTYRIC ACID	8	C3	III	8		LQ7	E1	P001 IBC03 LP01 R001		MP19	T4	TP1
2821	PHENOL SOLUTION	6.1	T1	II	6.1		LQ17	E4	P001 IBC02		MP15	T7	TP2
2821	PHENOL SOLUTION	6.1	T1	III	6.1		LQ7	E1	P001 IBC03 LP01 R001		MP19	T4	TP1
2822	2-CHLOROPYRIDINE	6.1	T1	II	6.1		LQ17	E4	P001 IBC02		MP15	T7	TP2
2823	CROTONIC ACID, SOLID	8	C4	III	8		LQ24	E1	P002 IBC08 LP02 R001	B3	MP10	T1	TP33

ADR tank		Vehicle for tank carriage	Transport category (Tunnel restriction code)	Special provisions for carriage				Hazard identifi- cation No.	UN No.	Name and description
Tank code	Special provisions			Packages	Bulk	Loading, unloading and handling	Operation			
4.3	4.3.5, 6.8.4	9.1.1.2	1.1.3.6 (8.6)	7.2.4	7.3.3	7.5.11	8.5	5.3.2.3		3.1.2
(12)	(13)	(14)	(15)	(16)	(17)	(18)	(19)	(20)	(1)	(2)
L4BH	TU15 TE19	AT	2 (E)			CV13 CV28	S9	60	2810	TOXIC LIQUID, ORGANIC, N.O.S.
S10AH L10CH	TU15 TE19	AT	1 (C/E)	V10 V12		CV1 CV13 CV28	S9 S14	66	2811	TOXIC SOLID, ORGANIC, N.O.S.
SGAH L4BH	TU15 TE19	AT	2 (D/E)	V11		CV13 CV28	S9 S19	60	2811	TOXIC SOLID, ORGANIC, N.O.S.
SGAH L4BH	TU15 TE19	AT	2 (E)		VV9	CV13 CV28	S9	60	2811	TOXIC SOLID, ORGANIC, N.O.S.
NOT SUBJECT TO ADR									2812	Sodium aluminate, solid
S10AN L10DH	TU4 TU14 TU22 TE21 TM2	AT	0 (E)	V1		CV23	S20	X423	2813	WATER-REACTIVE SOLID, N.O.S.
SGAN		AT	0 (D/E)	V1 V12		CV23		423	2813	WATER-REACTIVE SOLID, N.O.S.
SGAN		AT	0 (E)	V1	VV5	CV23		423	2813	WATER-REACTIVE SOLID, N.O.S.
			0 (E)			CV13 CV25 CV26 CV28	S3 S9 S15		2814	INFECTIOUS SUBSTANCE, AFFECTING HUMANS
			0 (E)			CV13 CV25 CV26 CV28	S3 S9 S15		2814	INFECTIOUS SUBSTANCE, AFFECTING HUMANS, in refrigerated liquid nitrogen
			0 (E)			CV13 CV25 CV26 CV28	S3 S9 S15	606	2814	INFECTIOUS SUBSTANCE, AFFECTING HUMANS (animal material only)
L4BN		AT	3 (E)					80	2815	N-AMINOETHYL- PIPERAZINE
L4DH	TU14 TE21	AT	2 (E)			CV13 CV28		86	2817	AMMONIUM HYDROGENDIFLUORIDE SOLUTION
L4DH	TU14 TE21	AT	3 (E)			CV13 CV28		86	2817	AMMONIUM HYDROGENDIFLUORIDE SOLUTION
L4BN		AT	2 (E)			CV13 CV28		86	2818	AMMONIUM POLYSULPHIDE SOLUTION
L4BN		AT	3 (E)			CV13 CV28		86	2818	AMMONIUM POLYSULPHIDE SOLUTION
L4BN		AT	3 (E)					80	2819	AMYL ACID PHOSPHATE
L4BN		AT	3 (E)					80	2820	BUTYRIC ACID
L4BH	TU15 TE19	AT	2 (D/E)			CV13 CV28	S9 S19	60	2821	PHENOL SOLUTION
L4BH	TU15 TE19	AT	2 (E)			CV13 CV28	S9	60	2821	PHENOL SOLUTION
L4BH	TU15 TE19	AT	2 (D/E)			CV13 CV28	S9 S19	60	2822	2-CHLOROPYRIDINE
SGAV L4BN		AT	3 (E)		VV9			80	2823	CROTONIC ACID, SOLID

UN No.	Name and description	Class	Classification code	Packing group	Labels	Special provisions	Limited and excepted quantities		Packaging			Portable tanks and bulk containers	
									Packing instructions	Special packing provisions	Mixed packing provisions	Instructions	Special provisions
	3.1.2	2.2	2.2	2.1.1.3	5.2.2	3.3	3.4.6	3.5.1.2	4.1.4	4.1.4	4.1.10	4.2.5.2 7.3.2	4.2.5.3
(1)	(2)	(3a)	(3b)	(4)	(5)	(6)	(7a)	(7b)	(8)	(9a)	(9b)	(10)	(11)
2826	ETHYL CHLOROTHIOFORMATE	8	CF1	II	8 +3		LQ22	E2	P001		MP15	T7	TP2
2829	CAPROIC ACID	8	C3	III	8		LQ7	E1	P001 IBC03 LP01 R001		MP19	T4	TP1
2830	LITHIUM FERROSILICON	4.3	W2	II	4.3		LQ11	E2	P410 IBC07		MP14	T3	TP33
2831	1,1,1-TRICHLOROETHANE	6.1	T1	III	6.1		LQ7	E1	P001 IBC03 LP01 R001		MP19	T4	TP1
2834	PHOSPHOROUS ACID	8	C2	III	8		LQ24	E1	P002 IBC08 LP02 R001	B3	MP10	T1	TP33
2835	SODIUM ALUMINIUM HYDRIDE	4.3	W2	II	4.3		LQ11	E2	P410 IBC04		MP14	T3	TP33
2837	BISULPHATES, AQUEOUS SOLUTION	8	C1	II	8	274	LQ22	E2	P001 IBC02		MP15	T7	TP2
2837	BISULPHATES, AQUEOUS SOLUTION	8	C1	III	8	274	LQ7	E1	P001 IBC03 LP01 R001		MP19	T4	TP1
2838	VINYL BUTYRATE, STABILIZED	3	F1	II	3		LQ4	E2	P001 IBC02 R001		MP19	T4	TP1
2839	ALDOL	6.1	T1	II	6.1		LQ17	E4	P001 IBC02		MP15	T7	TP2
2840	BUTYRALDOXIME	3	F1	III	3		LQ7	E1	P001 IBC03 LP01 R001		MP19	T2	TP1
2841	DI-n-AMYLAMINE	3	FT1	III	3 +6.1		LQ7	E1	P001 IBC03 R001		MP19	T4	TP1
2842	NITROETHANE	3	F1	III	3		LQ7	E1	P001 IBC03 LP01 R001		MP19	T2	TP1
2844	CALCIUM MANGANESE SILICON	4.3	W2	III	4.3		LQ12	E1	P410 IBC08 R001	B4	MP14	T1	TP33
2845	PYROPHORIC LIQUID, ORGANIC, N.O.S.	4.2	S1	I	4.2	274	LQ0	E0	P400		MP2	T22	TP2 TP7
2846	PYROPHORIC SOLID, ORGANIC, N.O.S.	4.2	S2	I	4.2	274	LQ0	E0	P404		MP13		
2849	3-CHLOROPROPANOL-1	6.1	T1	III	6.1		LQ7	E1	P001 IBC03 LP01 R001		MP19	T4	TP1
2850	PROPYLENE TETRAMER	3	F1	III	3		LQ7	E1	P001 IBC03 LP01 R001		MP19	T2	TP1
2851	BORON TRIFLUORIDE DIHYDRATE	8	C1	II	8		LQ22	E2	P001 IBC02		MP15	T7	TP2
2852	DIPICRYL SULPHIDE, WETTED with not less than 10% water, by mass	4.1	D	I	4.1	545	LQ0	E0	P406	PP24	MP2		
2853	MAGNESIUM FLUOROSILICATE	6.1	T5	III	6.1		LQ9	E1	P002 IBC08 LP02 R001	B3	MP10	T1	TP33
2854	AMMONIUM FLUOROSILICATE	6.1	T5	III	6.1		LQ9	E1	P002 IBC08 LP02 R001	B3	MP10	T1	TP33
2855	ZINC FLUOROSILICATE	6.1	T5	III	6.1		LQ9	E1	P002 IBC08 LP02 R001	B3	MP10	T1	TP33

ADR tank		Vehicle for tank carriage	Transport category (Tunnel restriction code)	Special provisions for carriage				Hazard identifi-cation No.	UN No.	Name and description
Tank code	Special provisions			Packages	Bulk	Loading, unloading and handling	Operation			
4.3	4.3.5, 6.8.4	9.1.1.2	1.1.3.6 (8.6)	7.2.4	7.3.3	7.5.11	8.5	5.3.2.3		3.1.2
(12)	(13)	(14)	(15)	(16)	(17)	(18)	(19)	(20)	(1)	(2)
L4BN		FL	2 (D/E)				S2	83	2826	ETHYL CHLOROTHIOFORMATE
L4BN		AT	3 (E)					80	2829	CAPROIC ACID
SGAN		AT	2 (D/E)	V1 V12		CV23		423	2830	LITHIUM FERROSILICON
L4BH	TU15 TE19	AT	2 (E)			CV13 CV28	S9	60	2831	1,1,1-TRICHLOROETHANE
SGAV		AT	3 (E)		VV9			80	2834	PHOSPHOROUS ACID
SGAN		AT	2 (D/E)	V1		CV23		423	2835	SODIUM ALUMINIUM HYDRIDE
L4BN		AT	2 (E)					80	2837	BISULPHATES, AQUEOUS SOLUTION
L4BN		AT	3 (E)					80	2837	BISULPHATES, AQUEOUS SOLUTION
LGBF		FL	2 (D/E)				S2 S20	339	2838	VINYL BUTYRATE, STABILIZED
L4BH	TU15 TE19	AT	2 (D/E)			CV13 CV28	S9 S19	60	2839	ALDOL
LGBF		FL	3 (D/E)				S2	30	2840	BUTYRALDOXIME
L4BH	TU15	FL	3 (D/E)			CV13 CV28	S2	36	2841	DI-n-AMYLAMINE
LGBF		FL	3 (D/E)				S2	30	2842	NITROETHANE
SGAN		AT	3 (E)	V1	VV5 VV7	CV23		423	2844	CALCIUM MANGANESE SILICON
L21DH	TU14 TC1 TE21 TM1	AT	0 (B/E)	V1			S20	333	2845	PYROPHORIC LIQUID, ORGANIC, N.O.S.
			0 (E)	V1			S20		2846	PYROPHORIC SOLID, ORGANIC, N.O.S.
L4BH	TU15 TE19	AT	2 (E)			CV13 CV28	S9	60	2849	3-CHLOROPROPANOL-1
LGBF		FL	3 (D/E)				S2	30	2850	PROPYLENE TETRAMER
L4BN		AT	2 (E)					80	2851	BORON TRIFLUORIDE DIHYDRATE
			1 (B)				S14		2852	DIPICRYL SULPHIDE, WETTED with not less than 10% water, by mass
SGAH L4BH	TU15 TE19	AT	2 (E)		VV9	CV13 CV28	S9	60	2853	MAGNESIUM FLUOROSILICATE
SGAH L4BH	TU15 TE19	AT	2 (E)		VV9	CV13 CV28	S9	60	2854	AMMONIUM FLUOROSILICATE
SGAH L4BH	TU15 TE19	AT	2 (E)		VV9	CV13 CV28	S9	60	2855	ZINC FLUOROSILICATE

UN No.	Name and description	Class	Classification code	Packing group	Labels	Special provisions	Limited and excepted quantities		Packaging			Portable tanks and bulk containers	
									Packing instructions	Special packing provisions	Mixed packing provisions	Instructions	Special provisions
	3.1.2	2.2	2.2	2.1.1.3	5.2.2	3.3	3.4.6	3.5.1.2	4.1.4	4.1.4	4.1.10	4.2.5.2 7.3.2	4.2.5.3
(1)	(2)	(3a)	(3b)	(4)	(5)	(6)	(7a)	(7b)	(8)	(9a)	(9b)	(10)	(11)
2856	FLUOROSILICATES, N.O.S.	6.1	T5	III	6.1	274	LQ9	E1	P002 IBC08 LP02 R001	B3	MP10	T1	TP33
2857	REFRIGERATING MACHINES containing non-flammable, non-toxic gases or ammonia solutions (UN 2672)	2	6A		2.2	119	LQ0	E0	P003	PP32	MP9		
2858	ZIRCONIUM, DRY, coiled wire, finished metal sheets, strip (thinner than 254 microns but not thinner than 18 microns)	4.1	F3	III	4.1	546	LQ9	E1	P002 LP02 R001		MP11		
2859	AMMONIUM METAVANADATE	6.1	T5	II	6.1		LQ18	E4	P002 IBC08	B4	MP10	T3	TP33
2861	AMMONIUM POLYVANADATE	6.1	T5	II	6.1		LQ18	E4	P002 IBC08	B4	MP10	T3	TP33
2862	VANADIUM PENTOXIDE, non-fused form	6.1	T5	III	6.1	600	LQ9	E1	P002 IBC08 LP02 R001	B3	MP10	T1	TP33
2863	SODIUM AMMONIUM VANADATE	6.1	T5	II	6.1		LQ18	E4	P002 IBC08	B4	MP10	T3	TP33
2864	POTASSIUM METAVANADATE	6.1	T5	II	6.1		LQ18	E4	P002 IBC08	B4	MP10	T3	TP33
2865	HYDROXYLAMINE SULPHATE	8	C2	III	8		LQ24	E1	P002 IBC08 LP02 R001	B3	MP10	T1	TP33
2869	TITANIUM TRICHLORIDE MIXTURE	8	C2	II	8		LQ23	E2	P002 IBC08	B4	MP10	T3	TP33
2869	TITANIUM TRICHLORIDE MIXTURE	8	C2	III	8		LQ24	E1	P002 IBC08 LP02 R001	B3	MP10	T1	TP33
2870	ALUMINIUM BOROHYDRIDE	4.2	SW	I	4.2 +4.3		LQ0	E0	P400		MP2	T21	TP7 TP33
2870	ALUMINIUM BOROHYDRIDE IN DEVICES	4.2	SW	I	4.2 +4.3		LQ0	E0	P002	PP13	MP2		
2871	ANTIMONY POWDER	6.1	T5	III	6.1		LQ9	E1	P002 IBC08 LP02 R001	B3	MP10	T1	TP33
2872	DIBROMOCHLORO-PROPANES	6.1	T1	II	6.1		LQ17	E4	P001 IBC02		MP15	T7	TP2
2872	DIBROMOCHLORO-PROPANES	6.1	T1	III	6.1		LQ7	E1	P001 IBC03 LP01 R001		MP19	T4	TP1
2873	DIBUTYLAMINOETHANOL	6.1	T1	III	6.1		LQ7	E1	P001 IBC03 LP01 R001		MP19	T4	TP1
2874	FURFURYL ALCOHOL	6.1	T1	III	6.1		LQ7	E1	P001 IBC03 LP01 R001		MP19	T4	TP1
2875	HEXACHLOROPHENE	6.1	T2	III	6.1		LQ9	E1	P002 IBC08 LP02 R001	B3	MP10	T1	TP33
2876	RESORCINOL	6.1	T2	III	6.1		LQ9	E1	P002 IBC08 LP02 R001	B3	MP10	T1	TP33
2878	TITANIUM SPONGE GRANULES or TITANIUM SPONGE POWDERS	4.1	F3	III	4.1		LQ9	E1	P002 IBC08 LP02 R001	B3	MP11	T1	TP33
2879	SELENIUM OXYCHLORIDE	8	CT1	I	8 +6.1		LQ0	E0	P001		MP8 MP17	T10	TP2

ADR tank		Vehicle for tank carriage	Transport category (Tunnel restriction code)	Special provisions for carriage				Hazard identifi-cation No.	UN No.	Name and description
Tank code	Special provisions			Packages	Bulk	Loading, unloading and handling	Operation			
4.3	4.3.5, 6.8.4	9.1.1.2	1.1.3.6 (8.6)	7.2.4	7.3.3	7.5.11	8.5	5.3.2.3		3.1.2
(12)	(13)	(14)	(15)	(16)	(17)	(18)	(19)	(20)	(1)	(2)
SGAH L4BH	TU15 TE19	AT	2 (E)		VV9	CV13 CV28	S9	60	2856	FLUOROSILICATES, N.O.S.
			3 (E)			CV9			2857	REFRIGERATING MACHINES containing non-flammable, non-toxic gases or ammonia solutions (UN 2672)
			3 (E)		VV1			40	2858	ZIRCONIUM, DRY, coiled wire, finished metal sheets, strip (thinner than 254 microns but not thinner than 18 microns)
SGAH	TU15 TE19	AT	2 (D/E)	V11		CV13 CV28	S9 S19	60	2859	AMMONIUM METAVANADATE
SGAH	TU15 TE19	AT	2 (D/E)	V11		CV13 CV28	S9 S19	60	2861	AMMONIUM POLYVANADATE
SGAH	TU15 TE19	AT	2 (E)		VV9	CV13 CV28	S9	60	2862	VANADIUM PENTOXIDE, non-fused form
SGAH	TU15 TE19	AT	2 (D/E)	V11		CV13 CV28	S9 S19	60	2863	SODIUM AMMONIUM VANADATE
SGAH	TU15 TE19	AT	2 (D/E)	V11		CV13 CV28	S9 S19	60	2864	POTASSIUM METAVANADATE
SGAV		AT	3 (E)		VV9			80	2865	HYDROXYLAMINE SULPHATE
SGAN		AT	2 (E)	V11				80	2869	TITANIUM TRICHLORIDE MIXTURE
SGAV		AT	3 (E)		VV9			80	2869	TITANIUM TRICHLORIDE MIXTURE
L21DH	TU14 TC1 TE21 TM1	AT	0 (E)	V1			S20	X333	2870	ALUMINIUM BOROHYDRIDE
			0 (E)	V1			S20		2870	ALUMINIUM BOROHYDRIDE IN DEVICES
SGAH L4BH	TU15 TE19	AT	2 (E)		VV9	CV13 CV28	S9	60	2871	ANTIMONY POWDER
L4BH	TU15 TE19	AT	2 (D/E)			CV13 CV28	S9 S19	60	2872	DIBROMOCHLORO-PROPANES
L4BH	TU15 TE19	AT	2 (E)			CV13 CV28	S9	60	2872	DIBROMOCHLORO-PROPANES
L4BH	TU15 TE19	AT	2 (E)			CV13 CV28	S9	60	2873	DIBUTYLAMINOETHANOL
L4BH	TU15 TE19	AT	2 (E)			CV13 CV28	S9	60	2874	FURFURYL ALCOHOL
SGAH L4BH	TU15 TE19	AT	2 (E)		VV9	CV13 CV28	S9	60	2875	HEXACHLOROPHENE
SGAH L4BH	TU15 TE19	AT	2 (E)		VV9	CV13 CV28	S9	60	2876	RESORCINOL
SGAV		AT	3 (E)		VV1			40	2878	TITANIUM SPONGE GRANULES or TITANIUM SPONGE POWDERS
L10BH		AT	1 (C/D)			CV13 CV28	S14	X886	2879	SELENIUM OXYCHLORIDE

UN No.	Name and description	Class	Classification code	Packing group	Labels	Special provisions	Limited and excepted quantities		Packaging			Portable tanks and bulk containers	
							quantities		Packing instructions	Special packing provisions	Mixed packing provisions	Instructions	Special provisions
	3.1.2	2.2	2.2	2.1.1.3	5.2.2	3.3	3.4.6	3.5.1.2	4.1.4	4.1.4	4.1.10	4.2.5.2 7.3.2	4.2.5.3
(1)	(2)	(3a)	(3b)	(4)	(5)	(6)	(7a)	(7b)	(8)	(9a)	(9b)	(10)	(11)
2880	CALCIUM HYPOCHLORITE, HYDRATED, or CALCIUM HYPOCHLORITE, HYDRATED MIXTURE, with not less than 5.5% but not more than 16% water	5.1	O2	II	5.1	313 314 322	LQ11	E2	P002 IBC08	B4 B13	MP10		
2880	CALCIUM HYPOCHLORITE, HYDRATED, or CALCIUM HYPOCHLORITE, HYDRATED MIXTURE, with not less than 5.5% but not more than 16% water	5.1	O2	III	5.1	313 314	LQ12	E1	P002 IBC08 R001	B4	MP10		
2881	METAL CATALYST, DRY	4.2	S4	I	4.2	274	LQ0	E0	P404		MP13	T21	TP7 TP33
2881	METAL CATALYST, DRY	4.2	S4	II	4.2	274	LQ0	E2	P410 IBC06		MP14	T3	TP33
2881	METAL CATALYST, DRY	4.2	S4	III	4.2	274	LQ0	E1	P002 IBC08 LP02 R001	B3	MP14	T1	TP33
2900	INFECTIOUS SUBSTANCE, AFFECTING ANIMALS only	6.2	I2		6.2	318	LQ0	E0	P620		MP5		
2900	INFECTIOUS SUBSTANCE, AFFECTING ANIMALS only, in refrigerated liquid nitrogen	6.2	I2		6.2 +2.2	318	LQ0	E0	P620		MP5		
2900	INFECTIOUS SUBSTANCE, AFFECTING ANIMALS only (animal material only)	6.2	I2		6.2	318	LQ0	E0	P620		MP5	BK1 BK2	
2901	BROMINE CHLORIDE	2	2TOC		2.3 +5.1 +8		LQ0	E0	P200		MP9	(M)	
2902	PESTICIDE, LIQUID, TOXIC, N.O.S.	6.1	T6	I	6.1	61 274 648	LQ0	E5	P001		MP8 MP17	T14	TP2 TP27
2902	PESTICIDE, LIQUID, TOXIC, N.O.S.	6.1	T6	II	6.1	61 274 648	LQ17	E4	P001 IBC02		MP15	T11	TP2 TP27
2902	PESTICIDE, LIQUID, TOXIC, N.O.S.	6.1	T6	III	6.1	61 274 648	LQ7	E1	P001 IBC03 LP01 R001		MP19	T7	TP2 TP28
2903	PESTICIDE, LIQUID, TOXIC, FLAMMABLE, N.O.S., flash-point not less than 23 °C	6.1	TF2	I	6.1 +3	61 274	LQ0	E5	P001		MP8 MP17	T14	TP2 TP27
2903	PESTICIDE, LIQUID, TOXIC, FLAMMABLE, N.O.S., flash-point not less than 23 °C	6.1	TF2	II	6.1 +3	61 274	LQ17	E4	P001 IBC02		MP15	T11	TP2 TP27
2903	PESTICIDE, LIQUID, TOXIC, FLAMMABLE, N.O.S., flash-point not less than 23 °C	6.1	TF2	III	6.1 +3	61 274	LQ7	E1	P001 IBC03 R001		MP19	T7	TP2
2904	CHLOROPHENOLATES, LIQUID or PHENOLATES, LIQUID	8	C9	III	8		LQ7	E1	P001 IBC03 LP01 R001		MP19		
2905	CHLOROPHENOLATES, SOLID or PHENOLATES, SOLID	8	C10	III	8		LQ24	E1	P002 IBC08 LP02 R001	B3	MP10	T1	TP33
2907	ISOSORBIDE DINITRATE MIXTURE with not less than 60% lactose, mannose, starch or calcium hydrogen phosphate	4.1	D	II	4.1	127	LQ8	E0	P406 IBC06	PP26 PP80 B12	MP2		
2908	RADIOACTIVE MATERIAL, EXCEPTED PACKAGE - EMPTY PACKAGING	7				290	LQ0	E0	See 1.7	See 4.1.9.1.3			

ADR tank		Vehicle for tank carriage	Transport category (Tunnel restriction code)	Special provisions for carriage				Hazard identifi- cation No.	UN No.	Name and description
Tank code	Special provisions			Packages	Bulk	Loading, unloading and handling	Operation			
4.3	4.3.5, 6.8.4	9.1.1.2	1.1.3.6 (8.6)	7.2.4	7.3.3	7.5.11	8.5	5.3.2.3		3.1.2
(12)	(13)	(14)	(15)	(16)	(17)	(18)	(19)	(20)	(1)	(2)
SGAN	TU3	AT	2 (E)	V11		CV24 CV35		50	2880	CALCIUM HYPOCHLORITE, HYDRATED, or CALCIUM HYPOCHLORITE, HYDRATED MIXTURE, with not less than 5.5% but not more than 16% water
SGAV	TU3	AT	3 (E)		VV8	CV24 CV35		50	2880	CALCIUM HYPOCHLORITE, HYDRATED, or CALCIUM HYPOCHLORITE, HYDRATED MIXTURE, with not less than 5.5% but not more than 16% water
		AT	0 (B/E)	V1			S20	43	2881	METAL CATALYST, DRY
SGAN		AT	2 (D/E)	V1 V12				40	2881	METAL CATALYST, DRY
SGAN		AT	3 (E)	V1	VV4			40	2881	METAL CATALYST, DRY
			0 (E)			CV13 CV25 CV26 CV28	S3 S9 S15		2900	INFECTIOUS SUBSTANCE, AFFECTING ANIMALS only
			0 (E)			CV13 CV25 CV26 CV28	S3 S9 S15		2900	INFECTIOUS SUBSTANCE, AFFECTING ANIMALS only, in refrigerated liquid nitrogen
			0 (E)			CV13 CV25 CV26 CV28	S3 S9 S15	606	2900	INFECTIOUS SUBSTANCE, AFFECTING ANIMALS only (animal material only)
PxBH(M)	TA4 TT9	AT	1 (C/D)			CV9 CV10 CV36	S14	265	2901	BROMINE CHLORIDE
L10CH	TU14 TU15 TE19 TE21	AT	1 (C/E)			CV1 CV13 CV28	S9 S14	66	2902	PESTICIDE, LIQUID, TOXIC, N.O.S.
L4BH	TU15 TE19	AT	2 (D/E)			CV13 CV28	S9 S19	60	2902	PESTICIDE, LIQUID, TOXIC, N.O.S.
L4BH	TU15 TE19	AT	2 (E)			CV13 CV28	S9	60	2902	PESTICIDE, LIQUID, TOXIC, N.O.S.
L10CH	TU14 TU15 TE19 TE21	FL	1 (C/E)			CV1 CV13 CV28	S2 S9 S14	663	2903	PESTICIDE, LIQUID, TOXIC, FLAMMABLE, N.O.S., flash-point not less than 23 °C
L4BH	TU15 TE19	FL	2 (D/E)			CV13 CV28	S2 S9 S19	63	2903	PESTICIDE, LIQUID, TOXIC, FLAMMABLE, N.O.S., flash-point not less than 23 °C
L4BH	TU15 TE19	FL	2 (D/E)			CV13 CV28	S2 S9	63	2903	PESTICIDE, LIQUID, TOXIC, FLAMMABLE, N.O.S., flash-point not less than 23 °C
L4BN		AT	3 (E)					80	2904	CHLOROPHENOLATES, LIQUID or PHENOLATES, LIQUID
SGAV L4BN		AT	3 (E)		VV9			80	2905	CHLOROPHENOLATES, SOLID or PHENOLATES, SOLID
			2 (B)	V11 V12			S14		2907	ISOSORBIDE DINITRATE MIXTURE with not less than 60% lactose, mannose, starch or calcium hydrogen phosphate
			4 (E)			CV33	S5 S13 S21		2908	RADIOACTIVE MATERIAL, EXCEPTED PACKAGE - EMPTY PACKAGING

UN No.	Name and description	Class	Classifi-cation code	Packing group	Labels	Special provi-sions	Limited and excepted quantities		Packaging			Portable tanks and bulk containers	
									Packing instruc-tions	Special packing provisions	Mixed packing provisions	Instruc-tions	Special provisions
	3.1.2	2.2	2.2	2.1.1.3	5.2.2	3.3	3.4.6	3.5.1.2	4.1.4	4.1.4	4.1.10	4.2.5.2 7.3.2	4.2.5.3
(1)	(2)	(3a)	(3b)	(4)	(5)	(6)	(7a)	(7b)	(8)	(9a)	(9b)	(10)	(11)
2909	RADIOACTIVE MATERIAL, EXCEPTED PACKAGE - ARTICLES MANUFACTURED FROM NATURAL URANIUM or DEPLETED URANIUM or NATURAL THORIUM	7				290	LQ0	E0	See 1.7	See 4.1.9.1.3			
2910	RADIOACTIVE MATERIAL, EXCEPTED PACKAGE - LIMITED QUANTITY OF MATERIAL	7				290	LQ0	E0	See 1.7	See 4.1.9.1.3			
2911	RADIOACTIVE MATERIAL, EXCEPTED PACKAGE - INSTRUMENTS or ARTICLES	7				290	LQ0	E0	See 1.7	See 4.1.9.1.3			
2912	RADIOACTIVE MATERIAL, LOW SPECIFIC ACTIVITY (LSA-I), non fissile or fissile-excepted	7			7X	172 317 325	LQ0	E0	See 2.2.7 and 4.1.9	See 4.1.9.1.3		T5	TP4
2913	RADIOACTIVE MATERIAL, SURFACE CONTAMINATED OBJECTS (SCO-I or SCO-II), non fissile or fissile-excepted	7			7X	172 317 336	LQ0	E0	See 2.2.7 and 4.1.9	See 4.1.9.1.3			
2915	RADIOACTIVE MATERIAL, TYPE A PACKAGE, non-special form, non fissile or fissile-excepted	7			7X	172 317 325	LQ0	E0	See 2.2.7 and 4.1.9	See 4.1.9.1.3			
2916	RADIOACTIVE MATERIAL, TYPE B(U) PACKAGE, non fissile or fissile-excepted	7			7X	172 317 337	LQ0	E0	See 2.2.7 and 4.1.9	See 4.1.9.1.3			
2917	RADIOACTIVE MATERIAL, TYPE B(M) PACKAGE, non fissile or fissile-excepted	7			7X	172 317 337	LQ0	E0	See 2.2.7 and 4.1.9	See 4.1.9.1.3			
2919	RADIOACTIVE MATERIAL, TRANSPORTED UNDER SPECIAL ARRANGEMENT, non fissile or fissile-excepted	7			7X	172 317	LQ0	E0	See 2.2.7 and 4.1.9	See 4.1.9.1.3			
2920	CORROSIVE LIQUID, FLAMMABLE, N.O.S.	8	CF1	I	8 +3	274	LQ0	E0	P001		MP8 MP17	T14	TP2 TP27
2920	CORROSIVE LIQUID, FLAMMABLE, N.O.S.	8	CF1	II	8 +3	274	LQ22	E2	P001 IBC02		MP15	T11	TP2 TP27
2921	CORROSIVE SOLID, FLAMMABLE, N.O.S.	8	CF2	I	8 +4.1	274	LQ0	E0	P002 IBC05		MP18	T6	TP33
2921	CORROSIVE SOLID, FLAMMABLE, N.O.S.	8	CF2	II	8 +4.1	274	LQ23	E2	P002 IBC08	B4	MP10	T3	TP33
2922	CORROSIVE LIQUID, TOXIC, N.O.S.	8	CT1	I	8 +6.1	274	LQ0	E0	P001		MP8 MP17	T14	TP2 TP27
2922	CORROSIVE LIQUID, TOXIC, N.O.S.	8	CT1	II	8 +6.1	274	LQ22	E2	P001 IBC02		MP15	T7	TP2
2922	CORROSIVE LIQUID, TOXIC, N.O.S.	8	CT1	III	8 +6.1	274	LQ7	E1	P001 IBC03 R001		MP19	T7	TP1 TP28
2923	CORROSIVE SOLID, TOXIC, N.O.S.	8	CT2	I	8 +6.1	274	LQ0	E0	P002 IBC05		MP18	T6	TP33
2923	CORROSIVE SOLID, TOXIC, N.O.S.	8	CT2	II	8 +6.1	274	LQ23	E2	P002 IBC08	B4	MP10	T3	TP33
2923	CORROSIVE SOLID, TOXIC, N.O.S.	8	CT2	III	8 +6.1	274	LQ24	E1	P002 IBC08 R001	B3	MP10	T1	TP33
2924	FLAMMABLE LIQUID, CORROSIVE, N.O.S.	3	FC	I	3 +8	274	LQ3	E0	P001		MP7 MP17	T14	TP2
2924	FLAMMABLE LIQUID, CORROSIVE, N.O.S.	3	FC	II	3 +8	274	LQ4	E2	P001 IBC02		MP19	T11	TP2 TP27
2924	FLAMMABLE LIQUID, CORROSIVE, N.O.S.	3	FC	III	3 +8	274	LQ7	E1	P001 IBC03 R001		MP19	T7	TP1 TP28
2925	FLAMMABLE SOLID, CORROSIVE, ORGANIC, N.O.S.	4.1	FC1	II	4.1 +8	274	LQ0	E2	P002 IBC06		MP10	T3	TP33
2925	FLAMMABLE SOLID, CORROSIVE, ORGANIC, N.O.S.	4.1	FC1	III	4.1 +8	274	LQ0	E1	P002 IBC06 R001		MP10	T1	TP33

ADR tank		Vehicle for tank carriage	Transport category (Tunnel restriction code)	Special provisions for carriage				Hazard identifi-cation No.	UN No.	Name and description
Tank code	Special provisions			Packages	Bulk	Loading, unloading and handling	Operation			
4.3	4.3.5, 6.8.4	9.1.1.2	1.1.3.6 (8.6)	7.2.4	7.3.3	7.5.11	8.5	5.3.2.3		3.1.2
(12)	(13)	(14)	(15)	(16)	(17)	(18)	(19)	(20)	(1)	(2)
			4 (E)			CV33	S5 S13 S21		2909	RADIOACTIVE MATERIAL, EXCEPTED PACKAGE - ARTICLES MANUFACTURED FROM NATURAL URANIUM or DEPLETED URANIUM or NATURAL THORIUM
			4 (E)			CV33	S5 S13 S21		2910	RADIOACTIVE MATERIAL, EXCEPTED PACKAGE - LIMITED QUANTITY OF MATERIAL
			4 (E)			CV33	S5 S13 S21		2911	RADIOACTIVE MATERIAL, EXCEPTED PACKAGE - INSTRUMENTS or ARTICLES
S2.65AN(+) L2.65CN(+)	TU36 TT7 TM7	AT	0 (E)		VV16	CV33	S6 S11 S13 S21	70	2912	RADIOACTIVE MATERIAL, LOW SPECIFIC ACTIVITY (LSA-I), non fissile or fissile-excepted
			0 (E)		VV17	CV33	S6 S11 S13 S21	70	2913	RADIOACTIVE MATERIAL, SURFACE CONTAMINATED OBJECTS (SCO-I or SCO-II), non fissile or fissile-excepted
			0 (E)			CV33	S6 S11 S12 S13 S21	70	2915	RADIOACTIVE MATERIAL, TYPE A PACKAGE, non-special form, non fissile or fissile-excepted
			0 (E)			CV33	S6 S11 S13 S21	70	2916	RADIOACTIVE MATERIAL, TYPE B(U) PACKAGE, non fissile or fissile-excepted
			0 (E)			CV33	S6 S11 S13 S21	70	2917	RADIOACTIVE MATERIAL, TYPE B(M) PACKAGE, non fissile or fissile-excepted
			0 (-)			CV33	S6 S11 S13 S21	70	2919	RADIOACTIVE MATERIAL, TRANSPORTED UNDER SPECIAL ARRANGEMENT, non fissile or fissile-excepted
L10BH		FL	1 (D/E)				S2 S14	883	2920	CORROSIVE LIQUID, FLAMMABLE, N.O.S.
L4BN		FL	2 (D/E)				S2	83	2920	CORROSIVE LIQUID, FLAMMABLE, N.O.S.
S10AN L10BH		AT	1 (E)	V10			S14	884	2921	CORROSIVE SOLID, FLAMMABLE, N.O.S.
SGAN L4BN		AT	2 (E)	V11				84	2921	CORROSIVE SOLID, FLAMMABLE, N.O.S.
L10BH		AT	1 (C/D)			CV13 CV28	S14	886	2922	CORROSIVE LIQUID, TOXIC, N.O.S.
L4BN		AT	2 (E)			CV13 CV28		86	2922	CORROSIVE LIQUID, TOXIC, N.O.S.
L4BN		AT	3 (E)			CV13 CV28		86	2922	CORROSIVE LIQUID, TOXIC, N.O.S.
S10AN L10BH		AT	1 (E)	V10		CV13 CV28	S14	886	2923	CORROSIVE SOLID, TOXIC, N.O.S.
SGAN L4BN		AT	2 (E)	V11		CV13 CV28		86	2923	CORROSIVE SOLID, TOXIC, N.O.S.
SGAV L4BN		AT	3 (E)		VV9	CV13 CV28		86	2923	CORROSIVE SOLID, TOXIC, N.O.S.
L10CH	TU14 TE21	FL	1 (C/E)				S2 S20	338	2924	FLAMMABLE LIQUID, CORROSIVE, N.O.S.
L4BH		FL	2 (D/E)				S2 S20	338	2924	FLAMMABLE LIQUID, CORROSIVE, N.O.S.
L4BN		FL	3 (D/E)				S2	38	2924	FLAMMABLE LIQUID, CORROSIVE, N.O.S.
SGAN		AT	2 (E)	V11 V12				48	2925	FLAMMABLE SOLID, CORROSIVE, ORGANIC, N.O.S.
SGAN		AT	3 (E)	V12				48	2925	FLAMMABLE SOLID, CORROSIVE, ORGANIC, N.O.S.

UN No.	Name and description	Class	Classifi-cation code	Packing group	Labels	Special provi-sions	Limited and excepted quantities		Packaging			Portable tanks and bulk containers	
									Packing instruc-tions	Special packing provisions	Mixed packing provisions	Instruc-tions	Special provisions
	3.1.2	2.2	2.2	2.1.1.3	5.2.2	3.3	3.4.6	3.5.1.2	4.1.4	4.1.4	4.1.10	4.2.5.2 7.3.2	4.2.5.3
(1)	(2)	(3a)	(3b)	(4)	(5)	(6)	(7a)	(7b)	(8)	(9a)	(9b)	(10)	(11)
2926	FLAMMABLE SOLID, TOXIC, ORGANIC, N.O.S.	4.1	FT1	II	4.1 +6.1	274	LQ0	E2	P002 IBC06		MP10	T3	TP33
2926	FLAMMABLE SOLID, TOXIC, ORGANIC, N.O.S.	4.1	FT1	III	4.1 +6.1	274	LQ0	E1	P002 IBC06 R001		MP10	T1	TP33
2927	TOXIC LIQUID, CORROSIVE, ORGANIC, N.O.S.	6.1	TC1	I	6.1 +8	274 315	LQ0	E5	P001		MP8 MP17	T14	TP2 TP27
2927	TOXIC LIQUID, CORROSIVE, ORGANIC, N.O.S.	6.1	TC1	II	6.1 +8	274	LQ17	E4	P001 IBC02		MP15	T11	TP2 TP27
2928	TOXIC SOLID, CORROSIVE, ORGANIC, N.O.S.	6.1	TC2	I	6.1 +8	274	LQ0	E5	P002 IBC05		MP18	T6	TP33
2928	TOXIC SOLID, CORROSIVE, ORGANIC, N.O.S.	6.1	TC2	II	6.1 +8	274	LQ18	E4	P002 IBC06		MP10	T3	TP33
2929	TOXIC LIQUID, FLAMMABLE, ORGANIC, N.O.S.	6.1	TF1	I	6.1 +3	274 315	LQ0	E5	P001		MP8 MP17	T14	TP2 TP27
2929	TOXIC LIQUID, FLAMMABLE, ORGANIC, N.O.S.	6.1	TF1	II	6.1 +3	274	LQ17	E4	P001 IBC02		MP15	T11	TP2 TP27
2930	TOXIC SOLID, FLAMMABLE, ORGANIC, N.O.S.	6.1	TF3	I	6.1 +4.1	274	LQ0	E5	P002 IBC05		MP18	T6	TP33
2930	TOXIC SOLID, FLAMMABLE, ORGANIC, N.O.S.	6.1	TF3	II	6.1 +4.1	274	LQ18	E4	P002 IBC08	B4	MP10	T3	TP33
2931	VANADYL SULPHATE	6.1	T5	II	6.1		LQ18	E4	P002 IBC08	B4	MP10	T3	TP33
2933	METHYL 2-CHLOROPROPIONATE	3	F1	III	3		LQ7	E1	P001 IBC03 LP01 R001		MP19	T2	TP1
2934	ISOPROPYL 2-CHLOROPROPIONATE	3	F1	III	3		LQ7	E1	P001 IBC03 LP01 R001		MP19	T2	TP1
2935	ETHYL 2-CHLOROPROPIONATE	3	F1	III	3		LQ7	E1	P001 IBC03 LP01 R001		MP19	T2	TP1
2936	THIOLACTIC ACID	6.1	T1	II	6.1		LQ17	E4	P001 IBC02		MP15	T7	TP2
2937	alpha-METHYLBENZYL ALCOHOL, LIQUID	6.1	T1	III	6.1		LQ7	E1	P001 IBC03 LP01 R001		MP19	T4	TP1
2940	9-PHOSPHABICYCLO-NONANES (CYCLOOCTADIENE PHOSPHINES)	4.2	S2	II	4.2		LQ0	E2	P410 IBC06		MP14	T3	TP33
2941	FLUOROANILINES	6.1	T1	III	6.1		LQ7	E1	P001 IBC03 LP01 R001		MP19	T4	TP1
2942	2-TRIFLUOROMETHYL-ANILINE	6.1	T1	III	6.1		LQ7	E1	P001 IBC03 LP01 R001		MP19		
2943	TETRAHYDROFURFURYL-AMINE	3	F1	III	3		LQ7	E1	P001 IBC03 LP01 R001		MP19	T2	TP1
2945	N-METHYLBUTYLAMINE	3	FC	II	3 +8		LQ4	E2	P001 IBC02		MP19	T7	TP1
2946	2-AMINO-5-DIETHYLAMINOPENTANE	6.1	T1	III	6.1		LQ7	E1	P001 IBC03 LP01 R001		MP19	T4	TP1

ADR tank		Vehicle for tank carriage	Transport category (Tunnel restriction code)	Special provisions for carriage				Hazard identifi-cation No.	UN No.	Name and description
Tank code	Special provisions			Packages	Bulk	Loading, unloading and handling	Operation			
4.3	4.3.5, 6.8.4	9.1.1.2	1.1.3.6 (8.6)	7.2.4	7.3.3	7.5.11	8.5	5.3.2.3		3.1.2
(12)	(13)	(14)	(15)	(16)	(17)	(18)	(19)	(20)	(1)	(2)
SGAN		AT	2 (E)	V11 V12		CV28		46	2926	FLAMMABLE SOLID, TOXIC, ORGANIC, N.O.S.
SGAN		AT	3 (E)	V12		CV28		46	2926	FLAMMABLE SOLID, TOXIC, ORGANIC, N.O.S.
L10CH	TU14 TU15 TE19 TE21	AT	1 (C/E)			CV1 CV13 CV28	S9 S14	668	2927	TOXIC LIQUID, CORROSIVE, ORGANIC, N.O.S.
L4BH	TU15 TE19	AT	2 (D/E)			CV13 CV28	S9 S19	68	2927	TOXIC LIQUID, CORROSIVE, ORGANIC, N.O.S.
S10AH	TU14 TU15 TE19 TE21	AT	1 (C/E)	V10		CV1 CV13 CV28	S9 S14	668	2928	TOXIC SOLID, CORROSIVE, ORGANIC, N.O.S.
SGAH L4BH	TU15 TE19	AT	2 (D/E)	V11 V12		CV13 CV28	S9 S19	68	2928	TOXIC SOLID, CORROSIVE, ORGANIC, N.O.S.
L10CH	TU14 TU15 TE19 TE21	FL	1 (C/D)			CV1 CV13 CV28	S2 S9 S14	663	2929	TOXIC LIQUID, FLAMMABLE, ORGANIC, N.O.S.
L4BH	TU15 TE19	FL	2 (D/E)			CV13 CV28	S2 S9 S19	63	2929	TOXIC LIQUID, FLAMMABLE, ORGANIC, N.O.S.
		AT	1 (C/E)	V10		CV1 CV13 CV28	S9 S14	664	2930	TOXIC SOLID, FLAMMABLE, ORGANIC, N.O.S.
SGAH L4BH	TU15 TE19	AT	2 (D/E)	V11		CV13 CV28	S9 S19	64	2930	TOXIC SOLID, FLAMMABLE, ORGANIC, N.O.S.
SGAH	TU15 TE19	AT	2 (D/E)	V11		CV13 CV28	S9 S19	60	2931	VANADYL SULPHATE
LGBF		FL	3 (D/E)				S2	30	2933	METHYL 2-CHLOROPROPIONATE
LGBF		FL	3 (D/E)				S2	30	2934	ISOPROPYL 2-CHLOROPROPIONATE
LGBF		FL	3 (D/E)				S2	30	2935	ETHYL 2-CHLOROPROPIONATE
L4BH	TU15 TE19	AT	2 (D/E)			CV13 CV28	S9 S19	60	2936	THIOLACTIC ACID
L4BH	TU15 TE19	AT	2 (E)			CV13 CV28	S9	60	2937	alpha-METHYLBENZYL ALCOHOL, LIQUID
SGAN		AT	2 (D/E)	V1 V12				40	2940	9-PHOSPHABICYCLO-NONANES (CYCLOOCTADIENE PHOSPHINES)
L4BH	TU15 TE19	AT	2 (E)			CV13 CV28	S9	60	2941	FLUOROANILINES
L4BH	TU15 TE19	AT	2 (E)			CV13 CV28	S9	60	2942	2-TRIFLUOROMETHYL-ANILINE
LGBF		FL	3 (D/E)				S2	30	2943	TETRAHYDROFURFURYL-AMINE
L4BH		FL	2 (D/E)				S2 S20	338	2945	N-METHYLBUTYLAMINE
L4BH	TU15 TE19	AT	2 (E)			CV13 CV28	S9	60	2946	2-AMINO-5-DIETHYLAMINOPENTANE

UN No.	Name and description	Class	Classifi-cation code	Packing group	Labels	Special provi-sions	Limited and excepted quantities		Packaging			Portable tanks and bulk containers	
									Packing instruc-tions	Special packing provisions	Mixed packing provisions	Instruc-tions	Special provisions
	3.1.2	2.2	2.2	2.1.1.3	5.2.2	3.3	3.4.6	3.5.1.2	4.1.4	4.1.4	4.1.10	4.2.5.2 7.3.2	4.2.5.3
(1)	(2)	(3a)	(3b)	(4)	(5)	(6)	(7a)	(7b)	(8)	(9a)	(9b)	(10)	(11)
2947	ISOPROPYL CHLOROACETATE	3	F1	III	3		LQ7	E1	P001 IBC03 LP01 R001		MP19	T2	TP1
2948	3-TRIFLUOROMETHYL-ANILINE	6.1	T1	II	6.1		LQ17	E4	P001 IBC02		MP15	T7	TP2
2949	SODIUM HYDROSULPHIDE, HYDRATED with not less than 25% water of crystallization	8	C6	II	8	523	LQ23	E2	P002 IBC08	B4	MP10	T7	TP2
2950	MAGNESIUM GRANULES, COATED, particle size not less than 149 microns	4.3	W2	III	4.3		LQ12	E1	P410 IBC08 R001	B4	MP14	T1 BK2	TP33
2956	5-tert-BUTYL-2,4,6-TRINITRO-m-XYLENE (MUSK XYLENE)	4.1	SR1	III	4.1	638	LQ0	E1	P409		MP2		
2965	BORON TRIFLUORIDE DIMETHYL ETHERATE	4.3	WFC	I	4.3 +3 +8		LQ0	E0	P401		MP2	T10	TP2 TP7
2966	THIOGLYCOL	6.1	T1	II	6.1		LQ17	E4	P001 IBC02		MP15	T7	TP2
2967	SULPHAMIC ACID	8	C2	III	8		LQ24	E1	P002 IBC08 LP02 R001	B3	MP10	T1	TP33
2968	MANEB, STABILIZED or MANEB PREPARATION, STABILIZED against self-heating	4.3	W2	III	4.3	547	LQ12	E1	P002 IBC08 R001	B4	MP14	T1	TP33
2969	CASTOR BEANS or CASTOR MEAL or CASTOR POMACE or CASTOR FLAKE	9	M11	II	9	141	LQ25	E2	P002 IBC08	PP34 B4	MP10	T3 BK1 BK2	TP33
2977	RADIOACTIVE MATERIAL, URANIUM HEXAFLUORIDE, FISSILE	7			7X +7E +8	172	LQ0	E0	See 2.2.7 and 4.1.9	See 4.1.9.1.3			
2978	RADIOACTIVE MATERIAL, URANIUM HEXAFLUORIDE, non fissile or fissile-excepted	7			7X +8	172 317	LQ0	E0	See 2.2.7 and 4.1.9	See 4.1.9.1.3			
2983	ETHYLENE OXIDE AND PROPYLENE OXIDE MIXTURE, not more than 30% ethylene oxide	3	FT1	I	3 +6.1		LQ0	E0	P001		MP7 MP17	T14	TP2 TP7
2984	HYDROGEN PEROXIDE, AQUEOUS SOLUTION with not less than 8% but less than 20% hydrogen peroxide (stabilized as necessary)	5.1	O1	III	5.1	65	LQ13	E1	P504 IBC02 R001	PP10 B5	MP15	T4	TP1 TP6 TP24
2985	CHLOROSILANES, FLAMMABLE, CORROSIVE, N.O.S.	3	FC	II	3 +8	274 548	LQ4	E2	P010		MP19	T14	TP2 TP7 TP27
2986	CHLOROSILANES, CORROSIVE, FLAMMABLE, N.O.S.	8	CF1	II	8 +3	274 548	LQ22	E2	P010		MP15	T14	TP2 TP7 TP27
2987	CHLOROSILANES, CORROSIVE, N.O.S.	8	C3	II	8	274 548	LQ22	E2	P010		MP15	T14	TP2 TP7 TP27
2988	CHLOROSILANES, WATER-REACTIVE, FLAMMABLE, CORROSIVE, N.O.S.	4.3	WFC	I	4.3 +3 +8	274 549	LQ0	E0	P401	RR7	MP2	T14	TP2 TP7
2989	LEAD PHOSPHITE, DIBASIC	4.1	F3	II	4.1		LQ8	E2	P002 IBC08	B4	MP11	T3	TP33
2989	LEAD PHOSPHITE, DIBASIC	4.1	F3	III	4.1		LQ9	E1	P002 IBC08 LP02 R001	B3	MP11	T1	TP33
2990	LIFE-SAVING APPLIANCES, SELF-INFLATING	9	M5		9	296 635	LQ0	E0	P905				

ADR tank		Vehicle for tank carriage	Transport category (Tunnel restriction code)	Special provisions for carriage				Hazard identification No.	UN No.	Name and description
Tank code	Special provisions			Packages	Bulk	Loading, unloading and handling	Operation			
4.3	4.3.5, 6.8.4	9.1.1.2	1.1.3.6 (8.6)	7.2.4	7.3.3	7.5.11	8.5	5.3.2.3		3.1.2
(12)	(13)	(14)	(15)	(16)	(17)	(18)	(19)	(20)	(1)	(2)
LGBF		FL	3 (D/E)				S2	30	2947	ISOPROPYL CHLOROACETATE
L4BH	TU15 TE19	AT	2 (D/E)			CV13 CV28	S9 S19	60	2948	3-TRIFLUOROMETHYL-ANILINE
SGAN L4BN		AT	2 (E)	V11				80	2949	SODIUM HYDROSULPHIDE, HYDRATED with not less than 25% water of crystallization
SGAN		AT	3 (E)	V1	VV5	CV23		423	2950	MAGNESIUM GRANULES, COATED, particle size not less than 149 microns
			3 (D)			CV14	S24		2956	5-tert-BUTYL-2,4,6-TRINITRO-m-XYLENE (MUSK XYLENE)
L10DH	TU4 TU14 TU22 TE21 TM2	FL	0 (B/E)	V1		CV23	S2 S20	382	2965	BORON TRIFLUORIDE DIMETHYL ETHERATE
L4BH	TU15 TE19	AT	2 (D/E)			CV13 CV28	S9 S19	60	2966	THIOGLYCOL
SGAV		AT	3 (E)		VV9			80	2967	SULPHAMIC ACID
SGAN		AT	0 (E)	V1	VV5	CV23		423	2968	MANEB, STABILIZED or MANEB PREPARATION, STABILIZED against self-heating
SGAV		AT	2 (E)	V11	VV3			90	2969	CASTOR BEANS or CASTOR MEAL or CASTOR POMACE or CASTOR FLAKE
			0 (C)			CV33	S6 S11 S13 S21	78	2977	RADIOACTIVE MATERIAL, URANIUM HEXAFLUORIDE, FISSILE
			0 (C)			CV33	S6 S11 S13 S21	78	2978	RADIOACTIVE MATERIAL, URANIUM HEXAFLUORIDE, non fissile or fissile-excepted
L10CH	TU14 TU15 TE21	FL	1 (C/E)			CV13 CV28	S2 S22	336	2983	ETHYLENE OXIDE AND PROPYLENE OXIDE MIXTURE, not more than 30% ethylene oxide
LGBV	TU3 TC2 TE8 TE11 TT1	AT	3 (E)			CV24		50	2984	HYDROGEN PEROXIDE, AQUEOUS SOLUTION with not less than 8% but less than 20% hydrogen peroxide (stabilized as necessary)
L4BH		FL	2 (D/E)				S2 S20	X338	2985	CHLOROSILANES, FLAMMABLE, CORROSIVE, N.O.S.
L4BN		FL	2 (D/E)				S2	X83	2986	CHLOROSILANES, CORROSIVE, FLAMMABLE, N.O.S.
L4BN		AT	2 (E)					X80	2987	CHLOROSILANES, CORROSIVE, N.O.S.
L10DH	TU14 TU26 TE21 TM2 TM3	FL	0 (B/E)	V1		CV23	S2 S20	X338	2988	CHLOROSILANES, WATER-REACTIVE, FLAMMABLE, CORROSIVE, N.O.S.
SGAN		AT	2 (E)	V11				40	2989	LEAD PHOSPHITE, DIBASIC
SGAV		AT	3 (E)		VV1			40	2989	LEAD PHOSPHITE, DIBASIC
			3 (E)						2990	LIFE-SAVING APPLIANCES, SELF-INFLATING

UN No.	Name and description	Class	Classification code	Packing group	Labels	Special provisions	Limited and excepted quantities		Packaging			Portable tanks and bulk containers	
									Packing instructions	Special packing provisions	Mixed packing provisions	Instructions	Special provisions
	3.1.2	2.2	2.2	2.1.1.3	5.2.2	3.3	3.4.6	3.5.1.2	4.1.4	4.1.4	4.1.10	4.2.5.2 7.3.2	4.2.5.3
(1)	(2)	(3a)	(3b)	(4)	(5)	(6)	(7a)	(7b)	(8)	(9a)	(9b)	(10)	(11)
2991	CARBAMATE PESTICIDE, LIQUID, TOXIC, FLAMMABLE, flash-point not less than 23 °C	6.1	TF2	I	6.1 +3	61 274	LQ0	E5	P001		MP8 MP17	T14	TP2 TP27
2991	CARBAMATE PESTICIDE, LIQUID, TOXIC, FLAMMABLE, flash-point not less than 23 °C	6.1	TF2	II	6.1 +3	61 274	LQ17	E4	P001 IBC02		MP15	T11	TP2 TP27
2991	CARBAMATE PESTICIDE, LIQUID, TOXIC, FLAMMABLE, flash-point not less than 23 °C	6.1	TF2	III	6.1 +3	61 274	LQ7	E1	P001 IBC03 R001		MP19	T7	TP2 TP28
2992	CARBAMATE PESTICIDE, LIQUID, TOXIC	6.1	T6	I	6.1	61 274 648	LQ0	E5	P001		MP8 MP17	T14	TP2 TP27
2992	CARBAMATE PESTICIDE, LIQUID, TOXIC	6.1	T6	II	6.1	61 274 648	LQ17	E4	P001 IBC02		MP15	T11	TP2 TP27
2992	CARBAMATE PESTICIDE, LIQUID, TOXIC	6.1	T6	III	6.1	61 274 648	LQ7	E1	P001 IBC03 LP01 R001		MP19	T7	TP2 TP28
2993	ARSENICAL PESTICIDE, LIQUID, TOXIC, FLAMMABLE, flash-point not less than 23 °C	6.1	TF2	I	6.1 +3	61 274	LQ0	E5	P001		MP8 MP17	T14	TP2 TP27
2993	ARSENICAL PESTICIDE, LIQUID, TOXIC, FLAMMABLE, flash-point not less than 23 °C	6.1	TF2	II	6.1 +3	61 274	LQ17	E4	P001 IBC02		MP15	T11	TP2 TP27
2993	ARSENICAL PESTICIDE, LIQUID, TOXIC, FLAMMABLE, flash-point not less than 23 °C	6.1	TF2	III	6.1 +3	61 274	LQ7	E1	P001 IBC03 R001		MP19	T7	TP2 TP28
2994	ARSENICAL PESTICIDE, LIQUID, TOXIC	6.1	T6	I	6.1	61 274 648	LQ0	E5	P001		MP8 MP17	T14	TP2 TP27
2994	ARSENICAL PESTICIDE, LIQUID, TOXIC	6.1	T6	II	6.1	61 274 648	LQ17	E4	P001 IBC02		MP15	T11	TP2 TP27
2994	ARSENICAL PESTICIDE, LIQUID, TOXIC	6.1	T6	III	6.1	61 274 648	LQ7	E1	P001 IBC03 LP01 R001		MP19	T7	TP2 TP28
2995	ORGANOCHLORINE PESTICIDE, LIQUID, TOXIC, FLAMMABLE, flash-point not less than 23 °C	6.1	TF2	I	6.1 +3	61 274	LQ0	E5	P001		MP8 MP17	T14	TP2 TP27
2995	ORGANOCHLORINE PESTICIDE, LIQUID, TOXIC, FLAMMABLE, flash-point not less than 23 °C	6.1	TF2	II	6.1 +3	61 274	LQ17	E4	P001 IBC02		MP15	T11	TP2 TP27
2995	ORGANOCHLORINE PESTICIDE, LIQUID, TOXIC, FLAMMABLE, flash-point not less than 23 °C	6.1	TF2	III	6.1 +3	61 274	LQ7	E1	P001 IBC03 R001		MP19	T7	TP2 TP28
2996	ORGANOCHLORINE PESTICIDE, LIQUID, TOXIC	6.1	T6	I	6.1	61 274 648	LQ0	E5	P001		MP8 MP17	T14	TP2 TP27
2996	ORGANOCHLORINE PESTICIDE, LIQUID, TOXIC	6.1	T6	II	6.1	61 274 648	LQ17	E4	P001 IBC02		MP15	T11	TP2 TP27
2996	ORGANOCHLORINE PESTICIDE, LIQUID, TOXIC	6.1	T6	III	6.1	61 274 648	LQ7	E1	P001 IBC03 LP01 R001		MP19	T7	TP2 TP28
2997	TRIAZINE PESTICIDE, LIQUID, TOXIC, FLAMMABLE, flash-point not less than 23 °C	6.1	TF2	I	6.1 +3	61 274	LQ0	E5	P001		MP8 MP17	T14	TP2 TP27

ADR tank		Vehicle for tank carriage	Transport category (Tunnel restriction code)	Special provisions for carriage				Hazard identifi-cation No.	UN No.	Name and description
Tank code	Special provisions			Packages	Bulk	Loading, unloading and handling	Operation			
4.3	4.3.5, 6.8.4	9.1.1.2	1.1.3.6 (8.6)	7.2.4	7.3.3	7.5.11	8.5	5.3.2.3		3.1.2
(12)	(13)	(14)	(15)	(16)	(17)	(18)	(19)	(20)	(1)	(2)
L10CH	TU14 TU15 TE19 TE21	FL	1 (C/E)			CV1 CV13 CV28	S2 S9 S14	663	2991	CARBAMATE PESTICIDE, LIQUID, TOXIC, FLAMMABLE, flash-point not less than 23 °C
L4BH	TU15 TE19	FL	2 (D/E)			CV13 CV28	S2 S9 S19	63	2991	CARBAMATE PESTICIDE, LIQUID, TOXIC, FLAMMABLE, flash-point not less than 23 °C
L4BH	TU15 TE19	FL	2 (D/E)			CV13 CV28	S2 S9	63	2991	CARBAMATE PESTICIDE, LIQUID, TOXIC, FLAMMABLE, flash-point not less than 23 °C
L10CH	TU14 TU15 TE19 TE21	AT	1 (C/E)			CV1 CV13 CV28	S9 S14	66	2992	CARBAMATE PESTICIDE, LIQUID, TOXIC
L4BH	TU15 TE19	AT	2 (D/E)			CV13 CV28	S9 S19	60	2992	CARBAMATE PESTICIDE, LIQUID, TOXIC
L4BH	TU15 TE19	AT	2 (E)			CV13 CV28	S9	60	2992	CARBAMATE PESTICIDE, LIQUID, TOXIC
L10CH	TU14 TU15 TE19 TE21	FL	1 (C/E)			CV1 CV13 CV28	S2 S9 S14	663	2993	ARSENICAL PESTICIDE, LIQUID, TOXIC, FLAMMABLE, flash-point not less than 23 °C
L4BH	TU15 TE19	FL	2 (D/E)			CV13 CV28	S2 S9 S19	63	2993	ARSENICAL PESTICIDE, LIQUID, TOXIC, FLAMMABLE, flash-point not less than 23 °C
L4BH	TU15 TE19	FL	2 (D/E)			CV13 CV28	S2 S9	63	2993	ARSENICAL PESTICIDE, LIQUID, TOXIC, FLAMMABLE, flash-point not less than 23 °C
L10CH	TU14 TU15 TE19 TE21	AT	1 (C/E)			CV1 CV13 CV28	S9 S14	66	2994	ARSENICAL PESTICIDE, LIQUID, TOXIC
L4BH	TU15 TE19	AT	2 (D/E)			CV13 CV28	S9 S19	60	2994	ARSENICAL PESTICIDE, LIQUID, TOXIC
L4BH	TU15 TE19	AT	2 (E)			CV13 CV28	S9	60	2994	ARSENICAL PESTICIDE, LIQUID, TOXIC
L10CH	TU14 TU15 TE19 TE21	FL	1 (C/E)			CV1 CV13 CV28	S2 S9 S14	663	2995	ORGANOCHLORINE PESTICIDE, LIQUID, TOXIC, FLAMMABLE, flash-point not less than 23 °C
L4BH	TU15 TE19	FL	2 (D/E)			CV13 CV28	S2 S9 S19	63	2995	ORGANOCHLORINE PESTICIDE, LIQUID, TOXIC, FLAMMABLE, flash-point not less than 23 °C
L4BH	TU15 TE19	FL	2 (D/E)			CV13 CV28	S2 S9	63	2995	ORGANOCHLORINE PESTICIDE, LIQUID, TOXIC, FLAMMABLE, flash-point not less than 23 °C
L10CH	TU14 TU15 TE19 TE21	AT	1 (C/E)			CV1 CV13 CV28	S9 S14	66	2996	ORGANOCHLORINE PESTICIDE, LIQUID, TOXIC
L4BH	TU15 TE19	AT	2 (D/E)			CV13 CV28	S9 S19	60	2996	ORGANOCHLORINE PESTICIDE, LIQUID, TOXIC
L4BH	TU15 TE19	AT	2 (E)			CV13 CV28	S9	60	2996	ORGANOCHLORINE PESTICIDE, LIQUID, TOXIC
L10CH	TU14 TU15 TE19 TE21	FL	1 (C/E)			CV1 CV13 CV28	S2 S9 S14	663	2997	TRIAZINE PESTICIDE, LIQUID, TOXIC, FLAMMABLE, flash-point not less than 23 °C

UN No.	Name and description	Class	Classifi- cation code	Packing group	Labels	Special provi- sions	Limited and excepted quantities		Packaging			Portable tanks and bulk containers	
									Packing instruc- tions	Special packing provisions	Mixed packing provisions	Instruc- tions	Special provisions
	3.1.2	2.2	2.2	2.1.1.3	5.2.2	3.3	3.4.6	3.5.1.2	4.1.4	4.1.4	4.1.10	4.2.5.2 7.3.2	4.2.5.3
(1)	(2)	(3a)	(3b)	(4)	(5)	(6)	(7a)	(7b)	(8)	(9a)	(9b)	(10)	(11)
2997	TRIAZINE PESTICIDE, LIQUID, TOXIC, FLAMMABLE, flash-point not less than 23 °C	6.1	TF2	II	6.1 +3	61 274	LQ17	E4	P001 IBC02		MP15	T11	TP2 TP27
2997	TRIAZINE PESTICIDE, LIQUID, TOXIC, FLAMMABLE, flash-point not less than 23 °C	6.1	TF2	III	6.1 +3	61 274	LQ7	E1	P001 IBC03 R001		MP19	T7	TP2 TP28
2998	TRIAZINE PESTICIDE, LIQUID, TOXIC	6.1	T6	I	6.1	61 274 648	LQ0	E5	P001		MP8 MP17	T14	TP2 TP27
2998	TRIAZINE PESTICIDE, LIQUID, TOXIC	6.1	T6	II	6.1	61 274 648	LQ17	E4	P001 IBC02		MP15	T11	TP2 TP27
2998	TRIAZINE PESTICIDE, LIQUID, TOXIC	6.1	T6	III	6.1	61 274 648	LQ7	E1	P001 IBC03 LP01 R001		MP19	T7	TP2 TP28
3005	THIOCARBAMATE PESTICIDE, LIQUID, TOXIC, FLAMMABLE, flash-point not less than 23 °C	6.1	TF2	I	6.1 +3	61 274	LQ0	E5	P001		MP8 MP17	T14	TP2
3005	THIOCARBAMATE PESTICIDE, LIQUID, TOXIC, FLAMMABLE, flash-point not less than 23 °C	6.1	TF2	II	6.1 +3	61 274	LQ17	E4	P001 IBC02		MP15	T11	TP2 TP27
3005	THIOCARBAMATE PESTICIDE, LIQUID, TOXIC, FLAMMABLE, flash-point not less than 23 °C	6.1	TF2	III	6.1 +3	61 274	LQ7	E1	P001 IBC03 R001		MP19	T7	TP2 TP28
3006	THIOCARBAMATE PESTICIDE, LIQUID, TOXIC	6.1	T6	I	6.1	61 274 648	LQ0	E5	P001		MP8 MP17	T14	TP2
3006	THIOCARBAMATE PESTICIDE, LIQUID, TOXIC	6.1	T6	II	6.1	61 274 648	LQ17	E4	P001 IBC02		MP15	T11	TP2 TP27
3006	THIOCARBAMATE PESTICIDE, LIQUID, TOXIC	6.1	T6	III	6.1	61 274 648	LQ7	E1	P001 IBC03 LP01 R001		MP19	T7	TP2 TP28
3009	COPPER BASED PESTICIDE, LIQUID, TOXIC, FLAMMABLE, flash-point not less than 23 °C	6.1	TF2	I	6.1 +3	61 274	LQ0	E5	P001		MP8 MP17	T14	TP2 TP27
3009	COPPER BASED PESTICIDE, LIQUID, TOXIC, FLAMMABLE, flash-point not less than 23 °C	6.1	TF2	II	6.1 +3	61 274	LQ17	E4	P001 IBC02		MP15	T11	TP2 TP27
3009	COPPER BASED PESTICIDE, LIQUID, TOXIC, FLAMMABLE, flash-point not less than 23 °C	6.1	TF2	III	6.1 +3	61 274	LQ7	E1	P001 IBC03 R001		MP19	T7	TP2 TP28
3010	COPPER BASED PESTICIDE, LIQUID, TOXIC	6.1	T6	I	6.1	61 274 648	LQ0	E5	P001		MP8 MP17	T14	TP2 TP27
3010	COPPER BASED PESTICIDE, LIQUID, TOXIC	6.1	T6	II	6.1	61 274 648	LQ17	E4	P001 IBC02		MP15	T11	TP2 TP27
3010	COPPER BASED PESTICIDE, LIQUID, TOXIC	6.1	T6	III	6.1	61 274 648	LQ7	E1	P001 IBC03 LP01 R001		MP19	T7	TP2 TP28
3011	MERCURY BASED PESTICIDE, LIQUID, TOXIC, FLAMMABLE, flash-point not less than 23 °C	6.1	TF2	I	6.1 +3	61 274	LQ0	E5	P001		MP8 MP17	T14	TP2 TP27
3011	MERCURY BASED PESTICIDE, LIQUID, TOXIC, FLAMMABLE, flash-point not less than 23 °C	6.1	TF2	II	6.1 +3	61 274	LQ17	E4	P001 IBC02		MP15	T11	TP2 TP27

ADR tank		Vehicle for tank carriage	Transport category (Tunnel restriction code)	Special provisions for carriage				Hazard identifi- cation No.	UN No.	Name and description
Tank code	Special provisions			Packages	Bulk	Loading, unloading and handling	Operation			
4.3	4.3.5, 6.8.4	9.1.1.2	1.1.3.6 (8.6)	7.2.4	7.3.3	7.5.11	8.5	5.3.2.3		3.1.2
(12)	(13)	(14)	(15)	(16)	(17)	(18)	(19)	(20)	(1)	(2)
L4BH	TU15 TE19	FL	2 (D/E)			CV13 CV28	S2 S9 S19	63	2997	TRIAZINE PESTICIDE, LIQUID, TOXIC, FLAMMABLE, flash-point not less than 23 °C
L4BH	TU15 TE19	FL	2 (D/E)			CV13 CV28	S2 S9	63	2997	TRIAZINE PESTICIDE, LIQUID, TOXIC, FLAMMABLE, flash-point not less than 23 °C
L10CH	TU14 TU15 TE19 TE21	AT	1 (C/E)			CV1 CV13 CV28	S9 S14	66	2998	TRIAZINE PESTICIDE, LIQUID, TOXIC
L4BH	TU15 TE19	AT	2 (D/E)			CV13 CV28	S9 S19	60	2998	TRIAZINE PESTICIDE, LIQUID, TOXIC
L4BH	TU15 TE19	AT	2 (E)			CV13 CV28	S9	60	2998	TRIAZINE PESTICIDE, LIQUID, TOXIC
L10CH	TU14 TU15 TE19 TE21	FL	1 (C/E)			CV1 CV13 CV28	S2 S9 S14	663	3005	THIOCARBAMATE PESTICIDE, LIQUID, TOXIC, FLAMMABLE, flash-point not less than 23 °C
L4BH	TU15 TE19	FL	2 (D/E)			CV13 CV28	S2 S9 S19	63	3005	THIOCARBAMATE PESTICIDE, LIQUID, TOXIC, FLAMMABLE, flash-point not less than 23 °C
L4BH	TU15 TE19	FL	2 (D/E)			CV13 CV28	S2 S9	63	3005	THIOCARBAMATE PESTICIDE, LIQUID, TOXIC, FLAMMABLE, flash-point not less than 23 °C
L10CH	TU14 TU15 TE19 TE21	AT	1 (C/E)			CV1 CV13 CV28	S9 S14	66	3006	THIOCARBAMATE PESTICIDE, LIQUID, TOXIC
L4BH	TU15 TE19	AT	2 (D/E)			CV13 CV28	S9 S19	60	3006	THIOCARBAMATE PESTICIDE, LIQUID, TOXIC
L4BH	TU15 TE19	AT	2 (E)			CV13 CV28	S9	60	3006	THIOCARBAMATE PESTICIDE, LIQUID, TOXIC
L10CH	TU14 TU15 TE19 TE21	FL	1 (C/E)			CV1 CV13 CV28	S2 S9 S14	663	3009	COPPER BASED PESTICIDE, LIQUID, TOXIC, FLAMMABLE, flash-point not less than 23 °C
L4BH	TU15 TE19	FL	2 (D/E)			CV13 CV28	S2 S9 S19	63	3009	COPPER BASED PESTICIDE, LIQUID, TOXIC, FLAMMABLE, flash-point not less than 23 °C
L4BH	TU15 TE19	FL	2 (D/E)			CV13 CV28	S2 S9	63	3009	COPPER BASED PESTICIDE, LIQUID, TOXIC, FLAMMABLE, flash-point not less than 23 °C
L10CH	TU14 TU15 TE19 TE21	AT	1 (C/E)			CV1 CV13 CV28	S9 S14	66	3010	COPPER BASED PESTICIDE, LIQUID, TOXIC
L4BH	TU15 TE19	AT	2 (D/E)			CV13 CV28	S9 S19	60	3010	COPPER BASED PESTICIDE, LIQUID, TOXIC
L4BH	TU15 TE19	AT	2 (E)			CV13 CV28	S9	60	3010	COPPER BASED PESTICIDE, LIQUID, TOXIC
L10CH	TU14 TU15 TE19 TE21	FL	1 (C/E)			CV1 CV13 CV28	S2 S9 S14	663	3011	MERCURY BASED PESTICIDE, LIQUID, TOXIC, FLAMMABLE, flash-point not less than 23 °C
L4BH	TU15 TE19	FL	2 (D/E)			CV13 CV28	S2 S9 S19	63	3011	MERCURY BASED PESTICIDE, LIQUID, TOXIC, FLAMMABLE, flash-point not less than 23 °C

UN No.	Name and description	Class	Classifi-cation code	Packing group	Labels	Special provi-sions	Limited and excepted quantities		Packaging			Portable tanks and bulk containers	
									Packing instruc-tions	Special packing provisions	Mixed packing provisions	Instruc-tions	Special provisions
	3.1.2	2.2	2.2	2.1.1.3	5.2.2	3.3	3.4.6	3.5.1.2	4.1.4	4.1.4	4.1.10	4.2.5.2 7.3.2	4.2.5.3
(1)	(2)	(3a)	(3b)	(4)	(5)	(6)	(7a)	(7b)	(8)	(9a)	(9b)	(10)	(11)
3011	MERCURY BASED PESTICIDE, LIQUID, TOXIC, FLAMMABLE, flash-point not less than 23 °C	6.1	TF2	III	6.1 +3	61 274	LQ7	E1	P001 IBC03 R001		MP19	T7	TP2 TP28
3012	MERCURY BASED PESTICIDE, LIQUID, TOXIC	6.1	T6	I	6.1	61 274 648	LQ0	E5	P001		MP8 MP17	T14	TP2 TP27
3012	MERCURY BASED PESTICIDE, LIQUID, TOXIC	6.1	T6	II	6.1	61 274 648	LQ17	E4	P001 IBC02		MP15	T11	TP2 TP27
3012	MERCURY BASED PESTICIDE, LIQUID, TOXIC	6.1	T6	III	6.1	61 274 648	LQ7	E1	P001 IBC03 LP01 R001		MP19	T7	TP2 TP28
3013	SUBSTITUTED NITROPHENOL PESTICIDE, LIQUID, TOXIC, FLAMMABLE, flash-point not less than 23 °C	6.1	TF2	I	6.1 +3	61 274	LQ0	E5	P001		MP8 MP17	T14	TP2 TP27
3013	SUBSTITUTED NITROPHENOL PESTICIDE, LIQUID, TOXIC, FLAMMABLE, flash-point not less than 23 °C	6.1	TF2	II	6.1 +3	61 274	LQ17	E4	P001 IBC02		MP15	T11	TP2 TP27
3013	SUBSTITUTED NITROPHENOL PESTICIDE, LIQUID, TOXIC, FLAMMABLE, flash-point not less than 23 °C	6.1	TF2	III	6.1 +3	61 274	LQ7	E1	P001 IBC03 R001		MP19	T7	TP2 TP28
3014	SUBSTITUTED NITROPHENOL PESTICIDE, LIQUID, TOXIC	6.1	T6	I	6.1	61 274 648	LQ0	E5	P001		MP8 MP17	T14	TP2 TP27
3014	SUBSTITUTED NITROPHENOL PESTICIDE, LIQUID, TOXIC	6.1	T6	II	6.1	61 274 648	LQ17	E4	P001 IBC02		MP15	T11	TP2 TP27
3014	SUBSTITUTED NITROPHENOL PESTICIDE, LIQUID, TOXIC	6.1	T6	III	6.1	61 274 648	LQ7	E1	P001 IBC03 LP01 R001		MP19	T7	TP2 TP28
3015	BIPYRIDILIUM PESTICIDE, LIQUID, TOXIC, FLAMMABLE, flash-point not less than 23 °C	6.1	TF2	I	6.1 +3	61 274	LQ0	E5	P001		MP8 MP17	T14	TP2 TP27
3015	BIPYRIDILIUM PESTICIDE, LIQUID, TOXIC, FLAMMABLE, flash-point not less than 23 °C	6.1	TF2	II	6.1 +3	61 274	LQ17	E4	P001 IBC02		MP15	T11	TP2 TP27
3015	BIPYRIDILIUM PESTICIDE, LIQUID, TOXIC, FLAMMABLE, flash-point not less than 23 °C	6.1	TF2	III	6.1 +3	61 274	LQ7	E1	P001 IBC03 R001		MP19	T7	TP2 TP28
3016	BIPYRIDILIUM PESTICIDE, LIQUID, TOXIC	6.1	T6	I	6.1	61 274 648	LQ0	E5	P001		MP8 MP17	T14	TP2 TP27
3016	BIPYRIDILIUM PESTICIDE, LIQUID, TOXIC	6.1	T6	II	6.1	61 274 648	LQ17	E4	P001 IBC02		MP15	T11	TP2 TP27
3016	BIPYRIDILIUM PESTICIDE, LIQUID, TOXIC	6.1	T6	III	6.1	61 274 648	LQ7	E1	P001 IBC03 LP01 R001		MP19	T7	TP2 TP28
3017	ORGANOPHOSPHORUS PESTICIDE, LIQUID, TOXIC, FLAMMABLE, flash-point not less than 23 °C	6.1	TF2	I	6.1 +3	61 274	LQ0	E5	P001		MP8 MP17	T14	TP2 TP27
3017	ORGANOPHOSPHORUS PESTICIDE, LIQUID, TOXIC, FLAMMABLE, flash-point not less than 23 °C	6.1	TF2	II	6.1 +3	61 274	LQ17	E4	P001 IBC02		MP15	T11	TP2 TP27

ADR tank		Vehicle for tank carriage	Transport category (Tunnel restriction code)	Special provisions for carriage				Hazard identifi-cation No.	UN No.	Name and description
Tank code	Special provisions			Packages	Bulk	Loading, unloading and handling	Operation			
4.3	4.3.5, 6.8.4	9.1.1.2	1.1.3.6 (8.6)	7.2.4	7.3.3	7.5.11	8.5	5.3.2.3		3.1.2
(12)	(13)	(14)	(15)	(16)	(17)	(18)	(19)	(20)	(1)	(2)
L4BH	TU15 TE19	FL	2 (D/E)			CV13 CV28	S2 S9	63	3011	MERCURY BASED PESTICIDE, LIQUID, TOXIC, FLAMMABLE, flash-point not less than 23 °C
L10CH	TU14 TU15 TE19 TE21	AT	1 (C/E)			CV1 CV13 CV28	S9 S14	66	3012	MERCURY BASED PESTICIDE, LIQUID, TOXIC
L4BH	TU15 TE19	AT	2 (D/E)			CV13 CV28	S9 S19	60	3012	MERCURY BASED PESTICIDE, LIQUID, TOXIC
L4BH	TU15 TE19	AT	2 (E)			CV13 CV28	S9	60	3012	MERCURY BASED PESTICIDE, LIQUID, TOXIC
L10CH	TU14 TU15 TE19 TE21	FL	1 (C/E)			CV1 CV13 CV28	S2 S9 S14	663	3013	SUBSTITUTED NITROPHENOL PESTICIDE, LIQUID, TOXIC, FLAMMABLE, flash-point not less than 23 °C
L4BH	TU15 TE19	FL	2 (D/E)			CV13 CV28	S2 S9 S19	63	3013	SUBSTITUTED NITROPHENOL PESTICIDE, LIQUID, TOXIC, FLAMMABLE, flash-point not less than 23 °C
L4BH	TU15 TE19	FL	2 (D/E)			CV13 CV28	S2 S9	63	3013	SUBSTITUTED NITROPHENOL PESTICIDE, LIQUID, TOXIC, FLAMMABLE, flash-point not less than 23 °C
L10CH	TU14 TU15 TE19 TE21	AT	1 (C/E)			CV1 CV13 CV28	S9 S14	66	3014	SUBSTITUTED NITROPHENOL PESTICIDE, LIQUID, TOXIC
L4BH	TU15 TE19	AT	2 (D/E)			CV13 CV28	S9 S19	60	3014	SUBSTITUTED NITROPHENOL PESTICIDE, LIQUID, TOXIC
L4BH	TU15 TE19	AT	2 (E)			CV13 CV28	S9	60	3014	SUBSTITUTED NITROPHENOL PESTICIDE, LIQUID, TOXIC
L10CH	TU14 TU15 TE19 TE21	FL	1 (C/E)			CV1 CV13 CV28	S2 S9 S14	663	3015	BIPYRIDILIUM PESTICIDE, LIQUID, TOXIC, FLAMMABLE, flash-point not less than 23 °C
L4BH	TU15 TE19	FL	2 (D/E)			CV13 CV28	S2 S9 S19	63	3015	BIPYRIDILIUM PESTICIDE, LIQUID, TOXIC, FLAMMABLE, flash-point not less than 23 °C
L4BH	TU15 TE19	FL	2 (D/E)			CV13 CV28	S2 S9	63	3015	BIPYRIDILIUM PESTICIDE, LIQUID, TOXIC, FLAMMABLE, flash-point not less than 23 °C
L10CH	TU14 TU15 TE19 TE21	AT	1 (C/E)			CV1 CV13 CV28	S9 S14	66	3016	BIPYRIDILIUM PESTICIDE, LIQUID, TOXIC
L4BH	TU15 TE19	AT	2 (D/E)			CV13 CV28	S9 S19	60	3016	BIPYRIDILIUM PESTICIDE, LIQUID, TOXIC
L4BH	TU15 TE19	AT	2 (E)			CV13 CV28	S9	60	3016	BIPYRIDILIUM PESTICIDE, LIQUID, TOXIC
L10CH	TU14 TU15 TE19 TE21	FL	1 (C/E)			CV1 CV13 CV28	S2 S9 S14	663	3017	ORGANOPHOSPHORUS PESTICIDE, LIQUID, TOXIC, FLAMMABLE, flash-point not less than 23 °C
L4BH	TU15 TE19	FL	2 (D/E)			CV13 CV28	S2 S9 S19	63	3017	ORGANOPHOSPHORUS PESTICIDE, LIQUID, TOXIC, FLAMMABLE, flash-point not less than 23 °C

UN No.	Name and description	Class	Classification code	Packing group	Labels	Special provisions	Limited and excepted quantities		Packaging			Portable tanks and bulk containers	
							quantities		Packing instructions	Special packing provisions	Mixed packing provisions	Instructions	Special provisions
	3.1.2	2.2	2.2	2.1.1.3	5.2.2	3.3	3.4.6	3.5.1.2	4.1.4	4.1.4	4.1.10	4.2.5.2 7.3.2	4.2.5.3
(1)	(2)	(3a)	(3b)	(4)	(5)	(6)	(7a)	(7b)	(8)	(9a)	(9b)	(10)	(11)
3017	ORGANOPHOSPHORUS PESTICIDE, LIQUID, TOXIC, FLAMMABLE, flash-point not less than 23 °C	6.1	TF2	III	6.1 +3	61 274	LQ7	E1	P001 IBC03 R001		MP19	T7	TP2 TP28
3018	ORGANOPHOSPHORUS PESTICIDE, LIQUID, TOXIC	6.1	T6	I	6.1	61 274 648	LQ0	E5	P001		MP8 MP17	T14	TP2 TP27
3018	ORGANOPHOSPHORUS PESTICIDE, LIQUID, TOXIC	6.1	T6	II	6.1	61 274 648	LQ17	E4	P001 IBC02		MP15	T11	TP2 TP27
3018	ORGANOPHOSPHORUS PESTICIDE, LIQUID, TOXIC	6.1	T6	III	6.1	61 274 648	LQ7	E1	P001 IBC03 LP01 R001		MP19	T7	TP2 TP28
3019	ORGANOTIN PESTICIDE, LIQUID, TOXIC, FLAMMABLE, flash-point not less than 23 °C	6.1	TF2	I	6.1 +3	61 274	LQ0	E5	P001		MP8 MP17	T14	TP2 TP27
3019	ORGANOTIN PESTICIDE, LIQUID, TOXIC, FLAMMABLE, flash-point not less than 23 °C	6.1	TF2	II	6.1 +3	61 274	LQ17	E4	P001 IBC02		MP15	T11	TP2 TP27
3019	ORGANOTIN PESTICIDE, LIQUID, TOXIC, FLAMMABLE, flash-point not less than 23 °C	6.1	TF2	III	6.1 +3	61 274	LQ7	E1	P001 IBC03 R001		MP19	T7	TP2 TP28
3020	ORGANOTIN PESTICIDE, LIQUID, TOXIC	6.1	T6	I	6.1	61 274 648	LQ0	E5	P001		MP8 MP17	T14	TP2 TP27
3020	ORGANOTIN PESTICIDE, LIQUID, TOXIC	6.1	T6	II	6.1	61 274 648	LQ17	E4	P001 IBC02		MP15	T11	TP2 TP27
3020	ORGANOTIN PESTICIDE, LIQUID, TOXIC	6.1	T6	III	6.1	61 274 648	LQ7	E1	P001 IBC03 LP01 R001		MP19	T7	TP2 TP28
3021	PESTICIDE, LIQUID, FLAMMABLE, TOXIC, N.O.S., flash-point less than 23 °C	3	FT2	I	3 +6.1	61 274	LQ3	E0	P001		MP7 MP17	T14	TP2 TP27
3021	PESTICIDE, LIQUID, FLAMMABLE, TOXIC, N.O.S., flash-point less than 23 °C	3	FT2	II	3 +6.1	61 274	LQ4	E2	P001 IBC02 R001		MP19	T11	TP2 TP27
3022	1,2-BUTYLENE OXIDE, STABILIZED	3	F1	II	3		LQ4	E2	P001 IBC02 R001		MP19	T4	TP1
3023	2-METHYL-2-HEPTANETHIOL	6.1	TF1	I	6.1 +3		LQ0	E5	P001		MP8 MP17	T20	TP2 TP35
3024	COUMARIN DERIVATIVE PESTICIDE, LIQUID, FLAMMABLE, TOXIC, flash-point less than 23 °C	3	FT2	I	3 +6.1	61 274	LQ3	E0	P001		MP7 MP17	T14	TP2 TP27
3024	COUMARIN DERIVATIVE PESTICIDE, LIQUID, FLAMMABLE, TOXIC, flash-point less than 23 °C	3	FT2	II	3 +6.1	61 274	LQ4	E2	P001 IBC02 R001		MP19	T11	TP2 TP27
3025	COUMARIN DERIVATIVE PESTICIDE, LIQUID, TOXIC, FLAMMABLE, flash-point not less than 23 °C	6.1	TF2	I	6.1 +3	61 274	LQ0	E5	P001		MP8 MP17	T14	TP2 TP27
3025	COUMARIN DERIVATIVE PESTICIDE, LIQUID, TOXIC, FLAMMABLE, flash-point not less than 23 °C	6.1	TF2	II	6.1 +3	61 274	LQ17	E4	P001 IBC02		MP15	T11	TP2 TP27
3025	COUMARIN DERIVATIVE PESTICIDE, LIQUID, TOXIC, FLAMMABLE, flash-point not less than 23 °C	6.1	TF2	III	6.1 +3	61 274	LQ7	E1	P001 IBC03 R001		MP19	T7	TP1 TP28
3026	COUMARIN DERIVATIVE PESTICIDE, LIQUID, TOXIC	6.1	T6	I	6.1	61 274 648	LQ0	E5	P001		MP8 MP17	T14	TP2 TP27

ADR tank		Vehicle for tank carriage	Transport category (Tunnel restriction code)	Special provisions for carriage				Hazard identifi-cation No.	UN No.	Name and description
Tank code	Special provisions			Packages	Bulk	Loading, unloading and handling	Operation			
4.3	4.3.5, 6.8.4	9.1.1.2	1.1.3.6 (8.6)	7.2.4	7.3.3	7.5.11	8.5	5.3.2.3		3.1.2
(12)	(13)	(14)	(15)	(16)	(17)	(18)	(19)	(20)	(1)	(2)
L4BH	TU15 TE19	FL	2 (D/E)			CV13 CV28	S2 S9	63	3017	ORGANOPHOSPHORUS PESTICIDE, LIQUID, TOXIC, FLAMMABLE, flash-point not less than 23 °C
L10CH	TU14 TU15 TE19 TE21	AT	1 (C/E)			CV1 CV13 CV28	S9 S14	66	3018	ORGANOPHOSPHORUS PESTICIDE, LIQUID, TOXIC
L4BH	TU15 TE19	AT	2 (D/E)			CV13 CV28	S9 S19	60	3018	ORGANOPHOSPHORUS PESTICIDE, LIQUID, TOXIC
L4BH	TU15 TE19	AT	2 (E)			CV13 CV28	S9	60	3018	ORGANOPHOSPHORUS PESTICIDE, LIQUID, TOXIC
L10CH	TU14 TU15 TE19 TE21	FL	1 (C/E)			CV1 CV13 CV28	S2 S9 S14	663	3019	ORGANOTIN PESTICIDE, LIQUID, TOXIC, FLAMMABLE, flash-point not less than 23 °C
L4BH	TU15 TE19	FL	2 (D/E)			CV13 CV28	S2 S9 S19	63	3019	ORGANOTIN PESTICIDE, LIQUID, TOXIC, FLAMMABLE, flash-point not less than 23 °C
L4BH	TU15 TE19	FL	2 (D/E)			CV13 CV28	S2 S9	63	3019	ORGANOTIN PESTICIDE, LIQUID, TOXIC, FLAMMABLE, flash-point not less than 23 °C
L10CH	TU14 TU15 TE19 TE21	AT	1 (C/E)			CV1 CV13 CV28	S9 S14	66	3020	ORGANOTIN PESTICIDE, LIQUID, TOXIC
L4BH	TU15 TE19	AT	2 (D/E)			CV13 CV28	S9 S19	60	3020	ORGANOTIN PESTICIDE, LIQUID, TOXIC
L4BH	TU15 TE19	AT	2 (E)			CV13 CV28	S9	60	3020	ORGANOTIN PESTICIDE, LIQUID, TOXIC
L10CH	TU14 TU15 TE21	FL	1 (C/E)			CV13 CV28	S2 S22	336	3021	PESTICIDE, LIQUID, FLAMMABLE, TOXIC, N.O.S., flash-point less than 23 °C
L4BH	TU15	FL	2 (D/E)			CV13 CV28	S2 S22	336	3021	PESTICIDE, LIQUID, FLAMMABLE, TOXIC, N.O.S., flash-point less than 23 °C
LGBF		FL	2 (D/E)				S2 S20	339	3022	1,2-BUTYLENE OXIDE, STABILIZED
L10CH	TU14 TU15 TE19 TE21	FL	1 (C/D)			CV1 CV13 CV28	S2 S9 S14	663	3023	2-METHYL-2-HEPTANETHIOL
L10CH	TU14 TU15 TE21	FL	1 (C/E)			CV13 CV28	S2 S22	336	3024	COUMARIN DERIVATIVE PESTICIDE, LIQUID, FLAMMABLE, TOXIC, flash-point less than 23 °C
L4BH	TU15	FL	2 (D/E)			CV13 CV28	S2 S22	336	3024	COUMARIN DERIVATIVE PESTICIDE, LIQUID, FLAMMABLE, TOXIC, flash-point less than 23 °C
L10CH	TU14 TU15 TE19 TE21	FL	1 (C/E)			CV1 CV13 CV28	S2 S9 S14	663	3025	COUMARIN DERIVATIVE PESTICIDE, LIQUID, TOXIC, FLAMMABLE, flash-point not less than 23 °C
L4BH	TU15 TE19	FL	2 (D/E)			CV13 CV28	S2 S9 S19	63	3025	COUMARIN DERIVATIVE PESTICIDE, LIQUID, TOXIC, FLAMMABLE, flash-point not less than 23 °C
L4BH	TU15 TE19	FL	2 (D/E)			CV13 CV28	S2 S9	63	3025	COUMARIN DERIVATIVE PESTICIDE, LIQUID, TOXIC, FLAMMABLE, flash-point not less than 23 °C
L10CH	TU14 TU15 TE19 TE21	AT	1 (C/E)			CV1 CV13 CV28	S9 S14	66	3026	COUMARIN DERIVATIVE PESTICIDE, LIQUID, TOXIC

UN No. 3.1.2	Name and description 3.1.2	Class 2.2	Classification code 2.2	Packing group 2.1.1.3	Labels 5.2.2	Special provisions 3.3	Limited and excepted quantities 3.4.6	Limited and excepted quantities 3.5.1.2	Packing instructions 4.1.4	Special packing provisions 4.1.4	Mixed packing provisions 4.1.10	Instructions 4.2.5.2 7.3.2	Special provisions 4.2.5.3
(1)	(2)	(3a)	(3b)	(4)	(5)	(6)	(7a)	(7b)	(8)	(9a)	(9b)	(10)	(11)
3026	COUMARIN DERIVATIVE PESTICIDE, LIQUID, TOXIC	6.1	T6	II	6.1	61 274 648	LQ17	E4	P001 IBC02		MP15	T11	TP2 TP27
3026	COUMARIN DERIVATIVE PESTICIDE, LIQUID, TOXIC	6.1	T6	III	6.1	61 274 648	LQ7	E1	P001 IBC03 LP01 R001		MP19	T7	TP1 TP28
3027	COUMARIN DERIVATIVE PESTICIDE, SOLID, TOXIC	6.1	T7	I	6.1	61 274 648	LQ0	E5	P002 IBC07		MP18	T6	TP33
3027	COUMARIN DERIVATIVE PESTICIDE, SOLID, TOXIC	6.1	T7	II	6.1	61 274 648	LQ18	E4	P002 IBC08	B4	MP10	T3	TP33
3027	COUMARIN DERIVATIVE PESTICIDE, SOLID, TOXIC	6.1	T7	III	6.1	61 274 648	LQ9	E1	P002 IBC08 LP02 R001	B3	MP10	T1	TP33
3028	BATTERIES, DRY, CONTAINING POTASSIUM HYDROXIDE SOLID, electric storage	8	C11		8	295 304 598	LQ0	E0	P801 P801a				
3048	ALUMINIUM PHOSPHIDE PESTICIDE	6.1	T7	I	6.1	153 648	LQ0	E5	P002 IBC07		MP18	T6	TP33
3054	CYCLOHEXYL MERCAPTAN	3	F1	III	3		LQ7	E1	P001 IBC03 LP01 R001		MP19	T2	TP1
3055	2-(2-AMINOETHOXY) ETHANOL	8	C7	III	8		LQ7	E1	P001 IBC03 LP01 R001		MP19	T4	TP1
3056	n-HEPTALDEHYDE	3	F1	III	3		LQ7	E1	P001 IBC03 LP01 R001		MP19	T2	TP1
3057	TRIFLUOROACETYL CHLORIDE	2	2TC		2.3 +8		LQ0	E0	P200		MP9	T50	TP21
3064	NITROGLYCERIN, SOLUTION IN ALCOHOL with more than 1% but not more than 5% nitroglycerin	3	D	II	3		LQ0	E0	P300		MP2		
3065	ALCOHOLIC BEVERAGES, with more than 70% alcohol by volume	3	F1	II	3		LQ5	E2	P001 IBC02 R001	PP2	MP19	T4	TP1
3065	ALCOHOLIC BEVERAGES, with more than 24% but not more than 70% alcohol by volume	3	F1	III	3	144 145 247	LQ7	E1	P001 IBC03 R001	PP2	MP19	T2	TP1
3066	PAINT (including paint, lacquer, enamel, stain, shellac, varnish, polish, liquid filler and liquid lacquer base) or PAINT RELATED MATERIAL (including paint thinning and reducing compound)	8	C9	II	8	163	LQ22	E2	P001 IBC02		MP15	T7	TP2 TP28
3066	PAINT (including paint, lacquer, enamel, stain, shellac, varnish, polish, liquid filler and liquid lacquer base) or PAINT RELATED MATERIAL (including paint thinning and reducing compound)	8	C9	III	8	163	LQ7	E1	P001 IBC03 R001		MP19	T4	TP1 TP29
3070	ETHYLENE OXIDE AND DICHLORODIFLUORO-METHANE MIXTURE with not more than 12.5% ethylene oxide	2	2A		2.2		LQ1	E1	P200		MP9	(M) T50	

ADR tank		Vehicle for tank carriage	Transport category (Tunnel restriction code)	Special provisions for carriage				Hazard identifi-cation No.	UN No.	Name and description
Tank code	Special provisions			Packages	Bulk	Loading, unloading and handling	Operation			
4.3	4.3.5, 6.8.4	9.1.1.2	1.1.3.6 (8.6)	7.2.4	7.3.3	7.5.11	8.5	5.3.2.3		3.1.2
(12)	(13)	(14)	(15)	(16)	(17)	(18)	(19)	(20)	(1)	(2)
L4BH	TU15 TE19	AT	2 (D/E)			CV13 CV28	S9 S19	60	3026	COUMARIN DERIVATIVE PESTICIDE, LIQUID, TOXIC
L4BH	TU15 TE19	AT	2 (E)			CV13 CV28	S9	60	3026	COUMARIN DERIVATIVE PESTICIDE, LIQUID, TOXIC
S10AH L10CH	TU14 TU15 TE19 TE21	AT	1 (C/E)	V10 V12		CV1 CV13 CV28	S9 S14	66	3027	COUMARIN DERIVATIVE PESTICIDE, SOLID, TOXIC
SGAH L4BH	TU15 TE19	AT	2 (D/E)	V11		CV13 CV28	S9 S19	60	3027	COUMARIN DERIVATIVE PESTICIDE, SOLID, TOXIC
SGAH L4BH	TU15 TE19	AT	2 (E)		VV9	CV13 CV28	S9	60	3027	COUMARIN DERIVATIVE PESTICIDE, SOLID, TOXIC
			3 (E)		VV14			80	3028	BATTERIES, DRY, CONTAINING POTASSIUM HYDROXIDE SOLID, electric storage
S10AH	TU15 TE19	AT	1 (C/E)	V10 V12		CV1 CV13 CV28	S9 S14	642	3048	ALUMINIUM PHOSPHIDE PESTICIDE
LGBF		FL	3 (D/E)				S2	30	3054	CYCLOHEXYL MERCAPTAN
L4BN		AT	3 (E)					80	3055	2-(2-AMINOETHOXY) ETHANOL
LGBF		FL	3 (D/E)				S2	30	3056	n-HEPTALDEHYDE
PxBH(M)	TA4 TT9	AT	1 (C/D)			CV9 CV10 CV36	S14	268	3057	TRIFLUOROACETYL CHLORIDE
			2 (B)				S2 S14		3064	NITROGLYCERIN, SOLUTION IN ALCOHOL with more than 1% but not more than 5% nitroglycerin
LGBF		FL	2 (D/E)				S2 S20	33	3065	ALCOHOLIC BEVERAGES, with more than 70% alcohol by volume
LGBF		FL	3 (D/E)				S2	30	3065	ALCOHOLIC BEVERAGES, with more than 24% but not more than 70% alcohol by volume
L4BN		AT	2 (E)					80	3066	PAINT (including paint, lacquer, enamel, stain, shellac, varnish, polish, liquid filler and liquid lacquer base) or PAINT RELATED MATERIAL (including paint thinning and reducing compound)
L4BN		AT	3 (E)					80	3066	PAINT (including paint, lacquer, enamel, stain, shellac, varnish, polish, liquid filler and liquid lacquer base) or PAINT RELATED MATERIAL (including paint thinning and reducing compound)
PxBN(M)	TA4 TT9	AT	3 (C/E)			CV9 CV10 CV36		20	3070	ETHYLENE OXIDE AND DICHLORODIFLUORO-METHANE MIXTURE with not more than 12.5% ethylene oxide

UN No. 3.1.2 (1)	Name and description 3.1.2 (2)	Class 2.2 (3a)	Classification code 2.2 (3b)	Packing group 2.1.1.3 (4)	Labels 5.2.2 (5)	Special provisions 3.3 (6)	Limited quantities 3.4.6 (7a)	Excepted quantities 3.5.1.2 (7b)	Packing instructions 4.1.4 (8)	Special packing provisions 4.1.4 (9a)	Mixed packing provisions 4.1.10 (9b)	Instructions 4.2.5.2 7.3.2 (10)	Special provisions 4.2.5.3 (11)
3071	MERCAPTANS, LIQUID, TOXIC, FLAMMABLE, N.O.S. or MERCAPTAN MIXTURE, LIQUID, TOXIC, FLAMMABLE, N.O.S.	6.1	TF1	II	6.1 +3	274	LQ17	E4	P001 IBC02		MP15	T11	TP2 TP27
3072	LIFE-SAVING APPLIANCES NOT SELF-INFLATING containing dangerous goods as equipment	9	M5		9	296 635	LQ0	E0	P905				
3073	VINYLPYRIDINES, STABILIZED	6.1	TFC	II	6.1 +3 +8		LQ17	E4	P001 IBC01		MP15	T7	TP2
3077	ENVIRONMENTALLY HAZARDOUS SUBSTANCE, SOLID, N.O.S.	9	M7	III	9	274 335 601	LQ27	E1	P002 IBC08 LP02 R001	PP12 B3	MP10	T1 BK1 BK2	TP33
3078	CERIUM, turnings or gritty powder	4.3	W2	II	4.3	550	LQ11	E2	P410 IBC07		MP14	T3	TP33
3079	METHACRYLONITRILE, STABILIZED	3	FT1	I	3 +6.1		LQ0	E0	P001		MP7 MP17	T14	TP2
3080	ISOCYANATES, TOXIC, FLAMMABLE, N.O.S. or ISOCYANATE SOLUTION, TOXIC, FLAMMABLE, N.O.S.	6.1	TF1	II	6.1 +3	274 551	LQ17	E4	P001 IBC02		MP15	T11	TP2 TP27
3082	ENVIRONMENTALLY HAZARDOUS SUBSTANCE, LIQUID, N.O.S.	9	M6	III	9	274 335 601	LQ7	E1	P001 IBC03 LP01 R001	PP1	MP19	T4	TP1 TP29
3083	PERCHLORYL FLUORIDE	2	2TO		2.3 +5.1		LQ0	E0	P200		MP9	(M)	
3084	CORROSIVE SOLID, OXIDIZING, N.O.S.	8	CO2	I	8 +5.1	274	LQ0	E0	P002		MP18	T6	TP33
3084	CORROSIVE SOLID, OXIDIZING, N.O.S.	8	CO2	II	8 +5.1	274	LQ23	E2	P002 IBC06		MP10	T3	TP33
3085	OXIDIZING SOLID, CORROSIVE, N.O.S.	5.1	OC2	I	5.1 +8	274	LQ0	E0	P503		MP2		
3085	OXIDIZING SOLID, CORROSIVE, N.O.S.	5.1	OC2	II	5.1 +8	274	LQ11	E2	P002 IBC06		MP2	T3	TP33
3085	OXIDIZING SOLID, CORROSIVE, N.O.S.	5.1	OC2	III	5.1 +8	274	LQ12	E1	P002 IBC08 R001	B3	MP2	T1	TP33
3086	TOXIC SOLID, OXIDIZING, N.O.S.	6.1	TO2	I	6.1 +5.1	274	LQ0	E5	P002		MP18	T6	TP33
3086	TOXIC SOLID, OXIDIZING, N.O.S.	6.1	TO2	II	6.1 +5.1	274	LQ18	E4	P002 IBC06		MP10	T3	TP33
3087	OXIDIZING SOLID, TOXIC, N.O.S.	5.1	OT2	I	5.1 +6.1	274	LQ0	E0	P503		MP2		
3087	OXIDIZING SOLID, TOXIC, N.O.S.	5.1	OT2	II	5.1 +6.1	274	LQ11	E2	P002 IBC06		MP2	T3	TP33
3087	OXIDIZING SOLID, TOXIC, N.O.S.	5.1	OT2	III	5.1 +6.1	274	LQ12	E1	P002 IBC08 R001	B3	MP2	T1	TP33
3088	SELF-HEATING SOLID, ORGANIC, N.O.S.	4.2	S2	II	4.2	274	LQ0	E2	P410 IBC06		MP14	T3	TP33
3088	SELF-HEATING SOLID, ORGANIC, N.O.S.	4.2	S2	III	4.2	274	LQ0	E1	P002 IBC08 LP02 R001	B3	MP14	T1	TP33
3089	METAL POWDER, FLAMMABLE, N.O.S.	4.1	F3	II	4.1	274 552	LQ8	E2	P002 IBC08	B4	MP11	T3	TP33
3089	METAL POWDER, FLAMMABLE, N.O.S.	4.1	F3	III	4.1	274 552	LQ9	E1	P002 IBC06 R001		MP11	T1	TP33
3090	LITHIUM METAL BATTERIES (including lithium alloy batteries)	9	M4	II	9	188 230 310 636	LQ0	E0	P903 P903a P903b				

ADR tank		Vehicle for tank carriage	Transport category (Tunnel restriction code)	Special provisions for carriage				Hazard identifi-cation No.	UN No.	Name and description
Tank code	Special provisions			Packages	Bulk	Loading, unloading and handling	Operation			
4.3	4.3.5, 6.8.4	9.1.1.2	1.1.3.6 (8.6)	7.2.4	7.3.3	7.5.11	8.5	5.3.2.3		3.1.2
(12)	(13)	(14)	(15)	(16)	(17)	(18)	(19)	(20)	(1)	(2)
L4BH	TU15 TE19	FL	2 (D/E)			CV13 CV28	S2 S9 S19	63	3071	MERCAPTANS, LIQUID, TOXIC, FLAMMABLE, N.O.S. or MERCAPTAN MIXTURE, LIQUID, TOXIC, FLAMMABLE, N.O.S.
			3 (E)						3072	LIFE-SAVING APPLIANCES NOT SELF-INFLATING containing dangerous goods as equipment
L4BH	TU15 TE19	FL	2 (D/E)			CV13 CV28	S2 S9 S19	638	3073	VINYLPYRIDINES, STABILIZED
SGAV LGBV		AT	3 (E)	V13	VV1	CV13		90	3077	ENVIRONMENTALLY HAZARDOUS SUBSTANCE, SOLID, N.O.S.
SGAN		AT	2 (D/E)	V1 V12		CV23		423	3078	CERIUM, turnings or gritty powder
L10CH	TU14 TU15 TE21	FL	1 (C/E)			CV13 CV28	S2 S22	336	3079	METHACRYLONITRILE, STABILIZED
L4BH	TU15 TE19	FL	2 (D/E)			CV13 CV28	S2 S9 S19	63	3080	ISOCYANATES, TOXIC, FLAMMABLE, N.O.S. or ISOCYANATE SOLUTION, TOXIC, FLAMMABLE, N.O.S.
LGBV		AT	3 (E)			CV13		90	3082	ENVIRONMENTALLY HAZARDOUS SUBSTANCE, LIQUID, N.O.S.
PxBH(M)	TA4 TT9	AT	1 (C/D)			CV9 CV10 CV36	S14	265	3083	PERCHLORYL FLUORIDE
S10AN L10BH		AT	1 (E)			CV24	S14	885	3084	CORROSIVE SOLID, OXIDIZING, N.O.S.
SGAN L4BN		AT	2 (E)	V11 V12		CV24		85	3084	CORROSIVE SOLID, OXIDIZING, N.O.S.
			1 (E)			CV24	S20		3085	OXIDIZING SOLID, CORROSIVE, N.O.S.
SGAN	TU3	AT	2 (E)	V11 V12		CV24		58	3085	OXIDIZING SOLID, CORROSIVE, N.O.S.
SGAN	TU3	AT	3 (E)			CV24		58	3085	OXIDIZING SOLID, CORROSIVE, N.O.S.
S10AH L10CH	TU14 TU15 TE19 TE21	AT	1 (C/E)			CV1 CV13 CV28	S9 S14	665	3086	TOXIC SOLID, OXIDIZING, N.O.S.
SGAH L4BH	TU15 TE19	AT	2 (D/E)	V11 V12		CV13 CV28	S9 S19	65	3086	TOXIC SOLID, OXIDIZING, N.O.S.
			1 (E)			CV24 CV28	S20		3087	OXIDIZING SOLID, TOXIC, N.O.S.
SGAN	TU3	AT	2 (E)	V11 V12		CV24 CV28		56	3087	OXIDIZING SOLID, TOXIC, N.O.S.
SGAN	TU3	AT	3 (E)			CV24 CV28		56	3087	OXIDIZING SOLID, TOXIC, N.O.S.
SGAV		AT	2 (D/E)	V1 V12				40	3088	SELF-HEATING SOLID, ORGANIC, N.O.S.
SGAV		AT	3 (E)	V1				40	3088	SELF-HEATING SOLID, ORGANIC, N.O.S.
SGAN		AT	2 (E)	V11				40	3089	METAL POWDER, FLAMMABLE, N.O.S.
SGAV		AT	3 (E)	V12	VV1			40	3089	METAL POWDER, FLAMMABLE, N.O.S.
			2 (E)						3090	LITHIUM METAL BATTERIES (including lithium alloy batteries)

UN No.	Name and description	Class	Classification code	Packing group	Labels	Special provisions	Limited and excepted quantities		Packaging			Portable tanks and bulk containers	
									Packing instructions	Special packing provisions	Mixed packing provisions	Instructions	Special provisions
	3.1.2	2.2	2.2	2.1.1.3	5.2.2	3.3	3.4.6	3.5.1.2	4.1.4	4.1.4	4.1.10	4.2.5.2 7.3.2	4.2.5.3
(1)	(2)	(3a)	(3b)	(4)	(5)	(6)	(7a)	(7b)	(8)	(9a)	(9b)	(10)	(11)
3091	LITHIUM METAL BATTERIES CONTAINED IN EQUIPMENT or LITHIUM METAL BATTERIES PACKED WITH EQUIPMENT (including lithium alloy batteries)	9	M4	II	9	188 230 636	LQ0	E0	P903 P903a P903b				
3092	1-METHOXY-2-PROPANOL	3	F1	III	3		LQ7	E1	P001 IBC03 LP01 R001		MP19	T2	TP1
3093	CORROSIVE LIQUID, OXIDIZING, N.O.S.	8	CO1	I	8 +5.1	274	LQ0	E0	P001		MP8 MP17		
3093	CORROSIVE LIQUID, OXIDIZING, N.O.S.	8	CO1	II	8 +5.1	274	LQ22	E2	P001 IBC02		MP15		
3094	CORROSIVE LIQUID, WATER-REACTIVE, N.O.S.	8	CW1	I	8 +4.3	274	LQ0	E0	P001		MP8 MP17		
3094	CORROSIVE LIQUID, WATER-REACTIVE, N.O.S.	8	CW1	II	8 +4.3	274	LQ22	E2	P001		MP15		
3095	CORROSIVE SOLID, SELF-HEATING, N.O.S.	8	CS2	I	8 +4.2	274	LQ0	E0	P002		MP18	T6	TP33
3095	CORROSIVE SOLID, SELF-HEATING, N.O.S.	8	CS2	II	8 +4.2	274	LQ23	E2	P002 IBC06		MP10	T3	TP33
3096	CORROSIVE SOLID, WATER-REACTIVE, N.O.S.	8	CW2	I	8 +4.3	274	LQ0	E0	P002		MP18	T6	TP33
3096	CORROSIVE SOLID, WATER-REACTIVE, N.O.S.	8	CW2	II	8 +4.3	274	LQ23	E2	P002 IBC06		MP10	T3	TP33
3097	FLAMMABLE SOLID, OXIDIZING, N.O.S.	4.1	FO				CARRIAGE PROHIBITED						
3098	OXIDIZING LIQUID, CORROSIVE, N.O.S.	5.1	OC1	I	5.1 +8	274	LQ0	E0	P502		MP2		
3098	OXIDIZING LIQUID, CORROSIVE, N.O.S.	5.1	OC1	II	5.1 +8	274	LQ10	E2	P504 IBC01		MP2		
3098	OXIDIZING LIQUID, CORROSIVE, N.O.S.	5.1	OC1	III	5.1 +8	274	LQ13	E1	P504 IBC02 R001		MP2		
3099	OXIDIZING LIQUID, TOXIC, N.O.S.	5.1	OT1	I	5.1 +6.1	274	LQ0	E0	P502		MP2		
3099	OXIDIZING LIQUID, TOXIC, N.O.S.	5.1	OT1	II	5.1 +6.1	274	LQ10	E2	P504 IBC01		MP2		
3099	OXIDIZING LIQUID, TOXIC, N.O.S.	5.1	OT1	III	5.1 +6.1	274	LQ13	E1	P504 IBC02 R001		MP2		
3100	OXIDIZING SOLID, SELF-HEATING, N.O.S.	5.1	OS				CARRIAGE PROHIBITED						
3101	ORGANIC PEROXIDE TYPE B, LIQUID	5.2	P1		5.2 +1	122 181 274	LQ14	E0	P520		MP4		
3102	ORGANIC PEROXIDE TYPE B, SOLID	5.2	P1		5.2 +1	122 181 274	LQ15	E0	P520		MP4		
3103	ORGANIC PEROXIDE TYPE C, LIQUID	5.2	P1		5.2	122 274	LQ14	E0	P520		MP4		
3104	ORGANIC PEROXIDE TYPE C, SOLID	5.2	P1		5.2	122 274	LQ15	E0	P520		MP4		
3105	ORGANIC PEROXIDE TYPE D, LIQUID	5.2	P1		5.2	122 274	LQ16	E0	P520		MP4		
3106	ORGANIC PEROXIDE TYPE D, SOLID	5.2	P1		5.2	122 274	LQ11	E0	P520		MP4		

ADR tank		Vehicle for tank carriage	Transport category (Tunnel restriction code)	Special provisions for carriage				Hazard identifi-cation No.	UN No.	Name and description
Tank code	Special provisions			Packages	Bulk	Loading, unloading and handling	Operation			
4.3	4.3.5, 6.8.4	9.1.1.2	1.1.3.6 (8.6)	7.2.4	7.3.3	7.5.11	8.5	5.3.2.3		3.1.2
(12)	(13)	(14)	(15)	(16)	(17)	(18)	(19)	(20)	(1)	(2)
			2 (E)						3091	LITHIUM METAL BATTERIES CONTAINED IN EQUIPMENT or LITHIUM METAL BATTERIES PACKED WITH EQUIPMENT (including lithium alloy batteries)
LGBF		FL	3 (D/E)				S2	30	3092	1-METHOXY-2-PROPANOL
L10BH		AT	1 (E)			CV24	S14	885	3093	CORROSIVE LIQUID, OXIDIZING, N.O.S.
L4BN		AT	2 (E)			CV24		85	3093	CORROSIVE LIQUID, OXIDIZING, N.O.S.
L10BH		AT	1 (D/E)				S14	823	3094	CORROSIVE LIQUID, WATER-REACTIVE, N.O.S.
L4BN		AT	2 (E)					823	3094	CORROSIVE LIQUID, WATER-REACTIVE, N.O.S.
S10AN		AT	1 (E)				S14	884	3095	CORROSIVE SOLID, SELF-HEATING, N.O.S.
SGAN		AT	2 (E)	V11 V12				84	3095	CORROSIVE SOLID, SELF-HEATING, N.O.S.
S10AN L10BH		AT	1 (E)				S14	842	3096	CORROSIVE SOLID, WATER-REACTIVE, N.O.S.
SGAN L4BN		AT	2 (E)	V11 V12				842	3096	CORROSIVE SOLID, WATER-REACTIVE, N.O.S.
		CARRIAGE PROHIBITED							3097	FLAMMABLE SOLID, OXIDIZING, N.O.S.
			1 (E)			CV24	S20		3098	OXIDIZING LIQUID, CORROSIVE, N.O.S.
			2 (E)			CV24			3098	OXIDIZING LIQUID, CORROSIVE, N.O.S.
			3 (E)			CV24			3098	OXIDIZING LIQUID, CORROSIVE, N.O.S.
			1 (E)			CV24 CV28	S20		3099	OXIDIZING LIQUID, TOXIC, N.O.S.
			2 (E)			CV24 CV28			3099	OXIDIZING LIQUID, TOXIC, N.O.S.
			3 (E)			CV24 CV28			3099	OXIDIZING LIQUID, TOXIC, N.O.S.
		CARRIAGE PROHIBITED							3100	OXIDIZING SOLID, SELF-HEATING, N.O.S.
			1 (B)	V1 V5		CV15 CV20 CV22 CV24	S9 S17		3101	ORGANIC PEROXIDE TYPE B, LIQUID
			1 (B)	V1 V5		CV15 CV20 CV22 CV24	S9 S17		3102	ORGANIC PEROXIDE TYPE B, SOLID
			1 (D)	V1		CV15 CV20 CV22 CV24	S8 S18		3103	ORGANIC PEROXIDE TYPE C, LIQUID
			1 (D)	V1		CV15 CV20 CV22 CV24	S8 S18		3104	ORGANIC PEROXIDE TYPE C, SOLID
			2 (D)	V1		CV15 CV22 CV24	S19		3105	ORGANIC PEROXIDE TYPE D, LIQUID
			2 (D)	V1		CV15 CV22 CV24	S19		3106	ORGANIC PEROXIDE TYPE D, SOLID

UN No.	Name and description	Class	Classifi-cation code	Packing group	Labels	Special provi-sions	Limited and excepted quantities		Packaging			Portable tanks and bulk containers	
									Packing instruc-tions	Special packing provisions	Mixed packing provisions	Instruc-tions	Special provisions
3.1.2	3.1.2	2.2	2.2	2.1.1.3	5.2.2	3.3	3.4.6	3.5.1.2	4.1.4	4.1.4	4.1.10	4.2.5.2 7.3.2	4.2.5.3
(1)	(2)	(3a)	(3b)	(4)	(5)	(6)	(7a)	(7b)	(8)	(9a)	(9b)	(10)	(11)
3107	ORGANIC PEROXIDE TYPE E, LIQUID	5.2	P1		5.2	122 274	LQ16	E0	P520		MP4		
3108	ORGANIC PEROXIDE TYPE E, SOLID	5.2	P1		5.2	122 274	LQ11	E0	P520		MP4		
3109	ORGANIC PEROXIDE TYPE F, LIQUID	5.2	P1		5.2	122 274	LQ16	E0	P520 IBC520		MP4	T23	
3110	ORGANIC PEROXIDE TYPE F, SOLID	5.2	P1		5.2	122 274	LQ11	E0	P520 IBC520		MP4	T23	TP33
3111	ORGANIC PEROXIDE TYPE B, LIQUID, TEMPERATURE CONTROLLED	5.2	P2		5.2 +1	122 181 274	LQ0	E0	P520		MP4		
3112	ORGANIC PEROXIDE TYPE B, SOLID, TEMPERATURE CONTROLLED	5.2	P2		5.2 +1	122 181 274	LQ0	E0	P520		MP4		
3113	ORGANIC PEROXIDE TYPE C, LIQUID, TEMPERATURE CONTROLLED	5.2	P2		5.2	122 274	LQ0	E0	P520		MP4		
3114	ORGANIC PEROXIDE TYPE C, SOLID, TEMPERATURE CONTROLLED	5.2	P2		5.2	122 274	LQ0	E0	P520		MP4		
3115	ORGANIC PEROXIDE TYPE D, LIQUID, TEMPERATURE CONTROLLED	5.2	P2		5.2	122 274	LQ0	E0	P520		MP4		
3116	ORGANIC PEROXIDE TYPE D, SOLID, TEMPERATURE CONTROLLED	5.2	P2		5.2	122 274	LQ0	E0	P520		MP4		
3117	ORGANIC PEROXIDE TYPE E, LIQUID, TEMPERATURE CONTROLLED	5.2	P2		5.2	122 274	LQ0	E0	P520		MP4		
3118	ORGANIC PEROXIDE TYPE E, SOLID, TEMPERATURE CONTROLLED	5.2	P2		5.2	122 274	LQ0	E0	P520		MP4		
3119	ORGANIC PEROXIDE TYPE F, LIQUID, TEMPERATURE CONTROLLED	5.2	P2		5.2	122 274	LQ0	E0	P520 IBC520		MP4	T23	
3120	ORGANIC PEROXIDE TYPE F, SOLID, TEMPERATURE CONTROLLED	5.2	P2		5.2	122 274	LQ0	E0	P520 IBC520		MP4	T23	TP33
3121	OXIDIZING SOLID, WATER-REACTIVE, N.O.S.	5.1	OW	CARRIAGE PROHIBITED									
3122	TOXIC LIQUID, OXIDIZING, N.O.S.	6.1	TO1	I	6.1 +5.1	274 315	LQ0	E5	P001		MP8 MP17		
3122	TOXIC LIQUID, OXIDIZING, N.O.S.	6.1	TO1	II	6.1 +5.1	274	LQ17	E4	P001 IBC02		MP15		
3123	TOXIC LIQUID, WATER-REACTIVE, N.O.S.	6.1	TW1	I	6.1 +4.3	274 315	LQ0	E5	P099		MP8 MP17		
3123	TOXIC LIQUID, WATER-REACTIVE, N.O.S.	6.1	TW1	II	6.1 +4.3	274	LQ17	E4	P001 IBC02		MP15		
3124	TOXIC SOLID, SELF-HEATING, N.O.S.	6.1	TS	I	6.1 +4.2	274	LQ0	E5	P002		MP18	T6	TP33

ADR tank		Vehicle for tank carriage	Transport category (Tunnel restriction code)	Special provisions for carriage				Hazard identifi-cation No.	UN No.	Name and description
Tank code	Special provisions			Packages	Bulk	Loading, unloading and handling	Operation			
4.3	4.3.5, 6.8.4	9.1.1.2	1.1.3.6 (8.6)	7.2.4	7.3.3	7.5.11	8.5	5.3.2.3		3.1.2
(12)	(13)	(14)	(15)	(16)	(17)	(18)	(19)	(20)	(1)	(2)
			2 (D)	V1		CV15 CV22 CV24			3107	ORGANIC PEROXIDE TYPE E, LIQUID
			2 (D)	V1		CV15 CV22 CV24			3108	ORGANIC PEROXIDE TYPE E, SOLID
L4BN(+)	TU3 TU13 TU30 TE12 TA2 TM4	AT	2 (D)	V1		CV15 CV22 CV24		539	3109	ORGANIC PEROXIDE TYPE F, LIQUID
S4AN(+)	TU3 TU13 TU30 TE12 TA2 TM4	AT	2 (D)	V1		CV15 CV22 CV24		539	3110	ORGANIC PEROXIDE TYPE F, SOLID
			1 (B)	V8		CV15 CV20 CV21 CV22 CV24	S4 S9 S16		3111	ORGANIC PEROXIDE TYPE B, LIQUID, TEMPERATURE CONTROLLED
			1 (B)	V8		CV15 CV20 CV21 CV22 CV24	S4 S9 S16		3112	ORGANIC PEROXIDE TYPE B, SOLID, TEMPERATURE CONTROLLED
			1 (D)	V8		CV15 CV20 CV21 CV22 CV24	S4 S8 S17		3113	ORGANIC PEROXIDE TYPE C, LIQUID, TEMPERATURE CONTROLLED
			1 (D)	V8		CV15 CV20 CV21 CV22 CV24	S4 S8 S17		3114	ORGANIC PEROXIDE TYPE C, SOLID, TEMPERATURE CONTROLLED
			1 (D)	V8		CV15 CV21 CV22 CV24	S4 S18		3115	ORGANIC PEROXIDE TYPE D, LIQUID, TEMPERATURE CONTROLLED
			1 (D)	V8		CV15 CV21 CV22 CV24	S4 S18		3116	ORGANIC PEROXIDE TYPE D, SOLID, TEMPERATURE CONTROLLED
			1 (D)	V8		CV15 CV21 CV22 CV24	S4 S19		3117	ORGANIC PEROXIDE TYPE E, LIQUID, TEMPERATURE CONTROLLED
			1 (D)	V8		CV15 CV21 CV22 CV24	S4 S19		3118	ORGANIC PEROXIDE TYPE E, SOLID, TEMPERATURE CONTROLLED
L4BN(+)	TU3 TU13 TU30 TE12 TA2 TM4	AT	1 (D)	V8		CV15 CV21 CV22 CV24	S4	539	3119	ORGANIC PEROXIDE TYPE F, LIQUID, TEMPERATURE CONTROLLED
S4AN(+)	TU3 TU13 TU30 TE12 TA2 TM4	AT	1 (D)	V8		CV15 CV21 CV22 CV24	S4	539	3120	ORGANIC PEROXIDE TYPE F, SOLID, TEMPERATURE CONTROLLED
CARRIAGE PROHIBITED									3121	OXIDIZING SOLID, WATER-REACTIVE, N.O.S.
L10CH	TU14 TU15 TE19 TE21	AT	1 (C/E)			CV1 CV13 CV28	S9 S14	665	3122	TOXIC LIQUID, OXIDIZING, N.O.S.
L4BH	TU15 TE19	AT	2 (D/E)			CV13 CV28	S9 S19	65	3122	TOXIC LIQUID, OXIDIZING, N.O.S.
L10CH	TU14 TU15 TE19 TE21	AT	1 (C/E)			CV1 CV13 CV28	S9 S14	623	3123	TOXIC LIQUID, WATER-REACTIVE, N.O.S.
L4BH	TU15 TE19	AT	2 (D/E)			CV13 CV28	S9 S19	623	3123	TOXIC LIQUID, WATER-REACTIVE, N.O.S.
S10AH L10CH	TU14 TU15 TE19 TE21	AT	1 (C/E)			CV1 CV13 CV28	S9 S14	664	3124	TOXIC SOLID, SELF-HEATING, N.O.S.

UN No.	Name and description	Class	Classification code	Packing group	Labels	Special provisions	Limited and excepted quantities		Packaging			Portable tanks and bulk containers	
									Packing instructions	Special packing provisions	Mixed packing provisions	Instructions	Special provisions
	3.1.2	2.2	2.2	2.1.1.3	5.2.2	3.3	3.4.6	3.5.1.2	4.1.4	4.1.4	4.1.10	4.2.5.2 7.3.2	4.2.5.3
(1)	(2)	(3a)	(3b)	(4)	(5)	(6)	(7a)	(7b)	(8)	(9a)	(9b)	(10)	(11)
3124	TOXIC SOLID, SELF-HEATING, N.O.S.	6.1	TS	II	6.1 +4.2	274	LQ18	E4	P002 IBC06		MP10	T3	TP33
3125	TOXIC SOLID, WATER-REACTIVE, N.O.S.	6.1	TW2	I	6.1 +4.3	274	LQ0	E5	P099		MP18	T6	TP33
3125	TOXIC SOLID, WATER-REACTIVE, N.O.S.	6.1	TW2	II	6.1 +4.3	274	LQ18	E4	P002 IBC06		MP10	T3	TP33
3126	SELF-HEATING SOLID, CORROSIVE, ORGANIC, N.O.S.	4.2	SC2	II	4.2 +8	274	LQ0	E2	P410 IBC05		MP14	T3	TP33
3126	SELF-HEATING SOLID, CORROSIVE, ORGANIC, N.O.S.	4.2	SC2	III	4.2 +8	274	LQ0	E1	P002 IBC08 R001	B3	MP14	T1	TP33
3127	SELF-HEATING SOLID, OXIDIZING, N.O.S	4.2	SO	CARRIAGE PROHIBITED									
3128	SELF-HEATING SOLID, TOXIC, ORGANIC, N.O.S.	4.2	ST2	II	4.2 +6.1	274	LQ0	E2	P410 IBC05		MP14	T3	TP33
3128	SELF-HEATING SOLID, TOXIC, ORGANIC, N.O.S.	4.2	ST2	III	4.2 +6.1	274	LQ0	E1	P002 IBC08 R001	B3	MP14	T1	TP33
3129	WATER-REACTIVE LIQUID, CORROSIVE, N.O.S.	4.3	WC1	I	4.3 +8	274	LQ0	E0	P402	RR7 RR8	MP2	T14	TP2 TP7
3129	WATER-REACTIVE LIQUID, CORROSIVE, N.O.S.	4.3	WC1	II	4.3 +8	274	LQ10	E2	P402 IBC01	RR7 RR8	MP15	T11	TP2
3129	WATER-REACTIVE LIQUID, CORROSIVE, N.O.S.	4.3	WC1	III	4.3 +8	274	LQ13	E1	P001 IBC02 R001		MP15	T7	TP1
3130	WATER-REACTIVE LIQUID, TOXIC, N.O.S.	4.3	WT1	I	4.3 +6.1	274	LQ0	E0	P402	RR4 RR8	MP2		
3130	WATER-REACTIVE LIQUID, TOXIC, N.O.S.	4.3	WT1	II	4.3 +6.1	274	LQ10	E2	P402 IBC01	RR4 RR8 BB1	MP15		
3130	WATER-REACTIVE LIQUID, TOXIC, N.O.S.	4.3	WT1	III	4.3 +6.1	274	LQ13	E1	P001 IBC02 R001		MP15		
3131	WATER-REACTIVE SOLID, CORROSIVE, N.O.S.	4.3	WC2	I	4.3 +8	274	LQ0	E0	P403		MP2	T9	TP7 TP33
3131	WATER-REACTIVE SOLID, CORROSIVE, N.O.S.	4.3	WC2	II	4.3 +8	274	LQ11	E2	P410 IBC06		MP14	T3	TP33
3131	WATER-REACTIVE SOLID, CORROSIVE, N.O.S.	4.3	WC2	III	4.3 +8	274	LQ12	E1	P410 IBC08 R001	B4	MP14	T1	TP33
3132	WATER-REACTIVE SOLID, FLAMMABLE, N.O.S.	4.3	WF2	I	4.3 +4.1	274	LQ0	E0	P403 IBC99		MP2		
3132	WATER-REACTIVE SOLID, FLAMMABLE, N.O.S.	4.3	WF2	II	4.3 +4.1	274	LQ11	E2	P410 IBC04		MP14	T3	TP33
3132	WATER-REACTIVE SOLID, FLAMMABLE, N.O.S.	4.3	WF2	III	4.3 +4.1	274	LQ12	E1	P410 IBC06		MP14	T1	TP33
3133	WATER-REACTIVE SOLID, OXIDIZING, N.O.S.	4.3	WO	CARRIAGE PROHIBITED									
3134	WATER-REACTIVE SOLID, TOXIC, N.O.S.	4.3	WT2	I	4.3 +6.1	274	LQ0	E0	P403		MP2		
3134	WATER-REACTIVE SOLID, TOXIC, N.O.S.	4.3	WT2	II	4.3 +6.1	274	LQ11	E2	P410 IBC05		MP14	T3	TP33
3134	WATER-REACTIVE SOLID, TOXIC, N.O.S.	4.3	WT2	III	4.3 +6.1	274	LQ12	E1	P410 IBC08 R001	B4	MP14	T1	TP33
3135	WATER-REACTIVE SOLID, SELF HEATING, N.O.S.	4.3	WS	I	4.3 +4.2	274	LQ0	E0	P403		MP2		
3135	WATER-REACTIVE SOLID, SELF HEATING, N.O.S.	4.3	WS	II	4.3 +4.2	274	LQ11	E2	P410 IBC05		MP14	T3	TP33

ADR tank		Vehicle for tank carriage	Transport category (Tunnel restriction code)	Special provisions for carriage				Hazard identifi-cation No.	UN No.	Name and description
Tank code	Special provisions			Packages	Bulk	Loading, unloading and handling	Operation			
4.3	4.3.5, 6.8.4	9.1.1.2	1.1.3.6 (8.6)	7.2.4	7.3.3	7.5.11	8.5	5.3.2.3		3.1.2
(12)	(13)	(14)	(15)	(16)	(17)	(18)	(19)	(20)	(1)	(2)
SGAH L4BH	TU15 TE19	AT	2 (D/E)	V11 V12		CV13 CV28	S9 S19	64	3124	TOXIC SOLID, SELF-HEATING, N.O.S.
S10AH L10CH	TU14 TU15 TE19 TE21	AT	1 (C/E)			CV1 CV13 CV28	S9 S14	642	3125	TOXIC SOLID, WATER-REACTIVE, N.O.S.
SGAH L4BH	TU15 TE19	AT	2 (D/E)	V11 V12		CV13 CV28	S9 S19	642	3125	TOXIC SOLID, WATER-REACTIVE, N.O.S.
SGAN		AT	2 (D/E)	V1				48	3126	SELF-HEATING SOLID, CORROSIVE, ORGANIC, N.O.S.
SGAN		AT	3 (E)	V1				48	3126	SELF-HEATING SOLID, CORROSIVE, ORGANIC, N.O.S.
CARRIAGE PROHIBITED									3127	SELF-HEATING SOLID, OXIDIZING, N.O.S
SGAN		AT	2 (D/E)	V1		CV28		46	3128	SELF-HEATING SOLID, TOXIC, ORGANIC, N.O.S.
SGAN		AT	3 (E)	V1		CV28		46	3128	SELF-HEATING SOLID, TOXIC, ORGANIC, N.O.S.
L10DH	TU14 TE21 TM2	AT	0 (B/E)	V1		CV23	S20	X382	3129	WATER-REACTIVE LIQUID, CORROSIVE, N.O.S.
L4DH	TU14 TE21 TM2	AT	0 (D/E)	V1		CV23		382	3129	WATER-REACTIVE LIQUID, CORROSIVE, N.O.S.
L4DH	TU14 TE21 TM2	AT	0 (E)	V1		CV23		382	3129	WATER-REACTIVE LIQUID, CORROSIVE, N.O.S.
L10DH	TU14 TE21 TM2	AT	0 (B/E)	V1		CV23 CV28	S20	X362	3130	WATER-REACTIVE LIQUID, TOXIC, N.O.S.
L4DH	TU14 TE21 TM2	AT	0 (D/E)	V1		CV23 CV28		362	3130	WATER-REACTIVE LIQUID, TOXIC, N.O.S.
L4DH	TU14 TE21 TM2	AT	0 (E)	V1		CV23 CV28		362	3130	WATER-REACTIVE LIQUID, TOXIC, N.O.S.
S10AN L10DH	TU4 TU14 TU22 TE21 TM2	AT	0 (E)	V1		CV23	S20	X482	3131	WATER-REACTIVE SOLID, CORROSIVE, N.O.S.
SGAN		AT	0 (D/E)	V1 V12		CV23		482	3131	WATER-REACTIVE SOLID, CORROSIVE, N.O.S.
SGAN		AT	0 (E)	V1		CV23		482	3131	WATER-REACTIVE SOLID, CORROSIVE, N.O.S.
			0 (B/E)	V1		CV23	S20		3132	WATER-REACTIVE SOLID, FLAMMABLE, N.O.S.
SGAN L4DH	TU14 TE21 TM2	AT	0 (D/E)	V1		CV23		423	3132	WATER-REACTIVE SOLID, FLAMMABLE, N.O.S.
SGAN L4DH	TU14 TE21 TM2	AT	0 (E)	V1		CV23		423	3132	WATER-REACTIVE SOLID, FLAMMABLE, N.O.S.
CARRIAGE PROHIBITED									3133	WATER-REACTIVE SOLID, OXIDIZING, N.O.S.
			0 (E)	V1		CV23 CV28	S20		3134	WATER-REACTIVE SOLID, TOXIC, N.O.S.
SGAN		AT	0 (D/E)	V1		CV23 CV28		462	3134	WATER-REACTIVE SOLID, TOXIC, N.O.S.
SGAN		AT	0 (E)	V1		CV23 CV28		462	3134	WATER-REACTIVE SOLID, TOXIC, N.O.S.
			1 (B/E)	V1		CV23	S20		3135	WATER-REACTIVE SOLID, SELF HEATING, N.O.S.
SGAN L4DH	TU14 TE21 TM2	AT	2 (D/E)	V1		CV23		423	3135	WATER-REACTIVE SOLID, SELF HEATING, N.O.S.

UN No.	Name and description	Class	Classifi-cation code	Packing group	Labels	Special provi-sions	Limited and excepted quantities		Packaging			Portable tanks and bulk containers	
									Packing instruc-tions	Special packing provisions	Mixed packing provisions	Instruc-tions	Special provisions
	3.1.2	2.2	2.2	2.1.1.3	5.2.2	3.3	3.4.6	3.5.1.2	4.1.4	4.1.4	4.1.10	4.2.5.2 7.3.2	4.2.5.3
(1)	(2)	(3a)	(3b)	(4)	(5)	(6)	(7a)	(7b)	(8)	(9a)	(9b)	(10)	(11)
3135	WATER-REACTIVE SOLID, SELF HEATING, N.O.S.	4.3	WS	III	4.3 +4.2	274	LQ12	E1	P410 IBC08	B4	MP14	T1	TP33
3136	TRIFLUOROMETHANE, REFRIGERATED LIQUID	2	3A		2.2	593	LQ1	E1	P203		MP9	T75	TP5
3137	OXIDIZING SOLID, FLAMMABLE, N.O.S.	5.1	OF	CARRIAGE PROHIBITED									
3138	ETHYLENE, ACETYLENE AND PROPYLENE MIXTURE, REFRIGERATED LIQUID containing at least 71.5% ethylene with not more than 22.5% acetylene and not more than 6% propylene	2	3F		2.1		LQ0	E0	P203		MP9	T75	TP5
3139	OXIDIZING LIQUID, N.O.S.	5.1	O1	I	5.1	274	LQ0	E0	P502		MP2		
3139	OXIDIZING LIQUID, N.O.S.	5.1	O1	II	5.1	274	LQ10	E2	P504 IBC02		MP2		
3139	OXIDIZING LIQUID, N.O.S.	5.1	O1	III	5.1	274	LQ13	E1	P504 IBC02 R001		MP2		
3140	ALKALOIDS, LIQUID, N.O.S. or ALKALOID SALTS, LIQUID, N.O.S.	6.1	T1	I	6.1	43 274	LQ0	E5	P001		MP8 MP17		
3140	ALKALOIDS, LIQUID, N.O.S. or ALKALOID SALTS, LIQUID, N.O.S.	6.1	T1	II	6.1	43 274	LQ17	E4	P001 IBC02		MP15		
3140	ALKALOIDS, LIQUID, N.O.S. or ALKALOID SALTS, LIQUID, N.O.S.	6.1	T1	III	6.1	43 274	LQ7	E1	P001 IBC03 LP01 R001		MP19		
3141	ANTIMONY COMPOUND, INORGANIC, LIQUID, N.O.S.	6.1	T4	III	6.1	45 274 512	LQ7	E1	P001 IBC03 LP01 R001		MP19		
3142	DISINFECTANT, LIQUID, TOXIC, N.O.S.	6.1	T1	I	6.1	274	LQ0	E5	P001		MP8 MP17		
3142	DISINFECTANT, LIQUID, TOXIC, N.O.S.	6.1	T1	II	6.1	274	LQ17	E4	P001 IBC02		MP15		
3142	DISINFECTANT, LIQUID, TOXIC, N.O.S.	6.1	T1	III	6.1	274	LQ7	E1	P001 IBC03 LP01 R001		MP19		
3143	DYE, SOLID, TOXIC, N.O.S. or DYE INTERMEDIATE, SOLID, TOXIC, N.O.S.	6.1	T2	I	6.1	274	LQ0	E5	P002 IBC07		MP18	T6	TP33
3143	DYE, SOLID, TOXIC, N.O.S. or DYE INTERMEDIATE, SOLID, TOXIC, N.O.S.	6.1	T2	II	6.1	274	LQ18	E4	P002 IBC08	B4	MP10	T3	TP33
3143	DYE, SOLID, TOXIC, N.O.S. or DYE INTERMEDIATE, SOLID, TOXIC, N.O.S.	6.1	T2	III	6.1	274	LQ9	E1	P002 IBC08 LP02 R001	B3	MP10	T1	TP33
3144	NICOTINE COMPOUND, LIQUID, N.O.S. or NICOTINE PREPARATION, LIQUID, N.O.S.	6.1	T1	I	6.1	43 274	LQ0	E5	P001		MP8 MP17		
3144	NICOTINE COMPOUND, LIQUID, N.O.S. or NICOTINE PREPARATION, LIQUID, N.O.S.	6.1	T1	II	6.1	43 274	LQ17	E4	P001 IBC02		MP15		
3144	NICOTINE COMPOUND, LIQUID, N.O.S. or NICOTINE PREPARATION, LIQUID, N.O.S.	6.1	T1	III	6.1	43 274	LQ7	E1	P001 IBC03 LP01 R001		MP19		
3145	ALKYLPHENOLS, LIQUID, N.O.S. (including C_2-C_{12} homologues)	8	C3	I	8	274	LQ0	E0	P001		MP8 MP17	T14	TP2

ADR tank		Vehicle for tank carriage	Transport category (Tunnel restriction code)	Special provisions for carriage				Hazard identification No.	UN No.	Name and description
Tank code	Special provisions			Packages	Bulk	Loading, unloading and handling	Operation			
4.3	4.3.5, 6.8.4	9.1.1.2	1.1.3.6 (8.6)	7.2.4	7.3.3	7.5.11	8.5	5.3.2.3		3.1.2
(12)	(13)	(14)	(15)	(16)	(17)	(18)	(19)	(20)	(1)	(2)
SGAN L4DH	TU14 TE21 TM2	AT	3 (E)	V1		CV23		423	3135	WATER-REACTIVE SOLID, SELF HEATING, N.O.S.
RxBN	TU19 TA4 TT9	AT	3 (C/E)	V5		CV9 CV11 CV36	S20	22	3136	TRIFLUOROMETHANE, REFRIGERATED LIQUID
CARRIAGE PROHIBITED									3137	OXIDIZING SOLID, FLAMMABLE, N.O.S.
RxBN	TU18 TA4 TT9	FL	2 (B/D)	V5		CV9 CV11 CV36	S2 S17	223	3138	ETHYLENE, ACETYLENE AND PROPYLENE MIXTURE, REFRIGERATED LIQUID containing at least 71.5% ethylene with not more than 22.5% acetylene and not more than 6% propylene
			1 (E)			CV24	S20		3139	OXIDIZING LIQUID, N.O.S.
			2 (E)			CV24			3139	OXIDIZING LIQUID, N.O.S.
			3 (E)			CV24			3139	OXIDIZING LIQUID, N.O.S.
L10CH	TU14 TU15 TE19 TE21	AT	1 (C/E)			CV1 CV13 CV28	S9 S14	66	3140	ALKALOIDS, LIQUID, N.O.S. or ALKALOID SALTS, LIQUID, N.O.S.
L4BH	TU15 TE19	AT	2 (D/E)			CV13 CV28	S9 S19	60	3140	ALKALOIDS, LIQUID, N.O.S. or ALKALOID SALTS, LIQUID, N.O.S.
L4BH	TU15 TE19	AT	2 (E)			CV13 CV28	S9	60	3140	ALKALOIDS, LIQUID, N.O.S. or ALKALOID SALTS, LIQUID, N.O.S.
L4BH	TU15 TE19	AT	2 (E)			CV13 CV28	S9	60	3141	ANTIMONY COMPOUND, INORGANIC, LIQUID, N.O.S.
L10CH	TU14 TU15 TE19 TE21	AT	1 (C/E)			CV1 CV13 CV28	S9 S14	66	3142	DISINFECTANT, LIQUID, TOXIC, N.O.S.
L4BH	TU15 TE19	AT	2 (D/E)			CV13 CV28	S9 S19	60	3142	DISINFECTANT, LIQUID, TOXIC, N.O.S.
L4BH	TU15 TE19	AT	2 (E)			CV13 CV28	S9	60	3142	DISINFECTANT, LIQUID, TOXIC, N.O.S.
S10AH L10CH	TU15 TE19	AT	1 (C/E)	V10 V12		CV1 CV13 CV28	S9 S14	66	3143	DYE, SOLID, TOXIC, N.O.S. or DYE INTERMEDIATE, SOLID, TOXIC, N.O.S.
SGAH L4BH	TU15 TE19	AT	2 (D/E)	V11		CV13 CV28	S9 S19	60	3143	DYE, SOLID, TOXIC, N.O.S. or DYE INTERMEDIATE, SOLID, TOXIC, N.O.S.
SGAH L4BH	TU15 TE19	AT	2 (E)		VV9	CV13 CV28	S9	60	3143	DYE, SOLID, TOXIC, N.O.S. or DYE INTERMEDIATE, SOLID, TOXIC, N.O.S.
L10CH	TU14 TU15 TE19 TE21	AT	1 (C/E)			CV1 CV13 CV28	S9 S14	66	3144	NICOTINE COMPOUND, LIQUID, N.O.S. or NICOTINE PREPARATION, LIQUID, N.O.S.
L4BH	TU15 TE19	AT	2 (D/E)			CV13 CV28	S9 S19	60	3144	NICOTINE COMPOUND, LIQUID, N.O.S. or NICOTINE PREPARATION, LIQUID, N.O.S.
L4BH	TU15 TE19	AT	2 (E)			CV13 CV28	S9	60	3144	NICOTINE COMPOUND, LIQUID, N.O.S. or NICOTINE PREPARATION, LIQUID, N.O.S.
L10BH		AT	1 (E)				S20	88	3145	ALKYLPHENOLS, LIQUID, N.O.S. (including C_2-C_{12} homologues)

UN No.	Name and description	Class	Classification code	Packing group	Labels	Special provisions	Limited and excepted quantities		Packaging			Portable tanks and bulk containers	
									Packing instructions	Special packing provisions	Mixed packing provisions	Instructions	Special provisions
	3.1.2	2.2	2.2	2.1.1.3	5.2.2	3.3	3.4.6	3.5.1.2	4.1.4	4.1.4	4.1.10	4.2.5.2 7.3.2	4.2.5.3
(1)	(2)	(3a)	(3b)	(4)	(5)	(6)	(7a)	(7b)	(8)	(9a)	(9b)	(10)	(11)
3145	ALKYLPHENOLS, LIQUID, N.O.S. (including C_2-C_{12} homologues)	8	C3	II	8	274	LQ22	E2	P001 IBC02		MP15	T11	TP2 TP27
3145	ALKYLPHENOLS, LIQUID, N.O.S. (including C_2-C_{12} homologues)	8	C3	III	8	274	LQ7	E1	P001 IBC03 LP01 R001		MP19	T7	TP1 TP28
3146	ORGANOTIN COMPOUND, SOLID, N.O.S.	6.1	T3	I	6.1	43 274	LQ0	E5	P002 IBC07		MP18	T6	TP33
3146	ORGANOTIN COMPOUND, SOLID, N.O.S.	6.1	T3	II	6.1	43 274	LQ18	E4	P002 IBC08	B4	MP10	T3	TP33
3146	ORGANOTIN COMPOUND, SOLID, N.O.S.	6.1	T3	III	6.1	43 274	LQ9	E1	P002 IBC08 LP02 R001	B3	MP10	T1	TP33
3147	DYE, SOLID, CORROSIVE, N.O.S. or DYE INTERMEDIATE, SOLID, CORROSIVE, N.O.S.	8	C10	I	8	274	LQ0	E0	P002 IBC07		MP18	T6	TP33
3147	DYE, SOLID, CORROSIVE, N.O.S. or DYE INTERMEDIATE, SOLID, CORROSIVE, N.O.S.	8	C10	II	8	274	LQ23	E2	P002 IBC08	B4	MP10	T3	TP33
3147	DYE, SOLID, CORROSIVE, N.O.S. or DYE INTERMEDIATE, SOLID, CORROSIVE, N.O.S.	8	C10	III	8	274	LQ24	E1	P002 IBC08 LP02 R001	B3	MP10	T1	TP33
3148	WATER-REACTIVE LIQUID, N.O.S.	4.3	W1	I	4.3	274	LQ0	E0	P402	RR8	MP2	T9	TP2 TP7
3148	WATER-REACTIVE LIQUID, N.O.S.	4.3	W1	II	4.3	274	LQ10	E2	P402 IBC01	RR8	MP15	T7	TP2
3148	WATER-REACTIVE LIQUID, N.O.S.	4.3	W1	III	4.3	274	LQ13	E1	P001 IBC02 R001		MP15	T7	TP1
3149	HYDROGEN PEROXIDE AND PEROXYACETIC ACID MIXTURE with acid(s), water and not more than 5% peroxyacetic acid, STABILIZED	5.1	OC1	II	5.1 +8	196 553	LQ10	E2	P504 IBC02	PP10 B5	MP15	T7	TP2 TP6 TP24
3150	DEVICES, SMALL, HYDROCARBON GAS POWERED or HYDROCARBON GAS REFILLS FOR SMALL DEVICES with release device	2	6F		2.1		LQ0	E0	P206		MP9		
3151	POLYHALOGENATED BIPHENYLS, LIQUID or POLYHALOGENATED TERPHENYLS, LIQUID	9	M2	II	9	203 305	LQ26	E2	P906 IBC02		MP15		
3152	POLYHALOGENATED BIPHENYLS, SOLID or POLYHALOGENATED TERPHENYLS, SOLID	9	M2	II	9	203 305	LQ25	E2	P906 IBC08	B4	MP10	T3	TP33
3153	PERFLUORO(METHYL VINYL ETHER)	2	2F		2.1		LQ0	E0	P200		MP9	(M) T50	
3154	PERFLUORO(ETHYL VINYL ETHER)	2	2F		2.1		LQ0	E0	P200		MP9	(M)	
3155	PENTACHLOROPHENOL	6.1	T2	II	6.1	43	LQ18	E4	P002 IBC08	B4	MP10	T3	TP33
3156	COMPRESSED GAS, OXIDIZING, N.O.S.	2	1O		2.2 +5.1	274	LQ0	E0	P200		MP9	(M)	
3157	LIQUEFIED GAS, OXIDIZING, N.O.S.	2	2O		2.2 +5.1	274	LQ0	E0	P200		MP9	(M)	

ADR tank		Vehicle for tank carriage	Transport category (Tunnel restriction code)	Special provisions for carriage				Hazard identifi- cation No.	UN No.	Name and description
Tank code	Special provisions			Packages	Bulk	Loading, unloading and handling	Operation			
4.3	4.3.5, 6.8.4	9.1.1.2	1.1.3.6 (8.6)	7.2.4	7.3.3	7.5.11	8.5	5.3.2.3		3.1.2
(12)	(13)	(14)	(15)	(16)	(17)	(18)	(19)	(20)	(1)	(2)
L4BN		AT	2 (E)					80	3145	ALKYLPHENOLS, LIQUID, N.O.S. (including C_2-C_{12} homologues)
L4BN		AT	3 (E)					80	3145	ALKYLPHENOLS, LIQUID, N.O.S. (including C_2-C_{12} homologues)
S10AH L10CH	TU14 TU15 TE19 TE21	AT	1 (C/E)	V10 V12		CV1 CV13 CV28	S9 S14	66	3146	ORGANOTIN COMPOUND, SOLID, N.O.S.
SGAH L4BH	TU15 TE19	AT	2 (D/E)	V11		CV13 CV28	S9 S19	60	3146	ORGANOTIN COMPOUND, SOLID, N.O.S.
SGAH L4BH	TU15 TE19	AT	2 (E)		VV9	CV13 CV28	S9	60	3146	ORGANOTIN COMPOUND, SOLID, N.O.S.
S10AN L10BH		AT	1 (E)	V10 V12			S20	88	3147	DYE, SOLID, CORROSIVE, N.O.S. or DYE INTERMEDIATE, SOLID, CORROSIVE, N.O.S.
SGAN L4BN		AT	2 (E)	V11				80	3147	DYE, SOLID, CORROSIVE, N.O.S. or DYE INTERMEDIATE, SOLID, CORROSIVE, N.O.S.
SGAV L4BN		AT	3 (E)		VV9			80	3147	DYE, SOLID, CORROSIVE, N.O.S. or DYE INTERMEDIATE, SOLID, CORROSIVE, N.O.S.
L10DH	TU14 TE21 TM2	AT	0 (B/E)	V1		CV23	S20	X323	3148	WATER-REACTIVE LIQUID, N.O.S.
L4DH	TU14 TE21 TM2	AT	0 (D/E)	V1		CV23		323	3148	WATER-REACTIVE LIQUID, N.O.S.
L4DH	TU14 TE21 TM2	AT	0 (E)	V1		CV23		323	3148	WATER-REACTIVE LIQUID, N.O.S.
L4BV(+)	TU3 TC2 TE8 TE11 TT1	AT	2 (E)			CV24		58	3149	HYDROGEN PEROXIDE AND PEROXYACETIC ACID MIXTURE with acid(s), water and not more than 5% peroxyacetic acid, STABILIZED
			2 (D)			CV9	S2		3150	DEVICES, SMALL, HYDROCARBON GAS POWERED or HYDROCARBON GAS REFILLS FOR SMALL DEVICES with release device
L4BH	TU15	AT	0 (D/E)		VV15	CV1 CV13 CV28	S19	90	3151	POLYHALOGENATED BIPHENYLS, LIQUID or POLYHALOGENATED TERPHENYLS, LIQUID
S4AH L4BH	TU15	AT	0 (D/E)	V11	VV15	CV1 CV13 CV28	S19	90	3152	POLYHALOGENATED BIPHENYLS, SOLID or POLYHALOGENATED TERPHENYLS, SOLID
PxBN(M)	TA4 TT9	FL	2 (B/D)			CV9 CV10 CV36	S2 S20	23	3153	PERFLUORO(METHYL VINYL ETHER)
PxBN(M)	TA4 TT9	FL	2 (B/D)			CV9 CV10 CV36	S2 S20	23	3154	PERFLUORO(ETHYL VINYL ETHER)
SGAH	TU15 TE19	AT	2 (D/E)	V11		CV13 CV28	S9 S19	60	3155	PENTACHLOROPHENOL
CxBN(M)	TA4 TT9	AT	3 (E)			CV9 CV10 CV36		25	3156	COMPRESSED GAS, OXIDIZING, N.O.S.
PxBN(M)	TA4 TT9	AT	3 (C/E)			CV9 CV10 CV36		25	3157	LIQUEFIED GAS, OXIDIZING, N.O.S.

UN No.	Name and description	Class	Classification code	Packing group	Labels	Special provisions	Limited and excepted quantities		Packaging			Portable tanks and bulk containers	
									Packing instructions	Special packing provisions	Mixed packing provisions	Instructions	Special provisions
	3.1.2	2.2	2.2	2.1.1.3	5.2.2	3.3	3.4.6	3.5.1.2	4.1.4	4.1.4	4.1.10	4.2.5.2 7.3.2	4.2.5.3
(1)	(2)	(3a)	(3b)	(4)	(5)	(6)	(7a)	(7b)	(8)	(9a)	(9b)	(10)	(11)
3158	GAS, REFRIGERATED LIQUID, N.O.S.	2	3A		2.2	274 593	LQ1	E1	P203		MP9	T75	TP5
3159	1,1,1,2-TETRAFLUOROETHANE (REFRIGERANT GAS R 134a)	2	2A		2.2		LQ1	E1	P200		MP9	(M) T50	
3160	LIQUEFIED GAS, TOXIC, FLAMMABLE, N.O.S.	2	2TF		2.3 +2.1	274	LQ0	E0	P200		MP9	(M)	
3161	LIQUEFIED GAS, FLAMMABLE, N.O.S.	2	2F		2.1	274	LQ0	E0	P200		MP9	(M) T50	
3162	LIQUEFIED GAS, TOXIC, N.O.S.	2	2T		2.3	274	LQ0	E0	P200		MP9	(M)	
3163	LIQUEFIED GAS, N.O.S.	2	2A		2.2	274	LQ1	E1	P200		MP9	(M) T50	
3164	ARTICLES, PRESSURIZED, PNEUMATIC or HYDRAULIC (containing non-flammable gas)	2	6A		2.2	283 594	LQ0	E0	P003		MP9		
3165	AIRCRAFT HYDRAULIC POWER UNIT FUEL TANK (containing a mixture of anhydrous hydrazine and methylhydrazine) (M86 fuel)	3	FTC	I	3 +6.1 +8		LQ0	E0	P301		MP7		
3166	Engine, internal combustion or vehicle, flammable gas powered or vehicle, flammable liquid powered	9	M11		NOT SUBJECT TO ADR								
3167	GAS SAMPLE, NON-PRESSURIZED, FLAMMABLE, N.O.S., not refrigerated liquid	2	7F		2.1	274	LQ0	E0	P201		MP9		
3168	GAS SAMPLE, NON-PRESSURIZED, TOXIC, FLAMMABLE, N.O.S., not refrigerated liquid	2	7TF		2.3 +2.1	274	LQ0	E0	P201		MP9		
3169	GAS SAMPLE, NON-PRESSURIZED, TOXIC, N.O.S., not refrigerated liquid	2	7T		2.3	274	LQ0	E0	P201		MP9		
3170	ALUMINIUM SMELTING BY-PRODUCTS or ALUMINIUM REMELTING BY-PRODUCTS	4.3	W2	II	4.3	244	LQ11	E2	P410 IBC07		MP14	T3 BK1 BK2	TP33
3170	ALUMINIUM SMELTING BY-PRODUCTS or ALUMINIUM REMELTING BY-PRODUCTS	4.3	W2	III	4.3	244	LQ12	E1	P002 IBC08 R001	B4	MP14	T1 BK1 BK2	TP33
3171	Battery-powered vehicle or Battery-powered equipment	9	M11		NOT SUBJECT TO ADR								
3172	TOXINS, EXTRACTED FROM LIVING SOURCES, LIQUID, N.O.S.	6.1	T1	I	6.1	210 274	LQ0	E5	P001		MP8 MP17		
3172	TOXINS, EXTRACTED FROM LIVING SOURCES, LIQUID, N.O.S.	6.1	T1	II	6.1	210 274	LQ17	E4	P001 IBC02		MP15		
3172	TOXINS, EXTRACTED FROM LIVING SOURCES, LIQUID, N.O.S.	6.1	T1	III	6.1	210 274	LQ7	E1	P001 IBC03 LP01 R001		MP19		
3174	TITANIUM DISULPHIDE	4.2	S4	III	4.2		LQ0	E1	P002 IBC08 LP02 R001	B3	MP14	T1	TP33
3175	SOLIDS or mixtures of solids (such as preparations and wastes) CONTAINING FLAMMABLE LIQUID, N.O.S. having a flash-point up to 60 °C	4.1	F1	II	4.1	216 274	LQ8	E2	P002 IBC06 R001	PP9	MP11	T3 BK1 BK2	TP33

ADR tank		Vehicle for tank carriage	Transport category (Tunnel restriction code)	Special provisions for carriage				Hazard identifi-cation No.	UN No.	Name and description
Tank code	Special provisions			Packages	Bulk	Loading, unloading and handling	Operation			
4.3	4.3.5, 6.8.4	9.1.1.2	1.1.3.6 (8.6)	7.2.4	7.3.3	7.5.11	8.5	5.3.2.3		3.1.2
(12)	(13)	(14)	(15)	(16)	(17)	(18)	(19)	(20)	(1)	(2)
RxBN	TU19 TA4 TT9	AT	3 (C/E)	V5		CV9 CV11 CV36	S20	22	3158	GAS, REFRIGERATED LIQUID, N.O.S.
PxBN(M)	TA4 TT9	AT	3 (C/E)			CV9 CV10 CV36		20	3159	1,1,1,2-TETRAFLUOROETHANE (REFRIGERANT GAS R 134a)
PxBH(M)	TU6 TA4 TT9	FL	1 (B/D)			CV9 CV10 CV36	S2 S14	263	3160	LIQUEFIED GAS, TOXIC, FLAMMABLE, N.O.S.
PxBN(M)	TA4 TT9	FL	2 (B/D)			CV9 CV10 CV36	S2 S20	23	3161	LIQUEFIED GAS, FLAMMABLE, N.O.S.
PxBH(M)	TU6 TA4 TT9	AT	1 (C/D)			CV9 CV10 CV36	S14	26	3162	LIQUEFIED GAS, TOXIC, N.O.S.
PxBN(M)	TA4 TT9	AT	3 (C/E)			CV9 CV10 CV36		20	3163	LIQUEFIED GAS, N.O.S.
			3 (E)			CV9			3164	ARTICLES, PRESSURIZED, PNEUMATIC or HYDRAULIC (containing non-flammable gas)
			1 (E)			CV13 CV28	S2 S19		3165	AIRCRAFT HYDRAULIC POWER UNIT FUEL TANK (containing a mixture of anhydrous hydrazine and methylhydrazine) (M86 fuel)
NOT SUBJECT TO ADR									3166	Engine, internal combustion or vehicle, flammable gas powered or vehicle, flammable liquid powered
			2 (D)			CV9	S2		3167	GAS SAMPLE, NON-PRESSURIZED, FLAMMABLE, N.O.S., not refrigerated liquid
			1 (D)			CV9	S2		3168	GAS SAMPLE, NON-PRESSURIZED, TOXIC, FLAMMABLE, N.O.S., not refrigerated liquid
			1 (D)			CV9			3169	GAS SAMPLE, NON-PRESSURIZED, TOXIC, N.O.S., not refrigerated liquid
SGAN		AT	2 (D/E)	V1 V12	VV3	CV23		423	3170	ALUMINIUM SMELTING BY-PRODUCTS or ALUMINIUM REMELTING BY-PRODUCTS
SGAN		AT	3 (E)	V1	VV1 VV5	CV23		423	3170	ALUMINIUM SMELTING BY-PRODUCTS or ALUMINIUM REMELTING BY-PRODUCTS
NOT SUBJECT TO ADR									3171	Battery-powered vehicle or Battery-powered equipment
L10CH	TU14 TU15 TE19 TE21	AT	1 (C/E)			CV1 CV13 CV28	S9 S14	66	3172	TOXINS, EXTRACTED FROM LIVING SOURCES, LIQUID, N.O.S.
L4BH	TU15 TE19	AT	2 (D/E)			CV13 CV28	S9 S19	60	3172	TOXINS, EXTRACTED FROM LIVING SOURCES, LIQUID, N.O.S.
L4BH	TU15 TE19	AT	2 (E)			CV13 CV28	S9	60	3172	TOXINS, EXTRACTED FROM LIVING SOURCES, LIQUID, N.O.S.
SGAN		AT	3 (E)	V1				40	3174	TITANIUM DISULPHIDE
			2 (E)	V11 V12	VV3			40	3175	SOLIDS or mixtures of solids (such as preparations and wastes) CONTAINING FLAMMABLE LIQUID, N.O.S. having a flash-point up to 60 °C

UN No.	Name and description	Class	Classifi-cation code	Packing group	Labels	Special provi-sions	Limited and excepted quantities		Packaging			Portable tanks and bulk containers	
									Packing instruc-tions	Special packing provisions	Mixed packing provisions	Instruc-tions	Special provisions
	3.1.2	2.2	2.2	2.1.1.3	5.2.2	3.3	3.4.6	3.5.1.2	4.1.4	4.1.4	4.1.10	4.2.5.2 7.3.2	4.2.5.3
(1)	(2)	(3a)	(3b)	(4)	(5)	(6)	(7a)	(7b)	(8)	(9a)	(9b)	(10)	(11)
3176	FLAMMABLE SOLID, ORGANIC, MOLTEN, N.O.S.	4.1	F2	II	4.1	274	LQ0	E0				T3	TP3 TP26
3176	FLAMMABLE SOLID, ORGANIC, MOLTEN, N.O.S.	4.1	F2	III	4.1	274	LQ0	E0				T1	TP3 TP26
3178	FLAMMABLE SOLID, INORGANIC, N.O.S.	4.1	F3	II	4.1	274	LQ8	E2	P002 IBC08	B4	MP11	T3	TP33
3178	FLAMMABLE SOLID, INORGANIC, N.O.S.	4.1	F3	III	4.1	274	LQ9	E1	P002 IBC08 LP02 R001	B3	MP11	T1	TP33
3179	FLAMMABLE SOLID, TOXIC, INORGANIC, N.O.S.	4.1	FT2	II	4.1 +6.1	274	LQ0	E2	P002 IBC06		MP10	T3	TP33
3179	FLAMMABLE SOLID, TOXIC, INORGANIC, N.O.S.	4.1	FT2	III	4.1 +6.1	274	LQ0	E1	P002 IBC06 R001		MP10	T1	TP33
3180	FLAMMABLE SOLID, CORROSIVE, INORGANIC, N.O.S.	4.1	FC2	II	4.1 +8	274	LQ0	E2	P002 IBC06		MP10	T3	TP33
3180	FLAMMABLE SOLID, CORROSIVE, INORGANIC, N.O.S.	4.1	FC2	III	4.1 +8	274	LQ0	E1	P002 IBC06 R001		MP10	T1	TP33
3181	METAL SALTS OF ORGANIC COMPOUNDS, FLAMMABLE, N.O.S.	4.1	F3	II	4.1	274	LQ8	E2	P002 IBC08	B4	MP11	T3	TP33
3181	METAL SALTS OF ORGANIC COMPOUNDS, FLAMMABLE, N.O.S.	4.1	F3	III	4.1	274	LQ9	E1	P002 IBC08 LP02 R001	B3	MP11	T1	TP33
3182	METAL HYDRIDES, FLAMMABLE, N.O.S.	4.1	F3	II	4.1	274 554	LQ8	E2	P410 IBC04	PP40	MP11	T3	TP33
3182	METAL HYDRIDES, FLAMMABLE, N.O.S.	4.1	F3	III	4.1	274 554	LQ9	E1	P002 IBC04 R001		MP11	T1	TP33
3183	SELF-HEATING LIQUID, ORGANIC, N.O.S.	4.2	S1	II	4.2	274	LQ0	E2	P001 IBC02		MP15		
3183	SELF-HEATING LIQUID, ORGANIC, N.O.S.	4.2	S1	III	4.2	274	LQ0	E1	P001 IBC02 R001		MP15		
3184	SELF-HEATING LIQUID, TOXIC, ORGANIC, N.O.S.	4.2	ST1	II	4.2 +6.1	274	LQ0	E2	P402 IBC02		MP15		
3184	SELF-HEATING LIQUID, TOXIC, ORGANIC, N.O.S.	4.2	ST1	III	4.2 +6.1	274	LQ0	E1	P001 IBC02 R001		MP15		
3185	SELF-HEATING LIQUID, CORROSIVE, ORGANIC, N.O.S.	4.2	SC1	II	4.2 +8	274	LQ0	E2	P402 IBC02		MP15		
3185	SELF-HEATING LIQUID, CORROSIVE, ORGANIC, N.O.S.	4.2	SC1	III	4.2 +8	274	LQ0	E1	P001 IBC02 R001		MP15		
3186	SELF-HEATING LIQUID, INORGANIC, N.O.S.	4.2	S3	II	4.2	274	LQ0	E2	P001 IBC02		MP15		
3186	SELF-HEATING LIQUID, INORGANIC, N.O.S.	4.2	S3	III	4.2	274	LQ0	E1	P001 IBC02 R001		MP15		
3187	SELF-HEATING LIQUID, TOXIC, INORGANIC, N.O.S.	4.2	ST3	II	4.2 +6.1	274	LQ0	E2	P402 IBC02		MP15		
3187	SELF-HEATING LIQUID, TOXIC, INORGANIC, N.O.S.	4.2	ST3	III	4.2 +6.1	274	LQ0	E1	P001 IBC02 R001		MP15		
3188	SELF-HEATING LIQUID, CORROSIVE, INORGANIC, N.O.S.	4.2	SC3	II	4.2 +8	274	LQ0	E2	P402 IBC02		MP15		
3188	SELF-HEATING LIQUID, CORROSIVE, INORGANIC, N.O.S.	4.2	SC3	III	4.2 +8	274	LQ0	E1	P001 IBC02 R001		MP15		
3189	METAL POWDER, SELF-HEATING, N.O.S.	4.2	S4	II	4.2	274 555	LQ0	E2	P410 IBC06		MP14	T3	TP33

ADR tank		Vehicle for tank carriage	Transport category (Tunnel restriction code)	Special provisions for carriage				Hazard identifi-cation No.	UN No.	Name and description
Tank code	Special provisions			Packages	Bulk	Loading, unloading and handling	Operation			
4.3	4.3.5, 6.8.4	9.1.1.2	1.1.3.6 (8.6)	7.2.4	7.3.3	7.5.11	8.5	5.3.2.3		3.1.2
(12)	(13)	(14)	(15)	(16)	(17)	(18)	(19)	(20)	(1)	(2)
LGBV	TU27 TE4 TE6	AT	2 (E)					44	3176	FLAMMABLE SOLID, ORGANIC, MOLTEN, N.O.S.
LGBV	TU27 TE4 TE6	AT	3 (E)					44	3176	FLAMMABLE SOLID, ORGANIC, MOLTEN, N.O.S.
SGAN		AT	2 (E)	V11				40	3178	FLAMMABLE SOLID, INORGANIC, N.O.S.
SGAV		AT	3 (E)		VV1			40	3178	FLAMMABLE SOLID, INORGANIC, N.O.S.
SGAN		AT	2 (E)	V11 V12		CV28		46	3179	FLAMMABLE SOLID, TOXIC, INORGANIC, N.O.S.
SGAN		AT	3 (E)	V12		CV28		46	3179	FLAMMABLE SOLID, TOXIC, INORGANIC, N.O.S.
SGAN		AT	2 (E)	V11 V12				48	3180	FLAMMABLE SOLID, CORROSIVE, INORGANIC, N.O.S.
SGAN		AT	3 (E)	V12				48	3180	FLAMMABLE SOLID, CORROSIVE, INORGANIC, N.O.S.
SGAN		AT	2 (E)	V11				40	3181	METAL SALTS OF ORGANIC COMPOUNDS, FLAMMABLE, N.O.S.
SGAV		AT	3 (E)		VV1			40	3181	METAL SALTS OF ORGANIC COMPOUNDS, FLAMMABLE, N.O.S.
SGAN		AT	2 (E)					40	3182	METAL HYDRIDES, FLAMMABLE, N.O.S.
SGAV		AT	3 (E)		VV1			40	3182	METAL HYDRIDES, FLAMMABLE, N.O.S.
L4DH	TU14 TE21	AT	2 (D/E)	V1				30	3183	SELF-HEATING LIQUID, ORGANIC, N.O.S.
L4DH	TU14 TE21	AT	3 (E)	V1				30	3183	SELF-HEATING LIQUID, ORGANIC, N.O.S.
L4DH	TU14 TE21	AT	2 (D/E)	V1		CV28		36	3184	SELF-HEATING LIQUID, TOXIC, ORGANIC, N.O.S.
L4DH	TU14 TE21	AT	3 (E)	V1		CV28		36	3184	SELF-HEATING LIQUID, TOXIC, ORGANIC, N.O.S.
L4DH	TU14 TE21	AT	2 (D/E)	V1				38	3185	SELF-HEATING LIQUID, CORROSIVE, ORGANIC, N.O.S.
L4DH	TU14 TE21	AT	3 (E)	V1				38	3185	SELF-HEATING LIQUID, CORROSIVE, ORGANIC, N.O.S.
L4DH	TU14 TE21	AT	2 (D/E)	V1				30	3186	SELF-HEATING LIQUID, INORGANIC, N.O.S.
L4DH	TU14 TE21	AT	3 (E)	V1				30	3186	SELF-HEATING LIQUID, INORGANIC, N.O.S.
L4DH	TU14 TE21	AT	2 (D/E)	V1		CV28		36	3187	SELF-HEATING LIQUID, TOXIC, INORGANIC, N.O.S.
L4DH	TU14 TE21	AT	3 (E)	V1		CV28		36	3187	SELF-HEATING LIQUID, TOXIC, INORGANIC, N.O.S.
L4DH	TU14 TE21	AT	2 (D/E)	V1				38	3188	SELF-HEATING LIQUID, CORROSIVE, INORGANIC, N.O.S.
L4DH	TU14 TE21	AT	3 (E)	V1				38	3188	SELF-HEATING LIQUID, CORROSIVE, INORGANIC, N.O.S.
SGAN		AT	2 (D/E)	V1 V12				40	3189	METAL POWDER, SELF-HEATING, N.O.S.

UN No.	Name and description	Class	Classification code	Packing group	Labels	Special provisions	Limited and excepted quantities		Packaging			Portable tanks and bulk containers	
							quantities		Packing instructions	Special packing provisions	Mixed packing provisions	Instructions	Special provisions
	3.1.2	2.2	2.2	2.1.1.3	5.2.2	3.3	3.4.6	3.5.1.2	4.1.4	4.1.4	4.1.10	4.2.5.2 7.3.2	4.2.5.3
(1)	(2)	(3a)	(3b)	(4)	(5)	(6)	(7a)	(7b)	(8)	(9a)	(9b)	(10)	(11)
3189	METAL POWDER, SELF-HEATING, N.O.S.	4.2	S4	III	4.2	274 555	LQ0	E1	P002 IBC08 LP02 R001	B3	MP14	T1	TP33
3190	SELF-HEATING SOLID, INORGANIC, N.O.S.	4.2	S4	II	4.2	274	LQ0	E2	P410 IBC06		MP14	T3	TP33
3190	SELF-HEATING SOLID, INORGANIC, N.O.S.	4.2	S4	III	4.2	274	LQ0	E1	P002 IBC08 LP02 R001	B3	MP14	T1	TP33
3191	SELF-HEATING SOLID, TOXIC, INORGANIC, N.O.S.	4.2	ST4	II	4.2 +6.1	274	LQ0	E2	P410 IBC05		MP14	T3	TP33
3191	SELF-HEATING SOLID, TOXIC, INORGANIC, N.O.S.	4.2	ST4	III	4.2 +6.1	274	LQ0	E1	P002 IBC08 R001	B3	MP14	T1	TP33
3192	SELF-HEATING SOLID, CORROSIVE, INORGANIC, N.O.S.	4.2	SC4	II	4.2 +8	274	LQ0	E2	P410 IBC05		MP14	T3	TP33
3192	SELF-HEATING SOLID, CORROSIVE, INORGANIC, N.O.S.	4.2	SC4	III	4.2 +8	274	LQ0	E1	P002 IBC08 R001	B3	MP14	T1	TP33
3194	PYROPHORIC LIQUID, INORGANIC, N.O.S.	4.2	S3	I	4.2	274	LQ0	E0	P400		MP2		
3200	PYROPHORIC SOLID, INORGANIC, N.O.S.	4.2	S4	I	4.2	274	LQ0	E0	P404		MP13	T21	TP7 TP33
3205	ALKALINE EARTH METAL ALCOHOLATES, N.O.S.	4.2	S4	II	4.2	183 274	LQ0	E2	P410 IBC06		MP14	T3	TP33
3205	ALKALINE EARTH METAL ALCOHOLATES, N.O.S.	4.2	S4	III	4.2	183 274	LQ0	E1	P002 IBC08 LP02 R001	B3	MP14	T1	TP33
3206	ALKALI METAL ALCOHOLATES, SELF-HEATING, CORROSIVE, N.O.S.	4.2	SC4	II	4.2 +8	182 274	LQ0	E2	P410 IBC05		MP14	T3	TP33
3206	ALKALI METAL ALCOHOLATES, SELF-HEATING, CORROSIVE, N.O.S.	4.2	SC4	III	4.2 +8	182 274	LQ0	E1	P002 IBC08 R001	B3	MP14	T1	TP33
3208	METALLIC SUBSTANCE, WATER-REACTIVE, N.O.S.	4.3	W2	I	4.3	274 557	LQ0	E0	P403 IBC99		MP2		
3208	METALLIC SUBSTANCE, WATER-REACTIVE, N.O.S.	4.3	W2	II	4.3	274 557	LQ11	E2	P410 IBC07		MP14	T3	TP33
3208	METALLIC SUBSTANCE, WATER-REACTIVE, N.O.S.	4.3	W2	III	4.3	274 557	LQ12	E1	P410 IBC08 R001	B4	MP14	T1	TP33
3209	METALLIC SUBSTANCE, WATER-REACTIVE, SELF-HEATING, N.O.S.	4.3	WS	I	4.3 +4.2	274 558	LQ0	E0	P403		MP2		
3209	METALLIC SUBSTANCE, WATER-REACTIVE, SELF-HEATING, N.O.S.	4.3	WS	II	4.3 +4.2	274 558	LQ11	E2	P410 IBC05		MP14	T3	TP33
3209	METALLIC SUBSTANCE, WATER-REACTIVE, SELF-HEATING, N.O.S.	4.3	WS	III	4.3 +4.2	274 558	LQ12	E1	P410 IBC08 R001	B4	MP14	T1	TP33
3210	CHLORATES, INORGANIC, AQUEOUS SOLUTION, N.O.S.	5.1	O1	II	5.1	274 605	LQ10	E2	P504 IBC02		MP2	T4	TP1
3210	CHLORATES, INORGANIC, AQUEOUS SOLUTION, N.O.S.	5.1	O1	III	5.1	274 605	LQ13	E1	P504 IBC02 R001		MP2	T4	TP1
3211	PERCHLORATES, INORGANIC, AQUEOUS SOLUTION, N.O.S.	5.1	O1	II	5.1	274	LQ10	E2	P504 IBC02		MP2	T4	TP1
3211	PERCHLORATES, INORGANIC, AQUEOUS SOLUTION, N.O.S.	5.1	O1	III	5.1	274	LQ13	E1	P504 IBC02 R001		MP2	T4	TP1

ADR tank		Vehicle for tank carriage	Transport category (Tunnel restriction code)	Special provisions for carriage				Hazard identifi-cation No.	UN No.	Name and description
Tank code	Special provisions			Packages	Bulk	Loading, unloading and handling	Operation			
4.3	4.3.5, 6.8.4	9.1.1.2	1.1.3.6 (8.6)	7.2.4	7.3.3	7.5.11	8.5	5.3.2.3		3.1.2
(12)	(13)	(14)	(15)	(16)	(17)	(18)	(19)	(20)	(1)	(2)
SGAN		AT	3 (E)	V1	VV4			40	3189	METAL POWDER, SELF-HEATING, N.O.S.
SGAN		AT	2 (D/E)	V1 V12				40	3190	SELF-HEATING SOLID, INORGANIC, N.O.S.
SGAN		AT	3 (E)	V1	VV4			40	3190	SELF-HEATING SOLID, INORGANIC, N.O.S.
SGAN		AT	2 (D/E)	V1		CV28		46	3191	SELF-HEATING SOLID, TOXIC, INORGANIC, N.O.S.
SGAN		AT	3 (E)	V1		CV28		46	3191	SELF-HEATING SOLID, TOXIC, INORGANIC, N.O.S.
SGAN		AT	2 (D/E)	V1				48	3192	SELF-HEATING SOLID, CORROSIVE, INORGANIC, N.O.S.
SGAN		AT	3 (E)	V1				48	3192	SELF-HEATING SOLID, CORROSIVE, INORGANIC, N.O.S.
L21DH	TU14 TC1 TE21 TM1	AT	0 (B/E)	V1			S20	333	3194	PYROPHORIC LIQUID, INORGANIC, N.O.S.
		AT	0 (B/E)	V1			S20	43	3200	PYROPHORIC SOLID, INORGANIC, N.O.S.
SGAN		AT	2 (D/E)	V1 V12				40	3205	ALKALINE EARTH METAL ALCOHOLATES, N.O.S.
SGAN		AT	3 (E)	V1				40	3205	ALKALINE EARTH METAL ALCOHOLATES, N.O.S.
SGAN		AT	2 (D/E)	V1				48	3206	ALKALI METAL ALCOHOLATES, SELF-HEATING, CORROSIVE, N.O.S.
SGAN		AT	3 (E)	V1				48	3206	ALKALI METAL ALCOHOLATES, SELF-HEATING, CORROSIVE, N.O.S.
			1 (E)	V1		CV23	S20		3208	METALLIC SUBSTANCE, WATER-REACTIVE, N.O.S.
SGAN		AT	2 (D/E)	V1 V12		CV23		423	3208	METALLIC SUBSTANCE, WATER-REACTIVE, N.O.S.
SGAN		AT	3 (E)	V1	VV5	CV23		423	3208	METALLIC SUBSTANCE, WATER-REACTIVE, N.O.S.
			1 (E)	V1		CV23	S20		3209	METALLIC SUBSTANCE, WATER-REACTIVE, SELF-HEATING, N.O.S.
SGAN		AT	2 (D/E)	V1		CV23		423	3209	METALLIC SUBSTANCE, WATER-REACTIVE, SELF-HEATING, N.O.S.
SGAN		AT	3 (E)	V1	VV5	CV23		423	3209	METALLIC SUBSTANCE, WATER-REACTIVE, SELF-HEATING, N.O.S.
L4BN	TU3	AT	2 (E)			CV24		50	3210	CHLORATES, INORGANIC, AQUEOUS SOLUTION, N.O.S.
LGBV	TU3	AT	3 (E)			CV24		50	3210	CHLORATES, INORGANIC, AQUEOUS SOLUTION, N.O.S.
L4BN	TU3	AT	2 (E)			CV24		50	3211	PERCHLORATES, INORGANIC, AQUEOUS SOLUTION, N.O.S.
LGBV	TU3	AT	3 (E)			CV24		50	3211	PERCHLORATES, INORGANIC, AQUEOUS SOLUTION, N.O.S.

UN No.	Name and description	Class	Classifi-cation code	Packing group	Labels	Special provi-sions	Limited and excepted quantities		Packaging			Portable tanks and bulk containers	
									Packing instruc-tions	Special packing provisions	Mixed packing provisions	Instruc-tions	Special provisions
	3.1.2	2.2	2.2	2.1.1.3	5.2.2	3.3	3.4.6	3.5.1.2	4.1.4	4.1.4	4.1.10	4.2.5.2 7.3.2	4.2.5.3
(1)	(2)	(3a)	(3b)	(4)	(5)	(6)	(7a)	(7b)	(8)	(9a)	(9b)	(10)	(11)
3212	HYPOCHLORITES, INORGANIC, N.O.S.	5.1	O2	II	5.1	274 559	LQ11	E2	P002 IBC08	B4	MP10	T3	TP33
3213	BROMATES, INORGANIC, AQUEOUS SOLUTION, N.O.S.	5.1	O1	II	5.1	274 604	LQ10	E2	P504 IBC02		MP2	T4	TP1
3213	BROMATES, INORGANIC, AQUEOUS SOLUTION, N.O.S.	5.1	O1	III	5.1	274 604	LQ13	E1	P504 IBC02 R001		MP15	T4	TP1
3214	PERMANGANATES, INORGANIC, AQUEOUS SOLUTION, N.O.S.	5.1	O1	II	5.1	274 608	LQ10	E2	P504 IBC02		MP2	T4	TP1
3215	PERSULPHATES, INORGANIC, N.O.S.	5.1	O2	III	5.1	274	LQ12	E1	P002 IBC08 LP02 R001	B3	MP10	T1	TP33
3216	PERSULPHATES, INORGANIC, AQUEOUS SOLUTION, N.O.S.	5.1	O1	III	5.1	274	LQ13	E1	P504 IBC02 R001		MP15	T4	TP1 TP29
3218	NITRATES, INORGANIC, AQUEOUS SOLUTION, N.O.S.	5.1	O1	II	5.1	270 274 511	LQ10	E2	P504 IBC02		MP15	T4	TP1
3218	NITRATES, INORGANIC, AQUEOUS SOLUTION, N.O.S.	5.1	O1	III	5.1	270 274 511	LQ13	E1	P504 IBC02 R001		MP15	T4	TP1
3219	NITRITES, INORGANIC, AQUEOUS SOLUTION, N.O.S.	5.1	O1	II	5.1	103 274	LQ10	E2	P504 IBC01		MP15	T4	TP1
3219	NITRITES, INORGANIC, AQUEOUS SOLUTION, N.O.S.	5.1	O1	III	5.1	103 274	LQ13	E1	P504 IBC02 R001		MP15	T4	TP1
3220	PENTAFLUOROETHANE (REFRIGERANT GAS R 125)	2	2A		2.2		LQ1	E1	P200		MP9	(M) T50	
3221	SELF-REACTIVE LIQUID TYPE B	4.1	SR1		4.1 +1	181 194 274	LQ14	E0	P520	PP21	MP2		
3222	SELF-REACTIVE SOLID TYPE B	4.1	SR1		4.1 +1	181 194 274	LQ15	E0	P520	PP21	MP2		
3223	SELF-REACTIVE LIQUID TYPE C	4.1	SR1		4.1	194 274	LQ14	E0	P520	PP21	MP2		
3224	SELF-REACTIVE SOLID TYPE C	4.1	SR1		4.1	194 274	LQ15	E0	P520	PP21	MP2		
3225	SELF-REACTIVE LIQUID TYPE D	4.1	SR1		4.1	194 274	LQ16	E0	P520		MP2		
3226	SELF-REACTIVE SOLID TYPE D	4.1	SR1		4.1	194 274	LQ11	E0	P520		MP2		
3227	SELF-REACTIVE LIQUID TYPE E	4.1	SR1		4.1	194 274	LQ16	E0	P520		MP2		
3228	SELF-REACTIVE SOLID TYPE E	4.1	SR1		4.1	194 274	LQ11	E0	P520		MP2		
3229	SELF-REACTIVE LIQUID TYPE F	4.1	SR1		4.1	194 274	LQ16	E0	P520 IBC99		MP2	T23	
3230	SELF-REACTIVE SOLID TYPE F	4.1	SR1		4.1	194 274	LQ11	E0	P520 IBC99		MP2	T23	
3231	SELF-REACTIVE LIQUID TYPE B, TEMPERATURE CONTROLLED	4.1	SR2		4.1 +1	181 194 274	LQ0	E0	P520	PP21	MP2		
3232	SELF-REACTIVE SOLID TYPE B, TEMPERATURE CONTROLLED	4.1	SR2		4.1 +1	181 194 274	LQ0	E0	P520	PP21	MP2		
3233	SELF-REACTIVE LIQUID TYPE C, TEMPERATURE CONTROLLED	4.1	SR2		4.1	194 274	LQ0	E0	P520	PP21	MP2		

ADR tank		Vehicle for tank carriage	Transport category (Tunnel restriction code)	Special provisions for carriage				Hazard identifi-cation No.	UN No.	Name and description
Tank code	Special provisions			Packages	Bulk	Loading, unloading and handling	Operation			
4.3	4.3.5, 6.8.4	9.1.1.2	1.1.3.6 (8.6)	7.2.4	7.3.3	7.5.11	8.5	5.3.2.3		3.1.2
(12)	(13)	(14)	(15)	(16)	(17)	(18)	(19)	(20)	(1)	(2)
SGAN	TU3	AT	2 (E)	V11		CV24		50	3212	HYPOCHLORITES, INORGANIC, N.O.S.
L4BN	TU3	AT	2 (E)			CV24		50	3213	BROMATES, INORGANIC, AQUEOUS SOLUTION, N.O.S.
LGBV	TU3	AT	3 (E)			CV24		50	3213	BROMATES, INORGANIC, AQUEOUS SOLUTION, N.O.S.
L4BN	TU3	AT	2 (E)			CV24		50	3214	PERMANGANATES, INORGANIC, AQUEOUS SOLUTION, N.O.S.
SGAV	TU3	AT	3 (E)		VV8	CV24		50	3215	PERSULPHATES, INORGANIC, N.O.S.
LGBV	TU3	AT	3 (E)			CV24		50	3216	PERSULPHATES, INORGANIC, AQUEOUS SOLUTION, N.O.S.
L4BN	TU3	AT	2 (E)			CV24		50	3218	NITRATES, INORGANIC, AQUEOUS SOLUTION, N.O.S.
LGBV	TU3	AT	3 (E)			CV24		50	3218	NITRATES, INORGANIC, AQUEOUS SOLUTION, N.O.S.
L4BN	TU3	AT	2 (E)			CV24		50	3219	NITRITES, INORGANIC, AQUEOUS SOLUTION, N.O.S.
LGBV	TU3	AT	3 (E)			CV24		50	3219	NITRITES, INORGANIC, AQUEOUS SOLUTION, N.O.S.
PxBN(M)	TA4 TT9	AT	3 (C/E)			CV9 CV10 CV36		20	3220	PENTAFLUOROETHANE (REFRIGERANT GAS R 125)
			1 (B)	V1		CV15 CV20 CV22	S9 S17		3221	SELF-REACTIVE LIQUID TYPE B
			1 (B)	V1		CV15 CV20 CV22	S9 S17		3222	SELF-REACTIVE SOLID TYPE B
			1 (D)	V1		CV15 CV20 CV22	S8 S18		3223	SELF-REACTIVE LIQUID TYPE C
			1 (D)	V1		CV15 CV20 CV22	S8 S18		3224	SELF-REACTIVE SOLID TYPE C
			2 (D)	V1		CV15 CV22	S19		3225	SELF-REACTIVE LIQUID TYPE D
			2 (D)	V1		CV15 CV22	S19		3226	SELF-REACTIVE SOLID TYPE D
			2 (D)	V1		CV15 CV22			3227	SELF-REACTIVE LIQUID TYPE E
			2 (D)	V1		CV15 CV22			3228	SELF-REACTIVE SOLID TYPE E
		AT	2 (D)	V1		CV15 CV22		40	3229	SELF-REACTIVE LIQUID TYPE F
		AT	2 (D)	V1		CV15 CV22		40	3230	SELF-REACTIVE SOLID TYPE F
			1 (B)	V8		CV15 CV20 CV21 CV22	S4 S9 S16		3231	SELF-REACTIVE LIQUID TYPE B, TEMPERATURE CONTROLLED
			1 (B)	V8		CV15 CV20 CV21 CV22	S4 S9 S16		3232	SELF-REACTIVE SOLID TYPE B, TEMPERATURE CONTROLLED
			1 (D)	V8		CV15 CV20 CV21 CV22	S4 S8 S17		3233	SELF-REACTIVE LIQUID TYPE C, TEMPERATURE CONTROLLED

UN No.	Name and description	Class	Classification code	Packing group	Labels	Special provisions	Limited and excepted quantities		Packaging			Portable tanks and bulk containers	
							quantities		Packing instructions	Special packing provisions	Mixed packing provisions	Instructions	Special provisions
	3.1.2	2.2	2.2	2.1.1.3	5.2.2	3.3	3.4.6	3.5.1.2	4.1.4	4.1.4	4.1.10	4.2.5.2 7.3.2	4.2.5.3
(1)	(2)	(3a)	(3b)	(4)	(5)	(6)	(7a)	(7b)	(8)	(9a)	(9b)	(10)	(11)
3234	SELF-REACTIVE SOLID TYPE C, TEMPERATURE CONTROLLED	4.1	SR2		4.1	194 274	LQ0	E0	P520	PP21	MP2		
3235	SELF-REACTIVE LIQUID TYPE D, TEMPERATURE CONTROLLED	4.1	SR2		4.1	194 274	LQ0	E0	P520		MP2		
3236	SELF-REACTIVE SOLID TYPE D, TEMPERATURE CONTROLLED	4.1	SR2		4.1	194 274	LQ0	E0	P520		MP2		
3237	SELF-REACTIVE LIQUID TYPE E, TEMPERATURE CONTROLLED	4.1	SR2		4.1	194 274	LQ0	E0	P520		MP2		
3238	SELF-REACTIVE SOLID TYPE E, TEMPERATURE CONTROLLED	4.1	SR2		4.1	194 274	LQ0	E0	P520		MP2		
3239	SELF-REACTIVE LIQUID TYPE F, TEMPERATURE CONTROLLED	4.1	SR2		4.1	194 274	LQ0	E0	P520		MP2	T23	
3240	SELF-REACTIVE SOLID TYPE F, TEMPERATURE CONTROLLED	4.1	SR2		4.1	194 274	LQ0	E0	P520		MP2	T23	
3241	2-BROMO-2-NITROPROPANE-1,3-DIOL	4.1	SR1	III	4.1	638	LQ0	E1	P520 IBC08	PP22 B3	MP2		
3242	AZODICARBONAMIDE	4.1	SR1	II	4.1	215 638	LQ0	E2	P409		MP2	T3	TP33
3243	SOLIDS CONTAINING TOXIC LIQUID, N.O.S.	6.1	T9	II	6.1	217 274	LQ18	E4	P002 IBC02	PP9	MP10	T3 BK1 BK2	TP33
3244	SOLIDS CONTAINING CORROSIVE LIQUID, N.O.S.	8	C10	II	8	218 274	LQ23	E2	P002 IBC05	PP9	MP10	T3 BK1 BK2	TP33
3245	GENETICALLY MODIFIED MICROORGANISMS or GENETICALLY MODIFIED ORGANISMS	9	M8		9	219 637	LQ0	E0	P904 IBC08		MP6		
3245	GENETICALLY MODIFIED MICROORGANISMS or GENETICALLY MODIFIED ORGANISMS, in refrigerated liquid nitrogen	9	M8		9 +2.2	219 637	LQ0	E0	P904 IBC08		MP6		
3246	METHANESULPHONYL CHLORIDE	6.1	TC1	I	6.1 +8		LQ0	E5	P001		MP8 MP17	T14	TP2
3247	SODIUM PEROXOBORATE, ANHYDROUS	5.1	O2	II	5.1		LQ11	E2	P002 IBC08	B4	MP2	T3	TP33
3248	MEDICINE, LIQUID, FLAMMABLE, TOXIC, N.O.S.	3	FT1	II	3 +6.1	220 221 274 601	LQ0	E2	P001		MP19		
3248	MEDICINE, LIQUID, FLAMMABLE, TOXIC, N.O.S.	3	FT1	III	3 +6.1	220 221 274 601	LQ7	E1	P001 R001		MP19		
3249	MEDICINE, SOLID, TOXIC, N.O.S.	6.1	T2	II	6.1	221 274 601	LQ18	E4	P002		MP10	T3	TP33
3249	MEDICINE, SOLID, TOXIC, N.O.S.	6.1	T2	III	6.1	221 274 601	LQ9	E1	P002 LP02 R001		MP10	T1	TP33
3250	CHLOROACETIC ACID, MOLTEN	6.1	TC1	II	6.1 +8		LQ0	E0				T7	TP3 TP28
3251	ISOSORBIDE-5-MONONITRATE	4.1	SR1	III	4.1	226 638	LQ0	E1	P409		MP2		
3252	DIFLUOROMETHANE (REFRIGERANT GAS R 32)	2	2F		2.1		LQ0	E0	P200		MP9	(M) T50	

ADR tank		Vehicle for tank carriage	Transport category (Tunnel restriction code)	Special provisions for carriage				Hazard identifi-cation No.	UN No.	Name and description
Tank code	Special provisions			Packages	Bulk	Loading, unloading and handling	Operation			
4.3	4.3.5, 6.8.4	9.1.1.2	1.1.3.6 (8.6)	7.2.4	7.3.3	7.5.11	8.5	5.3.2.3		3.1.2
(12)	(13)	(14)	(15)	(16)	(17)	(18)	(19)	(20)	(1)	(2)
			1 (D)	V8		CV15 CV20 CV21 CV22	S4 S8 S17		3234	SELF-REACTIVE SOLID TYPE C, TEMPERATURE CONTROLLED
			1 (D)	V8		CV15 CV21 CV22	S4 S18		3235	SELF-REACTIVE LIQUID TYPE D, TEMPERATURE CONTROLLED
			1 (D)	V8		CV15 CV21 CV22	S4 S18		3236	SELF-REACTIVE SOLID TYPE D, TEMPERATURE CONTROLLED
			1 (D)	V8		CV15 CV21 CV22	S4 S19		3237	SELF-REACTIVE LIQUID TYPE E, TEMPERATURE CONTROLLED
			1 (D)	V8		CV15 CV21 CV22	S4 S19		3238	SELF-REACTIVE SOLID TYPE E, TEMPERATURE CONTROLLED
		AT	1 (D)	V8		CV15 CV21 CV22	S4	40	3239	SELF-REACTIVE LIQUID TYPE F, TEMPERATURE CONTROLLED
		AT	1 (D)	V8		CV15 CV21 CV22	S4	40	3240	SELF-REACTIVE SOLID TYPE F, TEMPERATURE CONTROLLED
			3 (D)			CV14	S24		3241	2-BROMO-2-NITROPROPANE-1,3-DIOL
		AT	2 (D)			CV14	S24	40	3242	AZODICARBONAMIDE
SGAH	TU15 TE19	AT	2 (D/E)		VV10	CV13 CV28	S9 S19	60	3243	SOLIDS CONTAINING TOXIC LIQUID, N.O.S.
SGAV		AT	2 (E)		VV10			80	3244	SOLIDS CONTAINING CORROSIVE LIQUID, N.O.S.
			2 (E)			CV1 CV13 CV26 CV27 CV28	S17		3245	GENETICALLY MODIFIED MICROORGANISMS or GENETICALLY MODIFIED ORGANISMS
			2 (E)			CV1 CV13 CV26 CV27 CV28	S17		3245	GENETICALLY MODIFIED MICROORGANISMS or GENETICALLY MODIFIED ORGANISMS, in refrigerated liquid nitrogen
L10CH	TU14 TU15 TE19 TE21	AT	1 (C/E)			CV1 CV13 CV28	S9 S14	668	3246	METHANESULPHONYL CHLORIDE
SGAN	TU3	AT	2 (E)	V11		CV24		50	3247	SODIUM PEROXOBORATE, ANHYDROUS
L4BH	TU15	FL	2 (D/E)			CV13 CV28	S2 S19	336	3248	MEDICINE, LIQUID, FLAMMABLE, TOXIC, N.O.S.
L4BH	TU15	FL	3 (D/E)			CV13 CV28	S2	36	3248	MEDICINE, LIQUID, FLAMMABLE, TOXIC, N.O.S.
SGAH L4BH	TU15 TE19	AT	2 (D/E)			CV13 CV28	S9 S19	60	3249	MEDICINE, SOLID, TOXIC, N.O.S.
SGAH L4BH	TU15 TE19	AT	2 (E)		VV9	CV13 CV28	S9	60	3249	MEDICINE, SOLID, TOXIC, N.O.S.
L4BH	TU15 TC4 TE19	AT	0 (D/E)			CV13	S9 S19	68	3250	CHLOROACETIC ACID, MOLTEN
			3 (D)			CV14	S24		3251	ISOSORBIDE-5-MONONITRATE
PxBN(M)	TA4 TT9	FL	2 (B/D)			CV9 CV10 CV36	S2 S20	23	3252	DIFLUOROMETHANE (REFRIGERANT GAS R 32)

UN No.	Name and description	Class	Classification code	Packing group	Labels	Special provisions	Limited and excepted quantities		Packaging			Portable tanks and bulk containers	
									Packing instructions	Special packing provisions	Mixed packing provisions	Instructions	Special provisions
	3.1.2	2.2	2.2	2.1.1.3	5.2.2	3.3	3.4.6	3.5.1.2	4.1.4	4.1.4	4.1.10	4.2.5.2 7.3.2	4.2.5.3
(1)	(2)	(3a)	(3b)	(4)	(5)	(6)	(7a)	(7b)	(8)	(9a)	(9b)	(10)	(11)
3253	DISODIUM TRIOXOSILICATE	8	C6	III	8		LQ24	E1	P002 IBC08 LP02 R001	B3	MP10	T1	TP33
3254	TRIBUTYLPHOSPHANE	4.2	S1	I	4.2		LQ0	E0	P400		MP2	T21	TP2 TP7
3255	tert-BUTYL HYPOCHLORITE	4.2	SC1	CARRIAGE PROHIBITED									
3256	ELEVATED TEMPERATURE LIQUID, FLAMMABLE, N.O.S. with flash-point above 60 °C, at or above its flash-point	3	F2	III	3	274 560	LQ0	E0	P099 IBC99		MP2	T3	TP3 TP29
3257	ELEVATED TEMPERATURE LIQUID, N.O.S., at or above 100 °C and below its flash-point (including molten metals, molten salts, etc.), filled at a temperature higher than 190 °C	9	M9	III	9	274 580 643	LQ0	E0	P099 IBC99			T3	TP3 TP29
3257	ELEVATED TEMPERATURE LIQUID, N.O.S., at or above 100 °C and below its flash-point (including molten metals, molten salts, etc.), filled at or below 190 °C	9	M9	III	9	274 580 643	LQ0	E0	P099 IBC99			T3	TP3 TP29
3258	ELEVATED TEMPERATURE SOLID, N.O.S., at or above 240 °C	9	M10	III	9	274 580 643	LQ0	E0	P099 IBC99				
3259	AMINES, SOLID, CORROSIVE, N.O.S. or POLYAMINES, SOLID, CORROSIVE, N.O.S.	8	C8	I	8	274	LQ0	E0	P002 IBC07		MP18	T6	TP33
3259	AMINES, SOLID, CORROSIVE, N.O.S. or POLYAMINES, SOLID, CORROSIVE, N.O.S.	8	C8	II	8	274	LQ23	E2	P002 IBC08	B4	MP10	T3	TP33
3259	AMINES, SOLID, CORROSIVE, N.O.S. or POLYAMINES, SOLID, CORROSIVE, N.O.S.	8	C8	III	8	274	LQ24	E1	P002 IBC08 LP02 R001	B3	MP10	T1	TP33
3260	CORROSIVE SOLID, ACIDIC, INORGANIC, N.O.S.	8	C2	I	8	274	LQ0	E0	P002 IBC07		MP18	T6	TP33
3260	CORROSIVE SOLID, ACIDIC, INORGANIC, N.O.S.	8	C2	II	8	274	LQ23	E2	P002 IBC08	B4	MP10	T3	TP33
3260	CORROSIVE SOLID, ACIDIC, INORGANIC, N.O.S.	8	C2	III	8	274	LQ24	E1	P002 IBC08 LP02 R001	B3	MP10	T1	TP33
3261	CORROSIVE SOLID, ACIDIC, ORGANIC, N.O.S.	8	C4	I	8	274	LQ0	E0	P002 IBC07		MP18	T6	TP33
3261	CORROSIVE SOLID, ACIDIC, ORGANIC, N.O.S.	8	C4	II	8	274	LQ23	E2	P002 IBC08	B4	MP10	T3	TP33
3261	CORROSIVE SOLID, ACIDIC, ORGANIC, N.O.S.	8	C4	III	8	274	LQ24	E1	P002 IBC08 LP02 R001	B3	MP10	T1	TP33
3262	CORROSIVE SOLID, BASIC, INORGANIC, N.O.S.	8	C6	I	8	274	LQ0	E0	P002 IBC07		MP18	T6	TP33
3262	CORROSIVE SOLID, BASIC, INORGANIC, N.O.S.	8	C6	II	8	274	LQ23	E2	P002 IBC08	B4	MP10	T3	TP33
3262	CORROSIVE SOLID, BASIC, INORGANIC, N.O.S.	8	C6	III	8	274	LQ24	E1	P002 IBC08 LP02 R001	B3	MP10	T1	TP33
3263	CORROSIVE SOLID, BASIC, ORGANIC, N.O.S.	8	C8	I	8	274	LQ0	E0	P002 IBC07		MP18	T6	TP33
3263	CORROSIVE SOLID, BASIC, ORGANIC, N.O.S.	8	C8	II	8	274	LQ23	E2	P002 IBC08	B4	MP10	T3	TP33

ADR tank		Vehicle for tank carriage	Transport category (Tunnel restriction code)	Special provisions for carriage				Hazard identification No.	UN No.	Name and description
Tank code	Special provisions			Packages	Bulk	Loading, unloading and handling	Operation			
4.3	4.3.5, 6.8.4	9.1.1.2	1.1.3.6 (8.6)	7.2.4	7.3.3	7.5.11	8.5	5.3.2.3		3.1.2
(12)	(13)	(14)	(15)	(16)	(17)	(18)	(19)	(20)	(1)	(2)
SGAV		AT	3 (E)		VV9			80	3253	DISODIUM TRIOXOSILICATE
		AT	0 (B/E)	V1			S20	333	3254	TRIBUTYLPHOSPHANE
CARRIAGE PROHIBITED									3255	tert-BUTYL HYPOCHLORITE
LGAV	TU35 TE24	FL	3 (D/E)				S2	30	3256	ELEVATED TEMPERATURE LIQUID, FLAMMABLE, N.O.S. with flash-point above 60 °C, at or above its flash-point
LGAV	TU35 TC7 TE6 TE14 TE18 TE24	AT	3 (D)		VV12			99	3257	ELEVATED TEMPERATURE LIQUID, N.O.S., at or above 100 °C and below its flash-point (including molten metals, molten salts, etc.), filled at a temperature higher than 190 °C
LGAV	TU35 TC7 TE6 TE14 TE24	AT	3 (D)		VV12			99	3257	ELEVATED TEMPERATURE LIQUID, N.O.S., at or above 100 °C and below its flash-point (including molten metals, molten salts, etc.), filled at or below 190 °C
			3 (D)		VV13			99	3258	ELEVATED TEMPERATURE SOLID, N.O.S., at or above 240 °C
S10AN L10BH		AT	1 (E)	V10 V12			S20	88	3259	AMINES, SOLID, CORROSIVE, N.O.S. or POLYAMINES, SOLID, CORROSIVE, N.O.S.
SGAN L4BN		AT	2 (E)	V11				80	3259	AMINES, SOLID, CORROSIVE, N.O.S. or POLYAMINES, SOLID, CORROSIVE, N.O.S.
SGAV L4BN		AT	3 (E)		VV9			80	3259	AMINES, SOLID, CORROSIVE, N.O.S. or POLYAMINES, SOLID, CORROSIVE, N.O.S.
S10AN		AT	1 (E)	V10 V12			S20	88	3260	CORROSIVE SOLID, ACIDIC, INORGANIC, N.O.S.
SGAN		AT	2 (E)	V11				80	3260	CORROSIVE SOLID, ACIDIC, INORGANIC, N.O.S.
SGAV		AT	3 (E)		VV9			80	3260	CORROSIVE SOLID, ACIDIC, INORGANIC, N.O.S.
S10AN L10BH		AT	1 (E)	V10 V12			S20	88	3261	CORROSIVE SOLID, ACIDIC, ORGANIC, N.O.S.
SGAN L4BN		AT	2 (E)	V11				80	3261	CORROSIVE SOLID, ACIDIC, ORGANIC, N.O.S.
SGAV L4BN		AT	3 (E)		VV9			80	3261	CORROSIVE SOLID, ACIDIC, ORGANIC, N.O.S.
S10AN L10BH		AT	1 (E)	V10 V12			S20	88	3262	CORROSIVE SOLID, BASIC, INORGANIC, N.O.S.
SGAN L4BN		AT	2 (E)	V11				80	3262	CORROSIVE SOLID, BASIC, INORGANIC, N.O.S.
SGAV L4BN		AT	3 (E)		VV9			80	3262	CORROSIVE SOLID, BASIC, INORGANIC, N.O.S.
S10AN L10BH		AT	1 (E)	V10 V12			S20	88	3263	CORROSIVE SOLID, BASIC, ORGANIC, N.O.S.
SGAN L4BN		AT	2 (E)	V11				80	3263	CORROSIVE SOLID, BASIC, ORGANIC, N.O.S.

UN No.	Name and description	Class	Classification code	Packing group	Labels	Special provisions	Limited and excepted quantities		Packaging			Portable tanks and bulk containers	
									Packing instructions	Special packing provisions	Mixed packing provisions	Instructions	Special provisions
	3.1.2	2.2	2.2	2.1.1.3	5.2.2	3.3	3.4.6	3.5.1.2	4.1.4	4.1.4	4.1.10	4.2.5.2 7.3.2	4.2.5.3
(1)	(2)	(3a)	(3b)	(4)	(5)	(6)	(7a)	(7b)	(8)	(9a)	(9b)	(10)	(11)
3263	CORROSIVE SOLID, BASIC, ORGANIC, N.O.S.	8	C8	III	8	274	LQ24	E1	P002 IBC08 LP02 R001	B3	MP10	T1	TP33
3264	CORROSIVE LIQUID, ACIDIC, INORGANIC, N.O.S.	8	C1	I	8	274	LQ0	E0	P001		MP8 MP17	T14	TP2 TP27
3264	CORROSIVE LIQUID, ACIDIC, INORGANIC, N.O.S.	8	C1	II	8	274	LQ22	E2	P001 IBC02		MP15	T11	TP2 TP27
3264	CORROSIVE LIQUID, ACIDIC, INORGANIC, N.O.S.	8	C1	III	8	274	LQ7	E1	P001 IBC03 LP01 R001		MP19	T7	TP1 TP28
3265	CORROSIVE LIQUID, ACIDIC, ORGANIC, N.O.S.	8	C3	I	8	274	LQ0	E0	P001		MP8 MP17	T14	TP2 TP27
3265	CORROSIVE LIQUID, ACIDIC, ORGANIC, N.O.S.	8	C3	II	8	274	LQ22	E2	P001 IBC02		MP15	T11	TP2 TP27
3265	CORROSIVE LIQUID, ACIDIC, ORGANIC, N.O.S.	8	C3	III	8	274	LQ7	E1	P001 IBC03 LP01 R001		MP19	T7	TP1 TP28
3266	CORROSIVE LIQUID, BASIC, INORGANIC, N.O.S.	8	C5	I	8	274	LQ0	E0	P001		MP8 MP17	T14	TP2 TP27
3266	CORROSIVE LIQUID, BASIC, INORGANIC, N.O.S.	8	C5	II	8	274	LQ22	E2	P001 IBC02		MP15	T11	TP2 TP27
3266	CORROSIVE LIQUID, BASIC, INORGANIC, N.O.S.	8	C5	III	8	274	LQ7	E1	P001 IBC03 LP01 R001		MP19	T7	TP1 TP28
3267	CORROSIVE LIQUID, BASIC, ORGANIC, N.O.S.	8	C7	I	8	274	LQ0	E0	P001		MP8 MP17	T14	TP2 TP27
3267	CORROSIVE LIQUID, BASIC, ORGANIC, N.O.S.	8	C7	II	8	274	LQ22	E2	P001 IBC02		MP15	T11	TP2 TP27
3267	CORROSIVE LIQUID, BASIC, ORGANIC, N.O.S.	8	C7	III	8	274	LQ7	E1	P001 IBC03 LP01 R001		MP19	T7	TP1 TP28
3268	AIR BAG INFLATORS or AIR BAG MODULES or SEAT-BELT PRETENSIONERS	9	M5	III	9	280 289	LQ0	E0	P902 LP902				
3269	POLYESTER RESIN KIT	3	F1	II	3	236 340	LQ6	E0	P302 R001				
3269	POLYESTER RESIN KIT	3	F1	III	3	236 340	LQ7	E0	P302 R001				
3270	NITROCELLULOSE MEMBRANE FILTERS, with not more than 12.6% nitrogen, by dry mass	4.1	F1	II	4.1	237 286	LQ8	E2	P411		MP11		
3271	ETHERS, N.O.S.	3	F1	II	3	274	LQ4	E2	P001 IBC02 R001		MP19	T7	TP1 TP8 TP28
3271	ETHERS, N.O.S.	3	F1	III	3	274	LQ7	E1	P001 IBC03 LP01 R001		MP19	T4	TP1 TP29
3272	ESTERS, N.O.S.	3	F1	II	3	274 601	LQ4	E2	P001 IBC02 R001		MP19	T7	TP1 TP8 TP28
3272	ESTERS, N.O.S.	3	F1	III	3	274 601	LQ7	E1	P001 IBC03 LP01 R001		MP19	T4	TP1 TP29
3273	NITRILES, FLAMMABLE, TOXIC, N.O.S.	3	FT1	I	3 +6.1	274	LQ0	E0	P001		MP7 MP17	T14	TP2 TP27
3273	NITRILES, FLAMMABLE, TOXIC, N.O.S.	3	FT1	II	3 +6.1	274	LQ0	E2	P001 IBC02		MP19	T11	TP2 TP27
3274	ALCOHOLATES SOLUTION, N.O.S., in alcohol	3	FC	II	3 +8	274	LQ4	E2	P001 IBC02		MP19		

ADR tank		Vehicle for tank carriage	Transport category (Tunnel restriction code)	Special provisions for carriage				Hazard identification No.	UN No.	Name and description
Tank code	Special provisions	9.1.1.2	1.1.3.6 (8.6)	Packages 7.2.4	Bulk 7.3.3	Loading, unloading and handling 7.5.11	Operation 8.5	5.3.2.3		3.1.2
4.3	4.3.5, 6.8.4									
(12)	(13)	(14)	(15)	(16)	(17)	(18)	(19)	(20)	(1)	(2)
SGAV L4BN		AT	3 (E)		VV9			80	3263	CORROSIVE SOLID, BASIC, ORGANIC, N.O.S.
L10BH		AT	1 (E)				S20	88	3264	CORROSIVE LIQUID, ACIDIC, INORGANIC, N.O.S.
L4BN		AT	2 (E)					80	3264	CORROSIVE LIQUID, ACIDIC, INORGANIC, N.O.S.
L4BN		AT	3 (E)					80	3264	CORROSIVE LIQUID, ACIDIC, INORGANIC, N.O.S.
L10BH		AT	1 (E)				S20	88	3265	CORROSIVE LIQUID, ACIDIC, ORGANIC, N.O.S.
L4BN		AT	2 (E)					80	3265	CORROSIVE LIQUID, ACIDIC, ORGANIC, N.O.S.
L4BN		AT	3 (E)					80	3265	CORROSIVE LIQUID, ACIDIC, ORGANIC, N.O.S.
L10BH		AT	1 (E)				S20	88	3266	CORROSIVE LIQUID, BASIC, INORGANIC, N.O.S.
L4BN		AT	2 (E)					80	3266	CORROSIVE LIQUID, BASIC, INORGANIC, N.O.S.
L4BN		AT	3 (E)					80	3266	CORROSIVE LIQUID, BASIC, INORGANIC, N.O.S.
L10BH		AT	1 (E)				S20	88	3267	CORROSIVE LIQUID, BASIC, ORGANIC, N.O.S.
L4BN		AT	2 (E)					80	3267	CORROSIVE LIQUID, BASIC, ORGANIC, N.O.S.
L4BN		AT	3 (E)					80	3267	CORROSIVE LIQUID, BASIC, ORGANIC, N.O.S.
			4 (E)						3268	AIR BAG INFLATORS or AIR BAG MODULES or SEAT-BELT PRETENSIONERS
			2 (E)				S2 S20		3269	POLYESTER RESIN KIT
			3 (E)				S2		3269	POLYESTER RESIN KIT
			2 (E)						3270	NITROCELLULOSE MEMBRANE FILTERS, with not more than 12.6% nitrogen, by dry mass
LGBF		FL	2 (D/E)				S2 S20	33	3271	ETHERS, N.O.S.
LGBF		FL	3 (D/E)				S2	30	3271	ETHERS, N.O.S.
LGBF		FL	2 (D/E)				S2 S20	33	3272	ESTERS, N.O.S.
LGBF		FL	3 (D/E)				S2	30	3272	ESTERS, N.O.S.
L10CH	TU14 TU15 TE21	FL	1 (C/E)			CV13 CV28	S2 S22	336	3273	NITRILES, FLAMMABLE, TOXIC, N.O.S.
L4BH	TU15	FL	2 (D/E)			CV13 CV28	S2 S22	336	3273	NITRILES, FLAMMABLE, TOXIC, N.O.S.
L4BH		FL	2 (D/E)				S2 S20	338	3274	ALCOHOLATES SOLUTION, N.O.S., in alcohol

UN No.	Name and description	Class	Classifi- cation code	Packing group	Labels	Special provi- sions	Limited and excepted quantities		Packaging			Portable tanks and bulk containers	
									Packing instruc- tions	Special packing provisions	Mixed packing provisions	Instruc- tions	Special provisions
	3.1.2	2.2	2.2	2.1.1.3	5.2.2	3.3	3.4.6	3.5.1.2	4.1.4	4.1.4	4.1.10	4.2.5.2 7.3.2	4.2.5.3
(1)	(2)	(3a)	(3b)	(4)	(5)	(6)	(7a)	(7b)	(8)	(9a)	(9b)	(10)	(11)
3275	NITRILES, TOXIC, FLAMMABLE, N.O.S.	6.1	TF1	I	6.1 +3	274 315	LQ0	E5	P001		MP8 MP17	T14	TP2 TP27
3275	NITRILES, TOXIC, FLAMMABLE, N.O.S.	6.1	TF1	II	6.1 +3	274	LQ17	E4	P001 IBC02		MP15	T11	TP2 TP27
3276	NITRILES, TOXIC, LIQUID, N.O.S.	6.1	T1	I	6.1	274 315	LQ0	E5	P001		MP8 MP17	T14	TP2 TP27
3276	NITRILES, TOXIC, LIQUID, N.O.S.	6.1	T1	II	6.1	274	LQ17	E4	P001 IBC02		MP15	T11	TP2 TP27
3276	NITRILES, TOXIC, LIQUID, N.O.S.	6.1	T1	III	6.1	274	LQ7	E1	P001 IBC03 LP01 R001		MP19	T7	TP1 TP28
3277	CHLOROFORMATES, TOXIC, CORROSIVE, N.O.S.	6.1	TC1	II	6.1 +8	274 561	LQ17	E4	P001 IBC02		MP15	T8	TP2 TP28
3278	ORGANOPHOSPHORUS COMPOUND, TOXIC, LIQUID, N.O.S.	6.1	T1	I	6.1	43 274 315	LQ0	E5	P001		MP8 MP17	T14	TP2 TP27
3278	ORGANOPHOSPHORUS COMPOUND, TOXIC, LIQUID, N.O.S.	6.1	T1	II	6.1	43 274	LQ17	E4	P001 IBC02		MP15	T11	TP2 TP27
3278	ORGANOPHOSPHORUS COMPOUND, TOXIC, LIQUID, N.O.S.	6.1	T1	III	6.1	43 274	LQ7	E1	P001 IBC03 LP01 R001		MP19	T7	TP1 TP28
3279	ORGANOPHOSPHORUS COMPOUND, TOXIC, FLAMMABLE, N.O.S.	6.1	TF1	I	6.1 +3	43 274 315	LQ0	E5	P001		MP8 MP17	T14	TP2 TP27
3279	ORGANOPHOSPHORUS COMPOUND, TOXIC, FLAMMABLE, N.O.S.	6.1	TF1	II	6.1 +3	43 274	LQ17	E4	P001		MP15	T11	TP2 TP27
3280	ORGANOARSENIC COMPOUND, LIQUID, N.O.S.	6.1	T3	I	6.1	274 315	LQ0	E5	P001		MP8 MP17	T14	TP2 TP27
3280	ORGANOARSENIC COMPOUND, LIQUID, N.O.S.	6.1	T3	II	6.1	274	LQ17	E4	P001 IBC02		MP15	T11	TP2 TP27
3280	ORGANOARSENIC COMPOUND, LIQUID, N.O.S.	6.1	T3	III	6.1	274	LQ7	E1	P001 IBC03 LP01 R001		MP19	T7	TP1 TP28
3281	METAL CARBONYLS, LIQUID, N.O.S.	6.1	T3	I	6.1	274 315 562	LQ0	E5	P601		MP8 MP17	T14	TP2 TP27
3281	METAL CARBONYLS, LIQUID, N.O.S.	6.1	T3	II	6.1	274 562	LQ17	E4	P001 IBC02		MP15	T11	TP2 TP27
3281	METAL CARBONYLS, LIQUID, N.O.S.	6.1	T3	III	6.1	274 562	LQ7	E1	P001 IBC03 LP01 R001		MP19	T7	TP1 TP28
3282	ORGANOMETALLIC COMPOUND, TOXIC, LIQUID, N.O.S.	6.1	T3	I	6.1	274 562	LQ0	E5	P001		MP8 MP17	T14	TP2 TP27
3282	ORGANOMETALLIC COMPOUND, TOXIC, LIQUID, N.O.S.	6.1	T3	II	6.1	274 562	LQ17	E4	P001 IBC02		MP15	T11	TP2 TP27
3282	ORGANOMETALLIC COMPOUND, TOXIC, LIQUID, N.O.S.	6.1	T3	III	6.1	274 562	LQ7	E1	P001 IBC03 LP01 R001		MP19	T7	TP1 TP28
3283	SELENIUM COMPOUND, SOLID, N.O.S.	6.1	T5	I	6.1	274 563	LQ0	E5	P002 IBC07		MP18	T6	TP33
3283	SELENIUM COMPOUND, SOLID, N.O.S.	6.1	T5	II	6.1	274 563	LQ18	E4	P002 IBC08	B4	MP10	T3	TP33
3283	SELENIUM COMPOUND, SOLID, N.O.S.	6.1	T5	III	6.1	274 563	LQ9	E1	P002 IBC08 LP02 R001	B3	MP10	T1	TP33

ADR tank		Vehicle for tank carriage	Transport category (Tunnel restriction code)	Special provisions for carriage				Hazard identification No.	UN No.	Name and description
Tank code	Special provisions			Packages	Bulk	Loading, unloading and handling	Operation			
4.3	4.3.5, 6.8.4	9.1.1.2	1.1.3.6 (8.6)	7.2.4	7.3.3	7.5.11	8.5	5.3.2.3		3.1.2
(12)	(13)	(14)	(15)	(16)	(17)	(18)	(19)	(20)	(1)	(2)
L10CH	TU14 TU15 TE19 TE21	FL	1 (C/D)			CV1 CV13 CV28	S2 S9 S14	663	3275	NITRILES, TOXIC, FLAMMABLE, N.O.S.
L4BH	TU15 TE19	FL	2 (D/E)			CV13 CV28	S2 S9 S19	63	3275	NITRILES, TOXIC, FLAMMABLE, N.O.S.
L10CH	TU14 TU15 TE19 TE21	AT	1 (C/E)			CV1 CV13 CV28	S9 S14	66	3276	NITRILES, TOXIC, LIQUID, N.O.S.
L4BH	TU15 TE19	AT	2 (D/E)			CV13 CV28	S9 S19	60	3276	NITRILES, TOXIC, LIQUID, N.O.S.
L4BH	TU15 TE19	AT	2 (E)			CV13 CV28	S9	60	3276	NITRILES, TOXIC, LIQUID, N.O.S.
L4BH	TU15 TE19	AT	2 (D/E)			CV13 CV28	S9 S19	68	3277	CHLOROFORMATES, TOXIC, CORROSIVE, N.O.S.
L10CH	TU14 TU15 TE19 TE21	AT	1 (C/E)			CV1 CV13 CV28	S9 S14	66	3278	ORGANOPHOSPHORUS COMPOUND, TOXIC, LIQUID, N.O.S.
L4BH	TU15 TE19	AT	2 (D/E)			CV13 CV28	S9 S19	60	3278	ORGANOPHOSPHORUS COMPOUND, TOXIC, LIQUID, N.O.S.
L4BH	TU15 TE19	AT	2 (E)			CV13 CV28	S9	60	3278	ORGANOPHOSPHORUS COMPOUND, TOXIC, LIQUID, N.O.S.
L10CH	TU14 TU15 TE19 TE21	FL	1 (C/D)			CV1 CV13 CV28	S2 S9 S14	663	3279	ORGANOPHOSPHORUS COMPOUND, TOXIC, FLAMMABLE, N.O.S.
L4BH	TU15 TE19	FL	2 (D/E)			CV13 CV28	S2 S9 S19	63	3279	ORGANOPHOSPHORUS COMPOUND, TOXIC, FLAMMABLE, N.O.S.
L10CH	TU14 TU15 TE19 TE21	AT	1 (C/E)			CV1 CV13 CV28	S9 S14	66	3280	ORGANOARSENIC COMPOUND, LIQUID, N.O.S.
L4BH	TU15 TE19	AT	2 (D/E)			CV13 CV28	S9 S19	60	3280	ORGANOARSENIC COMPOUND, LIQUID, N.O.S.
L4BH	TU15 TE19	AT	2 (E)			CV13 CV28	S9	60	3280	ORGANOARSENIC COMPOUND, LIQUID, N.O.S.
L10CH	TU14 TU15 TE19 TE21	AT	1 (C/E)			CV1 CV13 CV28	S9 S14	66	3281	METAL CARBONYLS, LIQUID, N.O.S.
L4BH	TU15 TE19	AT	2 (D/E)			CV13 CV28	S9 S19	60	3281	METAL CARBONYLS, LIQUID, N.O.S.
L4BH	TU15 TE19	AT	2 (E)			CV13 CV28	S9	60	3281	METAL CARBONYLS, LIQUID, N.O.S.
L10CH	TU14 TU15 TE19 TE21	AT	1 (C/E)			CV1 CV13 CV28	S9 S14	66	3282	ORGANOMETALLIC COMPOUND, TOXIC, LIQUID, N.O.S.
L4BH	TU15 TE19	AT	2 (D/E)			CV13 CV28	S9 S19	60	3282	ORGANOMETALLIC COMPOUND, TOXIC, LIQUID, N.O.S.
L4BH	TU15 TE19	AT	2 (E)			CV13 CV28	S9	60	3282	ORGANOMETALLIC COMPOUND, TOXIC, LIQUID, N.O.S.
S10AH L10CH	TU14 TU15 TE19 TE21	AT	1 (C/E)	V10 V12		CV1 CV13 CV28	S9 S14	66	3283	SELENIUM COMPOUND, SOLID, N.O.S.
SGAH L4BH	TU15 TE19	AT	2 (D/E)	V11		CV13 CV28	S9 S19	60	3283	SELENIUM COMPOUND, SOLID, N.O.S.
SGAH L4BH	TU15 TE19	AT	2 (E)		VV9	CV13 CV28	S9	60	3283	SELENIUM COMPOUND, SOLID, N.O.S.

UN No.	Name and description	Class	Classifi-cation code	Packing group	Labels	Special provi-sions	Limited and excepted quantities		Packaging			Portable tanks and bulk containers	
									Packing instruc-tions	Special packing provisions	Mixed packing provisions	Instruc-tions	Special provisions
	3.1.2	2.2	2.2	2.1.1.3	5.2.2	3.3	3.4.6	3.5.1.2	4.1.4	4.1.4	4.1.10	4.2.5.2 7.3.2	4.2.5.3
(1)	(2)	(3a)	(3b)	(4)	(5)	(6)	(7a)	(7b)	(8)	(9a)	(9b)	(10)	(11)
3284	TELLURIUM COMPOUND, N.O.S.	6.1	T5	I	6.1	274	LQ0	E5	P002 IBC07		MP18	T6	TP33
3284	TELLURIUM COMPOUND, N.O.S.	6.1	T5	II	6.1	274	LQ18	E4	P002 IBC08	B4	MP10	T3	TP33
3284	TELLURIUM COMPOUND, N.O.S.	6.1	T5	III	6.1	274	LQ9	E1	P002 IBC08 LP02 R001	B3	MP10	T1	TP33
3285	VANADIUM COMPOUND, N.O.S.	6.1	T5	I	6.1	274 564	LQ0	E5	P002 IBC07		MP18	T6	TP33
3285	VANADIUM COMPOUND, N.O.S.	6.1	T5	II	6.1	274 564	LQ18	E4	P002 IBC08	B4	MP10	T3	TP33
3285	VANADIUM COMPOUND, N.O.S.	6.1	T5	III	6.1	274 564	LQ9	E1	P002 IBC08 LP02 R001	B3	MP10	T1	TP33
3286	FLAMMABLE LIQUID, TOXIC, CORROSIVE, N.O.S.	3	FTC	I	3 +6.1 +8	274	LQ0	E0	P001		MP7 MP17	T14	TP2 TP27
3286	FLAMMABLE LIQUID, TOXIC, CORROSIVE, N.O.S.	3	FTC	II	3 +6.1 +8	274	LQ0	E2	P001 IBC02		MP19	T11	TP2 TP27
3287	TOXIC LIQUID, INORGANIC, N.O.S.	6.1	T4	I	6.1	274 315	LQ0	E5	P001		MP8 MP17	T14	TP2 TP27
3287	TOXIC LIQUID, INORGANIC, N.O.S.	6.1	T4	II	6.1	274	LQ17	E4	P001 IBC02		MP15	T11	TP2 TP27
3287	TOXIC LIQUID, INORGANIC, N.O.S.	6.1	T4	III	6.1	274	LQ7	E1	P001 IBC03 LP01 R001		MP19	T7	TP1 TP28
3288	TOXIC SOLID, INORGANIC, N.O.S.	6.1	T5	I	6.1	274	LQ0	E5	P002 IBC07		MP18	T6	TP33
3288	TOXIC SOLID, INORGANIC, N.O.S.	6.1	T5	II	6.1	274	LQ18	E4	P002 IBC08	B4	MP10	T3	TP33
3288	TOXIC SOLID, INORGANIC, N.O.S.	6.1	T5	III	6.1	274	LQ9	E1	P002 IBC08 LP02 R001	B3	MP10	T1	TP33
3289	TOXIC LIQUID, CORROSIVE, INORGANIC, N.O.S.	6.1	TC3	I	6.1 +8	274 315	LQ0	E5	P001		MP8 MP17	T14	TP2 TP27
3289	TOXIC LIQUID, CORROSIVE, INORGANIC, N.O.S.	6.1	TC3	II	6.1 +8	274	LQ17	E4	P001 IBC02		MP15	T11	TP2 TP27
3290	TOXIC SOLID, CORROSIVE, INORGANIC, N.O.S.	6.1	TC4	I	6.1 +8	274	LQ0	E5	P002 IBC05		MP18	T6	TP33
3290	TOXIC SOLID, CORROSIVE, INORGANIC, N.O.S.	6.1	TC4	II	6.1 +8	274	LQ18	E4	P002 IBC06		MP10	T3	TP33
3291	CLINICAL WASTE, UNSPECIFIED, N.O.S. or (BIO) MEDICAL WASTE, N.O.S. or REGULATED MEDICAL WASTE, N.O.S.	6.2	I3	II	6.2	565	LQ0	E0	P621 IBC620 LP621		MP6	BK2	
3291	CLINICAL WASTE, UNSPECIFIED, N.O.S. or (BIO) MEDICAL WASTE, N.O.S. or REGULATED MEDICAL WASTE, N.O.S., in refrigerated liquid nitrogen	6.2	I3	II	6.2 +2.2	565	LQ0	E0	P621 IBC620 LP621		MP6		
3292	BATTERIES, CONTAINING SODIUM, or CELLS, CONTAINING SODIUM	4.3	W3	II	4.3	239 295	LQ0	E0	P408				

ADR tank		Vehicle for tank carriage	Transport category (Tunnel restriction code)	Special provisions for carriage				Hazard identifi-cation No.	UN No.	Name and description
Tank code	Special provisions			Packages	Bulk	Loading, unloading and handling	Operation			
4.3	4.3.5, 6.8.4	9.1.1.2	1.1.3.6 (8.6)	7.2.4	7.3.3	7.5.11	8.5	5.3.2.3		3.1.2
(12)	(13)	(14)	(15)	(16)	(17)	(18)	(19)	(20)	(1)	(2)
S10AH L10CH	TU14 TU15 TE19 TE21	AT	1 (C/E)	V10 V12		CV1 CV13 CV28	S9 S14	66	3284	TELLURIUM COMPOUND, N.O.S.
SGAH L4BH	TU15 TE19	AT	2 (D/E)	V11		CV13 CV28	S9 S19	60	3284	TELLURIUM COMPOUND, N.O.S.
SGAH L4BH	TU15 TE19	AT	2 (E)		VV9	CV13 CV28	S9	60	3284	TELLURIUM COMPOUND, N.O.S.
S10AH L10CH	TU14 TU15 TE19 TE21	AT	1 (C/E)	V10 V12		CV1 CV13 CV28	S9 S14	66	3285	VANADIUM COMPOUND, N.O.S.
SGAH L4BH	TU15 TE19	AT	2 (D/E)	V11		CV13 CV28	S9 S19	60	3285	VANADIUM COMPOUND, N.O.S.
SGAH L4BH	TU15 TE19	AT	2 (E)		VV9	CV13 CV28	S9	60	3285	VANADIUM COMPOUND, N.O.S.
L10CH	TU14 TU15 TE21	FL	1 (C/E)			CV13 CV28	S2 S22	368	3286	FLAMMABLE LIQUID, TOXIC, CORROSIVE, N.O.S.
L4BH	TU15	FL	2 (D/E)			CV13 CV28	S2 S22	368	3286	FLAMMABLE LIQUID, TOXIC, CORROSIVE, N.O.S.
L10CH	TU14 TU15 TE19 TE21	AT	1 (C/E)			CV1 CV13 CV28	S9 S14	66	3287	TOXIC LIQUID, INORGANIC, N.O.S.
L4BH	TU15 TE19	AT	2 (D/E)			CV13 CV28	S9 S19	60	3287	TOXIC LIQUID, INORGANIC, N.O.S.
L4BH	TU15 TE19	AT	2 (E)			CV13 CV28	S9	60	3287	TOXIC LIQUID, INORGANIC, N.O.S.
S10AH L10CH	TU14 TU15 TE19 TE21	AT	1 (C/E)	V10 V12		CV1 CV13 CV28	S9 S14	66	3288	TOXIC SOLID, INORGANIC, N.O.S.
SGAH L4BH	TU15 TE19	AT	2 (D/E)	V11		CV13 CV28	S9 S19	60	3288	TOXIC SOLID, INORGANIC, N.O.S.
SGAH L4BH	TU15 TE19	AT	2 (E)		VV9	CV13 CV28	S9	60	3288	TOXIC SOLID, INORGANIC, N.O.S.
L10CH	TU14 TU15 TE19 TE21	AT	1 (C/E)			CV1 CV13 CV28	S9 S14	668	3289	TOXIC LIQUID, CORROSIVE, INORGANIC, N.O.S.
L4BH	TU15 TE19	AT	2 (D/E)			CV13 CV28	S9 S19	68	3289	TOXIC LIQUID, CORROSIVE, INORGANIC, N.O.S.
S10AH L10CH	TU15 TE19	AT	1 (C/E)	V10		CV1 CV13 CV28	S9 S14	668	3290	TOXIC SOLID, CORROSIVE, INORGANIC, N.O.S.
SGAH L4BH	TU15 TE19	AT	2 (D/E)	V11 V12		CV13 CV28	S9 S19	68	3290	TOXIC SOLID, CORROSIVE, INORGANIC, N.O.S.
S4AH L4BH	TU15 TE19	AT	2 (-)	V1	VV11	CV13 CV25 CV28	S3	606	3291	CLINICAL WASTE, UNSPECIFIED, N.O.S. or (BIO) MEDICAL WASTE, N.O.S. or REGULATED MEDICAL WASTE, N.O.S.
			2 (-)	V1		CV13 CV25 CV28	S3		3291	CLINICAL WASTE, UNSPECIFIED, N.O.S. or (BIO) MEDICAL WASTE, N.O.S. or REGULATED MEDICAL WASTE, N.O.S., in refrigerated liquid nitrogen
			2 (E)	V1		CV23			3292	BATTERIES, CONTAINING SODIUM, or CELLS, CONTAINING SODIUM

UN No.	Name and description	Class	Classifi-cation code	Packing group	Labels	Special provi-sions	Limited and excepted quantities		Packaging			Portable tanks and bulk containers	
									Packing instruc-tions	Special packing provisions	Mixed packing provisions	Instruc-tions	Special provisions
	3.1.2	2.2	2.2	2.1.1.3	5.2.2	3.3	3.4.6	3.5.1.2	4.1.4	4.1.4	4.1.10	4.2.5.2 7.3.2	4.2.5.3
(1)	(2)	(3a)	(3b)	(4)	(5)	(6)	(7a)	(7b)	(8)	(9a)	(9b)	(10)	(11)
3293	HYDRAZINE, AQUEOUS SOLUTION with not more than 37% hydrazine, by mass	6.1	T4	III	6.1	566	LQ7	E1	P001 IBC03 LP01 R001		MP19	T4	TP1
3294	HYDROGEN CYANIDE, SOLUTION IN ALCOHOL with not more than 45% hydrogen cyanide	6.1	TF1	I	6.1 +3	610	LQ0	E5	P601		MP8 MP17	T14	TP2
3295	HYDROCARBONS, LIQUID, N.O.S.	3	F1	I	3	649	LQ3	E3	P001		MP7 MP17	T11	TP1 TP8
3295	HYDROCARBONS, LIQUID, N.O.S. (vapour pressure at 50 °C more than 110 kPa)	3	F1	II	3	640C 649	LQ4	E2	P001		MP19	T7	TP1 TP8 TP28
3295	HYDROCARBONS, LIQUID, N.O.S. (vapour pressure at 50 °C not more than 110 kPa)	3	F1	II	3	640D 649	LQ4	E2	P001 IBC02 R001		MP19	T7	TP1 TP8 TP28
3295	HYDROCARBONS, LIQUID, N.O.S.	3	F1	III	3		LQ7	E1	P001 IBC03 LP01 R001		MP19	T4	TP1 TP29
3296	HEPTAFLUOROPROPANE (REFRIGERANT GAS R 227)	2	2A		2.2		LQ1	E1	P200		MP9	(M) T50	
3297	ETHYLENE OXIDE AND CHLOROTETRAFLUORO-ETHANE MIXTURE with not more than 8.8% ethylene oxide	2	2A		2.2		LQ1	E1	P200		MP9	(M) T50	
3298	ETHYLENE OXIDE AND PENTAFLUOROETHANE MIXTURE with not more than 7.9% ethylene oxide	2	2A		2.2		LQ1	E1	P200		MP9	(M) T50	
3299	ETHYLENE OXIDE AND TETRAFLUOROETHANE MIXTURE with not more than 5.6% ethylene oxide	2	2A		2.2		LQ1	E1	P200		MP9	(M) T50	
3300	ETHYLENE OXIDE AND CARBON DIOXIDE MIXTURE with more than 87% ethylene oxide	2	2TF		2.3 +2.1		LQ0	E0	P200		MP9	(M)	
3301	CORROSIVE LIQUID, SELF-HEATING, N.O.S.	8	CS1	I	8 +4.2	274	LQ0	E0	P001		MP8 MP17		
3301	CORROSIVE LIQUID, SELF-HEATING, N.O.S.	8	CS1	II	8 +4.2	274	LQ22	E2	P001		MP15		
3302	2-DIMETHYLAMINOETHYL ACRYLATE	6.1	T1	II	6.1		LQ17	E4	P001 IBC02		MP15	T7	TP2
3303	COMPRESSED GAS, TOXIC, OXIDIZING, N.O.S.	2	1TO		2.3 +5.1	274	LQ0	E0	P200		MP9	(M)	
3304	COMPRESSED GAS, TOXIC, CORROSIVE, N.O.S.	2	1TC		2.3 +8	274	LQ0	E0	P200		MP9	(M)	
3305	COMPRESSED GAS, TOXIC, FLAMMABLE, CORROSIVE, N.O.S.	2	1TFC		2.3 +2.1 +8	274	LQ0	E0	P200		MP9	(M)	
3306	COMPRESSED GAS, TOXIC, OXIDIZING, CORROSIVE, N.O.S.	2	1TOC		2.3 +5.1 +8	274	LQ0	E0	P200		MP9	(M)	
3307	LIQUEFIED GAS, TOXIC, OXIDIZING, N.O.S.	2	2TO		2.3 +5.1	274	LQ0	E0	P200		MP9	(M)	
3308	LIQUEFIED GAS, TOXIC, CORROSIVE, N.O.S.	2	2TC		2.3 +8	274	LQ0	E0	P200		MP9	(M)	
3309	LIQUEFIED GAS, TOXIC, FLAMMABLE, CORROSIVE, N.O.S.	2	2TFC		2.3 +2.1 +8	274	LQ0	E0	P200		MP9	(M)	
3310	LIQUEFIED GAS, TOXIC, OXIDIZING, CORROSIVE, N.O.S.	2	2TOC		2.3 +5.1 +8	274	LQ0	E0	P200		MP9	(M)	

ADR tank		Vehicle for tank carriage	Transport category (Tunnel restriction code)	Special provisions for carriage				Hazard identifi-cation No.	UN No.	Name and description
Tank code	Special provisions			Packages	Bulk	Loading, unloading and handling	Operation			
4.3	4.3.5, 6.8.4	9.1.1.2	1.1.3.6 (8.6)	7.2.4	7.3.3	7.5.11	8.5	5.3.2.3		3.1.2
(12)	(13)	(14)	(15)	(16)	(17)	(18)	(19)	(20)	(1)	(2)
L4BH	TU15 TE19	AT	2 (E)			CV13 CV28	S9	60	3293	HYDRAZINE, AQUEOUS SOLUTION with not more than 37% hydrazine, by mass
L15DH(+)	TU14 TU15 TE19 TE21	FL	0 (C/D)			CV1 CV13 CV28	S2 S9 S14	663	3294	HYDROGEN CYANIDE, SOLUTION IN ALCOHOL with not more than 45% hydrogen cyanide
L4BN		FL	1 (D/E)				S2 S20	33	3295	HYDROCARBONS, LIQUID, N.O.S.
L1.5BN		FL	2 (D/E)				S2 S20	33	3295	HYDROCARBONS, LIQUID, N.O.S. (vapour pressure at 50 °C more than 110 kPa)
LGBF		FL	2 (D/E)				S2 S20	33	3295	HYDROCARBONS, LIQUID, N.O.S. (vapour pressure at 50 °C not more than 110 kPa)
LGBF		FL	3 (D/E)				S2	30	3295	HYDROCARBONS, LIQUID, N.O.S.
PxBN(M)	TA4 TT9	AT	3 (C/E)			CV9 CV10 CV36		20	3296	HEPTAFLUOROPROPANE (REFRIGERANT GAS R 227)
PxBN(M)	TA4 TT9	AT	3 (C/E)			CV9 CV10 CV36		20	3297	ETHYLENE OXIDE AND CHLOROTETRAFLUORO-ETHANE MIXTURE with not more than 8.8% ethylene oxide
PxBN(M)	TA4 TT9	AT	3 (C/E)			CV9 CV10 CV36		20	3298	ETHYLENE OXIDE AND PENTAFLUOROETHANE MIXTURE with not more than 7.9% ethylene oxide
PxBN(M)	TA4 TT9	AT	3 (C/E)			CV9 CV10 CV36		20	3299	ETHYLENE OXIDE AND TETRAFLUOROETHANE MIXTURE with not more than 5.6% ethylene oxide
PxBH(M)	TA4 TT9	FL	1 (B/D)			CV9 CV10 CV36	S2 S14	263	3300	ETHYLENE OXIDE AND CARBON DIOXIDE MIXTURE with more than 87% ethylene oxide
L10BH		AT	1 (E)				S14	884	3301	CORROSIVE LIQUID, SELF-HEATING, N.O.S.
L4BN		AT	2 (E)					84	3301	CORROSIVE LIQUID, SELF-HEATING, N.O.S.
L4BH	TU15 TE19	AT	2 (D/E)			CV13 CV28	S9 S19	60	3302	2-DIMETHYLAMINOETHYL ACRYLATE
CxBH(M)	TU6 TA4 TT9	AT	1 (C/D)			CV9 CV10 CV36	S14	265	3303	COMPRESSED GAS, TOXIC, OXIDIZING, N.O.S.
CxBH(M)	TU6 TA4 TT9	AT	1 (C/D)			CV9 CV10 CV36	S14	268	3304	COMPRESSED GAS, TOXIC, CORROSIVE, N.O.S.
CxBH(M)	TU6 TA4 TT9	FL	1 (B/D)			CV9 CV10 CV36	S2 S14	263	3305	COMPRESSED GAS, TOXIC, FLAMMABLE, CORROSIVE, N.O.S.
CxBH(M)	TU6 TA4 TT9	AT	1 (C/D)			CV9 CV10 CV36	S14	265	3306	COMPRESSED GAS, TOXIC, OXIDIZING, CORROSIVE, N.O.S.
PxBH(M)	TU6 TA4 TT9	AT	1 (C/D)			CV9 CV10 CV36	S14	265	3307	LIQUEFIED GAS, TOXIC, OXIDIZING, N.O.S.
PxBH(M)	TU6 TA4 TT9	AT	1 (C/D)			CV9 CV10 CV36	S14	268	3308	LIQUEFIED GAS, TOXIC, CORROSIVE, N.O.S.
PxBH(M)	TU6 TA4 TT9	FL	1 (B/D)			CV9 CV10 CV36	S2 S14	263	3309	LIQUEFIED GAS, TOXIC, FLAMMABLE, CORROSIVE, N.O.S.
PxBH(M)	TU6 TA4 TT9	AT	1 (C/D)			CV9 CV10 CV36	S14	265	3310	LIQUEFIED GAS, TOXIC, OXIDIZING, CORROSIVE, N.O.S.

UN No.	Name and description	Class	Classifi-cation code	Packing group	Labels	Special provi-sions	Limited and excepted quantities		Packaging			Portable tanks and bulk containers	
									Packing instruc-tions	Special packing provisions	Mixed packing provisions	Instruc-tions	Special provisions
	3.1.2	2.2	2.2	2.1.1.3	5.2.2	3.3	3.4.6	3.5.1.2	4.1.4	4.1.4	4.1.10	4.2.5.2 7.3.2	4.2.5.3
(1)	(2)	(3a)	(3b)	(4)	(5)	(6)	(7a)	(7b)	(8)	(9a)	(9b)	(10)	(11)
3311	GAS, REFRIGERATED LIQUID, OXIDIZING, N.O.S.	2	3O		2.2 +5.1	274	LQ0	E0	P203		MP9	T75	TP5 TP22
3312	GAS, REFRIGERATED LIQUID, FLAMMABLE, N.O.S.	2	3F		2.1	274	LQ0	E0	P203		MP9	T75	TP5
3313	ORGANIC PIGMENTS, SELF-HEATING	4.2	S2	II	4.2		LQ0	E2	P002 IBC08	B4	MP14	T3	TP33
3313	ORGANIC PIGMENTS, SELF-HEATING	4.2	S2	III	4.2		LQ0	E1	P002 IBC08 LP02 R001	B3	MP14	T1	TP33
3314	PLASTICS MOULDING COMPOUND in dough, sheet or extruded rope form evolving flammable vapour	9	M3	III	None	207 633	LQ27	E1	P002 IBC08 R001	PP14 B3 B6	MP10		
3315	CHEMICAL SAMPLE, TOXIC	6.1	T8	I	6.1	250	LQ0	E5	P099		MP8 MP17		
3316	CHEMICAL KIT or FIRST AID KIT	9	M11	II	9	251 340	LQ0	E0	P901				
3316	CHEMICAL KIT or FIRST AID KIT	9	M11	III	9	251 340	LQ0	E0	P901				
3317	2-AMINO-4,6-DINITROPHENOL, WETTED with not less than 20% water, by mass	4.1	D	I	4.1		LQ0	E0	P406	PP26	MP2		
3318	AMMONIA SOLUTION, relative density less than 0.880 at 15 °C in water, with more than 50% ammonia	2	4TC		2.3 +8	23	LQ0	E0	P200		MP9	(M) T50	
3319	NITROGLYCERIN MIXTURE, DESENSITIZED, SOLID, N.O.S. with more than 2% but not more than 10% nitroglycerin, by mass	4.1	D	II	4.1	272 274	LQ0	E0	P099 IBC99		MP2		
3320	SODIUM BOROHYDRIDE AND SODIUM HYDROXIDE SOLUTION, with not more than 12% sodium borohydride and not more than 40% sodium hydroxide by mass	8	C5	II	8		LQ22	E2	P001 IBC02		MP15	T7	TP2
3320	SODIUM BOROHYDRIDE AND SODIUM HYDROXIDE SOLUTION, with not more than 12% sodium borohydride and not more than 40% sodium hydroxide by mass	8	C5	III	8		LQ7	E1	P001 IBC03 LP01 R001		MP19	T4	TP2
3321	RADIOACTIVE MATERIAL, LOW SPECIFIC ACTIVITY (LSA-II), non fissile or fissile-excepted	7			7X	172 317 325 336	LQ0	E0	See 2.2.7 and 4.1.9	See 4.1.9.1.3		T5	TP4
3322	RADIOACTIVE MATERIAL, LOW SPECIFIC ACTIVITY (LSA-III), non fissile or fissile-excepted	7			7X	172 317 325 336	LQ0	E0	See 2.2.7 and 4.1.9	See 4.1.9.1.3		T5	TP4
3323	RADIOACTIVE MATERIAL, TYPE C PACKAGE, non fissile or fissile-excepted	7			7X	172 317	LQ0	E0	See 2.2.7 and 4.1.9	See 4.1.9.1.3			
3324	RADIOACTIVE MATERIAL, LOW SPECIFIC ACTIVITY (LSA-II), FISSILE	7			7X +7E	172 326 336	LQ0	E0	See 2.2.7 and 4.1.9	See 4.1.9.1.3			
3325	RADIOACTIVE MATERIAL, LOW SPECIFIC ACTIVITY, (LSA-III), FISSILE	7			7X +7E	172 326 336	LQ0	E0	See 2.2.7 and 4.1.9	See 4.1.9.1.3			
3326	RADIOACTIVE MATERIAL, SURFACE CONTAMINATED OBJECTS (SCO-I or SCO-II), FISSILE	7			7X +7E	172 336	LQ0	E0	See 2.2.7 and 4.1.9	See 4.1.9.1.3			
3327	RADIOACTIVE MATERIAL, TYPE A PACKAGE, FISSILE, non-special form	7			7X +7E	172 326	LQ0	E0	See 2.2.7 and 4.1.9	See 4.1.9.1.3			

ADR tank		Vehicle for tank carriage	Transport category (Tunnel restriction code)	Special provisions for carriage				Hazard identifi-cation No.	UN No.	Name and description
Tank code	Special provisions			Packages	Bulk	Loading, unloading and handling	Operation			
4.3	4.3.5, 6.8.4	9.1.1.2	1.1.3.6 (8.6)	7.2.4	7.3.3	7.5.11	8.5	5.3.2.3		3.1.2
(12)	(13)	(14)	(15)	(16)	(17)	(18)	(19)	(20)	(1)	(2)
RxBN	TU7 TU19 TA4 TT9	AT	3 (C/E)	V5		CV9 CV11 CV36	S20	225	3311	GAS, REFRIGERATED LIQUID, OXIDIZING, N.O.S.
RxBN	TU18 TA4 TT9	FL	2 (B/D)	V5		CV9 CV11 CV36	S2 S17	223	3312	GAS, REFRIGERATED LIQUID, FLAMMABLE, N.O.S.
SGAV		AT	2 (D/E)	V1				40	3313	ORGANIC PIGMENTS, SELF-HEATING
SGAV		AT	3 (E)	V1				40	3313	ORGANIC PIGMENTS, SELF-HEATING
			3 (D/E)		VV3			90	3314	PLASTICS MOULDING COMPOUND in dough, sheet or extruded rope form evolving flammable vapour
			1 (C/E)			CV1 CV13 CV28	S9 S14		3315	CHEMICAL SAMPLE, TOXIC
			2 (E)						3316	CHEMICAL KIT or FIRST AID KIT
			3 (E)						3316	CHEMICAL KIT or FIRST AID KIT
			1 (B)				S14		3317	2-AMINO-4,6-DINITROPHENOL, WETTED with not less than 20% water, by mass
PxBH(M)	TA4 TT9	AT	1 (C/D)			CV9 CV10	S14	268	3318	AMMONIA SOLUTION, relative density less than 0.880 at 15 °C in water, with more than 50% ammonia
			2 (B)				S14		3319	NITROGLYCERIN MIXTURE, DESENSITIZED, SOLID, N.O.S. with more than 2% but not more than 10% nitroglycerin, by mass
L4BN		AT	2 (E)					80	3320	SODIUM BOROHYDRIDE AND SODIUM HYDROXIDE SOLUTION, with not more than 12% sodium borohydride and not more than 40% sodium hydroxide by mass
L4BN		AT	3 (E)					80	3320	SODIUM BOROHYDRIDE AND SODIUM HYDROXIDE SOLUTION, with not more than 12% sodium borohydride and not more than 40% sodium hydroxide by mass
S2.65AN(+) L2.65CN(+)	TU36 TT7 TM7	AT	0 (E)			CV33	S6 S11 S13 S21	70	3321	RADIOACTIVE MATERIAL, LOW SPECIFIC ACTIVITY (LSA-II), non fissile or fissile-excepted
S2.65AN(+) L2.65CN(+)	TU36 TT7 TM7	AT	0 (E)			CV33	S6 S11 S13 S21	70	3322	RADIOACTIVE MATERIAL, LOW SPECIFIC ACTIVITY (LSA-III), non fissile or fissile-excepted
			0 (E)			CV33	S6 S11 S13 S21	70	3323	RADIOACTIVE MATERIAL, TYPE C PACKAGE, non fissile or fissile-excepted
			0 (E)			CV33	S6 S11 S13 S21	70	3324	RADIOACTIVE MATERIAL, LOW SPECIFIC ACTIVITY (LSA-II), FISSILE
			0 (E)			CV33	S6 S11 S13 S21	70	3325	RADIOACTIVE MATERIAL, LOW SPECIFIC ACTIVITY, (LSA-III), FISSILE
			0 (E)			CV33	S6 S11 S13 S21	70	3326	RADIOACTIVE MATERIAL, SURFACE CONTAMINATED OBJECTS (SCO-I or SCO-II), FISSILE
			0 (E)			CV33	S6 S11 S13 S21	70	3327	RADIOACTIVE MATERIAL, TYPE A PACKAGE, FISSILE, non-special form

UN No.	Name and description	Class	Classification code	Packing group	Labels	Special provisions	Limited and excepted quantities		Packaging			Portable tanks and bulk containers	
									Packing instructions	Special packing provisions	Mixed packing provisions	Instructions	Special provisions
3.1.2	3.1.2	2.2	2.2	2.1.1.3	5.2.2	3.3	3.4.6	3.5.1.2	4.1.4	4.1.4	4.1.10	4.2.5.2 7.3.2	4.2.5.3
(1)	(2)	(3a)	(3b)	(4)	(5)	(6)	(7a)	(7b)	(8)	(9a)	(9b)	(10)	(11)
3328	RADIOACTIVE MATERIAL, TYPE B(U) PACKAGE, FISSILE	7			7X +7E	172 337	LQ0	E0	See 2.2.7 and 4.1.9	See 4.1.9.1.3			
3329	RADIOACTIVE MATERIAL, TYPE B(M) PACKAGE, FISSILE	7			7X +7E	172 337	LQ0	E0	See 2.2.7 and 4.1.9	See 4.1.9.1.3			
3330	RADIOACTIVE MATERIAL, TYPE C PACKAGE, FISSILE	7			7X +7E	172	LQ0	E0	See 2.2.7 and 4.1.9	See 4.1.9.1.3			
3331	RADIOACTIVE MATERIAL, TRANSPORTED UNDER SPECIAL ARRANGEMENT, FISSILE	7			7X +7E	172	LQ0	E0	See 2.2.7 and 4.1.9	See 4.1.9.1.3			
3332	RADIOACTIVE MATERIAL, TYPE A PACKAGE, SPECIAL FORM, non fissile or fissile-excepted	7			7X	172 317	LQ0	E0	See 2.2.7 and 4.1.9	See 4.1.9.1.3			
3333	RADIOACTIVE MATERIAL, TYPE A PACKAGE, SPECIAL FORM, FISSILE	7			7X +7E	172	LQ0	E0	See 2.2.7 and 4.1.9	See 4.1.9.1.3			
3334	Aviation regulated liquid, n.o.s.	9	M11		NOT SUBJECT TO ADR								
3335	Aviation regulated solid, n.o.s.	9	M11		NOT SUBJECT TO ADR								
3336	MERCAPTANS, LIQUID, FLAMMABLE, N.O.S. or MERCAPTAN MIXTURE, LIQUID, FLAMMABLE, N.O.S.	3	F1	I	3	274	LQ3	E3	P001		MP7 MP17	T11	TP2
3336	MERCAPTANS, LIQUID, FLAMMABLE, N.O.S. or MERCAPTAN MIXTURE, LIQUID, FLAMMABLE, N.O.S. (vapour pressure at 50 °C more than 110 kPa)	3	F1	II	3	274 640C	LQ4	E2	P001		MP19	T7	TP1 TP8 TP28
3336	MERCAPTANS, LIQUID, FLAMMABLE, N.O.S. or MERCAPTAN MIXTURE, LIQUID, FLAMMABLE, N.O.S. (vapour pressure at 50 °C not more than 110 kPa)	3	F1	II	3	274 640D	LQ4	E2	P001 IBC02 R001		MP19	T7	TP1 TP8 TP28
3336	MERCAPTANS, LIQUID, FLAMMABLE, N.O.S. or MERCAPTAN MIXTURE, LIQUID, FLAMMABLE, N.O.S.	3	F1	III	3	274	LQ7	E1	P001 IBC03 LP01 R001		MP19	T4	TP1 TP29
3337	REFRIGERANT GAS R 404A (Pentafluoroethane, 1,1,1-trifluoroethane, and 1,1,1,2-tetrafluoroethane zeotropic mixture with approximately 44% pentafluoroethane and 52% 1,1,1-trifluoroethane)	2	2A		2.2		LQ1	E1	P200		MP9	(M) T50	
3338	REFRIGERANT GAS R 407A (Difluoromethane, pentafluoroethane, and 1,1,1,2-tetrafluoroethane zeotropic mixture with approximately 20% difluoromethane and 40% pentafluoroethane)	2	2A		2.2		LQ1	E1	P200		MP9	(M) T50	
3339	REFRIGERANT GAS R 407B (Difluoromethane, pentafluoroethane, and 1,1,1,2-tetrafluoroethane zeotropic mixture with approximately 10% difluoromethane and 70% pentafluoroethane)	2	2A		2.2		LQ1	E1	P200		MP9	(M) T50	

ADR tank		Vehicle for tank carriage	Transport category (Tunnel restriction code)	Special provisions for carriage				Hazard identifi- cation No.	UN No.	Name and description
Tank code	Special provisions			Packages	Bulk	Loading, unloading and handling	Operation			
4.3	4.3.5, 6.8.4	9.1.1.2	1.1.3.6 (8.6)	7.2.4	7.3.3	7.5.11	8.5	5.3.2.3		3.1.2
(12)	(13)	(14)	(15)	(16)	(17)	(18)	(19)	(20)	(1)	(2)
			0 (E)			CV33	S6 S11 S13 S21	70	3328	RADIOACTIVE MATERIAL, TYPE B(U) PACKAGE, FISSILE
			0 (E)			CV33	S6 S11 S13 S21	70	3329	RADIOACTIVE MATERIAL, TYPE B(M) PACKAGE, FISSILE
			0 (E)			CV33	S6 S11 S13 S21	70	3330	RADIOACTIVE MATERIAL, TYPE C PACKAGE, FISSILE
			0 (-)			CV33	S6 S11 S13 S21	70	3331	RADIOACTIVE MATERIAL, TRANSPORTED UNDER SPECIAL ARRANGEMENT, FISSILE
			0 (E)			CV33	S6 S11 S12 S13 S21	70	3332	RADIOACTIVE MATERIAL, TYPE A PACKAGE, SPECIAL FORM, non fissile or fissile-excepted
			0 (E)			CV33	S6 S11 S13 S21	70	3333	RADIOACTIVE MATERIAL, TYPE A PACKAGE, SPECIAL FORM, FISSILE
NOT SUBJECT TO ADR									3334	Aviation regulated liquid, n.o.s.
NOT SUBJECT TO ADR									3335	Aviation regulated solid, n.o.s.
L4BN		FL	1 (D/E)				S2 S20	33	3336	MERCAPTANS, LIQUID, FLAMMABLE, N.O.S. or MERCAPTAN MIXTURE, LIQUID, FLAMMABLE, N.O.S.
L1.5BN		FL	2 (D/E)				S2 S20	33	3336	MERCAPTANS, LIQUID, FLAMMABLE, N.O.S. or MERCAPTAN MIXTURE, LIQUID, FLAMMABLE, N.O.S. (vapour pressure at 50 °C more than 110 kPa)
LGBF		FL	2 (D/E)				S2 S20	33	3336	MERCAPTANS, LIQUID, FLAMMABLE, N.O.S. or MERCAPTAN MIXTURE, LIQUID, FLAMMABLE, N.O.S. (vapour pressure at 50 °C not more than 110 kPa)
LGBF		FL	3 (D/E)				S2	30	3336	MERCAPTANS, LIQUID, FLAMMABLE, N.O.S. or MERCAPTAN MIXTURE, LIQUID, FLAMMABLE, N.O.S.
PxBN(M)	TA4 TT9	AT	3 (C/E)			CV9 CV10 CV36		20	3337	REFRIGERANT GAS R 404A (Pentafluoroethane, 1,1,1-trifluoroethane, and 1,1,1,2-tetrafluoroethane zeotropic mixture with approximately 44% pentafluoroethane and 52% 1,1,1-trifluoroethane)
PxBN(M)	TA4 TT9	AT	3 (C/E)			CV9 CV10 CV36		20	3338	REFRIGERANT GAS R 407A (Difluoromethane, pentafluoroethane, and 1,1,1,2-tetrafluoroethane zeotropic mixture with approximately 20% difluoromethane and 40% pentafluoroethane)
PxBN(M)	TA4 TT9	AT	3 (C/E)			CV9 CV10 CV36		20	3339	REFRIGERANT GAS R 407B (Difluoromethane, pentafluoroethane, and 1,1,1,2-tetrafluoroethane zeotropic mixture with approximately 10% difluoromethane and 70% pentafluoroethane)

UN No.	Name and description	Class	Classifi-cation code	Packing group	Labels	Special provi-sions	Limited and excepted quantities		Packaging			Portable tanks and bulk containers	
									Packing instruc-tions	Special packing provisions	Mixed packing provisions	Instruc-tions	Special provisions
	3.1.2	2.2	2.2	2.1.1.3	5.2.2	3.3	3.4.6	3.5.1.2	4.1.4	4.1.4	4.1.10	4.2.5.2 7.3.2	4.2.5.3
(1)	(2)	(3a)	(3b)	(4)	(5)	(6)	(7a)	(7b)	(8)	(9a)	(9b)	(10)	(11)
3340	REFRIGERANT GAS R 407C (Difluoromethane, pentafluoroethane, and 1,1,1,2-tetrafluoroethane zeotropic mixture with approximately 23%difluoromethane and 25% pentafluoroethane)	2	2A		2.2		LQ1	E1	P200		MP9	(M) T50	
3341	THIOUREA DIOXIDE	4.2	S2	II	4.2		LQ0	E2	P002 IBC06		MP14	T3	TP33
3341	THIOUREA DIOXIDE	4.2	S2	III	4.2		LQ0	E1	P002 IBC08 LP02 R001	B3	MP14	T1	TP33
3342	XANTHATES	4.2	S2	II	4.2		LQ0	E2	P002 IBC06		MP14	T3	TP33
3342	XANTHATES	4.2	S2	III	4.2		LQ0	E1	P002 IBC08 LP02 R001	B3	MP14	T1	TP33
3343	NITROGLYCERIN MIXTURE, DESENSITIZED, LIQUID, FLAMMABLE, N.O.S. with not more than 30% nitroglycerin, by mass	3	D		3	274 278	LQ0	E0	P099		MP2		
3344	PENTAERYTHRITE TETRANITRATE (PENTAERYTHRITOL TETRANITRATE; PETN) MIXTURE, DESENSITIZED, SOLID, N.O.S. with more than 10% but not more than 20% PETN, by mass	4.1	D	II	4.1	272 274	LQ0	E0	P099		MP2		
3345	PHENOXYACETIC ACID DERIVATIVE PESTICIDE, SOLID, TOXIC	6.1	T7	I	6.1	61 274 648	LQ0	E5	P002 IBC07		MP18	T6	TP33
3345	PHENOXYACETIC ACID DERIVATIVE PESTICIDE, SOLID, TOXIC	6.1	T7	II	6.1	61 274 648	LQ18	E4	P002 IBC08	B4	MP10	T3	TP33
3345	PHENOXYACETIC ACID DERIVATIVE PESTICIDE, SOLID, TOXIC	6.1	T7	III	6.1	61 274 648	LQ9	E1	P002 IBC08 LP02 R001	B3	MP10	T1	TP33
3346	PHENOXYACETIC ACID DERIVATIVE PESTICIDE, LIQUID, FLAMMABLE, TOXIC, flash-point less than 23 °C	3	FT2	I	3 +6.1	61 274	LQ3	E0	P001		MP7 MP17	T14	TP2 TP27
3346	PHENOXYACETIC ACID DERIVATIVE PESTICIDE, LIQUID, FLAMMABLE, TOXIC, flash-point less than 23 °C	3	FT2	II	3 +6.1	61 274	LQ4	E2	P001 IBC02 R001		MP19	T11	TP2 TP27
3347	PHENOXYACETIC ACID DERIVATIVE PESTICIDE, LIQUID, TOXIC, FLAMMABLE, flash-point not less than 23 °C	6.1	TF2	I	6.1 +3	61 274	LQ0	E5	P001		MP8 MP17	T14	TP2 TP27
3347	PHENOXYACETIC ACID DERIVATIVE PESTICIDE, LIQUID, TOXIC, FLAMMABLE, flash-point not less than 23 °C	6.1	TF2	II	6.1 +3	61 274	LQ17	E4	P001 IBC02		MP15	T11	TP2 TP27
3347	PHENOXYACETIC ACID DERIVATIVE PESTICIDE, LIQUID, TOXIC, FLAMMABLE, flash-point not less than 23 °C	6.1	TF2	III	6.1 +3	61 274	LQ7	E1	P001 IBC03 R001		MP19	T7	TP2 TP28
3348	PHENOXYACETIC ACID DERIVATIVE PESTICIDE, LIQUID, TOXIC	6.1	T6	I	6.1	61 274 648	LQ0	E5	P001		MP8 MP17	T14	TP2 TP27

ADR tank		Vehicle for tank carriage	Transport category	Special provisions for carriage				Hazard identification No.	UN No.	Name and description
Tank code	Special provisions		(Tunnel restriction code)	Packages	Bulk	Loading, unloading and handling	Operation			
4.3	4.3.5, 6.8.4	9.1.1.2	1.1.3.6 (8.6)	7.2.4	7.3.3	7.5.11	8.5	5.3.2.3		3.1.2
(12)	(13)	(14)	(15)	(16)	(17)	(18)	(19)	(20)	(1)	(2)
PxBN(M)	TA4 TT9	AT	3 (C/E)			CV9 CV10 CV36		20	3340	REFRIGERANT GAS R 407C (Difluoromethane, pentafluoroethane, and 1,1,1,2-tetrafluoroethane zeotropic mixture with approximately 23%difluoromethane and 25% pentafluoroethane)
SGAV		AT	2 (D/E)	V1 V12				40	3341	THIOUREA DIOXIDE
SGAV		AT	3 (E)	V1				40	3341	THIOUREA DIOXIDE
SGAV		AT	2 (D/E)	V1 V12				40	3342	XANTHATES
SGAV		AT	3 (E)	V1				40	3342	XANTHATES
			0 (B)				S2 S14		3343	NITROGLYCERIN MIXTURE, DESENSITIZED, LIQUID, FLAMMABLE, N.O.S. with not more than 30% nitroglycerin, by mass
			2 (B)				S14		3344	PENTAERYTHRITE TETRANITRATE (PENTAERYTHRITOL TETRANITRATE; PETN) MIXTURE, DESENSITIZED, SOLID, N.O.S. with more than 10% but not more than 20% PETN, by mass
S10AH L10CH	TU14 TU15 TE19 TE21	AT	1 (C/E)	V10 V12		CV1 CV13 CV28	S9 S14	66	3345	PHENOXYACETIC ACID DERIVATIVE PESTICIDE, SOLID, TOXIC
SGAH L4BH	TU15 TE19	AT	2 (D/E)	V11		CV13 CV28	S9 S19	60	3345	PHENOXYACETIC ACID DERIVATIVE PESTICIDE, SOLID, TOXIC
SGAH L4BH	TU15 TE19	AT	2 (E)		VV9	CV13 CV28	S9	60	3345	PHENOXYACETIC ACID DERIVATIVE PESTICIDE, SOLID, TOXIC
L10CH	TU14 TU15 TE21	FL	1 (C/E)			CV13 CV28	S2 S22	336	3346	PHENOXYACETIC ACID DERIVATIVE PESTICIDE, LIQUID, FLAMMABLE, TOXIC, flash-point less than 23 °C
L4BH	TU15	FL	2 (D/E)			CV13 CV28	S2 S22	336	3346	PHENOXYACETIC ACID DERIVATIVE PESTICIDE, LIQUID, FLAMMABLE, TOXIC, flash-point less than 23 °C
L10CH	TU14 TU15 TE19 TE21	FL	1 (C/E)			CV1 CV13 CV28	S2 S9 S14	663	3347	PHENOXYACETIC ACID DERIVATIVE PESTICIDE, LIQUID, TOXIC, FLAMMABLE, flash-point not less than 23 °C
L4BH	TU15 TE19	FL	2 (D/E)			CV13 CV28	S2 S9 S19	63	3347	PHENOXYACETIC ACID DERIVATIVE PESTICIDE, LIQUID, TOXIC, FLAMMABLE, flash-point not less than 23 °C
L4BH	TU15 TE19	FL	2 (D/E)			CV13 CV28	S2 S9	63	3347	PHENOXYACETIC ACID DERIVATIVE PESTICIDE, LIQUID, TOXIC, FLAMMABLE, flash-point not less than 23 °C
L10CH	TU14 TU15 TE19 TE21	AT	1 (C/E)			CV1 CV13 CV28	S9 S14	66	3348	PHENOXYACETIC ACID DERIVATIVE PESTICIDE, LIQUID, TOXIC

UN No.	Name and description	Class	Classification code	Packing group	Labels	Special provisions	Limited and excepted quantities		Packaging			Portable tanks and bulk containers	
							quantities		Packing instructions	Special packing provisions	Mixed packing provisions	Instructions	Special provisions
	3.1.2	2.2	2.2	2.1.1.3	5.2.2	3.3	3.4.6	3.5.1.2	4.1.4	4.1.4	4.1.10	4.2.5.2 7.3.2	4.2.5.3
(1)	(2)	(3a)	(3b)	(4)	(5)	(6)	(7a)	(7b)	(8)	(9a)	(9b)	(10)	(11)
3348	PHENOXYACETIC ACID DERIVATIVE PESTICIDE, LIQUID, TOXIC	6.1	T6	II	6.1	61 274 648	LQ17	E4	P001 IBC02		MP15	T11	TP2 TP27
3348	PHENOXYACETIC ACID DERIVATIVE PESTICIDE, LIQUID, TOXIC	6.1	T6	III	6.1	61 274 648	LQ7	E1	P001 IBC03 LP01 R001		MP19	T7	TP2 TP28
3349	PYRETHROID PESTICIDE, SOLID, TOXIC	6.1	T7	I	6.1	61 274 648	LQ0	E5	P002 IBC07		MP18	T6	TP33
3349	PYRETHROID PESTICIDE, SOLID, TOXIC	6.1	T7	II	6.1	61 274 648	LQ18	E4	P002 IBC08	B4	MP10	T3	TP33
3349	PYRETHROID PESTICIDE, SOLID, TOXIC	6.1	T7	III	6.1	61 274 648	LQ9	E1	P002 IBC08 LP02 R001	B3	MP10	T1	TP33
3350	PYRETHROID PESTICIDE, LIQUID, FLAMMABLE, TOXIC, flash-point less than 23 °C	3	FT2	I	3 +6.1	61 274	LQ3	E0	P001		MP7 MP17	T14	TP2 TP27
3350	PYRETHROID PESTICIDE, LIQUID, FLAMMABLE, TOXIC, flash-point less than 23 °C	3	FT2	II	3 +6.1	61 274	LQ4	E2	P001 IBC02 R001		MP19	T11	TP2 TP27
3351	PYRETHROID PESTICIDE, LIQUID, TOXIC, FLAMMABLE, flash-point not less than 23 °C	6.1	TF2	I	6.1 +3	61 274	LQ0	E5	P001		MP8 MP17	T14	TP2 TP27
3351	PYRETHROID PESTICIDE, LIQUID, TOXIC, FLAMMABLE, flash-point not less than 23 °C	6.1	TF2	II	6.1 +3	61 274	LQ17	E4	P001 IBC02		MP15	T11	TP2 TP27
3351	PYRETHROID PESTICIDE, LIQUID, TOXIC, FLAMMABLE, flash-point not less than 23 °C	6.1	TF2	III	6.1 +3	61 274	LQ7	E1	P001 IBC03 R001		MP19	T7	TP2 TP28
3352	PYRETHROID PESTICIDE, LIQUID, TOXIC	6.1	T6	I	6.1	61 274 648	LQ0	E5	P001		MP8 MP17	T14	TP2 TP27
3352	PYRETHROID PESTICIDE, LIQUID, TOXIC	6.1	T6	II	6.1	61 274 648	LQ17	E4	P001 IBC02		MP15	T11	TP2 TP27
3352	PYRETHROID PESTICIDE, LIQUID, TOXIC	6.1	T6	III	6.1	61 274 648	LQ7	E1	P001 IBC03 LP01 R001		MP19	T7	TP2 TP28
3354	INSECTICIDE GAS, FLAMMABLE, N.O.S.	2	2F		2.1	274	LQ0	E0	P200		MP9	(M)	
3355	INSECTICIDE GAS, TOXIC, FLAMMABLE, N.O.S.	2	2TF		2.3 +2.1	274	LQ0	E0	P200		MP9	(M)	
3356	OXYGEN GENERATOR, CHEMICAL	5.1	O3	II	5.1	284	LQ0	E0	P500		MP2		
3357	NITROGLYCERIN MIXTURE, DESENSITIZED, LIQUID, N.O.S. with not more than 30% nitroglycerin, by mass	3	D	II	3	274 288	LQ0	E0	P099		MP2		
3358	REFRIGERATING MACHINES containing flammable, non-toxic, liquefied gas	2	6F		2.1	291	LQ0	E0	P003	PP32	MP9		
3359	FUMIGATED UNIT	9	M11			302							
3360	Fibres, vegetable, dry	4.1	F1				NOT SUBJECT TO ADR						
3361	CHLOROSILANES, TOXIC, CORROSIVE, N.O.S.	6.1	TC1	II	6.1 +8	274	LQ0	E4	P010		MP15	T14	TP2 TP7 TP27

ADR tank		Vehicle for tank carriage	Transport category (Tunnel restriction code)	Special provisions for carriage				Hazard identifi-cation No.	UN No.	Name and description
Tank code	Special provisions			Packages	Bulk	Loading, unloading and handling	Operation			
4.3	4.3.5, 6.8.4	9.1.1.2	1.1.3.6 (8.6)	7.2.4	7.3.3	7.5.11	8.5	5.3.2.3		3.1.2
(12)	(13)	(14)	(15)	(16)	(17)	(18)	(19)	(20)	(1)	(2)
L4BH	TU15 TE19	AT	2 (D/E)			CV13 CV28	S9 S19	60	3348	PHENOXYACETIC ACID DERIVATIVE PESTICIDE, LIQUID, TOXIC
L4BH	TU15 TE19	AT	2 (E)			CV13 CV28	S9	60	3348	PHENOXYACETIC ACID DERIVATIVE PESTICIDE, LIQUID, TOXIC
S10AH L10CH	TU14 TU15 TE19 TE21	AT	1 (C/E)	V10 V12		CV1 CV13 CV28	S9 S14	66	3349	PYRETHROID PESTICIDE, SOLID, TOXIC
SGAH L4BH	TU15 TE19	AT	2 (D/E)	V11		CV13 CV28	S9 S19	60	3349	PYRETHROID PESTICIDE, SOLID, TOXIC
SGAH L4BH	TU15 TE19	AT	2 (E)		VV9	CV13 CV28	S9	60	3349	PYRETHROID PESTICIDE, SOLID, TOXIC
L10CH	TU14 TU15 TE21	FL	1 (C/E)			CV13 CV28	S2 S22	336	3350	PYRETHROID PESTICIDE, LIQUID, FLAMMABLE, TOXIC, flash-point less than 23 °C
L4BH	TU15	FL	2 (D/E)			CV13 CV28	S2 S22	336	3350	PYRETHROID PESTICIDE, LIQUID, FLAMMABLE, TOXIC, flash-point less than 23 °C
L10CH	TU14 TU15 TE19 TE21	FL	1 (C/E)			CV1 CV13 CV28	S2 S9 S14	663	3351	PYRETHROID PESTICIDE, LIQUID, TOXIC, FLAMMABLE, flash-point not less than 23 °C
L4BH	TU15 TE19	FL	2 (D/E)			CV13 CV28	S2 S9 S19	63	3351	PYRETHROID PESTICIDE, LIQUID, TOXIC, FLAMMABLE, flash-point not less than 23 °C
L4BH	TU15 TE19	FL	2 (D/E)			CV13 CV28	S2 S9	63	3351	PYRETHROID PESTICIDE, LIQUID, TOXIC, FLAMMABLE, flash-point not less than 23 °C
L10CH	TU14 TU15 TE19 TE21	AT	1 (C/E)			CV1 CV13 CV28	S9 S14	66	3352	PYRETHROID PESTICIDE, LIQUID, TOXIC
L4BH	TU15 TE19	AT	2 (D/E)			CV13 CV28	S9 S19	60	3352	PYRETHROID PESTICIDE, LIQUID, TOXIC
L4BH	TU15 TE19	AT	2 (E)			CV13 CV28	S9	60	3352	PYRETHROID PESTICIDE, LIQUID, TOXIC
PxBN(M)	TA4 TT9	FL	2 (B/D)			CV9 CV10 CV36	S2 S20	23	3354	INSECTICIDE GAS, FLAMMABLE, N.O.S.
PxBH(M)	TU6 TA4 TT9	FL	1 (B/D)			CV9 CV10 CV36	S2 S14	263	3355	INSECTICIDE GAS, TOXIC, FLAMMABLE, N.O.S.
			2 (E)			CV24			3356	OXYGEN GENERATOR, CHEMICAL
			2 (B)				S2 S14		3357	NITROGLYCERIN MIXTURE, DESENSITIZED, LIQUID, N.O.S. with not more than 30% nitroglycerin, by mass
			2 (D)			CV9	S2		3358	REFRIGERATING MACHINES containing flammable, non-toxic, liquefied gas
			(-)						3359	FUMIGATED UNIT
NOT SUBJECT TO ADR									3360	Fibres, vegetable, dry
L4BH	TU15 TE19	AT	2 (D/E)			CV13 CV28	S9 S19	68	3361	CHLOROSILANES, TOXIC, CORROSIVE, N.O.S.

UN No.	Name and description	Class	Classifi-cation code	Packing group	Labels	Special provi-sions	Limited and excepted quantities		Packaging			Portable tanks and bulk containers	
									Packing instruc-tions	Special packing provisions	Mixed packing provisions	Instruc-tions	Special provisions
	3.1.2	2.2	2.2	2.1.1.3	5.2.2	3.3	3.4.6	3.5.1.2	4.1.4	4.1.4	4.1.10	4.2.5.2 7.3.2	4.2.5.3
(1)	(2)	(3a)	(3b)	(4)	(5)	(6)	(7a)	(7b)	(8)	(9a)	(9b)	(10)	(11)
3362	CHLOROSILANES, TOXIC, CORROSIVE, FLAMMABLE, N.O.S.	6.1	TFC	II	6.1 +3 +8	274	LQ0	E4	P010		MP15	T14	TP2 TP7 TP27
3363	Dangerous goods in machinery or dangerous goods in apparatus	9	M11			NOT SUBJECT TO ADR [see also 1.1.3.1 (b)]							
3364	TRINITROPHENOL (PICRIC ACID), WETTED with not less than 10% water, by mass	4.1	D	I	4.1		LQ0	E0	P406	PP24	MP2		
3365	TRINITROCHLORO-BENZENE (PICRYL CHLORIDE), WETTED with not less than 10% water, by mass	4.1	D	I	4.1		LQ0	E0	P406	PP24	MP2		
3366	TRINITROTOLUENE (TNT), WETTED with not less than 10% water, by mass	4.1	D	I	4.1		LQ0	E0	P406	PP24	MP2		
3367	TRINITROBENZENE, WETTED with not less than 10% water, by mass	4.1	D	I	4.1		LQ0	E0	P406	PP24	MP2		
3368	TRINITROBENZOIC ACID, WETTED with not less than 10% water, by mass	4.1	D	I	4.1		LQ0	E0	P406	PP24	MP2		
3369	SODIUM DINITRO-o-CRESOLATE, WETTED with not less than 10% water, by mass	4.1	DT	I	4.1 +6.1		LQ0	E0	P406	PP24	MP2		
3370	UREA NITRATE, WETTED with not less than 10% water, by mass	4.1	D	I	4.1		LQ0	E0	P406	PP78	MP2		
3371	2 –METHYLBUTANAL	3	F1	II	3		LQ4	E2	P001 IBC02 R001		MP19	T4	TP1
3373	BIOLOGICAL SUBSTANCE, CATEGORY B	6.2	I4		6.2	319	LQ0	E0	P650			T1	TP1
3373	BIOLOGICAL SUBSTANCE, CATEGORY B (animal material only)	6.2	I4		6.2	319	LQ0	E0	P650			T1 BK1 BK2	TP1
3374	ACETYLENE, SOLVENT FREE	2	2F		2.1		LQ0	E0	P200		MP9		
3375	AMMONIUM NITRATE EMULSION or SUSPENSION or GEL, intermediate for blasting explosives, liquid	5.1	O1	II	5.1	309	LQ0	E2	P099 IBC99		MP2	T1	TP1 TP9 TP17 TP32
3375	AMMONIUM NITRATE EMULSION or SUSPENSION or GEL, intermediate for blasting explosives, solid	5.1	O2	II	5.1	309	LQ0	E2	P099 IBC99		MP2	T1	TP1 TP9 TP17 TP32
3376	4-NITROPHENYL-HYDRAZINE, with not less than 30% water, by mass	4.1	D	I	4.1		LQ0	E0	P406	PP26	MP2		
3377	SODIUM PERBORATE MONOHYDRATE	5.1	O2	III	5.1		LQ12	E1	P002 IBC08 LP02 R001	B3	MP10	T1 BK1 BK2	TP33
3378	SODIUM CARBONATE PEROXYHYDRATE	5.1	O2	II	5.1		LQ11	E2	P002 IBC08	B4	MP10	T3 BK1 BK2	TP33
3378	SODIUM CARBONATE PEROXYHYDRATE	5.1	O2	III	5.1		LQ12	E1	P002 IBC08 LP02 R001	B3	MP10	T1 BK1 BK2	TP33
3379	DESENSITIZED EXPLOSIVE, LIQUID, N.O.S.	3	D	I	3	274 311	LQ0	E0	P099		MP2		
3380	DESENSITIZED EXPLOSIVE, SOLID, N.O.S.	4.1	D	I	4.1	274 311	LQ0	E0	P099		MP2		

ADR tank		Vehicle for tank carriage	Transport category (Tunnel restriction code)	Special provisions for carriage				Hazard identifi-cation No.	UN No.	Name and description
Tank code	Special provisions	9.1.1.2	1.1.3.6 (8.6)	Packages	Bulk	Loading, unloading and handling	Operation	5.3.2.3		3.1.2
4.3	4.3.5, 6.8.4			7.2.4	7.3.3	7.5.11	8.5			
(12)	(13)	(14)	(15)	(16)	(17)	(18)	(19)	(20)	(1)	(2)
L4BH	TU15 TE19	FL	2 (D/E)			CV13 CV28	S2 S9 S19	638	3362	CHLOROSILANES, TOXIC, CORROSIVE, FLAMMABLE, N.O.S.
NOT SUBJECT TO ADR [see also 1.1.3.1 (b)]									3363	Dangerous goods in machinery or dangerous goods in apparatus
			1 (B)				S14		3364	TRINITROPHENOL (PICRIC ACID), WETTED with not less than 10% water, by mass
			1 (B)				S14		3365	TRINITROCHLORO-BENZENE (PICRYL CHLORIDE), WETTED with not less than 10% water, by mass
			1 (B)				S14		3366	TRINITROTOLUENE (TNT), WETTED with not less than 10% water, by mass
			1 (B)				S14		3367	TRINITROBENZENE, WETTED with not less than 10% water, by mass
			1 (B)				S14		3368	TRINITROBENZOIC ACID, WETTED with not less than 10% water, by mass
			1 (B)			CV13 CV28	S14		3369	SODIUM DINITRO-o-CRESOLATE, WETTED with not less than 10% water, by mass
			1 (B)				S14		3370	UREA NITRATE, WETTED with not less than 10% water, by mass
LGBF		FL	2 (D/E)				S2 S20	33	3371	2 –METHYLBUTANAL
L4BH	TU15 TU37 TE19	AT	(-)				S3	606	3373	BIOLOGICAL SUBSTANCE, CATEGORY B
L4BH	TU15 TU37 TE19	AT	– (-)				S3	606	3373	BIOLOGICAL SUBSTANCE, CATEGORY B (animal material only)
			2 (D)			CV9 CV10 CV36	S2 S20		3374	ACETYLENE, SOLVENT FREE
LGAV(+)	TU3 TU12 TU39 TE10 TE23 TA1 TA3	AT	2 (E)			CV24	S9 S23	50	3375	AMMONIUM NITRATE EMULSION or SUSPENSION or GEL, intermediate for blasting explosives, liquid
SGAV(+)	TU3 TU12 TU39 TE10 TE23 TA1 TA3	AT	2 (E)			CV24	S9 S23	50	3375	AMMONIUM NITRATE EMULSION or SUSPENSION or GEL, intermediate for blasting explosives, solid
			1 (B)	V1			S14		3376	4-NITROPHENYL-HYDRAZINE, with not less than 30% water, by mass
SGAV	TU3	AT	3 (E)		VV8	CV24		50	3377	SODIUM PERBORATE MONOHYDRATE
SGAV	TU3	AT	2 (E)	V11	VV8	CV24		50	3378	SODIUM CARBONATE PEROXYHYDRATE
SGAV	TU3	AT	3 (E)		VV8	CV24		50	3378	SODIUM CARBONATE PEROXYHYDRATE
			1 (B)				S2 S14		3379	DESENSITIZED EXPLOSIVE, LIQUID, N.O.S.
			1 (B)				S14		3380	DESENSITIZED EXPLOSIVE, SOLID, N.O.S.

UN No.	Name and description	Class	Classification code	Packing group	Labels	Special provisions	Limited and excepted quantities		Packaging			Portable tanks and bulk containers	
							quantities		Packing instructions	Special packing provisions	Mixed packing provisions	Instructions	Special provisions
	3.1.2	2.2	2.2	2.1.1.3	5.2.2	3.3	3.4.6	3.5.1.2	4.1.4	4.1.4	4.1.10	4.2.5.2 7.3.2	4.2.5.3
(1)	(2)	(3a)	(3b)	(4)	(5)	(6)	(7a)	(7b)	(8)	(9a)	(9b)	(10)	(11)
3381	TOXIC BY INHALATION LIQUID, N.O.S. with an inhalation toxicity lower than or equal to 200 ml/m^3 and saturated vapour concentration greater than or equal to 500 LC$_{50}$	6.1	T1 or T4	I	6.1	274	LQ0	E5	P601		MP8 MP17	T22	TP2
3382	TOXIC BY INHALATION LIQUID, N.O.S. with an inhalation toxicity lower than or equal to 1000 ml/m^3 and saturated vapour concentration greater than or equal to 10 LC$_{50}$	6.1	T1 or T4	I	6.1	274	LQ0	E5	P602		MP8 MP17	T20	TP2
3383	TOXIC BY INHALATION LIQUID, FLAMMABLE, N.O.S. with an inhalation toxicity lower than or equal to 200 ml/m^3 and saturated vapour concentration greater than or equal to 500 LC$_{50}$	6.1	TF1	I	6.1 +3	274	LQ0	E5	P601		MP8 MP17	T22	TP2
3384	TOXIC BY INHALATION LIQUID, FLAMMABLE, N.O.S. with an inhalation toxicity lower than or equal to 1000 ml/m^3 and saturated vapour concentration greater than or equal to 10 LC$_{50}$	6.1	TF1	I	6.1 +3	274	LQ0	E5	P602		MP8 MP17	T20	TP2
3385	TOXIC BY INHALATION LIQUID, WATER-REACTIVE, N.O.S. with an inhalation toxicity lower than or equal to 200 ml/m^3 and saturated vapour concentration greater than or equal to 500 LC$_{50}$	6.1	TW1	I	6.1 +4.3	274	LQ0	E5	P601		MP8 MP17	T22	TP2
3386	TOXIC BY INHALATION LIQUID, WATER-REACTIVE, N.O.S. with an inhalation toxicity lower than or equal to 1000 ml/m^3 and saturated vapour concentration greater than or equal to 10 LC$_{50}$	6.1	TW1	I	6.1 +4.3	274	LQ0	E5	P602		MP8 MP17	T20	TP2
3387	TOXIC BY INHALATION LIQUID, OXIDIZING, N.O.S. with an inhalation toxicity lower than or equal to 200 ml/m^3 and saturated vapour concentration greater than or equal to 500 LC$_{50}$	6.1	TO1	I	6.1 +5.1	274	LQ0	E5	P601		MP8 MP17	T22	TP2
3388	TOXIC BY INHALATION LIQUID, OXIDIZING, N.O.S. with an inhalation toxicity lower than or equal to 1000 ml/m^3 and saturated vapour concentration greater than or equal to 10 LC$_{50}$	6.1	TO1	I	6.1 +5.1	274	LQ0	E5	P602		MP8 MP17	T20	TP2
3389	TOXIC BY INHALATION LIQUID, CORROSIVE, N.O.S. with an inhalation toxicity lower than or equal to 200 ml/m^3 and saturated vapour concentration greater than or equal to 500 LC$_{50}$	6.1	TC1 or TC3	I	6.1 +8	274	LQ0	E5	P601		MP8 MP17	T22	TP2
3390	TOXIC BY INHALATION LIQUID, CORROSIVE, N.O.S. with an inhalation toxicity lower than or equal to 1000 ml/m^3 and saturated vapour concentration greater than or equal to 10 LC$_{50}$	6.1	TC1 or TC3	I	6.1 +8	274	LQ0	E5	P602		MP8 MP17	T20	TP2

ADR tank		Vehicle for tank carriage	Transport category (Tunnel restriction code)	Special provisions for carriage				Hazard identifi-cation No.	UN No.	Name and description
Tank code	Special provisions			Packages	Bulk	Loading, unloading and handling	Operation			
4.3	4.3.5, 6.8.4	9.1.1.2	1.1.3.6 (8.6)	7.2.4	7.3.3	7.5.11	8.5	5.3.2.3		3.1.2
(12)	(13)	(14)	(15)	(16)	(17)	(18)	(19)	(20)	(1)	(2)
L10CH	TU14 TU15 TE19 TE21	AT	1 (C/D)			CV1 CV13 CV28	S9 S14	66	3381	TOXIC BY INHALATION LIQUID, N.O.S. with an inhalation toxicity lower than or equal to 200 ml/m^3 and saturated vapour concentration greater than or equal to 500 LC$_{50}$
L10CH	TU14 TU15 TE19 TE21	AT	1 (C/D)			CV1 CV13 CV28	S9 S14	66	3382	TOXIC BY INHALATION LIQUID, N.O.S. with an inhalation toxicity lower than or equal to 1000 ml/m^3 and saturated vapour concentration greater than or equal to 10 LC$_{50}$
L10CH	TU14 TU15 TE19 TE21	FL	1 (C/D)			CV1 CV13 CV28	S2 S9 S14	663	3383	TOXIC BY INHALATION LIQUID, FLAMMABLE, N.O.S. with an inhalation toxicity lower than or equal to 200 ml/m^3 and saturated vapour concentration greater than or equal to 500 LC$_{50}$
L10CH	TU14 TU15 TE19 TE21	FL	1 (C/D)			CV1 CV13 CV28	S2 S9 S14	663	3384	TOXIC BY INHALATION LIQUID, FLAMMABLE, N.O.S. with an inhalation toxicity lower than or equal to 1000 ml/m^3 and saturated vapour concentration greater than or equal to 10 LC$_{50}$
L10CH	TU14 TU15 TE19 TE21	AT	1 (C/D)			CV1 CV13 CV28	S9 S14	623	3385	TOXIC BY INHALATION LIQUID, WATER-REACTIVE, N.O.S. with an inhalation toxicity lower than or equal to 200 ml/m^3 and saturated vapour concentration greater than or equal to 500 LC$_{50}$
L10CH	TU14 TU15 TE19 TE21	AT	1 (C/D)			CV1 CV13 CV28	S9 S14	623	3386	TOXIC BY INHALATION LIQUID, WATER-REACTIVE, N.O.S. with an inhalation toxicity lower than or equal to 1000 ml/m^3 and saturated vapour concentration greater than or equal to 10 LC$_{50}$
L10CH	TU14 TU15 TE19 TE21	AT	1 (C/D)			CV1 CV13 CV28	S9 S14	665	3387	TOXIC BY INHALATION LIQUID, OXIDIZING, N.O.S. with an inhalation toxicity lower than or equal to 200 ml/m^3 and saturated vapour concentration greater than or equal to 500 LC$_{50}$
L10CH	TU14 TU15 TE19 TE21	AT	1 (C/D)			CV1 CV13 CV28	S9 S14	665	3388	TOXIC BY INHALATION LIQUID, OXIDIZING, N.O.S. with an inhalation toxicity lower than or equal to 1000 ml/m^3 and saturated vapour concentration greater than or equal to 10 LC$_{50}$
L10CH	TU14 TU15 TE19 TE21	AT	1 (C/D)			CV1 CV13 CV28	S9 S14	668	3389	TOXIC BY INHALATION LIQUID, CORROSIVE, N.O.S. with an inhalation toxicity lower than or equal to 200 ml/m^3 and saturated vapour concentration greater than or equal to 500 LC$_{50}$
L10CH	TU14 TU15 TE19 TE21	AT	1 (C/D)			CV1 CV13 CV28	S9 S14	668	3390	TOXIC BY INHALATION LIQUID, CORROSIVE, N.O.S. with an inhalation toxicity lower than or equal to 1000 ml/m^3 and saturated vapour concentration greater than or equal to 10 LC$_{50}$

UN No.	Name and description	Class	Classification code	Packing group	Labels	Special provisions	Limited and excepted quantities		Packaging			Portable tanks and bulk containers	
									Packing instructions	Special packing provisions	Mixed packing provisions	Instructions	Special provisions
	3.1.2	2.2	2.2	2.1.1.3	5.2.2	3.3	3.4.6	3.5.1.2	4.1.4	4.1.4	4.1.10	4.2.5.2 7.3.2	4.2.5.3
(1)	(2)	(3a)	(3b)	(4)	(5)	(6)	(7a)	(7b)	(8)	(9a)	(9b)	(10)	(11)
3391	ORGANOMETALLIC SUBSTANCE, SOLID, PYROPHORIC	4.2	S5	I	4.2	274	LQ0	E0	P404	PP86	MP2	T21	TP7 TP33
3392	ORGANOMETALLIC SUBSTANCE, LIQUID, PYROPHORIC	4.2	S5	I	4.2	274	LQ0	E0	P400	PP86	MP2	T21	TP2 TP7
3393	ORGANOMETALLIC SUBSTANCE, SOLID, PYROPHORIC, WATER-REACTIVE	4.2	SW	I	4.2 +4.3	274	LQ0	E0	P404	PP86	MP2	T21	TP7 TP33
3394	ORGANOMETALLIC SUBSTANCE, LIQUID, PYROPHORIC, WATER-REACTIVE	4.2	SW	I	4.2 +4.3	274	LQ0	E0	P400	PP86	MP2	T21	TP2 TP7
3395	ORGANOMETALLIC SUBSTANCE, SOLID, WATER-REACTIVE	4.3	W2	I	4.3	274	LQ0	E0	P403		MP2	T9	TP7 TP33
3395	ORGANOMETALLIC SUBSTANCE, SOLID, WATER-REACTIVE	4.3	W2	II	4.3	274	LQ11	E2	P410 IBC04		MP14	T3	TP33
3395	ORGANOMETALLIC SUBSTANCE, SOLID, WATER-REACTIVE	4.3	W2	III	4.3	274	LQ12	E1	P410 IBC06		MP14	T1	TP33
3396	ORGANOMETALLIC SUBSTANCE, SOLID, WATER-REACTIVE, FLAMMABLE	4.3	WF2	I	4.3 +4.1	274	LQ0	E0	P403		MP2	T9	TP7 TP33
3396	ORGANOMETALLIC SUBSTANCE, SOLID, WATER-REACTIVE, FLAMMABLE	4.3	WF2	II	4.3 +4.1	274	LQ11	E2	P410 IBC04		MP14	T3	TP33
3396	ORGANOMETALLIC SUBSTANCE, SOLID, WATER-REACTIVE, FLAMMABLE	4.3	WF2	III	4.3 +4.1	274	LQ12	E1	P410 IBC06		MP14	T1	TP33
3397	ORGANOMETALLIC SUBSTANCE, SOLID, WATER-REACTIVE, SELF-HEATING	4.3	WS	I	4.3 +4.2	274	LQ0	E0	P403		MP2	T9	TP7 TP33
3397	ORGANOMETALLIC SUBSTANCE, SOLID, WATER-REACTIVE, SELF-HEATING	4.3	WS	II	4.3 +4.2	274	LQ11	E2	P410 IBC04		MP14	T3	TP33
3397	ORGANOMETALLIC SUBSTANCE, SOLID, WATER-REACTIVE, SELF-HEATING	4.3	WS	III	4.3 +4.2	274	LQ12	E1	P410 IBC06		MP14	T1	TP33
3398	ORGANOMETALLIC SUBSTANCE, LIQUID, WATER-REACTIVE	4.3	W1	I	4.3	274	LQ0	E0	P402		MP2	T13	TP2 TP7
3398	ORGANOMETALLIC SUBSTANCE, LIQUID, WATER-REACTIVE	4.3	W1	II	4.3	274	LQ10	E2	P001 IBC01		MP15	T7	TP2 TP7
3398	ORGANOMETALLIC SUBSTANCE, LIQUID, WATER-REACTIVE	4.3	W1	III	4.3	274	LQ13	E1	P001 IBC02		MP15	T7	TP2 TP7
3399	ORGANOMETALLIC SUBSTANCE, LIQUID, WATER-REACTIVE, FLAMMABLE	4.3	WF1	I	4.3 +3	274	LQ0	E0	P402		MP2	T13	TP2 TP7
3399	ORGANOMETALLIC SUBSTANCE, LIQUID, WATER-REACTIVE, FLAMMABLE	4.3	WF1	II	4.3 +3	274	LQ10	E2	P001 IBC01		MP15	T7	TP2 TP7
3399	ORGANOMETALLIC SUBSTANCE, LIQUID, WATER-REACTIVE, FLAMMABLE	4.3	WF1	III	4.3 +3	274	LQ13	E1	P001 IBC02 R001		MP15	T7	TP2 TP7
3400	ORGANOMETALLIC SUBSTANCE, SOLID, SELF-HEATING	4.2	S5	II	4.2	274	LQ18	E2	P410 IBC06		MP14	T3	TP33

ADR tank		Vehicle for tank carriage	Transport category (Tunnel restriction code)	Special provisions for carriage				Hazard identification No.	UN No.	Name and description
Tank code	Special provisions			Packages	Bulk	Loading, unloading and handling	Operation			
4.3	4.3.5, 6.8.4	9.1.1.2	1.1.3.6 (8.6)	7.2.4	7.3.3	7.5.11	8.5	5.3.2.3		3.1.2
(12)	(13)	(14)	(15)	(16)	(17)	(18)	(19)	(20)	(1)	(2)
L21DH	TU4 TU14 TU22 TC1 TE21 TM1	AT	0 (B/E)	V1			S20	43	3391	ORGANOMETALLIC SUBSTANCE, SOLID, PYROPHORIC
L21DH	TU4 TU14 TU22 TC1 TE21 TM1	AT	0 (B/E)	V1			S20	333	3392	ORGANOMETALLIC SUBSTANCE, LIQUID, PYROPHORIC
L21DH	TU4 TU14 TU22 TC1 TE21 TM1	AT	0 (B/E)	V1			S20	X432	3393	ORGANOMETALLIC SUBSTANCE, SOLID, PYROPHORIC, WATER-REACTIVE
L21DH	TU4 TU14 TU22 TC1 TE21 TM1	AT	0 (B/E)	V1			S20	X333	3394	ORGANOMETALLIC SUBSTANCE, LIQUID, PYROPHORIC, WATER-REACTIVE
S10AN L10DH	TU4 TU14 TU22 TE21 TM2	AT	1 (B/E)	V1		CV23	S20	X423	3395	ORGANOMETALLIC SUBSTANCE, SOLID, WATER-REACTIVE
SGAN L4DH	TU14 TE21 TM2	AT	2 (D/E)	V1		CV23		423	3395	ORGANOMETALLIC SUBSTANCE, SOLID, WATER-REACTIVE
SGAN L4DH	TU14 TE21 TM2	AT	3 (E)	V1		CV23		423	3395	ORGANOMETALLIC SUBSTANCE, SOLID, WATER-REACTIVE
S10AN L10DH	TU4 TU14 TU22 TE21 TM2	AT	0 (B/E)	V1		CV23	S20	X423	3396	ORGANOMETALLIC SUBSTANCE, SOLID, WATER-REACTIVE, FLAMMABLE
SGAN L4DH	TU14 TE21 TM2	AT	0 (D/E)	V1		CV23		423	3396	ORGANOMETALLIC SUBSTANCE, SOLID, WATER-REACTIVE, FLAMMABLE
SGAN L4DH	TU14 TE21 TM2	AT	0 (E)	V1		CV23		423	3396	ORGANOMETALLIC SUBSTANCE, SOLID, WATER-REACTIVE, FLAMMABLE
S10AN L10DH	TU14 TE21 TM2	AT	1 (B/E)	V1		CV23	S20	X423	3397	ORGANOMETALLIC SUBSTANCE, SOLID, WATER-REACTIVE, SELF-HEATING
SGAN L4DH		AT	2 (D/E)	V1		CV23		423	3397	ORGANOMETALLIC SUBSTANCE, SOLID, WATER-REACTIVE, SELF-HEATING
SGAN L4DH		AT	3 (E)	V1		CV23		423	3397	ORGANOMETALLIC SUBSTANCE, SOLID, WATER-REACTIVE, SELF-HEATING
L10DH	TU4 TU14 TU22 TE21 TM2	AT	0 (B/E)	V1		CV23	S20	X323	3398	ORGANOMETALLIC SUBSTANCE, LIQUID, WATER-REACTIVE
L4DH	TU14 TE21 TM2	AT	0 (D/E)	V1		CV23		323	3398	ORGANOMETALLIC SUBSTANCE, LIQUID, WATER-REACTIVE
L4DH	TU14 TE21 TM2	AT	0 (E)	V1		CV23		323	3398	ORGANOMETALLIC SUBSTANCE, LIQUID, WATER-REACTIVE
L10DH	TU4 TU14 TU22 TE21 TM2	FL	0 (B/E)	V1		CV23	S2 S20	X323	3399	ORGANOMETALLIC SUBSTANCE, LIQUID, WATER-REACTIVE, FLAMMABLE
L4DH	TU4 TU14 TU22 TE21 TM2	FL	0 (D/E)	V1		CV23	S2	323	3399	ORGANOMETALLIC SUBSTANCE, LIQUID, WATER-REACTIVE, FLAMMABLE
L4DH	TU14 TE21 TM2	FL	0 (E)	V1		CV23	S2	323	3399	ORGANOMETALLIC SUBSTANCE, LIQUID, WATER-REACTIVE, FLAMMABLE
SGAN L4BN		AT	2 (D/E)	V1 V12				40	3400	ORGANOMETALLIC SUBSTANCE, SOLID, SELF-HEATING

UN No.	Name and description	Class	Classifi-cation code	Packing group	Labels	Special provi-sions	Limited and excepted quantities		Packaging			Portable tanks and bulk containers	
									Packing instruc-tions	Special packing provisions	Mixed packing provisions	Instruc-tions	Special provisions
3.1.2		2.2	2.2	2.1.1.3	5.2.2	3.3	3.4.6	3.5.1.2	4.1.4	4.1.4	4.1.10	4.2.5.2 7.3.2	4.2.5.3
(1)	(2)	(3a)	(3b)	(4)	(5)	(6)	(7a)	(7b)	(8)	(9a)	(9b)	(10)	(11)
3400	ORGANOMETALLIC SUBSTANCE, SOLID, SELF-HEATING	4.2	S5	III	4.2	274	LQ11	E1	P002 IBC08		MP14	T1	TP33
3401	ALKALI METAL AMALGAM, SOLID	4.3	W2	I	4.3	182 274	LQ0	E0	P403		MP2	T9	TP7 TP33
3402	ALKALINE EARTH METAL AMALGAM, SOLID	4.3	W2	I	4.3	183 274 506	LQ0	E0	P403		MP2	T9	TP7 TP33
3403	POTASSIUM METAL ALLOYS, SOLID	4.3	W2	I	4.3		LQ0	E0	P403		MP2	T9	TP7 TP33
3404	POTASSIUM SODIUM ALLOYS, SOLID	4.3	W2	I	4.3		LQ0	E0	P403		MP2	T9	TP7 TP33
3405	BARIUM CHLORATE SOLUTION	5.1	OT1	II	5.1 +6.1		LQ10	E2	P504 IBC02		MP2	T4	TP1
3405	BARIUM CHLORATE SOLUTION	5.1	OT1	III	5.1 +6.1		LQ13	E1	P001 IBC02		MP2	T4	TP1
3406	BARIUM PERCHLORATE SOLUTION	5.1	OT1	II	5.1 +6.1		LQ10	E2	P504 IBC02		MP2	T4	TP1
3406	BARIUM PERCHLORATE SOLUTION	5.1	OT1	III	5.1 +6.1		LQ13	E1	P001 IBC02		MP2	T4	TP1
3407	CHLORATE AND MAGNESIUM CHLORIDE MIXTURE SOLUTION	5.1	O1	II	5.1		LQ10	E2	P504 IBC02		MP2	T4	TP1
3407	CHLORATE AND MAGNESIUM CHLORIDE MIXTURE SOLUTION	5.1	O1	III	5.1		LQ13	E1	P504 IBC02		MP2	T4	TP1
3408	LEAD PERCHLORATE SOLUTION	5.1	OT1	II	5.1 +6.1		LQ10	E2	P504 IBC02		MP2	T4	TP1
3408	LEAD PERCHLORATE SOLUTION	5.1	OT1	III	5.1 +6.1		LQ13	E1	P001 IBC02		MP2	T4	TP1
3409	CHLORONITRO-BENZENES, LIQUID	6.1	T1	II	6.1	279	LQ17	E4	P001 IBC02		MP15	T7	TP2
3410	4-CHLORO-o-TOLUIDINE HYDROCHLORIDE SOLUTION	6.1	T1	III	6.1		LQ7	E1	P001 IBC03 R001		MP19	T4	TP1
3411	beta-NAPHTHYLAMINE SOLUTION	6.1	T1	II	6.1		LQ17	E4	P001 IBC02		MP15	T7	TP2
3411	beta-NAPHTHYLAMINE SOLUTION	6.1	T1	III	6.1		LQ7	E1	P001 IBC02		MP19	T7	TP2
3412	FORMIC ACID with not less than 10% but not more than 85% acid by mass	8	C3	II	8		LQ22	E2	P001 IBC02		MP15	T7	TP2
3412	FORMIC ACID with not less than 5% but less than 10% acid by mass	8	C3	III	8		LQ7	E1	P001 IBC03 LP01 R001		MP19	T4	TP1
3413	POTASSIUM CYANIDE SOLUTION	6.1	T4	I	6.1		LQ0	E5	P001		MP8 MP17	T14	TP2
3413	POTASSIUM CYANIDE SOLUTION	6.1	T4	II	6.1		LQ17	E4	P001 IBC02		MP15	T11	TP2 TP27
3413	POTASSIUM CYANIDE SOLUTION	6.1	T4	III	6.1		LQ7	E1	P001 IBC03 LP01 R001		MP19	T7	TP2 TP28
3414	SODIUM CYANIDE SOLUTION	6.1	T4	I	6.1		LQ0	E5	P001		MP8 MP17	T14	TP2
3414	SODIUM CYANIDE SOLUTION	6.1	T4	II	6.1		LQ17	E4	P001 IBC02		MP15	T11	TP2 TP27
3414	SODIUM CYANIDE SOLUTION	6.1	T4	III	6.1		LQ7	E1	P001 IBC03 LP01 R001		MP19	T7	TP2 TP28
3415	SODIUM FLUORIDE SOLUTION	6.1	T4	III	6.1		LQ7	E1	P001 IBC03 LP01 R001		MP19	T4	TP1
3416	CHLOROACETO-PHENONE, LIQUID	6.1	T1	II	6.1		LQ17	E4	P001 IBC02		MP15	T7	TP2
3417	XYLYL BROMIDE, SOLID	6.1	T2	II	6.1		LQ18	E4	P002 IBC08	B4	MP10	T3	TP33

ADR tank		Vehicle for tank carriage	Transport category (Tunnel restriction code)	Special provisions for carriage				Hazard identifi-cation No.	UN No.	Name and description
Tank code	Special provisions	9.1.1.2	1.1.3.6 (8.6)	Packages	Bulk	Loading, unloading and handling	Operation	5.3.2.3		3.1.2
4.3	4.3.5, 6.8.4			7.2.4	7.3.3	7.5.11	8.5			
(12)	(13)	(14)	(15)	(16)	(17)	(18)	(19)	(20)	(1)	(2)
SGAN L4BN		AT	3 (E)	V1				40	3400	ORGANOMETALLIC SUBSTANCE, SOLID, SELF-HEATING
L10BN(+)	TU1 TE5 TT3 TM2	AT	1 (B/E)	V1		CV23	S20	X423	3401	ALKALI METAL AMALGAM, SOLID
L10BN(+)	TU1 TE5 TT3 TM2	AT	1 (B/E)	V1		CV23	S20	X423	3402	ALKALINE EARTH METAL AMALGAM, SOLID
L10BN(+)	TU1 TE5 TT3 TM2	AT	1 (B/E)	V1		CV23	S20	X423	3403	POTASSIUM METAL ALLOYS, SOLID
L10BN(+)	TU1 TE5 TT3 TM2	AT	1 (B/E)	V1		CV23	S20	X423	3404	POTASSIUM SODIUM ALLOYS, SOLID
L4BN	TU3	AT	2 (E)			CV24 CV28		56	3405	BARIUM CHLORATE SOLUTION
LGBV	TU3	AT	3 (E)			CV24 CV28		56	3405	BARIUM CHLORATE SOLUTION
L4BN	TU3	AT	2 (E)			CV24 CV28		56	3406	BARIUM PERCHLORATE SOLUTION
LGBV	TU3	AT	3 (E)			CV24 CV28		56	3406	BARIUM PERCHLORATE SOLUTION
L4BN	TU3	AT	2 (E)			CV24		50	3407	CHLORATE AND MAGNESIUM CHLORIDE MIXTURE SOLUTION
LGBV	TU3	AT	3 (E)			CV24		50	3407	CHLORATE AND MAGNESIUM CHLORIDE MIXTURE SOLUTION
L4BN	TU3	AT	2 (E)			CV24 CV28		56	3408	LEAD PERCHLORATE SOLUTION
LGBV	TU3	AT	3 (E)			CV24 CV28		56	3408	LEAD PERCHLORATE SOLUTION
L4BH	TU15 TE19	AT	2 (D/E)			CV13 CV28	S9 S19	60	3409	CHLORONITRO-BENZENES, LIQUID
L4BH	TU15 TE19	AT	2 (E)			CV13 CV28	S9	60	3410	4-CHLORO-o-TOLUIDINE HYDROCHLORIDE SOLUTION
L4BH	TU15 TE19	AT	2 (D/E)			CV13 CV28	S9 S19	60	3411	beta-NAPHTHYLAMINE SOLUTION
L4BH	TU15 TE19	AT	2 (E)			CV13 CV28	S9	60	3411	beta-NAPHTHYLAMINE SOLUTION
L4BN		AT	2 (E)					80	3412	FORMIC ACID with not less than 10% but not more than 85% acid by mass
L4BN		AT	3 (E)					80	3412	FORMIC ACID with not less than 5% but less than 10% acid by mass
L10CH	TU14 TU15 TE19 TE21	AT	1 (C/E)			CV1 CV13 CV28	S9 S14	66	3413	POTASSIUM CYANIDE SOLUTION
L4BH	TU15 TE19	AT	2 (D/E)			CV13 CV28	S9 S19	60	3413	POTASSIUM CYANIDE SOLUTION
L4BH	TU15 TE19	AT	2 (E)			CV13 CV28	S9	60	3413	POTASSIUM CYANIDE SOLUTION
L10CH	TU14 TU15 TE19 TE21	AT	1 (C/E)			CV1 CV13 CV28	S9 S14	66	3414	SODIUM CYANIDE SOLUTION
L4BH	TU15 TE19	AT	2 (D/E)			CV13 CV28	S9 S19	60	3414	SODIUM CYANIDE SOLUTION
L4BH	TU15 TE19	AT	2 (E)			CV13 CV28	S9	60	3414	SODIUM CYANIDE SOLUTION
L4BH	TU15 TE19	AT	2 (E)			CV13 CV28	S9	60	3415	SODIUM FLUORIDE SOLUTION
L4BH	TU15 TE19	AT	2 (D/E)			CV13 CV28	S9 S19	60	3416	CHLOROACETO-PHENONE, LIQUID
SGAH L4BH	TU15 TE19	AT	2 (D/E)	V11		CV13 CV28	S9 S19	60	3417	XYLYL BROMIDE, SOLID

UN No.	Name and description	Class	Classification code	Packing group	Labels	Special provisions	Limited and excepted quantities		Packaging			Portable tanks and bulk containers	
									Packing instructions	Special packing provisions	Mixed packing provisions	Instructions	Special provisions
	3.1.2	2.2	2.2	2.1.1.3	5.2.2	3.3	3.4.6	3.5.1.2	4.1.4	4.1.4	4.1.10	4.2.5.2 7.3.2	4.2.5.3
(1)	(2)	(3a)	(3b)	(4)	(5)	(6)	(7a)	(7b)	(8)	(9a)	(9b)	(10)	(11)
3418	2,4-TOLUYLENEDIAMINE SOLUTION	6.1	T1	III	6.1		LQ7	E1	P001 IBC03 LP01 R001		MP19	T4	TP1
3419	BORON TRIFLUORIDE ACETIC ACID COMPLEX, SOLID	8	C4	II	8		LQ23	E2	P002 IBC08	B4	MP10	T3	TP33
3420	BORON TRIFLUORIDE PROPIONIC ACID COMPLEX, SOLID	8	C4	II	8		LQ23	E2	P002 IBC08	B4	MP10	T3	TP33
3421	POTASSIUM HYDROGENDIFLUORIDE SOLUTION	8	CT1	II	8 +6.1		LQ22	E2	P001 IBC02		MP15	T7	TP2
3421	POTASSIUM HYDROGENDIFLUORIDE SOLUTION	8	CT1	III	8 +6.1		LQ7	E1	P001 IBC03 R001		MP19	T4	TP1
3422	POTASSIUM FLUORIDE SOLUTION	6.1	T4	III	6.1		LQ7	E1	P001 IBC03 LP01 R001		MP19	T4	TP1
3423	TETRAMETHYL-AMMONIUM HYDROXIDE, SOLID	8	C8	II	8		LQ24	E2	P002 IBC08	B4	MP10	T3	TP33
3424	AMMONIUM DINITRO-o-CRESOLATE SOLUTION	6.1	T1	II	6.1		LQ17	E4	P001 IBC02		MP15	T7	TP2
3424	AMMONIUM DINITRO-o-CRESOLATE SOLUTION	6.1	T1	III	6.1		LQ7	E1	P001 IBC02		MP19	T7	TP2
3425	BROMOACETIC ACID, SOLID	8	C4	II	8		LQ23	E2	P002 IBC08	B4	MP10	T3	TP33
3426	ACRYLAMIDE SOLUTION	6.1	T1	III	6.1		LQ7	E1	P001 IBC03 LP01 R001		MP19	T4	TP1
3427	CHLOROBENZYL CHLORIDES, SOLID	6.1	T2	III	6.1		LQ9	E1	P002 IBC08 LP02 R001	B3	MP10	T1	TP33
3428	3-CHLORO-4-METHYLPHENYL ISOCYANATE, SOLID	6.1	T2	II	6.1		LQ18	E4	P002 IBC08	B4	MP10	T3	TP33
3429	CHLOROTOLUIDINES, LIQUID	6.1	T1	III	6.1		LQ7	E1	P001 IBC03 LP01 R001		MP19	T4	TP1
3430	XYLENOLS, LIQUID	6.1	T1	II	6.1		LQ17	E4	P001 IBC02		MP15	T7	TP2
3431	NITROBENZO-TRIFLUORIDES, SOLID	6.1	T2	II	6.1		LQ18	E4	P002 IBC08	B4	MP10	T3	TP33
3432	POLYCHLORINATED BIPHENYLS, SOLID	9	M2	II	9	305	LQ25	E2	P906 IBC08	B4	MP10	T3	TP33
3434	NITROCRESOLS, LIQUID	6.1	T1	III	6.1		LQ7	E1	P001 IBC03 LP01 R001		MP19	T4	TP1
3436	HEXAFLUOROACETONE HYDRATE, SOLID	6.1	T2	II	6.1		LQ18	E4	P002 IBC08	B4	MP10	T3	TP33
3437	CHLOROCRESOLS, SOLID	6.1	T2	II	6.1		LQ18	E4	P002 IBC08	B4	MP10	T3	TP33
3438	alpha-METHYLBENZYL ALCOHOL, SOLID	6.1	T2	III	6.1		LQ9	E1	P002 IBC08 LP02 R001	B3	MP10	T1	TP33
3439	NITRILES, TOXIC, SOLID, N.O.S.	6.1	T2	I	6.1	274	LQ0	E5	P002 IBC07		MP18	T6	TP33
3439	NITRILES, TOXIC, SOLID, N.O.S.	6.1	T2	II	6.1	274	LQ18	E4	P002 IBC08	B4	MP10	T3	TP33
3439	NITRILES, TOXIC, SOLID, N.O.S.	6.1	T2	III	6.1	274	LQ9	E1	P002 IBC08 LP02 R001	B3	MP10	T1	TP33

ADR tank		Vehicle for tank carriage	Transport category (Tunnel restriction code)	Special provisions for carriage				Hazard identifi-cation No.	UN No.	Name and description
Tank code	Special provisions			Packages	Bulk	Loading, unloading and handling	Operation			
4.3	4.3.5, 6.8.4	9.1.1.2	1.1.3.6 (8.6)	7.2.4	7.3.3	7.5.11	8.5	5.3.2.3		3.1.2
(12)	(13)	(14)	(15)	(16)	(17)	(18)	(19)	(20)	(1)	(2)
L4BH	TU15 TE19	AT	2 (E)			CV13 CV28	S9	60	3418	2,4-TOLUYLENEDIAMINE SOLUTION
SGAN L4BN		AT	2 (E)	V11				80	3419	BORON TRIFLUORIDE ACETIC ACID COMPLEX, SOLID
SGAN L4BN		AT	2 (E)	V11				80	3420	BORON TRIFLUORIDE PROPIONIC ACID COMPLEX, SOLID
L4DH	TU14 TE21	AT	2 (E)			CV13 CV28		86	3421	POTASSIUM HYDROGENDIFLUORIDE SOLUTION
L4DH	TU14 TE21	AT	3 (E)			CV13 CV28		86	3421	POTASSIUM HYDROGENDIFLUORIDE SOLUTION
L4BH	TU15 TE19	AT	2 (E)			CV13 CV28	S9	60	3422	POTASSIUM FLUORIDE SOLUTION
SGAN L4BN		AT	2 (E)	V11				80	3423	TETRAMETHYL-AMMONIUM HYDROXIDE, SOLID
L4BH	TU15 TE19	AT	2 (D/E)			CV13 CV28	S9 S19	60	3424	AMMONIUM DINITRO-o-CRESOLATE SOLUTION
L4BH	TU15 TE19	AT	2 (E)			CV13 CV28	S9	60	3424	AMMONIUM DINITRO-o-CRESOLATE SOLUTION
SGAN L4BN		AT	2 (E)	V11				80	3425	BROMOACETIC ACID, SOLID
L4BH	TU15 TE19	AT	2 (E)			CV13 CV28	S9	60	3426	ACRYLAMIDE SOLUTION
SGAH L4BH	TU15 TE19	AT	2 (E)		VV9	CV13 CV28	S9	60	3427	CHLOROBENZYL CHLORIDES, SOLID
SGAH L4BH	TU15 TE19	AT	2 (D/E)	V11		CV13 CV28	S9 S19	60	3428	3-CHLORO-4-METHYLPHENYL ISOCYANATE, SOLID
L4BH	TU15 TE19	AT	2 (E)			CV13 CV28	S9	60	3429	CHLOROTOLUIDINES, LIQUID
L4BH	TU15 TE19	AT	2 (D/E)			CV13 CV28	S9 S19	60	3430	XYLENOLS, LIQUID
SGAH L4BH	TU15 TE19	AT	2 (D/E)	V11		CV13 CV28	S9 S19	60	3431	NITROBENZO-TRIFLUORIDES, SOLID
S4AH L4BH	TU15	AT	0 (D/E)	V11	VV15	CV1 CV13 CV28	S19	90	3432	POLYCHLORINATED BIPHENYLS, SOLID
L4BH	TU15 TE19	AT	2 (E)			CV13 CV28	S9	60	3434	NITROCRESOLS, LIQUID
SGAH L4BH	TU15 TE19	AT	2 (D/E)	V11		CV13 CV28	S9 S19	60	3436	HEXAFLUOROACETONE HYDRATE, SOLID
SGAH L4BH	TU15 TE19	AT	2 (D/E)	V11		CV13 CV28	S9 S19	60	3437	CHLOROCRESOLS, SOLID
SGAH L4BH	TU15 TE19	AT	2 (E)		VV9	CV13 CV28	S9	60	3438	alpha-METHYLBENZYL ALCOHOL, SOLID
S10AH L10CH	TU14 TU15 TE19 TE21	AT	1 (C/E)	V10 V12		CV1 CV13 CV28	S9 S14	66	3439	NITRILES, TOXIC, SOLID, N.O.S.
SGAH L4BH	TU15 TE19	AT	2 (D/E)	V11		CV13 CV28	S9 S19	60	3439	NITRILES, TOXIC, SOLID, N.O.S.
SGAH L4BH	TU15 TE19	AT	2 (E)		VV9	CV13 CV28	S9	60	3439	NITRILES, TOXIC, SOLID, N.O.S.

UN No.	Name and description	Class	Classification code	Packing group	Labels	Special provisions	Limited and excepted quantities		Packaging			Portable tanks and bulk containers	
							quantities		Packing instructions	Special packing provisions	Mixed packing provisions	Instructions	Special provisions
	3.1.2	2.2	2.2	2.1.1.3	5.2.2	3.3	3.4.6	3.5.1.2	4.1.4	4.1.4	4.1.10	4.2.5.2 7.3.2	4.2.5.3
(1)	(2)	(3a)	(3b)	(4)	(5)	(6)	(7a)	(7b)	(8)	(9a)	(9b)	(10)	(11)
3440	SELENIUM COMPOUND, LIQUID, N.O.S.	6.1	T4	I	6.1	274 563	LQ0	E5	P001		MP8 MP17	T14	TP2 TP27
3440	SELENIUM COMPOUND, LIQUID, N.O.S.	6.1	T4	II	6.1	274 563	LQ17	E4	P001 IBC02		MP15	T11	TP2 TP27
3440	SELENIUM COMPOUND, LIQUID, N.O.S.	6.1	T4	III	6.1	274 563	LQ7	E1	P001 IBC03 R001		MP19	T7	TP1 TP28
3441	CHLORODINITRO-BENZENES, SOLID	6.1	T2	II	6.1	279	LQ18	E4	P002 IBC08	B4	MP10	T3	TP33
3442	DICHLOROANILINES, SOLID	6.1	T2	II	6.1	279	LQ18	E4	P002 IBC08	B4	MP10	T3	TP33
3443	DINITROBENZENES, SOLID	6.1	T2	II	6.1		LQ18	E4	P002 IBC08	B4	MP10	T3	TP33
3444	NICOTINE HYDROCHLORIDE, SOLID	6.1	T2	II	6.1	43	LQ18	E4	P002 IBC08	B4	MP10	T3	TP33
3445	NICOTINE SULPHATE, SOLID	6.1	T2	II	6.1		LQ18	E4	P002 IBC08	B4	MP10	T3	TP33
3446	NITROTOLUENES, SOLID	6.1	T2	II	6.1		LQ18	E4	P002 IBC08	B4	MP10	T3	TP33
3447	NITROXYLENES, SOLID	6.1	T2	II	6.1		LQ18	E4	P002 IBC08	B4	MP10	T3	TP33
3448	TEAR GAS SUBSTANCE, SOLID, N.O.S.	6.1	T2	I	6.1	274	LQ0	E5	P002		MP18	T6	TP33
3448	TEAR GAS SUBSTANCE, SOLID, N.O.S.	6.1	T2	II	6.1	274	LQ18	E4	P002 IBC08	B4	MP10	T3	TP33
3449	BROMOBENZYL CYANIDES, SOLID	6.1	T2	I	6.1	138	LQ0	E5	P002		MP18	T6	TP33
3450	DIPHENYLCHLORO-ARSINE, SOLID	6.1	T3	I	6.1		LQ0	E5	P002 IBC07		MP18	T6	TP33
3451	TOLUIDINES, SOLID	6.1	T2	II	6.1	279	LQ18	E4	P002 IBC08	B4	MP10	T3	TP33
3452	XYLIDINES, SOLID	6.1	T2	II	6.1		LQ18	E4	P002 IBC08	B4	MP10	T3	TP33
3453	PHOSPHORIC ACID, SOLID	8	C2	III	8		LQ24	E1	P002 IBC08 LP02 R001	B3	MP10	T1	TP33
3454	DINITROTOLUENES, SOLID	6.1	T2	II	6.1		LQ18	E4	P002 IBC08	B4	MP10	T3	TP33
3455	CRESOLS, SOLID	6.1	TC2	II	6.1 +8		LQ18	E4	P002 IBC08	B4	MP10	T3	TP33
3456	NITROSYLSULPHURIC ACID, SOLID	8	C2	II	8		LQ23	E2	P002 IBC08	B4	MP10	T3	TP33
3457	CHLORONITROTOLUENES, SOLID	6.1	T2	III	6.1		LQ9	E1	P002 IBC08 LP02 R001	B3	MP10	T1	TP33
3458	NITROANISOLES, SOLID	6.1	T2	III	6.1	279	LQ9	E1	P002 IBC08 LP02 R001	B3	MP10	T1	TP33
3459	NITROBROMOBENZENES, SOLID	6.1	T2	III	6.1		LQ9	E1	P002 IBC08 LP02 R001	B3	MP10	T1	TP33
3460	N-ETHYLBENZYL-TOLUIDINES, SOLID	6.1	T2	III	6.1		LQ9	E1	P002 IBC08 LP02 R001	B3	MP10	T1	TP33
3462	TOXINS, EXTRACTED FROM LIVING SOURCES, SOLID, N.O.S.	6.1	T2	I	6.1	210 274	LQ0	E5	P002 IBC07		MP18	T6	TP33
3462	TOXINS, EXTRACTED FROM LIVING SOURCES, SOLID, N.O.S.	6.1	T2	II	6.1	210 274	LQ18	E4	P002 IBC08	B4	MP10	T3	TP33
3462	TOXINS, EXTRACTED FROM LIVING SOURCES, SOLID, N.O.S.	6.1	T2	III	6.1	210 274	LQ9	E1	P002 IBC08 R001	B3	MP10	T1	TP33

| ADR tank | | Vehicle for tank carriage | Transport category (Tunnel restriction code) | Special provisions for carriage | | | | Hazard identifi-cation No. | UN No. | Name and description |
| Tank code | Special provisions | | | Packages | Bulk | Loading, unloading and handling | Operation | | | |
4.3	4.3.5, 6.8.4	9.1.1.2	1.1.3.6 (8.6)	7.2.4	7.3.3	7.5.11	8.5	5.3.2.3		3.1.2
(12)	(13)	(14)	(15)	(16)	(17)	(18)	(19)	(20)	(1)	(2)
L10CH	TU14 TU15 TE19 TE21	AT	1 (C/E)			CV1 CV13 CV28	S9 S14	66	3440	SELENIUM COMPOUND, LIQUID, N.O.S.
L4BH	TU15 TE19	AT	2 (D/E)			CV13 CV28	S9 S19	60	3440	SELENIUM COMPOUND, LIQUID, N.O.S.
L4BH	TU15 TE19	AT	2 (E)			CV13 CV28	S9	60	3440	SELENIUM COMPOUND, LIQUID, N.O.S.
SGAH L4BH	TU15 TE19	AT	2 (D/E)	V11		CV13 CV28	S9 S19	60	3441	CHLORODINITRO-BENZENES, SOLID
SGAH L4BH	TU15 TE19	AT	2 (D/E)	V11		CV13 CV28	S9 S19	60	3442	DICHLOROANILINES, SOLID
SGAH L4BH	TU15 TE19	AT	2 (D/E)	V11		CV13 CV28	S9 S19	60	3443	DINITROBENZENES, SOLID
SGAH	TU15 TE19	AT	2 (D/E)	V11		CV13 CV28	S9 S19	60	3444	NICOTINE HYDROCHLORIDE, SOLID
SGAH	TU15 TE19	AT	2 (D/E)	V11		CV13 CV28	S9 S19	60	3445	NICOTINE SULPHATE, SOLID
SGAH L4BH	TU15 TE19	AT	2 (D/E)	V11		CV13 CV28	S9 S19	60	3446	NITROTOLUENES, SOLID
SGAH L4BH	TU15 TE19	AT	2 (D/E)	V11		CV13 CV28	S9 S19	60	3447	NITROXYLENES, SOLID
S10AH L10CH	TU14 TU15 TE19 TE21	AT	1 (C/E)			CV1 CV13 CV28	S9 S14	66	3448	TEAR GAS SUBSTANCE, SOLID, N.O.S.
SGAH L4BH	TU15 TE19	AT	2 (D/E)	V11		CV13 CV28	S9 S19	60	3448	TEAR GAS SUBSTANCE, SOLID, N.O.S.
S10AH L10CH	TU15 TE19	AT	1 (C/E)			CV1 CV13 CV28	S9 S14	66	3449	BROMOBENZYL CYANIDES, SOLID
S10AH L10CH	TU15 TE19	AT	1 (C/E)	V10 V12		CV1 CV13 CV28	S9 S14	66	3450	DIPHENYLCHLORO-ARSINE, SOLID
SGAH L4BH	TU15 TE19	AT	2 (D/E)	V11		CV13 CV28	S9 S19	60	3451	TOLUIDINES, SOLID
SGAH L4BH	TU15 TE19	AT	2 (D/E)	V11		CV13 CV28	S9 S19	60	3452	XYLIDINES, SOLID
SGAV L4BN		AT	3 (E)		VV9			80	3453	PHOSPHORIC ACID, SOLID
SGAH L4BH	TU15 TE19	AT	2 (D/E)	V11		CV13 CV28	S9 S19	60	3454	DINITROTOLUENES, SOLID
SGAH L4BH	TU15 TE19	AT	2 (D/E)	V11		CV13 CV28	S9 S19	68	3455	CRESOLS, SOLID
SGAN L4BN		AT	2 (E)	V11				X80	3456	NITROSYLSULPHURIC ACID, SOLID
SGAH L4BH	TU15 TE19	AT	2 (E)		VV9	CV13 CV28	S9	60	3457	CHLORONITROTOLUENES, SOLID
SGAH L4BH	TU15 TE19	AT	2 (E)		VV9	CV13 CV28	S9	60	3458	NITROANISOLES, SOLID
SGAH L4BH	TU15 TE19	AT	2 (E)		VV9	CV13 CV28	S9	60	3459	NITROBROMOBENZENES, SOLID
SGAH L4BH	TU15 TE19	AT	2 (E)		VV9	CV13 CV28	S9	60	3460	N-ETHYLBENZYL-TOLUIDINES, SOLID
S10AH L10CH	TU15 TE19	AT	1 (C/E)	V10 V12		CV1 CV13 CV28	S9 S14	66	3462	TOXINS, EXTRACTED FROM LIVING SOURCES, SOLID, N.O.S.
SGAH L4BH	TU15 TE19	AT	2 (D/E)	V11		CV13 CV28	S9 S19	60	3462	TOXINS, EXTRACTED FROM LIVING SOURCES, SOLID, N.O.S.
SGAH L4BH	TU15 TE19	AT	2 (E)		VV9	CV13 CV28	S9	60	3462	TOXINS, EXTRACTED FROM LIVING SOURCES, SOLID, N.O.S.

UN No.	Name and description	Class	Classification code	Packing group	Labels	Special provisions	Limited and excepted quantities		Packaging			Portable tanks and bulk containers	
									Packing instructions	Special packing provisions	Mixed packing provisions	Instructions	Special provisions
	3.1.2	2.2	2.2	2.1.1.3	5.2.2	3.3	3.4.6	3.5.1.2	4.1.4	4.1.4	4.1.10	4.2.5.2 7.3.2	4.2.5.3
(1)	(2)	(3a)	(3b)	(4)	(5)	(6)	(7a)	(7b)	(8)	(9a)	(9b)	(10)	(11)
3463	PROPIONIC ACID with not less than 90% acid by mass	8	CF1	II	8 +3		LQ22	E2	P001 IBC02		MP15	T7	TP2
3464	ORGANOPHOSPHORUS COMPOUND, TOXIC, SOLID, N.O.S.	6.1	T2	I	6.1	43 274	LQ0	E5	P002 IBC07		MP18	T6	TP33
3464	ORGANOPHOSPHORUS COMPOUND, TOXIC, SOLID, N.O.S.	6.1	T2	II	6.1	43 274	LQ18	E4	P002 IBC08	B4	MP10	T3	TP33
3464	ORGANOPHOSPHORUS COMPOUND, TOXIC, SOLID, N.O.S.	6.1	T2	III	6.1	43 274	LQ9	E1	P002 IBC08 LP02 R001	B3	MP10	T1	TP33
3465	ORGANOARSENIC COMPOUND, SOLID, N.O.S.	6.1	T3	I	6.1	274	LQ0	E5	P002 IBC07		MP18	T6	TP33
3465	ORGANOARSENIC COMPOUND, SOLID, N.O.S.	6.1	T3	II	6.1	274	LQ18	E4	P002 IBC08	B4	MP10	T3	TP33
3465	ORGANOARSENIC COMPOUND, SOLID, N.O.S.	6.1	T3	III	6.1	274	LQ9	E1	P002 IBC08 LP02 R001	B3	MP10	T1	TP33
3466	METAL CARBONYLS, SOLID, N.O.S.	6.1	T3	I	6.1	274 562	LQ0	E5	P002 IBC07		MP18	T6	TP33
3466	METAL CARBONYLS, SOLID, N.O.S.	6.1	T3	II	6.1	274 562	LQ18	E4	P002 IBC08	B4	MP10	T3	TP33
3466	METAL CARBONYLS, SOLID, N.O.S.	6.1	T3	III	6.1	274 562	LQ9	E1	P002 IBC08 LP02 R001	B3	MP10	T1	TP33
3467	ORGANOMETALLIC COMPOUND, TOXIC, SOLID, N.O.S.	6.1	T3	I	6.1	274 562	LQ0	E5	P002 IBC07		MP18	T6	TP33
3467	ORGANOMETALLIC COMPOUND, TOXIC, SOLID, N.O.S.	6.1	T3	II	6.1	274 562	LQ18	E4	P002 IBC08	B4	MP10	T3	TP33
3467	ORGANOMETALLIC COMPOUND, TOXIC, SOLID, N.O.S.	6.1	T3	III	6.1	274 562	LQ9	E1	P002 IBC08 LP02 R001	B3	MP10	T1	TP33
3468	HYDROGEN IN A METAL HYDRIDE STORAGE SYSTEM or HYDROGEN IN A METAL HYDRIDE STORAGE SYSTEM CONTAINED IN EQUIPMENT or HYDROGEN IN A METAL HYDRIDE STORAGE SYSTEM PACKED WITH EQUIPMENT	2	1F		2.1	321	LQ0	E0	P099		MP9		
3469	PAINT, FLAMMABLE, CORROSIVE (including paint, lacquer, enamel, stain, shellac, varnish, polish, liquid filler and liquid lacquer base) or PAINT RELATED MATERIAL, FLAMMABLE, CORROSIVE (including paint thinning and reducing compound)	3	FC	I	3 +8	163	LQ3	E0	P001		MP7 MP17	T11	TP2 TP27
3469	PAINT, FLAMMABLE, CORROSIVE (including paint, lacquer, enamel, stain, shellac, varnish, polish, liquid filler and liquid lacquer base) or PAINT RELATED MATERIAL, FLAMMABLE, CORROSIVE (including paint thinning and reducing compound)	3	FC	II	3 +8	163	LQ4	E2	P001 IBC02		MP19	T7	TP2 TP8 TP28

ADR tank		Vehicle for tank carriage	Transport category (Tunnel restriction code)	Special provisions for carriage				Hazard identification No.	UN No.	Name and description
Tank code	Special provisions			Packages	Bulk	Loading, unloading and handling	Operation			
4.3	4.3.5, 6.8.4	9.1.1.2	1.1.3.6 (8.6)	7.2.4	7.3.3	7.5.11	8.5	5.3.2.3		3.1.2
(12)	(13)	(14)	(15)	(16)	(17)	(18)	(19)	(20)	(1)	(2)
L4BN		FL	2 (D/E)				S2	83	3463	PROPIONIC ACID with not less than 90% acid by mass
S10AH L10CH	TU14 TU15 TE19 TE21	AT	1 (C/E)	V10 V12		CV1 CV13 CV28	S9 S14	66	3464	ORGANOPHOSPHORUS COMPOUND, TOXIC, SOLID, N.O.S.
SGAH L4BH	TU15 TE19	AT	2 (D/E)	V11		CV13 CV28	S9 S19	60	3464	ORGANOPHOSPHORUS COMPOUND, TOXIC, SOLID, N.O.S.
SGAH L4BH	TU15 TE19	AT	2 (E)		VV9	CV13 CV28	S9	60	3464	ORGANOPHOSPHORUS COMPOUND, TOXIC, SOLID, N.O.S.
S10AH L10CH	TU14 TU15 TE19 TE21	AT	1 (C/E)	V10 V12		CV1 CV13 CV28	S9 S14	66	3465	ORGANOARSENIC COMPOUND, SOLID, N.O.S.
SGAH L4BH	TU15 TE19	AT	2 (D/E)	V11		CV13 CV28	S9 S19	60	3465	ORGANOARSENIC COMPOUND, SOLID, N.O.S.
SGAH L4BH	TU15 TE19	AT	2 (E)		VV9	CV13 CV28	S9	60	3465	ORGANOARSENIC COMPOUND, SOLID, N.O.S.
S10AH L10CH	TU14 TU15 TE19 TE21	AT	1 (C/E)	V10 V12		CV1 CV13 CV28	S9 S14	66	3466	METAL CARBONYLS, SOLID, N.O.S.
SGAH L4BH	TU15 TE19	AT	2 (D/E)	V11		CV13 CV28	S9 S19	60	3466	METAL CARBONYLS, SOLID, N.O.S.
SGAH L4BH	TU15 TE19	AT	2 (E)		VV9	CV13 CV28	S9	60	3466	METAL CARBONYLS, SOLID, N.O.S.
S10AH L10CH	TU14 TU15 TE19 TE21	AT	1 (C/E)	V10 V12		CV1 CV13 CV28	S9 S14	66	3467	ORGANOMETALLIC COMPOUND, TOXIC, SOLID, N.O.S.
SGAH L4BH	TU15 TE19	AT	2 (D/E)	V11		CV13 CV28	S9 S19	60	3467	ORGANOMETALLIC COMPOUND, TOXIC, SOLID, N.O.S.
SGAH L4BH	TU15 TE19	AT	2 (E)		VV9	CV13 CV28	S9	60	3467	ORGANOMETALLIC COMPOUND, TOXIC, SOLID, N.O.S.
			2 (D)			CV9 CV10 CV36	S2 S20		3468	HYDROGEN IN A METAL HYDRIDE STORAGE SYSTEM or HYDROGEN IN A METAL HYDRIDE STORAGE SYSTEM CONTAINED IN EQUIPMENT or HYDROGEN IN A METAL HYDRIDE STORAGE SYSTEM PACKED WITH EQUIPMENT
L10CH	TU14 TE21	FL	1 (C/E)				S2 S20	338	3469	PAINT, FLAMMABLE, CORROSIVE (including paint, lacquer, enamel, stain, shellac, varnish, polish, liquid filler and liquid lacquer base) or PAINT RELATED MATERIAL, FLAMMABLE, CORROSIVE (including paint thinning and reducing compound)
L4BH		FL	2 (D/E)				S2 S20	338	3469	PAINT, FLAMMABLE, CORROSIVE (including paint, lacquer, enamel, stain, shellac, varnish, polish, liquid filler and liquid lacquer base) or PAINT RELATED MATERIAL, FLAMMABLE, CORROSIVE (including paint thinning and reducing compound)

UN No.	Name and description	Class	Classifi-cation code	Packing group	Labels	Special provi-sions	Limited and excepted quantities		Packaging			Portable tanks and bulk containers	
									Packing instruc-tions	Special packing provisions	Mixed packing provisions	Instruc-tions	Special provisions
3.1.2	3.1.2	2.2	2.2	2.1.1.3	5.2.2	3.3	3.4.6	3.5.1.2	4.1.4	4.1.4	4.1.10	4.2.5.2 7.3.2	4.2.5.3
(1)	(2)	(3a)	(3b)	(4)	(5)	(6)	(7a)	(7b)	(8)	(9a)	(9b)	(10)	(11)
3469	PAINT, FLAMMABLE, CORROSIVE (including paint, lacquer, enamel, stain, shellac, varnish, polish, liquid filler and liquid lacquer base) or PAINT RELATED MATERIAL, FLAMMABLE, CORROSIVE (including paint thinning and reducing compound)	3	FC	III	3 +8	163	LQ7	E1	P001 IBC03 R001		MP19	T4	TP1 TP29
3470	PAINT, CORROSIVE, FLAMMABLE (including paint, lacquer, enamel, stain, shellac, varnish, polish, liquid filler and liquid lacquer base) or PAINT RELATED MATERIAL, CORROSIVE, FLAMMABLE (including paint thinning and reducing compound)	8	CF1	II	8 +3	163	LQ22	E2	P001 IBC02		MP15	T7	TP2 TP8 TP28
3471	HYDROGENDIFLUORIDES SOLUTION, N.O.S.	8	CT1	II	8 +6.1		LQ22	E2	P001 IBC02		MP15	T7	TP2
3471	HYDROGENDIFLUORIDES SOLUTION, N.O.S.	8	CT1	III	8 +6.1		LQ7	E1	P001 IBC03 R001		MP19	T4	TP1
3472	CROTONIC ACID, LIQUID	8	C3	III	8		LQ7	E1	P001 IBC03 LP01 R001		MP19	T4	TP1
3473	FUEL CELL CARTRIDGES or FUEL CELL CARTRIDGES CONTAINED IN EQUIPMENT or FUEL CELL CARTRIDGES PACKED WITH EQUIPMENT containing flammable liquids	3	F1		3	328	LQ13	E0	P004				
3474	1-HYDROXYBENZO-TRIAZOLE, ANHYDROUS, WETTED with not less than 20% water, by mass	4.1	D	I	4.1		LQ0	E0	P406	PP48	MP2		
3475	ETHANOL AND GASOLINE MIXTURE or ETHANOL AND MOTOR SPIRIT MIXTURE or ETHANOL AND PETROL MIXTURE, with more than 10% ethanol	3	F1	II	3	333	LQ4	E2	P001 IBC02		MP19	T4	TP1
3476	FUEL CELL CARTRIDGES or FUEL CELL CARTRIDGES CONTAINED IN EQUIPMENT or FUEL CELL CARTRIDGES PACKED WITH EQUIPMENT, containing water-reactive substances	4.3	W3		4.3	328 334	LQ10 LQ11	E0	P004				
3477	FUEL CELL CARTRIDGES or FUEL CELL CARTRIDGES CONTAINED IN EQUIPMENT or FUEL CELL CARTRIDGES PACKED WITH EQUIPMENT, containing corrosive substances	8	C11		8	328 334	LQ12 LQ13	E0	P004				

ADR tank		Vehicle for tank carriage	Transport category (Tunnel restriction code)	Special provisions for carriage				Hazard identifi-cation No.	UN No.	Name and description
Tank code	Special provisions			Packages	Bulk	Loading, unloading and handling	Operation			
4.3	4.3.5, 6.8.4	9.1.1.2	1.1.3.6 (8.6)	7.2.4	7.3.3	7.5.11	8.5	5.3.2.3		3.1.2
(12)	(13)	(14)	(15)	(16)	(17)	(18)	(19)	(20)	(1)	(2)
L4BN		FL	3 (D/E)				S2	38	3469	PAINT, FLAMMABLE, CORROSIVE (including paint, lacquer, enamel, stain, shellac, varnish, polish, liquid filler and liquid lacquer base) or PAINT RELATED MATERIAL, FLAMMABLE, CORROSIVE (including paint thinning and reducing compound)
L4BN		FL	2 (D/E)				S2	83	3470	PAINT, CORROSIVE, FLAMMABLE (including paint, lacquer, enamel, stain, shellac, varnish, polish, liquid filler and liquid lacquer base) or PAINT RELATED MATERIAL, CORROSIVE, FLAMMABLE (including paint thinning and reducing compound)
L4DH	TU14 TE21	AT	2 (E)			CV13 CV28		86	3471	HYDROGENDIFLUORIDES SOLUTION, N.O.S.
L4DH	TU14 TE21	AT	3 (E)			CV13 CV28		86	3471	HYDROGENDIFLUORIDES SOLUTION, N.O.S.
L4BN		AT	3 (E)					80	3472	CROTONIC ACID, LIQUID
			3 (E)				S2		3473	FUEL CELL CARTRIDGES or FUEL CELL CARTRIDGES CONTAINED IN EQUIPMENT or FUEL CELL CARTRIDGES PACKED WITH EQUIPMENT containing flammable liquids
			1 (B)				S17		3474	1-HYDROXYBENZO-TRIAZOLE, ANHYDROUS, WETTED with not less than 20% water, by mass
LGBF		FL	2 (D/E)				S2 S20	33	3475	ETHANOL AND GASOLINE MIXTURE or ETHANOL AND MOTOR SPIRIT MIXTURE or ETHANOL AND PETROL MIXTURE, with more than 10% ethanol
			3 (E)	V1		CV23			3476	FUEL CELL CARTRIDGES or FUEL CELL CARTRIDGES CONTAINED IN EQUIPMENT or FUEL CELL CARTRIDGES PACKED WITH EQUIPMENT, containing water-reactive substances
			3 (E)						3477	FUEL CELL CARTRIDGES or FUEL CELL CARTRIDGES CONTAINED IN EQUIPMENT or FUEL CELL CARTRIDGES PACKED WITH EQUIPMENT, containing corrosive substances

UN No.	Name and description	Class	Classifi-cation code	Packing group	Labels	Special provi-sions	Limited and excepted quantities		Packaging			Portable tanks and bulk containers	
									Packing instruc-tions	Special packing provisions	Mixed packing provisions	Instruc-tions	Special provisions
	3.1.2	2.2	2.2	2.1.1.3	5.2.2	3.3	3.4.6	3.5.1.2	4.1.4	4.1.4	4.1.10	4.2.5.2 7.3.2	4.2.5.3
(1)	(2)	(3a)	(3b)	(4)	(5)	(6)	(7a)	(7b)	(8)	(9a)	(9b)	(10)	(11)
3478	FUEL CELL CARTRIDGES or FUEL CELL CARTRIDGES CONTAINED IN EQUIPMENT or FUEL CELL CARTRIDGES PACKED WITH EQUIPMENT, containing liquefied flammable gas	2	6F		2.1	328 338	LQ1	E0	P004				
3479	FUEL CELL CARTRIDGES or FUEL CELL CARTRIDGES CONTAINED IN EQUIPMENT or FUEL CELL CARTRIDGES PACKED WITH EQUIPMENT, containing hydrogen in metal hydride	2	6F		2.1	328 339	LQ1	E0	P004				
3480	LITHIUM ION BATTERIES (including lithium ion polymer batteries)	9	M4	II	9	188 230 310 636	LQ0	E0	P903 P903a P903b				
3481	LITHIUM ION BATTERIES CONTAINED IN EQUIPMENT or LITHIUM ION BATTERIES PACKED WITH EQUIPMENT (including lithium ion polymer batteries)	9	M4	II	9	188 230 636	LQ0	E0	P903 P903a P903b				

ADR tank		Vehicle for tank carriage	Transport category (Tunnel restriction code)	Special provisions for carriage				Hazard identifi- cation No.	UN No.	Name and description
Tank code	Special provisions			Packages	Bulk	Loading, unloading and handling	Operation			
4.3	4.3.5, 6.8.4	9.1.1.2	1.1.3.6 (8.6)	7.2.4	7.3.3	7.5.11	8.5	5.3.2.3		3.1.2
(12)	(13)	(14)	(15)	(16)	(17)	(18)	(19)	(20)	(1)	(2)
			2 (B/D)			CV9 CV12	S2		3478	FUEL CELL CARTRIDGES or FUEL CELL CARTRIDGES CONTAINED IN EQUIPMENT or FUEL CELL CARTRIDGES PACKED WITH EQUIPMENT, containing liquefied flammable gas
			2 (B/D)			CV9 CV12	S2		3479	FUEL CELL CARTRIDGES or FUEL CELL CARTRIDGES CONTAINED IN EQUIPMENT or FUEL CELL CARTRIDGES PACKED WITH EQUIPMENT, containing hydrogen in metal hydride
			2 (E)						3480	LITHIUM ION BATTERIES (including lithium ion polymer batteries)
			2 (E)						3481	LITHIUM ION BATTERIES CONTAINED IN EQUIPMENT or LITHIUM ION BATTERIES PACKED WITH EQUIPMENT (including lithium ion polymer batteries)

3.2.2   **Table B: Alphabetic index of substances and articles of ADR**

This index is an alphabetical list of the substances and articles which are listed in the UN numerical order in Table A of 3.2.1. It does not form an integral part of ADR. It has been submitted neither to the Working Party on the Transport of Dangerous Goods of the Inland Transport Committee for checking and approval nor to the Contracting Parties to ADR for formal acceptance. It has been prepared, with all necessary care by the Secretariat of the United Nations Economic Commission for Europe, in order to facilitate the consultation of Annexes A and B, but it cannot be relied upon as a substitute for the careful study and observance of the actual provisions of those annexes which, in case of conflict, are deemed to be authoritative.

NOTE 1: For the purpose of determining the alphabetical order the following information has been ignored, even when it forms part of the proper shipping name: numbers; Greek letters; the abbreviations "sec" and "tert"; and the letters "N" (nitrogen), "n" (normal), "o" (ortho), "m" (meta), "p" (para) and "N.O.S." (not otherwise specified).

NOTE 2: The name of a substance or article in block capital letters indicates a proper shipping name (see 3.1.2).

NOTE 3: The name of a substance or article in block capital letters followed by the word "see" indicates an alternative proper shipping name or part of a proper shipping name (except for PCBs) (see 3.1.2.1).

NOTE 4: An entry in lower case letters followed by the word "see" indicates that the entry is not a proper shipping name; it is a synonym.

NOTE 5: Where an entry is partly in block capital letters and partly in lower case letters, the latter part is considered not to be part of the proper shipping name (see 3.1.2.1).

NOTE 6: A proper shipping name may be used in the singular or plural, as appropriate, for the purposes of documentation and package marking (see 3.1.2.3).

NOTE 7: For the exact determination of a proper shipping name, see 3.1.2.

Name and description	UN No.	Class	Remarks	Name and description	UN No.	Class	Remarks
Accumulators, electric, see	2794	8		Activated charcoal, see	1362	4.2	
	2795	8		ADHESIVES containing flammable liquid	1133	3	
	2800	8					
	3028	8		ADIPONITRILE	2205	6.1	
	3292	4.3		Aeroplane flares, see	0093	1	
ACETAL	1088	3			0403	1	
ACETALDEHYDE	1089	3			0404	1	
ACETALDEHYDE AMMONIA	1841	9			0420	1	
ACETALDEHYDE OXIME	2332	3			0421	1	
ACETIC ACID, GLACIAL	2789	8		AEROSOLS	1950	2	
ACETIC ACID SOLUTION, more than 10% but not more than 80% acid, by mass	2790	8		AGENT, BLASTING, TYPE B	0331	1	
				AGENT, BLASTING, TYPE E	0332	1	
				AIR BAG INFLATORS	0503	1	
ACETIC ACID SOLUTION, more than 80% acid, by mass	2789	8			3268	9	
				AIR BAG MODULES	0503	1	
ACETIC ANHYDRIDE	1715	8			3268	9	
Acetoin, see	2621	3		AIR, COMPRESSED	1002	2	
ACETONE	1090	3		Aircraft evacuation slides, see	2990	9	
ACETONE CYANOHYDRIN, STABILIZED	1541	6.1		AIRCRAFT HYDRAULIC POWER UNIT FUEL TANK (containing a mixture of anhydrous hydrazine and methylhydrazine) (M86 fuel)	3165	3	
ACETONE OILS	1091	3					
ACETONITRILE	1648	3		Aircraft survival kits, see	2990	9	
ACETYL BROMIDE	1716	8		AIR, REFRIGERATED LIQUID	1003	2	
ACETYL CHLORIDE	1717	3		ALCOHOLATES SOLUTION, N.O.S., in alcohol	3274	3	
ACETYLENE, DISSOLVED	1001	2					
ACETYLENE, SOLVENT FREE	3374	2		Alcohol, denatured, see	1986	3	
Acetylene tetrabromide, see	2504	6.1			1987	3	
Acetylene tetrachloride, see	1702	6.1		Alcohol, industrial, see	1986	3	
ACETYL IODIDE	1898	8			1987	3	
ACETYL METHYL CARBINOL	2621	3		ALCOHOLS, N.O.S.	1987	3	
Acid butyl phosphate, see	1718	8		ALCOHOLS, FLAMMABLE, TOXIC, N.O.S.	1986	3	
Acid mixture, hydrofluoric and sulphuric, see	1786	8		ALCOHOLIC BEVERAGES, with more than 24% but not more than 70% alcohol by volume	3065	3	
Acid mixture, nitrating acid, see	1796	8					
Acid mixture, spent, nitrating acid, see	1826	8		ALCOHOLIC BEVERAGES, with more than 70% alcohol by volume	3065	3	
Acraldehyde, inhibited, see	1092	6.1		Aldehyde, see	1989	3	
ACRIDINE	2713	6.1		ALDEHYDES, N.O.S.	1989	3	
ACROLEIN DIMER, STABILIZED	2607	3		ALDEHYDES, FLAMMABLE, TOXIC, N.O.S.	1988	3	
ACROLEIN, STABILIZED	1092	6.1		ALDOL	2839	6.1	
ACRYLAMIDE, SOLID	2074	6.1		ALKALI METAL ALCOHOLATES, SELF-HEATING, CORROSIVE, N.O.S.	3206	4.2	
ACRYLAMIDE, SOLUTION	3426	6.1					
ACRYLIC ACID, STABILIZED	2218	8		ALKALI METAL ALLOY, LIQUID, N.O.S.	1421	4.3	
ACRYLONITRILE, STABILIZED	1093	3					
Actinolite, see	2590	9		ALKALI METAL AMALGAM, LIQUID	1389	4.3	
Activated carbon, see	1362	4.2					

Name and description	UN No.	Class	Remarks	Name and description	UN No.	Class	Remarks
ALKALI METAL AMALGAM, SOLID	3401	4.3		ALLYL GLYCIDYL ETHER	2219	3	
ALKALI METAL AMIDES	1390	4.3		ALLYL IODIDE	1723	3	
ALKALI METAL DISPERSION	1391	4.3		ALLYL ISOTHIOCYANATE, STABILIZED	1545	6.1	
Alkaline corrosive battery fluid, see	2797	8		ALLYLTRICHLOROSILANE, STABILIZED	1724	8	
ALKALINE EARTH METAL ALCOHOLATES, N.O.S.	3205	4.2		Aluminium alkyls, see	3394	4.2	
ALKALINE EARTH METAL ALLOY, N.O.S.	1393	4.3		Aluminium alkyl halides, liquid, see	3394	4.2	
ALKALINE EARTH METAL AMALGAM, LIQUID	1392	4.3		Aluminium alkyl halides, solid, see	3393	4.2	
				Aluminium alkyl hydrides, see	3394	4.2	
ALKALINE EARTH METAL AMALGAM, SOLID	3402	4.3		ALUMINIUM BOROHYDRIDE	2870	4.2	
ALKALINE EARTH METAL DISPERSION	1391	4.3		ALUMINIUM BOROHYDRIDE IN DEVICES	2870	4.2	
ALKALOIDS, LIQUID, N.O.S.	3140	6.1		ALUMINIUM BROMIDE, ANHYDROUS	1725	8	
ALKALOIDS, SOLID, N.O.S.	1544	6.1		ALUMINIUM BROMIDE SOLUTION	2580	8	
ALKALOID SALTS, LIQUID, N.O.S.	3140	6.1		ALUMINIUM CARBIDE	1394	4.3	
ALKALOID SALTS, SOLID, N.O.S.	1544	6.1		ALUMINIUM CHLORIDE, ANHYDROUS	1726	8	
Alkyl aluminium halides, see	3394	4.2		ALUMINIUM CHLORIDE SOLUTION	2581	8	
ALKYLPHENOLS, LIQUID, N.O.S. (including C_2-C_{12} homologues)	3145	8		Aluminium dross, see	3170	4.3	
ALKYLPHENOLS, SOLID, N.O.S. (including C_2-C_{12} homologues)	2430	8		ALUMINIUM FERROSILICON POWDER	1395	4.3	
ALKYLSULPHONIC ACIDS, LIQUID with more than 5% free sulphuric acid	2584	8		ALUMINIUM HYDRIDE	2463	4.3	
				ALUMINIUM NITRATE	1438	5.1	
				ALUMINIUM PHOSPHIDE	1397	4.3	
ALKYLSULPHONIC ACIDS, LIQUID with not more than 5% free sulphuric acid	2586	8		ALUMINIUM PHOSPHIDE PESTICIDE	3048	6.1	
ALKYLSULPHONIC ACIDS, SOLID with more than 5% free sulphuric acid	2583	8		ALUMINIUM POWDER, COATED	1309	4.1	
				ALUMINIUM POWDER, UNCOATED	1396	4.3	
ALKYLSULPHONIC ACIDS, SOLID with not more than 5% free sulphuric acid	2585	8		ALUMINIUM REMELTING BY-PRODUCTS	3170	4.3	
				ALUMINIUM RESINATE	2715	4.1	
ALKYLSULPHURIC ACIDS	2571	8		ALUMINIUM SILICON POWDER, UNCOATED	1398	4.3	
Allene, see	2200	2		ALUMINIUM SMELTING BY-PRODUCTS	3170	4.3	
ALLYL ACETATE	2333	3					
ALLYL ALCOHOL	1098	6.1		Amatols, see	0082	1	
ALLYLAMINE	2334	6.1		AMINES, FLAMMABLE, CORROSIVE, N.O.S.	2733	3	
ALLYL BROMIDE	1099	3		AMINES, LIQUID, CORROSIVE, N.O.S.	2735	8	
ALLYL CHLORIDE	1100	3					
Allyl chlorocarbonate, see	1722	6.1		AMINES, LIQUID, CORROSIVE, FLAMMABLE, N.O.S.	2734	8	
ALLYL CHLOROFORMATE	1722	6.1					
ALLYL ETHYL ETHER	2335	3		AMINES, SOLID, CORROSIVE, N.O.S.	3259	8	
ALLYL FORMATE	2336	3					

Name and description	UN No.	Class	Remarks	Name and description	UN No.	Class	Remarks
Aminobenzene, see	1547	6.1		AMMONIUM HYDROGENDIFLUORIDE SOLUTION	2817	8	
2-Aminobenzotrifluoruride, see	2942	6.1					
3-Aminobenzotrifluoruride, see	2948	6.1		AMMONIUM HYDROGEN SULPHATE	2506	8	
Aminobutane, see	1125	3					
2-AMINO-4-CHLOROPHENOL	2673	6.1		Ammonium hydrosulphide solution (treat as ammonium sulphide solution), see	2683	8	
2-AMINO-5-DIETHYL-AMINOPENTANE	2946	6.1					
				AMMONIUM METAVANADATE	2859	6.1	
2-AMINO-4,6-DINITROPHENOL, WETTED with not less than 20% water, by mass	3317	4.1		AMMONIUM NITRATE with more than 0.2% combustible substances, including any organic substance calculated as carbon, to the exclusion of any other added substance	0222	1	
2-(2-AMINOETHOXY) ETHANOL	3055	8					
N-AMINOETHYLPIPERAZINE	2815	8		AMMONIUM NITRATE with not more than 0.2% total combustible material, including any organic substance calculated as carbon, to the exclusion of any other added substance	1942	5.1	
1-Amino-2-nitrobenzene, see	1661	6.1					
1-Amino-3-nitrobenzene, see	1661	6.1					
1-Amino-4-nitrobenzene, see	1661	6.1					
AMINOPHENOLS (o-, m-, p-)	2512	6.1		AMMONIUM NITRATE EMULSION, intermediate for blasting explosives, liquid	3375	5.1	
AMINOPYRIDINES (o-, m-, p-)	2671	6.1		AMMONIUM NITRATE EMULSION, intermediate for blasting explosives, solid	3375	5.1	
AMMONIA, ANHYDROUS	1005	2					
AMMONIA SOLUTION relative density between 0.880 and 0.957 at 15 °C in water, with more than 10% but not more than 35% ammonia	2672	8		Ammonium nitrate explosive, see	0082 0331	1 1	
				AMMONIUM NITRATE BASED FERTILIZER	2067	5.1	
AMMONIA SOLUTION, relative density less than 0.880 at 15 °C in water, with more than 35% but not more than 50% ammonia	2073	2		Ammonium nitrate based fertilizer, uniform mixtures of the nitrogen/phosphate, nitrogen/potash or nitrogen/phosphate/potash type, containing not more than 70% ammonium nitrate and not more than 0.4% total combustible/organic material calculated as carbon or with not more than 45% ammonium nitrate and unrestricted combustible material	2071	9	Not subject to ADR
AMMONIA SOLUTION, relative density less than 0.880 at 15 °C in water, with more than 50% ammonia	3318	2					
AMMONIUM ARSENATE	1546	6.1					
Ammonium bichromate, see	1439	5.1					
Ammonium bifluoride solid, see	1727	8					
Ammonium bifluoride solution, see	2817	8		AMMONIUM NITRATE GEL, intermediate for blasting explosives, liquid	3375	5.1	
Ammonium bisulphate, see	2506	8					
Ammonium bisulphite solution, see	2693	8		AMMONIUM NITRATE GEL, intermediate for blasting explosives, solid	3375	5.1	
AMMONIUM DICHROMATE	1439	5.1					
AMMONIUM DINITRO-o-CRESOLATE, SOLID	1843	6.1		AMMONIUM NITRATE, LIQUID hot concentrated solution, in a concentration of more than 80% but not more than 93%	2426	5.1	
AMMONIUM DINITRO-o-CRESOLATE, SOLUTION	3424	6.1					
AMMONIUM FLUORIDE	2505	6.1		AMMONIUM NITRATE SUSPENSION, intermediate for blasting explosives, liquid	3375	5.1	
AMMONIUM FLUORO-SILICATE	2854	6.1					
Ammonium hexafluorosilicate, see	2854	6.1		AMMONIUM NITRATE SUSPENSION, intermediate for blasting explosives, solid	3375	5.1	
AMMONIUM HYDROGENDIFLUORIDE, SOLID	1727	8					

Name and description	UN No.	Class	Remarks	Name and description	UN No.	Class	Remarks
AMMONIUM PERCHLORATE	0402	1		AMMUNITION, PROOF	0363	1	
	1442	5.1		AMMUNITION, SMOKE with or without burster, expelling charge or propelling charge	0015	1	
Ammonium permanganate, see	1482	5.1			0016	1	
					0303	1	
AMMONIUM PERSULPHATE	1444	5.1		Ammunition, smoke (water-activated contrivances), white phosphorus with burster, expelling charge or propelling charge, see	0248	1	
AMMONIUM PICRATE dry or wetted with less than 10% water, by mass	0004	1					
AMMONIUM PICRATE, WETTED with not less than 10% water, by mass	1310	4.1		Ammunition, smoke (water-activated contrivances), without white phosphorus or phosphides with burster, expelling charge or propelling charge, see	0249	1	
AMMONIUM POLYSULPHIDE SOLUTION	2818	8					
AMMONIUM POLYVANADATE	2861	6.1		AMMUNITION, SMOKE, WHITE PHOSPHORUS with burster, expelling charge or propelling charge	0245	1	
Ammonium silicofluoride, see	2854	6.1			0246	1	
AMMONIUM SULPHIDE SOLUTION	2683	8		Ammunition, sporting, see	0012	1	
Ammunition, blank, see	0014	1			0328	1	
	0326	1			0339	1	
	0327	1			0417	1	
	0338	1		AMMUNITION, TEAR-PRODUCING, NON-EXPLOSIVE without burster or expelling charge, non-fuzed	2017	6.1	
	0413	1					
Ammunition, fixed	0005	1					
Ammunition, semi-fixed	0006	1					
Ammunition, separate loading, see	0007	1		AMMUNITION, TEAR-PRODUCING with burster, expelling charge or propelling charge	0018	1	
	0321	1			0019	1	
	0348	1			0301	1	
	0412	1					
AMMUNITION, ILLUMINATING with or without burster, expelling charge or propelling charge	0171	1		AMMUNITION, TOXIC with burster, expelling charge or propelling charge	0020	1	Carriage prohibited
	0254	1					
	0297	1					
AMMUNITION, INCENDIARY, liquid or gel, with burster, expelling charge or propelling charge	0247	1		AMMUNITION, TOXIC with burster, expelling charge or propelling charge	0021	1	Carriage prohibited
AMMUNITION, INCENDIARY with or without burster, expelling charge or propelling charge	0009	1		Ammunition, toxic (water-activated contrivances) with burster, expelling charge or propelling charge, see	0248	1	
	0010	1			0249	1	
	0300	1					
Ammunition, incendiary (water-activated contrivances) with burster, expelling charge or propelling charge, see	0248	1		AMMUNITION, TOXIC, NON-EXPLOSIVE without burster or expelling charge, non-fuzed	2016	6.1	
	0249	1					
AMMUNITION, INCENDIARY, WHITE PHOSPHORUS with burster, expelling charge or propelling charge	0243	1		Amosite, see	2212	9	
	0244	1		AMYL ACETATES	1104	3	
				AMYL ACID PHOSPHATE	2819	8	
Ammunition, industrial, see	0275	1		Amyl aldehyde, see	2058	3	
	0276	1		AMYLAMINE	1106	3	
	0277	1					
	0278	1		AMYL BUTYRATES	2620	3	
	0323	1		AMYL CHLORIDE	1107	3	
	0381	1		n-AMYLENE, see	1108	3	
Ammunition, lachrymatory, see	0018	1		AMYL FORMATES	1109	3	
	0019	1					
	0301	1		AMYL MERCAPTAN	1111	3	
	2017	1					
AMMUNITION, PRACTICE	0362	1		n-AMYL METHYL KETONE	1110	3	
	0488	1					

Name and description	UN No.	Class	Remarks	Name and description	UN No.	Class	Remarks
AMYL NITRATE	1112	3		ARSENICAL PESTICIDE, LIQUID, TOXIC	2994	6.1	
AMYL NITRITE	1113	3		ARSENICAL PESTICIDE, LIQUID, TOXIC, FLAMMABLE, flash-point not less than 23 °C	2993	6.1	
AMYLTRICHLOROSILANE	1728	8					
Anaesthetic ether, see	1155	3		ARSENICAL PESTICIDE, SOLID, TOXIC	2759	6.1	
ANILINE	1547	6.1					
Aniline chloride, see	1548	6.1		ARSENIC BROMIDE	1555	6.1	
ANILINE HYDROCHLORIDE	1548	6.1		Arsenic (III) bromide, see	1555	6.1	
Aniline oil, see	1547	6.1		Arsenic chloride, see	1560	6.1	
Aniline salt, see	1548	6.1		ARSENIC COMPOUND, LIQUID, N.O.S., inorganic, including: Arsenates, n.o.s., Arsenites, n.o.s.; and Arsenic sulphides, n.o.s.	1556	6.1	
ANISIDINES	2431	6.1					
ANISOLE	2222	3					
ANISOYL CHLORIDE	1729	8		ARSENIC COMPOUND, SOLID, N.O.S., inorganic, including: Arsenates, n.o.s.; Arsenites, n.o.s.; and Arsenic sulphides, n.o.s.	1557	6.1	
Anthophyllite, see	2590	9					
Antimonous chloride, see	1733	8					
ANTIMONY COMPOUND, INORGANIC, LIQUID, N.O.S.	3141	6.1		Arsenic (III) oxide, see	1561	6.1	
				Arsenic (V) oxide, see	1559	6.1	
ANTIMONY COMPOUND, INORGANIC, SOLID, N.O.S.	1549	6.1		ARSENIC PENTOXIDE	1559	6.1	
Antimony hydride, see	2676	2		Arsenic sulphides, see	1556	6.1	
ANTIMONY LACTATE	1550	6.1			1557	6.1	
Antimony (III) lactate, see	1550	6.1		ARSENIC TRICHLORIDE	1560	6.1	
ANTIMONY PENTACHLORIDE, LIQUID	1730	8		ARSENIC TRIOXIDE	1561	6.1	
				Arsenious chloride, see	1560	6.1	
ANTIMONY PENTACHLORIDE SOLUTION	1731	8		Arsenites, n.o.s., see	1556	6.1	
					1557	6.1	
ANTIMONY PENTAFLUORIDE	1732	8		Arsenous chloride, see	1560	6.1	
Antimony perchloride, liquid, see	1730	8		ARSINE	2188	2	
ANTIMONY POTASSIUM TARTRATE	1551	6.1		ARTICLES, EEI, see	0486	1	
				ARTICLES, EXPLOSIVE, EXTREMELY INSENSITIVE	0486	1	
ANTIMONY POWDER	2871	6.1					
ANTIMONY TRICHLORIDE	1733	8		ARTICLES, EXPLOSIVE, N.O.S.	0349	1	
A.n.t.u., see	1651	6.1			0350	1	
ARGON, COMPRESSED	1006	2			0351	1	
					0352	1	
ARGON, REFRIGERATED LIQUID	1951	2			0353	1	
					0354	1	
					0355	1	
Arsenates, n.o.s., see	1556	6.1			0356	1	
	1557	6.1			0462	1	
ARSENIC	1558	6.1			0463	1	
					0464	1	
ARSENIC ACID, LIQUID	1553	6.1			0465	1	
					0466	1	
ARSENIC ACID, SOLID	1554	6.1			0467	1	
ARSENICAL DUST	1562	6.1			0468	1	
					0469	1	
Arsenical flue dust, see	1562	6.1			0470	1	
ARSENICAL PESTICIDE, LIQUID, FLAMMABLE, TOXIC, flash-point less than 23 °C	2760	3			0471	1	
					0472	1	

Name and description	UN No.	Class	Remarks	Name and description	UN No.	Class	Remarks
ARTICLES, PRESSURIZED, HYDRAULIC (containing non-flammable gas)	3164	2		BARIUM AZIDE, WETTED with not less than 50% water, by mass	1571	4.1	
ARTICLES, PRESSURIZED, PNEUMATIC (containing non-flammable gas)	3164	2		Barium binoxide, see	1449	5.1	
				BARIUM BROMATE	2719	5.1	
ARTICLES, PYROPHORIC	0380	1		BARIUM CHLORATE, SOLID	1445	5.1	
ARTICLES, PYROTECHNIC for technical purposes	0428	1		BARIUM CHLORATE, SOLUTION	3405	5.1	
	0429	1		BARIUM COMPOUND, N.O.S.	1564	6.1	
	0430	1		BARIUM CYANIDE	1565	6.1	
	0431	1		Barium dioxide, see	1449	5.1	
	0432	1		BARIUM HYPOCHLORITE with more than 22% available chlorine	2741	5.1	
ARYLSULPHONIC ACIDS, LIQUID with more than 5% free sulphuric acid	2584	8					
				BARIUM NITRATE	1446	5.1	
ARYLSULPHONIC ACIDS, LIQUID with not more than 5% free sulphuric acid	2586	8		BARIUM OXIDE	1884	6.1	
				BARIUM PERCHLORATE, SOLID	1447	5.1	
ARYLSULPHONIC ACIDS, SOLID with more than 5% free sulphuric acid	2583	8		BARIUM PERCHLORATE, SOLUTION	3406	5.1	
				BARIUM PERMANGANATE	1448	5.1	
ARYLSULPHONIC ACIDS, SOLID with not more than 5% free sulphuric acid	2585	8		BARIUM PEROXIDE	1449	5.1	
				Barium selenate, see	2630	6.1	
				Barium selenite, see	2630	6.1	
Asbestos, blue or brown, see	2212	9		Barium superoxide, see	1449	5.1	
Asbestos, white, see	2590	9		BATTERIES, CONTAINING SODIUM	3292	4.3	
Asphalt, with a flash-point not greater than 60 °C, see	1999	3					
				BATTERIES, DRY, CONTAINING POTASSIUM HYDROXIDE SOLID, electric storage	3028	8	
Asphalt, with a flash-point above 60 °C, at or above its flash-point, see	3256	3					
				BATTERIES, WET, FILLED WITH ACID, electric storage	2794	8	
Asphalt, at or above 100 °C and below its flash-point, see	3257	9		BATTERIES, WET, FILLED WITH ALKALI, electric storage	2795	8	
Aviation regulated liquid, n.o.s.	3334	9	Not subject to ADR	BATTERIES, WET, NON-SPILLABLE, electric storage	2800	8	
Aviation regulated solid, n.o.s.	3335	9	Not subject to ADR	BATTERY FLUID, ACID	2796	8	
				BATTERY FLUID, ALKALI	2797	8	
AZODICARBONAMIDE	3242	4.1		Battery-powered vehicle or Battery-powered equipment	3171	9	Not subject to ADR
Bag charges, see	0242	1					
	0279	1		BENZALDEHYDE	1990	9	
	0414	1		BENZENE	1114	3	
Ballistite, see	0160	1		BENZENESULPHONYL CHLORIDE	2225	8	
	0161	1					
Bangalore torpedoes, see	0136	1		Benzenethiol, see	2337	6.1	
	0137	1		BENZIDINE	1885	6.1	
	0138	1		Benzol, see	1114	3	
	0294	1		Benzolene, see	1268	3	
BARIUM	1400	4.3		BENZONITRILE	2224	6.1	
BARIUM ALLOYS, PYROPHORIC	1854	4.2		BENZOQUINONE	2587	6.1	
BARIUM AZIDE, dry or wetted with less than 50% water, by mass	0224	1		Benzosulphochloride, see	2225	8	

Name and description	UN No.	Class	Remarks	Name and description	UN No.	Class	Remarks
BENZOTRICHLORIDE	2226	8		Blasting cap assemblies, see	0360	1	
BENZOTRIFLUORIDE	2338	3			0361	1	
BENZOYL CHLORIDE	1736	8		Blasting caps, electric, see	0030	1	
BENZYL BROMIDE	1737	6.1			0255	1	
BENZYL CHLORIDE	1738	6.1			0456	1	
Benzyl chlorocarbonate, see	1739	8		Blasting caps, non electric, see	0029	1	
BENZYL CHLOROFORMATE	1739	8			0267	1	
Benzyl cyanide, see	2470	6.1			0455	1	
BENZYLDIMETHYLAMINE	2619	8		Bleaching powder, see	2208	5.1	
BENZYLIDENE CHLORIDE	1886	6.1		BLUE ASBESTOS (crocidolite)	2212	9	
BENZYL IODIDE	2653	6.1		BOMBS with bursting charge	0033	1	
BERYLLIUM COMPOUND, N.O.S.	1566	6.1			0034	1	
BERYLLIUM NITRATE	2464	5.1			0035	1	
BERYLLIUM POWDER	1567	6.1			0291	1	
Bhusa	1327	4.1	Not subject to ADR	Bombs, illuminating, see	0254	1	
				BOMBS, PHOTO-FLASH	0037	1	
					0038	1	
					0039	1	
BICYCLO[2.2.1]HEPTA-2,5-DIENE, STABILIZED	2251	3			0299	1	
Bifluorides, n.o.s., see	1740	8		BOMBS, SMOKE, NON-EXPLOSIVE with corrosive liquid, without initiating device	2028	8	
BIOLOGICAL SUBSTANCE, CATEGORY B	3373	6.2		Bombs, target identification, see	0171	1	
					0254	1	
(BIO) MEDICAL WASTE, N.O.S.	3291	6.2			0297	1	
BIPYRIDILIUM PESTICIDE, LIQUID, FLAMMABLE, TOXIC, flash-point less than 23 °C	2782	3		BOMBS WITH FLAMMABLE LIQUID with bursting charge	0399	1	
					0400	1	
				BOOSTERS WITH DETONATOR	0225	1	
BIPYRIDILIUM PESTICIDE, LIQUID, TOXIC	3016	6.1			0268	1	
				BOOSTERS without detonator	0042	1	
BIPYRIDILIUM PESTICIDE, LIQUID, TOXIC, FLAMMABLE, flash-point not less than 23 °C	3015	6.1			0283	1	
				Borate and chlorate mixture, see	1458	5.1	
				BORNEOL	1312	4.1	
BIPYRIDILIUM PESTICIDE, SOLID, TOXIC	2781	6.1		BORON TRIBROMIDE	2692	8	
				BORON TRICHLORIDE	1741	2	
BISULPHATES, AQUEOUS SOLUTION	2837	8		BORON TRIFLUORIDE ACETIC ACID COMPLEX, LIQUID	1742	8	
BISULPHITES, AQUEOUS SOLUTION, N.O.S.	2693	8		BORON TRIFLUORIDE ACETIC ACID COMPLEX, SOLID	3419	8	
				BORON TRIFLUORIDE	1008	2	
Bitumen, with a flash-point not greater than 60 °C, see	1999	3		BORON TRIFLUORIDE DIETHYL ETHERATE	2604	8	
Bitumen, with a flash-point above 60 °C, at or above its flash-point, see	3256	3		BORON TRIFLUORIDE DIHYDRATE	2851	8	
				BORON TRIFLUORIDE DIMETHYL ETHERATE	2965	4.3	
Bitumen, at or above 100 °C and below its flash-point, see	3257	9		BORON TRIFLUORIDE PROPIONIC ACID COMPLEX, LIQUID	1743	8	
BLACK POWDER, COMPRESSED	0028	1					
BLACK POWDER, granular or as a meal	0027	1		BORON TRIFLUORIDE PROPIONIC ACID COMPLEX, SOLID	3420	8	
BLACK POWDER, IN PELLETS	0028	1					

Name and description	UN No.	Class	Remarks	Name and description	UN No.	Class	Remarks
BROMATES, INORGANIC, N.O.S.	1450	5.1		BUTADIENES, STABILIZED, (1,2-butadiene)	1010	2	
BROMATES, INORGANIC, AQUEOUS SOLUTION, N.O.S	3213	5.1		BUTADIENES, STABILIZED, (1,3-butadiene)	1010	2	
BROMINE	1744	8		BUTANE	1011	2	
BROMINE CHLORIDE	2901	2		BUTANEDIONE	2346	3	
BROMINE PENTAFLUORIDE	1745	5.1		Butane-1-thiol, see	2347	3	
BROMINE SOLUTION	1744	8		BUTANOLS	1120	3	
BROMINE TRIFLUORIDE	1746	5.1		1-Butanol, see	1120	3	
BROMOACETIC ACID, SOLID	3425	8		Butan-2-ol, see	1120	3	
BROMOACETIC ACID, SOLUTION	1938	8		Butanol, secondary, see	1120	3	
BROMOACETONE	1569	6.1		Butanol, tertiary, see	1120	3	
omega-Bromoacetone, see	2645	6.4		Butanone, see	1193	3	
BROMOACETYL BROMIDE	2513	8		2-Butenal, see	1143	6.1	
BROMOBENZENE	2514	3		Butene, see	1012	2	
BROMOBENZYL CYANIDES, LIQUID	1694	6.1		Bute-1-ene-3-one, see	1251	3	
BROMOBENZYL CYANIDES, SOLID	3449	6.1		1,2-Buteneoxide, see	3022	3	
				2-Buten-1-ol, see	2614	3	
1-BROMOBUTANE	1126	3		BUTYL ACETATES	1123	3	
2-BROMOBUTANE	2339	3		Butyl acetate, secondary, see	1123	3	
BROMOCHLOROMETHANE	1887	6.1		BUTYL ACID PHOSPHATE	1718	8	
1-BROMO-3-CHLORO-PROPANE	2688	6.1		BUTYL ACRYLATES, STABILIZED	2348	3	
1-Bromo-2,3-epoxypropane, see	2558	6.1		Butyl alcohols, see	1120	3	
Bromoethane, see	1891	6.1		n-BUTYLAMINE	1125	3	
2-BROMOETHYL ETHYL ETHER	2340	3		N-BUTYLANILINE	2738	6.1	
BROMOFORM	2515	6.1		sec-Butyl benzene, see	2709	3	
Bromomethane, see	1062	2		BUTYLBENZENES	2709	3	
1-BROMO-3-METHYL-BUTANE	2341	3		n-Butyl bromide, see	1126	3	
BROMOMETHYLPROPANES	2342	3		n-Butyl chloride, see	1127	3	
2-BROMO-2-NITROPROPANE-1,3-DIOL	3241	4.1		n-BUTYL CHLOROFORMATE	2743	6.1	
2-BROMOPENTANE	2343	3		tert-BUTYLCYCLOHEXYL CHLOROFORMATE	2747	6.1	
BROMOPROPANES	2344	3		BUTYLENES MIXTURE or 1-BUTYLENE or CIS-2-BUTYLENE or TRANS-2-BUTYLENE	1012	2	
3-BROMOPROPYNE	2345	3					
BROMOTRIFLUORO-ETHYLENE	2419	2		1,2-BUTYLENE OXIDE, STABILIZED	3022	3	
BROMOTRIFLUORO-METHANE	1009	2		Butyl ethers, see	1149	3	
BROWN ASBESTOS (amosite, mysorite)	2212	9		Butyl ethyl ether, see	1179	3	
BRUCINE	1570	6.1		n-BUTYL FORMATE	1128	3	
BURSTERS, explosive	0043	1		tert-BUTYL HYPOCHLORITE	3255	4.2	Carriage prohibited
BUTADIENES AND HYDROCARBON MIXTURE, STABILIZED, having a vapour pressure at 70 °C not exceeding 1.1 MPa (11 bar) and a density at 50 °C not lower than 0.525 kg/l	1010	2		N,n-BUTYLIMIDAZOLE	2690	6.1	
				N,n-Butyliminazole, see	2690	6.1	
				n-BUTYL ISOCYANATE	2485	6.1	

Name and description	UN No.	Class	Remarks	Name and description	UN No.	Class	Remarks
tert-BUTYL ISOCYANATE	2484	6.1		Calcium bisulphite solution, see	2693	8	
Butyl lithium, see	3394	4.2		CALCIUM CARBIDE	1402	4.3	
BUTYL MERCAPTAN	2347	3		CALCIUM CHLORATE	1452	5.1	
n-BUTYL METHACRYLATE, STABILIZED	2227	3		CALCIUM CHLORATE, AQUEOUS SOLUTION	2429	5.1	
BUTYL METHYL ETHER	2350	3		CALCIUM CHLORITE	1453	5.1	
BUTYL NITRITES	2351	3		CALCIUM CYANAMIDE with more than 0.1% calcium carbide	1403	4.3	
Butylphenols, liquid, see	3145	8		CALCIUM CYANIDE	1575	6.1	
Butylphenols, solid, see	2430	8		CALCIUM DITHIONITE	1923	4.2	
BUTYL PROPIONATES	1914	3		CALCIUM HYDRIDE	1404	4.3	
p-tert-Butyltoluene, see	2667	6.1		CALCIUM HYDROSULPHITE, see	1923	4.2	
BUTYLTOLUENES	2667	6.1		CALCIUM HYPOCHLORITE, DRY with more than 39% available chlorine (8.8% available oxygen)	1748	5.1	
BUTYLTRICHLOROSILANE	1747	8					
5-tert-BUTYL-2,4,6-TRINITRO-m-XYLENE	2956	4.1		CALCIUM HYPOCHLORITE, HYDRATED with not less than 5.5% but not more than 16% water	2880	5.1	
BUTYL VINYL ETHER, STABILIZED	2352	3		CALCIUM HYPOCHLORITE, HYDRATED MIXTURE with not less than 5.5% but not more than 16% water	2880	5.1	
But-1-yne, see	2452	2					
1,4-BUTYNEDIOL	2716	6.1					
2-Butyne-1,4-diol, see	2716	6.1		CALCIUM HYPOCHLORITE MIXTURE, DRY with more than 10% but not more than 39% available chlorine	2208	5.1	
BUTYRALDEHYDE	1129	3					
BUTYRALDOXIME	2840	3					
BUTYRIC ACID	2820	8		CALCIUM HYPOCHLORITE MIXTURE, DRY with more than 39% available chlorine (8.8% available oxygen)	1748	5.1	
BUTYRIC ANHYDRIDE	2739	8					
Butyrone, see	2710	3					
BUTYRONITRILE	2411	3					
Butyroyl chloride, see	2353	3		CALCIUM MANGANESE SILICON	2844	4.3	
BUTYRYL CHLORIDE	2353	3		CALCIUM NITRATE	1454	5.1	
Cable cutters, explosive, see	0070	1		Calcium oxide	1910	8	Not subject to ADR
CACODYLIC ACID	1572	6.1					
CADMIUM COMPOUND	2570	6.1					
CAESIUM	1407	4.3		CALCIUM PERCHLORATE	1455	5.1	
CAESIUM HYDROXIDE	2682	8		CALCIUM PERMANGANATE	1456	5.1	
CAESIUM HYDROXIDE SOLUTION	2681	8		CALCIUM PEROXIDE	1457	5.1	
				CALCIUM PHOSPHIDE	1360	4.3	
CAESIUM NITRATE	1451	5.1		CALCIUM, PYROPHORIC	1855	4.2	
Caffeine, see	1544	6.1		CALCIUM RESINATE	1313	4.1	
Cajeputene, see	2052	3		CALCIUM RESINATE, FUSED	1314	4.1	
CALCIUM	1401	4.3		Calcium selenate, see	2630	6.1	
CALCIUM ALLOYS, PYROPHORIC	1855	4.2		CALCIUM SILICIDE	1405	4.3	
				Calcium silicon, see	1405	4.3	
CALCIUM ARSENATE	1573	6.1		Calcium superoxide, see	1457	5.1	
CALCIUM ARSENATE AND CALCIUM ARSENITE MIXTURE, SOLID	1574	6.1		Camphanone, see	2717	4.1	
				CAMPHOR OIL	1130	3	

Name and description	UN No.	Class	Remarks	Name and description	UN No.	Class	Remarks
CAMPHOR, synthetic	2717	4.1		CARTRIDGES FOR WEAPONS with bursting charge	0005	1	
CAPROIC ACID	2829	8			0006	1	
CARBAMATE PESTICIDE, LIQUID, FLAMMABLE, TOXIC, flash-point less than 23 °C	2758	3			0007	1	
					0321	1	
					0348	1	
					0412	1	
CARBAMATE PESTICIDE, LIQUID, TOXIC	2992	6.1		CARTRIDGES FOR WEAPONS, BLANK	0014	1	
					0326	1	
CARBAMATE PESTICIDE, LIQUID, TOXIC, FLAMMABLE, flash-point not less than 23 °C	2991	6.1			0327	1	
					0338	1	
					0413	1	
CARBAMATE PESTICIDE, SOLID, TOXIC	2757	6.1		CARTRIDGES FOR WEAPONS, INERT PROJECTILE	0012	1	
					0328	1	
Carbolic acid, see	1671	6.1			0339	1	
	2312	6.1			0417	1	
	2821	6.1		Cartridges, illuminating, see	0171	1	
					0254	1	
CARBON, animal or vegetable origin	1361	4.2			0297	1	
				CARTRIDGES, OIL WELL	0277	1	
CARBON, ACTIVATED	1362	4.2			0278	1	
Carbon bisulphide, see	1131	3		CARTRIDGES, POWER DEVICE	0275	1	
Carbon black (animal or vegetable origin), see	1361	4.2			0276	1	
					0323	1	
					0381	1	
CARBON DIOXIDE	1013	2		CARTRIDGES, SIGNAL	0054	1	
Carbon dioxide and ethylene oxide mixture, see	1041	2			0312	1	
	1952	2			0405	1	
	3300	2		CARTRIDGES, SMALL ARMS	0012	1	
CARBON DIOXIDE, REFRIGERATED LIQUID	2187	2			0339	1	
					0417	1	
Carbon dioxide, solid	1845	9	Not subject to ADR	CARTRIDGES, SMALL ARMS, BLANK	0014	1	
					0327	1	
					0338	1	
CARBON DISULPHIDE	1131	3		Cartridges, starter, jet engine, see	0275	1	
Carbonic anhydride, see	1013	2			0276	1	
	1845	9			0323	1	
	2187	2			0381	1	
CARBON MONOXIDE, COMPRESSED	1016	2		CASES, CARTRIDGE, EMPTY, WITH PRIMER	0055	1	
					0379	1	
Carbon oxysulphide, see	2204	2.3		CASES, COMBUSTIBLE, EMPTY, WITHOUT PRIMER	0446	1	
CARBON TETRABROMIDE	2516	6.1			0447	1	
CARBON TETRACHLORIDE	1846	6.1		Casinghead gasoline, see	1203	3	
Carbonyl chloride, see	1076	2		CASTOR BEANS	2969	9	
CARBONYL FLUORIDE	2417	2		CASTOR FLAKE	2969	9	
CARBONYL SULPHIDE	2204	2		CASTOR MEAL	2969	9	
Cartridge cases, empty, primed, see	0055	1		CASTOR POMACE	2969	9	
	0379	1		CAUSTIC ALKALI LIQUID, N.O.S.	1719	8	
Cartridges, actuating, for fire extinguisher or apparatus valve, see	0275	1					
	0276	1		Caustic potash, see	1814	8	
	0323	1		Caustic soda, see	1824	8	
	0381	1		Caustic soda liquor, see	1824	8	
Cartridges, explosive, see	0048	1		CELLS, CONTAINING SODIUM	3292	4.3	
CARTRIDGES, FLASH	0049	1		CELLULOID in block, rods, rolls, sheets, tubes, etc., except scrap	2000	4.1	
	0050	1					

Name and description	UN No.	Class	Remarks	Name and description	UN No.	Class	Remarks
CELLULOID, SCRAP	2002	4.2		CHLORIC ACID, AQUEOUS SOLUTION with not more than 10% chloric acid	2626	5.1	
Cement, see	1133	3		CHLORINE	1017	2	
CERIUM, slabs, ingots or rods	1333	4.1		CHLORINE PENTAFLUORIDE	2548	2	
CERIUM, turnings or gritty powder	3078	4.3		CHLORINE TRIFLUORIDE	1749	2	
Cer mishmetall, see	1323	4.1		CHLORITES, INORGANIC, N.O.S.	1462	5.1	
Charcoal, activated, see	1362	4.1		CHLORITE SOLUTION	1908	8	
Charcoal, non-activated, see	1361	4.2		Chloroacetaldehyde, see	2232	6.1	
CHARGES, BURSTING, PLASTICS BONDED	0457 0458 0459 0460	1 1 1 1		CHLOROACETIC ACID, MOLTEN	3250	6.1	
				CHLOROACETIC ACID, SOLID	1751	6.1	
CHARGES, DEMOLITION	0048	1		CHLOROACETIC ACID SOLUTION	1750	6.1	
CHARGES, DEPTH	0056	1		CHLOROACETONE, STABILIZED	1695	6.1	
Charges, expelling, explosive, for fire extinguishers, see	0275 0276 0323 0381	1 1 1 1		CHLOROACETONITRILE	2668	6.1	
				CHLOROACETOPHENONE, LIQUID	3416	6.1	
CHARGES, EXPLOSIVE, COMMERCIAL without detonator	0442 0443 0444 0445	1 1 1 1		CHLOROACETOPHENONE, SOLID	1697	6.1	
				CHLOROACETYL CHLORIDE	1752	6.1	
CHARGES, PROPELLING	0271 0272 0415 0491	1 1 1 1		CHLOROANILINES, LIQUID	2019	6.1	
				CHLOROANILINES, SOLID	2018	6.1	
				CHLOROANISIDINES	2233	6.1	
CHARGES, PROPELLING, FOR CANNON	0242 0279 0414	1 1 1		CHLOROBENZENE	1134	3	
				CHLOROBENZO-TRIFLUORIDES	2234	3	
CHARGES, SHAPED, FLEXIBLE, LINEAR	0237 0288	1 1		CHLOROBENZYL CHLORIDES, LIQUID	2235	6.1	
CHARGES, SHAPED, without detonator	0059 0439 0440 0441	1 1 1 1		CHLOROBENZYL CHLORIDES, SOLID	3427	6.1	
				1-Chloro-3-bromopropane, see	2688	6.1	
				1-Chlorobutane, see	1127	3	
CHARGES, SUPPLEMENTARY, EXPLOSIVE	0060	1		2-Chlorobutane, see	1127	3	
CHEMICAL KIT	3316	9		CHLOROBUTANES	1127	3	
CHEMICAL SAMPLE, TOXIC	3315	6.1		CHLOROCRESOLS, SOLUTION	2669	6.1	
Chile saltpetre, see	1498	5.1		CHLOROCRESOLS, SOLID	3437	6.1	
CHLORAL, ANHYDROUS, STABILIZED	2075	6.1		CHLORODIFLUORO-BROMOMETHANE	1974	2	
CHLORATE AND BORATE MIXTURE	1458	5.1		1-CHLORO-1,1-DIFLUORO-ETHANE	2517	2	
CHLORATE AND MAGNESIUM CHLORIDE MIXTURE, SOLID	1459	5.1		CHLORODIFLUORO-METHANE	1018	2	
CHLORATE AND MAGNESIUM CHLORIDE MIXTURE, SOLUTION	3407	5.1		CHLORODIFLUORO-METHANE AND CHLORO-PENTAFLUOROETHANE MIXTURE with fixed boiling point, with approximately 49% chlorodifluoromethane	1973	2	
CHLORATES, INORGANIC, N.O.S.	1461	5.1					
CHLORATES, INORGANIC, AQUEOUS SOLUTION, N.O.S.	3210	5.1		3-Chloro-1,2-dihydroxypropane, see	2689	6.1	
				Chlorodimethyl ether, see	1239	6.1	

Name and description	UN No.	Class	Remarks	Name and description	UN No.	Class	Remarks
CHLORODINITRO-BENZENES, LIQUID	1577	6.1		CHLOROPICRIN AND METHYL BROMIDE MIXTURE, with more than 2% chloropicrin	1581	2	
CHLORODINITRO-BENZENES, SOLID	3441	6.1		CHLOROPICRIN AND METHYL CHLORIDE MIXTURE	1582	2	
2-CHLOROETHANAL	2232	6.1		CHLOROPICRIN MIXTURE, N.O.S.	1583	6.1	
Chloroethane, see	1037	2					
Chloroethane nitrile, see	2668	6.1		CHLOROPLATINIC ACID, SOLID	2507	8	
2-Chloroethanol, see	1135	6.1		CHLOROPRENE, STABILIZED	1991	3	
CHLOROFORM	1888	6.1		1-CHLOROPROPANE	1278	3	
CHLOROFORMATES, TOXIC, CORROSIVE, N.O.S.	3277	6.1		2-CHLOROPROPANE	2356	3	
CHLOROFORMATES, TOXIC, CORROSIVE, FLAMMABLE, N.O.S.	2742	6.1		3-Chloro-propanediol-1,2, see	2689	6.1	
				3-CHLOROPROPANOL-1	2849	6.1	
				2-CHLOROPROPENE	2456	3	
Chloromethane, see	1063	2		3-Chloropropene, see	1100	3	
1-Chloro-3-methylbutane, see	1107	3		3-Chloroprop-1-ene, see	1100	3	
2-Chloro-2-methylbutane, see	1107	3					
CHLOROMETHYL CHLOROFORMATE	2745	6.1		2-CHLOROPROPIONIC ACID	2511	8	
Chloromethyl cyanide, see	2668	6.1		2-CHLOROPYRIDINE	2822	6.1	
CHLOROMETHYL ETHYL ETHER	2354	3		CHLOROSILANES, CORROSIVE, N.O.S.	2987	8	
Chloromethyl methyl ether, see	1239	6.1		CHLOROSILANES, CORROSIVE, FLAMMABLE, N.O.S.	2986	8	
3-CHLORO-4-METHYL-PHENYL ISOCYANATE, LIQUID	2236	6.1		CHLOROSILANES, FLAMMABLE, CORROSIVE, N.O.S.	2985	3	
3-CHLORO-4-METHYL-PHENYL ISOCYANATE, SOLID	3428	6.1					
3-Chloro-2-methylprop-1-ene, see	2554	3		CHLOROSILANES, TOXIC, CORROSIVE, N.O.S.	3361	6.1	
CHLORONITROANILINES	2237	6.1		CHLOROSILANES, TOXIC, CORROSIVE, FLAMMABLE, N.O.S.	3362	6.1	
CHLORONITROBENZENES LIQUID	3409	6.1					
CHLORONITROBENZENES SOLID	1578	6.1		CHLOROSILANES, WATER-REACTIVE, FLAMMABLE, CORROSIVE, N.O.S.	2988	4.3	
CHLORONITROTOLUENES, LIQUID	2433	6.1					
CHLORONITROTOLUENES, SOLID	3457	6.1		CHLOROSULPHONIC ACID (with or without sulphur trioxide)	1754	8	
CHLOROPENTAFLUORO-ETHANE	1020	2		1-CHLORO-1,2,2,2-TETRA-FLUOROETHANE	1021	2	
CHLOROPHENOLATES, LIQUID	2904	8		CHLOROTOLUENES	2238	3	
CHLOROPHENOLATES, SOLID	2905	8		4-CHLORO-o-TOLUIDINE HYDROCHLORIDE, SOLID	1579	6.1	
CHLOROPHENOLS, LIQUID	2021	6.1		4-CHLORO-o-TOLUIDINE HYDROCHLORIDE, SOLUTION	3410	6.1	
CHLOROPHENOLS, SOLID	2020	6.1		CHLOROTOLUIDINES LIQUID	3429	6.1	
CHLOROPHENYL-TRICHLOROSILANE	1753	8		CHLOROTOLUIDINES SOLID	3429	6.1	
CHLOROPICRIN	1580	6.1		1-CHLORO-2,2,2-TRIFLUORO-ETHANE	1983	2	
				Chlorotrifluoroethylene, see	1082	2	
				CHLOROTRIFLUORO-METHANE	1022	2	

Name and description	UN No.	Class	Remarks	Name and description	UN No.	Class	Remarks
CHLOROTRIFLUORO-METHANE AND TRIFLUOROMETHANE AZEOTROPIC MIXTURE with approximately 60% chlorotrifluoromethane	2599	2		COMPONENTS, EXPLOSIVE TRAIN, N.O.S.	0382 0383 0384 0461	1 1 1 1	
				Composition B, see	0118	1	
Chromic acid, solid, see	1463	5.1		COMPRESSED GAS, N.O.S.	1956	2	
CHROMIC ACID SOLUTION	1755	8		COMPRESSED GAS, FLAMMABLE, N.O.S.	1954	2	
Chromic anhydride, solid, see	1463	5.1		COMPRESSED GAS, OXIDIZING, N.O.S.	3156	2	
CHROMIC FLUORIDE, SOLID	1756	8					
CHROMIC FLUORIDE SOLUTION	1757	8		COMPRESSED GAS, TOXIC, N.O.S.	1955	2	
Chromic nitrate, see	2720	5.1		COMPRESSED GAS, TOXIC, CORROSIVE, N.O.S.	3304	2	
Chromium (VI) dichloride dioxide, see	1758	8		COMPRESSED GAS, TOXIC, FLAMMABLE, N.O.S.	1953	2	
Chromium (III) fluoride, solid, see	1756	8		COMPRESSED GAS, TOXIC, FLAMMABLE, CORROSIVE, N.O.S.	3305	2	
CHROMIUM NITRATE	2720	5.1					
Chromium (III) nitrate, see	2720	5.1		COMPRESSED GAS, TOXIC, OXIDIZING, N.O.S.	3303	2	
CHROMIUM OXYCHLORIDE	1758	8					
CHROMIUM TRIOXIDE, ANHYDROUS	1463	5.1		COMPRESSED GAS, TOXIC, OXIDIZING, CORROSIVE, N.O.S.	3306	2	
CHROMOSULPHURIC ACID	2240	8		CONTRIVANCES, WATER-ACTIVATED with burster, expelling charge or propelling charge	0248 0249	1 1	
Chryosotile, see	2590	9					
Cinene, see	2052	3					
Cinnamene, see	2055	3		COPPER ACETOARSENITE	1585	6.1	
Cinnamol, see	2055	3		COPPER ARSENITE	1586	6.1	
CLINICAL WASTE, UNSPECIFIED, N.O.S.	3291	6.2		Copper (II) arsenite, see	1586	6.1	
COAL GAS, COMPRESSED	1023	2		COPPER BASED PESTICIDE, LIQUID, FLAMMABLE, TOXIC, flash-point less than 23 °C	2776	3	
COAL TAR DISTILLATES, FLAMMABLE	1136	3					
Coal tar naphtha, see	1268	3		COPPER BASED PESTICIDE, LIQUID, TOXIC	3010	6.1	
Coal tar oil, see	1136	3		COPPER BASED PESTICIDE, LIQUID, TOXIC, FLAMMABLE, flash-point not less than 23 °C	3009	6.1	
COATING SOLUTION (includes surface treatments or coatings used for industrial or other purposes such as vehicle under coating, drum or barrel lining)	1139	3					
				COPPER BASED PESTICIDE, SOLID, TOXIC	2775	6.1	
COBALT NAPHTHENATES, POWDER	2001	4.1		COPPER CHLORATE	2721	5.1	
COBALT RESINATE, PRECIPITATED	1318	4.1		Copper (II) chlorate, see	2721	5.1	
				COPPER CHLORIDE	2802	8	
Cocculus, see	3172 3462	6.1 6.1		COPPER CYANIDE	1587	6.1	
Collodion cottons, see	0340 0341 0342 2059 2555 2556 2557	1 1 1 3 4.1 4.1 4.1		Copper selenate, see	2630	6.1	
				Copper selenite, see	2630	6.1	
				COPRA	1363	4.2	
				CORD, DETONATING, flexible	0065 0289	1 1	
				CORD, DETONATING, metal clad	0102 0290	1 1	

Name and description	UN No.	Class	Remarks	Name and description	UN No.	Class	Remarks
CORD, DETONATING, MILD EFFECT, metal clad	0104	1		COUMARIN DERIVATIVE PESTICIDE, LIQUID, TOXIC, FLAMMABLE, flash-point not less than 23 °C	3025	6.1	
CORD, IGNITER	0066	1					
Cordite, see	0160	1		COUMARIN DERIVATIVE PESTICIDE, SOLID, TOXIC	3027	6.1	
	0161	1					
CORROSIVE LIQUID, N.O.S.	1760	8		Creosote, see	2810	6.1	
CORROSIVE LIQUID, ACIDIC, INORGANIC, N.O.S.	3264	8		Creosote salts, see	1334	4.1	
				CRESOLS, LIQUID	2076	6.1	
CORROSIVE LIQUID, ACIDIC, ORGANIC, N.O.S.	3265	8		CRESOLS, SOLID	3455	6.1	
CORROSIVE LIQUID, BASIC, INORGANIC, N.O.S.	3266	8		CRESYLIC ACID	2022	6.1	
				Crocidolite, see	2212	9	
CORROSIVE LIQUID, BASIC, ORGANIC, N.O.S.	3267	8		CROTONALDEHYDE or CROTONALDEHYDE, STABILIZED	1143	6.1	
CORROSIVE LIQUID, FLAMMABLE, N.O.S.	2920	8					
CORROSIVE LIQUID, OXIDIZING, N.O.S.	3093	8		CROTONIC ACID, LIQUID	3472	8	
CORROSIVE LIQUID, SELF-HEATING, N.O.S.	3301	8		CROTONIC ACID, SOLID	2823	8	
				Crotonic aldehyde / Crotonic aldehyde, stabilized, see	1143	6.1	
CORROSIVE LIQUID, TOXIC, N.O.S.	2922	8		CROTONYLENE	1144	3	
CORROSIVE LIQUID, WATER-REACTIVE, N.O.S.	3094	8		Crude naphtha, see	1268	3	
				Cumene, see	1918	3	
CORROSIVE SOLID, N.O.S.	1759	8		Cupric chlorate, see	2721	5.1	
CORROSIVE SOLID, ACIDIC, INORGANIC, N.O.S.	3260	8		CUPRIETHYLENEDIAMINE SOLUTION	1761	8	
CORROSIVE SOLID, ACIDIC, ORGANIC, N.O.S.	3261	8		Cut backs, with a flash-point not greater than 60 °C, see	1999	3	
CORROSIVE SOLID, BASIC, INORGANIC, N.O.S.	3262	8		Cut backs, with a flash-point above 60 °C, at or above its flash-point, see	3256	3	
CORROSIVE SOLID, BASIC, ORGANIC, N.O.S.	3263	8		Cut backs, at or above 100 °C and below its flash-point, see	3257	9	
CORROSIVE SOLID, FLAMMABLE, N.O.S.	2921	8		CUTTERS, CABLE, EXPLOSIVE	0070	1	
CORROSIVE SOLID, OXIDIZING, N.O.S.	3084	8		CYANIDE SOLUTION, N.O.S.	1935	6.1	
CORROSIVE SOLID, SELF-HEATING, N.O.S.	3095	8		CYANIDES, INORGANIC, SOLID, N.O.S.	1588	6.1	
CORROSIVE SOLID, TOXIC, N.O.S.	2923	8		Cyanides, organic, flammable, toxic, n.o.s., see	3273	3	
CORROSIVE SOLID, WATER-REACTIVE, N.O.S.	3096	8		Cyanides, organic, toxic, n.o.s., see	3276	6.1	
					3439		
COTTON WASTE, OILY	1364	4.2		Cyanides, organic, toxic, flammable, n.o.s., see	3275	6.1	
COTTON, WET	1365	4.2		Cyanoacetonitrile, see	2647	6.1	
COUMARIN DERIVATIVE PESTICIDE, LIQUID, FLAMMABLE, TOXIC, flash-point less than 23 °C	3024	3		CYANOGEN	1026	2	
				CYANOGEN BROMIDE	1889	6.1	
				CYANOGEN CHLORIDE, STABILIZED	1589	2	
COUMARIN DERIVATIVE PESTICIDE, LIQUID, TOXIC	3026	6.1		CYANURIC CHLORIDE	2670	8	
				CYCLOBUTANE	2601	2	

Name and description	UN No.	Class	Remarks	Name and description	UN No.	Class	Remarks
CYCLOBUTYL CHLOROFORMATE	2744	6.1		CYCLOTRIMETHYLENE-TRINITRAMINE AND CYCLOTETRAMETHYLENE-TETRANITRAMINE MIXTURE, DESENSITIZED with not less than 10% phlegmatiser by mass	0391	1	
1,5,9-CYCLODODECA-TRIENE	2518	6.1					
CYCLOHEPTANE	2241	3					
CYCLOHEPTATRIENE	2603	3		CYCLOTRIMETHYLENE-TRINITRAMINE AND CYCLOTETRAMETHYLENE-TETRANITRAMINE MIXTURE, WETTED with not less than 15% water, by mass	0391	1	
1,3,5-Cycloheptatriene, see	2603	3					
CYCLOHEPTENE	2242	3					
1,4-Cyclohexadienedione, see	2587	6.1					
CYCLOHEXANE	1145	3					
Cyclehexanethiol, see	3054	3		CYCLOTRIMETHYLENE-TRINITRAMINE, DESENSITIZED	0483	1	
CYCLOHEXANONE	1915	3					
CYCLOHEXENE	2256	3					
CYCLOHEXENYLTRI-CHLOROSILANE	1762	8		CYCLOTRIMETHYLENE-TRINITRAMINE, WETTED with not less than 15% water, by mass	0072	1	
CYCLOHEXYL ACETATE	2243	3		CYMENES	2046	3	
CYCLOHEXYLAMINE	2357	8		Cymol, see	2046	3	
CYCLOHEXYL ISOCYANATE	2488	6.1		Deanol, see	2051	8	
CYCLOHEXYL MERCAPTAN	3054	3		Dangerous goods in machinery or dangerous goods in apparatus	3363	9	Not subject to ADR [see also 1.1.3.1 (b)]
CYCLOHEXYLTRICHLORO-SILANE	1763	8					
CYCLONITE AND CYCLOTETRAMETHYLENE-TETRANITRAMINE MIXTURE, WETTED with not less than 15% water, by mass or DESENSITIZED with not less than 10% phlegmatiser by mass, see	0391	1		DECABORANE	1868	4.1	
				DECAHYDRONAPHTHALENE	1147	3	
				Decalin, see	1147	3	
				n-DECANE	2247	3	
				DEFLAGRATING METAL SALTS OF AROMATIC NITRODERIVATIVES, N.O.S.	0132	1	
				Depth charge, see	0056	1	
CYCLONITE, DESENSITIZED, see	0483	1		DESENSITIZED EXPLOSIVE, LIQUID, N.O.S.	3379	3	
CYCLONITE, WETTED with not less than 15% water, by mass, see	0072	1		DESENSITIZED EXPLOSIVE, SOLID, N.O.S.	3380	4.1	
CYCLOOCTADIENES	2520	3		Detonating relays, see	0029	1	
CYCLOOCTADIENE PHOSPHINES, see	2940	4.2			0267	1	
					0360	1	
					0361	1	
CYCLOOCTATETRAENE	2358	3			0455	1	
CYCLOPENTANE	1146	3			0500	1	
CYCLOPENTANOL	2244	3		DETONATOR ASSEMBLIES, NON-ELECTRIC for blasting	0360	1	
CYCLOPENTANONE	2245	3			0361	1	
CYCLOPENTENE	2246	3			0500	1	
CYCLOPROPANE	1027	2		DETONATORS FOR AMMUNITION	0073	1	
CYCLOTETRAMETHYLENE-TETRANITRAMINE, DESENSITIZED	0484	1			0364	1	
					0365	1	
					0366	1	
CYCLOTETRAMETHYLENE-TETRANITRAMINE, WETTED with not less than 15% water, by mass	0226	1		DETONATORS, ELECTRIC for blasting	0030	1	
					0255	1	
					0456	1	

Name and description	UN No.	Class	Remarks	Name and description	UN No.	Class	Remarks
DETONATORS, NON-ELECTRIC for blasting	0029 0267 0455	1 1 1		Dichlorodifluoromethane and ethylene oxide mixture, see	3070	2	
DEUTERIUM, COMPRESSED	1957	2		DICHLORODIMETHYL ETHER, SYMMETRICAL	2249	6.1	Carriage prohibited
DEVICES, SMALL, HYDROCARBON GAS POWERED with release device	3150	2		1,1-DICHLOROETHANE	2362	3	
				1,2-Dichloroethane, see	1184	3	
DIACETONE ALCOHOL	1148	3		1,2-DICHLOROETHYLENE	1150	3	
DIALLYLAMINE	2359	3		Di(2-chloroethyl) ether, see	1916	6.1	
DIALLYL ETHER	2360	3		DICHLOROFLUORO-METHANE	1029	2	
4,4'-DIAMINODIPHENYL-METHANE	2651	6.1		alpha-Dichlorohydrin, see	2750	6.1	
1,2-Diaminoethane, see	1604	8		DICHLOROISOCYANURIC ACID, DRY	2465	5.1	
Diaminopropylamine, see	2269	8		DICHLOROISOCYANURIC ACID SALTS	2465	5.1	
DI-n-AMYLAMINE	2841	3		DICHLOROISOPROPYL ETHER	2490	6.1	
DIAZODINITROPHENOL, WETTED with not less than 40% water, or mixture of alcohol and water, by mass	0074	1		DICHLOROMETHANE	1593	6.1	
				1,1-DICHLORO-1-NITROETHANE	2650	6.1	
				DICHLOROPENTANES	1152	3	
Dibenzopyridine, see	2713	6.1		Dichlorophenol, see	2020 2021	6.1 6.1	
DIBENZYLDICHLORO-SILANE	2434	8		DICHLOROPHENYL ISOCYANATES	2250	6.1	
DIBORANE	1911	2					
1,2-DIBROMOBUTAN-3-ONE	2648	6.1		DICHLOROPHENYLTRI-CHLOROSILANE	1766	8	
DIBROMOCHLORO-PROPANES	2872	6.1					
1,2-Dibromo-3-chloropropane, see	2872	6.1		1,2-DICHLOROPROPANE	1279	3	
DIBROMODIFLUORO-METHANE	1941	9		1,3-DICHLOROPROPANOL-2	2750	6.1	
DIBROMOMETHANE	2664	6.1		1,3-Dichloro-2-propanone, see	2649	6.1	
DI-n-BUTYLAMINE	2248	8		DICHLOROPROPENES	2047	3	
DIBUTYLAMINOETHANOL	2873	6.1		DICHLOROSILANE	2189	2	
2-Dibutylaminoethanol, see	2873	6.1		1,2-DICHLORO-1,1,2,2-TETRAFLUOROETHANE	1958	2	
N,N-Di-n-butylaminoethanol, see	2873	6.1					
DIBUTYL ETHERS	1149	3		Dichloro-s-triazine-2,4,6-trione, see	2465	5.1	
DICHLOROACETIC ACID	1764	8		1,4-Dicyanobutane, see	2205	6.1	
1,3-DICHLOROACETONE	2649	6.1		Dicycloheptadiene, see	2251	3	
DICHLOROACETYL CHLORIDE	1765	8		DICYCLOHEXYLAMINE	2565	8	
DICHLOROANILINES, LIQUID	1590	6.1		Dicyclohexylamine nitrite, see	2687	4.1	
DICHLOROANILINES, SOLID	3442	6.1		DICYCLOHEXYL-AMMONIUM NITRITE	2687	4.1	
o-DICHLOROBENZENE	1591	6.1		DICYCLOPENTADIENE	2048	3	
2,2'-DICHLORODIETHYL ETHER	1916	6.1		1,2-DI-(DIMETHYLAMINO) ETHANE	2372	3	
DICHLORODIFLUORO-METHANE	1028	2					
				DIDYMIUM NITRATE	1465	5.1	
DICHLORODIFLUORO-METHANE AND DIFLUOROETHANE AZEOTROPIC MIXTURE with approximately 74% dichlorodifluoromethane	2602	2		DIESEL FUEL	1202	3	
				1,1-Diethoxyethane, see	1088	3	
				1,2-Diethoxyethane, see	1153	3	
				DIETHOXYMETHANE	2373	3	

Name and description	UN No.	Class	Remarks	Name and description	UN No.	Class	Remarks
3,3-DIETHOXYPROPENE	2374	3		Difluoromethane, pentafluoroethane, and 1,1,1,2-tetrafluoroethane zeotropic mixture with approximately 23%difluoromethane and 25% pentafluoroethane, see	3340	2	
DIETHYLAMINE	1154	3					
2-DIETHYLAMINOETHANOL	2686	8					
3-DIETHYLAMINO-PROPYLAMINE	2684	3		DIFLUOROPHOSPHORIC ACID, ANHYDROUS	1768	8	
N,N-DIETHYLANILINE	2432	6.1		2,3-DIHYDROPYRAN	2376	3	
DIETHYLBENZENE	2049	3		DIISOBUTYLAMINE	2361	3	
Diethylcarbinol, see	1105	3		DIISOBUTYLENE, ISOMERIC COMPOUNDS	2050	3	
DIETHYL CARBONATE	2366	3		alpha-Diisobutylene, see	2050	3	
DIETHYLDICHLOROSILANE	1767	8		beta-Diisobutylene, see	2050	3	
Diethylenediamine, see	2579	8		DIISOBUTYL KETONE	1157	3	
DIETHYLENEGLYCOL DINITRATE, DESENSITIZED with not less than 25% non-volatile, water-insoluble phlegmatizer, by mass	0075	1		DIISOOCTYL ACID PHOSPHATE	1902	8	
				DIISOPROPYLAMINE	1158	3	
				DIISOPROPYL ETHER	1159	3	
DIETHYLENETRIAMINE	2079	8		DIKETENE, STABILIZED	2521	6.1	
N,N-Diethylethanolamine, see	2686	3		1,1-DIMETHOXYETHANE	2377	3	
DIETHYL ETHER	1155	3		1,2-DIMETHOXYETHANE	2252	3	
N,N-DIETHYLETHYLENE-DIAMINE	2685	8		Dimethoxystrychnine, see	1570	6.1	
Di-(2-ethylhexyl) phosphoric acid, see	1902	8		DIMETHYLAMINE, ANHYDROUS	1032	2	
DIETHYL KETONE	1156	3		DIMETHYLAMINE AQUEOUS SOLUTION	1160	3	
DIETHYL SULPHATE	1594	6.1		2-DIMETHYLAMINO-ACETONITRILE	2378	3	
DIETHYL SULPHIDE	2375	3		2-DIMETHYLAMINO-ETHANOL	2051	8	
DIETHYLTHIOPHOSPHORYL CHLORIDE	2751	8		2-DIMETHYLAMINOETHYL ACRYLATE	3302	6.1	
Diethylzinc, see	3394	4.2		2-DIMETHYLAMINOETHYL METHACRYLATE	2522	6.1	
2,4-Difluoroaniline, see	2941	6.1		N,N-DIMETHYLANILINE	2253	6.1	
Difluorochloroethane, see	2517	2		Dimethylarsenic acid, see	1572	6.1	
1,1-DIFLUOROETHANE	1030	2		N,N-Dimethylbenzylamine, see	2619	8	
1,1-DIFLUOROETHYLENE	1959	2		2,3-DIMETHYLBUTANE	2457	3	
DIFLUOROMETHANE	3252	2		1,3-DIMETHYLBUTYLAMINE	2379	3	
Difluoromethane, pentafluoroethane, and 1,1,1,2-tetrafluoroethane zeotropic mixture with approximately 10% difluoromethane and 70% pentafluoroethane, see	3339	2		DIMETHYLCARBAMOYL CHLORIDE	2262	8	
				DIMETHYL CARBONATE	1161	3	
				DIMETHYLCYCLOHEXANES	2263	3	
Difluoromethane, pentafluoroethane, and 1,1,1,2-tetrafluoroethane zeotropic mixture with approximately 20% difluoromethane and 40% pentafluoroethane, see	3338	2		N,N-DIMETHYLCYCLO-HEXYLAMINE	2264	8	
				DIMETHYLDICHLORO-SILANE	1162	3	
				DIMETHYLDIETHOXY-SILANE	2380	3	
				DIMETHYLDIOXANES	2707	3	
				DIMETHYL DISULPHIDE	2381	3	

Name and description	UN No.	Class	Remarks	Name and description	UN No.	Class	Remarks
Dimethylethanolamine, see	2051	8		DIOXANE	1165	3	
DIMETHYL ETHER	1033	2		DIOXOLANE	1166	3	
N,N-DIMETHYLFORMAMIDE	2265	3		DIPENTENE	2052	3	
DIMETHYLHYDRAZINE, SYMMETRICAL	2382	6.1		DIPHENYLAMINE CHLOROARSINE	1698	6.1	
DIMETHYLHYDRAZINE, UNSYMMETRICAL	1163	6.1		DIPHENYLCHLOROARSINE, LIQUID	1699	6.1	
1,1-Dimethylhydrazine, see	1163	6.1		DIPHENYLCHLOROARSINE, SOLID	3450	6.1	
N,N-Dimethyl-4-nitrosoaniline, see	1369	4.2		DIPHENYLDICHLORO-SILANE	1769	8	
2,2-DIMETHYLPROPANE	2044	2		DIPHENYLMETHYL BROMIDE	1770	8	
DIMETHYL-N-PROPYL-AMINE	2266	3		DIPICRYLAMINE, see	0079	1	
DIMETHYL SULPHATE	1595	6.1		DIPICRYL SULPHIDE, dry or wetted with less than 10% water, by mass	0401	1	
DIMETHYL SULPHIDE	1164	3					
DIMETHYL THIOPHOSPHORYL CHLORIDE	2267	6.1		DIPICRYL SULPHIDE, WETTED with not less than 10% water, by mass	2852	4.1	
Dimethylzinc, see	3394	4.2					
DINGU, see	0489	1		DIPROPYLAMINE	2383	3	
DINITROANILINES	1596	6.1		Dipropylene triamine, see	2269	8	
DINITROBENZENES, LIQUID	1597	6.1		DI-n-PROPYL ETHER	2384	3	
DINITROBENZENES, SOLID	3443	6.1		DIPROPYL KETONE	2710	3	
Dinitrochlorobenzene, see	1577	6.1		DISINFECTANT, LIQUID, CORROSIVE, N.O.S.	1903	8	
	3441	6.1		DISINFECTANT, LIQUID, TOXIC, N.O.S.	3142	6.1	
DINITRO-o-CRESOL	1598	6.1					
DINITROGEN TETROXIDE	1067	2		DISINFECTANT, SOLID, TOXIC, N.O.S.	1601	6.1	
DINITROGLYCOLURIL	0489	1					
DINITROPHENOL, dry or wetted with less than 15% water, by mass	0076	1		DISODIUM TRIOXOSILICATE	3253	8	
DINITROPHENOL SOLUTION	1599	6.1		DIVINYL ETHER, STABILIZED	1167	3	
DINITROPHENOL, WETTED with not less than 15% water, by mass	1320	4.1		DODECYLTRICHLORO-SILANE	1771	8	
DINITROPHENOLATES, alkali metals, dry or wetted with less than 15% water, by mass	0077	1		Dry ice, see	1845	9	Not subject to ADR
				DYE INTERMEDIATE, LIQUID, CORROSIVE, N.O.S.	2801	8	
DINITROPHENOLATES, WETTED with not less than 15% water, by mass	1321	4.1		DYE INTERMEDIATE, LIQUID, TOXIC, N.O.S.	1602	6.1	
DINITRORESORCINOL, dry or wetted with less than 15% water, by mass	0078	1		DYE INTERMEDIATE, SOLID, CORROSIVE, N.O.S.	3147	8	
				DYE INTERMEDIATE, SOLID, TOXIC, N.O.S.	3143	6.1	
DINITRORESORCINOL, WETTED with not less than 15% water, by mass	1322	4.1		DYE, LIQUID, CORROSIVE, N.O.S.	2801	8	
DINITROSOBENZENE	0406	1		DYE, LIQUID, TOXIC, N.O.S.	1602	6.1	
Dinitrotoluene mixed with sodium chlorate, see	0083	1		DYE, SOLID, CORROSIVE, N.O.S.	3147	8	
DINITROTOLUENES, LIQUID	2038	6.1		DYE, SOLID, TOXIC, N.O.S.	3143	6.1	
DINITROTOLUENES, MOLTEN	1600	6.1		Dynamite, see	0081	1	
DINITROTOLUENES, SOLID	3454	6.1					

Name and description	UN No.	Class	Remarks	Name and description	UN No.	Class	Remarks
Electric storage batteries, see	2794	8		ENVIRONMENTALLY HAZARDOUS SUBSTANCE, LIQUID, N.O.S.	3082	9	
	2795	8					
	2800	8					
	3028	8		ENVIRONMENTALLY HAZARDOUS SUBSTANCE, SOLID, N.O.S.	3077	9	
Electrolyte (acid or alkaline) for batteries, see	2796	8					
	2797	8		EPIBROMOHYDRIN	2558	6.1	
ELEVATED TEMPERATURE LIQUID, N.O.S., at or above 100 °C and below its flash-point (including molten metals, molten salts, etc.)	3257	9		EPICHLOROHYDRIN	2023	6.1	
				1,2-Epoxybutane, stabilized, see	3022	3	
				Epoxyethane, see	1040	2	
				1,2-EPOXY-3-ETHOXYPROPANE	2752	3	
ELEVATED TEMPERATURE LIQUID, FLAMMABLE, N.O.S. with flash-point above 60 °C, at or above its flash-point	3256	3		2,3-Epoxy-1-propanal, see	2622	3	
				2,3-Epoxypropyl ethyl ether, see	2752	3	
				ESTERS, N.O.S.	3272	3	
ELEVATED TEMPERATURE SOLID, N.O.S., at or above 240 °C	3258	9		ETHANE	1035	2	
Empty battery-vehicle, uncleaned			See 4.3.2.4, 5.1.3 and 5.4.1.1.6	ETHANE, REFRIGERATED LIQUID	1961	2	
Empty IBC, uncleaned			See 4.1.1.11, 5.1.3 and 5.4.1.1.6	Ethanethiol, see	2363	3	
				ETHANOL	1170	3	
Empty large packaging, uncleaned			See 4.1.1.11, 5.1.3 and 5.4.1.1.6	ETHANOL AND GASOLINE MIXTURE or ETHANOL AND MOTOR SPIRIT MIXTURE or ETHANOL AND PETROL MIXTURE, with more than 10% ethanol	3475	3	
Empty MEGC, uncleaned			See 4.3.2.4, 5.1.3 and 5.4.1.1.6	ETHANOL SOLUTION	1170	3	
				ETHANOLAMINE	2491	8	
				ETHANOLAMINE SOLUTION	2491	8	
Empty packaging, uncleaned			See 4.1.1.11, 5.1.3 and 5.4.1.1.6	Ether, see	1155	3	
				ETHERS, N.O.S.	3271	3	
Empty receptacle, uncleaned			See 5.1.3 and 5.4.1.1.6	2-Ethoxyethanol, see	1171	3	
				2-Ethoxyethyl acetate, see	1172	3	
				Ethoxy propane-1, see	2615	3	
Empty tank, uncleaned			See 4.3.2.4, 5.1.3 and 5.4.1.1.6	ETHYL ACETATE	1173	3	
				ETHYLACETYLENE, STABILIZED	2452	2	
Empty vehicle, uncleaned			See 5.1.3 and 5.4.1.1.6	ETHYL ACRYLATE, STABILIZED	1917	3	
				ETHYL ALCOHOL, see	1170	3	
Enamel, see	1263	3		ETHYL ALCOHOL SOLUTION, see	1170	3	
	3066	8					
	3469	3		ETHYLAMINE	1036	2	
	3470	8		ETHYLAMINE, AQUEOUS SOLUTION with not less than 50% but not more than 70% ethylamine	2270	3	
Engines, internal combustion	3166	9	Not subject to ADR				
				ETHYL AMYL KETONE	2271	3	
Engines, rocket, see	0250	1		N-ETHYLANILINE	2272	6.1	
	0322	1		2-ETHYLANILINE	2273	6.1	
				ETHYLBENZENE	1175	3	

Name and description	UN No.	Class	Remarks	Name and description	UN No.	Class	Remarks
N-ETHYL-N-BENZYL-ANILINE	2274	6.1		ETHYLENE OXIDE	1040	2	
N-ETHYLBENZYL-TOLUIDINES, LIQUID	2753	6.1		ETHYLENE OXIDE AND CARBON DIOXIDE MIXTURE with more than 87% ethylene oxide	3300	2	
N-ETHYLBENZYL-TOLUIDINES, SOLID	3460	6.1		ETHYLENE OXIDE AND CARBON DIOXIDE MIXTURE with more than 9% but not more than 87% ethylene oxide	1041	2	
ETHYL BORATE	1176	3					
ETHYL BROMIDE	1891	6.1					
ETHYL BROMOACETATE	1603	6.1		ETHYLENE OXIDE AND CARBON DIOXIDE MIXTURE with not more than 9% ethylene oxide	1952	2	
2-ETHYLBUTANOL	2275	3					
2-ETHYLBUTYL ACETATE	1177	3					
ETHYL BUTYL ETHER	1179	3		ETHYLENE OXIDE AND CHLOROTETRAFLUORO-ETHANE MIXTURE with not more than 8.8% ethylene oxide	3297	2	
2-ETHYLBUTYRALDEHYDE	1178	3					
ETHYL BUTYRATE	1180	3					
ETHYL CHLORIDE	1037	2					
ETHYL CHLOROACETATE	1181	6.1		ETHYLENE OXIDE AND DICHLORODIFLUORO-METHANE MIXTURE with not more than 12.5% ethylene oxide	3070	2	
Ethyl chlorocarbonate, see	1182	6.1					
ETHYL CHLOROFORMATE	1182	6.1					
ETHYL 2-CHLORO-PROPIONATE	2935	3		ETHYLENE OXIDE AND PENTAFLUOROETHANE MIXTURE with not more than 7.9% ethylene oxide	3298	2	
Ethyl-alpha-chloropropionate, see	2935	3					
ETHYL CHLORO-THIOFORMATE	2826	8					
ETHYL CROTONATE	1862	3		ETHYLENE OXIDE AND PROPYLENE OXIDE MIXTURE, not more than 30% ethylene oxide	2983	3	
ETHYLDICHLOROARSINE	1892	6.1					
ETHYLDICHLOROSILANE	1183	4.3		ETHYLENE OXIDE AND TETRAFLUOROETHANE MIXTURE with not more than 5.6% ethylene oxide	3299	2	
ETHYLENE, ACETYLENE AND PROPYLENE MIXTURE, REFRIGERATED LIQUID containing at least 71.5% ethylene with not more than 22.5% acetylene and not more than 6% propylene	3138	2					
				ETHYLENE OXIDE WITH NITROGEN up to a total pressure of 1 MPa (10 bar) at 50 °C	1040	2	
ETHYLENE CHLOROHYDRIN	1135	6.1		ETHYLENE, REFRIGERATED LIQUID	1038	2	
ETHYLENE	1962	2		ETHYL ETHER, see	1155	3	
ETHYLENEDIAMINE	1604	8		ETHYL FLUORIDE	2453	2	
ETHYLENE DIBROMIDE	1605	6.1		ETHYL FORMATE	1190	3	
Ethylene dibromide and methyl bromide, liquid mixture, see	1647	6.1		2-ETHYLHEXYLAMINE	2276	3	
ETHYLENE DICHLORIDE	1184	3		2-ETHYLHEXYL CHLOROFORMATE	2748	6.1	
ETHYLENE GLYCOL DIETHYL ETHER	1153	3		Ethylidene chloride, see	2362	3	
ETHYLENE GLYCOL MONOETHYL ETHER	1171	3		ETHYL ISOBUTYRATE	2385	3	
				ETHYL ISOCYANATE	2481	3	
ETHYLENE GLYCOL MONOETHYL ETHER ACETATE	1172	3		ETHYL LACTATE	1192	3	
				ETHYL MERCAPTAN	2363	3	
ETHYLENE GLYCOL MONOMETHYL ETHER	1188	3		ETHYL METHACRYLATE, STABILIZED	2277	3	
ETHYLENE GLYCOL MONOMETHYL ETHER ACETATE	1189	3		ETHYL METHYL ETHER	1039	2	
				ETHYL METHYL KETONE	1193	3	
ETHYLENEIMINE, STABILIZED	1185	6.1		ETHYL NITRITE SOLUTION	1194	3	

Name and description	UN No.	Class	Remarks	Name and description	UN No.	Class	Remarks
ETHYL ORTHOFORMATE	2524	3		FERROUS ARSENATE	1608	6.1	
ETHYL OXALATE	2525	6.1		FERROUS METAL BORINGS in a form liable to self-heating	2793	4.2	
ETHYLPHENYL-DICHLOROSILANE	2435	8		FERROUS METAL CUTTINGS in a form liable to self-heating	2793	4.2	
1-ETHYLPIPERIDINE	2386	3		FERROUS METAL SHAVINGS in a form liable to self-heating	2793	4.2	
ETHYL PROPIONATE	1195	3		FERROUS METAL TURNINGS in a form liable to self-heating	2793	4.2	
ETHYL PROPYL ETHER	2615	3		FERTILIZER AMMONIATING SOLUTION with free ammonia	1043	2	
Ethyl silicate, see	1292	3		Fertilizer with ammonium nitrate, n.o.s., see	2067	5.1	
Ethyl sulphate, see	1594	6.1		Fibres, animal, burnt wet or damp	1372	4.2	Not subject to ADR
N-ETHYLTOLUIDINES	2754	6.1					
ETHYLTRICHLOROSILANE	1196	3		FIBRES, ANIMAL, N.O.S. with oil	1373	4.2	
EXPLOSIVE, BLASTING, TYPE A	0081	1		FIBRES IMPREGNATED WITH WEAKLY NITRATED NITROCELLULOSE, N.O.S.	1353	4.1	
EXPLOSIVE, BLASTING, TYPE B	0082	1					
	0331	1		FIBRES, SYNTHETIC, N.O.S. with oil	1373	4.2	
EXPLOSIVE, BLASTING, TYPE C	0083	1		Fibres, vegetable, burnt wet or damp	1372	4.2	Not subject to ADR
EXPLOSIVE, BLASTING, TYPE D	0084	1					
EXPLOSIVE, BLASTING, TYPE E	0241	1					
	0332	1		Fibres, vegetable, dry	3360	4.1	Not subject to ADR
Explosives, emulsion, see	0241	1					
	0332	1					
Explosive, seismic, see	0081	1		FIBRES, VEGETABLE, N.O.S. with oil	1373	4.2	
	0082	1					
	0083	1		Films, nitrocellulose base, from which gelatine has been removed; film scrap, see	2002	4.2	
	0331	1					
Explosive, slurry, see	0241	1					
	0332	1		FILMS, NITROCELLULOSE BASE, gelatin coated, except scrap	1324	4.1	
Explosive, water gel, see	0241	1					
	0332	1		Filler, liquid, see	1263	3	
EXTRACTS, AROMATIC, LIQUID	1169	3			3066	8	
EXTRACTS, FLAVOURING, LIQUID	1197	3			3469	3	
					3470	8	
FABRICS, ANIMAL, N.O.S. with oil	1373	4.2		FIRE EXTINGUISHER CHARGES, corrosive liquid	1774	8	
FABRICS IMPREGNATED WITH WEAKLY NITRATED NITROCELLULOSE, N.O.S.	1353	4.1		Fire extinguisher charges, expelling, explosive, see	0275	1	
					0276	1	
					0323	1	
FABRICS, SYNTHETIC, N.O.S. with oil	1373	4.2			0381	1	
FABRICS, VEGETABLE, N.O.S. with oil	1373	4.2		FIRE EXTINGUISHERS with compressed or liquefied gas	1044	2	
FERRIC ARSENATE	1606	6.1		FIRELIGHTERS, SOLID with flammable liquid	2623	4.1	
FERRIC ARSENITE	1607	6.1		FIREWORKS	0333	1	See 2.2.1.1.7
FERRIC CHLORIDE, ANHYDROUS	1773	8			0334	1	
					0335	1	
FERRIC CHLORIDE SOLUTION	2582	8			0336	1	
FERRIC NITRATE	1466	5.1			0337	1	
FERROCERIUM	1323	4.1		FIRST AID KIT	3316	9	
FERROSILICON with 30% or more but less than 90% silicon	1408	4.3					

Name and description	UN No.	Class	Remarks	Name and description	UN No.	Class	Remarks
Fish meal, stabilized	2216	9	Not subject to ADR	Flue dusts, toxic, see	1562	6.1	
				Fluoric acid, see	1790	8	
FISH MEAL, UNSTABILIZED	1374	4.2		FLUORINE, COMPRESSED	1045	2	
Fish scrap, stabilized, see	2216	9	Not subject to ADR	FLUOROACETIC ACID	2642	6.1	
				FLUOROANILINES	2941	6.1	
				2-Fluoroaniline, see	2941	6.1	
FISH SCRAP, UNSTABILIZED, see	1374	4.2		4-Fluoroaniline, see	2941	6.1	
Flammable gas in lighters, see	1057	2		o-Fluoroaniline, see	2941	6.1	
FLAMMABLE LIQUID, N.O.S.	1993	3		p-Fluoroaniline, see	2941	6.1	
FLAMMABLE LIQUID, CORROSIVE, N.O.S.	2924	3		FLUOROBENZENE	2387	3	
				FLUOROBORIC ACID	1775	8	
FLAMMABLE LIQUID, TOXIC, N.O.S.	1992	3		Fluoroethane, see	2453	2	
				Fluoroform, see	1984	2	
FLAMMABLE LIQUID, TOXIC, CORROSIVE, N.O.S.	3286	3		Fluoromethane, see	2454	2	
				FLUOROPHOSPHORIC ACID, ANHYDROUS	1776	8	
FLAMMABLE SOLID, CORROSIVE, INORGANIC, N.O.S.	3180	4.1					
				FLUOROSILICATES, N.O.S.	2856	6.1	
FLAMMABLE SOLID, CORROSIVE, ORGANIC, N.O.S.	2925	4.1		FLUOROSILICIC ACID	1778	8	
				FLUOROSULPHONIC ACID	1777	8	
FLAMMABLE SOLID, INORGANIC, N.O.S.	3178	4.1		FLUOROTOLUENES	2388	3	
FLAMMABLE SOLID, ORGANIC, N.O.S.	1325	4.1		FORMALDEHYDE SOLUTION with not less than 25% formaldehyde	2209	8	
FLAMMABLE SOLID, ORGANIC, MOLTEN, N.O.S.	3176	4.1					
FLAMMABLE SOLID, OXIDIZING, N.O.S.	3097	4.1	Carriage prohibited	FORMALDEHYDE SOLUTION, FLAMMABLE	1198	3	
				Formalin, see	1198	3	
					2209	8	
FLAMMABLE SOLID, TOXIC, INORGANIC, N.O.S.	3179	4.1		Formamidine sulphinic acid, see	3341	4.2	
FLAMMABLE SOLID, TOXIC, ORGANIC, N.O.S.	2926	4.1		FORMIC ACID with more than 85% acid by mass	1779	8	
FLARES, AERIAL	0093	1					
	0403	1		FORMIC ACID with not more than 85% acid by mass	3412	8	
	0404	1					
	0420	1		Formic aldehyde, see	1198	3	
	0421	1			2209	8	
Flares, aeroplane, see	0093	1		2-Formyl-3,4-dihydro-2H-pyran, see	2607	3	
	0403	1		FRACTURING DEVICES, EXPLOSIVE without detonator, for oil wells	0099	1	
	0404	1					
	0420	1					
	0421	1					
Flares, highway, Flares, distress, small, Flares, railway or highway, see	0191	1		FUEL, AVIATION, TURBINE ENGINE	1863	3	
	0373	1					
FLARES, SURFACE	0092	1		FUEL CELL CARTRIDGES	3478	2	
	0418	1			3479	2	
	0419	1			3473	3	
					3476	4.3	
Flares, water-activated, see	0248	1			3477	8	
	0249	1		FUEL CELL CARTRIDGES CONTAINED IN EQUIPMENT	3478	2	
FLASH POWDER	0094	1			3479	2	
	0305	1			3473	3	
					3476	4.3	
					3477	8	

Name and description	UN No.	Class	Remarks	Name and description	UN No.	Class	Remarks
FUEL CELL CARTRIDGES PACKED WITH EQUIPMENT	3478	2		GAS, REFRIGERATED LIQUID, OXIDIZING, N.O.S.	3311	2	
	3479	2					
	3473	3		GAS SAMPLE, NON-PRESSURIZED, FLAMMABLE, N.O.S., not refrigerated liquid	3167	2	
	3476	4.3					
	3477	8					
Fumaroyl dichloride, see	1780	3		GAS SAMPLE, NON-PRESSURIZED, TOXIC, N.O.S., not refrigerated liquid	3169	2	
FUMARYL CHLORIDE	1780	8					
FUMIGATED UNIT	3359	9		GAS SAMPLE, NON-PRESSURIZED, TOXIC, FLAMMABLE, N.O.S., not refrigerated liquid	3168	2	
FURALDEHYDES	1199	6.1					
FURAN	2389	3					
FURFURYL ALCOHOL	2874	6.1					
FURFURYLAMINE	2526	3		Gelatin, blasting, see	0081	1	
Furyl carbinol, see	2874	6.1		Gelatin, dynamites, see	0081	1	
FUSE, DETONATING, metal clad	0102	1		GENETICALLY MODIFIED MICROORGANISMS	3245	9	
	0290	1					
FUSE, DETONATING, MILD EFFECT, metal clad	0104	1		GENETICALLY MODIFIED ORGANISMS	3245	9	
FUSE, IGNITER, tubular, metal clad	0103	1		GERMANE	2192	2	
FUSE, NON-DETONATING	0101	1		Germanium hydride, see	2192	2	
FUSEL OIL	1201	3		Glycer-1,3-dichlorohydrin, see	2750	6.1	
FUSE, SAFETY	0105	1		GLYCEROL alpha-MONOCHLOROHYDRIN	2689	6.1	
Fuze, combination, percussion or time, see	0106	1		Glyceryl trinitrate, see	0143	1	
	0107	1			0144	1	
	0257	1			1204	3	
	0316	1			3064	3	
	0317	1					
	0367	1		GLYCIDALDEHYDE	2622	3	
	0368	1		GRENADES, hand or rifle, with bursting charge	0284	1	
FUZES, DETONATING	0106	1			0285	1	
	0107	1			0292	1	
	0257	1			0293	1	
	0367	1		Grenades, illuminating, see	0171	1	
FUZES, DETONATING with protective features	0408	1			0254	1	
	0409	1			0297	1	
	0410	1		GRENADES, PRACTICE, hand or rifle	0110	1	
FUZES, IGNITING	0316	1			0318	1	
	0317	1			0372	1	
	0368	1			0452	1	
GALLIUM	2803	8		Grenades, smoke, see	0015	1	
GAS CARTRIDGES without a release device, non-refillable, see	2037	2			0016	1	
					0245	1	
Gas drips, hydrocarbon, see	3295	3			0246	1	
					0303	1	
GAS OIL	1202	3		GUANIDINE NITRATE	1467	5.1	
GASOLINE	1203	3		GUANYLNITROSAMINO-GUANYLIDENE HYDRAZINE, WETTED with not less than 30% water, by mass	0113	1	
Gasoline and ethanol mixture, with more than 10% ethanol, see	3475	3					
Gasoline, casinghead, see	1203	3					
GAS, REFRIGERATED LIQUID, N.O.S.	3158	2		GUANYLNITROSAMINO-GUANYLTETRAZENE, WETTED with not less than 30% water, or mixture of alcohol and water, by mass	0114	1	
GAS, REFRIGERATED LIQUID, FLAMMABLE, N.O.S.	3312	2					

Name and description	UN No.	Class	Remarks	Name and description	UN No.	Class	Remarks
GUNPOWDER, COMPRESSED, see	0028	1		Hexahydrocresol, see	2617	3	
				Hexahydromethyl phenol, see	2617	3	
GUNPOWDER, granular or as a meal, see	0027	1		HEXALDEHYDE	1207	3	
GUNPOWDER, IN PELLETS, see	0028	1		HEXAMETHYLENEDIAMINE, SOLID	2280	8	
Gutta percha solution, see	1287	3		HEXAMETHYLENEDIAMINE SOLUTION	1783	8	
HAFNIUM POWDER, DRY	2545	4.2					
HAFNIUM POWDER, WETTED with not less than 25% water	1326	4.1		HEXAMETHYLENE DIISOCYANATE	2281	6.1	
Hay	1327	4.1	Not subject to ADR	HEXAMETHYLENEIMINE	2493	3	
				HEXAMETHYLENE-TETRAMINE	1328	4.1	
				Hexamine, see	1328	4.1	
HEATING OIL, LIGHT	1202	3		HEXANES	1208	3	
Heavy hydrogen, see	1957	2		HEXANITRODIPHENYL-AMINE	0079	1	
HELIUM, COMPRESSED	1046	2		HEXANITROSTILBENE	0392	1	
HELIUM, REFRIGERATED LIQUID	1963	2		Hexanoic acid, see	2829	8	
HEPTAFLUOROPROPANE	3296	2		HEXANOLS	2282	3	
n-HEPTALDEHYDE	3056	3		1-HEXENE	2370	3	
n-Heptanal, see	3056	3		HEXOGEN AND CYCLOTETRAMETHYLENE-TETRANITRAMINE MIXTURE, WETTED with not less than 15% water, by mass or DESENSITIZED with not less than 10% phlegmatiser by mass, see	0391	1	
HEPTANES	1206	3					
4-Heptanone, see	2710	3					
n-HEPTENE	2278	3					
HEXACHLOROACETONE	2661	6.1					
HEXACHLOROBENZENE	2729	6.1					
HEXACHLOROBUTADIENE	2279	6.1		HEXOGEN, DESENSITIZED, see	0483	1	
Hexachloro-1,3-butadiene, see	2279	6.1		HEXOGEN, WETTED with not less than 15% water, by mass, see	0072	1	
HEXACHLOROCYCLO-PENTADIENE	2646	6.1		HEXOLITE, dry or wetted with less than 15% water, by mass	0118	1	
HEXACHLOROPHENE	2875	6.1		HEXOTOL, dry or wetted with less than 15% water, by mass, see	0118	1	
Hexachloro-2-propanone, see	2661	6.1					
HEXADECYLTRICHLORO-SILANE	1781	8		HEXOTONAL	0393	1	
HEXADIENES	2458	3		HEXOTONAL, cast, see	0393	1	
HEXAETHYL TETRAPHOSPHATE	1611	6.1		HEXYL, see	0079	1	
				HEXYLTRICHLOROSILANE	1784	8	
HEXAETHYL TETRAPHOSPHATE AND COMPRESSED GAS MIXTURE	1612	2		HMX, see	0391	1	
				HMX, DESENSITIZED, see	0484	1	
				HMX, WETTED with not less than 15% water, by mass, see	0226	1	
HEXAFLUOROACETONE	2420	2		HYDRAZINE, ANHYDROUS	2029	8	
HEXAFLUOROACETONE HYDRATE, LIQUID	2552	6.1		HYDRAZINE AQUEOUS SOLUTION, with more than 37% hydrazine by mass	2030	8	
HEXAFLUOROACETONE HYDRATE, SOLID	3436	6.1					
HEXAFLUOROETHANE	2193	2		HYDRAZINE, AQUEOUS SOLUTION with not more than 37% hydrazine, by mass	3293	6.1	
HEXAFLUOROPHOSPHORIC ACID	1782	8					
HEXAFLUOROPROPYLENE	1858	2		Hydrides, metal, water-reactive, n.o.s., see	1409	4.3	

Name and description	UN No.	Class	Remarks	Name and description	UN No.	Class	Remarks
Hydriodic acid, anhydrous, see	2197	2		HYDROGEN CYANIDE, STABILIZED, containing less than 3% water and absorbed in a porous inert material	1614	6.1	
HYDRIODIC ACID	1787	8					
HYDROBROMIC ACID	1788	8		HYDROGENDIFLUORIDES, SOLID, N.O.S.	1740	8	
HYDROCARBON GAS MIXTURE, COMPRESSED, N.O.S.	1964	2		HYDROGENDIFLUORIDES SOLUTION, N.O.S.	3471	8	
HYDROCARBON GAS MIXTURE, LIQUEFIED, N.O.S. such as mixtures A, A01, A02, A0, A1, B1, B2, B or C	1965	2		HYDROGEN FLUORIDE, ANHYDROUS	1052	8	
				Hydrogen fluoride solution, see	1790	8	
HYDROCARBON GAS REFILLS FOR SMALL DEVICES with release device	3150	2		HYDROGEN IN A METAL HYDRIDE STORAGE SYSTEM	2	3468	
HYDROCARBONS, LIQUID, N.O.S.	3295	3		HYDROGEN IN A METAL HYDRIDE STORAGE SYSTEM CONTAINED IN EQUIPMENT	2	3468	
HYDROCHLORIC ACID	1789	8		HYDROGEN IN A METAL HYDRIDE STORAGE SYSTEM PACKED WITH EQUIPMENT	2	3468	
HYDROCYANIC ACID, AQUEOUS SOLUTION with not more than 20% hydrogen cyanide	1613	6.1					
HYDROFLUORIC ACID with more than 60% but not more than 85% hydrogen fluoride	1790	8		HYDROGEN IODIDE, ANHYDROUS	2197	2	
				Hydrogen iodide solution, see	1787	8	
HYDROFLUORIC ACID with more than 85% hydrogen fluoride	1790	8		HYDROGEN PEROXIDE AND PEROXYACETIC ACID MIXTURE with acid(s), water and not more than 5% peroxyacetic acid, STABILIZED	3149	5.1	
HYDROFLUORIC ACID with not more than 60% hydrogen fluoride	1790	8					
HYDROFLUORIC ACID AND SULPHURIC ACID MIXTURE	1786	8		HYDROGEN PEROXIDE, AQUEOUS SOLUTION with not less than 8% but less than 20% hydrogen peroxide (stabilized as necessary)	2984	5.1	
Hydrofluoroboric acid, see	1775	8					
Hydrofluorosilicic acid, see	1778	8					
HYDROGEN AND METHANE MIXTURE, COMPRESSED	2034	2		HYDROGEN PEROXIDE, AQUEOUS SOLUTION with not less than 20% but not more than 60% hydrogen peroxide (stabilized as necessary)	2014	5.1	
Hydrogen arsenide, see	2188	2					
HYDROGEN BROMIDE, ANHYDROUS	1048	2					
Hydrogen bromide solution, see	1788	8		HYDROGEN PEROXIDE, AQUEOUS SOLUTION, STABILIZED with more than 60% hydrogen peroxide and not more than 70% hydrogen peroxide	2015	5.1	
HYDROGEN CHLORIDE, ANHYDROUS	1050	2					
HYDROGEN CHLORIDE, REFRIGERATED LIQUID	2186	2	Carriage prohibited				
HYDROGEN, COMPRESSED	1049	2		HYDROGEN PEROXIDE, AQUEOUS SOLUTION, STABILIZED with more than 70% hydrogen peroxide	2015	5.1	
HYDROGEN CYANIDE, AQUEOUS SOLUTION with not more than 20% hydrogen cyanide, see	1613	6.1					
				HYDROGEN, REFRIGERATED LIQUID	1966	2	
HYDROGEN CYANIDE, SOLUTION IN ALCOHOL with not more than 45% hydrogen cyanide	3294	6.1		HYDROGEN SELENIDE, ANHYDROUS	2202	2	
				Hydrogen silicide, see	2203	2	
HYDROGEN CYANIDE, STABILIZED containing less than 3% water	1051	6.1		HYDROGEN SULPHIDE	1053	2	
				Hydroselenic acid, see	2202	2	
				Hydrosilicofluoric acid, see	1778	8	

Name and description	UN No.	Class	Remarks	Name and description	UN No.	Class	Remarks
1-HYDROXY-BENZOTRIAZOLE, ANHYDROUS, dry or wetted with less than 20% water, by mass	0508 3474	1 1		IRON SPONGE, SPENT obtained from coal gas purification	1376	4.2	
3-Hydroxybutan-2-one, see	2621	3		Iron swarf, see	2793	4.2	
HYDROXYLAMINE SULPHATE	2865	8		ISOBUTANE	1969	2	
1-Hydroxy-3-methyl-2-penten-4-yne, see	2705	8		ISOBUTANOL	1212	3	
				Isobutene, see	1055	2	
3-Hydroxyphenol, see	2876	6.1		ISOBUTYL ACETATE	1213	3	
HYPOCHLORITES, INORGANIC, N.O.S.	3212	5.1		ISOBUTYL ACRYLATE, STABILIZED	2527	3	
HYPOCHLORITE SOLUTION	1791	8		ISOBUTYL ALCOHOL, see	1212	3	
IGNITERS	0121	1		ISOBUTYL ALDEHYDE, see	2045	3	
	0314	1		ISOBUTYLAMINE	1214	3	
	0315	1		ISOBUTYLENE	1055	2	
	0325	1		ISOBUTYL FORMATE	2393	3	
	0454	1		ISOBUTYL ISOBUTYRATE	2528	3	
3,3'-IMINO-DIPROPYLAMINE	2269	8		ISOBUTYL ISOCYANATE	2486	3	
Indiarubber, see	1287	3		ISOBUTYL METHACRYLATE, STABILIZED	2283	3	
INFECTIOUS SUBSTANCE, AFFECTING ANIMALS only	2900	6.2		ISOBUTYL PROPIONATE	2394	3	
INFECTIOUS SUBSTANCE, AFFECTING HUMANS	2814	6.2		ISOBUTYRALDEHYDE	2045	3	
Ink, printer's, flammable, see	1210	3		ISOBUTYRIC ACID	2529	3	
INSECTICIDE GAS, N.O.S.	1968	2		ISOBUTYRONITRILE	2284	3	
INSECTICIDE GAS, FLAMMABLE, N.O.S.	3354	2		ISOBUTYRYL CHLORIDE	2395	3	
INSECTICIDE GAS, TOXIC, N.O.S.	1967	2		ISOCYANATES, FLAMMABLE, TOXIC, N.O.S.	2478	3	
INSECTICIDE GAS, TOXIC, FLAMMABLE, N.O.S.	3355	2		ISOCYANATES, TOXIC, N.O.S.	2206	6.1	
IODINE MONOCHLORIDE	1792	8		ISOCYANATES, TOXIC, FLAMMABLE, N.O.S.	3080	6.1	
IODINE PENTAFLUORIDE	2495	5.1		ISOCYANATE SOLUTION, FLAMMABLE, TOXIC, N.O.S.	2478	3	
2-IODOBUTANE	2390	3		ISOCYANATE SOLUTION, TOXIC, N.O.S.	2206	6.1	
Iodomethane, see	2644	6.1					
IODOMETHYLPROPANES	2391	3		ISOCYANATE SOLUTION, TOXIC, FLAMMABLE, N.O.S.	3080	6.1	
IODOPROPANES	2392	3					
alpha-Iodotoluene, see	2653	6.1		ISOCYANATO-BENZOTRIFLUORIDES	2285	6.1	
I.p.d.i., see	2290	6.1		3-Isocyanatomethyl-3,5,5-tri-methylcyclohexyl isocyanate, see	2290	6.1	
Iron chloride, anhydrous, see	1773	8					
Iron (III) chloride, anhydrous, see	1773	8		Isododecane, see	2286	3	
				ISOHEPTENE	2287	3	
Iron chloride solution, see	2582	8		ISOHEXENE	2288	3	
IRON OXIDE, SPENT obtained from coal gas purification	1376	4.2		Isooctane, see	1262	3	
IRON PENTACARBONYL	1994	6.1		ISOOCTENE	1216	3	
Iron perchloride, anhydrous, see	1773	8		Isopentane, see	1265	3	
Iron powder, pyrophoric, see	1383	4.2		ISOPENTENES	2371	3	
Iron sesquichloride, anhydrous, see	1773	8		Isopentylamine, see	1106	3	

Name and description	UN No.	Class	Remarks	Name and description	UN No.	Class	Remarks
Isopentyl nitrite, see	1113	3		Lacquer, see	1263	3	
ISOPHORONEDIAMINE	2289	8			3066	8	
ISOPHORONE DIISOCYANATE	2290	6.1			3469	3	
ISOPRENE, STABILIZED	1218	3			3470	8	
ISOPROPANOL	1219	3		Lacquer base, liquid, see	1263	3	
ISOPROPENYL ACETATE	2403	3			3066	8	
ISOPROPENYLBENZENE	2303	3			3469	3	
ISOPROPYL ACETATE	1220	3			3470	8	
ISOPROPYL ACID PHOSPHATE	1793	8		Lacquer base or lacquer chips, nitrocellulose, dry, see	2557	4.1	
ISOPROPYL ALCOHOL, see	1219	3		Lacquer base or lacquer chips, plastic, wet with alcohol or solvent, see	1263	3	
ISOPROPYLAMINE	1221	3			2059	3	
ISOPROPYLBENZENE	1918	3			2555	4.1	
ISOPROPYL BUTYRATE	2405	3			2556	4.1	
Isopropyl chloride, see	2356	3		LEAD ACETATE	1616	6.1	
ISOPROPYL CHLOROACETATE	2947	3		Lead (II) acetate, see	1616	6.1	
ISOPROPYL CHLOROFORMATE	2407	6.1		LEAD ARSENATES	1617	6.1	
ISOPROPYL 2-CHLORO-PROPIONATE	2934	3		LEAD ARSENITES	1618	6.1	
				LEAD AZIDE, WETTED with not less than 20% water, or mixture of alcohol and water, by mass	0129	1	
Isopropyl-alpha-chloropropionate, see	2934	3		Lead chloride, solid, see	2291	6.1	
Isopropyl ether, see	1159	3		LEAD COMPOUND, SOLUBLE, N.O.S.	2291	6.1	
Isopropylethylene, see	2561	3		LEAD CYANIDE	1620	6.1	
Isopropyl formate, see	1281	3		Lead (II) cyanide	1620	6.1	
ISOPROPYL ISOBUTYRATE	2406	3		LEAD DIOXIDE	1872	5.1	
ISOPROPYL ISOCYANATE	2483	3		LEAD NITRATE	1469	5.1	
Isopropyl mercaptan, see	2402	3		Lead (II) nitrate	1469	5.1	
ISOPROPYL NITRATE	1222	3		LEAD PERCHLORATE, SOLID	1470	5.1	
ISOPROPYL PROPIONATE	2409	3		LEAD PERCHLORATE, SOLUTION	3408	5.1	
Isolpropyltoluene, see	2046	3		Lead (II) perchlorate	1470	5.1	
Isopropyltoluol, see	2046	3			3408	5.1	
ISOSORBIDE DINITRATE MIXTURE with not less than 60% lactose, mannose, starch or calcium hydrogen phosphate	2907	4.1		Lead peroxide, see	1872	5.1	
				LEAD PHOSPHITE, DIBASIC	2989	4.1	
ISOSORBIDE-5-MONONITRATE	3251	4.1		LEAD STYPHNATE, WETTED with not less than 20% water, or mixture of alcohol and water, by mass	0130	1	
Isovaleraldehyde, see	2058	3		LEAD SULPHATE with more than 3% free acid	1794	8	
JET PERFORATING GUNS, CHARGED, oil well, without detonator	0124	1		Lead tetraethyl, see	1649	6.1	
	0494	1		Lead tetramethyl, see	1649	6.1	
Jet tappers, without detonator, see	0059	1		LEAD TRINITRO-RESORCINATE, WETTED with not less than 20% water, or mixture of alcohol and water, by mass, see	0130	1	
KEROSENE	1223	3					
KETONES, LIQUID, N.O.S.	1224	3					
KRYPTON, COMPRESSED	1056	2		LIFE-SAVING APPLIANCES NOT SELF-INFLATING containing dangerous goods as equipment	3072	9	
KRYPTON, REFRIGERATED LIQUID	1970	2					

Name and description	UN No.	Class	Remarks	Name and description	UN No.	Class	Remarks
LIFE-SAVING APPLIANCES, SELF-INFLATING	2990	9		LITHIUM ION BATTERIES PACKED WITH EQUIPMENT (including lithium ion polymer batteries)	3091	9	
LIGHTER REFILLS containing flammable gas	1057	2		LITHIUM METAL BATTERIES (including lithium alloy batteries)	3090	9	
LIGHTERS containing flammable gas	1057	2		LITHIUM METAL BATTERIES CONTAINED IN EQUIPMENT (including lithium alloy batteries)	3091	9	
LIGHTERS, FUSE	0131	1					
Limonene, inactive, see	2052	3		LITHIUM METAL BATTERIES PACKED WITH EQUIPMENT (including lithium alloy batteries)	3091	9	
LIQUEFIED GAS, N.O.S.	3163	2					
LIQUEFIED GAS, FLAMMABLE, N.O.S.	3161	2		LITHIUM BOROHYDRIDE	1413	4.3	
LIQUEFIED GASES, non-flammable, charged with nitrogen, carbon dioxide or air	1058	2		LITHIUM FERROSILICON	2830	4.3	
				LITHIUM HYDRIDE	1414	4.3	
LIQUEFIED GAS, OXIDIZING, N.O.S.	3157	2		LITHIUM HYDRIDE, FUSED SOLID	2805	4.3	
LIQUEFIED GAS, TOXIC, N.O.S.	3162	2		LITHIUM HYDROXIDE	2680	8	
LIQUEFIED GAS, TOXIC, CORROSIVE, N.O.S.	3308	2		LITHIUM HYDROXIDE SOLUTION	2679	8	
LIQUEFIED GAS, TOXIC, FLAMMABLE, N.O.S.	3160	2		LITHIUM HYPOCHLORITE, DRY	1471	5.1	
LIQUEFIED GAS, TOXIC, FLAMMABLE, CORROSIVE, N.O.S.	3309	2		LITHIUM HYPOCHLORITE MIXTURE	1471	5.1	
				Lithium in cartouches, see	1415	4.3	
LIQUEFIED GAS, TOXIC, OXIDIZING, N.O.S.	3307	2		LITHIUM NITRATE	2722	5.1	
				LITHIUM NITRIDE	2806	4.3	
LIQUEFIED GAS, TOXIC, OXIDIZING, CORROSIVE, N.O.S.	3310	2		LITHIUM PEROXIDE	1472	5.1	
				Lithium silicide, see	1417	4.3	
Liquefied petroleum gas, see	1075	2		LITHIUM SILICON	1417	4.3	
Liquid filler, see	1263	3		L.n.g., see	1972	2	
	3066	8		LONDON PURPLE	1621	6.1	
	3469	3					
	3470	8		L.p.g., see	1075	2	
Liquid lacquer base, see	1263	3		Lye, see	1823	8	
	3066	8		Lythene, see	1268	3	
	3469	3		MAGNESIUM in pellets, turnings or ribbons	1869	4.1	
	3470	8					
LITHIUM	1415	4.3		Magnesium alkyls, see	3394	4.2	
Lithium alkyls, liquid, see	3394	4.2		MAGNESIUM ALLOYS with more than 50% magnesium in pellets, turnings or ribbons	1869	4.1	
Lithium alkyls, solid, see	3393	4.2					
LITHIUM ALUMINIUM HYDRIDE	1410	4.3		MAGNESIUM ALLOYS POWDER	1418	4.3	
LITHIUM ALUMINIUM HYDRIDE, ETHEREAL	1411	4.3		MAGNESIUM ALUMINIUM PHOSPHIDE	1419	4.3	
LITHIUM ION BATTERIES (including lithium ion polymer batteries)	3090	9		MAGNESIUM ARSENATE	1622	6.1	
				Magnesium bisulphite solution, see	2693	8	
LITHIUM ION BATTERIES CONTAINED IN EQUIPMENT (including lithium ion polymer batteries)	3091	9		MAGNESIUM BROMATE	1473	5.1	
				MAGNESIUM CHLORATE	2723	5.1	

Name and description	UN No.	Class	Remarks	Name and description	UN No.	Class	Remarks
Magnesium chloride and chlorate mixture, see	1459 3407	5.1 5.1		MATCHES, "STRIKE ANYWHERE"	1331	4.1	
MAGNESIUM DIAMIDE	2004	4.2		MATCHES, WAX "VESTA"	1945	4.1	
Magnesium diphenyl, see	3393	4.2		MEDICAL WASTE, N.O.S.	3291	6.2	
MAGNESIUM FLUORO-SILICATE	2853	6.1		MEDICINE, LIQUID, FLAMMABLE, TOXIC, N.O.S.	3248	3	
MAGNESIUM GRANULES, COATED, particle size not less than 149 microns	2950	4.3		MEDICINE, LIQUID, TOXIC, N.O.S.	1851	6.1	
MAGNESIUM HYDRIDE	2010	4.3		MEDICINE, SOLID, TOXIC, N.O.S.	3249	6.1	
MAGNESIUM NITRATE	1474	5.1		p-Mentha-1,8-diene, see	2052	8	
MAGNESIUM PERCHLORATE	1475	5.1		MERCAPTANS, LIQUID, FLAMMABLE, N.O.S.	3336	3	
MAGNESIUM PEROXIDE	1476	5.1		MERCAPTANS, LIQUID, FLAMMABLE, TOXIC, N.O.S.	1228	3	
MAGNESIUM PHOSPHIDE	2011	4.3		MERCAPTANS, LIQUID, TOXIC, FLAMMABLE, N.O.S.	3071	6.1	
MAGNESIUM POWDER	1418	4.3					
Magnesium scrap, see	1869	4.1		MERCAPTAN MIXTURE, LIQUID, FLAMMABLE, N.O.S.	3336	3	
MAGNESIUM SILICIDE	2624	4.3		MERCAPTAN MIXTURE, LIQUID, FLAMMABLE, TOXIC, N.O.S.	1228	3	
Magnesium silicofluoride, see	2853	6.1					
Magnetized material	2807	9	Not subject to ADR	MERCAPTAN MIXTURE, LIQUID, TOXIC, FLAMMABLE, N.O.S.	3071	6.1	
MALEIC ANHYDRIDE	2215	8		2-Mercaptoethanol, see	2966	6.1	
MALEIC ANHYDRIDE, MOLTEN	2215	8		2-Mercaptopropionic acid, see	2936	6.1	
Malonic dinitrile, see	2647	6.1		5-MERCAPTOTETRAZOL-1-ACETIC ACID	0448	1	
Malonodinitrile, see	2647	6.1		MERCURIC ARSENATE	1623	6.1	
MALONONITRILE	2647	6.1		MERCURIC CHLORIDE	1624	6.1	
MANEB	2210	4.2		MERCURIC NITRATE	1625	6.1	
MANEB PREPARATION with not less than 60% maneb	2210	4.2		MERCURIC POTASSIUM CYANIDE	1626	6.1	
MANEB PREPARATION, STABILIZED against self-heating	2968	4.3		Mercuric sulphate, see	1645	6.1	
MANEB, STABILIZED against self-heating	2968	4.3		Mercurol, see	1639	6.1	
				Mercurous bisulphate, see	1645	6.1	
Manganese ethylene-di-dithiocarbamate, see	2210	4.2		MERCUROUS NITRATE	1627	6.1	
Manganese ethylene-1,2-dithiocarbamate, see	2210	4.2		Mercurous sulphate, see	1645	6.1	
MANGANESE NITRATE	2724	5.1		MERCURY	2809	8	
Manganese (II) nitrate, see	2724	5.1		MERCURY ACETATE	1629	6.1	
MANGANESE RESINATE	1330	4.1		MERCURY AMMONIUM CHLORIDE	1630	6.1	
Manganous nitrate, see	2724	5.1					
MANNITOL HEXANITRATE, WETTED with not less than 40% water, or mixture of alcohol and water, by mass	0133	1		MERCURY BASED PESTICIDE, LIQUID, FLAMMABLE, TOXIC, flash-point less than 23 °C	2778	3	
				MERCURY BASED PESTICIDE, LIQUID, TOXIC	3012	6.1	
MATCHES, FUSEE	2254	4.1					
MATCHES, SAFETY (book, card or strike on box)	1944	4.1		MERCURY BASED PESTICIDE, LIQUID, TOXIC, FLAMMABLE, flash-point not less than 23 °C	3011	6.1	

Name and description	UN No.	Class	Remarks	Name and description	UN No.	Class	Remarks
MERCURY BASED PESTICIDE, SOLID, TOXIC	2777	6.1		METALLIC SUBSTANCE, WATER-REACTIVE, SELF-HEATING, N.O.S.	3209	4.3	
MERCURY BENZOATE	1631	6.1		METAL POWDER, FLAMMABLE, N.O.S.	3089	4.1	
Mercury bichloride, see	1624	6.1					
MERCURY BROMIDES	1634	6.1		METAL POWDER, SELF-HEATING, N.O.S.	3189	4.2	
MERCURY COMPOUND, LIQUID, N.O.S.	2024	6.1		METAL SALTS OF ORGANIC COMPOUNDS, FLAMMABLE, N.O.S.	3181	4.1	
MERCURY COMPOUND, SOLID, N.O.S.	2025	6.1					
MERCURY CYANIDE	1636	6.1		METHACRYLALDEHYDE, STABILIZED	2396	3	
MERCURY FULMINATE, WETTED with not less than 20% water, or mixture of alcohol and water, by mass	0135	1		METHACRYLIC ACID, STABILIZED	2531	8	
				METHACRYLONITRILE, STABILIZED	3079	3	
MERCURY GLUCONATE	1637	6.1		METHALLYL ALCOHOL	2614	3	
MERCURY IODIDE	1638	6.1		Methanal, see	1198	3	
MERCURY NUCLEATE	1639	6.1			2209	8	
MERCURY OLEATE	1640	6.1		Methane and hydrogen mixture, see	2034	2	
MERCURY OXIDE	1641	6.1		METHANE, COMPRESSED	1971	2	
MERCURY OXYCYANIDE, DESENSITIZED	1642	6.1		METHANE, REFRIGERATED LIQUID	1972	2	
MERCURY POTASSIUM IODIDE	1643	6.1		METHANESULPHONYL CHLORIDE	3246	6.1	
MERCURY SALICYLATE	1644	6.1					
MERCURY SULPHATE	1645	6.1		METHANOL	1230	3	
MERCURY THIOCYANATE	1646	6.1		2-Methoxyethyl acetate, see	1189	3	
Mesitylene, see	2325	3		METHOXYMETHYL ISOCYANATE	2605	3	
MESITYL OXIDE	1229	3					
Metal alkyl halides, water-reactive, n.o.s. / Metal aryl halides, water-reactive, n.o.s., see	3394	4.2		4-METHOXY-4-METHYLPENTAN-2-ONE	2293	3	
				1-Methoxy-2-nitrobenzene, see	2730	6.1	
					3458	6.1	
Metal alkyl hydrides, water-reactive, n.o.s. / Metal aryl hydrides, water-reactive, n.o.s., see	3394	4.2		1-Methoxy-3-nitrobenzene, see	2730	6.1	
					3458	6.1	
Metal alkyls, water-reactive, n.o.s. / Metal aryls, water-reactive, n.o.s., see	3393	4.2		1-Methoxy-4-nitrobenzene, see	2730	6.1	
					3458	6.1	
METAL CARBONYLS, LIQUID, N.O.S.	3281	6.1		1-METHOXY-2-PROPANOL	3092	3	
				METHYL ACETATE	1231	3	
METAL CARBONYLS, SOLID, N.O.S.	3466	6.1		METHYLACETYLENE AND PROPADIENE MIXTURE, STABILIZED such as mixture P1 or mixture P2	1060	2	
METAL CATALYST, DRY	2881	4.2					
METAL CATALYST, WETTED with a visible excess of liquid	1378	4.2		beta-Methyl acrolein, see	1143	6.1	
METALDEHYDE	1332	4.1		METHYL ACRYLATE, STABILIZED	1919	3	
METAL HYDRIDES, FLAMMABLE, N.O.S.	3182	4.1		METHYLAL	1234	3	
METAL HYDRIDES, WATER-REACTIVE, N.O.S.	1409	4.3		Methyl alcohol, see	1230	3	
				Methyl allyl alcohol, see	2614	3	
METALLIC SUBSTANCE, WATER-REACTIVE, N.O.S.	3208	4.3		METHYLALLYL CHLORIDE	2554	3	

Name and description	UN No.	Class	Remarks	Name and description	UN No.	Class	Remarks
METHYLAMINE, ANHYDROUS	1061	2		METHYLCYCLOHEXANOLS, flammable	2617	3	
METHYLAMINE, AQUEOUS SOLUTION	1235	3		METHYLCYCLOHEXANONE	2297	3	
METHYLAMYL ACETATE	1233	3		METHYLCYCLOPENTANE	2298	3	
Methyl amyl alcohol, see	2053	3		METHYL DICHLORO-ACETATE	2299	6.1	
Methyl amyl ketone, see	1110	3		METHYLDICHLOROSILANE	1242	4.3	
N-METHYLANILINE	2294	6.1		Methylene bromide, see	2664	6.1	
Methylated spirit, see	1986	3		Methylene chloride, see	1593	6.1	
	1987	3		Methylene chloride and methyl chloride mixture, see	1912	2	
alpha-METHYLBENZYL ALCOHOL, LIQUID	2937	6.1		Methylene cyanide, see	2647	6.1	
alpha-METHYLBENZYL ALCOHOL, SOLID	3438	6.1		p,p'-Methylene dianiline, see	2651	6.1	
				Methylene dibromide, see	2664	6.1	
METHYL BROMIDE with not more than 2% chloropicrin	1062	2		2,2'-Methylene-di-(3,4,6-trichlorophenol), see	2875	6.1	
Methyl bromide and chloropicrin mixture, with more than 2% chloropicrin, see	1581	2		Methyl ethyl ether, see	1039	2	
				METHYL ETHYL KETONE, see	1193	3	
METHYL BROMIDE AND ETHYLENE DIBROMIDE MIXTURE, LIQUID	1647	6.1		2-METHYL-5-ETHYLPYRIDINE	2300	6.1	
				METHYL FLUORIDE	2454	2	
METHYL BROMOACETATE	2643	6.1		METHYL FORMATE	1243	3	
2-METHYLBUTANAL	3371	3		2-METHYLFURAN	2301	3	
3-METHYLBUTAN-2-ONE	2397	3		Methyl glycol, see	1188	3	
2-METHYL-1-BUTENE	2459	3		Methyl glycol acetate, see	1189	3	
2-METHYL-2-BUTENE	2460	3		2-METHYL-2-HEPTANE-THIOL	3023	6.1	
3-METHYL-1-BUTENE	2561	3		5-METHYLHEXAN-2-ONE	2302	3	
N-METHYLBUTYLAMINE	2945	3		METHYLHYDRAZINE	1244	6.1	
METHYL tert-BUTYL ETHER	2398	3		METHYL IODIDE	2644	6.1	
METHYL BUTYRATE	1237	3		METHYL ISOBUTYL CARBINOL	2053	3	
METHYL CHLORIDE	1063	2		METHYL ISOBUTYL KETONE	1245	3	
Methyl chloride and chloropicrin mixture, see	1582	2		METHYL ISOCYANATE	2480	6.1	
METHYL CHLORIDE AND METHYLENE CHLORIDE MIXTURE	1912	2		METHYL ISOPROPENYL KETONE, STABILIZED	1246	3	
				METHYL ISOTHIOCYANATE	2477	6.1	
METHYL CHLOROACETATE	2295	6.1		METHYL ISOVALERATE	2400	3	
Methyl chlorocarbonate, see	1238	6.1		METHYL MAGNESIUM BROMIDE IN ETHYL ETHER	1928	4.3	
Methyl chloroform, see	2831	6.1					
METHYL CHLOROFORMATE	1238	6.1		METHYL MERCAPTAN	1064	2	
METHYL CHLOROMETHYL ETHER	1239	6.1		Methyl mercapto-propionaldehyde, see	2785	6.1	
METHYL 2-CHLORO-PROPIONATE	2933	3		METHYL METHACRYLATE MONOMER, STABILIZED	1247	3	
Methyl alpha-chloropropionate, see	2933	3		4-METHYLMORPHOLINE	2535	3	
METHYLCHLOROSILANE	2534	2		N-METHYLMORPHOLINE, see	2535	3	
Methyl cyanide, see	1648	3		METHYL NITRITE	2455	2	Carriage prohibited
METHYLCYCLOHEXANE	2296	3		METHYL ORTHOSILICATE	2606	6.1	

Name and description	UN No.	Class	Remarks	Name and description	UN No.	Class	Remarks
METHYLPENTADIENE	2461	3		MIXTURES OF 1,3-BUTADIENE AND HYDROCARBONS, STABILIZED, having a vapour pressure at 70 °C not exceeding 1.1 MPa (11 bar) and a density at 50 °C not lower than 0.525 kg/l	1010	2	
Methylpentanes, see	1208	3					
2-METHYLPENTAN-2-OL	2560	3					
4-Methylpentan-2-ol, see	2053	3					
3-Methyl-2-penten-4ynol, see	2705	8		Mixture P1 or mixture P2, see	1060	2	
METHYLPHENYL-DICHLOROSILANE	2437	8		MOLYBDENUM PENTACHLORIDE	2508	8	
2-Methyl-2-phenylpropane, see	2709	3		Monochloroacetic acid, see	1750	6.1	
1-METHYLPIPERIDINE	2399	3			1751	6.1	
METHYL PROPIONATE	1248	3		Monochlorobenzene, see	1134	3	
Methylpropylbenzene, see	2046	3		Monochlorodifluoromethane, see	1018	2	
METHYL PROPYL ETHER	2612	3		Monochlorodifluoromethane and monochloropentafluoroethane mixture, see	1973	2	
METHYL PROPYL KETONE	1249	3					
Methyl pyridines, see	2313	3		Monochlorodifluoromonobromo-methane, see	1974	2	
Methylstyrene, inhibited, see	2618	3					
alpha-Methylstyrene, see	2303	3		Monochloropentafluoroethane and monochlorodifluoromethane mixture, see	1973	2	
Methyl sulphate, see	1595	6.1					
Methyl sulphide, see	1164	3		Monoethylamine, see	1036	2	
METHYLTETRAHYDRO-FURAN	2536	3		MONONITROTOLUIDINES, see	2660	6.1	
METHYL TRICHLORO-ACETATE	2533	6.1		Monopropylamine, see	1277	3	
METHYLTRICHLOROSILANE	1250	3		MORPHOLINE	2054	8	
alpha-METHYLVALERAL-DEHYDE	2367	3		MOTOR FUEL ANTI-KNOCK MIXTURE	1649	6.1	
Methyl vinyl benzene, inhibited, see	2618	3		MOTOR SPIRIT	1203	3	
METHYL VINYL KETONE, STABILIZED	1251	6.1		Motor spirit and ethanol mixture, with more than 10% ethanol, see	3475	3	
M.i.b.c., see	2053	3		Muriatic acid, see	1789	8	
MINES with bursting charge	0136	1		MUSK XYLENE, see	2956	4.1	
	0137	1		Mysorite, see	2212	9	
	0138	1		Naphta, see	1268	3	
	0294	1					
Mirbane oil, see	1662	6.1		Naphta, petroleum, see	1268	3	
Missiles, guided, see	0180	1		Naphta, solvent, see	1268	3	
	0181	1		NAPHTHALENE, CRUDE	1334	4.1	
	0182	1		NAPHTHALENE, MOLTEN	2304	4.1	
	0183	1		NAPHTHALENE, REFINED	1334	4.1	
	0295	1		alpha-NAPHTHYLAMINE	2077	6.1	
	0397	1					
	0398	1		beta-NAPHTHYLAMINE, SOLID	1650	6.1	
	0436	1		beta-NAPHTHYLAMINE, SOLUTION	3411	6.1	
	0437	1					
	0438	1		NAPHTHYLTHIOUREA	1651	6.1	
Mixtures A, A01, A02, A0, A1, B1, B2, B or C, see	1965	2		1-Naphthylthiourea, see	1651	6.1	
				NAPHTHYLUREA	1652	6.1	
Mixture F1, mixture F2 or mixture F3, see	1078	2		1-Naphthylthiourea, see	1651	6.1	
				NAPHTHYLUREA	1652	6.1	
				NATURAL GAS, COMPRESSED with high methane content	1971	2	

Name and description	UN No.	Class	Remarks	Name and description	UN No.	Class	Remarks
NATURAL GAS, REFRIGERATED LIQUID with high methane content	1972	2		NITRATING ACID MIXTURE, SPENT, with not more than 50% nitric acid	1826	8	
Natural gasoline, see	1203	3		NITRIC ACID, other than red fuming, with at least 65% but not more than 70% nitric acid	2031	8	
Neohexane, see	1208	3					
NEON, COMPRESSED	1065	2		NITRIC ACID, other than red fuming, with less than 65% nitric acid	2031	8	
NEON, REFRIGERATED LIQUID	1913	2					
Neothyl, see	2612	3		NITRIC ACID, other than red fuming, with more than 70% nitric acid	2031	8	
NICKEL CARBONYL	1259	6.1					
NICKEL CYANIDE	1653	6.1		NITRIC ACID, RED FUMING	2032	8	
Nickel (II) cyanide, see	1653	6.1		NITRIC OXIDE, COMPRESSED	1660	2	
NICKEL NITRATE	2725	5.1		NITRIC OXIDE AND DINITROGEN TETROXIDE MIXTURE	1975	2	
Nickel (II) nitrate, see	2725	5.1					
NICKEL NITRITE	2726	5.1		NITRIC OXIDE AND NITROGEN DIOXIDE MIXTURE, see	1975	2	
Nickel (II) nitrite, see	2726	5.1					
Nickelous nitrate, see	2725	5.1		NITRILES, FLAMMABLE, TOXIC, N.O.S.	3273	3	
Nickelous nitrite, see	2726	5.1					
Nickel tetracarbonyl, see	1259	6.1		NITRILES, TOXIC, LIQUID, N.O.S.	3276	6.1	
NICOTINE	1654	6.1					
NICOTINE COMPOUND, LIQUID, N.O.S	3144	6.1		NITRILES, TOXIC, SOLID, N.O.S.	3439	6.1	
NICOTINE COMPOUND, SOLID, N.O.S.	1655	6.1		NITRILES, TOXIC, FLAMMABLE, N.O.S.	3275	6.1	
				NITRITES, INORGANIC, N.O.S.	2627	5.1	
NICOTINE HYDROCHLORIDE, LIQUID	1656	6.1		NITRITES, INORGANIC, AQUEOUS SOLUTION, N.O.S.	3219	5.1	
NICOTINE HYDROCHLORIDE, SOLID	3444	6.1		NITROANILINES (o-, m-, p-)	1661	6.1	
NICOTINE HYDROCHLORIDE, SOLUTION	1656	6.1		NITROANISOLES, LIQUID	2730	6.1	
				NITROANISOLES, SOLID	3458	6.1	
NICOTINE PREPARATION, LIQUID, N.O.S.	3144	6.1		NITROBENZENE	1662	6.1	
				Nitrobenzene bromide, see	2732	6.1	
NICOTINE PREPARATION, SOLID, N.O.S.	1655	6.1		NITROBENZENESULPHONIC ACID	2305	8	
NICOTINE SALICYLATE	1657	6.1		Nitrobenzol, see	1662	6.1	
NICOTINE SULPHATE, SOLID	3445	6.1		5-NITROBENZOTRIAZOL	0385	1	
NICOTINE SULPHATE, SOLUTION	1658	6.1		NITROBENZO-TRIFLUORIDES, LIQUID	2306	6.1	
NICOTINE TARTRATE	1659	6.1		NITROBENZOTRIFLUO-RIDES, SOLID	3431	6.1	
NITRATES, INORGANIC, N.O.S.	1477	5.1					
NITRATES, INORGANIC, AQUEOUS SOLUTION, N.O.S.	3218	5.1		NITROBROMOBENZENES, LIQUID	2732	6.1	
NITRATING ACID MIXTURE with more than 50% nitric acid	1796	8		NITROBROMOBENZENES, SOLID	3459	6.1	
NITRATING ACID MIXTURE with not more than 50% nitric acid	1796	8		NITROCELLULOSE, dry or wetted with less than 25% water (or alcohol), by mass	0340	1	
NITRATING ACID MIXTURE, SPENT, with more than 50% nitric acid	1826	8					

Name and description	UN No.	Class	Remarks	Name and description	UN No.	Class	Remarks
NITROCELLULOSE, unmodified or plasticized with less than 18% plasticizing substance, by mass	0341	1		NITROGLYCERIN, DESENSITIZED with not less than 40% non-volatile water-insoluble phlegmatizer, by mass	0143	1	
NITROCELLULOSE MEMBRANE FILTERS, with not more than 12.6% nitrogen, by dry mass	3270	4.1		NITROGLYCERIN MIXTURE, DESENSITIZED, LIQUID, N.O.S. with not more than 30% nitroglycerin, by mass	3357	3	
NITROCELLULOSE, with not more than 12.6% nitrogen, by dry mass, MIXTURE WITH PLASTICIZER, WITH PIGMENT	2557	4.1		NITROGLYCERIN MIXTURE, DESENSITIZED, LIQUID, FLAMMABLE, N.O.S. with not more than 30% nitroglycerin, by mass	3343	3	
NITROCELLULOSE, with not more than 12.6% nitrogen, by dry mass, MIXTURE WITH PLASTICIZER, WITHOUT PIGMENT	2557	4.1		NITROGLYCERIN MIXTURE, DESENSITIZED, SOLID, N.O.S. with more than 2% but not more than 10% nitroglycerin, by mass	3319	4.1	
NITROCELLULOSE, with not more than 12.6% nitrogen, by dry mass, MIXTURE WITHOUT PLASTICIZER, WITH PIGMENT	2557	4.1		NITROGLYCERIN, SOLUTION IN ALCOHOL with more than 1% but not more than 5% nitroglycerin	3064	3	
NITROCELLULOSE, with not more than 12.6% nitrogen, by dry mass, MIXTURE WITHOUT PLASTICIZER, WITHOUT PIGMENT	2557	4.1		NITROGLYCERIN SOLUTION IN ALCOHOL with more than 1% but not more than 10% nitroglycerin	0144	1	
NITROCELLULOSE, PLASTICIZED with not less than 18% plasticizing substance, by mass	0343	1		NITROGLYCERIN SOLUTION IN ALCOHOL with not more than 1% nitroglycerin	1204	3	
NITROCELLULOSE SOLUTION, FLAMMABLE with not more than 12.6% nitrogen, by dry mass, and not more than 55% nitrocellulose	2059	3		NITROGUANIDINE, dry or wetted with less than 20% water, by mass	0282	1	
NITROCELLULOSE, WETTED with not less than 25% alcohol, by mass	0342	1		NITROGUANIDINE, WETTED with not less than 20% water, by mass	1336	4.1	
NITROCELLULOSE WITH ALCOHOL (not less than 25% alcohol, by mass, and not more than 12.6% nitrogen, by dry mass)	2556	4.1		NITROHYDROCHLORIC ACID	1798	8	Carriage prohibited
				NITROMANNITE, WETTED, see	0133	1	
NITROCELLULOSE WITH WATER (not less than 25% water, by mass)	2555	4.1		NITROMETHANE	1261	3	
				Nitromuriatic acid, see	1798	8	
Nitrochlorobenzenes, see	1578 3409	6.1		NITRONAPHTHALENE	2538	4.1	
				NITROPHENOLS (o-, m-, p-)	1663	6.1	
3-NITRO-4-CHLOROBENZO-TRIFLUORIDE	2307	6.1		4-NITROPHENYL-HYDRAZINE, with not less than 30% water, by mass	3376	4.1	
NITROCRESOLS, LIQUID	3434	6.1		NITROPROPANES	2608	3	
NITROCRESOLS, SOLID	2446	6.1		p-NITROSODIMETHYL-ANILINE	1369	4.2	
NITROETHANE	2842	3		NITROSTARCH, dry or wetted with less than 20% water, by mass	0146	1	
NITROGEN, COMPRESSED	1066	2		NITROSTARCH, WETTED with not less than 20% water, by mass	1337	4.1	
NITROGEN DIOXIDE, see	1067	2		NITROSYL CHLORIDE	1069	2	
NITROGEN, REFRIGERATED LIQUID	1977	2		NITROSYLSULPHURIC ACID, LIQUID	2308	8	
NITROGEN TRIFLUORIDE	2451	2		NITROSYLSULPHURIC ACID, SOLID	3456	8	
NITROGEN TRIOXIDE	2421	2	Carriage prohibited	NITROTOLUENES, LIQUID	1664	6.1	

Name and description	UN No.	Class	Remarks	Name and description	UN No.	Class	Remarks
NITROTOLUENES, SOLID	3446	6.1		ORGANIC PEROXIDE TYPE B, SOLID, TEMPERATURE CONTROLLED	3112	5.2	
NITROTOLUIDINES	2660	6.1					
NITROTRIAZOLONE	0490	1		ORGANIC PEROXIDE TYPE C, LIQUID	3103	5.2	
NITRO UREA	0147	1					
NITROUS OXIDE	1070	2		ORGANIC PEROXIDE TYPE C, LIQUID, TEMPERATURE CONTROLLED	3113	5.2	
NITROUS OXIDE, REFRIGERATED LIQUID	2201	2					
NITROXYLENES, LIQUID	1665	6.1		ORGANIC PEROXIDE TYPE C, SOLID	3104	5.2	
NITROXYLENES, SOLID	3447	6.1		ORGANIC PEROXIDE TYPE C, SOLID, TEMPERATURE CONTROLLED	3114	5.2	
Non-activated carbon, see	1361	4.2					
Non-activated charcoal, see	1361	4.2		ORGANIC PEROXIDE TYPE D, LIQUID	3105	5.2	
NONANES	1920	3					
NONYLTRICHLOROSILANE	1799	8		ORGANIC PEROXIDE TYPE D, LIQUID, TEMPERATURE CONTROLLED	3115	5.2	
2,5-NORBORNADIENE, STABILIZED, see	2251	3					
Normal propyl alcohol, see	1274	3		ORGANIC PEROXIDE TYPE D, SOLID	3106	5.2	
NTO, see	0490	1		ORGANIC PEROXIDE TYPE D, SOLID, TEMPERATURE CONTROLLED	3116	5.2	
OCTADECYLTRICHLORO-SILANE	1800	8					
OCTADIENE	2309	3		ORGANIC PEROXIDE TYPE E, LIQUID	3107	5.2	
OCTAFLUOROBUT-2-ENE	2422	2		ORGANIC PEROXIDE TYPE E, LIQUID, TEMPERATURE CONTROLLED	3117	5.2	
OCTAFLUOROCYCLO-BUTANE	1976	2					
OCTAFLUOROPROPANE	2424	2		ORGANIC PEROXIDE TYPE E, SOLID	3108	5.2	
OCTANES	1262	3					
OCTOGEN, see	0226	1		ORGANIC PEROXIDE TYPE E, SOLID, TEMPERATURE CONTROLLED	3118	5.2	
	0391	1					
	0484	1					
OCTOL, dry or wetted with less than 15% water, by mass, see	0266	1		ORGANIC PEROXIDE TYPE F, LIQUID	3109	5.2	
OCTOLITE, dry or wetted with less than 15% water, by mass	0266	1		ORGANIC PEROXIDE TYPE F, LIQUID, TEMPERATURE CONTROLLED	3119	5.2	
OCTONAL	0496	1		ORGANIC PEROXIDE TYPE F, SOLID	3110	5.2	
OCTYL ALDEHYDES	1191	3					
tert-Octyl mercaptan, see	3023	6.1		ORGANIC PEROXIDE TYPE F, SOLID, TEMPERATURE CONTROLLED	3120	5.2	
OCTYLTRICHLOROSILANE	1801	8					
Oenanthol, see	3056	3					
OIL GAS, COMPRESSED	1071	2		Organic peroxides, see 2.2.52.4 for an alphabetic list of currently assigned organic peroxides and see	3101 to 3120	5.2	
Oleum, see	1831	8					
ORGANIC PEROXIDE TYPE B, LIQUID	3101	5.2		ORGANIC PIGMENTS, SELF-HEATING	3313	4.2	
ORGANIC PEROXIDE TYPE B, LIQUID, TEMPERATURE CONTROLLED	3111	5.2		ORGANOARSENIC COMPOUND, LIQUID, N.O.S.	3280	6.1	
ORGANIC PEROXIDE TYPE B, SOLID	3102	5.2		ORGANOARSENIC COMPOUND, SOLID, N.O.S.	3465	6.1	

Name and description	UN No.	Class	Remarks	Name and description	UN No.	Class	Remarks
ORGANOCHLORINE PESTICIDE, LIQUID, FLAMMABLE, TOXIC, flash-point less than 23 °C	2762	3		ORGANOPHOSPHORUS COMPOUND, TOXIC, LIQUID, N.O.S.	3278	6.1	
ORGANOCHLORINE PESTICIDE, LIQUID, TOXIC	2996	6.1		ORGANOPHOSPHORUS COMPOUND, TOXIC, SOLID N.O.S.	3464	6.1	
ORGANOCHLORINE PESTICIDE, LIQUID, TOXIC, FLAMMABLE, flash-point not less than 23 °C	2995	6.1		ORGANOPHOSPHORUS COMPOUND, TOXIC, FLAMMABLE, N.O.S.	3279	6.1	
ORGANOCHLORINE PESTICIDE, SOLID, TOXIC	2761	6.1		ORGANOPHOSPHORUS PESTICIDE, LIQUID, FLAMMABLE, TOXIC, flash-point less than 23 °C	2784	3	
ORGANOMETALLIC COMPOUND, TOXIC, LIQUID, N.O.S.,	3282	6.1					
ORGANOMETALLIC COMPOUND, TOXIC, SOLID, N.O.S.,	3467	6.1		ORGANOPHOSPHORUS PESTICIDE, LIQUID, TOXIC	3018	6.1	
Organometallic compound, solid, water-reactive, flammable, n.o.s., see	3396	4.3		ORGANOPHOSPHORUS PESTICIDE, LIQUID, TOXIC, FLAMMABLE, flash-point not less than 23 °C	3017	6.1	
Organometallic compound or Organometallic compound solution or Organometallic compound dispersion, water-reactive, flammable, n.o.s., see	3399	4.3		ORGANOPHOSPHORUS PESTICIDE, SOLID, TOXIC	2783	6.1	
				ORGANOTIN COMPOUND, LIQUID, N.O.S.	2788	6.1	
ORGANOMETALLIC SUBSTANCE, LIQUID, PYROPHORIC	3392	4.2		ORGANOTIN COMPOUND, SOLID, N.O.S.	3146	6.1	
ORGANOMETALLIC SUBSTANCE, SOLID, PYROPHORIC	3391	4.2		ORGANOTIN PESTICIDE, LIQUID, FLAMMABLE, TOXIC, flash-point less than 23 °C	2787	3	
ORGANOMETALLIC SUBSTANCE, SOLID, SELF-HEATING	3400	4.2		ORGANOTIN PESTICIDE, LIQUID, TOXIC	3020	6.1	
ORGANOMETALLIC SUBSTANCE, LIQUID, PYROPHORIC, WATER-REACTIVE	3394	4.2		ORGANOTIN PESTICIDE, LIQUID, TOXIC, FLAMMABLE, flash-point not less than 23 °C	3019	6.1	
ORGANOMETALLIC SUBSTANCE, SOLID, PYROPHORIC, WATER-REACTIVE	3393	4.2		ORGANOTIN PESTICIDE, SOLID, TOXIC	2786	6.1	
				Orthophospohoric acid, see	1805	8	
ORGANOMETALLIC SUBSTANCE, LIQUID, WATER-REACTIVE	3398	4.3		OSMIUM TETROXIDE	2471	6.1	
				OXIDIZING LIQUID, N.O.S.	3139	5.1	
ORGANOMETALLIC SUBSTANCE, SOLID, WATER-REACTIVE	3395	4.3		OXIDIZING LIQUID, CORROSIVE, N.O.S.	3098	5.1	
ORGANOMETALLIC SUBSTANCE, LIQUID, WATER-REACTIVE, FLAMMABLE	3399	4.3		OXIDIZING LIQUID, TOXIC, N.O.S.	3099	5.1	
				OXIDIZING SOLID, N.O.S.	1479	5.1	
				OXIDIZING SOLID, CORROSIVE, N.O.S.	3085	5.1	
ORGANOMETALLIC SUBSTANCE, SOLID, WATER-REACTIVE, FLAMMABLE	3396	4.3		OXIDIZING SOLID, FLAMMABLE, N.O.S.	3137	5.1	Carriage prohibited
ORGANOMETALLIC SUBSTANCE, SOLID, WATER-REACTIVE, SELF-HEATING	3397	4.3		OXIDIZING SOLID, SELF-HEATING, N.O.S.	3100	5.1	Carriage prohibited
				OXIDIZING SOLID, TOXIC, N.O.S.	3087	5.1	
				OXIDIZING SOLID, WATER-REACTIVE, N.O.S.	3121	5.1	Carriage prohibited

Name and description	UN No.	Class	Remarks	Name and description	UN No.	Class	Remarks
Oxirane, see	1040	2		Pentafluoroethane, 1,1,1-trifluoroethane, and 1,1,1,2-tetrafluoroethane zeotropic mixture with approximately 44% pentafluoroethane and 52% 1,1,1-trifluoroethane, see	3337	2	
OXYGEN, COMPRESSED	1072	2					
OXYGEN DIFLUORIDE, COMPRESSED	2190	2					
OXYGEN GENERATOR, CHEMICAL	3356	5.1		PENTAMETHYLHEPTANE	2286	3	
OXYGEN, REFRIGERATED LIQUID	1073	2		Pentanal, see	2058	3	
				PENTANE-2,4-DIONE	2310	3	
1-Oxy-4-nitrobenzene, see	1663	6.1		PENTANES, liquid	1265	3	
PAINT (including paint, lacquer, enamel, stain, shellac, varnish, polish, liquid filler and liquid lacquer base)	1263	3		n-Pentane, see	1265	3	
	3066	8		PENTANOLS	1105	3	
	3469	3		3-Pentanol, see	1105	3	
	3470	8		1-PENTENE	1108	3	
PAINT RELATED MATERIAL (including paint thinning and reducing compound)	1263	3		1-PENTOL	2705	8	
	3066	8		PENTOLITE, dry or wetted with less than 15% water, by mass	0151	1	
	3469	3					
	3470	8		Pentyl nitrite, see	1113	3	
Paint thinning and reducing compound, see	1263	3		PERCHLORATES, INORGANIC, N.O.S.	1481	5.1	
	3066	8					
	3469	3		PERCHLORATES, INORGANIC, AQUEOUS SOLUTION, N.O.S.	3211	5.1	
	3470	8					
PAPER, UNSATURATED OIL TREATED, incompletely dried (including carbon paper)	1379	4.2		PERCHLORIC ACID with more than 50% but not more than 72% acid, by mass	1873	5.1	
Paraffin, see	1223	3		PERCHLORIC ACID with not more than 50% acid, by mass	1802	8	
PARAFORMALDEHYDE	2213	4.1					
PARALDEHYDE	1264	3		Perchlorobenzene, see	2729	6.1	
PCBs, see	2315	9		Perchlorocyclopentadiene, see	2646	6.1	
	3432	9		Perchloroethylene, see	1897	6.1	
PENTABORANE	1380	4.2		PERCHLOROMETHYL MERCAPTAN	1670	6.1	
PENTACHLOROETHANE	1669	6.1					
PENTACHLOROPHENOL	3155	6.1		PERCHLORYL FLUORIDE	3083	2	
PENTAERYTHRITE TETRANITRATE with not less than 7% wax, by mass	0411	1		Perfluoroacetylchloride, see	3057	2	
				PERFLUORO (ETHYL VINYL ETHER)	3154	2	
PENTAERYTHRITE TETRANITRATE, DESENSITIZED with not less than 15% phlegmatizer, by mass	0150	1		PERFLUORO (METHYL VINYL ETHER)	3153	2	
				Perfluoropropane, see	2424	2	
PENTAERYTHRITE TETRANITRATE MIXTURE, DESENSITIZED, SOLID, N.O.S. with more than 10% but not more than 20% PETN, by mass	3344	4.1		PERFUMERY PRODUCTS with flammable solvents	1266	3	
				PERMANGANATES, INORGANIC, N.O.S.	1482	5.1	
PENTAERYTHRITE TETRANITRATE, WETTED with not less than 25% water, by mass	0150	1		PERMANGANATES, INORGANIC, AQUEOUS SOLUTION, N.O.S.	3214	5.1	
PENTAERYTHRITOL TETRANITRATE, see	0150	1		PEROXIDES, INORGANIC, N.O.S.	1483	5.1	
	0411	1		PERSULPHATES, INORGANIC, N.O.S.	3215	5.1	
	3344	4.1					
PENTAFLUOROETHANE	3220	2					

Name and description	UN No.	Class	Remarks	Name and description	UN No.	Class	Remarks
PERSULPHATES, INORGANIC, AQUEOUS SOLUTION, N.O.S.	3216	5.1		PHENOXYACETIC ACID DERIVATIVE PESTICIDE, LIQUID, TOXIC, FLAMMABLE, flash-point not less than 23 °C	3347	6.1	
PESTICIDE, LIQUID, FLAMMABLE, TOXIC, N.O.S., flash-point less than 23 °C	3021	3		PHENOXYACETIC ACID DERIVATIVE PESTICIDE, SOLID, TOXIC	3345	6.1	
PESTICIDE, LIQUID, TOXIC, N.O.S.	2902	6.1		PHENYLACETONITRILE, LIQUID	2470	6.1	
PESTICIDE, LIQUID, TOXIC, FLAMMABLE, N.O.S., flash-point not less than 23 °C	2903	6.1		PHENYLACETYL CHLORIDE	2577	8	
				Phenylamine, see	1547	6.1	
PESTICIDE, SOLID, TOXIC, N.O.S.	2588	6.1		1-Phenylbutane, see	2709	3	
				2-Phenylbutane, see	2709	3	
Pesticide, toxic, under compressed gas, n.o.s, see	1950	2		PHENYLCARBYLAMINE CHLORIDE	1672	6.1	
PETN, see	0150	1		PHENYL CHLOROFORMATE	2746	6.1	
	0411	1		Phenyl cyanide, see	2224	6.1	
	3344	4.1		PHENYLENEDIAMINES (o-, m-, p-)	1673	6.1	
PETN/TNT, see	0151	1		Phenylethylene, see	2055	3	
PETROL	1203	3		PHENYLHYDRAZINE	2572	6.1	
Petrol and ethanol mixture, with more than 10% ethanol, see	3475	3		PHENYL ISOCYANATE	2487	6.1	
PETROLEUM CRUDE OIL	1267	3		Phenylisocyanodichloride, see	1672	6.1	
PETROLEUM DISTILLATES, N.O.S.	1268	3		PHENYL MERCAPTAN	2337	6.1	
				PHENYLMERCURIC ACETATE	1674	6.1	
Petroleum ether, see	1268	3		PHENYLMERCURIC COMPOUND, N.O.S.	2026	6.1	
PETROLEUM GASES, LIQUEFIED	1075	2		PHENYLMERCURIC HYDROXIDE	1894	6.1	
Petroleum naphtha, see	1268	3					
Petroleum oil, see	1268	3		PHENYLMERCURIC NITRATE	1895	6.1	
PETROLEUM PRODUCTS, N.O.S.	1268	3		PHENYLPHOSPHORUS DICHLORIDE	2798	8	
Petroleum raffinate, see	1268	3					
Petroleum spirit, see	1268	3		PHENYLPHOSPHORUS THIODICHLORIDE	2799	8	
PHENACYL BROMIDE	2645	6.1		2-Phenylpropene, see	2303	3	
PHENETIDINES	2311	6.1		PHENYLTRICHLOROSILANE	1804	8	
PHENOLATES, LIQUID	2904	8		PHOSGENE	1076	2	
PHENOLATES, SOLID	2905	8		9-PHOSPHABICYCLO-NONANES	2940	4.2	
PHENOL, MOLTEN	2312	6.1		PHOSPHINE	2199	2	
PHENOL, SOLID	1671	6.1		Phosphoretted hydrogen, see	2199	2	
PHENOL SOLUTION	2821	6.1		PHOSPHORIC ACID, SOLUTION	1805	8	
PHENOLSULPHONIC ACID, LIQUID	1803	8		PHOSPHORIC ACID, SOLID	3453	8	
				Phosphoric acid, anhydrous, see	1807	8	
PHENOXYACETIC ACID DERIVATIVE PESTICIDE, LIQUID, FLAMMABLE, TOXIC, flash-point less than 23 °C	3346	3		PHOSPHOROUS ACID	2834	8	
				PHOSPHORUS, AMORPHOUS	1338	4.1	
PHENOXYACETIC ACID DERIVATIVE PESTICIDE, LIQUID, TOXIC	3348	6.1		Phosphorus bromide, see	1808	8	
				Phosphorus chloride, see	1809	6.1	

Name and description	UN No.	Class	Remarks	Name and description	UN No.	Class	Remarks
PHOSPHORUS HEPTASULPHIDE, free from yellow and white phosphorus	1339	4.1		PICRYL CHLORIDE, see	0155	1	
				PICRYL CHLORIDE, WETTED, see	3365	4.1	
PHOSPHORUS OXYBROMIDE	1939	8		alpha-PINENE	2368	3	
PHOSPHORUS OXYBROMIDE, MOLTEN	2576	8		PINE OIL	1272	3	
PHOSPHORUS OXYCHLORIDE	1810	8		PIPERAZINE	2579	8	
PHOSPHORUS PENTABROMIDE	2691	8		PIPERIDINE	2401	8	
PHOSPHORUS PENTACHLORIDE	1806	8		Pivaloyl chloride, see	2438	6.1	
PHOSPHORUS PENTAFLUORIDE	2198	2		Plastic explosives, see	0084	1	
PHOSPHORUS PENTASULPHIDE, free from yellow and white phosphorus	1340	4.3		PLASTICS MOULDING COMPOUND in dough, sheet or extruded rope form evolving flammable vapour	3314	9	
PHOSPHORUS PENTOXIDE	1807	8		PLASTICS, NITROCELLULOSE-BASED, SELF-HEATING, N.O.S.	2006	4.2	
PHOSPHORUS SESQUISULPHIDE, free from yellow and white phosphorus	1341	4.1		Polish, see	1263 3066 3469 3470	3 8 3 8	
Phosphorus (V) sulphide, free from yellow and white phosphorus, see	1340	4.3					
Phosphorus sulphochloride, see	1837	8		POLYAMINES, FLAMMABLE, CORROSIVE, N.O.S.	2733	3	
PHOSPHORUS TRIBROMIDE	1808	8		POLYAMINES, LIQUID, CORROSIVE, N.O.S.	2735	8	
PHOSPHORUS TRICHLORIDE	1809	6.1		POLYAMINES, LIQUID, CORROSIVE, FLAMMABLE, N.O.S.	2734	8	
PHOSPHORUS TRIOXIDE	2578	8					
PHOSPHORUS TRISULPHIDE, free from yellow and white phosphorus	1343	4.1		POLYAMINES, SOLID, CORROSIVE, N.O.S.	3259	8	
PHOSPHORUS, WHITE, DRY	1381	4.2		POLYCHLORINATED BIPHENYLS, LIQUID	2315	9	
PHOSPHORUS, WHITE IN SOLUTION	1381	4.2		POLYCHLORINATED BIPHENYLS, SOLID	3432	9	
PHOSPHORUS, WHITE, MOLTEN	2447	4.2		POLYESTER RESIN KIT	3269	3	
PHOSPHORUS, WHITE, UNDER WATER	1381	4.2		POLYHALOGENATED BIPHENYLS, LIQUID	3151	9	
PHOSPHORUS, YELLOW, DRY	1381	4.2		POLYHALOGENATED BIPHENYLS, SOLID	3152	9	
PHOSPHORUS, YELLOW, IN SOLUTION	1381	4.2		POLYHALOGENATED TERPHENYLS, LIQUID	3151	9	
PHOSPHORUS, YELLOW, UNDER WATER	1381	4.2		POLYHALOGENATED TERPHENYLS, SOLID	3152	9	
Phosphoryl chloride, see	1810	8		POLYMERIC BEADS, EXPANDABLE, evolving flammable vapour	2211	9	
PHTHALIC ANHYDRIDE with more than 0.05% of maleic anhydride	2214	8					
PICOLINES	2313	3		Polystyrene beads, expandable, see	2211	9	
PICRAMIDE, see	0153	1		POTASSIUM	2257	4.3	
PICRIC ACID, WETTED, see	1344 3364	4.1 4.1		POTASSIUM ARSENATE	1677	6.1	
				POTASSIUM ARSENITE	1678	6.1	
PICRITE, see	0282	1		Potassium bifluoride, see	1811	8	
PICRITE, WETTED, see	1336	4.1		Potassium bisulphate, see	2509	8	
Picrotoxin, see	3172 3462	6.1 6.1					

Name and description	UN No.	Class	Remarks	Name and description	UN No.	Class	Remarks
Potassium bisulphite solution, see	2693	8		POTASSIUM PERCHLORATE	1489	5.1	
POTASSIUM BOROHYDRIDE	1870	4.3		POTASSIUM PERMANGANATE	1490	5.1	
POTASSIUM BROMATE	1484	5.1		POTASSIUM PEROXIDE	1491	5.1	
POTASSIUM CHLORATE	1485	5.1		POTASSIUM PERSULPHATE	1492	5.1	
POTASSIUM CHLORATE, AQUEOUS SOLUTION	2427	5.1		POTASSIUM PHOSPHIDE	2012	4.3	
Potassium chlorate mixed with mineral oil, see	0083	1		Potassium selenate, see	2630	6.1	
				Potassium selenite, see	2630	6.1	
POTASSIUM CUPROCYANIDE	1679	6.1		Potassium silicofluoride, see	2655	6.1	
POTASSIUM CYANIDE, SOLID	1680	6.1		POTASSIUM SODIUM ALLOYS, LIQUID	1422	4.3	
POTASSIUM CYANIDE, SOLUTION	3413	6.1		POTASSIUM SODIUM ALLOYS, SOLID	3404	4.3	
Potassium dicyanocuprate (I), see	1679	6.1		POTASSIUM SULPHIDE with less than 30% water of crystallization	1382	4.2	
POTASSIUM DITHIONITE	1929	4.2					
POTASSIUM FLUORIDE, SOLID	1812	6.1		POTASSIUM SULPHIDE, ANHYDROUS	1382	4.2	
POTASSIUM FLUORIDE, SOLUTION	3422	6.1		POTASSIUM SULPHIDE, HYDRATED with not less than 30% water of crystallization	1847	8	
POTASSIUM FLUOROACETATE	2628	6.1					
POTASSIUM FLUOROSILICATE	2655	6.1		POTASSIUM SUPEROXIDE	2466	5.1	
Potassium hexafluorosilicate, see	2655	6.1		Potassium tetracyanomercurate (II), see	1626	6.1	
Potassium hydrate, see	1814	8					
POTASSIUM HYDROGENDIFLUORIDE, SOLID	1811	8		POWDER CAKE, WETTED with not less than 17% alcohol, by mass	0433	1	
POTASSIUM HYDROGENDIFLUORIDE, SOLUTION	3421	8		POWDER CAKE, WETTED with not less than 25% water, by mass	0159	1	
				POWDER PASTE, see	0159	1	
POTASSIUM HYDROGEN SULPHATE	2509	8			0433	1	
POTASSIUM HYDROSULPHITE, see	1929	4.2		POWDER, SMOKELESS	0160	1	
					0161	1	
Potassium hydroxide, liquid, see	1814	8		Power devices, explosive, see	0275	1	
POTASSIUM HYDROXIDE, SOLID	1813	8			0276	1	
					0323	1	
					0381	1	
POTASSIUM HYDROXIDE SOLUTION	1814	8		PRIMERS, CAP TYPE	0044	1	
					0377	1	
					0378	1	
POTASSIUM METAL ALLOYS, LIQUID	1420	4.3		Primers, small arms, see	0044	1	
POTASSIUM METAL ALLOYS, SOLID	3403	4.3		PRIMERS, TUBULAR	0319	1	
					0320	1	
					0376	1	
POTASSIUM METAVANADATE	2864	6.1		PRINTING INK, flammable or PRINTING INK RELATED MATERIAL (including printing ink thinning or reducing compound), flammable	1210	3	
POTASSIUM MONOXIDE	2033	8					
POTASSIUM NITRATE	1486	5.1					
Potassium nitrate and sodium nitrate mixture, see	1499	5.1		Projectiles, illuminating, see	0171	1	
					0254	1	
POTASSIUM NITRATE AND SODIUM NITRITE MIXTURE	1487	5.1			0297	1	
				PROJECTILES, inert with tracer	0345	1	
POTASSIUM NITRITE	1488	5.1			0424	1	
					0425	1	

Name and description	UN No.	Class	Remarks	Name and description	UN No.	Class	Remarks
PROJECTILES with burster or expelling charge	0346	1		PROPYL FORMATES	1281	3	
	0347	1		n-PROPYL ISOCYANATE	2482	6.1	
	0426	1		Propyl mercaptan, see	2402	3	
	0427	1		n-PROPYL NITRATE	1865	3	
	0434	1		PROPYLTRICHLOROSILANE	1816	8	
	0435	1		Pyrazine hexahydride, see	2579	8	
PROJECTILES with bursting charge	0167	1		PYRETHROID PESTICIDE, LIQUID, FLAMMABLE, TOXIC, flash-point less than 23 °C	3350	3	
	0168	1					
	0169	1					
	0324	1		PYRETHROID PESTICIDE, LIQUID, TOXIC	3352	6.1	
	0344	1					
PROPADIENE, STABILIZED	2200	2		PYRETHROID PESTICIDE, LIQUID, TOXIC, FLAMMABLE, flash-point not less than 23 °C	3351	6.1	
Propadiene and methyl acetylene mixture, stabilized, see	1060	2					
PROPANE	1978	2		PYRETHROID PESTICIDE, SOLID, TOXIC	3349	6.1	
PROPANETHIOLS	2402	3					
n-PROPANOL	1274	3		PYRIDINE	1282	3	
PROPELLANT, LIQUID	0495	1		PYROPHORIC ALLOY, N.O.S.	1383	4.2	
	0497	1		Pyrophoric organometallic compound, water-reactive, n.o.s., liquid, see	3394	4.2	
PROPELLANT, SOLID	0498	1					
	0499	1					
	0501	1		Pyrophoric organometallic compound, water-reactive, n.o.s., solid, see	3393	4.2	
Propellant with a single base, Propellant with a double base, Propellant with a triple base, see	0160	1					
	0161	1		PYROPHORIC LIQUID, INORGANIC, N.O.S.	3194	4.2	
Propene, see	1077	2		PYROPHORIC LIQUID, ORGANIC, N.O.S.	2845	4.2	
PROPIONALDEHYDE	1275	3					
PROPIONIC ACID with not less than 10% and less than 90% acid by mass	1848	8		PYROPHORIC METAL, N.O.S.	1383	4.2	
				PYROPHORIC SOLID, INORGANIC, N.O.S.	3200	4.2	
PROPIONIC ACID with not less than 90% acid by mass	3463	8		PYROPHORIC SOLID, ORGANIC, N.O.S.	2846	4.2	
PROPIONIC ANHYDRIDE	2496	8		PYROSULPHURYL CHLORIDE	1817	8	
PROPIONITRILE	2404	3		Pyroxylin solution, see	2059	3	
PROPIONYL CHLORIDE	1815	3		PYRROLIDINE	1922	3	
n-PROPYL ACETATE	1276	3		QUINOLINE	2656	6.1	
PROPYL ALCOHOL, NORMAL, see	1274	3		Quinone, see	2587	6.1	
PROPYLAMINE	1277	3		RADIOACTIVE MATERIAL, EXCEPTED PACKAGE - ARTICLES MANUFACTURED FROM NATURAL URANIUM or DEPLETED URANIUM or NATURAL THORIUM	2909	7	
n-PROPYLBENZENE	2364	3					
Propyl chloride, see	1278	3					
n-PROPYL CHLOROFORMATE	2740	6.1					
PROPYLENE	1077	2		RADIOACTIVE MATERIAL, EXCEPTED PACKAGE - EMPTY PACKAGING	2908	7	
PROPYLENE CHLOROHYDRIN	2611	6.1					
1,2-PROPYLENEDIAMINE	2258	8					
Propylene dichloride, see	1279	3		RADIOACTIVE MATERIAL, EXCEPTED PACKAGE - INSTRUMENTS or ARTICLES	2911	7	
PROPYLENEIMINE, STABILIZED	1921	3					
PROPYLENE OXIDE	1280	3					
PROPYLENE TETRAMER	2850	3					
Propylene trimer, see	2057	3					

Name and description	UN No.	Class	Remarks	Name and description	UN No.	Class	Remarks
RADIOACTIVE MATERIAL, EXCEPTED PACKAGE - LIMITED QUANTITY OF MATERIAL	2910	7		RADIOACTIVE MATERIAL, TYPE B(U) PACKAGE, non fissile or fissile-excepted	2916	7	
RADIOACTIVE MATERIAL, LOW SPECIFIC ACTIVITY (LSA-I), non fissile or fissile-excepted	2912	7		RADIOACTIVE MATERIAL, TYPE C PACKAGE, FISSILE	3330	7	
RADIOACTIVE MATERIAL, LOW SPECIFIC ACTIVITY (LSA-II), FISSILE	3324	7		RADIOACTIVE MATERIAL, TYPE C PACKAGE, non fissile or fissile-excepted	3323	7	
RADIOACTIVE MATERIAL, LOW SPECIFIC ACTIVITY (LSA-II), non fissile or fissile-excepted	3321	7		RADIOACTIVE MATERIAL, URANIUM HEXAFLUORIDE, FISSILE	2977	7	
RADIOACTIVE MATERIAL, LOW SPECIFIC ACTIVITY, (LSA-III), FISSILE	3325	7		RADIOACTIVE MATERIAL, URANIUM HEXAFLUORIDE, non fissile or fissile-excepted	2978	7	
RADIOACTIVE MATERIAL, LOW SPECIFIC ACTIVITY (LSA-III), non fissile or fissile-excepted	3322	7		Rags, oily	1856	4.2	Not subject to ADR
RADIOACTIVE MATERIAL, SURFACE CONTAMINATED OBJECTS (SCO-I or SCO-II), FISSILE	3326	7		RDX, see	0072 0391 0483	1 1 1	
RADIOACTIVE MATERIAL, SURFACE CONTAMINATED OBJECTS (SCO-I or SCO-II), non fissile or fissile-excepted	2913	7		RECEPTACLES, SMALL, CONTAINING GAS without a release device, non-refillable	2037	2	
RADIOACTIVE MATERIAL, TRANSPORTED UNDER SPECIAL ARRANGEMENT, FISSILE	3331	7		Red phosphorus, see	1338	4.1	
				REFRIGERANT GAS, N.O.S., such as mixture F1, mixture F2 or mixture P2	1078	2	
RADIOACTIVE MATERIAL, TRANSPORTED UNDER SPECIAL ARRANGEMENT, non fissile or fissile-excepted	2919	7		REFRIGERANT GAS R 12, see	1028	2	
				REFRIGERANT GAS R 12B1, see	1974	2	
RADIOACTIVE MATERIAL, TYPE A PACKAGE, FISSILE, non-special form	3327	7		REFRIGERANT GAS R 13, see	1022	2	
				REFRIGERANT GAS R 13B1, see	1009	2	
				REFRIGERANT GAS R 14, see	1982	2	
RADIOACTIVE MATERIAL, TYPE A PACKAGE, non-special form, non fissile or fissile-excepted	2915	7		REFRIGERANT GAS R 21, see	1029	2	
				REFRIGERANT GAS R 22, see	1018	2	
RADIOACTIVE MATERIAL, TYPE A PACKAGE, SPECIAL FORM, FISSILE	3333	7		REFRIGERANT GAS R 23, see	1984	2	
				REFRIGERANT GAS R 32, see	3252	2	
RADIOACTIVE MATERIAL, TYPE A PACKAGE, SPECIAL FORM, non fissile or fissile-excepted	3332	7		REFRIGERANT GAS R 40, see	1063	2	
				REFRIGERANT GAS R 41, see	2454	2	
				REFRIGERANT GAS R 114, see	1958	2	
RADIOACTIVE MATERIAL, TYPE B(M) PACKAGE, FISSILE	3329	7		REFRIGERANT GAS R 115, see	1020	2	
				REFRIGERANT GAS R 116, see	2193	2	
				REFRIGERANT GAS R 124, see	1021	2	
RADIOACTIVE MATERIAL, TYPE B(M) PACKAGE, non fissile or fissile-excepted	2917	7		REFRIGERANT GAS R 125, see	3220	2	
				REFRIGERANT GAS R 133a, see	1983	2	
RADIOACTIVE MATERIAL, TYPE B(U) PACKAGE, FISSILE	3328	7		REFRIGERANT GAS R 134a, see	3159	2	
				REFRIGERANT GAS R 142b, see	2517	2	
				REFRIGERANT GAS R 143a, see	2035	2	
				REFRIGERANT GASR 152a, see	1030	2	
				REFRIGERANT GAS R 161, see	2453	2	

Name and description	UN No.	Class	Remarks	Name and description	UN No.	Class	Remarks
REFRIGERANT GAS R 218, see	2424	2		RUBBER SCRAP, powdered or granulated	1345	4.1	
REFRIGERANT GAS R 227, see	3296	2		RUBBER SHODDY, powdered or granulated	1345	4.1	
REFRIGERANT GAS R 404A	3337	2		RUBBER SOLUTION	1287	3	
REFRIGERANT GAS R 407A	3338	2		RUBIDIUM	1423	4.3	
REFRIGERANT GAS R 407B	3339	2		RUBIDIUM HYDROXIDE	2678	8	
REFRIGERANT GAS R 407C	3340	2		RUBIDIUM HYDROXIDE SOLUTION	2677	8	
REFRIGERANT GAS R 500, see	2602	2		Saltpetre, see	1486	5.1	
REFRIGERANT GAS R 502, see	1973	2		SAMPLES, EXPLOSIVE, other than initiating explosive	0190	1	
REFRIGERANT GAS R 503, see	2599	2					
REFRIGERANT GAS R 1132a, see	1959	2		Sand acid, see	1778	8	
REFRIGERANT GAS R 1216, see	1858	2		SEAT-BELT PRETENSIONERS	0503	1	
REFRIGERANT GAS R 1318, see	2422	2			3268	9	
REFRIGERANT GAS RC 318, see	1976	2		SEED CAKE with more than 1.5% oil and not more than 11% moisture	1386	4.2	
REFRIGERATING MACHINES containing flammable, non-toxic, liquefied gas	3358	2		SEED CAKE with not more than 1.5% oil and not more than 11% moisture	2217	4.2	
REFRIGERATING MACHINES containing non-flammable, non-toxic, gases or ammonia solutions (UN 2672)	2857	2		Seed expellers, see	1386	4.2	
					2217	4.2	
REGULATED MEDICAL WASTE, N.O.S.	3291	6.2		SELENATES	2630	6.1	
RELEASE DEVICES, EXPLOSIVE	0173	1		SELENIC ACID	1905	8	
RESIN SOLUTION, flammable	1866	3		SELENITES	2630	6.1	
Resorcin, see	2876	6.1		SELENIUM COMPOUND, LIQUID, N.O.S.	3440	6.1	
RESORCINOL	2876	6.1		SELENIUM COMPOUND, SOLID, N.O.S.	3283	6.1	
RIVETS, EXPLOSIVE	0174	1					
ROCKET MOTORS	0186	1		SELENIUM DISULPHIDE	2657	6.1	
	0280	1		SELENIUM HEXAFLUORIDE	2194	2	
	0281	1		SELENIUM OXYCHLORIDE	2879	8	
ROCKET MOTORS, LIQUID FUELLED	0395	1		SELF-HEATING LIQUID, CORROSIVE, INORGANIC, N.O.S.	3188	4.2	
	0396	1					
ROCKET MOTORS WITH HYPERGOLIC LIQUIDS with or without expelling charge	0250	1		SELF-HEATING LIQUID, CORROSIVE, ORGANIC, N.O.S.	3185	4.2	
	0322	1					
ROCKETS with bursting charge	0180	1		SELF-HEATING LIQUID, INORGANIC, N.O.S.	3186	4.2	
	0181	1					
	0182	1		SELF-HEATING LIQUID, ORGANIC, N.O.S.	3183	4.2	
	0295	1					
ROCKETS with expelling charge	0436	1		SELF-HEATING LIQUID, TOXIC, INORGANIC, N.O.S.	3187	4.2	
	0437	1					
	0438	1		SELF-HEATING LIQUID, TOXIC, ORGANIC, N.O.S.	3184	4.2	
ROCKETS with inert head	0183	1					
	0502	1		SELF-HEATING SOLID, CORROSIVE, INORGANIC, N.O.S.	3192	4.2	
ROCKETS, LINE-THROWING	0238	1					
	0240	1					
	0453	1					
ROCKETS, LIQUID FUELLED with bursting charge	0397	1		SELF-HEATING SOLID, CORROSIVE, ORGANIC, N.O.S.	3126	4.2	
	0398	1					
ROSIN OIL	1286	3					

Name and description	UN No.	Class	Remarks	Name and description	UN No.	Class	Remarks
SELF-HEATING SOLID, INORGANIC, N.O.S.	3190	4.2		Shellac, see	1263	3	
					3066	8	
SELF-HEATING SOLID, ORGANIC, N.O.S.	3088	4.2			3469	3	
					3470	8	
SELF-HEATING SOLID, OXIDIZING, N.O.S	3127	4.2	Carriage prohibited	SIGNAL DEVICES, HAND	0191	1	
					0373	1	
SELF-HEATING SOLID, TOXIC, INORGANIC, N.O.S.	3191	4.2		SIGNALS, DISTRESS, ship	0194	1	
					0195	1	
					0505	1	
SELF-HEATING SOLID, TOXIC, ORGANIC, N.O.S.	3128	4.2			0506	1	
SELF-REACTIVE LIQUID TYPE B	3221	4.1		Signals, distress, ship, water-activated, see	0249	1	
SELF-REACTIVE LIQUID TYPE B, TEMPERATURE CONTROLLED	3231	4.1		SIGNALS, RAILWAY TRACK, EXPLOSIVE	0192	1	
					0193	1	
					0492	1	
SELF-REACTIVE LIQUID TYPE C	3223	4.1			0493	1	
SELF-REACTIVE LIQUID TYPE C, TEMPERATURE CONTROLLED	3233	4.1		SIGNALS, SMOKE	0196	1	
					0197	1	
					0313	1	
SELF-REACTIVE LIQUID TYPE D	3225	4.1			0487	1	
SELF-REACTIVE LIQUID TYPE D, TEMPERATURE CONTROLLED	3235	4.1			0507	1	
				SILANE	2203	2	
SELF-REACTIVE LIQUID TYPE E	3227	4.1		Silicofluoric acid, see	1778	8	
SELF-REACTIVE LIQUID TYPE E, TEMPERATURE CONTROLLED	3237	4.1		Silicofluorides, n.o.s., see	2856	6.1	
				Silicon chloride, see	1818	8	
				SILICON POWDER, AMORPHOUS	1346	4.1	
SELF-REACTIVE LIQUID TYPE F	3229	4.1					
SELF-REACTIVE LIQUID TYPE F, TEMPERATURE CONTROLLED	3239	4.1		SILICON TETRACHLORIDE	1818	8	
SELF-REACTIVE SOLID TYPE B	3222	4.1		SILICON TETRAFLUORIDE	1859	2	
SELF-REACTIVE SOLID TYPE B, TEMPERATURE CONTROLLED	3232	4.1		SILVER ARSENITE	1683	6.1	
SELF-REACTIVE SOLID TYPE C	3224	4.1		SILVER CYANIDE	1684	6.1	
SELF-REACTIVE SOLID TYPE C, TEMPERATURE CONTROLLED	3234	4.1		SILVER NITRATE	1493	5.1	
SELF-REACTIVE SOLID TYPE D	3226	4.1		SILVER PICRATE, WETTED with not less than 30% water, by mass	1347	4.1	
SELF-REACTIVE SOLID TYPE D, TEMPERATURE CONTROLLED	3236	4.1		SLUDGE ACID	1906	8	
SELF-REACTIVE SOLID TYPE E	3228	4.1		SODA LIME with more than 4% sodium hydroxide	1907	8	
SELF-REACTIVE SOLID TYPE E, TEMPERATURE CONTROLLED	3238	4.1		SODIUM	1428	4.3	
				Sodium aluminate, solid	2812	8	Not subject to ADR
SELF-REACTIVE SOLID TYPE F	3230	4.1		SODIUM ALUMINATE SOLUTION	1819	8	
SELF-REACTIVE SOLID TYPE F, TEMPERATURE CONTROLLED	3240	4.1		SODIUM ALUMINIUM HYDRIDE	2835	4.3	
SHALE OIL	1288	3		SODIUM AMMONIUM VANADATE	2863	6.1	
Shaped charges, see	0059	1		SODIUM ARSANILATE	2473	6.1	
	0439	1		SODIUM ARSENATE	1685	6.1	
	0440	1		SODIUM ARSENITE, AQUEOUS SOLUTION	1686	6.1	
	0441	1					
				SODIUM ARSENITE, SOLID	2027	6.1	
				SODIUM AZIDE	1687	6.1	

Name and description	UN No.	Class	Remarks	Name and description	UN No.	Class	Remarks
Sodium bifluoride, see	2439	8		Sodium hydrogen 4-amino-phenylarsenate, see	2473	6.1	
Sodium binoxide, see	1504	5.1		SODIUM HYDROGEN-DIFLUORIDE	2439	8	
Sodium bisulphite solution, see	2693	8		SODIUM HYDROSULPHIDE with less than 25% water of crystallization	2318	4.2	
SODIUM BOROHYDRIDE	1426	4.3					
SODIUM BOROHYDRIDE AND SODIUM HYDROXIDE SOLUTION, with not more than 12% sodium borohydride and not more than 40% sodium hydroxide by mass	3320	8		SODIUM HYDROSULPHIDE, HYDRATED with not less than 25% water of crystallization	2949	8	
				SODIUM HYDROSULPHITE, see	1384	4.2	
SODIUM BROMATE	1494	5.1		SODIUM HYDROXIDE, SOLID	1823	8	
SODIUM CACODYLATE	1688	6.1		SODIUM HYDROXIDE SOLUTION	1824	8	
SODIUM CARBONATE PEROXYHYDRATE	3378	5.1		Sodium metasilicate pentahydrate, see	3253	8	
SODIUM CHLORATE	1495	5.1		SODIUM METHYLATE	1431	4.2	
SODIUM CHLORATE, AQUEOUS SOLUTION	2428	5.1		SODIUM METHYLATE SOLUTION in alcohol	1289	3	
Sodium chlorate mixed with dinitrotoluene, see	0083	1		SODIUM MONOXIDE	1825	8	
SODIUM CHLORITE	1496	5.1		SODIUM NITRATE	1498	5.1	
SODIUM CHLOROACETATE	2659	6.1		SODIUM NITRATE AND POTASSIUM NITRATE MIXTURE	1499	5.1	
SODIUM CUPROCYANIDE, SOLID	2316	6.1					
SODIUM CUPROCYANIDE SOLUTION	2317	6.1		SODIUM NITRITE	1500	5.1	
SODIUM CYANIDE, SOLID	1689	6.1		Sodium nitrite and potassium nitrate mixture, see	1487	5.1	
SODIUM CYANIDE, SOLUTION	3414	6.1		SODIUM PENTACHLORO-HENATE	2567	6.1	
Sodium dicyanocuprate (I), solid, see	2316	6.1		SODIUM PERBORATE MONOHYDRATE	3377	5.1	
Sodium dicyanocuprate (I) solution, see	2317	6.1		SODIUM PERCHLORATE	1502	5.1	
Sodium dimethylarsenate, see	1688	6.1		SODIUM PERMANGANATE	1503	5.1	
SODIUM DINITRO-o-CRESOLATE, dry or wetted with less than 15% water, by mass	0234	1		SODIUM PEROXIDE	1504	5.1	
				SODIUM PEROXOBORATE, ANHYDROUS	3247	5.1	
SODIUM DINITRO-o-CRESOLATE, WETTED with not less than 10% water, by mass	3369	4.1		SODIUM PERSULPHATE	1505	5.1	
				SODIUM PHOSPHIDE	1432	4.3	
SODIUM DINITRO-o-CRESOLATE, WETTED with not less than 15% water, by mass	1348	4.1		SODIUM PICRAMATE, dry or wetted with less than 20% water, by mass	0235	1	
Sodium dioxide, see	1504	5.1		SODIUM PICRAMATE, WETTED with not less than 20% water, by mass	1349	4.1	
SODIUM DITHIONITE	1384	4.2					
SODIUM FLUORIDE, SOLID	1690	6.1		Sodium potassium alloys, liquid, see	1422	4.3	
SODIUM FLUORIDE, SOLUTION	3415	6.1		Sodium selenate, see	2630	6.1	
SODIUM FLUOROACETATE	2629	6.1		Sodium selenite, see	2630	6.1	
SODIUM FLUOROSILICATE	2674	6.1		Sodium silicofluoride, see	2674	6.1	
Sodium hexafluorosilicate, see	2674	6.1		SODIUM SULPHIDE, ANHYDROUS	1385	4.2	
Sodium hydrate, see	1824	8					
SODIUM HYDRIDE	1427	4.3					

Name and description	UN No.	Class	Remarks	Name and description	UN No.	Class	Remarks
SODIUM SULPHIDE with less than 30% water of crystallization	1385	4.2		SUBSTANCES, EVI, N.O.S., see	0482	1	
SODIUM SULPHIDE, HYDRATED with not less than 30% water	1849	8		SUBSTANCES, EXPLOSIVE, N.O.S.	0357	1	
					0358	1	
					0359	1	
SODIUM SUPEROXIDE	2547	5.1			0473	1	
SOLIDS CONTAINING CORROSIVE LIQUID, N.O.S.	3244	8			0474	1	
					0475	1	
					0476	1	
SOLIDS or mixtures of solids (such as preparations and wastes) CONTAINING FLAMMABLE LIQUID, N.O.S. having a flash-point up to 60 °C	3175	4.1			0477	1	
					0478	1	
					0479	1	
					0480	1	
					0481	1	
					0485	1	
SOLIDS CONTAINING TOXIC LIQUID, N.O.S.	3243	6.1		SUBSTANCES, EXPLOSIVE, VERY INSENSITIVE, N.O.S.	0482	1	
Solvents, flammable, n.o.s., see	1993	3		Substances liable to spontaneous combustion, n.o.s., see	2845	4.2	
Solvents, flammable, toxic, n.o.s., see	1992	3			2846	4.2	
SOUNDING DEVICES, EXPLOSIVE	0204	1			3194	4.2	
	0296	1			3200	4.2	
	0374	1		SUBSTITUTED NITROPHENOL PESTICIDE, LIQUID, FLAMMABLE, TOXIC, flash-point less than 23 °C	2780	3	
	0375	1					
Squibs, see	0325	1					
	0454	1		SUBSTITUTED NITROPHENOL PESTICIDE, LIQUID, TOXIC	3014	6.1	
Stain, see	1263	3					
	3066	8		SUBSTITUTED NITROPHENOL PESTICIDE, LIQUID, TOXIC, FLAMMABLE, flash-point not less than 23 °C	3013	6.1	
	3469	3					
	3470	8					
STANNIC CHLORIDE, ANHYDROUS	1827	8					
				SUBSTITUTED NITROPHENOL PESTICIDE, SOLID, TOXIC	2779	6.1	
STANNIC CHLORIDE PENTAHYDRATE	2440	8					
				SULPHAMIC ACID	2967	8	
STANNIC PHOSPHIDES	1433	4.3		SULPHUR	1350	4.1	
Steel swarf, see	2793	4.2		SULPHUR CHLORIDES	1828	8	
STIBINE	2676	2		Sulphur dichloride, see	1828	8	
Straw	1327	4.1	Not subject to ADR	SULPHUR DIOXIDE	1079	2	
				Sulphuretted hydrogen, see	1053	2	
Strontium alloys, pyrophoric, see	1383	4.2		SULPHUR HEXAFLUORIDE	1080	2	
STRONTIUM ARSENITE	1691	6.1		SULPHURIC ACID with more than 51% acid	1830	8	
STRONTIUM CHLORATE	1506	5.1		SULPHURIC ACID with not more than 51% acid	2796	8	
Strontium dioxide, see	1509	5.1					
STRONTIUM NITRATE	1507	5.1		SULPHURIC ACID, FUMING	1831	8	
STRONTIUM PERCHLORATE	1508	5.1		SULPHURIC ACID, SPENT	1832	8	
STRONTIUM PEROXIDE	1509	5.1		Sulphuric and hydrofluoric acid mixture, see	1786	8	
STRONTIUM PHOSPHIDE	2013	4.3					
STRYCHNINE	1692	6.1		SULPHUR, MOLTEN	2448	4.1	
STRYCHNINE SALTS	1692	6.1		Sulphur monochloride, see	1828	8	
STYPHNIC ACID, see	0219	1		SULPHUROUS ACID	1833	8	
	0394	1		SULPHUR TETRAFLUORIDE	2418	2	
STYRENE MONOMER, STABILIZED	2055	3		SULPHUR TRIOXIDE, STABILIZED	1829	8	

Name and description	UN No.	Class	Remarks	Name and description	UN No.	Class	Remarks
SULPHURYL CHLORIDE	1834	8		TETRAHYDROTHIOPHENE	2412	3	
SULPHURYL FLUORIDE	2191	2		Tetramethoxysilane, see	2606	6.1	
Talcum with tremolite and/or actinolite, see	2590	9		TETRAMETHYLAMMONIUM HYDROXIDE SOLID	3423	8	
TARS, LIQUID, including road asphalt and oils, bitumen and cut backs, with a flash-point not greater than 60 °C	1999	3		TETRAMETHYLAMMONIUM HYDROXIDE SOLUTION	1835	8	
				Tetramethylene, see	2601	2	
				Tetramethylene cyanide, see	2205	6.1	
Tars, liquid, with a flash-point above 60 °C, at or above its flash-point, see	3256	3		Tetramethyl lead, see	1649	6.1	
				TETRAMETHYLSILANE	2749	3	
Tars, liquid, at or above 100 °C and below its flash-point, see	3257	9		TETRANITROANILINE	0207	1	
				TETRANITROMETHANE	1510	5.1	
Tartar emetic, see	1551	6.1		TETRAPROPYL ORTHOTITANATE	2413	3	
TEAR GAS CANDLES	1700	6.1		TETRAZENE, WETTED with not less than 30% water, or mixture of alcohol and water, by mass, see	0114	1	
TEAR GAS SUBSTANCE, LIQUID, N.O.S.	1693	6.1					
TEAR GAS SUBSTANCE, SOLID, N.O.S.	3448	6.1		TETRAZOL-1-ACETIC ACID	0407	1	
TELLURIUM COMPOUND, N.O.S.	3284	6.1		1H-TETRAZOLE	0504	1	
TELLURIUM HEXAFLUORIDE	2195	2		TETRYL, see	0208	1	
TERPENE HYDROCARBONS, N.O.S.	2319	3		Textile waste, wet	1857	4.2	Not subject to ADR
TERPINOLENE	2541	3					
TETRABROMOETHANE	2504	6.1		THALLIUM CHLORATE	2573	5.1	
1,1,2,2-TETRACHLORO-ETHANE	1702	6.1		Thallium (I) chlorate, see	2573	5.1	
TETRACHLOROETHYLENE	1897	6.1		THALLIUM COMPOUND, N.O.S.	1707	6.1	
TETRAETHYL DITHIO-PYROPHOSPHATE	1704	6.1		THALLIUM NITRATE	2727	6.1	
				Thallium (I) nitrate, see	2727	6.1	
TETRAETHYLENE-PENTAMINE	2320	8		Thallous chlorate, see	2573	5.1	
Tetraethyl lead, see	1649	6.1		4-THIAPENTANAL	2785	6.1	
TETRAETHYL SILICATE	1292	3		Thia-4-pentanal, see	2785	6.1	
Tetraethyoxysilane, see	1292	3		THIOACETIC ACID	2436	3	
Tetrafluorodichloroethane, see	1958	2		THIOCARBAMATE PESTICIDE, LIQUID, FLAMMABLE, TOXIC, flash-point less than 23 °C	2772	3	
1,1,1,2-TETRAFLUORO-ETHANE	3159	2					
TETRAFLUOROETHYLENE, STABILIZED	1081	2		THIOCARBAMATE PESTICIDE, LIQUID, TOXIC	3006	6.1	
TETRAFLUOROMETHANE	1982	2		THIOCARBAMATE PESTICIDE, LIQUID, TOXIC, FLAMMABLE, flash-point not less than 23 °C	3005	6.1	
1,2,3,6-TETRAHYDRO-BENZALDEHYDE	2498	3					
TETRAHYDROFURAN	2056	3		THIOCARBAMATE PESTICIDE, SOLID, TOXIC	2771	6.1	
TETRAHYDRO-FURFURYLAMINE	2943	3					
				THIOGLYCOL	2966	6.1	
Tetrahydro-1,4-oxazine, see	2054	3		THIOGLYCOLIC ACID	1940	8	
TETRAHYDROPHTHALIC ANHYDRIDES with more than 0.05% of maleic anhydride	2698	8		THIOLACTIC ACID	2936	6.1	
				THIONYL CHLORIDE	1836	8	
1,2,3,6-TETRAHYDRO-PYRIDINE	2410	3		THIOPHENE	2414	3	

Name and description	UN No.	Class	Remarks	Name and description	UN No.	Class	Remarks
Thiophenol, see	2337	6.1		TORPEDOES, LIQUID FUELLED with inert head	0450	1	
THIOPHOSGENE	2474	6.1		TORPEDOES, LIQUID FUELLED with or without bursting charge	0449	1	
THIOPHOSPHORYL CHLORIDE	1837	8		TOXIC BY INHALATION LIQUID, N.O.S. with an inhalation toxicity lower than or equal to 200 ml/m^3 and saturated vapour concentration greater than or equal to 500 LC$_{50}$	3381	6.1	
THIOUREA DIOXIDE	3341	4.2					
Tin (IV) chloride, anhydrous, see	1827	8					
Tin (IV) chloride pentahydrate, see	2440	8					
TINCTURES, MEDICINAL	1293	3		TOXIC BY INHALATION LIQUID, N.O.S. with an inhalation toxicity lower than or equal to 1000 ml/m^3 and saturated vapour concentration greater than or equal to 10 LC$_{50}$	3382	6.1	
Tin tetrachloride, see	1827	8					
TITANIUM DISULPHIDE	3174	4.2					
TITANIUM HYDRIDE	1871	4.1					
TITANIUM POWDER, DRY	2546	4.2		TOXIC BY INHALATION LIQUID, CORROSIVE, N.O.S. with an inhalation toxicity lower than or equal to 200 ml/m^3 and saturated vapour concentration greater than or equal to 500 LC$_{50}$	3389	6.1	
TITANIUM POWDER, WETTED with not less than 25% water	1352	4.1					
TITANIUM SPONGE GRANULES	2878	4.1					
TITANIUM SPONGE POWDERS	2878	4.1					
TITANIUM TETRACHLORIDE	1838	8		TOXIC BY INHALATION LIQUID, CORROSIVE, N.O.S. with an inhalation toxicity lower than or equal to 1000 ml/m^3 and saturated vapour concentration greater than or equal to 10 LC$_{50}$	3390	6.1	
TITANIUM TRICHLORIDE MIXTURE	2869	8					
TITANIUM TRICHLORIDE MIXTURE, PYROPHORIC	2441	4.2					
TITANIUM TRICHLORIDE, PYROPHORIC	2441	4.2		TOXIC BY INHALATION LIQUID, FLAMMABLE, N.O.S. with an inhalation toxicity lower than or equal to 200 ml/m^3 and saturated vapour concentration greater than or equal to 500 LC$_{50}$	3383	6.1	
TNT, see	0209	1					
	0388	1					
	0389	1					
TNT mixed with aluminium, see	0390	1		TOXIC BY INHALATION LIQUID, FLAMMABLE, N.O.S. with an inhalation toxicity lower than or equal to 1000 ml/m^3 and saturated vapour concentration greater than or equal to 10 LC$_{50}$	3384	6.1	
TNT, WETTED with not less than 30% water, by mass, see	1356	4.1					
TNT, WETTED with not less than 10% water, by mass, see	3366	4.1					
Toe puffs, nitrocellulose base, see	1353	4.1		TOXIC BY INHALATION LIQUID, OXIDIZING, N.O.S. with an inhalation toxicity lower than or equal to 200 ml/m^3 and saturated vapour concentration greater than or equal to 500 LC$_{50}$	3387	6.1	
TOLUENE	1294	3					
TOLUENE DIISOCYANATE	2078	6.1					
TOLUIDINES, LIQUID	1708	6.1					
TOLUIDINES, SOLID	3451	6.1		TOXIC BY INHALATION LIQUID, OXIDIZING, N.O.S. with an inhalation toxicity lower than or equal to 1000 ml/m^3 and saturated vapour concentration greater than or equal to 10 LC$_{50}$	3388	6.1	
Toluol, see	1294	3					
2,4-TOLUYLENEDIAMINE, SOLID	1709	6.1					
2,4-TOLUYLENEDIAMINE, SOLUTION	3418	6.1					
Toluylene diisocyanate, see	2078	6.1		TOXIC BY INHALATION LIQUID, WATER-REACTIVE, N.O.S. with an inhalation toxicity lower than or equal to 200 ml/m^3 and saturated vapour concentration greater than or equal to 500 LC$_{50}$	3385	6.1	
Tolylene diisocyanate, see	2078	6.1					
Tolylethylene, inhibited, see	2618	3					
TORPEDOES with bursting charge	0329	1					
	0330	1					
	0451	1					

Name and description	UN No.	Class	Remarks	Name and description	UN No.	Class	Remarks
TOXIC BY INHALATION LIQUID, WATER-REACTIVE, N.O.S. with an inhalation toxicity lower than or equal to 1000 ml/m^3 and saturated vapour concentration greater than or equal to 10 LC$_{50}$	3386	6.1		TRIAZINE PESTICIDE, SOLID, TOXIC	2763	6.1	
				Tribromoborane, see	2692	8	
				TRIBUTYLAMINE	2542	6.1	
				TRIBUTYLPHOSPHANE	3254	4.2	
TOXIC LIQUID, CORROSIVE, INORGANIC, N.O.S.	3289	6.1		Trichloroacetaldehyde, see	2075	6.1	
TOXIC LIQUID, CORROSIVE, ORGANIC, N.O.S.	2927	6.1		TRICHLOROACETIC ACID	1839	8	
TOXIC LIQUID, FLAMMABLE, ORGANIC, N.O.S.	2929	6.1		TRICHLOROACETIC ACID SOLUTION	2564	8	
TOXIC LIQUID, INORGANIC, N.O.S.	3287	6.1		Trichlororaceticaldehyde, see	2075	6.1	
TOXIC LIQUID, ORGANIC, N.O.S.	2810	6.1		TRICHLOROACETYL CHLORIDE	2442	8	
TOXIC LIQUID, OXIDIZING, N.O.S.	3122	6.1		TRICHLOROBENZENES, LIQUID	2321	6.1	
				TRICHLOROBUTENE	2322	6.1	
TOXIC LIQUID, WATER-REACTIVE, N.O.S.	3123	6.1		1,1,1-TRICHLOROETHANE	2831	6.1	
TOXIC SOLID, CORROSIVE, INORGANIC, N.O.S.	3290	6.1		TRICHLOROETHYLENE	1710	6.1	
TOXIC SOLID, CORROSIVE, ORGANIC, N.O.S.	2928	6.1		TRICHLOROISOCYANURIC ACID, DRY	2468	5.1	
TOXIC SOLID, FLAMMABLE, ORGANIC, N.O.S.	2930	6.1		Trichloronitromethane, see	1580	6.1	
TOXIC SOLID, INORGANIC, N.O.S.	3288	6.1		TRICHLOROSILANE	1295	4.3	
				1,3,5-Trichloro-s-triazine-2,4,6-trione, see	2468	5.1	
TOXIC SOLID, ORGANIC, N.O.S.	2811	6.1		2,4,6-Trichloro-1,3,5- triazine, see	2670	8	
TOXIC SOLID, OXIDIZING, N.O.S.	3086	6.1		TRICRESYL PHOSPHATE with more than 3% ortho isomer	2574	6.1	
TOXIC SOLID, SELF-HEATING, N.O.S.	3124	6.1		TRIETHYLAMINE	1296	3	
				Triethyl borate, see	1176	3	
TOXIC SOLID, WATER-REACTIVE, N.O.S.	3125	6.1		TRIETHYLENETETRAMINE	2259	8	
				Triethyl orthoformate, see	2524	3	
TOXINS, EXTRACTED FROM LIVING SOURCES, LIQUID, N.O.S.	3172	6.1		TRIETHYL PHOSPHITE	2323	3	
				TRIFLUOROACETIC ACID	2699	8	
TOXINS, EXTRACTED FROM LIVING SOURCES, SOLID, N.O.S.	3462	6.1		TRIFLUOROACETYL CHLORIDE	3057	2	
				Trifluorobromomethane, see	1009	2	
				Trifluorochloroethane, see	1983	2	
TRACERS FOR AMMUNITION	0212	1		TRIFLUOROCHLORO-ETHYLENE, STABILIZED	1082	2	
	0306	1		Trifluorochloromethane, see	1022	2	
Tremolite, see	2590	9		1,1,1-TRIFLUOROETHANE	2035	2	
TRIALLYLAMINE	2610	3		TRIFLUOROMETHANE	1984	2	
TRIALLYL BORATE	2609	6.1		TRIFLUOROMETHANE, REFRIGERATED LIQUID	3136	2	
TRIAZINE PESTICIDE, LIQUID, FLAMMABLE, TOXIC, flash-point less than 23 °C	2764	3		2-TRIFLUOROMETHYL-ANILINE	2942	6.1	
				3-TRIFLUOROMETHYL-ANILINE	2948	6.1	
TRIAZINE PESTICIDE, LIQUID, TOXIC	2998	6.1		TRIISOBUTYLENE	2324	3	
				TRIISOPROPYL BORATE	2616	3	
TRIAZINE PESTICIDE, LIQUID, TOXIC, FLAMMABLE, flash-point not less than 23 °C	2997	6.1		TRIMETHYLACETYL CHLORIDE	2438	6.1	

Name and description	UN No.	Class	Remarks	Name and description	UN No.	Class	Remarks
TRIMETHYLAMINE, ANHYDROUS	1083	2		TRINITROPHENOL (PICRIC ACID), WETTED with not less than 30% water, by mass	1344	4.1	
TRIMETHYLAMINE, AQUEOUS SOLUTION, not more than 50% trimethylamine, by mass	1297	3		TRINITROPHENOL WETTED with not less than 10% water, by mass	3364	4.1	
1,3,5-TRIMETHYLBENZENE	2325	3		TRINITROPHENYL-METHYLNITRAMINE	0208	1	
TRIMETHYL BORATE	2416	3		TRINITRORESORCINOL, dry or wetted with less than 20% water, or mixture of alcohol and water, by mass	0219	1	
TRIMETHYLCHLOROSILANE	1298	3					
TRIMETHYLCYCLOHEXYL-AMINE	2326	8					
Trimethylene chlorobromide, see	2688	6.1		TRINITRORESORCINOL, WETTED with not less than 20% water, or mixture of alcohol and water, by mass	0394	1	
TRIMETHYLHEXA-METHYLENEDIAMINES	2327	8					
TRIMETHYLHEXA-METHYLENE DIISOCYANATE	2328	6.1		TRINITROTOLUENE (TNT), dry or wetted with less than 30% water, by mass	0209	1	
2,4,4-Trimethylpentene-1, see	2050	3					
2,4,4-Trimethylpentene-2, see	2050	3		TRINITROTOLUENE AND HEXANITROSTILBENE MIXTURE	0388	1	
TRIMETHYL PHOSPHITE	2329	3					
TRINITROANILINE	0153	1		TRINITROTOLUENE MIXTURE CONTAINING TRINITROBENZENE AND HEXANITROSTILBENE	0389	1	
TRINITROANISOLE	0213	1					
TRINITROBENZENE, dry or wetted with less than 30% water, by mass	0214	1					
TRINITROBENZENE, WETTED with not less than 10% water, by mass	3367	4.1		TRINITROTOLUENE AND TRINITROBENZENE MIXTURE	0388	1	
				TRINITROTOLUENE, WETTED with not less than 10% water, by mass	3366	4.1	
TRINITROBENZENE, WETTED with not less than 30% water, by mass	1354	4.1					
TRINITROBENZENE-SULPHONIC ACID	0386	1		TRINITROTOLUENE, WETTED with not less than 30% water, by mass	1356	4.1	
TRINITROBENZOIC ACID, dry or wetted with less than 30% water, by mass	0215	1		TRIPROPYLAMINE	2260	3	
				TRIPROPYLENE	2057	3	
TRINITROBENZOIC ACID, WETTED with not less than 10% water, by mass	3368	4.1		TRIS-(1-AZIRIDINYL) PHOSPHINE OXIDE SOLUTION	2501	6.1	
TRINITROBENZOIC ACID, WETTED with not less than 30% water, by mass	1355	4.1		TRITONAL	0390	1	
				Tropilidene, see	2603	3	
TRINITROCHLOROBENZENE	0155	1		TUNGSTEN HEXAFLUORIDE	2196	2	
TRINITROCHLOROBENZENE WETTED with not less than 10% water, by mass	3365	4.1		TURPENTINE	1299	3	
				TURPENTINE SUBSTITUTE	1300	3	
				UNDECANE	2330	3	
TRINITRO-m-CRESOL	0216	1		UREA HYDROGEN PEROXIDE	1511	5.1	
TRINITROFLUORENONE	0387	1		UREA NITRATE, dry or wetted with less than 20% water, by mass	0220	1	
TRINITRONAPHTHALENE	0217	1					
TRINITROPHENETOLE	0218	1		UREA NITRATE, WETTED with not less than 10% water, by mass	3370	4.1	
TRINITROPHENOL, dry or wetted with less than 30% water, by mass	0154	1		UREA NITRATE, WETTED with not less than 20% water, by mass	1357	4.1	
				Valeral, see	2058	3	
				VALERALDEHYDE	2058	3	

Name and description	UN No.	Class	Remarks	Name and description	UN No.	Class	Remarks
n-Valeraldehyde, see	2058	3		WATER-REACTIVE LIQUID, N.O.S.	3148	4.3	
Valeric aldehyde, see	2058	3		WATER-REACTIVE LIQUID, CORROSIVE, N.O.S.	3129	4.3	
VALERYL CHLORIDE	2502	8		WATER-REACTIVE LIQUID, TOXIC, N.O.S.	3130	4.3	
VANADIUM COMPOUND, N.O.S.	3285	6.1					
Vanadium (IV) oxide sulphate, see	2931	6.1		WATER-REACTIVE SOLID, N.O.S.	2813	4.3	
Vanadium oxysulphate, see	2931	6.1		WATER-REACTIVE SOLID, CORROSIVE, N.O.S.	3131	4.3	
VANADIUM OXYTRICHLORIDE	2443	8		WATER-REACTIVE SOLID, FLAMMABLE, N.O.S.	3132	4.3	
VANADIUM PENTOXIDE, non-fused form	2862	6.1		WATER-REACTIVE SOLID, OXIDIZING, N.O.S.	3133	4.3	Carriage prohibited
VANADIUM TETRACHLORIDE	2444	8					
VANADIUM TRICHLORIDE	2475	8		WATER-REACTIVE SOLID, SELF-HEATING, N.O.S.	3135	4.3	
VANADYL SULPHATE	2931	6.1		WATER-REACTIVE SOLID, TOXIC, N.O.S.	3134	4.3	
Varnish, see	1263	3					
	3066	8		White arsenic, see	1561	6.1	
	3469	3					
	3470	8		WHITE ASBESTOS (chrysotile, actinolite, anthophyllite, tremolite)	2590	9	
Vehicle, flammable gas powered or vehicle, flammable liquid powered	3166	9	Not subject to ADR				
				White spirit, see	1300	3	
Villiaumite, see	1690	6.1		WOOD PRESERVATIVES, LIQUID	1306	3	
VINYL ACETATE, STABILIZED	1301	3					
Vinylbenzene, see	2055	3		Wool waste, wet	1387	4.2	Not subject to ADR
VINYL BROMIDE, STABILIZED	1085	2					
VINYL BUTYRATE, STABILIZED	2838	3		XANTHATES	3342	4.2	
VINYL CHLORIDE, STABILIZED	1086	2		XENON	2036	2	
VINYL CHLOROACETATE	2589	6.1		XENON, REFRIGERATED LIQUID	2591	2	
VINYL ETHYL ETHER, STABILIZED	1302	3					
				XYLENES	1307	3	
VINYL FLUORIDE, STABILIZED	1860	2		XYLENOLS, LIQUID	3430	6.1	
VINYLIDENE CHLORIDE, STABILIZED	1303	3		XYLENOLS, SOLID	2261	6.1	
				XYLIDINES, LIQUID	1711	6.1	
VINYL ISOBUTYL ETHER, STABILIZED	1304	3		XYLIDINES, SOLID	3452	6.1	
VINYL METHYL ETHER, STABILIZED	1087	2		Xylols, see	1307	3	
				XYLYL BROMIDE, LIQUID	1701	6.1	
VINYLPYRIDINES, STABILIZED	3073	6.1		XYLYL BROMIDE, SOLID	3417	6.1	
VINYLTOLUENES, STABILIZED	2618	3					
VINYLTRICHLOROSILANE	1305	3		ZINC AMMONIUM NITRITE	1512	5.1	
Warheads for guided missiles, see	0286	1		ZINC ARSENATE	1712	6.1	
	0287	1		ZINC ARSENATE AND ZINC ARSENITE MIXTURE	1712	6.1	
	0369	1					
	0370	1		ZINC ARSENITE	1712	6.1	
	0371	1		ZINC ASHES	1435	4.3	
WARHEADS, ROCKET with burster or expelling charge	0370	1		Zinc bisulphite solution, see	2693	8	
	0371	1		ZINC BROMATE	2469	5.1	
WARHEADS, ROCKET with bursting charge	0286	1		ZINC CHLORATE	1513	5.1	
	0287	1					
	0369	1		ZINC CHLORIDE, ANHYDROUS	2331	8	
WARHEADS, TORPEDO with bursting charge	0221	1					

Name and description	UN No.	Class	Remarks	Name and description	UN No.	Class	Remarks
ZINC CHLORIDE SOLUTION	1840	8		ZIRCONIUM, DRY, coiled wire, finished metal sheets, strip (thinner than 254 microns but not thinner than 18 microns)	2858	4.1	
ZINC CYANIDE	1713	6.1					
ZINC DITHIONITE	1931	9					
ZINC DUST	1436	4.3		ZIRCONIUM, DRY, finished sheets, strip or coiled wire	2009	4.2	
ZINC FLUOROSILICATE	2855	6.1					
Zinc hexafluorosilicate, see	2855	6.1		ZIRCONIUM HYDRIDE	1437	4.1	
ZINC HYDROSULPHITE, see	1931	9		ZIRCONIUM NITRATE	2728	5.1	
ZINC NITRATE	1514	5.1		ZIRCONIUM PICRAMATE, dry or wetted with less than 20% water, by mass	0236	1	
ZINC PERMANGANATE	1515	5.1					
ZINC PEROXIDE	1516	5.1		ZIRCONIUM PICRAMATE, WETTED with not less than 20% water, by mass	1517	4.1	
ZINC PHOSPHIDE	1714	4.3					
ZINC POWDER	1436	4.3					
ZINC RESINATE	2714	4.1		ZIRCONIUM POWDER, DRY	2008	4.2	
Zinc selenate, see	2630	4.1		ZIRCONIUM POWDER, WETTED with not less than 25% water	1358	4.1	
Zinc selenite, see	2630	4.1					
Zinc silicofluoride, see	2855	6.1		ZIRCONIUM SCRAP	1932	4.2	
				ZIRCONIUM SUSPENDED IN A FLAMMABLE LIQUID	1308	3	
				ZIRCONIUM TETRACHLORIDE	2503	8	